LIPPERT, Summer '92

S0-ARB-603

Montgomery's AUDITING

Eleventh Edition

COLLEGE VERSION

PHILIP L. DEFLIESE, CPA
Professor Emeritus, Graduate School of Business,
Columbia University

HENRY R. JAENICKE, Ph.D., CPA
C.D. Clarkson Professor of Accounting,
College of Business and Administration,
Drexel University

VINCENT M. O'REILLY, CPA
Deputy Chairman, Accounting and Auditing,
Coopers & Lybrand

MURRAY B. HIRSCH, CPA
Vice Chairman, Auditing, Coopers & Lybrand

JOHN WILEY & SONS
New York Chichester Brisbane Toronto Singapore

This book contains quotations and adaptations from publications copyrighted by the American Institute of Certified Public Accountants, Inc. and the Financial Accounting Standards Board. Those materials have been reprinted or adapted with the permission of those organizations, from whom copies of the complete documents are available.

Material from Uniform CPA Examination Questions and Unofficial Answers, copyright © 1947 through 1989 by the American Institute of Certified Public Accountants, Inc., is reprinted or adapted with permission.

Copyright © 1990 by Coopers & Lybrand (United States)
Published by John Wiley & Sons, Inc.

All rights reserved. Published simultaneously in Canada.

Reproduction or translation of any part of this work beyond that permitted by Section 107 or 108 of the 1976 United States Copyright Act without the permission of the copyright owner is unlawful. Requests for permission or further information should be addressed to the Permissions Department, John Wiley & Sons, Inc.

Library of Congress Cataloging in Publication Data:

Montgomery, Robert Hiester, 1872–1953.
Montgomery's Auditing.

Includes index.
1. Auditing. I. Defliese, Philip L. II. Title.
III. Title: Auditing.

ISBN 0471-50706-7

Printed in the United States of America

10 9 8 7 6 5 4 3 2 1

About the Authors

Philip L. Defliese, D.C.S. (Hon.) and CPA, is a co-author of the 8th, 9th, and 10th editions of this book. He is the retired Chairman of Coopers & Lybrand, former Chairman of the AICPA, former Chairman of the Accounting Principles Board, former Chairman of the Auditing Standards Board, and former Chairman of the Audit Committee for New York City. He is Professor Emeritus at Columbia University and a member of the Governmental Accounting Standards Board. He was elected to the Accounting Hall of Fame and is a recipient of the AICPA Gold Medal for Distinguished Service to the Accounting Profession.

Henry R. Jaenicke, Ph.D. and CPA, is the C.D. Clarkson Professor of Accounting at Drexel University. He was the principal research consultant to the Commission on Auditors' Responsibilities and authored the commission's research study on *The Effect of Litigation on Independent Auditors*. He was the Project Director of the AICPA's Special Committee on Governance and Structure of the Institute and the Profession. He won the American Accounting Association's Wildman Medal for his FASB research study, *Survey of Present Practices in Recognizing Revenues, Expenses, Gains, and Losses*. He is also co-author of *Evaluating Internal Control*, published by John Wiley & Sons, and of *A Framework for Evaluating an Internal Audit Function*, published by the Institute of Internal Auditors.

Vincent M. O'Reilly, CPA, is Deputy Chairman, Accounting and Auditing, and a member of the Executive Committee at Coopers & Lybrand. Previously he was the Regional Managing Partner responsible for the firm's Northeast operations. He is a member of the SEC Practice Section Executive Committee of the AICPA and also a member of the Accounting Education Change Commission.

Murray B. Hirsch, CPA, is Vice Chairman, Auditing, at Coopers & Lybrand. He is a member of the Auditing Standards Board of the AICPA and of Coopers & Lybrand's International Accounting and Auditing Committee. He is also a member of the Accreditation Management Committee of the American Assembly of Collegiate Schools of Business. He was formerly National Director of Professional Education and Regional Managing Partner in the Actuarial, Benefits, and Compensation Consulting Division of Coopers & Lybrand.

Historical Perspective

Robert H. Montgomery (1872–1953) together with William M. Lybrand (1867–1960), Adam Ross (1869–1929), and T. Edward Ross (1867–1963) founded the firm of Lybrand, Ross Bros. & Montgomery (now Coopers & Lybrand) in 1898, two years after the first CPA law was passed. The four had for some time previously practiced public accounting in Philadelphia.

Montgomery was a prolific writer and leader of his profession. He was instrumental in the organization of what is now the American Institute of Certified Public Accountants and served as its president. Earlier, he also taught at Columbia University, New York University, and the University of Pennsylvania.[1] He saw the need for a practical book on auditing and in 1905 and 1909 published American editions of Dicksee's *Auditing*, a British work. Noting the radical departure of American practice from Dicksee's work, however, he wrote the first American book on the subject, *Auditing: Theory and Practice*, in 1912. Nine subsequent editions followed from 1916 through 1985. For the seventh edition, co-authors Alvin R. Jennings and Norman J. Lenhart joined him and the book was renamed *Montgomery's Auditing*. The eighth edition, published after his death, was co-authored by Norman J. Lenhart and Philip L. Defliese in 1957. The ninth edition, published in 1975, was co-authored by Philip L. Defliese, Kenneth P. Johnson, and Roderick K. Macleod. The tenth edition, co-authored by Jerry D. Sullivan, Richard A. Gnospelius, Philip L. Defliese, and Henry R. Jaenicke, was published in 1985; college versions of the tenth edition (adapted for classroom use) were also begun at this time. Comparisons of the various editions reveal the development of accounting and auditing in the United States.

In 1956, in recognition of the growing needs of international practice, Cooper Bros. & Co. in the United Kingdom and other countries (founded in 1854), MacDonald Currie & Co. in Canada (founded in 1910), and Lybrand, Ross Bros. & Montgomery formed the multinational firm of Coopers & Lybrand. Dropping the Montgomery name from a firm that had so long celebrated his contributions was not easy. The continued association of the Montgomery name, however, with his major contribution to the literature of the profession is a proper tribute to his memory.

[1]For a full account of Montgomery's contributions, see his autobiography, *Fifty Years of Accountancy* (New York: The Ronald Press Co., 1939).

Preface

Before the profession formalized the standard-setting process following the landmark *McKesson & Robbins* case in 1938, auditing practice was governed by views expressed in books and articles. Montgomery was a pioneer among the writers of the time, and his *Auditing* was revered as the practitioner's manual. There was no professional standard-setting organization or process at that time, and Montgomery's views were his own, based on many years of practice and observation. Auditing standard-setting today—50 years later—has evolved into a formal and complex process, in which pronouncements reflect a consensus, arrived at after healthy debate, among the appointed members of the profession's standard-setting board. This process brings together the collective wisdom of those individuals, often aiding in articulating and fine-tuning pronouncements.

We have just passed through a period of reexamination and revision of some of the basic standards—most visibly a radical change in the wording of the auditor's standard report on financial statements, the first such change in 40 years. The standard on detecting fraudulent financial reporting is the fourth during that period, each reflecting an attempt to clarify earlier thinking and refocus the emphasis in keeping with the times. The standard on internal control is a replacement for a Statement on Auditing Procedure issued in 1972; the standard on analytical procedures supersedes one originally issued in 1978; the standards on communicating internal control deficiencies and on "going concern uncertainties" replace standards issued in 1977 and 1981.

Other standards—those on auditing accounting estimates and communicating with audit committees—are new pronouncements that recognized the need for guidance in areas previously not specifically covered in official pronouncements. Underscoring the growing importance of another area—testing and reporting on compliance with laws and regulations—the Auditing Standards Board issued a standard on compliance auditing.

Much of the Auditing Standards Board's recent efforts was inspired by the same series of events that led to the creation of the National Commission on Fraudulent Financial Reporting (Treadway Commission), a two-year, private-sector study by knowledgeable lawyers, bankers, financiers, and accountants. Its objective was to make recommendations that would stem the tide of misleading financial reporting. Most of the 49 recommendations in the 1987

Treadway report focused on the role of management, regulators, and educators rather than on the auditing profession. Treadway's major points for the profession suggested a clarification of and greater emphasis on the auditor's role in detecting fraudulent financial reporting and in communicating with the public; the new auditing standards in these areas were developed contemporaneously with those recommendations and harmonized well with them. Both the new auditing standards and the Treadway recommendations in these areas were responsive to the gap between the assurance that an audit actually provides and the public's perception that an audit provides absolute assurance of the quality of an entity's financial statements and the ongoing viability of its business operations—two things an audit could never give.

The Treadway Commission recognized this, as Montgomery had in the early years of this century. The limitations of auditing remain with us today, as the following quotes from the Treadway report show:

> The responsibility for reliable financial reporting resides first and foremost at the corporate level. Top management—starting with the chief executive officer—sets the tone and establishes the financial reporting environment. Therefore, reducing the risk of fraudulent financial reporting must start within the reporting company. . . .
>
> Prior efforts to reduce the risk of fraudulent financial reporting have tended to focus heavily on the independent public accountant and, as such, were inherently limited. Independent public accountants play a crucial, but secondary role. They are not guarantors. Their role, however, can be enhanced, particularly with respect to detecting fraudulent financial reporting, and financial statement preparers and users should be made to understand the enhanced role. . . .
>
> Yet, implementing all 49 of the Commission's recommendations would still not guarantee that fraudulent financial reporting will disappear. Similarly, failure to implement some or all of the recommendations should not automatically establish liability if fraudulent financial reporting occurs. Those who allege that fraud has occurred must still offer affirmative proof of any actual wrong doing.
>
> A further word of caution also is in order. While increased awareness of fraudulent financial reporting within the business and professional community and among the investing public generally is important, it is equally important that public expectations not be raised unduly because even full implementation of the Commission's recommendations will not completely eradicate fraudulent financial reporting. Fraudulent financial reporting must not be assumed merely because a business fails. The public must recognize and understand the clear line that distinguishes the failure of the top management to manage well from the intentional or reckless conduct that amounts to fraud. . . .

Since fraudulent financial reporting will never be completely eradicated, an auditor signing an opinion will always be taking a risk even when the audit has been conducted in accordance with generally accepted auditing standards and an appropriately low level of audit risk has been achieved. The consideration of this exposure and the assessment of audit risk are not new ideas, nor were they new with the 1983 standard on audit risk. Montgomery's second edition (1916) described audit risk in the following way:

> Opportunities for wrong-doing vary, as a rule, with the size of the undertaking. In a small business the details are apt to be supervised by one or all of the proprietors, while in a large business much of the detail is necessarily left to subordinates. The auditor must be governed by the circumstances surrounding each engagement and then determine the amount of detail to be covered. (p. 13)

In the preface to the tenth edition, the authors stated that "the more things change, the more they remain the same," and quoted excerpts from prefaces of earlier editions of this book as evidence that basic audit concepts and objectives remained largely unchanged, while techniques, terminology, and approaches varied from time to time. Many of the events of the intervening five years seem to substantiate that view. Careful analysis of the new standards will reveal that the underlying conceptual basis of auditing continues to be sound and unchanged. What was needed were new ways for the professional literature to respond to the challenges posed by the current business environment and, in particular, the "expectation gap," a large part of which may be perhaps better described as a "communication gap," between the public's expectations for audits and its perception of auditors' performance.

The current business environment poses another challenge to the profession. We expressed our concern in the preface to the tenth edition over the increased competition within the accounting profession and the resulting lower fees and emphasis on audit efficiency. The recent mergers in the accounting profession can also trace their roots to the competitive environment. With the greater competition comes a concern for maintaining the level of audit quality. Regardless of size and competitive pressures, the auditing profession has a responsibility to the public to perform high-quality audits. The profession has taken many steps to create incentives to achieve and maintain that quality. In the final analysis, however, quality work is the result of a sense of professionalism on the part of individual auditors and an environment of professionalism created by individual firms.

Preface to the College Version

Except for two short-lived college versions published in 1915 and 1923, when Montgomery was teaching at Columbia University, a college text based on the professional reference book known as *Montgomery's Auditing* was not available until 1984 when an adaptation of the tenth edition tailored to the needs of college courses in auditing was published. A revised edition of that book followed in 1987.

Like the earlier editions, this college version of the eleventh edition emphasizes the development of judgment by the auditor and provides aids for enhancing decision-making skills. The book covers and explains all current authoritative pronouncements, including the recently issued "expectation gap" standards, relevant to the audit process. It expounds an approach to auditing based on what the authors believe is the best of practice, but it also incorporates alternative viewpoints. While the authors are or have been associated with Coopers & Lybrand, the text is not limited to that firm's policies and practices. The intent was to cover all viewpoints objectively.

Many readers will use this book in studying for the CPA examination and as a reference work after they embark on their professional careers. Accordingly, the authoritative auditing literature is heavily referenced and cited, and the problem material presented at the end of each chapter includes an ample selection of CPA examination questions.

The problem material is divided into four categories, as follows:

- *Review Questions* (numbered 1 through 29): These are designed to assist students in reviewing and testing their comprehension of the chapter. They serve as a form of refresher to determine whether the student has grasped the salient points made.
- *Discussion Questions* (numbered 30 through 39): These are designed to provide topics for class discussion. They assist in applying the principles or practices described in the text, and thus often introduce business practices or situations not explicitly covered in the chapter.
- *AICPA Multiple Choice Questions* (numbered 40 through 59): These are taken from the Auditing part of Uniform CPA Examinations and provide

a test of the ability to discriminate, from several choices, among practical applications of the concepts covered in the chapter.

- *Problems and Cases* (numbered starting with 60): These are longer problems involving, in many instances, the preparation of audit working papers and analytical treatment of case material. They vary in length and complexity and may be assigned as time permits depending on the length and level of the course. A case study (Quinn Hardware) is begun in Chapter 6 and continued in Chapters 8, 10, 12, 13, 14, 17, and 18, providing students with a comprehensive, integrated view of the audit process. The case is lengthy, as its purpose is to provide a realistic setting in which audit decisions are made. If the case is assigned, an additional audit case or "practice set" might prove redundant. On the other hand, the case has been designed so that it does not have to be used in its entirety; with the exception of Problem 6–62, which provides background for the other parts, each part of the case can stand on its own. (The Quinn Hardware problem in Chapter 8 requires students to prepare a systems flowchart for part of a buying cycle. The instructor may assign that problem as part of the coverage of Chapter 8 or, alternatively, in combination with the continuation of the case in Chapter 13, "Auditing the Buying Cycle.") The Lemco case (8–64) in Chapter 8 includes illustrations of certain forms related to the buying cycle—purchase order, receiving report, invoice, voucher, and perpetual inventory record—that will be helpful to students who would otherwise be unfamiliar with such forms.

The numbering system for the problem material was devised to enable students and instructors to identify the type of problem by its number. For example, any problem with a number between 40 and 59 is an AICPA multiple choice question. Of course, not all numbers are used in each chapter.

In addition to the multiple choice questions, questions from Uniform CPA Examinations have been used as discussion questions and problems, and are labeled "AICPA adapted." That designation indicates that the authors have not felt constrained in taking considerable liberties with the questions, including but not limited to updating them to reflect revised terminology, dividing questions among two or more chapters, and deleting parts of questions.

Organization of the Text

This book has been organized into four parts, with the chapters for the most part arranged to follow the sequence in a typical audit. The four parts are

Part 1: The Audit Environment. The four chapters in Part 1 provide an overview of auditing (Chapter 1), the professional structure and organization into which auditing has evolved (Chapter 2), and the standards and responsibilities to which auditors are held (Chapters 3 and 4). These provide an understanding of the environment in which the auditor operates.

Part 2: Theory and Concepts. These seven chapters provide the conceptual basis for an understanding of the way in which audits are planned and conducted. Chapter 5 presents an overview of the audit process, including the types of evidence and tests that constitute that process. Chapter 6 considers how audit risk, materiality, and other factors enter into engagement strategy. The internal control structure is described in depth in Chapter 7; assessing inherent and control risks, including tests of controls, is covered in Chapter 8. Both of those chapters have been rewritten from the previous edition to expand on SAS No. 55 dealing with the control structure and assessing control risk. Chapter 9 discusses substantive testing, including analytical procedures. Audit sampling, both statistical and nonstatistical, is covered in Chapter 10. Finally, auditing in an EDP environment is the topic of Chapter 11. Throughout Part 2, the topics are covered at the conceptual level rather than in the context of specific cycles or account balances, although numerous realistic illustrations of the application of those concepts are provided.

Part 3: Auditing Specific Cycles and Accounts. These chapters apply the concepts from Part 2 to the audit of specific transaction cycles and account balances that form the body of the financial statements that are the subject matter of an audit. The five chapters in Part 3 cover all the areas required to be audited. Three segments of the audit are presented using the cycle approach, and six, covered in two chapters, using the account balance approach.

The text stresses the need for audit efficiency as well as audit effectiveness, and the reader is constantly reminded of the need to inject efficiency considerations into testing decisions for each particular audit. Efficiency considerations and the resultant strategy will determine whether, in auditing a particular cycle or group of accounts for a particular client, the auditor will test specific internal control procedures as a basis for restricting substantive tests, or will perform primarily substantive tests, including analytical procedures. On many audits, there are three areas for which the auditor is likely to choose a strategy that includes tests of control procedures as the most efficient way of achieving the necessary audit assurance. They are the revenue cycle, buying cycle, and production cycle, and are the subject matter of Chapters 12, 13, and 14, respectively. On the other hand, more often than not the most efficient audit of other areas or accounts in the financial statements can be accomplished by performing primarily analytical procedures and substantive tests of the details of transactions and balances. Chapters 15 and 16 cover the audit of such accounts: cash, property, investments, prepayments and accruals, income taxes, and debt and equity. In Chapters 12, 13, and 14, the text describes typical transactions, accounting systems, and control procedures; audit objectives; risk assessment; and typical tests of controls and substantive tests.

Chapters 15 and 16 describe substantive tests that are performed to meet the audit objectives for specific accounts. In all of the chapters in Part 3, the selection of tests is linked to the audit strategy; the tests associated with specific accounts are also linked to the audit of other, related accounts.

Part 4: Completing the Work and Reporting the Results. The auditor's work culminates in drafting the report—the primary manifestation of the audit that the financial statement reader sees. Completing the audit, which entails evaluating the overall findings, is a prerequisite to the report and is covered in Chapter 17. Chapter 18 deals with the auditor's standard report on financial statements. Other engagements—special reporting situations, attestation engagements, and compliance audits—are discussed in Chapter 19. Coverage of the latter two topics incorporates the attestation standards and SAS No. 63 on compliance auditing.

The sequence of some of the chapters can be rearranged to some extent without affecting continuity. Chapter 18 on the auditor's report, for example, could be assigned early in the course. Although the material in Chapters 3 and 4 on professional ethics and legal liability, respectively, could be moved to the end of the course, as is frequently done, it would probably be best to assign the first parts of each of those chapters—on auditing standards and on responsibility for detecting misstatements, respectively—early in the course. The chapters in Part 3 could be assigned in virtually any order without causing problems in continuity. Even though this college version has been condensed from the professional reference book, many opportunities still exist for deleting or covering lightly chapters that cannot be covered in depth because of time constraints. Among those are one or two of the cycle chapters and one or more sections of the account balance chapters in Part 3, and Chapter 19.

Users should also be aware that the professional version of the book contains more detailed discussion of several topics condensed or deleted in the college version, particularly in Chapters 15 and 16. Adopters of this book may reproduce and distribute, for classroom use only, pages from Chapters 1 to 25 of the professional version that cover topics not included or treated less extensively in the present version. In addition, some instructors may want to supplement the text with other materials, for example, Statements on Auditing Standards or other AICPA materials such as industry audit guides or auditing procedure studies.

Major Changes to the Eleventh Edition

Most of the changes to the text have been driven by changes in ethical and technical standards, principally the Code of Professional Conduct adopted by the AICPA membership in 1988 and Statemens on Auditing Standards issued by the Auditing Standards Board in 1988 and 1989. Other significant events since the Revised College Version of tenth edition was published in 1987 include the publication in the United States of the Report of the National Commission on Fraudulent Financial Reporting (also known as the Treadway Commission) and the publication in Canada of the Report of the Commission to Study the Public's Expectations of Audits (also known as the Macdonald Commission). Those pronouncements and publications, together with other changes in the environment in which audits are performed, are reflected in this edition.

- Chapter 1 discusses the various "gaps" identified by the report of the Macdonald Commission and sets the stage for the discussion in Chapter 4 of the auditor's responsibility to detect financial statement errors and irregularities. Chapter 4 also tracks significant recent legal cases and other developments that affect the common law relationship between the auditor and third parties.
- The new AICPA Code of Professional Conduct is covered in Chapter 3, as is the impact on professional services of the accord between the AICPA and the Federal Trade Commission with respect to contingent fees and commissions. The coverage of the AICPA's practice-monitoring programs has been expanded to include the new Quality Review Program.
- Chapters 7 and 8 have been completely rewritten to reflect SAS No. 55, *Consideration of the Internal Control Structure in a Financial Statement Audit.*
- The coverage of analytical procedures and auditing accounting estimates in Chapter 9 has been expanded to reflect the new SASs on those topics.
- Chapters 12, 13, and 14 (the three "transaction cycle" chapters) have been rewritten to acknowledge how accounting systems of different degrees of sophistication and subject to different control procedures are likely to affect the auditor's assessment of control risk. These chapters provide practical guidance in applying SAS No. 55.
- Chapter 18, "The Auditor's Report," has been rewritten to reflect the new standard report adopted by the ASB in SAS No. 58.
- The attestation standards, including standards for prospective financial information, and compliance auditing have been added to Chapter 19. That chapter now covers the wide variety of attest and related services CPAs are likely to perform that extend well beyond audits of historical-based financial information.

Acknowledgments

We acknowledge with thanks the permission granted to us by the American Institute of Certified Public Accountants and the Financial Accounting Standards Board to quote or paraphrase passages from their publications. Copies of the complete documents can be obtained from those organizations.

This book represents the efforts and ideas of many people. The following individuals, presently or formerly associated with Coopers & Lybrand, contributed to various portions of the book: Alan M. Bangser, Bhaskar H. Bhave, Robert Chakrin, David J. Checkosky, Raymond L. Dever, Stephen J. Emanuel, Michael R. Galper, John F. Garry, James S. Gerson, Lynford E. Graham, Jr., Edward R. Hansen, James A. Hogan, Stephen J. Lis, Martin S. McDermut, David L. McLean, James C. Meehan, Frank C. Munn, Ronald J. Murray, Dennis E. Peavey, William J. Powers, Jane S. Pressly, James J. Quinn, Walter G. Ricciardi, Gregory C. Scates, Christopher S. Stafford, Richard M. Steinberg, J. Donald Warren, Jr., David T. Wright.

We are deeply indebted to our co-author of the tenth edition and the former Director of Audit Policy at Coopers & Lybrand, Jerry D. Sullivan, for his major contribution to this revision. As Chairman of the Auditing Standards Board from 1985 to 1988, he was a driving force behind the Board's recently issued "expectation gap" standards. The authors of this edition are the beneficiaries of his insights into the thinking behind those standards. We are greatly appreciative of his efforts in drafting and reviewing the manuscript of this edition.

We owe a special acknowledgment to A. J. Lorie, partner at Coopers & Lybrand, for his invaluable assistance in drafting sections of this book and for his careful and thoughtful review of the entire manuscript. His scrutiny of the book from beginning to end provided a needed continuity to an undertaking of this scope. Our thanks are also due to Myra D. Cleary, who was the senior editor of the book and managed the administrative aspects of its creation. In that role, she endeavored, by editing and rewriting the manuscript, to shape it into a coherent work. Finally, we are grateful to Jill Spelman, who copyedited the manuscript, for her efforts to streamline the writing and enhance the readability of the book. To all those individuals, and any who were inadvertently omitted, go not only our thanks, but also the usual absolution from blame for errors and omissions.

P.L.D.
H.R.J.
V.M.O.
M.B.H.

Contents

PART 1 THE AUDIT ENVIRONMENT

Chapter 1 An Overview of Auditing 3

Chapter 2 The Organization and Structure of the Auditing Profession 29

Chapter 3 Auditing Standards and Professional Conduct 51

Chapter 4 Professional Responsibility and Legal Liability 101

PART 2 THEORY AND CONCEPTS

Chapter 5 The Audit Process 149

Chapter 6 Audit Risk, Materiality, and Engagement Strategy 187

Chapter 7 The Internal Control Structure 219

Chapter 8 Assessing Inherent and Control Risk 259

Chapter 9 Controlling Detection Risk: Substantive Tests 323

PART 3 AUDITING SPECIFIC CYCLES AND ACCOUNTS

Abbreviations and References

Abbreviations

References in this book to names of organizations, committees, and publications are often abbreviated, as follows:

AAA	American Accounting Association
AcSEC	Accounting Standards Executive Committee
AAER	Accounting and Auditing Enforcement Release
AICPA	American Institute of Certified Public Accountants
ALI	American Law Institute
APB	Accounting Principles Board
ARB	Accounting Research Bulletin
ASB	Auditing Standards Board
ASR	Accounting Series Release
AudSEC	Auditing Standards Executive Committee
EITF	Emerging Issues Task Force
FASB	Financial Accounting Standards Board
FRR	Financial Reporting Release
GAO	General Accounting Office
GASB	Governmental Accounting Standards Board
IAPC	International Auditing Practices Committee
IFAC	International Federation of Accountants
IIA	Institute of Internal Auditors
IRS	Internal Revenue Service
SAB	Staff Accounting Bulletin
SAP	Statement on Auditing Procedure
SAS	Statement on Auditing Standards
SEC	Securities and Exchange Commission
SFAS	Statement of Financial Accounting Standards
SOP	Statement of Position
SSARS	Statement on Standards for Accounting and Review Services
SSAE	Statement on Standards for Attestation Engagements
SSMAS	Statement on Standards for Management Advisory Services

References

References in this book to AICPA and FASB pronouncements are current as of September 1, 1989. In addition to citations to original AICPA or FASB pronouncements (or later codifications, where applicable), second references are provided wherever possible. For pronouncements contained in *AICPA Professional Standards*, second references are to the appropriate section in that publication. Second references for accounting pronouncements are to the General Standards volume of the *Current Text* of FASB Accounting Standards; however, all quotations from the accounting literature are taken from the original pronouncements.

PART 1

The Audit Environment

1

An Overview of Auditing

This book covers auditing—what auditors do and should do when they perform an audit—and the auditing profession—the institutional framework within which the practice of auditing takes place. An understanding of what an audit is and how it is performed is needed to understand the social function of an audit and the professional responsibilities auditors assume when they fill that function. To understand the background and logic behind the methods and techniques auditors use and the care they exercise in conducting an audit, one must also understand the environment and institutions within which an audit occurs. Knowing what constitutes an audit performed with due professional care and why particular auditing procedures are followed enables the auditor to adapt to changing circumstances in order to meet social, legal, and professional responsibilities. This book is based on the premise that an auditor who understands the theory and concepts of auditing—discussed in detail in Part 2 of this book—is more effective and efficient than an auditor who has merely memorized a series of steps to be performed. That understanding is enhanced by the broad overview of the audit function that this chapter provides.

DEFINITION OF AUDITING

Different types of audits and the purposes of audits have evolved over many years, and this evolution is still taking place. Accordingly, auditing should be defined broadly enough to cover the various types and purposes of audits. The definition of auditing that appeared in *A Statement of Basic Auditing Concepts*, published in 1973 by the American Accounting Association (AAA) Committee on Basic Auditing Concepts, embraces both the process and purposes of auditing.

> Auditing is a systematic process of objectively obtaining and evaluating evidence regarding assertions about economic actions and events to ascertain the degree of correspondence between those assertions and established criteria and communicating the results to interested users. (p. 2)

The AAA Committee noted that its definition was intentionally quite broad to cover "the many different purposes for which an audit might be conducted and the variety of subject matter that might be focused on in a specific audit engagement" (p. 2). The following discussion of each key phrase in the definition is couched primarily in the context of an audit of the financial statements of a business organization, usually referred to as a financial audit. Chapter 2 discusses compliance audits and performance audits as well as financial audits.

Assertions About Economic Actions and Events. The assertions of management that are embodied in a set of financial statements are the subject matter of an audit of those statements. For example, the item "inventories . . . $5,426,000" in a balance sheet of a manufacturing company embodies the following assertions, among others: The inventories physically exist; they are held for sale or use in operations; they include all products and materials; $5,426,000 is the lower of their cost or market value (as both terms are defined under generally accepted accounting principles); they are properly classified on the balance sheet; and appropriate disclosures related to inventories have been made, such as their major categories and amounts pledged or assigned. Comparable assertions are embodied in all the other specific items and amounts in financial statements.

The assertions are made by the preparer of the financial statements—management—and communicated to the readers of the statements; they are not assertions by the auditor. The auditor's responsibility is to express an opinion on management's assertions in the context of the financial statements taken as a whole, and to communicate that opinion to the readers in the form of the auditor's report. Similar assertions are also the subject matter of compliance and performance audits.

Degree of Correspondence Between Assertions and Established Criteria. Everything that takes place during an audit has one primary objective: the formation of an opinion by the auditor on the assertions about economic actions and events that have been audited. The auditor's opinion will specify how well those assertions conform to established criteria or standards. In financial audits, generally accepted accounting principles (GAAP) are the established criteria against which the assertions are measured; GAAP require that inventories exist and be owned by the enterprise before they can be included among its assets. If the inventories exist and are owned by the reporting enterprise, and if the other assertions implicit in the item "inventories . . . $5,426,000" also conform to generally accepted accounting principles, the auditor will conclude that there is complete correspondence between those assertions and established criteria.

GAAP are, for the most part, explicit and precisely defined. The same may be true in the case of many compliance audits. For example, the established criteria against which the assertions on a tax return are measured are the tax laws, regulations, and rulings that pertain to the particular tax return. In other instances, such as a performance audit of an enterprise's capital budgeting system, the criteria are far less precise and are generally ill defined. In those situations, the auditor and the client will have to agree on the criteria to be used, and those criteria should be explicitly stated in the auditor's report.

Objectively Obtaining and Evaluating Evidence. In essence, auditing consists of obtaining and evaluating evidence that will support the auditor's opinion that the assertions conform to established criteria. "The types of evidence obtained and the criteria employed to evaluate evidence may vary from audit to audit, but all audits center on the process of obtaining and evaluating evidence" (*A Statement of Basic Auditing Concepts*, p. 2). In a financial audit, for example, evidence about the degree of correspondence between assertions in the financial statements and generally accepted accounting principles consists of underlying accounting data (such as journals, ledgers, and files) and corroborating information (such as invoices, checks, and information obtained by inquiry, observation, physical inspection of assets, and correspondence with customers). To continue with the inventory example, the auditor may examine purchase contracts or paid invoices to ascertain that the enterprise owns the inventory, observe an inventory count to determine that it exists, and retotal the perpetual inventory ledger to ascertain the mathematical accuracy of the dollar amount of inventory reported on the balance sheet.

The auditor must also interpret and evaluate the evidence obtained before reaching the conclusion that the assertions conform to objective criteria. The judgments required are often extremely difficult and call for significant analytical and interpretive skills. For example, judging whether inventories are properly valued at the lower of cost or market requires the auditor to understand and evaluate how the enterprise determined cost. This may be particularly difficult if sophisticated last-in, first-out costing methods are used or if a standard cost system is employed, to cite just two examples. That same inventory valuation assertion also requires the auditor to evaluate how management determined replacement cost, estimated selling price, and normal profit margins in the course of ascertaining "market" value. Finally, the auditor must evaluate whether provisions for losses on obsolete and slow-moving items are adequate. Conclusive evidence is rarely available to support these judgments, but they are crucial to an audit of financial statements.

The definition of auditing specifies that the process of obtaining and evaluating evidence must be carried out objectively. Objectivity in the process of obtaining and evaluating evidence is not the same as objectivity of the evidence itself. Objectivity of evidence relates to how useful the evidence will be in achieving the auditor's purpose. Objectivity of the process refers to the auditor's ability to maintain an impartial attitude in selecting and evaluating evidence. That impartial attitude is part of the concept of auditor independence.

Systematic Process. The word "systematic" implies that planning the audit and formulating an audit strategy are important parts of the audit process. Moreover, evidence should be selected and evaluated in relation to specific audit objectives, many of which are interrelated. This requires the auditor to make many decisions in the course of planning and performing an audit.

A Statement of Basic Auditing Concepts notes that the phrase "systematic process" suggests that "auditing is based, in part at least, on the discipline and philosophy of scientific method" (p. 2). Most auditors, however, do not think of themselves as applying the scientific method, probably because the term implies a more highly structured method of inquiry than is possible or even desirable in most audits. Certainly an audit should be founded on a carefully conceived audit strategy, but that strategy is subject to extensive modification during an audit as the auditor obtains and evaluates evidence relating to specific assertions about the various, often interrelated components of financial statements.

Communicating the Results to Interested Users. The end and aim of all audits is a report that communicates to the reader the degree to which the client's assertions meet the agreed-upon criteria. In an audit of financial statements, the communication, called an auditor's report, states the conclusions reached on whether or not the financial statements conform to generally accepted accounting principles. (This kind of report is discussed briefly later in this chapter and at length in Chapter 18.) In other types of audits, the auditor similarly reports the findings to interested parties.

Relationship Between Accounting and Auditing. It should be clear from the definition of auditing and the references to various types of possible audits that there *need not* be any relationship between auditing and accounting. Virtually any information that is quantifiable and verifiable can be audited, as long as the auditor and the auditee agree on the criteria to be used as the basis for determining the degree of correspondence. For example, an auditor for the United States General Accounting Office may be requested to audit the effectiveness of a particular airplane. The criteria for measuring effectiveness, which will have to be agreed on before the audit takes place, will most likely be concerned with speed, acceleration, cruising altitude, number and type of armaments, and so on. None of these criteria involve accounting data.

The subject matter of most audits, however, and all financial audits, is usually accounting data that is contained in the books, records, and financial statements of the audited entity. The assertions about economic actions and events that the auditor is concerned with are often assertions about accounting transactions and the resulting account balances. The established criteria that accounting assertions are ordinarily measured by are generally accepted accounting principles. Thus, while an accountant need not be knowledgeable about auditing, an auditor must be knowledgeable about accounting. The accounting process creates financial statements and other useful information; auditing generally does not create accounting data or other information. Rather, auditing enhances the value of the information created by the accounting process by critically evaluating that information and communicating the resulting opinion to interested parties.

ORIGINS AND EARLY HISTORY OF AUDITING[1]

Historians believe that record keeping originated about 4000 B.C., when ancient civilizations in the Near East began to establish organized governments

[1]Much of the material in this section is based on Richard Brown, *A History of Accounting and Accountants* (Edinburgh: T. C. and E. C. Jack, 1905); and Michael Chatfield, *A History of Accounting Thought*, rev. ed. (Huntington, NY: Robert E. Kreiger Publishing Company, 1977).

and businesses. From the beginning, governments were concerned with accounting for receipts and disbursements and collecting taxes. An integral part of this concern was establishing controls, including audits, to reduce errors and fraud on the part of incompetent or dishonest officials. Several "modern" forms of internal control are described in the Bible, which is generally viewed as covering the period between 1800 B.C. and A.D. 95, and the explanation of the logic behind instituting controls—that if employees have an opportunity to steal they may take advantage of it—reflects the same professional skepticism expected of auditors today. Specifically, the Bible discusses dual custody of assets, the need for competent and honest employees, restricted access, and segregation of duties.

The government accounting system of the Zhao dynasty (1122–256 B.C.) in China included an elaborate budgetary process and audits of all government departments. In fifth-century B.C. Athens, the popular Assembly controlled the receipt and disbursement of public funds. The public finance system included government auditors who examined the records of all officeholders at the expiration of their terms. In the private sector, managers of estates conducted audits of the accounts. Public finance in the Roman Republic was under control of the Senate, and public accounts were examined by a staff of auditors supervised by the treasurer. The Romans maintained segregation of duties between the officials who authorized taxes and expenditures and those who handled receipts and payments, and, like the Greeks, devised an elaborate system of checks and counterchecks.

The oldest surviving accounting records and references to audits in English-speaking countries are those of the Exchequers of England and Scotland, which date back to 1130. There are references to auditors and auditing in the thirteenth century in both England and Italy, and a French work on estate management written in the same century recommends an annual audit of the accounts. The City of London was audited at least as early as the 1200s, and in the early fourteenth century auditors were among the elected officials. From that time on, there is extensive evidence that the value of audits was widely recognized and that the accounts of municipalities, private landholdings, and craft guilds were audited regularly.

The early audits in Great Britain were of two types. Audits of cities and towns were held publicly before the governing officials and citizens and consisted of the auditors' hearing the accounts[2] read by the treasurer. Similarly, audits of guilds were heard before the membership. By the middle of the sixteenth century, auditors of cities often annotated the accounts with phrases such as "heard by the auditors undersigned." Reporting by auditors can be traced to this preliminary form of "audit certificate." The second type of audit involved a detailed examination of the "charge and discharge" accounts

[2]The practice of "hearing the accounts," which originated in the days when few people could read, continued until the seventeenth century. The word "audit," in fact, derives from the Latin word for a hearing.

maintained by the financial officers of large manors, followed by a "declaration of audit," that is, an oral report before the lord of the manor and the council. Typically, the auditor was a member of the manorial council, and thus was the precursor of the modern internal auditor.

Both types of audits performed in Great Britain before the seventeenth century were directed primarily at ensuring the accountability of funds entrusted to public or private officials. Those audits were not designed to test the quality of the accounts, except insofar as inaccuracies might point to the existence of fraud. The economic changes between 1600 and 1800—which saw the growth of towns in place of manors, and factories in place of guilds, and the beginning of widespread commerce—introduced new accounting concerns. These focused on the ownership of property and the calculation of profits and losses in a business sense. Auditing also began to evolve from a listening process to a close examination of written records and testing of supporting evidence. At the end of the seventeenth century, the first law was enacted (in Scotland) prohibiting certain officials from serving as auditors of a town, thus introducing the modern notion of auditor independence to the Western world.

Despite these advances in auditing practices, it was not until well into the nineteenth century—which brought the construction of railways and the growth of insurance companies, banks, and other joint-stock companies—that the professional auditor became an important part of the business scene. The railroad industry in the United States was among the first employers of internal auditors. By the latter part of the nineteenth century, so-called traveling auditors visited widely dispersed ticket agencies to evaluate management's accountability for assets and its reporting systems.

HISTORICAL DEVELOPMENT OF EXTERNAL AUDITING IN THE UNITED STATES[3]

Independent audits in the United States up to the turn of the twentieth century were modeled on British practices. The audit work consisted of detailed scrutinies of clerical data relating to the balance sheet. Robert H. Montgomery, in the first edition of this book, called the early American audits "bookkeeper audits," and he estimated that three quarters of the audit time was spent on footings and postings. Since there were no statutory requirements for audits in America, and since most audits were performed by auditors from Britain who were sent by British investors in U.S. companies, the profession grew slowly at first. Only a small amount of auditing literature was published in the United States prior to the 1900s. In 1905 and again in 1909, Montgomery published American editions of *Auditing: A Practical Manual for Auditors*,

[3]A more comprehensive history of American auditing appears in C. A. Moyer, "Early Developments in American Auditing," *The Accounting Review* (January 1951), pp. 3–8.

written by Lawrence R. Dicksee in England, and in 1912, recognizing the departures of U.S. practice from the British, he wrote the first American auditing book, *Auditing: Theory and Practice,* subsequently to be retitled *Montgomery's Auditing*.

Gradually, American audits evolved into "test audits" as procedures were adapted to rapidly expanding American business, which considered British-style detailed checking of footings and postings too time-consuming and expensive. In addition to increased use of testing methods, auditors began to obtain evidence from outside clients' records as a means of examining transactions. Because of investors' concerns, they began to pay closer attention to the valuations of assets and liabilities. These developments reflected a broadening of audit objectives beyond checking clerical accuracy. Independent auditing in the modern sense was emerging in the United States, motivated largely by the demands of creditors, especially banks, for reliable financial information on which to base credit decisions.

Financial statement users in the early years of this century continued to focus on the balance sheet as the primary indicator of a company's health, and, for the most part, auditors emphasized the balance sheet in their work. The first U.S. authoritative auditing pronouncement, prepared by the American Institute of Accountants (now the American Institute of Certified Public Accountants [AICPA]) at the request of the Federal Trade Commission, was published in 1917 and referred to "balance-sheet audits." A revised pamphlet was published in 1929, under the title "Verification of Financial Statements." Although the pamphlet still emphasized the balance sheet audit, it discussed income statement accounts in detail, thus reflecting the growing interest in results of operations. The 1929 pamphlet also covered reporting practices and stressed reliance on internal controls. The 1936 edition of the pamphlet was entitled "Examination of Financial Statements by Independent Public Accountants," and was influenced by a number of significant events of the previous few years, most notably the AICPA's collaboration with the New York Stock Exchange in an effort to improve reporting standards and the enactment of the Securities Act of 1933 and the Securities Exchange Act of 1934, which required listed companies to file audited financial statements.

The modern era of audit standard-setting began in 1939, when the AICPA created the Committee on Auditing Procedure and that committee issued the first Statement on Auditing Procedure (SAP). Fifty-four SAPs were issued through 1972, at which time the name of the committee was changed to the Auditing Standards Executive Committee (later renamed the Auditing Standards Board), which codified all the SAPs in Statement on Auditing Standards (SAS) No. 1; that series of statements continues to the present.

The 1970s and 1980s were marked by heightened public interest in the responsibilities and performance of auditors. The period was marked by a succession of alleged audit failures, followed by congressional hearings, the creation of special commissions to determine the role and responsibilities of auditors, the conclusion that a gap existed between the public's perception of what an audit was supposed to do and the limitations of the actual audit process, and heightened activity by the Auditing Standards Board to help close that gap.

THE ROLE OF INDEPENDENT AUDITS

The social purpose that independent audits serve today has been concisely stated by the Financial Accounting Standards Board in Statement of Financial Accounting Concepts No. 1, *Objectives of Financial Reporting by Business Enterprises*, as follows:

> The effectiveness of individuals, enterprises, markets, and government in allocating scarce resources among competing uses is enhanced if those who make economic decisions have information that reflects the relative standing and performance of business enterprises to assist them in evaluating alternative courses of action and the expected returns, costs, and risks of each. . . . Independent auditors commonly examine or review financial statements and perhaps other information, and both those who provide and those who use that information often view an independent auditor's opinion as enhancing the reliability or credibility of the information. (para. 16)

Users of audited financial information are often actual or potential investors and creditors. Members of the public at large generally are also interested in audited financial information, however, because their present and future income and wealth may also depend on reliable financial information. Accordingly, this book will refer to "the public" as a way of acknowledging the large number of individuals who are served by reliable financial reporting, in addition to those who use financial information to make investing and lending decisions.

By enhancing the credibility of financial information, an audit reduces the "information risk" to financial statement users. "Information risk" is the risk that information, in this case information contained in financial reports, is incorrect. Information risk is distinguishable from business risk, which is the risk that, even with correct information, the return on an investment will be less than expected because of some unforeseen circumstance or event. Investors and lenders demand, and the "market" pays, a return for assuming risk. Reducing the information risk in financial information reduces the risk premium that must be paid by an enterprise. This lowers the audited enterprise's cost of capital, thereby promoting the efficient allocation of scarce economic resources among competing uses. Of course, audits are not the only way to reduce information risk. Accounting standard-setting bodies in both the public sector (the Securities and Exchange Commission) and the private sector (the Financial Accounting Standards Board and the Governmental Accounting Standards Board) promote uniformity of accounting measurement principles and full disclosure of relevant financial information.

There has been considerable research in recent years on the value of annual financial statements to investment and credit decision makers. That research, with its focus on the "efficient market hypothesis," seems to suggest that annual financial statements have little effect on security prices. Information is available to investors in the financial press and from investment analysts and is acted on before the annual financial statements are published. There is widespread agreement, however, that *audited* financial statements do have "information content," that is, they contain *new* information merely by virtue of their having been audited. The Commission on Auditors' Responsibilities, also known as the Cohen Commission, after its chairman, Manuel C. Cohen, concluded that "audited financial statements provide a means of confirming or correcting the information received earlier by the market. In effect, the audited statements help to assure the efficiency of the market by limiting the life of inaccurate information or by deterring its dissemination."[4]

In addition to the credibility dimension, the AAA Committee on Basic Auditing Concepts considered the control dimension as another aspect of the value an audit adds to financial information.

> The addition of the audit function serves as a *control* over the quality of information because:
>
> 1. It provides an independent check on the accounting information against established criteria presumably reflecting the user's needs and desires.
> 2. It motivates the preparer of the information to carry out the accounting process under his control in a way that conforms to the user's criteria since he (the preparer) knows his efforts will be subjected to independent, expert review.[5]

The motivational aspect of an audit has long been recognized: Knowing that an audit will be performed is a strong deterrent to disseminating erroneous information.

Objectives of Audits of Financial Statements. In contrast to the social role filled by an audit of financial statements, the AICPA has stated, in SAS No. 1, *Codification of Auditing Standards and Procedures*, the immediate objective of an audit, as follows:

> The objective of the ordinary audit of financial statements by the independent auditor is the expression of an opinion on the fairness with which they present . . . , in all material respects, financial position, results of operations, and its cash flows in conformity with generally accepted accounting principles. (para. 110.01)

Thus, meeting the needs of the people who require an entity to present audited financial statements can be thought of as the immediate objective of an audit.

[4]*Report, Conclusions, and Recommendations*, 1978, p. 6.

[5]*A Statement of Basic Auditing Concepts*, 1973, p. 13.

Several groups or organizations have the power or authority to require that specific entities be audited. (The authors are not suggesting that without those specific requirements audits would not occur.) Those groups include creditors and potential creditors, the SEC and the various stock exchanges acting on behalf of actual and potential investors, and government agencies that require nonbusiness organizations to file audited financial statements.

Lending institutions, such as banks and insurance companies, frequently want audited financial statements of borrowers and prospective borrowers. Other creditors, such as vendors, may request audited financial statements to help them make credit and lending decisions. All of those organizations may want audited financial statements throughout the life of the credit or loan agreement. To a great extent, audits are performed because lenders and creditors demand them. In addition, the Securities Act of 1933 and the Securities Exchange Act of 1934 require that companies (with several exceptions) that issue securities to the public or seek to have their securities publicly traded on the various securities exchanges and in the securities market must file audited financial statements with the SEC. Since 1933, the New York Stock Exchange has required independently audited financial statements to be filed with listing applications and to be published annually after a security has been listed for trading on the exchange.

An additional objective of financial statement audits is to provide the client with information about its internal control structure. Auditors are required to inform the audit committee (or its equivalent) about significant deficiencies in the design or operation of the internal control structure that come to their attention in the course of an audit. In practice, auditors often extend that communication to include less significant deficiencies as well, along with suggestions for improving the internal control structure. The latter communication is ordinarily in writing, although it is customary to review its contents with management before the document, known as either a "management letter" or an "internal control letter," is finalized. The management letter is provided to the client as a service and is an important by-product or secondary objective of an audit. Performing an audit also gives the auditor substantial knowledge of the client's business and financial operations. That knowledge often enables the auditor to provide other, nonaudit services, such as tax planning advice and recommendations on the financial statement effects of alternative acceptable accounting principles.

Expectations of Users of Financial Information. The National Commission on Fraudulent Financial Reporting, also known as the Treadway Commission, after its chairman, James C. Treadway, Jr., stated that

> The financial statements are first and foremost the responsibility of the management of the reporting entity. But the independent public accountant plays a crucial role in the financial reporting process.
>
> Users of financial statements expect auditors to bring to the reporting process technical competence, integrity, independence, and objectivity. Users also expect

> auditors to search for and detect material misstatements, whether intentional or unintentional, and to prevent the issuance of misleading financial statements.[6]

Recent survey research in Canada indicates, however, that

> The public at large and even some quite sophisticated members of the financial community have only a vague understanding of the responsibilities undertaken and work done by the auditor. To the public it is the end result, the financial disclosure, that is important. The auditor is quite likely to be the first to be blamed for errors or inadequacies in financial disclosure almost without regard to his or her audit responsibility.[7]

The Canadian survey results parallel those of earlier surveys taken in the United States and other countries, and are confirmed by views expressed in Congress, in the media, and in the 1987 report of the Treadway Commission.

Inaccurate or misleading financial reporting happens in one of two ways. First, financial statements or other financial information may be misstated unintentionally because of errors in processing or recording transactions (such as failure to record an authorized sale that actually took place) or because of incorrect judgments in interpreting facts or presenting them in conformity with GAAP. For example, management may truly believe a particular lease is an operating lease when, in fact, under GAAP it should be classified as a capital lease.

Second, the financial reporting may be deficient because of deliberate financial statement misrepresentations by management or because assets have been stolen or otherwise misappropriated and the loss not properly shown in the financial statements. Examples of these types of fraud are, respectively, the deliberate recording of sales that never occurred, and the undiscovered theft of customers' remittances.

The public's concern about being misinformed by financial statements stems from an awareness of the inherent potential conflict of interest between preparers and users of financial statements. This is not to say that there is or must be a conflict of interest; nor does it suggest that managements are dishonest. It merely suggests that preparers may have certain biases in preparing financial information, as do those who use the information. Audits have a restraining influence in that auditors serve as independent third-party intermediaries between preparers and users of financial information.

Addressing User Expectations. In performing audits aimed at meeting financial statement users' expectations, independent auditors perform two functions. One of them is serving as an expert gatherer and evaluator of evidence to

[6] *Report of the National Commission on Fraudulent Financial Reporting* (Treadway Commission), 1987, p. 49.

[7] *Report of the Commission to Study the Public's Expectations of Audits* (Macdonald Commission) (Toronto: Canadian Institute of Chartered Accountants, 1988), p. 11.

corroborate the completeness, genuineness, and arithmetical accuracy of the information presented in the financial statements. For example, the item "accounts receivable—trade" shown in a balance sheet implies that the accounts receivable exist, that the enterprise owns them, and that all existing and owned trade accounts receivable are included in the total. It also implies that the computations behind the amount shown are mechanically accurate—that is, the arithmetic involved in preparing customer invoices, posting the invoice amounts to individual customer accounts, and summarizing the individual accounts was done correctly—and that the effects of transactions with non-trade debtors (e.g., enterprise officers and other related parties) have not been included. An auditor will obtain and evaluate evidence to corroborate those assertions.

The auditor's other function involves management's assertions concerning financial statement disclosures and valuations in conformity with generally accepted accounting principles. To make the financial statements useful or, at a minimum, ensure that they are not misleading, certain disclosures about the accounts receivable may be necessary. Also, generally accepted accounting principles require that accounts receivable be valued net of appropriate allowances, such as for uncollectible accounts and returns. Deciding what to disclose and estimating the necessary allowances require the financial statement preparer to exercise considerable judgment. An integral part of the auditor's function is to interpret the facts supporting the preparer's judgments and evaluate the judgments made. To do this, the auditor must have a thorough understanding of the client's business as well as of generally accepted accounting principles.

Over the years, and particularly in the last two decades, the evidence-gathering function has become less important and the interpreting/evaluating function more so. This is not to suggest that the former is unimportant or that it is not time-consuming, but merely that the more judgmental function has taken on greater significance. In part, this has resulted from management's increasing success in developing internal control structures that ensure mechanically correct accounting information. Auditors often find it more efficient to test the client's internal control structure to obtain evidence that it is designed and operating effectively than to test the output of the accounting system. Another reason for this change in audit emphasis is the proliferation of complex and innovative transactions and the need to evaluate how management has chosen to account for them. Still another reason is the increase in both the number and level of specificity of accounting standards, especially disclosure requirements, in recent years. These all demand increased time and effort from the auditor to obtain the facts defining the underlying substance—rather than merely the legal form—of the transactions and evaluate the judgments management made in accounting for them.

The Limitations of Auditing. No audit provides complete assurance that the financial statements are free from material misstatement. Errors can exist, because of either incorrect processing of accounting data or incorrect judgments in selecting and applying accounting principles, and not be found even though the audit was performed according to generally accepted auditing standards. As the Cohen Commission noted,

> Audited financial statements cannot be perfectly accurate, in part because of the ambiguity of the accounting concepts they reflect. . . . [Also,] accounting results—the financial statements—cannot be more accurate and reliable than the underlying accounting measurement methods permit. For example, no one, including accountants, can foresee the results of many uncertain future events. To the extent that the accuracy of an accounting presentation is dependent on an unpredictable future event, the accounting presentation will be inaccurate. The *audited* accounting presentation can be no more accurate, for the auditor cannot add certainty where it does not exist.[8]

Moreover, accounting measurement principles frequently provide more than one way to account for a given transaction or event. For example, there are several acceptable ways of accounting for the flow of inventory costs through an enterprise and for the depreciation of tangible assets. Neither the authoritative accounting literature nor logic supports one alternative over another. This flexibility of generally accepted accounting principles allows enterprises to influence the financial information they present. Also, reasonable financial statement preparers and auditors can disagree about the interpretation and application of accounting principles.

In addition to limitations imposed by the existing accounting framework, there are limitations imposed by management's decisions about the accounting and control procedures to use in processing transactions. Management makes decisions, based largely on weighing costs and benefits, about the design of its internal control structure. No cost-effective control structure can provide absolute assurance that management's financial reporting objectives will be met with 100 percent accuracy. Similarly, the audit process itself and auditing technology limit the assurance that can be attained from an audit. Ideally, an auditor would like to have sufficient firsthand evidence to provide absolute assurance about every assertion implicit in a set of financial statements, but that is usually impracticable if not impossible. For one thing, even if that goal could be achieved, it would probably not be worth the cost, to either the client or the financial statement user. Accordingly, in corroborating an assertion about an account balance or a class of transactions, the auditor will often examine less than 100 percent of the items involved. Moreover, the auditor cannot audit the results of events and transactions that were never recorded. If control procedures to ensure the completeness of processing and recording data are nonexistent or ineffective, it may be impossible to audit some aspects of the financial statements or even the statements as a whole. In addition, the need for judgment and the fact that much of the evidence available to the

[8] *Report, Conclusions, and Recommendations*, *op. cit.*, p. 7.

auditor is persuasive, rather than conclusive, preclude the auditor from attaining absolute assurance.

Generally accepted auditing standards recognize these limitations by requiring only that the auditor obtain sufficient evidence to provide a reasonable basis for forming an opinion on the financial statements. The auditor's standard report acknowledges this by stating that auditing standards "require that we plan and perform the audit to obtain reasonable assurance about whether the financial statements are free of material misstatements."

THE EXPECTATION GAP—AN ONGOING CONCERN

The limitations of auditing are generally well known to auditors, but not to most users of audited financial information. In addition, the public probably perceives the quality of auditor performance as lower than it actually is, because of the mistaken assumption that fraudulent financial reporting (and, by implication, an audit failure) is involved whenever there is a business failure. As a result, the public's expectations for audits greatly exceed its perception of auditors' performance, thereby creating what has come to be called the expectation gap.

The 1988 Report of the Commission to Study the Public's Expectations of Audits (Macdonald Commission) illustrated the expectation gap, its components, and the conceptual means of resolving it, as shown in Figure 1.1. The shaded horizontal line represents the full gap possible between the highest expectations from audits (point A) to public perceptions of what audits actually provide (point E). Point C represents auditor performance and financial information quality called for by present standards. The line segment A to C (labeled the "Standards Gap") represents public expectations that go beyond existing auditing and accounting standards. The line segment C to E (labeled the "Performance Gap") represents public perceptions that auditor performance or audited financial information falls short of what is required by existing standards.

The Macdonald Commission Report notes that

> The emphasis in this diagram [Figure 1.1] is on public expectations and public perceptions. Those expectations may or may not be reasonable, and those perceptions may or may not be realistic. An unrealistic expectation that is disappointed, or an erroneous perception of performance, can be just as damaging to the public's trust in auditors and audited information as real shortcomings in auditing and accounting standards or performance. It is, nevertheless, important to appraise the realism of public expectations and perceptions when the profession seeks remedies to the expectation gap. If the public has reasonable expectations not met by existing professional standards (line segment B to C) or the profession's performance falls short of its standards (line segment C to D), then it can and should act to improve standards or improve performance. On the

Figure 1.1 Components of the Expectation Gap

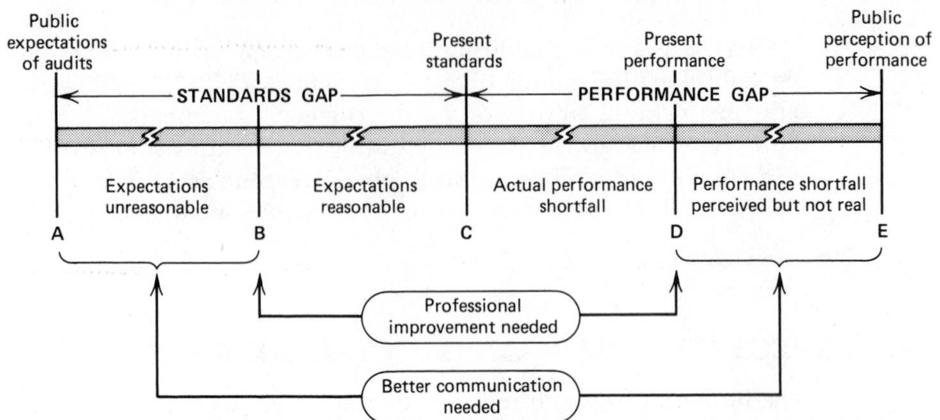

Source: Reprinted, with permission, from *Report of the Commission to Study the Public's Expectations of Audits*, The Canadian Institute of Chartered Accountants, Toronto, 1988, p. 6.

> other hand, if the problem is that the public's expectations are unreasonable (line segment A to B) or its perceptions of performance are mistaken (line segment D to E), then the logical course is to attempt to improve public understanding. Should that not be feasible, the profession must be prepared to cope with the consequences.[9]

The Commission also recognized that the figure "does not illustrate separately expectation gaps related to the quality of work the auditor does, which is the subject of auditing standards, and gaps related to the quality of financial information with which the auditor is associated, which is the subject of accounting standards." (The Canadian Institute of Chartered Accountants is responsible for developing both authoritative accounting and auditing standards. In the United States, the Financial Accounting Standards Board and the Governmental Accounting Standards Board are the private-sector bodies responsible for developing authoritative accounting standards, while the Auditing Standards Board is responsible for developing authoritative auditing standards.)

Efforts have been made to reduce the actual performance shortfall. This book details, particularly in Chapters 3 and 4, what steps the auditing profession in the United States has taken to maintain the level of audit quality, and what sanctions are imposed when audit failures do occur. In 1988, the Auditing Standards Board issued nine new authoritative auditing pronouncements designed to narrow the expectation gap by raising performance and reporting standards. Those "standards gap" pronouncements, as well as others in various stages of development, are discussed throughout the book, starting in Chapter 4.

[9]*Report of the Commission to Study the Public's Expectations of Audits, op. cit.*, pp. 6–7.

AN OVERVIEW OF AN AUDIT OF FINANCIAL STATEMENTS

An audit is based on a single premise: The auditor's objective is to understand the subject matter under audit in sufficient detail and depth to express an informed opinion on it. Every step in the audit process should enhance that understanding. The process of performing a financial statement audit is expanded on throughout this book. The steps in that process are described briefly in this section and summarized in Figure 1.2.

1. Obtain (or, for a continuing client, update) and document information about the client and its control structure and consider how that information may affect the audit testing plan.

This step consists, among other things, of learning about the client's business and matters affecting the business or the industry in which it operates, such as the business environment and legal constraints, and about the internal control structure—the control environment and management and accounting policies, practices, and methods; the accounting system; and significant control procedures. The auditor obtains that information through review of prior-year working papers and research in business and professional publications and publications of the client enterprise, such as annual reports and news releases; through interviews of knowledgeable client, audit firm, and other personnel; by plant and office tours; by reviewing the client's procedures and policy manuals; by reading the minutes of meetings of the board of directors and the stockholders; and by studying and comparing relationships among various financial and operational data.

The auditor obtains (or updates) an understanding of the client's control structure mainly through observing and inquiring of client personnel, referring to relevant policy and procedures manuals, and inspecting books, records, forms, and reports. In obtaining the understanding of the control structure, the auditor identifies the critical points in the accounting system where significant errors or irregularities could occur and determines whether policies and procedures to prevent or detect such errors or irregularities have been designed and placed in operation at those critical points.

The information obtained (or updated) by the auditor is used to make preliminary judgments about materiality, assess the risk that certain management assertions may be materially misstated, and consider where it may be appropriate to seek evidence from tests of the client's control structure policies and procedures to reduce the assurance needed from tests of account balances. Sometimes the auditor tests certain policies and procedures concurrently with obtaining an understanding of their design.

2. Assess the risk that the financial statements may contain material misstatements and, based on the assessment, develop an effective and efficient audit testing plan.

Figure 1.2 Summary of the Audit Process for Audits of Financial Statements

1. *Information-Gathering Phase:*
   - Obtain (or update) and document information about the client and related risk factors.
   - Understand and document principal features of the client's internal control structure.

2. *Planning Phase:*
   - Make preliminary materiality judgments and assess the risk that various management assertions may be materially misstated.
   - Determine whether to test the effectiveness of control structure policies and procedures in order to reduce the assurance needed from tests of account balances.
   - Select and document the appropriate audit strategy for each account balance or group of account balances.

3. *Performance Phase:*
   - Obtain, evaluate, and document evidence to corroborate whether the management assertions embodied in account balances and financial statement disclosures are reasonable.
   - Revise audit strategy as appropriate.

4. *Reporting Phase:*
   - Prepare auditor's report on financial statements.
   - Prepare communication on the internal control structure.

An effective audit provides the auditor with the reasonable assurance required under generally accepted auditing standards for the purpose of expressing an opinion on financial statements. The auditor's objective is to limit to an appropriately low level the risk that he or she may unknowingly issue an unqualified opinion when the financial statements are materially misstated. The audit should also be designed to provide the auditor with the desired assurance most efficiently, that is, at the lowest practicable cost. Planning the audit to achieve those ends requires the auditor to assess the risk of material misstatement associated with each of management's assertions and then choose an audit strategy that is effective in light of those risks and, among equally effective alternatives, the most efficient. A key element in determining the audit strategy is the decision whether to test the effectiveness of internal control structure policies and procedures in order to reduce the scope of tests of account balances. Audit planning is not confined solely to the early stages of an audit, but is an ongoing process that may result in changes to the audit strategy as additional knowledge that warrants a reassessment of various risks is obtained in the course of the audit.

The audit testing plan specifies the nature, timing, and extent of auditing procedures to be carried out in obtaining and evaluating the audit evidence that forms the basis for expressing an opinion on financial statements. The nature of auditing procedures refers to the kinds of work the auditor performs to obtain and evaluate evidence—such as confirming balances due from customers; timing refers to when in the audit the evidence is gathered—either before the end of the client's accounting year or after year-end; the extent of auditing procedures refers to how much of any kind of work—for example, the number of customers' accounts to be confirmed—the auditor performs for the purpose of formulating a judgment about each management assertion embodied in the financial statements.

3. Obtain, evaluate, and document sufficient competent evidence to corroborate whether the management assertions embodied in individual account balances and in the financial statements as a whole, including the disclosures, are reasonable.

That evidence consists of information derived from the auditor's risk assessments, including evidence from testing the client's internal control structure, and information underlying the auditor's conclusions about the reasonableness of management's assertions embodied in specific account balances. In the course of obtaining and evaluating evidence regarding the client's account balances and the effectiveness of its internal control structure, the auditor may find that the audit strategy needs to be revised. Auditing procedures are interrelated; the results of tests of the client's internal control structure provide a basis for assessing the risk that account balances may be materially misstated, and obtaining and evaluating evidence about account balances may reveal deficiencies in the client's internal control structure. It is only after all of the steps in the audit have been completed that the auditor can reach a conclusion regarding the opinion that should be expressed on the financial statements as a whole. Therefore, tentative conclusions reached during the earlier stages of an audit may have to be revised, and the audit strategy initially contemplated or preliminary judgments about materiality may have to be changed, based on the results of subsequent auditing procedures.

4. Formulate and prepare the auditor's report and communicate deficiencies in the internal control structure to the client.

This is the reporting phase of an audit, and it results in two reports: the auditor's report on the financial statements, discussed later in this chapter, and a communication to management or the audit committee of the board of directors (or both) about the deficiencies in the client's internal control structure. Although the auditor's report is the primary objective of an audit, the communication about control structure deficiencies provides a useful and relatively inexpensive client service, which auditors are particularly well qualified to perform after developing an understanding of the client's business and control structure for audit purposes. Depending on the significance of the deficiencies the auditor finds in the course of the audit, that communication may be required by professional auditing standards.

The auditor must apply significant judgment throughout the audit process just described. How the interrelationships among auditing procedures require the auditor to make certain decisions has already been explained. The need for other decisions arises at every stage of the audit. All of these decisions require the exercise of judgment; they cannot be made by rote or by formula.

AUDIT REPORTS

The auditor's report is discussed briefly in this section; it is considered in greater detail in Chapter 18. The discussion here is restricted to the level of detail needed to understand the document that is the end result of an audit of financial statements.

The auditor's report that appears in Figure 1.3 indicates the wording of the standard "short form" report. The opening paragraph of the report identifies the financial statements that were audited and states that management is responsible for them. Since an annual report or prospectus contains much more than the financial statements, the reader must be told specifically what has been audited (the financial statements and the related notes that are, as stated on each page of the body of the financial statements, an "integral part of the financial statements") and what, by implication, has not been audited, such as the letter from the president and chairman of the board, financial ratios, and information about stock prices. The second, or scope, paragraph describes the auditor's basis for forming the opinion on the financial statements. It also includes a thumbnail sketch of what an audit entails.

The opinion paragraph of the auditor's report—usually the third, and final, paragraph—states the auditor's conclusions reached from the work performed. The auditor's opinion represents a judgment made after evaluating evidence about the assertions implicit in the financial statements; the phrase "in our opinion" is intended to convey this element of judgment, as opposed to a statement of fact. (As discussed later, in some cases the auditor may be unable to form an opinion.) The conclusion the auditor reaches in most audits of financial statements, and in the example presented, is that the financial statements "present fairly, in all material respects, . . . in conformity with generally accepted accounting principles." The opinion illustrated here is called an unqualified opinion—that is, it is not qualified by any exceptions.

An independent auditor will issue a standard, unqualified, three-paragraph report if

Figure 1.3 Auditor's Standard Report

Independent Auditor's Report

To the Board of Directors and Stockholders of X Company:

We have audited the accompanying balance sheets of X Company as of December 31, 19X2 and 19X1, and the related statements of income, retained earnings, and cash flows for the years then ended. These financial statements are the responsibility of the Company's management. Our responsibility is to express an opinion on these financial statements based on our audits.

We conducted our audits in accordance with generally accepted auditing standards. Those standards require that we plan and perform the audit to obtain reasonable assurance about whether the financial statements are free of material misstatement. An audit includes examining, on a test basis, evidence supporting the amounts and disclosures in the financial statements. An audit also includes assessing the accounting principles used and significant estimates made by management, as well as evaluating the overall financial statement presentation. We believe that our audits provide a reasonable basis for our opinion.

In our opinion, the financial statements referred to above present fairly, in all material respects, the financial position of X Company as of [at] December 31, 19X2 and 19X1, and the results of its operations and its cash flows for the years then ended in conformity with generally accepted accounting principles.

[Signature]
[Address]
[Date]

1. The audit was conducted with due professional care by independent persons with adequate training and proficiency.
2. Sufficient evidence was obtained and evaluated to enable the auditor to conclude that the financial statements are presented fairly, in all material respects, in conformity with GAAP.
3. None of the conditions discussed below are present that would require that explanatory language be added after the third paragraph.

If those circumstances are not present, a standard, three-paragraph, unqualified report will not be issued. Other types of auditor's reports disclaim the ability to form an opinion, state that the financial statements are not presented fairly, in all material respects, in conformity with GAAP, or contain qualifying language. Such reports express disclaimers of opinion, adverse opinions, and qualified opinions, respectively. Also, explanatory language will be added to the standard, unqualified report if there is a material uncertainty affecting the financial statements or if GAAP have not been applied on a consistent basis.

Disclaimers of opinion state that the auditor does not express an opinion on the financial statements or any part of them. This form of report is used when the auditor is unable to obtain sufficient evidence to form an opinion on the financial statements, either because of restrictions imposed by the client or because of circumstances beyond either the client's or the auditor's control.

Adverse opinions state that the financial statements are not presented fairly in conformity with GAAP. Such an opinion is used when the auditor believes that inappropriate accounting principles have been applied or the disclosures in the notes to the financial statements are inadequate or otherwise misleading, and that the effect on the statements is so pervasive that, taken as a whole, they are misleading. Unlike a disclaimer of opinion, an adverse opinion is given only when the auditor has knowledge, after sufficient evidence has been evaluated, that the financial statements are not presented fairly in conformity with GAAP.

Qualified opinions state that "except for" the effect of a specified matter, the financial statements are presented fairly, in all material respects, in conformity with GAAP. A qualified opinion would be used in the following circumstances, provided that the auditor believed that the financial statements taken as a whole were otherwise presented fairly in conformity with GAAP:

1. There is a lack of sufficient competent evidence or there are restrictions on the scope of the audit that preclude expressing an unqualified opinion. (Example: In accordance with the terms of the engagement, the auditor did not examine records supporting the client's investment in a foreign company or its equity in that company's earnings.)
2. The financial statements contain a departure from GAAP, the effect of which is material. (Examples: The enterprise excluded from its balance sheet lease obligations that, to conform with GAAP, should have been classified as capital leases and capitalized; the enterprise declined to disclose the basis of valuing inventories or of depreciating plant and equipment.)

Explanatory language will be added at the end of an auditor's report containing an unqualified opinion if the financial statements are presented fairly in conformity with GAAP and either or both of the following conditions are present:

1. *Significant uncertainties* that affect the financial statements but are not susceptible to reasonable estimation have not been resolved as of the date of the auditor's report. (Example: A lawsuit against the enterprise is unresolved and the likelihood of an adverse resolution is greater than remote.)
2. There was a material *change in an accounting principle* or in the method of applying it between periods. (Example: During the current year, the

client changed from the last-in, first-out method to the first-in, first-out method for determining the cost of its inventories.)

The auditor's decision on whether to include explanatory language, or to issue a qualified opinion, a disclaimer of opinion, or an adverse opinion is grounded in materiality considerations that are discussed in Chapter 18.

Review Questions[10]

1–1. The terms accounting, auditing, and financial reporting are often mistakenly used interchangeably. Define and contrast these three terms.

1–2. Compare and contrast the responsibilities of enterprise management and of the auditor regarding financial statements.

1–3. What are some examples of established criteria against which assertions can be measured in various types of audits?

1–4. How do auditors communicate their results to interested users in financial audits? Give examples of interested users.

1–5. What are some of the limitations of a financial audit?

1–6. What are the four major types of reports that can be given under generally accepted auditing standards? Explain how they differ.

1–7. Nature, timing, and extent of audit tests and procedures are specified in the audit testing plan. What objectives does an audit testing plan seek to accomplish?

1–8. Obtaining and evaluating evidence is the essence of auditing. What does audit evidence consist of in a financial audit? What are some of the difficulties encountered in evaluating audit evidence?

1–9. In recent years the relative importance of the two aspects of auditing has shifted from the gathering of audit evidence to interpeting facts and evaluating accounting judgments. Why has this shift occurred?

1–10. What are four phases involved in every financial statement audit?

Discussion Questions

1–30. The following two statements are representative of attitudes and opinions sometimes encountered by CPAs in their professional practice:

1. Today's audit consists of test checking. This is a dangerous practice because test checking depends on the auditor's judgment, which may be defective. An audit can be relied on only if every transaction is verified.
2. Audits by CPAs are essentially negative and contribute to neither the gross

[10]See *Preface to College Version* for an explanation of the numbering system used for end-of-chapter questions and problems.

national product nor the general well-being of society. Auditors do not create; they merely check what someone else has done.

Required:

Evaluate each of the above statements and indicate

a. Areas of agreement with the statement, if any.
b. Areas of misconception, incompleteness, or fallacious reasoning included in the statement, if any.

Complete your discussion of each statement (both parts a and b) before going on to the next statement.

(AICPA adapted)

1–31. Many people believe that auditing is an exact science, using standard procedures that are applied by rote. Do you agree or disagree? State why.

1–32. Borgman, the sole owner of a small hardware business, has been told that the business should have financial statements reported on by an independent CPA. Borgman, having some bookkeeping experience, has personally prepared the company's financial statements and does not understand why such statements should be audited by a CPA. Borgman discussed the matter with Davies, a CPA, and asked Davies to explain why an audit is considered important.

Required:

a. Describe the objectives of an independent audit.
b. Identify the ways in which an independent audit may be beneficial to Borgman.

(AICPA adapted)

1–33. On completion of the audit of a client's financial statements, the CPA must either express an opinion or disclaim an opinion on the statements taken as a whole. The opinion may be unqualified, qualified, or adverse.

Required:

a. Under what general conditions may a CPA express an unqualified opinion on a set of financial statements?
b. Define and distinguish among (1) a qualified opinion, (2) an adverse opinion, and (3) a disclaimer of opinion on the statements taken as a whole.

(AICPA adapted)

1–34. A CPA's report on financial statements includes an opinion on whether the statements are presented in conformity with generally accepted accounting principles. In evaluating the general acceptability of an accounting principle, the CPA must determine whether the principle has substantial authoritative support.

Required:

a. Describe the procedure that the CPA should follow in forming an opinion on whether to accept an accounting principle proposed by a client for use in preparing the current year's financial statements. Assume that the principle has been consistently applied.

b. Cite primary sources and authorities that the CPA might consult in determining whether an accounting principle has substantial authoritative support. (A source is primary if it is sufficient evidence by itself to constitute substantial authoritative support.)
c. Cite secondary sources and authorities that the CPA might consult in determining whether an accounting principle has substantial authoritative support. (A source is secondary if it must be combined with one or more other secondary sources to constitute substantial authoritative support.)

(AICPA adapted)

AICPA Multiple Choice Questions

These questions are taken from the Auditing part of Uniform CPA Examinations. Choose the single most appropriate answer.

1-40. The essence of the attest function is to

a. Detect fraud.
b. Examine individual transactions so that the auditor may certify as to their validity.
c. Determine whether the client's financial statements are fairly stated.
d. Assure the consistent application of correct accounting procedures.

1-41. Which of the following is responsible for the fairness of the representations made in financial statements?

a. Client's management.
b. Independent auditor.
c. Audit committee.
d. AICPA

1-42. The first standard of reporting requires that "the report shall state whether the financial statements are presented in accordance with generally accepted accounting principles." This should be construed to require

a. A statement of fact by the auditor.
b. An opinion by the auditor.
c. An implied measure of fairness.
d. An objective measure of compliance.

Problems and Cases

1-60. On completion of all field work on September 23, 1990, the following "short form" report was rendered by Steven Turner to the directors of Sidco Corporation.

To the Directors of Sidco Corporation:

We have examined the balance sheet and the related statement of income and retained earnings of Sidco Corporation as of July 31, 1990. In accordance with your instructions, a complete audit was conducted.

In many respects, this was an unusual year for Sidco Corporation. The weakening of the economy in the early part of the year and the strike of plant employees in the summer of 1990 led to a decline in sales and net income. After making several tests of sales records, nothing came to our attention that would indicate that sales have not been properly recorded.

In our opinion, with the explanation given above, and with the exception of some minor errors that are considered immaterial, the aforementioned financial statements present fairly the financial position of Sidco Corporation at July 31, 1990, and the results of its operations for the year then ended, in conformity with pronouncements of the Accounting Principles Board and the Financial Accounting Standards Board applied consistently throughout the period.

Steven Turner, CPA
September 23, 1990

Required:

List and explain deficiencies and omissions in the auditor's report. The type of opinion (unqualified, qualified, adverse, or disclaimer) is of no consequence and need not be discussed.

Organize your answer by paragraph of the auditor's report.

(AICPA adapted)

2

The Organization and Structure of the Auditing Profession

Although the focus of this book is on financial audits, the definition of auditing is sufficiently broad to include other types of audits. This chapter describes financial, compliance, and performance audits, and relates them to the various groups of auditors who perform them. It also describes the typical organization of a firm of CPAs and outlines the major organizations of the auditing profession, the certification and licensing systems in effect, and the professional pronouncements issued by the various standard-setting bodies.

TYPES OF SERVICES

Auditors are often called on to express opinions on the reliability of information other than historical financial statements. Some of these services continue to be referred to as "audits," while others—particularly some of the newer ones—are called "attest engagements."

Financial Audits. In a financial audit, the auditor seeks evidence about assertions related mainly to financial information, usually contained in a set of financial statements or some component thereof. The established criteria that information is measured against are generally accepted accounting principles or some other specified basis of accounting (such as might be stipulated in a rental agreement). Generally, the information will be used by parties other than the management of the entity that prepared it. Sometimes, however, the information is intended to be used primarily by management for internal decision-making purposes. In that event, it may include nonfinancial as well as financial data. While financial audits are most often associated with independent auditors whose work results in an opinion on financial statements, both internal auditors and government auditors also perform financial audits, often in conjunction with compliance or performance audits.

Compliance Audits. Compliance audits are intended to determine whether an entity has complied with specified policies, procedures, laws, regulations, or contracts that affect operations or reports. Examples of compliance audits include auditing a tax return by an Internal Revenue Service agent, auditing components of financial statements to determine compliance with a bond indenture, auditing a researcher's expenditures under a government grant to determine compliance with the terms of the grant, and auditing an entity's hiring policies to determine whether the Equal Employment Opportunity Act has been complied with. As with all audits, a compliance audit requires established criteria (such as those contained in a law or regulation) to measure the relevant assertions against. Compliance audits are performed by independent auditors and by internal and government auditors (often as part of a performance audit).

If a policy, contract, law, or regulation has a direct and material effect on the entity's financial statements, determining the extent of compliance with it will usually be an integral part of a financial statement audit. For example, an auditor reviews an enterprise's conformity with the restrictive covenants in a long-term debt agreement to ascertain that a violation of the covenant has not made the entire bond issue due and payable at the lender's option, which might require that the debt be reclassified as a current liability. Independent auditors do not, however, plan their audits of financial statements to provide assurance about an enterprise's compliance with policies, contracts, laws, and regulations that do not have a direct and material effect on the financial statements.

Performance Audits. Performance audits, also referred to as operational audits, include economy and efficiency audits and program audits. *Government Auditing Standards: Standards for Audit of Governmental Organizations, Programs, Activities, and Functions*, issued by the U.S. General Accounting Office in 1988, defines those audits as follows:

> Economy and efficiency audits include determining (1) whether the entity is acquiring, protecting, and using its resources (such as personnel, property, and space) economically and efficiently, (2) the causes of inefficiencies or uneconomical practices, and (3) whether the entity has complied with laws and regulations concerning matters of economy and efficiency.
>
> Program audits include determining (1) the extent to which the desired results or benefits established by the legislature or other authorizing body are being achieved, (2) the effectiveness of organizations, programs, activities, or functions, and (3) whether the entity has complied with laws and regulations applicable to the program.

Using resources economically means achieving a specified output or performance level at the lowest possible cost. An enterprise that met or exceeded the specified level at the lowest cost would be using its resources economically. Using resources efficiently means attaining the highest possible output or performance level at a specified cost. If output or performance can be increased without incurring additional costs, the implication is that a more efficient use of resources is possible. The achievement of desired results or benefits refers to the extent to which a program meets objectives and goals that are proper, suitable, or relevant. Results that are consistent with established objectives and goals indicate that the program is being carried out effectively.

Objectives and goals may be established by federal or state legislatures or granting agencies or they may be set by management of an enterprise. As noted in Chapter 1, the subject matter of auditing usually is quantifiable information about economic actions and events. Some quantifiable objectives and goals may not relate to economic actions and events, however, which raises the question of whether their evaluation falls within the definition of auditing. For example, in an "audit" of program results in a state's prison system, program objectives and goals will almost surely not be stated in terms of economic actions or events; instead, they may be stated in terms of the number of prisoners rehabilitated and released, the number of repeat offenders, or the percentage of prison capacity utilized. While such program audits may at times stretch the definition of auditing, they are widely performed, particularly by government auditors, and are almost always referred to as audits.

Attest Engagements. An attest engagement is defined in Statement on Standards for Attestation Engagements, *Attestation Standards* (AT Section 100), as "one in which a practitioner is engaged to issue or does issue a written communication that expresses a conclusion about the reliability of a written assertion that is the responsibility of another party." The scope of services covered by this definition is similar, if not identical, to that in the American Accounting Association's definition of auditing, which was discussed in Chapter 1. Examples of attest services include testing and reporting on representations about the characteristics of computer software, investment performance statistics, internal control structures, prospective financial information, and historical occupancy data for hospitals.

The profession has not yet reached a consensus about which services should be called audits and which attest engagements. For the foreseeable future, however, it is clear that attest services related to historical financial statements will continue to be called audits.

TYPES OF AUDITORS

A popular classification of auditors uses three categories: independent, internal, and government.

Independent auditors are also referred to as external auditors, and frequently as CPAs, public accountants, or "outside" auditors. Independent auditors are never owners or employees of the organization that retains them to perform an audit (their client), although they receive a fee from the client for their services. Independent auditors perform financial statement audits to meet the needs of investors and creditors and the requirements of regulatory bodies like the Securities and Exchange Commission (SEC). The audits result in an opinion on whether the financial statements are fairly stated, in all material respects, in conformity with generally accepted accounting principles. Occasionally, independent auditors perform performance audits. Increasingly, they perform attest engagements.

Internal auditors are employed by the enterprise they audit. The Institute of Internal Auditors has defined internal auditing as "an independent appraisal function established within an organization to examine and evaluate its activities as a service to the organization. The objective of internal auditing is to assist members of the organization in the effective discharge of their responsibilities. . . . The internal auditing department is an integral part of the organization and functions under the policies established by management and the board [of directors]."[1] The primary function of internal auditors is to examine their organization's internal control structure and evaluate how adequate and effective it is. In performing that function, internal auditors often conduct performance (or operational) audits that are broadly designed to accomplish financial and compliance audit objectives as well.

The independence of internal auditors is different from that of independent (i.e., external) auditors. Internal auditors' independence comes from their organizational status—essentially, their function and to whom they report—and their objectivity. For external auditors, independence derives instead from the absence of any obligation to or financial interest in their client, its management, or its owners.

Government auditors are employed by agencies of federal, state, and local governments. When the audit is of the government agency or department that employs them, they function as internal auditors; when they audit recipients of government funds (including other government agencies), they act as external auditors. For example, auditors employed by the U.S. Department of Agriculture may audit the internal operations of that department; they may also audit the economy, efficiency, and program results of research funded by the Department of Agriculture but performed by others, such as colleges and universities. Most audits performed by government auditors are performance audits of economy, efficiency, and programs, which include determining whether the entity being audited has complied with laws and regulations concerning economy and efficiency as well as those applicable to the program. Some audits, such as those by the Internal Revenue Service, are performed almost exclusively for compliance purposes.

There are many different groups of government auditors; virtually every level of government and every government agency has its own auditors. One group in particular warrants further discussion—the General Accounting Office (GAO). A nonpolitical agency headed by the Comptroller General of the United States, it was created by and reports directly to Congress. The GAO has the authority to audit virtually every federal agency and expenditure. The GAO formulated the notion of and standards for economy, efficiency, and program audits, which are the major part of its activities.

As suggested by the foregoing discussion, the work performed by independent, internal, and government auditors is not mutually exclusive. The classification scheme used in this book is of necessity limited, and does not fully describe the three branches of the auditing profession. There is considerable overlap in the types of audits they perform, and all possess varying degrees of independence.

[1]*Standards for the Professional Practice of Internal Auditing.* The Institute of Internal Auditors, Inc., 1978, p. 1.

THE ORGANIZATION OF AN ACCOUNTING FIRM

Accounting firms range in size from an individual CPA in business as a sole practitioner to large firms with an international practice, hundreds of offices worldwide, and thousands of partners and employees. In between these two extremes are countless small and medium-sized firms of professional accountants. In general, the larger firms offer a broader range of services to clients than do the smaller ones. The majority of medium-sized and large accounting firms are multicapability firms, meaning that they serve clients in several major practice areas, including accounting and auditing, taxation, management consulting, and actuarial, benefits, and compensation consulting. Although the structure of individual firms varies, it is possible to make some generalizations about the services typically offered by the majority of accounting firms.

Auditing Services. The most basic practice area of a CPA firm is accounting and auditing, which consists primarily of performing independent audits of companies' financial statements. In addition, a number of audit-related services are generally offered to clients, either in conjunction with an audit or as separate engagements. One of these services is a communication to management containing recommendations for improvements in the internal control structure and other matters, such as comments on operating efficiencies and profitability. Additional audit-related services include acquisition audits of entities that clients are contemplating acquiring, and issuing letters reporting whether a client is in compliance with the covenants of debt instruments. Some of these services qualify as attest engagements. While attest engagements are typically undertaken by audit personnel, at times they are performed by personnel specializing in some of the "other services" offered by accounting firms, as described below.

An audit requires personnel with a blend of skills and technical expertise. For example, if the engagement is extremely complex technically, the audit team may require members who have industry expertise, a high level of knowledge of computer auditing, tax expertise, or the ability to understand difficult actuarial computations. A team with such expertise will frequently find and recommend ways to improve the client's financial and operating policies, a client service that is derived from the audit process.

Compilation and Review Services. CPAs also perform compilation and review services. A compilation consists of presenting information in the form of financial statements without expressing any opinion on them. A review consists of applying certain limited procedures to financial statements so as to express limited assurance that there are no material modifications that should be made to them. Compilation and review services for nonpublic entities were defined by the American Institute of Certified Public Accountants (AICPA) in 1978 in the first of a series of Statements on Standards for Accounting and Review Services (SSARSs). Those statements resulted from the AICPA's recognition of the need for professional services that are less than an audit, but that provide some assurance about the reliability of a nonpublic entity's financial statements. The SSARSs establish guidelines for performing and reporting on compilation and review engagements. Compilations and reviews are discussed further in Chapter 19.

Other Services. Another major service provided by accounting firms is in the area of taxation—tax and business planning and compliance services offered to corporations, other businesses, and individuals. Tax services offered to businesses by accounting firms cover a broad spectrum, including preparing federal, state, and local tax returns; advising on merger or acquisition approaches to minimize taxes and on structuring operations to take advantage of tax opportunities; and reviewing tax returns for compliance with applicable laws and regulations. Services to individuals include tax, financial, and estate planning.

A firm's tax practice often includes one or more special service groups that address complex issues related to taxation. For instance, some accounting firms maintain support groups composed of senior tax professionals who monitor new tax laws, regulations, rulings, cases, and other related developments and communicate this specialized knowledge to the rest of the firm. Many firms employ lawyers and engineers to advise clients on tax aspects of various transactions. Other groups that combine both tax and financial accounting expertise may be established to provide tax services relating to state and local tax matters; mergers, acquisitions, divestitures, sales of businesses, and related financing transactions; specialized industries that are affected by legislative, regulatory, and judicial proceedings; and international tax developments that concern multinational clients.

Management advisory services (MAS), sometimes called management consulting services, are offered in several diversified areas, such as strategic planning, finance, inventory and supply, transportation, computers, and human resources. For example, professionals working in the MAS practice area of an accounting firm may undertake work and make recommendations to client management in one or more of the following areas:

- Establishing long-range strategic planning programs.
- Analyzing and improving administration—organization, methods, procedures, and productivity.
- Developing data processing strategy, equipment and software evaluation and selection, and telecommunications network and security evaluation.
- Designing and implementing information systems.
- Applying techniques, such as just-in-time inventory planning, to improve profits.
- Improving materials controls, from consumer goods sales forecasting to manufacturing planning and control.

Actuarial, benefits, and compensation consulting professionals employed by accounting firms can advise clients about

- Planning executive compensation arrangements, conducting salary surveys, and devising wage programs.
- Designing pension and profit-sharing plans, performing annual actuarial valuations, and implementing medical, life, and disability insurance programs.
- Communicating benefits and compensation policies to employees.
- Developing benefits and compensation administration systems.
- Determining compliance with government reporting requirements.

Those consultants may also provide technical support to audit engagement teams.

Firm Structure. It is difficult to generalize about the organization of accounting firms because each one has its own structure and no two are exactly alike. Some multioffice firms are organized by groups or regions, with one partner designated overall responsibility for the practice offices in each group or region. The group or regional partners may report to a number of vice chairmen or other designated partners. Each practice office is headed by a partner, often called the managing partner or partner in charge of the office, who is responsible for day-to-day operations. Within each practice office, there may be separate units for auditing, tax, MAS, and perhaps one or more specialized practice areas. In addition to professional personnel, each practice office may have an administrative staff to handle personnel management, including recruiting, and to support the office's accounting and reporting function.

In addition to their practice offices, many large accounting firms have a number of specialized departments, usually organized as part of a national office, that provide support to the practice. Examples of such resource groups are industry specialization, marketing and planning, professional education, and accounting and auditing policy setting, research, and consulting. Firms that practice in different countries are further organized under an international structure usually governed by a committee of representatives from the various member firms or geographic areas.

The Audit Engagement Team. Each audit is staffed by a team headed by a partner who signs the audit report and is ultimately responsible for the audit and its results. Especially on large or complex engagements, there may be more than one partner, or the partner may delegate many functions to one or more managers; however, one partner retains responsibility for the quality of the audit and thus should be actively involved in its planning and in evaluating the results, as documented and summarized by the members of the engagement team. The team usually includes a manager (or more than one on a large engagement) and other personnel with varying degrees of experience and professional expertise and competence. Firms establish staff classifications through which employees progress and policies that set forth the responsibilities of audit personnel on each level. While these responsibilities vary from one firm to another, the typical functions and duties of each classification can be described generally.

Partner. The partner has primary responsibility for accounting and auditing services and is usually the direct contact with the client. The partner is responsible for all decisions made in the course of the engagement, including those about the scope of services, the audit strategy, and the resolution of significant accounting and auditing technical issues. In short, the partner is responsible for ensuring that the audit has been planned, conducted, and reported on in accordance with the firm's policies and professional standards. As noted in Chapter 3, firms that are members of the AICPA's Practice Section are required to assign a second, or concurring, partner on SEC engagements to provide additional assurance that those objectives are achieved. Because of the perceived benefits of such additional partner review, many firms assign a concurring partner to other engagements as well.

The concurring partner on an engagement generally assesses the audit strategy, including auditing procedures to be performed in sensitive or high-risk areas, and may suggest additional matters to be addressed or recommend ways of enhancing audit efficiency. The concurring partner reviews the draft audit report, related financial information and disclosures, and, where applicable, published reports and filings to be made with the SEC and other regulatory bodies. In some circumstances, the concurring partner's review may be more detailed and include inquiring of members of the engagement team and reviewing working papers to determine that the scope of auditing procedures and related documentation comply with the firm's policies and professional standards.

Manager. Under the direction of a partner, a manager is responsible for administering all aspects of an engagement, including planning and coordinating activities with client personnel, delegating duties to team members, coaching them, supervising and reviewing their work, controlling engagement time and expenses, and overseeing billings and collections. A manager is expected to have attained a degree of technical competence in accounting and auditing sufficient to ensure that an audit complies with all applicable professional standards and firm policies. The manager is also responsible for keeping the partner informed of all significant developments throughout the audit. Among other things, the manager is often delegated the responsibility for reviewing the report to management covering control structure related matters, the financial statements, the engagement documentation, and proposed changes in the audit program.

Other Personnel. One or more experienced accountants are responsible, under the manager's direction, for the overall quality, timeliness, and efficiency of the field work in an audit. This involves assisting the manager with administrative matters during the planning phase of the engagement as well as during and after the field work. During the field work, these individuals are responsible for understanding the client's business, industry, and control structure; assessing risk; reviewing working papers prepared by other engagement team personnel; drafting the report on control structure related matters and the proposed audit report; and preparing a summary of audit findings for the partner's attention.

Less experienced personnel are responsible for completing assigned tasks under supervision. Their assignments, which vary with the size and complexity of the engagement, generally include preparing documentation of the understanding of the client and its control structure, performing various types of audit tests and documenting the results, and keeping higher-level personnel informed of all findings.

The Audit Pyramid. The engagement team members at the various levels are commonly viewed as forming a "staffing pyramid." There are generally large numbers of less experienced personnel on an engagement team, with proportionately fewer people at each higher level and one partner, with ultimate responsibility for the audit, at the top. The exact shape of the pyramid varies both by the size and organization of the accounting firm and by the circumstances of the client's business and industry. For example, on multilocation, technically complex engagements, there may be several individuals with differing amounts of experience; those less experienced will be assigned responsibility for specific aspects of the field work, under the supervision of a more experienced individual who will direct the overall field work. The specific needs of the engagement, as determined by the client's operations and industry, also affect the shape of the pyramid. For instance, if the audit work includes extensive detailed testing, such as counting securities or confirming customers' accounts receivable, a larger number of less experienced personnel may be necessary than on an engagement in which detailed testing is limited.

THE ORGANIZATION OF THE AUDITING PROFESSION

The auditing profession in the United States has formed numerous voluntary groups with various purposes, among them the AICPA, state societies or institutes of CPAs, and the Institute of Internal Auditors, all of which have broadly based memberships. In addition, there are more specialized organizations of government auditors, computer auditors, teachers of auditing, and internal auditors with particular industry interests. The designation "Certified Public Accountant" is granted by state boards of accountancy, discussed in the next section of this chapter.

American Institute of CPAs. The mission of the AICPA is "to act on behalf of its members and provide necessary support to assure that CPAs serve the public interest in performing quality professional services." Just under half of the AICPA's approximately 280,000 members, who are required to be CPAs, are in public practice either with CPA firms or as sole practitioners. (The rest are in business and industry, government, or education; or are retired.) The AICPA provides a broad range of services to members, including continuing professional education, technical accounting and auditing assistance, auditing standards, self-regulation of the profession, and assistance in managing an accounting practice.

Ultimate authority over the AICPA is vested in its Council. Its 21-member Board of Directors, which includes 3 non-Institute members who represent the public, administers resources and sets policy. Pronouncements in the form of technical and ethical standards are issued by senior technical committees composed of Institute members in public practice and, to some extent, in industry, government, and academe. The Institute's bylaws authorize eight senior technical committees to make public statements, sometimes in the form of authoritative pronouncements, on matters related to their areas of practice, without clearance by Council or the Board of Directors. Those senior technical committees and the public statements they issue are shown in Figure 2.1.

In addition, the AICPA has four voluntary membership divisions. Three are for individual members with a special interest in tax, management advisory services, or personal financial planning. The fourth is the Division for CPA Firms.

Through its Continuing Professional Education Division, the AICPA provides programs covering a wide range of technical and professional subjects of interest to members in public practice, business, teaching, and government. The Institute also publishes the *Journal of Accountancy* and *The Tax Adviser* monthly, which are available to nonmembers as well as members; several newsletters of interest to practicing members; and numerous pamphlets, reports, and studies. The Institute's Board of Examiners prepares, administers, and grades the semiannual CPA examinations on behalf of the 50 states and other licensing jurisdictions. Through its Professional Ethics Division, the AICPA issues interpretations of the Principles and Rules of the Code of Professional Conduct, investigates complaints against members regarding unethical practices, and assists in investigating and presenting ethics cases referred to the Joint Trial Board.

State Societies of CPAs. In addition to belonging to the AICPA, most CPAs belong to a state society of CPAs. The purpose of the state societies is also to improve the profession and help their members better serve the public interest. To accomplish this, the state societies offer members continuing professional education courses, provide consultation services, maintain liaison with members of state legislatures and relevant administrative agencies of state governments, publish professional journals, clarify and enforce professional technical and ethical standards, and provide other services to members, such as various types of group insurance. Members of a state society are automatically members of a specific local chapter within the state, which holds regular meetings and coordinates its activities with those of the state society.

Figure 2.1 Public Statements Issued by AICPA Senior Technical Committees

Senior Technical Committee[a]	*Public Statements Issued*
Accounting and Review Services Committee	Statements on Standards for Accounting and Review Services[b] Accounting and Review Services Interpretations Statements on Standards for Attestation Engagements[b]
Accounting Standards Executive Committee	Statements of Position Issues Papers Practice Bulletins
Auditing Standards Board	Statements on Auditing Standards[b] Auditing Interpretations Statements on Standards for Attestation Engagements[b] Interpretations of Attestation Standards Statements on Standards for Accountants' Services on Prospective Financial Information[b] Notices to Practitioners Statements of Position
Federal Taxation Executive Committee	Statements on Responsibilities in Tax Practice
Management Advisory Services Executive Committee	Statements on Standards for Management Advisory Services[b] Statements on Standards for Attestation Engagements[b]
Professional Ethics Executive Committee	Interpretations of Rules of Conduct[b] Ethics Rulings[b]
Quality Review Executive Committee	Standards for Performing and Reporting on Quality Reviews

[a]The Personal Financial Planning Executive Committee has also been designated as a senior technical committee and is authorized to make public statements on matters related to its area of practice. At the time of this writing, however, it has not issued any public statements.

[b]The Rules of the AICPA Code of Professional Conduct and implementing resolutions of Council require AICPA members to comply with standards contained in these pronouncements; departures therefrom must be justified by those members who do not follow them.

The Institute of Internal Auditors. The Institute of Internal Auditors (IIA) was formed in 1941 to promote the professionalism and education of internal auditors. The organization now has more than 32,000 members in over 180 chapters throughout the world. The Institute actively sponsors training seminars, conferences, research, and books and other publications, including a bimonthly professional journal entitled *The Internal Auditor*. The Institute's International Board of Directors and other international committees set Institute policy. The IIA offers a certification program leading to the professional designation of Certified Internal Auditor (CIA). IIA achievements include codifying ethics, developing professional standards, and identifying a common body of practitioner knowledge.

Other Organizations. Auditors with specialized interests have formed various organizations, usually with more precisely defined objectives than the broadly based AICPA and IIA. Among those groups are computer, insurance company, government, and bank auditors. Members of the American Accounting Association who are interested in auditing research and teaching have established an Auditing Section of the Association, which publishes *Auditing: A Journal of Practice and Theory.* Membership in some of these organizations is limited to auditors practicing in a specific field or industry.

PROFESSIONAL CERTIFICATION AND LICENSING

The main professional designations relating to the practice of auditing are "Certified Public Accountant," "Certified Internal Auditor," and "Certified Information Systems Auditor."

Certified Public Accountant (CPA). The semiannual, two-and-one-half-day CPA examination is prepared by the Board of Examiners of the AICPA and is given uniformly throughout the United States in May and November. Only individuals who pass the CPA examination and meet the education and experience requirements of their state boards are granted a license to practice by the state and are entitled to use the designation "Certified Public Accountant" or "CPA." The CPA certificate is granted to qualified candidates to ensure the professional competence of those who offer their services to the public as professional accountants.

The examination in all states currently consists of the following four parts:

- Accounting Theory—tests the candidate's conceptual knowledge of accounting.
- Accounting Practice—tests the candidate's ability to apply accounting concepts, authoritative accounting pronouncements, cost accounting concepts, and federal tax accounting principles and procedures.
- Auditing—tests the candidate's knowledge of professional responsibilities, auditing standards and procedures, and standards relating to nonauditing services provided by CPAs.
- Business Law—tests the candidate's knowledge of the legal implications of business transactions, particularly as they relate to accounting and auditing, and auditors' legal liability.

Some states may require candidates to be tested in other subjects as well.

All state boards of accountancy use the AICPA Uniform CPA Examination and Advisory Grading Service. Even though the papers are graded by the AICPA, the state boards are responsible for the quality, composition, and grading of the examination and for licensing individuals, and thus may review the Institute's grading. Education and experience requirements differ from state to state. Although in some states individuals receive a CPA certificate on passing the examination, most states require a period of experience before they issue a license to practice.

Additional information concerning a state's regulations and requirements can be obtained from the following sources:

- The appropriate state education department or state board of accountancy.
- National Association of State Boards of Accountancy, 545 Fifth Avenue, New York, New York 10017.
- American Institute of Certified Public Accountants, 1211 Avenue of the Americas, New York, New York 10036.
- The appropriate state society of certified public accountants.

Publications that may have information about the CPA examination and state accountancy laws include

- *Information for CPA Candidates*, published by the American Institute of Certified Public Accountants.
- *Digest of State Accountancy Laws and State Board Regulations*, which includes a listing of the state boards of accountancy, published by the National Association of State Boards of Accountancy and the AICPA.
- *Accountancy Law Reporter*, published by Commerce Clearing House.

Certified Internal Auditor (CIA). The Certified Internal Auditor examination measures technical competence in the practice of internal auditing and is administered by the Board of Regents of the Institute of Internal Auditors (IIA). The IIA's Director of Professional Practices is responsible for preparing, administering, and grading the examination within the guidelines established by IIA's Board of Regents and Board of Directors. The Certified Internal Auditor examination is open to internal auditors and others who have the required professional qualifications. To maintain the CIA designation, a holder of a CIA certificate must meet specific CPE requirements. The certificate confers professional recognition, but does not include a license to practice. Because CIAs do not offer their services to the public, states do not license them.

Additional information relating to the experience and education requirements for the CIA examination can be obtained by writing to The Institute of

Internal Auditors, Inc., 249 Maitland Avenue, Altamonte Springs, Florida 32701.

Certified Information Systems Auditor (CISA). In 1979, the EDP Auditors Foundation engaged Educational Testing Service to develop a certification examination for Certified Information Systems Auditor (CISA), to test knowledge and skills in the various fields of EDP auditing. The EDP Auditors Foundation appointed a Certification Board to supervise and control the program and the content of the test. To retain certification, a CISA must meet certain CPE requirements or retake the examination. The CISA program is also one of professional recognition rather than state licensure.

Additional information about the experience and education requirements for the CISA examination can be obtained by writing to the EDP Auditors Foundation, Inc., 455 East Kehoe Boulevard, Suite 106, Carol Stream, Illinois 60188.

PROFESSIONAL STANDARDS AND STANDARD-SETTING BODIES

Auditing standards, in the broadest sense, are guidelines for performing professionally responsible audits. The AICPA, IIA, and General Accounting Office have all formulated auditing standards to guide their members.

Generally Accepted Auditing Standards. The membership of the AICPA has approved and adopted ten broad statements collectively entitled "generally accepted auditing standards," often abbreviated as "GAAS." Nine of them were originally adopted in 1948 and have not changed basically since (although our understanding of several of them has changed significantly over the years). The tenth was adopted some years later, but the basic principle had existed before. Two of the standards were amended in 1988. Of the ten standards, three are concerned with personal qualities that the auditor should possess (general standards), three with how an audit should be conducted (field work standards), and four with the form and content of the auditor's report (reporting standards). The ten GAAS are discussed in detail in Chapter 3.

The authority to amplify and interpret the ten original GAAS resides in a senior technical committee of the AICPA. From 1939 to 1972, that committee was called the Committee on Auditing Procedure and issued 54 pronouncements called Statements on Auditing Procedure. The Committee on Auditing Procedure was replaced in 1972 by the Auditing Standards Executive Committee, and in 1978 the Auditing Standards Board (ASB) was formed to succeed the Executive Committee. The ASB is now responsible for promulgating auditing standards and procedures to be observed by AICPA members in accordance with the Institute's Code of Professional Conduct. The pronouncements of the Auditing Standards Executive Committee and the Auditing Standards Board are called Statements on Auditing Standards (SASs). They define the nature and extent of auditors' responsibilities and provide guidance to auditors in carrying out their duties. From 1972 through mid-1989 the two committees issued 63 Statements on Auditing Standards. While statements issued by all three committees are technically amplifications and interpretations of the ten original GAAS, they and the ten GAAS are frequently referred to collectively as generally accepted auditing standards.

In addition to issuing SASs, the Auditing Standards Board approves for publication auditing interpretations of the SASs; the interpretations are prepared by the staff of the Auditing Standards Division of the AICPA. As they are issued, Statements on Auditing Standards, auditing interpretations, and other AICPA professional standards are incorporated in the AICPA's looseleaf service, *Professional Standards*, which results in a continuous codification of those pronouncements. Once a year, a bound version of the latest *Professional Standards* is published for Institute members by the AICPA and for non-Institute members by Commerce Clearing House.

In an effort to promote international uniformity in auditing, the International Auditing Practices Committee (IAPC) of the International Federation of Accountants (IFAC) issues guidelines on generally accepted auditing practices and audit reports. The guidelines are not authoritative in the way AICPA professional standards are in the United States, but IAPC members have agreed to work toward implementing them to the extent practicable. Twenty-seven international guidelines have been issued through mid-1989; for the most part, their provisions conform with comparable U.S. GAAS. If a guideline is issued that deviates significantly from GAAS, the Auditing Standards Board considers ways of resolving the differences.

The Role of the SEC and the Courts in Setting Auditing Standards. The various federal acts that the Securities and Exchange Commission administers give it broad powers. Those powers probably include promulgating auditing standards and may extend even to prescribing specific steps to be followed by auditors of financial statements filed with the Commission. The Commission has, however, adopted the general policy of relying on the public accounting profession to establish auditing standards, largely because of the profession's willingness to address issues the SEC deems significant. The policy stated by the Commission in 1940 in Accounting Series Release No. 19 continues to be effective.

> Until experience should prove the contrary, we feel that this program is preferable to its alternative—the detailed prescription of the scope of and procedures to be followed in the audit for the various types of issuers of securities who file statements with us—and will allow for further consideration of varying audit procedures and for the development of different treatment for specific types of issuers.

This is not to suggest that the SEC has not or will not influence the development of auditing standards. Indeed, it has done so on several occasions and is likely to continue doing so. That influence takes essentially two forms: stimulating the Auditing Standards Board to issue a pronouncement when the Commission believes one is needed (as occurred with SAS No. 36, *Review of Interim Financial Information* [AU Section 722]) and informing the Auditing Standards Board of its views during the standard-setting process. The Auditing Standards Board must continually acknowledge the presence of the SEC throughout its deliberations, but must not sacrifice the independence and objectivity that are essential to its standard-setting function.

Despite numerous opportunities to interpret auditing standards when auditors have been the subject of litigation, only rarely have the courts failed to apply the profession's own auditing standards, and then it was primarily in areas involving reporting standards. Conformity with promulgated professional auditing standards has generally been an effective defense for auditors.

Attestation Standards. In March 1986, the AICPA's Auditing Standards Board and its Accounting and Review Services Committee (ARSC) jointly issued Statement on Standards for Attestation Engagements (SSAE), *Attestation Standards* (AT Section 100), the first in a new series of statements. (The AICPA's Management Advisory Services Executive Committee is also authorized to issue SSAEs.) The attestation standards provide guidance and establish a broad framework for performing and reporting on attest services generally. The standards do not supersede any existing SASs or other authoritative standards, but are a natural extension of the ten GAAS. Because of their breadth, the attestation standards can serve as a basis for establishing interpretive standards for a wide range of services in the future, while at the same time setting reasonable boundaries around the attest function. The attestation standards are discussed in Chapter 19.

Standards for Tax Practice. The AICPA's Tax Division issues Statements on Responsibilities in Tax Practice, which provide guidance on tax practice and accountants' responsibilities in this area. They are not as authoritative as SASs because they are not enforceable under the Rules of the AICPA Code of Professional Conduct. Rather, they constitute advice on standards of good tax practice, covering the CPA's responsibility to his or her client, the public, the government, and the accounting profession.

Standards for MAS Practice. In 1981, the AICPA's Management Advisory Services Executive Committee issued Statement on Standards for Management Advisory Services (SSMAS) No. 1, which defines two types of management advisory services—MAS engagements and MAS consultations—and sets forth a number of general and technical standards for MAS practice. Two subsequent statements provide guidance on the application of the standards in SSMAS No. 1 and establish additional standards. Compliance with the MAS

Figure 2.2 Standards for MAS Practice

General Standards:

Professional competence. A member shall undertake only those engagements which he or his firm can reasonably expect to complete with professional competence.

Due professional care. A member shall exercise due professional care in the performance of an engagement.

Planning and supervision. A member shall adequately plan and supervise an engagement.

Sufficient relevant data. A member shall obtain sufficient relevant data to afford a reasonable basis for conclusions or recommendations in relation to an engagement.

Forecasts. A member shall not permit his name to be used in conjunction with any forecast of future transactions in a manner that may lead to the belief that the member vouches for the achievability of the forecast.

Technical Standards:

Role of MAS practitioner. In performing an MAS engagement (consultation), an MAS practitioner should not assume the role of management or take any positions that might impair the MAS practitioner's objectivity.

Understanding with client. An oral or written understanding should be reached with the client concerning the nature, scope, and limitations of the MAS engagement (consultation) to be performed.

Client benefit. Since the potential benefits to be derived by the client are a major consideration in MAS engagements (consultations), such potential benefits should be viewed objectively and the client should be notified of reservations regarding them. In offering and providing MAS engagements (consultations), results should not be explicitly or implicitly guaranteed. When estimates of quantifiable results are presented, they should be clearly identified as estimates and the support for such estimates should be disclosed.

Communication of results. Significant information pertinent to the results of an MAS engagement (consultation), together with any limitations, qualifications, or reservations needed to assist the client in making its decision, should be communicated to the client orally or in writing.

standards is required under the Code of Professional Conduct. The MAS general and technical standards, adapted from *AICPA Professional Standards* MS Sections 11.05, 11.06, and 31.11, are summarized in Figure 2.2.

Standards for Internal Auditing. The Institute of Internal Auditors in 1978 adopted a series of *Standards for the Professional Practice of Internal Auditing*. Those standards address the independence of internal auditors, their professional proficiency, the scope and performance of their work, and the management of internal auditing departments. The IIA standards differ somewhat in their philosophy from the AICPA standards for external auditors in that the former represent the practice of internal auditing as it *should be*, whereas to a large extent Statements on Auditing Standards represent the Auditing Standards

Board's view of the consensus among practitioners—what is "generally accepted." That difference should not be exaggerated, however; the IIA standards are also a consensus, but of the best of practice rather than of what is minimally acceptable. The IIA also periodically issues Statements on Internal Auditing Standards to provide guidance on issues of interest to internal auditors.

Standards for Government Auditing. The General Accounting Office, the largest employer of government auditors in the United States, has issued a set of *Government Auditing Standards: Standards for Audit of Governmental Organizations, Programs, Activities, and Functions,* popularly referred to as the "Yellow Book." The standards were first published in 1972 and have been revised several times since then, most recently in 1988. Adherence to the standards is required not only for audits of federal organizations, programs, activities, and functions but also for federal funds received by nonprofit organizations and other nongovernmental entities. The GAO recommends that the standards be followed for state and local government audits performed by government auditors or CPAs, and several state and local audit agencies have adopted them. The GAO standards incorporate the AICPA's auditing standards and are compatible with the standards issued by the IIA.

The GAO standards define two types of government audits: financial audits (which include financial statements and financial-related audits) and performance audits (which include economy and efficiency audits and program audits). The standards consist of general standards, including independence and due professional care, and field work and reporting standards. The GAO standards are discussed further in Chapter 19.

Review Questions

2-1. Audits can generally be classified into three types. How do they differ in their objectives?

2-2. Auditors can generally be classified into three types. What are they?

2-3. How does an internal auditor's independence differ from an external auditor's independence?

2-4. Describe several audit-related services that may be offered to clients.

2-5. Describe several nonaudit services that may be offered to clients.

2-6. What is an acquisition audit?

2-7. What is the major responsibility of the partner on an engagement and how is that responsibility met?

2-8. What are the responsibilities of an audit manager?

2-9. What is the major responsibility of an experienced staff accountant?

2–10. What is meant by the audit pyramid?

2–11. What types of services does the AICPA provide to its members?

2–12. Name the four parts of the CPA examination and describe what they are designed to test.

2–13. What is the responsibility of the Auditing Standards Board?

2–14. What is the SEC? Briefly describe its jurisdiction.

2–15. What is the purpose of state societies of CPAs and how do they accomplish their purpose?

2–16. What is the Institute of Internal Auditors and what do its standards address?

2–17. Who is responsible for administering the CIA examination?

2–18. What is the General Accounting Office? Describe its Yellow Book.

Discussion Questions

2–30. In the early 1970s, the responsibility for setting *accounting* standards was transferred from the AICPA to the FASB. Furthermore, the SEC has often intervened directly in the accounting standard-setting process, particularly with respect to disclosure standards. The responsibility for setting *auditing* standards continues to rest with the AICPA, and although the SEC has the authority to do so, it has only rarely intervened directly in the auditing standard-setting process.

Required:

a. Discuss the pros and cons of transferring responsibility for setting auditing standards to an organization other than the AICPA.
b. Why do you think the SEC has only rarely intervened directly in the auditing standard-setting process?

2–31. Medium-sized and large accounting firms generally categorize their staffs as audit, tax, and management advisory services. Some accounting firms also have an actuarial, benefits, and compensation consulting group.

Required:

a. Briefly describe the types of service each group would provide clients.
b. Most audit engagements require that people from each of the firm's practice areas join the engagement team to assist in the audit. Describe the roles each of those groups could play (interacting with the auditors) in fulfilling the requirements of an audit.

2–32. You are meeting with executives of Townsend Paper Products to arrange your firm's engagement to audit the corporation's financial statements for the year ended December 31, 1991. One executive suggested that the audit work be divided among three audit staff members so that one person would examine asset accounts, the second would examine liability accounts, and the third would examine income and expense accounts to minimize audit time, avoid duplication of staff effort, and curtail interference with company operations.

Required:

a. To what extent should a CPA follow a client's suggestions for the conduct of an audit? Discuss.

b. List and discuss the reasons why audit work should not be assigned solely according to asset, liability, and income and expense categories.

(AICPA adapted)

AICPA Multiple Choice Questions

These questions are taken from the Auditing part of Uniform CPA Examinations. Choose the single most appropriate answer.

2–40. A CPA certificate is evidence of

a. Recognition of independence.
b. Basic competence at the time the certificate is granted.
c. Culmination of the educational process.
d. Membership in the AICPA.

2–41. An individual just entering upon an auditing career must obtain professional experience primarily in order to achieve a

a. Positive quality control review.
b. Seasoned judgment.
c. Favorable peer review.
d. Specialty designation by the AICPA.

2–42. Governmental audits consist of financial audits and audits of efficiency, effectiveness, and

a. Internal control.
b. Evaluation.
c. Accuracy.
d. Programs.

2–43. Performance audits generally have been conducted by internal auditors and governmental audit agencies but may be performed by certified public accountants. A primary purpose of a performance audit is to provide

a. A means of assurance that the internal control structure is functioning as planned.
b. Aid to the independent auditor, who is conducting the audit of the financial statements.
c. The results of internal examinations of financial and accounting matters to a company's top-level management.
d. A measure of management performance in meeting organizational goals.

2–44. The primary purpose of a management advisory services engagement is to help the client

a. Become more profitable by relying upon the CPA's existing personal knowledge about the client's business.
b. Improve the use of its capabilities and resources to achieve its objectives.
c. Document and quantify its future plans without impairing the CPA's objectivity or allowing the CPA to assume the role of management.
d. Obtain benefits that are guaranteed implicitly by the CPA.

3

Auditing Standards and Professional Conduct

All professions have technical and ethical standards to guide their members in carrying out their duties and in their relationships with the various groups with which they come in contact. Also, all professions have means for enforcing those standards. This chapter presents and elaborates on the public accounting profession's technical standards relating to the conduct of an audit (generally accepted auditing standards) and the ethical standards that guide members of professional auditing organizations in their working relationships with clients, colleagues, and the public. Compliance with the profession's technical and ethical standards is enforced through various mechanisms created by the AICPA and by state societies of CPAs, state boards of accountancy, the Securities and Exchange Commission (SEC), the courts, and accounting firms themselves, all of which are discussed below. The chapter concludes with a discussion of ways of enhancing auditor independence.

AUDITING AS A PROFESSION

While various writers and organizations have different criteria for defining an activity as a profession, there seems to be widespread agreement that the following characteristics must be present:

1. Formal recognition of professional status by means of a license issued by a government body after admission standards have been met.
2. A body of specialized knowledge, usually acquired through formal education.
3. A code of ethics to provide standards of conduct, and a means of enforcing compliance with the code.
4. Informal recognition and acceptance of professional status by the public, and public interest in the work performed.
5. Recognition by the professionals of a social obligation beyond the service performed for a particular client.

There can be little doubt that auditing has the attributes necessary to qualify as a profession. In a majority of jurisdictions in the United States, the privilege of practicing as a public accountant is limited by the statutes of the various states and territories to those who have been granted the designation of Certified Public Accountant (CPA) by a particular state or territory. The certification is granted only to those who have passed the CPA examination and, in many jurisdictions, who have also met specified education and experience requirements. At least in part because the CPA examination is uniform throughout all licensing jurisdictions and has a well-deserved reputation of being difficult, the public has come to expect a high level of expertise in accounting and auditing from a person who is a CPA.

The specialized knowledge of accounting and auditing that an auditor must have is usually acquired initially through an academic program at the undergraduate level, the graduate level, or both. The necessary knowledge is also acquired through on-the-job training and continuing education courses, sometimes to meet licensing or membership requirements of various bodies. For example, many states require an average of 40 hours of annual continuing education credits for CPAs to keep their license to practice; the AICPA's membership requirements also stipulate that members in public practice meet a similar level of professional education, with fewer credits required for members not in public practice. CPAs must also supplement their knowledge through an ongoing program of reading and self-study to keep current with new professional standards and stay abreast of economic and business issues.

As discussed later in this chapter, membership in the AICPA requires adherence to the Institute's Code of Professional Conduct. The Institute of Internal Auditors also has such a code, adherence to which is required of those internal auditors who have qualified as Certified Internal Auditors by virtue of having met examination, education, and experience requirements. The AICPA's Code of Professional Conduct and its enforcement are designed to ensure that CPAs who are members of the AICPA accept and achieve a high level of responsibility to the public, clients, and colleagues.

It is apparent that the public considers public accountancy a profession. Universities have established schools and programs of professional accountancy, and a mechanism is in place for separate accreditation of those programs by the American Assembly of Collegiate Schools of Business (AACSB). There is a high level of public interest in the work performed by CPAs, particularly auditing services. It is unusual for someone other than a CPA to be asked to attest to financial or other information that will be disseminated outside the enterprise.

Lastly, it is clear that the profession has long recognized an obligation to the public at large that extends well beyond the services performed for a particular client. While auditors realize that they have an obligation or responsibility to the client that has retained them, they are also aware that their audience is much larger. Audited financial statements are read, used, and relied on by many other groups—present and potential investors and creditors, suppliers, employees, customers, and government agencies. Testimony before legislative bodies at all levels of government and other less formal recommendations regarding tax laws, securities acts, and other relevant legislation have indicated a concern for the public interest that extends far beyond the parochial interests of auditors whose livelihood could be enhanced or diminished by the proposed legislation. Often, the positions an auditor takes publicly on such matters conflict with the specific interests of one or more clients, but professionals should place the interests of the public ahead of their own or those of a particular client. Above all, however, CPAs have an awareness of a professional's responsibilities to the public at large, an awareness that is continually enhanced by Congress, the media, the courts, the SEC, the AICPA, and other organizations, such as the Commission on Auditors' Responsibilities (the Cohen Commission) and the National Commission on Fraudulent Financial Reporting (the Treadway Commission).

GENERALLY ACCEPTED AUDITING STANDARDS

Professions set technical standards to ensure a specified minimum level of performance and quality, primarily because they recognize that the public has an interest in and relies on the work of professionals—and this is undoubtedly true for the auditing profession. Standards set the minimum level of performance and quality that auditors are expected, by their clients and the public, to achieve. In contrast to auditing procedures—which are steps to be performed and vary depending on factors unique to each audit, such as client size, industry, accounting system, and other circumstances—standards are measures of the quality of performance. Auditing standards should be unvarying over a wide spectrum of audit engagements over long periods of time.

The balance between the exercise of professional judgment and the establishment of specific rules to guide professional conduct pervades every aspect of accounting and auditing. The auditing profession has clearly rejected the two extremes: On the one hand, "cookbook" rules are not and never will be sufficient to cover every possible combination of circumstances and thereby allow auditors to shed their responsibility to exercise professional judgment; on the other hand, a framework exists to provide guidance for exercising judgment in all significant aspects of audit practice. It is between the two extremes that tensions and controversies arise: for example, how much uniformity should be required in auditing practice versus how much flexibility should be permitted, or to what extent standard sample sizes and auditing procedures should be spelled out versus the extent to which an auditor's pragmatic judgments should be required. Although the specific subject matter of debate changes from time to time, it is likely that the philosophical debate itself will never be concluded. It should be noted that this same tension between rules and individual judgment pervades most professions.

The membership of the AICPA officially adopted ten generally accepted auditing standards in 1948. AICPA pronouncements—Statements on Auditing Procedure and Statements on Auditing Standards—have amplified and interpreted the ten GAAS. Fifty-four Statements on Auditing Procedure (SAPs) were issued between 1939 and 1972; 63 Statements on Auditing Standards (SASs) have been issued since then, and others are in draft. Statement on Auditing Standards No. 1 codified the 54 SAPs; updated codifications of SAPs and SASs that are still effective are issued annually by the AICPA.

Practitioners and others who need to understand auditors' work and reports should be thoroughly familiar with the SASs, for they constitute the authoritative professional auditing literature. The ten generally accepted auditing standards—the source of all subsequent SAPs and SASs—are found in AU Section 150 of *AICPA Professional Standards*, as follows:

General Standards

1. The audit is to be performed by a person or persons having adequate technical training and proficiency as an auditor.
2. In all matters relating to the assignment, an independence in mental attitude is to be maintained by the auditor or auditors.
3. Due professional care is to be exercised in the performance of the audit and the preparation of the report.

Standards of Field Work

1. The work is to be adequately planned and assistants, if any, are to be properly supervised.
2. A sufficient understanding of the internal control structure is to be obtained to plan the audit and to determine the nature, timing, and extent of tests to be performed.
3. Sufficient competent evidential matter is to be obtained through inspection, observation, inquiries, and confirmations to afford a reasonable basis for an opinion regarding the financial statements under audit.

Standards of Reporting

1. The report shall state whether the financial statements are presented in accordance with generally accepted accounting principles.
2. The report shall identify those circumstances in which such principles have not been consistently observed in the current period in relation to the preceding period.
3. Informative disclosures in the financial statements are to be regarded as reasonably adequate unless otherwise stated in the report.
4. The report shall either contain an expression of opinion regarding the financial statements, taken as a whole, or an assertion to the effect that an opinion cannot be expressed. When an overall opinion cannot be expressed, the reasons therefor should be stated. In all cases where an auditor's name is associated with financial statements, the report should contain a clear-cut indication of the character of the auditor's work, and the degree of responsibility the auditor is taking.

General Standards

The general standards relate to the qualifications of an auditor and the quality of the audit work. They are personal in nature and are distinct from the standards governing the performance of field work and reporting.

Training and Proficiency. The first general standard suggests that the auditor must have proper education and experience in the field of auditing to meet the profession's requirements for adequate training and proficiency. Training begins with formal education and continues with proper supervision and review on the job, as well as formal continuing professional education and self-study. Formal continuing education and self-study are necessary parts of this standard, especially as new developments in accounting, auditing, finance, data processing, taxes, and other aspects of business management continue to force change on practitioners. The need for formal continuing education and self-study, however, does not diminish the importance of on-the-job training, planned development of well-rounded experience, and adequate supervision and review in maintaining proficiency.

Independence. The second general standard requires that the auditor not be biased toward the client. Furthermore, to safeguard the confidence of the public and users of financial statements in auditor independence, auditors must also be "recognized" as independent. SAS No. 1 (AU Section 220.03) provides the following amplification of this:

> To *be* independent, the auditor must be intellectually honest; to be *recognized* as independent, he must be free from any obligation to or interest in the client, its management, or its owners. For example, an independent auditor auditing a company of which he was also a director might be intellectually honest, but it is unlikely that the public would accept him as independent since he would be in effect auditing decisions which he had a part in making. Likewise, an auditor with a substantial financial interest in a company might be unbiased in expressing his opinion on the financial statements of the company, but the public would be reluctant to believe that he was unbiased. Independent auditors should not only be independent in fact; they should avoid situations that may lead outsiders to doubt their independence.

The distinction drawn in this quotation is often referred to as that of "independence in fact" contrasted with "independence in appearance." The former—intellectual honesty—cannot be ensured by rules or prohibitions. The latter—avoiding potentially compromising situations—can, at least partially, be. To guard against any appearance or "presumption" of loss of independence, the AICPA has established specific rules on independence in its Code of Professional Conduct, as discussed in the next section of this chapter. Likewise, the Securities and Exchange Commission has emphasized the importance of independence and has issued rules relating to it.

Due Care. SAS No. 1 (AU Section 230.04) notes that due care relates to what independent auditors do and how well they do it. Due care imposes a responsibility on each person in an auditing firm to exercise the skills he or she possesses with reasonable care and diligence; due care also requires critical review of the work done and of the judgments made. For example, due care is not exercised if the auditor fails to corroborate representations of client management that are significant to the financial statements, such as representations regarding the collectibility of long-outstanding accounts receivable.

Standards of Field Work

The standards of field work cover planning and supervising the audit, understanding the internal control structure, and obtaining audit evidence.

Adequate Planning and Supervision. Planning an audit engagement involves both technical and administrative considerations. The technical aspect of planning entails formulating an overall audit strategy for the engagement. Implementing the audit strategy includes numerous planning decisions of an administrative nature, such as scheduling the work, assigning personnel, and similar matters.

Early appointment of the independent auditor facilitates audit planning. In particular, it makes it possible to consider performing certain auditing procedures during the year rather than at year-end. This increases both audit efficiency and the likelihood of identifying problems at an early date. In the planning stage, analytical procedures are performed to help determine the nature, timing, and extent of other auditing procedures by identifying significant matters the auditor should address.

SAS No. 22, *Planning and Supervision* (AU Section 311.11), states that supervision involves directing the work of assistants and determining whether the objectives of that work were accomplished. On many engagements, as much as one-fifth to one-fourth of the total audit time is spent on supervision. The time is well spent, because the total audit time is likely to be much greater without effective supervision.

Supervision starts with assigning tasks and ensuring that each task and its objectives are understood. It continues with frequent discussions between supervisor and assistants for the purpose of both keeping informed, especially about significant problems encountered, and providing ongoing advice and direction to assistants. That means discussions among the partner, manager, and staff members on an engagement; on large audits personal visits to many different groups and locations may be required. Supervision also entails dealing with differences of opinion among staff members concerning accounting and auditing issues. A final element of supervision is reviewing the completed work of assistants, discussing the review with them, and evaluating their performance.

Understanding the Internal Control Structure. The importance of the second standard of field work has increased as the role of the control environment in preventing and detecting fraud and error has received increasing recognition, as specialists have learned to construct highly reliable computerized accounting systems, and as auditors have become concerned with conducting efficient as well as effective audits. This standard requires the auditor to obtain a sufficient understanding of the client's control structure to adequately plan the tests of transactions and account balances to be performed; the standard does not require that the entire control structure, or even a part of it, be tested *unless* the auditor plans to use the knowledge obtained from such tests to restrict the testing of transactions and account balances. Subsequent chapters discuss the elements of the control structure, how the auditor assesses it, and how that assessment affects the tests the auditor applies to account balances and underlying transactions.

Obtaining Competent Evidence. A detailed understanding of the third standard of field work is important to all phases of auditing. The standard covers both the "competence" and the "sufficiency" of evidence. The competence of evidence relates to its relevance and reliability; sufficiency depends on the amount of assurance the auditor believes is needed to support an opinion that the financial statements are not materially misstated.

Standards of Reporting

Four standards of reporting govern this aspect of the audit effort.

Adherence to Generally Accepted Accounting Principles. The auditor is required first to be thoroughly familiar with generally accepted accounting principles, and second to determine whether the financial statements reported on "present fairly" the client's financial position, results of operations, and cash flows in conformity with those principles. Chapter 18, "The Auditor's Report," deals in depth with the auditor's reporting responsibilities relating to generally accepted accounting principles and fairness, and presents examples of appropriate auditors' reports in cases of departures from generally accepted accounting principles.

Consistent Application. The consistency standard requires the auditor to identify in the auditor's report circumstances in which generally accepted accounting principles have not been applied consistently from period to period. The objective is to ensure either that changes in accounting principles or methods of applying them do not materially affect the comparability of financial statements between periods or that the effect is disclosed.

Adequate Disclosure. The intent of the third standard of reporting is that issuers of financial statements and auditors have a responsibility to ensure that disclosures are adequate, regardless of whether a specific authoritative pronouncement covers the matter. It is thus the auditor's responsibility to identify matters of potential interest to users of the financial statements and to form a conclusion about whether and how they should be disclosed. If the client does not make the necessary disclosures, the auditor must qualify the opinion.

Expression of Opinion. An auditor's report must be painstakingly precise in spelling out the opinion expressed. Leaving the meaning of an auditor's opinion open to readers' inferences is both inappropriate and dangerous. In some instances, an auditor's failure to state the reasons for disclaiming an opinion has permitted inferences that were either more or less favorable to a client than was warranted. In other instances, financial statement users cited ambiguity in an auditor's report as grounds for claims against the auditor. From the time of its adoption, the fourth standard of reporting has been accompanied by detailed recommendations for reporting in all conceivable circumstances. The intention of those detailed prescriptions is to ensure that all auditors use precisely the same words in the same circumstances to prevent misinterpretation of their opinions and the responsibility they assume.

THE AICPA CODE OF PROFESSIONAL CONDUCT

The Code of Professional Conduct of the American Institute of Certified Public Accountants covers both the profession's responsibility to the public and the CPA's responsibility to clients and colleagues. While the AICPA Code is directly enforceable only against individual AICPA members, in reality its applicability is much more pervasive. Most of the significant portions of the Code have been adopted by the various state societies or institutes of CPAs and in many cases have also been incorporated into state statutes or the regulations of state boards of accountancy that license CPAs to practice before the public. In effect, all of these organizations enforce ethical behavior by CPAs.

Codes of ethical conduct are not unique to the practice of accounting. All professionals, including doctors, lawyers, and actuaries, to name a few, have deemed it essential to promulgate codes of professional conduct and to establish means for ensuring their observance. Such codes define the type of behavior that the public has a right to expect from the professionals, and thereby enhance the public's confidence in the quality of professional services rendered.

Most codes of professional conduct, including the AICPA's, contain general ethical principles that are aspirational in character and represent the objectives toward which every member of the profession should strive. The codes also usually contain a set of specific, mandatory rules that state the minimum level of conduct the professional must maintain to avoid being subject to disciplinary action. In the past, some sections of many codes of conduct have also had an ancillary effect of reducing competition, through prohibitions against advertising, solicitation of clients, and encroachment on the practice of a fellow professional. In recent years, however, the courts have deemed such prohibitions to be illegal. Accordingly, most professional associations, including the AICPA, have revised their codes to permit advertising and other forms of solicitation, so long as the professional does not seek to obtain clients by false, misleading, or deceptive advertising or other forms of solicitation.

The AICPA's ethical standards fall into four categories: Principles, Rules, Interpretations of the Rules, and Ethics Rulings. The Principles and Rules comprise the Code of Professional Conduct, the latest version of which was adopted by vote of the AICPA membership in 1988. The Principles express the basic tenets of ethical and professional conduct. The Rules consist of enforceable ethical standards to which AICPA members must adhere: Members must be prepared to justify departures from the Rules. Interpretations of the Rules have been adopted by the AICPA to provide guidelines on the scope and application of the Rules. Ethics Rulings summarize the application of the Rules and Interpretations to a particular set of factual circumstances. The Code as a whole is intended to provide guidance and rules for all AICPA members in the performance of their professional responsibilities, regardless of whether the members are in the public practice of accountancy, in industry, in government, or in academe. Some of the Rules, however, are specifically relevant and stated to be applicable only to CPAs in public practice.

The Preamble to the Principles of Professional Conduct emphasizes the professional's responsibility to the public, clients, and colleagues. The Principles of the Code of Professional Conduct are goal oriented, describing general ideals accountants should aspire to, while the Rules set forth minimum levels of acceptable conduct. The high level of conduct for which CPAs should strive is embodied in the more philosophical Principles, which "call for an unswerving commitment to honorable behavior, even at the sacrifice of personal advantage."

The six Principles of the Code are as follows:

Responsibilities. In carrying out their responsibilities as professionals, members should exercise sensitive professional and moral judgments in all their activities.

The Public Interest. Members should accept the obligation to act in a way that will serve the public interest, honor the public trust, and demonstrate commitment to professionalism.

Integrity. To maintain and broaden public confidence, members should perform all professional responsibilities with the highest sense of integrity.

Objectivity and Independence. A member should maintain objectivity and be free of conflicts of interest in discharging professional responsibilities. A member in public practice should be independent in fact and appearance when providing auditing and other attestation services.

Due Care. A member should observe the profession's technical and ethical standards, strive continually to improve competence and the quality of services, and discharge professional responsibility to the best of the member's ability.

Scope and Nature of Services. A member in public practice should observe the Principles of the Code of Professional Conduct in determining the scope and nature of services to be provided.

A discussion of each of the Rules, along with the related Interpretations and Rulings, follows.

Independence, Integrity, and Objectivity

According to the Principles of the Code of Professional Conduct,

> Integrity is an element of character fundamental to professional recognition. It is the quality from which the public trust derives and the benchmark against which a member must ultimately test all decisions. . . . Integrity also requires a member to observe the principles of objectivity and independence and of due care.
>
> Objectivity is a state of mind, a quality that lends value to a member's services. It is a distinguishing feature of the profession. The principle of objectivity imposes the obligation to be impartial, intellectually honest, and free of conflicts of interest. Independence precludes relationships that may appear to impair a member's objectivity in rendering attestation services.

The importance of independence is indicated by the prevalence of the subject in the profession's authoritative literature. It is found not only in the Principles of the Code of Professional Conduct and Rule 101, but also in the corresponding rules of professional conduct of the various state societies and state regulatory agencies; in SAS No. 1 (AU Section 220) (discussed in an earlier section of this chapter); in Statement on Quality Control Standards No. 1, *System of Quality Control for a CPA Firm* (QC Section 10); and in Rule 2-01 of SEC Regulation S-X. Independence enhances the auditor's ability to act with integrity and objectivity.

Rule 101 (Independence) requires AICPA members in public practice to be independent in the performance of auditing and other attestation services. Auditors, like practitioners in other professions, offer clients specialized technical skills and knowledge based on training and experience, but that is not all. Clients and others rely on auditors because of their belief in the auditors' professional integrity, independence, and objectivity. Clearly, the published opinion of an auditor has little value unless it rests unquestionably on those qualities. They are personal, inward qualities not susceptible to precise determination or definition, and are best maintained by the individual auditor's own conscience and the recognition that a professional's principal asset is a reputation for integrity, independence, and objectivity. It is also important to the public's confidence in an auditor's opinion that the auditor's respect for those qualities be as apparent as possible.

The Code of Professional Conduct, like SAS No. 1, emphasizes *appearing* to be independent as well as *being* independent. Both the accounting profession and the SEC have spelled out detailed prohibitions, not only against those activities or relationships that might actually erode the mental attitude of independence but also against those that might even suggest or imply a possibility of lack of independence.

Interpretation 101-1 (ET Section 101.02) provides examples of situations that impair independence.

> **Interpretation of Rule 101.** Independence shall be considered to be impaired if, for example, a member had any of the following transactions, interests, or relationships:
>
> A. During the period of a professional engagement or at the time of expressing an opinion, a member or a member's firm
>
> 1. Had or was committed to acquire any direct or material indirect financial interest in the enterprise.
> 2. Was a trustee of any trust or executor or administrator of any estate if such trust or estate had or was committed to acquire any direct or material indirect financial interest in the enterprise.
> 3. Had any joint, closely held business investment with the enterprise or with any officer, director, or principal stockholders thereof that was material in relation to the member's net worth or to the net worth of the member's firm.
> 4. Had any loan to or from the enterprise or any officer, director, or principal stockholder of the enterprise. This proscription does not apply to the following loans from a financial institution when made under normal lending procedures, terms, and requirements:
>   a. Loans obtained by a member or a member's firm that are not material in relation to the net worth of such borrower.
>   b. Home mortgages.
>   c. Other secured loans, except loans guaranteed by a member's firm which are otherwise unsecured.
>
> B. During the period covered by the financial statements, during the period of the professional engagement, or at the time of expressing an opinion, a member or a member's firm
>
> 1. Was connected with the enterprise as a promoter, underwriter or voting trustee, as a director or officer, or in any capacity equivalent to that of a member of management or of an employee.
> 2. Was a trustee for any pension or profit-sharing trust of the enterprise.
>
> The above examples are not intended to be all-inclusive.

Many of the foregoing prohibitions reach extremes that might appear ridiculous to a nonprofessional, but they reflect the profession's concern about the appearance of independence. For example, no partner in an auditing firm or member of the partner's immediate family is permitted to own even one share of stock of a client or affiliated company or even to participate in an investment club that holds such shares, no matter what the individual's personal net worth, the size of the company, or the partner's distance from the actual audit work. Some firms also prohibit ownership of a client's stock by any staff member, regardless of what office is performing the audit. As another example, an auditing firm may not have its employees' pension fund managed by an investment counselor that also manages a mutual fund client; even though there is no actual financial relationship, there might be an appearance of lack of independence. In addition, other Interpretations and Ethics Rulings under Rule 101 outline specific prohibitions in this area.

The AICPA's and SEC's prohibitions relating to independence are not entirely free of social costs. Weighing the costs and benefits of prohibitions on individual or firm conduct in order to enhance independence is a matter of public policy and social choice.

Accounting Services. Interpretation 101-3 (ET Section 101.05) permits members to provide bookkeeping or data processing services to audit clients only if the following requirements are met:

- There must be no relationship or conflict of interest between the CPA and the client that would impair the CPA's integrity and objectivity.
- The client's management must accept responsibility for the financial statements.
- The CPA must not assume the role of an employee or management of the client.
- In auditing the financial statements, the CPA must comply with generally accepted auditing standards, i.e., must perform sufficient audit tests of statements prepared from records that the CPA has maintained or processed.

The SEC has noted that an accountant's maintaining the records of an SEC registrant either manually or through EDP equipment may be indicative of a lack of independence. (Many of the SEC's independence requirements extend to the entire period covered by the financial statements, which generally cover three years of operations and cash flows.)

Family Relationships. Interpretation 101-9 (ET Section 101.10) addresses two categories of family relationships that may affect the independence of members. The first category comprises a member's spouse, dependent children, and any other dependent person living in the same household as or supported by the member. The financial interests and business relationships of such individuals are ascribed to the member and thus are governed by Rule 101. The second category is nondependent close relatives, defined as nondependent children, brothers and sisters, grandparents, parents, parents-in-law, and the spouses of any of those individuals. Relatives in this category are not permitted to have a material financial interest or investment in or business relationship with a client of a member, nor may they hold a position with a client in which they can exercise significant influence over its operating, financial, or accounting policies.

Past-Due Fees. Ethics Ruling 52 (ET Section 191.103–.104) addresses the effect of past-due fees on the independence of a member's firm. The Ruling states that independence may be impaired if more than one year's fees are unpaid when the member issues a report on the client's financial statements for the current year. The reason for this ruling is that past-due fees may make it appear that the auditor is providing working capital for the client and that collecting the past-due fees may depend on the nature of the auditor's report on the financial statements. (The SEC's rules in this regard are more restrictive than those of the AICPA.)

Conflicts of Interest. Rule 101 on independence is applicable only to members in public practice. That Rule (and the Interpretations under it) are intended, according to the Principles of the Code of Professional Conduct, to preclude "relationships that may appear to impair a member's objectivity in rendering attestation services." Rule 102 is intended to prohibit members, whether or not in public practice, from subordinating their judgment to others when performing *any* professional service.

Rule 102 (Integrity and Objectivity) states

> In the performance of any professional service, a member shall maintain objectivity and integrity, shall be free of conflicts of interest, and shall not knowingly misrepresent facts or subordinate his or her judgment to others.

General and Technical Standards

The Rules require adherence to standards related to the conduct of the CPA's work.

General Standards. Rule 201 sets forth the following general standards:

> A member shall comply with the following standards and with any interpretations thereof by bodies designated by Council.
>
> A. *Professional Competence.* Undertake only those professional services that the member or the member's firm can reasonably expect to be completed with professional competence.
>
> B. *Due Professional Care.* Exercise due professional care in the performance of professional services.
>
> C. *Planning and Supervision.* Adequately plan and supervise the performance of professional services.

D. *Sufficient Relevant Data.* Obtain sufficient relevant data to afford a reasonable basis for conclusions or recommendations in relation to any professional services performed.

Technical Standards. Rules 202 and 203 are as follows:

Compliance With Standards. A member who performs auditing, review, compilation, management advisory, tax, or other professional services shall comply with standards promulgated by bodies designated by Council.

Accounting Principles. A member shall not (1) express an opinion or state affirmatively that the financial statements or other financial data of any entity are presented in conformity with generally accepted accounting principles or (2) state that he or she is not aware of any material modifications that should be made to such statements or data in order for them to be in conformity with generally accepted accounting principles, if such statements or data contain any departure from an accounting principle promulgated by bodies designated by Council to establish such principles that has a material effect on the statements or data taken as a whole. If, however, the statements or data contain such a departure and the member can demonstrate that due to unusual circumstances the financial statements or data would otherwise have been misleading, the member can comply with the rule by describing the departure, its approximate effects, if practicable, and the reasons why compliance with the principle would result in a misleading statement.

Rules 202 and 203 were adopted to require compliance with the profession's practice standards and accounting principles. There is a strong presumption that adherence to accounting principles promulgated by the FASB and the Governmental Accounting Standards Board (GASB) will result in financial statements that are not misleading.

Rule 203 and Interpretation 203-1 also recognize that occasionally there may be unusual circumstances in which the literal application of pronouncements on accounting principles would have the effect of rendering financial statements misleading. In such unusual cases, the proper accounting treatment is one that will render the financial statements not misleading. Chapter 18 discusses the appropriate wording of the auditor's report in these circumstances.

Responsibilities to Clients

The Principles of the Code of Professional Conduct note that a CPA has responsibilities to clients as well as to the public. CPAs should serve their clients with competence and with regard for the clients' interests. They must also, however, maintain their obligation to the public as evidenced by their independence, integrity, and objectivity.

A fundamental responsibility of the CPA concerns the confidentiality of client information. Rule 301 states that "a member in public practice shall not disclose any confidential information without the specific consent of the client."[1]

Need for Confidentiality. Both common sense and the independence concept dictate that the auditor, not the client, should decide what information the auditor needs to conduct an effective audit. That decision should not be influenced by a client's belief that certain information is confidential. An efficient and effective audit requires that the client have the necessary trust in the auditor to be extremely candid in supplying information. Therefore, the client must be assured of confidentiality and that, except for disclosures required by generally accepted accounting principles, information shared with the auditor will go no further without explicit permission.

Despite the profession's emphasis on confidentiality, executives of some companies are concerned about losing control of sensitive material through an auditor's staff. They may believe that certain material is so sensitive that they cannot be comfortable with an auditor's general assurances about the character and training of the audit staff. If access to the material is necessary to the auditor's opinion, the client's executives have no alternative but to grant access; if they wish to limit that access to specified individuals on the audit team, that condition should be respected. Although awareness of clients' sensibilities is important, the authors have observed that clients' fears generally tend to subside as the working relationship is strengthened, confidence grows, and mutually satisfactory arrangements are made.

Confidentiality Versus Privilege. Except as noted earlier, communications between the client and the auditor are confidential; that is, the auditor should not reveal the information contained in the communication without the client's permission. Under common law, however, that information is not "privileged." Information is privileged if the client can prevent a court or government agency from gaining access to it through a summons or subpoena. Information given to an auditor by a client is often not privileged; it is subject

[1]Rule 301 states that "this rule shall not be construed (1) to relieve a member of his or her professional obligations under rules 202 and 203, (2) to affect in any way the member's obligation to comply with a validly issued and enforceable subpoena or summons, (3) to prohibit review of a member's professional practice under AICPA or state CPA society authorization, or (4) to preclude a member from initiating a complaint with or responding to any inquiry made by a recognized investigative or disciplinary body."

In 1989, the Professional Ethics Executive Committee adopted an Interpretation (301–2) under Rule 301 that provides that "exemption (2) is interpreted to provide that Rule 301 should not be construed to prohibit or interfere with a member's compliance with applicable laws and government regulations"; and also specifies that the recognized investigative or disciplinary bodies noted in exemption (4) are only AICPA bodies or other participants in the Joint Ethics Enforcement Program.

to summons or subpoena in many jurisdictions, including the federal courts. (In those states where an auditor–client privilege does exist, it can be waived only by the client. While it exists for the client's benefit, it also serves to enhance full and honest disclosure between client and auditor.) Auditors and their professional organizations generally support clients' legal resistance to summonses and subpoenas to produce documents or other communications given to or received from their auditors, when it appears that there are legitimate reasons for maintaining confidentiality.

One particularly sensitive area involves the auditor's review of the client's analysis of the provision for income taxes. As a result of Internal Revenue Service subpoenas of auditors' tax provision working papers, and several lawsuits resulting from CPA firms' refusal to comply, many clients are reluctant to provide the auditor with such tax analyses. Regardless of a client's fears, however, the auditor must review sufficient evidential matter to conclude that the tax provision is adequate. Fortunately for the public as well as for the profession, the courts have placed significant limitations on the extent to which these working papers may be subpoenaed.

Insider Information. Auditors and their staff have the same responsibilities as management for handling insider information: not to turn it to personal profit or to disclose it to others who may do so. Those responsibilities are clearly covered by the general injunctions of the Code of Professional Conduct: Independence forbids personal profit, and confidentiality forbids aiding others in that pursuit. The ways in which insider information may be used, even inadvertently, are many and subtle; society's heightened standards of accountability have focused attention on the responsibility of all insiders to use insider information only for the benefit of the enterprise.

Problems Involving Confidentiality. Some clients' fears that secrets will be passed on to competitors are so great that they refuse to engage an auditor whose clients include a competitor; others are satisfied with assurances that the staff on their engagement has no contact with a competitor's personnel. The price paid by a client for so high a degree of confidentiality is the loss of industry expertise that can be provided by auditors who are familiar with more than one company in an industry. Experience suggests that the risk of leakage of information that has competitive value is extremely slight.

A more difficult and quite common dilemma results if two of an auditor's clients do business with each other. For example, an auditor of a commercial bank is likely also to have clients among the bank's depositors and borrowers. Suppose the auditor observes the September 30th physical inventory of a company that is also a borrower at the client bank, and finds a substantial shortage. Under the terms of the company's loan agreement with the bank, audited financial statements are not due at the bank until the next March 31. The client understandably wants time to determine the cause of the shortage. What does the auditor do? This is a practical dilemma quite apart from problems of potential formal legal liability or expression of an opinion on either set of financial statements. On the one hand, the auditor must not use insider information from one client to profit by improving his or her relationship with the other client. On the other hand, it is absurd for the auditor to pretend not to know something that he or she does know. One party will be unhappy if the auditor does nothing; the other party will be upset if the auditor does anything.

The solution to the dilemma is clear in principle, though following it in practice may be difficult. Court cases have clarified the client's responsibility: As soon as a significant event—good or bad—happens, it should be disclosed to all concerned. Neither the client bank nor the client borrower has priority, and the incidental fact of their parallel relationship with the auditor should not affect the handling of the matter. The auditor's duty is to persuade the client borrower to make the necessary prompt disclosures—to the other party if it affects only the two, and publicly if it affects the public.

Before information is publicly disclosed, however, the auditor needs to obtain and document all available pertinent facts, discuss them with the client, and evaluate their effect on the financial statements. All of this takes time, but the resulting delay in making the disclosure is justified: Disclosing information prematurely or inappropriately, that is, before it has been adequately investigated, may create more problems than it solves.

If the client's management refuses to disclose information that the auditor has concluded should be disclosed, the auditor must decide whether it is possible to continue to serve the client. The auditor may want to seek legal counsel in this situation. Usually the auditor will consider going to the board of directors, and in some cases to the SEC and the stock exchanges, and to anyone else known to be affected. Those are very serious steps, and whether to take them is as difficult a decision as an auditor can ever be called on to make. The auditor would risk even more serious problems, however, by favoring a client over other concerned parties. The courts have made clear, as indicated by the *Fund of Funds*[2] case, that an auditor who has reason to believe, from whatever source, that a client's financial statements are materially misstated cannot issue an unqualified opinion.

Another problem of confidentiality may result if a client that is considering acquiring another company engages its own auditor to audit that company. What happens to the auditor's findings and to whom is the duty of confidentiality owed? Common practice in those circumstances is to obtain written confirmations from the chief executives of both companies regarding the extent and limitations of the auditor's responsibilities to each. The confirmation letter to the company to be acquired often includes a statement that the auditor has no responsibility to that company other than the obvious requirement to act in a professional manner. Usually the confirmations approve

[2]*Fund of Funds, Ltd.* v. *Arthur Andersen & Co.*, 545 F. Supp. 1314 (S.D.N.Y. 1982).

delivering the findings to the acquiring company, but only after discussing them with the company to be acquired.

Responsibilities to Colleagues

While there are currently no specific Rules governing a CPA's responsibility to colleagues, the Principles set forth the fundamental tenet of cooperation among members of the profession by stating that AICPA members should "cooperate with each other to improve the art of accounting, maintain the public's confidence, and carry out the profession's special responsibilities for self-governance."

Other Responsibilities and Practices

Acts Discreditable to the Profession. Rule 501 states: "A member shall not commit an act discreditable to the profession." Interpretations under Rule 501 (ET Section 501.01–.05) provide examples of specific acts that would be discreditable to the profession.

1. Retention of client records after a demand is made for them.
2. Discrimination based on race, color, religion, sex, age, or national origin in hiring, promotion, or salary practices.
3. Failure to follow government audit standards, guides, procedures, statutes, rules, and regulations (in addition to generally accepted auditing standards) that may be specified in an audit of government grants, government units, or other recipients of government monies if an engagement has been accepted under those conditions.
4. Negligence in the preparation of financial statements or records (thus explicitly including CPAs who are not in public practice and who serve as preparers rather than auditors of financial statements).

Form of Practice and Name and Ownership of Practice Units. Rule 505 states, in part,

> A member shall not practice public accounting under a firm name that is misleading. Names of one or more past partners or shareholders may be included in the firm name of a successor partnership or corporation. Also, a partner or shareholder surviving the death or withdrawal of all other partners or shareholders may continue to practice under such name which includes the name of past partners or shareholders for up to two years after becoming a sole practitioner.

The current rule revises a previous rule that prohibited a firm name that included a fictitious name or indicated specialization. The previous rule was revised because the prohibition against fictitious names was vulnerable to antitrust attack and was inconsistent with the rule on advertising and solicitation, which prohibits only claims that are false, misleading, or deceptive. Since a member may advertise a specialty, there is no reason a firm should not be allowed to do so in its name, provided the false, misleading, or deceptive test is met.

Appendix B to the Code contains a resolution of AICPA Council that specifies the characteristics that a professional corporation must have to comply with Rule 505. That resolution restricts ownership of a professional corporation to persons engaged in the practice of public accounting, and is intended to make the owners of practice units subject to the Institute's technical, ethical, and practice-monitoring requirements and its self-regulatory and disciplinary processes.

The contrary view, which has been expressed by the Federal Trade Commission (FTC), is that this rule may deter the use of more efficient forms of practice and thereby restrain competition. The ownership question raises complex economic and social issues, which are likely to be of significant concern to the SEC, other regulatory bodies, and congressional oversight committees. At the time of this writing, the FTC is consulting with those bodies.

Marketing Professional Services

Traditionally, CPAs marketed their services by performing quality work and relying on word of mouth to inform potential clients about their professional qualifications. Until the late 1970s, the AICPA code of ethics prohibited members from advertising and using all forms of direct solicitation, including competitive bidding. Such activities were viewed as potentially encroaching on the practice of other members, which was considered unprofessional.

The Rules of the AICPA Code of Professional Conduct presently address the marketing of professional services in three ways. Rule 302 generally prohibits performing services for contingent fees; Rule 502 sets restraints on advertising and solicitation; and Rule 503 prohibits paying or receiving commissions or referral fees. Each of those rules is discussed below. Since those rules, or related interpretations, are currently being questioned by the FTC, the discussion concludes with a summary of the AICPA's consent agreement with the FTC.

Contingent Fees. Rule 302 states

> Professional services shall not be offered or rendered under an arrangement whereby no fee will be charged unless a specified finding or result is attained, or

> where the fee is otherwise contingent upon the finding or results of such services. However, a member's fees may vary depending, for example, on the complexity of services rendered.

There is a presumption that a CPA will perform professional services in a competent manner and that the fee charged will not depend on the CPA's findings or the outcome of the work. For example, specific Ethics Rulings prohibit fees as a percentage of a bond issue, finder's fees based on a percentage of the acquisition price, and fees as an expert witness based on the amount awarded the plaintiff.

Fees are not regarded as being contingent if, for any type of engagement, they are fixed by courts or other public authorities or, in tax matters, if they are determined based on the results of court decisions or the resolution of controversies with government agencies. An Ethics Ruling explicitly states, however, that basing a fee for preparing a tax return on the amount of tax savings to the client would violate Rule 302.

Advertising and Solicitation. Following U.S. Supreme Court rulings that the Virginia bar association's minimum fee schedule was a violation of the Sherman Act[3] and that the Arizona bar association's restrictions on advertising violated the right of free speech guaranteed by the First Amendment to the U.S. Constitution,[4] the AICPA in 1978 lifted the ban on advertising by accountants. One year later, the AICPA removed its prohibition against direct solicitation of clients when it abolished Rule 401 (Encroachment). That Rule stated that "a member shall not endeavor to provide a person or entity with a professional service which is currently provided by another public accountant."

The present Rule 502 on advertising and solicitation is as follows: "A member in public practice shall not seek to obtain clients by advertising or other forms of solicitation in a manner that is false, misleading, or deceptive. Solicitation by the use of coercion, over-reaching, or harassing conduct is prohibited." There are no restrictions on the type of advertising media or frequency of placement.

Commissions and Referral Fees. Rule 503 states

> The acceptance by a member in public practice of a payment for the referral of products or services of others to a client is prohibited. Such action is considered to create a conflict of interest that results in a loss of objectivity and independence.
>
> A member shall not make a payment to obtain a client. This rule shall not prohibit payments for the purchase of an accounting practice or retirement

[3]*Goldfarb* v. *Virginia State Bar*, 421 U.S. 773 (1975).

[4]*Bates* v. *State Bar of Arizona,* 433 U.S. 350 (1977).

payments to individuals formerly engaged in the practice of public accounting or payments to their heirs or estates.

AICPA–FTC Consent Agreement. In 1989, the FTC approved for public comment a consent agreement with the AICPA under which the Institute agreed to cease and desist from enforcing some portions of its Code of Professional Conduct relating to contingent fees, commissions, referral fees, solicitation, advertising, and the use of "trade names" in designating a practice unit.

An important aspect of the consent agreement that many auditors believe constitutes a major victory for the profession is that the Institute can continue to prohibit members from receiving commissions or contingent fees for services performed for audit and other attest *clients* (even if such commissions or contingent fees are not related to such an *engagement*); and can require members to disclose to clients any permissible referral fees or commissions they do receive. The AICPA's keeping and exercising those rights could mitigate the perception that CPAs will now be able to act with less objectivity and independence than previously.

At the time of this writing, significant issues relating to the AICPA–FTC consent agreement are still unsettled. Most significantly, because the FTC has not issued a final Rule, the AICPA has not yet promulgated new Rules on commissions, contingent fees, and referral fees consistent with the consent agreement. In addition, the codes of conduct of many state societies of CPAs and the rules of many state boards of accountancy proscribe the same types of activities the FTC consent agreement would bar the AICPA from proscribing.[5] Those state proscriptions are not directly affected by the consent agreement and thus may still serve to restrain CPAs from engaging in activities that may be acceptable under a revised AICPA Code of Professional Conduct.

INCENTIVES FOR MAINTAINING AUDIT QUALITY

Introduction

Audit quality embraces the concepts of professional competence and the meeting or exceeding of professional standards (both technical and ethical) in expressing an opinion on audited financial statements, reporting on prospective financial information, being associated with unaudited financial statements, and providing other types of accounting services.

[5]At least one state (California) has passed legislation that may, depending on its interpretation and enforcement, also proscribe those activities, and similar legislation has been introduced in several other states.

Audit quality proceeds primarily from a firm's enlightened self-interest and from the concept of integrity. The first step in ensuring the quality of a firm's accounting and audit practice is to incorporate quality control measures into the audit itself—requirements, at the engagement level, for documentation, the use of practice aids, and reviews by various knowledgeable personnel. While each firm's specific policies concerning documentation, use of practice aids, consultation, and review, and its means of enforcing them, depend largely on its size, organizational structure, and style or philosophy of management, each of those elements must be present in one way or another. In addition to building audit quality into individual engagements as a means of achieving and maintaining a reputation for professional excellence, incentives for maintaining audit quality are provided through regulatory mechanisms and other means.

The regulatory mechanisms include both the self-regulatory system of the profession and the disciplinary systems provided by government agencies like the SEC and individual state boards of accountancy. The self-regulatory system of the profession imposes penalties for performance or conduct that departs from professional standards. In addition, the profession has developed recommendations for quality control systems to provide reasonable assurance that CPA firms conform with professional standards in the conduct of their accounting and auditing practices.

Furthermore, since 1988 the AICPA has required members engaged in the practice of public accounting in the United States or its territories to practice as proprietors, partners, shareholders, or employees of firms enrolled in an approved practice-monitoring program in order to retain their membership in the Institute beyond specified periods. There are two approved practice-monitoring programs.

- The peer review programs of the AICPA Division for CPA Firms.
- The quality review program the AICPA has established in cooperation with state CPA societies.

Both of those programs are discussed later in the chapter.

Other incentives for maintaining audit quality also exist. For one thing, firms are increasingly exposed to litigation in the conduct of their audit practices and to sanctions by the SEC. In addition, clients, and particularly audit committees, are putting increasing pressure on firms to maintain high audit quality. Audit quality is also a significant factor in a firm's ability to attract and retain clients and high-caliber personnel. Furthermore, through the efforts of financial writers and other news media, there is increasing public awareness of a firm's image and of the events that shape it.

The remainder of this section describes the profession's quality control and practice-monitoring programs, and the disciplinary systems of the profession and the state boards of accountancy.

Quality Controls

The objectives of quality control policies and procedures are to improve individual and firm performance and to ensure compliance with technical and ethical standards. The relationship of generally accepted auditing standards to quality control standards is discussed in SAS No. 25, *The Relationship of Generally Accepted Auditing Standards to Quality Control Standards* (AU Section 161.03).

> Generally accepted auditing standards relate to the conduct of individual audit engagements; quality control standards relate to the conduct of a firm's audit practice as a whole. Thus, generally accepted auditing standards and quality control standards are related, and the quality control policies and procedures that a firm adopts may affect both the conduct of individual audit engagements and the conduct of a firm's audit practice as a whole.

Statement on Quality Control Standards (SQCS) No. 1, *System of Quality Control for a CPA Firm* (QC Section 10), requires CPA firms to have a system of quality control. SQCS No. 1 describes nine elements of quality control and requires that a firm consider each of them, to the extent applicable to its practice, in establishing its quality control policies and procedures. The nine elements of quality control, as listed below, are interrelated (e.g., a firm's hiring practices affect its policies relating to training).

1. *Acceptance and continuance of clients.* Policies and procedures should be established for deciding whether to accept or continue a client in order to minimize the likelihood of association with a client whose management lacks integrity.
2. *Assigning personnel to engagements.* Policies and procedures for assigning personnel to engagements should be established to provide the firm with reasonable assurance that work will be performed by persons having the required degree of technical training and proficiency.

3. *Supervision.* Policies and procedures for the conduct and supervision of work at all organizational levels should be established to provide the firm with reasonable assurance that the work performed meets the firm's standards of quality.
4. *Hiring.* Policies and procedures for hiring should be established to provide the firm with reasonable assurance that employees possess the appropriate characteristics to enable them to perform competently.
5. *Professional development.* Policies and procedures for professional development should be established to provide the firm with reasonable assurance that personnel will have the knowledge required to enable them to fulfill their responsibilities.
6. *Advancement.* Policies and procedures for advancing personnel should be established to provide the firm with reasonable assurance that those

selected for advancement will have the qualifications necessary to fulfill the responsibilities they will be called on to assume.

7. *Consultation.* Policies and procedures for consultation should be established to provide the firm with reasonable assurance that personnel will seek assistance, to the extent required, from persons having appropriate levels of knowledge, competence, judgment, and authority.
8. *Independence.* Policies and procedures should be established to provide the firm with reasonable assurance that persons at all organizational levels maintain independence to the extent required by the AICPA's Code of Professional Conduct.
9. *Inspection.* Policies and procedures for inspection should be established to provide the firm with reasonable assurance that the procedures relating to the other elements of quality control are being effectively applied.

The element relating to accepting clients formalizes a long-standing practice by auditors of seeking to ascertain the reputation and business integrity of potential clients as a means of protecting their own reputation and avoiding inadvertently accepting an audit of high or unknown risk. The extent of the inquiry varies with the circumstances. It will be informal and brief, for example, if the potential client is well known in the community or can be easily investigated through mutual business associates. In other instances, more extreme and formal inquiries are called for, as often happens with companies having new management or diverse private ownership, or companies in industries or areas with which the auditor is relatively unfamiliar.

The inspection element is performed internally by individuals acting on behalf of the firm's management, as contrasted with peer reviews, discussed below, which are conducted by individuals not associated with the firm being reviewed. SQCS No. 1 (QC Section 10.10) also requires firms to maintain a monitoring function, of which inspection is one aspect. In monitoring the effectiveness of its system of quality control, a firm should modify its policies and procedures in a timely manner to address not only findings from its inspection program and peer review but also changed circumstances in its practice and new authoritative pronouncements.

Practice-Monitoring Programs

AICPA Division for CPA Firms. The AICPA Division for CPA Firms comprises two sections, one for SEC practice and the other for private company practice. The principal objective of each section is to improve the quality of CPA firms' practice by establishing requirements for member firms and an effective system of self-regulation. Following are requirements that have the most direct effect on audit quality.

Requirements common to both sections:

- Adhere to quality control standards established by the AICPA Quality Control Standards Committee.
- Submit to peer reviews of the firm's accounting and audit practice every three years or at such additional times as designated by the section's executive committee. The reviews will be conducted in accordance with review standards established by the section's peer review committee.
- Ensure that all professionals in the firm achieve at least the minimum hours of continuing professional education prescribed by the section.

Additional SEC Practice Section Requirements for All SEC Engagements[6]:

- Periodically rotate partners.
- Have a partner other than the audit partner in charge review and concur with the audit report on the financial statements before it is issued.
- Refrain from performing certain management advisory services. Such services include psychological testing; public opinion polls; merger and acquisition assistance for a finder's fee; recruitment for managerial, executive, or director positions; and, in certain situations, actuarial services to insurance companies.
- Communicate at least annually with the audit committee or, if there is no audit committee, with the board of directors (or its equivalent in a partnership) the total fees received from the client for management advisory services during the year under audit and a description of the types of such services rendered.[7]
- Report to the Quality Control Inquiry Committee (described below) any litigation (including criminal indictments) against the firm or its personnel or any proceeding or investigation publicly announced by a regulatory agency that alleges deficiencies in the conduct of an audit of the financial statements or reporting thereon of a present or former SEC client. Any allegations made in such formal litigation, proceeding, or investigation that the firm or its personnel have violated the federal securities laws in connection with services other than audit services must also be reported.
- Communicate in writing to all professional firm personnel the broad principles that influence the firm's quality control and operating policies and procedures on, as a minimum, matters related to the recommenda-

[6]The section's definition of an SEC engagement includes audits of certain banks and other lending institutions and certain sponsors or managers of investment funds, even though they are not registered with the SEC.

[7]In addition, SAS No. 61 requires auditors of SEC clients and other entities that have an audit committee or its equivalent to communicate certain other matters to the committee, as discussed in Chapter 17.

tion and approval of accounting principles, present and potential client relationships, and the types of services provided; and inform professional firm personnel periodically that compliance with those principles is mandatory.

- Notify the Chief Accountant of the SEC within five business days when the auditor–client relationship with an SEC registrant ceases (because the auditor has resigned, declined to stand for reelection, or been dismissed).

There are no significant additional requirements for membership in the Private Companies Practice Section.

Each section is governed by an executive committee composed of representatives from member firms that establishes the section's general policies and oversees its activities. Each section also has a peer review committee that administers its peer review program. The Executive Committee of the SEC Practice Section has in addition organized a Quality Control Inquiry Committee to identify corrective measures, if any, that should be taken by a member firm involved in a specific alleged audit failure. The activities of the SEC Practice Section are also subject to review by an independent Public Oversight Board that issues public reports.

Peer Review. Peer reviews must be conducted in conformity with the confidentiality requirements in the AICPA Code of Professional Conduct. (Rule 301 contains an exception that allows a peer review of a member's practice.) Information obtained concerning a reviewed firm or any of its clients is confidential and should not be disclosed by review team members to anyone not "associated with the review." (The executive and peer review committees and the Public Oversight Board are encompassed by the phrase "associated with the review.") While the AICPA Code of Professional Conduct does not deal specifically with independence in relationships between reviewers, reviewed firms, and clients of reviewed firms, the concepts of independence expressed in the Code are considered in regard to these relationships. The firm under review has the option of either having the Peer Review Committee appoint the review team or engaging another member firm to conduct the review; however, reciprocal reviews are not permitted.

The peer review team evaluates whether the reviewed firm's quality control system met the objectives of the quality control standards established by the AICPA, whether it was complied with to provide reasonable assurance of conforming with professional standards, and whether the firm was in compliance with the membership requirements of the section. Some tests made by the review team are performed at the practice office level, others on a firm-wide basis, and still others on an individual engagement basis. The review is of the firm's accounting and auditing practice, but other segments, such as tax, are covered in the review (1) to the extent that personnel from those segments assist on accounting and auditing engagements, and (2) as to compliance with

Figure 3.1 Unqualified Peer Review Report

[AICPA or Other Appropriate Letterhead]

September 15, 19____

To the Partners
Jones, Smith & Co.

We have reviewed the system of quality control for the accounting and auditing practice of Jones, Smith & Co. (the firm) in effect for the year ended June 30, 19____. Our review was conducted in conformity with standards for peer reviews promulgated by the peer review committee of the SEC Practice Section of the AICPA Division for CPA Firms (the section). We tested compliance with the firm's quality control policies and procedures (at the firm's executive office and at selected practice offices in the United States)* and with the membership requirements of the section to the extent we considered appropriate. These tests included the application of the firm's policies and procedures on selected accounting and auditing engagements. (We tested the supervision and control of portions of engagements performed outside the United States.)**

In performing our review, we have given consideration to the general characteristics of a system of quality control as described in quality control standards issued by the AICPA. Such a system should be appropriately comprehensive and suitably designed in relation to the firm's organizational structure, its policies, and the nature of its practice. Variance in individual performance can affect the degree of compliance with a firm's prescribed quality control policies and procedures. Therefore, adherence to all policies and procedures in every case may not be possible. (As is customary in a peer review, we are issuing a letter under this date that sets forth comments related to certain policies and procedures or compliance with them. None of these matters were considered to be of sufficient significance to affect the opinion expressed in this report.)***

membership requirements.[8] At the completion of the peer review, the review team furnishes the reviewed firm with a formal peer review report and, if applicable, a letter of comments on matters that may require action by the firm, both of which are available to the public. The SEC Practice Section manual presents an example of an unqualified peer review report, which is reproduced in Figure 3.1.

[8]The Division for CPA Firms has defined a firm's accounting and auditing practice as being "limited to all auditing, and all accounting, review, and compilation services covered by generally accepted auditing standards, standards for accounting and review services, standards for accountants' services on prospective financial information, and standards for financial and compliance audits contained in *Standards for Audit of Governmental Organizations, Programs, Activities, and Functions* issued by the U.S. General Accounting Office."

Figure 3.1 *Continued*

In our opinion, the system of quality control for the accounting and auditing practice of Jones, Smith & Co. in effect for the year ended June 30, 19____, met the objectives of quality control standards established by the AICPA and was being complied with during the year then ended to provide the firm with reasonable assurance of conforming with professional standards. Also, in our opinion the firm was in conformity with the membership requirements of the section in all material respects.

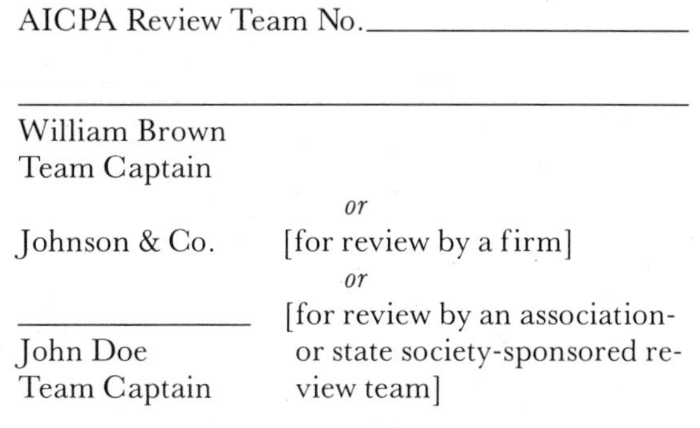

AICPA Review Team No.________________

____

William Brown
Team Captain

or

Johnson & Co. [for review by a firm]

or

________________ [for review by an association- or state society-sponsored review team]
John Doe
Team Captain

*To be included, as appropriate, for reviews of multioffice firms.

**To be included for reviewed firms with offices, correspondents, or affiliates outside the United States. Appropriately modified wording should be used if the reviewed firm uses correspondents or affiliates domestically, if that is significant to the scope of the review.

***To be included if the review team issues a letter of comments along with the unqualified report.

With respect to member firms with SEC clients, a procedure has been established to enable the SEC to make its own evaluation of whether the peer review process and the Public Oversight Board's oversight of it are adequate. The procedure permits the SEC access, during a limited period following the Peer Review Committee's acceptance of the peer review report, to defined areas of the peer review working papers, with appropriate safeguards to prevent the SEC from identifying the clients whose audit working papers were reviewed. After their review of the working papers on a specific peer review, the SEC representatives discuss with representatives of the Public Oversight Board and the Peer Review Committee any matters that they believe the committee should consider.

The following circumstances ordinarily would require a modified report:

- The scope of the review is limited by conditions that preclude the application of one or more review procedures considered necessary.
- The system of quality control as designed fails to meet one or more applicable objectives of quality control standards established by the

AICPA, resulting in a condition in which the firm did not have reasonable assurance of conforming with professional standards.
- The degree of noncompliance with the reviewed firm's quality control policies and procedures was such that the reviewed firm did not have reasonable assurance of conforming with professional standards.
- The reviewed firm did not comply with the membership requirements of the Section in all material respects.

The objective of the letter of comments is to report to the reviewed firm matters that resulted in a modified report or that the review team believes created a condition in which there is more than a remote (i.e., slight) possibility that the firm would not conform with professional standards on accounting and auditing engagements. The letter should include appropriate comments regarding the design of the reviewed firm's system of quality control, its compliance with that system (including professional standards), and its compliance with the membership requirements of the Section. The review team may also communicate orally to senior management of the reviewed firm comments that were not deemed significant enough to be included in the letter of comments.

Quality Review Program. The quality review program, which applies to firms that are not members of the Division, is similar to the peer review program of the Private Companies Practice Section of the Division for CPA Firms. There are some differences, however, between the two programs, particularly in the reporting requirements and distribution of review reports.

Standards for the quality review program are applicable to firms enrolled in the program, individuals and firms that perform and report on reviews, state societies that participate in the administration of the program, associations of CPA firms that assist their members in arranging and carrying out quality reviews, and the AICPA Quality Review Division itself. Specifically, the standards

- Provide distinctly different performance and reporting standards for two types of quality reviews—an on-site review for firms that examine historical or prospective financial statements, and an off-site review for firms that issue compilation or review reports but perform no examinations of historical or prospective financial statements.
- Provide guidance on general considerations applicable to all quality reviews.
- Describe how review teams are formed and what qualifications they must possess.
- Define the responsibilities of the review team, the reviewed firm, and the entity administering the review, and provide standards, procedures, and guidelines to be followed by each participant in the process.

Disciplinary System

The AICPA (in conjunction with state societies of CPAs), state boards of accountancy, the courts, and the SEC may impose sanctions on individuals and firms for performance or conduct that violates professional standards or civil or criminal laws. The paragraphs that follow discuss disciplinary actions of the profession and state boards of accountancy.

Disciplinary System Within the Profession for Individuals. The AICPA's self-disciplinary mechanism for individual members consists of the Institute's Professional Ethics Division (the Division) and the Joint Trial Board.

The Division is responsible for interpreting the Code of Professional Conduct and proposing amendments to it. The Division is also responsible for investigating alleged violations of the Code for possible disciplinary or rehabilitative action, including hearings before panels of the Joint Trial Board. The Division may initiate an investigation on the basis of complaints from individuals, state societies of CPAs, or government agencies, or on the basis of information from news media, the SEC *Docket*, or the IRS *Bulletin*.

The Executive Committee of the Division can take the following types of disciplinary actions against individual members:

- If the Executive Committee concludes that a prima facie violation of the Code of Professional Conduct or bylaws is not of sufficient gravity to warrant further formal action, it may direct the member or members concerned to complete specified continuing professional education courses or to take other remedial or corrective action. There is no publication of that action in the Institute's principal membership periodical, *The CPA Letter*. The member has the right to reject the direction. If he or she does, the Executive Committee determines whether to bring the matter to a panel of the Joint Trial Board for a hearing.
- Presentation of a prima facie case to a panel of the Joint Trial Board, a proceeding that is used for serious violations that may require suspension or expulsion from membership or public censure. Publication of the names of members found guilty of the charges is required.

The AICPA's bylaws provide for automatic termination of membership (with publication of name) if a member is convicted of (1) a crime punishable by imprisonment for more than one year, (2) the willful failure to file any income tax return that he or she is required to file as an individual taxpayer, (3) filing a false or fraudulent income tax return on the member's own or a client's behalf, or (4) the willful aiding in the preparation and presentation of a false and fraudulent income tax return of a client.

Disciplinary System Within the Profession for Firms. The executive committee of each section of the AICPA Division for CPA Firms has the authority to impose sanctions on member firms for failing to meet membership requirements, either on its own initiative or on the basis of recommendations from that Section's Peer Review Committee. The following types of sanctions may be imposed on member firms:

Peer

- Corrective measures by the firm, including consideration by the firm of appropriate actions with respect to individual firm personnel.
- Additional requirements for continuing professional education.
- Accelerated or special peer reviews.
- Admonishments, censures, or reprimands.
- Monetary fines.
- Suspension or expulsion from membership.

State Boards of Accountancy. A state board of accountancy is charged with enforcing laws that regulate the practice of public accounting in that state. Generally, a board has the power to revoke or suspend the certificates of CPAs; to revoke, suspend, or refuse to renew permits to practice; and to censure the holders of licenses or permits to practice.[9] Those penalties can be imposed for a wide variety of acts or omissions specified in accountancy laws. Several states also require the registration of firms, issue permits for firms to practice in the state, and have the power to revoke or suspend those permits. An increasing number of states have required firms to participate in "Positive Enforcement Programs"—a type of quality review—as a condition for practicing within those states.

ENHANCING THE INDEPENDENCE OF AUDITORS

Generally accepted auditing standards, the AICPA Code of Professional Conduct, the Securities and Exchange Commission, and individual accounting firms require auditors to maintain an attitude of independence and prohibit certain relationships with clients. Nevertheless, some people believe that there are potential threats to auditor independence because the client selects the auditor and pays the fee and because the auditor may undertake nonaudit services for the client. Since auditors are often selected and paid, retained, or replaced at the sole discretion of the management on whose representations they are expected to report, many people believe that total professional independence is impossible. While "total" independence may be impossible, auditors are extremely conscious that their independence is vital and that they must preserve the standards of the profession for the sake of their own reputation.

[9]It should be noted that the AICPA has no such powers, since it does not issue certificates or permits to practice. AICPA disciplinary actions are related only to membership in the Institute.

The profession, the SEC, and responsible leaders of the financial community have recognized this alleged threat and have taken steps to deal with it. Some companies require that the selection and retention of auditors be ratified by the stockholders. In the case of companies whose securities are publicly traded, the SEC requires public notice of the termination of auditors, disclosure of any accounting or auditing disputes within two years between the client and the former auditor, and a letter from the former auditor concurring in such disclosure. Those are worthwhile steps, but they mitigate rather than eliminate the threat to auditor independence.

Another alleged threat to auditor independence arises from the various types of nonaudit services provided to audit clients by public accounting firms. Such services include tax services (such as tax return preparation, tax planning advice, and representation before the IRS); management services, some that are related to accounting and auditing (such as advice on systems, control procedures, data processing, and cost accounting) and some that are not (for instance, market studies or studies of factory layout); and accounting services (such as compilations and reviews for nonpublic companies and advice on selection and application of accounting principles and the accounting implications of proposed management decisions). There is no general proscription by either the SEC or the AICPA against performing nonauditing services for audit clients. The SEC has at times in the past monitored such relationships and required their disclosure, and the AICPA Division for CPA Firms prohibits members of its SEC Practice Section from providing certain management advisory services.

Many proposals have been made to strengthen auditor independence. They fall into two broad categories.

- Protecting the auditor from management influence, through the use of audit committees, requiring that a successor auditor communicate with the predecessor auditor, SEC scrutiny of auditor changes, and rotation of audit personnel.
- Other proposals to increase auditor independence, including transfer of the audit function to the public sector, auditor selection of generally accepted accounting principles for clients, and prohibiting auditors from performing management advisory services for audit clients.

The Cohen Commission considered and evaluated those proposals in its 1978 report; several of them were restudied by the Treadway Commission in its 1987 report. The remainder of this chapter discusses and evaluates each of the proposals.

Protecting the Auditor from Management Influence

Neither audit effectiveness nor audit efficiency would be strengthened if the auditor were isolated from client management. An auditor must work with management because management's active and positive cooperation is required in conducting an audit, and that in turn requires the auditor and management to have a high degree of confidence in one another. Yet auditor independence must be maintained despite the need for cooperation. Another difficulty auditors face in maintaining their independence is that they are members of a profit-making firm that depends on fees over which client management may exert considerable control. Several proposals to increase the auditor's ability to resist pressure from management are discussed next.

Audit Committees. Over the years, several professional and regulatory bodies have suggested requiring companies to have audit committees of boards of directors as a means of reinforcing auditors' independence from management. The SEC endorsed the establishment of audit committees composed of outside directors in 1972 (ASR No. 123) and subsequently adopted nonbinding rules underscoring this commitment. The AICPA recommended in 1967 that audit committees be established for all publicly held companies. In 1978, the New York Stock Exchange mandated that domestic companies with listed securities establish audit committees made up entirely of outside directors; in 1979, the American Stock Exchange strongly recommended similar action. A special House subcommittee in 1976 also noted the desirability of audit committees. The Cohen Commission strongly endorsed the use of audit committees to recommend to shareholders the appointment of independent auditors and to evaluate the relationship between auditor and management. The Institute of Internal Auditors also endorsed the establishment of audit committees consisting of outside directors by both public companies and other organizations, such as not-for-profit and governmental bodies. Finally, the Treadway Commission recommended that the SEC require all public companies to establish audit committees composed solely of outside directors. It also provided guidance on how audit committees could serve as "informed, vigilant, and effective overseers of the financial reporting process and the company's internal controls."[10]

Today, although not universally required, audit committees are an important part of our corporate structure. They oversee a company's accounting and financial reporting policies and practices, help the board of directors fulfill its corporate reporting responsibilities, and help maintain a direct line of communication between the board and the company's external and internal auditors. Although occasionally the entire board may turn to the independent auditors for assistance in reviewing the financial statements or other data, contact between the board and the auditors is generally through the audit committee.

Over the years, the AICPA and the New York Stock Exchange have issued general guidelines for audit committees but have not mandated specific duties,

[10]*Report of the National Commission on Fraudulent Financial Reporting* (Treadway Commission), 1987, p. 41.

responsibilities, or activities. Since specific functions have not been prescribed for audit committees, their activities vary from one company to the next. Effective committees, however, should generally perform at least the following:

- Recommend the appointment of the independent auditor and review the fee arrangements.
- Review the proposed scope of the independent audit.
- Communicate with the internal auditors and review their activities, effectiveness, and recommendations for improving the company's control structure.
- Review the financial statements and the results of the independent audit.
- Review the report by management containing management's opinion on the effectiveness of the company's control structure and the basis for that opinion.
- Consider the selection of accounting policies.
- Scrutinize the required communications from the independent auditor regarding deficiencies in the company's control structure, irregularities discovered in the course of the audit, and many other matters related to the audit.
- Oversee or conduct special investigations or other functions on behalf of the board of directors.

In the authors' opinion, the trend toward establishing audit committees of outside directors has been beneficial to management, directors, stockholders, and the auditing profession. Auditors and outside directors have common interests that are vastly strengthened by interaction between the two groups. An active and involved audit committee serves to protect corporate interests by overseeing the activities of the auditor and, at least to some extent in matters of financial reporting, company management. The existence of an audit committee of outside directors demonstrates that all parties with responsibility for reliable financial reporting—management, the independent auditors, and the board of directors acting in an oversight capacity—are diligently carrying out their duties to the stockholders. An audit committee reinforces the auditor's independence, while the auditor provides an independent source of information to the directors; management's support of the relationship demonstrates a sense of accountability.

Communicating with Predecessor Auditors. SAS No. 7, *Communications Between Predecessor and Successor Auditors* (AU Section 315.01–.09), issued in 1975, requires a successor auditor to attempt to communicate with the predecessor as part of the process of determining whether to accept an engagement. The SAS outlines, in paragraph 6 (AU Section 315.06), the procedures to be followed by a successor auditor.

> The successor auditor should make specific and reasonable inquiries of the predecessor regarding matters that the successor believes will assist him in determining whether to accept the engagement. His inquiries should include specific questions regarding, among other things, facts that might bear on the integrity of management; on disagreements with management as to accounting principles, auditing procedures, or other similarly significant matters; and on the predecessor's understanding as to the reasons for the change of auditors.

AU Section 315 indicates that the predecessor auditor is obligated to "respond promptly and fully" to any "reasonable" question, but it also recognizes that, in unusual situations such as when litigation is or may be involved, the predecessor may need to advise the successor that the response is limited. In that event, the successor auditor should consider whether the information obtained from all sources is adequate to support accepting the client. If the client refuses to allow the successor auditor to talk to the predecessor auditor, the successor auditor should also consider whether to accept the engagement.

After a successor auditor has been appointed, there are two occasions when communications between the predecessor and the successor auditors are appropriate. One reflects the successor's need to review the prior auditor's working papers, and the other arises if the successor believes that there is an error in the financial statements on which the predecessor auditor expressed an opinion.

Working papers are the property of the auditor who prepared them, who is under no compulsion to share them with a successor auditor. In the absence of unusual circumstances, however, such as litigation between the client and the predecessor auditor or amounts owed to the predecessor auditor by the client, predecessor auditors customarily allow successor auditors access to at least certain working papers.

Scrutiny of Auditor Changes. Management sometimes threatens to dismiss the auditor when there is a disagreement on accounting principles. Management might then "shop around" for a more compliant auditor. Requiring auditor changes to be ratified by an audit committee is one way of relieving pressure on the auditor from management. Outside scrutiny of the dismissal of an auditor also inhibits the tendency to apply such pressure. The scrutiny of auditor changes has been enhanced by SEC requirements to disclose potential "opinion shopping" situations and disagreements between the client and the auditor when there is a change in auditors.

Opinion Shopping. An auditor may be asked by another accountant's client for professional advice on an accounting or auditing technical matter. In some situations, the client and its auditor may have disagreed about the matter in question. When the client's purpose in seeking another professional opinion is to find an accountant willing to support a proposed accounting treatment that would favor a particular reporting objective but that is not necessarily in conformity with GAAP and is not supported by the client's auditor, the practice is commonly referred to as "opinion shopping." SAS No. 50, *Reports on the Application of Accounting Principles* (AU Section 625), contains standards to be followed by an accountant who is asked to give an opinion on GAAP to another auditor's client (see discussion in Chapter 19).

The SEC has noted that the search for an auditor who would support a proposed accounting treatment may indicate an effort by management to avoid the requirement for an independent audit, and that an auditor's willingness to support a proposed accounting treatment that may frustrate reliable reporting may suggest a lack of professional skepticism and independence on the part of the auditor. The SEC requires disclosure of possible opinion shopping situations in connection with a change in auditors if the registrant consulted the newly engaged auditor within approximately two years before the engagement.[11] (The SEC rule specifies the matters covered by the consultation and the information required to be disclosed.)

Disagreements with Clients. Since 1971, the SEC has required disclosure in a timely Form 8-K filing of a change in auditors made by the registrant, including disclosure of certain disagreements between the registrant and the predecessor auditor during the two most recent fiscal years and any subsequent interim period. The predecessor auditor provides a letter, which is generally filed by the company with its Form 8-K, either concurring with the company's disclosures or setting forth any disagreements that were omitted or require further explanation. In addition, if the predecessor auditor objected to an accounting method or disclosure that had a material effect on the financial statements and the successor auditor agrees to it, the SEC requires the registrant to disclose the disagreement and the effect on the financial statements that would have resulted if the method advocated by the former auditor had been followed.

The SEC rules emphasize that the term "disagreements" should be interpreted broadly to include any differences of opinion regarding accounting principles or practices, financial statement disclosure, or auditing scope or procedure that, if not resolved to the satisfaction of the former auditor, would have caused him or her to refer to the disagreement in the audit report. Further, the rules indicate that a disagreement means a difference of opinion, not necessarily an argument. Both disagreements that were resolved to the former auditor's satisfaction and those that were not are required to be reported. However, initial differences of opinion based on incomplete facts or preliminary information that were later resolved to the former auditor's satisfaction (before his or her dismissal or resignation) are not disagreements.

Certain other events also require the same disclosures as for disagreements, when there is a change in auditors (even if the registrant and the former auditor did not have a difference of opinion regarding the event). These reportable

[11]SEC Financial Reporting Release No. 31, April 7, 1988.

events include situations in which the former auditor advised the registrant that

- Internal controls necessary for the registrant to develop reliable financial statements did not exist.
- He or she was unwilling to rely on management's representations or be associated with the registrant's financial statements.
- He or she would have had to significantly expand the scope of the audit and was not permitted to do so.
- Information came to his or her attention that he or she has concluded materially affects the fairness or reliability of either a prior audit report or the underlying financial statements, or the current financial statements, and, for whatever reason, the issue was not resolved.

The registrant must also disclose whether

- The former auditor resigned, declined to stand for reelection, or was dismissed.
- The audit committee of the board of directors or the board discussed the subject matter of each disagreement or reportable event with the former auditor.
- The registrant has authorized the former auditor to respond fully to the inquiries of the successor auditor regarding the subject matter of each disagreement or reportable event.

Members of the SEC Practice Section of the AICPA Division for CPA Firms must report disagreements (as defined) to the audit committee or board of directors of SEC clients, even when there has not been a change in auditors. As previously noted, members of the SEC Practice Section must also notify the Chief Accountant of the SEC within five business days when the auditor–client relationship with an SEC registrant ceases, regardless of whether the client has reported a change in auditors in a Form 8-K filing.

Rotation of Audit Personnel. To decrease the auditor's incentive for yielding to pressure from management, some people have proposed mandatory rotation of auditors, with a new auditor to be appointed every three to five years. Also, some argue that a new auditor would bring a fresh viewpoint to the engagement. Rotation would considerably increase audit costs, however, because of the start-up and learning time necessary on a new engagement. In addition, the Cohen Commission, noting that most cases of substandard performance by auditors were first- or second-year audits, stated, "Once an auditor becomes well acquainted with the operation of a client, audit risks are reduced" (p. 109).

Because of this, the Cohen Commission concluded that rotation of audit firms should not be required. The Commission also pointed out that the primary advantage of rotation—the fresh viewpoint—can be achieved if the personnel assigned to an engagement are systematically rotated.[12] This recommendation is reflected in the membership requirement of the SEC Practice Section of the AICPA Division for CPA Firms that certain personnel on audits of SEC engagements be periodically rotated.

Other Proposals to Enhance Independence

Over the years, there have been many other proposals to enhance auditor independence, several of which would require a sweeping change in the relationship between auditor and client. They have not been supported, however, by the AICPA, the SEC, the Cohen and Treadway Commissions, or the authors of this book. Three of the more frequently presented of those proposals are discussed next.

Transfer to the Public Sector. In order to sever the ties between auditor and management, proposals have been made to have independent auditors approved, assigned, or compensated by a government agency or by the stock exchanges or to have audits conducted by a group of government auditors. The Cohen Commission concluded that having auditors approved, assigned, or compensated by the government is not warranted either by the magnitude of deficiencies in present practice or by the promise of potential improvements. It also noted that the government may use accounting information to accomplish its own economic or political objectives, which suggests that increased government involvement in audits may well create problems of independence and objectivity.[13]

Auditor Selection of GAAP for Clients. Traditionally, management has had the primary responsibility for the financial statements, including selecting what accounting principles to use and what disclosures to make. Proposals have been made to require the auditor to assume those responsibilities. The authors believe that the present division of responsibility is sound and should not be changed. Management, with firsthand knowledge of what has occurred, should be responsible for ensuring that events and transactions are properly reported. Furthermore, management is in the best position to make the judgments and estimates necessary to prepare the financial statements, and the auditor is in the best position to challenge and evaluate those judgments and estimates.

[12] *Report, Conclusions, and Recommendations*, 1978, pp. 108–9.

[13] *Ibid.*, p. 105.

Occasionally, an issue involving reporting standards or the application of generally accepted accounting principles becomes a "disagreement" between management and the auditor. Such disagreements are frequently resolved by the auditor's convincing management of the propriety of an accounting principle or the necessity and justification for a particular disclosure. If, however, the auditor is not successful, a qualification results. Probably the most effective way of avoiding this is for the client to seek the auditor's early involvement and consultation in the formative stages of nonroutine transactions. In that way, neither party is faced with an unavoidable accounting or auditing outcome that is unsatisfactory to the client.

The linkage between selecting accounting principles and accumulating and classifying accounting data is very close. If auditors were responsible for selecting accounting principles and disclosures, they would lose the independent evaluation function that they perform today. Auditors should use their expertise to advise and counsel management in preparing financial statements, with management retaining the ultimate responsibility for the presentation.

Prohibition of Management Advisory Services. The potential adverse effect on auditor independence of performing management advisory services for audit clients has been debated for more than three decades. The Treadway Commission noted that

> Some argue that the independent public accountant's performance of management advisory services improves the quality of audits. They claim that in the process of advising management the independent public accountant acquires a deeper understanding of the client's business. Many in the public accounting profession also maintain that benefits accrue to the audit process when the independent public accountant is already familiar with the company's operations.
>
> Others believe that some management advisory services place independent public accountants in the role of management, add commercial pressures to the audit examination and, as a result, impair independence. These individuals also argue that, at the very least, the public accountant's performance of management advisory services raises the perception of impaired independence. (p. 43)

Like the Cohen Commission before it, the Treadway Commission reviewed previous studies of the issue and sponsored its own research study. Neither commission found any actual case in which an auditor's independence was compromised by providing management advisory services. The Treadway Commission cited several empirical studies, however, that indicated that "a substantial percentage of members of key public groups involved in the financial reporting process believe that performing certain management advisory services can impair a public auditor's objectivity and independence."[14]

[14]Treadway Commission, p. 44.

The Treadway Commission concluded that the existence of that perception should not be ignored. It noted that members of the SEC Practice Section of the AICPA's Division for CPA Firms must disclose to the audit committee or board of directors the total fees received from an SEC audit client for management advisory services during the past year and a description of the types of such services rendered. The Treadway Commission recommended that the audit committee should oversee management judgments relating to management advisory services and the auditor's independence.

Review Questions

3-1. What attributes of auditing qualify it as a profession?

3-2. What requirements generally must be met for certification as a CPA?

3-3. What are auditing standards? How do they differ from auditing procedures?

3-4. Name the ten generally accepted auditing standards and classify them into three basic categories.

3-5. What is the auditor's responsibility for understanding the internal control structure?

3-6. What is the objective of the consistency standard of reporting?

3-7. Why must an auditor's report be painstakingly precise in spelling out the opinion expressed?

3-8. What are the six broad Principles embodied in the AICPA Code of Professional Conduct?

3-9. Distinguish between the appearance of independence and the fact of independence. Give examples of how an auditor could be independent in fact but not in appearance, and vice versa. Do professional standards require the auditor to possess independence in both appearance and fact? Why?

3-10. What are some examples of activities that will result in an auditor's independence being considered impaired?

3-11. How does the existence of past-due fees affect an auditor's independence and how does the auditor resolve the issue?

3-12. What should be done if an auditor does not possess the competence to perform the services needed by the client?

3-13. What should the auditor do when the literal application of a pronouncement on accounting principles would have the effect of rendering the financial statements misleading?

3-14. What is the difference between confidential information and privileged information?

3-15. What are a CPA's responsibilities regarding insider information?

3-16. Describe the past and present position of the AICPA regarding advertising and solicitation.

3-17. What specific acts are considered discreditable to the profession? Which acts provide for automatic termination of membership under the AICPA bylaws? Who can revoke a CPA's certificate?

3–18. What are the elements of quality control described by SQCS No. 1?

3–19. What is a peer review and how is it accomplished?

3–20. What types of sanctions may be imposed on member firms for failure to comply with the membership requirements of the AICPA Division for CPA Firms?

3–21. What is the role of the audit committee of the board of directors? How does an audit committee act as a check on the auditor?

3–22. What developments have increased the scrutiny of auditor changes?

3–23. What type of inquiries should a successor auditor make of a predecessor?

3–24. What types of disagreements with the client or other events must a replaced auditor report to the SEC?

Discussion Questions

3–30. Give some examples of due professional care not being exercised in the course of an ordinary audit.

3–31. Mary De Haven, CPA, has audited the financial statements of Forsythe Corporation for several years. Forsythe's president has now asked De Haven to install an inventory control system for the company.

Required:

Discuss the factors that De Haven should consider in determining whether to accept this engagement.

(AICPA adapted)

3–32. In your audit of Client A you discover information that, if known, would have an adverse effect on the financial statements of Client B. Explain how you would proceed in this situation, considering the auditor's responsibility concerning confidentiality.

3–33. Some critics of the profession feel that auditors should not render management advisory services to clients being audited by them. Discuss the profession's position on this subject, including the conclusions of the Commission on Auditors' Responsibilities and the Treadway Commission on this subject.

3–34. Discuss CPAs' responsibilities to their clients and to the public at large.

3–35. Discuss the pros and cons of proposals to enhance auditor independence by transferring the audit function to the public sector or by making auditors responsible for selecting accounting principles for their clients.

3–36. Rotation of auditors has frequently been recommended by critics of the profession. Discuss the profession's attitude toward rotation, including the conclusion of the Commission on Auditors' Responsibilities on this subject.

AICPA Multiple Choice Questions

These questions are taken from the Auditing part of Uniform CPA Examinations. Choose the single most appropriate answer.

3–40. Which of the following *best* describes what is meant by generally accepted auditing standards?

a. Acts to be performed by the auditor.
b. Measures of the quality of the auditor's performance.
c. Procedures to be used to gather evidence to support financial statements.
d. Audit objectives generally determined on audit engagements.

3–41. The third general standard states that due care is to be exercised in the performance of the audit. This standard means that a CPA who undertakes an engagement assumes a duty to perform each audit

a. As a professional possessing the degree of skill commonly possessed by others in the field.
b. In conformity with generally accepted accounting principles.
c. With reasonable diligence and without fault or error.
d. To the satisfaction of governmental agencies and investors who rely upon the audit.

3–42. The fourth reporting standard requires the auditor's report to contain either an expression of opinion regarding the financial statements, taken as a whole, or an assertion to the effect that an opinion cannot be expressed. The objective of the fourth standard is to prevent

a. The CPA from reporting on one basic financial statement and *not* the others.
b. Misinterpretations regarding the degree of responsibility the auditor is assuming.
c. The CPA from expressing different opinins on each of the basic financial statements.
d. Management from reducing its final responsibility for the basic financial statements.

3–43. A CPA, while performing an audit, strives to achieve independence in appearance in order to

a. Reduce risk and liability.
b. Become independent in fact.
c. Maintain public confidence in the profession.
d. Comply with the generally accepted standards of field work.

3–44. An independent auditor must be without bias with respect to the financial statements of a client in order to

a. Comply with the laws established by governmental agencies.
b. Maintain the appearance of separate interests on the part of the auditor and the client.
c. Protect against criticism and possible litigation from stockholders and creditors.
d. Ensure the impartiality necessary for an expression of the auditor's opinion.

3–45. A violation of the profession's ethical standards would most likely have occurred when a CPA

a. Purchased a bookkeeping firm's practice of monthly write-ups for a percentage of fees received over a three-year period.
b. Made arrangements with a bank to collect notes issued by a client in payment of fees due.
c. Named Smith formed a partnership with two other CPAs and use "Smith & Co." as the firm name.
d. Issued an unqualified opinion on the 1990 financial statements when fees for the 1989 audit were unpaid.

3–46. Before accepting an audit engagement, a successor auditor should make specific inquiries of the predecessor auditor regarding the predecessor's

a. Awareness of the consistency in the application of generally accepted accounting principles between periods.
b. Evaluation of all matters of continuing accounting significance.
c. Opinion of any subsequent events occurring since the predecessor's audit report was issued.
d. Understanding as to the reasons for the change of auditors.

3–47. Smith, CPA, issued an "except for" opinion on the financial statements of Wald Company for the year ended December 31, 1991. Wald has engaged another firm of CPAs to make a second audit. The local bank has knowledge of Smith's audit and has asked Smith to explain why the financial statements and his opinion have *not* been made available.

a. Smith *cannot* provide the bank with information about Wald under any circumstances.
b. If Wald consents, Smith may provide the bank with information concerning Wald.
c. If the other firm of CPAs consents, Smith may provide the bank with information concerning Wald.
d. The only way the bank can obtain information concerning Smith's audit is to obtain it by subpoena.

3–48. Richard, CPA, performs accounting services for Norton Corporation. Norton wishes to offer its shares to the public and asks Richard to audit the financial statements prepared for registration purposes. Richard refers Norton to Cruz, CPA, who is more competent in the area of registration statements. Cruz performs the audit of Norton's financial statements and subsequently thanks Richard for the referral by giving Richard a portion of the audit fee collected. Richard accepts the fee. Who, if anyone, has violated professional ethics?

a. Only Richard.
b. Both Richard and Cruz.
c. Only Cruz.
d. Neither Richard nor Cruz.

3–49. According to the profession's ethical standards, an auditor would be considered independent in which of the following instances?

a. The auditor's checking account, which is fully insured by a federal agency, is held at a client financial institution.
b. The auditor is also an attorney who advises the client as its general counsel.
c. An employee of the auditor donates service as treasurer of a charitable organization that is a client.
d. The client owes the auditor fees for two consecutive annual audits.

3–50. Working papers prepared by a CPA in connection with an audit engagement are owned by the CPA, subject to certain limitations. The rationale for this rule is to

a. Protect the working papers from being subpoenaed.
b. Provide the basis for excluding admission of the working papers as evidence because of the privileged communication rule.
c. Provide the CPA with evidence and documentation that may be helpful in the event of a lawsuit.
d. Establish a continuity of relationship with the client whereby indiscriminate replacement of CPAs is discouraged.

3–51. In pursuing its quality-control objectives with respect to assigning personnel to engagements, a firm of independent auditors may use policies and procedures such as

a. Designating senior qualified personnel to provide advice on accounting or auditing questions throughout the engagement.
b. Requiring timely identification of the staffing requirements of specific engagements so that enough qualified personnel can be made available.
c. Establishing at entry levels a policy for recruiting that includes minimum standards of academic preparation and accomplishment.
d. Requiring auditing personnel to have current accounting and auditing literature available for research and reference purposes throughout the engagement.

3–52. Williams & Co., a large international CPA firm, is to have an "external peer review." The peer review will most likely be performed by

a. Employees and partners of Williams & Co., who are *not* associated with the particular audits being reviewed.
b. Audit review staff of the Securities and Exchange Commission.
c. Audit review staff of the American Institute of Certified Public Accountants.
d. Employees and partners of another CPA firm.

3–53. The SEC has strengthened auditor independence by requiring that management

a. Engage auditors to report in accordance with the Foreign Corrupt Practices Act.
b. Report the nature of disagreements with former auditors.
c. Select auditors through audit committees.
d. Acknowledge their responsibility for the fairness of the financial statements.

3–54. The CPA firm of Knox & Knox has been subpoenaed to testify and produce its correspondence and working papers in connection with a lawsuit brought by a third party against one of its clients. Knox considers the subpoenaed documents to be privileged communication and therefore seeks to avoid admission of such evidence in the lawsuit. Which of the following is correct?

a. Federal law recognizes such a privilege if the accountant is a Certified Public Accountant.
b. The privilege is available regarding the working papers since the CPA is deemed to own them.
c. The privileged communication rule as it applies to the CPA–client relationship is the same as that of attorney–client.
d. In the absence of a specific statutory provision, the law does *not* recognize the existence of the privileged communication rule between a CPA and his client.

3–55. A CPA is permitted to disclose confidential client information without the consent of the client to

I. Another CPA who has purchased the CPA's tax practice.
II. A successor CPA firm if the information concerns suspected tax return irregularities.
III. A voluntary quality control review board.

a. I and III only.
b. II and III only.
c. II only.
d. III only.

Problems and Cases

3–60. a. Lewis & Stern, CPAs, were engaged for several years by Custom Cabinet Corporation, manufacturers of wood cabinets, to conduct an annual audit. Foremost Cabinet Company, a competitor of Custom, now seeks to engage Lewis & Stern to install a more advanced accounting system and to conduct an annual audit. The officers of Foremost approached Lewis & Stern because of its outstanding reputation in the community and its acknowledged expertise in the wood products industry.

Required:
May Lewis & Stern accept the Foremost Cabinet Company as a client? Explain.

b. Continuing the facts in *a*) Subsequently, one of the officers of Foremost offered to pay Lewis & Stern a substantial bonus if they would disclose confidential information about Custom's operations to permit the officer to make a comparative study of the operating performance of the two companies.

Required:
May Lewis & Stern accept this offer? Explain.

(AICPA adapted)

3–61. For each of the following unrelated cases, state whether there has been a violation of the AICPA's Code of Professional Conduct, and, if so, explain why the rule is necessary.

a. Wills, CPA, and Michaels, CPA, have combined their practices and have incorporated to practice public accounting. They are the only shareholders.
b. Lawles, CPA, has installed a medium-sized computer in his office, which he uses to service audit and nonaudit clients not large enough to support computers of their own. In many instances, the data processing provided includes maintenance of the general ledger and the preparation of financial statements, on which Lawles (after auditing) expresses unqualified opinions.
c. Michaels, CPA, has retired and sold his audit practice to Blum, CPA, who has taken over Michaels' office and files and begun routine work on the practice. Michaels, fearful of the loss of clients because of the change, has not advised his clients, but intends to introduce Blum as his successor as each engagement commences.
d. Brown, CPA, has obtained licenses as a real estate broker and insurance agent, and combines his practices in one office. In many instances, his audit clients are also his insurance and real estate clients.
e. Sacks, CPA, having recently been granted his certificate, has begun practice and is advertising in the local paper as "Accountant and Auditor." He is sending fliers to the heads of all local businesses indicating his availability for services.
f. Blum, CPA, specializes in taxes and includes on his letterhead and business card the designation "Tax Expert."
g. Evans, CPA, and Michaels, CPA, were fellow panelists at a seminar conducted by the local chapter of their state society of CPAs. Impressed by Michaels' expertise, Evans offered Michaels a position with his firm at a salary greater than that which she was receiving as a staff member of another firm.
h. Miller, CPA, an SEC specialist, has written an article for publication. The publisher insists on including among her credits the fact that Miller is the SEC specialist for her firm.
i. Thomas, a real estate broker and insurance agent, regularly refers his clients to Davis, CPA, for tax return preparation. Pursuant to their arrangement, Davis pays Thomas 5 percent of all fees collected from Thomas' clients.

3-62. Laura Greene, CPA, has audited Tory Tools, Inc. for the last ten years. It was recently discovered that Tory's top management has been engaged in some questionable financial activities since the last audited financial statements were issued.

Subsequently, Tory was sued in state court by its major competitor, General Hardware. In addition, the SEC commenced an investigation against Tory for possible violations of the federal securities laws.

Both General and the SEC have subpoenaed all of Greene's working papers relating to her audits of Tory for the last ten years. There is no evidence either that Greene did anything improper or that any questionable financial activities by Tory occurred prior to this year.

Greene estimates that the cost for her photocopying of all of the working papers would be $25,000 (approximately one year's audit fee). Tory has instructed Greene not to turn over the working papers to anyone.

Required:

Answer the following, setting forth reasons for any conclusions stated.

a. If Greene practices in a state that has a statutory accountant–client privilege, may the state's accountant–client privilege be successfully asserted to avoid turning over the working papers to the SEC?
b. Assuming Greene, with Tory's permission, turns over to General working papers for the last two audit years, may the state's accountant–client privilege be successfully asserted to avoid producing the working papers for the first eight years?
c. Other than asserting an accountant–client privilege, what major defenses might Greene raise against the SEC and General in order to resist turning over the subpoenaed working papers?

(AICPA adapted)

3–63. For many years the financial and accounting community has recognized the importance of the use of audit committees and has endorsed their formation.

At this time, the use of audit committees has become widespread. Independent auditors have become increasingly involved with audit committees and consequently have become familiar with their nature and function.

Required:

a. Describe what an audit committee is.
b. Identify the reasons why audit committees have been formed and are currently in operation.
c. What are the functions of an audit committee?

(AICPA adapted)

3–64. Diane Pitman, CPA, has been requested by an audit client to perform a nonrecurring engagement involving the implementation of an EDP information and accounting system. The client requests that in setting up the new system and during the period prior to conversion to the new system Pitman

- Counsel on potential expansion of business activity plans.
- Search for and interview new personnel.
- Hire new personnel.
- Train personnel.

In addition, the client requests that during the three months after the conversion Pitman

- Supervise the operation of the new system.
- Monitor client-prepared source documents and make changes in basic EDP-generated data as she may deem necessary without concurrence of the client.

Pitman responds that she may perform some of the services requested, but not all of them.

Required:

Which of these services may Pitman perform and which of these services may she not perform?

(AICPA adapted)

3–65. Henley, the owner of a small company, asked O'Brien, CPA, to conduct an audit of the company's records. Henley told O'Brien that the audit was to be completed in time to submit audited financial statements to a bank as part of a loan application. O'Brien immediately accepted the engagement and agreed to provide an auditor's report within three weeks. Henley agreed to pay O'Brien a fixed fee plus a bonus if the loan was granted.

O'Brien hired two accounting students to conduct the audit and spent several hours telling them exactly what to do. O'Brien told the students not to spend time reviewing the control structure, but instead to concentrate on proving the mathematical accuracy of the ledger accounts and summarizing the data in the accounting records that support Henley's financial statements. The students followed O'Brien's instructions and after two weeks gave O'Brien the financial statements, which did not include footnotes. O'Brien reviewed the statements and prepared an unqualified auditor's report. The report, however, did not refer to generally accepted accounting principles.

Required:

Briefly describe each of the generally accepted auditing standards and indicate how O'Brien's action(s) resulted in a failure to comply with each standard.

Organize your answer as follows:

Brief Description of Generally Accepted Auditing Standards	O'Brien's Actions Resulting in Failure to Comply with Generally Accepted Auditing Standards

(AICPA adapted)

3–66. Simmons Company is suing Precision Products, Inc., your client, in the state court system, alleging a breach of contract. The contract provided for Precision to construct a piece of highly technical equipment at Precision's cost plus a fixed fee. Specifically, Simmons alleges that Precision has calculated costs incorrectly, loading the contract billings with inappropriate costs. Simmons seeks to recover the excess costs.

Timothy Burns, your CPA firm's partner in charge of the Precision account, has been subpoenaed by Simmons to testify. Neither Burns nor the firm wishes to become involved in the litigation. Furthermore, if Burns testifies, some of the facts he would reveal might be prejudicial to the client.

Required:

a. Must Burns testify? Explain.
b. If the cause of the action had been such that the suit would have been brought in a federal court, would Burns have had to testify? Explain.

(AICPA adapted)

4

Professional Responsibility and Legal Liability

The terms "auditors' responsibility" and "auditors' legal liability" are often confused by nonauditors. The distinction is subtle, yet it must be drawn in order for auditors and nonauditors to communicate with each other. This entire book, with the exception of the second section of this chapter, "Auditors' Legal Liability," is concerned with auditors' responsibilities.

An appropriate way of viewing the relationship between responsibility and liability is to think of "responsibilities" as synonymous with "professional duties," and "legal liabilities" as relating to society's means of enforcing adherence to those professional duties—that is, compliance with professional standards—and providing compensation to victims of wrongful conduct. The concept of auditor responsibility usually arises in two related contexts: responsibility for what, and to whom? Answers to both questions are found primarily in the technical and ethical standards of the public accounting profession; they are also occasionally specified in state and federal statutes and court decisions. All of these sources provide guidance to auditors on how to conduct audits with due professional care and thus meet their professional responsibilities, and on the duties that auditors owe to their clients and third parties.

Chapter 3 described the various mechanisms the AICPA and state boards of accountancy have for maintaining the quality of audit practice. The legal process is another mechanism that helps ensure that auditors meet their responsibilities. Litigation and threats of litigation serve as enforcers of duties; they also help define auditors' responsibilities and, on rare occasions, create what some perceive to be new responsibilities. The Commission on Auditors' Responsibilities (Cohen Commission) noted that "court decisions are particularly useful [in defining auditors' responsibilities] because they involve consideration of competing theories of responsibility. However, they must be considered carefully because a decision is usually closely related to the facts of a particular case. Consequently, the language used in a particular decision may not be the best expression of the technical issues involved."[1] The outcome of a specific legal case also may not be a reliable indicator of auditors' responsibilities because it is often impossible to discern the rationale of a jury verdict, and appellate decisions are often clouded by procedural rules, such as the requirement that factual determinations not be disturbed.

AUDITORS' PROFESSIONAL RESPONSIBILITY

To a great degree, auditors' responsibilities reflect the expectations of users of audited financial statements. Users expect an auditor to evaluate the measurements and disclosures made by management and determine whether the financial statements contain material misstatements, either unintentional or not. Auditors have long accepted the responsibility to design their audits to

[1] *Report, Conclusions, and Recommendations,* 1978, p. 2.

detect material unintentional errors in financial statements; after all, if that is not a purpose of an audit, what is? The auditor's responsibility for designing audits to detect deliberate misstatements in financial statements has been less clear over the years, mainly because of the difficulty, or even impossibility, of detecting skillfully contrived employee or management fraud, particularly if any form of collusion is present.[2] Although management fraud is only one of several categories of misstatements affecting financial statements, it has probably received more attention from the public and been alleged in more instances of litigation involving auditors than any other category.

Responding to Public Expectations

In 1978, the Cohen Commission concluded that a gap existed between the performance of auditors and the expectations of financial statement users, and that, with certain exceptions, the users' expectations were generally reasonable. The Commission recommended a number of ways to respond to user expectations by clarifying and tightening auditing standards and improving communication of the auditor's role and work to the public. Several of those recommendations were acted on by the auditing profession, but others were either rejected or ignored.

By the mid-1980s, the "expectation gap" not only continued to exist but was exacerbated by difficult economic times in certain industries and several notable bankruptcies traceable to questionable business practices or to management's lack of awareness of the risks it was incurring. Unfortunately, many investors mistakenly believe that a business failure equates with an audit failure. Also, highly publicized instances of fraudulent financial reporting and illegal corporate activities had raised questions about auditors' responsibility for detecting and reporting fraud and illegalities, and also about their role in assessing an entity's policies and procedures that might prevent such irregularities. In addition, senior management and directors of major corporations were expressing a desire for the independent auditor to provide them with more assistance in meeting their responsibilities for overseeing the corporate financial reporting process.

The expectation gap and the expressed needs of corporate officers and directors resulted in efforts by three diverse bodies to consider how independent auditors can better meet and communicate their responsibilities. First, the House Subcommittee on Oversight and Investigations, chaired by Congressman John Dingell of Michigan, conducted a series of hearings regarding auditing and financial reporting problems under the federal securities laws. The Subcommittee focused public attention on several notorious business failures and frauds.

[2]"Management" as used in this chapter includes both top management and all lower levels of management that may have reasons to deceive top management.

Second, the National Commission on Fraudulent Financial Reporting (Treadway Commission) was established under the sponsorship of the AICPA, American Accounting Association, Financial Executives Institute, Institute of Internal Auditors, and National Association of Accountants. The Commission's objectives were to develop initiatives for the prevention and detection of fraud and, in particular, to determine what the role of the independent auditor should be in detecting management fraud. The Treadway Commission's recommendations were published in October 1987. The five sponsoring organizations have set up a committee—the Treadway Oversight Implementation Committee—to monitor the business community's reaction to the Commission's recommendations.

Third, the AICPA's Auditing Standards Board (ASB) issued nine new Statements on Auditing Standards (SASs) that represent a major attempt to respond to the public's expectations of auditors and to the needs of senior management and corporate directors. In addition, the ASB has issued guidance on implementing various aspects of the new SASs. It is also likely that additional SASs will be issued in response to regulatory rule-making, research, and other activities undertaken as a result of the Treadway Commission's recommendations.

The authors of this book believe that the recently issued SASs address in many significant respects the needs of financial statement users, senior management and boards of directors, and the public. It is clear, however, that the issues surrounding the expectations of those groups do not simply concern auditor performance and responsibilities, but are far more complex. There are, for example, fundamental concerns about the accounting measurement and disclosure principles that enter into the preparation of financial statements, about business ethics and conduct, and about the responsibilities of corporate directors and management. The ASB can address only the auditor's performance and responsibilities. The authors believe it has done so in a way that will help to close the expectation gap and that is also responsive to many of the concerns of the Dingell Committee and the Treadway Commission relating to auditors' responsibilities in performing an audit and communicating their findings.

Responsibility for Detecting Misstatements

The authoritative auditing literature for many years reflected the view that auditors were not responsible for detecting deliberate financial statement misstatements unless the application of generally accepted auditing standards (GAAS) would result in such detection. Many financial statement users, however, believe that one of the primary purposes of an audit is to detect management fraud or other intentional misstatements in *all* circumstances. The Securities and Exchange Commission (SEC) has long taken the position that an audit can be expected to detect certain kinds of fraud, stating in

Accounting Series Release (ASR) No. 19, "In the Matter of McKesson & Robbins, Inc.," issued in 1940

> Moreover, we believe that, even in balance sheet examinations for corporations whose securities are held by the public, accountants can be expected to detect gross overstatements of assets and profits whether resulting from collusive fraud or otherwise. We believe that alertness on the part of the entire [audit] staff, coupled with intelligent analysis by experienced accountants of the manner of doing business, should detect overstatements in the accounts, regardless of their cause, long before they assume the magnitude reached in this case. Furthermore, an examination of this kind should not, in our opinion, exclude the highest officers of the corporation from its appraisal of the manner in which the business under review is conducted. Without underestimating the important service rendered by independent public accountants in their review of the accounting principles employed in the preparation of financial statements filed with us and issued to stockholders, we feel that the discovery of gross overstatements in the accounts is a major purpose of such an audit even though it be conceded that it might not disclose every minor defalcation.

AICPA Professional Requirements. Many commentators both inside and outside the accounting profession believe that until 1988, official pronouncements on auditors' responsibilities were broad, vague, and sometimes overly defensive and self-serving. However, the latest AICPA pronouncement on the auditor's responsibility to detect financial statement misstatements, SAS No. 53, *The Auditor's Responsibility to Detect and Report Errors and Irregularities* (AU Section 316.05 and .08), issued in April 1988, explicitly states

> The auditor should assess the risk that errors and irregularities may cause the financial statements to contain a material misstatement. Based on that assessment, the auditor should design the audit to provide reasonable assurance of detecting errors and irregularities that are material to the financial statements. . . .
>
> The auditor should exercise (a) due care in planning, performing, and evaluating the results of audit procedures, and (b) the proper degree of professional skepticism to achieve reasonable assurance that material errors or irregularities will be detected.

On the other hand, the SAS makes it clear (as was stated in prior pronouncements) that the auditor is not an insurer or guarantor that the financial statements are free of material misstatement.

> Since the auditor's opinion on the financial statements is based on the concept of reasonable assurance, the auditor is not an insurer and his report does not constitute a guarantee. Therefore, the subsequent discovery that a material misstatement exists in the financial statements does not, in and of itself, evidence inadequate planning, performance, or judgment on the part of the auditor. (AU Section 316.08)

The reason for this is that even a properly designed and executed audit may not detect material irregularities, because of their multifaceted characteristics. For example, an irregularity may involve forgery and collusion. Auditors are not trained to authenticate signatures or documents, and skillful collusion between client personnel and third parties or among management or employees may make otherwise appropriate auditing procedures totally ineffective. Also, auditing procedures that are effective for detecting an unintentional misstatement may be ineffective when the same misstatement is intentional, cleverly executed, or concealed through collusion.

Definitions. As used in SAS No. 53, the terms "errors" and "irregularities" are precisely defined (AU Section 316.02 - .04).

> The term *errors* refers to *unintentional* misstatements or omissions of amounts or disclosures in financial statements. Errors may involve—
>
> - Mistakes in gathering or processing accounting data from which financial statements are prepared.
> - Incorrect accounting estimates arising from oversight or misinterpretation of facts.
> - Mistakes in the application of accounting principles relating to amount, classification, manner of presentation, or disclosure.
>
> The term *irregularities* refers to *intentional* misstatements or omissions of amounts or disclosures in financial statements. Irregularities include fraudulent financial reporting undertaken to render financial statements misleading, sometimes called *management fraud*, and misappropriation of assets, sometimes called *defalcations*. Irregularities may involve acts such as the following:
>
> - Manipulation, falsification, or alteration of accounting records or supporting documents from which financial statements are prepared.
> - Misrepresentation or intentional omission of events, transactions, or other significant information.
> - Intentional misapplication of accounting principles relating to amounts, classification, manner of presentation, or disclosure.
>
> The primary factor that distinguishes errors from irregularities is whether the underlying cause of a misstatement in financial statements is intentional or unintentional. Intent, however, is often difficult to determine, particularly in matters involving accounting estimates or the application of accounting principles. For example, an unreasonable accounting estimate may result from unintentional bias or may be an intentional attempt to misstate the financial statements.

Management fraud often involves the deliberate misapplication of accounting principles, such as the failure to provide for uncollectible accounts receivable or the deliberate overstatement of inventory. Often it is done to further a management goal, such as higher reported earnings, rather than for direct personal enrichment. Such irregularities are likely to have a significant effect on financial statements. Management fraud sometimes includes misappropriation of assets or services. That type of management fraud is difficult to detect, because it involves management override of control structure policies and procedures, and is less likely than other types of management fraud to be material to the financial statements.

Employee defalcations are generally less significant than management fraud. Clever concealment of defalcations can result in overstatements of assets (paid receivables reported as still due) or understatements of liabilities (cash misappropriated and reported as payments made). In many instances of defalcation, however, the financial statements are not actually misstated, because the asset that has been misappropriated is no longer included in the balance sheet and total expenses on the income statement are correct, although amounts related to the misappropriation are misclassified. (For example, inventory that was stolen may have been properly removed from the balance sheet, but charged to cost of sales rather than to a loss account.)

Considering the Risk of Irregularities. As cited above, SAS No. 53 states that the auditor's responsibility under GAAS is to "design the audit to provide reasonable assurance of detecting errors and irregularities that are material to the financial statements," and to "exercise (a) due care in planning, performing, and evaluating the results of audit procedures, and (b) the proper degree of professional skepticism. . . ." Neither SAS No. 53 nor any other auditing standards, however, describe specific procedures that should be performed to accomplish these objectives. Instead, the emphasis is placed on the auditor's awareness of factors that influence the risk of material misstatements in the client's particular situation. Those factors may be related to particular account balances or classes of transactions, or they may have effects that are pervasive to the financial statements taken as a whole. As an example of the former, a management that places undue stress on increased earnings may be disinclined to provide adequate allowances for uncollectible accounts receivable or unsalable inventory. To illustrate the latter, pressure on divisional executives to meet unrealistic budgets, or a downturn in the economy, may lead to recording sales in advance of shipments, nonrecognition of expenses, unreasonably low estimates of annual depreciation, or other means of artificially inflating income.

A management orientation toward a favorable earnings trend, however, or the imposition of tight budgets on divisions, does not necessarily mean there is a likelihood of management fraud. Also, while a perceived reluctance by management to segregate responsibilities appropriately among employees, or an accounting function that is distinctly less effective than one would expect in a particular organization, may increase the possibility of errors, management fraud, and defalcations, it does not necessarily imply that they are probable. However, when factors are present that increase the risk of material errors or irregularities, the auditor should respond to that higher risk. For example, more experienced personnel could be assigned to the audit, the extent of procedures applied in particular areas (for example, the size of the sample in a particular test) could be increased, or the type of procedure used could be changed to obtain evidence that is more persuasive than would have otherwise been appropriate. A higher risk should also cause the auditor to exercise a heightened degree of professional skepticism in conducting the audit.

Management Integrity and Professional Skepticism. An auditor should neither assume that management is dishonest nor assume unquestioned honesty. As SAS No. 53 (AU Section 316.17) points out,

> A presumption of management dishonesty . . . would be contrary to the accumulated experience of auditors. Moreover, if dishonesty were presumed, the auditor would potentially need to question the genuineness of all records and documents obtained from the client and would require conclusive rather than persuasive evidence to corroborate all management representations. An audit conducted on these terms would be unreasonably costly and impractical.

The way the auditor meets the obligation to not assume unquestioningly that management is honest is by maintaining an attitude of professional skepticism throughout the audit, especially when gathering and evaluating evidence, including management's answers to audit inquiries. For example, the auditor may detect conditions or circumstances that serve as "red flags," that is, that indicate a material misstatement could exist. Typically, these are conditions or circumstances that differ from the auditor's expectations; for example, errors are detected in an audit test that apparently were known to management but were not voluntarily disclosed to the auditor. Professional skepticism requires that when such "red flags" appear, the auditor should reconsider the audit testing plan in order to obtain sufficient competent evidence that the financial statements are free of material misstatements.

Illegal Acts by Clients. Illegal acts by clients are violations of laws or government regulations, perpetrated by an entity or by management or employees acting on behalf of the entity; they do not include personal misconduct unrelated to the client's business.

Some laws and regulations have a direct and material effect on the determination of amounts in financial statement line items. For example, tax laws affect the provision for income taxes and the related tax liability; federal laws and regulations may affect the amount of revenue that should be recognized under a government contract. The auditor, however, considers such laws and regulations from the perspective of their known relation to audit objectives and the corresponding financial statement assertions, rather than from the perspective of legality per se. The auditor's responsibility to detect misstatements resulting from illegal acts that have a direct and material effect on financial statement amounts is the same as for errors and irregularities.

SAS No. 54, *Illegal Acts by Clients* (AU Section 317.06), explains, however, that there is another class of illegal acts for which the auditor has far less detection responsibility.

> Entities may be affected by many other laws or regulations, including those related to securities trading, occupational safety and health, food and drug administration, environmental protection, equal employment, and price-fixing or other antitrust violations. Generally, these laws and regulations relate more to an entity's operating aspects than to its financial and accounting aspects, and their financial statement effect is indirect. An auditor ordinarily does not have sufficient basis for recognizing possible violations of such laws and regulations. Their indirect effect is normally the result of the need to disclose a contingent liability because of the allegation or determination of illegality. For example, securities may be purchased or sold based on inside information. While the direct effects of the purchase or sale may be recorded appropriately, their indirect effect, the possible contingent liability for violating securities laws, may not be appropriately disclosed. Even when violations of such laws and regulations can have consequences material to the financial statements, the auditor may not become aware of the existence of the illegal act unless he is informed by the client, or there is evidence of a governmental agency investigation or enforcement proceeding in the records, documents, or other information normally inspected in an audit of financial statements.

The auditor should be aware of the possibility that these kinds of illegal acts may have occurred. Normally, an audit performed in accordance with generally accepted auditing standards does not include procedures specifically designed to detect these illegal acts. Only if specific information comes to the auditor's attention indicating that such acts might exist and might need to be disclosed in the financial statements, should the auditor apply procedures specifically directed to ascertaining whether such an illegal act has occurred. An audit conducted in accordance with generally accepted auditing standards provides no assurance that this type of illegal act will be detected or that any resultant contingent liabilities will be disclosed.

Procedures that would otherwise be applied, however, for the purpose of forming an opinion on the financial statements, may bring possible illegal acts to the auditor's attention. Such procedures include reading minutes of directors' meetings; inquiring of the client's management and legal counsel concerning litigation, claims, and assessments; and performing tests of the various account balances. The auditor may also make inquiries of management concerning the client's

- Compliance with laws and regulations.
- Policies relating to the prevention of illegal acts.
- Communications to, and the receipt of representations from, its own management at appropriate levels of authority concerning compliance

with laws and regulations. Those representations often include statements, signed annually by all levels of management, that they have not violated company policy—which is usually defined to cover all of the actions proscribed by the Foreign Corrupt Practices Act, as well as conflicts of interest—and that they are not aware of any such violations.

Finally, through the performance of procedures (including communication with attorneys) to determine the existence of loss contingencies, the auditor may uncover violations of laws.

Responsibilities on Discovering an Error, Irregularity, or Illegal Act. An auditor who becomes aware of an error or a possible irregularity or illegal act should determine the potential effect on the financial statements being audited. The auditor must be aware of the sensitivity of these matters and the need for substantial evidence before making any allegations of irregularities or illegal acts. If the auditor concludes that the financial statements are materially misstated, because of either errors or possible irregularities or illegal acts, or that loss contingencies or the potential effects of an illegal act on the entity's operations are inadequately disclosed, the auditor should insist that the statements be revised. If they are not, he or she should express a qualified or an adverse opinion on the financial statements. In addition, the auditor should bring immaterial irregularities to the attention of management at a level high enough to be able to deal appropriately with the matter, including further investigation if considered necessary. This level should be at least one level above those involved. Also, the auditor should be sure that the audit committee has been informed about all irregularities and illegal acts of which the auditor becomes aware, unless they are clearly inconsequential.

Disclosure of irregularities or illegal acts to parties other than the client's senior management and its audit committee, however, is not ordinarily part of the auditor's responsibility (unless the matter affects the opinion on the financial statements), and would be precluded by the auditor's ethical and legal obligation of confidentiality. There are four circumstances, however, in which a duty to notify parties outside the client may exist: (a) disclosure to the SEC when an auditor change is reported, (b) disclosure to a successor auditor upon appropriate inquiry, (c) disclosure in response to a subpoena, and (d) disclosure to a governmental agency in accordance with requirements for audits of entities that receive financial assistance from a governmental agency. The SASs note that "because potential conflicts with the auditor's ethical and legal obligations for confidentiality may be complex, the auditor may wish to consult with legal counsel before discussing [irregularities or illegal acts] with parties outside the client" (AU Sections 316.29 and 317.23).

SAS No. 53 indicates that in some cases the auditor may not be able to determine the extent of a possible irregularity. If the auditor is precluded by the client from applying necessary procedures or is otherwise unable to conclude whether irregularities may materially affect the financial statements, an opinion qualified because of a scope limitation or a disclaimer of opinion should be issued. SAS No. 54 contains similar guidance with respect to an illegal act. The auditor could be precluded by the client from evaluating whether a possible illegal act is, in fact, illegal and material to the financial statements. In those instances, the auditor should generally disclaim an opinion on the financial statements. If, however, the auditor's inability to determine whether an act is illegal does not result from client-imposed restrictions, a scope qualification, or explanatory language because of an uncertainty, may be appropriate.

If the client refuses to accept the auditor's report as modified for the reasons described above, the auditor should withdraw from the engagement and indicate the reasons for withdrawal to the audit committee or board of directors. Withdrawal might also be appropriate in other circumstances, such as when the client continues to retain a known perpetrator of an irregularity in a position with a significant role in the entity's internal control structure, or when the client refuses to take remedial action the auditor considers appropriate when an illegal act has occurred. Withdrawal from an engagement would cause a change of auditors, which, for a publicly traded company, would trigger the SEC Form 8-K filing discussed in Chapter 3, thereby publicizing the reasons for the withdrawal.

Engagement Letters. Most auditors recognize the need for a written communication to the client specifying the responsibilities of both the client and auditor. That communication, called an "engagement letter," is not required by generally accepted auditing standards, but is widely employed to avoid misunderstandings about the auditor's responsibility for discovering errors, irregularities, and illegal acts, and to remind clients of the inherent limitations of an audit. (Some auditors also include fee terms and other arrangements in the letter, and may wish to include a statement that consistent application of generally accepted accounting principles is assumed unless otherwise stated in the auditor's report.) A typical engagement letter (for an entity that has an audit committee) is shown in Figure 4.1. Some auditors ask clients to sign and return a copy of the engagement letter to indicate their acceptance of, and agreement with, its contents.

AUDITORS' LEGAL LIABILITY

Beyond the disciplinary system of the profession discussed in the previous chapter, auditors,[3] in common with other professionals, are subject to legal and other sanctions as a consequence of deficiencies, that is, failure to meet

[3]In this section of the chapter, the words "auditor" and "auditors" apply to both individuals, whether sole practitioners or employees of CPA firms, and auditing firms, unless otherwise specified or indicated by context.

Figure 4.1 Typical Engagement Letter

Audit Committee
X Corporation

This letter sets forth our understanding of the terms and objectives of our engagement, and the nature and scope of the services we will provide.

We will audit your financial statements as of and for the year ended December 31, 19XX, in accordance with generally accepted auditing standards. The objective of an audit is the expression of our opinion on whether the financial statements present fairly, in all material respects, the financial position, results of operations, and cash flows in conformity with generally accepted accounting principles.

As a part of our audit, we will consider the Company's internal control structure, as required by generally accepted auditing standards, for the purpose of establishing a basis for determining the nature, timing, and extent of auditing procedures necessary for expressing our opinion on the financial statements. We will also read information included in the annual report to shareholders and consider whether such information, including the manner of its presentation, is consistent with information appearing in the financial statements.

Our audit will include procedures designed to provide reasonable assurance of detecting errors and irregularities that are material to the financial statements. As you are aware, however, there are inherent limitations in the auditing process. For example, audits are based on the concept of selective testing of the data being examined and are, therefore, subject to the limitation that such matters, if they exist, may not be detected. Also, because of the characteristics of irregularities, including attempts at concealment through collusion and forgery, a properly designed and executed audit may not detect a material irregularity.

Similarly, in performing our audit we will be aware of the possibility that illegal acts may have occurred. However, it should be recognized that our audit provides no assurance that illegal acts, other than those having a direct and material effect on the determination of financial statement amounts, will be detected. We will inform you with respect to illegal acts or material errors and irregularities that come to our attention during the course of our audit.

You recognize that the financial statements and the establishment and maintenance of an internal control structure are the responsibility of management. Appropriate supervisory review procedures are necessary to provide reasonable assurance that adopted policies and prescribed procedures are adhered to and to identify errors and irregularities or illegal acts. As part of our aforementioned consideration of the Company's internal control structure, we will inform you of matters that come to our attention that represent significant deficiencies in the design or functioning of the internal control structure.

Generally accepted auditing standards require that we communicate certain additional matters to you or, alternatively, assure ourselves that management has appropriately made you aware of those matters. Such matters specifically

Figure 4.1 ***Continued***

include (1) the initial selection of and changes in significant accounting policies and their application; (2) the process used by management in formulating particularly sensitive accounting estimates and the basis for our conclusions regarding the reasonableness of those estimates; (3) audit adjustments that could, in our judgment, either individually or in the aggregate, have a significant effect on your financial reporting process; (4) any disagreements with management, whether or not satisfactorily resolved, about matters that individually or in the aggregate could be significant to the financial statements or our report; (5) our views about matters that were the subject of management's consultation with other accountants about auditing and accounting matters; (6) major issues that were discussed with management in connection with the retention of our services, including, among other matters, any discussions regarding the application of accounting principles and auditing standards; and (7) serious difficulties that we encountered in dealing with management related to the performance of the audit.

At the conclusion of the engagement, we will be supplied with a representation letter that, among other things, will confirm management's responsibility for the preparation of the financial statements in conformity with generally accepted accounting principles, the availability of financial records and related data, the completeness and availability of all minutes of board of directors (and committee) meetings, and the absence of irregularities involving management or those employees who have significant roles in the control structure.

We shall be pleased to discuss this letter with you.

[Firm name, manually signed]

professional standards in the performance of their work. Unlike some other professionals, however, whose liability is limited to their clients and patients, independent auditors are also liable to growing numbers of nonclient third parties, mainly investors and creditors, who rely on audited financial statements in making decisions that expose them to substantial potential losses. As a result, auditors' exposure to possible loss is great, and the amount of potential loss is usually indeterminate at the time the audit is performed. This section of the chapter examines auditors' civil liabilities to clients and third parties, as well as criminal liability and civil regulatory remedies. It starts with an overview of the American legal system.

The American legal system consists of state and federal courts and administrative agencies. Auditors' legal liability under that system derives from both common and statutory law as applied by the courts and the rulings of administrative agencies. Common law evolves from judicial rulings on matters of law in specific cases. Statutory law may codify or change common law. Judicial interpretation of statutory law, in turn, leads to the development of case law precedents. This interaction permits the courts to continually redefine the auditor's role and duties. Administrative agencies, which are created by state legislatures and Congress, have the power to enact and enforce regulations affecting auditors.

Common law includes contract law, which concerns the enforcement of promises, and the law of torts, which involves the duty to not cause harm to others. The law of torts covers negligence, which is the failure to conform one's conduct to the standard of a reasonable person, and fraud, which is an intentional misstatement made for the purpose of monetary gain. Professional malpractice, the failure of a licensed professional to conform his or her conduct to professional standards, falls under the law of negligence. For auditors, professional standards are contained in generally accepted auditing standards. In almost all cases, a licensed professional must testify that there has been a deviation from professional standards in order to support a charge of professional malpractice. Thus, unless a violation is so egregious that it would be obvious to a lay person, a plaintiff generally must retain an "expert" witness in order to prevail in a malpractice claim.

The Litigation Explosion

Few lawsuits were brought against accountants prior to 1965. In the late 1960s, several court decisions signaled dramatic changes in the attitude of the courts and the expectations of the public concerning auditors' responsibilities and their legal liability to third parties. By the mid-1970s, hundreds of lawsuits were pending against accountants. Lawsuits against accountants received new impetus in the early 1980s, with jury awards of damages in the tens of millions of dollars, including an $80 million award in 1981. Such awards initiated a new wave of litigation against accountants.

The extent of litigation facing accounting firms is reflected also by the size of their internal legal staffs. The first time a lawyer joined an accounting firm to provide legal advice was in 1968. In 1983, 40 lawyers were employed for such purposes by the 11 largest accounting firms. By 1989, 103 lawyers were providing legal advice to the 14 largest accounting firms. In addition, in 1988, the eight largest accounting firms spent over $100 million in out-of-pocket expenses, including attorney's fees paid to outside lawyers, in defending litigation. This amount does not include the cost of verdicts or settlements, or of liability insurance, when it is available.[4] Moreover, it is estimated there are over $1 billion in claims pending against accountants. Undoubtedly, auditors' legal liability is one of the most important issues currently facing the profession.

[4]An October 10, 1988, article in *Crain Business Insurance* (M. Bradford, "Accountants E&O Market Stable—for Now," p. 14) included an estimate that small firms pay from $1000 to $2500 per professional for liability insurance, while the largest firms pay at least twice that amount. Some small firms have difficulty obtaining professional liability insurance.

A number of factors have contributed to the increase in litigation against auditors since the 1960s, including technical legal developments that made legal remedies available to third parties (discussed in a later section) and social changes that influenced the public's expectations of auditors. Most notable of these social changes are the growth of consumerism and the perception of auditors as "insurers" of the reliability of a company's financial statements.

Consumerism. It was inevitable with the passage of the federal securities laws in the early 1930s and the growth of the securities markets that investors and creditors would make increased use of audited financial statements. Paralleling this development has been the growth of an attitude that just as consumers of the products and services of American business are entitled to expect more from their purchases than they did in the past, so too are investors and creditors, as consumers of financial information. When people's expectations are not met, they are increasingly likely to contact legal counsel, especially since many attorneys are willing to take cases on a contingency basis.

This attitude has been buttressed by the access that disappointed consumers of financial information have to new and far-reaching remedies, perhaps the most significant of which from the auditor's point of view is the class action lawsuit (discussed later in this chapter). The result of these developments has been a heightening of the public's expectations of auditors and their work, and a far greater willingness on the part of investors and creditors who relied on that work to seek recovery from auditors for losses suffered. Rightly or wrongly, many people believe auditors can act to prevent investor and creditor losses and are thus a logical choice to bear those losses.

Auditors as "Insurers." A second important influence on the legal environment is the public's perception of auditors as "guarantors" of the reliability of a company's financial statements. The public, perhaps because of the perceived precision of financial statements and the prominence of the auditor's report accompanying them, often does not recognize that a company's management has primary responsibility for its financial statements and that the auditor's role inherently involves numerous difficult judgments.

Thus, when the "guarantor" is viewed as a large, successful organization with substantial resources (including professional liability insurance), and frequently in troubled situations is also the only financially viable entity available to sue, it should not be surprising that auditors are looked to for their "deep pockets" and are sued by injured persons primarily because of their ability to pay, regardless of culpability. The fact that an auditor's fees for an engagement rarely bear any reasonable relationship to the auditor's potential liability, and that the auditor derived no "equity" benefit from the operations of the entity, rarely elicits sympathy from disappointed investor-plaintiffs.

Substantial numbers of lawsuits against auditors alleging inadequacies in their professional services will probably continue to be a fact of life, at least for the foreseeable future. The nine auditing pronouncements issued in 1988 in an attempt to narrow the "expectation gap," and other efforts by the profession to articulate its objectives, responsibilities, and the limitations of those responsibilities, may have an effect on the public's expectations and perception of auditors. In the meantime, an auditor's best protection against liability (in addition to adequate malpractice insurance, when available) is to do competent work and to keep in mind an understanding of how the courts perceive the professional's role and responsibilities, as expressed in judicial rulings under common law and as codified in the securities laws.

Liability to Clients

An auditor's liability to clients is based on the direct contractual relationship between them, referred to as "privity," and on the law of torts. Under common law, a professional is liable to a client for breach of contract (e.g., an auditor's issuing an unqualified opinion without conducting an audit in accordance with GAAS when that has been contracted for) and also, under tort law, for ordinary negligence. Obviously, if an auditor is liable to a client for ordinary negligence, gross negligence and fraud on the part of the auditor are also grounds for liability to a client.

Most lawsuits by clients are brought on grounds of ordinary negligence, which is defined as the failure to exercise due professional care. For auditors, due care essentially means adhering to generally accepted auditing standards. Gross negligence is the lack of even slight care. The client has a cause for action against the auditor if the financial statements contain a misrepresentation of a material fact—that is, a material error or irregularity—that was not detected because of the auditor's failure to exercise due care, and that injured the client.

Suits by clients arise in a variety of contexts, but certain patterns are evident. Many instances of litigation against auditors involve the situation in which an audit does not detect an ongoing embezzlement by an employee of the client, and additional money is taken after the audit is completed. The client contends the losses occurring after the audit would have been prevented if the auditor had detected the embezzlement. A client may also contend that internal control deficiencies enabled losses to go undetected, and the auditor failed to bring such deficiencies to the attention of management.

Clients often have fidelity bond coverage to protect against such losses. In many circumstances, after a fidelity bond carrier pays on a loss, it becomes "subrogated" to the client's claim against the auditor, that is, it "steps into the shoes" of the client and may assert the client's rights.[5]

[5]In 1945, the predecessor of the American Institute of Certified Public Accountants reached an agreement with the industry trade group representing the surety bond companies. The agreement provided that accountants would encourage their clients to rely on fidelity bond coverage to protect themselves from losses from embezzlements. In exchange, a number of fidelity bond carriers agreed not to sue an accountant for failing to detect such losses unless they could first prove to an independent panel that the accountant was grossly negligent. A number of courts have enforced the agreement.

Clients also bring suits against their accountants in a variety of other contexts. For example, suits by clients may arise out of business acquisitions, when the accountant has performed a review prior to the acquisition. The purchase price may be based on the assets of the acquired company as reflected by the financial statements. If the client determines later that the assets were overstated, a suit against the accountant may result. Clients have also sued when they discovered that certain divisions they thought were profitable based on the financial statements were actually losing money. The client contends it would have closed the unprofitable divisions had it known about the losses and thereby would have prevented additional injury.

A claim by a client for failing to detect an embezzlement scheme or an overstatement of assets or income is generally based on negligence. It is alleged the accountant failed to comply with professional standards; had such standards been followed, the subsequent losses would have been prevented. Since such a claim is brought by the client, privity is satisfied. The person who embezzled the money or who sold the business is also made a party to such litigation in most cases. By the time the loss is discovered, however, the embezzler has often spent the stolen funds and will be "judgment-proof," that is, will lack assets to collect a court judgment against. In addition, the seller may have been released from liability by the buyer as part of the sale contract.

Besides defending the quality of their audits, auditors also defend themselves in such cases by pointing to negligence on the part of officers and employees of the client—in selecting or supervising the embezzler or in evaluating the acquisition. This concept is known as contributory negligence. In addition, auditors point to management's primary responsibility for the financial statements and the internal control structure. In states where contributory negligence is still the rule, proof of such negligence will completely bar the client's claim.

Today, however, most states follow the concept of comparative negligence, and the client's negligence will not bar the claim. Instead, it will be compared with any negligence of the auditor on a percentage basis, and liability will be apportioned based on the parties' relative degrees of fault. Most of those states, however, also follow the rule of "joint and several liability," under which claimants can collect all or part of their damages from any defendant found liable, irrespective of that defendant's proportionate fault. In many cases, the other defendants are "judgment-proof" because they have few assets and no insurance, leaving the auditor, who usually has "deep pockets," responsible for all the damages awarded. Many auditors believe that the prevailing rule of "joint and several liability" should be replaced by a "several liability" rule, under which defendants would not be required to pay more than their proportionate share of the claimant's losses.

At some point, fraud by a client company may become so pervasive that it will bar any claim against the accountant. In *Cenco Inc.* v. *Seidman & Seidman*,[6] managerial employees of the client engaged in a massive fraud that involved

[6]686 F.2d 449 (7th Cir.), *cert. denied*, 459 U.S. 880 (1982).

the overstatement of inventories. The inflated value of inventory increased the price of the client's stock, and enabled the company to buy other companies cheaply, obtain overstated insurance recoveries for lost inventory, and borrow money at lower rates. The chairman and president were aware of the fraud, but seven of the nine members of the board were not. The company brought a negligence claim against the accountant for failing to detect the fraud. The court held that the company could not recover against the accountants "if the fraud permeates the top management of the company and if, moreover, the managers are not stealing from the company—that is, from its current stockholders—but instead are turning the company into an engine of theft against outsiders—creditors, prospective stockholders, insurers, etc."

An accounting firm may be liable for a loss resulting from an embezzlement, even if it provides only review or compilation services and does not conduct an audit. In *Robert Wooler Co.* v. *Fidelity Bank*[7] the court held that the accounting firm, which had not performed an audit, nevertheless had an obligation "to warn its client of known deficiencies in the client's internal operating procedures which enhanced opportunities for employee defalcations." In *1136 Tenants' Corp.* v. *Max Rothenberg & Co.*,[8] an accountant engaged to perform nonaudit accounting services was liable for failing to inform the client of missing invoices, which enabled an employee's embezzlement to go unnoticed.

Auditors should try to avoid misunderstandings with clients about their responsibility for detecting errors or irregularities and illegal acts. Because this is a sensitive area, most auditors discuss these matters with their clients and follow up with a written communication spelling out a mutual understanding of functions, objectives, and responsibilities regarding the audit (see Figure 4.1). Such communications do not, however, relieve the auditor of legal liability for failing to exercise due professional care.

Potential liability also arises from the auditor's quasi-fiduciary relationship with a client. As discussed in Chapter 3, the auditor has a professional responsibility not to disclose confidential information obtained during an audit unless disclosure is required to fairly present the client's financial information in conformity with generally accepted accounting principles. In *Fund of Funds, Ltd.* v. *Arthur Andersen & Co.*,[9] the auditors were found liable as a result of, among other things, failing to use information they obtained from another client to determine which of the two clients' financial statements accurately portrayed the facts of the same transaction. Thus, there may be a legal precedent for holding an auditor liable for not disclosing and using information obtained from services rendered to one client that is relevant to the audit of another client. The auditor's professional responsibility in this situation is discussed in Chapter 3.

[7]479 A.2d 1027 (Pa. App. 1984).

[8]36 A.D.2d 804 (App. Div. 1971), *aff'd*, 281 N.E.2d 846 (N.Y. 1972).

[9]545 F. Supp. 1314 (S.D.N.Y. 1982).

Civil Liability to Third Parties Under Common Law

Most civil suits brought by third parties against auditors under common law allege losses resulting from reliance on financial statements. Such suits arise when lenders or investors lose money on a loan to or an investment in a company and contend, with the benefit of hindsight, that the financial statements materially misstated the company's financial condition. Suits of this type have increased as a result of a number of judicial decisions beginning in the 1960s that expanded the class to whom the auditor owed a duty of care and also raised the level of care owed to third parties. Today an auditor may be liable for ordinary negligence to any reasonably limited and reasonably definable class of persons the auditor might reasonably expect to rely on the opinion. Liability for gross negligence and fraud extends to all third parties.

Privity of Contract Doctrine. Unlike the auditor–client relationship, there is no privity of contract between the auditor and third parties. Traditionally, claims by third parties under common law were based on the law of torts, and only fraud, not ordinary negligence from failure to exercise due care, was considered a wrongful act by an auditor. The first case to test the privity of contract doctrine involving auditors was *Ultramares Corp. v. Touche*[10] in 1931. The plaintiff, without the defendant's knowledge, had relied on financial statements audited by the defendant to make loans to a company that later became insolvent. The plaintiff alleged that the auditors were guilty of negligence and fraudulent misrepresentation in not detecting fictitious amounts included in accounts receivable and accounts payable. The court upheld the doctrine of privity of contract as a limitation on the auditors' liability to the unforeseen third party for ordinary negligence, based, at least in part, on Judge Cardozo's reasoning that auditors' liability for negligence should not be extended to third parties because doing so would have the potential effect of deterring people from entering the profession, which would be detrimental to society. Cardozo described the consequences of extending the auditor's duty to third parties as follows:

> If liability for negligence exists, a thoughtless slip or blunder, the failure to detect a theft or forgery beneath the cover of deceptive entries, may expose accountants to a liability in an indeterminate amount for an indeterminate time to an indeterminate class. The hazards of a business conducted on these terms are so extreme as to enkindle doubt whether a flaw may not exist in an implication of a duty that exposes to these consequences.

Primary Benefit Rule. Subsequently, however, courts in some states have attempted to increase the auditor's liability to third parties for ordinary negligence by undermining the privity doctrine. The first crack in the privity

[10]255 N.Y. 170 (1931).

rule occurred in the *Ultramares* case itself with the formulation of the "primary benefit rule," which held that an auditor would be liable to a third party for ordinary negligence if the auditor knew that the audit was being performed for the primary benefit of a specifically identified third party. Before the mid-1960s, however, most third-party plaintiffs bringing suit against auditors pursuant to the primary benefit rule were not successful, even in cases in which the auditor knew specific persons might rely on the opinion. For example, in *State St. Trust Co.* v. *Ernst*[11] the auditor was found not liable to a lender for negligence, even though the auditor knew the particular lender intended to rely on the audited financial statements.

Further weakening of the privity of contract doctrine in cases of professionals' liability did not occur until 1963, 32 years after *Ultramares*. It began with a series of cases that represented an attack on the primary benefit rule. The *Hedley Byrne* case[12] was decided by the highest court of England, the House of Lords, in 1963. The case did not involve auditors, but a negligently stated accommodation credit report by a bank on which a third person relied, to his damage. In their opinions, the justices stated that "where there is a relationship equivalent to contract . . . , there is a duty of care." The court's finding, however, was intended to have somewhat limited application in that it extended the duty of care to only a restricted class of third parties, as in *Ultramares*.

Foreseen Third Parties. In 1965, the American Law Institute (ALI) issued its Second Restatement of the Law of Torts, a compendium of tort principles. Partly in reliance on *Hedley Byrne*, the ALI interpreted the law of negligent misrepresentations by professionals to third parties more broadly than before. The Restatement provides that an accountant is liable to a person who justifiably relies on false information when the accountant fails to exercise reasonable care in obtaining or communicating the information, if: (1) the loss is suffered "by the person or one of a limited group of persons for whose benefit and guidance . . . [the accountant] knows that the recipient intends to supply" the information; and (2) the loss is suffered "through reliance upon" the information in a transaction that the accountant knows the recipient intends the information to influence or in a substantially similar transaction. Thus, the Restatement extended liability to a member of a limited group that the accountant is aware will receive information that is provided with regard to a transaction the accountant is aware of or a substantially similar transaction. This can be described as a "foreseen" class of recipients, as opposed to a "foreseeable" class, defined as an unlimited class of persons not identified by the auditor who may foreseeably be expected to rely on information.

The distinction in the Restatement's interpretation of a professional's duty to third parties between *foreseen* and *foreseeable* persons is critical to an under-

[11]278 N.Y. 104 (1938).

[12]*Hedley Byrne & Co. Ltd.* v. *Heller & Partners, Ltd.*, 1964 A.C. 465 [1963] 2 *All E.R.* 575 (H.L. 1963).

standing of post-1965 legal decisions based on common law. In several significant cases, courts accepted the foreseen class concept of the Restatement. In *Rusch Factors, Inc.* v. *Levin*,[13] the court ruled that the auditor could be liable to the third-party plaintiff, a lender of the client, for negligence. In this case, the audit was performed at the specific request of the plaintiff-lender. In another case, *Rhode Island Hospital Trust National Bank* v. *Swartz, Bresenoff, Yavner & Jacobs*,[14] the court found the auditors liable for negligence to a foreseen party; the auditors knew that the plaintiff-bank required audited financial statements of the client, even though they did not know the specific identity of the plaintiff.

Foreseeable Third Parties. Until 1983, auditors' common law liability for negligence extended no further than foreseen third parties. In that year, the New Jersey Supreme Court ruled in a motion for partial summary judgment that an auditor has a duty to reasonably foreseeable but unidentifiable third-party users who may rely on financial statements for appropriate business purposes.[15] The plaintiffs had alleged that they relied on financial statements audited by the defendants in making an investment that subsequently proved to be worthless, after the financial statements were found to be misstated. The plaintiffs were not members of an identifiable group of users to whom the financial statements were intended to be furnished. In handing down the opinion, the court quoted the court's opinion in *Rusch Factors*, which questioned the wisdom of the *Ultramares* decision, as follows:

> Why should an innocent reliant party be forced to carry the weighty burden of an accountant's professional malpractice? Isn't the risk of loss more easily distributed and fairly spread by imposing it on the accounting profession, which can pass the cost of insuring against the risk onto its customers, who can in turn pass the cost onto the entire consuming public? Finally, wouldn't a rule of foreseeability elevate the cautionary techniques of the accounting profession?[16]

The court added its own belief that

> When the independent auditor furnishes an opinion with no limitation in the certificate as to whom the company may disseminate the financial statements, he has a duty to all those whom that auditor should reasonably foresee as recipients from the company of the statements for its proper business purposes, provided that the recipients rely on the statements pursuant to those business purposes.

The key distinction between the Restatement rule and the liberalized standard recognized in New Jersey is the accountant's knowledge at the time the

[13]284 F. Supp. 85 (D.R.I. 1968).

[14]482 F.2nd 1000 (4th Cir. 1973).

[15]*H. Rosenblum, Inc.* v. *Adler*, 93 N.J. 324 (1983).

[16]*Rusch Factors, Inc.* v. *Levin*, 284 F. Supp. 85 (D.R.I. 1968).

audit is performed with regard to who will be supplied with financial statements and for what purpose. Under the Restatement rule, the accountant must have been aware of a limited group of parties and the particular or a substantially similar transaction in which it was intended that a party would rely on the financial statements. For example, if a certain investor was considering purchasing a company, the accountant would have to have known about the investor's intended reliance on the financial statements in connection with the proposed purchase. Under the liberalized test, the accountant would be liable for negligence to an unforeseen investor with regard to an unexpected transaction if such an event was foreseeable.

Soon after the decision by the New Jersey Supreme Court in *Rosenblum*, the Wisconsin Supreme Court reached the same result in *Citizens State Bank* v. *Timm, Schmidt & Co.*[17] In the *Timm* case, the court stated that "the fundamental principle of Wisconsin negligence law is that a tortfeasor is fully liable for all foreseeable consequences of his act." The court rejected any policy consideration that might have justified a more restrictive rule of liability for accountants.

In 1985, however, the highest court in New York rigorously adhered to the *Ultramares* rule in *Credit Alliance Corp.* v. *Arthur Andersen & Co.*[18] The court in *Credit Alliance* set forth three "prerequisites that must be satisfied before accountants would be held liable in negligence to third parties who rely to their detriment on inaccurate financial reports: (1) the accountants must have been aware that the financial reports were to be used for a particular purpose or purposes; (2) in the furtherance of which a known party or parties was intended to rely; and (3) there must have been some conduct on the part of the accountants linking them to that party or parties, which evinces the accountants' understanding of that party or parties' reliance."

Since the decision in *Credit Alliance*, other state courts have taken various positions. In 1986, in *International Mortgage Co.* v. *John P. Butler Accountancy Corp.*[19] an intermediate appellate court in California rejected the New York rule and followed New Jersey and Wisconsin, holding that an accountant was liable to a lender for failing to detect that a preexisting mortgage was not reflected on a real estate firm's financial statements, even though the lender first contacted the real estate firm after the report was issued.

In 1988 the highest court in New York reaffirmed the test set forth in *Credit Alliance* and applied it in the context of a review of financial statements.[20] A year later, in *Law Offices of Lawrence J. Stockler, P.C.* v. *Rose*,[21] the Michigan Court of Appeals followed the Restatement test, holding that the accountant

[17] 113 Wis. 2d 376 (1983).

[18] 65 N.Y. 2d 536 (1985).

[19] 177 Cal. App. 3d 806 (1986).

[20] *William Iselin & Co.* v. *Mann Judd Landau*, 71 N.Y. 2d 420 (1988).

[21] 174 Mich. App. 14 (1989).

could be liable for negligence to the purchaser of a company that relied on the financial statements. In this case, the accountant was aware, at the time the report was issued, that the purchaser would rely on the financial statements for purposes of purchasing the company. The court rejected the "foreseeable" test followed by California, New Jersey, and Wisconsin on the following ground:

> The reasons for taking this more restricted approach in third party actions against the accountant have been a recognition that the financial statements themselves are the representations of the client (with the auditor's liability arising from the opinion rendered concerning the accuracy of the client's records) and the accountant's inability to control the distribution of the report or the content of some of the statements he is assessing.

In 1989 the Idaho and Nebraska supreme courts and the intermediate court of appeals in Florida adopted the *Ultramares* rule.[22]

At the time of this writing, the following jurisdictions, in addition to those cited above, appear to be adhering to the *Ultramares* rule: Arkansas, Delaware, Indiana, Kansas, and Pennsylvania. The following jurisdictions are apparently following the Restatement approach: Georgia, Hawaii, Iowa, Minnesota, Missouri, New Hampshire, New Mexico, North Carolina, Ohio, Tennessee, Texas, Utah, and Washington. The only court to join New Jersey, California, and Wisconsin since the California decision in 1986 was the supreme court of Mississippi in August 1987. In that case the accountant provided a copy of the financial statements to a third party.

An interesting development on this issue occurred in 1987, when the Illinois legislature enacted a statute that codified the *Ultramares* rule.[23] More recently, Arkansas and Kansas enacted similar statutes.[24] These statutes provide that accountants are not liable for negligence to anyone other than their clients, unless it can be established that the auditor knew of and acceded to third parties' reliance on the auditor's report. In addition, the Illinois and Arkansas statutes provide a mechanism by which accountants may limit their liability by formally identifying in writing to the third parties and the client the third parties they know to be relying on the report. That communication is known as a "privity letter." Accountants are in the process of lobbying other states for similar relief.

Some third parties have attempted to satisfy the privity requirement imposed by common law, such as *Credit Alliance*, or the above statutes by notifying the accountants in writing *after* the report has been issued that they are relying on it. Accountants have been advised to respond to such letters by commu-

[22]*Idaho Bank & Trust Co.* v. *First Bancorp*, Idaho LEXIS 68 (1989); *Citizens National Bank* v. *Kennedy & Coe*, 232 Neb. 477 (1989); *First Florida Bank* v. *Max Mitchell & Co.*, 541 So.2d 155 Fla. App. (1989).

[23]Ill. Rev. Stat. ch. 111 ¶5535.1 (1987).

[24]Ark. Stat. Ann.§ 16-114-302 (Supp. 1987); Kan. Stat. Ann. §1-402 (Supp. 1988).

nicating in writing that they were not aware at the time the report was issued that the parties would be relying on it.

Scienter Requirement. In addition to actions on the grounds of negligence, third parties may bring suit against auditors on the grounds of fraud or constructive fraud that is inferred from evidence of gross negligence. Constructive fraud differs from actual fraud in that the former involves the lack of a reasonable basis for believing that a representation is true, whereas the latter involves actual knowledge that a representation is false. Actions grounded in fraud (actual or constructive) require the plaintiff to prove some form of knowledge on the auditor's part of the falsity (or its equivalent) of a representation. This knowledge is commonly referred to as "scienter" and the requirement to prove it as the "scienter" requirement. Essentially, it is a requirement to prove an intent to injure. In some jurisdictions, scienter may be established by proof of any one of the following three elements:

1. Actual knowledge of the falsity of the representation.
2. A lack of knowledge of the truth of the representation.
3. A reckless disregard for the truth or falsity of the representation.

Under common law, the distinction between negligence and fraud rests essentially on the requirement for scienter. If a jury were to find that the defendant-auditors expressed an unqualified opinion on the financial statements when they had no knowledge of the facts, and if this would support an allegation of fraud in other respects,[25] then liability for the tort of deceit (fraud) could extend to all injured third parties. Without scienter, the case would not involve fraud. The question of the requirement to prove scienter and the elements that constitute scienter are further explored in the discussion, later in the chapter, of the auditor's liability under Section 10(b) of the Securities Exchange Act of 1934 and related Rule 10b-5.

Civil Liability to Third Parties Under the Federal Securities Acts

The principal provisions of the federal securities acts that have determined the auditor's civil liability are Section 11 of the Securities Act of 1933 and Section 10(b) of the Securities Exchange Act of 1934 and related Rule 10b-5. Class action suits against auditors under the federal securities laws became common after 1966, when the procedural rules governing them were liberalized. Class actions are litigations in which one or a relatively small number of plaintiffs sue on behalf of a very large number of allegedly injured persons. One of the

[25] Those "other respects" include proof of false representation that was relied on by and caused damages to the plaintiff.

prerequisites of a class action is that the number of potential claimants is so large that it would be impracticable for each of them to sue individually. The dollar amount of potential liability in class actions can run into the hundreds of millions of dollars, thereby making the class action technique a formidable weapon.

The Securities Act of 1933. The Securities Act of 1933 regulates public offerings of securities and contains provisions intended to protect purchasers of securities. Section 11(a) reads, in part, as follows:

> In case any part of the registration statement . . . contained an untrue statement of a material fact or omitted to state a material fact required to be stated therein or necessary to make the statements therein not misleading, any person acquiring such security . . . may . . . sue . . . every accountant . . . who has with his consent been named as having . . . certified any part of the registration statement . . . with respect to the statement in such registration statement . . . which purports to have been . . . certified by him.

Thus, Section 11 of the Securities Act of 1933 imposes civil liability on auditors for misrepresentations or omissions of material facts in a registration statement. The measure of damages under the civil provisions of the 1933 Act is based on the difference between the amount the plaintiff paid for the security and either the market price at the time of the suit or, if the security was sold, the selling price.

Section 11 expands the elements of an auditor's liability to third parties beyond that of common law in the following significant ways:

1. Privity with the plaintiff is not a necessary element; unnamed third parties, that is, the purchasers of securities in a public offering, may sue auditors.
2. Liability to third parties does not require proof of fraud or gross negligence; ordinary negligence is a basis for liability.
3. The burden of proof of negligence is shifted from the plaintiff to the defendant. The plaintiff has to prove only a material misstatement of fact.
4. The auditor is held to a standard of care described as the exercise of "due diligence"—a reasonable investigation leading to a belief that the financial statements are neither false nor misleading.
5. The plaintiff need not prove reliance on the financial statements or the auditor's report on them, but the defendant-auditor will prevail if the plaintiff's knowledge of the "untruth or omission" is proved.

The first, and still the most significant, judicial interpretation of Section 11, *Escott* v. *BarChris Construction Corp.*,[26] did not occur until 1968. The *BarChris*

[26] 283 F. Supp. 643 (S.D.N.Y. 1968).

case was a class action against a bowling alley construction corporation that had issued debentures and subsequently declared bankruptcy, and against its auditors. The suit was brought by the purchasers of the debentures for damages sustained as a result of false statements and material omissions in the prospectus contained in the registration statement. The court ruled that the auditors were liable on the grounds that they had not met the minimum standard of "due diligence" in their review for subsequent events occurring to the effective date of the registration statement (required under the 1933 Act and known as an S-1 review) because the auditor performing the review failed to appropriately follow up management's answers to his inquiries.

A defense to a Section 11 action against auditors would require demonstrating that a reasonable investigation (defined in Section 11[c]) had been made and that the auditors had reasonable grounds for believing and did believe that the financial statements were true and not misleading. In the *BarChris* case, the court stated that "accountants should not be held to a higher standard than that recognized in their profession," but held that the individual accountant responsible for the S-1 review, who had little practical auditing experience, had not met even that standard. As a direct result of this case, professional standards governing auditing procedures in the subsequent period were made stricter, and auditing firms began to place more emphasis on staff members' knowledge of a client's business and industry.

A controversial aspect of the 1933 Act concerns the issues of reliance and causation. An auditor is liable to purchasers of securities who may not have relied on the financial statements or the auditor's opinion or who may not even have known of their existence. If the auditor can prove, however, that something other than the misleading financial statements caused the plaintiff's loss, the amount of loss related to those other factors is not recoverable. Section 11 thus provides a causation defense, but it clearly places the burden of proof on the defendant-auditor; it requires the defendant to prove that factors other than the misleading statements caused the loss (in whole or in part). The courts have rarely considered the causation defense in Section 11 cases against auditors because damages in such cases have usually been determined in out-of-court settlements, as happened in *BarChris*.

The Securities Exchange Act of 1934. Many more suits alleging civil liability against auditors have been brought under the Securities Exchange Act of 1934 than under the 1933 Act. The 1934 Act, which requires all companies whose securities are traded to file annual audited financial statements and quarterly and other financial information, regulates trading of securities and thus has broad applicability. Auditors' liability under the 1934 Act, however, is not as extensive as under the 1933 Act in the following significant respects:

1. As established by the *Hochfelder* case (described below) in 1976, ordinary negligence is not a basis for liability to third parties under Section 10(b) and Rule 10b-5. Thus the auditor's liability to unforeseen third parties

under the 1934 Act is essentially the same as it is under common law following *Ultramares* and *Credit Alliance*.

2. The burden of proof of both reliance on the financial statements and causation (i.e., that the loss was caused by reliance on the statements, known as "proximate cause") rests with the plaintiff, as it does under common law.

On the other hand, the 1934 Act is accessible to both buyers and sellers of securities; Section 11 of the 1933 Act applies only to buyers.

Damages recoverable under the civil provisions of the 1934 Act are the plaintiff's "out of pocket" losses, determined by the difference between the contract price of the securities and their actual value on the date of the transaction. Actual value is ordinarily considered to be the market value on the date the misrepresentation or omission is discovered and rectified.

The majority of civil lawsuits against auditors have been based on Section 10(b) and Rule 10b-5. Their provisions apply to any purchase or sale of any security, and thus they can be used by a plaintiff with respect to both registered public offerings (also covered by the 1933 Act) and most other transactions in securities. Rule 10b-5 states, in part, that

> It shall be unlawful for any person . . . (a) To employ any device, scheme, or artifice to defraud, (b) To make any untrue statement of a material fact or to omit to state a material fact necessary in order to make the statements made, in light of the circumstances under which they were made, not misleading, or (c) To engage in any act, practice, or course of business which operates or would operate as a fraud or deceit upon any person, in connection with the purchase or sale of any security.

Section 10(b) and Rule 10b-5 do not provide a good-faith defense; rather, the defendant must refute the specific charges brought by the plaintiff. On the other hand, in a Rule 10b-5 action, the burden of proof that the auditor acted fraudulently rests with the plaintiff; under Section 11 of the 1933 Act, the burden of proof that the auditor was not culpable rests with the defendant-auditor.

The SEC enacted Rule 10b-5 in 1942 as a disciplinary measure for its own use against fraudulent purchasers of securities. A series of judicial interpretations subsequently made the rule accessible to private claimants who were able to prove damages resulting from their reliance on financial statements containing misrepresentations or omissions. Unfortunately, Rule 10b-5 is not at all precise in defining standards for liability, and it does not include a due-diligence defense. Between the time of its enactment and the *Hochfelder* ruling in 1976 (discussed below), the courts interpreted the rule in disparate ways. Thus, in some jurisdictions auditors were found liable to third parties for ordinary negligence (absence of due diligence) in rendering their opinions; in other jurisdictions the courts held that an element of knowledge of the wrongful act or an intent to commit fraud (scienter) was required. Much of the controversy was resolved by the U.S. Supreme Court in 1976 with its decision in *Ernst & Ernst* v. *Hochfelder.*[27]

The complaint in *Hochfelder* charged that the auditors had violated Rule 10b-5 by their failure to conduct proper audits and thereby aided and abetted a fraud perpetrated by the president of a securities firm. The plaintiff's case rested on a charge of negligence and did not allege fraud or intentional misconduct on the part of the auditors. The Supreme Court ruled that a private suit for damages under Section 10(b) and Rule 10b-5 required an allegation of scienter. The Court's opinion stated, in part,

> When a statute speaks so specifically in terms of manipulation and deception, and of implementing devices and contrivances—the commonly understood terminology of intentional wrongdoing—and when its history reflects no more expansive intent, we are quite unwilling to extend the scope of the statute to negligent conduct.

The Court noted in *Hochfelder* that ''in certain areas of the law, recklessness is considered to be a form of intentional conduct for purposes of imposing liability for some act.'' Thus, although the Court declined to address the question of reckless behavior in that case, most courts have since held that recklessness is sufficient to meet the scienter test.

In an action under Section 10(b), a buyer or seller of a security must also demonstrate reliance on the misstatement. This defense can be important in cases where the plaintiff did not know of the misstatement, such as when he or she never read the financial statements. One exception to the reliance requirement is the ''fraud on the market'' theory of liability, which the Supreme Court adopted in 1988 in *Basic, Inc.* v. *Levinson.*[28] This doctrine provides that a misstatement or omission that has a general effect on the market price of the security can result in liability, even without actual reliance by the plaintiff. The rule is based on the theory that the purchaser or seller relies on the integrity of the market price, which should reflect all relevant information available in the market. However, at least for the present, the doctrine is limited to securities traded on the national public markets, such as the New York or American Stock Exchange.

A party can also be held liable for aiding and abetting a violation of Section 10(b). In *Roberts* v. *Peat, Marwick, Mitchell & Co.*,[29] the U.S. Court of Appeals for the Ninth Circuit ruled that an accounting firm could be liable for aiding and abetting a violation of Section 10(b). In that case the offering documents indicated that the accounting firm agreed to perform accounting services for the partnership, and the plaintiffs alleged that the firm knew that the docu-

[27] 425 U.S. 185 (1976).
[28] 485 U.S. 224 (1988).
[29] 857 F.2d 646 (9th Cir. 1988).

ments were false and that it furthered the fraud by consenting to the inclusion of its name in the offering material. According to the court, "the investors relied on Peat, Marwick's reputation when deciding to invest and . . . they would not have invested had Peat, Marwick disclosed the alleged fraud."

RICO

Since the early 1980s, more and more suits have been brought against accountants for violations of the Racketeer Influenced and Corrupt Organizations (RICO) statute of the Organized Crime Control Act of 1970. In general, RICO provides a remedy of triple damages and attorney's fees to any person injured by reason of the operation of an enterprise through "a pattern of racketeering." The statute defines a pattern of racketeering as two violations of a list of statutes, including mail fraud, wire fraud, and securities fraud. In 1989, the U.S. Supreme Court held that such a "pattern" of racketeering activities may be satisfied by a series of actions that are part of a single fraudulent scheme.[30]

Although the statute, which provides a remedy to any victim of a common-law fraud, was designed to attack organized crime, courts have generally followed the literal language of the statute. Moreover, the Supreme Court has stated that there is no record that Congress intended its use to be limited to organized crime activities. In 1988, it was estimated that over 50 such claims were pending against accountants, and the first RICO case to go to trial against an accountant resulted in a verdict against the accountant.[31] The accounting profession, and others, are currently lobbying Congress for a change in the RICO statute.

Criminal Liability

Violations of the securities acts that give rise to civil liability for association with misleading financial statements also subject auditors to criminal penalties (fines of up to $10,000 or imprisonment for not more than five years, or both) under Section 24 of the Securities Act of 1933 and Section 32 of the Securities Exchange Act of 1934 if the violations can be shown to be willful or intentional. Auditors are also exposed to criminal penalties under the federal mail fraud and conspiracy statutes.

Perhaps because of the availability of other legal remedies (including injunctions, administrative proceedings, and civil suits by third parties) and the

[30] *H. J. Inc.* v. *Northwestern Bell Telephone Co.*, 109 S. Ct. 2893 (1989).

[31] *The Wall Street Journal*, May 9, 1988, p. 43. The case was settled for $15 million after the defendant said it would appeal a jury verdict in the amount of $60 million.

absence of the element of personal gain, there have been few criminal actions against auditors. Four of the most widely publicized criminal prosecutions were *Continental Vending,*[32] *Four Seasons,*[33] *National Student Marketing,*[34] and *Equity Funding,*[35] which together produced the conviction of eight individuals. Those cases demonstrate that auditors' errors of judgment in not insisting on appropriate accounting, including adequate disclosure, of certain matters known to them may result in criminal liability in certain circumstances, even though no motive can be proved and no personal gain can be shown to have resulted.

John C. Burton, former Chief Accountant of the SEC, stated the Commission's position on bringing criminal charges against auditors.

> While virtually all Commission cases are civil in character, on rare occasions it is concluded that a case is sufficiently serious that it should be referred to the Department of Justice for consideration of criminal prosecution. Referrals in regard to accountants have only been made when the Commission and the staff believed that the evidence indicated that a professional accountant certified financial statements that he knew to be false when he reported on them. The Commission does not make criminal references in cases that it believes are simply matters of professional judgment even if the judgments appear to be bad ones.[36]

The consequences of criminal prosecution to an auditor may go beyond the obvious ones of the costs of defense and the resulting fines and imprisonment. A successful criminal prosecution may help to establish civil liability and will generally preclude the individual from continuing to practice as an auditor.

Other SEC Sanctions

Auditors are also subject under the federal securities acts to legal sanctions that do not involve criminal penalties or the payment of damages. The SEC, as the principal government regulatory agency charged with enforcing financial reporting standards, has two civil remedies available to it: civil injunctive actions and disciplinary (administrative) proceedings under Rule 2(e) of its Rules of Practice. Either remedy may be sought against an individual auditor or an entire firm.

Injunctive Proceedings. The SEC has the authority under Section 20 of the 1933 Act and Section 21 of the 1934 Act to initiate injunctive actions in the courts to restrain future violations of the provisions of those acts (including

[32] *United States* v. *Simon*, 425 F.2d 796 (2d Cir. 1969), *cert. denied*, 397 U.S. 1006 (1970).

[33] *United States* v. *Clark*, 360 F. Supp. 936 (S.D.N.Y. 1973).

[34] *United States* v. *Natelli*, 527 F.2d 311 (2d Cir. 1975), *cert. denied*, 425 U.S. 934 (1976).

[35] *United States* v. *Weiner*, 578 F.2d 757 (9th Cir.), *cert. denied*, 439 U.S. 981 (1978).

[36] John C. Burton, "SEC Enforcement and Professional Accountants: Philosophy, Objectives and Approach," *Vanderbilt Law Review* 28 (January 1975), p. 28.

Section 10[b] of the 1934 Act). Under currently prevailing standards, discussed below, such injunctions are available only against those the SEC can persuade a court are likely to violate the federal securities laws again if not enjoined. In a case tried in 1980, *Aaron* v. *SEC*,[37] the Supreme Court held that injunctions under Section 10(b) of the 1934 Act (and one subsection of Section 17[a] of the 1933 Act) require scienter.[38]

The consequences of an injunction may extend far beyond an admonition to obey the law in the future. The injunction can be useful to plaintiffs in subsequent civil suits for damages, and the person enjoined is exposed to civil and criminal contempt proceedings. Moreover, an injunction resulting from a consent decree, in which guilt is neither admitted nor denied, may require the auditor or firm to adopt and comply with certain procedures to prevent future violations.

Requests for permanent injunctions are tried publicly before a judge without a jury. Thus, the injunctions are granted or denied largely at the discretion of the trial judge. The SEC must prove not only that a violation of the securities laws has occurred but also that there is a reasonable likelihood that future violations will occur if an injunction is not imposed. For example, in *SEC* v. *Geotek*,[39] the court found there was no evidence of a past violation. The issue of what constitutes a "reasonable likelihood" of future violations remains unresolved. On the one hand, the courts tend to give great weight to the SEC's expert judgment of the immediate need for an injunction. On the other hand, however, in *SEC* v. *Bausch & Lomb, Inc.*,[40] the court ruled against enjoining the auditors, on the grounds of insufficient evidence that they were likely to commit further violations.

Administrative (Rule 2[e]) Proceedings. Rule 2(e) of the SEC's Rules of Practice states that the Commission

> May deny, temporarily or permanently, the privilege of appearing or practicing before it in any way to any person who is found . . . (i) not to possess the requisite qualifications to represent others, (ii) to be lacking in character or integrity or have engaged in unethical or improper professional conduct, or (iii) to have willfully violated or willfully aided and abetted the violation of any provision of the federal securities laws . . . or the rules and regulations thereunder.

Before 1989, proceedings under Rule 2(e) were generally conducted in private hearings. Such proceedings are now public, unless the SEC directs otherwise in a particular case. In addition, the resulting Accounting and Auditing

[37]446 U.S. 680 (1980).

[38]The Supreme Court decided, however, that injunctions under two other subsections of Section 17(a) do not require scienter.

[39]426 F. Supp. 715 (N.D. Cal. 1976), *aff'd sub nom. SEC* v. *Arthur Young & Co.*, 590 F. 2d 785 (9th Cir. 1979).

[40]420 F. Supp. 1226 (S.D.N.Y. 1976), *aff'd*, 565 F. 2d 8 (2d Cir. 1977).

Enforcement Releases, which set forth the SEC's allegations and the terms of settlement, attract a great deal of publicity. Rule 2(e) gives the SEC the explicit authority to suspend from appearing or practicing before it auditors who have been permanently enjoined from violation of the securities laws or convicted of a felony or of a misdemeanor involving immoral conduct.

Over the years, the SEC has devised imaginative, often sweeping sanctions against auditing firms under Rule 2(e), many of which involved agreements to institute new or improved control procedures and to subject those procedures to an independent review. Some of the more innovative procedures required by the SEC in settlement of Rule 2(e) proceedings are evidence of the Commission's ability to create or influence specific professional standards. This has taken basically two forms.

1. Language in a proceeding indicating auditing responsibilities not prescribed by the profession. (An example is the view expressed in ASR No. 153 [1974] that successor auditors must review the work of predecessor auditors, and that a refusal by the client to permit the necessary communication should be grounds for rejecting the engagement. Professional literature at the time did not make predecessor–successor communications mandatory. Moreover, present standards, while requiring such communication, leave room for the exercise of professional judgment on the effect of a prospective client's forbidding such communication.)
2. Language in a consent decree requiring an auditing firm to develop specific auditing procedures not addressed in the professional literature. (An example is the auditing firm's consent in ASR No. 153 to develop and submit to the SEC procedures for the audit of related party transactions. An SAS on the subject did not exist at the time of ASR No. 153.)

As discussed in Chapter 2, the SEC has traditionally left the specific implementation and interpretation of GAAS to the auditing profession. At the least, Rule 2(e) proceedings and the accompanying consent decrees provide a vehicle for selective departure from that policy.

The Profession's Responses to the Litigious Environment

The litigious environment has encouraged the public accounting profession as a whole and individual firms to reexamine and strengthen auditing standards and ways of encouraging compliance with them. Since the increase in litigation against auditors, the AICPA has issued a great many authoritative auditing pronouncements (48 SASs were promulgated between 1977 and March 1989) and has twice revised its code of ethics. The Institute has also devoted considerable attention to the design and implementation of quality control reviews of firms. Individual firms have devoted increasingly more resources to their own policies and procedures for maintaining and raising the quality of practice.

Authoritative Pronouncements. Many of the Statements on Auditing Procedure (SAPs) and SASs were issued following audit failures that led to litigation. In addition, other auditing pronouncements originated from accounting pronouncements that, in turn, can be traced to alleged misconduct of one kind or another that led to litigation. For example, SAPs No. 47, *Subsequent Events*, and No. 48, *Letters for Underwriters* (both issued in 1971), can be traced to the *BarChris* case, discussed earlier. SAS No. 7, *Communications Between Predecessor and Successor Auditors* (1975), was related to the *U.S. Financial*[41] case. The origin of SAP No. 44 (1971), *Reports Following a Pooling of Interests*, was Accounting Principles Board Opinion No. 16, *Business Combinations* (1970). This in turn had its source in the deterioration of accounting principles evidenced at least in part by litigation, like the *Westec*[42] case, that raised questions of the propriety of the accounting principles selected and applied to account for particular combinations. Moreover, a number of auditing pronouncements further refined or clarified previous pronouncements that were traceable to litigation involving auditors. For example, several subsequent pronouncements further clarified the auditor's responsibilities set forth in SAP No. 1, *Extensions of Auditing Procedure*, which had its source in the *McKesson & Robbins*[43] case.

Other auditing pronouncements, while not individually traceable to specific audit failures that led to litigation, represent part of the accounting profession's program to close the "expectation gap," discussed both in Chapter 1 and earlier in this chapter, which had its roots in several audit failures and attendant litigation and investigations. SAS Nos. 53 through 61, issued in 1988, were all responsive to the issues underlying the expectation gap, namely, a series of business failures that revealed material misstatements in audited financial statements.

Increased Attention to Quality Control. Both the auditing profession and individual firms have recognized the need for more effective controls over the quality of audit practice. Statement on Quality Control Standards No. 1, *System of Quality Control for a CPA Firm* (QC Section 10), requires CPA firms to establish quality control policies and procedures. Efforts by the AICPA to improve and monitor the quality of audit practice are described in Chapter 3.

Measures to Protect Against Legal Liability. Individual firms have also designed and implemented programs for monitoring their audit practices, including, among other things

- Increased resources devoted to continuing education.
- Institution of second-partner and interoffice reviews of working papers and reports.

[41] *In re U.S. Financial Securities Litigation*, 609 F.2d 411 (9th Cir. 1979), *cert. denied*, 446 U.S. 929 (1980).

[42] *In re Westec Corp.*, 434 F.2d 195 (5th Cir. 1970).

[43] ASR No. 19, "In the Matter of McKesson & Robbins, Inc." (1940).

- Practice bulletins directed at both accounting and auditing issues.
- Policy statements on internal quality control programs.
- Engagement of other auditing firms to conduct independent quality reviews.
- Increased emphasis on research in auditing theory and applications, including the use of sophisticated technology to enhance the quality of audit performance.

The practice many auditing firms have adopted of having a second-partner review of engagements has been traced directly to the *Continental Vending* case.[44] As mentioned earlier, most auditors follow the practice of setting forth the scope and inherent limitations of an audit in an engagement letter to the client. Many of the points covered in a typical engagement letter are also addressed in the representation letter from management, which SAS No. 19, *Client Representations* (AU Section 333), requires the auditor to obtain. Management's representation letter provides written evidence of, among other matters, inquiries made by the auditor and management's responses to them. Both the engagement letter and the management representation letter may constitute important evidence in the event of a lawsuit.

In very general terms, the best protection against legal liability for both CPA firms and individual practitioners is meticulous adherence to the technical and ethical standards of the profession, described in Chapter 3, and establishing and implementing policies and procedures designed to ensure that all audits are systematically planned and performed, that the work is done with a high degree of professional skepticism by people who understand the client's business circumstances, that appropriate evidence is obtained and objectively evaluated, and that all work done is carefully documented. These objectives are the underlying structure of the theory and practice of auditing described throughout this book.

Review Questions

4–1. During the course of an audit, what factors or circumstances may lead an auditor to believe that irregularities may exist?

4–2. Explain the difference between errors and irregularities. Give examples of each.

4–3. What client management policies should the auditor recognize as conducive to the possibility of irregularities?

4–4. What responsibility does the auditor have to detect errors and irregularities?

4–5. What should an auditor do on becoming aware of a possible irregularity or illegal act?

[44]A. A. Sommer, Jr., "Legal Liability of Accountants," *Financial Executive* 42 (March 1974), p. 24.

4–6. How should auditors convey their responsibilities for detecting errors, irregularities, and illegal acts to their clients? What information should be included?

4–7. What is ordinary negligence? To whom is the auditor liable for ordinary negligence under common law?

4–8. What is gross negligence? To whom is the auditor liable for gross negligence under common law?

4–9. What is the present position of the courts concerning an auditor's liability for ordinary negligence to foreseeable but unidentifiable third-party users who rely on financial statements?

4–10. Define the term "scienter." How is scienter established?

4–11. How does Section 11 of the Securities Act of 1933 expand the auditor's liability to third parties beyond that of common law?

4–12. What defenses does an auditor have against liability under the 1933 Act?

4–13. How does the 1934 Act differ from the 1933 Act in its impact on auditor liability?

4–14. What is a class action and how does it arise?

4–15. Name the types of sanctions that may be imposed by the SEC on auditing firms.

4–16. What measures have accounting firms undertaken to protect themselves against legal liability?

4–17. What is the RICO statute and what effect has it had on accounting malpractice actions?

Discussion Questions

4–30. Finley Manufacturing applied for a substantial bank loan from First National Bank. In connection with its application, Finley engaged Gregory & Co., CPAs, to audit its financial statements. Gregory completed the audit and rendered an unqualified opinion. On the basis of the financial statements and Gregory's opinion, First National granted Finley a loan of $500,000.

Within three months after the loan was granted, Finley filed for bankruptcy. First National promptly brought suit against Gregory for damages, claiming that it had relied to its detriment on misleading financial statements and the unqualified opinion of Gregory.

Gregory's audit working papers reveal negligence and possible other misconduct in the performance of the audit. Nevertheless, Gregory believes it can defend against liability to First National based on the privity defense.

Required:

Answer the following, setting forth reasons for any conclusions stated.

a. Explain the privity defense and evaluate its application to Gregory.
b. What exceptions to the privity defense might First National argue?

(AICPA adapted)

4–31. Reed, CPA, accepted an engagement to audit the financial statements of Smith Company. Reed's discussions with Smith's new management and the predecessor auditor indicated the possibility that Smith's financial statements may be misstated due to the possible occurrence of errors, irregularities, and illegal acts.

Required:

a. Identify and describe Reed's responsibilities to detect Smith's errors and irregularities. Do *not* identify specific auditing procedures.
b. Identify and describe Reed's responsibilities to report Smith's errors and irregularities in the auditor's report and in other ways.
c. Describe Reed's responsibilities to detect Smith's material illegal acts. Do not identify specific auditing procedures.

(AICPA adapted)

4-32. A CPA has been asked to audit the financial statements of a publicly held company for the first time. All preliminary verbal discussions and inquiries have been completed among the CPA, the company, the predecessor auditor, and all other necessary parties. The CPA is now preparing an engagement letter.

Required:

List the items that should be included in the typical engagement letter in these circumstances and describe the benefits derived from preparing an engagement letter.

(AICPA adapted)

4-33. Sam Maxwell was a junior staff member of an accounting firm. He began the audit of Park Jewelry, Inc., which manufactured and sold gold jewelry. He quit in the middle of the audit. The accounting firm hired another person to continue the audit of Park. Due to the changeover and the time pressure to finish the audit, the firm violated certain generally accepted auditing standards when it did not follow adequate procedures with respect to the physical inventory. Had the proper procedures been used during the audit, it would have been discovered that jewelry worth more than $20,000 was missing. The employee who was stealing the jewelry was able to steal an additional $30,000 worth before the thefts were discovered six months after the completion of the audit.

Required:

Discuss the legal problems of the accounting firm as a result of these facts.

(AICPA adapted)

4-34. Briefly discuss the auditor's liability to third parties

a. Under common law.
b. Under the Securities Act of 1933.
c. Under the Securities Exchange Act of 1934.

4-35. Adams & Good, CPAs, audited Windsor Corporation. Their audit was deficient in several respects.

- Adams & Good failed to substantiate properly certain receivables that later proved to be fictitious.
- With respect to other receivables, although they made a cursory check, they did not detect many accounts that were long overdue and obviously uncollectible.
- No physical inventory was taken of the securities claimed to be in Windsor's possession, which in fact had been sold. Both the securities and cash received from the sales were listed on the balance sheet as assets.

There is no indication that Adams & Good actually believed that the financial statements were false. Subsequent creditors, not known to Adams & Good, are now suing based on the deficiencies in the audit. Adams & Good moved to dismiss the lawsuit against them on the basis that the firm did not have actual knowledge of falsity and therefore did not commit fraud.

Required:

Answer the following, setting forth reasons for any conclusions stated.

May the creditors recover without demonstrating that Adams & Good had actual knowledge of falsity?

(AICPA adapted)

AICPA Multiple Choice Questions

These questions are taken from the Auditing and the Business Law parts of Uniform CPA Examinations. Choose the single most appropriate answer.

4-40. Under Statements on Auditing Standards, which of the following would be classified as an error?

a. Misappropriation of assets for the benefit of management.
b. Misinterpretation by management of facts that existed when the financial statements were prepared.
c. Preparation of records by employees to cover a fraudulent scheme.
d. Intentional omission of the recording of a transaction to benefit a third party.

4-41. An independent auditor has the responsibility to design the audit to provide reasonable assurance of detecting errors and irregularities that are material to the financial statements. Which of the following, if material, would be an *irregularity* as defined in Statements on Auditing Standards?

a. Misappropriation of an asset or groups of assets.
b. Clerical mistakes in the accounting data underlying the financial statements.
c. Mistakes in the application of accounting principles.
d. Misinterpretation of facts that existed when the financial statements were prepared.

4-42. Which of the following statements best describes the auditor's responsibility regarding the detection of material errors and irregularities?

a. The auditor is responsible for the failure to detect material errors and irregularities only when such failure results from the nonapplication of generally accepted accounting principles.
b. Extended auditing procedures are required to detect material errors and irregularities if the audit indicates that they may exist.
c. The auditor is responsible for the failure to detect material errors and irregularities only when the auditor fails to confirm receivables or observe inventories.
d. Extended auditing procedures are required to detect unrecorded transactions even if there is *no* evidence that material errors and irregularities may exist.

4–43. If an audit of financial statements causes the auditor to believe that material errors or irregularities exist the auditor should

a. Consider the implications and discuss the matter with appropriate levels of management.
b. Make the investigation necessary to determine whether the errors or irregularities have in fact occurred.
c. Request that the management investigate to determine whether the errors or irregularities have in fact occurred.
d. Consider whether the errors or irregularities were the result of a failure by employees to comply with existing internal control policies and procedures.

4–44. An audit performed in accordance with generally accepted auditing standards generally should

a. Be expected to provide assurance that illegal acts will be detected where the internal control structure is effective.
b. Be relied upon to disclose violations of truth-in-lending laws.
c. Encompass a plan to actively search for illegalities that relate to operating aspects.
d. *Not* be relied upon to provide assurance that illegal acts will be detected.

4–45. If as a result of auditing procedures an auditor believes that the client may have committed illegal acts, which of the following actions should be taken immediately by the auditor?

a. Consult with the client's counsel and the auditor's counsel to determine how the suspected illegal acts will be communicated to the stockholders.
b. Extend normal auditing procedures to ascertain whether the suspected illegal acts may have a material effect on the financial statements.
c. Inquire of the client's management and consult with the client's legal counsel or other specialists, as necessary, to obtain an understanding of the nature of the acts and their possible effects on the financial statements.
d. Notify each member of the audit committee of the board of directors of the nature of the acts and request that they give guidance with respect to the approach to be taken by the auditor.

4–46. An auditor who finds that the client has committed an illegal act would be most likely to withdraw from the engagement when the

a. Illegal act affects the auditor's ability to rely on management representations.
b. Illegal act has material financial statement implications.
c. Illegal act has received widespread publicity.
d. Auditor can *not* reasonably estimate the effect of the illegal act on the financial statements.

4–47. Hall purchased Eon Corp. bonds in a public offering subject to the Securities Act of 1933. Kosson and Co., CPAs, rendered an unqualified opinion on Eon's financial statements, which were included in Eon's registration statement. Kosson is being sued by Hall based upon misstatements contained in the financial statements. In order to be successful, Hall must prove

	Damages	Materiality of the misstatement	Kosson's scienter
a.	Yes	Yes	Yes
b.	Yes	Yes	No
c.	Yes	No	No
d.	No	Yes	Yes

4-48. DMO Enterprises, Inc., engaged the accounting firm of Martin, Seals & Anderson to perform its annual audit. The firm performed the audit in a competent, nonnegligent manner and billed DMO for $16,000, the agreed fee. Shortly after delivery of the audited financial statements, Hightower, the assistant controller, disappeared, taking with him $28,000 of DMO's funds. It was then discovered that Hightower had been engaged in a highly sophisticated, novel defalcation scheme during the past year. He had previously embezzled $35,000 of DMO funds. DMO has refused to pay the accounting firm's fee and is seeking to recover the $63,000 that was stolen by Hightower. Which of the following is correct?

a. The accountants can *not* recover their fee and are liable for $63,000.
b. The accountants are entitled to collect their fee and are *not* liable for $63,000.
c. DMO is entitled to rescind the audit contract and thus is *not* liable for the $16,000 fee, but it can *not* recover damages.
d. DMO is entitled to recover the $28,000 defalcation, and is *not* liable for the $16,000 fee.

4-49. Doe and Co., CPAs, issued an unqualified opinion on the 1990 financial statements of Marx Corp. These financial statements were included in Marx's annual report and Form 10-K filed with the SEC. Doe did not detect material misstatements in the financial statements as a result of negligence in the performance of the audit. Based upon the financial statements, Fitch purchased stock in Marx. Shortly thereafter, Marx became insolvent, causing the price of the stock to decline drastically. Fitch has commenced legal action against Doe for damages based upon Section 10(b) and Rule 10b-5 of the Securities Exchange Act of 1934. Doe's best defense to such an action would be that

a. Fitch lacks privity to sue.
b. The engagement letter specifically disclaimed all liability to third parties.
c. There is *no* proof of scienter.
d. There has been no subsequent sale for which a loss can be computed.

4-50. Sharp & Co., CPAs, was engaged by Radar Corp. to audit its financial statements. Sharp issued an unqualified opinion on Radar's financial statements. Radar has been accused of making negligent misrepresentations in the financial statements which Wisk relied upon when purchasing Radar stock. Sharp was not aware of the misrepresentations nor was it negligent in performing the audit. If Wisk sues Sharp for damages based upon Section 10(b) and Rule 10b-5 of the Securities Exchange Act of 1934, Sharp will

a. Lose, since the statements contained negligent misrepresentations.
b. Lose, since Wisk relied upon the financial statements.
c. Prevail, since some element of scienter must be proved.
d. Prevail, since Wisk was *not* in privity of contract with Sharp.

4-51. West & Co., CPAs, rendered an unqualified opinion on the financial statements of Pride Corp., which were included in Pride's registration statement filed with the SEC. Subsequently, Hex purchased 500 shares of Pride's preferred stock, which were acquired as part of a public offering subject to the Securities Act of 1933. Hex has commenced an action against West based on the Securities Act of 1933 for losses resulting from misstatements of facts in the financial statements included in the registration statement.

(1) Which of the following elements must Hex prove to hold West liable?

a. West rendered its opinion with knowledge of material misstatements.
b. West performed the audit negligently.
c. Hex relied on the financial statements included in the registration statement.
d. The misstatements were material.

(2) Which of the following defenses would be *least* helpful to West in avoiding liability to Hex?

a. West was *not* in privity of contract with Hex.
b. West conducted the audit in accordance with GAAS.
c. Hex's losses were caused by factors other than the misstatements.
d. Hex knew of the misstatements when Hex acquired the preferred stock.

4-52. Major, Major & Sharpe, CPAs, are the auditors of MacLain Industries. In connection with the public offering of $10 million of MacLain securities, Major expressed an unqualified opinion as to the financial statements. Subsequent to the offering, certain misstatements and omissions were revealed. Major has been sued by the purchasers of the stock offered pursuant to the registration statement, which included the financial statements audited by Major. In the ensuing lawsuit by the MacLain investors, Major will be able to avoid liability if

a. The errors and omissions were caused primarily by MacLain.
b. It can be shown that at least some of the investors did *not* actually read the audited financial statements.
c. It can prove due diligence in the audit of the financial statements of MacLain.
d. MacLain had expressly assumed any liability in connection with the public offering.

4-53. In general, the third party (primary) beneficiary rule as applied to a CPA's legal liability in conducting an audit is relevant to which of the following causes of action against a CPA?

	Fraud	*Constructive fraud*	*Negligence*
a.	Yes	Yes	No
b.	Yes	No	No
c.	No	Yes	Yes
d.	No	No	Yes

4-54. Mead Corp. orally engaged Dex & Co., CPAs, to audit its financial statements. The management of Mead informed Dex that it suspected that the accounts receivable were materially overstated. Although the financial statements audited by Dex did, in fact, include a materially overstated accounts receivable balance, Dex issued an unqualified opinion. Mead relied on the financial statements in deciding to obtain a loan from City Bank to expand its operations. City relied on the financial statements in making the loan to Mead. As a result of the overstated accounts receivable balance, Mead has defaulted on the loan and has incurred a substantial loss.

(1) If Mead sues Dex for negligence in failing to discover the overstatement, Dex's best defense would be that

a. No engagement letter had been signed by Dex.
b. The audit was performed by Dex in accordance with generally accepted auditing standards.
c. Dex was *not* in privity of contract with Mead.
d. Dex did *not* perform the audit recklessly or with an intent to deceive.

(2) If City sues Dex for fraud, Dex would most likely avoid liability if it could prove that

a. Dex was *not* in privity of contract with City.
b. Dex did *not* perform the audit recklessly or with an intent to deceive.
c. Mead should have provided more specific information concerning its suspicions.
d. Mead was contributorily negligent.

(3) If City sues Dex for fraud, could Dex be compelled to furnish City with the audit working papers?

a. No, because of the privileged communication rule, which is recognized in a majority of jurisdictions.
b. No, because City was *not* in privity of contract with Dex.
c. Yes, if the working papers are relevant to the action.
d. Yes, provided that Mead does *not* object.

4–55. Starr Corp. approved a plan of merger with Silo Corp. One of the determining factors in approving the merger was the strong financial statements of Silo, which were audited by Cox & Co., CPAs. Starr had engaged Cox to audit Silo's financial statements. While performing the audit, Cox failed to discover certain irregularities that have subsequently caused Starr to suffer substantial losses. In order for Cox to be liable under common law, Starr at a minimum must prove that Cox

a. Acted recklessly or with a lack of reasonable grounds for belief.
b. Knew of the irregularities.
c. Failed to exercise due care.
d. Was grossly negligent.

4–56. If a CPA recklessly departs from the standards of due care when conducting an audit, the CPA will be liable to third parties who were unknown to the CPA based on

a. Strict liability.
b. Gross negligence.
c. Negligence.
d. Breach of contract.

Problems and Cases

4-60. Dill Corp. was one of three major suppliers who sold raw materials to Fogg & Co. on credit. Dill became concerned over Fogg's ability to pay its debts. Payments had been consistently late and some checks had been returned, marked "insufficient funds." In addition, there were rumors concerning Fogg's solvency. Dill decided it would make no further sales to Fogg on credit unless it received a copy of Fogg's current, audited financial statements. It also required Fogg to assign its accounts receivable to Dill to provide security for the sales to Fogg on credit.

Clark & Wall, CPAs, was engaged by Fogg to perform an audit of Fogg's financial statements on which they subsequently issued an unqualified opinion. Several months later, Fogg defaulted on its obligations to Dill. At this point Dill was owed $240,000 by Fogg. Subsequently, Dill discovered that only $60,000 of the accounts receivable that Fogg had assigned to Dill as collateral was collectible.

Dill has commenced a lawsuit against Clark & Wall. The complaint alleges that Dill has incurred a $180,000 loss as a result of negligent or fraudulent misrepresentations contained in the audited financial statements of Fogg. Specifically, it alleges negligence, gross negligence, and actual and/or constructive fraud on the part of Clark & Wall in the conduct of the audit and the issuance of an unqualified opinion.

State law applicable to this action follows the majority rule with respect to the accountant's liability to third parties for negligence. In addition, there is no applicable state statute that creates an accountant-client privilege. Dill demanded to be provided a copy of the Fogg working papers from Clark & Wall, who refused to comply with the request, claiming that they are privileged documents. Clark & Wall has asserted that the entire action should be dismissed because Dill has no standing to sue the firm because of the absence of any contractual relationship with it, i.e., a lack of privity.

Required:

Answer the following, setting forth reasons for any conclusions stated.

a. Will Clark & Wall be able to avoid production of the Fogg working papers based on the assertion that they represent privileged communications?
b. What elements must be established by Dill to show negligence on the part of Clark & Wall?
c. What is the significance of compliance with GAAS in determining whether the audit was performed negligently?
d. What elements must be established by Dill to show actual or constructive fraud on the part of Clark & Wall?

(AICPA adapted)

4-61. Maybrook & Company is a brokerage firm registered under the Securities Exchange Act of 1934. The Act requires such a brokerage firm to file audited financial statements with the SEC annually. Wilson & Wilson, Maybrook's CPAs, performed the annual audit for the year ended December 31, 1989, and rendered an unqualified opinion, which was filed with the SEC along with Maybrook's financial statements. During 1989, Stevens, the president of Maybrook & Company, engaged in a huge embezzlement scheme that eventually bankrupted the firm. As a result, substantial losses were suffered by customers and shareholders of Maybrook & Company, including John Fowler, who had recently purchased several shares of stock of Maybrook & Company after reviewing the company's 1989 audit report. Wilson & Wilson's audit was deficient; if they had complied with generally accepted auditing standards, the embezzlement would have been discovered. However, Wilson & Wilson had no knowledge of the embezzlement nor could their conduct be categorized as reckless.

Required:

Answer the following, setting forth reasons for any conclusions stated.

a. What liability to Fowler, if any, does Wilson & Wilson have under the Securities Exchange Act of 1934?
b. What theory or theories of liability, if any, are available to Maybrook & Company's customers and shareholders under common law?

(AICPA adapted)

4–62. Jingles Corporation manufactured children's games. Because its cash position was deteriorating, Jingles sought a loan from A&C Financial Company. A&C had previously extended $25,000 credit to Jingles but refused to lend any additional money without obtaining copies of Jingles' audited financial statements.

Jingles contacted the CPA firm of Metz & Halsey to perform the audit. In arranging for the audit, Jingles clearly indicated that its purpose was to satisfy A&C Financial on the Corporation's sound financial condition and thus to obtain an additional loan of $50,000. Metz & Halsey accepted the engagement, performed the audit in a negligent manner, and rendered an unqualified auditor's opinion. If an adequate audit had been performed, the financial statements would have been found to be misleading.

Jingles submitted the audited financial statements to A&C Financial and obtained an additional loan of $35,000. A&C refused to lend more than that amount. After several other finance companies also refused, Jingles finally was able to persuade Rainbow Toy Stores, one of its customers, to lend the additional $15,000. Rainbow relied on the financial statements audited by Metz & Halsey.

Jingles is now in bankruptcy and A&C seeks to collect from Metz & Halsey the $60,000 it lent Jingles. Rainbow seeks to recover from Metz & Halsey the $15,000 it lent Jingles.

Required:

a. Will A&C recover? Explain.
b. Will Rainbow recover? Explain.

(AICPA adapted)

4–63. The Glengate Corporation decided to raise additional long-term capital by issuing $3,000,000 of 8 percent subordinated debentures to the public. Barber, Drake & Co., CPAs, the company's auditors, were engaged to audit the June 30, 1990 financial statements, which were included in the bond registration statement.

Barber, Drake & Co. completed its audit and submitted an unqualified auditor's report dated July 15, 1990. The registration statement was filed and became effective on September 1, 1990. Two weeks prior to the effective date, one of the partners of Barber, Drake & Co. called on Glengate Corporation and had lunch with the financial vice president and the controller. The partner questioned both officials on the company's operations since June 30 and inquired whether there had been any material changes in the company's financial position since that date. Both officers assured the partner that everything had proceeded normally and that the financial condition of the company had not changed materially.

Unfortunately, the officers' representation was not true. On July 30, a substantial debtor of the company failed to pay the $400,000 due on its account receivable and indicated to Glengate that it would probably be forced into bankruptcy. This receivable was shown as a collateralized loan on the June 30 financial statements. It was secured by stock of the debtor corporation, which had a value in excess of the loan at the time the financial statements were prepared but was virtually worthless at the effective date of the registration statement. This $400,000 account receivable was material to the financial condition of Glengate Corporation, and the market price of the subordinated debentures decreased by nearly 50 percent after the foregoing facts were disclosed.

The debenture holders of Glengate are seeking recovery of their loss against all parties connected with the debenture registration.

Required:

Is Barber, Drake & Co. liable to the Glengate debenture holders? Explain.

(AICPA adapted)

4–64. The CPA firm of Daniels & Forman was expanding very rapidly. Consequently, it hired several junior accountants, including a man named Richards. The partners of the firm eventually became dissatisfied with Richards' production and warned him that they would be forced to discharge him unless his output increased significantly.

At that time Richards was engaged in audits of several clients. He decided that to avoid being fired, he would reduce or omit entirely some of the standard auditing procedures listed in audit programs prepared by the partners. One of the CPA firm's clients, Stonewall Corporation, was in serious financial difficulty and had adjusted several of the accounts being audited by Richards so that they would appear to be financially sound. Richards prepared fictitious working papers in his home at night to support purported completion of auditing procedures assigned to him, although he in fact did not examine the adjusting entries. The CPA firm rendered an unqualified opinion on Stonewall's financial statements, which were grossly misstated. Several creditors, relying on the audited financial statements, subsequently extended large sums of money to Stonewall Corporation.

Required:

Would the CPA firm be liable to the creditors who extended the money because of their reliance on the erroneous financial statements if Stonewall Corporation should fail to pay the debts? Explain.

(AICPA adapted)

4–65. Beeline Bargains, Inc., is a chain store discount outlet that sells women's clothes. It has an excessively large inventory on hand and is in urgent need of additonal cash. It is bordering on bankruptcy, especially if the inventory has to be liquidated by sale to other stores instead of the public. Furthermore, about 15 percent of the inventory is not resalable except at a drastic discount below cost. Faced with this financial crisis, Beeline approached several of the manufacturers from whom it purchases. Elegant Fashions, Inc., one of the parties approached, indicated a willingness to lend Beeline $300,000 under certain conditions. First, Beeline was to submit audited financial statements for the express purpose of providing the correct financial condition of the company. The loan was to be predicated on these financial statements, and Beeline's engagement letter with Rose & Harris, its CPAs, expressly indicated this.

The second condition insisted on by Elegant Fashions was that it obtain a secured position in all unsecured inventory, accounts receivable, and other related personal property. In due course, a security agreement was executed and a financing statement properly filed and recorded.

In preparing the financial statements, Beeline valued the inventory at cost, which was approximately $100,000 over the current fair market value. Also, Beeline failed to disclose two secured creditors to whom substantial amounts are owed and who take priority over Elegant Fashions' security interests.

Rose & Harris issued an unqualified opinion on the financial statements of Beeline, which they believed were fairly presented.

Six months later Beeline filed a voluntary bankruptcy petition. Elegant Fashions received $125,000 as its share of the bankrupt's estate. It is suing Rose & Harris for the loss of $175,000. Rose & Harris deny liability based on lack of privity and lack of negligence.

Required:

Answer the following, setting forth reasons for any conclusions stated.

Is Elegant Fashions entitled to recover its loss from Rose & Harris?

(AICPA adapted)

4–66. Penn, CPA, is the auditor for Clayton Corporation, a privately owned company that has a June 30 fiscal year-end. Clayton arranged for a substantial bank loan, which was dependent on the bank receiving, by September 30, audited financial statements that showed a current ratio of at least 2 to 1. On September 25, just before the audit report was to be issued, Penn received an anonymous letter on Clayton's stationery indicating that a five-year lease by Clayton, as lessee of a factory building that was accounted for in the financial statements as an operating lease, was in fact a capital lease. The letter stated that there was a secret written agreement with the lessor modifying the lease and creating a capital lease.

Penn confronted the president of Clayton, who admitted that a secret agreement existed but said it was necessary to treat the lease as an operating lease to meet the current ratio requirement of the pending loan and that nobody would ever discover the secret agreement with the lessor. The president said that if Penn did not issue the report by September 30, Clayton would sue Penn for substantial damages that would result from not getting the loan. Under this pressure and because the working papers contained a copy of the five-year lease agreement, which supported the operating lease treatment, Penn issued the report with an unqualified opinion on September 29.

In spite of the fact that the loan was received, Clayton went bankrupt within two years. The bank is suing Penn to recover its losses on the loan and the lessor is suing Penn to recover uncollected rents.

Required:

Answer the following, setting forth reasons for any conclusions stated.

a. Is Penn liable to the bank?
b. Is Penn liable to the lessor?

(AICPA adapted)

PART 2

Theory and Concepts

5

The Audit Process

Most of the auditor's work in forming an opinion on financial statements consists of obtaining and evaluating evidence about management's assertions that are embodied in those statements. To be able to express an opinion on financial statements, the auditor must establish specific audit objectives related to those assertions and then design and perform audit tests to obtain and evaluate evidence about whether the objectives have been met. Throughout the process, the auditor must make decisions about whether the evidence obtained is competent and sufficient for formulating an opinion.

The approach the auditor takes can be broken down into a series of systematic steps. The steps are usually the same in every audit, but the types of tests performed and the evidence obtained vary with each engagement. This chapter explores the concepts of audit objectives, risk, and evidence, and presents an overall framework for viewing the steps in an audit. It concludes with a discussion of working papers—the principal means of documenting the work performed, the evidence obtained, and the conclusions reached.

AUDIT ASSERTIONS, OBJECTIVES, AND PROCEDURES

An entity's financial statements can be thought of as embodying a set of assertions by management. SAS No. 31, *Evidential Matter* (AU Section 326), groups financial statement assertions into the following broad categories:

- Existence or occurrence.
- Completeness.
- Rights and obligations.
- Valuation or allocation.
- Presentation and disclosure.

Many auditors find it helpful to consider explicitly two additional categories of assertions that are implicit in the SAS No. 31 list, namely

- Accuracy.
- Cutoff.

Assertions about existence relate to whether assets, liabilities, and ownership interests exist at a specific date. These assertions pertain to both physical items—such as inventory, plant and equipment, and cash—and accounts without physical substance—such as accounts receivable and accounts payable. Assertions about occurrence are concerned with whether recorded transactions, such as purchases and sales, represent economic events that actually occurred during a certain period. Assertions about existence and occurrence state that transactions and balances recorded in the accounts have real-world counterparts, for example, that there are real-world asset equivalents to the financial statement accounts representing the assets.

Assertions about completeness pertain to whether all transactions and other events and circumstances that occurred during a specific period and should have been recognized in that period have in fact been recorded. For example, *all* purchases of goods and services should be recorded and included in the financial statements. The completeness assertion also states that all recognizable financial statement items are in fact included in the financial statements. For example, management asserts that accounts payable reported on the balance sheet include all such obligations of the enterprise.

Assertions about rights and obligations relate to whether assets are the rights, and liabilities are the obligations, of the entity at a given date. For example, the reporting of capitalized leases in the balance sheet is an assertion that the amount capitalized is the unamortized cost of rights to leased property and that the amount of the lease liability is the unamortized obligation of the enterprise.

Assertions about valuation or allocation pertain to whether financial statement items are recorded at appropriate amounts in conformity with generally accepted accounting principles. For example, the financial statements represent that depreciation expense for the year and the carrying value of property, plant, and equipment are based on the systematic amortization of the historical cost of the assets, and that trade accounts receivable are stated at their net realizable value.

Assertions about presentation and disclosure relate to the proper classification, description, and disclosure of items in the financial statements; for example, that the settlement of long-term liabilities will not require the use of assets classified as current, and that the accounting policy note to the financial statements includes the disclosures required by generally accepted accounting principles.

Assertions about accuracy relate to the mathematical correctness of recorded transactions that are reflected in the financial statements and the appropriate summarization and posting of those transactions to the general ledger. For example, the financial statements represent that accounts payable reflect purchases of goods and services that are based on correct prices and quantities and on invoices that have been accurately computed.

Assertions about cutoff relate to the recording of transactions in the proper accounting period. For example, a check to a vendor that is mailed on December 31 should be recorded in December and not, through either oversight or intent, in January.

SAS No. 31 is written in terms of financial statement assertions; auditors generally translate those assertions into audit objectives that they seek to achieve by performing auditing procedures. For each assertion embodied in each item in the financial statements, the auditor develops a corresponding audit objective. Then the auditor designs procedures for obtaining sufficient

assertions → aud. objectives → audit procedures

competent evidential matter to either corroborate or contradict each assertion and thereby achieve the related audit objective or reveal a deficiency in the financial statements.

Chapter 1 discussed two functions that auditors perform: first, gathering and evaluating evidence about verifiable "facts" and, second, interpreting those facts once they are known, which includes evaluating accounting estimates and judgments made by the client's management. Although the two functions of auditing are distinguishable by the type of assertion for which evidence is primarily gathered, in practice they are interrelated. Moreover, the auditor must evaluate all evidence obtained, regardless of why it was gathered. Hence, the function of interpreting/evaluating permeates all audit work.

In developing audit objectives and related auditing procedures for certain categories of assertions—existence or occurrence, completeness, accuracy, cutoff, and rights and obligations—the auditor's function is primarily evidence gathering. Interpreting and evaluating relate mainly to formulating audit objectives and designing auditing procedures to test the assertions relating to valuation or allocation and presentation and disclosure. These assertions reflect the client's selection and application of accounting measurement and disclosure principles, including the estimates that are an inherent part of the accounting process.

Figure 5.1 illustrates how auditors consider these seven broad categories of assertions in formulating audit objectives and designing auditing procedures to obtain evidence supporting them. In the figure, a single auditing procedure is linked to each stated audit objective. In an actual audit, a combination of auditing procedures will generally be necessary to achieve a single objective, and some auditing procedures will relate to more than one objective. For example, in addition to observing physical inventory counts by client personnel to obtain evidence that inventories included in the balance sheet physically exist, the auditor may also confirm the existence and amount of inventories stored in public warehouses or with other custodians at locations outside the entity's premises. Moreover, observing inventory counts also provides evidence that the inventory quantities include all products, materials, and supplies on hand (completeness objective).

Relating the evidence obtained from auditing procedures to the audit objectives is an iterative process of accumulating, analyzing, and interpreting information in light of the auditor's expectations, past experience with the client, generally accepted accounting principles, and good management practices. Procedures performed to meet one audit objective for one account frequently generate information that requires further action by the auditor to achieve that particular audit objective or other audit objectives related to that particular account or other accounts. Evidence that raises questions, for example, about revenues recorded may also raise questions about the adequacy of the allowance for inventory obsolescence, which in turn will require the auditor to accumulate and analyze additional evidence.

Figure 5.1 Examples of Audit Objectives and Procedures

Management Assertion	*Example of Audit Objective*	*Example of Auditing Procedure*	*Primary Audit Function*
Existence or occurrence	Inventories in the balance sheet physically exist.	Observe physical inventory counts by client personnel.	Evidence gathering
Completeness	Sales revenues include all items shipped to customers.	Review the client's periodic accounting for the numerical sequence of shipping documents and invoices.	Evidence gathering
Accuracy	Accounts receivable reflect sales transactions that are based on correct prices and quantities and are accurately computed.	Compare prices on invoices with master price list and quantities with customer's sales order and client's shipping records; recalculate amounts on invoices.	Evidence gathering
Cutoff	Sales transactions are reported in the proper period.	Compare shipping dates with dates of journal entries for sales recorded in the last several days of the old year and the first several days of the new year.	Evidence gathering
Rights and obligations	Real estate in the balance sheet is owned by the entity.	Inspect deeds, purchase contracts, settlement papers, insurance policies, minutes, and related correspondence.	Evidence gathering
Valuation or allocation	Receivables are stated at net realizable value.	Review client's aging of receivables to evaluate adequacy of allowance for uncollectible accounts.	Interpreting/evaluating
Presentation and disclosure	Loss contingencies not required to be recorded are appropriately disclosed.	Inquire of the client's lawyers concerning litigation, claims, and assessments and evaluate the related disclosures.	Interpreting/evaluating

AUDIT RISK

Audit risk is the risk that the auditor will issue an inappropriate opinion on financial statements. Although an auditor could conceivably report that financial statements are not fairly presented when they are, for practical purposes audit risk refers to the risk of reporting that financial statements are fairly presented when they are not. The auditor's objective is to design and perform auditing procedures that will restrict audit risk to a low level.

Audit risk has two components: the risk that the financial statements contain misstatements and the risk that the auditor will not detect them. The former risk is not under the auditor's control; the auditor assesses the risks that are associated with the entity, but cannot in any way change them. The latter risk, called detection risk, is controlled by the auditor through the selection and performance of tests directed at specific assertions relating to specific transactions and account balances. The auditor's assessment of the risk of the financial statements containing misstatements determines the level of detection risk he or she can accept, and still restrict audit risk to an appropriately low level.

The risk of misstatement occurring in the financial statements has two aspects—inherent risk and control risk. Inherent risk is the susceptibility of an account balance or a class of transactions to material misstatements, without consideration of the control structure. That susceptibility may result from either conditions affecting the entity as a whole or characteristics of specific transactions or accounts. Control risk is the risk that the control structure will not prevent or detect material misstatements on a timely basis. The auditor assesses inherent risk conditions and characteristics to identify areas where the risk of material misstatement may be high. In assessing control risk, the auditor considers the elements of the entity's control structure and, if appropriate, tests them to determine to what extent they are designed and operating effectively and thus can be expected to prevent or detect misstatements. The resulting evidence reduces the evidence the auditor needs from tests of transactions and account balances to restrict audit risk to an acceptably low level.

AUDIT EVIDENCE AND AUDIT TESTS

The third standard of field work states

> Sufficient competent evidential matter is to be obtained through inspection, observation, inquiries, and confirmations to afford a reasonable basis for an opinion regarding the financial statements under audit. (AU Section 326.01)

The evidence necessary to either corroborate or contradict the assertions in the financial statements and thus provide the auditor with a basis for an opinion is obtained by designing and performing auditing procedures. This section of the chapter describes the various kinds of evidence that are available to the auditor and the types of procedures that the auditor performs to obtain evidence.

Types of Evidence

SAS No. 31 (AU Section 326) points out that evidential matter necessary to support the assertions in the financial statements consists of *underlying accounting data* and all *corroborating information* available to the auditor. Underlying evidence for the most part is available to the auditor from within the client company. It consists of the accounting data from which the financial statements are prepared, and includes journals, ledgers, and computer files; accounting manuals; and memoranda and worksheets supporting such items as cost allocations, computations, and reconciliations.

Corroborating evidence is information that supports the underlying evidence, and generally is available to the auditor from both the client and outside sources. Client sources include documentary material closely related to accounting data, such as checks, invoices, contracts, minutes of meetings, correspondence, written representations by knowledgeable employees of the client, and information obtained by the auditor by inquiry of officers and employees and observation of employees at work. Additional types of corroborating evidence include confirmations of amounts due or assets held by third parties (such as customers and custodians), correspondence with experts such as attorneys and engineers, and physical examination or inspection of assets such as marketable securities and inventories.

Examination of underlying accounting data alone is not sufficient to meet the third standard of field work. The auditor must obtain satisfaction about the quality of the underlying evidence through corroborating evidence. For example, an auditor usually finds it necessary to confirm open accounts receivable to support receivable balances in the accounts receivable subsidiary ledger. To cite another example, the auditor should ordinarily corroborate lists of inventory items counted by client personnel by observing the client's physical inventory counting procedures and making some test counts.

Auditors use various methods, or procedures—inquiry, observation, inspecting assets, confirmation, examination of documents, reperformance, and analytical procedures—to obtain sufficient competent evidential matter. How the evidence is classified is not very important; what is important is the auditor's ability to evaluate each kind of evidence in terms of its relevance and reliability, as discussed later in this chapter.

Inquiry. Inquiry means asking questions. The questions may be oral or written and may be directed to the client or to third parties. At the planning stage of the audit, the auditor needs to develop an understanding of the client's business and its internal control structure; one of the easiest ways to do this initially is through inquiry. (Later in the audit, the understanding is either corroborated or contradicted by the results of other tests.) At various stages in the audit, the auditor may ask the client's employees specific questions about matters arising in the course of the audit work. The auditor makes inquiries of management as part of evaluating accounting principles and estimates. Requesting a representation letter from client management as to the recording of all known liabilities, the existence of contingent liabilities, and the existence and carrying value of inventory is a form of inquiry. The auditor may also inquire of third parties, such as the client's outside legal counsel regarding legal matters, on matters outside the auditor's expertise. In all instances, the auditor's evaluation of responses is an integral part of the inquiry process.

Observation. Observation involves direct visual viewing of client employees in their work environment, and of other facts and events. It is a useful technique that can be employed in many phases of an audit. The auditor should consider, however, that employees may not perform in the same way when the auditor is not present. At the beginning of the audit, the auditor may tour the client's facilities as part of gaining an understanding of the client's business. That tour may also provide possible indications of slow-moving or obsolete goods. Observation of the client's employees taking a physical inventory can provide firsthand knowledge to help the auditor assess the adequacy of the inventory taking. Watching employees whose functions have accounting significance perform their assigned tasks can help the auditor assess whether specific control procedures are operating effectively.

Inspection and Counting of Assets. The auditor may obtain evidence by inspecting or counting assets. For example, the auditor may count cash or marketable securities on hand to ascertain that the assets in the accounts actually exist and are accurately recorded.

Confirmation. Confirmation involves obtaining a representation of a fact or condition from a third party, preferably in writing. Examples are a confirmation from a bank of the amount on deposit or of a loan outstanding, or a confirmation from a customer of the existence of a receivable balance at a certain date. Auditors most often associate confirmations with cash (confirmation from a bank) and accounts receivable (confirmation from customers). Confirmation, however, has widespread applicability; depending on the circumstances, virtually any transaction, event, or account balance can be confirmed with a third party. For example, creditors can confirm accounts and notes payable; both customers and creditors can confirm specific transactions; insurance companies can confirm insurance premiums paid during the year and balances due at year-end, as well as borrowings on life insurance policies; transfer agents and registrars can confirm shares of stock outstanding; trustees can confirm balances due under long-term borrowings and payments required and made under bond sinking fund requirements.

Examination of Documents and Records. Examining documents includes reading, tracing, looking at supporting documentation, comparing, and reconciling. The auditor may read the minutes of the board of directors' meetings for authorization of new financing. The auditor may trace postings from customers' sales invoices to individual customer accounts, or may examine invoices, purchase orders, and receiving reports to ascertain that the charges to a particular asset or expense account are adequately supported. The auditor may look at evidence in the form of signatures or initials on a purchase invoice, indicating that the invoice has been compared, by appropriate client personnel, with the corresponding purchase order and receiving report, and that the footings and extensions on the invoice have been recalculated. The auditor may compare purchase invoices with related receiving reports for evidence that merchandise has been received for bills rendered by creditors. The auditor may examine the client's reconciliation of accounts receivable subsidiary ledgers with control accounts.

Reperformance. Reperformance involves repeating, either in whole or in part, the same procedures performed by the client's employees, particularly recalculations to ensure mathematical accuracy. Reperformance may involve some of the other techniques previously mentioned, such as comparing or counting. For example, comparing a vendor's invoice with the corresponding purchase order and receiving report, where there is evidence in the form of initials on a document that the client's employees previously made that comparison, is reperformance. Reperformance may also involve recounting some of the client's physical inventory counts, recalculating the client's extensions and footings on sales invoices and inventory listings, repeating the client's calculations of depreciation expense, and reconstructing a client-prepared bank reconciliation. In addition, in evaluating management's accounting estimates and its choice and application of accounting principles, the auditor may "reperform" the processes followed by management.

Analytical Procedures. Analytical procedures are reasonableness tests of financial information made by studying and comparing relationships among data and trends in the data. Analytical procedures include scanning or scrutinizing accounting records, such as entries to an inventory control account for a period, looking for evidence of unusual amounts or unusual sources of input, which, if found, would be further investigated. Other examples of analytical procedures typically performed in an audit include fluctuation analyses, ratio analyses, comparisons of accounting data with operating data, and comparisons of recorded amounts with expectations developed by the auditor. Analytical procedures are performed early in the audit to help the auditor in planning other auditing procedures, as substantive tests to obtain evidence about specific assertions and accounts, and at the end of the audit as an overall review of the financial statements.

Competence of Evidential Matter

The third standard of field work requires the auditor to obtain evidential matter that is both competent and sufficient. In other words, the auditor must reach a decision, based on experience and judgment, on whether the evidence obtained is good or useful (competent evidential matter) and whether enough useful evidence has been obtained (sufficient evidential matter).

To be competent, evidence must be both relevant and reliable. To be relevant, evidence must affect the auditor's ability to accept or reject a specific financial statement assertion. The auditor reaches a conclusion on the financial statements taken as a whole through a series of judgments made throughout the audit about specific financial statement assertions. Each piece of evidence obtained is evaluated in terms of its usefulness either in corroborating or contradicting an assertion by management or in the auditor's evaluation of evidence obtained at other stages of the audit. Evidence is relevant to the extent that it serves either of those purposes.

An example or two will illustrate the concept of relevance of evidence. Confirming accounts receivable by requesting the client's customers to inform the auditor about any differences between their records of amounts they owe the client and the client's records of open balances is a commonly performed auditing procedure. When considered in conjunction with other evidence, a signed confirmation returned to the auditor indicating agreement with the open balance on the client's books can provide support for the implicit management assertion that the account receivable exists and is not overstated. Confirmations, however, do not provide evidence about collectibility, completeness, or rights and obligations. A confirmed account may not be collectible because the debtor does not intend or is unable to pay; receivables may exist that have not been recorded and therefore cannot possibly be selected for confirmation; or the client may have sold the receivables to another party and may be merely acting as a collection agent for that party. Similarly, physically inspecting and counting inventory gives the auditor evidence about its existence, but not about its valuation or about the client's title to it. Using irrelevant evidence to support an audit conclusion about a management assertion is a major source of "nonsampling error," as discussed in Chapter 10.

Evidence must also be reliable if it is to be useful to the auditor. The FASB's definition of reliability is also appropriate in the context of audit evidence. Reliability is "the quality of information that assures that information is reasonably free from error and bias and faithfully represents what it purports to represent."[1] Synonyms for reliability are "dependability" and "trustworthiness." The reliability of audit evidence is influenced by several factors.

- *Independence of the source.* Evidential matter obtained by the auditor from independent sources outside the entity being audited is usually more reliable

[1]Statement of Financial Accounting Concepts No. 2, "Glossary of Terms."

than that from within the entity. Examples of evidence from independent sources include a confirmation from a state agency of the number of shares of common stock authorized to be issued, and a confirmation from a bank of a cash balance, a loan balance, or securities held as collateral. (The high level of reliability that such evidence provides does not mean that errors in confirmations of this nature never occur.) In contrast, evidence arising from inquiries of the client or from inspecting documents provided by the client is usually considered less reliable from the auditor's viewpoint.

- *Qualifications of the source.* For audit evidence to be reliable, it must be obtained from people who are competent and have the qualifications to make the information free from error. (The independence-of-the-source criterion addresses the possibility of deliberate errors in the evidence; the qualifications-of-the-source criterion addresses the possibility of unintentional errors in the evidence.) For instance, confirmations provided by business customers are usually more reliable than confirmations provided by individuals. Answers to inquiries about pending litigation from client counsel are usually more reliable than answers from persons not working in the legal department. The auditor should not necessarily assume that the higher a person is in the client's organization, the better qualified that person is to provide evidence. The accounts payable clerk probably knows the "true" routine in the accounts payable section of the accounting department better than the corporate controller does. Furthermore, auditors should challenge their own qualifications when evaluating evidence they have gathered. When inspecting or counting precious gems in a jeweler's inventory, for example, the auditor is probably not qualified to distinguish between diamonds and pieces of glass.
- *Internal control structure.* Underlying accounting data developed within a satisfactory internal control structure is more reliable than similar data developed within a less adequate internal control structure. The auditor does not accept the client's description of the control structure without corroboration. Instead, if the auditor plans to look to the control structure as a source of audit evidence, he or she observes the activities of company personnel and performs other tests of policies and procedures that are part of the control structure to determine that they are designed and operating effectively.
- *Objectivity of the evidence.* Evidence is objective if it requires little judgment to evaluate its reliability. Evidence obtained by an auditor's direct, personal knowledge through counting, observing, calculating, or examining documents is generally more objective than evidence based on the opinions of others, such as the opinion of an appraiser about the value of an asset acquired by the client in a nonmonetary transaction, the opinion of a lawyer about the outcome of pending litigation, or the opinion of the client's credit manager about the collectibility of outstanding receivables. Sometimes, however, more objective evidence is not attainable.

The auditor's twofold objective in performing an audit in accordance with generally accepted auditing standards is to achieve the necessary assurance to support the audit opinion and to perform the audit as efficiently as possible. Thus, in addition to considering the relevance and reliability of evidence, the auditor must also consider its availability, timeliness, and cost. Sometimes a desirable form of evidence is simply not available. For example, an auditor who is retained by the client after its accounting year-end cannot be present to observe and test-count the ending inventory. Also, time constraints may not permit an auditor to consider a particular source of evidence. For example, confirming a foreign account receivable might delay the completion of the audit by weeks or even months. Different types of evidence have different costs associated with them, and the auditor must consider cost–benefit trade-offs.

Fortunately, auditors usually have available more than one source or method of obtaining evidence to corroborate a particular financial statement assertion. If one source or method is not practicable to use, another can often be substituted. For example, a customer who may not be able to confirm an account receivable balance may be able to confirm specific sales transactions and cash remittances. Or a more costly source of evidence may be substituted for a less costly source that is not as reliable. For instance, a petroleum engineer who is independent of the client could be retained instead of the auditor's relying on engineers employed by the client for estimates of proven oil reserves. The auditor should choose the type of evidence (corroborating evidence often is sought using more than one method) that meets the audit objectives at the lowest cost.

What the auditor normally expects to achieve through this process of gathering and evaluating audit evidence is the assurance needed to support an unqualified opinion on the financial statements. The auditor cannot be satisfied with anything less and still express such an opinion. The type of evidence, the amount needed, and the timing of the procedures used to obtain the evidence, however, can all be varied to fit the circumstances of the individual engagement and thus enhance efficiency.

Sufficiency of Evidential Matter

Determining the sufficiency of evidential matter is a question of deciding how much evidence is enough to achieve the reasonable assurance necessary to support the auditor's opinion. The sufficiency of evidence depends partly on the thoroughness of the auditor's search for it and partly on the auditor's ability to evaluate it objectively. For some auditing procedures, the amount of evidence needed corresponds precisely with the decision to use a certain procedure at all: The auditor either performs or does not perform the procedure. For example, in the audit of a client with a single cash fund, a decision to count cash on hand is a decision to count *all* cash on hand. If the client had numerous cash funds, however, the auditor could count only some of the cash funds. In that case, the question of sufficiency becomes one of determining the extent of testing. The extent of testing, including the use of sampling, is discussed in Chapter 10.

Types of Audit Tests

The types of evidence and the procedures for obtaining it described previously could also be classified according to the purpose for which the evidence is gathered. Viewed in terms of their purpose, auditing procedures can for the most part be classified as one of two major types: *tests of controls* and *substantive tests*. These two types of audit tests and their respective purposes are discussed at length in Chapters 8 and 9. They are described briefly here to set the stage for the overview of an audit that is presented later in this chapter.

Tests of controls are performed to provide the auditor with evidence about the effectiveness of the design and operation of internal control structure policies and procedures. That evidence supports an assessment of control risk below the maximum for one or more assertions. Based on that assessment, the assurance needed from substantive tests, which are tests of transactions and account balances, is reduced. To illustrate a test of controls, consider a client's internal control structure that requires the accounts payable clerk to recalculate the extensions and footings on vendors' invoices as a means of determining that the vendors' calculations are mathematically accurate. As evidence that the control procedure has been applied, the clerk initials the invoice after performing the calculations. To test the effectiveness of the control procedure, the auditor should inspect the invoice for the presence of the clerk's initials and may reperform the calculations that the clerk was supposed to have made. If the initials are present and the extensions and footings are correct, the auditor would conclude that the control procedure operated effectively in that specific instance.

Substantive tests consist of tests of the details of transactions and account balances, and analytical procedures. The purpose of substantive tests is to provide the auditor with evidence supporting management's assertions that are implicit in the financial statements or, conversely, to discover errors or irregularities in the financial statements. Analytical procedures used as substantive tests are discussed in detail in Chapter 9. An example of a test of the details of transactions is the auditor's examination of underlying documents that support purchases, sales, and retirements of property, plant, and equipment during the year. The auditor examines them as a means of forming a conclusion about the assertions concerning existence, rights and obligations, and accuracy that are implicit in the balance reported for that account in the balance sheet. An example of a test of the details of an account balance is the confirming of accounts receivable in order to form a conclusion about their existence.

Other key auditing procedures, which do not fit the literal definition of substantive tests, include reading minutes of meetings of the board of directors and its important committees, obtaining letters from outside counsel regarding legal matters, and obtaining a letter of representation from management about the completeness of recorded liabilities.

Audit Evidence Decisions

The amount and kinds of evidence that the auditor decides are necessary to provide a reasonable basis for forming an opinion on the financial statements taken as a whole, and the timing of procedures used to obtain the evidence, are matters of professional judgment. The auditor makes these decisions only after carefully deliberating on the circumstances of a particular engagement and considering the various risks related to the audit. The goal in every audit should be to perform the work in an effective and efficient manner.

Usually an auditor finds it necessary to rely on evidence that is persuasive rather than convincing. In deciding how much persuasive evidence is enough, by necessity the auditor must work within time constraints, considering the cost of obtaining evidence and evaluating the usefulness of the evidence obtained. In making these decisions, the auditor cannot ignore the risk of issuing an inappropriate opinion or justify omitting a particular test solely because it is difficult or expensive to perform. While an auditor is seldom convinced beyond all doubt with respect to all the assertions embodied in the financial statements, he or she must achieve the level of assurance necessary to support the opinion given.

An unqualified opinion requires that the auditor have reasonable assurance about the fairness of presentation of all material items in the financial statements. The auditor must refrain from forming an opinion until sufficient competent evidential matter has been obtained to remove all substantial doubt. For example, if the auditor tries to communicate with a customer to confirm a material amount owed to the entity and the customer fails to respond after repeated requests, the auditor should use alternative procedures—such as examining evidence of subsequent cash receipts, cash remittance advices, the customer's purchase orders, and sales and shipping documents—to obtain satisfaction that the account receivable exists and the balance is accurate.

In deciding on the nature, timing, and extent of auditing procedures to be performed, the auditor can choose from a number of alternative strategies. For example, for some audit objectives for specific accounts, the auditor might decide to perform tests of controls. The tests would be designed to provide evidence that the accounting system from which the account balances were derived and the other elements of the internal control structure were operating consistently and effectively, and would be combined with limited substantive tests of the account balances themselves. For other audit objectives or accounts, the auditor might decide to obtain evidence mainly from substantive tests. These decisions will be influenced by answers to such questions as: which approach provides the needed assurance most efficiently; are the accounting system and related control procedures satisfactory; what are the principal risks of the client's business; and what are the significant account balances in the financial statements? These questions are not all-inclusive, but are indicative of the kinds of considerations and judgments the auditor must make. They are discussed throughout this book and particularly in Chapter 6.

THE STEPS IN AN AUDIT

Every audit includes the following major steps:

1. Carrying out such initial audit activities as staffing and budgeting.
2. Obtaining (or updating) and documenting information about the client and its control structure as a basis for assessing inherent and control risk, including, in many situations, performing some tests of controls.
3. Developing the audit testing plan.
4. For specific audit objectives and account balances, where appropriate, performing additional tests of controls to further reduce the assurance needed from substantive tests.
5. Performing substantive tests to obtain, evaluate, and document sufficient competent evidence to corroborate that the management assertions embodied in account balances and in the financial statements as a whole, including the disclosures, are reasonable and thus to determine that the corresponding audit objectives have been met.
6. Performing final analytical and other procedures, and reviewing and evaluating the audit findings.
7. Formulating the auditor's report and communicating deficiencies in the control structure.

The nature, timing, and extent of the work in each step vary from one audit client to another and may vary from year to year for a given client. Moreover, the steps seldom appear as separate, isolated, specifically identifiable activities. These steps are elaborated on in this section and graphically displayed in Figure 5.2. With the exception of the reporting phase of the audit process, all the steps involve activities that affect audit strategy decisions. As depicted in the figure, strategy considerations are most intense during the risk assessment activities and when the auditor evaluates the results of those activities and develops the audit testing plan. The key strategy decision made at that time is whether to perform additional tests of controls to further reduce the assurance needed from substantive tests or to proceed directly to the substantive testing step.

Figure 5.2 Summary of the Audit Process

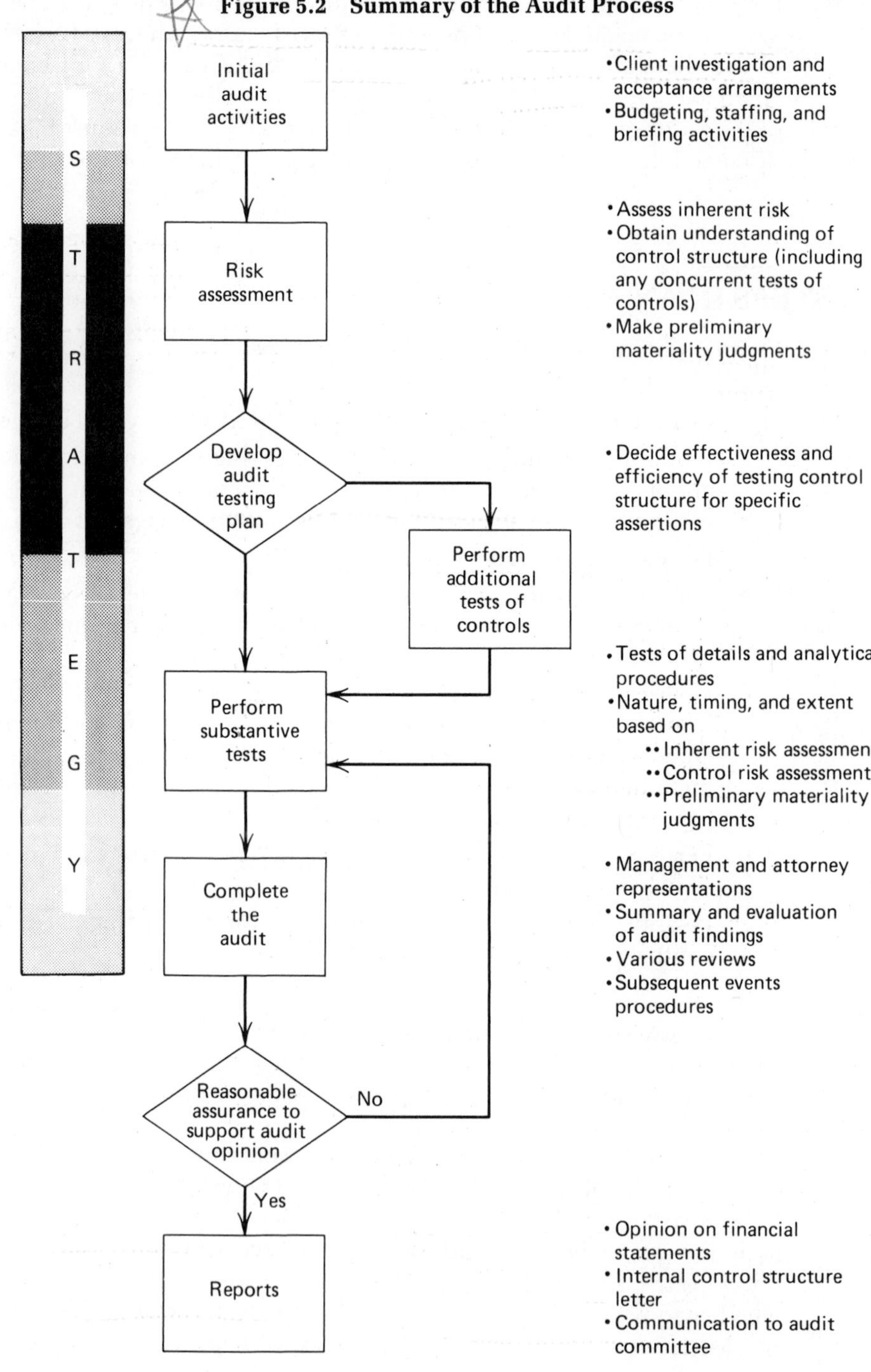
S
T
R
A
T
E
G
Y
Initial audit activities
•Client investigation and acceptance arrangements
•Budgeting, staffing, and briefing activities
Risk assessment
•Assess inherent risk
•Obtain understanding of control structure (including any concurrent tests of controls)
•Make preliminary materiality judgments
Develop audit testing plan
•Decide effectiveness and efficiency of testing control structure for specific assertions
Perform additional tests of controls
Perform substantive tests
•Tests of details and analytical procedures
•Nature, timing, and extent based on
••Inherent risk assessment
••Control risk assessment
••Preliminary materiality judgments
Complete the audit
•Management and attorney representations
•Summary and evaluation of audit findings
•Various reviews
•Subsequent events procedures
Reasonable assurance to support audit opinion
No
Yes
Reports
•Opinion on financial statements
•Internal control structure letter
•Communication to audit committee

Initial Audit Activities

Before a new client or a recurring engagement is accepted, appropriate information is gathered and evaluated as a basis for deciding whether to accept or retain the engagement. Once the engagement has been accepted, the terms and engagement goals have to be established. A number of administrative and strategy decisions also need to be made, namely, whether to use the work of internal auditors and specialists (for example, actuaries, appraisers), determining whether to use the work and reports of other firms that have been engaged to audit one or more components of the client, assigning staff, preparing time budgets, and other similar scheduling and administrative activities. In addition, opportunities to improve client relations and to maximize the quality of client services may be identified at this initial stage of the audit.

Obtaining and Documenting Information About the Client

At an early stage in the audit, the auditor obtains (or updates) information about the client. This information is used to assess inherent and control risk as a basis for developing the audit testing plan. Among other things, the auditor gathers information about

- The nature, size, and organization of the enterprise and its operations.
- Matters affecting the business and industry in which the enterprise operates, such as
  - —The business environment
  - —Legal constraints and requirements.
- The control environment and significant management and accounting policies, practices, and methods.
- The accounting system and significant control procedures.
- Significant accounts or groups of accounts and the interrelationships among significant financial and operating data.

- Important dates, such as
  - —Dates of the auditor's meetings with the audit committee of the board of directors
  - —Dates by which the client will have assembled the data, records, and documents required by the auditor
  - —Date or dates on which the client plans to physically count inventories or other assets
  - —Deadlines for issuing the report on the financial statements and any other audit-related reports.

The information is obtained in a number of ways. The auditor may begin by consulting such materials as the client's recent annual reports and interim earnings or other news releases; general business or industry publications; industry accounting and auditing guides developed by the AICPA, the auditor's firm, and others; and trade association materials. For a recurring engagement, prior years' working papers and current correspondence files are also valuable sources of information. For an initial engagement, the auditor makes inquiries and reviews preceding years' working papers of the predecessor auditor, if the client has been audited in the past. The auditor supplements this knowledge by interviewing officers and employees of the client and others knowledgeable about and experienced in the industry. Additionally, the auditor typically reviews the company's policy and procedures manuals; tours its major plants and offices; reads the minutes of recent meetings of the board of directors, its important committees, and the stockholders; reads the client's significant contracts and other agreements; and compares the client's significant financial and operating data with that of its competitors, analyzing relationships and trends in the data.

Understanding the Control Structure. Generally accepted auditing standards require the auditor to obtain an understanding of the client's control structure, which comprises the control environment, accounting system, and control procedures. On a recurring engagement, the auditor should focus on aspects of the control structure that have been added, changed, or assumed increased importance since the previous audit. At a minimum, the understanding must be sufficient for planning the audit, that is, for the auditor to identify and respond to the risk of material misstatements in the financial statements and design appropriate substantive tests to detect them. In obtaining the understanding of the control structure, the auditor identifies the critical points in the accounting system where significant errors or irregularities could occur and determines whether policies and procedures to prevent or detect such errors or irregularities have been designed and placed in operation at those critical points.

The auditor obtains (or updates) an understanding of the client's control structure mainly through observing and inquiring of client personnel, referring to relevant policy and procedures manuals, and inspecting books, records, forms, and reports. As a practical matter, the auditor generally does not "relearn" or redocument the client's control structure in each year's engagement. Most audits are recurring engagements, for which the auditor carries forward the knowledge and documentation developed in prior years and updates them for significant changes since the preceding year's audit. Most (if not all) of those changes generally come to the auditor's attention through continuing contact with the client between one year's audit and the next. If the auditor is concerned that the documented understanding of the client's accounting system may be incorrect or incomplete, perhaps because of changes since the preceding audit, it may be efficient to trace one or a few representative transactions through the system (sometimes called a transaction review or "walkthrough") before formalizing the audit testing plan.

A record of the information obtained by the auditor is needed to plan and control the audit and document the auditor's compliance with generally accepted auditing standards. Some auditors document all the information in narrative form; others prefer to use narratives for general information about the industry and company, and overview flowcharts to describe the accounting system and key control procedures. How much information is necessary to design and carry out subsequent auditing procedures depends on whether there have been significant changes in matters affecting the client, its business, or its control structure since the preceding audit, as well as on the audit testing plan contemplated.

Concurrent Tests of Controls. The auditor uses the information about the client to make preliminary materiality judgments and assess inherent and control risk. As part of the assessment of control risk, the auditor often performs tests of controls concurrently with obtaining the understanding of the control structure. Those tests of controls provide evidence about whether control structure policies and procedures have been properly designed to prevent or detect errors on a timely basis and have operated effectively and continuously. They may include inquiring of client personnel who apply policies and procedures, as well as others in a position to be aware of control breakdowns; observing how the policies and procedures are applied; examining records and documents for evidence that they have been applied; and reperforming control procedures by duplicating the actions of the client's personnel. If the results of the tests of controls are positive, the auditor then considers whether, based on the work done so far, he or she can reduce the assurance needed from substantive tests for specific accounts and audit objectives. This will ordinarily be possible.

Developing the Audit Testing Plan

The auditor's materiality judgments and risk assessments determine the nature, timing, and extent of auditing procedures for each account or group of accounts. The auditor's aim is to choose an audit strategy that will most efficiently limit audit risk—that is, the risk that he or she will unknowingly fail to modify the opinion appropriately if the financial statements are materially misstated—to a low level.

As explained in Chapter 1, the auditor typically tests less than 100 percent of the items in an account balance or class of transactions. Most auditors start with the presumption that it will not be necessary to perform substantive tests on every item that supports an account balance in the financial statements. From information gathered or updated about the client (particularly about its control environment and accounting system), and from any concurrent tests of controls performed, the auditor usually has some evidence that the client has established policies and procedures that reduce the risk of material misstatement, either in particular accounts or groups of accounts or in the financial statements as a whole.

After the auditor has completed the risk assessment activities, he or she develops the audit testing plan. Concurrent tests of controls may have been performed as part of obtaining the understanding of the control structure, and the auditor may have assessed control risk at below the maximum. He or she then considers whether additional evidence about the effectiveness of control structure policies and procedures is likely to be available and whether it would be efficient to obtain it in order to further reduce substantive tests for specific audit objectives. If so, the auditor will perform additional tests of controls.

Performing Additional Tests of Controls

Performing additional tests of controls will be efficient only if the audit time and effort saved by reducing substantive testing exceeds the time and effort spent in performing the tests of controls. Therefore, additional tests of controls are generally performed only when achieving the relevant audit objectives solely by substantive testing would require substantial audit time and effort. Moreover, tests of controls are usually performed only on those policies and procedures that the auditor has assessed as potentially capable of limiting control risk to a low level. The auditor should not automatically decide to perform additional tests of controls, even if it appears that they will provide the necessary evidence, without considering whether performing them will be efficient.

The auditor should discuss with appropriate client personnel any significant deficiencies in the design of control structure policies and procedures and any significant breakdowns in their operation. The auditor should also consider how such deficiencies and breakdowns affect the risk that account balances could be materially misstated, and should plan the nature, timing, and extent of substantive procedures accordingly.

The basic audit strategy alternatives are either to perform additional tests of controls and thus significantly reduce substantive procedures, or to perform substantive tests without significant restriction based on tests of controls. The auditor usually adopts different strategies for different parts of the audit. Thus, it is possible to achieve one or more audit objectives for an account or a group of accounts by performing additional tests of controls and restricting substantive tests, while achieving other audit objectives entirely by performing substantive procedures. This flexibility also applies to different client locations, subsidiaries, and components of business activities.

Regardless of the audit strategy chosen, auditors have traditionally focused more on audit objectives related to balance sheet accounts than on their income statement counterparts, since that is frequently the most efficient way to conduct an audit. Emphasizing balance sheet accounts is also conceptually sound: Balance sheet accounts represent the enterprise's economic resources and claims to those resources at a point in time, reflecting the cumulative effects of transactions and other events and circumstances on the enterprise. Income statement accounts reflect the enterprise's performance during a period between two points in time, measuring its revenues, expenses, gains, and losses that occurred during the period. Income statement accounts are logically and inextricably related to one or more balance sheet accounts. Often, evidence that helps achieve an audit objective for a balance sheet account also helps achieve a corresponding audit objective for an income statement account. For example, evidence about the existence of trade accounts receivable at the beginning and end of a period is also a source of assurance about the occurrence of sales transactions during the period. In some cases, however, it may be more efficient to achieve audit objectives for balance sheet accounts by achieving the corresponding audit objectives for related income statement accounts. For example, the completeness of trade accounts receivable at the end of a period may be audited most efficiently by auditing the completeness of sales recorded for the period.

The audit strategy selected for each part of the audit and the significant reasons for choosing that strategy should be documented. The accounting system and control procedures and related tests of controls are documented on various forms, such as systems flowcharts, questionnaires, or other practice aids. Audit strategy documentation should also include the decisions made about certain other aspects of the audit plan, such as locations where work will be performed, analyses to be prepared by the client, the need to use the work of other auditing firms or specialists (such as actuaries), and the effects of an internal audit function on the audit strategy. The audit plan as initially determined and documented should be reviewed, and revised if necessary, as the audit progresses and new information becomes available.

The auditor may decide on the audit strategy for each account or group of accounts, develop the audit program, and plan and schedule the work, particularly for recurring engagements, before performing additional tests of controls. If those tests then indicate that control structure elements may not have operated effectively throughout the period, the auditor may have to reassess the risk that account balances could be materially misstated, and revise the audit plan accordingly. In formulating the audit plan before completing tests of controls, the auditor assumes the test results will be satisfactory. On a new engagement, the basis for that assumption is generally derived from knowledge (which may perhaps be limited in scope) obtained through inquiries, observation, and inspection of documents, records, and reports undertaken as part of developing an understanding of the control structure and from any concurrent tests of controls performed at that time. On a recurring engagement, that assumption is also supported by the prior year's audit experience, preliminary inquiries of knowledgeable client personnel, and the auditor's recognition that, except in extraordinary circumstances, a client's control structure generally does not deteriorate markedly from one year to the next.

Performing Substantive Tests

Substantive tests provide evidence about management's assertions and the corresponding audit objectives. In the substantive testing phase, the auditor obtains, evaluates, and documents evidence to corroborate management's assertions embodied in the accounts and other information in the financial statements and related notes. The auditor's purpose in performing substantive tests is to determine whether the audit objectives have been achieved. Substantive procedures include tests of details of account balances and transactions, and analytical comparisons and other procedures. The nature of substantive tests, when they are performed, and the extent to which they are performed depend on the auditor's materiality judgments and risk assessments. Furthermore, the assurance required from substantive tests may be obtained from tests of details, analytical procedures, or some combination of both, with the assurance obtained from one reducing the assurance needed from the other.

Substantive tests may also provide evidence about the control structure, such as when a misstatement discovered through a substantive test is, upon further investigation, found to have resulted from a deficiency in the control structure. In that situation, the auditor may have to reassess his or her prior conclusions about the control structure.

Completing the Audit

After all the previous steps in the audit have been performed, the auditor performs final analytical and certain other procedures, such as reading minutes of recent board and committee meetings and obtaining representation letters. Then he or she makes final materiality judgments, summarizes and evaluates the audit findings, reviews the working papers and reviews the financial statement presentation and disclosures for adequacy, and considers subsequent events. Those procedures require the exercise of considerable professional judgment and thus are generally performed by the senior members of the engagement team.

Formulating the Auditor's Report and Communicating Control Structure Deficiencies

Finally, the auditor prepares the audit report and generally also communicates to management and the audit committee significant control structure deficiencies noted during the course of the audit.

WORKING PAPERS

Statement on Auditing Standards No. 41, *Working Papers* (AU Section 339), specifies that the auditor should prepare and maintain working papers as a record of the work done and conclusions reached on significant matters. Working papers also help the auditor in planning, conducting, and supervising the work.

More specifically, the working papers document

- The understanding of the client's business.
- The consideration of inherent risk.
- The understanding of the internal control structure.
- The basis for the conclusion about whether control structure policies and procedures are designed and operating effectively.
- The audit strategy decisions made.
- Tests of controls performed.
- Substantive procedures applied to transactions, account balances, and other information presented in the financial statements.
- That the work of any assistants was supervised and reviewed.
- Resolution of exceptions and unusual matters.
- Recommendations for improving control structure policies and procedures, as noted throughout the engagement.
- Support for the auditor's opinion on the financial statements.[2]

In addition, the working papers provide information needed for SEC reports, tax returns, and reports to other government agencies, and they serve as a source of information for succeeding audits.

Working papers are the property of the auditor and not a substitute for the client's accounting records. (In some cases, as an accommodation to the client, working papers are transmitted to and accepted by the client as a substitute for a record that it would otherwise prepare.) The auditor should adopt reasonable procedures for the safekeeping and retention of working papers long enough to meet his or her own practice needs and to satisfy any pertinent legal requirements for records retention.

Form and Content of Working Papers

Working papers include audit programs, trial balances, schedules, analyses, memoranda, letters of confirmation, representative abstracts of company

[2]As noted in footnote 3 to AU Section 339.01, however, "there is no intention to imply that the auditor would be precluded from supporting his report by other means in addition to working papers."

documents, narratives, flowcharts, questionnaires, and various other forms and practice aids. They may be handwritten, typewritten, or in the form of computer printouts or data stored on electronic media. Often, portions of working papers are prepared by client personnel according to auditor-determined specifications; the auditor should, of course, test the accuracy of client-prepared working papers.

The *content* of working papers generally cannot be standardized. Certain types of working papers, however, lend themselves to standardization, such as a summary of accounts receivable confirmation coverage and results. Working papers should be legible, complete, readily understandable, and designed to fit the circumstances and needs of the auditor for the particular engagement and subject matter under audit.

Unnecessary or irrelevant working papers that do not serve a useful purpose should not be prepared. If such working papers are inadvertently prepared, they should generally not be kept.

Although the content of working papers varies with the engagement, there are several advantages to adopting a standardized approach to their *format*. It facilitates the systematic organization of working papers for use during an engagement, enhances their ready access for reference or review, and aids in their orderly filing for future reference. Thus, every working paper should be headed, dated, and initialed by the preparer at the time the work is performed.

Every working paper should contain an explanation of the procedures followed (unless the information is included elsewhere in the working papers, such as in an audit program) and the results of those procedures. Sometimes the procedures are obvious from the computations or other data recorded; sometimes a narrative explanation is required. When an explanation is required, it is frequently placed at the end of the working paper and assigned a symbol or "tick mark," which is placed next to the appropriate item (generally a dollar amount) in the body of the working paper. For example, a working paper listing the details of notes receivable at a particular date may have the letter "E" after the details of each note, with the following explanation at the end of the working paper—"E = note examined," meaning that the auditor physically inspected the notes. Some auditors use a standardized set of symbols to document procedures.

Each working paper or set of working papers covering an audit objective should contain a clear record of all work performed. This record should include an explanation of exceptions noted by the auditor as a result of the procedures performed and identification of proposed adjustments to account balances. Language such as "are fairly stated" and "appear to be fairly stated" should be avoided, however, because the conclusion could be misinterpreted as having been reached in the context of the financial statements taken as a whole. That inference would be inappropriate and unsupportable since the conclusion is based on only a portion of the work done during the audit of the overall financial statements.

Most working papers contain quantitative information. Some working papers, however, are prepared based on inquiry or observation procedures and contain no quantitative information. For example, the auditor may inquire of management about the existence of transactions with related parties or observe the physical condition of inventory during the client's year-end inventory count. In these instances, the auditor should prepare working papers that clearly document the inquiries made, the client personnel involved, any tests resulting from the inquiry, or a description of the condition observed and the conclusion reached.

Working Paper Organization

There are no rigid guidelines for organizing a set of audit working papers. What follows should be viewed as general guidance that is subject to substantial modification by individual auditors and firms.

Detailed working papers are often summarized through the use of lead schedules for each financial statement caption. This technique provides an overview of an entire audit area for the preparer, as well as reviewers. In addition, a lead schedule enables a reviewer to look at as much or as little detail as is considered necessary in the circumstances.

Detailed support for lead schedules or other summary working papers is often filed behind the summary in order of relative significance or other meaningful sequence. There should always be an easy-to-follow trail between the detailed working papers and the amounts in the financial statements. Each working paper should be able to stand on its own; that is, it should be complete and understandable in itself. Reference may be made to other working papers to document audit findings. Cross-referencing of working papers should be specific rather than general. The "to-from" technique is used to make the "direction" of referencing apparent; that is, it shows which number is the source and which is the summary (see Figure 5.3).

Typical Working Papers

As suggested above, the variety of conditions encountered in practice generates a wide variety of working papers. Nevertheless, some types of working papers have common characteristics, which are explained in this section of the chapter.

The Trial Balance. The trial balance is the key working paper in many audits because it is the one where data from all underlying working papers is integrated, referenced, and summarized into the amounts appearing in the financial statements. There are a number of ways to prepare the trial balance, and

Figure 5.3 Working Paper Organization

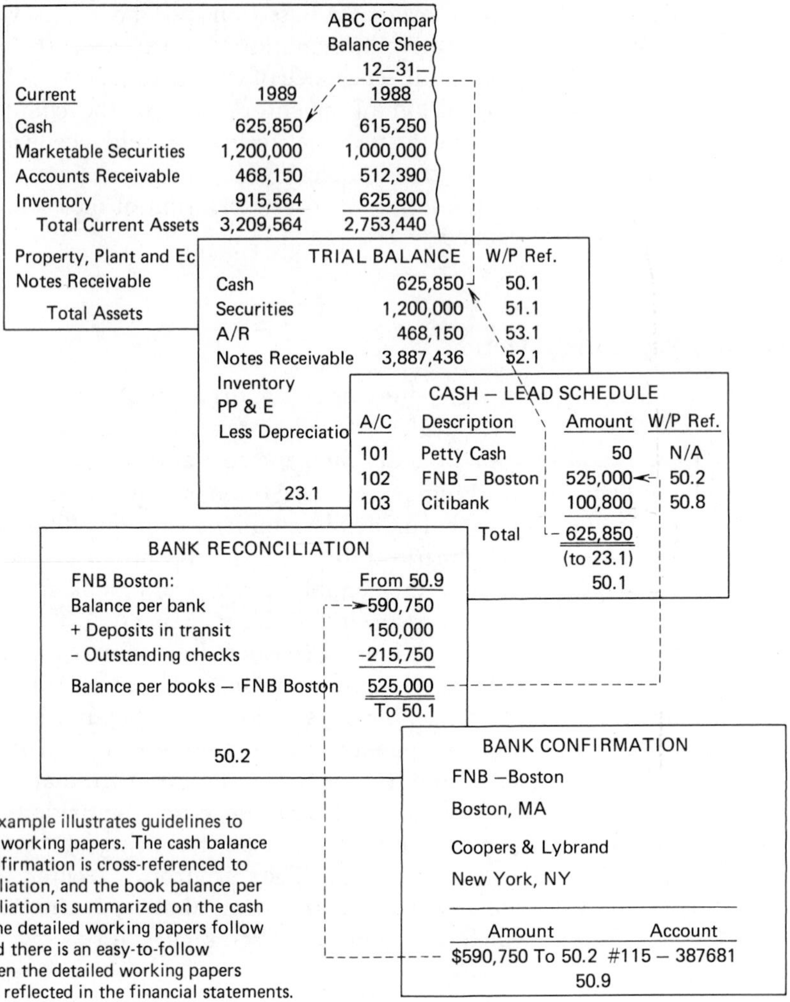

ABC Compar
Balance Shee
12–31–

Current	1989	1988
Cash	625,850	615,250
Marketable Securities	1,200,000	1,000,000
Accounts Receivable	468,150	512,390
Inventory	915,564	625,800
Total Current Assets	3,209,564	2,753,440
Property, Plant and Ec		
Notes Receivable		
Total Assets		

TRIAL BALANCE		W/P Ref.
Cash	625,850	50.1
Securities	1,200,000	51.1
A/R	468,150	53.1
Notes Receivable	3,887,436	52.1
Inventory		
PP & E		
Less Depreciatio		

23.1

CASH – LEAD SCHEDULE

A/C	Description	Amount	W/P Ref.
101	Petty Cash	50	N/A
102	FNB – Boston	525,000	50.2
103	Citibank	100,800	50.8
	Total	625,850	
		(to 23.1)	

50.1

BANK RECONCILIATION

FNB Boston:	From 50.9
Balance per bank	590,750
+ Deposits in transit	150,000
- Outstanding checks	-215,750
Balance per books – FNB Boston	525,000
	To 50.1

50.2

BANK CONFIRMATION

FNB –Boston
Boston, MA

Coopers & Lybrand
New York, NY

Amount	Account
$590,750 To 50.2	#115 – 387681

50.9

This simplified example illustrates guidelines to better organized working papers. The cash balance per the bank confirmation is cross-referenced to the bank reconciliation, and the book balance per the bank reconciliation is summarized on the cash lead schedule. The detailed working papers follow the summary and there is an easy-to-follow audit trail between the detailed working papers and the amounts reflected in the financial statements.

each of them has its advantages. Often it is prepared in a form that compares the current figures with those of the previous period. It may be prepared in balance sheet and income statement order, and amounts may be grouped into subtotals to make it easier to identify trial balance amounts with those in the financial statements. Client adjustments made as a result of the audit and financial statement reclassification entries (made only on the trial balance) are shown in additional columns. The adjusted trial balance is usually cross-referenced to supporting working papers. Figure 5.4 is an example of a partial trial balance before adjustments and reclassifications have been posted.

Figure 5.4 Trial Balance (Partial)

Date Prepared 1/10/90
Prepared by ST

COOPERS CABINET COMPANY
TRIAL BALANCE
12/31/89

ACCOUNT NUMBER	ACCOUNT DESCRIPTION	BALANCE 12/31/88 DR <CR>	BALANCE 12/31/89 DR <CR>	W/P REFERENCE	ADJUSTMENTS DR	ADJUSTMENTS CR	RECLASSIFICATIONS DR	RECLASSIFICATIONS CR	ADJUSTED BALANCE DR <CR>	PER FINANCIAL STATEMENTS DR <CR>
101	PETTY CASH	500.00	500.00							
103	CASH-COMMERCIAL ACCOUNT	20,438.00	26,675.00							
104	CASH-PAYROLL ACCOUNT	500.00	500.00							
110	ACCOUNTS RECEIVABLE	90,000.00	103,500.00							
111	ALLOWANCE FOR DOUBTFUL ACCOUNTS	<2,000.00>	<2,000.00>							
116	NOTES RECEIVABLE	15,000.00	17,500.00							
117	ACCRUED INTEREST RECEIVABLE	600.00	700.00							
120	MARKETABLE SECURITIES	55,000.00	43,000.00							
121	DIVIDENDS RECEIVABLE	1,650.00	925.00							
132	DEPOSITS	1,000.00	1,000.00							
134	PREPAID INSURANCE	7,848.00	10,953.00							
136	PREPAID TAXES	1,300.00	1,500.00							
138	PREPAID-OTHER	450.00	300.00							
140	INVENTORY	81,000.00	124,719.00							
150	LAND	81,950.00	99,700.00							
151	BUILDING	170,000.00	170,000.00							
152	MACHINERY AND EQUIPMENT	134,300.00	146,700.00							
153	VEHICLES	39,525.00	41,760.00							
155	ACCUMULATED DEPRECIATION	<94,061.00>	<104,100.00>							
123	SECURITIES VALUATION ALLOWANCE	-	<1,200.00>							
	TOTAL ASSETS	605,000.00	682,632.00							
		P	G/L							

P - Agreed to prior year's working papers
G/L - Agreed to the general ledger

Schedules and Analyses. Auditing procedures are documented on a variety of schedules and analyses, as well as in narrative form.

- *Tests of controls* may be documented in narrative form by describing what tests were performed and which control structure policies and procedures were tested. Sometimes a test of controls requires preparing a list of items to be extracted from the files or compared with data in another location. If so, the schedule or listing prepared can serve as the working paper. (In some instances, tests of controls are documented on the same form—for example, a questionnaire—that lists what policies and procedures were tested.) Figure 5.5 is an illustration of a working paper for a test of controls.

- *Substantive tests* are most often evidenced by some kind of analysis; the form depends on the nature of the auditing procedures performed. For example, the working papers might include an analysis showing the composition of the ending balance in a particular account, or perhaps a summary of the account. They also might include an analysis of the activity in the particular account for the period, showing the beginning balance, a summary of the transactions during the period (logically classified so that relationships with related accounts are apparent), and the ending balance. The working papers should present both the account information and an indication of what evidence was examined and what other auditing procedures were performed; sometimes the dollar amount or the percentage of the total tested is also shown. Figure 5.6 illustrates a working paper analyzing federal income taxes payable. Figure 5.7 indi-

Figure 5.5 Payroll Test of Controls, 19X2

Change Notice #	*Dept. Head Authorized*	*Per. Mgr. Authorized*	*Change Notice #*	*Dept. Head Authorized*	*Per. Mgr. Authorized*
4142	A	B✓	4322	A	B✓
4172	A	B✓	4352	A	B✓
4202	A	B✓	4382	A	B✓
4232	A	B✓	4412	A	B✓
4262	A	B✓	4442	A	C✓
4292	A	B✓	4472	A	B✓

Legend

A—Examined payroll change notice for signature of appropriate department head, indicating proper authorization.

B—Examined payroll change notice for signature of personnel manager, indicating proper authorization and segregation of duties.

C—Payroll change notice not signed by personnel manager. Personnel manager indicated this was an oversight. See working paper XX.2 for evaluation of sample results.

✓—Agreed payroll change notice to payroll master file change report, indicating accounting supervisor had accurately compared change notice with the master file change report.

Figure 5.6 XYZ Industries: Analysis of Federal Income Taxes Payable (A/C 3231)

Prepared ____________

Reviewed ____________

	Total	1989	1988	1987	Miscellaneous
Balance 1/1/89	36,000 T		18,500 T	8,100 T	9,400 T
Payment with automatic extension 3/15/89	(17,000) V		(17,000)		
Final payment with tax return	(2,700)		(1,500) TR, V		(1,200)
Estimated payments for 1989	(60,000) CR	(60,000) (2)			
Payment of additional assessment re: 1987	(6,300) RAR(1)			(8,100)	1,800
1989 current provisions	193,200 W/P	193,200			
Balance 12/31/89	✓✓ 143,200	133,200	0	0	10,000 (A)
	✓✓	✓✓	✓✓		✓✓

Legend

T—Traced to prior year's working papers
V—Examined canceled check
TR—Agrees with tax return examined
✓✓—Checked calculations
CR—Traced 1st and 3rd quarter payments to check register
RAR—Agrees with revenue agent's report
W/P—Traced to working paper source reference

(1) $2,300 interest on the assessment was separately charged to interest expense.
(2) No underpayment penalty because $60,000 exceeded last year's tax.
(A) Represents miscellaneous underaccruals and overaccruals not taken into income—not material.

Figure 5.7 Analysis of Notes Receivable and Related Interest Accounts

Date Prepared: 3/10/89
Prepared By:
a) C&L EF
b) Client and Examined By ______
Reviewed By:
C&L Sr Sup ______

COOPERS CABINET COMPANY
NOTES RECEIVABLE
12/31/88

⑦ DEBTOR	INTEREST RATE		NOTE DATE / DUE DATE	PRINCIPAL-A/C 116: BALANCE 12/31/87	ADDITIONS	RECEIPTS	BALANCE 12/31/88	CURRENT PORTION	LONG-TERM PORTION	ACCRUED INTEREST-A/C 117: BALANCE 12/31/87	INTEREST INCOME	RECEIPTS	BALANCE 12/31/88
				P				├── ø ──┤		P	R		
④ WATTS ENGINEERING	c	15	6/30/85 DEMAND	3,275 00			② 3,275 00	3,275		245 62	491 26	491 26	245 62
④ MATCHOMATIC	c	16 ①	4/4/86 4/4/91 Payable $1570 annually, plus interest		② 7,850 00		③ ⑨ 1/31/87 7,850 00	1,570	6,280		1015 58		1015 58
④ POWER BELT CONVEYORS	c	12	3/7/85 3/7/88 Payable $2125 annually, plus interest	6,375 00			⑥ ⑨ 6,375 00	4,250	2,125	98 38	765 00	724 58	138 80
④ BORLAND PLUMBING	c	8	3/2/78 DEMAND	5,350 00		⑤ 5,350 00	–			856 00	38 16	② 894 16	
				15,000 00	7,850 00	5,350 00	17,500 00 cf	9,095	8,405	1,200 00	2,310 00	2,110 00	1,400 00
				✓	✓	✓	✓ T/B	⑧		✓	✓	✓	✓ T/B

✓-Footed cf-cross footed
P-Agreed to prior year's W/P's
T/B-Agreed to the trial balance
c-Agreed all details to confirmation on W/P's 52.2 to 52.5
ø-Recomputed classifications based on terms of the notes
R-Recomputed; appears reasonable
①-Agreed to copy of executed note in permanent file. Reviewed note for unusual terms, collateral arrangements and significant requirements, restrictions or other covenants. None noted other than the note is collateralized by inventory (See confirmation on 52.3)
②-Agreed to customer remittance advice paid 2/3/86, totaling $6,244.16 including interest
Traced to cash receipts journal and agreed to deposit slip on 2/3/88
③-Agreed to remittance advice for collection of note installment and/or interest, date indicated next to tickmark.
④-Reviewed stated interest rate for reasonableness
⑤-Note not collected at 3/10/89. Discussion with treasurer disclosed that demand for payment will be 6/1/89. D&B report of Watts Engineering indicates good credit rating. Balance appears collectible; no allowance deemed necessary.
⑥-First installment due 3/7/88 was made on 2/3/89. Client indicated customer has experienced a cash flow problem in early 1988, which has now been remedied. Customer has indicated the second installment will be paid on time. D&B report of Power Belt indicates improved rating. Balance appears collectible; no allowance deemed necessary.
⑦-Per review of the notes and discussion with Treasurer, none of these are related parties as defined by SAS No. 45
⑧-Reclassification entry for financial statements:
116 Notes receivable - short term 8405
116 Notes receivable - long term 8405
A&E No. 47
⑨-For footnote disclosure, notes collateralized by inventory. See confirmations 52.1

cates the variety of auditing procedures performed on notes receivable and related interest accounts that can be documented on a single working paper.

- *Analytical procedures* involve a study and comparison of relationships among data; they are often evidenced by computations the auditor makes as part of the comparison. The working paper evidence usually consists of a narrative description of the procedures, their results, further investigation of matters identified as having a significant effect on the audit, and any resulting changes in the scope of the audit of related accounts.

Memoranda. Questions, errors discovered by procedures performed, or unusual matters that arise during the audit should be documented. A memorandum should explain what steps were taken to resolve them (such as additional auditing procedures, consultation with the client, the auditor's own research and reasoning), what people were involved in the resolution, and the resulting conclusions. It is undesirable simply to check off a question or record a cryptic answer such as "cleared." Explanations of material matters should be complete and conclusive.

Permanent Working Papers. Working papers for recurring engagements usually contain files that are carried forward from preceding years' audits; these are often referred to as permanent files. These files should include data having continuing use and not subject to frequent change. Examples of such data include copies or abstracts of the certificate of incorporation, bylaws, bond and note indentures, union agreements, important contracts having historical significance, organization charts, the client's accounting policies and procedures, key personnel, and location of plants. The file may also include activity schedules not maintained by the client, for example, schedules of future amortization or depreciation (sometimes referred to as "lapse schedules"), and analyses and other working papers that have historical significance, such as analyses of various capital accounts. Audit programs, descriptions of the accounting system, flowcharts, and questionnaires or other documentation of the control structure are also often kept in the permanent files.

Common Working Paper Deficiencies

Deficiencies in working papers often result in confusion and wasted time at several stages—carrying out auditing procedures, assisting new staff in the following year's audit, and reconstructing at a later date the work performed and judgments made. Those deficiencies are generally discovered during the working paper review process. Some of the more common working paper deficiencies are listed in Figure 5.8.

Figure 5.8 Common Working Paper Deficiencies

- Working paper not initialed and dated by preparer or reviewer.
- Working paper not properly "headed."
- Cross-referencing too general; reviewer unable to find referenced working papers.
- Reason for cross-referencing missing or not apparent.
- Tick marks appearing on the working paper without a descriptive legend.
- Purpose of working paper not apparent; no explanation given.
- Working papers sloppy or cluttered.
- Exceptions or unusual items not properly explained or evaluated.
- Working paper content illogical.
- Amounts not in agreement with trial balance.
- Poor quality, illegible photocopy placed in the working papers.
- Detailed explanation given for insignificant items or differences, for which a simple notation, such as "Amounts insignificant; no audit work deemed necessary," would be sufficient.
- Arrangement of working papers not logical.
- Too much reliance placed on the prior year's working papers, which resulted in a lack of focus on unusual items or changes in significant account balances.
- Preparing a working paper because the client-prepared working paper was not in the exact format preferred by the auditor.
- Nature of auditing procedures performed not described fully and clearly.
- Use of similar tick marks to denote different procedures.

Review Questions

5–1. For an opinion to be expressed, the auditor must determine the degree to which management's assertions embodied in the statements conform with GAAP. What are the categories into which these assertions are classified?

5–2. What do each of the above assertions relate to?

5–3. What does the third standard of field work require?

5–4. For which of the assertions does the auditor perform primarily the evidence-gathering function, as opposed to the interpreting/evaluating function?

5–5. What function does the auditor perform with respect to the assertions of valuation or allocation and presentation and disclosure?

5–6. How does underlying evidence differ from corroborating evidence?

5–7. Name and describe the basic methods used by auditors to obtain competent evidential matter.

5–8. What purposes are served in performing analytical procedures?

5–9. Compare, contrast, and illustrate the two basic types of tests in auditing.

5–10. What are the major steps in every financial audit?

5–11. What is meant by audit strategy? What are the basic audit strategy alternatives?

5–12. Specify some of the considerations that should enter into the strategy decisions.

5–13. What control structure policies and procedures should be tested?

5–14. How is the selection of substantive tests made?

5–15. What are the functions of working papers?

5–16. To whom do working papers belong?

5–17. What types of working papers are there? What types of information should all working papers contain?

5–18. What is the key working paper in most audits and why is it important?

5–19. What are some common working paper deficiencies?

Discussion Questions

5–30. How does an auditor know when enough evidence has been collected? How does an auditor determine whether documentation in the working papers is adequate?

5–31. Auditors frequently refer to the terms "standards" and "procedures." Standards deal with measures of the quality of the auditor's performance. Standards specifically refer to the ten generally accepted auditing standards. Procedures relate to those acts that are performed by the auditor while trying to gather evidence. Procedures specifically refer to the methods or techniques used by the auditor in the conduct of the audit.

Required:

Describe several different types of procedures that an auditor would use during an audit of financial statements. For example, the observation of activities and conditions is a type of procedure that an auditor would frequently use. Do not discuss specific accounts.

(AICPA adapted)

5–32. Analytical procedures are useful in various stages of an audit.

Required:

a. Explain how analytical procedures may be used as substantive tests.
b. Explain how analytical procedures may be useful in the initial audit planning stage.
c. Give examples of the analytical procedures that one might expect a CPA to use during an audit performed in accordance with generally accepted auditing standards.

(AICPA adapted)

5–33. The first major step in the performance of an audit is obtaining and documenting information about the client's business and its control structure. When and how should an auditor obtain that information?

5–34. Auditors normally associate counting inventory with inspection. What other items might be subject to inspection?

5-35. Why is it necessary for working papers to be kept under the control of the auditor?

5-36. What are some techniques for improving the organization of working papers and keeping working paper preparation time to a minimum?

AICPA Multiple Choice Questions

These questions are taken from the Auditing part of Uniform CPA Examinations. Choose the single most appropriate answer.

5-40. Audit evidence can come in different forms with different degrees of persuasiveness. Which of the following is the *least* persuasive type of evidence?

a. Bank statement obtained from the client.
b. Computations made by the auditor.
c. Prenumbered client sales invoices.
d. Vendor's invoice.

5-41. Which of the following statements is generally correct about the competence of evidential matter?

a. The auditor's direct personal knowledge, obtained through observation and inspection, is more persuasive than information obtained indirectly from independent outside sources.
b. To be competent, evidential matter must be either valid or relevant, but need *not* be both.
c. Accounting data alone may be considered sufficient competent evidential matter to issue an unqualified opinion on financial statements.
d. Competence of evidential matter refers to the amount of corroborative evidence to be obtained.

5-42. Which of the following procedures would an auditor most likely rely on to verify management's assertion of completeness?

a. Compare a sample of vendors' invoices with related purchase orders.
b. Compare a sample of shipping documents with related sales invoices.
c. Observe the client's distribution of payroll checks.
d. Confirm a sample of recorded receivables by direct communication with the debtors.

5-43. An example of an analytical procedure is the comparison of

a. Financial information with similar information regarding the industry in which the entity operates.
b. Recorded amounts of major disbursements with appropriate invoices.
c. Results of a statistical sample with the expected characteristics of the actual population.
d. EDP generated data with similar data generated by a manual accounting system.

5-44. An audit working paper that reflects the major components of an amount reported in the financial statements is referred to as a (an)

a. Lead schedule.
b. Supporting schedule.
c. Audit control account.
d. Working trial balance.

5-45. Working papers that record the procedures used by the auditor to gather evidence should be

a. Considered the primary support for the financial statements being audited.
b. Viewed as the connecting link between the books of account and the financial statements.
c. Designed to meet the circumstances of the particular engagement.
d. Destroyed when the audited entity ceases to be a client.

Problems and Cases

5-60. The purpose of all auditing procedures is to gather sufficient competent evidence for an auditor to form an opinion regarding the financial statements taken as a whole.

Required:

a. In addition to the example below, identify and describe five means or techniques of gathering audit evidence used to evaluate a client's inventory balance.

Technique	*Description*
Observation	An auditor watches the performance of some function, such as a client's annual inventory count.

b. Identify the audit objectives regarding a client's inventory balance and describe one *different* substantive auditing procedure for each objective. Use the format illustrated below.

Audit Objective	*Substantive Auditing Procedure*

(AICPA adapted)

5-61. You are the auditor of the Petersen Company; you have obtained the following data:

a. A trial balance taken from the books of Petersen one month prior to year-end follows:

	Dr. (Cr.)
Cash in bank	$ 87,000
Trade accounts receivable	345,000
Notes receivable	125,000
Inventories	317,000
Land	66,000
Buildings, net	350,000
Furniture, fixtures, and equipment, net	325,000
Trade accounts payable	(235,000)
Mortgages payable	(400,000)
Capital stock	(300,000)
Retained earnings	(510,000)
Sales	(3,130,000)
Cost of sales	2,300,000
General and administrative expenses	622,000
Legal and professional fees	3,000
Interest expense	35,000

b. There are no inventories consigned either in or out.
c. All notes receivable are due from outsiders and held by Petersen.

Required:
Which accounts could be confirmed with outside sources? Briefly describe with whom they could be confirmed and the information that could be confirmed. Organize your answer in the following format:

Account Name	*With Whom Confirmed*	*Information to Be Confirmed*

(AICPA adapted)

5-62. During the current year, your client borrowed $800,000 from its bank to finance plant expansion. The long-term note agreement provided for the annual payment of principal and interest over five years. The existing plant was pledged as security for the loan. The borrowed funds were invested in securities until they were needed to pay for the construction work.

Required:
a. What are the audit objectives in the audit of long-term debt?
b. How could you obtain assurance that the securities held by your client at year-end actually exist?

(AICPA adapted)

5-63. The partnership of Stanley, Grossman, & May, a CPA firm, has been the auditor of Hawkins, Inc., for many years. During the annual audit of the financial statements for the year ended December 31, 1989, a dispute developed over whether certain disclosures should be made in the financial statements. The dispute resulted in Stanley, Grossman, & May's being dismissed and Hawkins' engaging another firm. Hawkins demanded that Stanley, Grossman, & May turn over all working papers applicable to the Hawkins audits or face a lawsuit. Stanley, Grossman, & May refused. Hawkins has instituted a suit against Stanley, Grossman, & May to obtain the working papers.

Required:

a. Will Hawkins succeed in its suit? Explain.
b. Discuss the rationale underlying the rule of law applicable to the ownership of working papers.

(AICPA adapted)

5-64. In auditing financial statements, auditors must judge the reliability of the audit evidence they obtain.

Required:

a. In the course of an audit, an auditor asks many questions of client officers and employees.
   1. Describe the factors that the auditor should consider in evaluating oral evidence provided by client officers and employees.
   2. Discuss the reliability and limitations of oral evidence.
b. An audit may include computation of various balance sheet and operating ratios for comparison with prior years and industry averages. Discuss the reliability and limitations of such analytical procedures.
c. In connection with the audit of the financial statements of a manufacturing company, an auditor observes the physical inventory of finished goods, which consists of expensive, highly complex electronic equipment. Discuss the reliability and limitations of the audit evidence provided by this procedure.

(AICPA adapted)

5-65. An important part of every audit of financial statements is the preparation of audit working papers.

Required:

a. Discuss the relationship of audit working papers to each of the standards of field work.
b. You are instructing an inexperienced staff person on how to audit an account on his or her first auditing assignment. An analysis of the account has been prepared by the client for inclusion in the audit working papers. Prepare a list of the comments, commentaries, and notations that the staff person should make or have made on the account analysis to provide an adequate audit working paper. (Do not include a description of auditing procedures applicable to the account.)

(AICPA adapted)

5-66. The preparation of working papers is an integral part of a CPA's audit of financial statements. On a recurring engagement, a CPA reviews the audit programs and working papers from the prior audit while planning the current audit to determine their usefulness for the current engagement.

Required:

a. What are the purposes or functions of audit working papers?
b. What records may be included in audit working papers?
c. What factors affect the CPA's judgment of the type and content of the working papers for a particular engagement?

(AICPA adapted)

5–67. In an audit of financial statements, the CPA is concerned with the examination and accumulation of accounting evidence.

Required:

a. What is the objective of the CPA's examination and accumulation of accounting evidence during the course of the audit?
b. The source of the accounting evidence is of primary importance in the CPA's evaluation of its quality. Accounting evidence may be classified according to source. For example, one class originates within the client's organization, passes through the hands of third parties, and returns to the client, where it may be examined by the auditor. List the classifications of accounting evidence according to source, briefly discussing the effect of the source on the reliability of the evidence.
c. In evaluating the quality of the accounting evidence, the CPA also considers factors other than the sources of the evidence. Briefly discuss these other factors.

(AICPA adapted)

6

Audit Risk, Materiality, and Engagement Strategy

The first standard of field work requires that the audit be adequately planned; good management practices require that it be controlled to ensure that it is performed efficiently and on a timely basis as well as in accordance with professional standards—that is, effectively. Planning and control are closely related aspects of engagement management. Engagement management is a continuous activity that involves determining the strategy to use on an audit, planning how to implement that strategy, and controlling the way the audit is performed in accordance with the audit plan. Throughout the audit, the auditor makes numerous decisions, ranging from determining the overall strategy to choosing specific auditing procedures and deciding how to implement them. The most significant factor in all those decisions is the auditor's assessment of the principal risks associated with the client's financial statements. The chapter begins with a discussion of the components of audit risk and then explains the concept of materiality, which is an integral part of the auditor's consideration of audit risk. Following that, audit strategy and planning considerations are described.

AUDIT RISK

Generally accepted auditing standards (GAAS), user expectations, and sound business practices require the auditor to design and perform auditing procedures that will permit expressing an opinion on the financial statements with a low risk that the opinion will be inappropriate. The complement of that risk is an expression of the level of assurance that the opinion will be appropriate. Stated another way, the auditor seeks to have a low risk that the opinion expressed is inappropriate or a high level of assurance that the financial statements are free from material misstatements. Obtaining audit assurance and restricting audit risk are alternative ways of looking at the same process.

There is no practical way to reduce audit risk to zero. The auditor's determination of how much risk is acceptable is a business decision constrained by users' expectations. To users, an audit opinion indicates that professional standards were adhered to and sufficient evidence was accumulated and evaluated to support the opinion. The auditor should design the audit so that the risk of an inappropriate opinion is sufficiently low to meet those expectations.

The auditor varies the nature, timing, and extent of auditing procedures in response to his or her perception of risk. Thus, when risk is perceived to be high, more reliable evidence (see Chapter 5), larger sample sizes, and procedures timed at or near the end of the period under audit are common. Risk analysis is also used to balance the mix of tests of controls, substantive tests of details, and analytical procedures to achieve an efficient audit.

The term "overall audit risk" is used to describe the risk that the auditor will issue an inappropriate opinion. That opinion may be either that the financial statements taken as a whole are fairly stated when they are not, or that they are not fairly stated when they are.[1] For practical reasons, auditors are particularly attuned to the risk of issuing a ''clean'' opinion on materially misstated financial statements. Issuing a qualified or an adverse opinion on fairly stated financial statements is considered unlikely, because client concern over the adverse consequences of such opinions normally leads to a protracted study and investigation that would probably clear up the misperception before the auditor issued such an opinion. Nevertheless, both aspects of overall audit risk have cost implications for auditors.[2]

Overall audit risk is the combination of the various audit risks for each assertion related to each account balance or group of account balances. Considering overall audit risk in relation to the financial statements taken as a whole is usually impracticable. It ordinarily is practicable, however, to consider audit risk for particular assertions associated with particular account balances, groups of account balances, or related classes of transactions, because they are likely to have different patterns of risk, and the auditing procedures applied to them are likely to have different relative costs.

The primary objective in engagement management is limiting the audit risk in individual balances or classes of transactions so that, at the completion of the audit, overall audit risk is limited to a level sufficiently low—or conversely, that the level of assurance is sufficiently high—to permit the auditor to express an opinion on the financial statements taken as a whole. A secondary objective is to achieve the desired assurance as efficiently as possible.

Many attempts have been made to develop mathematically based risk assessment models, but there is no requirement that audit risk or its components be quantified. In fact, it may not be practicable to objectively quantify certain components of audit risk because of the large number of variables affecting them and the subjective nature of many of those variables. Accordingly, many auditors do not attempt to assign specific values to risk factors. The auditor should always consider audit risk for each assertion related to each significant account or class of transactions.

[1]Statement on Auditing Standards No. 47, *Audit Risk and Materiality in Conducting an Audit* (AU Section 312), defines audit risk as ''the risk that the auditor may unknowingly fail to appropriately modify his opinion on financial statements that are materially misstated.'' Even though this definition does not include the risk that the auditor might erroneously conclude that the financial statements are materially misstated when they are not, it logically follows that the auditor should obtain sufficient evidence to give the proper opinion in all circumstances.

[2]SAS No. 47 (footnote to AU Section 312.02) notes that

> In addition to audit risk, the auditor is also exposed to loss or injury to his professional practice from litigation, adverse publicity, or other events arising in connection with financial statements that he has audited and reported on. This exposure is present even though the auditor has performed his audit in accordance with generally accepted auditing standards and has reported appropriately on those financial statements. Even if an auditor assesses this exposure as low, he should not perform less extensive procedures than would otherwise be appropriate under generally accepted auditing standards.

Audit exposure is one aspect of the business risk an accountant faces in accepting any engagement to perform professional services.

The Components of Audit Risk

Audit risk at the account-balance or class-of-transactions level has the following two major components for each assertion:

- The risk (consisting of inherent risk and control risk) that misstatements (from either errors or irregularities) that are material, either individually or in the aggregate, are contained within the financial statements. *Inherent risk* is the susceptibility of an account balance or a class of transactions to material misstatements, without consideration of the control structure. *Control risk* is the risk that the client's control structure policies and procedures will not prevent or detect material misstatements on a timely basis.
- The risk (called *detection risk*) that misstatements that are material, either individually or in the aggregate, in the financial statements will not be detected by the auditor's substantive tests (including both tests of details and analytical procedures).

Inherent and control risks differ from detection risk in that the auditor can only assess them but cannot control them. The auditor's assessment of inherent and control risks leads to a better understanding of them, but does not reduce or otherwise change them. The auditor can, however, control detection risk by varying the nature, timing, and extent of specific substantive tests.

Inherent Risk. Financial statement misstatements may be caused by a condition (referred to in this book as an "inherent risk condition") that exists at the macroeconomic, industry, or company level or by a characteristic of an account balance or a class of transactions (referred to in this book as an "inherent risk characteristic"). The auditor's understanding of inherent risk conditions and characteristics comes from knowing the client's business and industry, performing analytical procedures, studying prior years' audit results, and understanding the entity's transactions, their flow through the accounting system, and the account balances they generate.

Inherent Risk Conditions. Some aspects of inherent risk are not limited to specific transactions or accounts but stem from factors outside the entity that are related to its business environment. These *inherent risk conditions* usually cannot be controlled by the enterprise; they include changes in general business conditions, new governmental regulations, and other economic factors. Examples of the latter are a declining industry characterized by bankruptcies, other indications of financial distress, and a lack of financial flexibility, which might either affect the realization of assets or incurrence of liabilities, or influence client management or other personnel to deliberately misstate financial statements. Conversely, overrapid expansion (with or without concomitant demand) can create quality failures resulting in potential sales returns or unsalable inventory.

The audit objectives most likely to be affected by inherent risk conditions are valuation, rights and obligations, and presentation and disclosure. Certain inherent risk conditions might have such a pervasive effect on the client's financial statements as a whole as to warrant special audit attention. For example, a severe recession might lead to substantial doubt about a company's ability to continue to operate as a going concern. The auditor's responsibility in this situation is described in Chapter 18.

While inherent risk conditions cannot be controlled by the enterprise, the control environment set by management (the "tone at the top") can help ensure that the financial statements reflect the underlying economic realities that those conditions create. In addition, the client may establish special control procedures or perform special year-end procedures in response to inherent risk conditions. Examples include special reviews of inventory obsolescence or the provision for uncollectible accounts receivable.

Inherent Risk Characteristics. Other aspects of inherent risk are peculiar to the specific class of transactions or account being audited (i.e., they are *characteristics* of the transaction or account). The risk of errors or irregularities is greater for some classes of transactions or accounts than others. In general, transactions that require considerable accounting judgment by the client are more likely to produce errors. Similarly, some assets are more susceptible to theft than others; cash is more prone to misappropriation than are steel beams. Account balances derived from accounting estimates are more likely to be misstated than account balances composed of more factual data. The characteristics of accounts with generic titles differ from one company to another and even within a company. For example, not all inventories are the same. Consequently, in assessing risk, the auditor considers the characteristics of the specific items underlying the particular account. In some instances the auditor is mainly concerned with whether the inventory exists, while in other situations the auditor might be more concerned with its valuation.

Inherent risk characteristics should be, and usually are, addressed by the entity's control structure. If so, and if, based on efficiency considerations, the auditor plans to test the effectiveness of control structure policies or procedures, then the assessment of the inherent risk characteristics becomes inseparable from the assessment of control risk, and only a joint assessment of the two is useful. For example, the auditor may determine in planning the audit that an asset (such as cash) with characteristics (liquidity and transferability) that make it extremely prone to theft is nevertheless subject to extremely effective control structure policies and procedures. In effect, the enterprise has designed specific policies and procedures in light of the asset's characteristics. In this environment the auditor may find it efficient to test how well the policies and procedures are designed and operating. If they are effective, the auditor may then be able to assess the risk of misappropriation—and thus the risk of a financial statement misstatement—as low.

Control Risk. There are likely to be errors in the accounting process that the client does not detect because no affordable control structure can be 100 percent effective. Therefore, some risk is normally associated with every control structure; effective structures carry a relatively lower risk, less effective structures, a relatively higher risk.

The auditor may be able to assess control risk as low by determining whether the policies and procedures an enterprise applies to transactions and balances have been appropriately designed and testing whether they are operating effectively. If those tests indicate that appropriately designed policies and procedures are operating effectively, the auditor will be able to conclude that the risk of misstatement occurring is low.

Some assertions and some transactions and balances are not specifically addressed—either intentionally or otherwise—by the client's control structure. For example, discretionary bonuses and unusual transactions may not be subject to control procedures; in addition, management override of control procedures is always possible. If control risk for transactions or accounts is at the maximum—either because the transactions or accounts are not specifically addressed by the control structure or because the auditor does not plan, for reasons of efficiency or otherwise, to seek evidence to support an assessment below the maximum—the risk of misstatement occurring is determined by inherent risk only.

Detection Risk. Detection risk is the possibility that misstatements, in a cumulatively material amount, will go undetected by both analytical procedures and substantive tests of details. Since analytical procedures and substantive tests of details complement each other, the assurance derived from one reduces proportionately the assurance the auditor needs from the other to reduce detection risk to the desired level. In other words, the risks associated with them are multiplicative, as the following illustrates. As a conceptual exercise—recalling that it is not practicable to try to assign specific values to the various risk factors—suppose an auditor performs no substantive tests of details or analytical procedures. If there is an error in the financial statements, there is a 100 percent chance that it will not be detected (detection risk is 100 percent). On the other hand, if both substantive tests of details and analytical procedures are performed and there is a 40 percent risk that analytical procedures will not detect cumulatively material misstatements and a 20 percent risk that substantive tests of details will not detect them, the chance that neither procedure will detect the error is the product of 40 percent and 20 percent—8 percent. For a misstatement in the financial statements to go undetected by the auditor, both substantive tests of details and analytical procedures must fail to detect it.

Summary of the Risk Model

The components of overall audit risk and of audit risk associated with specific accounts and specific assertions are summarized in Figure 6.1. For a given

Figure 6.1 Basic Audit Risk Components

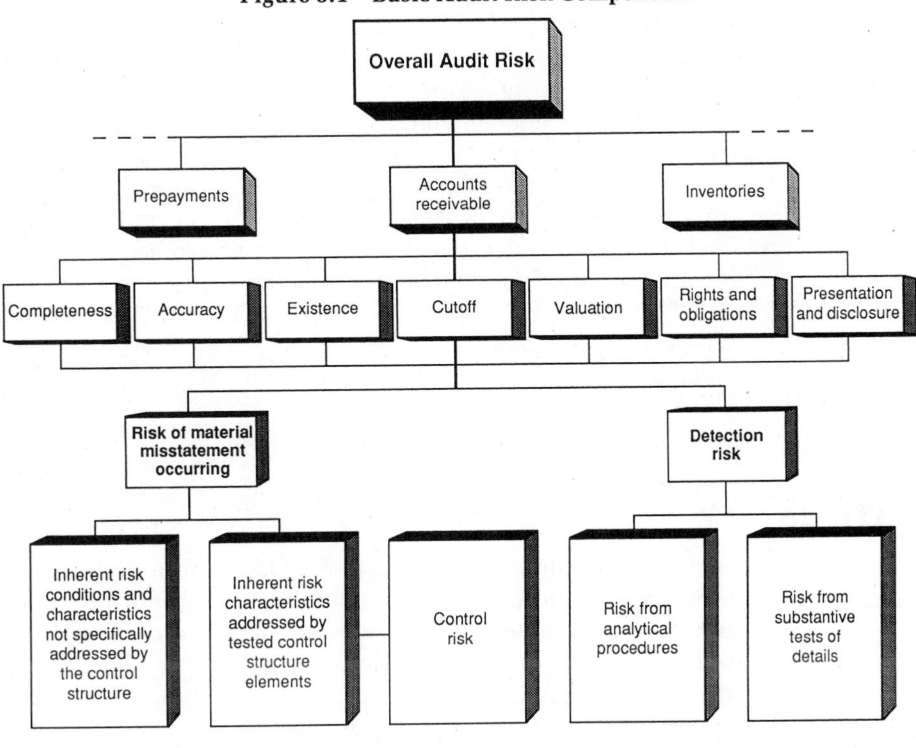

desired level of audit risk, the acceptable level of detection risk varies inversely with the auditor's assessment of the risk of material misstatement occurring. That is, the higher the perceived risk of material irregularities or errors, the more assurance the auditor needs from substantive tests (i.e., the lower the acceptable level of detection risk) to achieve a specified (presumably low) level of audit risk, and vice versa. Similarly, given the assurance desired from substantive tests, the assurance the auditor needs from substantive tests of details will vary inversely with the assurance obtained from analytical procedures. In high-risk situations where a great deal of assurance is needed, the auditor may choose to perform a combination of tests of details and analytical procedures aimed at the same accounts and assertions.

Various combinations of audit effort devoted to risk assessment activities, analytical procedures, and substantive tests of details can restrict audit risk to the same low level, but some combinations will be more efficient (i.e., less costly) than others. Based on his or her expectations about inherent and control risks, the auditor formulates an audit strategy that will, in a cost-effective manner, provide sufficient competent evidence to (1) confirm those expectations about inherent and control risk, and (2) reduce detection risk sufficiently to achieve a low level of audit risk.

Before issuing an unqualified opinion, the auditor should be satisfied that *overall* audit risk is appropriately low. In considering overall audit risk, the individual audit risks for the various account balances and assertions should be combined. To date, however, no single, simple, generally agreed-on mathematical approach to combining these risks has been developed. Nor has the profession been able to agree on what an appropriately low level of overall risk is. While the auditor may at times think in quantitative terms when considering alternative audit strategies and assessing risk, risk management ultimately requires seasoned judgment based on experience, training, and business sense. The way the audit results of each component of the financial statements are combined depends on how the auditor apportions materiality and combines risk. Normative models for apportioning materiality and combining risk for the financial statements taken as a whole have been a subject of academic research for some years, but do not seem likely to yield practical benefits in the foreseeable future.

MATERIALITY

A concept of materiality is a practical necessity in both auditing and accounting. Allowing immaterial items to complicate and clutter up the auditing process or financial statements is uneconomical and diverts users' attention from significant matters in the financial statements. Materiality judgments influence audit planning and, in the evaluation of audit results, are critical to determining whether the financial statements are fairly presented. Inherent in rendering an audit opinion is the recognition that financial statements cannot "precisely" or "exactly" present financial position, results of operations, and cash flows. Such precision is unattainable because of limitations in the accounting measurement process and constraints imposed by the audit process and auditing technology, as discussed in Chapter 1. Since 1988, the wording of the standard auditor's report has explicitly recognized this by stating that the financial statements are presented fairly, in all material respects.

Materiality is "the magnitude of an omission or misstatement of accounting information that, in the light of surrounding circumstances, makes it probable that the judgment of a reasonable person relying on the information would have been changed or influenced by the omission or misstatement" (FASB Statement of Financial Concepts No. 2, *Qualitative Characteristics of Accounting Information*). Ultimately, the user of financial statements determines what is material. There are many users, however, including enterprise management, shareholders, creditors, audit committees, financial analysts, investors, and labor unions, and each may have a different view of what is important.

SEC Regulation S-X (Rule 1-02) defines "materiality" as follows:

> The term "material," when used to qualify a requirement for the furnishing of information as to any subject, limits the information required to those matters about which an average prudent investor ought reasonably to be informed.

This definition has been reinforced by court decisions such as the *BarChris* case[3] in which the judge clearly indicated that the materiality issue involved amounts he believed would motivate the "average prudent investor," not the average banker or security analyst. In developing a standard of materiality for a particular situation, other court cases refer to the "reasonable shareholder"[4]; FASB Concepts Statement No. 2, to the "reasonable person"; and an American Accounting Association publication,[5] to the "informed investor." Thus, the consensus seems to be that materiality is determined by the user, who may be informed, but is not necessarily sophisticated, about financial statements.

Materiality has both qualitative and quantitative aspects. A financial statement misstatement may be quantitatively immaterial, but may nevertheless warrant disclosure in the financial statements. SAS No. 47, *Audit Risk and Materiality in Conducting an Audit* (AU Section 312.07), cites as an example "an illegal payment of an otherwise immaterial amount [that] could be material if there is a reasonable possibility that it could lead to a material contingent liability or a material loss of revenue." Moreover, such matters may have broad implications regarding the integrity of management, and thus may warrant further investigation. The auditor may need to assess the possible pervasiveness of the problem, reassess the effectiveness of the control structure, and report the findings to appropriate company officials. Similarly, qualitatively innocuous mistakes in the form of small unintentional errors can add up to quantitatively material dollar misstatements that would cause the auditor to qualify the opinion if adjustments were not made to the accounts. Materiality judgments also influence items that are or should be disclosed without directly affecting the financial statement amounts. Because of the dual influence of qualitative and quantitative factors in determining materiality, the concept is difficult to operationalize, and trying to establish a single, agreed-on quantitative standard is an exercise in futility.

The assessment of materiality takes place throughout an audit, particularly during planning and when evaluating the results of auditing procedures. SAS No. 47 (AU Section 312.10) requires the auditor, in planning an engagement, to consider a "preliminary judgment about materiality levels for audit purposes." That preliminary judgment may include assessments of what constitutes materiality for significant captions in the balance sheet, income statement, and statement of cash flows individually, and for the financial statements taken as a whole. One purpose of this preliminary materiality judgment is to focus the auditor's attention on the more significant financial statement items while he or she is determining the audit strategy. As a practical matter, however, SAS No. 47 indicates that the preliminary judgment about

[3]*Escott* v. *BarChris Construction Corp.*, 283 F. Supp. 643 (S.D.N.Y. 1968).

[4]For example, *TSC Industries* v. *Northway, Inc.*, 44 U.S.L.W. 4852 (1976).

[5]*Accounting and Reporting Standards for Corporate Financial Statements* (Evanston, IL: American Accounting Association, 1957).

materiality for the financial statements taken as a whole is generally the smallest aggregate level of errors that could be considered material to any one of the financial statements (AU Section 312.12).

As an example of how an auditor might set materiality levels in planning the audit, he or she may consider misstatements aggregating less than $100,000 not to be material to net income, but may establish a higher materiality threshold for misstatements that affect only the balance sheet (such as misclassifications). This would be because the relatively higher magnitude of the balance sheet components might cause the $100,000 to be immaterial to the balance sheet. Similarly, when planning procedures at the line item level (such as receivables or inventories), the auditor must consider that immaterial misstatements in separate line items might aggregate to a material amount. Thus, auditing procedures in one area—for example, receivables—might have to be designed to detect income statement misstatements of much less than $100,000, because of possible misstatements in other areas of the balance sheet. The auditor should consider materiality levels in planning the nature, timing, and extent of all auditing procedures.

To perform an effective and efficient audit, the auditor must continually assess the results of procedures performed and repeatedly reevaluate whether, based on those results, the scope of procedures planned for the various accounts is adequate, or possibly excessive. For example, individually immaterial misstatements of certain expenses may aggregate to a material amount. As audit work progresses, the auditor may find that the individually immaterial misstatements do not offset each other but cause income to be overstated. In these circumstances, the auditor may need to adjust the scope of procedures for the expenses remaining to be examined, to gain assurance that a material aggregate misstatement will be detected if it exists. It may also be necessary to apply additional procedures to areas that have already been audited.

New facts and circumstances may also change the amount the auditor considers material to individual financial statement line items or to the financial statements taken as a whole. For example, if adjustments are made to the accounts during the course of the audit, the parameters the auditor used to determine materiality in the planning stage (e.g., amounts for net income, revenues, and shareholders' equity) may change. By the end of the audit, materiality may be different than at the planning stage. An auditor who does not continually reassess materiality and audit scope as the engagement progresses assumes a greater risk of performing an inefficient or ineffective audit. Materiality assessments and audit planning should be viewed as dynamic rather than static auditing concepts.

To keep track of misstatements discovered through the various tests and procedures performed during an audit and to help in drawing conclusions about their effect on the financial statements, the auditor often maintains a summary of potential audit adjustments. This practice tool assists the auditor in accumulating known misstatements found through audit tests, misstatements based on projections developed from sampling procedures, and misstatements relating to client accounting estimates that the auditor believes are unreasonable. Ordinarily, management adjusts the records for many of the known misstatements. The auditor then considers the effect of the remaining unadjusted items on the financial statements. Sometimes the auditor believes that further adjustments are necessary for an unqualified opinion to be given. The summary also assists in evaluating whether misstatements, if uncorrected, would affect only the balance sheet, only the income statement, or both. The summary of adjustments is discussed in further detail and illustrated in the section on "Summarizing and Evaluating the Audit Findings" in Chapter 17.

AUDIT STRATEGY

From the time an engagement is first considered—even before it is accepted—until the results are summarized and evaluated at the end of the engagement, the auditor makes numerous decisions, which collectively constitute the audit strategy for the engagement. Formulating the audit strategy involves making broad-level planning decisions, such as whether to use the work of the client's internal auditors; whether the assistance of a specialist is needed; whether, in the audit of a multilocation or multicomponent client, to vary the locations or components visited each year; and whether to use the work of other independent auditors who have audited any of the client's components. Formulating the audit strategy also involves making detailed decisions about the nature, timing, and extent of auditing procedures for each significant account balance or class of transactions in the financial statements.

Generally, the most significant and sophisticated strategy decision the auditor makes is whether, and to what extent, to perform tests of controls to reduce the assurance needed from substantive tests. This aspect of audit strategy results in an audit testing plan for each account balance and each assertion, based on the auditor's assessment of inherent and control risk.

As indicated in the overview of the audit process in Chapter 5 and explained in detail in Chapter 8, during the risk assessment phase the auditor often performs some tests of controls concurrently with obtaining the required understanding of the control structure. If the results of those tests are positive, the auditor will be able to reduce the amount of assurance needed from substantive tests. After evaluating the results of concurrent tests of controls, the auditor makes a strategy decision about whether to perform additional tests of controls to support a further, significant reduction in substantive tests. Because additional tests of controls require substantial audit effort, performing them is efficient only if they can be expected to support a significant reduction in substantive tests.

Several factors determine the audit testing plan that will most efficiently enable the auditor to achieve the audit objectives related to each account balance. The most important of these is the auditor's assessment of inherent and control risk in the context of materiality. Other factors include

- *The cost of performing specific tests of controls versus the cost of performing specific substantive procedures.* "Cost" includes more than simply the number of hours of auditor time; it also involves optimal staff utilization, on-the-job training, and similar factors, as well as the level of client support needed. All of these influence what combination and timing of auditing procedures the auditor will choose. Cost is also affected by the availability of computer resources. Instead of performing tests manually, the auditor may use computer-assisted audit techniques, which are often more cost effective.
- *Prior decisions about the nature, timing, and extent of specific procedures.* For example, if the client wants the audit report shortly after year-end, the auditor might decide to perform substantive tests of details early and then to perform tests of controls and analytical procedures to obtain satisfaction about account balances at year-end. As another example, the decision to use negative rather than positive confirmations may ultimately lead the auditor to confirm more receivables or perform certain analytical procedures, because negative confirmations that are not returned are less conclusive evidence than positive confirmations.
- *Client expectations about the auditor's consideration of the control structure.* In setting the audit strategy, the auditor should consider whether additional responsibilities arise from requests of the client (e.g., a request for a review of the control structure beyond what the auditor believes is required for planning the audit), or because the company is subject to special regulatory or other requirements.
- *The auditor's ability to obtain corroborating evidence from outside the accounting system.* For example, the auditor may be able to obtain reliable information from operating personnel directly involved in sales or purchasing activities, or from knowledgeable third parties.

Audit strategy decisions are normally made by experienced staff members because such decisions require a high degree of professional judgment; approval of the audit testing plan should rest with the partner.

Audit strategy documentation varies in form and substance among auditing firms. Professional standards require the auditor to document his or her understanding of the control structure elements and the assessment of control risk. In addition, the auditor normally documents the understanding of the client's business, the assessment of inherent risk conditions, judgments about materiality, and the audit strategy adopted for major account balances and classes of transactions in the financial statements. Many auditors incorporate other materials in the planning section of the working papers, for example, detailed time budgets, the audit timetable, and certain audit-related correspondence such as communications with internal auditors.

PLANNING AND CONTROLLING THE AUDIT

Audit planning and control are essential to managing an engagement so that it both meets generally accepted auditing standards and is performed efficiently and within the client's time constraints.

Implementation Planning

Planning is the process of implementing the audit strategy decisions. Planning takes place throughout the audit, especially during the risk assessment activities and when the auditor develops the audit testing plan and formalizes it in a detailed audit program. The activities involved in planning the audit and the order in which they are done vary with the engagement; often the various activities overlap.

The auditor should establish a timetable for completing the principal segments of the engagement. The timetable sets forth the planned audit work and provides a way of controlling the engagement. The client's scheduling requirements should be considered in establishing the timetable.

The auditor should then prepare an audit program listing the detailed procedures to be undertaken on the engagement. The audit program is the basis for the detailed time and expense budgets. Preliminary budgets are sometimes prepared based on the initial audit activities and certain risk assessments, and revised, if necessary, when the audit strategy is finalized. Budgets help keep the work within the client's and the auditor's time requirements and are the basis for establishing the audit fee. The budgets should cover all the different tasks and levels of personnel to be employed on the engagement. They should be sufficiently detailed so that staff members can complete tasks in relatively short periods and thereby manage their time efficiently. The complexity of audits of multilocation and multinational companies makes detailed time and expense budgets critical to the timely and efficient conduct of those engagements. Both during the field work and at the end of the audit, time or expense overruns should be evaluated. If they were caused by inefficiencies, the evaluation can help ensure that they will not be repeated in the following year. If overruns were caused by the discovery of client errors or irregularities, the evaluation serves as a reminder to the auditor to determine that the matter has been properly disposed of. Finally, the evaluation helps ensure that next year's budget will be realistic, and also promotes more efficient use of staff.

Personnel for the engagement must be identified and assigned. In assigning people to a particular engagement, the manager and partner generally consider: how technically complex the engagement is and whether it calls for industry expertise; the continuity of the engagement team; personnel career development; and staff commitments to other engagements. Staff availability and cost considerations sometimes lead to adjustments in the timing of certain procedures and other strategy decisions.

If the client uses computers in significant accounting applications, the audit team may need specialized audit skills. AU Section 311.10 specifies that if the work of a professional with such skills (whether a member of the audit team or an outside professional) is used, the auditor must have sufficient computer-related knowledge to communicate audit objectives to that professional, evaluate whether the procedures he or she applies meet the auditor's objectives, and determine how the results of those procedures affect the nature, timing, and extent of other planned auditing procedures. A computer audit professional who is a member of the audit team requires the same supervision and review as any other member.

Personnel to whom work is delegated should be told what their responsibilities are, what objectives their procedures are meant to achieve, and when their work should be completed within the overall audit timetable. They should also be informed about matters that may affect the nature, timing, and extent of auditing procedures, such as the nature of the client's business and potential accounting and auditing problems. The audit plan should be communicated to the audit team, including other offices involved in the engagement. The principal auditor should establish communication links with other independent auditors involved in the engagement. Timetables, procedures to be performed, and the type of report the principal auditor needs should be communicated early in the audit.

The auditor usually should discuss the general audit strategy with the client's management. Some planning details (e.g., when to observe inventory, what schedules and analyses the client's staff should prepare, and what other ways client personnel can assist the auditor; and considering using the work of internal auditors) will almost inevitably need to be discussed and agreed on beforehand.

Using the Work of Internal Auditors

In some companies, the internal audit department operates with few or no restrictions and reports to the board of directors or audit committee on a wide range of matters. In other companies, the department may be limited in its duties and may not enjoy organizational independence. Internal audit departments can operate in a variety of ways. They may

- Perform specific control procedures, focusing heavily on activities like surprise cash counts and inventory counts.
- Function essentially parallel with the external audit function as described in this book, examining and evaluating control structure policies and procedures and substantiating account balances.
- Have broad responsibility for evaluating compliance with company policies and practices.

- Conduct performance audits, which are described in Chapter 2, in addition to financial and compliance audits.
- Work on special projects or be responsible for specific aspects of the control structure.

SAS No. 55 (AU Section 319.09) categorizes the internal audit function as part of the control environment, specifically, one of management's ways of monitoring whether the other aspects of the control structure—the accounting system and internal control procedures—are appropriately designed and operating effectively. For example, an entity may have a control procedure that calls for an employee to perform bank reconciliations. The internal auditor might evaluate how well the reconciliation process is designed and whether it is effectively performed by the employee, and report on it to management. In some organizations, internal auditors perform the reconciliations as part of their review of cash disbursements procedures; although not an internal audit function, this enhances the control environment by formalizing separation of duties.

As part of obtaining an understanding of the control structure as required by SAS No. 55, the external auditor considers the activities performed by the internal auditors to determine whether their work is related to areas of interest to the external auditor and whether he or she can use that work in assessing control risk.[6] In making that determination, the external auditor should first obtain an understanding of the operation of the internal audit function. The principal matters considered in obtaining that understanding are

- The standing and responsibilities of the person(s) to whom the head of internal audit reports and the resulting objectivity of internal audit personnel.
- The responsibilities assigned to the internal auditors. These responsibilities are frequently set forth in an internal audit department charter.
- The size and professional competence of the internal audit department, taking into consideration the complexity of the control structure. For example, if the circumstances require tests of general computer control procedures, the internal auditors should have an adequate knowledge of computer audit techniques. Hiring, training, advancement, assignment, and consultation practices of the internal audit function also should be considered.

[6]SAS No. 9, *The Effect of an Internal Audit Function on the Scope of the Independent Audit* (AU Section 322), provides guidance on the factors that affect the external auditor's consideration of the work of internal auditors. At the time of this writing, the Auditing Standards Board is considering whether SAS No. 9 should be revised. The guidance presented in this section reflects the authors' views on how SAS No. 9 should be applied in light of subsequent SASs, including SAS No. 47 (AU Section 312) and SAS No. 55.

- The extent of supervision and review of work. For example, the work carried out by the internal auditors should be supervised by senior internal audit personnel.
- The extent, if any, to which the internal auditors' access to records, documentation, and personnel is restricted.
- The adequacy of the evidence of the work done by the internal auditors.
- The nature, timing, and extent of the internal audit coverage.
- The nature and frequency of, and response to, reports issued by the internal auditors.

If, based on the understanding, the external auditor believes that it may be possible to use the work of the internal auditors, he or she should seek additional evidence of the effectiveness of that work. This usually involves reviewing internal audit working papers and related reports with respect to the internal control structure to determine whether the internal auditors' work appears to be adequately supervised and appears to support the external auditor's assessment of the internal audit function and the role it plays in the control structure.

If the external auditor concludes that he or she can use the internal auditors' work in assessing control risk, the following techniques may enhance the efficiency of the audit effort:

- Preparing integrated audit testing plans.
- Exchanging reports.
- Holding regularly scheduled coordination meetings.
- Granting free and open access to each other's working papers.
- Providing the internal auditors with audit software and training, or requesting that the internal auditors write computer programs for the external auditor's use.
- Making joint presentations to the audit committee or the board of directors.
- Adopting common documentation techniques and establishing common user files.

Using the Work of a Specialist

In considering evidence to corroborate management's assertions, an auditor may occasionally encounter a matter that requires special expertise. The auditor cannot be expected to have or develop the expertise of a person in another profession or occupation, and may thus decide to arrange for a specialist to help obtain competent evidential matter. The need to do so should be established in the planning stage of the audit, so that the necessary arrangements can be made on a timely basis.

Specialists may be used on a recurring basis or only for special matters. An actuary will ordinarily be engaged to perform certain calculations in determining pension plan costs. An appraiser may be used to establish fair market value of real estate collateralizing bank loans. Lawyers may be used as specialists in matters outside of litigation, claims, or assessments. Petroleum engineers may be used to estimate oil reserves, and gemologists to appraise precious gems.

The auditor should be satisfied with the competence, reputation, and standing of the specialist in the particular field. The specialist's competence may be demonstrated by professional certification, license, or other formal recognition. Peers or others familiar with the specialist's work may be able to vouch for the individual's reputation and standing.

As indicated in paragraph 6 of SAS No. 11, *Using the Work of a Specialist* (AU Section 336.06), the "work of a specialist unrelated to the client will usually provide the auditor with greater assurance of reliability because of the absence of a relationship that might impair objectivity." The auditor should take steps to ascertain the nature of any relationship the specialist may have with the client. Specialists are not required to be "independent" in the same sense as auditors are; however, the auditor must evaluate whether any relationship is material. If the specialist has a relationship with the client that might impair the specialist's objectivity, the auditor should consider performing additional procedures with respect to some or all of the specialist's assumptions, methods, or findings to determine that the findings are not unreasonable.

The work of a specialist may be used as an auditing procedure to obtain competent evidential matter, but it is not sufficient in itself. Additional auditing procedures must be performed to meet the requirements of particular circumstances. The procedures should not duplicate any of the specialist's work, but are generally needed to corroborate accounting data the client provides to the specialist. The specialist is responsible for the appropriateness, reasonableness, and application of any methods or assumptions used. The auditor must understand the methods or assumptions used, however, to determine whether the specialist's findings are suitable for corroborating the related information in the financial statements. The auditor is not required to conclude that the specialist's findings are reasonable, but only that they are not unreasonable. For example, an appraisal of real estate owned may indicate a 25 percent increase in fair market value over the previous year. This finding would appear to be unreasonable if current market conditions generally indicated a decline in values of comparable real estate during the same period. An auditor who believes that the specialist's findings are unreasonable should perform additional procedures, including inquiry of the specialist.

If the auditor is not able to resolve a matter after performing additional procedures, he or she should consider obtaining the opinion of another specialist. An unresolved matter will result in a qualified opinion or a disclaimer of opinion because the inability to obtain sufficient competent evidential matter constitutes a scope limitation (paragraphs 40 and 41 of SAS No. 58, *Reports on Audited Financial Statements* [AU Sections 508.40 and .41]). The auditor should not mention the work or findings of a specialist when expressing an unqualified opinion on financial statements.

Rotating Audit Emphasis

If the auditor has assessed the control environment as highly effective, it may be practical to rotate the audit emphasis from year to year and limit the number of locations where auditing procedures are performed in a specific engagement. This strategy may enhance audit efficiency and make a complex engagement (such as a multilocation audit) less costly. The way to accomplish this varies with the circumstances of the engagement. The auditor must ensure, however, that each year's audit work is adequate to support a conclusion on the fairness of the financial statements for that year. Subject to audit risk considerations, auditors may vary both the locations visited and the strategies employed at various locations. In a large multilocation engagement, often only a few, if any, locations are individually material to a specific account balance or class of transactions. For example, a retail chain store operation might consist of 300 separate stores of varying size, none of which is individually material to the enterprise in terms of its sales volume or inventory.

Using the Work of Other Auditors

In reporting on the financial statements of a company or group of companies, an auditor may use the work and report of other auditors who have audited one or more components (subsidiaries or divisions) of the entity. Other auditors may also be used to carry out part of an engagement on grounds of efficiency. Physical distance and language barriers among components of an entity may also be overcome most economically through these arrangements. When more than one auditor is involved in the engagement, one usually serves as principal auditor. Determining who is the principal auditor involves considering what proportion of the entire engagement each auditor performs and the auditor's overall knowledge of the engagement.

Even though each auditor has individual responsibility for the work performed and the opinion rendered, the principal auditor should apply certain procedures in order to be able to use another auditor's report and express an opinion on the overall financial statements. SAS No. 1 (AU Section 543) contains guidelines about what procedures should be performed. They include inquiring about the other auditor's professional reputation and ascertaining that the other auditor is independent; is aware of the intended use of the financial statements and report; is familiar with GAAP, GAAS, and other (e.g., SEC) reporting requirements; and has been informed about matters affecting the elimination of intercompany transactions and the uniformity of accounting principles among the components. In some circumstances, the principal auditor may review the other auditor's audit programs or working papers, read summaries of the work performed and conclusions reached by the other auditor, or attend key meetings between the other auditor and management. The principal auditor may also visit the other auditor's premises or obtain written representations about various matters. The need for such steps should be considered early in the planning process and continually reviewed during the engagement. When another auditor's work is used, the opinion may or may not refer to the other auditor's involvement. That issue is discussed in Chapter 18, "The Auditor's Report."

Using a Report on Internal Control at a Service Organization

A client may use a service organization, such as a data processing center, to record certain transactions, process data, or even execute transactions and maintain the related accounting records and assets such as securities. Transactions may flow through an accounting system that is, wholly or partially, separate from the client's organization, and the auditor may find it necessary or efficient in understanding and assessing the client's control structure to consider procedures performed at the service organization. To do that, the auditor may obtain a report prepared by the service organization's auditor covering aspects of internal control at the service organization.

SAS No. 44, *Special-Purpose Reports on Internal Accounting Control at Service Organizations* (AU Section 324), provides guidance on the auditor's use of a special-purpose report of another independent auditor on internal control at a service organization. In deciding whether to obtain such a report, the auditor considers both the nature of the procedures the service organization provides and their relationship to the client's control structure.

The service organization may both record significant classes of client transactions and process related data. In that situation, the auditor often considers it necessary, in order to obtain a sufficient understanding of the flow of transactions and to plan substantive tests, to obtain a report prepared by the service organization's auditor on the *design* of its internal control structure. If accounting and control procedures located at the service organization are essential to achieve one or more of the client's control objectives, and the auditor seeks to assess control risk at less than the maximum, he or she will find it necessary to obtain a report from the service organization's auditor about the *effectiveness* of its control structure or specific control procedures therein as well. In these circumstances, the auditor should assess control risk based on the combination of control structure policies and procedures of both the client and the service organization.

If the service organization executes transactions and maintains the related accounts, the client will be unable to maintain independent records of the transactions. In these circumstances, the auditor will need either to obtain a report from the service organization's auditor about the effectiveness of the control structure as a basis for evaluating whether relevant control objectives have been achieved, or to apply (or ask the service organization's auditor to apply) substantive tests at the service organization in order to meet the related audit objectives.

The decision to use a report on the service organization's internal control, along with appropriate inquiries and other steps necessary to implement that decision, should be made during the planning phase of the audit. Reporting considerations when a service organization's auditor's report is used are discussed in Chapter 19. SAS No. 44 also provides guidance on the responsibilities of the auditor who issues a report on internal control at a service organization.

Controlling the Engagement

Supervision and review are essential parts of managing an engagement. The partner is ultimately responsible for forming and expressing an opinion on the financial statements and cannot delegate this responsibility. The manager or other experienced individual is usually responsible for supervising and monitoring the work done to ensure that it is in accordance with the audit testing plan. Supervision also entails comparing the completed work with established timetables and budgets, training and coaching, and identifying differences in professional judgment among personnel and referring them to the appropriate level for resolution, as well as directly reviewing the work performed. The work done by each member of the audit team is supervised, reviewed, and approved by another, more experienced member. Queries raised during the review process should be followed up and resolved before completing the engagement and issuing the audit opinion.

Review Questions

6–1. What are the key aspects of engagement management?

6–2. What is meant by audit strategy formulation?

6–3. What is the most significant decision made in planning an audit?

6–4. What is meant by overall audit risk?

6–5. Aside from audit risk, what other factors are considered in determining audit strategy?

6–6. As used in auditing, what is materiality?

6–7. What is the relationship between materiality and audit risk?

6–8. What is an audit program and what is its purpose?

6–9. Why are audit budgets prepared? Why should actual hours be summarized and reviewed at the end of the audit?

6–10. What does supervision of the audit entail and whose responsibility is it?

6–11. Why is it necessary for an auditor to understand the client's internal audit function?

6–12. Give examples of techniques through which internal and external auditors may interact in the course of an engagement.

6–13. When would a principal auditor use the work of another auditor?

6–14. What are the major components of audit risk? Describe them.

6–15. In what circumstances does an auditor perform tests of controls?

6–16. When in the audit should the auditor's assessment of materiality take place?

6–17. Is obtaining the work of a specialist sufficient to preclude auditing procedures in that area?

Discussion Questions

6–30. The increasing use of internal auditors by clients has had an effect on the approach external auditors take toward the formulation of their strategies and programs. Discuss how internal and external auditors may interact on an engagement, giving recognition to the following:

a. The degree of independence exhibited by internal auditors.
b. The background, training, and competence of internal auditors.
c. The effect of internal audit activities on the nature, timing, and extent of tests and procedures performed by external auditors.

6–31. During the course of an audit engagement, an independent auditor gives serious consideration to the concept of materiality. This concept of materiality is inherent in the work of the independent auditor and is important for planning, preparing, and modifying audit programs. The concept of materiality underlies the application of all the generally accepted auditing standards, particularly the standards of field work and reporting.

Required:

a. Briefly describe what is meant by the independent auditor's concept of materiality.
b. What are some common relationships and other considerations used by the auditor in judging materiality?
c. Identify how the planning and execution of an audit program might be affected by the independent auditor's concept of materiality.

(AICPA adapted)

6–32. What are some of the things an auditor should do to ensure that the audit team fulfills the responsibility to exercise due care in the conduct of the audit?

6–33. What factors, in addition to dollar amount, should be considered in determining materiality?

6–34. Briefly list the circumstances or types of activity that might indicate possible errors or irregularities in the following accounts:

- Accounts receivable
- Inventory

6–35. Why are time budgets important in all phases of an audit?

6–36. Audit risk and materiality should be considered when planning and performing an audit of financial statements in accordance with generally accepted auditing standards. Audit risk and materiality should also be considered together in determining the nature, timing, and extent of auditing procedures and in evaluating the results of those procedures.

Required:

a. 1. Define audit risk.
   2. Describe its components of inherent risk, control risk, and detection risk.
   3. Explain how these components are interrelated.

b. 1. Define materiality.
   2. Discuss the factors affecting its determination.
   3. Describe the relationship between materiality for planning purposes and materiality for evaluation purposes.

(AICPA adapted)

6–37. The CPA firm of Jarvis & Sands has audited the consolidated financial statements of Sampan Company. Jarvis & Sands performed the audit of the parent company and all subsidiaries except for Sampan-National, which was audited by the CPA firm of Brown & Leeds. Sampan-National constituted approximately ten percent of the consolidated assets and six percent of the consolidated revenue.

Brown & Leeds issued an unqualified opinion on the financial statements of Sampan-National. Jarvis & Sands will be issuing an unqualified opinion on the consolidated financial statements of Sampan.

Required:

a. What procedures should Jarvis & Sands consider performing with respect to Brown & Leeds' audit of Sampan-National's financial statements that will be appropriate whether or not reference is to be made to other auditors?

b. Describe the various circumstances under which Jarvis & Sands could take responsibility for the work of Brown & Leeds and make no reference to Brown & Leeds' audit of Sampan-National in Jarvis & Sands' auditor's report on the consolidated financial statements of Sampan.

(AICPA adapted)

AICPA Multiple Choice Questions

These questions are taken from the Auditing part of Uniform CPA Examinations. Choose the single most appropriate answer.

6–40. The risk that an auditor's procedures will lead to the conclusion that a material error does *not* exist in an account balance when, in fact, such error does exist is referred to as

a. Audit risk.
b. Inherent risk.
c. Control risk.
d. Detection risk.

6–41. The element of the audit planning process most likely to be agreed upon with the client before implementation of the audit strategy is the determination of the

a. Methods of statistical sampling to be used in confirming accounts receivable.
b. Pending legal matters to be included in the inquiry of the client's attorney.
c. Evidence to be gathered to provide a sufficient basis for the auditor's opinion.
d. Schedules and analyses to be prepared by the client's staff.

6–42. Which of the following elements underlies the application of generally accepted auditing standards, particularly the standards of field work and reporting?

a. Internal control structure.
b. Corroborating evidence.
c. Quality control.
d. Materiality and relative risk.

6–43. Which of the following is an effective audit planning and control procedure that helps prevent misunderstandings and inefficient use of audit personnel?

a. Arrange to make copies, for inclusion in the working papers, of those client supporting documents examined by the auditor.
b. Arrange to provide the client with copies of the audit programs to be used during the audit.
c. Arrange a preliminary conference with the client to discuss audit objectives, fees, timing, and other information.
d. Arrange to have the auditor prepare and post any necessary adjusting or reclassification entries prior to final closing.

6–44. Rogers & Co., CPAs, policies require that all members of the audit staff submit weekly time reports to the audit manager, who then prepares a weekly summary work report regarding variance from budget for Rogers' review. This provides written evidence of Rogers & Co.'s professional concern regarding compliance with which of the following generally accepted auditing standards?

a. Quality control.
b. Due professional care.
c. Adequate review.
d. Adequate planning.

6–45. When considering the objectivity of internal auditors, an independent auditor should

a. Evaluate the quality control program in effect for the internal auditors.
b. Examine documentary evidence of the work performed by the internal auditors.

c. Test a sample of the transactions and balances that the internal auditors examined.
d. Determine the organizational level to which the internal auditors report.

6-46. Which of the following statements concerning the auditor's use of the work of a specialist is correct?

a. If the specialist is related to the client, the auditor is *not* permitted to use the specialist's findings as corroborative evidence.
b. The specialist may be identified in the auditor's report only when the auditor issues a qualified opinion.
c. The specialist should have an understanding of the auditor's corroborative use of the specialist's findings.
d. If the auditor believes that the determinations made by the specialist are unreasonable, only an adverse opinion may be issued.

6-47. An auditor who uses the work of a specialist may refer to and identify the specialist in the auditor's report if the

a. Specialist is also considered to be a related party.
b. Auditor indicates a division of responsibility related to the work of the specialist.
c. Specialist's work provides the auditor greater assurance of reliability.
d. Auditor expresses an "except for" qualified opinion or an adverse opinion related to the work of the specialist.

Problems and Cases

6-60. Parker is the staff member with administrative responsibilities for the upcoming annual audit of FGH Company, a continuing audit client. Parker will supervise two assistants on the engagement and will visit the client before the field work begins.

Parker has started the planning process by preparing a list of procedures to be performed prior to the beginning of field work. The list includes:

1. Review correspondence and permanent files.
2. Review prior years' audit working papers, financial statements, and auditor's reports.
3. Discuss with CPA firm personnel responsible for audit and nonaudit services to the client, matters that may affect the engagement.
4. Discuss with management current business developments affecting the client.

Required:

Complete Parker's list of procedures to be performed prior to the beginning of field work.

(AICPA adapted)

6-61. You are an experienced staff member in a CPA firm. In late spring of 1989 you are advised of a new assignment to a recurring annual audit of a major client. You are given the engagement letter for the audit covering the calendar year ending December 31, 1989, and a list of personnel assigned to this engagement. It is your responsibility to plan and supervise the field work for the engagement.

Required:

Discuss the necessary preparation and planning for the annual audit *prior to* beginning field work at the client's office. In your discussion include the sources you should consult, the type of information you should seek, the preliminary plans and preparation you should make for the field work, and any actions you should take relative to the staff assigned to the engagement. *Do not write an audit program.*

(AICPA adapted)

6–62. You have been assigned to the Quinn Hardware audit engagement. Review the client background information that follows and answer the following questions.

a. Identify the risk factors that should be considered by the engagement team in determining an effective and efficient engagement strategy for the audit of Quinn Hardware for the year ended May 31, 1991. Support your responses with information obtained from your review of the client background information and analytical procedures performed on the financial information. Identify which audit objectives these risk factors affect and the impact of the risk factors on the audit strategy and auditing procedures.
b. Identify other considerations that should enter into the audit strategy.
c. What specific additional information not contained in the client background information would you need to assist you in determining the audit strategy?

QUINN HARDWARE
DESCRIPTION OF THE BUSINESS

Company History

The Company was founded in 1947 by the present chairman, Harvey Quinn. The business began in Chicago as a wholesale distributor of building materials and of heavy mining and industrial equipment to large industrial companies in the Chicago area. The wholesale business has grown rapidly and the Company now distributes a very wide range of hardware products all across the United States.

In 1959, the Company opened its first retail hardware outlet under the name of "Quinn's Hardware Store." The retail hardware business has grown and the Company now operates six company-owned retail hardware stores and a hardware dealers' franchise system with over 200 franchised dealerships. Negotiations are currently in progress for a term loan to expand the franchise system. In 1967, a wholly owned subsidiary company, Quinn Hardware Stores, Inc., was established to carry on the retail business and to provide managerial and marketing expertise to the franchised dealerships in what is now a very competitive industry. A significant portion of Quinn's wholesale business is with Company-franchised dealerships, which have credit terms similar to those with other customers. Quinn also supplies several U.S. Government agencies with various products, such as industrial and mining equipment and building supplies. Discussions with Quinn's management disclosed that during the past year the Company lost six franchised dealerships (in Oklahoma, Louisiana, and Texas) because of bankruptcy; it was the first such loss of any of its franchises.

Organization

The Company employs 612 people, who participate in its defined contribution pension plan.

Head Office:		
Executive Staff	30	
Purchasing Department	45	
Finance and Accounting	24	
Data Processing	34	
Internal Audit	6	
Other	4	
		143
Marketing:		
Eastern region	40	
Great Lakes region	44	
Central region	20	
Western region	20	
Southern region	25	
		149
Branch Operations:		
New York	46	
Pittsburgh	20	
Chicago	92	
Detroit	32	
Houston	26	
Los Angeles	42	
		258
Retail Stores		62
Total Employees		612

Organization charts are shown on pages 213 and 214.

Products

In addition to heavy mining, building materials, and industrial equipment, the Company buys and sells over 35,000 different hardware products on a wholesale basis. These products are purchased from over 3500 different vendors in the United States. Hardware products may be generally categorized as follows:

1. Housewares
2. Sporting goods
3. Hand tools
4. Machine tools
5. Building materials
6. Architectural hardware
7. Paint
8. Plumbing materials
9. Lawn and garden supplies (new line started as of March 1990)

The Company has been made aware of new government safety regulations relating to mining and industrial equipment. Quinn is conducting an evaluation of the inventory

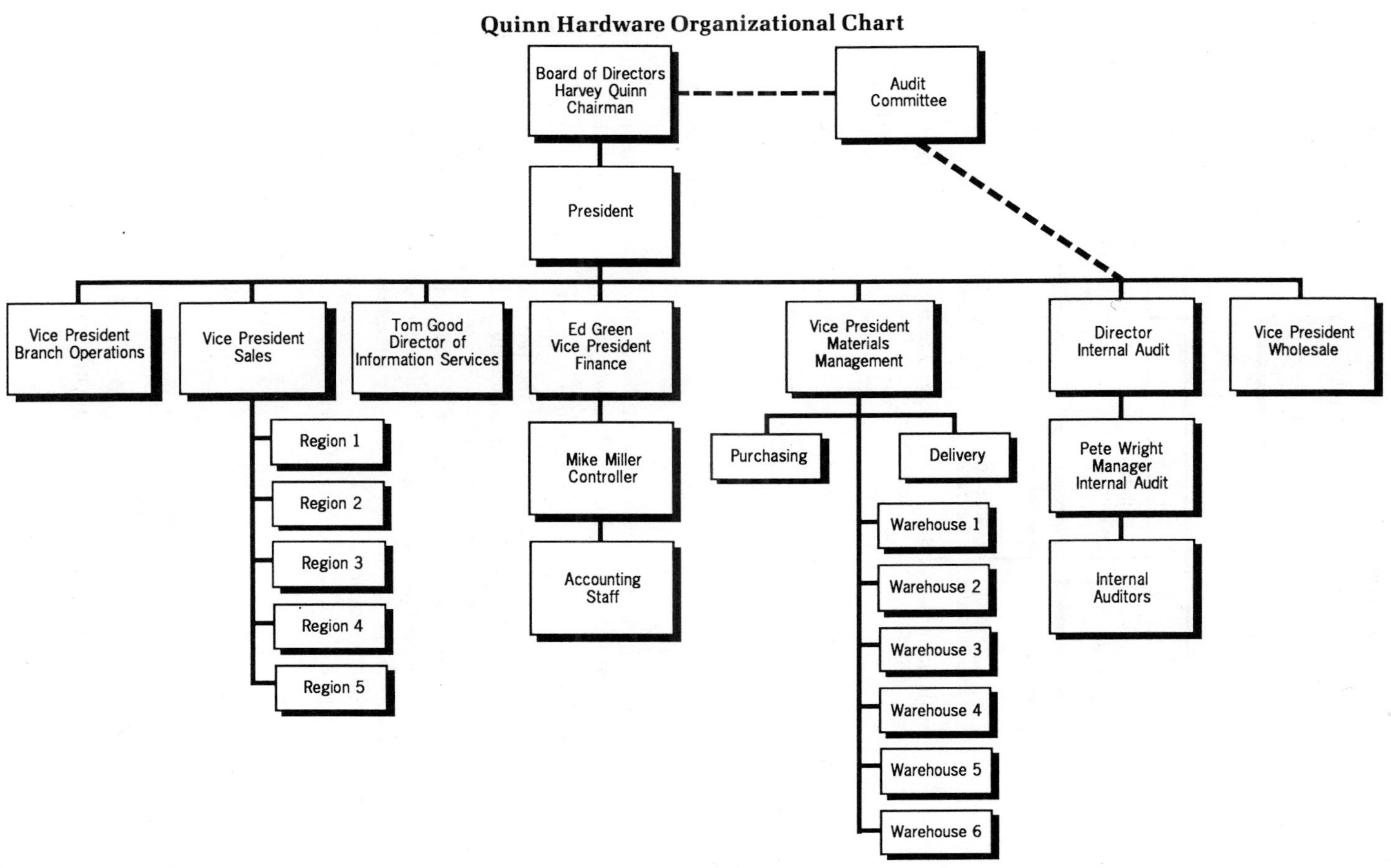
Quinn Hardware Organizational Chart
Board of Directors Harvey Quinn Chairman
Audit Committee
President
Vice President Branch Operations
Vice President Sales
Tom Good Director of Information Services
Ed Green Vice President Finance
Vice President Materials Management
Director Internal Audit
Vice President Wholesale
Region 1
Region 2
Region 3
Region 4
Region 5
Mike Miller Controller
Accounting Staff
Purchasing
Delivery
Warehouse 1
Warehouse 2
Warehouse 3
Warehouse 4
Warehouse 5
Warehouse 6
Pete Wright Manager Internal Audit
Internal Auditors

Quinn Hardware Relevant EDP Organizational Chart

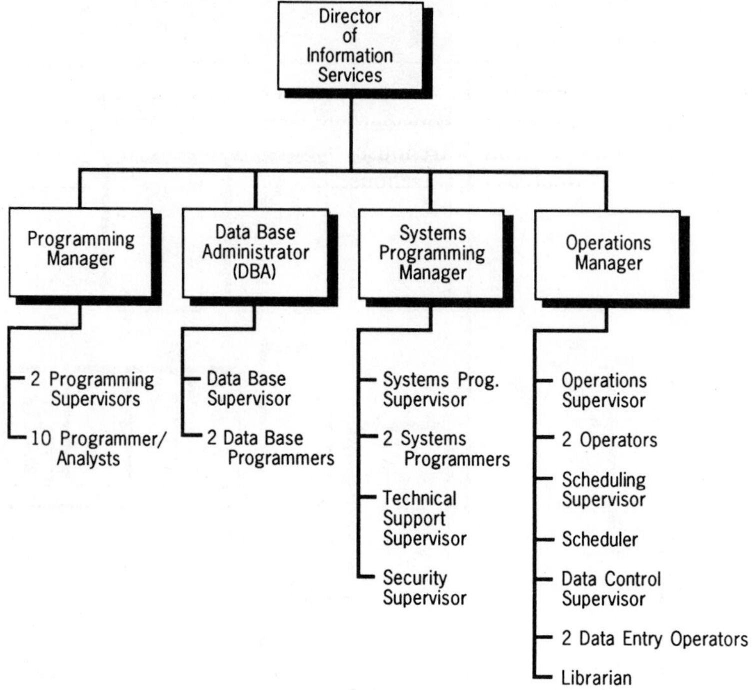

items impacted by these regulations. Additionally, the overall downturn in the mining industry has caused Quinn to more closely evaluate inventory obsolescence.

Purchasing

All purchasing is done centrally by the purchasing department in Chicago. The purchasing department employs approximately 30 buyers, each of whom is responsible for purchasing from certain vendors of hardware merchandise.

The purchasing function, which is considered critical to the successful overall operation of the Company, is highly complex because of the large number of different inventory products, the different types of customers, and varying product mixes at the various warehouse locations.

Information about the volume of purchase and cash disbursement transactions is as follows:

Transactions	*Approximate Annual Volume*
Purchase Orders/Receiving Memos	180,000
Check Disbursements	150,000
Vendor Invoices	180,000
Standing Data Amendments	
• price	120,000
• product	20,000
• vendor	2,000

Warehousing/Distribution

The Company maintains a warehouse at the location of each of the six branch operations. Three are company owned and three are leased from H. Quinn under operating leases. Two of the warehouse managers were terminated during the year because they were unable to maintain operating schedules.

Inventory mix varies considerably from warehouse to warehouse. For example, the Chicago and Detroit warehouses handle primarily heavy industrial hardware and equipment, whereas the warehouses in other metropolitan centers handle mainly small hardware items and building materials. Quinn Hardware uses an extensive cycle counting process to update the perpetual inventory records. A complete physical inventory is taken each year at the end of March when inventory is historically at the lowest level.

The Company has its own fleet of delivery trucks for local deliveries at each warehouse location. All deliveries to points further than 100 miles from distribution points are made via commercial carriers.

Marketing

Quinn Hardware sells to approximately 9000 customers in the retail, government, and wholesale markets. The Company employs a sales force of 149 salespeople, operating from 30 sales offices in 5 marketing regions.

Annual Sales

Annual sales by major customer category for the year ended May 31, 1990 were as follows:

	No. of Customers	*Sales ($000s)*	%
Retail division			
Hardware chain stores	4,500	$ 63,856	25
Independents	2,000	25,543	10
Department stores	35	35,760	14
	6,535	125,159	49
Industrial division	2,300	56,194	22
Mining division	215	38,314	15
Building division	150	35,759	14
	9,200	$255,426	100

Credit sales from the warehouse are made on a 1/10 net 30 day basis. Cash sales represent 10 percent of the hardware chain stores' volume. The hardware chain stores' established credit terms are net 30.

Operating Results

(See Attached Financial Statements)

Operating results of the Company for the last four years and the nine months ended February 28, 1991 (in $000s) are as follows:

	Nine Months Ended February 28, 1991		*Year Ended May 31*		
		1990	*1989*	*1988*	*1987*
Sales	$219,097*	$255,426	$230,118	$225,895	$191,444
Cost of goods sold	158,486	186,684	171,062	163,682	142,023
Gross profit	60,611	68,742	59,056	62,213	49,421
Selling, general, and administrative expenses	34,938	40,732	41,274	32,129	27,711
Operating profit	$ 25,673	$ 28,010	$ 17,782	$ 30,084	$ 21,710

*1991 sales include sales of $16,850,000 to DAP Mining Company in which H. Quinn, Quinn Hardware's President, is a significant stockholder.

Litigation

The Company is currently being sued by three vendors for nonpayment on certain contractual obligations. Quinn has stated that there are counterclaims and offsets in excess of amounts claimed by these vendors. The Company and its counsel are unable to determine the outcome that may result from this litigation; however, they believe that the cases are without merit and intend to defend them vigorously. No trial dates have been set at this time.

Auditors

Your firm has been the auditor of the Company since it was founded and has been retained by Quinn to audit its financial statements for the year ended May 31, 1991. Quinn requested that it receive the audit report no later than July 10, 1991, in order to meet proposed closing schedules for a new term loan. The letter to management and the audit committee communicating significant deficiencies in the control structure is usually issued by July 15.

Your past audit strategy included performing tests of control procedures and assessing control risk as low in the buying cycle, and substantive procedures in the revenue cycle. The control environment was assessed as favorable.

Management Personnel

Mr. Green was hired in July 1989 as Vice President of Finance and is the third to hold that position within the last six years. Mr. Miller, Controller, has been with the Company for two years; Mr. Wright, Manager, Internal Auditing, for four years; and Mr. Good, Director of Information Services, for three years. Although they are not long-term employees, the financial personnel have a good knowledge of Quinn's accounting system and are aware of the need for a strong internal control structure.

Your firm has found few audit adjustments in prior years. All estimates and valuation reserves are prepared by accounting personnel and reviewed and approved by the controller. Additionally, the controller has designated an accounting department employee who is responsible for reconciling all general ledger accounts. These reconciliations are prepared monthly and are reviewed and approved by the controller.

Control Environment

The following is a summary of key points relating to Quinn's control environment.

- Organizational structure of the Company appears appropriate for the size and nature of the business.
- Key personnel are knowledgeable of Quinn's systems but are not long-term employees of the Company.
- The majority of the Board of Directors are not members of Company management or key stockholders.
- There is an audit committee composed entirely of outside directors.
  - They meet with the external independent auditors at least twice a year to discuss the scope and results of the audit.
- Internal audit formally reports to the president of the Company.
  - The Director of Internal Audit has access to the audit committee and meets alone with the committee twice a year.
  - The internal audit plan is reviewed annually by both the external independent auditors and the audit committee and is approved by the audit committee.
  - The Company has six internal auditors, including one EDP auditor. The staff appears to possess the skills necessary to competently carry out their plans.
- Some suggestions for improvements to the internal control structure have been vetoed by Mr. Quinn on grounds of cost effectiveness.
- Personnel at appropriate levels of middle management are involved in the development of the budgets.
  - Budgets are communicated to all appropriate personnel.
  - "Budget vs. actual" analysis is done on a monthly basis.
  - Deviations are analyzed and reported to appropriate levels of management.
  - Plans for corrective action are developed as appropriate.
- The Company has developed an employee handbook that sets forth a code of conduct.
- A written policies and procedures manual, developed and updated as necessary by each department, has been distributed to all employees in the respective departments.
  - The section related to the accounting department requires documentation of all investigation and review procedures. Initials and dates are required as evidence supporting completion of tasks.
- Division of duties is appropriate.
- The EDP department appears to be organized in an appropriate fashion and has sufficient skills.
  - Quinn Hardware uses an IBM mainframe system.
  - Accounting applications and system software are purchased packages.

QUINN HARDWARE, INC.
CONSOLIDATED BALANCE SHEETS
FEBRUARY 28, 1991 AND MAY 31, 1990 AND 1989
(in 000s)

ASSETS	1991	1990	1989
	(Unaudited)		
Current Assets:			
Cash	$ 3,542	$ 12,919	$ 9,539
Accounts Receivable	43,831	37,074	30,573
Merchandise Inventory	59,327	48,637	50,603
Other Current Assets	6,430	6,675	5,838
Total Current Assets	113,130	105,305	96,553
Property, Plant, and Equipment, at Cost:			
Land	2,206	1,804	1,804
Buildings and Improvements	44,605	44,749	42,722
Furniture and Fixtures	105,316	92,530	94,414
Automotive Equipment	15,320	14,780	12,410
	167,447	153,863	151,350
Less: Accumulated Depreciation	74,217	66,819	63,505
Total Property, Plant, and Equipment	93,230	87,044	87,845
Buildings and Improvements Held for Sale	7,232	5,772	7,025
	$213,592	$198,121	$191,423

LIABILITIES AND STOCKHOLDERS' EQUITY	1991	1990	1989
	(Unaudited)		
Current Liabilities:			
Accounts Payable and Accrued Liabilities	$ 30,030	$ 39,645	$ 30,390
Income Taxes Payable	1,385	1,431	1,182
Total Current Liabilities	31,415	41,076	31,572
Long-term Indebtedness	39,280	30,280	39,191
Deferred Income Taxes	14,100	13,400	10,360
	84,795	84,756	81,123
Stockholders' Equity:			
Preferred Stock, $1.00 Par Value, Nonparticipating, 9% Cumulative Preference, 500,000 Shares Authorized, 250,000 Shares Issued and Outstanding	250	250	250
Common Stock, No Par Value, 1,250,000 Shares Authorized, 500,000 Shares Issued and Outstanding	5,000	5,000	5,000
Additional Paid-in Capital	27,168	27,168	27,168
Retained Earnings	96,379	80,947	77,882
Total Stockholders' Equity	128,797	113,365	110,300
	$213,592	$198,121	$191,423

7

The Internal Control Structure

An enterprise's internal control structure comprises three elements: the control environment, the accounting system, and control procedures. Each of these elements consists of policies, procedures, methods, and records designed by management to safeguard its assets, generate reliable financial information, promote operational efficiency, and encourage adherence to prescribed managerial policies. Collectively, the elements of the internal control structure operate within an enterprise to reduce its unintended exposure to business, financial, and accounting risks.

RELEVANCE OF AN ENTITY'S INTERNAL CONTROL STRUCTURE TO AN AUDIT

The auditor's responsibility regarding a client's internal control structure is formalized in the second standard of field work, stated in paragraph 1 of Statement on Auditing Standards No. 55, *Consideration of the Internal Control Structure in a Financial Statement Audit* (AU Section 319), as follows:

> A sufficient understanding of the internal control structure is to be obtained to plan the audit and to determine the nature, timing, and extent of tests to be performed.

In addition, as discussed in Chapter 6, the auditor assesses control risk to determine the acceptable level of detection risk with respect to financial statement assertions related to account balances. (Those assertions are described in Chapter 5.) For some assertions, the auditor will assess control risk at the maximum level, but is often able to assess it at below the maximum by performing tests that provide evidence that the control structure is designed and operating effectively. The auditor can then limit the substantive tests applied to account balances for those assertions. For example, if the auditor is satisfied, based on the results of tests performed in assessing control risk related to revenue, that control procedures applied to sales transactions are adequate to ensure that all authorized shipments of products, and only authorized shipments, are accurately billed and recorded, the auditor can reduce the substantive tests related to the completeness, accuracy, and existence of sales and the related charges to accounts receivable.

An entity establishes internal control structure policies and procedures for a variety of reasons, only some of which may be relevant to an audit of its financial statements. In general, the policies and procedures that are relevant to an audit concern the entity's ability to record, process, summarize, and report financial information consistent with the assertions embodied in the financial statements. Other policies and procedures, however, may also be relevant to an audit if they are related to information the auditor uses in performing auditing procedures, even though the information itself is not part of the financial statements. An example might be policies and procedures related to production statistics that are used by the auditor in certain analytical procedures.

Still other control structure policies and procedures are not relevant to an audit of financial statements, but relate to the effectiveness and efficiency of certain management decision-making processes. Although auditors have no responsibility to do so, they often report deficiencies in such policies and procedures as a client service, when they become aware of them in the course of an audit. For example, an auditor who noticed that the monthly sales analysis used by management was prepared from an ancillary system that did not include all adjustments made in the general ledger might suggest that the client reexamine how the sales analysis is prepared.

AN OVERVIEW OF THE CONTROL STRUCTURE

Internal control structure policies and procedures can generally be classified into three elements—the control environment, the accounting system, and control procedures.[1] Whether individual control structure policies and procedures are relevant to an audit is determined not by what category they fall in, but by whether they affect, directly or indirectly, financial statement assertions or the auditor's ability to form judgments about those assertions.

The *control environment* comprises the attitudes, abilities, awareness, and actions of an enterprise's personnel, especially its management, as they affect the overall operation and control of the business. In the words of the National Commission on Fraudulent Financial Reporting (Treadway Commission), it is the "tone at the top." The control environment represents the collective effect of various factors (described in detail later) on the effectiveness of specific control structure policies and procedures. Management's actions in enforcing the company's code of conduct, for example, would be one aspect of the control environment.

The *accounting system* consists of the procedures established to identify, assemble, classify, analyze, and record an entity's transactions, as well as the documents produced as a result of those procedures. These procedures and documents help management operate the business effectively and enable it to prepare proper financial statements. For example, the way in which a purchase

[1]In this book, the term "internal control *structure policies and procedures*" or "control *structure policies and procedures*" will be used to denote the totality of an entity's control structure. In contrast, policies and procedures that constitute the third element of the control structure will be referred to as "control *procedures*."

transaction is recorded and posted to ledger accounts is part of the accounting system.

Control procedures are the policies and procedures, in addition to those that are part of the control environment and accounting system, that have been established to provide reasonable assurance that the entity's objectives regarding the processing of transactions, the preservation of related data on files, and the safeguarding (or protection) of assets will be achieved. While control procedures are conceptually separate from the control environment and accounting system, they may at times be integrated into various components of the latter two elements. For example, recording a sale of merchandise based on a prenumbered invoice is a procedure that is part of the accounting system. Accounting for the numerical sequence of the invoices is a control procedure to ensure that all items billed to customers have been recorded.

The Concept of "Reasonable Assurance"

Auditors have long recognized the inherent limitations on the effectiveness of an internal control structure. SAS No. 55 notes the following factors that may reduce or eliminate the effectiveness of the internal control structure:

> Misunderstanding of instructions, mistakes of judgment, personal carelessness, distraction, or fatigue on the part of the person responsible for performing a control procedure.
>
> Collusion among individuals, circumventing control procedures whose effectiveness depends on segregation of duties.
>
> Management override of certain policies or procedures.

In view of these as well as cost limitations, an internal control structure can provide reasonable, but not absolute, assurance that its objectives will be accomplished. This is recognized by SAS No. 55, the Foreign Corrupt Practices Act of 1977 (the Act), and sound financial management. Management will always have to make economic judgments about relative benefits and costs. SAS No. 55 expresses it in this way.

> The concept of reasonable assurance recognizes that the cost of an entity's internal control structure should not exceed the benefits that are expected to be derived. Although the cost-benefit relationship is a primary criterion that should be considered in designing an internal control structure, the precise measurement of costs and benefits usually is not possible. Accordingly, management makes both quantitative and qualitative estimates and judgments in evaluating the cost-benefit relationship. (AU Section 319.14)

TRANSACTION CYCLES

The approach to the internal control structure described in this book views business activities in terms of "cycles" into which related transactions can be conveniently grouped and for which specific policies and procedures are established by an entity's management.[2]

Each cycle comprises several transaction classes that vary with the operations of a particular business. For example, sales of goods and services, cash receipts, and customer returns may be three distinct transaction classes making up the revenue cycle. Further, each class of transactions may have two or more subclasses; for instance, sales of goods and services may be subdivided into cash sales and credit sales, or into foreign sales and domestic sales. Transaction classes and subclasses are distinguished from each other primarily by differences in the control structure policies and procedures applied to them.

Three major transaction cycles are identified in this book and discussed in detail in Chapters 12 through 14. They are the revenue, buying, and production cycles, and may be described as follows[3]:

> *Revenue Cycle*—Transactions relating to revenue generating and collecting, and related control structure policies and procedures applied to such activities as recording sales orders, shipping, and cash collection.
>
> *Buying Cycle*—Transactions relating to purchases and payments, and related control structure policies and procedures applied to such activities as ordering and receiving purchases, payroll functions, and cash disbursements.
>
> *Production Cycle*—Transactions relating to producing goods or services, and related control structure policies and procedures applied to such activities as maintaining inventory balances, inventory transfers, and charges to production for labor and overhead.

The essence of the cycle concept is its focus on whether appropriate control structure policies and procedures are applied to each class of transactions as they flow through the processing system. The auditor considers each transaction class or subclass to determine whether adequate control structure policies and procedures have been designed and are operating effectively to achieve their intended objectives.

[2]The FASB defines a "transaction" as "an external event involving transfer of something of value . . . between two (or more) entities" (Statement of Financial Accounting Concepts No. 3, para. 77). The term is used more broadly in this book to include all events and circumstances that require accounting recognition. In the context of computerized systems, the term is used even more broadly to encompass any change to the computerized records.

[3]Other transaction cycles—for example, determining, recording, and paying income taxes—may be identified, if the client has created specific control structure policies and procedures unique to classes of transactions.

CONTROL OBJECTIVES

Control structure policies and procedures that are relevant to an audit are established to meet specific objectives related to

- Processing transactions,
- Preserving the integrity of files on which those transactions and related data are stored, and
- Protecting assets.

Processing Transactions

Five control objectives relate to transaction processing. They are referred to as

Completeness of input—that all transactions that occurred are initially entered into the accounting records and accepted for processing.

Accuracy of input—that transactions are initially recorded at the correct amount, in the appropriate account, and on a timely basis.

Authorization of transactions—that all recorded transactions represent economic events that actually occurred and relate to the organization, and were approved by designated personnel.

Completeness of updating—that the data files and the records and reports generated at each stage of processing reflect all transactions that have occurred.

Accuracy of updating—that transactions are accurately recorded at each stage of their processing.

Maintaining Files

The five objectives outlined above also apply to storing recorded accounting data on files.[4] For ease of reference, in discussing files the above five control objectives have been grouped together and designated as

File control objective—that the transactions and related data contained on a file continue to be complete, accurate, and authorized until they are affected by subsequent transactions that are similarly complete, accurate, and authorized.

[4]A file is an accumulation of transactions or other data and may be in the form of a computerized file or a manual journal or ledger.

Protecting Assets

An additional control objective relates to the safeguarding of assets and is referred to as

> *Asset protection*—that access to assets and to the documents that control their movement and the records of their existence is suitably restricted to authorized personnel.

Conceptually, the seven control objectives fit every enterprise and apply to all transactions into which it enters (and the related files and assets), regardless of the specific control structure policies and procedures established to achieve them. For purposes of this chapter, however, the control objectives will be considered only as they apply to major classes and subclasses of transactions, such as sales, purchases, cash receipts, and cash disbursements. Those are generally the high-volume transactions within transaction cycles; in addition, certain entities may enter into other high-volume transactions, depending on the nature of their business.

In considering how the control objectives apply to classes or subclasses of transactions, the auditor formulates control objectives specific to each class or subclass of transactions. For example, Figure 7.1 identifies the specific control objectives for credit sales transactions processed by computer in the revenue cycle.

Two pervasive aspects of the control structure facilitate achieving the control objectives, namely,

- Arrangements to segregate duties so that the same person is not responsible for both accounting or control procedures for a particular transaction and the safeguarding of related assets.
- Arrangements to ensure that employees are adequately supervised.

ELEMENTS OF THE INTERNAL CONTROL STRUCTURE—A CLOSER LOOK

The three elements of the internal control structure and their relevance to an audit are discussed in the following sections. Although all three elements contribute to the achievement of the control objectives, those objectives are generally met more directly by the accounting system and control procedures than by the control environment.

Control Environment

An enterprise's management can foster an environment that encourages maintaining an effective accounting system and control procedures. Such a control

Figure 7.1 Control Objectives for Credit Sales Transactions

Control Objective	*Specific Control Objective for Credit Sales Transactions in a Computerized Accounting System*
Completeness of input	All credit sales transactions are input and accepted for processing.
Accuracy of input	Sales are correctly recorded as to amounts, quantities, dates, and customers in the proper period; are accurately converted into computer-readable form; and are accurately input to the computer.
Authorization of transactions	All recorded sales transactions represent actual shipments of goods or rendering of services to nonfictitious customers of the entity and were approved by responsible personnel.
Completeness of updating	The sales and accounts receivable data files are updated by all sales transaction data input and accepted for processing.
Accuracy of updating	The sales and accounts receivable data files are accurately updated by the data input.
File control	The integrity of both individual accounts receivable in the subsidiary ledger and the general ledger control account, after sales transactions have been accumulated in them, is preserved.
Asset protection	Only authorized personnel have access to accounts receivable records or data stored on files.

environment can have a "significant impact on the selection and effectiveness of a company's . . . control procedures and techniques"[5] and, in accordance with SAS No. 55, is required to be considered in planning an audit engagement.

Knowledge about the control environment enables the auditor to determine (1) whether it appears to be conducive to maintaining an effective accounting system and control procedures, and (2) whether it minimizes the incentives and opportunities for management to deliberately distort the financial statements.

Various factors that affect an enterprise's control environment can have a pervasive effect on the management assertions underlying the financial statements. These factors typically include

1. Management's philosophy and operating style.
2. The organizational structure of the entity.

[5]*Report of the Special Advisory Committee on Internal Accounting Control* (New York: American Institute of Certified Public Accountants, 1979), p. 12.

3. The composition and activities of the board of directors and its committees, particularly the audit committee.
4. Methods of assigning authority and responsibility.
5. The control methods used by management for monitoring and following up on performance, including an internal audit function.
6. The personnel policies and practices of the entity.
7. Various external influences that affect an entity's operations and practices.

The following paragraphs discuss each of these factors and indicate their relevance to the audit.

Management's Philosophy and Operating Style. Management's philosophy and operating style are expressed through its attitudes toward a broad range of matters, including taking business risks, reporting financial information, adhering to an appropriate code of conduct, and achieving financial or operating goals. In addition, management's integrity, which has a pervasive influence on the control environment, is an integral part of its philosophy and operating style. If management is dominated by one or a few individuals, their philosophy and operating style are likely to have a particularly significant influence on the control environment.

Management's attitude about adhering to standards of ethical behavior is reflected in its establishment and enforcement of a formal or informal code of conduct. By demonstrating its own compliance with the code, management sets an example for employees to follow. Management further communicates its expectations by the way it monitors employees' behavior and reacts to violations of the code.

Direct indications of management's philosophy and operating style can often be found in how candidly management discusses matters with the auditor, whether management has previously tried to materially misstate financial information, and whether there are frequent disputes over the application of accounting principles. Management's philosophy and operating style are indirectly reflected in events such as frequent turnover of operating management personnel, which may result from top management's overemphasis on unreasonable operating or financial goals, possibly through tying a significant portion of operating management's compensation to meeting those goals. This type of pressure to meet unreasonable expectations may also encourage management to intentionally misstate financial information.

The attitudes and attributes of management that characterize its philosophy and operating style have a significant impact on both the entity's ability to maintain an effective accounting system and control procedures, and the likelihood of attempts by management to deliberately distort the financial statements. Accordingly, the auditor needs to identify those attitudes and attributes and develop an understanding of them. Because they are subjective, it may take more judgment and experience on the part of the auditor to understand them than any of the other factors.

Organizational Structure. All business entities have an organizational structure within which their operations are planned, executed, controlled, and monitored. Defining key areas of responsibility and establishing appropriate lines of reporting are significant aspects of the organizational structure. For example, the director of internal audit should report to a higher level than the individuals responsible for the areas under audit. Without the appropriate line of reporting, the internal audit department's work, including recommendations for corrective action, may lack objectivity.

The appropriateness of an entity's organizational structure, for example, whether it is centralized or decentralized, depends, in part, on the size and nature of the entity. A highly structured arrangement, including formal documentation of reporting lines and responsibilities, may be appropriate for a larger entity, but could impede the necessary flow of information and thus be inappropriate in a small entity, such as an owner-operated business. The auditor should judge the effectiveness of the entity's organizational structure in light of the size and nature of the entity.

Composition and Activities of the Board of Directors and Committees. The effectiveness of the board of directors and committees, especially the audit committee, is an important factor in the control environment. The more effective the board and audit committee are in overseeing the entity's policies and practices, the less likely management is to have the opportunity to misappropriate resources, involve the entity in illegal acts, subject the entity or its assets to inordinate risk, or materially misstate financial information. The effectiveness of the board of directors and audit committee is evidenced by whether board members are independent from management, how frequently the board and the audit committee hold meetings, and how well they analyze relevant accounting and financial information. In addition, the presence of an audit committee that fosters a direct line of communication between the board and the external and internal auditors is a further indication that the board of directors is monitoring management appropriately.

The auditor should consider how effectively the board of directors appears to be overseeing the entity's accounting and financial reporting policies and practices. If the board does not exercise adequate oversight, management may have greater opportunity to override control structure policies and procedures, and thereby render them ineffective. An active and involved audit committee of independent directors, in particular, is often a good indication that management is effectively monitored.

Assigning Authority and Responsibility. To ensure that the activities of the business are properly carried out, individuals within the organization must have an adequate understanding of their authority and responsibilities. Adequately communicating expectations to personnel and monitoring their achievement help to ensure that the business will be run properly. Ways of doing this in large entities include written codes of conduct, job descriptions, policy bulletins, and operating manuals. In smaller entities, codes of conduct may be implicit in the operating style of the owner-manager. Whether disseminated formally or informally, policies governing the delegation of authority, responsibilities, and reporting relationships must be effectively communicated to employees. As discussed earlier, management's attitude about adhering to these policies is an important aspect of its philosophy and operating style.

Considering whether the appropriate methods are used to assign and communicate authority and responsibilities, including ethical responsibilities, will help the auditor judge whether personnel understand their responsibilities and therefore can be expected to carry them out properly. If management does not effectively communicate its expectations, control structure policies and procedures may not be complied with.

Control Methods Used by Management. Management uses various methods to monitor the entity's activities, including the performance of individuals in authority and the systems used to process and report information. These methods include establishing an internal audit function that evaluates and reports on the effectiveness of other control structure policies and procedures. Management also exercises control by comparing actual financial and operating results with benchmarks or predetermined expectations and investigating variances. For this aspect of the control environment to be effective, management must also follow up on findings and implement corrective action where needed. Management's follow-up includes identifying the specific activities and individuals affected by the matter in question.

Understanding the process by which management institutes systems for developing and reporting performance and financial information, and reviews the resulting reports, helps the auditor judge whether management is likely to become aware of material misstatements in financial information. In particular, management's comparison of financial data, such as an aged accounts receivable listing, with benchmarks, goals, or expectations based on knowledge of the business may provide the auditor with evidence of how reliable the financial information is. The auditor's identification of those key management reports may also be useful in designing audit tests.

Personnel Policies and Practices. To operate effectively, the entity needs appropriate policies and procedures to hire, train, supervise, and evaluate employees to ensure that they have sufficient knowledge and experience to carry out their assigned responsibilities. Further, there must be a sufficient number of employees, and the employees must have adequate equipment. The entity's personnel policies and practices should be directed toward achieving those goals. For example, the proper functioning of computer operations and processing depends on EDP personnel with appropriate skills and on adequate computer equipment to meet the entity's processing needs.

If the auditor concludes that the entity's personnel policies and practices appear to be adequate, the personnel who operate the accounting system and apply control procedures are likely to be competent. That, in turn, reduces the likelihood that financial information will contain misstatements.

External Influences. Outside parties, while generally not subject to management's control, may have an influence on the entity. Management may react to such external influences with a heightened awareness of the need to monitor and report certain entity operations, or by deciding to establish specific control structure policies or procedures. For example, the Securities and Exchange Commission's requirements for quarterly securities counts by broker-dealers may focus management's attention more closely on control procedures relating to securities.

Knowing management is focusing special attention on certain aspects of operations can help the auditor determine what areas are most likely to have effective control structure policies and procedures. On the other hand, knowing the entity is subject to scrutiny by regulatory agencies may cause the auditor to seek additional evidence that relevant control structure policies and procedures are effective.

After considering the factors that contribute to the control environment, the auditor should be able to reach an overall conclusion about whether the environment is conducive to maintaining an effective accounting system and control procedures, and how much it reduces the incentives and opportunities for intentional distortion of the financial statements by management. If the auditor concludes that the control environment is favorable, there is a lower risk that control structure policies and procedures will be overridden or neglected and that misstatements may occur. That conclusion helps the auditor determine the nature, timing, and extent of other auditing procedures. In addition, knowledge about the control environment provides the auditor with certain information that can be helpful in developing the audit testing plan, for example, significant reports and procedures that management uses to control the business.

Accounting System

All active businesses enter into transactions and use resources, and have some form of accounting system consisting of a series of procedures to gather data and to process and record transactions. Such procedures may be performed manually, for example, the manual recording of goods received or the manual calculation of invoices. Accounting procedures may also be performed by computer, for example, the automatic generation of checks to pay suppliers or the computerized preparation of invoices. These computerized accounting procedures are referred to as *programmed accounting procedures*. A computerized system normally comprises a series of both manual and computerized procedures that record transactions from their inception to their entry in the general ledger.

An effective accounting system includes appropriate methods and records to

1. Identify and record all authorized transactions.
2. Describe the transaction on a timely basis, in sufficient detail to classify it properly for financial reporting.
3. Measure the value of the transaction so that its monetary value can be recorded in the financial statements.
4. Determine when the transaction occurred, to ensure that it is recorded in the proper accounting period.
5. Present the transaction and related disclosures properly in the financial statements.

The documents produced by the accounting system provide third parties, management, and employees with information about the processing and recording of transactions. These documents, for example, checks, bills of lading, and accounts receivable aging schedules, are often subject to scrutiny by those users, who may detect errors in the information resulting from the failure of accounting procedures or related control procedures to operate effectively.

Two principal types of data are used by the accounting system: *standing data* (also called *master file data*) and *transaction data*. Standing data is data of a permanent or semipermanent nature that is used repeatedly during processing. Examples are rates of pay used to calculate salaries, and customer credit limits used to decide whether to accept customer orders. Transaction data relates to individual transactions, for example, the number of hours an individual employee worked in a particular week, which is used to calculate that person's salary. Errors in standing data are likely to be of greater significance than errors in transaction data, because errors in standing data will affect many transactions until they are corrected. This is particularly true of computerized systems in which standing data is usually reviewed only when originally set up on files and not each time it is used.

Conceptually, the accounting system is separate from the control procedures that constitute the third element of the control structure. However, it is generally not practical to separate the contribution of the accounting system toward achieving the control objectives from that of the control procedures that are applied to the transactions that flow through the accounting system. That is because the appropriateness of control procedures depends on the attributes of the accounting system, such as the means of processing, volume of transactions, level of sophistication, and so forth. A simple manual accounting system and a sophisticated computerized one may both contribute toward meeting the control objectives, if the control procedures applied to transactions processed by each system are appropriate to that system.

For example, a manual accounting system for processing sales invoices may contribute toward meeting the completeness control objective for sales and accounts receivable if all invoices and shipping documents are prenumbered and the numerical sequence is accounted for; missing or unmatched items are investigated and followed up by persons independent of the shipping and invoicing functions; and supervisory personnel review and approve the performance of the above procedures. For a sophisticated computerized system, appropriate control procedures would generally include computer matching of shipping orders to an outstanding order file and sales transaction file, the generation of an exception report by the computer, and control procedures applied to ensure program and data file security, in addition to follow-up and supervision by responsible personnel. The appropriateness of the control procedures, in each instance, is determined by the attributes of the accounting system.

Control Procedures

In contrast to the policies and procedures that are part of the control environment and accounting system, which relate to all relevant transactions an entity enters into, control procedures are generally established only for high-volume or high-risk classes of transactions. The design of control procedures is influenced by the size, complexity, and nature of the business as well as the nature of the entity's control environment and accounting system, including the method of data processing. For example, for a large entity with a complex data processing environment, it is usually necessary to establish formal approved vendor or customer lists, credit policies, and program and data file security control procedures. For a small entity with a relatively simple data processing environment, such control procedures may not always be considered necessary to meet the control objectives.

Entities meet the control objectives by designing and applying control procedures at various organizational and data processing levels. Some control procedures are applied directly to transactions, files, data, records, and assets. The effectiveness of those control procedures is enhanced if they are routinely overseen or reviewed and if functions are assigned in ways that help protect assets and prevent or detect misstatements in the accounts. In computerized environments, there are control procedures, commonly called general control procedures, that do not relate to specific transactions or files but have a pervasive effect on an entire transaction cycle or more than one cycle, or on the entity as a whole. General control procedures, which are increasingly being referred to by the more descriptive term "information technology control procedures," are discussed in detail in Chapter 11.

As discussed in SAS No. 55, control procedures fall into several broad categories, including, but not limited to

- Proper authorization of transactions and activities.
- Segregation of duties so that a person's opportunity to both perpetrate

and conceal errors or irregularities in the normal course of his or her duties is reduced—for example, assigning the responsibilities for authorizing transactions, recording transactions, and safeguarding assets to different people.

- Design and use of adequate documents and records to help ensure the proper recording of transactions and events, such as monitoring the use of prenumbered shipping documents.
- Adequate safeguards over access to and use of assets and records, such as secured facilities and authorization for access to computer programs and data files.
- Independent (including supervisory) reviews of performance and of the valuation of recorded amounts, such as clerical checks, reconciliations, comparison of assets with recorded amounts, control procedures performed by a computer, management review of reports that summarize the detail of account balances (e.g., an aged trial balance of accounts receivable), and user review of computer-generated reports.

In noncomputerized environments, all control procedures are, of course, performed manually. In computerized environments, certain control procedures are carried out by computer programs. These control procedures are referred to as *programmed control procedures*; an example is the computer matching of purchase invoices with goods received records held on file. To be effective, control procedures must cover the entire processing system from the initial recording of transactions to their ultimate recording and storage in manual ledgers or computer files. In a computerized environment, this requires a combination of programmed control procedures that generate reports, and manual operations that are applied to those reports. For example, before a vendor's invoice is paid on its due date, a computer program may match all open invoices due on that date with the file of open receiving reports. If there is a match, the computer removes both the invoices and the receiving reports from their respective files, puts them into a paid invoice file, and prints out the vendor's check. If there is no match, either because there is no receiving report or because the data on the receiving report differs from the data on the invoice, the computer does not print out the check but instead prints out an ''exception report'' of invoices due for which no receiving report exists or for which the data on the two documents does not agree. An accounting supervisor reviews and ''clears'' the exception report by determining that, in fact, the goods have not been received and no receiving report should have been created, or that the data does not otherwise agree and the vendor should not be paid. The computerized matching and the generation of the exception report are programmed control procedures; the review and clearing of the exception report is a manual control procedure. Both operations are necessary for the control objective to be achieved—in this case, that all payments to vendors are authorized.

In computerized systems, computer programs can create certain transactions without specific manual intervention. Examples of computer-generated transactions include

- Automatic posting of standard journal entries during month-end processing.
- Automatic reversal of monthly accrual or prepaid accounts in a subsequent month.
- Automatic payment of recurring operating expenditures (e.g., rents, royalties, etc.).

From a control perspective, the stored (i.e., standing) data that processes those transactions should be complete, accurate, and authorized, and the parameters, conditions, and programs used to initiate the transactions should be appropriately set up and maintained.

As noted earlier, entities design and implement control procedures to ensure that all transactions that actually occurred are authorized and are recorded completely and accurately, that errors in execution or recording are detected as soon as possible (regardless of whether the error is the processing of an unauthorized transaction, the failure to process an authorized one, or the failure to process it accurately), that the integrity of recorded accounting data is preserved on computer files and in ledgers, and that access to assets and related records is restricted. That is, the control procedures ensure that the control objectives of completeness, accuracy, authorization, file control, and asset protection are achieved and reliable financial information is thereby generated. The following paragraphs discuss different ways of achieving those objectives.

Completeness. *Completeness-of-input* control procedures in a computerized environment are designed to ensure that all transactions are initially input and accepted for processing. The initial recording of transactions frequently involves manual procedures performed before transactions are entered into the computer, although in many on-line systems, transactions are input at terminals as they occur, with no prior manual recording. In a manual system, control procedures are designed to ensure that all transactions that occur are entered on a control document (e.g., a receiving report or shipping advice) and then recorded. Without adequate completeness control procedures, there is a possibility that documents may be lost or misplaced, and this could result in a failure to record transactions that occurred. Regardless of the means of processing, control procedures should be established for correcting and resubmitting rejected items. Examples of control procedures designed to ensure completeness are described below.

- *Numbering all transactions as soon as they originate (or, preferably, prenumbering them) and then accounting for all the transactions after they have been processed.* Numbering documents is an accounting procedure; the control procedure is the act of reviewing to see that all numbered documents complete the expected processing. In a computer-based system, a technique known as a computer sequence check can be used to have the computer ascertain that the sequence of serially numbered documents is maintained and to report missing or duplicate numbers for manual investigation. The possibility of purposeful or accidental errors in the numbering process is reduced if the numerical sequence is printed in advance on the forms. If the risk of error or misuse is not considered significant, the numbering is often originated simultaneously with the document.

- *Determining that all data is processed by using "control totals."* This can be done in a computerized system by batching source documents and controlling batch totals, or in a manual system by totaling the critical numbers for a batch of transactions before and after processing; the assumption is that the processing is correct if the two totals agree. There is, of course, a possibility of one error exactly offsetting another error or omission, but the possibility is slight. Control totals do not provide control in themselves; they provide information for exercising control. The control procedure is comparing two totals and searching out and correcting errors that caused differences. Control totals appear in many forms. The double-entry system provides control totals in the sense that the totals of the debits must always equal the totals of the credits, both in individual entries and in the accounts as a whole.
- *Matching data from different sources.* Examples are computer matching of transactions input to other data within the system (such as matching the receipt of goods to the open purchase order file), and periodic reviews, either manual or by computer, of unmatched documents (such as receiving reports or vendors' invoices) and the investigation of long-outstanding items to ascertain that a document has not been lost in the processing.
- *Determining that all transactions are entered in a register.* For example, in a manual system, all chargeable service hours may be recorded in a service register that is reconciled to the hours that customers are billed for.
- *One-for-one comparison of input with retained source documents.* This technique is often used for standing data in a computerized system, because of the limited volume of changes and the importance of the data. An example is comparing changes in wage rates used to calculate employees' salaries with an approved listing of wage rate changes.

Completeness control procedures are also needed to ensure that information is properly summarized and financial reports are properly prepared for both internal and external purposes. Such control procedures are particularly important if general ledger entries come from sources other than books of original entry. For example, it is relatively easy to ascertain the completeness of postings to the general ledger for sales transactions if the postings are made directly from the summarized totals in the sales journal. A simple review to ensure that there are 12 monthly postings in the general ledger may suffice. If, however, general ledger entries arise from other sources as well, additional control procedures may be needed to ensure that all transactions are summarized and posted. Using standard journal entry numbers, with reviews to determine that all appropriate standard journal entries were made, may facilitate achieving this control objective.

Control procedures that relate to *completeness of updating* in computerized systems are designed to ensure that all transaction data input and accepted for processing updates the appropriate data file. In some cases the completeness-of-input control procedures might also control completeness of updating. Examples are a one-for-one comparison carried out on a report produced after updating or, where updating takes place at the same time as input, a sequence check carried out on an updated file. More commonly, some form of control total is used to ensure completeness of updating. This may include manual batch totals reconciled to updated file totals, or computer-generated totals and control records that report out-of-balance situations. Completeness of updating of computer-generated data should also be controlled, including calculations and summarizations of transaction data that are carried out by programmed accounting procedures as the data is processed. Examples are programmed accounting procedures that calculate sales invoices from a transaction file of goods shipped and that summarize invoices for posting to the accounts receivable control account.

Accuracy. Control procedures are necessary to ensure that each transaction is recorded at the correct amount, in the right account, and on a timely basis.  Accuracy of amount and account is most frequently achieved by establishing control procedures to review calculations, extensions, additions, and account classifications. Such reviews might be performed and evidenced by the performer's initialing sales invoices, credit memoranda, or payroll summaries. In manual systems, where there is a possibility of random error in processing transactions, occasionally an additional "double check" is made by another individual who repeats the calculations, extensions, and additions, and reviews the account classifications.

In a computerized environment, *accuracy-of-input* controls are designed to ensure that data is accurately recorded and accurately input to the computer. Although the control procedures are usually applied mainly to key financial data that directly affects balances in the financial statements, reference data such as customer number or invoice date may also be subject to control procedures.

Control procedures to ensure that transactions are recorded on a timely basis are also essential to achieve the accuracy objective. This requires procedures to establish what date a transaction took place. (Those procedures also help to ensure a proper "cutoff," that is, that transactions are recorded and reported in the proper accounting period.) As an example, goods received are inspected and recorded at the time of their receipt. Usually the receiving records are matched to related vendors' invoices as part of a subsequent control procedure to ensure the timely recording of transactions.

Various procedures for processing transactions through the accounting system may generate "exception reports" that are used by management for operational purposes. These reports may also provide evidence that certain types of errors are absent. For example, before cash receipts from customers are credited to their accounts, they may be matched to specific sales charged to the customers' accounts and an exception report of unmatched receipts may be generated. The purpose of the match and the exception report is to ensure that the full amount of specific invoices is collected. The matching of receipts to sales on the accounts receivable file and the follow-up of the exception report, however, also provide evidence of the accuracy and genuineness of the sales transactions. Furthermore, as noted earlier, management's review and follow-up of exception reports is itself an important aspect of an effective control structure.

Certain techniques used to ensure completeness of input may also ensure accuracy of input of some types of data. Examples are one-for-one comparison, establishing batch totals for certain data, and computer matching of data. Specific techniques to achieve accuracy usually include a wide range of edit checks, many of which may be carried out directly at terminals as transactions are input. These edit checks depend on the operation of programmed control procedures, for example, matching a customer number input at a terminal to the customer master file, followed by the system displaying the customer name on the screen for visual checking.

Control procedures that relate to *accuracy of updating* in a computerized environment are designed to ensure that the appropriate files are accurately updated by the data input. Accuracy of the most significant data, for example, monetary amount and date for open accounts receivable balances, is often ensured by control procedures used for completeness of updating. Except for the most significant data, accuracy of updating is often not specifically controlled, and the client relies on the effective operation of relevant programmed procedures.

Authorization. Recorded transactions can be controlled in various ways to ensure that they represent economic events that actually occurred. The most elementary control procedure to do this consists of requiring transactions to be approved by persons having the authority to do so, as specified by the entity's established policies and procedures. In more sophisticated systems, control procedures to ensure authorization are built into the system so that transactions are automatically tested against predetermined expectations; exceptions must then be reviewed by someone who is authorized to approve them. Control procedures to ensure that fictitious transactions are not recorded include segregating responsibilities for processing transactions (such as credit sales) from responsibilities for corresponding with other parties to the transaction (such as mailing monthly statements and opening customer correspondence).

Typical authorization techniques include approval by a responsible official, exception reporting (such as reporting employees working more than a given number of hours in a week, with a subsequent review by a responsible official), computer matching to authorized standing or transaction data (for example, matching customers' orders to authorized credit limits or matching goods received to authorized orders), and procedures that restrict access to programs and data files to authorized users. A responsible official can give approval online by inputting an appropriate password and authorization code at a terminal. Except for manual authorization, the effectiveness of the above techniques is likely to depend on the operation of programmed control procedures and on the security procedures applied to files.

Some authorization control procedures are designed to ensure that only transactions that actually occurred are recorded, and that no transactions are recorded more than once. For example,

- Accounting procedures are normally established to record goods received on receiving reports, and goods shipped on shipping reports. Control procedures designed to ensure the authorization of these transactions include inspecting the related goods to determine that their description, condition, and quantities are correct and comparing that information with data on sales and vendors' invoices. (Any significant discrepancies noted must also be investigated and resolved if these control procedures are to be effective.)
- Canceling the voucher and related documents supporting a purchase transaction at the time of payment prevents their being recorded a second time and being reused to support a duplicate payment or a payment for a nonexistent purchase.

Other authorization control procedures are designed to ensure that individual transactions are approved by responsible personnel in accordance with established guidelines. Such authorization can be general or specific. A general authorization may take the form of giving a department or function permission to enter into transactions against some budgeted amount. Budget approval for a capital expenditure, for example, in effect serves as authorization for expenditures up to the budgeted amount. Another example, from the retail industry, is the "open to buy" concept in which a buyer is authorized to buy merchandise up to a specified amount. A specific authorization, on the other hand, would grant permission to a person to enter into a specific transaction, for example, to buy a specific amount of raw material needed to produce a made-to-order item.

Control procedures to ensure the authorization of transactions are increasingly being automated by specifying in advance the conditions under which a transaction will be automatically authorized and executed. For example, a production order can be automatically authorized when the on-hand amount of an inventory item falls to a predetermined point and needs replenishing. Even in nonautomated systems, general authorizations can be used to accomplish the same objective.

File Control. File control procedures are designed to ensure that transaction data and standing data contained on files continue to be complete, accurate, and authorized until the files are updated by subsequent transactions that are similarly complete, accurate, and authorized. Examples of techniques for ensuring the integrity of files are reconciling the accounts receivable detail ledger to the general ledger, matching cash receipts to the accounts receivable file, and reconciling an inventory count to the recorded inventory. If file control procedures are absent or ineffective, the files may be incomplete or inaccurate, or may contain unauthorized data. For example, if an entity failed to periodically reconcile subsidiary ledgers to the general ledger control account, misstatements that management would not be aware of could exist in either the control account or the detailed accounts.

In a manual accounting system, the file control objective is achieved largely by periodically reconciling subsidiary ledgers to general ledgers. In a computerized accounting system, achieving file control means ensuring the integrity of stored data on computer files, at both the file total level and the detail level. File control in a computerized system also requires procedures to ensure that transactions are processed using only the most recently updated files and that the current files can be recovered in the event of a computer failure.

Some control procedures that achieve one or more transaction processing control objectives also achieve the file control objective. For example, matching cash receipts to the accounts receivable file is performed mainly to ensure that cash receipts are accurately posted, but it also serves to ensure the integrity of the detail of unpaid balances on the accounts receivable file; that is, that all unpaid accounts receivable remain on the file and the details of individual accounts (customer name, invoice number, and dollar amount) remain accurate on the file. That matching procedure, or other similar procedures, would be likely to disclose errors in files if transaction processing was disrupted for any reason, although the errors might not be revealed on a timely basis. In a computerized environment, file control at the file total level might be ensured by the general control procedures within computer operations (as discussed in Chapter 11), especially those pertaining to recovery from processing failures and to the use of correct files.

As an illustration of how account balances could be misstated if file control procedures were not effective, assume that during the year a company disposed of some spoiled raw materials. The quantities disposed of were removed from the detailed perpetual inventory records, but the control account was inadvertently not adjusted. In this situation, an adequate transaction processing control procedure for raw material disposal was not sufficient to prevent misstatement of the inventory balance. File control procedures, such as reconciling the perpetual inventory records to the control account and investigating differences, would also have been necessary. And if the materials disposed of were not removed from either the detailed perpetual inventory records *or* the control account, neither one would properly reflect the existing assets. Physically counting the inventory, reconciling the count to the accounting records, and investigating differences would be the appropriate file control procedures.

Asset Protection. Control procedures designed to safeguard assets are based on restricting access to assets to authorized personnel. Effective asset protection depends on adequate division of duties. To prevent theft or simply well-intended activity not consistent with established policies and procedures, it is necessary to restrict access to anything that could be used to initiate or process a transaction. Asset protection is most commonly thought of in connection with negotiable assets—cash, securities, and sometimes inventory and other items easily convertible to cash or personal use. But the concept of limited access applies equally to the books and records and the means of altering them, such as unused forms, unissued checks, check signature plates, files, and ledgers.

In its simplest form, asset protection is evidenced by such things as a safe, a vault, a locked door, a storeroom with a custodian, a guarded fence, or other means of preventing unauthorized persons from gaining access to assets and records. Control procedures should also protect assets and records from physical harm such as accidental destruction, deterioration, or simply being mislaid.

In computerized systems, control procedures to limit access to data stored on files to authorized persons are especially important because assets can be moved by manipulating data (for example, transactions generating an automatic check payment), and fraud or theft can be obscured by processing unauthorized transactions. Control procedures to ensure the security of computer programs and stored data are of key importance in computerized systems where there may be potentially wide access to programs and data through terminals. Such control is normally achieved by general control procedures relating to program and data file security, as discussed further in Chapter 11.

Segregation of Duties. If the internal control structure is to be effective, there needs to be an adequate division of duties among those who perform accounting and control procedures and handle assets. Although division of duties relates to all three elements of the control structure, it is most prevalent in the performance of control procedures. It consists of assigning different people to authorize a particular class of transactions, perform control procedures when the transactions are processed, supervise those procedures, maintain the related accounting records, and handle the related assets. Such arrangements reduce the risk of error and limit opportunities to misappropriate assets or conceal other intentional misrepresentations in the financial statements. For example, to reduce the risk of error, management may establish procedures for monthly reconciliations of a control account to be reviewed and approved by someone who did not perform the reconciliations.

If two accounting procedures related to a single transaction are handled by different people, each serves as a control mechanism on the other; a further control procedure should be applied to the transaction by a third person. For example, one bookkeeper can process a day's cash receipts received through the mail, and another can post the receipts to the accounts receivable records. A third person's comparison of the total of the postings with the total receipts provides evidence that each operation was accurately performed. If the comparison of the postings total with the total receipts is not performed by a third person, there is an increased risk of misstatement in the accounting records.

Segregation of duties also serves as a deterrent to fraud or concealment of error because of the need to recruit another individual's cooperation (collusion) to conceal it. For example, separating responsibility for physically protecting assets from the related record keeping is a significant control mechanism over the fraudulent conversion of the assets. Similarly, the treasurer who signs checks should not be able to make entries in the disbursements records and thereby hide unauthorized disbursements. Control is even further enhanced if neither the treasurer nor the bookkeeper is responsible for periodically comparing cash on hand and in the bank with the cash records and taking appropriate action if there are any differences. In a computerized system, for example, personnel responsible for sensitive standing data should not be responsible for processing transaction data.

Supervision. Supervisory control procedures lower the risk that accounting and control procedures are not functioning as designed at all times, as opposed to solely in those instances observed by the auditor. Supervisory control procedures also help ensure that errors that do occur are detected on a timely basis. Supervising the manual aspects of accounting and control procedures has an obvious effect on the quality of the accounting records. With effective supervision, personnel performing accounting and control procedures can be directed to make necessary modifications when new types of transactions occur, take corrective action when errors are revealed, and follow up when deficiencies in those procedures become evident.

Many supervisory control procedures consist of specific, observable administrative routines for regularly assuring supervisors that the prescribed control procedures are operating. These routines must be documented, for example, by means of checklists; exception reports; initials evidencing review of batch controls, bank reconciliations, and vouchers; log books for review routines; and written reports.

RELEVANCE OF CONTROL OBJECTIVES TO THE ACHIEVEMENT OF AUDIT OBJECTIVES

As indicated at the beginning of this chapter, the auditor is required by generally accepted auditing standards to assess control risk, that is, to reach a conclusion about how effective the entity's control structure policies and procedures are in reducing the risk that the financial statements will contain misstatements. To whatever extent the auditor concludes that control structure policies and procedures achieve the control objectives, he or she can restrict substantive tests for the related account balances and audit objectives. This section of the chapter discusses briefly the relationship between control objectives and audit objectives. It also discusses the relevance of the control objectives to the auditor's assessment of risk.

The control objectives of completeness, accuracy, and authorization are closely related to the audit objectives of completeness, accuracy, and existence/occurrence. For example, control procedures related to the control objective of accuracy are designed to prevent or detect sales transaction processing errors that could arise because incorrect prices were used, invoices were improperly computed, or shipments were billed to the wrong customer. From the auditor's point of view, these procedures reduce the risk that sales in the income statement and accounts receivable in the balance sheet are not accurate. Clearly, if there are control procedures to ensure the accuracy of recorded transactions and related files and the auditor has tested the control procedures and found them to be effective, that reduces the amount of assurance the auditor must obtain from substantive tests to meet the audit objective of accuracy.

While the control objectives of completeness and authorization are related to the audit objectives of completeness and existence/occurrence, the relationship is more complex than it is with the accuracy objective. This is primarily because of the double-entry system, which records two aspects of every transaction. Consider sales transactions: If a sale is made and goods are shipped, but the transaction is not recorded, the control objective of completeness of transaction processing is not achieved, resulting in both sales in the income statement and accounts receivable in the balance sheet being incomplete. If, however, ineffective control procedures permit the incomplete recording of cash receipts from charge customers, but the receipts have been properly deposited, then the cash account is not complete and accounts receivable contain nonexistent receivables. In this instance, an ineffective completeness control procedure has resulted in a misstatement with respect to existence.

The same type of analysis for the authorization objective leads to the conclusion that while ineffective control procedures that permit unauthorized transactions to be recorded may lead to recording nonexistent assets (for example, a fictitious sale that generates a nonexistent account receivable), in some circumstances those procedures may result in assets or liabilities being omitted from the balance sheet (for example, removing a receivable due from an employee by recording a fictitious sales return). Delineating the relationship between control objectives and audit objectives for all classes of transactions and related accounts is not practicable, because of the immense number of possible combinations of transactions and errors that could occur. In practice, auditors determine what could go wrong in the processing of specific transactions or in their preservation on files (ineffective control procedures), determine how that could affect specific audit objectives and accounts in the financial statements, and then design and perform substantive tests to detect possible financial statement misstatements.

Control procedures to ensure completeness may have an especially significant effect on the conduct of an audit. Auditors often find it particularly difficult to obtain sufficient evidence regarding the completeness of transaction recording. Because the control objectives of accuracy and authorization are concerned mainly with *recorded* transactions and balances, the auditor can usually obtain sufficient evidence about their accuracy and existence, even if control procedures are inadequate, by performing substantive tests of those balances or of the underlying transactions, for example, examining supporting documentation and reperforming accounting procedures.

When assessing the completeness of transaction processing and the resultant accounting records, the auditor is concerned with the possibility of *unrecorded* transactions, for which there is usually no evidence. For example, if prenumbered documents are used to record transactions, the auditor can account for the numerical sequence of documents and thus obtain evidence that all transactions for which a prenumbered document was prepared have been recorded. However, this will not detect unrecorded transactions if documents were not prepared for all transactions. The auditor should therefore pay particular attention to control procedures designed to ensure that all transactions are recorded on a document, for example, a requirement that a shipping document be prepared before a storeroom clerk releases merchandise for shipment.

Authoritative auditing literature notes that "in the great majority of cases, the auditor finds it necessary to rely on evidence that is persuasive rather than convincing" (SAS No. 31, *Evidential Matter* [AU Section 326.19]). This is particularly true for evidence supporting the completeness of recording of transactions that have occurred. In most instances, persuasive evidence about completeness can be obtained, but in extreme circumstances where completeness control procedures are absent or particularly ineffective, the auditor should question the auditability of the accounting records. Not all classes of transactions of a particular enterprise may be auditable; at the extreme, the significance of unauditable classes of transactions may be so great as to make the enterprise as a whole unauditable.

As discussed earlier, the file control objective is concerned with preserving the integrity of files that contain accumulated transactions and related accounting data. Accordingly, an entity's failure to achieve the file control objective could lead to account balances that are incomplete, inaccurate, or nonexistent. For example, if an entity fails to periodically reconcile the accounts receivable subsidiary ledger to the general ledger control account, the accounts receivable balance may be missing receivables for which goods were shipped, or may include receivables that were already paid or were fictitious. This increases the amount of assurance the auditor must obtain from substantive tests to achieve the completeness, accuracy, and existence audit objectives.

Inadequate control procedures to protect assets and the documents that control their movement might allow unauthorized access to those assets and could result in unrecorded loss of assets. In that situation, assets that did not exist would continue to be recorded, thus affecting the auditor's achievement of the existence audit objective.

The absence of adequate control procedures to safeguard assets and records affects the timing and extent of substantive tests. For example, the absence of adequate control procedures to limit physical access to inventories may mean that a complete inventory count must be performed at the balance sheet date, even if other control procedures applied to the inventory records are adequate. If adequate control procedures to protect assets and records exist, the auditor may either (1) observe and make some test counts of the client's cycle counts of portions of the inventory or (2) observe a physical inventory count at an interim date and then roll forward inventory balances on the balance sheet date based on recorded activity.

The relationships between control objectives and audit objectives discussed in the preceding paragraphs are summarized in Figure 7.2. Note that several of the audit objectives discussed in Chapter 5—namely, cutoff, valuation, rights and obligations, and presentation and disclosure—are not included in that figure. That is because those objectives, with the exception of the cutoff objective, are rarely specifically addressed by an entity's control procedures. The cutoff objective is sometimes addressed, in part, by control procedures related to the completeness and accuracy of transactions occurring near the year-end. The audit objectives not addressed by control procedures (and all audit objectives for accounts that are not related to a major class of transactions) may be achieved, to varying degrees in different entities, through many of the factors that make up the control environment. For example, management's review of operating reports may provide evidence relevant to meeting the valuation objective for certain accounts.

Figure 7.2 Relationship of Control Objectives to Audit Objectives

Audit Objectives	Control Objectives: Completeness	Accuracy	Authorization	File Control	Asset Protection
Completeness	X		X	X	
Accuracy		X		X	
Existence	X		X	X	X

MANAGEMENT'S RESPONSIBILITY FOR INTERNAL ACCOUNTING CONTROL UNDER THE FOREIGN CORRUPT PRACTICES ACT

Changes in the business and legal environment and in particular the Foreign Corrupt Practices Act of 1977 (the Act) have magnified the importance of the internal control structure to management. The Act, which amended the Securities Exchange Act of 1934, has two parts: One deals with specific acts and penalties associated with certain corrupt practices; the second, with standards relating to internal accounting controls (i.e., internal control procedures).

Illegal Payments

The Act prohibits any domestic company—or its officers, directors, employees, agents, or stockholders—from paying or offering to pay a foreign official to obtain, retain, or direct business to any person. Specifically, the law prohibits payments to foreign officials, political parties, and candidates for the purpose of obtaining or retaining business by influencing any act or decision of foreign parties in their official capacity, or by inducing such foreign parties to use their influence with a foreign government to sway any act or decision of such government. This section of the Act applies to virtually all U.S. businesses, and noncompliance with its provisions, as amended in August 1988, can result in fines of up to $2 million for corporations and up to $100,000 for individuals who willfully participate in the bribery of a foreign official. Violators may also be subject to imprisonment for up to five years.

Internal Accounting Control

The section of the Act addressing internal accounting control imposes additional legal obligations on publicly held companies. Failure by such companies to maintain appropriate books and records and internal accounting controls violates the Securities Exchange Act of 1934. In addition, the 1988 amendments to the Act created criminal liability for failing to comply with the internal accounting control provisions if an individual knowingly circumvents or knowingly fails to implement a system of internal accounting controls or knowingly falsifies any book, record, or account.

Specifically, the Foreign Corrupt Practices Act establishes a legal requirement that every SEC registrant

(A) Make and keep books, records and accounts, which, in reasonable detail, accurately and fairly reflect the transactions and dispositions of the assets of the issuer; and

(B) Devise and maintain a system of internal accounting controls sufficient to provide reasonable assurances that the following four objectives are met:—

(i) transactions are executed in accordance with management's general or specific authorization;

(ii) transactions are recorded as necessary (I) to permit preparation of financial statements in conformity with generally accepted accounting principles or any other criteria applicable to such statements, and (II) to maintain accountability for assets;

(iii) access to assets is permitted only in accordance with management's general or specific authorization; and

(iv) the recorded accountability for assets is compared with the existing assets at reasonable intervals and appropriate action is taken with respect to any differences.

The requirements in (B) are compatible with the control objectives discussed earlier in this chapter. (The language dealing with internal accounting control was taken directly from the relevant authoritative auditing literature [AU Section 320] in effect when the Act was drafted. AU Section 320 was superseded by SAS No. 55.) The 1988 amendments to the Act clarified the terms "reasonable detail" and "reasonable assurances" by describing them as the level of detail and degree of assurance that would satisfy prudent officials in the conduct of their own affairs.

It is clear from the legislative history of the Act that Congress' primary intent was to prevent corrupt payments to foreign officials, and that the requirements for accurate books and records and for internal accounting controls were intended mainly to help accomplish that objective. But those requirements are considerably more far reaching, since they cover all transactions, not only those related to illegal foreign payments. The SEC has enforced these provisions of the law in connection with domestic improprieties as well as illegal foreign payments.

While the Act has necessitated more direct management involvement in designing and maintaining the internal control structure, it does not specifically affect the auditor's responsibility. The auditor's responsibility with respect to the control structure remains as prescribed by the second standard of field work in SAS No. 55. This was explicitly articulated in an AICPA interpretation dealing with illegal acts by clients, which noted that the Foreign Corrupt Practices Act created new responsibilities for *companies* subject to the Securities Exchange Act of 1934, but not for their *auditors*.

Review Questions

7-1. What is the purpose of the required "understanding of the internal control structure"?

7-2. What are the three elements of the internal control structure? What is the difference between the accounting system and control procedures?

7-3. Which of the three control structure elements contributes less directly than the other two to achieving specific control objectives?

7-4. What are the major transaction cycles into which most business activities can be grouped?

7-5. Name the objectives of control structure policies and procedures that are relevant to an audit.

7-6. Explain why an internal control structure, no matter how effective it is, cannot provide complete assurance that errors and irregularities will be prevented or detected.

7-7. What is meant by the concept of reasonable assurance with respect to the internal control structure?

7-8. Name five factors that affect an entity's control environment.

7-9. Illustrate how each of the following control objectives might be achieved: completeness, accuracy, authorization, file control.

7-10. How would the absence of effective asset protection affect an audit?

7-11. What major purposes are served by segregation of duties?

7-12. What is the major purpose of supervisory control procedures?

7-13. What are the basic requirements of the Foreign Corrupt Practices Act (FCPA) of 1977? What companies are affected by the FCPA?

7-14. What effect does the FCPA have on the independent auditor's responsibilities?

Discussion Questions

7-30. Travis Lumber Company does not prelist cash receipts before they are recorded and has other deficiencies in processing collections of trade receivables, the company's largest asset. In discussing the matter with the controller, Marie Edwards, you find she is chiefly interested in economy when she assigns duties to the 15 office personnel. She feels the main considerations are that the work should be done by people who are most familiar with it, capable of doing it, and available when it has to be done.

The controller says she has excellent control over trade receivables because receivables are pledged as security for a continually renewable bank loan and the bank sends out positive confirmation requests occasionally, based on a list of pledged receivables furnished by the company each week. You learn that the bank's internal auditor is satisfied with an acceptable response on 70 percent of the requests.

Required:

a. Explain how prelisting of cash receipts strengthens control procedures with respect to cash.

b. Discuss the advisability of Marie's approach to assigning responsibilities among employees and her reliance on the bank's internal auditor to obtain assurance regarding Travis' accounts receivable.

(AICPA adapted)

7-31. Phebe Meyers is the bookkeeper for Madison Landscaping Company and is the sole office employee. She handles all billing, cash, and payroll activities, as well as the general ledger, financial statements, and tax returns. The proprietor, Norman Thompson, knows little about accounting and trusts Ms. Meyers implicitly because she is meticulous in her clerical operations, has been functioning in her capacity for ten years, and appears well systemized (e.g., prenumbered bills, checks, etc.). Because he is quite active in the supervision of the business, Mr. Thompson always signs a substantial number of regular and payroll checks in advance so that timely disbursements can be made. Mr. Thompson intends to expand his business and his bank requires an audit as a condition for a loan.

Required:

a. Discuss the independent auditor's approach to assessing control risk in these circumstances and give some indication of how to proceed with the audit.
b. What simple changes in procedures could you suggest to improve the internal control structure?

7-32. Evaluate the effectiveness of control procedures and state possible errors or irregularities that may result from each of the following unrelated situations:

1. The same person prepares purchase orders and receiving reports.
2. The same person prepares purchase orders and approves invoices for payment.
3. The same person prepares receiving reports and approves invoices for payment.
4. Amendments to payroll standing data are not authorized in writing.
5. The petty cash custodian is prohibited from making disbursements in excess of $100, cashing checks, or making advances in excess of one-half of an employee's weekly pay.

7-33. It is your client's policy to have invoices and supporting documents accompany all checks presented for signature. The signing officer insists that the invoices and documents be marked "paid" before she will review them and sign the checks. Her objective is to preclude resubmission of the same invoices and documents in support of another check. Do you believe this procedure is effective? Explain.

7-34. In a small corporation that publishes fiction and other nontechnical books, four salespeople sell to about 1000 retail bookstores. Because of his knowledge of the bookstores, Ben Jones, the sales manager, is required to approve each order before shipment is made. In the case of delinquent accounts the sales manager decides whether to extend further credit or to grant approval for any write-offs. One bookkeeper and two billing clerks handle the accounting records. The other personnel consist of three editors and their secretaries, and one production person who contracts with printers for the manufacture of the books. Shipments are made from the printers' warehouses directly to the bookstores.

Required:

Evaluate the control procedures for granting credit and writing off delinquent accounts.

AICPA Multiple Choice Questions

These questions are taken or adapted from the Auditing part of Uniform CPA Examinations. Choose the single most appropriate answer.

7-40. Which of the following is *not* an element of an entity's internal control structure?

a. Control risk.
b. Control procedures.
c. The accounting system.
d. The control environment.

7-41. What is the independent auditor's principal reason for understanding the internal control structure?

a. To comply with generally accepted accounting principles.
b. To obtain a measure of assurance of management's efficiency.
c. To maintain a state of independence in mental attitude in all matters relating to the audit.
d. To determine the nature, timing, and extent of tests to be performed.

7-42. Which of the following would be *least* likely to suggest to an auditor that the client's management may have overridden specific control procedures?

a. Differences are always disclosed on a computer exception report.
b. Management does *not* correct control deficiencies that it knows about.
c. There have been two new controllers this year.
d. There are numerous delays in preparing timely internal financial reports.

7-43. Proper segregation of functional responsibilities in an effective internal control structure calls for separation of the functions of

a. Authorization, execution, and payment.
b. Authorization, recording, and custody.
c. Custody, execution, and reporting.
d. Authorization, payment, and recording.

7-44. Which of the following is a control structure deficiency for a company whose inventory of supplies consists of a large number of individual items?

a. Supplies of relatively little value are expensed when purchased.
b. The cycle basis is used for physical counts.
c. The storekeeper is responsible for maintenance of perpetual inventory records.
d. Perpetual inventory records are maintained only for items of significant value.

7-45. In a properly designed internal control structure, the same employee may be permitted to

a. Receive and deposit checks, and also approve write-offs of customer accounts.
b. Approve vouchers for payment, and also sign checks.
c. Reconcile the bank statements, and also receive and deposit cash.
d. Sign checks, and also cancel supporting documents.

7-46. Which of the following is an effective control procedure for cash payments?

a. Signed checks should be mailed under the supervision of the check signer.
b. Spoiled checks that have been voided should be disposed of immediately.
c. Checks should be prepared only by persons responsible for cash receipts and cash disbursements.
d. A check-signing machine with two signatures should be utilized.

7-47. For an effective internal control structure, the accounts payable department should compare the information on each vendor's invoice with the

a. Receiving report and the purchase order.
b. Receiving report and the voucher.
c. Vendor's packing slip and the purchase order.
d. Vendor's packing slip and the voucher.

7-48. For an effective internal control structure, employees maintaining the accounts receivable subsidiary ledger should *not* also approve

a. Employee overtime wages.
b. Credit granted to customers.
c. Write-offs of customer accounts.
d. Cash disbursements.

7-49. While obtaining the understanding of a small business client's internal control structure, the auditor discovered that the accounts receivable clerk approves credit memos and has access to cash. Which of the following control procedures would be most effective in offsetting this deficiency?

a. The owner reviews errors in billings to customers and postings to the subsidiary ledger.
b. The controller receives the monthly bank statement directly and reconciles the checking accounts.
c. The owner reviews credit memos after they are recorded.
d. The controller reconciles the total of the detail accounts receivable accounts to the amount shown in the ledger.

7-50. The Foreign Corrupt Practices Act requires that

a. Auditors engaged to audit the financial statements of publicly held companies report all illegal payments to the SEC.
b. Publicly held companies establish independent audit committees to monitor the effectiveness of their internal control structure.
c. U.S. firms doing business abroad report sizeable payments to non-U.S. citizens to the Justice Department.
d. Publicly held companies devise and maintain an adequate internal control structure.

Problems and Cases

7-60. In 1989, Fieldstone Company purchased over $10 million of office equipment under its "special" ordering system, with individual orders ranging from $5000 to $30,000. "Special" orders entail low-volume items that have been included in an authorized user's budget. Department heads include in their annual budget requests the types of equipment and their estimated cost. The budget, which limits the types and dollar amounts of office equipment a department can requisition, is approved at the beginning of the year by the board of directors. Department heads prepare a purchase requisition form for equipment and forward the requisition to the purchasing department. Fieldstone's "special" ordering system functions as follows:

Purchasing:

Upon receiving a purchase requisition, one of five buyers verifies that the person requesting the equipment is a department head. The buyer then selects the appropriate vendor by searching the various vendor catalogs on file. The buyer then phones the vendor, requesting a price quotation, and gives the vendor a verbal order. A prenumbered purchase order is then processed, with the original sent to the vendor, a copy to the department head, a copy to receiving, a copy to accounts payable, and a copy filed in the open requisition file. When the buyer is orally informed by the receiving department that the item has been received, the buyer transfers the purchase order from the unfilled file to the filled file. Once a month the buyer reviews the unfilled file to follow up and expedite open orders.

Receiving:

The receiving department receives a copy of the purchase order. When equipment is received, the receiving clerk stamps the purchase order with the date received, and, if applicable, in red pen prints any differences between quantity on the purchase order and quantity received. The receiving clerk forwards the stamped purchase order and equipment to the requisitioning department head and notifies the purchasing department orally.

Accounts Payable:

Upon receipt of a purchase order, the accounts payable clerk files the purchase order in the open purchase order file. When a vendor invoice is received, the invoice is matched with the applicable purchase order, and a payable is set up by debiting the equipment account of the department requesting the items. Unpaid invoices are filed by due date and, at due date, a check is prepared. The invoice and purchase order are filed by purchase order number in a paid invoice file, and then the check is forwarded to the treasurer for signature.

Treasurer:

Checks received daily from the accounts payable department are sorted into two groups: those over $10,000 and those $10,000 and less. Checks for $10,000 and less are machine-signed. The cashier maintains the key and signature plate to the check-signing machine, and maintains a record of usage of the check-signing machine. All checks over $10,000 are signed by the treasurer or the controller.

Required:

Describe the deficiencies in the control procedures relating to purchases and payments of "special" orders of Fieldstone Company for each of the following functions:

a. Purchasing.
b. Receiving.
c. Accounts payable.
d. Treasurer.

(AICPA adapted)

7-61. Flawless Instruments, Inc., is a manufacturer of high-priced precision microscopes in which the specifications of component parts are vital to the manufacturing process. Flawless buys valuable lenses and large quantities of sheet metal and screws. Screws and lenses are ordered by Flawless and are billed by the vendors on the basis of weight. The receiving clerk is responsible for documenting the quality and quantity of merchandise received.

A review of the internal control structure indicates that the following procedures are being performed:

Receiving Report:

1. Properly approved purchase orders, which are prenumbered, are filed numerically. The copy sent to the receiving clerk is an exact duplicate of the copy sent to the vendor. Receipts of merchandise are recorded on the duplicate copy by the receiving clerk.

Sheet Metal:

2. The company receives sheet metal by railroad. The railroad independently weighs the sheet metal and reports the weight and date of receipt on a bill of lading (waybill), which accompanies all deliveries. The receiving clerk only checks the weight on the waybill to the purchase order.

Screws:

3. The receiving clerk opens cartons containing screws, then inspects and weighs the contents. The weight is converted to number of units by means of conversion charts. The receiving clerk then checks the computed quantity to the purchase order.

Lenses:

4. Each lens is delivered in a separate corrugated carton. Cartons are counted as they are received by the receiving clerk and the number of cartons is checked to purchase orders.

Required:

a. Explain why the control procedures—as they apply individually to receiving reports and the receipt of sheet metal, screws, and lenses—are adequate or inadequate. *Do not discuss recommendations for improvement.*
b. What financial statement misstatements may arise because of the inadequacies in Flawless' internal control structure, and how may they occur?

(AICPA adapted)

7-62. The Longmeadow Company is engaged in manufacturing. You are to consider the control procedures for each of the activities as described and point out the existing deficiencies, if any, in them, including an explanation of the errors or irregularities that might occur in view of each deficiency and your recommendations as to changes in procedures that could be made to correct the deficiency.

1. When materials are ordered, a duplicate of the purchase order is sent to the receiving department. When the materials are received, the receiving clerk records the receipt on the copy of the order, which is then sent to the accounting department to support the entry to accounts payable and material purchases.

The materials are then taken to stores where the quantity is entered on bin records.

2. Time cards of employees are sent to a computer processing department, which prepares magnetic tapes for use in the preparation of payrolls, payroll checks, and labor cost distribution records. The payroll checks are compared with the payrolls and signed by an official of the company, who returns them to the supervisor of the processing department for distribution to employees.
3. The company has an employee bond subscription plan under which employees subscribe to bonds and pay in installments by deductions from their salaries. The cashier keeps the supply of unissued bonds in a safe, together with the records showing each employee's subscription and payments to date. The amounts of unissued bonds in the hands of the cashier and the balances due from employees are controlled on the general ledger, kept in another department. However, the employees may, if they desire, pay any remaining balance to the cashier and receive their bonds.

   When an employee makes a payment, the cashier notes the amount in the records, delivers the bond, and receives a receipt from the employee for the amount of the bond. The cashier deposits bond cash received in an employee bond bank account and submits a report showing the transaction to the general ledger department; this report is used as a basis for the necessary adjustments of the control accounts. Periodic surprise counts of bonds on hand are made by independent employees, who compare the amounts of unissued bonds and employees' unpaid balances with the control accounts.

   During the cashier's lunch hour or at other times when the cashier is required to be absent, another employee, with keys to the safe in which unissued bonds and employee bond payment records are kept, comes in and carries out the same procedures as described above.
4. A sales branch of the company has an office force consisting of the manager and one assistant. The branch has a local bank account that is used to pay branch expenses. This is in the name of "The Longmeadow Company, Special Account." Checks drawn on the account require the manager's signature or the signature of the treasurer of the company. Bank statements and canceled checks are returned by the bank to the manager, who retains them in the files after making the reconciliation. Reports of disbursements are prepared by the manager and submitted to the home office on scheduled dates.

(AICPA adapted)

7-63. The National Bronze Company, a client of your firm, has come to you with the following problem: It has three clerical employees who must perform the following functions:

1. Maintain general ledger.
2. Maintain accounts payable ledger.
3. Maintain accounts receivable ledger.
4. Prepare checks for signature.
5. Maintain disbursements journal.
6. Issue credits on returns and allowances.
7. Reconcile the bank account.
8. Handle and deposit cash receipts.

Assuming that there is no problem regarding the ability of any of the employees, the company requests that you assign these functions to the three employees in such a manner as to strengthen the internal control structure to the greatest extent possible. It may be assumed that these employees will perform no other accounting functions than the ones listed and that any accounting functions not listed will be performed by persons other than these three employees.

Required:

a. State how you would distribute these functions among the three employees. Assume that with the exception of the simple jobs of the bank reconciliation and the issuance of credits on returns and allowances, all functions require an equal amount of time.
b. List four unsatisfactory combinations of the functions.

(AICPA adapted)

7-64. For each of the following situations, indicate whether there are deficiencies in control procedures and, if so, indicate the errors or irregularities that could occur (consider each independently):

a. Sales are authorized by the sales order department without reference to the credit department.
b. Sales invoices are not reexamined for correct prices and extensions.
c. Accounts receivable write-offs are authorized by the credit department.
d. Complete purchase orders are furnished to receiving department personnel who count incoming shipments and prepare receiving reports.
e. Incoming mail is opened by the cashier, who lists checks received, makes deposits, and records cash receipts.
f. Reconciliation between the accounts receivable subsidiary ledger and the control account is performed monthly by the general ledger bookkeeper, who also posts cash receipts.
g. Monthly statements to customers are prepared and mailed by the cashier.
h. A payroll clerk prepares payroll checks, has them signed by the Comptroller, and distributes them to the foremen of each department.
i. Disbursement checks to vendors are prepared by the cashier and signed by the Comptroller, who returns them to the cashier for mailing.
j. Supporting documents (purchase order, receiving report, invoice) are not canceled at the time of disbursement.
k. Monthly bank statements are reconciled to the cash book and general ledger by the Comptroller.

7-65. The division of the following duties is meant to provide the best possible control structure for the Durable Products Company, a small wholesale store.

a. Assemble supporting documents for disbursements and prepare checks for signature.
b. Sign general disbursement checks.
c. Record checks written in the cash disbursements and payroll journals.
d. Cancel supporting documents to prevent their reuse and mail disbursement checks to suppliers.
e. Approve credit for customers.
f. Bill customers and record the invoices in the sales journal and subsidiary ledger.

g. Open the mail and prepare a prelisting of cash receipts.
h. Record cash receipts in the cash journal and subsidiary ledger.
i. Prepare daily cash deposits.
j. Deliver daily cash deposits to the bank.
k. Assemble the payroll time cards and prepare the payroll checks.
l. Sign payroll checks.
m. Post the journals to the general ledger.
n. Reconcile the accounts receivable subsidiary account with the control account.
o. Prepare monthly statements for customers by copying the subsidiary ledger account.
p. Reconcile the monthly statements from vendors with the subsidiary accounts payable account.
q. Reconcile the bank account.

Required:

You are to divide the accounting-related duties a through q among Janet Dennis, Dan Bergman, and Sarah Longman. All of the responsibilities are assumed to take about the same amount of time and must be divided equally between the two employees, Dennis and Bergman. Both employees are equally competent. Longman, who is president of the Company, is willing to perform a maximum of three of the functions, provided that no great amount of details is involved. She prefers not to sign checks.

(AICPA adapted)

7-66. Identify control structure deficiencies in the following case and suggest ways of correcting them.

The Magic Carpet Company, Ltd., is engaged in selling worldwide vacation packages. Salespeople are paid on a commission basis, selling the trips based on standard prices established by the marketing department.

Salespeople may negotiate special cut rates; however, these are subject to approval by the marketing manager, Mr. Fenimore. Special commitments obtained by the salespeople are submitted to Mr. Fenimore, who signs them to indicate his approval and then returns them to the salespeople. Specially priced commitments and regularly priced commitments are then forwarded by the salespeople to the data input department, where a clerk reviews the special commitments for the presence of Mr. Fenimore's signature and batches the input, using total trips sold as the batch control total.

The computer processes each commitment by extending the number of trips by the standard price stored on the pricing file or, in specially negotiated situations, by the price on the input document. The sales file, accounts receivable file, and a reservation file are updated and invoices produced. A report of special prices is produced by data processing and sent to the salespeople to ensure that the specially negotiated commitments were processed correctly.

7-67. The Prime Quality Processing Company buys and processes livestock for sale to supermarkets. In connection with your audit of the company's financial statements, you have prepared the following notes based on your review of procedures:

1. Each livestock buyer submits a daily report of purchases to the plant superintendent. This report shows the dates of purchase and expected delivery, the vendor,

and the number, weights, and type of livestock purchased. As shipments are received, any available plant employee counts the number of each type received and places a check mark beside this quantity on the buyer's report. When all shipments listed on the report have been received, the report is returned to the buyer.

2. Vendors' invoices, after a clerical check, are sent to the buyer for approval and returned to the accounting department. A disbursement voucher and a check for the approved amount are prepared in the accounting department. Checks are forwarded to the treasurer for signature. The treasurer's office sends signed checks directly to the buyer for delivery to the vendor.
3. Livestock carcasses are processed by lots. Each lot is assigned a number. At the end of each day a tally sheet reporting the lots processed, the number and type of animals in each lot, and the carcass weight is sent to the accounting department, where a perpetual inventory record of processed carcasses and their weights is maintained.
4. Processed carcasses are stored in a refrigerated cooler located in a small building adjacent to the employee parking lot. The cooler is locked when the plant is not open, and a company guard is on duty when the employees report for work and leave at the end of their shifts. Supermarket truck drivers wishing to pick up their orders have been instructed to contact someone in the plant if no one is in the cooler.
5. Substantial quantities of by-products are produced and stored, either in the cooler or elsewhere in the plant. By-products are initially accounted for as they are sold. At this time the sales manager prepares a two-part form; one copy serves as authorization to transfer the goods to the customer and the other becomes the basis for billing the customer.

Required:

For each of the numbered notes 1 to 5, state

a. What the specific control objective(s) should be at the stage of the operating cycle described by the note.
b. The control deficiencies in the present procedures, if any, and suggestions for improvement, if any.

(AICPA adapted)

7-68. You are auditing the Michigan branch of National Housewares, Inc. This branch has substantial annual sales, which are billed and collected locally. As a part of your audit, you find that the procedures for handling cash receipts are as follows:

Cash collections on over-the-counter sales and C.O.D. sales are received from the customer or delivery service by the cashier. On receipt of cash, the cashier stamps the sales ticket "paid" and files a copy for future reference. The only record of C.O.D. sales is a copy of the sales ticket that is given to the cashier to hold until the cash is received from the delivery service.

Mail is opened by the secretary to the credit manager, and remittances are given to the credit manager for review. The credit manager then places the remittances in a tray on the cashier's desk. At the daily deposit cutoff time, the cashier delivers the checks and cash on hand to the assistant credit manager, who prepares remittance lists, makes up the bank deposit, and takes it to the bank. The assistant credit manager also posts remittances to the accounts receivable ledger cards and verifies the cash discount allowable.

You also ascertain that the credit manager obtains approval from the executive office of National Housewares, located in New York, to write off uncollectible accounts, and that some remittances that were received on various days during the last month are in the custody of the credit manager as of the end of the fiscal year.

Required:

a. Describe the irregularities that might occur under the procedures now in effect for handling cash collections and remittances.
b. Give procedures that you would recommend to strengthen the control structure for cash collections and remittances.

(AICPA adapted)

8

Assessing Inherent and Control Risk

The two major components of audit risk were discussed in Chapter 6 in connection with planning and controlling an engagement. The first component, the risk that the financial statements contain material misstatements, is beyond the auditor's ability to control or change; however, the auditor can and should assess that risk as a basis for determining the nature, timing, and extent of auditing procedures. This chapter discusses the ways auditors assess risk, including the performance of tests of controls, under different audit strategies. It also describes and illustrates different means of documenting risk assessment procedures and their results. The following chapter deals with the second component of audit risk—detection risk—and the substantive tests the auditor performs to reduce it to an acceptably low level.

Risk assessment is the process of arriving at an informed judgment of the risk that the financial statements contain material misstatements. That risk has two aspects, inherent risk and control risk, and the auditor assesses them within the context of materiality as a basis for determining the assurance he or she will need from substantive tests. Inherent and control risks should be assessed at the account balance and class of transactions level, and the assessment should address individual financial statement assertions and corresponding audit objectives.

Risk assessment aids the auditor in identifying

- Inherent risk conditions and characteristics that create a high risk of material misstatement and thus require emphasis on particular audit objectives and accounts.
- Internal control structure policies and procedures that may reduce the risk of material misstatement and enable the auditor to restrict substantive tests for particular audit objectives and accounts.
- Accounts that can be subjected to limited substantive tests because the risk of material misstatement is low.

The basis for the auditor's assessment of inherent and control risk is information about various aspects of the client and its business. Much of that information is general and relates to the nature of the entity's business; the industry it operates in, including legal and regulatory requirements peculiar to the industry; and the entity's significant accounts and interrelationships among financial and operating data. The auditor is also required to obtain an understanding of the entity's control structure in order to assess control risk as part of planning the audit.

OBTAINING INFORMATION TO ASSESS INHERENT AND CONTROL RISK

As discussed in Chapter 6, inherent risks result from both conditions that are not under the entity's control and the characteristics of its transactions and related account balances. Inherent risk *conditions* exist at the macroeconomic, industry, and company level, and sometimes relate to factors outside the entity.

These conditions may relate to changes in the general business environment, government regulations, and other economic factors. Inherent risk *characteristics* relate to the particular attributes of the entity's transactions and related accounts. The auditor considers both aspects of inherent risk in planning the audit. Information about inherent risk conditions comes mostly from outside sources. Inherent risk conditions generally are not addressed by specific accounting and control procedures; however, an effective control environment provides evidence of management's ability to monitor inherent risk conditions and respond to changes in them. In contrast, management designs control structure policies and procedures in response to the particular characteristics of its classes of transactions and account balances, so that inherent risk characteristics often are addressed by all three control structure elements. For that reason, inherent risk characteristics are ordinarily assessed concurrently with control risk, as discussed later in the chapter.

For a recurring audit engagement, much of the general information relevant to assessing inherent and control risk is available from prior years' working papers and needs only to be updated, not gathered all over again. Both client personnel and the auditor must be careful not to treat changed circumstances perfunctorily. A client's personnel can easily forget changes that took place during the year because they have become routine by the time the auditor makes inquiries; the auditor can easily treat significant changes as trivial if their implications are not thoroughly considered. An auditor approaching a recurring engagement must remember that changed conditions can make last year's risk assessments obsolete and a misleading guide to the nature and extent of procedures required. The auditor should not perform auditing procedures based on the previous year's assessments before reviewing changed circumstances.

The information needed to assess inherent and control risk is obtained from many sources and is documented in a number of places in the audit working papers. Most of the information-gathering procedures are performed during the early stages of the audit; however, the auditor is likely to obtain additional information about the client throughout the engagement and should consider that information in determining the nature, timing, and extent of auditing procedures.

Information about the client's business and industry, recent financial information, and a knowledge of applicable accounting, auditing, and regulatory standards are useful for identifying inherent risk conditions, inherent risk characteristics, and the control structure policies and procedures the client may have implemented in response to those characteristics. The paragraphs that follow describe how the auditor gathers or updates that information.

Obtaining Knowledge of the Client's Business and Industry

Relevant information about the client's business includes its product lines, sources and methods of supply, marketing and distribution methods, sources of financing, and production methods. The auditor should also obtain information about the locations and relative size of the client's operating plants, divisions, and subsidiaries, and the extent to which management is decentralized. Concerning the client's industry, the auditor needs to know such matters as industry characteristics and the client's position in the industry. Industry conditions that can affect a client include its market share and relative size, industry practices (for example, with regard to quantity discounts and consignment sales), and its competition. If the client operates in more than one industry, the auditor should obtain information about each industry in which the client has significant activities. The auditor can do this through a variety of information sources, including government statistics; economic, financial, industry, and trade journals; client publications and brochures; internal audit reports, where applicable; and reports prepared on the entity, its competitors, or its industry by underwriters, merchant bankers, and securities dealers and analysts.

The auditor should also learn about economic conditions that affect the client's business and industry. Economic conditions affect an entity's continuing ability to generate and collect revenues, operate profitably, and provide a return to investors. Unfavorable economic conditions may raise questions about whether the entity's assets are recoverable, how its liabilities should be measured, and, ultimately, whether it can remain in business. Unfavorable economic conditions may also increase the likelihood of intentional financial statement misrepresentations.

Analyzing Recent Financial Information

SAS No. 56, *Analytical Procedures* (AU Section 329), requires the auditor to use analytical procedures in planning the audit. In meeting that requirement, the auditor typically reviews recent financial statements and other available financial information and performance indicators to highlight changes in the client's business, to identify which account balances and classes of transactions are material and which are immaterial, and to identify unusual or unexpected relationships among accounts. Such relationships may indicate material misstatements in specific account balances, or inherent risk conditions such as declining liquidity or poor operating performance, that may have a pervasive effect on the financial statements. In addition, comparing recent financial information with prior-year financial data and with budgets for the current period may alert the auditor to favorable or unfavorable operating trends, significant deviations from expected results, recent financing or investment activities, and other changes in the entity's business. Unusual or unexpected balances or relationships among data aggregated at a high level, such as financial statement line items or their major components, could serve as an early warning of specific risks. Also, comparing a client's financial results with those of other companies in its industry group as a whole may be a useful way to determine whether the client's performance is consistent with that of other similar entities. Information compiled by services like Dun & Bradstreet, Robert Morris Associates, or Standard & Poor's can give the auditor standard "benchmarks" against which to measure performance. Auditors are increasingly using computers to access such information from public data bases. The nature and extent of analytical procedures depend on how large and complex the client's business is and what financial information is available.

In addition to financial data, analytical procedures used in planning the audit are sometimes based on relationships between financial and nonfinancial information, particularly for enterprises in industries in which an "average" rate has meaning. For example, in the hotel industry, the overall reasonableness of revenue from room occupancy may be tested by considering the result of multiplying the number of rooms by the occupancy rate by the average room rate.

Updating Knowledge of Applicable Accounting, Auditing, and Regulatory Standards

The auditor's understanding of the business also includes knowledge of the client's accounting policies and practices. The auditor should evaluate whether those policies and practices are appropriate for the way the client conducts its business and in light of generally accepted accounting principles. If the client has changed any accounting policies or practices during the current year, the auditor should determine whether those changes were made in response to changes in its methods of doing business or in accounting or regulatory standards, or to better reflect operating results, and should consider their possible effects on the audit.

The auditor should identify any accounting and auditing standards that warrant special attention in the current year, such as standards that have become applicable or have taken on increased significance because of changes in the client's business or because of significant, unusual, or nonrecurring transactions. The client may not be aware that such standards apply to its financial statements or may not fully understand how to apply the standards. New or changed regulatory standards may have a similar impact on the client's financial statements. The auditor should consider discussing such standards with management at the earliest possible date so that it can take action to address them properly and on a timely basis.

Related Party Transactions

In understanding the client's business, the auditor has a specific responsibility to consider the client's relationships and transactions with related parties. Statement of Financial Accounting Standards (SFAS) No. 57, *Related Party*

Disclosures (Accounting Standards Section R36), sets forth disclosure requirements with regard to related parties and contains (in Section R36.406) the following definition of related parties:

> Affiliates of the enterprise; entities for which investments are accounted for by the equity method by the enterprise; trusts for the benefit of employees, such as pension and profit-sharing trusts that are managed by or under the trusteeship of management; principal owners of the enterprise; its management; members of the immediate families of principal owners of the enterprise and its management; and other parties with which the enterprise may deal if one party controls or can significantly influence the management or operating policies of the other to an extent that one of the transacting parties might be prevented from fully pursuing its own separate interests. Another party also is a related party if it can significantly influence the management or operating policies of the transacting parties or if it has an ownership interest in one of the transacting parties and can significantly influence the other to an extent that one or more of the transacting parties might be prevented from fully pursuing its own separate interests.

The terms "affiliates," "control," "immediate family," "management," and "principal owners" are further defined in SFAS No. 57.

Under AU Section 334, *Related Parties*, the auditor has the responsibility to understand the client's business activities well enough to evaluate whether the client's disclosures regarding related parties are appropriate, including the propriety of any client representations that related party transactions took place at terms equivalent to arm's-length transactions. AU Section 334 sets forth specific auditing procedures the auditor should consider in determining the existence of related parties, procedures to help identify material transactions with related parties, and procedures the auditor should consider when examining any related party transactions identified.

The client has the ultimate responsibility for identifying, recording, and disclosing related party transactions, and the auditor should obtain specific representation from client management that it is aware of, and has fulfilled, that responsibility. The auditor's procedures, however, should extend beyond inquiry of, and obtaining such representations from, management. The auditor should also review other potential sources of information, such as proxy material, stockholder listings, and minutes of meetings of the board of directors and executive or operating committees. As far as possible, related parties should be identified at the beginning of the audit and their names distributed to all members of the audit team, including those responsible for auditing other divisions or subsidiaries of the enterprise, to help them identify related party transactions in the course of their work. The auditor should assess the client's procedures for identifying related parties and transactions to determine the nature and extent of auditing procedures he or she will have to perform to identify such transactions.

OBTAINING AN UNDERSTANDING OF THE CONTROL STRUCTURE ELEMENTS

The previous section described how the auditor obtains general information to assess inherent and control risk as part of planning an audit. The second standard of field work specifically requires that the auditor obtain a sufficient understanding of the client's internal control structure for planning purposes. A "sufficient" understanding of the control structure is one that, when considered together with other information about the client, such as that from prior years' experience, enables the auditor to identify what types of misstatements could occur, consider the risks of their occurring, and design appropriate substantive tests to detect them. The auditor develops this understanding by determining the *design* of relevant policies and procedures *in each element of the control structure* and whether they have been *placed in operation,* that is, whether the entity is actually using them. The auditor is *not required*, as part of developing the *understanding* of the control structure, to obtain evidence about whether those policies and procedures are *effectively designed* or are *operating effectively*. (Tests designed to provide evidence about effectiveness are discussed later in the chapter.) Often, however, in the course of developing the understanding of control structure policies and procedures, particularly those that are part of the accounting system or control environment, the auditor also obtains evidence about their effectiveness. The auditor considers that evidence when assessing control risk with respect to relevant assertions and account balances.

The understanding of the control structure required for audit planning (that is, for identifying and responding to the risk of material misstatements) is obtained by considering previous experience with the entity, reviewing prior-year audit results, interviewing client personnel and observing them in the performance of their duties, and examining client-prepared descriptions of policies and procedures and other appropriate documentation. As explained in Chapter 5, observation involves direct viewing of client employees in the work environment. Inquiry (interviewing) entails asking specific questions of the client's management and employees, which may be done informally or in formal interviews. The auditor examines records, documents, reconciliations, and reports for evidence that a policy or procedure has been properly applied. What procedures the auditor performs to obtain the necessary understanding of the control structure, and the extent to which they are performed on a particular audit, vary according to the client's size and complexity, the auditor's previous experience with the client, the particular policy or procedure, and the client's documentation. As a result of prior years' experience with the client, the auditor will likely have some idea of the level at which control risk will be assessed in the current audit. This may in some cases also affect the nature and extent of procedures performed in updating the understanding of the control structure.

Developing an Understanding of the Control Environment and Accounting System

The auditor obtains information about the control environment to determine whether it appears to be conducive to maintaining an effective accounting system and control procedures and whether it minimizes the incentives and opportunities for management to deliberately distort the financial statements. An understanding of the flow of transactions through the accounting system gives the auditor a general knowledge of the various classes of transactions, their volume and typical dollar values, and the procedures for authorizing, executing, initially recording, and subsequently processing them, including the methods of data processing. While obtaining an understanding of the accounting system, the auditor should consider whether client personnel who use the information the system generates would be likely to detect and report potential errors in data underlying the financial statements. In a recurring engagement, much of the relevant information about the control environment and the flow of transactions is already available in the prior years' working papers. The auditor should use this information as much as possible; however, it should be thoroughly reviewed and updated each year.

Reviewing Prior Years' Audit Results. Reviewing prior years' audit results can help the auditor determine the likelihood of material misstatements in current-year account balances. For example, if the control environment was found to be effective in prior years and there have been no changes in the people and procedures that generate information that management uses to monitor business activities, the auditor should consider this when planning substantive tests of accounts requiring management estimates and judgments.

Prior-year working papers the auditor ordinarily reviews include financial information, the understanding of the client's business and industry, and risk assessments. The auditor should also refer to the prior year's documentation of matters brought to the attention of the partner, particularly significant accounting and auditing matters such as the nature, cause, and amounts of errors the auditor found—both those that were material and resulted in adjustment of the financial statements and those that were not.

If a client changes auditors, professional courtesy calls for the predecessor auditor to make certain information in the working papers available to the successor auditor. The predecessor auditor's working papers can be a convenient source of information about the accounting system, control procedures, and accounting principles used by the client, as well as the composition of beginning balances of individual accounts, although most of this information can also be obtained from the client.

Interviews and Client Manuals. Interviewing is one of the most effective ways to gain an initial understanding of the client's accounting system and related control procedures. Interviews with client personnel who are knowledgeable about the accounting system and control procedures can give the auditor an understanding of how the company's accounting, internal control, and related activities are carried out. Interviewing personnel who are immediately responsible for performing procedures enables the auditor to learn about the main features of the accounting system and control procedures and about potential problem areas with implications for the internal control structure or the financial statements. In those interviews, questions and answers can be highly detailed, specific, and directed because both the auditor and knowledgeable client personnel know what information the auditor needs.

Many companies, particularly large and complex ones, maintain extensive manuals of policies and procedures. The auditor should normally obtain or have access to a complete set of procedures manuals covering accounting and internal control activities; familiarity with those manuals will help the auditor conduct more insightful interviews with client accounting personnel. Manuals of activities peripheral to accounting, such as purchasing and personnel policies, may also be useful. But although those manuals can often help clarify a particular phase of a client's operations, they are often too detailed and extensive to contribute effectively to the auditor's initial effort to understand the client's accounting system and control procedures. Instead, these manuals often serve as reference sources as the audit progresses.

Computerized Systems. Presuming that the client's accounting system is computerized, the auditor also needs a general understanding of the principles of computers and computer processing and how those principles are applied in the client's system. The auditor should become familiar with the hardware and software used to process financially significant transactions. This information serves as a basis for ascertaining the likelihood that the client will have appropriate general control procedures, and determining whether audit software can be used in the audit. The auditor generally obtains this information by inquiry of data processing management. The auditor should also consider whether specialized skills are needed to assess the effect of the computer environment on the audit.

Transaction Reviews. In some situations, the auditor may be concerned that his or her understanding of the design of the accounting system may not be correct or complete enough to provide an adequate basis for planning the audit. In that event, the auditor may decide to trace one or a few transactions of each relevant class of transactions completely through the system to determine whether relevant accounting procedures have been placed in operation. This process is sometimes referred to as a "transaction review" or "walk-through." By revealing what types of misstatements could occur because of absent or ineffective procedures or documents, a transaction review can help the auditor in designing substantive tests to detect those misstatements. To decide whether to perform transaction reviews to obtain evidence that accounting procedures have been placed in operation, the auditor considers whether it would be more efficient to obtain that evidence by other means, such as examining documents and information produced by the system.

Developing an Understanding of Control Procedures

In developing an understanding of control procedures, the auditor is concerned with whether such procedures have been designed and placed in operation to determine whether the entity's objectives for processing transactions, storing data on files, and safeguarding assets will be met. That information helps the auditor to design and carry out more efficient substantive tests to detect possible misstatements.

Some of the procedures that achieve the control objectives may be integrated into components of the control environment and the accounting system. Accordingly, the auditor is likely to obtain some information about the presence or absence of control procedures as part of obtaining an understanding of the control environment and accounting system. The auditor should consider that information in determining what, if any, additional understanding of control procedures is necessary to plan the audit. In addition, the auditor may want to obtain an understanding of certain control procedures in order to understand the accounting system. SAS No. 55 (AU Section 319) notes that audit planning ordinarily does not require an understanding of all control procedures related to an individual account balance or audit objective.

DOCUMENTING THE UNDERSTANDING OF THE CONTROL STRUCTURE

Professional standards require the auditor to document the understanding of the control structure elements, but do not specify the form and extent of documentation. Thus, the documentation will vary with the size and complexity of the entity and the nature of its control structure. In general, the more complex the control structure, the more detailed the documentation will be.

The documentation of accounting systems that process financially significant transactions usually includes a record of the significant classes of transactions and principal accounting procedures, files, ledgers, and reports. It may be in the form of narratives or flowcharts. Flowcharts are symbolic diagrams that show procedures in graphic form and thus make it easy to understand and communicate information. Commonly used flowcharting symbols are depicted and explained in Figure 8.1. Flowcharts usually flow from top to bottom or from left to right and should be clear and simple. Only procedures, documents, and reports that have audit significance need be shown.

Auditors frequently document accounting systems on a type of flowchart called an *overview flowchart*, which illustrates the flow of significant classes of transactions from initiation, through processing, to the reports generated by

Figure 8.1 Flowcharting Symbols

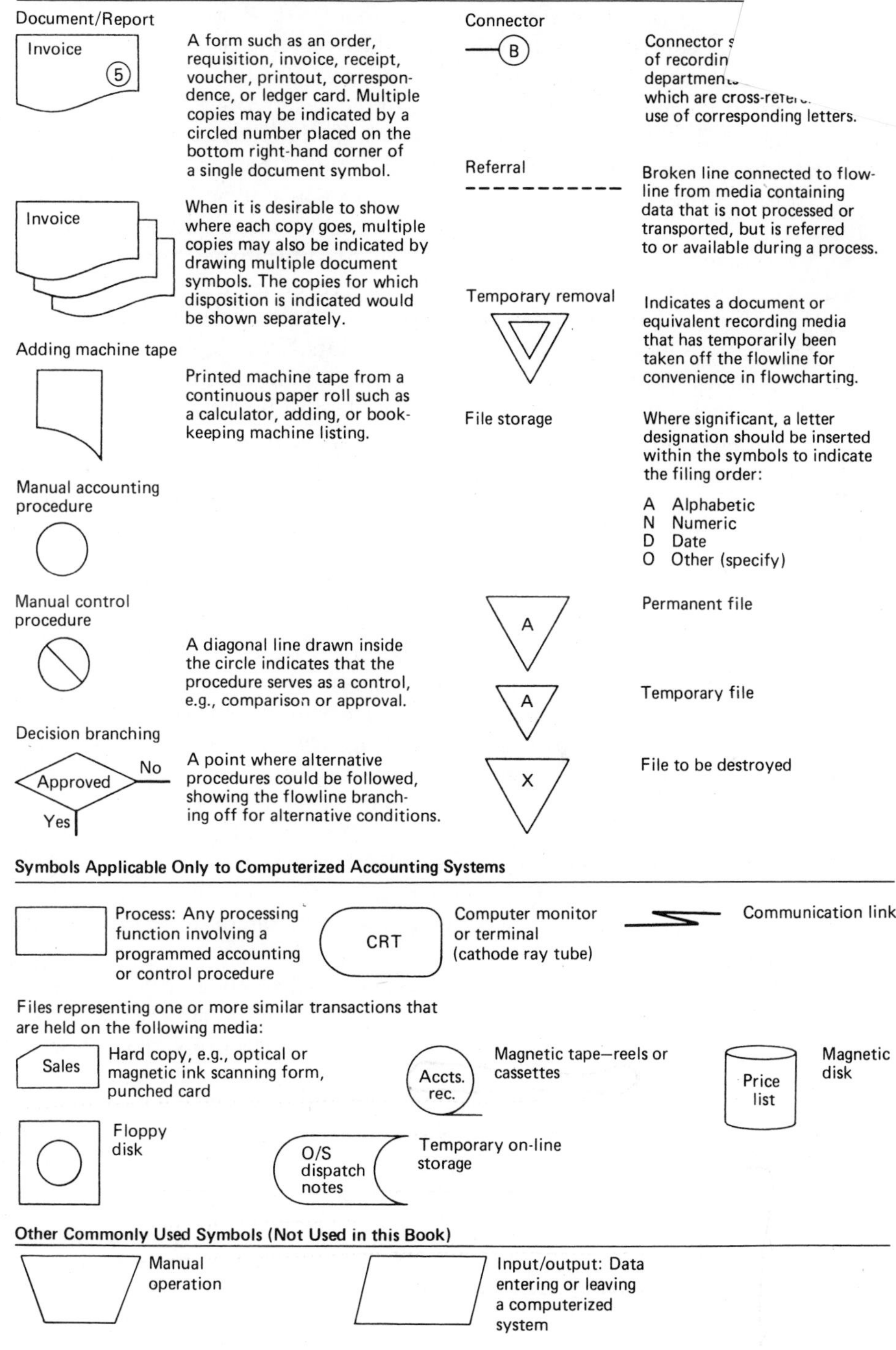
Symbols Applicable to All Accounting Systems
Document/Report
Invoice
5
A form such as an order, requisition, invoice, receipt, voucher, printout, correspondence, or ledger card. Multiple copies may be indicated by a circled number placed on the bottom right-hand corner of a single document symbol.
Invoice
When it is desirable to show where each copy goes, multiple copies may also be indicated by drawing multiple document symbols. The copies for which disposition is indicated would be shown separately.
Adding machine tape
Printed machine tape from a continuous paper roll such as a calculator, adding, or bookkeeping machine listing.
Manual accounting procedure
Manual control procedure
A diagonal line drawn inside the circle indicates that the procedure serves as a control, e.g., comparison or approval.
Decision branching
Approved
No
Yes
A point where alternative procedures could be followed, showing the flowline branching off for alternative conditions.
Connector
B
Connector s
of recordin
departmen
which are cross-refer
use of corresponding letters.
Referral
Broken line connected to flowline from media containing data that is not processed or transported, but is referred to or available during a process.
Temporary removal
Indicates a document or equivalent recording media that has temporarily been taken off the flowline for convenience in flowcharting.
File storage
Where significant, a letter designation should be inserted within the symbols to indicate the filing order:
A Alphabetic
N Numeric
D Date
O Other (specify)
A
Permanent file
A
Temporary file
X
File to be destroyed
Symbols Applicable Only to Computerized Accounting Systems
Process: Any processing function involving a programmed accounting or control procedure
CRT
Computer monitor or terminal (cathode ray tube)
Communication link
Files representing one or more similar transactions that are held on the following media:
Sales
Hard copy, e.g., optical or magnetic ink scanning form, punched card
Accts. rec.
Magnetic tape—reels or cassettes
Price list
Magnetic disk
Floppy disk
O/S dispatch notes
Temporary on-line storage
Other Commonly Used Symbols (Not Used in this Book)
Manual operation
Input/output: Data entering or leaving a computerized system

the system, including those that are used to update the general ledger. The degree of detail required in an overview flowchart varies, depending on the entity's accounting system and whether the auditor plans to test the effectiveness of control procedures. While the overview flowchart is used primarily to document the accounting system, it may also be a convenient place to document the auditor's understanding of the design of key control procedures, if he or she does not plan to specifically test their effectiveness. On the other hand, if the auditor plans to test control procedures, they will be documented on other forms (discussed below) and generally will not be indicated on the overview flowchart. In any event, an overview flowchart should contain sufficient information to facilitate the design of substantive tests. An example of an overview flowchart for a computerized revenue cycle is shown in Figure 8.2.

Flowcharts are appropriate for all engagements, regardless of size or complexity. On many recurring engagements, flowcharts will already have been prepared; they should be reviewed and updated annually and used as long as they continue to be relevant. A complete redrawing of flowcharts annually is usually unnecessary unless the underlying procedures have changed or previous amendments have impaired a flowchart's clarity. Supporting documentation—such as copies of (or extracts from) accounting records, procedures manuals, and filled-in specimen forms or documents—should be cross-referenced to and filed with the flowcharts to help the auditor understand the accounting system.

The auditor may need to prepare more than one flowchart to cover an entire transaction cycle. For example, within the buying cycle, separate flowcharts may be necessary to show goods or services purchased and wages paid. The decision to prepare separate flowcharts depends on how significant the transactions are and whether the accounting procedures and reports generated are different for different classes of transactions.

It is not necessary to include on the flowchart every transaction that is processed by a particular system. Only significant transactions should be documented. Transactions outside the main flow of information, such as adjustments, standing data amendments, and the like, may be documented in supplementary narratives as necessary. Such a narrative is illustrated in Figure 8.3.

An overview flowchart displays, normally on one or two pages, the accounting system for a transaction cycle in summary form. It provides the auditor with information about the nature of transactions that flow through the system. An overview flowchart should depict the principal features of the accounting system, including the following:

1. The nature and source of significant transactions.
2. The key processes and flow of significant transactions.
3. Principal files or ledgers supporting account balances and the process by which they are updated.

Figure 8.2 Overview Flowchart

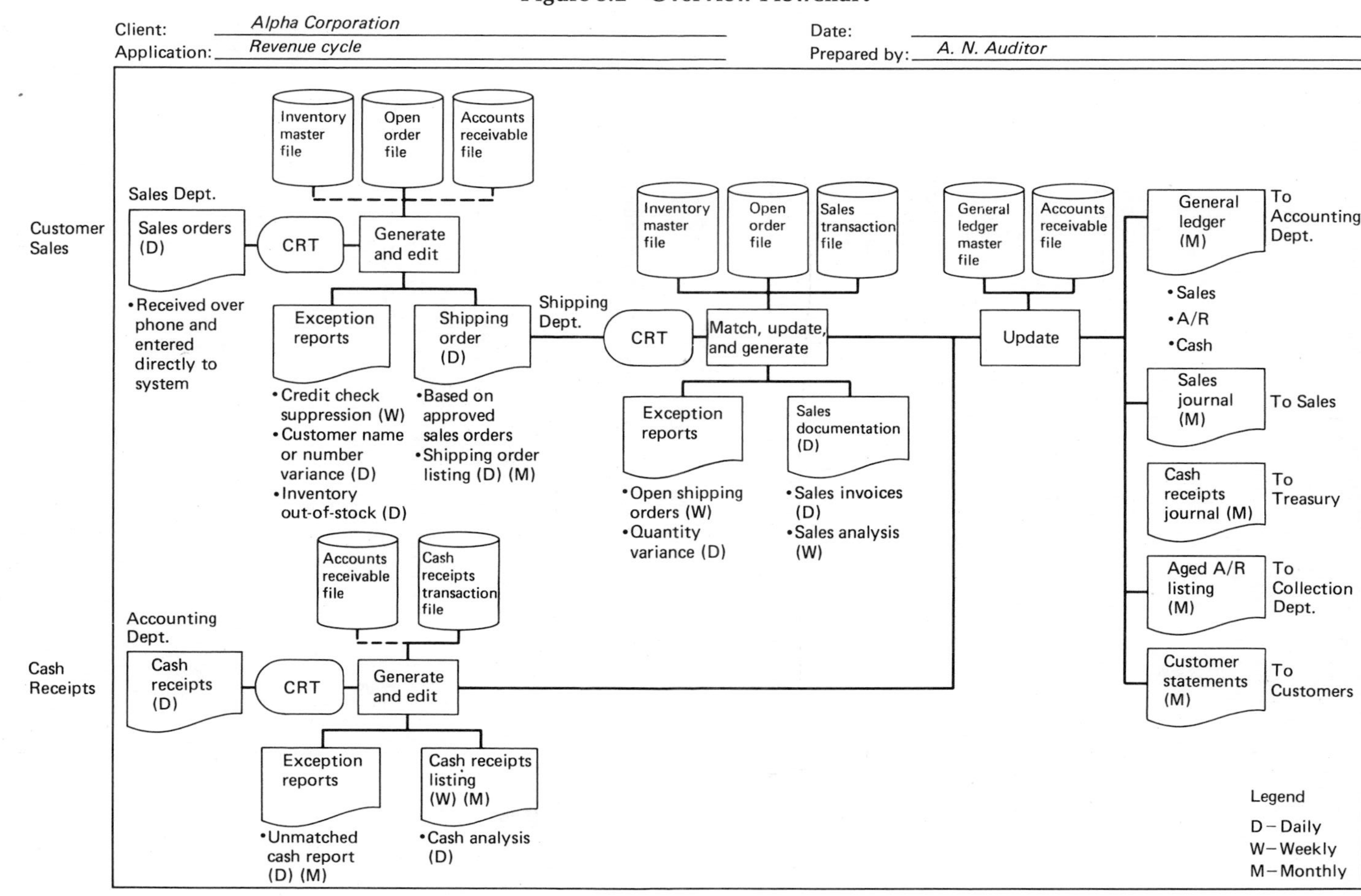

Figure 8.3 Supplementary Narrative to Overview Flowchart

Client: *Alpha Corporation*
Application: *Revenue cycle*

Adjustments to Accounts Receivable
Adjustments to accounts receivable balances are made by processing credit memos (which are initiated by the sales department, entered directly to the system, and processed similar to sales orders) or by processing accounts receivable adjustment sheets for account write-offs (which are initiated by the accounting department based on discussions with the collection department and processed directly against the accounts receivable and general ledger master files).

Standing Data Amendments
Unit sales price data stored on the inventory master file is updated monthly by the accounting department based on the price change list received from the sales department.

4. Reports of accounting significance produced, their frequency and distribution, and the files from which they are derived.

Each of those features is described below with reference to the computerized revenue cycle accounting system flowcharted in Figure 8.2 and the supplementary narrative shown in Figure 8.3.

Nature and source of significant transactions—The significant transactions flowcharted for the revenue cycle are customer sales and cash receipts. Other revenue cycle transactions outside the main flow of information, such as adjustments to accounts receivable and standing data amendments, are described in the supplementary narrative to the flowchart. The flowchart shows that customer sales transactions originate with the input of sales orders from customers and the automatic generation and further processing of shipping orders. This information helps the auditor identify what source documents to use in designing substantive tests and which information processing points might have completeness control procedures related to customer sales.

Key processes and flow of significant transactions—The flowchart shows how sales transactions flow from initiation (when the sales order is received over the phone and recorded on a sales order document), through processing (when the sales order is input to the system and used in connection with master file data to generate a shipping order and sales invoice), to updating significant accounting files and producing the ultimate reports from the system (the general ledger, sales journal, and aged accounts receivable listing). Also shown are the processes, called editing and matching, that compare sales orders and shipping orders with data on file to determine whether there are exceptions that must be cleared by a responsible person before processing can continue. This information helps the auditor understand how certain key files are updated and reports produced, so that he or she can design substantive tests or identify control procedures relating to transaction processing.

Principal files or ledgers supporting account balances and the process by which they are updated—The flowchart shows the principal file supporting the accounts receivable balance (the accounts receivable file) and how it is updated (e.g., by accessing data on the sales and cash receipts transaction files). This information helps the auditor identify key files that should be subjected to manual or automated substantive tests. It also helps identify key files that should be subject to control procedures and therefore be considered when testing the effectiveness of the control procedures.

Reports of accounting significance produced, their frequency and distribution, and the files from which they are derived—The flowchart shows how significant accounting reports (e.g., the aged accounts receivable listing and the general ledger) are produced, where they are distributed and how frequently, and what files they were derived from (the accounts receivable and general ledger master files). This information helps the auditor identify reports to use in designing substantive tests. The flowchart also shows how and when exception reports are produced. This helps identify documents the client may use in performing certain control procedures.

Figure 8.4 Computer Environment Form

PART 1: PROCESSING ENVIRONMENT

MIS Organization

MIS Contact name and title:__________ Phone:______

Installation address: __________

Size and structure of the department:__________

____

____

Hardware

Computer manufacturer and model:__________

Magnetic Storage Media:

Magnetic tape__________

Magnetic disk__________

Diskettes__________

Other (specify)__________

Software

Operating system:__________

Communications software:__________

Major programming languages:__________

Inquiry/report writer packages available:__________

____

____

If the client's operations are computerized, the auditor should obtain an understanding and record information about computer hardware and software used in financially significant applications. Some auditors document the relevant information on a form designed to record, concisely and in one place, the organization of the EDP installation, the hardware and software in use, the configuration of the network, and the details of the application environment, such as packages used, type of processing, access security software, and so on. Part of such a form is illustrated in Figure 8.4.

Generally, the auditor documents the understanding of the control environment and the design of many control procedures as part of documenting the assessment of control risk, as described later in this chapter. However, the auditor's understanding of the design of certain key control procedures may be documented on the overview flowchart by a narrative description, or by notations in the audit program, particularly if the auditor does not plan to test those control procedures as part of the process of assessing control risk. Often these are key control procedures that must be understood before the auditor can design efficient substantive tests; for example, the matching of shipping documents to invoices to ensure the completeness of recorded sales, and client procedures relating to physical inventory counts.

ASSESSING CONTROL RISK

Both SAS No. 47 and SAS No. 55 require the auditor to assess control risk to determine what level of detection risk is acceptable in an audit. Assessing control risk is defined in SAS No. 55 (AU Section 319.29) as the "process of evaluating the effectiveness of an entity's internal control structure policies and procedures in preventing or detecting material misstatements in the financial statements." The conclusion reached from this process is referred to as the "assessed level of control risk" and is a combined judgment, based on evidence obtained about all three control structure elements. While SAS No. 55 does not require the auditor to evaluate separately the effectiveness of each of the elements of the control structure, in most cases it is practical to do so in arriving at an assessed level of control risk. Figure 8.5 depicts the assessment of control risk in flowchart form, including the various decisions the auditor makes and their consequences for the audit strategy. The steps in the flowchart are expanded on in the following sections of the chapter.

Risk Assessment and Audit Strategy

Control risk should be assessed in relation to the audit objectives derived from the financial statement assertions. The auditor may assess control risk at the maximum level (that is, 100 percent) for all or certain audit objectives and

Figure 8.5 Control Risk Assessment*

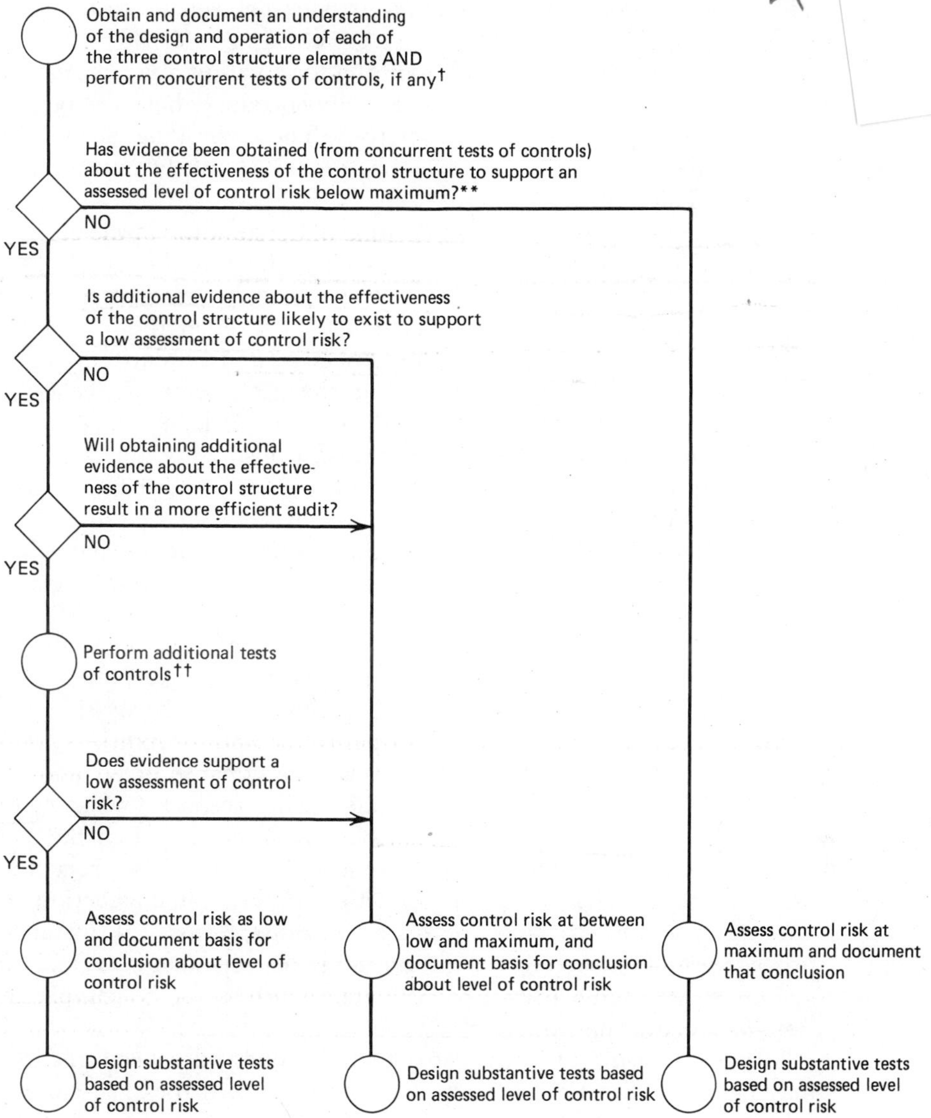

Obtain and document an understanding of the design and operation of each of the three control structure elements AND perform concurrent tests of controls, if any†

Has evidence been obtained (from concurrent tests of controls) about the effectiveness of the control structure to support an assessed level of control risk below maximum?**

NO

YES

Is additional evidence about the effectiveness of the control structure likely to exist to support a low assessment of control risk?

NO

YES

Will obtaining additional evidence about the effective-ness of the control structure result in a more efficient audit?

NO

YES

Perform additional tests of controls††

Does evidence support a low assessment of control risk?

NO

YES

Assess control risk as low and document basis for conclusion about level of control risk

Assess control risk at between low and maximum, and document basis for conclusion about level of control risk

Assess control risk at maximum and document that conclusion

Design substantive tests based on assessed level of control risk

Design substantive tests based on assessed level of control risk

Design substantive tests based on assessed level of control risk

*Relevant management assertions/audit objectives related to specific account balances or classes of transactions should be considered separately in assessing control risk and designing substantive tests.

†Conceptually it would be possible for the auditor not to perform any tests of controls until after obtaining the understanding of the control structure. In practice, however, the auditor is unlikely to plan to perform tests of controls after obtaining the understanding without having performed some concurrent tests of controls.

**Evidence about the effectiveness of control structure policies and procedures may result from auditing procedures *planned* as concurrent tests of controls; alternatively, such evidence may be obtained from concurrent tests of controls that are *incidental* to auditing procedures directed at obtaining the understanding.

††On a recurring audit engagement where the auditor intends to again perform additional tests of controls, he or she may begin at this point and update the understanding and perform tests of controls simultaneously.

decide to proceed directly to substantive tests to obtain assurance for those audit objectives, without doing any further work related to the control structure.

Assessing control risk at the maximum for an audit objective can result from a belief that control structure policies and procedures have not been effectively designed or have not operated effectively. The auditor can arrive at that belief based on the information gathered or updated about the client and the understanding of its control structure.

In order to assess control risk at below the maximum level, the auditor must be able to *identify* specific control structure policies and procedures that are in place and are likely to prevent or detect material misstatements in specific financial statement assertions, and must *test* whether those policies and procedures are designed and operating effectively.[1] In identifying control structure policies and procedures relevant to specific assertions, the auditor should keep in mind that some policies and procedures have a pervasive effect on many account balances or classes of transactions and on numerous assertions, while others have a specific effect on only one account or class of transactions and one assertion.

The effect of policies and procedures varies with the particular control structure element. The control environment and accounting system often have a pervasive effect on many account balances or classes of transactions and thus frequently affect several assertions. For example, the conclusion that an entity's decentralized accounting system is highly effective may affect the auditor's decision about the number of locations where he or she will perform auditing procedures or whether to perform certain auditing procedures in some locations at an interim date. Those decisions, in turn, affect the way in which auditing procedures are applied with respect to the completeness, accuracy, and existence/occurrence assertions, even though the auditor may not specifically consider each of those assertions. Control procedures, on the other hand, often have a specific effect on an individual assertion related to a particular account balance or class of transactions. For instance, control procedures established to ensure that all items reported on a receiving report log are included in accounts payable relate directly to the completeness assertion for accounts payable.

The relationship of control structure policies and procedures to assertions may be either direct or indirect. The degree of directness, or closeness, of the relationship determines, in part, how likely a specific policy or procedure is to have an effect on a particular assertion for a specific account balance or class of transactions. For example, accounting for the numerical sequence of sales

[1]The auditor may believe that such "tests of controls" (defined later) could lead to an assessment of control risk below the maximum level but that it would not be efficient to perform those tests. As noted in the section of the chapter on "Tests of Controls," however, tests of controls performed concurrently with developing the required understanding of the control structure will usually support an assessment of control risk at below the maximum for one or more specific assertions and account balances.

invoices is directly related to the completeness assertion for accounts receivable and sales, while management's review of monthly sales analyses indirectly relates to the completeness assertion for those account balances.

The tests the auditor performs to support an assessment of control risk at less than the maximum level are directed at the *effectiveness* of *both* the design *and* the operation of control structure policies and procedures. Those tests are referred to as "tests of controls" in SAS No. 55 and are discussed in a later section of this chapter. Effective design relates to whether the policy or procedure is suitably designed to prevent or detect material misstatements with respect to specific assertions. Effective operation is concerned with how the policy or procedure was applied, whether it was consistently applied throughout the period, and the person(s) who applied it. (As used in this chapter in the context of the operation of policies and procedures, the terms "effectiveness" and "effective" incorporate the concept of consistent, or continuous, operation.)

Assessing the Control Environment

In assessing the control environment, the auditor considers factors that contribute to its quality, tests whether those factors are operating effectively, and forms an overall conclusion about the environment. The factors that affect an enterprise's control environment were described in Chapter 7. Some of them affect the entity's ability to maintain an effective accounting system and control procedures. Others affect management's ability to make the informed judgments and estimates necessary to prepare financial statements. Still other factors affect the entity's ability to restrict the opportunity for management fraud. All of those factors are interrelated. The auditor should consider them both individually and collectively in assessing the extent to which they contribute to the control environment.

Management's review of various operating reports is an aspect of the control environment that the auditor frequently considers important and tests because it may provide evidence about the entity's accounting system and control procedures. (Knowing what reports management reviews may also serve as a basis for designing substantive tests.) In assessing how useful their reviews are, the auditor should consider

- The competence of the individuals reviewing the reports. They should have an adequate level of business knowledge and technical expertise and be familiar with the entity's operations.
- The authority of the individuals performing the reviews to take corrective action. They should be adequately positioned within the organization to act effectively.

- The objectivity of the individuals performing the reviews. The individuals should be independent of those who perform the work, both functionally (that is, there should be adequate segregation of duties) and motivationally (for example, an officer's review might be of less value from the auditor's standpoint if the officer's compensation is based on operating results being reviewed).

The objectivity of the manager who reviews operating reports is particularly important in audits of small businesses that are dominated by owner-managers or others who have the authority to establish policies and make decisions about how to pursue business objectives. On the one hand, owner-manager reviews may enhance the control structure because of the close attention with which they are carried out. They may also provide an additional level of segregation of duties in the accounting function. On the other hand, if there is no level of review above that of management (such as a review by nonmanagement members of the board of directors), the contribution of management reviews to the control environment may be limited because of a possible lack of objectivity. This would be particularly true if management's objectives regarding the financial statements did not coincide with those of the auditor—as would be the case if management's primary concern were maximizing (or minimizing) reported earnings rather than fair presentation in conformity with GAAP.

After testing the various policies and procedures that contribute to the control environment and assessing their effectiveness, the auditor reaches an overall conclusion about to what extent the environment is conducive to maintaining an effective accounting system and control procedures, and reduces the likelihood that management would intentionally distort the financial statements. If the auditor concludes that the control environment is favorable, there is a lower risk that other control structure policies and procedures will be overridden or bypassed and that misstatements may occur. That conclusion helps the auditor determine the nature, timing, and extent of other auditing procedures, including both tests of control procedures and substantive tests.

Auditors sometimes document the assessment of the control environment on a form that lists the various factors that make up the control environment and provides space for the auditor's comments and conclusions about each factor. Figure 8.6 illustrates part of such a form, dealing with the availability and reliability of information for management to use in reviewing and evaluating its operations.

Assessing the Accounting System

As described earlier in the chapter, the auditor obtains an understanding of the flow of transactions through the client's accounting system. That understanding covers the significant classes of transactions and key accounting procedures, files, ledgers, and reports. In the process of obtaining and documenting the understanding, the auditor considers whether the accounting system

Figure 8.6 Assessment of Control Environment

SECTION D: AVAILABILITY AND RELIABILITY OF MANAGEMENT INFORM

To monitor effectively the activities of the business, management must have sufficient, reliable information on a timely basis to review and evaluate its operations. In addition, appropriate actions must be taken as a result of mana reviews and evaluations. In evalu whether appropriate reliable man information exists, consider the fo factors:

Factors	*Comments*
The adequacy of financial, statistical, or other information used by management with respect to: • its relevance to the respective managers' responsibilities • its sufficiency • the frequency and timeliness with which it is received • its reliability (e.g., the adequacy of the accounting procedures to ensure the reliability of periodic financial statements—see also factors below) • its informational value (e.g., the appropriateness of its level of detail or aggregation).	Monthly Management Package* is given to each manager responsible for analyzing performance. —Reports are generated within ten working days —Reports are generated by the system or by accounting clerks and reviewed by the controller before going to users —Operating reports are produced in both detail and aggregated versions appropriate for various levels of management. (Note: There is no report that analyzes inventory levels.)
The comparison of current conditions or results with appropriate benchmarks (e.g., the preceding year's conditions or results, or a practicably achievable budget or plan).	Compared with prior year and month.
The explanations obtained for current variations from reasonable benchmarks and implementation of corrective action.	They obtain explanations for the differences in results between the prior year and prior month.
With respect to the explanations and corrective actions: • documentation of explanations • evaluation of explanations by the appropriate levels of management or the board of directors • implementation of corrective actions by the appropriate levels of management and follow-up by senior management.	Due to structure/size of company, explanations are seldom documented. They are discussed among management monthly and with Board quarterly. Corrective actions are agreed upon at those meetings. Corrective action plans are monitored and progress is reported at the next regularly scheduled meeting.

(*Continued*)

Figure 8.6 ***Continued***

Personal involvement of managers in activities relating to their respective areas of responsibility, and their accessibility to subordinates.	Key management personnel make periodic reports to the Board describing actions they have taken to meet the objectives of their department.
Other factors considered (list): —Close scrutiny of A/R status by key management	—Communications throughout the company are informal but effective based on prior audits and conversations with key/middle management. —President, Treasurer, and V.P.-Sales meet to review weekly aged A/R listing, at which time they decide whether to put delinquent accounts on a cash basis for future orders and adjust credit limits for other accounts. V.P.-Sales continuously receives input from salespeople on business climate in their territories and apparent health of customers' operations. On V.P.-Sales' instructions, salespeople visit delinquent accounts and press for payment.

Conclusions

It appears that management generally receives the type and level of information necessary to make informed judgments about the operations of the entity. In addition, the information is timely and corrective action, when necessary, seems appropriate. However, they do not monitor inventory levels on a current basis and obsolescence is considered only at year-end.

*Package Contains:
- Financial Statements
- Monthly Financial Statement Analysis
- Production, Cost, and Sales Information by Product
- Past Due A/R Analysis by Customer

appears to be effectively designed and operated. The auditor's review of prior-year working papers, interviews of accounting personnel, and transaction reviews (if performed) provide evidence about the accounting system. In addition, tests performed in assessing the control environment and control procedures provide evidence about the effectiveness of accounting procedures as well. In practice, the auditor does not make a separate assessment of the accounting system because it is not feasible to isolate the effect of the accounting system on specific assertions and account balances. Instead, the auditor incorporates the assessment of the accounting system into the overall assessment of control risk relating to specific assertions for particular account balances and classes of transactions.

Assessing Control Procedures

In assessing control procedures, the auditor identifies the specific procedures designed and placed in operation by the client to achieve the control objectives of completeness, accuracy, authorization, file control, and asset protection for a particular transaction cycle. The auditor then develops and performs appropriate tests of the effectiveness of the design and operation of those control procedures. As a practical matter, tests of control procedures are normally restricted to major transaction classes, because other transactions are relatively low volume and the related accounts can be more efficiently audited by substantive tests.

TESTS OF CONTROLS

The auditor performs tests of controls to determine whether the policies and procedures to prevent or detect misstatements have been effectively designed and have operated effectively throughout the period under audit.

Concurrent Tests of Controls

The auditor may perform some tests of controls concurrently with developing an understanding of the design of control structure policies and procedures and whether they have been placed in operation. Those tests are referred to in this book as "concurrent tests of controls." Evidence about the effectiveness of control structure policies and procedures may result from auditing procedures *planned* as concurrent tests of controls; alternatively, such evidence may be obtained from concurrent tests of controls that are *incidental* to auditing procedures directed at obtaining the understanding. In both situations, the auditor will ordinarily have obtained, concurrent with the understanding of the control structure, evidence to support an assessment of control risk at below the maximum for one or more specific assertions and account balances. Concurrent tests of controls are more likely to focus on the control environment and accounting system than on specific control procedures (the third element of the control structure). Because of the audit effort involved in testing control procedures, concurrent tests of control procedures are generally limited or in some cases not performed at all.

The authors believe that, because of evidence from concurrent tests of controls, auditors are rarely in a position where they must assess control risk at the maximum level for all audit objectives for all account balances. SAS No. 55 (AU Section 319.41) cites, as an example of concurrent tests of controls (although the term itself is not used in the SAS), the following procedures: inquiry about management's use of budgets, observing management's comparison of monthly budgeted with actual expenses, and inspecting reports of the investigation of variances between budgeted and actual amounts. Although those auditing procedures were directed at ascertaining the *design* of the entity's budgeting policies and whether they had been *placed in operation*, the procedures may also provide evidence about *how effectively the policies are designed and operating* to prevent or detect material misstatements in classifying expenses. In some circumstances, that evidence may support an assessment of control risk that is below the maximum level for the presentation and disclosure objective relating to expenses in the income statement.

Another example of how procedures performed in obtaining the required understanding of the control structure can also provide evidence of its effectiveness involves division of duties. In the course of obtaining an understanding of the accounting system, the auditor usually observes whether duties over cash receipts and deposits are adequately segregated. In doing this, the auditor will at the same time have obtained evidence about how effectively the separation procedure is designed and operating. This evidence may support a control risk assessment below the maximum level for, in this instance, the existence objective relating to cash. A third example involves the accounting system. In inquiring about how the accounting system for a particular class of transactions is designed and how the transactions flow through it, the auditor generally obtains evidence as well about whether the system is operating effectively. The authors believe that in most situations such evidence will support an assessment of control risk below the maximum.

Additional Tests of Controls

After evaluating the evidence about the effectiveness of the control structure that was obtained concurrently with obtaining the understanding of the control structure, the auditor decides whether to seek additional evidence through "additional tests of controls." Conceptually, the decision to perform tests of controls might not be made until after the understanding of the control structure has been obtained. In practice, however, the auditor is not likely to consider performing additional tests of controls unless he or she has obtained evidence of the effectiveness of the control structure concurrently with developing the understanding. The purpose of performing additional tests of controls is to support a further reduction in the assessed level of control risk for certain audit objectives and account balances. The decision is based mainly on the auditor's judgment about what evidence is likely to be available (discussed later) and whether testing the control structure in order to further restrict substantive tests of accounts in a particular transaction cycle will be efficient, as compared with proceeding directly to substantive testing. On a recurring engagement where the auditor intends to again perform additional tests of controls, he or she may update the understanding of the control structure and perform tests of controls simultaneously. Because of the substantial audit effort involved in performing additional tests of controls, it is usually not efficient to undertake them unless the auditor believes that they will support a low control risk assessment for specific assertions and account balances.

SAS No. 55 (AU Section 319.44) discusses audit efficiency considerations as follows:

> In considering efficiency, the auditor recognizes that additional evidential matter that supports a further reduction in the assessed level of control risk for an assertion would result in less audit effort for the substantive tests of that assertion. The auditor weighs the increase in audit effort associated with the additional tests of controls that is necessary to obtain such evidential matter against the resulting decrease in audit effort associated with the reduced substantive tests. When the auditor concludes it is inefficient to obtain additional evidential matter for specific assertions, the auditor uses the assessed level of control risk based on the understanding of the internal control structure in planning the substantive tests for those assertions.

The auditor usually decides that it would not be efficient to seek a further reduction in the assessed level of control risk when one or more of the following circumstances are present:

1. Volumes of transactions are low, or inherent risk characteristics make substantive tests relatively easy to apply.
2. The client has a manual system, or its computerized systems are neither complex nor pervasive.
3. The necessary tests of controls entail testing a large number of control procedures, as might be the case, for example, if relevant general control procedures in a computerized system do not ensure the effectiveness of programmed control procedures.

In these circumstances, the auditor designs and performs substantive tests for all relevant audit objectives and account balances, taking into consideration the results of the materiality and risk assessment activities already carried out.

Outside of the situations just described, the auditor may consider it efficient to perform additional tests of controls in one or more transaction cycles in order to further reduce the assessed level of control risk for specific assertions and account balances. In most instances, this strategy will enable the auditor to further reduce the assurance needed from substantive tests with respect to the audit objectives of completeness, accuracy, and existence/occurrence (and, in some cases, cutoff) for accounts that are derived from transaction cycles. This strategy will be particularly effective if it is possible to also obtain indirect evidence about the ongoing effective operation of control structure policies and procedures from such factors as management reviews of accounting reports and the absence of recurring problems in using data produced by those policies and procedures.

For large clients with pervasive, complex, and integrated computerized systems, it may be readily apparent that performing additional tests of control structure policies and procedures in all transaction cycles is an efficient strategy. For such clients, the auditor usually expects to be able to significantly reduce the assurance needed from substantive tests of accounts derived from transaction cycles, although some specific deficiencies in control structure policies and procedures may have to be taken into consideration.

Other enterprises, whether large or small, may have relatively complex computerized accounting systems, but the number and expertise of computer personnel may be limited. In other instances, there may be extensive control structure policies and procedures, but some general control procedures may be informal and not well documented. There are frequently deficiencies in control procedures related to program and data file security, although some of these deficiencies may be mitigated if the client uses purchased accounting packages for which the source code is not readily available (that is, the client's personnel are effectively unable to amend the programs). On these types of engagements it is often more difficult for the auditor to decide whether to perform additional tests of controls to support a further reduction in the assessed level of control risk.

Tests of controls focused on the control environment and accounting system do not require as much audit effort as tests of specific control procedures (the third element of the control structure). The evidence obtained from tests of the control environment and accounting system relates to several assertions and accounts, and thus is not sufficient in itself to support a low control risk assessment for specific assertions and account balances. To assess control risk as low for a particular assertion and account, the auditor will almost always have to perform additional tests of relevant control procedures and may also perform additional tests of controls directed at the control environment and accounting system.

In most engagements the auditor may believe he or she needs evidence of the effective operation of certain key control procedures in order to design efficient substantive tests with respect to a particular audit objective. The auditor then plans, at an early stage, to assess the effectiveness of those control procedures. Even if the results of such tests are not expected to support a low control risk assessment, they may affect the nature, timing, and extent of substantive tests. Examples of such key control procedures are physical inventory cycle count procedures, which the auditor might test to help establish the accuracy of inventory quantities, and cash reconciliations, tests of which might help establish the accuracy of the cash account balance.

The auditor's expectation when he or she performs tests of individual control procedures is that the tests will support a low risk assessment; that is, an assessment that all the control structure elements interacting together reduce to a low level the risk of material misstatement relating to an audit objective. This aggregate assessment will influence the auditor's decision about what specific tests to perform on which individual control procedures, what techniques to use, when to perform them, and how much testing to do. If the auditor assesses control risk as low for one or more assertions related to an account balance or class of transactions, he or she may be able to eliminate or significantly curtail substantive tests. SAS No. 55 cautions that regardless of the assessed level of control risk, some substantive tests should be performed for every significant account balance and class of transactions. However, if the auditor assesses the risk of material misstatement related to an assertion as low, it is not necessary to direct substantive tests to that particular assertion.

Figure 12.2 on pages 488 to 489 provides an example of the control objectives applicable to a client's sales of goods and services and of the control procedures an entity may have established to achieve the objectives.[2] As the figure indicates, one or more control procedures that the auditor expects will support a restriction of substantive tests would be identified for each control objective as a basis for designing tests of controls.

Sources of Evidence and Techniques Used to Test Controls

The evidence needed to support a specific assessed level of control risk is a matter of auditor judgment. In determining the evidence that is sufficient to support a specific assessed level of control risk below the maximum level, the auditor should consider the source of evidence, its timeliness, and whether related evidence exists. Those considerations in turn determine what specific techniques the auditor will use in performing tests of controls to obtain the needed evidence.

The techniques used in testing control structure policies and procedures are observation, inquiry of client personnel, examination of documents and records, and, in some cases, reperformance of the application of policies and procedures. (With the exception of reperformance, the techniques used in performing tests of controls are the same as those used in obtaining the understanding of the control structure elements, as described earlier in the chapter.)

There may be no client documentation of the design or operation of some policies or procedures, such as certain control environment factors and arrangements for segregating duties. In that event, evidence may be obtained through observation. In general, evidence the auditor obtains directly, for example, by observation, is more reliable than that obtained indirectly, such as by inquiry. However, this must be weighed against the possibility that the

[2]Figures 12.3, 13.2, 13.3, 13.4, and 14.2 illustrate the same principles for other classes of transactions.

observed procedure may not be performed in the same way when the auditor is not present.

During the inquiry process, the auditor should, wherever possible, corroborate the explanations received by inspecting procedures manuals and reports or other similar documents evidencing control structure policies and procedures. The auditor also may make corroborative inquiries of individuals other than those implementing the policies and procedures. SAS No. 55 states that inquiry alone generally does not provide sufficient evidence to support a conclusion about whether a specific policy or procedure is effective. Accordingly, if the auditor believes a policy or procedure may have a significant effect in reducing control risk to a low level for a specific assertion, he or she usually must perform tests in addition to inquiry to obtain sufficient evidence that it is designed and operating effectively.

For aspects of the control structure that are performed manually (such as the follow-up of items contained in computer-generated exception reports), the auditor should examine documents and records of the application when they may reasonably be expected to exist (for example, there may be written explanations, check marks, or other indications of performance on a copy of a report used in applying a control procedure). The auditor generally examines documentation of the performance of supervisory control procedures.

Tests based on observation, inquiry, and examination of documents ordinarily provide sufficient evidence about the effective design of a control structure policy or procedure, and often provide evidence about its operating effectiveness as well. That is, these tests provide evidence of how the policy or procedure was applied, whether it was applied consistently throughout the period, and the person(s) who applied it. However, in some instances, the auditor may also have to reperform the application of the policy or procedure to obtain adequate evidence that it is operating effectively. When the auditor believes a control structure policy or procedure is so significant that further evidence of its effectiveness is necessary, it is appropriate to reperform its application. For example, a bank's control procedure designed to ensure the completeness and accuracy of updating a standing data file of interest rates may be so significant to the accuracy of interest charged to loan customers that the auditor may wish to reperform the updating procedure a few times to gain additional evidence that it is operating as prescribed. If extensive reperformance of control procedures is likely to be necessary, the auditor should reconsider whether it is still efficient to perform tests of controls in order to restrict the scope of substantive testing.

Timeliness of Evidence. If observation is used as a test of controls, the auditor should consider that the evidence obtained from that test is relevant only to the time when the observation took place. Accordingly, the evidence may not be sufficient to assess effectiveness for untested periods. In that situation, the auditor may decide to perform other tests of controls to obtain evidence about whether the policy or procedure was operating during the entire period under audit. For example, the auditor may observe cycle counting of inventory at a point in time and examine documents evidencing the counting procedure during other time periods.

In considering evidence to support the assessment of the control structure in the current year, the auditor may consider prior-year audit evidence. In determining whether such evidence is relevant to the current audit, the auditor should consider the audit objective involved, the specific policies and procedures, the degree to which they were assessed in prior years, the results of the tests of controls performed, and the evidence about design or operation that may be expected from substantive tests in the current audit. The auditor should obtain information currently about whether changes in the control structure have occurred and, if so, their nature and extent. All of these considerations may support either increasing or decreasing the evidence needed in the current period.

Continuous Operation of Control Structure Policies and Procedures. When assessing whether tests of controls can reduce the assessed level of control risk sufficiently to permit the planned restriction of substantive tests, the auditor needs to determine that relevant control structure policies and procedures have operated continuously during the period.

Manually applied control structure policies and procedures are prone to random failures. When assessing those policies and procedures, the auditor should obtain evidence of their application, and if necessary reperform them, for control events occurring at different times during the period of assessment. These tests need not necessarily be extensive. Supervisory control procedures that the auditor can test may provide evidence that underlying manually performed control procedures were operating continuously.

Spreading tests throughout the period is not always necessary to obtain evidence about continuous operation. For example, if a control procedure involves reviewing and following up an exception report that is cumulative, transactions or circumstances meeting specified criteria continue to be reported and reviewed as long as the criteria are met (examples would be reports of "goods shipped but not billed" or "goods received but not invoiced"). For such control procedures, tests that provide evidence that a procedure operated effectively at a point in time will also provide evidence about the proper operation of the underlying accounting procedures throughout the period up to that point in time.

Accounting and control procedures performed by a computer program are not subject to random failures or deterioration over time, provided that the relevant general computer control procedures, including those for program maintenance, are operating effectively. This suggests that if general control procedures appear to be operating appropriately and effectively, the auditor could choose to test them as a basis for determining that accounting and control procedures performed by a computer program operated continuously throughout the period.

In addition, users of information affected by control structure policies and procedures would become aware of control breakdowns and report them to appropriate levels of management. Thus, the auditor can sometimes obtain indirect evidence, from the ongoing operation of business activities, that policies and procedures operated continuously.

Dual-Purpose Tests. Tests of controls normally precede substantive tests, because the results of tests of controls affect the auditor's decision about the appropriate nature, timing, and extent of substantive tests. Sometimes, however, to achieve greater audit efficiency, the two types of tests may be performed simultaneously using the same document or record. For example, the same accounts receivable balances selected for confirmation (a substantive test) may be used to determine that the customers' files contain documents showing that the sales orders were appropriately approved (a test of controls). Moreover, a test of controls may provide evidence about dollar errors in the accounts. Also, a substantive test may provide evidence about the control structure if no errors were found as a result of the substantive test or if errors that were found were investigated and determined to be the result of a control structure deficiency.

Interrelationship of Evidence. In assessing control risk for a specific audit objective, the auditor should consider evidence in its entirety: Evidence provided by tests of one element of the control structure should be considered in relation to evidence about the other elements. Evidence produced by different tests of controls should be considered in combination. Evidence from various tests that supports the same conclusion is more reliable than evidence obtained from a single test. When audit evidence from more than one source leads to different conclusions, however, the auditor should reconsider his or her original assessment. For example, if tests of the control environment indicate that it should prevent or detect unauthorized changes in a computer program, but tests of the effective operation of the program reveal that unauthorized changes were made and were not detected, the auditor would reassess the conclusion about the control environment.

Evaluating the Results of Tests of Controls. The auditor should review the results of the tests of controls and consider whether the expected reduction in the assessed level of control risk has been attained. If the auditor finds that the risk of material misstatement for a particular financial statement assertion is higher than originally expected, he or she will have to reconsider the assurance needed from substantive tests.

If the tests of controls reveal a departure from or breakdown in prescribed policies and procedures, the auditor should consider its cause and document his or her conclusions. What amendments need to be made to planned substantive tests will depend in part on the reasons for the departure. For example, the appropriate audit response to control structure breakdowns should be different if the cause was a poorly trained clerk who substituted for a highly trained clerk during the latter's three-week vacation than if the cause was incompetent work or ineffective supervision throughout the year. The auditor can sometimes ascertain the reason for a control breakdown by inquiring and examining the circumstances; in other cases, the auditor may have to extend the testing. Before extending the testing, however, the auditor should ensure that it will help determine the cause and extent of the breakdown. Depending on the nature of the policy or procedure, if a departure or breakdown is corrected long enough before year-end, and this is confirmed by appropriate tests, no amendment to other audit tests will normally be necessary.

Departures from and breakdowns in control structure policies and procedures should be considered for reporting to the client, as discussed later. Also, the documentation of the control structure should be amended as required.

DOCUMENTING THE ASSESSMENT AND TESTS

Professional standards require the auditor to document the basis for the conclusions reached concerning the assessed level of control risk for specific audit objectives related to the account balances and classes of transactions reflected in the financial statements. (For audit objectives for which control risk is assessed at the maximum level, however, the basis for the conclusion does not have to be documented.) The nature and extent of documentation will vary according to the assessed level of control risk and the nature of the control structure and the entity's related documentation.

Techniques for documenting the understanding of the control environment and the accounting system were discussed earlier in this chapter. This section presents several alternative formats for documenting the assessment of control procedures, provides examples, and explains when each could be used. Individual auditors and firms often express a preference for one type of documentation by means of their internal policy pronouncements and the practice aids (for example, forms, checklists, and questionnaires) they provide, which may be either required or optional. Regardless of the type of documentation the auditor uses, it must provide a means for recording in the working papers a description of the relevant control procedures and the tests the auditor performed to assess how effectively they were designed and operating.

Documenting Control Procedures

Control procedures are typically documented by narratives, flowcharts, control matrices, questionnaires, or other forms designed for this purpose.

Narratives. While many auditors prefer flowcharting as the means of documenting the design and assessment of the accounting system and related control procedures, narratives are often useful and, particularly for unsophisticated control structures, may be more cost effective. When narratives are used, the auditor should ensure that they contain all relevant information.

Flowcharts. Control procedures are sometimes documented on a flowchart, often called a *systems flowchart*, that depicts, for each significant class of transactions, the path of a transaction from its inception (that is, the point where the transaction first enters the accounting system) to the update of the general ledger. It provides, in a convenient form, a combined description of the accounting system and related control procedures and contains information necessary for the auditor to design tests of those control procedures. A systems flowchart typically contains, for each significant class of transactions,

1. The details of significant accounting and control procedures, including division of duties and supervision.
2. The job titles of the people performing the procedures.
3. The frequency of the operation of the procedures.

The information is usually organized by area of responsibility within the system. Depending on the responsibilities involved, an organizational unit may vary from a large department (such as a sales department) to one individual (the credit manager). The names of the organizational units the transactions flow through should be shown at the top of the flowchart. The flow of transactions usually is from top left to bottom right. Control procedures should be distinctly marked on the flowchart by a diagonal line inside a procedure symbol and may include a narrative supplement noting the nature of the control procedure (e.g., "approval").

Systems flowcharts need not be excessively detailed, as only significant procedures should be depicted. One or more accounting and related control procedures may be depicted by one symbol, with a narrative explanation of each significant procedure provided separately on the flowchart. This normally makes it possible to show each transaction cycle on one or two pages. An illustration of part of a systems flowchart for the sales order and billing portions of a computerized revenue cycle is provided in Figure 8.7.

Control Matrices. Some auditors capture information about the principal control procedures and any apparent deficiencies in them (such as omitted procedures) through the use of control matrices. Control matrices may be designed to record control procedures related to transaction processing, file control, asset protection, or any other relevant types of control procedures, whether computerized or manual. Figure 8.8 shows a control matrix covering the processing of transactions relating to both shipments and cash receipts in a computerized revenue cycle. It describes the principal control procedures the client designed to meet the control objectives relating to transaction processing and serves as an aid in understanding those procedures and designing tests of controls. It may even serve as a substitute for an internal control questionnaire or other similar form of documentation, as discussed later.

Figure 8.7 Systems Flowchart—Revenue Cycle, Shipping and Billing

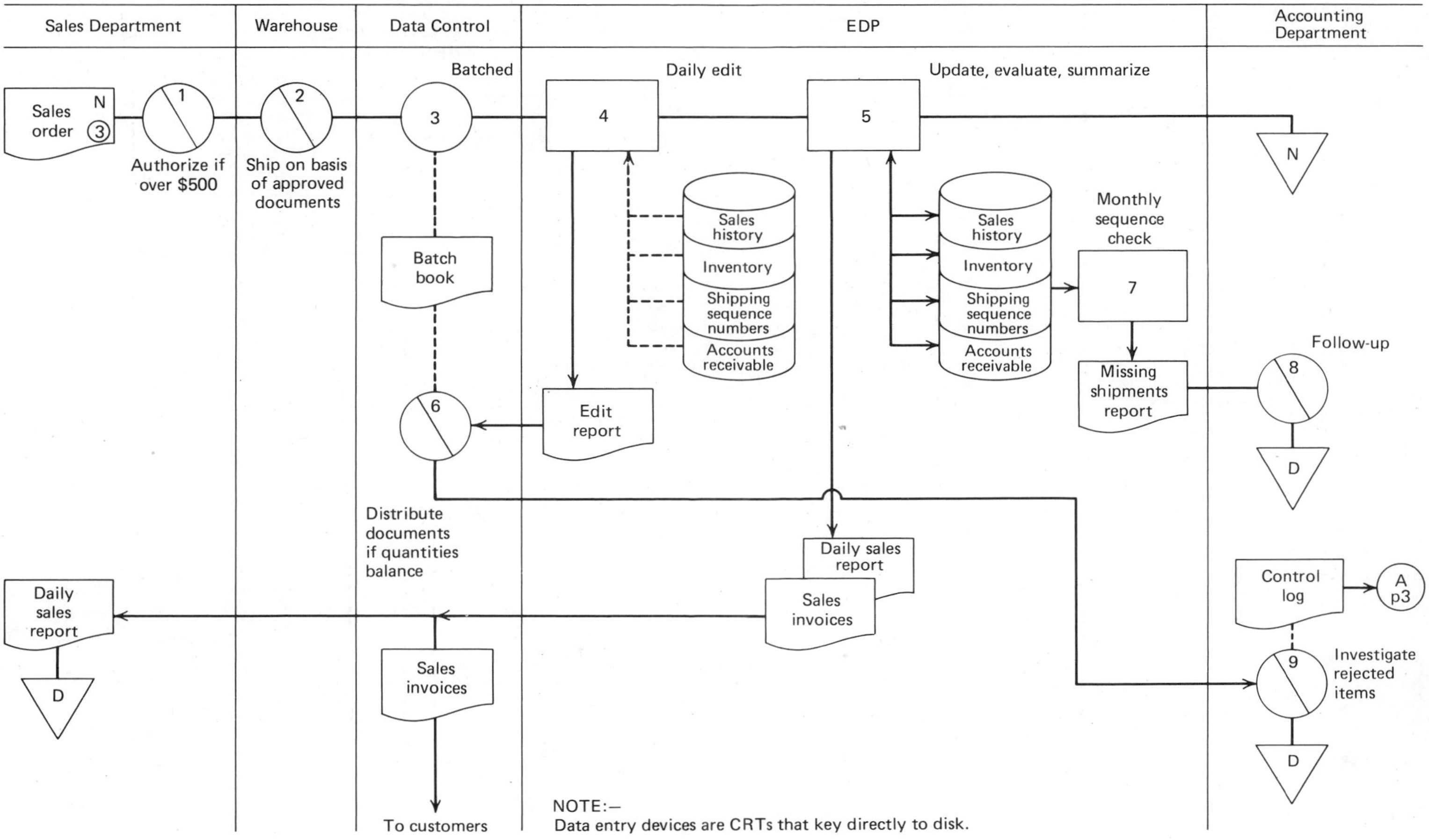

NOTE:—
Data entry devices are CRTs that key directly to disk.

Figure 8.8 Transaction Control Matrix

Client/Location Alpha Corporation/Middlebury
Application/Class of transactions Revenue Cycle

Prepared by/Date ______
Reviewed by/Date ______

Significant transactions/Key files receiving initial input (volumes)	*Input/Generation*				*Updates*		
	Completeness	*Accuracy (specify fields)*	*Standing data used*	*Authorization*	*Key file(s)*	*Completeness and accuracy*	*Division of duties*
Shipments Open order file Sales transaction file (160,000 shipments per year)	Shipments matched against open order file; numerically sequenced invoices generated; shipments recorded on sales transaction file. Investigation of long-outstanding open orders and review for integrity of numerical sequence of invoices & bills of lading on sales transaction listing.	Matching sales order to inventory master file and A/R file • customer no. • product code • price Matching shipping order to open order file • customer no. • product code • quantity	Product no. Price Customer no.	As orders are input, they are matched against preestablished credit limits and sales terms. Orders outside preestablished limits are investigated before being updated to the open order file.	A/R file, G/L master file	Comparison of A/R balance with G/L master file. Comparison of sales with monthly activity on G/L master file. Sequence check of invoice numbers.	Initiate order; approve order; input shipment; compare account activity & balances with G/L master file; follow-up on exceptions.
Cash remittances Cash receipts transaction file (45,000 cash remittances per year)	Cash receipts listing reconciled to bank's deposit control report.	Matching cash remittances to open invoices on A/R file	N/A	N/A	A/R file, G/L master file	Comparison of A/R balance with G/L master file. Comparison of cash receipts listings with deposits recorded on bank statements.	Receipt of cash; deposit of cash; input of cash remittance; comparison of A/R with G/L & comparison of cash receipts listing with bank deposits; follow-up on exceptions.

An explanation of the columns in the illustrated control matrix follows.

- The *significant transactions/key files receiving initial input (volumes)* column describes briefly each significant class of transactions (manually initiated or computer generated), including amendments to standing data, with an estimate of the annual volume of transactions processed. Significant transactions are transactions that could have a material effect on the key data file(s) that support account balances.
- The *completeness of input/generation* column identifies the principal control procedures used to ensure that all such transactions are initiated, recorded, and accepted for further processing.
- The *accuracy of input/generation* column identifies the principal control procedures used to ensure that the key data fields are accurately recorded.
- The *input/generation—standing data used* column indicates the key data file(s) involved.
- The *authorization for input/generation* column identifies and records the principal control procedures used to prevent or detect unauthorized transactions.
- The *updates—key file(s)* column records the key file(s) updated by the key transaction fields.
- The *completeness and accuracy of updates* column records the principal control procedures used to ensure that the key file(s) listed in the previous column are completely and accurately updated by the transaction.
- The *division of duties* column records what duties are performed by separate persons, i.e., showing that those responsible for control procedures related to transaction processing are separate from those who have access to the related assets.

Internal Control Questionnaires. Since control objectives and the means of achieving them are much the same from one control structure to another, some auditors find it efficient to design an internal control questionnaire (ICQ) that identifies and lists expected control procedures and then use the questionnaire to document control procedures on all or most engagements. The questionnaire is usually divided into transaction cycles that cover the main transaction flows, and is organized in terms of the control objectives that should be achieved by the client's control procedures at each stage of transaction processing. The questions relating to each control objective are sometimes further subdivided between

1. Those that seek information concerning *accounting procedures* that are not in themselves control procedures, but that form the basis for the exercise of control procedures.
2. Those that seek to determine whether or not *control procedures* are present.

A portion of this type of questionnaire for a manual revenue cycle is illustrated in Figure 8.9. Questions in an ICQ also frequently indicate the type of control procedure being addressed: transaction processing, file control, asset protection, segregation of duties, supervisory, or general computer. While it is not necessary to have this degree of subdivision for an ICQ to be effective, it may allow for a better understanding of the internal control structure and is helpful in designing both tests of controls and substantive tests.

The ICQ is also a convenient way of documenting the specific internal control procedures that the auditor intends to test. If systems flowcharts have

Figure 8.9 Internal Control Questionnaire

Control Procedures Applied to Goods Shipped and Services Performed	*Flowchart Reference*	*Yes*	*No*
Completeness			
Accounting Procedures—Basis for Control Procedures			
1. Are the accounting records maintained in such a way that it can subsequently be established whether all the related transactions have been accounted for (e.g., by sequentially prenumbering delivery slips) in respect of:			
(a) Goods?			
(b) Services?			
2. Are records maintained of goods shipped and services performed that have not been matched with the related sales invoices in respect of:			
(a) Goods?			
(b) Services?			
Control Procedures			
3. If sequentially prenumbered forms are used, are all numbers accounted for as part of the procedure for ascertaining unmatched items in respect of:			
(a) Goods?			
(b) Services?			
4. Are unmatched records of goods shipped and services performed reviewed on a regular basis (e.g., monthly) to determine the reasons for any such items that have not been matched within a reasonable period of time in respect of:			
(a) Goods?			
(b) Services?			
5. Are the results of the procedure in question 4 reviewed and approved by a responsible official?			

been prepared, the information contained in them should be used, as much as possible, in answering the ICQ questions. The questions in the ICQ are usually phrased so that they may be answered "Yes" or "No" to indicate, respectively, the presence or absence of a control procedure. If a question does not apply to a specific client or location, the appropriate response is N/A (Not Applicable).

The ICQ is often completed concurrently with obtaining the understanding of the design of control procedures, which is in part the basis for the auditor's decision to perform tests of controls. The auditor should reconsider the answers to the ICQ questions during subsequent stages of the audit, particularly after performing tests of controls and substantive tests. Departures from or deficiencies in prescribed control procedures may be disclosed by substantive tests. In that event, the ICQ should be amended to reflect the new information.

Documenting Tests of Control Procedures

When tests of controls are performed, they must be documented, and auditors use many different means of doing so. The choice, once again, depends on such factors as the type of test (for example, observing that a control procedure is operating versus reperforming it) and the policies of the particular CPA firm. Some tests of controls can conveniently be recorded directly on control matrices or internal control questionnaires, in which case the matrices and ICQs, with minor adaptations, document both the control procedures identified and the tests performed to ensure that they are operating effectively. (Conceptually, tests of controls can also be documented as part of a narrative description of accounting and control procedures or on a flowchart, but those documentation methods can make it difficult for a reviewer to evaluate the tests performed.) Alternatively, separate working papers could be used to document the tests performed; this method is particularly useful when a test consists of examining evidence of the operation of a control procedure (such as authorization of payroll changes by department heads and personnel managers) or reperformance of a control procedure (such as reperforming, at year-end, the client's monthly follow-up of all unmatched cash receipts included in a suspense account, for evidence that the receipts were credited to the proper account).

Some auditing firms have designed forms specifically for both recording the client's control procedures and documenting the results of tests of those procedures. The form may be organized like an ICQ; that is, it may be divided into sections by control objectives and list under each control objective questions related to the control procedures that achieve that objective. The auditor indicates a "Yes" or "No" answer to each question and describes, either directly on the form or on an attached working paper, the relevant control procedure and the tests of controls performed.

Control procedures should be described in sufficient detail to support the auditor's conclusion as to whether the control objective has been achieved. Similarly, tests of controls should be recorded in enough detail to support the auditor's conclusion about whether the procedures are operating effectively. A question may be included at the end of each section that prompts the auditor to draw an overall conclusion about whether the control procedures, taken as a whole, are appropriately designed to achieve the control objective and are operating effectively, and to document the reasons for the conclusion.

Figure 8.10 shows part of a form used to document control procedures and tests of controls. The two pages illustrated relate to the completeness-of-input control objective for shipments in a computerized revenue cycle. The control procedures described are based on the same set of facts recorded on the control matrix shown in Figure 8.8.

Documenting Control Deficiencies

It is often helpful for the auditor to prepare a document summarizing the deficiencies found in the design or operation of control procedures. This permits the auditor to consider the effect of the deficiencies on planned substantive tests. It also facilitates preparing the communication on control structure deficiencies (discussed in the next section). The documentation should be amended whenever pertinent information is found in the course of the audit, whether in performing tests of controls or substantive tests. The working paper documentation will usually include a description of the nature of the deficiency and its possible effect on the financial statements, a decision on whether the deficiency could give rise to material misstatement in the financial statements and the justification for this decision, and an explanation of the audit response to the deficiency, including any amendment to the nature, timing, or extent of substantive procedures.

COMMUNICATING CONTROL STRUCTURE DEFICIENCIES

While management has primary responsibility for reliable financial reporting, the board of directors, generally acting through its audit committee (if there is one), is responsible for overseeing the financial reporting process. That responsibility can be most effectively carried out if the board or audit committee is informed of deficiencies in the internal control structure that the auditor becomes aware of. Management also is usually interested in the auditor's observations about internal control deficiencies and ways of remedying them, and in suggestions the auditor may have for improving the enterprise's operations and profitability.

SAS No. 60, *Communication of Internal Control Structure Related Matters Noted in an Audit* (AU Section 325.02), requires the auditor to communicate to the audit committee of the board of directors, or its equivalent, matters coming to his or her attention in the course of the audit that represent "significant deficiencies" in the design or operation of any of the elements of the internal control structure that could adversely affect the organization's ability to "record, process, summarize, and report financial data consistent with the assertions of management in the financial statements." The SAS refers to these matters as "reportable conditions," and expresses a preference that they be communicated in writing rather than orally. The SAS explicitly permits the auditor to comment on other matters that do not meet the criteria of "reportable conditions" but that the auditor deems to be of value to the audit committee, and those comments may be segregated from observations about reportable conditions. Figure 8.11 presents an example of a report to an audit committee on internal control structure related matters.

Although the auditor is required to communicate reportable conditions only to the audit committee or its equivalent, the authors believe it is good practice to communicate such matters to management as well. If there is no audit committee or board of directors or the equivalent, the communication would be made only to management (which is likely to be an owner-manager) or to the party that engaged the auditor.

The auditor may come across matters other than reportable conditions in the course of an audit that would be helpful to management in carrying out its duties. These are matters that either may be below the threshold of significance for reporting to the audit committee, or may be financial and business suggestions that would enhance operational efficiency and profitability. The auditor usually discusses such matters with management and may also communicate them in writing. Similarly, management may request the auditor to be alert to certain matters that might not be considered reportable conditions and to submit a report on the findings. These agreed-upon arrangements, which may be particularly useful to the client, do not relieve the auditor of the basic responsibility to communicate reportable conditions.

It is good practice for the auditor to discuss all comments on the internal control structure with the client before drafting a written communication. If the auditor's understanding of the control structure was mistaken in some respect, discussing the comments will clarify the misunderstanding and save the auditor the embarrassment of discovering it later. In many instances, management's responses to the auditor's suggestions are included in the communication. The best time to discuss deficiencies in the control structure and related problems and to draft a written communication is at the conclusion of tests of controls. Ideally, that point occurs when both auditor and management have time to consider the auditor's findings. It should preferably take place far enough before year-end to permit corrective action that could affect the auditor's remaining work.

Figure 8.10 Record of Control Procedures and Tests

Control Objective 3—Revenue Cycle (Shipments)—Completeness of Input

Questions and control procedures	*Yes*	*No*	*Tests*
Transactions controlled by matching 3.1 Are the procedures for setting up and maintaining expected transactions on the control file adequate to ensure that the matching process could ensure completeness of processing? Shipments are matched against the items flagged on the open order file as having generated a bill of lading.	✓		Information provided by Jim Miller (Controller) and the EDP Manager
3.2 Is the matching process adequate to: (a) form a basis for identifying all unmatched transactions. (b) identify duplicates and other mismatching transactions? Twice a day, a list summarizing orders entered since the last transmission and a bill of lading for each order are generated. The items in the open order file are flagged as having generated a bill of lading. After shipment, the shipping input clerk enters the sales order number and quantity shipped via CRT. The customer and item number are compared with the order information appearing on the CRT. (a) Items flagged as having generated a bill of lading that have not been confirmed as shipped are reported on the unmatched bill of lading report. (b) Invoices are generated for items confirmed as shipped and the order is flagged as completed on the open order file.	✓		On 4/4/X3 we discussed the review of the unmatched bill of lading report with Jake O'Leary, accounts receivable supervisor. He indicated that normally the items are the result of orders received late in the day, which they were unable to ship until the following day. We examined the reports for the following days: June 8 and 15, September 17 and 19, November 10 and 25, and April 1 and noted fewer than 10 items appeared on each day (see workpapers 101.9–101.15). All orders were noted as being shipped the following day. The orders did not appear on the next day's report. O'Leary had approved the reports.
3.3 Are all changes and deletions to the control file of expected transactions approved?			The sales manager indicated that changes to the open order file normally result from changes to

Figure 8.10 *Continued*

Questions and control procedures	*Yes*	*No*	*Tests*
Changes to and deletions from the open order file require the approval of the sales manager prior to input. A report listing all the changes is generated, and a one-for-one comparison is performed.	✓		orders that were on backorder, had price overrides, or had credit limit overrides. We examined the file of daily change order reports for the month of March, noting that only 10 changes had been made that month. All reports were approved. We examined the March 12 report, noting that it contained only one item, which was a change in the order quantity that was made to keep the customer within its credit limit. Notations on the report indicated that the customer had been contacted and wished to reduce its order.
3.4 Is a report of long outstanding transactions or aged analysis produced at regular intervals? The unmatched bill of lading report is produced daily. The unmatched order report is cumulative; therefore any correction not made would reappear as an exception on the next day's report.	✓		During our performance of step 3.2 we observed that the client's files contained daily cumulative reports.
3.5 Are there adequate procedures to investigate and, if necessary, correct: (a) long outstanding items: (b) all duplicates, mismatches, and rejections? (a) Items appearing on the unmatched bill of lading report are investigated each day. The report and corrections are approved by the accounts receivable supervisor. (b) The integrity of the numerical sequence of the invoices and the bills of lading on the sales transaction listing is reviewed monthly. Mismatched bills of lading are investigated in (a).	✓		(a) See testing of 3.2. (b) We discussed the procedure with the accounts receivable supervisor and examined the June and November reports. One duplicate invoice and two missing bill of lading numbers were identified on the reports. We noted that the items were corrected and the supervisor had approved the reports and corrections.

Figure 8.11 Report on Internal Control Structure Related Matters

April 12, 19XY

Audit Committee of the Board of Directors
ABC Manufacturing Co., Inc.
123 Industrial Road
Anytown, U.S.A. 12345

Gentlemen:

In planning and performing our audit of the financial statements of the ABC Manufacturing Co., Inc., for the year ended December 31, 19XX, we considered its internal control structure in order to determine our auditing procedures for the purpose of expressing our opinion on the financial statements and not to provide assurance on the internal control structure. However, we noted certain matters involving the internal control structure and its operation that we consider to be reportable conditions under standards established by the American Institute of Certified Public Accountants. Reportable conditions involve matters coming to our attention relating to significant deficiencies in the design or operation of the internal control structure that, in our judgment, could adversely affect the organization's ability to record, process, summarize, and report financial data consistent with the assertions of management in the financial statements.

Access Controls to Data by Terminals Can Be Bypassed

At the present time, there is a critical "file protect" system that prohibits the access of production data by remote terminal users. Our review disclosed a method (special coding of a control card) by which this system can be bypassed and remote terminal users can access and/or alter financial data in computer files. Unauthorized access to data files can result in inaccurate financial data being reported by the systems or confidential data being available to unauthorized personnel. Management is currently studying various means of correcting this situation.

The Director of Internal Audit Reports to the Controller

The objectivity of the internal audit function is enhanced when the director of internal audit reports to an individual or group in the company with sufficient authority to promote independence, provide adequate consideration of findings and recommendations in audit reports, ensure that appropriate action is taken on audit recommendations, and resolve conflicts between internal auditors and various levels of management. At ABC Manufacturing Co., Inc., the director

Figure 8.11 ***Continued***

of internal audit for each subsidiary reports to the subsidiary controller; the corporate director of internal audit reports to the corporate controller. We believe that the directors' objectivity would be enhanced if they reported to the vice-president and treasurer of each subsidiary and the corporate vice-president and treasurer, respectively, with summaries of all internal audit reports presented to the audit committee of the board of directors.

Inadequate Systems for Preparing Consolidated Satements

The accounting department does not presently have sufficient staff to prepare consolidated reports of worldwide operations in time to meet the company's requirements for preparing quarterly and year-end financial information. Those requirements are presently met, in part, through the assistance of both the internal auditors and ourselves. Preparing consolidated financial statements is not an appropriate service for either the internal or external auditors to provide. Financial management agrees with our views and is currently undertaking to add sufficient competent personnel and appropriate computer software to the accounting department to enable it to prepare consolidated quarterly and year-end financial statements on a timely basis.

This report is intended solely for the information and use of the audit committee, management, and others within the organization.

Very truly yours,

Smith and Jones, CPAs

The auditor has no obligation to extend auditing procedures in order to search for reportable conditions, but merely an obligation to report those coming to his or her attention as a result of procedures that are performed as part of the audit. Many practitioners believe that reports on the internal control structure that are based solely on what the auditor learns in the course of an audit are likely to be often misunderstood or misinterpreted by the public at large, who may read into them a greater degree of assurance than is warranted. Accordingly, the SAS specifies that "the report should state that the communication is intended solely for the information and the use of the audit committee, management, and others within the organization" (AU Section 325.10). The report may also discuss the inherent limitations of internal control in general and the specific nature and extent of the auditor's consideration of the internal control structure.

Determining whether a deficiency in the design or operation of an entity's control environment, accounting system, or control procedures is a reportable condition requires considerable judgment on the part of the auditor. In making that judgment, the auditor considers various factors relating to the specific client, such as its organizational structure, ownership characteristics, size, complexity, and diversity of operations.

Reportable conditions may be of such magnitude as to be considered material weaknesses in the internal control structure. A material weakness is "a reportable condition in which the design or operation of the specific internal control structure elements do not reduce to a relatively low level the risk that errors or irregularities in amounts that would be material in relation to the financial statements being audited may occur and not be detected within a timely period by employees in the normal course of performing their assigned functions." Although not required to do so, an auditor may choose to separately identify those reportable conditions that meet this definition. Or, if it is appropriate to do so, the auditor may state that none of the reportable conditions communicated were believed to be a material weakness. However, the auditor should not issue a written representation that no reportable conditions were noted during the audit, because of the potential for misinterpretation of the limited degree of assurance that such a report would provide.

The client may already be aware of the existence of reportable conditions related to internal control structure design or operation, and may have decided to accept the accompanying degree of control risk because of cost or other considerations. If the audit committee has acknowledged that it understands and has considered a deficiency and the related risks, the auditor need not continue to report the matter after it has been initially reported to the committee. Changes in management or in the audit committee, or merely the passage of time, may nevertheless make continued reporting of such matters appropriate and timely.

Many auditors believe that all recommendations for improvements in the control structure that are communicated to any level of management should be brought to the attention of the client's audit committee. One way to do this would be to include a statement in the report to the audit committee that the auditor has, in a separate communication to management, made suggestions for control structure improvements that do not involve reportable conditions. A copy of that communication could also be sent to the audit committee.

Review Questions

8–1. Define inherent risk conditions and give some examples.

8–2. From what general sources does an auditor obtain the information to assess inherent risk and control risk?

8–3. Explain how analytical procedures aid in assessing inherent risk.

8–4. What are related parties and what are the auditor's responsibilities with respect to related party transactions?

8–5. What two aspects of control structure policies and procedures are covered by the required understanding of the control structure?

8–6. How does the auditor obtain an understanding of the control environment and the accounting system?

8–7. What is a transaction review and why do auditors sometimes perform such a review?

8–8. What are the principal features of an accounting system that an overview flowchart should depict?

8–9. How does risk assessment affect audit strategy?

8–10. What are tests of controls and what factors does the auditor consider in deciding whether to perform them?

8–11. What factors should the auditor consider in assessing the usefulness of management's review of operating reports?

8–12. What is the rationale behind the auditor's decision about which specific control procedures should be tested?

8–13. Name the techniques used in performing tests of controls.

8–14. When is reperformance of a control policy or procedure considered appropriate?

8–15. Describe and illustrate a dual-purpose test.

8–16. How does using an internal control questionnaire enhance audit effectiveness and efficiency?

8–17. What are the auditor's responsibilities regarding deficiencies in the internal control structure that are discovered in the course of an audit?

8–18. What are material weaknesses, as specified in SAS No. 60?

Discussion Questions

8–30. After obtaining an understanding of the internal control structure and assessment of inherent and control risks in an audit engagement, you are about to prepare a draft of the required communication to the audit committee about the control structure. Certain reportable conditions, as well as other matters calling for comments and recommendations, were noted during this work.

Required:

a. Draft the required communication, assuming the reportable conditions are not separately identified from the other comments and recommendations.

b. Draft the required communication, assuming the reportable conditions are separately identified from the other comments and recommendations.

8–31. An entity's internal control structure consists of the policies and procedures established to provide reasonable assurance that specific entity objectives will be achieved. For purposes of an audit of financial statements, the internal control structure consists of the control environment, the accounting system, and control procedures.

Required:

a. What is the purpose of the auditor's understanding of the internal control structure?
b. What are the minimum requirements for this understanding?
c. How is the auditor's understanding of the internal control structure documented?

(AICPA adapted)

8–32. Adherence to generally accepted auditing standards requires, among other things, an understanding of the internal control structure. The most common approaches to understanding the internal control structure include the use of a questionnaire, preparation of a memorandum, preparation of a flowchart, preparation of a control matrix, and combinations of these methods.

Required:

Discuss the advantages to a CPA of obtaining an understanding of the internal control structure by using:

a. An internal control questionnaire.
b. The memorandum (or narrative) approach.
c. A flowchart.
d. A control matrix.

(AICPA adapted)

8–33. Temple, CPA, is auditing the financial statements of Ford Lumber Yards, Inc., a privately held corporation with 300 employees and 5 stockholders, 3 of whom are active in management. Ford has been in business for many years, but has never had its financial statements audited. Temple suspects that the substance of some of Ford's business transactions differs from their form because of the pervasiveness of related party relationships and transactions in the local building supplies industry.

Required:

Describe the auditing procedures Temple should apply to identify related party relationships and transactions.

(AICPA adapted)

AICPA Multiple Choice Questions

These questions are taken or adapted from the Auditing part of Uniform CPA Examinations. Choose the single most appropriate answer.

8–40. To help plan the nature, timing, and extent of substantive auditing procedures, preliminary analytical procedures should focus on

a. Enhancing the auditor's understanding of the client's business and events that have occurred since the last audit date.
b. Developing plausible relationships that corroborate anticipated results with a measurable amount of precision.
c. Applying ratio analysis to externally generated data such as published industry statistics or price indices.
d. Comparing recorded financial information to the results of other tests of transactions and balances.

8–41. The auditor's communication of significant deficiencies in the internal control structure is

a. Required to enable the auditor to state that the audit has been conducted in accordance with generally accepted auditing standards.
b. The principal reason for assessing the internal control structure.
c. Incidental to the auditor's objective of forming an opinion as to the fair presentation of the financial statements.
d. Required to be documented in a written report to the chief executive officer.

8–42. When erroneous data is detected by programmed control procedures, such data may be excluded from processing and printed on an error report. The error report should most probably be reviewed and followed up by the

a. User department control group.
b. System analyst.
c. Supervisor of computer operations.
d. Computer programmer.

8–43. Which of the following is *not* a medium that can normally be used by an auditor to record information concerning a client's internal control structure?

a. Narrative memorandum.
b. Procedures manual.
c. Flowchart.
d. Decision table.

8–44. Which of the following is *least* likely to be evidence the auditor examines to determine whether control structure policies and procedures are being applied as prescribed?

a. Records documenting usage of EDP programs.
b. Canceled supporting documents.
c. Confirmations of accounts receivable.
d. Signatures on authorization forms.

8–45. Which of the following symbolic representations indicates that a sales invoice has been filed?

a. 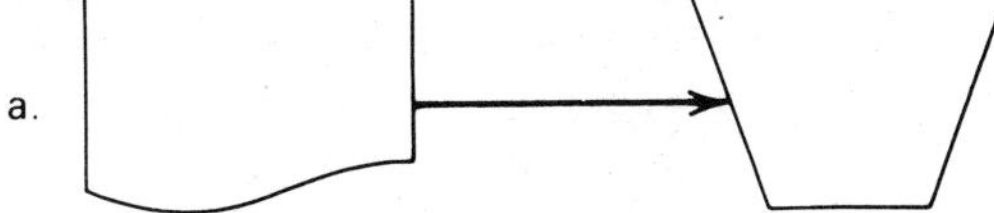

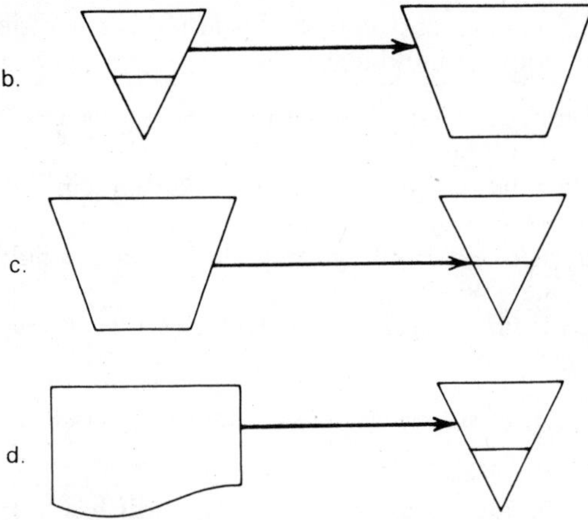

8–46. Tests of controls are performed in order to determine whether or not

a. Control procedures are functioning as designed.
b. Necessary control procedures are absent.
c. Incompatible functions exist.
d. Material dollar errors exist.

8–47. Which of the following would be *least* likely to be included in an auditor's tests of controls?

a. Inspection.
b. Observation.
c. Inquiry.
d. Confirmation.

8–48. A procedure that would most likely be used by an auditor in performing tests of control procedures that involve segregation of functions and that leave *no* transaction trail is

a. Inspection.
b. Observation.
c. Reperformance.
d. Reconciliation.

8–49. Which of the following is *not* a reason an auditor should obtain an understanding of the elements of an entity's internal control structure in planning an audit?

a. Identify the types of potential misstatements that can occur.
b. Design substantive tests.
c. Consider the operating effectiveness of the internal control structure.
d. Consider factors that affect the risk of material misstatements.

8–50. Which of the following statements is correct concerning related party transactions?

a. In the absence of evidence to the contrary, related party transactions should be assumed to be outside the ordinary course of business.

b. An auditor should determine whether a particular transaction would have occurred if the parties had *not* been related.
c. An auditor should substantiate that related party transactions were consummated on terms equivalent to those that prevail in arm's-length transactions.
d. The auditing procedures directed toward identifying related party transactions should include considering whether transactions are occurring, but are *not* being given proper accounting recognition.

8–51. Which of the following statements is correct concerning an auditor's communication of internal control structure related matters (reportable conditions) noted in an audit?

a. The auditor may issue a written report to the audit committee representing that *no* reportable conditions were noted during the audit.
b. Reportable conditions should be recommunicated each year even if the audit committee has acknowledged its understanding of such deficiencies.
c. Reportable conditions may *not* be communicated in a document that contains suggestions regarding activities that concern other topics such as business strategies or administrative efficiencies.
d. The auditor may choose to communicate significant internal control structure related matters either during the course of the audit or after the audit is concluded.

Problems and Cases

8–60. You have been approached by a young entrepreneur, Mr. Kent, who is starting a new business called Sooperman, Inc. The business will purchase television sets and radios from Krypto, Inc., at a favorable price for resale to small retailers throughout the United States. Mr. Kent is confident of success as the products are competitively priced.

To carry out this business, Mr. Kent will use the warehouse and offices that he uses for his existing business. However, the areas will be strictly segregated for the new operations. Mr. Kent needs advice in setting up an accounting system and procedures to ensure that he can control the new business. He realizes that he has no idea where to start, and has approached you for general advice about an accounting system.

Required:

Outlined on page 308 is a general description of how Mr. Kent intends to operate the business of buying and selling the equipment. Using this information:

a. List the books, documents, and other records that will be required to record transactions for purchases and payments.
b. List the books, documents, and other records that will be required to record sales transactions and collections.
c. Write out in narrative form a basic accounting system for the buying and revenue cycles of Sooperman, Inc. The accounting system should focus on the books, documents, and other records identified in Parts a and b. (Do not consider control procedures in your narrative.)

Buying Cycle

TVs and radios will be received bimonthly from Krypto, Inc., and invoiced at that time for payment 30 days later. At the end of each quarter, a bulk discount will be granted based on the number of units purchased during the quarter.

The discount will be calculated by Krypto, Inc., and remitted by check 10 days after the end of each quarter.

Orders must be sent to Krypto in writing and delivery will be made within two weeks.

All deliveries will be made to Sooperman's warehouse, and never directly to its customers.

Mr. Kent wishes to pay all his suppliers at the same time. Although Krypto will be his sole supplier for goods for resale, he knows that there will be expenses for stationery, utilities, fixtures, traveling, and entertaining. Mr. Kent will have two warehouse employees and a sales manager, in addition to a bookkeeper and six other administrative and secretarial personnel.

Revenue Cycle

Mr. Kent intends to sell the sets via sales agents in nine major cities. The agents will communicate the orders they receive to the company, and shipments will be made to the customers.

At present, Mr. Kent has a list of interested customers, but he is leaving the development of new customers to the agents and the sales manager. Agents will be paid a base salary and a commission on each sale in the month in which the goods are delivered.

Mr. Kent also appreciates that cash flow will be very important in the early days of the new business, so he intends to bill customers on delivery with 30-day payment terms, offering a 2 percent cash discount to customers who pay within 10 days.

All sets are guaranteed by the manufacturer, and warranty claims will be made directly to Krypto, Inc., by customers.

8–61. You are reviewing audit working papers containing a narrative description of the Thornwood Company's factory payroll system. A portion of that narrative is as follows:

> Factory employees punch time clock cards each day when entering or leaving the shop. At the end of each week the timekeeping department collects the time cards and prepares duplicate batch-control slips by department showing total hours and number of employees. The time cards and original batch-control slips are sent to the payroll accounting section. The second copies of the batch-control slips are filed by date.
>
> In the payroll accounting section payroll transaction cards are keypunched from the information on the time cards, and a batch total card for each batch is keypunched from the batch-control slip. The time cards and batch-control slips are then filed by batch for possible reference. The payroll transaction cards and batch total card are sent to data processing, where they are sorted by employee number within batch. Each batch is edited by a computer program that checks the validity of employee number against a master employee tape file and the total hours and number of employees against the batch total card. A detailed printout by batch and employee number is produced that indicates batches that do not balance and invalid employee numbers. This printout is returned to payroll accounting to resolve all differences.

In searching for documentation you found a flowchart of the payroll system that included all appropriate symbols (American National Standards Institute, Inc.) but was only partially labeled. The portion of this flowchart described by the foregoing narrative appears below.

Required:

a. Number your answer 1 through 17. Next to the corresponding number of your answer, supply the appropriate labeling (document name, process description, or file order) applicable to each numbered symbol on the flowchart.
b. Flowcharts are one of the aids an auditor may use to document an understanding of the client's internal control structure. List advantages of using flowcharts in this context.

(AICPA adapted)

8-62. The figure on page 310 illustrates a manual system for executing purchases and cash disbursements transactions.

Required:

Indicate what each of the letters "A" through "L" represents. Do not discuss adequacies or inadequacies in the control procedures.

(AICPA adapted)

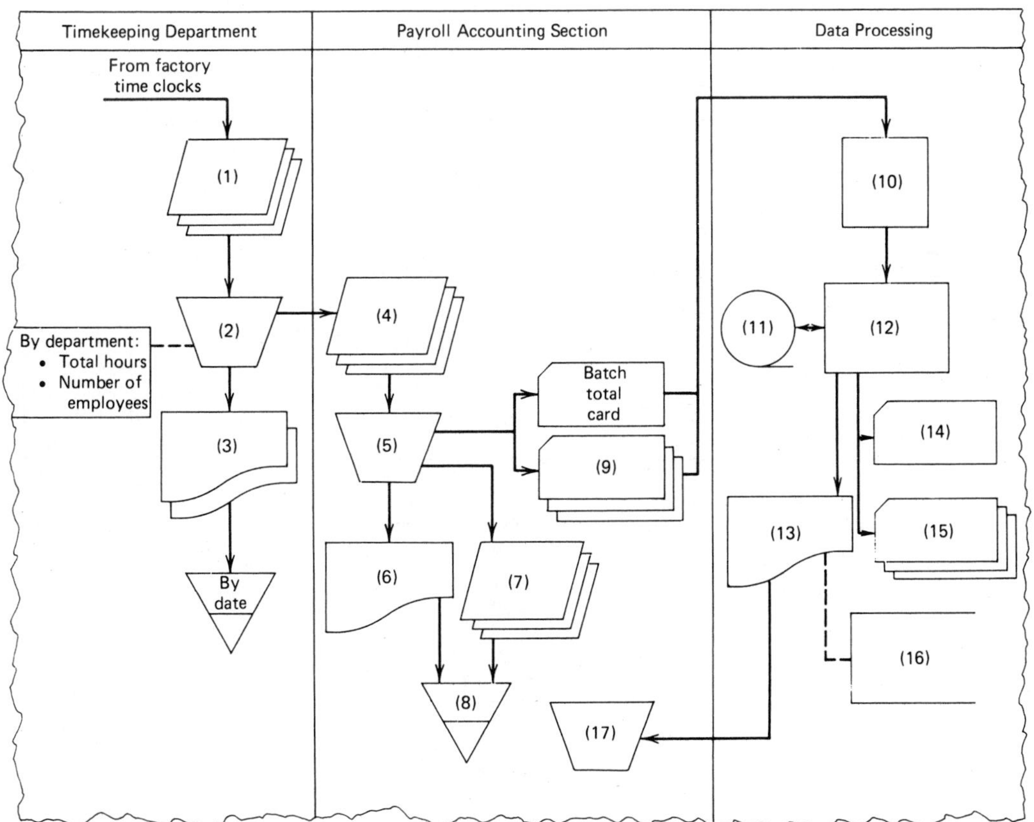

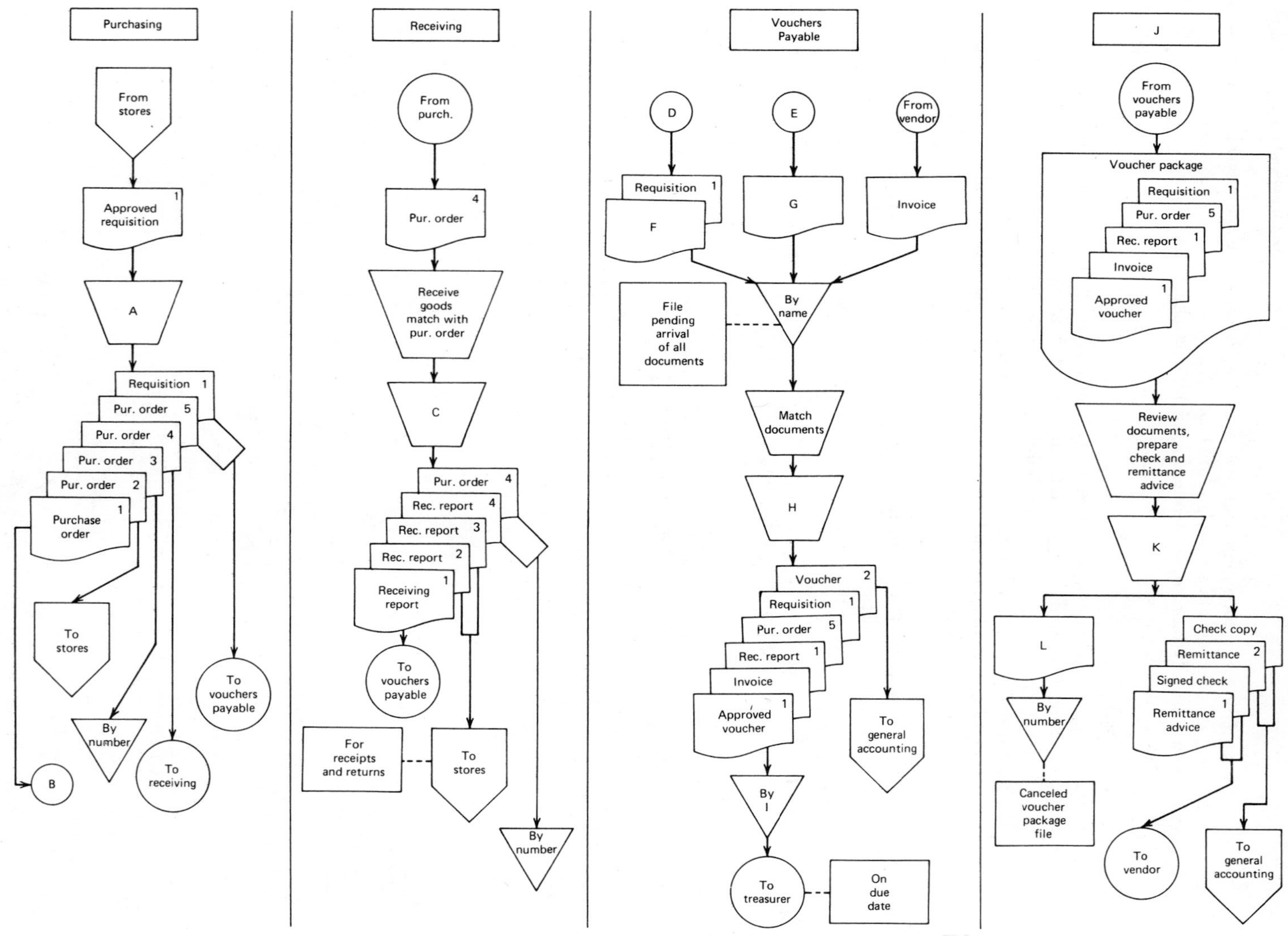

Purchasing
From stores
Approved requisition 1
A
Requisition 1
Pur. order 5
Pur. order 4
Pur. order 3
Pur. order 2
Purchase order 1
To stores
By number
To receiving
To vouchers payable
B
Receiving
From purch.
Pur. order 4
Receive goods match with pur. order
C
Pur. order 4
Rec. report 4
Rec. report 3
Rec. report 2
Receiving report 1
To vouchers payable
For receipts and returns
To stores
By number
Vouchers Payable
D
E
From vendor
Requisition 1
F
G
Invoice
By name
File pending arrival of all documents
Match documents
H
Voucher 2
Requisition 1
Pur. order 5
Rec. report 1
Invoice
Approved voucher 1
To general accounting
By I
To treasurer
On due date
J
From vouchers payable
Voucher package
Requisition 1
Pur. order 5
Rec. report 1
Invoice
Approved voucher 1
Review documents, prepare check and remittance advice
K
L
By number
Canceled voucher package file
Check copy
Remittance 2
Signed check
Remittance advice 1
To vendor
To general accounting

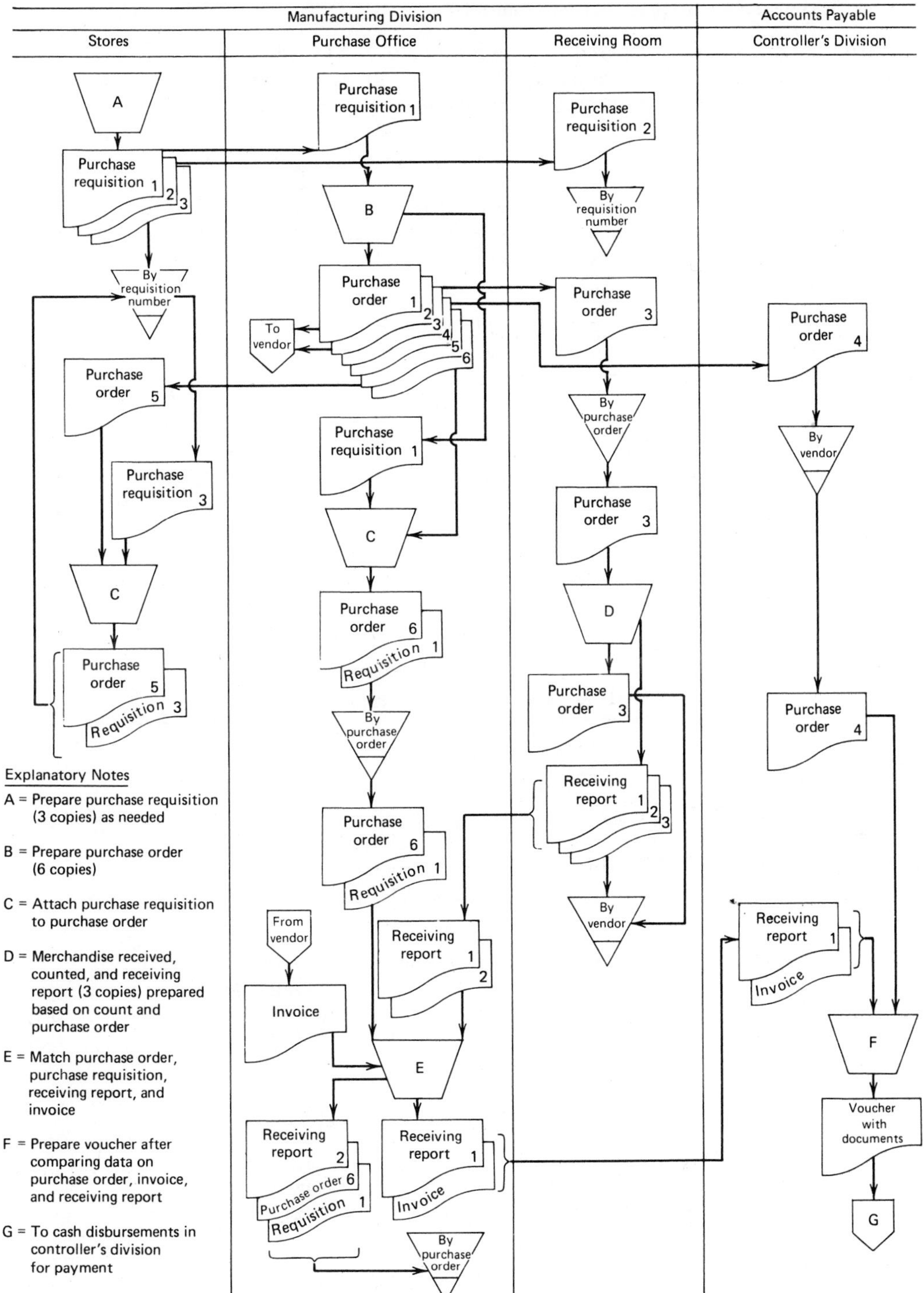
Manufacturing Division
Accounts Payable
Stores
Purchase Office
Receiving Room
Controller's Division
A
Purchase requisition 1 2 3
By requisition number
Purchase order 5
Purchase requisition 3
C
Purchase order 5
Requisition 3
Purchase requisition 1
B
Purchase order 1 2 3 4 5 6
To vendor
To vendor
Purchase requisition 1
C
Purchase order 6
Requisition 1
By purchase order
Purchase order 6
Requisition 1
From vendor
Invoice
Receiving report 1 2
E
Receiving report 2
Purchase order 6
Requisition 1
Receiving report 1
Invoice
By purchase order
Purchase requisition 2
By requisition number
Purchase order 3
By purchase order
Purchase order 3
D
Purchase order 3
Receiving report 1 2 3
By vendor
Purchase order 4
By vendor
Purchase order 4
Receiving report 1
Invoice
F
Voucher with documents
G
Explanatory Notes
A = Prepare purchase requisition (3 copies) as needed
B = Prepare purchase order (6 copies)
C = Attach purchase requisition to purchase order
D = Merchandise received, counted, and receiving report (3 copies) prepared based on count and purchase order
E = Match purchase order, purchase requisition, receiving report, and invoice
F = Prepare voucher after comparing data on purchase order, invoice, and receiving report
G = To cash disbursements in controller's division for payment

8–63. Stanton, CPA, prepared the flowchart on page 311, which portrays the raw materials purchasing function of one of Stanton's clients, a medium-sized manufacturing company, from the preparation of initial documents through the transmittal of invoices to accounts payable.

Required:

Identify and explain the deficiencies in control procedures evident from the flowchart. Include the deficiencies resulting from activities performed or not performed. All documents are prenumbered.

(AICPA adapted)

8–64. In the course of obtaining an understanding of the accounting system of the Lemco Manufacturing Co. Inc., you have gathered the five documents shown below and on pages 313 to 316 as examples of the flow of transactions through the accounting system.

Required:

a. What significant information concerning Lemco Manufacturing can be obtained from the purchase order, receiving report, invoice, and perpetual inventory record?

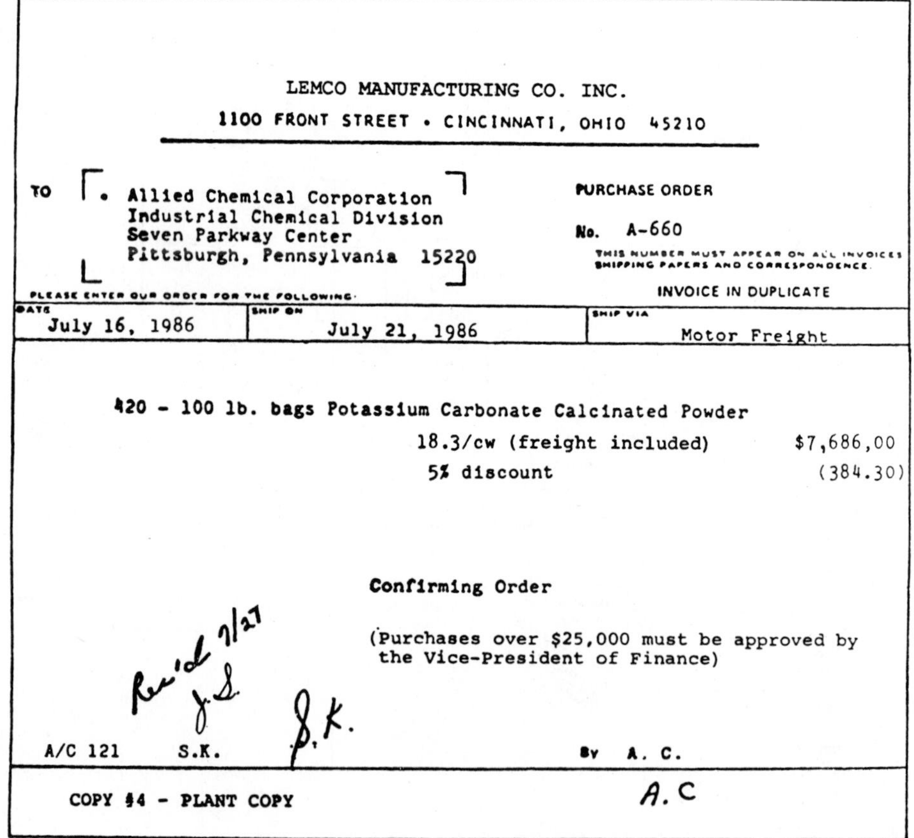

LEMCO MANUFACTURING CO. INC.
1100 FRONT STREET • CINCINNATI, OHIO 45210

TO Allied Chemical Corporation
Industrial Chemical Division
Seven Parkway Center
Pittsburgh, Pennsylvania 15230

PURCHASE ORDER
No. A-660
THIS NUMBER MUST APPEAR ON ALL INVOICES SHIPPING PAPERS AND CORRESPONDENCE.
INVOICE IN DUPLICATE

PLEASE ENTER OUR ORDER FOR THE FOLLOWING:

DATE	SHIP ON	SHIP VIA
July 16, 1986	July 21, 1986	Motor Freight

420 - 100 lb. bags Potassium Carbonate Calcinated Powder

18.3/cw (freight included)	$7,686,00
5% discount	(384.30)

Confirming Order

(Purchases over $25,000 must be approved by the Vice-President of Finance)

Rec'd 7/27 J.S.

S.K.

A/C 121 S.K. BY A. C.

COPY #4 - PLANT COPY A. C

LEMCO MANUFACTURING CO. INC.

RECEIVING REPORT

FROM: Allied Chemical Corp. Industrial Chemical Division Seven Parkway Center Pittsburgh, Penn. 15220		Receiving Report No. R-660 (Identify damaged stock specifically)
Purchase Order Date: July 16, 1986	Requested Ship Date: July 21, 1986	Requested Shipping: Motor Freight

Goods ordered:

420- 100 lb bags Potassium Carbonate Calcinated Powder

18.3/CW <freight included> $7,686.00

5% Discount <384.30>

Goods received:

400- 100 lb bags <18.3/CW> received in good condition. Stock stored at Public Warehouse Co. <9th and Main St.>

Damaged Goods	Received by	Date Received
- 20 bags sent back	Jim Smith	July 27, 1986

b. What is the purpose of the voucher?

c. What documents might a voucher package contain?

d. What is the significance of the purchase order and receiving report from an accounting control perspective? (Discuss each document separately.)

8-65. Grayman, Inc., a new audit client of yours, processes its sales and cash receipts documents in the following manner:

1. *Payment on account.* The mail is opened each morning by a mail clerk in the sales department. The mail clerk prepares a remittance advice (showing customer and amount paid) if one is not received. The checks and remittance advices are then forwarded to the sales department supervisor, who reviews each check and forwards the checks and remittance advices to the accounting department supervisor.

The accounting department supervisor, who also functions as credit manager in approving new credit and all credit limits, reviews all checks for payments on past-due accounts and then forwards the checks and remittance advices to the accounts receivable clerk, who arranges the advices in alphabetical order. The remittance advices are posted directly to the accounts receivable ledger cards. The checks are endorsed by stamp and totaled. The total is posted to the cash receipts journal. The remittance advices are filed chronologically.

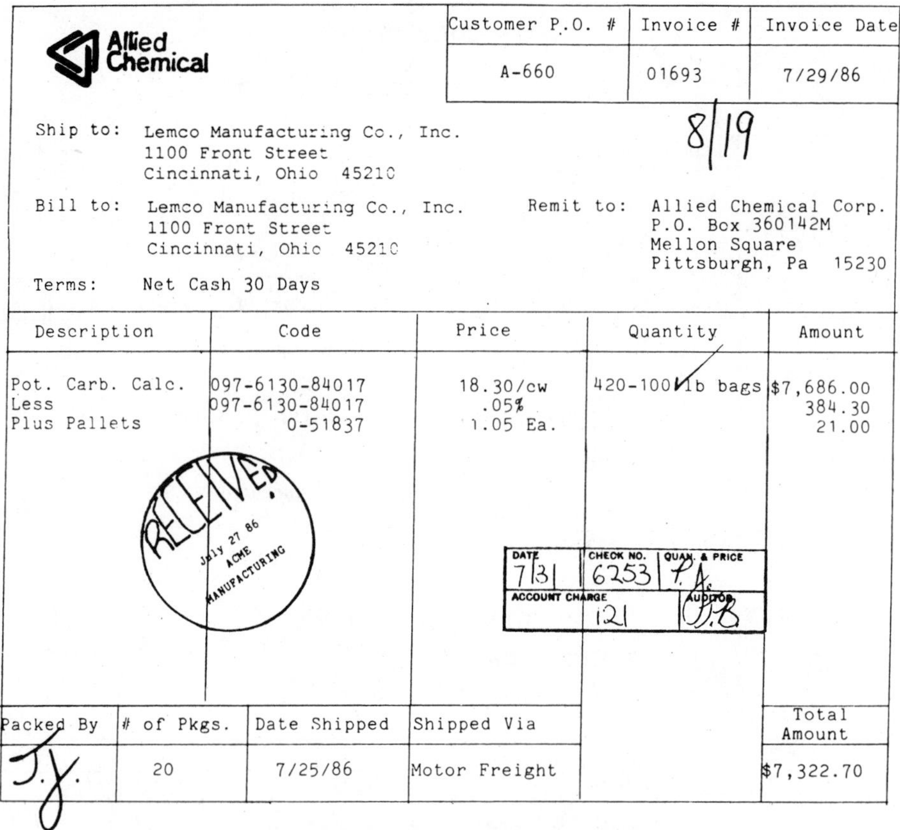

Allied Chemical

Customer P.O. #	Invoice #	Invoice Date
A-660	01693	7/29/86

8/19

Ship to: Lemco Manufacturing Co., Inc.
1100 Front Street
Cincinnati, Ohio 45210

Bill to: Lemco Manufacturing Co., Inc.
1100 Front Street
Cincinnati, Ohio 45210

Remit to: Allied Chemical Corp.
P.O. Box 360142M
Mellon Square
Pittsburgh, Pa 15230

Terms: Net Cash 30 Days

Description	Code	Price	Quantity	Amount
Pot. Carb. Calc.	097-6130-84017	18.30/cw	420-100 lb bags	$7,686.00
Less	097-6130-84017	.05%		384.30
Plus Pallets	0-51837	1.05 Ea.		21.00

RECEIVED July 27 86 ACME MANUFACTURING

DATE	CHECK NO.	QUAN. & PRICE
7/31	6253	P.A.
ACCOUNT CHARGE	121	AUDITOR J.B.

Packed By	# of Pkgs.	Date Shipped	Shipped Via		Total Amount
J.Y.	20	7/25/86	Motor Freight		$7,322.70

After receiving the cash from the previous day's cash sales, the accounts receivable clerk prepares the daily deposit slip in triplicate. The third copy of the deposit slip is filed by date and the second copy and the original accompany the bank deposit.

2. *Sales*. Sales clerks prepare sales invoices in triplicate. The original and second copy are presented to the cashier. The third copy is retained by the sales clerk in the sales book. When the sale is for cash, the customer pays the sales clerk, who presents the money to the cashier with the invoice copies.

A credit sale is approved by the cashier from an approved credit list after the sales clerk prepares the three-part invoice. After receiving the cash or approving the invoice, the cashier validates the original copy of the sales invoice and gives it to the customer. At the end of each day the cashier recaps the sales and cash received and forwards the cash and the second copy of all sales invoices to the accounts receivable clerk.

The accounts receivable clerk balances the cash received with cash sales invoices and prepares a daily sales summary. The credit sales invoices are posted to the accounts receivable ledger and then all invoices are sent to the inventory control clerk in the sales department for posting to the inventory control cards. After posting, the inventory control clerk files all invoices numerically. The accounts receivable clerk posts the daily sales summary to the cash receipts journal and sales journal and files the sales summaries by date.

LEMCO MANUFACTURING CO. INC.

1100 FRONT STREET CINCINNATI, OHIO 45210

DATE 8/19/86 Check No. 6253

AMOUNT $7,322.70

PAY TO THE ORDER OF Allied Chemical Corporation
P.O. Box 360142M
Mellon Square
Pittsburgh, Pa 15230

VOID 90 DAYS AFTER DATE

NOT NEGOTIABLE

THE FIRST NATIONAL BANK
CINCINNATI, OHIO
ELMWOOD PLACE OFFICE

AUTHORIZED SIGNATURE

DETACH THIS REMITTANCE ADVICE BEFORE DEPOSITING CHECK

ENTRY DATE	REFERENCE	AMOUNT	DISCOUNT	PREVIOUS	BALANCE	A/C DIST.	DESCRIPTION
7/31/86	01693	$7,707.00	$384.30	-0-	$7,322.70	121	Pot. Powder
COPY 2 - ACCOUNTING							6253

H.M.

The cash from cash sales is combined with the cash received on account, and this constitutes the daily bank deposit.

3. *Bank deposits*. The bank validates the deposit slip and returns the second copy to the accounting department where it is filed by date by the accounts receivable clerk.

Monthly bank statements are reconciled promptly by the accounting department supervisor and filed by date.

Required:

Flowchart the sales and cash receipts function of Grayman, Inc.

(AICPA adapted)

8-66. The following internal control procedures are employed by Stevensville Corporation:

1. Shipments of goods are authorized by the sales manager, who initials the sales order prepared by the sales personnel after approving terms and credit.
2. Sequentially prenumbered sales order forms are accounted for; sales order forms are matched with copies of invoices and shipping documents (bills of lading) on a monthly basis, and unmatched records are reviewed.
3. The accounts receivable subsidiary ledger is reconciled monthly to the control account in the general ledger.

INVENTORY RECORD

Item Description POTASSIUM CARBONATE CALCINATED POWDER

Unit Size 100 LB. BAGS

ORDER				GOODS ON HAND			
Date	P.O.#	Quantity	Estimated Receipt Date	Date	Material Requisition Number	Quantity	Cumulative Balance
				6/3		520	520
				6/30	8623	<500>	20
7/16	A-660	420	7/21	7/21	-	400	420

4. Checks received through the mail are restrictively endorsed immediately on receipt.
5. Customers in the company cafeteria are given a receipt printed out by the cash register when they pay for their food; if the receipt has a star imprinted on it (as is the case 2 percent of the time), the meal is free.
6. All purchases of raw materials are made using purchase orders prepared by a purchasing agent; purchase orders over $2000 are reviewed and initialed by the vice-president–purchasing.
7. Goods received are inspected and counted or weighed by the receiving department and recorded on a receiving report.
8. Prenumbered receiving reports are matched with purchase orders and invoices; unmatched receiving reports are periodically investigated.
9. Supporting documents are canceled by the controller when she signs checks made out to vendors.

10. The numbers of sequentially prenumbered checks are periodically accounted for.

Required:

For each of the control procedures described

a. State the specific control objective that the procedure is designed to achieve.
b. Describe an error or irregularity that could occur if the control were absent or ineffective.
c. Describe a test that the auditor could perform to determine whether the control procedure is designed and operating effectively.

8-67. While auditing Blackwell Products, Inc., the auditor prepared the flowchart of credit sales activities on page 318. (In this flowchart Code Letter "A" represents CUSTOMER.)

Required:

Indicate what each of the code letters "B" through "P" represents. Do *not* discuss adequacies or inadequacies in the control procedures.

(AICPA adapted)

8-68. ***Quinn Hardware*** (Documenting Control Procedures)

Note:

Before proceeding with this case, review the client background information for Quinn Hardware in Problem 6-62 in Chapter 6.

Required:

Part 1: Prepare a systems flowchart of the *ordering and receiving* segment of the Quinn Hardware buying cycle (steps 1 through 15 in the narrative that follows). Cross-reference the numbered paragraphs in the narrative to the manual or computer procedure symbols in your flowchart.

Part 2: a. List the significant programmed procedures in the *ordering and receiving* segment (steps 1 through 15) of Quinn Hardware's buying cycle. (Use the systems flowchart to assist you.)

b. Identify and describe the purpose of any reports generated from the programmed procedures identified in Part 2 (a).

Summary of Auditor's Understanding (Narrative)

Ordering and Receiving Segment

1. Purchase orders are prepared by either of the following methods:

   a. Quinn's computer generates a stock requirement report (SRR) weekly based on economic order quantity (EOQ) criteria.

   b. A purchase order requisition (POR) is prepared by a buyer, as required, and processed by a purchasing agent with other items not covered on the SRR.

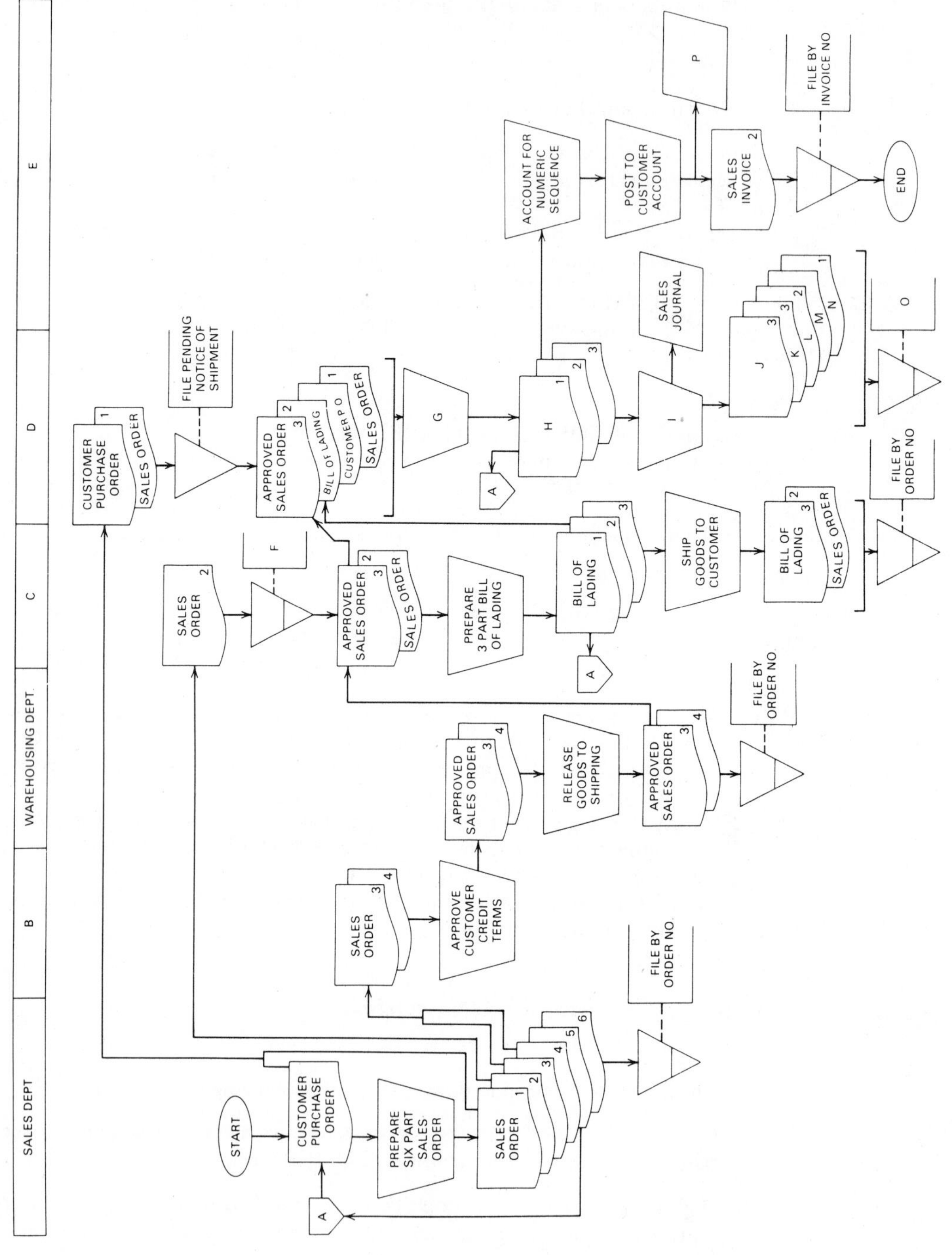
SALES DEPT
B
WAREHOUSING DEPT.
C
D
E
START
CUSTOMER PURCHASE ORDER
PREPARE SIX PART SALES ORDER
SALES ORDER 1 2 3 4 5 6
FILE BY ORDER NO.
A
SALES ORDER 3 4
APPROVE CUSTOMER CREDIT TERMS
APPROVED SALES ORDER 3 4
RELEASE GOODS TO SHIPPING
APPROVED SALES ORDER 3 4
FILE BY ORDER NO
SALES ORDER 2
F
APPROVED SALES ORDER 2 3
SALES ORDER
PREPARE 3 PART BILL OF LADING
BILL OF LADING 1 2 3
A
SHIP GOODS TO CUSTOMER
BILL OF LADING 2 3
SALES ORDER
FILE BY ORDER NO
CUSTOMER PURCHASE ORDER
SALES ORDER 1
FILE PENDING NOTICE OF SHIPMENT
APPROVED SALES ORDER 2 3
BILL OF LADING
CUSTOMER P O
SALES ORDER 1
G
H 1 2 3
A
I
SALES JOURNAL
J 3
K 3
L 2
M
N 1
O
ACCOUNT FOR NUMERIC SEQUENCE
POST TO CUSTOMER ACCOUNT
P
SALES INVOICE 2
FILE BY INVOICE NO
END

2. The SRR is reviewed by the buyer, who can change quantities. The buyer confirms prices and estimated receiving dates for items on the SRR and POR with suppliers and notes those details on the documents.
3. A purchasing clerk then uses a terminal in the purchasing section to perform the following functions:

   a. Amend quantity details, as necessary, on SRR-generated information.
   b. Input POR information.
   c. Record estimated delivery dates for SRR and PORs.

   At the same time, the following computer operations are performed:

   - Matching of product number to the Product Number Table to ensure that the product number exists.
   - Matching of vendor number to the Vendor Master File to ensure that the vendor number exists.

   Invalid matches of product numbers or vendor numbers are rejected on the screen for the purchasing clerk to correct.
4. The system then generates a five-part prenumbered purchase order (PO) and, at the end of each day, a Purchase Order Listing. PO sequence numbers are allocated by the computer on the basis of the last PO number plus one. The Purchase Order Listing contains details of all POs generated that day and indicates whether the PO was generated from an SRR or POR.

   POs contain the following details:

   - Quantities ordered.
   - Prices agreed with supplier.
   - Any other charges or discounts.

   At the same time as the POs are generated, the following computerized functions take place:

   - Updating of the "Outstanding Purchase Order File" with details of POs.
   - Earmarking stock items on the Inventory Master File to show that the item has been ordered.

   [Note: When step 3 is successfully completed, the computer automatically completes step 4. Steps 3 and 4 may be combined on your flowchart.]

5. Both POs and the Purchase Order Listing are reviewed by the buyer and initialed to indicate approval. The Purchase Order Listing and SRR are permanently filed by date, and the five-part POs are handled as follows:

   1. To vendor.
   2. To warehouse receiving department and temporarily filed by vendor number.

3. To central accounts payable department and temporarily filed alphabetically.
4. Permanently filed alphabetically.
5. Permanently filed numerically.

6. When goods are received at the warehouse receiving department, the second part of the PO is matched with the packing slip. The goods are inspected and counted by the receiver. The packing slip and PO are attached and are now called a receiving memo (R/M). The date received is entered on the R/M and the R/M is initialed and dated by the receiver.

   If goods are refused, they are sent back to the vendor with the packing slip. If only partial shipment is received, the quantity received is entered on the PO, which is returned to the temporary file. A partial shipment form is completed and treated in the same manner as a normal receipt. There is a separate numerical sequence for partial receipt forms. The original PO is submitted when the final shipment is made. Partial shipment forms must be approved by the buyer. (Partial shipments represent an immaterial transaction volume; therefore, you need not include them on your flowchart.)
7. A clerk in the warehouse uses a terminal (located in the warehouse) to input R/M details.
8. The following edit checks are performed by the computer as each R/M is input:

   a. The PO number is matched to the Outstanding Purchase Order File to ensure that is a valid PO number.
   b. For each line item on the R/M, the product number is matched to a Product Number Table to ensure that the product number exists.
   c. For each line item on the R/M, the quantity is matched to the Outstanding Purchase Order File. If the quantities differ, the system requests the clerk to confirm the quantity input.
   d. The date received is matched to calendar date.
   e. The vendor number is matched to the vendor number on the Outstanding Purchase Order File to ensure that it is a valid vendor number.

   If any of the above edit checks fail, the transaction is rejected on the terminal. It is the responsibility of the warehouse clerk to determine the reason for the rejection. Errors are corrected and re-input in the same fashion as new input.
9. On accepting the R/Ms, the computer updates the following files:

   - Inventory Master File.
   - Receipts History File (at standard costs per the Inventory Master File).
   - Outstanding Receipts File (at standard cost per the Inventory Master File).

   Accepted receiving memos are written directly to the Outstanding Receipts File and Receipts History File, priced at the standard cost recorded on the Inventory Master File.

   At the same time as the Inventory Master File is referred to for the extraction of standard cost, the "quantity on hand" and the "date of last receipt" fields are updated. (The SRR is generated based on EOQ criteria after the quantity on hand has been updated.)

The Outstanding Purchase Order File is updated to reflect filled purchase orders (PO deleted). Partial deliveries do not delete the related PO but earmark them as such.

The computer also generates the following *daily* output:

a. Daily Edit Report, containing the following information:

- Differences in quantities recorded on PO and input from R/Ms.
- Details and totals at standard cost of R/Ms accepted and R/Ms deleted as a result of purchase invoices being matched against R/Ms.

b. Daily transaction tape of R/Ms, which is filed in the library for three generations.
c. Receipts Update Report showing (at standard cost):

- Opening balance of the Outstanding Receipts File.
- Updates to the Outstanding Receipts File arising from the matching of R/Ms to the Outstanding Purchase Order File and deletions of R/Ms as a result of purchase invoices being processed.
- The theoretical balance of the Outstanding Receipts File, which is determined by adding/subtracting updates to/from the opening balance.
- The actual closing balance of the Outstanding Receipts File, which is determined by accumulating the value of all outstanding R/Ms on file.
- The difference, if any, between the theoretical and actual closing balances of the Outstanding Receipts File.

The system also produces the following general ledger entry on the basis of items written to the Outstanding Receipts File:

Inventory	Recorded at Standard Cost	
Accrued Liabilities		Recorded at Standard Cost

The system interfaces with the general ledger system. Posting to the General Ledger Master File is done daily, and the foregoing information is shown on the General Ledger Posting Summary. This report is sent to the controller's department.

10. At the conclusion of overnight processing, the edit reports are transmitted to the warehouses. The edit reports containing the differences in quantities are investigated by the warehouse clerk. The clerk identifies the reason for the discrepancy by reference to the original documents. The edit report is stamped "corrected" and the corrections are reentered along with the regular transactions for the day.
11. Daily, the warehouse clerk performs the following functions with respect to the Receipts Update Report:

    a. Agrees the opening balance to the closing balance on the prior day's report.
    b. Agrees the "updates" figure on the Receipts Update Report to the "accepted" totals on the Daily Edit Report.
    c. Follows up any differences between the theoretical and actual closing balances by reference to the Daily Edit Report.

12. The warehouse supervisor reviews the reconciliation of the Receipts Update Report to the Daily Edit Report and initials the reports and reconciliations as evidence. The Receipts Update Report and reconciliation are filed daily. The Daily Edit Report is reviewed, and initialed as evidence, to ensure that rejections have been followed up. This report is filed daily.
13. Weekly, the computer department generates a listing of all outstanding POs (i.e., not flagged as received). This report is sent to the purchasing department.
14. An expediter in the purchasing department investigates the listing of outstanding POs. The reported items are agreed to the POs, overdue orders are investigated, and corrections are entered and each item on the listing is marked.
15. A buyer reviews the report on a monthly basis and initials it to evidence the review. It is then filed by date.

9

Controlling Detection Risk: Substantive Tests

As stated in earlier chapters of this book, the primary purpose of an audit is the expression of an opinion on whether the entity's financial statements are presented fairly, in all material respects, in conformity with generally accepted accounting principles. The auditor needs a high level of assurance that the opinion is appropriate; that is, audit risk must be limited to a low level. Audit risk was defined in Chapter 6 as consisting of the risk of material misstatement occurring (comprising inherent and control risks), and the risk, known as detection risk, of not detecting a material misstatement that is contained in the financial statements. The auditor assesses inherent and control risks as part of developing the audit testing plan, and controls detection risk by performing substantive tests to gain the necessary assurance regarding the various assertions embodied in the financial statements. This chapter covers the substantive testing phase of the audit. To fit that phase into the perspective of the overall audit process, some of the underlying concepts and earlier steps in the process, which were discussed in detail in previous chapters, are first reviewed and summarized.

REVIEW: AUDIT OBJECTIVES, RISK ASSESSMENT, AND AUDIT STRATEGY DECISIONS

Audit Objectives

Each auditing procedure performed on an engagement should be designed to meet one or more specific audit objectives that, in turn, correspond with specific assertions embodied in the financial statements. Seven categories of management assertions and corresponding audit objectives were identified in Chapter 5: existence or occurrence, completeness, accuracy, cutoff, rights and obligations, valuation or allocation, and presentation and disclosure. The audit objectives are the same for all engagements; the emphasis given to particular objectives for specific account balances and classes of transactions varies according to the auditor's materiality judgments and risk assessments. Accordingly, the nature, timing, and extent of auditing procedures performed to achieve the audit objectives also vary.

Risk Assessment and Audit Strategy Decisions

The process by which inherent and control risks are assessed was described in Chapter 8. The results of those assessments have an inverse relationship to the acceptable level of detection risk. That is, the lower the risk of a material misstatement occurring, the higher the level of detection risk the auditor can accept in planning substantive tests to gain the assurance needed to limit audit risk to a sufficiently low level. Conversely, the greater the risk of a material misstatement occurring, the lower the acceptable level of detection risk.

Each of the auditor's risk assessment activities—assessing inherent risk conditions and characteristics and assessing, for purposes of audit planning, the elements of the control structure (including any concurrent tests of controls performed)—can result in a reduction in the perceived level of risk that a material misstatement has occurred, which in turn reduces the assurance needed from substantive tests. As discussed in Chapter 8, in most situations those risk assessment activities would enable the auditor to reduce to some degree the assurance needed from substantive tests. Beyond that, the auditor makes a key strategy decision about whether to perform additional tests of controls, particularly of control procedures, to support a further reduction in the assessed level of control risk. Those additional tests of controls would generally be directed toward completeness, accuracy, or existence. As explained in Chapter 7, those are the audit objectives that can often be related to control objectives specifically addressed by an entity's control structure. A key factor in the decision to perform additional tests of controls is whether it will be more efficient than performing substantive tests without seeking to further reduce the assessed level of control risk.

Both additional tests of controls and substantive tests help the auditor achieve specific audit objectives for specific accounts. For example, a set of financial statements generally includes management's assertion that accounts receivable exist and are the result of sales of goods and services to customers. The auditor seeks evidence to support this assertion, which corresponds with the audit objective of existence/occurrence. The audit objective may be achieved, in part, by confirming accounts receivable (a substantive test), or by testing the control procedures the client has established to ensure that only authorized sales of goods and services, and all cash collections, are properly processed and recorded (a test of controls).

The audit strategy for each significant class of transactions or account balance will depend both on the auditor's judgment about how effectively the relevant control procedures are designed and are operating and whether it will be more efficient to test the control procedures or to test the account balances themselves. The auditor *may* choose to obtain evidence entirely from substantive tests of account balances, but, as stated in Statement on Auditing Standards (SAS) No. 55 (AU Section 319.63), *may not* choose to omit substantive tests entirely for *all* of the audit objectives relevant to significant account balances or transaction classes. The evidence obtained from performing substantive tests will either confirm or contradict the conclusions the auditor reached when assessing inherent and control risks. If the auditor learns those risks are higher than was previously thought, the decision about how much assurance is needed from substantive tests should be reconsidered. Chapter 8 described tests of controls; this chapter covers substantive tests performed to obtain assurance about financial statement assertions.

DESIGNING AND PERFORMING SUBSTANTIVE TESTS

Substantive tests consist of tests of details of account balances and related transactions, and analytical procedures. The nature, timing, and extent of the substantive tests to be performed to meet specific audit objectives for each account balance and class of transactions are determined primarily by the results of the auditor's risk assessment activities. Assessing how much assurance can be attained from a particular substantive procedure is a matter of professional judgment and cannot be specified without knowledge of the full context in which the procedure is to be performed. This chapter describes many substantive procedures. Auditors rarely perform all of them on an engagement. Instead, after considering the evidence obtained from tests of controls and from other risk assessment activities, they select the specific procedures, for each audit objective relevant to each financial statement account and disclosure, that will provide the evidence needed in the particular circumstances. This section of the chapter describes the major considerations that determine what substantive tests should be performed in varying circumstances.

The key to selecting appropriate substantive tests is the auditor's understanding of management's assertions and the corresponding audit objectives. The auditor identifies specific audit objectives for each significant account balance and designs auditing procedures to provide the necessary assurance that those objectives have been achieved. Figure 9.1 illustrates the audit objectives that may be applicable to an entity's trade accounts receivable and sales, and provides examples (which are not intended to be exhaustive) of substantive tests the auditor may perform to satisfy the objectives.

Figure 9.1 Audit Objectives for Trade Accounts Receivable and Sales

Audit Objective	*Specific Audit Objectives for Trade Accounts Receivable and Sales*	*Illustrative Substantive Tests*[a]
Completeness	Trade accounts receivable represent all amounts owed to the entity at the balance sheet date arising from sales transactions. All shipments or services rendered during the period covered by the financial statements and all returns or allowances provided are reflected in the financial statements.	On a test basis, compare records of goods shipped and services performed with recorded transactions.
Accuracy	Sales transactions are based on correct prices and quantities and are accurately computed and classified in the appropriate general ledger and accounts receiv-	On a test basis, compare shipping documents and invoices with supporting documents and recorded transactions. (Confirmation of customers' accounts to

Figure 9.1 *Continued*

Audit Objective	*Specific Audit Objectives for Trade Accounts Receivable and Sales*	*Illustrative Substantive Tests*[a]
	able subsidiary ledger accounts. The accounts receivable subsidiary ledger is mathematically correct and agrees with the general ledger.	some extent also indicates the accuracy of the balances.) Using audit software, calculate invoice amounts and total the accounts receivable subsidiary ledger.
Existence or Occurrence	Recorded accounts receivable represent amounts owed to the entity at the balance sheet date. Recorded sales transactions represent goods actually shipped or services actually rendered during the period covered by the financial statements.	Select customers' accounts for confirmation and the method of confirmation (positive, negative, or a combination), investigate any discrepancies reported or questions raised, and determine whether any adjustments are necessary. For positive confirmations not responded to, agree amounts to subsequent cash receipts or supporting sales documents.
Cutoff	Sales transactions, cash receipts, and returns and claims are recorded in the proper period.	Perform cutoff tests: (a) Determine that sales invoices are recorded as sales in the proper period by comparing the related records of goods shipped and services performed with recorded sales for several days before and after year-end. (b) Determine that credit memos are recorded in the proper period by examining the related records of returns and claims from customers for several days before and after year-end. (*Note*: Improper cutoff of cash receipts is generally a low risk, since only the composition of current assets could be in error.)
Valuation or Allocation	Accounts receivable are stated at net realizable value (i.e., net of appropriate allowances for uncollectible accounts, discounts, returns, and similar items). Revenue is recognized only when ap-	Determine whether the allowance for uncollectible accounts is adequate by reviewing the aged trial balances, discussing the allowance and composition of the receivable balance with manage-

(*Continued*)

Figure 9.1 *Continued*

Audit Objective	*Specific Audit Objectives for Trade Accounts Receivable and Sales*	*Illustrative Substantive Tests*[a]
	propriate accounting recognition and measurement criteria are met.	ment, and identifying significant old receivables and receivables in dispute or changes in the collectibility of current receivables. Review cash collections after the balance sheet date and examine related remittance advices or other supporting documentation to ascertain that payments relate to the balance that was due at the balance sheet date. Determine the adequacy of collateral, if any. Review relevant credit file information, such as customer financial data and correspondence. Discuss all significant potentially uncollectible accounts with management.
Rights and Obligations	Accounts receivable are legal rights of the entity at the balance sheet date (i.e., customer accounts that have been sold or factored are excluded from the accounts receivable balance).	Make inquiries and read agreements relating to the possible sale of receivables that the client continues to service.
Presentation and Disclosure	Accounts receivable, sales, and related accounts are properly described and classified in the financial statements. Accounts receivable pledged as collateral are properly disclosed.	Identify liens, security interests, and assets pledged as loan collateral by reviewing debt and lease agreements; confirmation replies, particularly from financial institutions; and minutes of directors' meetings. Inquire of management about those items.

[a]Analytical procedures, such as analysis of monthly sales trends compared with prior years and budget, may be designed to provide assurance relating to audit objectives for trade accounts receivable and sales.

Types of Accounts

The nature, timing, and extent of substantive tests appropriate for a particular audit objective and account vary with the type of account. Accounts may be classified into three types.

1. Accounts that are derived from a major class of transactions within a transaction cycle that typically involves high volumes of transactions. These accounts are commonly subjected to control procedures that address the control objectives of completeness, accuracy, and authorization of transactions and files. Examples are cash, accounts receivable, inventory, accounts payable, purchases, salaries and wages, and sales. Decisions about whether the audit strategy for these accounts should include additional tests of controls are generally related to whether that would be the most efficient way to achieve the completeness, accuracy, and existence/occurrence audit objectives.

2. Accounts that reflect internal allocations of revenues or expenses over time through the accrual, deferral, amortization, or valuation of assets or liabilities. These accounts often require management to exercise judgment in determining the period or method of allocation and also in selecting and applying accounting measurement and recognition principles. While the transactions that form the basis for these accounts are sometimes subjected to control procedures, it is usually more efficient not to perform additional tests of controls related to these accounts. Examples of such accounts include accrued receivables and payables, deferred charges and credits, and asset valuation and estimated liability accounts.

3. Accounts that typically reflect a relatively small number of material transactions in an accounting period. These accounts are carried forward from one year to the next, unless transactions affecting them take place. Examples of these accounts include bonds payable, property and equipment, and contributed capital accounts. Because transactions affecting these accounts occur infrequently, control procedures may not be established to ensure their completeness, accuracy, and authorization. Even when the transactions affecting these accounts are subject to control procedures, it is usually not efficient to perform tests of controls for these accounts.

For the first type, accounts derived from a major class of transactions, the auditor will often face a strategy decision with respect to achieving the completeness, accuracy, and existence/occurrence audit objectives. For other accounts, however, the risks associated with completeness, accuracy, and existence/occurrence, and for all accounts, the risks associated with the audit objectives of valuation, rights and obligations, and presentation and disclosure, may not be addressed by control procedures, although policies and procedures that are part of the control environment and accounting system may affect the achievement of those audit objectives. Even if they do, the auditor is still likely to require a significant amount of assurance from substantive tests directed at the valuation, rights and obligations, and presentation and disclosure objectives. Although an enterprise may have control procedures to ensure a proper cutoff of purchases, sales, cash receipts, and cash disbursements, the auditor generally finds it more efficient not to perform additional tests of controls with respect to the cutoff objective but instead to obtain evidence primarily from substantive tests.

Tests of Details and Their Relationship to Audit Objectives

Tests of details of account balances and transactions are most commonly thought of in connection with providing assurance about specific audit objectives. This section discusses the different techniques used in performing tests of details and when they can be performed. Chapter 10 discusses the extent of testing—how many items to test.

Substantive tests of details of transactions and account balances or of other information in the financial statements normally involve the techniques of inquiry, observation, examining documents and records, reperformance, inspecting assets, and confirmation. The following paragraphs describe each of these and suggest how they relate to the audit objectives.

Frequently, one of the auditor's first steps in testing an account balance or class of transactions is making *inquiries* of client management and employees; the responses are then corroborated by other tests. At various stages in the audit, discussions with management or employees and subsequent follow-up may bring errors to the auditor's attention. As an example, the auditor inquires about management's plans as part of considering the entity's ability to continue as a going concern, as discussed in Chapter 18. In addition, the auditor obtains letters from the client's lawyers regarding legal matters and letters of representation from management concerning the recording of known liabilities, the existence of contingent liabilities, and the existence and carrying value of inventory. Inquiries may provide evidence about many audit objectives, depending on the specific accounts or transactions involved. Lawyers' and client representation letters provide assurance relating especially to rights and obligations, and presentation and disclosure.

The auditor may *observe* the client's employees as they perform various tasks, like counting inventory. The auditor's observation of how the client conducts a physical inventory can provide firsthand knowledge of the reliability of the inventory count.

The auditor often *examines documents or records* supporting a transaction or item in the financial statements and *reperforms*, usually on a test basis, the client's related procedures in order to determine that the transaction was both authorized and accurately accounted for. Accordingly, examining documentation often provides assurance that recorded assets or liabilities are accurate and, depending on the specific transaction under consideration, exist or are complete. The cutoff objective is often achieved by examining documentation for transactions recorded shortly before and after the client's year-end. The auditor normally examines documents to obtain evidence that the client has performed all prescribed procedures, reperforms those procedures (on a test basis, if appropriate), and determines that no aspects of the transaction appear unreasonable (such as a supplier's invoice not addressed to the client). That evidence may have been generated wholly or partly by entities outside the client (such as suppliers' invoices, customers' orders, signed contracts) or by the client itself (such as purchase orders, receiving reports, marketing plans). If external evidence is available, it is usually considered more reliable than internal evidence. One specific form of internal documentation the auditor reads at various stages in the audit is minutes of meetings of the board of directors and its important committees.

In many instances an account balance may represent the result of a computation or an accumulation of computations. To substantiate the accuracy of such an account balance, the auditor often reperforms some or all of the detailed computations or otherwise makes an overall evaluation of the balance. If judgment is the basis of a computation, such as in the valuation of accounts receivable, the auditor reperforming the computation must also understand and evaluate the reasoning process underlying the judgment. For example, if the provision for uncollectible accounts is based on a formula (giving appropriate consideration to past experience) related to the age of the receivables, the auditor should consider the reasonableness of the formula as well as reperform the mathematical calculations. (The auditor would also perform other procedures regarding the collectibility of accounts receivable in reviewing the adequacy of the provision for uncollectible accounts.)

If the client compares accounting records with physical assets, such as inventory, or with documents, such as an invoice, the auditor may be able to use these comparisons and their documentation in performing substantive tests. That is, the auditor may choose to test the client's matching procedures, which is what typically happens during the client's physical inventory count, rather than perform similar or duplicative procedures. If the client has supervisory control procedures over those comparisons, as part of the substantive tests the auditor may examine the documentation of those procedures to obtain evidence that they operated effectively. As an example, the auditor's tests of the client's physical inventory count would ordinarily include tests of the client's supervision of its counting personnel. In addition, management's review of reports, which is an aspect of the client's control environment that the auditor often tests in assessing control risk, can also serve as the basis for a substantive procedure, depending on the type of report involved. For example, management's review of reports of write-offs or dispositions of obsolete inventory could be one source of evidence that the financial statements do not reflect inventory carried at more than its net realizable value.

Inspecting assets involves counting or examining physical items represented by accounts in the financial statements. This procedure is generally performed by client personnel, with the auditor participating or observing, although on occasion the auditor actually performs the function. A typical example of inspection, combined with observation, is the tests of the client's counting procedures and recounting of some of the client's counts during a physical inventory. Other items subject to inspection (which may be counted or examined directly by the auditor) include cash, marketable securities, and property, plant, and equipment. Inspecting assets is a principal source of assurance about their existence and about the accuracy of the related accounts, and may provide some assurance about completeness, that is, that all items counted were recorded.

Confirmation consists of obtaining a representation of a fact or condition from a third party, preferably in writing. Although many facts can be confirmed, this procedure is generally applied to items making up an account balance and often serves as the principal test of details related to that balance. Confirmations obtained from parties that are independent of the client frequently provide strong support for the existence of the relevant fact or account balance and often provide some evidence with respect to the accuracy objective as well. For example, a customer's acknowledgment that it owes the client $1500 is strong evidence that the debt exists and that it is not overstated (absent valuation considerations). Confirmations also provide some evidence that the transactions underlying the account balances were recorded in the proper period. Confirmation provides little or no evidence, however, with respect to completeness, valuation, rights and obligations, or presentation and disclosure of receivables.

The level in the organization at which a fact or an account balance is confirmed is also relevant to how much assurance the confirmation provides. For example, an auditor seeking to confirm the existence and terms of a major contract between the client and a supplier would consider to whom the confirmation should appropriately be addressed. On receiving the signed confirmation, the auditor would note whether the signature was that of someone in a position to know and understand the details of the contract.

Many substantive tests of the details of transactions and account balances involve procedures, such as examining documents or reperforming calculations, that are the same as procedures used in performing tests of controls. This is not surprising; whether a particular procedure is a test of controls or a substantive test depends not on the procedure itself, but on the purpose for which it is performed. For example, footing and extending a purchase invoice could be part of a test of controls performed to obtain evidence about whether a control procedure designed to prevent purchase transactions from being recorded inaccurately was operating effectively; it could also be a substantive test of the accuracy of recorded machinery and equipment. Similarly, reperforming the client's bank reconciliation could be a test of the client's performance of periodic reconciliations of the cash account (a test of controls); the auditor's reconciliation at year-end would be a substantive test of the accuracy and existence of the cash balance. As a general rule, tests of details of transactions to which control procedures are applied are tests of controls; tests of details of ending balances of balance sheet accounts are substantive tests. Regardless of the purpose for performing a particular test, however, many tests provide evidence that serves the other purpose as well.

Timing of Tests of Details

It is often desirable to perform tests of details before year-end (early substantive testing), particularly if the client wants the audit to be completed shortly after year-end. This may be done in appropriate circumstances without impairing the effectiveness of the audit, although before doing so the auditor should assess the difficulty of controlling the incremental audit risk (AU Section 313.04–.07).

It is usually efficient to perform substantive tests on related accounts as of a common date. Therefore, when considering early substantive testing of a specific account, the auditor should consider the relationship of that account to others in the financial statements and the extent to which a single substantive test may apply to more than one account. For example, a cutoff test of shipments relates to sales, accounts receivable, cost of sales, and inventory accounts.

If early substantive testing is done, the auditor will have to obtain satisfaction that, for the balances tested early, the risk of material misstatement is low during the intervening period between the early testing date and year-end. Generally, the auditor obtains that satisfaction by performing tests of controls directed at the design and operation of relevant control structure policies and procedures during the intervening period.[1] Such tests of controls might include reviewing reconciliations of individual ledger balances to control accounts and investigating any unusual items in the reconciliations. The auditor should also perform analytical and other substantive procedures, as described later, to obtain assurance that transactions were properly recorded during the intervening period.

In certain circumstances, the auditor might obtain satisfaction about transactions during the intervening period by examining evidence of the operation of special procedures established by the client for that period. As an example, a management review of sales transactions recorded around year-end performed to ensure a proper cutoff would provide some evidence about the authorization and accuracy of sales recorded after an early accounts receivable confirmation.

If early substantive testing is performed, the auditor should link the balances tested early to year-end balances by one or more of the following procedures, as appropriate in light of the assessment of control risk:

- Review key performance indicators and management information for unexpected variations in account balances at the balance sheet date, and investigate any material fluctuations in account balances and any unusual activity since the time of the early substantive tests.

[1]AU Section 313.05 states that "assessing control risk at below the maximum is not required in order to have a reasonable basis for extending audit conclusions from an interim date to the balance-sheet date; however, if the auditor assesses control risk at the maximum during the remaining period, he should consider whether the effectiveness of certain of the substantive tests to cover that period will be impaired." The authors believe an auditor would rarely have the required "reasonable basis" if control risk was assessed at the maximum. However, as noted in Chapter 8, the authors also believe it would be rare for an auditor to assess control risk at the maximum for the completeness, accuracy, and authorization objectives for accounts derived from transaction cycles.

- Scan entries in the relevant general ledger accounts (including control accounts) or review summaries of recorded transactions to determine whether any expected entries have been omitted and whether the entries appear to be reasonable in relation to the normal level of activity.
- Review any special procedures the client has carried out on the year-end figures.
- Review reconciliations of individual ledger balances to control accounts, and investigate any unusual items in the reconciliations.
- Ensure that any relevant matters brought forward from the early substantive testing date have been satisfactorily resolved.
- Reassess any valuation accounts (e.g., allowance for uncollectible accounts) in light of the latest available information.

In most instances, early substantive testing is not appropriate unless the auditor has obtained evidence, through tests of controls, that control structure policies and procedures related to transactions and account balances tested early are effective. In addition, early substantive testing is not usually done for all assertions relating to an account balance. For example, the existence of accounts receivable may be confirmed at an early date, but their valuation tested at year-end. In particular, if control procedures necessary to safeguard assets (such as inventories) are ineffective, early substantive testing (such as observing early physical inventory counts) is normally not appropriate, because the auditor will be unable to obtain evidence that those assets were safeguarded in the intervening period, and will therefore not have evidence about their existence at year-end.

Significant changes in the client's circumstances after the date of early substantive testing may require the auditor to perform additional procedures. To avoid unnecessary work, the auditor should consider the possibility of such changes when determining the audit testing plan. AU Section 313 contains the authoritative guidance on performing substantive tests before the balance sheet date.

Analytical Procedures

Analytical procedures are an integral part of the audit process. They are reasonableness tests of account balances and classes of transactions and, as stated in SAS No. 56, *Analytical Procedures* (AU Section 329.02), "consist of evaluations of financial information made by a study of plausible relationships among both financial and nonfinancial data." Examples of analytical procedures routinely performed in an audit include fluctuation analyses, ratio analyses, comparisons of financial statements, and scanning accounting records for unusual entries or entries that do not meet the auditor's expectations. SAS No. 56 requires analytical procedures to be used in the planning and overall review stages of the audit, and encourages their use as substantive tests to provide assurance with respect to specific audit objectives for particular account balances or classes of transactions. Analytical procedures, together with tests of controls and substantive tests of details of transactions and balances, provide the evidential matter required by the third standard of field work.

Developing Expectations. The basic premise underlying analytical procedures is that relationships among data may reasonably be expected to exist and continue in the absence of known conditions to the contrary. Examples of those conditions include specific unusual transactions or events, accounting changes, business changes, random fluctuations, and errors or irregularities. Changes in relationships among data in the absence of conditions known to the auditor could suggest that the financial statements were misstated because of unknown errors or irregularities.

In performing analytical procedures, the auditor first develops expectations of recorded amounts or ratios derived therefrom, by considering plausible relationships among data. The bases for the auditor's expectations are knowledge obtained about the nature of the entity's business, the industry in which it operates, inherent risk conditions, and the characteristics of individual account balances and classes of transactions. The auditor then compares the expectations with the recorded amounts or ratios. The comparisons may be simple or complex, and may involve single or multiple relationships.

Typically, the auditor uses the following sources of information, either individually or in combination, in developing expectations:

a. Financial information of comparable prior periods, adjusted for known current changes. (For example, an expectation of current year's sales might be formed from the prior period's sales adjusted for known price and volume increases. That expectation would then be compared with the current period's recorded sales.)
b. Anticipated results. (For example, expectations could be developed from budgets, forecasts, and extrapolations of interim results, which would then be compared with recorded results.)
c. Relationships among elements of financial information within the period. (For example, an expectation of commission expense in relation to sales could be developed from knowledge of the entity's commission policies, and then compared with the relationship between recorded commission expense and recorded sales.)
d. Information regarding the industry in which the client operates. (For example, expectations of gross margin could be developed from industry-wide statistics for particular product lines.)
e. Relationships between financial information and relevant nonfinancial information. (For example, expectations might be developed concerning

available square footage related to revenue in a retail operation, labor hours related to labor costs, average rent related to rent revenue, or number of properties related to real estate tax expense.)

Unexpected relationships or other items that appear to be unusual should be investigated if the auditor believes they indicate matters that may have a significant effect on the audit. In investigating unusual items, the auditor generally considers them in the light of the information obtained about the client and its business, and makes inquiries of management. The auditor then seeks additional evidence to corroborate management's replies. Analytical procedures are effective only if the auditor exercises skepticism in evaluating management's explanations of unexpected results and seeks relevant and reliable evidence to support those explanations.

Using Analytical Procedures to Achieve Audit Objectives. A major decision the auditor makes in designing substantive tests is whether to perform an analytical procedure, a test of details, or a combination of the two. That decision is based on the auditor's judgment about the expected effectiveness and efficiency of available procedures, considering the total assurance sought from substantive tests with respect to a specific audit objective for a particular account balance or class of transactions. In many situations, it is possible to design analytical procedures that, when considered in combination with other auditing procedures, will provide relatively large amounts of assurance, so that the auditor will need less assurance from other substantive procedures. In designing and performing both analytical procedures and tests of details, the auditor should consider the relationship among accounts and the likelihood that evidence obtained about one or more audit objectives with respect to a particular account balance or class of transactions may also provide assurance about other account balances or classes of transactions.

The effectiveness and efficiency of an analytical procedure in identifying potential errors or irregularities depends on, among other things, (a) the plausibility and predictability of the relationship among the data analyzed, (b) the availability and reliability of the data used to develop the expectation, (c) the precision of the expectation, and (d) the nature of the account balances or classes of transactions and the particular audit objectives.

Plausibility and Predictability of the Relationship. It is important for the auditor to understand what makes relationships among data plausible. Data sets sometimes appear to be related when they are not, which could lead the auditor to erroneous conclusions.

Relationships in a stable environment are usually more predictable than relationships in a dynamic or unstable environment. Relationships among income statement accounts tend to be more predictable since they represent transactions over a period of time, whereas relationships among balance sheet accounts tend to be less predictable because a balance at a point in time may be subject to many random influences. Relationships involving transactions subject to management discretion are usually less predictable; for example, management may influence the timing of maintenance or advertising expenditures.

Availability and Reliability of the Data Used to Develop the Expectation. The availability of the data needed to develop expectations for a particular assertion will vary. SAS No. 56 notes, as an example, that for some entities expected sales might be developed from production statistics or from square feet of selling space as a means of testing the completeness of sales. For other entities, however, data relevant to that assertion may not be readily available, and it may be more effective or efficient to perform substantive tests of details on the entity's shipping records.

The auditor should also consider whether the underlying financial and nonfinancial data used to develop the expectation is reliable. In considering the likelihood of misstatements in such data, the auditor considers, among other things, knowledge obtained during previous audits, the results of the assessment of control risk, and the results of tests of details of account balances and transactions. How reliable data used in analytical procedures must be depends on how much assurance the auditor desires from the procedure. For example, in analytical procedures used in planning the audit, untested industry data may be appropriate for developing an expectation about the level of business activity. Expectations developed using information from a variety of independent sources may be more reliable than expectations developed using data from a single source.

Precision of the Expectation. The precision of the expectation depends on, among other things, how thoroughly the auditor considers the factors that affect the amount being audited, and the level of detail of the data used to develop the expectation.

Many factors affect financial relationships. For example, sales may be affected by prices, volume, and product mix, each of which, in turn, may be affected by a number of factors. In developing expectations, the auditor should consider the factors that might have a significant impact on the relationship. The more assurance desired from analytical procedures, the more thoroughly factors affecting the relationship should be considered.

Analytical procedures based on expectations developed at a more detailed level have a greater chance of detecting misstatements of a given amount—and thus provide greater assurance—than do broader comparisons. Comparisons of monthly amounts may be more effective than those of annual amounts, and comparisons by location or lines of business may be more effective than companywide comparisons. What level of detail is appropriate may be influenced by the nature of the entity, its size and complexity, and the level of detail available in its records. Generally, the possibility that material misstatements could be obscured by offsetting factors increases as an entity's operations become more complex and more diversified. For example, the auditor's expectations regarding profit margins on sales in a diversified business will be more precise if they are based on an analysis using disaggregated data, such as gross profit margin by facility or product line, rather than on an analysis of the consolidated gross profit margin.

Nature of the Account Balance and Audit Objective. For some accounts, analytical procedures may be the most effective means for achieving certain audit objectives and may sometimes be the only procedure performed. For example, in some situations, two common analytical procedures, comparing the allowance for uncollectible accounts as a percentage of accounts receivable and as a percentage of overdue receivables with expectations developed from similar percentages for the prior years, might provide sufficient evidence with respect to the valuation objective for accounts receivable. (However, in other situations some substantive tests of details, such as investigating specific overdue items, might also be done.) Or, in auditing accrued payroll at year-end the auditor may test the reasonableness of the accrual by multiplying the gross pay for the weekly, semi-monthly, and monthly payrolls by the ratio of days accrued at year-end to total number of days for the pay periods. Analytical procedures may also be particularly effective when potential misstatements would not be detectable by examining details of transactions, especially when the relevant audit objective is the completeness of recorded transactions.

On the other hand, examining documentation (a test of details) may be the most appropriate means of obtaining assurance regarding the accuracy of fixed asset additions. In obtaining assurance regarding the accuracy of depreciation expense, a combination of analytical procedures and tests of details (such as recalculation of individually significant amounts) may be appropriate. Like other auditing procedures, analytical procedures that are directed specifically at one or more audit objectives for a particular account balance or class of transactions may simultaneously address other accounts or objectives as well; the auditor should take this into consideration when deciding how to obtain the necessary assurance for a particular account or objective.

Other Considerations in Using Analytical Procedures. Many companies, as part of controlling the operation of their business, perform analytical procedures to identify unusual transactions, balances, or relationships on a timely basis. Depending on how relevant and reliable those procedures and the underlying data are, the information generated may be useful to the auditor. In addition, when assessing the control environment, the auditor may identify key performance indicators and management and budgetary information that management reviews and that may be useful in performing analytical procedures. Examples include operating budgets and results, sales analyses, inventory turnover and obsolescence reports, cash flow analyses, and forecasts.

The auditor may choose to use analytical procedures to help determine sample size, to stratify a population, or to assist in the design of other substantive tests. In determining the sample size necessary for auditing procedures related to inventory obsolescence, for example, the auditor may examine the change in inventory turnover rates for various components of inventory to decide which inventory items should be given more attention. Analytical procedures provide corroborative evidence about the accounting treatment of transactions and balances, and can also be good detectors of changes in accounting principles, but of course they will not alert the auditor to a misstatement if an inappropriate accounting principle remains unchanged. Analytical procedures may be particularly useful in helping the auditor to identify transactions that have not been recorded. Similarly, as discussed earlier, if the auditor performs substantive tests of details before year-end, analytical procedures can often provide evidence about the proper recording of transactions in the period between early testing and year-end.

The results of analytical procedures may possibly lead the auditor to extend testing. For example, the auditor might calculate the number of days' sales outstanding and observe that it had increased significantly, and he or she might not be satisfied with management's explanation of that trend. In those circumstances, the auditor might decide to confirm more customer accounts than planned and to confirm them at the end of the year to ensure that fictitious receivables had not been created. The auditor might also expand tests for collectibility, to ensure that the allowance for uncollectible accounts was adequate.

Scanning can be a particularly effective analytical procedure, provided the auditor has a thorough understanding of the account or schedule being scanned and the types of misstatements that could occur. For example, in scanning an inventory listing, the auditor needs to know how the listing is categorized (that is, what items have been grouped together) and what constitutes a reasonable set of parameters for both quantity and price for each group. A larger than expected quantity of an inventory item might indicate an error in transferring information from the count sheets to the listing, or it might be indicative of slow-moving merchandise that needs to be considered in the valuation allowance. In addition, the auditor would investigate any price that was unexpectedly high or low. Similarly, an auditor scanning accounts receivable would be alert to negative amounts that might indicate the misapplication of cash or incomplete recording of sales, and would also be watchful for account balances with related parties. Scanning a listing of monthly charges to expense accounts can alert the auditor to abnormal items that may reflect errors. Scanning may also be used to test the remaining portion of an account balance after the auditor has examined several large items that constitute a significant portion of the balance.

Analytical procedures may be performed using monetary amounts, physical quantities, ratios, or percentages; they may be applied to overall financial information of the entity, to financial information of components such as subsidiaries or divisions, and to individual elements of financial information. Some auditors have developed specialized software programs to extract appropriate client data from computer files and perform standardized procedures. Other software packages require the auditor to input client data to a computer (often a microcomputer), which processes the data and generates analytical reports.

Testing Accounting Judgments and Estimates

The auditor has a responsibility to perform substantive tests as part of evaluating accounting judgments and estimates made by management, which was described in Chapter 5 as the interpreting/evaluating function. The substantive tests performed to do this consist of a combination of tests of details and analytical procedures.

Evaluating Accounting Judgments. The auditor's responsibility entails more than merely substantiating facts about specific transactions and other events and circumstances in order to achieve specific audit objectives for relevant accounts. The auditor also has the responsibility to evaluate how the client has translated those facts into appropriate accounting presentations. As part of that process, the auditor should evaluate what accounting principles are selected and how they are applied. He or she should evaluate accounting judgments to address the risk that generally accepted accounting principles (GAAP) could be misused, intentionally or unintentionally, with respect to how transactions are accounted for and measured and how they are presented and disclosed in the financial statements. This is a pervasive aspect of audit risk that the auditor should keep in mind at all times.

The auditor's evaluation of the selection and application of GAAP requires consideration of the industry involved, the client environment, economic conditions, and numerous other intangible factors. Meeting that responsibility requires an extensive knowledge of accounting principles and of the ways in which they should be applied to produce financial statements that reflect, in all material respects, the substance of the client's transactions and present a picture of the enterprise that is not misleading. Many audit failures in the past have resulted from the auditor's failure to evaluate whether GAAP were properly applied, even when all of the relevant facts were available. The valuation and the presentation and disclosure audit objectives are pervasive; accordingly, the auditor should keep them in mind throughout the audit, not only when performing specific substantive tests directly related to those objectives.

Auditing Accounting Estimates. An important aspect of evaluating the application of accounting principles, particularly as they relate to the valuation objective for many accounts, involves evaluating accounting estimates. Accounting estimates are financial statement approximations that are necessary because the measurement of an account is uncertain until the outcome of future events is known, or because relevant data concerning events that have already occurred cannot be accumulated on a timely, cost-effective basis. Examples of the first type of accounting estimates include uncollectible receivables, obsolete inventory, useful lives of equipment, actuarial assumptions in pension plans, and warranty claims. Examples of the second type of accounting estimates include allocating passenger ticket revenues to airlines other than those issuing the tickets, and telephone company revenues from long distance calls involving more than one company. SAS No. 57, *Auditing Accounting Estimates* (AU Section 342), provides guidance to the auditor in auditing both types of estimates.

Management is responsible for making the necessary accounting estimates; the auditor is responsible for evaluating their reasonableness. Even when management's estimating process involves competent personnel using relevant and reliable data and the most likely assumptions about the factors that affect an accounting estimate, the subjectivity that enters into those estimates introduces the potential for bias. As a result, the auditor should evaluate accounting estimates with an attitude of professional skepticism. The auditor's objective in evaluating accounting estimates is to obtain sufficient competent evidence to provide reasonable assurance that all material accounting estimates have been developed, are reasonable, and are presented and disclosed in conformity with GAAP.

In evaluating the reasonableness of an estimate, the auditor should use one or a combination of three basic approaches.

1. Review and test the process management used to develop the estimate.
2. Independently develop an expectation of the estimate to corroborate the reasonableness of management's estimate.
3. Review events or transactions occurring after the date of the financial statements (but before the audit is completed) that provide an actual amount to compare the estimate with.

When following the first of these approaches, the auditor should

- Obtain an understanding of the process management established to develop each significant accounting estimate.
- Assess the inherent and control risks related to management's process for developing the estimate.
- Identify and evaluate the key factors and assumptions management used to formulate the estimate, concentrating on those key factors and assumptions that are
  - Material to the estimate.
  - Sensitive to variations.
  - Deviations from historical patterns.
  - Subjective, and therefore susceptible to misstatement and bias.

- Assess the reliability of the underlying data that enters into the estimate.
- Determine that the calculations used to translate the underlying data and assumptions into the accounting estimate are accurate.

The first two and last two of the above steps do not need further clarification here, since they involve procedures that are discussed throughout the book. However, procedures helpful in identifying and evaluating the key factors and assumptions are unique to auditing accounting estimates. They may involve some or all of the following steps:

- Identifying the sources of information that management used to formulate the assumptions and considering, based on information gathered from other audit tests, whether the information is relevant, reliable, and sufficient for the purpose.
- Considering whether there are additional key factors or alternative assumptions.
- Evaluating whether the assumptions are consistent with one another, with the supporting data, and with relevant historical data.
- Analyzing historical data used in developing the assumptions to assess whether it is comparable and consistent with data of the period under audit, and determining whether it is sufficiently reliable.
- Considering whether changes in the business or industry or in other facts or circumstances may cause factors different from those considered in the past to become significant to the accounting estimate.
- Reviewing available documentation of the assumptions used in developing the accounting estimate, and inquiring about any other relevant plans, goals, and objectives of the entity; and considering their relationship to the assumptions.
- Considering using the work of a specialist (SAS No. 11, *Using the Work of a Specialist* [AU Section 336]).

Evaluating the Results of Substantive Tests

Substantive tests may reveal errors or irregularities in account balances or classes of transactions. As explained in Chapter 17, auditors often maintain a summary of all misstatements found as a result of their auditing procedures. At the completion of the audit, the summary is evaluated to determine whether adjustments to account balances are needed before the auditor can conclude that the financial statements are presented fairly, in all material respects, in conformity with generally accepted accounting principles.

When errors or irregularities are found as a result of substantive tests, the auditor should ascertain the reason for them and consider the implications. If the nature or frequency of errors or irregularities indicates the possibility of a significant misstatement in the account balance in which they were found or in related account balances, the auditor should consider whether to increase the extent of substantive tests or to change their nature or timing. The auditor should also consider the implications of a misstatement in terms of the client's control structure and the auditor's assessment of control risk. For example, if the auditor's tests indicate that, contrary to expectations formed as a result of assessing control risk, not all transactions have been recorded, the auditor should reevaluate the assessed level of control risk. In addition, if substantive tests reveal a deficiency not previously identified in assessing control risk, the relevant documentation should be amended.

AUDIT PROGRAMS

Auditing procedures are compiled into a document referred to as an audit program. An audit program is a list of steps to be performed in the course of an audit. It typically specifies the nature and extent of the audit work, aids in scheduling and assigning the work, guards against possible omissions and duplications, and provides part of the documentation of the work done. An audit program is necessary for adequate planning and supervision of an engagement under the first standard of field work and is required by SAS No. 22, *Planning and Supervision* (AU Section 311). The audit program should be revised as new information is gathered during subsequent stages of the audit.

The audit program should be organized in a way that will provide for the efficient performance of the procedures listed. More specifically, the program should be organized so that when a particular document is examined, as many of the planned auditing procedures as possible are performed on it. For example, assume that one auditing procedure calls for examining vendor invoices for initials indicating the invoice was reviewed for mathematical accuracy and matched to a purchase order and receiving document, and that another auditing procedure calls for examining vendor invoices for evidence that they were authorized for payment. Combining these auditing procedures into one audit program step will enhance audit efficiency. Since the authors believe that audit programs should be tailored to the specific circumstances of individual clients, a "complete" audit program as such is not presented in this book, although specific tests of controls and substantive tests are presented and discussed in Part 3 in the context of auditing the various transaction cycles and account balances.

Auditors differ among themselves over the degree of detail that should be included in an audit program. Some auditors believe that an audit program should be as general as possible and that someone wanting to know what detailed audit steps were performed can find that information by looking at the working papers that report the results of the audit tests. At the extreme, such an audit program might, for example, include the step: "Perform tests of controls applied to shipments." Other auditors believe that the audit program should be as detailed and specific as possible. The advantage of this is that two people reading the audit program would perform exactly the same audit tests on the same number of transactions or balances. An audit program that reflected this attitude to the extreme might contain the step: "Examine 75 shipping documents for signature of individual authorized to release merchandise from warehouse." The disadvantage of this approach is that it could eliminate much judgment from the audit process and make that process somewhat mechanical. Either approach may be consistent with an efficient and effective audit as long as the work is planned and supervised appropriately for the particular type of audit program, and the education and training of the auditor performing the procedures are adequate to enable the individual to make the necessary judgments.

Review Questions

9–1. How do inherent risk and control risk differ from detection risk?

9–2. In what two ways may an auditor achieve the specific audit objectives related to specific accounts?

9–3. Can substantive tests be relied on to the exclusion of tests of controls? Can tests of controls be performed to the exclusion of substantive tests?

9–4. Name the two major categories of substantive tests.

9–5. What determines the nature, timing, and extent of substantive tests?

9–6. Name the three types of accounts that require different approaches to substantive tests.

9–7. Name the techniques generally used for substantive tests of details. What audit objectives is each of these techniques designed to achieve?

9–8. When is early substantive testing feasible?

9–9. When early substantive testing is followed, what additional procedures are necessary?

9–10. When are analytical procedures performed?

9–11. What are the various types of analytical procedures?

9–12. What are the various techniques by which financial information can be compared with expected results?

9–13. What factors does the effectiveness of analytical procedures depend on?

9–14. What factors should be considered in evaluating accounting judgments?

9–15. What approaches can be used in evaluating accounting estimates?

9–16. How does an audit program aid in performing an effective and efficient audit?

Discussion Questions

9–30. How do the inherent risk characteristics of an account affect the extent of substantive procedures? What balance sheet (and related income statement) accounts are usually audited by relying principally on substantive procedures?

9–31. If an auditor decides to perform tests of control structure policies and procedures and interim substantive procedures as a basis for reducing year-end substantive procedures, and those tests and procedures at the interim date prove satisfactory, what additional procedures are likely to be performed at year-end?

9–32. Assume that a comparison between last year's and the current year's number of days' sales in accounts receivable outstanding shows a significant increase. Sales terms did not change during the year. What effect would this have on an audit testing plan that calls for performing tests of controls?

9–33. What would be the effect on audit strategy of the discovery of an unexpected change in the gross margin ratio determined by analytical procedures?

9–34. When performing analytical procedures, should an auditor be satisfied with explanations that appear to account for observed trends? Explain.

9–35. In performing analytical procedures on fluctuations in payroll and payroll-related accounts, what might be the effect on audit strategy if all amounts are comparable with those of the prior year?

9–36. The first generally accepted standard of field work requires, in part, that "the work is to be adequately planned." An effective tool that aids the auditor in adequately planning the work is an audit program.

Required:

What is an audit program, and what purpose does it serve?

(AICPA adapted)

AICPA Multiple Choice Questions

These questions are taken from the Auditing part of Uniform CPA Examinations. Choose the single most appropriate answer.

9–40. Each of the following might, in itself, form a valid basis for an auditor to decide to omit a test *except* the

a. Relative risk involved.
b. Relationship between the cost of obtaining evidence and its usefulness.
c. Difficulty and expense involved in testing a particular item.
d. Auditor's assessment of control risk.

9–41. As a result of analytical procedures, the independent auditor determines that the gross profit percentage has declined from 30 percent in the preceding year to 20 percent in the current year. The auditor should

a. Express an opinion that is qualified due to inability of the client company to continue as a going concern.
b. Evaluate management's performance in causing this decline.
c. Require footnote disclosure.
d. Consider the possibility of a misstatement in the financial statements.

9–42. Which of the following ratios would be the *least* useful in reviewing the overall profitability of a manufacturing company?

a. Net income to net worth.
b. Net income to total assets.
c. Net income to sales.
d. Net income to working capital.

9–43. An entity's financial statements were misstated over a period of years due to large amounts of revenue being recorded in journal entries that involved debits and credits to an illogical combination of accounts. The auditor could most likely have been alerted to this irregularity by

a. Scanning the general journal for unusual entries.
b. Performing a revenue cutoff test at year-end.
c. Tracing a sample of journal entries to the general ledger.
d. Examining documentary evidence of sales returns and allowances recorded after year-end.

9–44. Which of the following is *not* a typical analytical procedure?

a. Study of relationships of the financial information with relevant nonfinancial information.
b. Comparison of the financial information with similar information regarding the industry in which the entity operates.
c. Comparison of recorded amounts of major disbursements with appropriate invoices.
d. Comparison of the financial information with budgeted amounts.

9–45. An inventory turnover analysis is useful to the auditor because it may detect

a. Inadequacies in inventory pricing.
b. Methods of avoiding cyclical holding costs.
c. The optimum automatic reorder points.
d. The existence of obsolete merchandise.

9–46. The controller of Excello Manufacturing Inc. wants to use ratio analysis to identify the possible existence of idle equipment or the possibility that equipment has been disposed of without having been written off. Which of the following ratios would best accomplish this objective?

a. Depreciation expense/book value of manufacturing equipment.
b. Accumulated depreciation/book value of manufacturing equipment.
c. Repairs and maintenance cost/direct labor costs.
d. Gross manufacturing equipment cost/units produced.

9–47. A basic premise underlying analytical procedures is that

a. These procedures can *not* replace tests of balances and transactions.
b. Statistical tests of financial information may lead to the discovery of material misstatements in the financial statements.
c. The study of financial ratios is an acceptable alternative to the investigation of unusual fluctuations.

d. Relationships among data may reasonably be expected to exist and continue in the absence of known conditions to the contrary.

9-48. Which of the following would be *least* likely to be comparable between similar corporations in the same industry line of business?

a. Earnings per share.
b. Return on total assets before interest and taxes.
c. Accounts receivable turnover.
d. Operating cycle.

9-49. To test for unsupported entries in the ledger, the direction of audit testing should be from the

a. Journal entries.
b. Ledger entries.
c. Original source documents.
d. Externally generated documents.

Problems and Cases

9-60. In auditing the financial statements of a manufacturing company that were prepared from data processed by electronic data processing equipment, the CPA has found that the traditional "audit trail" has been obscured. As a result the CPA may place increased emphasis on overall tests of the data under audit. These overall tests, which are also applied in auditing visibly posted accounting records, include the computation of ratios, which are compared with prior-year ratios or with industrywide norms. Examples of such overall tests or ratios are the computation of the rate of inventory turnover and the computation of the number of days' sales in receivables.

Required:

a. Discuss the advantages to the CPA of the use of ratios as overall tests in an audit.
b. In addition to the computations mentioned, list the ratios that a CPA could compute during an audit as overall tests of balance sheet and related income statement accounts. For each ratio listed, name the two (or more) accounts used in its computation.
c. On discovering that there has been a significant change in a ratio when compared with the prior year's ratio, the CPA considers the possible reasons for the change. Give the possible reasons for the following significant changes in ratios:
   1. The rate of inventory turnover (ratio of cost of sales to average inventory) has decreased from the prior year's rate.
   2. The number of days' sales in receivables (ratio of average daily accounts receivable to sales, times 365) has increased over the prior year.

(AICPA adapted)

9-61. A CPA accumulates various kinds of evidence on which the auditor's opinion on the fairness of financial statements audited will be based. Among this evidence are confirmations from third parties and written representations from the client.

Required:

a. 1. What is an audit confirmation?
   2. What characteristics should an audit confirmation possess if a CPA is to consider it as reliable evidence?

b. 1. What is a written representation?
   2. What information should a written representation contain?
   3. What effect does a written representation have on a CPA's audit of a client's financial statements?

c. 1. Distinguish between a positive confirmation and a negative confirmation in the audit of accounts receivable.
   2. In confirming an audit client's accounts receivable, what characteristics should be present in the accounts if the CPA is to use negative confirmations?

(AICPA adapted)

9–62. *Part a.*

Between the time trade accounts receivable confirmations were sent and year-end (a two-month period), the chief executive officer of a client implemented a new sales policy that resulted in an immediate, marked increase in reported sales. The chief executive called customers to obtain their consent to accept shipments of the company's product "on approval." Under the terms offered by the chief executive, the company would ship goods without customers' orders and bill those shipments as though they were sales. However, customers were not obligated to pay for the goods they received unless and until they decided to purchase them. The chief executive assured customers that they had an unconditional right to return any goods accepted "on approval" at any time. The company recorded those "on approval" shipments as sales without waiting for customers to decide which of the goods so shipped, if any, they would purchase. The new policy improved not only the company's sales, but also the chief executive's sales-dependent bonus.

Required:

What analytical procedures could you perform that have the potential to identify the irregularity described?

Part b.

Assume you performed the analytical procedures in your answer to Part a and discovered the unusual sales activity during the last two months of the year. You discussed this with management and learned that the sales increase near year-end is common in the industry. You questioned this response because, while you agree that the trend is consistent with the industry, you noted the *absence* of similar activity in the prior year.

Required:

What additional analytical procedures could you design to specifically address the irregularity in the sales and accounts receivable accounts?

9–63. The auditing procedures listed herein are procedures that an auditor might employ in an audit of a client's revenue cycle.

1. For selected sales, compare the date that sales invoices are recorded with the date that goods were shipped, as found on shipping documents.
2. Divide sales commissions by gross sales and compare the result with the client's stated commission rate.

3. Mail itemized statements to customers along with a request that they indicate whether the balances due are correct or incorrect.
4. For selected sales, compare customers' sales orders, invoices, and shipping documents for consistency of quantities, prices, customers' names, and other data.
5. Examine supervisor's initials indicating review of sales orders, invoices, and shipping documents for consistency before the invoices are mailed and recorded.
6. Examine shipping documents, copies of sales invoices, and customers' sales orders for evidence supporting unpaid balances in accounts receivable.
7. Review the aged trial balance of accounts receivable, identify old receivables, and evaluate their collectibility.
8. Calculate "days' sales outstanding" (average accounts receivable divided by average daily sales) and compare it with comparable figures for the past three years.
9. Examine reports indicating review of shipping documents for which no invoice has been prepared.
10. Examine documentation supporting credit memos issued after the balance sheet date and determine when the sales took place.
11. For a sample of invoices, recalculate extensions and footings.
12. Observe that a record of goods shipped is maintained.

Required:

a. For each of the foregoing auditing procedures:
   1. State whether it is a test of controls or a substantive test, or whether it could be either, depending on its purpose.
   2. Classify it according to whether it involves confirmation, observation, inspecting assets, reperformance, examining evidence (inspecting documents), or inquiry. (An auditing procedure may involve more than one type of evidence.)
b. If the procedure is a test of controls:
   1. State the control objective that is being met if the test indicates that the control procedure is designed and operating effectively.
   2. Identify a misstatement that could result if the control procedure is absent or ineffective.
   3. State a substantive test that the auditor could use that would provide evidence of the dollar amount of misstatement.
c. If the procedure is a substantive test, state the audit objective that the procedure is designed to meet.

9-64. What are the general objectives or purposes of the CPA's observation of the taking of a physical inventory? (Do not discuss the procedures or techniques involved in making the observation.)

(AICPA adapted)

9-65. The inspection of the minutes of meetings is an integral part of a CPA's audit of a corporation's financial statements.

Required:

a. A CPA should determine if there is any disagreement between transactions recorded in the corporate records and actions approved by the corporation's board of directors. Why is this so and how is it accomplished?

b. Discuss the effect each of the following situations would have on specific steps in a CPA's audit and on the auditor's opinion.
   1. The minute book does not show approval for the sale of an important manufacturing division, which was consummated during the year.
   2. Some details of a contract negotiated during the year with the labor union are different from the outline of the contract included in the minutes of a meeting of the board of directors.
   3. The minutes of a meeting of directors held after the balance sheet date have not yet been written, but the corporation's secretary shows the CPA notes from which the minutes are to be prepared when the secretary has time.

c. What corporate actions should be approved by stockholders and recorded in the minutes of the stockholders' meetings?

(AICPA adapted)

9-66. Your client, Fenton, Inc., fabricates electronic components for the automotive industry. Based on your knowledge of this client's operations, its competitors, the economy, and current activity in the automotive industry, you expected the gross margin for a particular product line, a climate control system, to remain relatively flat or increase only slightly from the prior year.

Just before performing substantive tests of details, you analyze the gross margin for this particular product line and identify an increase of 20 percent over the previous year. You discuss this with both the company controller and the individual responsible for this product line and learn that the purchase of several new machines resulting in significant labor efficiencies was responsible for the increase in the gross margin.

Required:

a. How would you follow up and corroborate management's explanation for the increase in the gross margin of this particular product line?
b. Would the fact that new equipment is included on the schedule of fixed assets, in itself, corroborate management's explanation of the increase in the gross margin of this particular product line? Why or why not?

9-67. The following errors and irregularities were found by the auditor as a result of performing substantive tests:

1. Goods shipped were not billed because the shipping document (bill of lading) was lost.
2. A cash payment from a customer was stolen by a clerk in the mailroom before any record was made of it.
3. Equipment repairs were unintentionally recorded as an equipment purchase.
4. A vendor's invoice was paid twice; the second payment was stolen by the accounts payable clerk after the treasurer had signed the checks. No entries were made for the second payment.
5. A check for $4321 was recorded as $1234.
6. The plant supervisor submitted a time card for a fictitious employee, received the check, endorsed it with the fictitious name, and deposited it in her bank account.

Required:

For each of those errors or irregularities:

a. State the financial statement assertion that is relevant to the error or irregularity. Be specific.
b. State the substantive test that the auditor probably used to detect the error or irregularity.
c. State the control objective that is not being met. Be specific.
d. Specify one or more control procedures that the client could install that would prevent or detect the error or irregularity.
e. Specify tests of controls that could be used to test the effectiveness of the control procedures specified in d.

9-68. Comparative balance sheets and statements of income and retained earnings (deficit) for Pennington Company at June 30, 1990 and 1989 and for the two years then ended are presented on pages 352 and 353. Prior years' financial statements include the following information relative to the year ended June 30, 1988:

Accounts receivable, net, totaled $5,001,000
Inventories totaled $5,003,000

Required:
Compute the following for 1990 and 1989, based on the Pennington Company's financial data. (Use end-of-year data if necessary.)

- Current ratio
- Accounts receivable turnover
- Inventory turnover
- Return on common stock equity
- Return on total assets
- Gross profit percentage
- Net income to sales
- Long-term debt to equity ratio

What does your analysis of Pennington's financial statements indicate?

9-69. Identify the accounts and other factors that, singly or in combination, might help to explain a fluctuation in each of the accruals listed below.

- Accrued hourly and salaried payroll
- Accrued sales commissions
- Accrued vacation pay
- Income and social security taxes withheld and accrued
- Accrued general and automobile insurance
- Accrued real and personal property taxes
- Accrued utilities (electricity and gas)
- Accrued rent
- Accrued bonus payable
- Accrued interest payable
- Accrued pension liability
- Accrued royalties payable

Pennington Company
Balance Sheets
June 30, 1990 and 1989

(Client prepared)

Assets	*1990*	*1989*
Current assets:		
Cash	$ 10,000	$ 100,000
Marketable securities	40,000	500,000
Accounts receivable, net of allowance for doubtful accounts of $409,000 in 1990 and $286,000 in 1989	6,000,000	5,000,000
Inventories	10,000,000	5,000,000
Prepaid expenses	50,000	200,000
Total current assets	16,100,000	10,800,000
Property, plant, and equipment, net of accumulated depreciation of $9,000,000 in 1990 and $6,000,000 in 1989	37,000,000	17,000,000
Other assets, net of accumulated amortization of $20,000 in 1990 and $15,000 in 1989	45,000	50,000
Total assets	$53,145,000	$27,850,000

Liabilities	*1990*	*1989*
Current liabilities:		
Bank loans	$ 2,500,000	
Accounts payable	9,000,000	$ 4,000,000
Accrued liabilities	3,000,000	1,000,000
Notes payable, current portion	3,000,000	1,000,000
Income taxes payable		1,500,000
Dividends payable		2,000,000
Total current liabilities	17,500,000	9,500,000
Notes payable, net of current portion	30,000,000	11,000,000
Deferred income taxes	500,000	500,000
Stockholders' Equity		
Preferred stock, 5% non-cumulative, 100,000 shares authorized, issued, and outstanding	1,000,000	1,000,000
Common stock, 500,000 shares authorized, issued, and outstanding	5,000,000	5,000,000
Retained earnings (deficit)	(855,000)	850,000
Total stockholders' equity	5,145,000	6,850,000
Total liabilities and stockholders' equity	$53,145,000	$27,850,000

Pennington Company
Statements of Income and Retained Earnings (Deficit)
For the Years Ended June 30, 1990 and 1989

(Client prepared)

	1990	*1989*
Net sales	$40,000,000	$45,000,000
Cost of sales	31,000,000	32,000,000
Gross profit	9,000,000	13,000,000
Selling, general, and administrative expenses	8,505,000	8,700,000
Income from operations	495,000	4,300,000
Other income (expense)		
Interest	(4,000,000)	(1,000,000)
Loss on sale of machinery and equipment	—	(100,000)
Gain on sale of marketable securities	300,000	100,000
	(3,700,000)	(1,000,000)
Income (loss) before provision for income taxes	(3,205,000)	3,300,000
Recovery of (provision for) income taxes	1,500,000	(1,500,000)
Net income (loss)	(1,705,000)	1,800,000
Retained earnings at beginning of the year	850,000	1,050,000
Dividends[a]	—	(2,000,000)
Retained earnings (deficit) at end of the year	$ (855,000)	$ 850,000

[a]No preferred stock dividends were declared in 1990.

10

The Extent of Testing: Audit Sampling

This book has noted on several occasions that the auditor has several decisions to make in gathering evidence about each assertion implicit in the individual measurements and disclosures in a set of financial statements. Those decisions include how much evidence to acquire, that is, decisions about the extent of audit tests. This chapter addresses those decisions. Audit sampling is defined, and procedures that do not involve sampling are discussed; then audit risk is described in the context of sampling, and the determinants of sample size are outlined. Those discussions provide background for guidance on applying statistical and nonstatistical sampling techniques in both tests of controls and substantive testing.

In the first edition of this book, published in 1912, Montgomery recognized as an "obvious conclusion" the notion that "no audit can or should embrace a complete verification of all the transactions of the period under review."[1] If for every procedure selected by the auditor for gathering evidence, or even if for a few of those procedures, the auditor were to examine every item that could possibly be selected for examination, it would be virtually impossible to complete an audit on a timely basis, not to mention at a reasonable cost. Neither the client nor the public expects the auditor to examine every transaction. Consequently, the auditor is continually faced with the question: How much testing is enough?

In some instances, that question is answered by deciding not to perform a specific procedure at all. For example, if control procedures applied to payroll disbursements are tested and found to be effective, the auditor may decide neither to prepare a reconciliation of the payroll bank account at year-end nor even to review the client's year-end reconciliation. (In that situation, the decisions about what kind of evidence and how much evidence to acquire are identical.) In other instances, the question is answered by deciding to perform some procedure, but not to apply it to all the items in an account or to all transactions of a specific class. For example, the auditor may decide to confirm accounts receivable, but to limit the procedure to only a portion of receivables under $10,000. Testing less than the entire population for the purpose of evaluating it is referred to as audit sampling.

Statement on Auditing Standards (SAS) No. 39, *Audit Sampling* (AU Section 350.01), provides a formal definition of audit sampling: "Audit sampling is the application of an audit procedure to less than 100 percent of the items within an account balance or class of transactions for the purpose of evaluating some characteristic of the balance or class."

Based on the results of applying an auditing procedure to a representative sample of items, the auditor can make an inference (by projecting or extrapolating the sample results) about the entire population from which the sample was selected. In fact, SAS No. 39 requires that the items be selected in such a way that the sample can be expected to be representative of the population. After performing the necessary auditing procedures, the auditor is required to

[1]R. H. Montgomery, *Auditing Theory and Practice* (New York: Ronald Press, 1912), p. 81.

project the sample results to the population. When evaluating whether the financial statements as a whole may be materially misstated, the auditor should aggregate all projected misstatements (discussed later) determined from sampling applications and other likely misstatements[2] determined from nonsampling procedures.

Audit sampling is used by auditors in both tests of controls and substantive tests. It is especially useful when the auditor's selection of items to be tested is drawn from a large population and the auditor has no specific knowledge about the characteristics of the population being tested, such as the frequency, size, and direction of misstatements. For example, accounts receivable, inventory, and accounts payable balances could be overstated or understated as a result of using incorrect quantities or prices or because of errors in posting or arithmetical extensions and footings.

PROCEDURES NOT INVOLVING SAMPLING

SAS No. 39 promulgated professional standards for all uses of audit sampling. Although in the past the term "sampling" was used to describe virtually all forms of detailed audit testing in which not every item was examined, the definition of sampling in SAS No. 39, cited earlier, excludes several types of tests frequently performed in an audit. To clarify the circumstances in which an auditor's examination of less than 100 percent of the items in a class of transactions or an account balance would not be considered audit sampling, in January 1985 the ASB issued an auditing interpretation of SAS No. 39 (AU Section 9350.01-.02).

The auditor's purpose in applying a procedure is the governing factor in determining whether the procedure constitutes sampling. Sampling is not involved if the auditor does not intend to extend the conclusion reached by performing the procedure to the remainder of the items in the class or account balance. Thus, sampling does not generally apply to procedures performed to obtain an understanding of the control structure. For example, the auditor might trace one or two transactions through the client's accounting system only for the purpose of understanding the flow of transactions through the system, and not for assessing the effectiveness of specific control procedures. Similarly, auditors sometimes reperform calculations or trace journal entries to ledger accounts on a test basis for the purpose of obtaining additional evidence relating to a financial statement assertion. SAS No. 39 does not apply in those situations because the auditor's intent is not to evaluate a characteristic of all

[2]In addition to projected misstatement, likely misstatement includes known misstatements specifically identified by the auditor in nonsampling procedures and differences between unreasonable estimates in the financial statements and the closest reasonable amount in a range of acceptable amounts.

transactions passing through the system or all balances in the account. Other auditing procedures, for example, reading the minutes of meetings of the board of directors, also do not involve sampling.

Furthermore, sampling is not involved when the auditor separates a class of transactions or an account balance into two groups based on specific criteria and then examines 100 percent of the items in one group and tests the other by other means or does not test it at all because it is immaterial. For example, in what is known as the "high dollar coverage" approach, the auditor might divide the accounts receivable balance into two groups: (1) several large items that constitute a significant portion of the balance, and (2) the remaining (smaller) items. All the accounts in the first group may be confirmed, while assurance for those in the second group, which may be material in the aggregate, may be obtained from other auditing procedures, for example, analytical procedures using scanning techniques. The auditor would be using sampling only if an auditing procedure were applied to individual items that constituted less than 100 percent of the population in the second group for the purpose of drawing a conclusion about all of the items in that group.

Sampling does not apply to many tests of controls, such as tests of control structure policies and procedures based on segregation of duties or other procedures that provide no documentary evidence of performance. In addition, sampling may not apply to tests of certain documented control structure policies and procedures. Those tests often consist of inquiry and observation. An example is an auditor's observation of a client's physical inventory count procedures, such as inventory movement and counting procedures. (Audit sampling may be involved in certain tests of inventory, such as tracing selected test counts into inventory records.) Generally, sampling applies less often to tests of controls directed at the control environment and accounting system than to tests of control procedures.

A substantive testing method in which less than 100 percent of an account balance is examined and that is similar to, but is not, sampling is referred to as "accept-reject" testing. It is used when projecting a misstatement amount (discussed later) is not practical, for example, test counts made as part of a physical inventory observation and tests of reconciling items. In those circumstances, the auditor either "accepts" that the test supports its objective (that is, no or few misstatements are found) or "rejects" the test (more than negligible misstatements are found) and performs other procedures to achieve the objective. However, the auditor still must consider the extent of testing (that is, assurance needed and materiality) in planning to use "accept-reject" testing and must adequately document the test results.

Other examples of auditing procedures that usually do not involve sampling are cutoff tests in which the auditor examines all significant transactions around the cutoff date and analytical procedures. Also, sampling may not always be necessary in testing control procedures that operate repeatedly throughout the period. Sometimes, if such a control procedure operates cumulatively, the auditor can achieve the test objective by examining a single item. For example, a review of the year-end bank reconciliation may be sufficient to achieve the auditor's objective with respect to control procedures for bank reconciliations generally. Similarly, examination of other year-end cumulative reconciliations (such as a reconciliation of the accounts receivable subsidiary ledger to the control account) may be sufficient to achieve the relevant test objectives.

Generally accepted auditing standards do not require auditors to use sampling (statistical or nonstatistical); they do require that auditors obtain sufficient competent evidence to afford a reasonable basis for an opinion regarding the financial statements, and that auditors document their sources of audit evidence, regardless of whether sampling is employed.

AUDIT RISK AND SAMPLING

Having decided that a particular auditing procedure will be applied to a sample of an audit population, the auditor must then determine the minimum sample size that is needed to control the risk of an undetected material misstatement in the financial statements. That risk—referred to as audit risk—is the risk that an improper conclusion may be reached about the client's financial statements. Audit risk was discussed in Chapter 6 in the context of formulating the audit strategy on an overall basis. How that discussion relates to sampling is explained here.

Nonsampling Risk

Nonsampling risk encompasses all risks that are not specifically the result of sampling. Nonsampling risk is the risk that any factor other than the size of the sample selected will cause the auditor to draw an incorrect conclusion about an account balance or about the effectiveness of a control structure policy or procedure. Examples of nonsampling risk are

- Omitting necessary auditing procedures (e.g., failing to review management or board minutes).
- Applying auditing procedures improperly (e.g., giving confirmation requests to the client for mailing).
- Applying auditing procedures to an inappropriate or incomplete population (e.g., excluding an entire class of purchases from the process of selecting a sample for substantive tests of the accuracy of recorded transactions and then concluding that all purchase transactions have been accurately recorded).
- Failing to recognize a deviation in a control procedure when it is encountered in a test of controls.

- Failing to detect that accounting recognition, measurement, or disclosure principles have been improperly selected or applied.
- Failing to take action either in response to audit findings or because factors requiring attention have been overlooked.

Sample size is not a consideration in assessing nonsampling risk. Analyses of past alleged audit failures indicate that such nonsampling risk factors as failure to understand business situations or risks, errors in interpreting accounting principles, mistakes in interpreting and applying standards, and misstatements caused by client fraud are among the most significant audit risk factors and sources of auditor liability. Since sample size is irrelevant if the auditor fails to apply appropriate auditing procedures or examines an inappropriate population, adequate control over nonsampling risk is a prerequisite to controlling sampling risk.

Most auditors deal with nonsampling risk, in part, by carefully planning the audit and maintaining high standards of audit quality. Quality standards address matters such as independence and professional development of staff, independent review of working papers, and senior and managerial personnel's supervision of the performance of procedures. These are covered in detail in Chapter 3.

Sampling Risk

Sampling risk is the risk that, when an audit test is restricted to a sample, the conclusion reached from the test will differ from the conclusion that would have been reached if the same test had been applied to all items in the population rather than to just a sample. It is the chance that the test will indicate that a control structure policy or procedure is effective or an account is not materially misstated when the opposite is true, or that the policy or procedure is not effective or an account is materially misstated when the opposite is true. Sampling risk can also be viewed as the complement of the desired level of assurance from a particular sample. Thus, if the auditor seeks a high level of assurance from a test, a low sampling risk should be specified.  Sampling risk is inversely related to sample size (i.e., with all other factors remaining the same, the larger the sample, the lower the sampling risk).

Sampling risk has the following aspects:

1. In the context of tests of controls
   a) The *risk of assessing control risk too low* is the risk that the auditor will conclude, based on the sample, that the control structure policy or procedure is operating more effectively than it actually is.[3]

[3]SAS No. 39 (AU Section 350.12) describes this risk as the risk that the auditor will conclude, based on a sample, that the assessed level of control risk is less than the true operating effectiveness of the control structure policy or procedure. This type of risk is sometimes referred to in statistical literature as the *beta* risk.

b) The *risk of assessing control risk too high* is the risk that the auditor will conclude, based on the sample, that the control structure policy or procedure is operating less effectively than it actually is.[4]

2. In the context of substantive tests of account balances

a) The *risk of incorrect acceptance* is the risk that the auditor will conclude, based on a sample, that the recorded account balance is not materially misstated when examination of every item in the population would reveal that it is materially misstated.[5]

b) The *risk of incorrect rejection* is the risk that the auditor will conclude, based on a sample, that the recorded account balance is materially misstated when examination of every item in the population would reveal that it is not materially misstated.[6]

The risks of assessing control risk too high and of incorrect rejection relate primarily to audit efficiency. For example, if the auditor initially concludes, based on an evaluation of an audit sample, that an account balance is materially misstated when it is not, performing additional auditing procedures and considering other audit evidence would ordinarily lead the auditor to the correct audit conclusion. Similarly, if the auditor's evaluation of a sample leads to a higher assessed level of control risk for an assertion than is necessary, substantive tests are likely to be increased to compensate for the perceived control structure ineffectiveness. Although the audit might be less efficient in those circumstances, it would nevertheless be effective.

The risks of incorrect acceptance and of assessing control risk too low are of greater concern to the auditor, since they relate directly to the effectiveness of an audit in detecting material misstatements. It is thus necessary to ensure that the extent of testing (sample size) is adequate to keep those risks from exceeding acceptable levels. The complement of the risks of assessing control risk too low and of incorrect acceptance is the desired level of assurance, which is sometimes referred to as the "reliability" or "confidence level." For example, an auditor's willingness to accept a 5 percent risk of assessing control risk too low for a test of a particular control procedure could also be expressed as seeking a confidence level of 95 percent.

DETERMINANTS OF SAMPLE SIZE

In planning a sampling application, an auditor must consider three factors: how much risk can be accepted that the sample results will be misleading

[4]SAS No. 39 (AU Section 350.12) describes this risk as the risk that the auditor will conclude, based on a sample, that the assessed level of control risk is greater than the true operating effectiveness of the control structure policy or procedure. This type of risk is sometimes referred to in statistical literature as the *alpha* risk.

[5]This type of risk is sometimes referred to in statistical literature as the *beta* risk.

[6]This type of risk is sometimes referred to in statistical literature as the *alpha* risk.

(sampling risk), how much misstatement can be accepted (tolerable misstatement), and how much misstatement there might be in the population (expected misstatement). The auditor then determines an appropriate sample size, either by applying statistical sampling techniques, described later in this chapter, that incorporate those factors, or on a nonstatistical[7] basis by applying professional judgment in considering each factor's relative impact on sample size. The population size is sometimes important to the statistical computations, but when the population is large (e.g., over 2000 items), the effect on the computations is often minimal. For small samples taken from large populations, the population size has the least influence of all the relevant factors on sample size. This emphasis on the planning aspects of sampling applications means that the auditor must thoroughly develop the sampling strategy before the testing begins.

Sampling Risk

As noted previously, sampling risk is inversely related to sample size. The auditor determines the acceptable level of sampling risk after considering the evidence obtained from other procedures performed on the account or control structure policy or procedure being tested. Thus, a higher level of sampling risk may be accepted for detailed substantive tests when control risk for the financial statement assertion being tested has been assessed as low.

The following example will illustrate these relationships. If an auditor has assessed control risk as low and is performing extensive analytical procedures for a specific assertion, then a high sampling risk (small sample size) is acceptable for related substantive tests of details (or perhaps it may not even be necessary to perform any detailed tests). On the other hand, if the auditor has assessed control risk as high and is not performing extensive analytical procedures for an assertion, then a low sampling risk (large sample size) is required. Very low levels of sampling risk are normally attainable only with very large sample sizes (i.e., several hundred items).

Tolerable Deviation Rate or Misstatement Amount

The *tolerable deviation rate* (usually shortened to "tolerable rate") is the rate of deviation from a prescribed procedure that can be found, as a result of performing tests of controls, without causing the auditor to either revise the

[7]The term "nonstatistical sampling" is used in SAS No. 39 to describe what many auditors previously referred to as "judgmental sampling." Statistical sampling procedures involve the exercise of substantial amounts of audit judgment, as, of course, does nonstatistical sampling.

assessed level of control risk or modify planned substantive tests.[8] The *tolerable misstatement amount* (usually shortened to "tolerable misstatement") is the amount of dollar misstatement in an account balance that may be discovered as a result of performing a substantive test and not require performing other auditing procedures or affect the auditor's opinion on the financial statements. For substantive test samples, the tolerable misstatement cannot be larger than the smaller of the materiality amount for the individual item or for the financial statements taken as a whole (which is the smaller of balance sheet or income statement materiality). For example, if balance sheet materiality is \$200,000 and income statement materiality is \$100,000, the tolerable misstatement should be no larger than \$100,000 or the materiality amount for the individual item, if smaller. Determining materiality levels is discussed in Chapter 6.

The chance of the true misstatement in every sampling application equaling tolerable misstatement is remote, and thus auditors normally plan auditing procedures so that the sum of the individual tolerable misstatements exceeds the amount considered "tolerable" (material) for the financial statements as a whole. In other words, tolerable misstatement for an account balance is usually set somewhere between overall materiality and a proportional allocation of overall tolerable misstatement to that account.

As the tolerable rate or misstatement amount increases, the sample size required to achieve the auditor's objective at a given level of sampling risk (or of its complement, reliability) decreases. (This conclusion is derived from the sample size table for statistical samples, Table 10.1, on page 371; the same concept applies to nonstatistical samples.) Thus, with all other factors remaining the same, sample size can be almost halved if the tolerable rate or misstatement amount is doubled (e.g., from 5 percent to 10 percent) at a confidence level of 95 percent with an expected deviation rate or misstatement amount (discussed later) of one-half of 1 percent. For tests of controls using statistical sampling, the examples in SAS No. 39 suggest a range of possible tolerable deviation rates between 5 percent and 10 percent. No such guidelines can be given for substantive tests, however, since tolerable misstatement for a specific account must be determined judgmentally based on a number of factors—overall materiality, account balance materiality, and type and amount of individual items within an account balance—that are not precisely definable. For example, if inventory has a larger account balance than accounts receivable, then inventory may be allocated a larger tolerable misstatement than accounts receivable.

Designing a sample with a high tolerable rate or misstatement may produce evidence that is too imprecise to support a conclusion at a low risk level that the

[8]Some auditors use the term "tolerable misstatement rate" instead of "tolerable deviation rate." Although an ineffective control structure policy or procedure *may* cause financial statement misstatements, it does not necessarily do so. Thus, the word "deviation" is used in this book in referring to a departure from a prescribed policy or procedure.

account and the financial statements taken as a whole are not materially misstated. Also, a large sample can generally detect both frequent and infrequent deviations or misstatements that aggregate to a material amount, but a small sample can be relied on to detect only frequent deviations or misstatements. At the extreme, some items in an account may individually be so material or may have such a high likelihood of misstatement that the auditor should be unwilling to accept any sampling risk; those items should not be sampled but should be examined 100 percent.

Expected Deviation Rate or Misstatement Amount

Expected deviation rate or misstatement amount also has an impact on sample size. As the expected rate or amount increases, the sample size necessary to meet the auditor's specified sampling risk at a given tolerable deviation rate or misstatement amount increases as well. The auditor's specification of the expected deviation rate or misstatement amount in the population to be sampled is the best estimate of the true deviation rate or misstatement amount in that population. Auditors commonly use the results of prior years' tests of controls to estimate the expected deviation rate; if those results are not available, a small preliminary sample from the current year's population can be used for that purpose, or the auditor's ''best guess'' can be used. The estimate need not be exact, since it affects only the determination of sample size and not the auditor's evaluation of sample results.

In a statistical sampling context, the relationship between the increase in expected deviation rate or misstatement amount and the increase in sample size is not proportionate. For example, if the auditor estimates the expected deviation rate at 2 percent for a particular test of controls and specifies a tolerable deviation rate of 5 percent at a 95 percent confidence level, the appropriate minimum statistical sample size is 190. If, given the same circumstances, the expected rate were estimated at 3 percent, the sample size would be 370. (This can be seen by referring to Table 10.1 on page 371.) When the expected deviation rate is close to the tolerable deviation rate, very large sample sizes are often necessary. On the other hand, if the auditor sets an expected deviation rate that is below the true deviation rate, the sample is likely not to be large enough to support, at the desired level of reliability, a conclusion that the true deviation rate does not exceed the tolerable rate.

Figures 10.1 and 10.2 summarize the effect of the factors discussed previously on sample size.

Other Planning Considerations

SAS No. 39 (AU Section 350.17) requires the auditor to ''determine that the population from which he draws the sample is appropriate for the specific audit

Figure 10.1 Factors Influencing Sample Size in a Test of Controls

	Conditions Leading to	
	Smaller Sample Size	*Larger Sample Size*
Desired assessed level of control risk	Higher	Lower
Expected deviation rate	Lower	Higher
Tolerable deviation rate	Higher	Lower
Number of items in population	Virtually no effect on sample size unless population is very small (fewer than 2000 items)	

objective. For example, an auditor would not be able to detect understatements of an account due to omitted items by sampling the recorded items. An appropriate sampling plan for detecting such understatements would involve selecting from a source in which the omitted items are included.'' In general, audit sampling (or any testing) directed at a recorded balance will not provide assurance as to the completeness of the balance. To test the completeness of an account balance (e.g., accounts receivable), it is often necessary to test some other source in which the potentially omitted items are included (e.g., the shipping log).

Figure 10.2 Factors Influencing Sample Size in a Substantive Test of Details

	Conditions Leading to	
	Smaller Sample Size	*Larger Sample Size*
Assessed level of control risk	Lower	Higher
Stratification[a]	Greater	Lesser
Expected misstatement:		
Size of expected individual misstatement	Smaller	Larger
Frequency and aggregate amount of expected misstatement	Lower	Higher[b]
Tolerable misstatement	Higher	Lower
Assurance from other substantive tests (e.g., analytical procedures)	Significant	Little or none
Number of items in population	Virtually no effect on sample size unless population is very small (fewer than 2000 items)	

[a]Stratification is the separation of population items into groups or strata on the basis of some characteristic related to the specific audit objective.

[b]If the auditor's assessment of the amount of expected misstatement exceeds an acceptable level of materiality, it may be inadvisable to perform the test on a sample basis.

CHOOSING STATISTICAL OR NONSTATISTICAL METHODS

SAS No. 39 explicitly recognizes that both statistical and nonstatistical approaches to audit sampling, when properly applied, can provide sufficient evidential matter. Moreover, the guidance in SAS No. 39 applies equally to both approaches. Both approaches have advantages and disadvantages, and the auditor should choose between them after considering those advantages and disadvantages.

The major advantages of statistical sampling are the opportunity to determine the minimum sample size needed to meet the objectives of audit tests and the opportunity to express the results quantitatively. In statistical sampling, sampling risk can be measured in quantitative terms and objectively evaluated and controlled. This is because the process of determining the appropriate sample size entails specifying a level of reliability[9] and a desired degree of precision.[10]

There are also disadvantages to using statistical sampling, however, and they can result in practical problems that might make the use of statistical techniques less efficient than nonstatistical sampling procedures. For example, the statistical sampler *must* use random sample selection techniques, which can be more time-consuming than the unsystematic (haphazard) techniques available to the nonstatistical sampler. In selecting a random sample, the auditor may have practical problems establishing a correlation between a table or computer printout of random numbers and the population under audit. For example, an auditor who plans to use random number selection of unpaid invoices in the audit of accounts receivable may face a population that is made up of invoices from three client locations, with the invoice numbers assigned at each location without regard to the numbers assigned at the other locations. Not only will problems be caused by missing numbers in the population as a result of paid invoices, but duplicate numbers could also exist because of the lack of coordination among locations in assigning invoice numbers. Thus, the auditor might have to renumber the population in order to use random number selection.

[9]As noted on page 361, reliability may be thought of as the auditor's level of assurance or confidence—expressed as a percentage—that the statistical results provide correct information about the true population value. A 95 percent reliability level is considered a high level of audit assurance for substantive tests of details. If control risk is assessed below the maximum or if additional assurance is obtained from other substantive tests such as analytical procedures, the auditor often designs a substantive test sample at a level below 95 percent.

[10]Precision may be defined as the difference between the rates or amounts specified for tolerable misstatement and expected misstatement (both of which were explained on pages 362–364) in planning a sample. For example, if tolerable misstatement is set at 5 percent and expected misstatement is set at 1 percent, the desired precision of the test is 4 percent. In some types of sampling, such as attributes sampling used in tests of controls, precision is stated in terms of a rate of occurrence (e.g., 5 percent). In other types, such as variables sampling used in substantive tests of details, it is expressed as a dollar amount (e.g., $25,000). SAS No. 39 (AU Section 350) uses the concepts of "tolerable misstatement" and an "allowance for sampling risk" instead of precision.

The use of specialized audit software to extract a sample from a population stored in machine-readable form may greatly reduce the costs of selecting a statistical sample. When appropriate audit software is used, statistical samples may not be more costly than nonstatistical samples. As a result, the availability of computerized sample selection and evaluation programs is often a deciding factor in determining whether it is efficient to use statistical sampling techniques. Before deciding whether to use a statistical sampling procedure in a particular circumstance, the auditor should make a cost-benefit analysis, weighing the additional costs of determining sample size, extracting the sample, and evaluating the results using appropriate formulas against the benefits of knowing the reliability and precision associated with the sample results.

STATISTICAL TESTS OF CONTROLS

A statistical technique called *attributes sampling* that deals with proportions and rates may be used for tests of controls. Attributes sampling techniques are used to estimate the true proportion (not dollar value) of an attribute in a population. The auditor must carefully define the attribute being measured—such as proper approval of an invoice for payment—because the person who examines each sample item must have criteria for determining whether the sample item possesses that attribute or not. The sample results are then projected to the population and statistical computations made to measure the precision and reliability associated with the sample results.

In tests of controls, departures from prescribed procedures (i.e., deviations) are generally measured in rates of incidence. For example, in a sample of 50 disbursement checks, the absence of evidence of proper authorization of 1 check is generally expressed as a 2 percent sample deviation rate (1/50). Since the control procedure either operates or not, percentages are a convenient way to express test sample results.

The true deviation rate in the population is likely to be higher or lower than the rate found in a sample. The statistical sampler can make a statement about how high the true deviation rate could be, at a given level of reliability. For example, an auditor, having evaluated a statistical sample, could state

> One deviation was found in a random sample of 50 items (a 2 percent deviation rate); thus, there is a 90 percent level of reliability (10 percent sampling risk) that the true deviation rate in the population is less than 8 percent.

In the authors' view, a mathematical statement of risk based on statistical attributes sampling often has limited applicability in assessing the effectiveness of a control procedure in a typical engagement. Since statistical procedures (e.g., formal random selection) introduce additional expense, and statistical and nonstatistical procedures may provide essentially equivalent audit information, the extra expense is rarely justified. Additionally, because of the existence of other, corroborative sources of audit evidence and the interrelatedness of many auditing procedures, a single test is rarely the sole source of audit evidence about whether a control procedure is effective. Furthermore, even after assessing the effectiveness of a control procedure statistically, the auditor must still exercise judgment to determine whether, and to what extent, the control procedure contributes to a low control risk assessment. As noted in Chapter 8, the assessment of control risk for a specific audit objective should be based on evidence provided by tests of controls in their entirety. The statistical measurement of sampling risk associated with a test of controls does not diminish the need to consider the interrelationships among elements of the control structure. However, in environments such as engagements to determine compliance with governmental laws and regulations (see Chapter 19), the precise measurement of risk that statistical attributes sampling provides may be more appropriate, since a specific test may more often be the sole source of evidence about compliance with a regulation.

Basic Concepts of Attributes Sampling

If the true deviation rate in a population were known, the exact (discrete) probability of obtaining a specific sample result (such as 1 deviation in a sample of 50 items) could be computed. The auditor does not, however, know the true deviation rate and thus can only infer what it could be, based on sample results. Because the auditor samples from a finite population and removes each item from the population as it is sampled (i.e., sampled items are not replaced), the auditor must use the appropriate statistical formulas to compute the reliability and precision of the sample results.

To illustrate the attributes sampling technique, consider a simple example in which the true population deviation rate is known. The example is later varied to resemble more closely a realistic audit situation. Assume the following:

Population	= 1000 invoices
Properly approved invoices	= 950 items
Improperly approved invoices	= 50 items

The attribute being measured by the auditor is the approval of invoices for payment. In assessing the approval control procedure to reduce the amount of substantive testing, the auditor might use the following decision rule: If no deviations were found in a sample of five items, the control procedure would be considered effective, but if one or more deviations were found in the sample (a 20 percent or more sample deviation rate), the control procedure would not be considered effective. (Small sample sizes are used to illustrate the concepts and computations and are not indicative of suggested sample sizes.) What is the chance the auditor would find no deviations in a random sample of five items from this population?

If a sample of five invoices is taken from the population, one item at a time, there will be 950 chances out of the total population of 1000 of drawing a properly approved invoice as the first sample item. If the first invoice was properly approved and is not placed back into the population, there will be 949 properly approved invoices out of the total of 999 items in the population available for the second draw. The probability of a sample of five invoices from this population containing no deviations is

$$\frac{950}{1000} \times \frac{949}{999} \times \frac{948}{998} \times \frac{947}{997} \times \frac{946}{996} = .7734$$

That is, there is a 77 percent chance of finding no deviations in a sample of five items when the true deviation rate in the population is 5 percent (50/1000).[11]

Ordinarily, the auditor would not know the true deviation rate in the population. Assume that the auditor would not consider the control procedure to be effective if he or she believed that the true deviation rate exceeded 5 percent. In other words, a 5 percent deviation rate is "tolerable," but a greater deviation rate is not. In this case, having drawn a sample of five invoices, all of which were found to be properly approved, the auditor would be accepting a 77 percent sampling risk (the risk of assessing control risk too low, as defined in SAS No. 39) that the true deviation rate might not be acceptable, even if no deviations were found in the sample of five items. The complement of the sampling risk (100% − 77% = 23%) is the reliability level of the test. Stated another way, the auditor obtained from the sample of five items a 23 percent level of reliability that the true deviation rate does not exceed 5 percent.

Increasing the sample size will reduce the sampling risk and thus increase the reliability of the test. For example, if one more item were added to the sample, the sampling risk would be reduced from 77 percent to 73 percent ($.7734 \times 945/995 = .7345$). To achieve a 90 percent reliability level (10 percent sampling risk) for the conclusion that the true deviation rate does not exceed 5 percent, a sample of approximately 45 items would be required, with no exceptions noted. Thus, by setting a tolerable deviation rate (5 percent) and a reliability level (90 percent) in the planning stage of the sampling application, the auditor could estimate, using statistical formulas, the minimum required sample size (45) to satisfy a stated audit objective.

[11]The proper general formula for computing probabilities in this situation is the hypergeometric formula, which can be found in most introductory statistics books. In certain circumstances, calculations using the binomial and Poisson probability distributions can yield approximations close to the exact hypergeometric probabilities. Normal distribution theory, however, is often inappropriate for attributes sampling in auditing because it approximates the hypergeometric probabilities only when deviation rates are between 30 and 70 percent. Generally, much lower deviation rates are found in audit populations. The mean-per-unit estimation technique, discussed later in this chapter, is an appropriate application of normal distribution theory.

The relationship among reliability, tolerable deviation rate, and sample size is particularly significant. For a given sample size (e.g., 60) and a tolerable deviation rate (e.g., 5 percent), only a certain level of reliability (in this case, 95 percent) can be obtained. To obtain a higher level of reliability or to be able to set a lower tolerable deviation rate (or both), the sample size must be increased. That is the price that must be paid by the auditor to reduce the risk of assessing control risk too low (the *beta* risk).

The auditor may also buy "insurance" that the sample will not contain so many deviations that control risk will be assessed too high (the *alpha* risk). This insurance is bought at the cost of a larger sample size. To control this risk (i.e., the risk that the sample will indicate that the deviation rate in the population may be unacceptable when, in reality, it is acceptable), the auditor must take a larger sample. By specifying a conservative (higher) expected deviation rate, the auditor protects somewhat against concluding that the control structure is operating less effectively than it actually is when one or more deviations appear in the sample. Another way to control this risk is for the auditor to specify an acceptable deviation rate, lower than the tolerable deviation rate, at which the risk of assessing control risk too high is to be controlled, and a reliability level commensurate with that specified risk. For example, the auditor may wish to be able to conclude at a 90 percent reliability level (10 percent risk) that the true deviation rate does not exceed the tolerable deviation rate of 5 percent, and may also wish to be assured at an 80 percent reliability level that, if the population deviation rate is actually 2 percent (the lower acceptable deviation rate), the sample results will not include so many deviations that they will lead to the conclusion that the population may contain an unacceptable deviation rate, that is, more than 5 percent. The closer the lower acceptable rate is set to the tolerable rate, and the higher the associated reliability level is set, the larger will be the sample size necessary to protect against the risk of assessing control risk too high. In practice, controlling that risk at a meaningful level is often inefficient, given the significant flexibility available to the auditor in designing additional substantive procedures when sample results may indicate that control risk is higher than was desired. Controlling this risk is covered in more advanced statistical sampling discussions.

Determining Sample Sizes in Statistical Attributes Tests

When designing an attributes test, the auditor should decide if it is necessary to estimate the range within which the true deviation rate lies (i.e., whether upper and lower deviation limits are relevant) or if it is sufficient to test whether the true deviation rate either exceeds or falls below a certain tolerable level. (For example, the auditor may only need to know whether the true deviation rate exceeds the tolerable rate.) That decision affects the size of the sample that is appropriate for performing the test. A sample in which the auditor is concerned with both the upper and lower limits is evaluated on a two-sided basis; if only one limit is of interest, the sample is evaluated on a one-sided basis. A possible conclusion for a two-sided estimate is

- The auditor can be 95 percent assured that the true deviation rate is between 2 percent and 8 percent.

A possible conclusion for a one-sided test is

- The auditor can be 95 percent assured that the true deviation rate is not greater than 8 percent.

Usually the auditor needs assurance only that the true deviation rate does not exceed the tolerable rate. Knowing the lower limit of the true rate would not add to the audit usefulness of the information from a sample. Sometimes, however, the client asks the auditor to estimate the range within which the true deviation rate may lie. Internal auditors may appropriately design two-sided estimates for internal reporting purposes to aid in making the cost–benefit determinations associated with improving the control structure.

If the auditor needs only a one-sided evaluation, the sample should be designed accordingly. One-sided testing is efficient because it is generally possible to use a smaller sample size to meet the same reliability level and tolerable deviation rate for one-sided tests than for two-sided estimates. Most standard attributes tables and some computer programs designed for audit use assume a one-sided testing plan. If a two-sided plan is desired, the documentation for the one-sided computer program or table usually explains how to make the conversion.

Table 10.1 is an abbreviated table for sample sizes at the 95 percent reliability level. To use the table, the auditor specifies a tolerable deviation rate

Table 10.1 Determination of Sample Size (Reliability = 95%)

Expected Deviation Rate	*Tolerable Deviation Rate (Percent)*											
(Percent)	*1*	*2*	*3*	*4*	*5*	*6*	*7*	*8*	*9*	*10*	*12*	*14*
0.00	300	150	100	75	60	50	45	40	35	30	25	20
0.50		320	160	120	95	80	70	60	55	50	40	35
1.0			260	160	95	80	70	60	55	50	40	35
2.0				300	190	130	90	80	70	50	40	35
3.0					370	200	130	95	85	65	55	35
4.0						430	230	150	100	90	65	45
5.0							480	240	160	120	75	55
6.0									270	180	100	65
7.0										300	130	85
8.0											200	100

and an expected population deviation rate, and locates the column for the tolerable rate along the top of the table and the row for the expected rate along the left-hand side of the table. The intersection of the row and column indicates the minimum necessary sample size. For example, if the tolerable rate is 6 percent and the expected rate is 1 percent, the minimum sample size is 80 items.

Reliability levels for tests of controls are generally set high (e.g., as high as 90 percent or 95 percent) if the test is the auditor's primary source of evidence about whether a control structure policy or procedure is effective. However, lower reliability levels are usually warranted, because additional evidence about the effectiveness of the policy or procedure will ordinarily be obtained through extensive observation and inquiries, tests of controls of related policies or procedures, and examination of the control aspects of sample items selected for substantive tests. Tolerable deviation rates of between 5 percent and 10 percent are common; the more critical the policy or procedure and the more likely that a deviation will cause a financial statement misstatement, the lower the tolerable deviation rate should be set. Appendix A contains tables for determining sample size (one-sided tests) in statistical attributes sampling at reliability levels of 60, 80, 90, and 95 percent. Because of rounding in those and other tables, however, the auditor should consider using computer software to determine the most efficient sample size. Computer programs may be particularly helpful in determining sample sizes in situations not covered by tables or where the population size is small, requiring more precise computations than are possible using tables.

Selecting the Sample

A statistical sample must be selected randomly, regardless of whether it is expensive, inconvenient, or time-consuming to do so. (A nonstatistical sample does not have to be selected randomly; however, knowing how to select a true random sample may help an auditor using nonstatistical sampling to select a representative sample.) Random sample selection is any method of selection in which every item (element) in the population has an equal (or, more technically, calculable) probability of being included in the sample. The two most common methods of achieving a random sample are random number selection and systematic selection.

For random number selection, the auditor needs a source of random numbers, such as random number tables or a computer program for generating random numbers, and a scheme establishing a one-to-one correspondence between each random number selected and a particular population item. The correspondence scheme is simple if the documents are numbered and can be retrieved based on the numbers. If documents are unnumbered or are filed other than numerically, the auditor may have to assign sequential numbers to them. If it is not easy to make the numbers correspond, or the auditor cannot determine the size of the population, it may be difficult to conclude that the population is complete.

In systematic sample selection, the auditor calculates a sampling interval (n) by dividing population size by sample size, randomly identifies a starting point between 1 and n, and then methodically selects every nth item in the entire population to be sampled. Alternatively, the auditor may use multiple random starts to overcome any possible nonrandomness in the population arrangement and to avoid potential criticism about the randomness of a sampling population. Using computer programs to generate random numbers or batch programs to select items randomly is often an efficient way of selecting specific items for examination.

Often the auditor finds it efficient to perform more than one test of controls using the same sample. For example, the auditor may wish to reperform, using a reliability level of 95 percent, an expected deviation rate of 1 percent, and a tolerable deviation rate of 8 percent, a control procedure the client applies to ensure the mathematical accuracy of cash disbursement vouchers. Using Table 10.1, the auditor can determine that the appropriate sample size is 60. If a sample of 80 disbursements had already been selected to test a control procedure relating to authorization, the auditor could randomly (or systematically) select 60 items from the initial 80 items for purposes of testing the control procedure relating to mathematical accuracy. Or, both tests may be performed using 80 items (the larger of the two sample sizes) when it is not too costly to do so.

Evaluating Statistical Attributes Sample Results

After the auditor has performed the auditing procedures, the results must be evaluated, using mathematical formulas, tables, or computer programs, to determine the upper (and, if desired, lower) deviation rate limits for a specified reliability level, based on the sample results. To determine the upper limit on the deviation rate, the auditor must have four pieces of information.

- The reliability level (which is selected judgmentally).
- The sample size.
- The number of observed deviations in the sample.
- The population size.

Table 10.2 is an abbreviated table for evaluating sample results at a desired reliability level of 95 percent in a large population. The sample size used is located along the left-hand column and the number of deviations found in the sample is located along the sample size row. The achieved upper deviation rate limit is read from the top of the column. The auditor compares this with the tolerable deviation rate to determine whether the objective of the test has been

Table 10.2 Evaluation of Results Based on Number of Observed Deviations (Reliability = 95%)

Sample Size	*Achieved Upper Deviation Rate Limit (Percent)*											
	1	*2*	*3*	*4*	*5*	*6*	*7*	*8*	*9*	*10*	*12*	*14*
30										0		
35									0			1
40								0			1	
45							0				1	2
50						0				1		2
55						0			1		2	3
60					0			1			2	3
65					0			1		2	3	4
70					0		1		2		3	4
75				0			1		2		4	5
80				0		1		2		3	4	5
85				0		1		2	3		5	6
90				0		1	2		3	4	5	6
95				0	1		2	3		4	5	7
100			0		1		2	3	4		6	8

met. Alternatively, some auditors may seek to know the achieved reliability of the test for a fixed tolerable deviation rate; this would require using several tables for varying reliability levels. Appendix B contains tables for evaluating sample results in attributes sampling at reliability levels of 60, 80, 90, and 95 percent.

Continuing with the earlier example, suppose in the test of 80 disbursement checks for proper authorization, 1 deviation was found. By using Table 10.2, the auditor determines an upper deviation rate limit of 6 percent. If the tolerable rate is 6 percent, the objective of the test has been met. If, however, 2 deviations were found in the test of disbursement vouchers for mathematical accuracy, from a sample of 60 items, the upper deviation rate limit would be 12 percent, which would exceed the specified tolerable deviation rate of 8 percent. In this instance, the auditor does not have the assurance sought from the test, and the assessed level of control risk is higher than planned.

Discovery Sampling

Discovery sampling is a special application of attributes sampling and is used when the attribute being tested is of such critical importance that a single exception in the sample may have audit significance. This single instance is a "red flag" that indicates the existence of a problem or a need for further investigation. Some examples of such significant attributes are

- Inaccuracies in an inventory of securities held in trust.
- Fraudulent transactions.
- Illegal payments.
- Circumvented control procedures.
- Fictitious employees.

When setting a discovery sample size, the auditor determines how many items to examine to gain assurance at a high level of reliability (e.g., 95 percent) that, if the true deviation rate in the population is at some low level (e.g., 1 percent), one or more instances will be found in the sample. Since the attribute being examined is critical, auditors often use high reliability levels (95 percent or above) and low "tolerable" deviation rates (less than 5 percent). The procedure for determining sample size is the same for discovery sampling as for attributes sampling in general, except that since no deviations are expected, the expected deviation rate is assumed to be zero.

To find an appropriate sample size, the auditor may use tables or computer programs. For example, in a population of over 10,000 items, the auditor would require a sample of about 300 items to be assured at a 95 percent reliability level that if the population incidence was 1 percent or more, 1 instance would appear in the sample (see Table 10.1).

Evaluating discovery sampling results is straightforward: If no instances of the critical attribute appear in the sample, the auditor has the assurance specified when the sample was designed. No evaluation tables or computer programs are necessary.

Although discovery sampling has been described in terms of tests of controls, the auditor may use any random sample of items—whether selected for tests of controls or for substantive testing—to gain assurance that a deviation from, or an instance of, a defined critical attribute would have appeared in the sample under certain conditions. For example, in a random sample of 300 accounts receivable selected for confirmation from a population of 2000 or more, the auditor may use computer programs or standard tables to determine that, at a 95 percent level of reliability, the sample would have contained at least 1 instance of a fictitious receivable if 1 percent of the items in the population were fictitious.

Sequential Sampling

In the previous discussion of attributes sampling, the sample was designed using a fixed-size sampling plan. Another form of attributes sampling is *sequential sampling*, in which the auditor selects the sample in several stages, using computer programs or tables specifically designed for sequential sampling to determine the sample size for each stage. After selecting items in the first stage of the sample and performing tests, the auditor evaluates the results and either (1) concludes that the sample meets or does not meet the criteria for reliability and tolerable deviation rate, and discontinues sampling, or (2) determines that a conclusion cannot be reached and selects and evaluates additional items (this is the second stage of the process). The sampling continues until a decision is ultimately reached. Sequential plans may be designed to include any number of stages. The risk of assessing control risk too high may or may not be specifically controlled, and the sample sizes at each stage may be varied; for example, some plans have larger initial sample sizes and smaller second-stage sizes, while others have smaller initial sample sizes and larger second-stage sample sizes. Regardless of the plan adopted, the auditor must follow the rules established for the plan to obtain the desired level of assurance.

An excerpt of a two-stage sequential sampling plan is presented in Table 10.3. The sampling plan was designed for a 95 percent level of reliability. By following the decision rules, the auditor will be able to determine whether the specified criteria have been met or not. In the illustration, the auditor stops testing after the first-stage sample if no deviations or if two or more deviations are found, but goes on to the second stage if one deviation is found. Separate sample evaluation tables are unnecessary, because the decision rules are an integral part of the sampling plan. Appendix C contains tables for two-stage sequential sampling plans at reliability levels of 80, 85, 90, and 95 percent. percent.

A sequential plan allows the auditor to examine additional sample items if an unexpected deviation is found in the sample, or to stop the work after examining a small number of items if no deviations are found in the first sample. Thus, it may be efficient for the auditor to use a sequential sampling plan if a zero or very low deviation rate is expected or if it is difficult to

Table 10.3 Two-Stage Sequential Sampling Plan (Reliability = 95%)

Tolerable Deviation Rate (Percent)	*Initial Sample Size*	*Second-Stage Sample Size*
10	31	23
9	34	29
8	39	30
7	45	33
6	53	38
5	65	42

Decision Rules

	No Deviations	*One Deviation*	*Two or More Deviations*
Initial sample	Stop—achieved goal	Go to next stage	Stop—failed
Second stage	Stop—achieved goal	Stop—failed	Stop—failed

estimate an expected deviation rate. In a fixed sample plan, if unfavorable results were obtained from the first sample, the auditor would be precluded from simply extending the sample and evaluating the combined results using a fixed sample table as though they were a single sample. To evaluate the results of a sequential plan properly, the exact plan and all the decision rules must be specified before the sample sizes are determined.

STATISTICAL SUBSTANTIVE TESTING

A group of statistical techniques called *variables sampling* can be used in substantive testing. Variables sampling techniques are used to estimate the true dollar value of a population or the total misstatement amount in the population and thereby permit the auditor to conclude that a recorded balance is not materially misstated. Since variables techniques deal with dollar values, their use in substantive testing is common. Although a variety of variables techniques may be used, two—monetary unit sampling and stratified mean-per-unit sampling—are particularly effective in auditing and are widely used. Two others—difference and ratio estimation techniques—are also effective in certain circumstances.

From a statistical variables sampling test, the following type of conclusion can usually be drawn:

> The amount of population misstatement projected from the sample is $20,000. It can be stated with a 95 percent level of reliability, however, that the true amount of misstatement in the population is between $10,000 and $30,000.

This means that the direct projection, or point estimate, of the misstatement in this account or class of transactions is $20,000, but the true misstatement amount at a 95 percent level of reliability may be anywhere between $10,000 and $30,000. The auditor must decide whether a $30,000 misstatement would be material to the account or class of transactions being examined. If it is not material, the auditor may conclude, exclusive of the results of other tests, that there is a 95 percent reliability level that no material misstatement exists in the population. If an amount less than $30,000 but greater than $20,000 could be material, the auditor's assurance that a material misstatement does not exist is reduced to less than a 95 percent level of reliability. After considering the results of this and all other tests performed, if the auditor still does not have reasonable assurance that the account or class is not materially misstated, he or she may have to perform additional auditing procedures.

Some variables techniques project sample results in terms of audited amounts; others project sample results in terms of the amount of misstatement—or difference (recorded amount minus audited amount)—as in the foregoing example. If the results are in terms of the misstatement amount, it must be added to or subtracted from the total recorded amount to produce an estimate of the total audited amount.

Applying Variables Sampling

An auditor using variables sampling relies on statistical theory (including the auditor judgments that must be made) to draw conclusions about whether material misstatement is present in the population sampled. SAS No. 39 (AU Section 350) requires that before sampling, the auditor remove from the population for 100 percent examination those items for which, based on auditor judgment, potential misstatements could individually equal or exceed tolerable misstatement. Those items are not considered as sample items. In some circumstances, the auditor may be able to achieve high dollar coverage of the population by examining a relatively small number of items, and by doing so may reduce the risk of an undetected material misstatement to an acceptably low level. Examining items to achieve a specified level of dollar coverage is not sampling according to the definition in SAS No. 39. If risk is reduced to an acceptably low level by nonsampling procedures, sampling the remaining items may not be necessary.

In general, variables sampling may be an efficient sampling approach in any of the following situations:

- The population consists of a large number of items.
- High dollar coverage cannot be achieved by examining an economical number of items.
- The auditor is unable to determine which specific items in the population should be examined to meet the audit objectives.
- The auditor desires a quantitative evaluation of sampling risk from the audit test, as might be appropriate in an unusually high-risk situation.

As in attributes sampling, the auditor can buy "insurance" against concluding that the population may be materially misstated when examining all items in the population would reveal that the population was not materially misstated—the *alpha* risk. Controlling this risk requires the auditor to increase the sample size, which is determined by setting an acceptable, less than material, amount of misstatement and an associated reliability level.

Monetary Unit Sampling (MUS)

In this statistical technique, the individual monetary unit in the population (i.e., the dollar) is the sampling unit. Thus, the sample is composed of random dollars, not random items, in the population. When a particular dollar is identified for examination, the auditor examines the entire item or transaction of which the identified dollar is a part and determines an audited value for the entire transaction. The ratio of the misstatement amount, if any, found in the transaction to the recorded amount is used to "taint" the sample dollar. For example, a recorded transaction value of $200 with an audited value of $150 yields a 25 percent tainting of the identified dollar. This tainted dollar information is used to project a point estimate of the misstatement and create an upper (and, if desired, a lower) misstatement limit at a specified reliability level.

Since the sample in monetary unit sampling is randomly selected from a population of dollars, large value transactions have more chances of being selected and are more likely to enter the sample than are small value transactions. Consequently, a transaction containing an understatement would have relatively fewer chances of being selected than would a properly stated transaction or a transaction containing an overstatement. MUS is one of the variables sampling evaluation methods that utilizes a probability-proportional-to-size (PPS) sample selection technique. This selection method is often appropriate in an audit, because large value transactions are often of greater concern to auditors than small value transactions.[12] Common applications where MUS may be an effective audit tool include

- Selecting accounts for confirmation of receivables.
- Testing the pricing of inventory.
- Determining the accuracy of recorded amounts of fixed assets.
- Selecting employees for payroll tests.

There are both advantages and disadvantages to MUS. Some of its advantages are

- The sample sizes used with MUS are generally efficient.
- It is usually easy to apply.
- It is an effective statistical technique for substantiating that an expected low misstatement population is not materially misstated.

The disadvantages of MUS are

- It requires that the population be cumulatively totaled so that random dollars can be identified.
- It is less likely to detect understated balances than overstated ones.
- It cannot select zero-value items for examination.

[12]Stratification can be used with an item-based sample selection method to accomplish a similar objective. Stratification is discussed later in this chapter in connection with mean-per-unit estimation.

- Either credit balance items must be sampled as a separate population or the selection of sample items must be based on the absolute recorded value of the population items.

Determining Sample Size. Determining sample size for an MUS sample is similar to the method used for attributes sampling in tests of controls, as discussed previously. The auditor must specify the dollar value of the population, a level of reliability, a maximum tolerable misstatement rate expressed as a percentage of the dollar value of the population, and an expected misstatement rate expressed as a percentage of the dollar value of the population. The auditor may use the same tables or computer programs as for attributes sampling to determine sample size.

For example, assume that accounts receivable has a balance of $1,000,000 as of the confirmation date and the auditor has specified a reliability level of 95 percent. If the maximum tolerable misstatement amount is $50,000, the maximum tolerable misstatement rate is 5 percent $\left(\frac{\$50{,}000}{\$1{,}000{,}000}\right)$. If the expected misstatement amount is $10,000, the expected misstatement rate is 1 percent $\left(\frac{\$10{,}000}{\$1{,}000{,}000}\right)$. Using Table 10.1 on page 371, the auditor can determine that the sample size is 95. Before determining sample size, the auditor should consider whether any population items exceed the maximum tolerable misstatement amount—in this case, $50,000. Any items in excess of that amount should be segregated from the population for 100 percent examination, and their value should be subtracted from the total population value.

Selecting the Sample. To determine which items in the population contain the selected dollar units, the population is cumulatively totaled by item. If the records are computerized, those totals should be easy to obtain; however, if the records are manual, this process may be time-consuming. MUS sample selection can then be made using random or systematic selection to identify unique dollars in the cumulatively subtotaled population, resulting in a random selection of dollar units from the population since each item has a chance of selection proportional to its dollar value.

The most common method of MUS sample selection is systematic selection with at least one random starting point between $1 and the sampling interval (the population value divided by sample size—in the illustration, $1,000,000 divided by 95, or $10,526). When using systematic selection, the auditor is assured that all items in the population greater in value than the sampling interval will be selected; those items should be treated as items selected for 100 percent examination, because there is no chance that they will not be selected. Alternatively, the auditor may remove these large value items from the population before selecting the sample items, reducing the population by the dollar value of the items removed.

Figure 10.3 Calculation of Misstatement-Tainting Amounts

	Amount			
Error	*Recorded*	*Audited*	*Difference*	*Tainting*
1	$100	$ 60	$40	.40
2	200	180	20	.10
3	80	76	4	.05

Evaluating MUS Results. After selecting the sample, the auditor applies the planned auditing procedures to the sample items, determines an audited value for each item examined, and evaluates the results. The first step in the evaluation is to calculate the "tainting" of the misstatements found in the sample. The tainting is determined by computing the ratio of each misstatement amount found in the sample items to the recorded amount.[13] To continue with the earlier illustration of accounts receivable confirmations, the three misstatements in Figure 10.3 are assumed to have been found in a population of $1,000,000 from which a sample of 95 items had been chosen.

The next step is to calculate the projected misstatement for the population. This is done by dividing the sum of the individual tainting factors by the sample size, in this case (.40 + .10 + .05) ÷ 95, or .0058, and multiplying the result by the population amount ($1,000,000), yielding the point estimate of the misstatement amount, in this case $5800. (Had all three errors been 100 percent tainted—that is, had the audited amounts been zero in each case—the point estimate of the misstatement amount for the population would have been $31,579, derived as follows: [(1.00 + 1.00 + 1.00) ÷ 95] x $1,000,000).

The last step is to compute an upper misstatement dollar limit. This requires two calculations. First, the auditor uses the table for evaluating the results of an attributes sample to calculate an upper misstatement rate limit for 3 misstatements in a sample of 95 items at a 95 percent reliability level.[14] Since the misstatements were not 100 percent taintings, a more precise upper misstatement rate limit can be obtained by using a "building block" approach, that is, by multiplying the increment in the upper misstatement rate limit for each misstatement by the individual tainting factors and adding the products to calculate the upper misstatement rate limit, as illustrated in Figure 10.4.

[13]Misstatement amounts found in sample items are those differences between recorded values and audited values that the auditor determines, after applying auditing procedures to the sample items, are in fact misstatements. For example, a response to a confirmation request might indicate that the recorded balance of an account receivable is incorrect because the balance had been paid before the confirmation was received. The auditor should determine whether a payment for that amount was in fact received within several days of the mailing of the confirmation. If it was, the audited value of the customer's balance and the recorded value would be in agreement as of the date of the confirmation and no misstatement would exist.

[14]More precise results may be obtained by using other tables or computer programs that are less subject to rounding errors than the attributes evaluation tables. Another method of computing the upper misstatement dollar limit that uses a different set of tables is illustrated in the AICPA Audit and Accounting Guide, *Audit Sampling* (New York: AICPA, March 1983).

Figure 10.4 Calculation of Upper Misstatement Rate Limit

Number of Misstatements	*Upper Misstatement Rate Limit*[a]	*Increment*	*Tainting*	*Product*
0	.04	.04	1.00	.0400
1	.05	.01	.40	.0040
2	.07	.02	.10	.0020
3	.08	.01	.05	.0005
		Upper misstatement rate limit		.0465

[a]Determined by reference to Table 10.2, "Evaluation of Results Based on Number of Observed Deviations (Reliability = 95%)," on p. 374.

For conservatism, the misstatements are arranged in descending order according to the size of the tainting. Also, an allowance for possible, but unfound, misstatements is labeled "0" and is conservatively assigned a tainting of 1.00. (This is done to consider the possibility that misstatements existed in the population, even if no misstatements had been found in the sample.)

Next, the auditor converts the upper misstatement rate limit to a dollar amount by multiplying it by the total population amount, in this case $1,000,000 x .0465, or $46,500. (Had all three misstatements been 100 percent tainted misstatements, the auditor would have used the attributes evaluation table [Table 10.2] to determine an upper misstatement rate limit of 8 percent, which would have been converted directly to dollars by multiplying it by the population dollar amount [$1,000,000 x 8%, or $80,000].)

In the foregoing example, the auditor can conclude that, at a 95 percent level of reliability, the true amount of misstatement in the population is less than $46,500.[15] This upper misstatement dollar limit of $46,500 is then compared with the tolerable misstatement amount used in determining the sample size, $50,000. If at the specified reliability level the tolerable misstatement is greater than the upper misstatement dollar limit, the results support accepting the recorded amount as not being materially misstated. If at the specified reliability level the tolerable misstatement is less than the upper misstatement dollar limit, the true population misstatement amount could exceed the tolerable misstatement.[16] When the tolerable misstatement is only slightly below the upper misstatement dollar limit (i.e., there is a higher than desired sampling risk that the true misstatement amount may exceed the tolerable misstatement), the auditor may wish to recalculate the upper misstatement dollar limit at successively lower reliability levels until the tolerable misstatement and upper

[15]Other ways to state this conclusion are as follows:

1. The auditor is 95 percent confident that the true amount of the population is at least $1,000,000 – $46,500, or $953,500.
2. The auditor is 95 percent confident that the true amount of misstatement in the population is not more than $5800 + $40,700.

[16]If at the specified reliability level the tolerable misstatement is also less than the point estimate, there is a high risk (greater than 50 percent) of misstatement.

misstatement dollar limit are approximately equal, to determine the additional risk implied by the test results. This may help the auditor choose among several possible courses of action, among them to (1) reconsider additional assurance obtained or obtainable from other substantive tests, such as analytical procedures; (2) modify planned substantive procedures; (3) select highly suspect elements in the population for more work by the client; and (4) request the client to correct the misstatements found or considered likely in the population.

In any event, misstatements found in the sample should always be considered for adjustment. Any additional amount relating to projected misstatements proposed as an adjustment is a matter of auditor judgment. Knowing the upper misstatement dollar limit and point estimate may help the auditor determine the appropriate amount of any proposed adjustment.

Considering Other Techniques. Although it would be cost effective to be able to use one variables technique in all audit situations, the auditor should be knowledgeable about several techniques to be able to choose the technique that will yield the most precise and relevant statistical results in a particular sampling application. For example, some audit tests, such as those involving samples from accounts payable, have as their specific objective to detect and evaluate understated amounts within the population of recorded accounts. In other cases, such as some inventory pricing tests, a number of understatements may be expected, even if the primary audit objective is to detect and evaluate overstatements. Because MUS is more likely to detect overstatements, its use in situations in which understatements are suspected may not be desirable. Furthermore, MUS methods of evaluating understatements found in the sample and methods that suggest netting them with overstatements in the sample remain an area of controversy and require further research. MUS may also sometimes be less efficient than other statistical techniques in situations where expected misstatement rates are high.

The following techniques are based on normal distribution theory. Although their use in auditing has diminished as a result of advancements in MUS technology, they remain important and effective techniques.

Mean-Per-Unit Estimation

In the mean-per-unit (MPU) technique, the auditor selects a random sample of accounts or items from the population, and, using the audited values of the sample items or balances, projects the average (or mean) value of the audited sample values to the population to create a population point estimate. For example, if the auditor selected a sample of 50 items from a population of 10,000 items and found their average audited value to be $20.25, the point estimate of the population amount would be $202,500 ($20.25 x 10,000). The auditor would have very little confidence, however, that the point estimate of $202,500 was the true population amount. Confidence can be expressed only in terms of the upper and lower precision limits that are determined in a statistical test. If upper and lower precision[17] limits have been calculated, the auditor can make the following type of statement:

> I am 95 percent confident that the true amount of the population falls within the interval of $202,500 plus or minus 10 percent (or, plus or minus $20,250).

One advantage of MPU is that it can be used on populations that do not have detailed recorded amounts. For example, it may be used to estimate the audited value of an inventory where only quantity information is recorded. Although MPU can be an effective technique in a wide variety of audit situations (e.g., those in which expected misstatement rates might be either low or high and those in which understatement is as likely as overstatement), the large sample sizes necessary to achieve the precision that is commonly sought in many audit tests may not always make it the most efficient statistical technique to use, unless the auditor stratifies (explained later in this chapter) the population.

A key factor in determining how close the point estimate of the population value will be to the true population value is the degree of variability (also referred to as dispersion) in the population. For example, if the average audited value of $20.25 in the foregoing example was developed from 50 invoices that were each valued at exactly $20.25, the auditor would intuitively be more comfortable with the point estimate than if the sample revealed 20 zero-value items, 20 items valued at $1.00, and 10 items valued at $99.25. Statistical computations of the upper and lower precision limits for the population (or misstatement) amount at a given level of reliability take into consideration the observed variability in the sample data. The more variable the sample data, the wider the range between the upper and lower precision limits will be (i.e., precision deteriorates as variability increases).

Because of the key role that sample values and their variability play in determining the point estimate and upper and lower precision limits, the sample should be as representative of the population as possible. Very small samples cannot be relied on to provide representative sample values, since the selection of one or several unusually large or small items in the sample would significantly affect the point estimate.

Basic MPU Concepts. SAS No. 39 requires the auditor to project sample results to the population as a basis for considering whether material misstatement exists in the population. In meeting this requirement, the auditor uses the information obtained from a sample to estimate the extent of misstatement in the population or the true value of the population.

To make statistical inferences about the dollar value or misstatements in a population from a sample, the auditor must compute the sample mean and the sample standard deviation. For example, an auditor, not knowing the audited

[17]SAS No. 39 uses the term "allowance for sampling risk" rather than "precision."

values of the population of 10,000 accounts receivable, might take a random sample of 100 items totaling $3318.73. The sample mean is computed by dividing $3318.73 by 100, to get $33.19, which is multiplied by the number of items in the population ($33.19 x 10,000) to compute an estimate, or projection, of the total value of the population ($331,900).

It is extremely unusual for any one sample mean to be exactly the same as the true mean in the population. Each different random sample of items from the population would most likely yield a different sample mean. For audit purposes, it is desirable for the sample mean to be close to the true mean. This is accomplished by both taking a representative sample from the population and choosing an adequate sample size.

A second measure that must be computed for the mean-per-unit technique is the sample standard deviation, which is a measure of the variability of particular item values around the mean value of the sample and serves as an estimate of the population standard deviation. In a sample whose values are very close to each other, and thus to the mean, the standard deviation will be very small. If there are both very large and very small values in the sample, however, the standard deviation will be larger. The sample standard deviation is computed using the following formula:

$$\text{Sample standard deviation} = \sqrt{\frac{\text{Sum of squared differences between sample audited values and mean value}}{\text{Sample size} - 1}}$$

Applying the Concepts. The calculation of a sample standard deviation is illustrated in Figure 10.5. The example assumes that a sample of 100 items drawn from a population of 10,000 items produced a sample mean of $33.19.

Figure 10.5 Calculation of a Sample Standard Deviation

Sample Observation	*(1) Audited Value*	*(2) Mean Value*	*(3) Difference*	*(4) Difference Squared*
1	$ 80.29	$33.19	$47.10	$ 2,218.41
2	6.97	33.19	- 26.22	687.49
•	•	•	•	•
•	•	•	•	•
•	•	•	•	•
100	10.30	33.19	- 22.89	523.95
Totals	$3,318.73			$76,120.85

$$\sqrt{\frac{\$76{,}120.85}{100-1}} = \$27.729$$

The individual sample audited values are listed in Column (*1*). In Column (*2*), the average or mean value of the sample items is shown, and in Column (*3*), the differences between the individual audited sample values and the mean value are computed. In Column (*4*), the differences are squared and totaled. [The differences are squared to keep them from netting out to zero, as they do in Column (*3*).] The total of the squared differences is divided by the sample size minus one, and the square root of the result is taken, giving the standard deviation of the sample, in this case $27.729.

The calculations involved in computing the standard deviation can be confusing, but it is important that the auditor grasp the mathematical relationships involved. The standard deviation decreases as the variability of the sample values around the mean value decreases (holding sample size constant), and it also decreases as the sample size increases (holding the variability constant). (As mentioned earlier, very small sample sizes do not generally give reliable information about the total population, because small samples sometimes contain one or more items that are unrepresentative of the population and that can significantly distort the point estimate of the population value and the calculations of variability among items.)

The standard deviation (a sample statistic) is used to compute the standard error (a statistic related to the population value). The standard error, in turn, determines the upper and lower precision limits of the point estimate of the population value, which in this example is $331,900 (mean value of $33.19 x population size of 10,000 items). The standard error of the estimate is the population size multiplied by the sample standard deviation divided by the square root of the sample size,[18] as follows:

$$\text{Standard error} = \frac{10{,}000 \times \$27.729}{\sqrt{100}} = \$27{,}729$$

The upper and lower precision limits can then be computed by multiplying the standard error ($27,729) by a reliability factor (discussed later) appropriate for the desired level of reliability (e.g., the factor for 95 percent reliability is 1.96; for 90 percent reliability, 1.64), and calculating an interval on either side (plus or minus) of the projected population value (in this example, $331,900 ± [1.96 × $27,729]). The conclusion, at a 95 percent reliability level, is that the lower precision limit is $277,551 and the upper precision limit is $386,249.

The statistical sampling results can be summarized by the statement that the total population amount is between $277,551 and $386,249 with 95 percent

[18]The sample standard deviation should also be multiplied by a finite population correction factor $\left(\sqrt{1 - \frac{\text{size of sample}}{\text{size of population}}}\right)$ when computing the standard error. However, when the sample size is small relative to the population (less than 10 percent), the factor has little influence on the computations. For many audit sampling applications this factor will not be significant and therefore is not illustrated in this chapter.

reliability. Thus, there is only a 5 percent risk (the complement of reliability) that the true value falls outside this range. SAS No. 39 refers to this risk for substantive test sampling applications as the risk of incorrect acceptance. If the true value of the population can be in the interval between $277,551 and $386,249 without causing the auditor to conclude that material misstatement exists in the population, then the auditor can say with 95 percent confidence that no material misstatement exists in this population. The limits are of primary importance when MPU sampling is employed. Point estimates are less important; they are used to compute the interval, or limits, on the population value. A reliability percentage can be associated only with computed upper and lower precision limits. No statistical statement or reliability level can be associated with point estimates.

In the preceding calculations, a 95 percent reliability level has been used. Sampling results, especially in the audit environment, do not always require a 95 percent level of reliability. Auditors often have information in addition to their sample results that they can rely on in reaching audit conclusions, and thus a reliability level of less than 95 percent frequently is appropriate for audit applications. The Appendix to SAS No. 39 contains an illustration leading to a substantive test sampling application with a desired reliability level of less than 50 percent. For practical purposes, if sampling is such a minor element in the auditor's strategy or if the sampling effort is minimal, it is rarely economical to perform a statistical procedure to be able to measure precisely the reliability of the sample.

Reliability Factors. The concept of reliability factors, as illustrated earlier, is derived from statistical theory based on the known mathematical properties of the normal, or bell-shape, distribution. The theory is that if repeated large samples from the population are taken and the frequency distribution of the point estimates of the population value from each sample is plotted (with the values along the horizontal axis and the frequency along the vertical axis), the distribution of the point estimates would create the distribution commonly referred to as the normal distribution. The normal, or bell-shape, distribution is illustrated in Figure 10.6.

The properties of the normal distribution that are used in the MPU technique have the following effect: If repeated samples were taken from the population and a point estimate of the population value from each sample was computed, 68 percent of the point estimates would lie at less than 1 standard

Figure 10.6 Normal Distribution

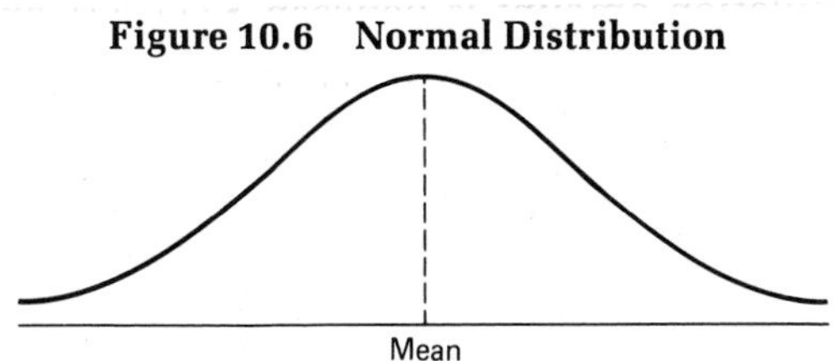

error on either side of the true population value and 95 percent of the point estimates would lie at less than 1.96 standard errors on either side of the true population value. That result is adapted to fit the audit situation (i.e., the auditor takes a single sample and makes inferences about the true population value from that sample). Thus, the auditor can determine, at a particular reliability level, upper and lower precision limits between which the true population value is expected to lie.

Reliability factors associated with different reliability levels are shown in Figure 10.7. Thus, if the auditor wanted to evaluate sample results at a 90 percent level of reliability and if a two-sided evaluation was appropriate (see subsequent discussion), the standard error would be multiplied by 1.645 to measure the allowance for sampling risk, or precision. Similarly, for a 99 percent reliability level, the auditor would multiply the standard error by 2.576 to measure the allowance for sampling risk.

When designing a statistical test, the auditor should consider whether a two-sided estimate is needed, or whether a one-sided test is sufficient to determine whether the true value either exceeds or falls below a certain tolerable level. By designing a one-sided evaluation, the auditor may be able to draw the desired conclusion using a smaller sample size than that necessary for a two-sided evaluation. Alternatively, for the same sample size and reliability level, a one-sided evaluation yields greater precision (a smaller allowance for sampling risk). For example, the auditor may use statistical techniques in lieu of determining exact amounts for inventory values. In that event, the auditor may

Figure 10.7 Factors for Different Reliability Levels

Two-Sided Evaluation

Reliability	*Factor*
60%	.842
70%	1.036
80%	1.282
85%	1.440
90%	1.645
95%	1.960
99%	2.576

One-Sided Evaluation

Reliability	*Factor*
60%	.253
70%	.524
80%	.842
85%	1.036
90%	1.282
95%	1.645
99%	2.326

desire a two-sided estimate, using the "plus and minus" as a benchmark for evaluating the precision of the sample result. However, when the auditor assesses the principal risk as either overstatement or understatement, such as in evaluating accounts receivable (in which the principal risk is generally overstatement), a one-sided test may be sufficient for audit purposes. Other procedures may be applied (e.g., analytical procedures) to assess the risk of understatement.

Stratified Mean-Per-Unit Estimation. One method of improving the precision of the mean-per-unit technique without increasing the sample size is to stratify the population and sample each stratum independently. In stratification, the auditor segments the population into groups of items that are likely to be close to each other in audited value. After the mean and standard error in each stratum have been calculated, the results for the individual strata can be combined to create an overall estimate. The first several strata dramatically reduce the required sample size (or reduce the allowance for sampling risk for the same sample size). Although increasing the number of strata generally improves the precision of the estimate (or reduces the required sample size necessary to achieve a specific precision), diminishing returns and other factors often lead the auditor to use between three and ten strata in most circumstances.

Research has shown the stratified mean-per-unit technique to be a very effective audit tool. It can be used in suspected low-misstatement and high-misstatement situations and, with the use of a sufficient number of strata, can often result in relatively efficient sample sizes. Since, unlike MUS, the technique requires a random selection of items, zero (recorded) value items have a chance for selection. The technique can be equally effective for evaluating overstatements and understatements of recorded values and net misstatement amounts.

Despite the advantages of stratified MPU, however, there are a number of significant constraints on its efficiency. Stratifying the population often requires reorganizing the underlying data, which, unless there is extensive computer assistance in data manipulation and sample selection, can be expensive. To compute the sample size required to meet the auditor's objectives, estimates of the variability among audited values need to be developed. Since estimates are somewhat difficult to develop, auditors often use the recorded values to estimate the necessary sample size and then include a safety factor (add extra sample items to the computed sample size). If the auditor performed a statistical application in the prior year, past experience is often a useful guide in estimating variability.

The steps required to apply stratified mean-per-unit estimation are summarized in the following paragraphs. Some of the steps in the evaluation process require the use of computations discussed earlier in the chapter. The steps are as follows:

1. Determine the number of strata to be used.
2. Determine stratum boundaries (the high and low population values for each stratum).
3. Determine an appropriate overall sample size.
4. Allocate the overall sample size to the individual strata.
5. Randomly select the sample items from each stratum.
6. Perform auditing procedures to determine an audited value for each sample item.
7. Compute an overall point estimate (projection) of the population value.
8. Compute the overall upper and lower precision limits at the desired reliability level.

As previously indicated, between three and ten strata are generally sufficient to meet audit objectives efficiently. A number of formulas (or judgment) can be used to satisfy steps 2, 3, and 4. One formula option for steps 2 and 4 determines stratum boundaries so that each stratum contains an approximately equal proportion of population dollars, and allocates sample size so that each stratum is allocated approximately the same sample size. Another option attempts to minimize the overall sample size by determining stratum boundaries and allocating sample size in such a way that the overall standard error is minimized.[19] As a rule of thumb, the auditor should plan for at least 20 to 25 items in each stratum so that representative results for each stratum are more likely.

The computations in steps 3 and 4 are often based on recorded values or small preliminary samples from the population. (As noted, because these figures may not be exactly representative of the final sample audited values, the auditor may want to add a "cushion" [10 percent is common] to the computed stratum sample sizes to ensure that the desired precision of the sample will be achieved.) Computer software can be designed to accomplish steps 2 through 5, 7, and 8 with a minimum of effort on the auditor's part, except for supplying the key judgments or information (such as reliability, precision, population size, and other options). Computer software can efficiently analyze a population, stratify it, determine sample sizes, allocate them to different strata, select a valid random sample from each stratum, and evaluate sample results. In this as well as other statistical sampling applications, manual computations of the formulas are often unnecessary and inefficient, given the current availability of timesharing and microcomputer software.

To evaluate the results of a stratified sample, the auditor calculates a sample mean, sample standard deviation, point estimate, and standard error for each stratum; finally, the auditor combines the results from the individual strata (steps 7 and 8). The combined (overall) point estimate is simply the sum of the

[19]For more details, see Donald M. Roberts, *Statistical Auditing* (New York: AICPA, 1978).

individual point estimates. The combined standard error is computed as the square root of the sum of the squared individual standard errors.

To illustrate, assume the following facts:

	Stratum 1	*Stratum 2*
Population	4,000	1,200
Sample size	50	50
Sample mean	$343.19	$989.91
Standard deviation	$21.98	$85.42
Point estimate	$1,372,760	$1,187,892
Standard error	$12,434	$14,496

Based on these facts, the results of the two strata can be combined as follows:

1. Combining of sample results
   (a) Point estimate = $1,372,760 + $1,187,892 = $2,560,652
   (b) (Standard error)^2 = $154,604,356 + $210,134,016 = $364,738,372
   Standard error = $\sqrt{\$364,738,372}$ = $19,098
2. Calculation of two-sided precision limits and total audited amount, 95% reliability
   $2,560,652 ± 1.96 ($19,098)
   $2,560,652 ± $37,432
3. Summary of misstatement limits

Recorded value	$2,787,200	$2,787,200
Lower precision limit	2,523,220	
Upper precision limit		2,598,084
Misstatement limits	$ 263,980	$ 189,116

Although the recorded value lies outside the computed precision limits of $2,523,220 and $2,598,084, the auditor may be able to accept it if the difference between the recorded value ($2,787,200) and the farthest limit ($2,523,220) is not material. Another way to arrive at the same conclusion is to compare the computed upper misstatement limit ($263,980) with the tolerable misstatement amount used in planning the sample. Even if the sample supports accepting the recorded amount, the auditor may propose that the accounts be adjusted for misstatements found in the sample as well as misstatements identified as a result of other procedures performed on the account.

Difference and Ratio Estimation

Difference and ratio estimation techniques are other variables sampling techniques also based on random item selection. They have many features in common with mean-per-unit sampling and can be used in stratified or unstratified populations, but are most effective when stratification is employed.

These techniques have long been used in audit tests because of their apparent ability to generate precise results with relatively small sample sizes. Research has demonstrated, however, that they may not be dependable (i.e., the auditor may believe the sample yielded a 95 percent level of reliability when it actually yielded a lower reliability) in populations with low misstatement rates or when used in unstratified form with small sample sizes.[20] For this reason, their use is recommended only when high misstatement rates are expected, such as in some inventory pricing situations (even if the misstatement rates are high, the amounts may still be small and offsetting) or for conversions of inventory bases (such as FIFO to LIFO conversions in which each item can be expected to show a "difference"). Either technique can be used in tests for both overstatements and understatements. Whether one technique is superior to the other in producing a more precise estimate depends on the characteristics of the misstatements found in the sample.

The computations used in these techniques are based on the differences between the recorded and audited amounts of the sample items. The techniques require estimating a standard deviation and, if stratification is used, employ similar formulas for obtaining stratum limits and combining them to obtain overall limits.

In the difference estimation approach, the auditor calculates the point estimate of the population misstatement amount (or difference) by computing the average sample misstatement and multiplying it by the number of items in the population. In the ratio approach, the point estimate of the population value is based on the ratio of the audited amount to the recorded amount of the sample items. In both approaches, the auditor should ascertain that the sample contains differences that are representative of those in the population. Unlike mean-per-unit sampling, difference and ratio estimation techniques require that each population item have a recorded amount.

These techniques are most effective if many small differences are expected between the recorded and audited amounts of the sample items. As a rule of thumb, 20 or more differences are considered sufficient. If no differences are found in the sample, these techniques cannot be used, and the auditor should consider evaluating the sample as a mean-per-unit sample.

An example of how an auditor might evaluate a sample using difference estimation at a 95 percent reliability level and with two-sided limits is summarized here.

1. Assumed facts
   (a) Population

Size	100,000
Amount	$1,700,000

   (b) Sample

Size	100
Audited amount	$1,500

[20]See John Neter and James K. Loebbecke, *Behavior of Major Statistical Estimators in Sampling Accounting Populations*, Auditing Research Monograph No. 2 (New York: AICPA, 1975).

Recorded amount	$1,600
Difference amount	– $100
Mean difference	– $1
Standard deviation of sample differences[21]	$2

2. Calculations
   (a) Point estimate of difference
   Population size × mean difference
   100,000 × – $1 = – $100,000
   (b) Standard error

$$\frac{\text{Population size} \times \text{standard deviation of sample differences}}{\text{Square root of sample size}}$$

$$\frac{100{,}000 \times \$2}{\sqrt{100}} = \$20{,}000$$

   (c) Upper and lower error limits
   Point estimate ± standard error × reliability factor
   $100,000 ± $20,000 × 1.96
   $100,000 ± $39,200

Thus, the true amount of misstatement is indicated as falling between $60,800 and $139,200 at a 95 percent reliability level. Provided these possible misstatement amounts do not exceed the tolerable misstatement for the account, the auditor may be able to conclude at the desired reliability level that the balance is not materially misstated.

An example of a ratio estimation computation is not presented, but the calculations would be similar to those for difference estimation. The ratio technique point estimate is based on a ratio of the audited sample values to the recorded sample values (using the foregoing example, $1500/$1600 x $1,700,000 = $1,593,750; $1,700,000 – $1,593,750 = $106,250 projected misstatement amount), and the precision is calculated by measuring the variability of the sample ratios, using a computational formula.[22]

[21]The standard deviation of sample differences is a measure of variability of *differences* between recorded values and audit values around the mean of those *differences*. In the earlier discussion of MPU estimation, the sample standard deviation was a measure of variability of audited *values* around the mean of those *values*.

[22]One such computational formula to measure the variability of the sample ratios (i.e., the standard deviation [SD_R] for an unstratified ratio estimator) is

$$SD_R = \sqrt{\frac{\Sigma x_i^2 + \hat{R}^2\Sigma y_i^2 - 2\hat{R}\Sigma x_i y_i}{n-1}}$$

where:

x_i = individual sample audited values
y_i = individual sample recorded values
$\hat{R}$ = the computed overall sample ratio $\left(\frac{\Sigma x_i}{\Sigma y_i}\right)$
n = sample size
Σ = summation.

The difference estimation technique is often more precise when all the differences found in the sample are of a similar amount and are not related to the recorded values for the items containing the misstatements. The ratio estimation technique may be more precise when the differences in the sample are roughly proportional to the recorded values of the items containing the misstatements (i.e., when large items contain the large differences and small items contain the small differences).

NONSTATISTICAL SAMPLING

The auditor is faced with the same decisions in applying both nonstatistical and statistical sampling, namely, determining an appropriate sample size, selecting the sample, performing the tests, and evaluating the results. This section provides guidance to the auditor in applying nonstatistical sampling techniques. Much of that guidance is, of course, based on statistical sampling principles and techniques.

Determining Sample Size

If the sampling application involves nonstatistical sampling, only the most general guidance can be given regarding the appropriate sample size in different circumstances. No rule of thumb is appropriate for all applications. Many auditors, in an effort to provide some uniformity among nonstatistical sampling applications throughout their practice, have developed more specific guidance for nonstatistical sampling applications, in some cases based on sample sizes used in similar circumstances on other engagements, and in other cases based on statistical sampling concepts and technology.

The guidance that follows represents the authors' views on appropriate sample sizes in nonstatistical applications, also based in part on experience and in part on conclusions reached in statistical sampling applications. This discussion, however, is clearly only one approach to providing guidance for the auditor's judgment process.

Some auditors establish a minimum sample size for tests of controls because they believe that there is some amount of testing below which the assessment of control risk will be unaffected. No minimum sample size can be established for substantive tests of details since the extent of these tests depends on the assessed level of control risk and on the extent of analytical procedures and other substantive tests of details. Therefore, a small sample size may be appropriate if a low level of assurance from the sample is acceptable.

A sample size of 260 for both tests of controls and substantive tests of details is a practical ceiling above which diminishing returns limit the incremental value of a few additional sample items. An auditor contemplating selecting more than 260 items for a nonstatistical sample should either consider using statistical sampling to increase the efficiency and effectiveness of the sampling application or ascertain that the cost–benefit trade-off of sampling versus other auditing procedures has been fully assessed. Experience has demonstrated that in many audit situations statistical samples of fewer than 260 items will achieve the audit objectives.

Selecting Representative Samples

Whenever sampling is used in an audit, SAS No. 39 requires that sample items be selected in such a way that they can be expected to be representative of the population from which they are drawn. The dictionary defines "representative" as "typical of a group or class." If each item in a population or subpopulation has a chance (not necessarily an equal chance) of being selected, the resulting sample is potentially representative of the characteristics contained in the population or subpopulation. For example, a sample cannot be relied on to be representative if it is made up of one or a few blocks of items in sequence (such as all items in a particular time period, on a particular page, or in a particular alphabetical section of a ledger) or if it is not drawn from the whole population. As another example, sample items that will be used to evaluate the reasonableness of a client's entire accounts receivable balance should be selected from the details of that entire balance, so that each item in the population has a chance of being selected. Conversely, sample items that will be used exclusively to evaluate balances outstanding for more than 90 days should be potentially representative of that group of balances, but may not necessarily be representative of the entire accounts receivable balance. Other procedures or a separate sample may be necessary to draw conclusions about the remainder of the receivables.

The auditor may achieve representative samples through either unsystematic, systematic, or dollar-weighted selection techniques. In the first two methods, the population may be stratified or unstratified. Unsystematic sample selection (sometimes referred to as haphazard sample selection) attempts to avoid personal bias in selecting items for testing. It is called haphazard selection because auditors intend it to approximate random sample selection; the term does not imply any element of carelessness. It can be affected by personal bias toward selecting certain items, however, such as a subconscious tendency to favor items in a particular location on each page or never to pick the first or last items in a listing. In its purest hypothetical form, unsystematic selection would involve blindfolded selection from a thoroughly mixed pile of all the records. More commonly, an auditor will choose a number of items from throughout the ledger or other records, after gaining satisfaction about the completeness of the population from which the sample is selected.

The only difference between the nonstatistical and statistical sampler's use of systematic sample selection is that the nonstatistical sampler often does not specifically identify a random starting point. Systematic selection is currently a commonly used nonstatistical sample selection method and in all likelihood will continue to be, because it is usually a cost-effective approach to extracting a potentially representative sample.

For substantive tests of details, sampling risk can be reduced without increasing sample size by stratifying the population by size or nature in order to permit different intensities of sampling for different strata. This technique may be effectively used to help ensure representative samples in either statistical or nonstatistical sampling applications. Often the auditor can use strata already inherent in the client data (e.g., location or product line). The sample sizes would be varied in accordance with the auditor's assessment of the risk of material misstatement associated with each stratum; that is, a larger number of sample items should be apportioned to those strata in which the auditor has assessed a higher risk of material misstatement. Either systematic or unsystematic selection methods can be used with a stratified population.

Evaluating Sample Results

Regardless of whether statistical or nonstatistical techniques are applied, the auditor should extrapolate (project) the sample results to the whole population. Because conclusions based on sample results apply only to the population from which the sample items were drawn, it is important that the auditor carefully define the population (i.e., the aggregate of items about which information is desired) and keep it in mind when evaluating the sample results. For example, conclusions about the entire accounts receivable balance cannot be supported on the basis of a sample selected only from accounts outstanding for more than 90 days.

Tests of Controls. Sample results for tests of controls are appropriately stated as deviation rates, which are determined by dividing the number of sample deviations by the sample size. The deviation rate in the sample is the best estimate of the deviation rate in the population from which the sample was selected.

The auditor should follow up on identified deviations from control structure policies and procedures to determine if they are "isolated incidents," such as a clerk's being on vacation, or indications of a possible control structure deficiency. Isolated incidents should always be included as sample deviations and projected to the population; their impact on the assessment of control risk should be carefully evaluated. If the projected deviation rate exceeds the tolerable rate, the auditor should reconsider the control risk assessment. Either a single instance of a control structure deficiency (e.g., circumvention of a control procedure) or the aggregate effect of a number of instances (whether "isolated" or not) may be sufficient to change the assessed level of control risk.

Substantive Tests. There are several acceptable methods of projecting the impact of dollar misstatements in a substantive test sample to the population. In the *ratio approach*, for example, the projected population misstatement is determined by multiplying the total dollar amount of the population by a misstatement rate obtained by dividing the total dollar amount of sample misstatements by the total dollar amount of the sample, as follows:

$$\underset{\text{(population amount)}}{\$1{,}000{,}000} \times \frac{\$100 \text{ (sample misstatements)}}{\$1000 \text{ (sample amount)}} = \$100{,}000 \text{ (projected population misstatement)}$$

In the *average-difference approach*, the total number of items in the population is multiplied by the average misstatement amount obtained by dividing the total dollar amount of sample misstatements by the number of sample items, as follows:

$$\underset{\text{(population items)}}{15{,}000} \times \frac{\$1000 \text{ (sample misstatements)}}{140 \text{ (sample items)}} = \$107{,}143 \text{ (projected population misstatement)}$$

The ratio approach is generally the more appropriate technique when the misstatement amounts are roughly proportional to the recorded values of the sample items (i.e., the larger dollar misstatements are from the larger sample items). The average-difference approach is more appropriate when the misstatement amounts are disproportionate to the recorded values of the sample items (e.g., large items have small dollar misstatements and small items have large dollar misstatements, or the dollar misstatements are all about the same size regardless of recorded amount).

Another acceptable (but infrequently used) method is the *projection of average audit values*. This approach is used, for example, in constructing a balance sheet value for inventory if recorded values are not available and only quantity (not price) information can be obtained from the client.[23] This approach may also be most appropriate if there are recorded amounts but the general ledger control account does not agree with the sum of the individual recorded amounts. In the average-audit-value approach, the total number of items in the population is multiplied by the quotient obtained by dividing the total "audited" dollar amount of the sample items by the number of sample items, as follows:

$$\underset{\text{(population items)}}{150{,}000} \times \frac{\$900 \text{ (total sample audited value)}}{150 \text{ (sample items)}} = \$900{,}000 \text{ (projected population amount)}$$

[23]In developing estimated amounts for financial reporting or tax reporting purposes, statistical samples are generally employed.

In this technique, the misstatement projection is the difference between the recorded and projected population dollar amounts.

Other methods of projection may also be appropriate. It is important to remember that different projection techniques often result in different projected misstatement amounts. Auditors may find the ratio approach useful for a wide variety of situations, but no one method of projecting the misstatement is necessarily "better" than the others in all circumstances.

To ascertain the total projected misstatement for the account balance being examined, the projected misstatement from the sample results should be added to any known misstatements discovered as a result of nonsampling procedures performed, such as misstatements identified in 100 percent examinations of selected items or from high dollar coverage tests. Since, by definition, the dollar amount of the projection of sample results already includes the sample misstatements found, those misstatements should not be separately added to the projected misstatement. Similarly, misstatements affecting the account balance that were found in related tests of controls should also not be separately added to the projected misstatement.

An auditor using stratification in the sampling plan should project the results for each stratum separately and then add the stratum projections to determine the projected misstatement for the account or class of transactions being examined.

The auditor should compare the projected misstatement obtained from sampling procedures and other likely misstatements with the tolerable misstatement. (If the tolerable misstatement was not quantified for purposes of determining sample size, the auditor may find it useful to use overall financial statement materiality or some smaller amount for this comparison.) Even if the projected misstatement from sampling procedures plus other likely misstatements are less than tolerable misstatement—the misstatement the auditor can accept before modifying the opinion—the auditor should post the projected misstatement to a working paper that summarizes misstatements and potential adjustments, discussed in Chapter 17, to determine whether all likely misstatements discovered during the audit equal or exceed the auditor's determination of materiality. The auditor should also evaluate the nature of the misstatements and discuss them with the client. In some circumstances it may be practicable for client personnel to review the remaining population for items having characteristics similar to those in the sample that were found to contain misstatements. When adjustments are made to the recorded balance, the related projected misstatement should be reduced by the amount of the adjustments. For example, if the auditor calculated a projected overstatement of $20,000 in an inventory balance based on misstatements found in the sample, but by investigating a few instances of a particular problem was able to identify $11,000 of overstatement that the client agreed to record as an adjustment to the recorded inventory balance, the projected misstatement would be reduced to $9000.

If the projected misstatement from sampling combined with other likely misstatements is greater than the tolerable misstatement (or financial statement materiality), the auditor must consider the implications for the audit opinion and audit testing plan and take appropriate action. Possible auditor actions include

- Asking the client to adjust for all of the known and some or all of the projected misstatements.
- Asking the client to perform additional work either to identify the sources of misstatements in the account balance and correct the account balance or to justify the balance.
- Extending the planned auditing procedures to identify and correct the misstatements or to demonstrate that the account balance is not materially misstated. Since extended sampling of the same population is usually not cost effective, this would likely involve designing other auditing procedures. For example, additional samples may "target" high-misstatement segments of the original test population.
- Concluding that the financial statements are materially misstated and modifying the audit report accordingly.

Allowance for Sampling Risk. Even if the projected misstatement or deviation rate is less than the tolerable misstatement or deviation rate, the auditor still must consider the risk that the true misstatement in the population exceeds the tolerable misstatement or rate. Thus, an allowance for sampling risk, defined as a margin for inaccuracy or imprecision in the sample result, must be determined. (The concept is similar to "precision," a term defined earlier in connection with statistical sampling applications.) When statistical sampling is applied, the allowance for sampling risk is computed. However, the nonstatistical sampler must rely on rules of thumb and judgment to consider the allowance for sampling risk. For example, assume that the tolerable misstatement in an account balance of $2,000,000 is $80,000 and that the total projected misstatement based on an appropriately sized sample is $20,000. A statistical test might result in a computed precision of plus or minus $40,000 for a specified level of reliability, such as 95 percent. Since the projected misstatement (i.e., $20,000) plus the allowance for sampling risk (i.e., $40,000) does not exceed the tolerable misstatement, the auditor may conclude that there is an acceptably low sampling risk (i.e., 5 percent, the complement of the 95 percent reliability level) that the true population misstatement does not exceed the tolerable misstatement. In part because of the difference between the $20,000 projected misstatement and the $80,000 tolerable misstatement, the nonstatistical sampler, not knowing the exact precision, would make a judgment that he or she may be reasonably assured that there is an acceptably low sampling risk that the true monetary misstatement in the population exceeds the tolerable misstatement. On the other hand, if the total projected misstatement approaches or exceeds the tolerable misstatement, the auditor may conclude that there is a higher-than-planned sampling risk that the true monetary misstatement in the population exceeds the tolerable misstatement.

A possible rule of thumb for the nonstatistical sampler when considering an allowance for sampling risk is: If the deviation rate or number or amount of misstatements actually identified in the sample does not exceed the expected rate or misstatement used in determining the sample size, the auditor can generally conclude that the risk that the true deviation rate or misstatement amount exceeds the tolerable rate or amount is consistent with the risk considered acceptable when the sample was initially planned. For example, if an auditor performing a test of controls had established expected and tolerable deviation rates of 1 percent and 5 percent, respectively, a deviation rate approximating 1 percent would be a satisfactory result consistent with the risk considered acceptable when the sample was planned. Conversely, if the deviation rate identified in the sample exceeds the expected deviation rate used in determining the sample size, the auditor should generally conclude that there is a higher-than-planned sampling risk that the true rate exceeds the tolerable rate.

If, based on this rule of thumb, the auditor concludes that there is an unacceptably high risk that the true deviation rate or misstatement amount in the population exceeds the tolerable deviation rate or misstatement amount (or financial statement materiality), appropriate action is necessary. For tests of controls, the auditor should consider revising the control risk assessment. For substantive tests, the auditor's possible actions are the same as those discussed in the preceding section as being appropriate when projected misstatement exceeds tolerable misstatement. In using this rule of thumb for substantive tests, the auditor may encounter situations in which the acceptability of the achieved sampling risk for a particular account balance or class of transactions is not clear—for example, if the sampling risk indicated by the sample only slightly exceeds the level the auditor originally desired from the test, and other auditing procedures have not yet been applied to the account or related accounts. In these cases, the auditor should consider deferring further action until the aggregation and evaluation of misstatements for the remaining areas in the financial statements have been completed.

Aggregating Misstatements. The auditor should consider the aggregate of all projected misstatement results from all sampling applications and all other likely misstatements from nonsampling applications and other relevant auditing procedures in evaluating whether the financial statements taken as a whole may be materially misstated. The aggregation and the disposition of the misstatements should be documented in the working papers. The summary discussed in Chapters 6 and 17 is an effective way of doing the aggregation.

After the projected misstatements have been aggregated, the auditor must determine an appropriate overall allowance for sampling risk to compensate for the fact that sample results may indicate the absence of material misstatements even though the true misstatements in the populations exceed the tolerable amount (financial statement materiality). This overall allowance is not the sum of the allowances for individual samples, because it is very unlikely that the true amount of misstatement in each sample is the extreme high or low of the range of possible values and because misstatements may be offsetting. Practically, the auditor must decide if the dollar difference between the aggregation of projected misstatements plus other likely misstatements and the amount deemed material to the financial statements is large enough to provide an adequate overall allowance for sampling risk.

For nonstatistical applications, the allowance should be based on the number of individual sampling applications and the size of the samples. For example, if the amount of misstatement material to the financial statements as a whole is $1,000,000 and there are net projected misstatements of $800,000 from sampling procedures and other likely misstatements of $20,000 from nonsampling procedures, the auditor must judge whether $180,000 ($1,000,000 – $820,000) is an adequate allowance for sampling risk. If a total of 1000 to 1200 items were examined in numerous (e.g., 8 to 10) sampling applications, $180,000 may be adequate, because those sample sizes would be likely to yield quite precise results. Alternatively, if the auditor examined 100 to 200 items in the same number of sampling applications, $180,000 might not be adequate, because the smaller sample sizes would produce less precise results. The deciding factor in determining the allowance for sampling risk in nonstatistical sampling is the probable preciseness of the results of individual samples, which is generally related to sample size.

If the auditor judges the allowance for sampling risk to be adequate, he or she should document that decision in the working papers and conclude that the financial statements as a whole are not materially misstated. Conversely, if the allowance for sampling risk is considered inadequate, the auditor's actions may include

- Requesting the client to perform additional work in those areas that were subject to large misstatement projections and to adjust for all or some of the misstatements.
- Extending the tests in those areas that were subject to large misstatement projections.

DOCUMENTING AUDIT SAMPLING

Documentation of the sampling applications used on an audit must satisfy the professional standards for working papers promulgated in Statement on Auditing Standards No. 41, *Working Papers* (AU Section 339). Working paper documentation of auditing procedures is discussed in Chapter 5 of this book. The

Figure 10.8 Summary of Audit Sampling Documentation

	Documentation Needed	
Type of Information	*Related to Planning the Sample*	*Related to Performing and Evaluating the Results of the Sample*
Objective and description of test	X	
Definition of misstatements (deviations)	X	
Population:		
1. Definition	X	
2. Description of how completeness was ensured	X	
3. Identification of items for 100 percent examination, if any	X	
Sample size determination factors:		
1. Degree of assurance/sampling risk	X	
2. Tolerable misstatement	X	
3. Expected misstatement	X	
4. Other factors, if any	X	
Sample size, including how determined	X	
Description of sample selection methods, including stratification	X	
Evaluation of sample results:		
1. Projection of misstatements		X
2. Aggregation with items examined 100 percent		X
3. Investigation of misstatement sources (causes)		X
4. Consideration of allowance for sampling risk		X
5. Conclusion on test		X
Aggregation with other test results and consideration of overall allowance for sampling risk		X

documentation should relate to planning the sampling application, and performing it and evaluating the results. Figure 10.8 identifies and categorizes information that should be documented.

Review Questions

10–1. What is meant by the concept of audit sampling?

10–2. Describe some auditing procedures that do not involve sampling.

10–3. Describe tests of controls that do not lend themselves to sampling.

10–4. Define "accept–reject" testing.

10–5. Define nonsampling risk.

10–6. How can an auditor assess and control nonsampling risk on an engagement?

10–7. What is sampling risk? How is sampling risk related to sample size?

10–8. What factors must an auditor consider in planning a sampling application?

10–9. Define the statistical term precision as it relates to determining sample size.

10–10. Define the statistical term confidence level (reliability) as it relates to determining sample size.

10–11. How do auditors estimate the expected deviation rate in attributes sampling?

10–12. What is the relationship between sample size and reliability? Between sample size and tolerable deviation rate? How do these relationships affect the auditor's approach to statistical sampling?

10–13. What are the similarities and dissimilarities between statistical sampling and nonstatistical sampling?

10–14. What are the major advantages and disadvantages of using statistical sampling?

10–15. What methods of sample selection are appropriate in statistical sampling applications?

10–16. Distinguish between evaluating an attributes test statistical sample on a one-sided basis and evaluating a sample on a two-sided basis. Give an example of a possible audit conclusion for each.

10–17. What information must the auditor have to determine the upper limit on the deviation rate for attributes sampling?

10–18. What is sequential sampling and how does it work?

10–19. What is discovery sampling and how does it work?

10–20. What is variables sampling and when is it used?

10–21. What is monetary unit sampling and when is it an effective audit tool?

10–22. How are monetary unit sampling results evaluated?

10–23. How is the mean-per-unit estimation technique used?

10–24. Define standard deviation and give the formula for sample standard deviation.

10–25. How is the standard deviation used in statistical sampling?

10–26. Define stratification and explain its usefulness to the auditor.

10–27. What are the steps required to apply stratified mean-per-unit estimation?

10–28. Specify the acceptable methods of projection in a nonstatistical substantive test sample.

Discussion Questions

10–30. a. In an application of nonstatistical sampling, projected misstatement exceeds tolerable misstatement. What courses of action may the auditor take?

b. If projected misstatement was between tolerable misstatement and expected misstatement, what actions could the auditor take?

10–31. Describe and illustrate the acceptable methods for projecting the sample results to the population from which the sample was drawn.

10–32. The following is a list of substantive test procedures that might be performed during an audit. Identify those that could involve sampling and thus be covered by SAS No. 39.

a. Performing analytical procedures on inventory statistics.
b. Reviewing all accounts receivable over 90 days old for collectibility.
c. Performing sales cutoff tests.
d. Observing physical inventory procedures.
e. Performing a reasonableness test of depreciation expense.
f. Confirming all accounts receivable over $100,000.
g. Reviewing minutes of board of directors' meetings.
h. Examining all disbursements over $50,000 after the balance sheet date for payment of unrecorded liabilities.
i. Recomputing commissions paid to salespeople.
j. Comparing market prices of selected marketable securities with an independent source.

10–33. Explain how the auditor may be able to test a variety of attributes from a sample of disbursement voucher packages. Explain how the auditor would approach the evaluation of results from this procedure.

10–34. The use of statistical sampling techniques in an audit of financial statements does not eliminate judgmental decisions.

Required:

a. Identify and explain four areas where a CPA may exercise judgment in planning a statistical sampling test.
b. Assume that a CPA's sample shows an unacceptable misstatement rate. Describe the various actions that the CPA may take based on this finding.
c. A nonstratified sample of 80 accounts payable vouchers is to be selected from a population of 3200. The vouchers are numbered consecutively from 1 to 3200 and are listed, 40 to a page, in the voucher register. Describe four different techniques for selecting a random sample of vouchers for review.

(AICPA adapted)

10–35. Michaels, CPA, is planning to use attributes sampling in order to determine the effectiveness of an audit client's internal control structure relating to sales. Michaels has begun to develop an outline of the main steps in the sampling plan:

1. State the objective(s) of the audit test (e.g., to test the effectiveness of the control structure for sales).
2. Define the population (define the period covered by the test, the sampling unit, and the completeness of the population).
3. Define the sampling unit (e.g., client copies of sales invoices).

Required:

a. What are the remaining steps in the outline that Michaels should include in the statistical test of sales invoices? *Do not present a detailed analysis of tasks that must be performed to carry out the objectives of each step. Parenthetical examples need not be provided.*
b. How does statistical methodology help the auditor to develop a satisfactory sampling plan?

(AICPA adapted)

10–36. In determining a sample size for a nonstatistical sample, a tolerable misstatement of $50,000 was considered along with an expected misstatement of $10,000 in arriving at a sample size of 100 items. The results of the test were that five misstatements were found that totaled to an overstatement of $15 of the total sample value of $1100.

a. What is the direct projection of the misstatement in the population book value of $1,000,000 if the ratio approach is used?
b. What is the allowance for sampling risk?
c. Is the allowance adequate?

10–37. What are the benefits of stratifying the population in a sampling application?

AICPA Multiple Choice Questions

These questions are taken from the Auditing part of Uniform CPA Examinations. Choose the single most appropriate answer.

10–40. A number of factors influences the sample size for a substantive test of details of an account balance. All other factors being equal, which of the following would lead to a larger sample size?

a. A lower planned assessment of control risk.
b. Greater reliance on analytical procedures.
c. Smaller expected frequency of misstatements.
d. Smaller measure of tolerable misstatement.

10–41. An accounts receivable aging schedule was prepared on 300 pages with each page containing the aging data for 50 accounts. The pages were numbered from 1 to 300 and the accounts listed on each were numbered from 1 to 50.

Godla, an auditor, selected accounts receivable for confirmation using a table of numbers as illustrated:

Procedures performed by Godla

Select column from table of numbers	*Separate 5 digits: First 3 digits Last 2 digits*	
02011	020-11	x
85393	853-93	*
97265	972-65	*
61680	616-80	*
16656	166-56	*
42751	427-51	*
69994	699-94	*
07942	079-42	y
10231	102-31	z
53988	539-88	*

x Mailed confirmation to account 11 listed on page 20
y Mailed confirmation to account 42 listed on page 79
z Mailed confirmation to account 31 listed on page 102
* Rejected

This is an example of which of the following sampling methods?

a. Acceptance sampling.
b. Systemic sampling.
c. Sequential sampling.
d. Random sampling.

10-42. Which of the following best illustrates the concept of sampling risk?

a. A randomly chosen sample may *not* be representative of the population as a whole on the characteristic of interest.
b. An auditor may select auditing procedures that are *not* appropriate to achieve the specific objective.
c. An auditor may fail to recognize misstatements in the documents examined for the chosen sample.
d. The documents related to the chosen sample may *not* be available for inspection.

10-43. When performing a test of controls with respect to control over cash receipts, an auditor may use a systematic sampling technique with a start at any randomly selected item. The biggest disadvantage of this type of sampling is that the items in the population

a. Must be systematically replaced in the population after sampling.
b. May systematically occur more than once in the sample.
c. Must be recorded in a systematic pattern before the sample can be drawn.
d. May occur in a systematic pattern, thus destroying the sample randomness.

10-44. In which of the following cases would the auditor be most likely to conclude that all of the items in an account under consideration should be examined rather than tested on a sample basis?

	The measure of tolerable misstatement is	*Misstatement frequency is expected to be*
a.	Large	Low
b.	Small	High
c.	Large	High
d.	Small	Low

10-45. When assessing the tolerable rate, the auditor should consider that, while deviations from control procedures increase the risk of material misstatements, such deviations do not necessarily result in misstatements. This explains why

a. A recorded disbursement that does *not* show evidence of required approval may nevertheless be a transaction that is properly authorized and recorded.
b. Deviations would result in misstatements in the accounting records only if the deviations and the misstatements occurred on different transactions.
c. Deviations from pertinent control procedures at a given rate ordinarily would be expected to result in misstatements at a higher rate.
d. A recorded disbursement that is properly authorized may nevertheless be a transaction that contains a material misstatement.

10-46. An example of sampling for attributes would be estimating the

a. Quantity of specific inventory items.
b. Probability of losing a patent infringement case.

c. Percentage of overdue accounts receivable.
d. Dollar value of accounts receivable.

10–47. Which of the following factors does an auditor generally need to consider in planning a particular audit sample for a test of controls?

a. Number of items in the population.
b. Total dollar amount of the items to be sampled.
c. Acceptable level of risk of assessing control risk too low.
d. Tolerable misstatement.

10–48. Auditors who prefer statistical sampling to nonstatistical sampling may do so because statistical sampling helps the auditor

a. Measure the sufficiency of the evidential matter obtained.
b. Eliminate subjectivity in the evaluation of sampling results.
c. Reduce the level of tolerable misstatement to a relatively low amount.
d. Minimize the failure to detect a material misstatement due to nonsampling risk.

10–49. An auditor is performing substantive tests of pricing and extensions of perpetual inventory balances consisting of a large number of items. Past experience indicates numerous pricing and extension errors. Which of the following statistical sampling approaches is most appropriate?

a. Unstratified mean-per-unit.
b. Probability-proportional-to-size.
c. Stop or go.
d. Ratio estimation.

10–50. Hill has decided to use Probability Proportional to Size (PPS) sampling, sometimes called dollar-unit sampling, in the audit of a client's accounts receivable balances. Hill plans to use the following PPS sampling table:

TABLE
Reliability Factors for Overstatements

Number of over-statements	*Risk of Incorrect Acceptance*				
	1%	*5%*	*10%*	*15%*	*20%*
0	4.61	3.00	2.31	1.90	1.61
1	6.64	4.75	3.89	3.38	3.00
2	8.41	6.30	5.33	4.72	4.28
3	10.05	7.76	6.69	6.02	5.52
4	11.61	9.16	8.00	7.27	6.73

Additional Information

Tolerable misstatement (net of effect of expected misstatement)	$ 24,000
Risk of incorrect acceptance	20%
Number of misstatements allowed	1
Recorded amount of accounts receivable	$240,000
Number of accounts	360

What sample size should Hill use?

a. 120
b. 108
c. 60
d. 30

10–51. Which of the following statistical sampling plans does *not* use a fixed sample size for the purpose of performing a test of controls?

a. Dollar-unit sampling.
b. Sequential sampling.
c. PPS sampling.
d. Variables sampling.

10–52. An auditor selects a preliminary sample of 100 items out of a population of 1000 items. The sample statistics generate an arithmetic mean of $120, a standard deviation of $12, and a standard error of $1200. If the sample was adequate for the auditor's purposes and the auditor's desired precision was plus or minus $2000, the *minimum* acceptable dollar value of the population would be

a. $122,000.
b. $120,000.
c. $118,000.
d. $117,600.

10–53. In an audit of financial statements a CPA generally will find stratified sampling techniques to be most applicable to

a. Recomputing net wage and salary payments to employees.
b. Tracing hours worked from the payroll summary back to the individual time cards.
c. Confirming accounts receivable for residential customers at a large electric utility.
d. Reviewing supporting documentation for additions to plant and equipment.

Problems and Cases

10–60. The auditor in charge of the engagement has asked you to select a representative sample of accounts receivable for positive confirmation. The nonstatistical sampling plan indicates 100 accounts should be selected using systematic selection. The accounts receivable trial balance lists 1000 accounts (including credit balances) that total $2,546,381. The listing on page 409 is the first page of the trial balance.

a. Describe how you would determine whether the accounts receivable trial balance is an appropriate source for selecting accounts for confirmation.
b. Determine the sampling interval.
c. Select the accounts from the trial balance on page 409 that would be confirmed. Assume that credit balances will be confirmed if they are selected and the selection process will begin with account number 753.

ACCOUNTS RECEIVABLE TRIAL BALANCE

Account Numbers	Amounts
752	$ 177
753	8,873
754	6,109
755	2,437
756	1,550
757	(3,961)
758	21,119
760	1,632
761	163
762	124
763	768
764	4,085
765	(12,230)
766	15,037
768	3,392
771	3,076
772	210
773	3,601
774	2,735
775	2,070
776	(279)
777	110
778	12,370
779	3,690
780	2,721
782	3,657
783	1,172
784	3,536
785	6,995
786	8,951
787	9,500
788	17,129
789	3,146
790	5,120
791	169
792	(2,887)
793	22,825
794	897
795	679
796	1,021
Total, page 1	$161,489

10-61. A nonstatistical sample of 200 accounts receivable from a total of 5000 accounts was drawn for confirmation at December 31, 1989. The accounts ranged in size from $1000 to $2500. "Positive" confirmations were mailed. All responses indicated agreement with the balances reported by the client, with a few exceptions. The exceptions, and the results of the auditor's investigation, are reported here.

1. "The balance indicated includes your invoice No. 8769 dated December 30, 1989, for $1725; we did not receive the merchandise until January 5, 1990." (The auditor's investigation showed that shipment was made on December 31, 1989; the terms were F.O.B. shipping point.)
2. "Your balance is overstated by $2375; our records show that payment of that amount was sent to you on December 27, 1989." (The auditor's investigation showed that payment was received and recorded on January 2, 1990.)
3. "Your balance includes $500 of merchandise received on December 15, 1989, on invoice No. 8524, which was returned to you because of an error in part number; a credit memo has not been received." (The auditor's investigation showed that the returned merchandise was received on December 22, 1989, and a credit memo issued on January 5, 1990; in the meantime the credit was held in a suspense account pending determination of whose error it was.)
4. "Your balance includes $1500 for invoice No. 8643 dated December 5, 1989. We have never received these goods." (The auditor's investigation showed that shipment was made on December 4, 1989, as evidenced by receipted bill of lading. A tracer was sent.)
5. "Your balance is overstated by $1100. Apparently you failed to consider your credit memo for that amount dated October 10, 1989, for damaged merchandise." (The auditor's investigation showed that the customer's assertion was correct.)
6. "Your balance includes an $800 overcharge on invoice No. 8623 dated December 18, 1989, because of incorrect pricing; you were notified immediately." (The auditor's investigation showed that the prices used were correct, but the customer had not been notified of price increases.)
7. "We regret we cannot confirm your receivable balance. We use an accounts payable voucher system." (The auditor's investigation substantiated shipment of the merchandise.)
8. "The balance indicated, $2365, is not owing. Per your request we advanced $3000 to cover our purchase." (The auditor's investigation showed that the $3000 had been credited to a liability account, "Customers' Advances.")
9. "Your balance of $2450 is correct. However, these goods were sent on consignment and have not been sold." (The auditor's investigation showed the customer's assertion to be correct.)

Required:

For each exception, indicate

a. Whether you would treat the exception noted as misstatement to be used in projecting the population misstatement. (Give reasons for your answers.)
b. The misstatement amount you would assign for the projection.

10-62. You are confirming accounts receivable using nonstatistical sampling. The population of accounts receivable is as follows:

Number of accounts	12,620
Total recorded book value	$41,710,000

The sample was designed to include the 50 largest accounts, which total $8,132,800, and a random selection of 150 of the remaining accounts.

The sample, when audited, contained 20 misstatements totaling a $9400 overstatement, none of which are in the 50 largest accounts. Misstatements totaling $2316 were found in the 50 largest accounts.

Required:

Calculate the most likely total population misstatement amount using the average-difference projection technique.

10–63. The following population and sample data is available to the auditor:

Number of items in the population	10,000
Total population amount	$2,000,000
Number of items sampled	200
Total recorded amount in sample	$45,000
Total misstatements found in the sample	$1,200

Required:

a. From the data provided, compute the projected population dollar misstatement using the (1) ratio approach, (2) average-difference approach, and (3) projection-of-average-audit-values approach.
b. In what circumstances is each of the three approaches the most appropriate one?

10–64. In determining a sample size for a nonstatistical sample, a tolerable misstatement of $100,000 was considered along with an expected misstatement of $20,000 in arriving at a sample size of 50 items (based on judgment). The results of the test were that ten misstatements were found, which amounted to an overstatement of $200 of the total sample value of $10,000.

Required:

a. What is the projection of the misstatement amount in the population of 4000 items with a book value of $1,000,000 if the average-difference approach is used?
b. Project the misstatement amount in the population using the same fact set, but using the average-audit-value approach. Why do the two projections differ?
c. Discuss the circumstances in which one approach might be preferable to the other. If the recorded amounts were considered to be good indicators of the audited values in this case, which projection method would be preferable?

10–65. Edwards has decided to use Probability Proportional to Size (PPS) sampling, sometimes called dollar-unit sampling, in the audit of a client's accounts receivable balance. Few, if any, overstatements of account balances are expected.

Edwards plans to use the following PPS sampling table:

TABLE
Reliability Factors for Overstatements

Number of Over-statements	*Risk of Incorrect Acceptance* 1%	5%	10%	15%	20%
0	4.61	3.00	2.31	1.90	1.61
1	6.64	4.75	3.89	3.38	3.00
2	8.41	6.30	5.33	4.72	4.28
3	10.05	7.76	6.69	6.02	5.52
4	11.61	9.16	8.00	7.27	6.73

Required:

a. Identify the advantages of using PPS sampling over classical variables sampling.

Note: Requirements b and c are *not* related.

b. Calculate the sampling interval and the sample size Edwards should use given the following information:

Tolerable misstatement	$15,000
Risk of incorrect acceptance	5%
Number of misstatements allowed	0
Recorded amount of accounts receivable	$300,000

Note: Requirements b and c are *not* related.

c. Calculate the total projected misstatement if the following three misstatements were discovered in a PPS sample:

	Recorded Amount	*Audit Amount*	*Sampling Interval*
1st misstatement	$ 400	$ 320	$1000
2nd misstatement	500	0	1000
3rd misstatement	3000	2500	1000

(AICPA adapted)

10–66. The following data is available (assume a large population):

- Desired level of assurance (level of reliability) — 90 percent
- Sample size — 100
- Deviations found — 2

Required:

a. Use Appendix B to determine the upper deviation rate limit.
b. What evaluation statement can be made from this test?
c. What evaluation statement could you make if the sample had been obtained using nonstatistical sampling?

10–67. Sampling for attributes is often used to allow an auditor to reach a conclusion concerning a rate of occurrence in a population. A common use in auditing is to test the rate of deviation from a prescribed internal control procedure to determine the extent to which the procedure is operating effectively.

Required:

a. When an auditor samples for attributes, identify the factors that should influence the auditor's judgment concerning the determination of

1. Acceptable level of risk of assessing control risk too low,
2. Tolerable deviation rate, and
3. Expected population deviation rate.

b. State the effect on sample size of an increase in each of the following factors, assuming all other factors are held constant:

1. Acceptable level of risk of assessing control risk too low,
2. Tolerable deviation rate, and
3. Expected population deviation rate.

c. Evaluate the sample results of a test for attributes if authorizations are found to be missing on 7 check requests out of a sample of 100 tested. The population consists of 2500 check requests and the tolerable deviation rate is 8%. The risk of assessing control risk too low has been set at a low level.

d. How may the use of statistical sampling assist the auditor in evaluating the sample results described in c, above?

(AICPA adapted)

10–68. An auditor is designing a sample to evaluate whether a priced inventory of automobile parts may be materially overstated as a result of overstated inventory quantities. The inventory is physically located in a central warehouse, and price and quantity information for each part is available to the auditor. The auditor wants to test the physical counts. Based on prior experience, little or no deviation from the recorded quantities is expected to appear in the sample.

Required:

a. Evaluate the suitability of the following techniques in the circumstances described:

- Attributes sampling
- Monetary unit sampling
- Mean-per-unit estimation
- Difference or ratio estimation

b. How would your evaluation of the appropriate technique change if

1. Many differences between the recorded and audited quantities were anticipated?
2. Understatements of quantities are likely to be found in the sample?
3. The inventory quantities are unpriced and the audit objective is to estimate the inventory value?

(Consider each situation separately.)

10–69. Assume the following facts in a substantive test of inventory pricing:

Number of inventory items	312,000
Recorded value of inventory items	$4,267,000
Size of sample	121 items
Recorded amount of sample	$1950
Audited amount of sample	$1705
Standard deviation of sample differences	$5

Required:

Using the difference estimation approach, calculate the upper and lower misstatement limits at a 90 percent reliability level and with two-sided limits.

10–70. An auditor selected a sample of 150 receivable invoices from a $3,000,000 aged trial balance of accounts receivable for confirmation. Monetary unit sampling was contemplated in the sample design, a valid random sample of dollars from the recorded total value of the receivables was selected, and a confirmation was prepared for each invoice containing the selected random dollar. Based on direct confirmation responses and the performance of acceptable alternative procedures for unreturned confirmations, all but three invoices were determined to be "as recorded." The three exceptions and explanations are as follows:

Exception	*Recorded*	*Audited*	*Explanation*
1	$150	$125	Improperly added shipping charges to this customer's bill
2	200	100	Billed for entire order, but only in-stock items shipped
3	75	0	Shipment never arrived at customer location

Required:

a. Using monetary unit sampling, determine at a 90 percent level of reliability the upper misstatement limit amount for the possible overstatement of the accounts receivable balance.

b. If a tolerable misstatement of $150,000 had been established for the accounts receivable balance, what would your conclusion be regarding whether this test alone indicated a possible financial statement misstatement requiring auditor action?

c. Describe circumstances in which you would feel comfortable evaluating or accepting sample results at a level of reliability of less than 90 percent.

10–71. Fryers, Inc., sells both wholesale and retail in the gourmet cookware industry. Its computerized accounts receivable system processes approximately 80,000 invoices related to 13,000 customer accounts annually. The year-end accounts receivable balance has historically been approximately 35 percent of total assets. Because the auditor's assessment is that Fryers has an effective internal control structure, the planned audit strategy for the revenue cycle is to perform tests of controls with the objective of reducing substantive procedures.

You have been asked to select a representative sample of customer invoices for examination of certain attributes. The audit work to be performed on the sample items is to determine that

1. Each invoice is supported by an authorized shipping document.
2. The invoice date is no more than three business days after the shipping date.
3. The invoice is mathematically accurate.

In prior years, the deviation rates discovered by these tests of controls have been low (1 to 2 percent), with the exception of *invoice dating*, which has been as high as 3 percent.

Required:

a. Determine the sample size for each attribute to be tested. (*Note:* You will have to make certain judgments in solving this problem.) Use the format indicated below.

	Shipping Documents	*Invoice Dating*	*Mathematical Accuracy*
Population:			
Tolerable deviation rate:			
Reliability (level of assurance):			
Estimated deviation rate:			
Risk:			
Sample size:			

b. Assuming that you will use one sample (i.e., use the same invoices) for all three attributes, determine the sample size and reliability level you would use.

10–72. Items 1 through 5 apply to an audit, by Andrea Manning, CPA, of the financial statements of Halling Brothers, Inc. for the year ended December 31, 1990. Halling manufactures two products: Product A and Product B. Product A requires raw materials that have a very low per-item cost, and Product B requires raw materials that have a very high per-item cost. Raw materials for both products are stored in a single warehouse. In 1989 Halling established the total value of raw materials stored in the warehouse by physically inventorying an unrestricted random sample of items selected without replacement.

Ms. Manning is evaluating the statistical validity of alternative sampling plans Halling is considering for 1990. Manning knows the size of the 1989 sample and that Halling did *not* use stratified sampling in 1989. Assumptions about the population, variability, tolerable misstatement rate, and specified reliability (confidence level) for a possible 1990 sample are given in each of the following five items.

Required:

In each case, indicate the effect on the size of the 1990 sample compared with the 1989 sample. Each of the five cases is independent of the other four and is to be considered separately. Your answer choice for each item 1 through 5 should be selected from the following responses:

a. Larger than the 1989 sample size.
b. Equal to the 1989 sample size.
c. Smaller than the 1989 sample size.
d. Of a size that is indeterminate based on the information given.

1. Halling wants to use stratified sampling in 1990 (the total population will be divided into two strata, one each for the raw materials for Product A and Product B). Compared with 1989, the population size of the raw materials inventory is approximately the same, and the variability of the items in the inventory is approximately the same. The specified tolerable misstatement rate and specified reliability are to remain the same.

Under these assumptions, what should be the required sample size for 1990?

2. Halling wants to use stratified sampling in 1990. Compared with 1989, the population size of the raw materials inventory is approximately the same, and the variability of the items in the inventory is approximately the same. Halling specified the same tolerable misstatement rate but wishes to change the specified reliability from 90 percent to 95 percent.

Under these assumptions, what should be the required sample size for 1990?

3. Halling wants to use unrestricted random sampling without replacement in 1990. Compared with 1989, the population size of the raw materials inventory is approximately the same, and the variability of the items in the inventory is approximately the same. Halling specifies the same tolerable misstatement rate but wishes to change the specified reliability from 90 percent to 95 percent.

Under these assumptions, what should be the required sample size for 1990?

4. Halling wants to use unrestricted random sampling without replacement in 1990. Compared with 1989, the population size of the raw materials inventory has increased, and the variability of the items in the inventory has increased. The specified tolerable misstatement rate and specified reliability are to remain the same.

Under these assumptions, what should be the required sample size for 1990?

5. Halling wants to use unrestricted random sampling without replacement in 1990. Compared with 1989, the population size of the raw materials inventory has increased, but the variability of the items in the inventory has decreased. The specified tolerable misstatement rate and specified reliability are to remain the same.

Under these assumptions, what should be the required sample size for 1990?

(AICPA adapted)

10-73. ***Quinn Hardware*** This problem is a continuation of the Quinn Hardware case. Before proceeding further, review the client background information for Quinn Hardware in Problem 6-62 in Chapter 6.

At March 31, 1991, Quinn Hardware has accounts receivable consisting of 4200 accounts aggregating $49,015,000. Approximately 4175 customer accounts have balances equal to or less than $200,000. The other 25 accounts have balances ranging from $200,001 to $950,000 and represent $17,500,000 of the total accounts receivable at March 31, 1991.

Planning materiality is $300,000 on a pretax basis for the consolidated income statement and $1,000,000 for the consolidated balance sheet. Tolerable misstatement for this application is $250,000 and expected misstatement has been estimated to be $100,000.

Assume that as a result of tests of controls performed in the revenue cycle, control risk has been determined to be low with respect to the completeness, existence, and accuracy audit objectives. Positive confirmation procedures will, therefore, be performed as of the interim date (March 31, 1991). The sampling plan, determined by judgment, calls for confirming all accounts receivable over $200,000 and 25 accounts with balances equal to or less than $200,000.

The accounts receivable trial balance has been reconciled to the general ledger at March 31, 1991. The trial balance is in numerical order of customer account numbers. The client has agreed to record all known misstatements.

The sample of accounts circularized, aggregating $1,285,000, yielded two misstatements resulting in an overstatement of $1200. The reasons for the misstatements were not specifically determinable. Two misstatements were also found in the accounts examined 100 percent, for an overstatement of $12,000.

Required:

a. Using the ratio method, compute the projected population dollar misstatement.
b. Management has indicated that all actual misstatements discovered as part of the audit will be recorded. Discuss (1) the financial statement impact of the known and projected misstatements, and (2) the adequacy of the allowance for sampling risk.

11

Auditing in an EDP Environment

Changes in computer technology have been accompanied by changes in auditing standards. When the AICPA issued Statement on Auditing Standards (SAS) No. 3, *The Effects of EDP on the Auditor's Study and Evaluation of Internal Control*, in December 1974, it was still possible to consider the impact of computers on an audit in relative isolation. With the issuance of SAS No. 48, *The Effects of Computer Processing on the Examination of Financial Statements*, in July 1984, the profession integrated guidance on the effects of EDP (electronic data processing) on financial statement audits with other SASs, thereby formally acknowledging that computers had so permeated organizations that they must be considered throughout the audit. Subsequent SASs have continued to recognize that conclusion.

In early computerized systems that printed out all results of processing, the auditor's assurance about the accuracy of computer-generated data was frequently attained by obtaining detailed printouts (hardcopy) that included the calculations performed, data used, and all exceptions and rejections, and then reperforming the computerized procedures. Since this in essence bypassed the computer, it was called "auditing around the computer." Today, auditing this way is often impossible because of the large volume of transactions processed and the number of locations where processing may take place. Moreover, modern systems generally do not print out calculations in detail, and some systems do not generate all output in hardcopy form. (A common exception is microcomputer applications in small organizations, which in some cases still may print processing details.)

Using the computer itself in the audit, by testing general control procedures or using computer software to test the programmed procedures that carry out accounting and control activities, is today the usual method of conducting an audit. Originally called "auditing through the computer," this technique has become all but essential in modern processing systems. It entails audit strategy decisions about whether and to what extent to test control procedures, and about the nature, timing, and extent of substantive tests of computer-generated data. In addition, virtually all audit strategies in a computer environment present opportunities to increase audit efficiency by "auditing with the computer": Whether using the client's or the auditor's computer, the auditor can use computer software to perform many tests that would be too time-consuming and perhaps not even possible to do manually.

FEATURES OF COMPUTER ENVIRONMENTS

Computerized systems and their configurations vary widely from one computer environment to another. Even when the same type of mainframe from the same vendor is used, there is an almost infinite variety of combinations of types of peripheral devices, software options, telecommunications networks, and application software.

Computer Operations

To provide some background about different computer environments, an overview of computer processing concepts and terminology is presented here. Detailed discussion is beyond the scope of this book and is available in works dealing specifically with EDP.

Hardware. Computers basically consist of a central processing unit, internal storage (memory) and external storage, input/output devices, and other peripheral equipment. External storage can be on magnetic tape, disk, or both, depending on the system. Input/output devices consist mainly of terminals with screens and keyboards, and printers for hardcopy output. Other devices whose use is increasing in certain types of operations are scanners, point-of-sale registers, optical character readers, mark sense readers, and light guns. Other peripheral equipment includes telecommunications devices like modems, which translate digital computer signals into analog form for transmission over phone lines and retranslate them at the other end, as well as devices like multiplexors and controllers, which handle complex communications message requirements, directing the information to the appropriate part of the system or computer. The current trend—which can be expected to accelerate—is toward machines that communicate with each other and share data and programs via telecommunications and area networks. In many of these so-called paperless systems, such as those for telephone order entry, there is no printed documentation of transactions.

Software. The programs that run the system and direct its operations are called the *system software*. System software includes the *operating system*, which directs internal operations and makes it possible for specific *application software programs* to be run. Among other components of system software in a modern system are *utilities*, which include report generators and powerful editors used to write or change programs; *telecommunications software; file and program access software;* and *data base management system software.*

Originally, software had to be created specifically for each application program, such as accounts receivable or payroll, to accomplish particular tasks. Most organizations still develop some custom-designed applications in-house. They are developed by EDP department staffs of system analysts and programmers, who use a standard system development methodology intended to ensure that applications are appropriate, are adequately controlled, and meet management and user needs.

Because the system development process is obviously expensive and time-consuming, however, outside vendors have developed standard applications, referred to as purchased systems or packaged software. Many organizations use these packages as an alternative to developing their own software. Purchased systems are normally sold with a maintenance agreement that provides program "fixes" as required to correct programming errors or add enhancements to the programs. To make these systems more efficient to use, vendors often build in numerous customizing features, called options, that allow users to tailor the software to their own needs without having to rewrite it.

Depending on the vendor, purchased systems may be available with or without source code. Source code is the series of instructions written so the programmer can understand them. They need to be "compiled," or translated, into machine language (object code) so that the computer can execute them. If the source code is not available to users, they cannot make changes to the programs easily. (Users can, however, change some program functions through other methods, such as "user exits," which allow the insertion of user programs, or selecting different options provided by the program.)

Data Base Management Systems. Data base management systems (DBMS) eliminate much of the redundancy of data that exists when each program requires its own file structure. In a standard file structure, each program has data available to it in files specifically designed for that program. (A file consists of records, which in turn contain data fields or elements.) For example, in a payroll system, the payroll program would use an employee master file containing, for each employee, data fields for employee name, number, social security number, address, and pay rate. The personnel department would typically have another program, with its own file that duplicated much of the information held in the payroll system. In a DBMS, on the other hand, all data elements are held in a central data base and are called on as required by the particular application program. In the foregoing example, a "human resources data base" would contain elements used by the payroll, personnel, and other applicable departments.

Integrated Systems. In today's environment, accounting systems are increasingly integrated with operational systems. These types of systems generate information used for both accounting and management decision-making purposes. An example is a manufacturer's accounting system that generates cost accounting information used for product pricing along with information for external financial reporting.

Organization of the EDP Department

The organization of the EDP department depends largely on the extent of computer processing, the number of employees, and the control techniques used. The department can range from one or two employees responsible for running a self-standing minicomputer to a large organization consisting of hundreds of people responsible for developing, maintaining, and executing applications on a multi-mainframe operation linked to a data telecommunications network.

Regardless of the size and complexity of the organization, there are a number of specific functions in an EDP installation.

Information systems management. Develop long-range plans and direct application development and computer operations.

System analysis. Design systems, prepare specifications for programmers, and serve as intermediary between users and programmers.

Programming. Develop logic, write computer programs, and prepare supporting documentation.

Technical support. Select, implement, and maintain system software, including operating systems, network software, DBMS, and so forth.

Data base administration (DBA). Design, implement, and maintain the data base in a DBMS.

Network management. Manage the operation of the organization's communication networks (including network utilization, routing, and problem management).

Computer operations. Operate computer in accordance with manually supplied and computer-generated instructions.

Data entry operations. Convert data into machine-readable form primarily using terminals or cathode ray tube (CRT) devices. Maintain and exercise control over the completeness, accuracy, and distribution of input and output.

Security administration. Control the security of the system, including the use of access controls and maintenance of user IDs and associated password files. (This function is normally found only in large installations.)

Tape library. Receive, maintain, and issue magnetic media files (data and programs) on tapes or disks; maintain systems libraries.

How duties are segregated within the EDP department is an important aspect of the control structure. To the extent possible, the aforementioned functions should be performed by different people, so that there is adequate separation of duties. For example, programmers should not have the ability to access programs actually in use. In general, the more sophisticated the system and the larger the department, the greater the opportunity to segregate incompatible functions. In small organizations, the same person may perform more than one function, which can present control problems with respect to incompatible duties, as, for example, when one person does almost all the work related to the operation of a departmental minicomputer.

Segregation of duties in computer environments, as in manual systems, also involves separating incompatible functions outside of the EDP department. This can be accomplished by permitting, normally via user IDs and passwords, user department operators access to only the functions required to perform their jobs. For example, if the payroll and personnel departments are among the users of a common data base, the payroll clerk should be able to access only the program that posts time sheets and enters paycheck-initiation transactions, while the appropriate personnel clerk should be able to access only the program that processes changes in pay status.

Supervisory control procedures in computerized systems are similar to those in noncomputerized systems. For example, in a user department, a responsible official should periodically determine that data rejected by the computer is being investigated as prescribed. Similarly, in the EDP department, a responsible manager should review and approve the adequacy of procedures for implementing and testing program changes. Supervisory control procedures can also be performed by the computer through its ability to match newly input information to preset tables or other files. Other supervisory tasks, such as recalculating invoices, are also performed by the computer; once appropriate formulas have been set up in the programs, and assuming that the programs are adequately controlled, the computer will do the calculations the same way every time.

Decentralized and Distributed Data Processing

The earliest EDP operations took place in centralized departments to which organizational users submitted requests for new and changed application systems and for job processing. Personnel in the EDP department designed, developed, operated, and maintained all of the organization's application systems. As the number of requests, together with the complexity of the systems, increased, however, many user departments sought alternatives to the centralized EDP function.

At the same time, technology advances made possible smaller, more powerful, and less expensive computer systems than the giant first-generation systems. Users began to buy and install these minicomputer systems throughout the organization, particularly at the departmental level. This was followed very quickly by a second phase of user computing resulting from the widespread availability and use of microcomputers. This form of computer use is referred to as decentralized or distributed data processing or computing. The most significant difference between decentralized computing and distributed computing is the extent of integration of the systems. Decentralized computing tends to be less integrated than distributed processing. In a decentralized environment, minicomputers and microcomputers generally operate independently of the centralized computer system. In a distributed system, there is usually a coordinating facility with responsibility for unifying the mainframe systems, minicomputers, and microcomputers, together with software, communications, and data base technology, into an organization-wide information system.

Distributed and decentralized environments have created new problems for both organizations and their auditors. For organizations, both the volume of requests for information and the amount of support required by users of these complex and sophisticated systems have increased dramatically. Other difficulties involve achieving compatibility of both hardware and software among different departments, conforming organizational and departmental standards, and establishing and implementing control structure policies and procedures. As noted later in this chapter, the existence of differing policies and procedures for different departments and applications may require the auditor to understand and test separate general control procedures for each application with audit relevance.

CONTROL PROCEDURES AND CONTROL OBJECTIVES IN COMPUTERIZED SYSTEMS

There are two types of control procedures associated with computerized systems: general control procedures, which for the most part apply to data processing as a whole, and control procedures that are applied to specific classes of transactions (such as cash collections from customers). The latter procedures are designed to ensure that all transactions are authorized and are processed and recorded completely and accurately; that the integrity of data on files is preserved; and that assets and related documents and records are protected from physical loss or theft and from unauthorized manipulation. Those control objectives and procedures for meeting them are discussed and illustrated in Chapter 7.

In computerized systems, processing is done by computer application programs, which are precise instructions to the computer to perform specific steps, referred to as *programmed procedures*, to achieve a particular task. There are two types of programmed procedures.

- *Programmed accounting procedures*, for example, calculating and producing sales invoices, updating master files, and generating data within the computer.
- *Programmed control procedures* that ensure the completeness, accuracy, and authorization of data being processed and stored, for example, matching sales orders against a master file containing credit information and reporting orders from customers not on the file or in excess of credit limits.

The consistency with which both programmed accounting and programmed control procedures process data is one of the benefits of the computer and is made possible in part by general control procedures. If the programmed accounting and control procedures are subject to adequate general control procedures, their performance should not vary unpredictably. Accordingly, random errors, which might occur in a manual accounting system, are virtually eliminated in a computerized system.

Control procedures designed to meet the control objectives for specific classes of transactions in a computerized system consist of a combination of programmed control procedures and manual procedures, called *user control procedures*. Programmed control procedures typically generate reports (known as exception reports) of instances when the computer, for one reason or another, is unable to complete the prescribed operation. The effectiveness of those programmed control procedures depends on two things. First, there must be adequate general control procedures to ensure the proper implementation, maintenance, and continued operation of the programmed procedures and that only authorized changes are made to programs and data. Otherwise, there is no assurance that the exception reports are accurate and complete. General control procedures are discussed extensively in this chapter. Second, a user control procedure, which commonly consists of the follow-up of items in exception reports, is also necessary. User control procedures are described and illustrated in Chapter 7.

For example, to ensure that only accurate data is entered into the system, the computer may be programmed to match cash receipts from customers to specific invoices in the open accounts receivable file, to print out an exception report of cash receipts that cannot be matched to specific invoices, and to create a file of unmatched cash receipts. The user control procedure consists of a person with the appropriate knowledge and authority investigating and following up on the exception report.

GENERAL CONTROL OBJECTIVES AND PROCEDURES

General control procedures are designed to ensure that the programmed (accounting and control) procedures within a computerized system are appropriately implemented, maintained, and operated and that only authorized changes are made to programs and data. Some auditors call general control procedures "information technology control procedures" because they believe that term better describes the purpose served by the procedures. This section describes those procedures and their objectives; a later section discusses methods of testing their effectiveness as a basis for reducing the assurance needed from substantive tests.

Overview of General Control Procedures

There are seven categories of general control procedures.

- *Implementation control procedures* are designed to ensure that programmed procedures for new systems or major enhancements to existing systems are effectively designed and implemented.

- *File conversion control procedures* are designed to ensure that when a significant new system is introduced or an existing system is modified, the conversion process does not give rise to data file errors.
- *Maintenance control procedures* are designed to ensure that changes to programmed procedures are effectively designed and implemented.
- *Computer operations control procedures* are designed to ensure the continuity of processing (that is, that the correct data files are used and recovery procedures are provided) and the consistent application of programmed procedures.
- *Data file security control procedures* are designed to prevent or detect unauthorized changes to stored data or the initiation of unauthorized transactions.
- *Program security control procedures* are designed to prevent or detect unauthorized amendments to programs.
- *System software control procedures* are designed to ensure that system software is effectively implemented, maintained, and protected from unauthorized changes.

The first four categories are necessary for the effective operation of programmed control procedures. The next two categories ensure that only properly approved changes are made to stored data and to programs. The last category relates to system functions and, therefore, can affect both programmed procedures and data files. System software procedures are particularly important because of their impact on the effectiveness of other control procedures. For example, the password verification procedures that permit access to data files are usually incorporated into system software.

Implementation

Implementation control procedures help guard against financially significant errors in new applications. The procedures cover the authorization and design of new computer applications, testing of new application programs, and procedures for putting approved programs into use; they apply to both internally developed and vendor-supplied applications. In the latter situation, the principal concerns are the original selection of the package, any modifications required to the package, and the testing and implementation of the package in the client's environment.

System Design and Program Preparation. Control procedures for program preparation ensure that appropriate programmed procedures are designed and coded into computer language and that the appropriate user control procedures are designed as part of the system. General design requirements are converted into detailed system specifications. Once detailed specifications have been developed and approved in both the user and computer departments, which may be done in modules or for the system as a whole, programming can begin. The computer programs can be generated in a variety of ways, ranging from purchasing or customizing application software packages to writing programs in-house. In any event, the programs should be documented in enough detail to facilitate subsequent testing, appropriate future modifications, and training of personnel.

Program and System Testing. Testing is normally carried out in three distinct stages: program testing, system testing, and parallel running.

Program testing consists of verifying the logic of individual programs, usually through *desk checking* and computer processing of *test data*. Desk checking involves determining visually that the program coding is consistent with the program specifications; it is generally done by a programmer other than the one who wrote the code. Desk checking is normally performed in conjunction with computer processing of hypothetical test data. Test data is designed to cover all elements of data in all classes of transactions that are likely to be encountered and for which input specifications have been written.

System testing consists of determining that the programs are logically compatible with each other and do not have an adverse impact on the system as a whole. Processing test data is the principal technique used in system testing; adjustments and reruns are performed until all observed logic failures have been corrected. The user and system analysts are the principal parties involved in the system testing process; programmers primarily correct program errors.

Parallel running involves operating the system under conditions that approximate the anticipated "live" environment, while the old system (computer or manual) continues to operate. Results of operating the new system are compared with those of the old system, with appropriate follow-up of inconsistencies. Parallel running is a means of testing the logic, programming, and implementation of a complete system, including all user control procedures. One of its objectives is to confirm the system's ability to cope with actual conditions and volumes of transactions. Operating and user instructions may be reviewed and approved by a responsible official as part of the parallel running process, or this may be done as part of the final acceptance procedures.

Cataloguing. Cataloguing is the process of incorporating computer programs into various program libraries, which may contain programs in source code, object code, or load module form. *Source code* or language refers to the high-level computer languages that programmers use (such as COBOL); *object code*, also known as object modules, is the output of the compiler, in machine code or language. Ordinarily, a program is written in source language form, which is then incorporated into a test source library. The program is subsequently compiled by the computer into an object module and catalogued into a test library. To be executable, the various object modules that make up a program are brought together in a process called link-editing. This process creates the *load module* that is actually used by the computer for program execution.

Program testing is performed using the program in a *test library*. After a program has been completely tested, the test source program is transferred to the production source library. The program in the production source library is used for cataloguing into the *production library*. This ensures that the production program is completely equivalent to the tested and approved source program.

It is important that cataloguing be effectively controlled. For example, it is preferable for programmers to have access to the test library only, and for testing and documentation to be satisfactorily completed before programs are incorporated into production libraries. At an appropriate cutoff point, a formal procedure transfers programs from test to production status.

File Conversion

Conversion of data files may be necessary when a computerized system is developed to replace a manual system or an existing computerized system, or an existing computerized system is significantly enhanced and the existing files need to be "rebuilt." To ensure that newly created or converted data files contain correct data, organizations typically develop a conversion plan, which generally covers

- Design of the conversion process.
- Documentation of any data conversion programs to be written.
- Techniques to be used to test the results of conversion (e.g., file balancing, one-to-one comparisons).
- Conversion timetable.
- Assignment of user and data processing responsibilities.

Data processing management involved in the process (e.g., the data base administrator and other programming project leaders) and user management (or its designee) review and approve the plan.

Normally, the conversion process is designed to ensure that

- Specifications for all master files and transaction files to be converted/created are identified.
- Specifications for new files are reviewed and approved by appropriate user and data processing management.
- Specifications for each new file are compared with those of existing files to determine the effect of any format changes to existing fields; new fields, if any, needed as a result of the new or modified system; and existing fields, if any, that will be eliminated from the converted files.
- Techniques are designed and responsibilities assigned to ensure that the newly created data files are complete and accurate.
- Data created for new files is appropriately reviewed and approved before being input to those files, e.g., one-for-one checks.

The final results of the conversion process are reviewed and approved by appropriate user and data processing management.

Maintenance

Maintenance control procedures cover the same areas as implementation procedures, but relate to program amendments rather than entirely new applications. Procedures ensure that amendments are properly designed, tested, approved, incorporated within the application, and updated to the live program file, and that change requests are handled appropriately.

Program changes occur frequently in most data processing installations. They vary in complexity, ranging from relatively simple changes in editing procedures to major overhauls of large systems. Control procedures for program changes are similar to those for new systems. Requests for changes are formalized and include enough details to facilitate authorization and to enable the changes to be designed. Testing of the changed program follows a process similar to that for new systems, and changes are appropriately approved before implementation.

Typically, maintenance policies and procedures require that

- All system change requests are properly approved and communicated to data processing, generally on a standard change request form.
- A cost-benefit analysis is performed to ensure efficient use of resources (personnel and hardware).
- Approved changes are tracked throughout the change process.
- The final design of changes is reviewed and approved by both user and data processing management.
- All changes, including those initiated within data processing, are subject to appropriate testing, and test results are reviewed and approved by user and data processing management.
- Implementation of tested changes is approved by the requestor.
- Data processing departments affected by the changes are notified, e.g., computer operations, data base administration.
- Documentation (such as operations runbooks, user manuals, program narratives, and system description) is prepared or updated.

Policies and procedures also ensure that an "owner" is defined for each system. An owner is the individual or department user of the system with the authority to request (or approve) changes in the system. System owners should be identified so that data processing management can ensure that changes are requested by the owner. In larger clients, because of the complexity and interrelationship of systems, a user committee reviews and coordinates changes. Once a request has been received and accepted by data processing, detailed specifications describing the requested change are developed by data processing personnel (e.g., programming, data base administration, or telecommunications specialists).

Users may inappropriately attempt to bypass formal change procedures by initiating program changes through direct contact with programmers. This can cause problems involving, for example, unauthorized changes, inappropriate installation dates, inadequate testing, and inconsistent application of accounting principles. In addition, EDP personnel may believe that there is no need to inform users of proposed program changes that are viewed as purely technical matters that users cannot comprehend and will not be affected by. Examples of such modifications are file reorganizations, changes from tape to disk, and optimizing restart procedures. All such changes should be appropriately communicated to users; although they may defer in-depth technical review to data processing management, they should at least be aware that the system is being modified so as to have an opportunity to determine whether output data is affected.

Computer Operations

Computer operations control procedures ensure the use of correct data files, including their correct version, and provide recovery procedures for processing failures; they also help ensure that programmed accounting and control procedures are consistently applied. Computer operations procedures cover both processing of data and computer department operations, and may be applied at a central location or at local installations.

Procedures to ensure the use of correct data files include software checking of information on files and manual checks of external file labels by operators. Control over recovery from processing failures requires that data is regularly copied as backup, that processing status at the time of failure can be established, and that proper recovery takes place. The consistent operation of programmed procedures is ensured by procedures that schedule jobs for processing, set them up, and execute them. Procedures also cover the actions of computer operators, such as supervision and review of their work. In on-line systems, data files normally are available to users at all times, so that relatively little operator intervention is required; in those systems, operations are controlled largely by the system software. In batch systems, jobs are grouped into job streams and are set up with the required files by operators. More operator intervention is required, and computer operations control procedures may be of greater concern.

Computer Processing Procedures. The computer operations department or function usually controls the day-to-day functioning of data processing hardware and software. In many organizations, it is assisted by a production control department. Computer operations is responsible for the physical running of the computer system (e.g., mounting files and printer forms and making decisions about computer hardware, such as whether to discontinue using a device in the event of a failure). The production control department is responsible for job scheduling and setup.

Production control frequently uses a job scheduling system and a tape management system to control the submission of jobs to the computer and ensure that the correct files are used for those jobs. Production control normally provides standards (e.g., job classes, use of tape and disk storage devices, printer classes, routing of output) for developing or updating run instructions for new or modified systems. Those standards consider time constraints and processing sequences that apply to each system. Effective control procedures for implementing and modifying systems (discussed earlier) normally include review and approval of operating parameters and job schedules by application owners and production control or computer operations management.

In many data processing installations, job scheduling, setup, and execution are not formally controlled by software or a production control department; instead, they are controlled manually. In those environments, manual procedures should be supervised by computer operations supervisors or other computer operations management.

Backup and Recovery Procedures. In the event of a computer failure, backup arrangements are needed so that the recovery process for production programs, system software, and data files does not introduce errors into the system. The principal techniques that may be employed are

- A facility for restarting at an intermediate stage of processing, for use if programs are intentionally or unintentionally terminated before their normal ending.
- A system to copy or store master files and associated transaction data, which makes it possible to restore files lost or damaged during disruption.
- Procedures to ensure that copies of operating instructions, run instructions, and other documentation are available if originals are lost.
- Formal instructions for resuming processing or transferring it to other locations, usually called a contingency plan.

Data File Security

Data file security control procedures are designed to protect data from unauthorized access that could result in their modification, disclosure, or destruction or that could inappropriately move assets, like cash or inventory, by manipulating data or processing unauthorized transactions. Data file security procedures are particularly important for master file data, since it is used repeatedly in processing transactions and may not be reviewed often enough to ensure timely identification of errors. Data file security control procedures are also necessary to protect files from accidental destruction or erasure. The extent of data file security needed depends on the sensitivity of the entity's data, characteristics of the related assets, and effectiveness of other control procedures.

Data file security control procedures usually involve techniques that restrict access to, use of, and ability to change data files to authorized users and ensure that the level of access is consistent with the users' responsibilities. The principal techniques are the use of software and physical security procedures. Access control software may entail the use of passwords, specialized security software, and tables that control the access rights of individuals. Where passwords are used, procedures are required to ensure that they are appropriately selected, kept secret, and regularly changed. Physical security procedures cover access to the computer room and terminals as well as the storage of data files held off-line. Data file security control procedures can enforce division of duties by limiting the functions or data to which specific users have access.

On-line environments provide greater opportunity for many users to gain access to data files and usually do not allow data processing to be adequately controlled by physical security procedures. Thus, system software is generally used to control data file security in on-line environments. Communications software and data base management packages often have password facilities. Security or access control software packages enhance the protection of data files.

Security procedures normally address such matters as

- The information classification scheme for information both stored on computers and located outside of data processing, including security categories (e.g., research, accounting, marketing) and security levels (e.g., top secret, confidential, internal use only, unclassified).
- The data in each information class and individuals or functions authorized to use it, and control and protection requirements.
- The types or classes of sensitive assets and the potential threats and protection requirements for each.
- The responsibilities of management, security administration, resource owners, computer operations, system users, and internal auditors.
- The consequences of noncompliance with policies and procedures.
- Any security implementation plan.

Where packaged application systems are used, data file access controls may be defined in option tables. Those tables may be maintained by user departments or by a security officer or administration function within data processing.

Program Security

In the absence of program security control procedures, the enterprise could be subject to the risk of defalcations or management fraud from unauthorized program changes. The risk of unauthorized amendment of programs is less where vendor-supplied packages are used and the user does not have access to the source code that would allow changes to the program. In on-line environments, users may be able to access program files, increasing the risk that unauthorized changes may be made to programs in order to misappropriate assets and modify reporting routines to conceal them. There is also a risk of unauthorized changes to options in purchased systems.

Features of system software are generally used to control program security in on-line environments. Communications software, data base management, and librarian packages commonly include password facilities. Librarian packages may also have other security features, such as the recording of program version numbers and the ability to secure production programs from alteration. Access control software packages are used to protect programs.

Program security control procedures may be similar to those used to achieve data file security or may be built into software used to maintain libraries of computer programs on file. Security procedures are also needed for system maintenance programs, for example, for correcting data files after a processing failure. These programs, commonly referred to as utility programs, can often make changes directly to programs or data, frequently without leaving any record of the changes.

System Software

System software control procedures ensure that system software is properly implemented, maintained, and protected from unauthorized changes. System software consists of various programs that direct computer functions and are not restricted to any one application. System software includes the operating system, utilities, sorts, compilers, file management systems, library management packages, time-sharing software, telecommunications software, job accounting software, data base management systems, and security software packages.

System software is typically acquired from computer or software vendors, rather than written by the user organization. Control procedures relate to selecting and implementing the appropriate software and options within it, including vendor-supplied amendments or "fixes," and to security and backup of system software. Control procedures for implementing system software are similar to those for packaged systems, except that the work is performed by the technical support group (i.e., system programmers), not application programmers. The "owners" are the management of various data processing functions, like the data base administrator, security administrator, and network or telecommunications administrator.

If an organization's technical support group develops some aspects of system software or adds functions to vendor-supplied system software (by making use of "exit" routines), appropriate system design procedures will be followed. When system software is supplied by a vendor, the user organization tests the integration of a particular package into the existing environment, including the selection of options and any subroutines added via exits by the technical support group.

Maintenance of system software deals primarily with changes supplied by the vendor. On rare occasions, the user may modify system software. All such modifications are controlled in much the same way as changes to application programs. Vendor-supplied system software is periodically modified by the vendor, and introduced as new programs or amendments to existing programs. New or amended system software is tested to ensure that it operates as intended within the organization's unique data processing environment. Tests of system software that interacts with application programs, such as the operating system, simulate the production environment. Normally, those tests involve running the system software with copies of proven application programs to identify anomalies associated with the modified system software.

In many organizations, neither the technical expertise nor the tools exist to make amendments to system software. This is often true of the operating system, which may be provided by the vendor in a low-level code like machine code or microcode, or in code built into the computer. In those circumstances the risk of unauthorized amendments to the system software is minimal. Where the technical expertise and tools do exist to change the system software, the organization establishes control procedures similar to those for the security of application programs. The technical support group is generally smaller than the application programming group, giving individual system programmers a greater opportunity to become familiar with a broader array of system software. The technical support group needs access to system software not only to perform routine maintenance but also when there are processing failures and other emergencies. Consequently, organizations normally enforce a division of duties to prevent technical support personnel from obtaining a detailed understanding of the applications processed and of user control procedures for key files and transactions in those applications. Also, the work of technical support staff is closely supervised.

COMPUTER FRAUD AND ABUSE

As computers become more sophisticated and pervasive, the potential for an entity to be harmed by computer fraud and abuse increases. While the distinctions are not always clear, computer fraud (or computer crime) usually refers to use of a computer to commit a crime; in computer abuse, the computer and related software are the objects of the crime. Instances of computer fraud and abuse, when discovered, frequently make sensational headlines; often the auditor is criticized for failing to detect fraud. Accordingly, auditors should be knowledgeable about control procedures to prevent computer fraud and abuse and about their responsibilities under GAAS to detect such acts.

Computer abuse encompasses the physical destruction and theft of computer hardware, software, or data and the unauthorized interception or alteration of software or data. Examples include sabotage of computers and software, unauthorized use of confidential records, unauthorized use of computer time for personal purposes, unauthorized alteration of data on file (such as student grades), the theft of portable computers, and the unauthorized copying of software.

Computer fraud involves using the computer to misappropriate assets (defalcations) or deliberately misstate an enterprise's financial statements (management fraud). Both types of fraud can be perpetrated by creating or altering computer programs and data on computer files or manipulating transaction data (altering, omitting, or creating unauthorized transactions), or both. For example,

- At a bank, a program was written to round downward to the nearest penny interest credited to depositors' accounts, accumulate the amounts rounded off, and credit them to the programmer's account—a case of a defalcation via unauthorized transactions generated by an unauthorized program.
- An employee of an insurance company who had clearance to process customer claims made unauthorized payments to himself and his children and then deleted the transactions from the files—a case of a defalcation by entering unauthorized transactions.
- Top management created nonexistent receivables and revenues by entering fictitious transactions; they then wrote a program to suppress the fictitious receivables when the auditor selected a sample from the accounts receivable file for the purpose of confirming them—a case of management fraud through entering fictitious transactions and creating a fraudulent program.

In most instances of computer fraud, it is clear that the fraud could have occurred in a manual system as well—particularly when the fraud was perpetrated by the inappropriate entry of transactions. Even many of the frauds involving the unauthorized creation or alteration of computer programs would be possible in manual systems, as, for example, crediting fractional cents of interest to an unauthorized account. In most instances, however, an enterprise uses a computer because of large transaction volumes. It is the combination of the existence of the computer and the large volumes of transactions that makes it possible for a person (or collusive group of people) to use the computer to assist in stealing assets or to intentionally misstate financial statements, and then to conceal those actions.

The incidence of defalcations can be reduced, at a price, through the effective design and operation of transaction processing and file control procedures and general control procedures relating to computer program and data file security. (As with any type of fraud, computer fraud can never be completely eliminated; even if it could, the cost of doing so would usually be far greater than the benefits derived.) Management fraud, however, whether perpetrated in a manual or computer environment, is less susceptible to prevention or detection by means of control procedures because of management's ability to override those procedures.

The auditor's responsibility for detecting computer fraud is the same as the responsibility for detecting other types of irregularities. Defalcations rarely result in material financial statement misstatements; management fraud, which typically is material to the financial statements, is often difficult to detect because it ordinarily involves control override and collusion. As discussed in Chapter 4, auditors have the responsibility to design their audits to provide reasonable assurance of detecting material fraud and to exercise due care and professional skepticism in performing them. They also have the responsibility under SAS No. 60, *Communication of Internal Control Structure Related Matters Noted in an Audit* (AU Section 325), to inform the client of significant deficiencies in the design or operation of the internal control structure—whether computer-related or otherwise—that come to their attention in the course of the audit.

AUDITING THROUGH AND WITH THE COMPUTER

To plan an effective and efficient audit, the auditor of an enterprise with a computerized accounting system needs to obtain, or update, and document the same kinds of information about the client's control structure as the auditor of an entity whose systems do not involve the use of EDP. Knowledge of the accounting system provides the auditor with information about the flow of significant classes of transactions through both manually operated and computerized elements of the system. That information, in turn, enables the auditor to identify the significant EDP accounting applications and understand such matters as the mode in which they operate (such as batch, on-line, or real-time), what accounting functions they perform (that is, the principal programmed accounting procedures), who operates them (including the relationships among users, operators, and programmers), how significant data used in processing those applications originates (for example, whether it is input through remote terminals or extracted from previously generated data files), the significant data files generated or updated by the processing, and information about reports produced—when and how they are produced, when and to whom they are distributed, and how they are used. All of that information generally enables the auditor to identify specific transaction processing, file, and asset protection control procedures that may prove useful in maximizing audit efficiency.

Information about the client's control environment relevant to the EDP department includes its organizational structure, the number of employees, and the extent of segregation of duties. The understanding of the control environment also helps the auditor assess the risk of computer fraud or abuse. As part of obtaining the understanding of the accounting system and control environment, the auditor also obtains some information about the client's general control procedures. Based on that information, the auditor considers what additional information is needed to plan the audit.

Audit Testing Plan

Audit objectives and the basis for the audit testing plan do not change because significant applications within the accounting system are computerized. As with manual systems, the auditor is concerned with whether particular audit objectives for individual accounts or groups of accounts can be achieved most efficiently by performing tests of controls as a basis for restricting substantive procedures, or by performing substantive procedures without significant reduction based on the effectiveness of the control structure. What does change when the accounting system is computerized are the points within the system where errors or irregularities can occur, the ways they can occur, and the ways they can be prevented or detected. Also, in a computerized environment the auditor may be able to use the computer to efficiently perform auditing procedures that would otherwise be prohibitively time-consuming and costly.

Audit strategy decisions in a computerized environment typically focus first on the effectiveness of general control procedures, because they ensure the proper implementation, maintenance, and operation of programmed accounting and programmed control procedures, and then on transaction processing and file control procedures. The auditor determines which categories of general control procedures to test by considering the risks associated with the different categories (risk of errors versus risk of irregularities), the programmed control procedures applied to transactions and files and what control objectives they relate to, and the likelihood that tests of controls will enable the auditor to assess control risk as low for specific control objectives.

The effectiveness of programmed control procedures relating to the completeness, accuracy, and authorization of transactions and files depends on the operation of general control procedures for implementation, file conversion, maintenance, and computer operations. Evidence that those programmed control procedures are effective may support a low assessment of control risk for the completeness, accuracy, and authorization transaction processing and file control objectives. The asset protection control objective is met, at least in part, by data file and program security general control procedures and by access control procedures that are part of system software, as well as by an appropriate division of duties. Evidence of the effectiveness of those procedures enables the auditor to assess control risk as low with respect to the protection of assets.

Typically in a computerized environment, one of the following audit testing plans results:

- The auditor tests all categories of general control procedures, and the results support the expected reduction in the assessed level of control risk for all relevant control objectives.
- The auditor's tests of general control procedures support the expected reduction in the assessed level of control risk for the completeness, accuracy, and authorization of transaction processing and files; however, the auditor determines that evidence of the effectiveness of certain categories of general control procedures, like those relating to program or data file security, is not available or not efficient to obtain. In this situation, the auditor assesses the risk of financial statement misstatements associated with those categories, by considering such factors as the susceptibility of relevant assets to theft, the sensitivity of stored data, and the adequacy and interrelationship of other relevant elements of the control structure, including the control environment, the accounting system, and other control procedures. Often, the auditor will not be able to conclude that the assessed level of control risk is low for asset protection; in that event, substantive procedures should be designed to provide the required assurance that related audit objectives have been achieved (principally the existence of assets and the classification of expenses and losses).
- The auditor determines that the general control procedures are not effective, and designs an audit testing plan that includes few tests of control procedures.

Transaction processing and file control procedures that depend on programmed control procedures are typically not tested unless the audit plan includes tests of related general control procedures. This is because obtaining evidence of the effectiveness of programmed control procedures by testing those procedures themselves is not likely to be efficient. In these circumstances, the auditor would obtain the necessary assurance from substantive tests instead. There may be some circumstances in which the auditor does not test general control procedures, but nevertheless wishes to test the effective operation of programmed accounting procedures directly. Those tests will be costly because of the sheer volume of such procedures in a typical computerized accounting system, although it might be possible to use software to facilitate the testing. Those tests are discussed later in the chapter.

Tests of Controls

The auditor's purpose in performing tests of controls, both of general control procedures and of user procedures, in EDP systems is the same as in manual systems, namely, to test the effectiveness of the control procedures as a basis for significantly restricting substantive tests. The same techniques are used in tests of controls regardless of whether the system is computerized or manual, that is, inquiry, observation, examination of evidence, and, where appropriate, reperformance. In computerized environments, however, the auditor may be able to use software to assist in performing the tests. Whenever the auditor uses the client's data files in performing tests, he or she should be sure the files are backed up so that the client's data will not be inadvertently lost or altered.

Testing General Control Procedures. Two current trends have affected the way the auditor approaches the testing of general control procedures. First, as noted earlier, many EDP functions are moving away from centralized systems toward decentralized or distributed data processing systems. Second, where large centralized systems still exist, their size and complexity have been increasing. While some general control procedures are still common to all applications, application-specific procedures have become more prevalent. For example, the applications for each major user may be supported by different system analysis and programming functions, which may be subject to different control procedures. In that situation, the auditor would have to test control procedures for applications in each of those user areas that have different functions and control procedures.

In some sophisticated computer environments, computer software can help the auditor test the client's general control procedures. For example, user procedures for reviewing and authorizing proposed changes to programs may be performed on-line without creating any tangible documentation. The auditor can use software to reperform such procedures. Although software can facilitate such tests of controls involving reperformance, the auditor should still consider carefully whether it might be more efficient to perform substantive tests than to reperform general control procedures.

Testing Control Procedures Applied to Classes of Transactions. As noted earlier, if the auditor intends to test control procedures related to classes of transactions as a basis for restricting substantive testing, he or she needs evidence that both relevant programmed control procedures and user control procedures operated effectively. Tests of user control procedures are described and illustrated in Chapter 8. Evidence about the effectiveness of programmed control procedures can be obtained either from tests of relevant general control procedures, as discussed earlier, or by seeking evidence about the effectiveness of the programmed procedures themselves. As already noted, however, testing programmed procedures is costly, and the auditor usually uses alternative means of obtaining evidence of their effectiveness.

Particularly in computerized systems where general control procedures may be less pervasive or sophisticated, or programmed accounting and control procedures are few, the auditor may be able to obtain indirect evidence about the effectiveness of control procedures applied to classes of transactions. Material misstatements that should have been prevented or detected by control procedures relating to the client's principal activities (such as sales, purchases, and receipt and disbursement of cash) may also be detected through management's use of the related data in managing the business. For example, material failures to bill for goods shipped or services rendered would generally come to management's attention through the adverse effect on profitability. Other misstatements affect relations with employees, customers, suppliers, or others. For instance, overbillings for goods shipped or services rendered would generally provoke unfavorable reactions from customers, including nonpayment of excess billings. The auditor may obtain evidence about whether such circumstances have arisen during the period by inquiring of client personnel, performing analytical procedures, or examining various management reports. The absence of such occurrences provides some evidence that the control procedures are effective.

After considering, in light of all relevant sources of evidence, whether a significant risk of material misstatement exists as a result of the failure of programmed accounting and control procedures to operate effectively, the auditor determines whether additional evidence is needed. If so, tests of specific programmed procedures may be necessary. Testing techniques using audit software are described briefly later in connection with substantive tests of programmed accounting procedures. Before undertaking such tests, however, the auditor should consider whether it would be more efficient to perform additional substantive tests directed at the relevant audit objective.

Substantive Tests Using Computer Software

In a computerized system, many substantive tests can be most efficiently performed using audit software on either the client's or the auditor's computer. Auditing with the computer can increase efficiency by mechanizing auditing procedures and enabling the auditor to test large numbers of transactions. Software is available or can be developed by the auditor to test transactions, master file and reference data, historical data, programs, activity logs—in fact, almost any information that is stored in a computerized system. The auditor can also perform various auditing procedures with the help of audit software designed specifically for that purpose. Auditors can use a microcomputer, a terminal connected to a large computer, or a micro-mainframe link in many phases of the audit—planning, engagement management, performing audit tests (including analytical procedures), and documenting the audit work.

The same software tools may be used in more than one testing technique; in certain circumstances these tools could also be used in performing tests of controls. Sometimes a combination of different types of software is required to meet a single audit objective. Audit software can assist in calculating, summarizing, selecting, sorting, and comparing data, and producing reports to the auditor's specifications. Sometimes, such as when generalized audit software packages (discussed later) are used, data can be accessed and processed by the same software tools. For example, the auditor can use software to examine all data on a file, to identify data that meets a particular condition (e.g., a total of debtors' balances that exceed their credit limits), and to print out selected data, like the results of tests or items selected for investigation. Figure 11.1 lists typical functions used by auditors in processing data.

Software tools that the auditor may use to access and process data include generalized audit software packages, application audit software packages, customized audit software, inquiry programs, and systems utility software and service aids.

Generalized Audit Software Packages. The most widely used computer-assisted audit techniques employ generalized software packages specifically designed for audit purposes. Audit tasks performed on client files include totaling a file, identifying exceptions, selecting items for manual review, and formatting reports. Generalized audit software packages help the auditor carry out those tasks on a variety of files at different installations. Their use eliminates much of the work involved in writing individual computer programs to accomplish those functions.

To use audit software, the auditor defines what computer configuration the program is to be run on and which files to use. The program logic is controlled by simplified procedural statements or parameters. The packages normally

Figure 11.1 Common Audit Software Processing Functions

Function	*Example*
Total	Add invoice amounts on the accounts receivable open item file and agree to the control total.
Compute	Multiply inventory quantities by unit costs.
Sort Summarize	Sort the file into customer number sequence and summarize to obtain customers' outstanding balances.
Analyze	Produce a frequency distribution.
Create	Produce a file for later comparison with another file.
Select	Produce a list of customers whose balances outstanding over 90 days are greater than $10,000.
Sample	Statistically sample the file for customer accounts to be confirmed.
Compare	Compare the file created at the confirmation date with the file at the balance sheet date and print out accounts with large percentage changes.
Format reports	Print confirmation letters and working papers.

have special functions to facilitate using the program to generate the kind of audit evidence and documentation desired. These include report formatting (page numbering, page breaking, column placement, and headings), totaling and subtotaling data, automatic production of processing statistics (number of records read and processed, and number of positive, negative, and zero-value records), and sorting and summarizing data.

Generalized audit software packages permit programs for specific applications to be developed in a relatively short time by people with somewhat limited programming skills. The use of generalized packages also reduces the auditor's reliance on the client's EDP staff, though client assistance is usually required to install the package and develop instructions to operate it. The main disadvantage of generalized packages is that there are usually limitations on the number and structure of files that can be accessed. Often the auditor can overcome those limitations by using a generalized audit software package in combination with customized software or utilities.

Application Audit Software Packages. Certain auditing procedures and requirements are so similar from one audit to another that the same programs can be applied with only minor changes, even though the data files vary. Some auditing firms have developed application audit software packages to achieve common audit objectives in several areas, like accounts receivable, accounts payable, and payroll. For example, application audit software can be used to analyze the accounts receivable ledger by age, select items for audit testing, produce confirmation letters, and match subsequent collections received. To run the software, the auditor converts the data files into a compatible format, determines the appropriate parameters, and executes the software. Some audit tests are unique to certain industries and to applications within those industries; some firms have also developed packages for these specialized areas.

Customized Audit Software. Although generalized and application software packages are useful in many situations, the auditor normally requires the ability to develop software for special needs beyond the capabilities of packaged software. For example, software packages may not be available for the client's computer, the output required may be very specialized, or the computations and data handling may be particularly intricate. In those circumstances, the auditor may use the computer languages available on the client's system to develop customized audit software. In addition, many generalized audit software packages allow additional routines written in computer languages to be integrated into the package, affording increased flexibility and wider applicability. If no compatible language is available, or if for other reasons it is impractical to integrate additional routines, an EDP audit specialist or a computer programmer can write programs to order.

Inquiry Programs. When available, standard data inquiry (or interrogation) programs, which extract or display data without updating or otherwise changing it, can be an economical audit tool. Relatively easy-to-use interrogation methods exist for many smaller computers, and are often built into larger data base management systems. A disadvantage of using inquiry programs is that they are often unique to a particular computer or data base, which means that the auditor may have to read manuals and learn the particular program.

Systems Utility Software and Service Aids. Systems utilities and service aids are provided by computer manufacturers and software vendors to perform limited, predefined tasks. Utilities and service aids are normally used to enhance system functioning or for programming. The auditor may use them to examine processing activity, interrogate data, and test programs and operational procedures. For example, one utility can copy and rearrange sequential files; another can extract particular records from one file and create a subset file for audit testing.

The auditor often needs utilities to set up and execute computerized auditing procedures. Some utilities may substitute for procedures that would otherwise be performed by generalized audit software or specially written programs. Most utilities come with a user manual that describes their functions. In smaller systems, utilities may allow the auditor access to many powerful, easy-to-use techniques. In larger systems, they may be much more difficult to use. Utilities are usually specific to a particular computer and operating system, so that the auditor must learn how to use separate ones for the different computers and systems that are audited.

Substantive Tests of Programmed Accounting Procedures

If the auditor needs evidence of the effective operation of programmed accounting procedures, it may be obtained by testing those procedures directly throughout the period, generally using various types of audit software. (In certain circumstances manual techniques may be appropriate; they are discussed later.) As noted earlier, however, testing specific programmed procedures is costly and the auditor usually chooses an alternative audit strategy. Therefore, only a brief description of some of the techniques used for testing client programs is presented here.

Flowcharting Programs. This software helps the auditor understand the programmed procedures by producing flowcharts and other documentation of the program being analyzed. The voluminous flowcharts produced, however, may contain more detail than is needed for that understanding. Lists of commands and data names in the program are also generated and are often helpful in program code analysis (described below).

Program Tracing and Mapping. These techniques involve processing test data through application programs and are used primarily by programmers when developing and testing programs. Program tracing identifies the actual steps executed; program mapping identifies any unexecuted program instructions. These techniques are only occasionally used by auditors because of the technical skills needed to analyze the results.

Program Code Analysis. This technique involves analyzing computer programs. Its main purpose is to confirm the existence of programmed procedures in a program or series of programs. Program code analysis consists of

- Identifying the program to be examined, by reference to the company's documentation.
- Selecting the form of code to be examined, which is normally the source code. The auditor must know the programming language and make sure that the source version examined is equivalent to the production program in use.
- Analyzing the selected coding. It is usually difficult to follow another person's coding, but adherence to standard programming methods may make this task a little easier. Software aids, such as flowcharting programs, can produce additional documentation. In subsequent periods, comparison programs can be used to indicate changes.

Test Data and Integrated Test Facility (ITF). The test data method tests the client's transaction processing control procedures. The audit software tools discussed earlier test actual client data; in the test data method, client programs are used to process test data. The output of the processing is then compared with predetermined results.

There are two methods of running test data.

- Test data can be processed using the company's operational programs, but separately from the company's data, and using either copies of master files or dummy files set up for testing purposes.
- Test data can be included in the company's regular data processing, with approval from a responsible official.

The latter method is referred to as an Integrated Test Facility (ITF). If specific records on the master files are reserved or created for this purpose and consistently processed during testing at regularly established intervals, an ITF is also referred to as a "Base Case System Evaluation."

Manual Testing. The auditor can use techniques for testing programmed procedures manually if adequate visible evidence is available. Data that must be tested to test the programmed procedures can be voluminous, however, making manual testing techniques impractical and inefficient. Although some visible evidence of the operation of programmed procedures is usually available, the results of processing are rarely printed out in detail (except in some microcomputer systems). Instead, totals and analyses are printed out without supporting details, thus rendering it impossible for the auditor to determine the correctness of a total or an analysis. Exception reports and rejection listings that are produced do not provide evidence that all items that should have been reported or rejected were properly treated. In those instances, the auditor may request and sometimes obtain reports generated specifically to meet audit needs.

Sometimes visible evidence not readily provided by the system can be recreated. Methods to achieve this are known collectively as "manual simulation techniques" and include

- Reassembling processed data into the same condition that existed when the programmed procedure was applied (e.g., reassembling batches of sales invoices to test the batch totals posted to the sales ledger control account).
- Using current data before processing by computer (e.g., testing the additions of batches before they are sent for processing, to determine that accurate batch totals are established to control subsequent processing).
- Selecting a small number of items from those submitted for processing and processing them in a separate run (e.g., splitting a batch into two batches, one large and one small, processing the small batch separately, and agreeing the resulting computer-produced total to manually precalculated results).
- Simulating a condition that will produce a report if the programmed procedure is working properly (e.g., altering a batch total to an incorrect figure so that the batch should be rejected, or withholding a document to see whether it is reported as missing); this approach requires careful planning and coordination with user departments.
- Requesting a special printout of items processed (e.g., a listing of sales invoices included in a sales total produced by the computer).

Manual tests cannot be performed if visible evidence of the operation of a programmed procedure neither exists nor can be produced, and the appropriate condition cannot be simulated. This often occurs in systems where transactions are entered directly through terminals without source documents.

Statistical Sampling Software

Statistical sampling applications, in both tests of controls and substantive tests, are particularly well suited to assistance from audit software. Using software reduces the need to make calculations manually and relieves the auditor of the need to understand fully some of the mathematical methods and concepts involved in sampling. In fact, many statistical sampling applications would be impractical without computer power.

A number of statistical sampling software packages are available to the auditor, some of which require almost no understanding of statistics. Most such packages support a limited number of statistical methodologies—usually those most frequently used by the accounting firm that developed the software. Other packages provide a wider selection of statistical methods, permitting the auditor to select the method best suited to the objective under consideration. Many of these packages can be used on microcomputers.

Two types of statistical sampling programs are generally available.

- Programs designed to develop strata boundaries, determine sample sizes, perform sample selection, and evaluate sampling results for variables sampling applications.
- Programs to calculate sample sizes and evaluate attributes sampling results.

Audit Documentation Software

Software packages are available that automate some of the labor-intensive tasks associated with auditing financial statements, including footing the trial balance and financial statements, ensuring the arithmetical accuracy and consistency of account groupings, and listing relevant financial statement ratios for subsequent analysis. Documentation programs can also be used to prepare opening and closing trial balances, lead schedules showing both current and prior-period information, financial statements, and other working papers. Software can be used to produce and format reports so they can be used as audit working papers. Auditors can use documentation software packages, instead of preparing working papers, to document the use of other audit software. The audit software packages—both for audit documentation and for the other purposes described in this chapter—are often designed to be used on the auditor's microcomputer at the client's office, a practice that is becoming increasingly common.

Analytical Procedures Software

Software can be used to calculate absolute dollar and percentage change ratios, and trends, and to highlight significant changes, enabling the auditor concentrate on evaluating the differences and obtaining explanations for them. This software is available on microcomputers, or by using utilities or software packages on minicomputers and mainframes. Auditors are increasingly using computers to compare client data with industry data using public data bases and microcomputer software. Virtually all of the analytical techniques discussed in Chapter 9 can be performed using software.

AUDIT MANAGEMENT

Computers can contribute to efficient engagement management, particularly in planning, budgeting, and scheduling. Extremely time-consuming when performed manually, these tasks can be expedited considerably by software like calculation worksheets, or "spread sheets." Once a spread sheet is set up, the user can input and change data, conditions, and formulas, and the results are recalculated automatically. Software can facilitate the effective use of, and control over, audit resources by determining the cost of assigned staff and evaluating alternatives, allocating staff and available chargeable hours to assignments, and scheduling staff by client, tasks to be performed, expected utilization, and available hours.

Accounting firms also use computers in a number of other ways to enhance the efficiency of their practices. Some of these computer applications are

- *Word processing.* Many standard letters and documents can be maintained in word processing libraries, including engagement and representation letters, financial reports, audit programs, and audit reports.
- *Audit statistics.* In performing analytical procedures on clients' financial results, the auditor often makes comparisons with industry results. Industry statistics and key business ratios can be collected and maintained on computer files.
- *Electronic mail.* Electronic mail has the benefits of speed and ease of response. It can be sent by telecommunications systems to and from geographically dispersed locations, thereby improving communications within a firm.
- *Audit department accounting and management.* Many accounting firms have management information systems to record budgets and time charges, facilitate prompt billing and revenue collection, and produce management and exception reports, such as staff utilization rates and overdue accounts. In some firms this processing is done on a centralized basis. In he future, accounting firms will probably follow the trend in the iness community toward decentralizing systems using mini- or computers at the local level that process local data and then input to, and retrieve reports from, the central processing site(s).

Review Questions

11–1. Distinguish among "auditing around the computer," "auditing through the computer," and "auditing with the computer."

11–2. Distinguish between programmed accounting procedures and programmed control procedures found in an EDP environment.

11–3. Explain how computers can perform some supervisory control procedures.

11–4. Describe the organization of a typical EDP department.

11–5. Describe how purchased software affects the risk of misstatement occurring.

11–6. Briefly describe the seven basic categories of general control procedures.

11–7. What is program testing and how is it performed?

11–8. What is system testing and how is it performed?

11–9. What is parallel running and what is its primary purpose?

11–10. What is the process of cataloguing and how should it be controlled?

11–11. How are program changes controlled and why is controlling them important?

11–12. What are the purposes of data file security control procedures and how are they achieved?

11–13. What are the objectives of computer operations control procedures?

11–14. Why are backup arrangements important and what techniques are used?

11–15. Explain how general control procedures and control procedures applied to classes of transactions affect audit strategy.

11–16. Explain how computer software can be used in testing general control procedures.

11–17. Illustrate how evidence obtained from other auditing procedures can assist in testing control procedures applied to classes of transactions.

11–18. Explain how the computer can be used to assist and expedite the auditing process.

11–19. What software tools are available to the auditor in using the computer in performing substantive tests?

11–20. Explain the two methods of running test data to evaluate a programmed procedure.

11–21. Explain how the computer can assist in the use of statistical sampling techniques.

11–22. Explain how the auditor can use the computer in engagement administration.

Discussion Questions

11–30. An auditor wishes to restrict computer auditing procedures to testing general control procedures. Discuss whether this is possible and, if so, how it is possible.

11–31. If the auditor's assessed level of control risk is planned to be low as a result of testing general control procedures, should some programmed procedures also be tested? Explain.

11–32. Since programmed procedures can be tested directly, why should general control procedures be tested?

11–33. What may happen in the event of deficiencies in computer program security? Describe various ways of achieving program security.

11–34. The following five topics are part of the relevant body of knowledge for CPAs having field work or immediate supervisory responsibility in audits.

1. Electronic data processing (EDP) equipment and its capabilities.
2. Organization and management of the data processing function.
3. Characteristics of computer-based systems.
4. Fundamentals of computer programming.
5. Computer center operations.

CPAs should possess certain general knowledge with respect to each of these five topics. For example, on the subject of EDP equipment and its capabilities, the auditor should have a general understanding of computer equipment and should be familiar with the uses and capabilities of the central processor and the peripheral equipment.

Required:

For each of the topics numbered 2 through 5 above, describe the general knowledge that should be possessed by CPAs.

(AICPA adapted)

11–35. When auditing an electronic data processing (EDP) accounting system, the independent auditor should have a general familiarity with the effects of the use of EDP on the various elements of the control structure and on the auditor's assessment and tests of it. The independent auditor must be aware of control procedures, commonly referred to as "general" control procedures, that relate to all EDP activities and control procedures that are applied to specific classes of transactions.

Required:

a. What are the general control procedures that should exist in EDP-based accounting systems?
b. What are the purposes of each of the following categories of control procedures that are applied to specific classes of transactions?
   1. Input control procedures.
   2. Authorization control procedures.
   3. Updating control procedures.

(AICPA adapted)

11–36. In the past, the records to be evaluated in an audit have been printed reports, listings, documents, and written papers, all of which are visible output. However, in fully computerized systems that employ daily updating of transaction files, output and files are frequently in machine-readable form such as cards, tapes, or disks. Thus, they often present the auditor with an opportunity to use the computer in performing an audit.

Required:

Discuss how the computer can be used to aid the auditor in auditing accounts receivable in such a fully computerized system.

(AICPA adapted)

11–37. Specify the type of general control procedure into which each of the following control procedures falls. Your selection should be made from the following categories of general control procedures:

a. Implementation
b. File conversion
c. Maintenance
d. Computer operations
e. Data file security
f. Program security
g. System software

Client Control Procedure

1.____ Documentation guide depicting new or revised system documents (e.g., user guide, program documentation)

2.____ Written policies and procedures regarding computer operations, particularly rules relating to:
- Organizational structure
- Division of duties
- Supervision and review
- Proper control/sequence processing

3.____ Establishment of test plans and documentation of results of testing of systems software implementation or changes, including supervisory review procedures

4.____ Access to terminals is physically restricted

5.____ Written policies and procedures regarding authorized movement of programs into production, including appropriate division of duties

6.____ List of personnel authorized to approve access to files

7.____ Review and approval of system output by supervisory personnel

8.____ Listing or log of failed and successful data access attempts

9.____ A statement of system or application requirements, approved by both user department personnel and data processing personnel for a new system or application

10.____ Regular changing of passwords

11.____ A reconciliation of old data converted to data on new file

12.____ Change request forms approved by user and/or data processing department

13.____ Approval of the results of testing new application by user departments and data processing personnel

14.____ A conversion plan that lists the timetable and methodology for data transfer, approved by the user and data processing departments

15.____ Written policies and procedures regarding the maintenance process, which includes rules on implementation and program change approvals

AICPA Multiple Choice Questions

These questions are taken from the Auditing part of Uniform CPA Examinations. Choose the single most appropriate answer.

11–40. Which of the following characteristics distinguishes computer processing from manual processing?

a. Computer processing virtually eliminates the occurrence of computational error normally associated with manual processing.
b. Errors or irregularities in computer processing will be detected soon after their occurrences.
c. The potential for systematic error is ordinarily greater in manual processing than in computerized processing.
d. Most computer systems are designed so that transaction trails useful for audit purposes do *not* exist.

11–41. Which of the following would be a deficiency in the internal control structure?

a. The computer librarian maintains custody of computer program instructions and detailed program listings.
b. Computer operators have access to operator instructions and detailed program listings.
c. The control group maintains sole custody of all computer output.
d. Computer programmers write and debug programs that perform routines designed by the systems analyst.

11–42. Which of the following would most likely be a deficiency in the internal control structure of a client that utilizes microcomputers rather than a larger computer system?

a. Employee collusion possibilities are increased because microcomputers from one vendor can process the programs of a system from a different vendor.
b. The microcomputer operators may be able to remove hardware and software components and modify them at home.
c. Programming errors result in all similar transactions being processed incorrectly when those transactions are processed under the same conditions.
d. Certain transactions may be automatically initiated by the microcomputers and management's authorization of these transactions may be implicit in its acceptance of the system design.

11–43. Errors in data processed in a batch computer system may *not* be detected immediately because

a. Transaction trails in a batch system are available only for a limited period of time.
b. There are time delays in processing transactions in a batch system.
c. Errors in some transactions cause rejection of other transactions in the batch.
d. Random errors are more likely in a batch system than in an on-line system.

11–44. Which of the following is *not* a major reason why an accounting audit trail should be maintained for a computer system?

a. Monitoring purposes.
b. Analytical procedures.
c. Query answering.
d. Deterrent to irregularities.

11-45. When EDP programs or files can be accessed from terminals, users should be required to enter a(an)

a. Parity check.
b. Personal identification code.
c. Self-diagnosis test.
d. Echo check.

11-46. The two requirements crucial to achieving audit efficiency and effectiveness with a microcomputer are selecting

a. The appropriate audit tasks for microcomputer applications and the appropriate software to perform the selected audit tasks.
b. The appropriate software to perform the selected audit tasks and client data that can be accessed by the auditor's microcomputer.
c. Client data that can be accessed by the auditor's microcomputer and audit procedures that are generally applicable to several clients in a specific industry.
d. Audit procedures that are generally applicable to several clients in a specific industry and the appropriate audit tasks for microcomputer applications.

11-47. Which of the following statements is *not* true of the test data approach when testing a computerized accounting system?

a. The test data need consist of only those valid and invalid conditions which interest the auditor.
b. Only one transaction of each type need be tested.
c. The test data must consist of all possible valid and invalid conditions.
d. Test data is processed by the client's computer programs under the auditor's control.

11-48. Which of the following computer-assisted auditing techniques allows fictitious and real transactions to be processed together without client operating personnel being aware of the testing process?

a. Parallel simulation.
b. Generalized audit software programming.
c. Integrated test facility.
d. Test data approach.

11-49. The primary purpose of a generalized computer audit program is to allow the auditor to

a. Use the client's employees to perform routine audit checks of the electronic data processing records that otherwise would be done by the auditor's staff accountants.
b. Test the logic of computer programs used in the client's electronic data processing systems.

c. Select larger samples from the client's electronic data processing records than would otherwise be selected without the generalized program.
d. Independently process client electronic data processing records.

11-50. Which of the following is likely to be of *least* importance to an auditor in assessing the internal control structure in a company with automated data processing?

a. The segregation of duties within the EDP center.
b. The control over source documents.
c. The documentation maintained for accounting applications.
d. The cost-benefit ratio of data processing operations.

Problems and Cases

11-60. A client uses a computer-generated report as the basis for writing the following monthly journal entry:

	Debit	*Credit*
Work in Process	$XXXX	
Raw Materials Inventory		$XXXX
(To record monthly issues of raw materials on a FIFO basis.)		

A review of the journal entry as written for the more recent months disclosed that the computer had erroneously priced the detail transactions supporting the entry on a moving average rather than a FIFO basis. A review of earlier journal entries indicated that the supporting transactions had been correctly priced on a FIFO basis.

The auditor received the following comments from members of the Data Processing and Accounting Departments.

Programmer—In order to improve processing efficiency, a number of computer files were restructured and the affected software was modified accordingly. In the case of the cost accounting system, the files were converted from magnetic tape to disk. It was also determined that the FIFO pricing procedure, requiring specific lot identity, resulted in a more extensive master file than would be required for a system using only cumulative totals for pricing, that is, a moving average basis. Consequently, the new files were redesigned to eliminate the individual lot data, and the pricing programs were modified to cost the issued raw material on a moving average basis. Since the printed report format had not changed, it was felt that the system had not changed from the user's perspective. Therefore, it was considered unnecessary to involve the Cost Accounting Department in the modification process. In fact, the moving average method appeared to present a more equitable method of distributing inventory costs.

Data Processing Manager—Company policy requires that changes directly affecting users be approved by the users. Changes affecting only internal activities of the Data Processing Department are considered to be purely technical items outside the responsibility and the expertise of users, and therefore do not require their approval. The file reorganization effort was inadvertently considered by Data Processing Management to be such a project. Unfortunately, since the general appearance of the report had not changed, it was considered unnecessary to inform the Cost Accounting Department of the program modification effort. The programmer assigned to the modification task was the person most familiar within the department with respect to the cost accounting application. It was felt that minimum supervision was required in the circumstances.

Cost Accounting Manager—Since the Company's financial statements were prepared on a FIFO basis, it was inappropriate to incorporate moving average pricing into the computer program. Because the report contained only one line of dollarized totals for each product, it was impossible for the recipient of the report to readily determine that the supporting details had been correctly priced on an individual basis. The programmed procedures for the FIFO calculation were extensively checked by the Cost Accounting Department at the time the system was originally implemented. Consequently, there was no reason for the Cost Accounting Department to believe that the calculations would not be performed correctly on a continuing basis.

Required:

Identify the control deficiencies that contributed to the foregoing situation and discuss how such problems could be avoided.

11-61. All user department requests for program modifications at Citywide Company are submitted to data processing on a program change request form. These forms are logged on receipt by data processing and assigned a sequential control number. Before the request form is sent to data processing by the user department, the manager of the user department approves the modification request. Data processing will not accept or log a modification request without a user department manager's signature.

The data processing clerk receiving and logging the modification requests distributes them to the responsible programmer. The programmer then obtains the production program documentation binder and a copy of the source version of the program from the production library, makes the coding changes, and tests the modified program. Test results are reviewed with the requesting user and a formal approval of the test results is obtained from the user.

The programmer uses the formal approval of the test results as authorization to have the modified program put into production. Placing the program into production is the responsibility of a production library control clerk. This clerk receives a copy of the user approval of the test results and the source version of the modified program from the programmer. As part of the control procedures for placing modified programs into production, this clerk recompiles the modified version of the source program and places the resulting object program on the production library. A form is sent to the user department notifying it when the modified program will begin to be used as part of normal production. A copy of this form is returned to the clerk who originally logged the request and that clerk notes the request as completed.

Required:

a. What control deficiencies, if any, may be present in this situation?
b. Explain how financial statement misstatements could result from those deficiencies.
c. Given those deficiencies, explain how the auditor could determine whether any unauthorized production program changes were made.

11–62. A CPA's client, Outdoors Products, is a medium-sized manufacturer of products for the leisure time activities market (camping equipment, scuba gear, bows and arrows, etc.). During the past year, a computerized system was installed, and inventory records of finished goods and parts were converted to computer processing. The inventory master file is maintained on a disk. Each record of the file contains the following information:

Item or part number
Description
Size
Unit of measure code
Quantity on hand
Cost per unit
Total value of inventory on hand at cost
Date of last sale or usage
Quantity used or sold this year
Economic order quantity
Code number of major vendor
Code number of secondary vendor

In preparation for year-end inventory, the client has two identical sets of preprinted inventory count cards. One set is for the client's inventory counts and the other is for the CPA's use to make audit test counts. The following information has been keypunched into the cards and interpreted on their face:

- Item or part number
- Description
- Size
- Unit of measure code

In taking the year-end inventory, the client's personnel will write the actual counted quantity on the face of each card. When all counts are complete, the counted quantity will be keypunched into the cards. The cards will be processed against the disk file, and quantity-on-hand figures will be adjusted to reflect the actual count. A computer listing will be prepared to show any missing inventory count cards and all quantity adjustments of more than $100 in value. These items will be investigated by client personnel, and all required adjustments will be made. When adjustments have been completed, the final year-end balances will be computed and posted to the general ledger.

The CPA has available a general-purpose computer audit software package that will run on the client's computer and can process both card and disk files.

Required:

a. In general and without regard to the foregoing facts, discuss the nature of general-purpose computer audit software packages and list the various types and uses of such packages.
b. List and describe at least five ways a general-purpose computer audit software package can be used to assist in all aspects of the audit of the inventory of Outdoors Products. (For example, the package can be used to read the disk inventory master file and list items and parts with a high unit cost or total value.

Such items can be included in the test counts to increase the dollar coverage of the audit verification.)

(AICPA adapted)

11-63. Greg Jamison, CPA, has audited the financial statements of Melgate Corporation for several years and is making preliminary plans for the audit for the year ended June 30, 1990. During this audit Mr. Jamison plans to use a set of generalized computer audit programs. Melgate's EDP manager has agreed to prepare special tapes of data from company records for the CPA's use with the generalized programs.

The following information is applicable to Mr. Jamison's audit of Melgate's accounts payable and related procedures:

1. The formats of pertinent tapes are on page 458.
2. The following monthly runs are prepared:
   a. Cash disbursements by check number.
   b. Outstanding payables.
   c. Purchase journals arranged (1) by account charged and (2) by vendor.
3. Vouchers and supporting invoices, receiving reports, and purchase order copies are filed by vendor code. Purchase orders and checks are filed numerically.
4. Company records are maintained on magnetic tapes. All tapes are stored in a restricted area within the computer room. A grandfather-father-son policy is followed for retaining and safeguarding tape files.

Required:

a. Explain the grandfather-father-son policy. Describe how files could be reconstructed when this policy is used.
b. Discuss whether company policies for retaining and safeguarding the tape files provide adequate protection against losses of data.
c. Describe the controls that the CPA should maintain over
   1. Preparing the special tape.
   2. Processing the special tape with the generalized computer audit programs.
d. Prepare a schedule for the EDP manager outlining the data that should be included on the special tape for the CPA's audit of accounts payable and related procedures. This schedule should show the
   1. Client tape from which the item should be extracted.
   2. Name of the item of data.

(AICPA adapted)

11-64. A client has established a data processing department for processing its financial applications. The department is relatively small, with personnel consisting of a supervisor, a programmer, a computer operator, and two data entry operators. The following observations were made during the initial stages of the audit:

- The supervisor develops the applications, which includes consulting with the users.
- In some cases the programs are written by the programmer and in other situations programs are purchased from software vendors and customized to accommodate the client's requirements.
- Programs may be defined, developed, or modified on the basis of written

Master File—Vendor Name

Vendor code	Recd type	Space	Blank	Vendor name	Blank	Card code 100

Master File—Vendor Address

Vendor code	Recd type	Space	Blank	Address—line 1	Address—line 2	Address—line 3	Blank	Card code 120

Transaction File—Expense Detail

Vendor code	Recd type	Voucher number	Blank	Batch	Voucher number	Voucher date	Vendor code	Invoice date	Due date	Invoice number	Purchase order number	Debit account	Prd type	Product code	Blank	Amount	Quantity	Card code 150

Transaction File—Payment Detail

Vendor code	Recd type	Voucher number	Blank	Batch	Voucher number	Voucher date	Vendor code	Invoice date	Due date	Invoice number	Purchase order number	Check number	Check date	Blank	Amount	Blank	Card code 170

specifications or oral communication, depending on the complexity or urgency of the requirements.

- The supervisor determines the nature and extent of testing.
- The programmer is responsible for maintaining the operating system software and may operate the computer when the operator is absent.
- The operator is aware of all the computer programs in production status and determines when it is necessary to initiate the production runs.
- The data entry operators convert transactions into machine-readable form through key-driven devices maintained in the data processing department.
- All magnetic disk files are maintained in the computer room where they are directly available to the operator for use on production runs.

Management has stated that since the business is relatively stable, major changes are not likely to occur in either the composition of personnel or the equipment configuration during the next two or three years. Management is content with the organization of the department and feels that the personnel assignments provide a good level of flexibility at a reasonable cost. It also feels that deemphasizing formality, both within and outside the department, results in a significant reduction of administrative cost.

Required:

a. What are some general observations that might be made concerning potential control deficiencies within the computer environment?

b. What are some practical considerations that the auditor must take into account with respect to communicating observations and recommendations to management?

11-65. Jendale is a medium-sized manufacturer that has approximately 1500 customers. Each month the EDP department produces a detailed listing of customers, an aged list of individual accounts, and monthly statements.

Each year, the auditor confirms the accounts receivable. This involves two audit assistants for two days each to

- Add the listing.
- Tie the information on the listing into the balance in the control account.
- Test the individual balances to source documents.
- Select accounts for confirmation.
- Prepare audit working papers.
- Draft confirmation letters.
- Coordinate the typing, proofing, and mailing of the letters.

The partner has requested that you investigate the feasibility of computerizing some of these auditing procedures, all of which are now performed manually. Your generalized audit software package is already loaded on the system.

Required:

a. What information do you need to make a preliminary judgment on the feasibility of using the generalized audit software package? What further information, if any, would you need to prepare the software?

b. Would it be efficient to computerize any or all of these procedures? Why or why not? You should consider the cost and time involved, the usefulness of the technique in performing the procedures, and any possible extra benefits.

11–66. You are the auditor of a large insurance company. Each month the company calculates its earned and unearned income. This calculation is extremely complex, involving a large number of variables. Your audit objective is to ensure that the correct amount of income is recognized.

The company has a large amount of long-term debt outstanding. Interest on the debt is paid every six months. The calculation for the interest payment is extremely simple. Your audit objective is to ensure that the interest payment to individual bondholders is correctly calculated.

Both of these objectives are to be achieved by ensuring the effective operation of the programmed procedures that perform the calculations.

After discussion and investigation, you determine that there are two possible testing techniques.

1. Using test data.
2. Using generalized audit software to simulate processing.

Required:

a. What particular problems are associated with each of the techniques? What additional steps must be performed when they are used?
b. Which technique(s) would you recommend given the particular circumstances and why?

11–67. Ajax, Inc., an audit client, recently installed a new EDP system to process more efficiently the shipping, billing, and accounts receivable records. During interim work, an assistant obtained the understanding of the accounting system and the control procedures. The assistant determined the following information concerning the new EDP system and the processing and control of shipping notices and customer invoices.

Each major computerized function, i.e., shipping, billing, accounts receivable, etc., is permanently assigned to a specific computer operator who is responsible for making program changes, running the program, and reconciling the computer log. Responsibility for the custody of the magnetic tapes and system documentation is randomly rotated among the computer operators on a monthly basis to prevent any one person from having access to the tapes and documentation at all times. Each computer programmer and computer operator has access to the computer room via a magnetic card and a digital code that is different for each card. The systems analyst and the supervisor of the computer operators do not have access to the computer room.

The EDP system documentation consists of the following items: program listing, error listing, logs, and record layout. To increase efficiency, batch totals and processing controls are omitted from the system.

Ajax ships its products directly from two warehouses, which forward shipping notices to general accounting. There, the billing clerk enters the price of the item and accounts for the numerical sequence of the shipping notices. The billing clerk also prepares daily adding machine tapes of the units shipped and the sales amounts. Shipping notices and adding machine tapes are forwarded to the computer department for processing. The computer output consists of:

- A three-copy invoice that is forwarded to the billing clerk, and
- A daily sales register showing the aggregate totals of units shipped and sales amounts that the computer operator compares with the adding machine tapes.

The billing clerk mails two copies of each invoice to the customer and retains the third copy in an open invoice file that serves as a detail accounts receivable record.

Required:

Describe one specific recommendation for correcting each deficiency in control procedures in the new EDP system and for correcting each deficiency or inefficiency in the procedures for processing and controlling shipping notices and customer invoices.

(AICPA adapted)

PART 3

Auditing Specific Cycles and Accounts

12

Auditing the Revenue Cycle

Revenue transactions that are completed within a relatively short time—when sale, delivery, and collection occur within a few weeks or months of each other—are the most common revenue transactions and are the subject of this chapter. Accounts encompassed by the revenue cycle are defined and described. Typical revenue transactions, accounting systems, and control procedures are then presented in detail, followed by a discussion of audit objectives, risk assessment, and the audit testing plan for the revenue cycle. Subsequent sections of the chapter present specific tests of controls and substantive tests that may be used in auditing revenue transactions and related account balances, including auditing procedures for specialized types of revenues.

DEFINITIONS AND ACCOUNTS RELATED TO THE REVENUE CYCLE

Revenues are generally given descriptive labels in financial statements. For example, a manufacturing or retail enterprise calls revenue transactions "sales." On the other hand, revenues in a service organization may be referred to as fees, commissions, rents, royalties, tuition, dues, or even more generally as "revenues" or "service revenues." In governmental or not-for-profit organizations, revenues may be referred to as grants or appropriations; in not-for-profit organizations, they may also be referred to as donations and contributions. Accounts related to ancillary revenue transactions include rents, dividends, interest (including lease finance income), by-product sales, and gains from the sale of nonproduct assets, like property.

Most companies have one or more major sources of revenues and several less significant types of miscellaneous revenues, commonly referred to as "other income." The term used for a given type of revenue usually depends on whether it is derived from one of the enterprise's principal business activities. For example, sales of transformers by an electrical supply company would be "sales," while such transactions would be "other income" to an electric utility. Conversely, interest and dividends from investments would be "other income" to almost all enterprises except investment companies, for which interest and dividends are a primary source of revenues.

If sales of products are the primary source of revenues, certain marketing and collection techniques are often used to increase sales and speed up the collection period. For example, returns may be allowed if the customer is not completely satisfied, or an allowance may be given if the goods are damaged; discounts may be available to customers who pay promptly. Management monitors such policies by establishing accounts for sales discounts, returns, and allowances. Additional techniques often used to increase sales include providing guarantees or warranties.

Numerous balance sheet and income statement accounts are affected by transactions in the revenue cycle. The most significant of these is accounts receivable. Accounts receivable are generally short-term assets, often outstanding for little more than the amount of time needed for sellers and buyers to process transactions—shipping, billing, receiving, processing the invoice for payment, and processing and recording the cash receipt.

Accounts receivable that are completely and accurately recorded may not be fully collectible. Accordingly, the allowance for uncollectible accounts and related bad debt expense accounts are additional accounts in the revenue cycle. Accounts receivable, net of the allowance for uncollectible accounts, provides an estimate of the net realizable value of the receivables. Bad debt expense represents the amount charged to income in the current period for uncollectible accounts. (Other allowance accounts may be necessary if estimated discounts, returns, and allowances are material to the financial statements.)

The unearned revenue and deferred income accounts reflect various kinds of advance receipts for goods and services not yet delivered, such as prepayments from customers for goods to be delivered in the future, advance payments on transportation or entertainment ticket sales, and magazine subscriptions.

T-accounts are presented in Figure 12.1 to illustrate the transactions and accounts encompassed by a typical revenue cycle.

TYPICAL TRANSACTIONS, ACCOUNTING SYSTEMS, AND CONTROL PROCEDURES

The revenue cycle in most contemporary businesses can be divided into three typical classes of transactions.

- Sales of goods and services.
- Payments received for goods and services.
- Goods returned by and claims received from customers.

Sales of Goods and Services

The process of selling goods and services generally includes the following activities:

- Receiving and recording customers' orders.
- Authorizing credit terms and shipments.
- Confirming orders.
- Executing shipping orders for goods or work orders for the performance of services.
- Recording the shipments or services performed.

Figure 12.1 Revenue Cycle Accounts

Balance Sheet Accounts

Cash	
Beginning balance Cash sales Collections from customers Advances by customers	

Accounts Receivable	
Beginning balance Sales on account Ending balance	Payments by customers Return of merchandise Write-off of uncollectible accounts

Allowance for Uncollectible Accounts	
Write-off of uncollectible accounts	Beginning balance Estimated bad debt expense for year Ending balance

Unearned Revenue	
Delivery of goods previously paid for	Beginning balance Advances by customers Ending balance

Income Statement Accounts

Sales	
	Cash sales Sales on account Sales previously paid for

Sales Discounts	
Discounts allowed for prompt payment	

Sales Returns and Allowances	
Return of merchandise	

Bad Debt Expense	
Estimated bad debt expense for year	

Note: Inventory and cost of sales accounts are covered in Chapter 14. Figure 12.1 assumes that the periodic inventory system is used.

In considering the accounting system that processes revenue transactions and the control procedures applied to them, the auditor is interested mainly in procedures to ensure that all sales transactions that actually occurred are authorized and are recorded accurately; that is, that the control objectives of completeness, accuracy, and authorization of transaction processing and files are met. Those control objectives are closely related to the audit objectives of completeness, accuracy, and existence of revenue cycle accounts, particularly sales and accounts receivable. Other control procedures, while not directly related to those audit objectives, may also be of interest to the auditor. For example, the fact that credit checks are performed may provide evidence the auditor can use to evaluate whether the allowance for uncollectible accounts is adequate, which affects the valuation audit objective for accounts receivable.

The paragraphs that follow describe the various activities involved in the sale of goods, and the control procedures typically applied in processing the transactions. (Later sections discuss the audit relevance of those procedures.) Some of the activities described in this section also apply to sales of services, while others, like requisitioning, packing, and shipping, do not. To the extent that the processes are similar for both goods and services, the discussion of control procedures applies to sales of services as well.

Receiving and Recording Customers' Orders. For the selling enterprise, receipt of a customer's order, either by mail, telephone, or other electronic means, starts the revenue cycle. When customer orders are received, they may be logged in a sales order record or similar document, recorded on prenumbered forms, batched for further processing, or, increasingly, entered directly into a computer.

Typically in a computerized environment, an open order file is generated when orders are input. Completeness of input of orders may be ensured by numerical sequencing or controlling batch totals. Completeness of processing of sales orders is then controlled by subsequently matching shipments against open orders and deleting or flagging fully processed orders. In a manual system, completeness of processing of sales orders may be controlled by accounting for the numerical sequence of prenumbered sales order forms, maintaining a holding file of control copies of order forms, and periodically removing fully processed orders. Alternatively, the enterprise could use a sales order record on which orders processed are subsequently noted. In each case, the control procedure consists of periodic review of the sequencing, control totals, open order or holding file, or sales order record by a responsible person. Control procedures designed to ensure completeness of input of customer orders, for example, the use of batch controls, may also help ensure that orders were accurately input.

The objective of control procedures applied to customer orders when they are received is to ensure that all orders received are considered for shipment. Although the absence or ineffectiveness of such control procedures could not result in financial statement misstatements, the auditor may still be interested in the procedures applied to sales orders before shipping orders (described below) are generated. Those procedures may indicate, for example, that management coordinates inventory requirements and production orders with product demand. They may also help ensure that all shipments are recorded; for example, the periodic review and follow-up of open orders should identify shipments that have not yet been recorded, as well as orders not yet shipped.

Authorizing Credit Terms and Shipments. Management establishes procedures to determine how much credit to extend to customers, communicates the information appropriately, revises it periodically, and monitors adherence to established credit limits. In some organizations that perform the credit approval function manually, customers' orders are sent to the credit department before they are recorded. In other entities, authorization takes place after orders have been recorded. Procedures for authorizing credit limits, other terms, and sales prices vary among companies, but certain practices are similar in most credit departments. Orders from repeat customers with a good record of payment, unless in excess of authorized credit limits, are usually routinely processed. Periodically, the credit department determines, by referring to published sources or requesting audited financial statements, that customers' financial condition has not deteriorated. The same means are used to ascertain new customers' creditworthiness. Many companies establish minimum sales order amounts before a credit check will be performed and credit extended. In any event, credit approval is usually evidenced in writing by the credit manager or other designated individual.

Where the authorization process is computerized, the input of sales orders generates a computer match of relevant customer information to master files of predetermined credit limits, other terms, and sales prices. If an order is in excess of the customer's limit or is for a customer not on the system, or if the sales terms or price is outside predetermined limits, a shipping or production order will not be generated and the sales order may not be accepted for further processing. Instead, an exception report will be produced for follow-up by a responsible individual. In some systems the computer also matches sales orders against an inventory master file to ascertain whether the goods are on hand to fill the order.

After all necessary approvals have been obtained, the shipment of goods or the production order is authorized. In a computerized system, when the goods are available for shipping, a shipping order is automatically generated. In a manual system, authorization may be noted on the sales order form or on a shipping order. The authorization process is usually subject to a supervisory control procedure, which in computerized systems covers the initial entry of and changes to predetermined credit limits, terms, and sales prices.

Confirming Orders. Inaccurately transcribed or lost orders can cause customer dissatisfaction and loss of revenues. To avoid errors or misunderstandings, many companies confirm orders with customers. This procedure may simply entail a telephone call or sending the customer a copy of the internally prepared sales order form or a computer-generated confirmation form. In many businesses, the substantial cost of changing or canceling an order after it has been processed makes the confirmation procedure a sound business practice; in other companies, however, order processing time is so short that confirming orders is not practicable.

Executing Shipping Orders. The steps in executing an order for goods are usually requisitioning, packing, and shipping. The instructions for all of those steps may be prepared on one form, or several different forms may be used. The execution instructions may be generated either manually or by computer.

If considerable work is involved in execution, such as fabrication to a customer's specifications, it may be necessary to prepare execution instructions in several stages. For items that are manufactured specifically for customers, work orders may be generated, either manually or by computer, and a file of open work orders maintained for follow-up. For other items, customers' orders may be requisitioned from finished goods inventory, from the factory by means of a production order, or from suppliers by means of a purchase order. The shipping orders are then usually matched against the inventory master file to determine whether the inventory exists to fill the order, or this match may have been done when the orders were received, as mentioned earlier.

In some organizations, a copy of the authorized sales order or a shipping order is used to instruct the various departments involved in physically executing shipments and to evidence the actual shipments. In other organizations, a "picking list" is generated, possibly by computer, and used by the warehouse or production department to gather and prepare orders for shipment. A packing slip or a bill of lading may be used by the shipping department in packing and shipping orders. Whatever form is used to document shipments, it will show the quantity shipped and the initials of the various people responsible for executing the shipment and the dates of their performance. Each department needs enough copies of the instructions to enable it to both advise other relevant departments of its action and retain evidence of performance in its own files.

Completeness of shipments (that is, the recording of all goods shipped) may be ensured by accounting for the numerical sequence of shipping orders or prenumbered bills of lading. An exception report listing outstanding shipping orders would identify authorized orders not yet input as shipped. In a computerized system, executed shipping orders are usually matched to the open order file to ensure that shipments input to the sales transaction file (and inventory master file) contain the quantities that were shipped. In a manual system, a holding file may be used; if execution involves a number of steps, a holding file is preferable because it affords ready access to information on uncompleted transactions. In many systems, it is useful to prepare and partially complete the invoice (described below) as part of preparing the execution instructions; the invoice can then serve as a holding file for the other execution steps. Sometimes invoices are not prepared until requisitioning, packing, and shipping have been completed; then a copy of the shipping order serves as a holding file. Either way, the control procedure consists of periodically matching notices of performance by each of the executing departments against the holding file to discover and investigate uncompleted transactions.

Recording Shipments. The recording of shipments generally initiates the formal recording of sales transactions for accounting purposes. In a computerized system, the input of executed shipping orders to the sales transaction file automatically generates a sales invoice. The control procedures of matching executed shipping orders to the open order file, as previously discussed, and of inputting executed shipping orders only when appropriate supporting documentation (for instance, initialed and dated shipping orders or supporting bills of lading) exists, are designed to ensure the complete and accurate recording of accounts receivable. In a manual system, invoices are authorized by a designated individual who ascertains that the supporting documents—sales and shipping orders and bills of lading, for example—exist and are appropriate.

Since invoices (and the sales transaction file in a computerized system) are the basis for recording sales and accounts receivable, control procedures to ensure that their processing is complete and accurate are imperative. Numerical sequencing is generally used for individual invoices; control totals are used for posting to the accounts receivable control account; and invoices or the sales transaction file is used for posting to the detailed accounts receivable listing (the accounts receivable subledger or subsidiary ledger). A typical control technique used to ensure the completeness of recorded sales transactions is periodic accounting for prenumbered shipping documents and sales invoices, with investigation of unmatched items by a person independent of the shipping and invoicing functions. Many computerized systems produce "missing item," or exception, reports of items like open shipping orders or missing bill of lading numbers, which are used for follow-up. Batch totals can also be used, for example, total units shipped and total units invoiced. Whether manual or automated, the investigation and resolution process is documented and periodically reviewed by supervisory personnel.

The final activity in a sales transaction is updating the general ledger accounts and the detailed accounts receivable listing. In computerized systems, there may be a matching procedure to ensure the completeness and accuracy of updating if the control account and detailed account are updated separately. It is also necessary to ensure that the accounts receivable control account and the detailed accounts receivable listing continue to be in agreement between postings, or transaction updates. A file control procedure commonly used to ensure this is the periodic comparison of the detailed listing with the general ledger control account by a person independent of the invoicing and cash receipts functions, with supervisory review of the comparison.

An inadequately designed accounting system or ineffective control procedures relating to invoicing and updating the accounts can result in critical misstatements. For example,

- Goods shipped but not invoiced could cause an understatement of revenues and accounts receivable.
- Unauthorized transactions could be recorded, causing a possibly uncollectible account.
- Errors on invoices could go undetected, causing an under- or overstatement of revenues and receivables.
- Errors in recording transactions in the detailed and control accounts

could result in the misstatement of related balances. (Errors or delays in posting could also affect the collectibility of receivables.)

If customers detect errors, their confidence in the entity may be adversely affected.

Variations in Typical Sales Transactions. The activities described above are usually necessary, to the extent that they apply, in all sales transactions. Following are some common examples of variations in those activities.

- In over-the-counter retail sales, the above activities may be condensed into a short personal encounter. The customer orders orally, and the clerk accepts the order, reviewing authorized sales terms and often determining the customer's credit standing within the company or at a financial institution, like the issuer of a credit card, via a remote access computer terminal. The sales slip combines all the paperwork, sometimes including the stock withdrawal notice and possibly the reorder notice (or the tag removed from the goods may serve those purposes); the clerk physically executes the sale; the customer pays or the sales slip is forwarded to the billing department or the financial institution for invoicing. The control procedure consists of accounting for the prenumbered sales slips or the cash register tapes and following up on missing items.
- In contract sales, there may be requests for proposals, bid preparation, bidding, and extended contract negotiations.
- In providing continuing services, such as electric or telephone services, the activities are performed once for each customer and execution is continuous thereafter until the customer either cancels the service or fails to pay for it. The revenue process from rents, royalties, and interest is similar. A procedure for periodic reporting of the amount of service delivered is needed to initiate billing.
- In transportation services, billing and collection may come before physical execution and at a different time from the receipt, authorization, and confirmation of the order. A customer buys a ticket or a token and uses it at a later time.

Payments Received for Goods and Services

Payments received for goods and services generally include the following activities:

- Receiving the cash and depositing it in the bank.
- Comparing amounts remitted with recorded amounts.
- Authorizing discounts and allowances.
- Recording cash receipts, discounts, and allowances.

Receiving the Cash and Depositing It in the Bank. Cash may be received by company personnel or directly by the bank. Asset protection is a significant control objective in the receipt stage. The procedures to accomplish this objective will differ depending on whether cash is received by the bank or by the company. Other control procedures applied to cash receipts are similar, regardless of where cash is received.

When cash is received by the company through the mail, it is usually in the form of checks; currency or checks may be received over the counter, by collectors, or by salespeople. Customer remittances received by the bank generally are through a lockbox or a wire transfer.

A lockbox system is a service offered by many banks to reduce cash transit time, thus increasing funds available to the company. Customers send their remittances to a post office box under control of the bank, which records the deposits and furnishes the company with the details. A lockbox provides improved protection of cash receipts because company personnel do not have access to them.

When funds are remitted by wire transfer, no currency or checks are involved. The customer provides details of the transfer (amount and bank account numbers) to its bank, which then executes the transfer. The receiving bank (the bank used by the company) notifies the company of the details of the transfer. Wire transfers are normally used only when large sums of money are being remitted. Cash transit time is significantly reduced; in fact, the funds normally are available for use by the company the same day the transfer is made. As with a lockbox, protection of cash receipts is improved because company personnel do not have access to them.

When cash is received through a lockbox or wire transfer, the bank provides some form of detail of the deposit. This may be remittance advices, statement stubs, or other correspondence from customers; alternatively, it may be a manual or computer-readable listing showing customers' names, amounts, and invoices being paid. This detail is used later to record cash receipts and for performing control procedures designed to ensure their complete and accurate processing.

Cash received by the company by mail is normally delivered from the mail room to an individual (e.g., a cashier) responsible for listing the receipts, endorsing checks, and preparing a deposit ticket. Listing (or, as it is frequently called, "prelisting") the cash receipts is the first step in establishing control over them. The listing usually includes names, amounts, and the invoices being paid (the customer's bill stub is commonly used for that purpose). Receipts over the counter may be listed on cash register tapes or counter sales slips prepared in the presence of customers; cash received from collectors or salespeople and not accompanied by listings is also listed upon receipt. Like the bank's detail of deposits, the company's cash receipts listing is used later to ensure the complete and accurate processing of cash receipts. Prenumbering counter sales slips, cashiers' receipts, and collectors' receipts and subsequently accounting for the numerical sequence help meet the transaction processing control objectives for cash receipts. Preparing the listing of receipts and accounting for the numerical sequence by an individual independent of other cash functions address asset protection, completeness, and accuracy of cash receipts.

Control procedures to ensure protection of cash received by the company include endorsing checks as soon as they are received and promptly depositing them in a bank account. Typically, an endorsement stamp including the notation "For Deposit Only" is used, and each day's cash receipts are deposited intact and without delay by an individual independent of other cash functions. Items not suitable for immediate deposit, like postdated checks or checks containing errors, typically are listed separately from the items ready for deposit, and later the two lists are reconciled with the deposit.

Often, cash is received from more than one source and at various times during the day. If more than one list or batch of cash receipts is prepared in a day, they usually are identified, for example, by batch number. Lists of receipts are totaled, usually at least daily, and the totals are compared with the corresponding deposit slip totals. If receipts flow from a number of sources, such as branch offices, collection departments, cash registers, lockboxes, and wire transfers, typically a control form or checklist is used to highlight missing entries and ensure the prompt reporting and inclusion of receipts from all locations daily.

Deposit or collection items charged back by a bank as uncollectible generally are delivered to and investigated by someone who has no responsibility for either handling or recording cash. Cash receipts of branch offices may be deposited in a bank account subject to withdrawal only by the main office.

Comparing Amounts Remitted with Recorded Amounts. This procedure, if done manually, is generally performed by the person responsible for maintaining the accounts receivable subsidiary ledger. In a computerized system, receipts may be matched against the accounts receivable detail file as they are input to ensure that the entity and its customer agree on the details of the invoice(s) being paid as well as the total amount. An exception report is then generated listing all cash receipts that could not be matched against an open invoice on the accounts receivable file. The comparison, whether performed manually or by computer, identifies credits taken for sales returns or allowances and whether they were authorized. The comparison also discloses whether discounts taken by customers were within the discount period, whether the receipt was applied to the right customer's account, and whether there are any potential disputes about amounts due. It also identifies cash receipts that were inaccurately input or that should not be applied against accounts receivable, for example, receipts from transactions outside the revenue cycle (such as the sale of a fixed asset). In addition, errors in the updating of sales to the accounts receivable file may be identified. For example, if certain sales were not updated to the accounts receivable file, investigation of the unmatched cash receipt would identify the error. Discrepancies, whether identified manually or by a computer match, are investigated and documentation of the resolution and any necessary corrections is reviewed by supervisory personnel.

Authorizing Discounts and Allowances. Discounts and allowances represent noncash reductions of the recorded invoice and receivable amounts. Discounts taken by customers are reviewed to ascertain that they are within the stated terms and for the proper amount. In some companies, discounts are routine, and the approval and recording function is well systematized. In a computerized environment, the discount terms and amount may be matched against the invoice or a master file containing discount information, at the time the cash receipt is input. An exception report of unauthorized discounts taken is generated for follow-up, investigation, and necessary corrections.

Allowances, on the other hand, are less frequent, more difficult to ascertain, and often based on evaluations of customer complaints. Allowances are generally controlled by policies specifying who may authorize them and under what conditions. Forms and reporting procedures are used to establish prompt authorization, approval, and documentation of allowances. Investigation of uncollected receivables may reveal unrecorded allowances.

Nonroutine discounts and allowances taken by customers are usually approved by supervisory personnel independent of people who receive cash and maintain the accounts receivable subsidiary ledger. Documentation of approval is ordinarily noted on prenumbered credit memos whose numerical sequence is reviewed for missing numbers to ensure completeness of input.

Recording Cash Receipts, Discounts, and Allowances. Cash receipts may be recorded before being compared with invoices, after any discounts or allowances taken have been approved, or at the same time as the comparison and identification of any discounts or allowances taken. In any event, the process of recording cash receipts is the same. In a manual system, cash received is generally entered by source (such as cash sale or payment from customer) in a cash receipts journal or other book of original entry that later serves as the basis for posting to the general ledger. The detailed lists prepared when the cash was received are used as the source documents for updating the subsidiary ledgers. In a computerized environment, the detailed listings are normally used as source documents for inputting cash receipts. If the bank provides details of lockbox receipts in machine-readable form, such as magnetic tape, inputting receipts may entail merely loading the tape onto the computer for processing. Typically a daily cash receipts report is generated, listing all receipts input. Once entered, the total cash receipts recorded for the day usually are reconciled to the original listings or batch totals and to authenticated duplicate deposit slips or other bank notices. This reconciliation, normally performed by an individual independent of those who enter the receipts, ensures that all cash receipts have been entered.

The final activity in processing payments for goods and services is updating the general ledger. In a manual system, the totals in the cash receipts journal and approved journal entries for discounts and allowances are posted to the general ledger periodically (usually monthly). When these transactions are processed by computer, the cash receipts file (which may also contain authorized discounts) is used to update the general ledger. The detailed accounts receivable file is relieved when the cash receipts and discounts are input and accepted for processing. Allowances and discounts, when not part of the routine transaction processing, are normally input separately and update the detailed accounts receivable file, if accepted for processing. Numerically sequenced credit memos are generated and the credit memo file is updated. This file is then used to update the general ledger.

Posting to the detailed accounts receivable ledger generally is performed by people independent of cash functions; the general ledger is ordinarily posted by computer or by someone other than the person who updates the accounts receivable subsidiary ledger or file. This segregation of duties meets both authorization and accuracy objectives; its effectiveness is typically ensured by periodic reconciliation of the general ledger to the detailed accounts receivable ledger. Periodic mailing of customer statements also helps ensure that all cash receipts, discounts, and allowances have been accurately recorded.

Goods Returned by and Claims Received from Customers

The third class of transactions in the revenue cycle is the processing of returns and claims. These transactions are often less well controlled than sales or cash receipts transactions: Returns and claims are likely to be sporadic and lacking in common characteristics. Accordingly, establishing control over them as early as possible enhances the achievement of the completeness, accuracy, and authorization control objectives. Since returned goods represent an asset to the company, many of the control procedures described in Chapter 13 for receiving goods are relevant.

Typically, goods returned by customers and the processing of claims are handled in the following steps:

- Receiving and accepting goods or claims.
- Preparing receiving reports.
- Authorizing credits.
- Preparing and mailing credit memos.
- Recording returns and claims.

Receiving and Accepting Goods or Claims. The receiving department handles goods returned for credit. Returned goods may go through the same receiving routine as other receipts of goods or may be processed through a separate receiving area, inspection procedure, and paperwork system. In either case, counting, inspecting, and noting quantities and condition serve as a basis for later determining the credit to give the customer and whether the goods need repair or can be placed back in stock.

Preparing Receiving Reports. Receiving reports typically are used for documenting and establishing control over goods returned. Generally, they are completed when goods are received. They are commonly prepared on prenumbered reports by the receiving department, which is independent of the shipping function. All pertinent data is recorded for later processing. If appropriate, reports may be completed in the presence of the customer to ensure that all customer complaints are recognized. The subsequent control procedure of accounting for the numerical sequence and investigating missing or duplicate receiving reports is performed by people independent of the shipping and receiving functions and is designed to ensure that all goods returned are recorded.

Authorizing Credits. The sales department is generally responsible for final authorization of credits. This approval is based on receiving reports and careful independent and documented inspection of goods, and is evidenced on the receiving and inspection reports. Credit memos initiated by the sales department are usually independently reviewed.

Preparing and Mailing Credit Memos. Credit memos generally are prepared only on the basis of authorized receiving and inspection reports, by individuals (preferably in the sales department) other than those who receive cash and record accounts receivable. Credit memos are usually in numerical sequence, and quantities, terms, prices, and extensions are reviewed for accuracy before mailing, by someone other than the preparer. Listings of credit memos issued, containing all pertinent data, normally are prepared to support the appropriate journal entry and for posting the accounts receivable subsidiary ledger. In a computerized system, credits for returned goods may be processed in the same way as allowances. Approved receiving reports may be used as source documents for computing the credits. Numerically sequenced credit memos are generated, and the accounts receivable file and credit memo file updated.

Recording Returns and Claims. There is a natural inclination to delay the processing of returns and claims; periodic review of the open file of receiving reports is a useful control procedure for identifying unprocessed claims. Understanding the reason for returns may help management determine whether they are a symptom of a problem such as defective production or a malfunctioning order entry system. In addition, achievement of the completeness control objective is enhanced by accounting for the numerical sequence of recorded credit memos, with appropriate follow-up of duplicate or missing items.

DETERMINING THE AUDIT STRATEGY

The audit strategy for each account balance and class of transactions in the revenue cycle is based primarily on the auditor's assessment of inherent and control risk relating to specific audit objectives and on efficiency considerations.

Audit Objectives

The audit objectives applicable to the accounts in the revenue cycle are

Completeness

- Accounts receivable represent all amounts owed to the entity at the balance sheet date arising from sales transactions.
- Unearned revenues represent all amounts received for which shipment or services have not been rendered.
- All shipments or services rendered during the period covered by the financial statements and all returns or allowances provided are reflected in the financial statements.

Accuracy

- Sales transactions are based on correct prices and quantities and are accurately computed and classified in the appropriate general ledger and accounts receivable subsidiary ledger accounts.
- Unearned revenues represent the correct amount received for shipments or services to be rendered in future periods and are classified in the appropriate general ledger account.
- The accounts receivable subsidiary ledger is mathematically correct and agrees with the general ledger.

Existence/Occurrence

- Recorded accounts receivable represent amounts owed to the entity at the balance sheet date.
- Recorded sales transactions represent goods actually shipped or services actually rendered during the period covered by the financial statements.
- Unearned revenues represent amounts received by the entity for future sales transactions.

Cutoff

- Sales transactions, cash receipts, and returns and claims are recorded in the proper period.

Valuation

- Accounts receivable are stated at net realizable value (i.e., net of appropriate allowances for uncollectible accounts, discounts, returns, and similar items).
- Revenue is recognized only when appropriate accounting recognition and measurement criteria are met.

Rights and Obligations

- Accounts receivable are legal rights of the entity at the balance sheet date (i.e., customer accounts that have been sold or factored are excluded from the accounts receivable balance).
- Unearned revenues reflect the amounts received for which the entity is obligated to provide future shipments or services.

Presentation and Disclosure

- Accounts receivable, sales, and related accounts are properly described and classified in the financial statements.
- Accounts receivable pledged as collateral are properly disclosed.

The auditor achieves these objectives by performing substantive tests or a combination of substantive tests and tests of control structure policies and procedures. The auditor frequently tests an entity's control procedures to obtain evidence that they are designed and operating effectively as a basis for significantly reducing the assurance needed from substantive tests directed at the completeness, accuracy, and existence audit objectives. The auditor generally achieves the remaining audit objectives (with the exception of cutoff) by performing substantive tests, supplemented by the evidence obtained through assessing the entity's inherent risk conditions, control environment, and accounting system. For example, the auditor's awareness of an economic decline in an industry in which the entity has many customers may cause concern about the valuation audit objective for accounts receivable.

The auditor usually performs substantive tests to achieve the cutoff objective, because companies frequently do not establish control procedures related to cutoff. In some situations, however, management may implement special control procedures designed to achieve proper cutoff at year-end. The auditor may then decide to test those special control procedures in conjunction with other tests of control structure policies and procedures.

Risk Assessment

As discussed in Chapter 8, the auditor gathers or updates information about various aspects of the client and its business as a basis for assessing inherent and control risk.

Analytical Procedures. Analytical procedures frequently highlight relationships between accounts and risks not otherwise apparent during the risk assessment phase of the audit. Analytical procedures can, for example, indicate trends in sales, returns, and collection of receivables that may assist the auditor in assessing risk. Relationships among revenue accounts and between revenue and other accounts should be reviewed and compared with those of prior periods and those anticipated in budgets or forecasts. Those relationships include the ratios of accounts receivable to sales, various allowance accounts to sales, and cost of goods sold to sales. It may also be useful to relate sales of certain product lines to one another. The ratios and the balances in the accounts themselves are often compared from month to month and with the corresponding period of the prior year. Trends and fluctuations (seasonal and other) should be noted and explanations sought for unusual patterns. Sometimes sales can be related to units sold or produced and the trend of an "average unit price" examined.

The auditor should consider management's performance of analytical procedures as part of its reviews of reports and other internal documentation. The auditor may obtain an understanding of the reviews performed by management and consider using the results of those procedures, to the extent necessary, to supplement his or her own analytical procedures. Management typically reviews various internal sales and budgetary reports and data, such as the following:

- Actual sales compared with historical trends and budgets or forecasts.
- Actual gross margins compared with historical trends and budgets.
- Actual write-offs, credit memos, and other noncash reductions of receivables compared with budgets and historical information.
- Accounts receivable aging.
- Unfilled sales commitments.

Management's review of reports such as these may help identify material misstatements in the processing of sales transactions. For example, investigation of significant differences between reported sales and budgeted and historical sales could identify incomplete updating of shipments to the general ledger.

The way the client responds to the auditor's inquiries resulting from analytical procedures may give some indication of the quality of the client's control environment. For example, prompt, logical, and meaningful answers to questions about fluctuations in gross margins from the prior to the current year would provide some indication, in the absence of evidence to the contrary, that the company's management is "in control" and that the accounting system and control procedures appear to be functioning as intended. Analytical procedures, however, may also indicate trends, even in well-controlled companies, that may lead the auditor to extend substantive tests; for example, trends that raise questions about the collectibility of accounts receivable. Analytical procedures performed as substantive tests are discussed later in this chapter.

Control Risk. The auditor also is required, at a minimum, to obtain an understanding of the entity's control structure sufficient to plan the audit. This understanding is used to identify the types of misstatements that might occur and the risk of their occurring, and to design substantive tests. The understanding is obtained, or updated, by considering previous experience with the entity, reviewing prior-year audit results, interviewing client personnel, observing personnel as they perform their duties, reviewing client-prepared descriptions of policies and procedures, and inspecting documents and records. These procedures normally reveal information about all significant cycles and account balances.

In addition to information about the client's overall control environment, how transactions are processed (manually or by computer) and how sophisticated these systems are, and other general characteristics of the control structure, the auditor should consider the following types of information, as appropriate, related to the revenue cycle:

- The entity's main source(s) of revenues.
- The volume and dollar amount of sales and the number of customers it sells to.
- The usual terms of sales, which would determine when it is proper to record revenue.
- The usual credit and discount terms.
- The flow of revenue cycle transactions through the accounting system.

The auditor should also obtain an understanding of control procedures applied to sales orders, shipping documents, invoices, and cash collections, and the extent to which duties are segregated among the people performing those procedures. Based on all the above information, the auditor determines whether control structure policies and procedures for specific classes of transactions are appropriately designed and have been placed in operation.

In the course of obtaining the understanding of the control structure, the auditor may perform concurrent tests of controls (either incidental or planned) and thereby obtain evidence that control structure policies and procedures have been properly designed and are operating effectively. That evidence would enable the auditor to assess control risk at below the maximum for relevant audit objectives. For example, when inquiring about management's review of sales reports, the auditor may also observe personnel performing the review or examine reports or documents that provide evidence of it. If operating effectively, management's review provides some evidence with respect to the completeness and accuracy of sales. The auditor considers the level of detail reviewed and the likelihood that the reviewer would detect a material misstatement.

The auditor next considers whether he or she wishes to obtain additional evidence of the effectiveness of policies and procedures as a basis for a low assessment of control risk, and then whether such evidence is likely to be available and efficient to obtain. If so, the auditor would usually perform additional tests of controls for specific audit objectives—commonly, completeness, accuracy, and existence/occurrence of accounts receivable and sales.

Audit Testing Plan

As discussed in Chapter 5, the basic audit strategy decision the auditor makes for each significant account balance is whether to perform additional tests of controls to support a low assessed level of control risk for specific audit objectives, or to perform substantive tests directed at all relevant audit objectives, without significant restriction based on tests of controls.

Professional judgment is needed to assess risks and translate that assessment into the various decisions that determine the audit plan. The following two situations describe the testing decisions an auditor might make in developing an appropriate audit strategy for the revenue cycle.

The first situation is a small manufacturing company with a manual accounting system for sales and cash receipts. The volume of transactions is low. Customer orders are received by phone by the sales clerk, who prepares an order form containing the customer's name and address, item, quantity, and price. The sales clerk retains a copy of the order and forwards the original to the controller for credit approval. The sales clerk's copies of the orders are used to total the orders received each day. This information is used by the sales manager to track performance and anticipate sales volumes. The company does not have formal control procedures to ensure that all approved orders are shipped. It does not consider such procedures necessary because of the low volume of sales and the fact that there has never been a problem with lost orders.

The controller approves orders for shipment by initialling them. Unless the customer has a poor payment history or a large accounts receivable balance outstanding, credit is extended. The order is then forwarded to the warehouse for shipment. The warehouse employees prepare a numerically sequenced packing slip, and package and ship the goods. A copy of the packing slip, with the original order attached, is forwarded to the accounts receivable clerk in the accounting department. The clerk prepares an invoice (using numerically sequenced forms) and records the sale in the sales journal and accounts receivable subsidiary ledger. Periodically the clerk accounts for the numerical sequence of the packing slips to identify any shipments that were not invoiced. The invoice package (invoice, packing slip, and order) is reviewed by the controller before being mailed to the customer.

Customer remittances are received by mail. The mail is opened by the receptionist, who prepares the bank deposit slip and a listing (showing customer's name, invoice being paid, and amount) of the day's remittances, attaching the customer remittance advices. The deposit slip and checks are given to the controller, who makes the daily deposit. The listing, with the remittance advices, is given to the accounts receivable clerk, who records the remittances in the cash receipts journal and accounts receivable subsidiary ledger.

At the end of the month, the accounts receivable clerk summarizes the sales journal and cash receipts journal and prepares the monthly entries to the general ledger. The controller reviews the subsidiary ledgers and approves the general ledger entries. The controller's review consists of scanning the subsidiary ledgers to account for the numerical sequencing of invoices and determine that an entry was made each business day. An accounting clerk posts the general ledger entries and prepares the financial statements for the controller's review. This clerk also performs the monthly bank reconciliation and reconciles the accounts receivable subsidiary ledger to the general ledger; the controller then reviews the reconciliations. The sales and production managers review the financial statements and identify any unexpected results.

In this situation, the auditor, based on his or her understanding of the control structure and any concurrent tests of controls performed, would probably assess control risk at below the maximum and decide not to perform additional tests of controls. Substantive tests of details would be directed at all assertions. In addition to the substantive tests described later in the chapter, the auditor might need to perform additional tests with respect to the accuracy of accounts receivable and sales. Those tests might include tracing prices to approved price lists, determining that the account classifications are proper, and ascertaining that the posting to the subsidiary and general ledgers was done correctly. The tests of details would be performed as of year-end.

The above strategy decisions are based on the following factors:

- Low transaction volume, which makes substantive testing efficient.
- Manual accounting system, which increases the risk of random errors.
- Limited control procedures; for example, no control procedure that addresses accuracy of input, and no independent review to determine that all shipments have been approved by the controller.

The auditor's decision might have been different if the company had

- A higher volume of transactions.

- A computerized accounting system that used packaged software developed and maintained by third-party vendors.
- Increased segregation of duties, for example, if the person responsible for accounting for the numerical sequencing of packing slips and investigating missing items were independent from the clerk who recorded sales.
- Effective transaction processing and file control procedures; for example, matching of shipments to an open order file, investigation of unmatched items by accounting clerks, and investigation of long-outstanding orders by the sales department.

In those circumstances, the auditor might have decided to perform additional tests of control procedures to reduce the assurance needed from substantive tests for the completeness, accuracy, and possibly existence audit objectives.

In the second situation, the client is a large manufacturing company with a computerized accounting system for sales and cash receipts. The company has a large highly skilled EDP department with effective general control procedures and division of duties. The EDP department typically develops software internally, but sometimes modifies packaged software. Control procedures for implementing new systems, maintaining existing systems, and the operations functions are effective, as are program and data file security control procedures. (These general control procedures are discussed in detail in Chapter 11.) Control procedures applied to sales and cash receipts are designed to ensure that authorized transactions are completely and accurately input and updated.

In this situation, the auditor will likely have performed tests of controls concurrently with obtaining an understanding of the control structure. The auditor is also likely to consider it efficient to perform additional tests of controls relating to the completeness, accuracy, and authorization control objectives for sales and cash receipts transactions, as a basis for assessing control risk as low. If the additional tests of controls support a low assessment of control risk, substantive tests directed at the completeness, accuracy, and existence audit objectives could be reduced. (Except for the need to confirm some receivables as required by GAAS, they might even be limited to analytical procedures.) The auditor would be likely to perform any tests of details prior to year-end.

ADDITIONAL TESTS OF CONTROLS

Concurrent tests of controls often provide evidence to support an assessment of control risk at below the maximum for one or more audit objectives. However, concurrent tests of controls are generally directed mainly at policies and procedures that are part of the control environment and accounting system, as opposed to specific control procedures, and therefore usually relate to several audit objectives and affect several accounts. Thus, concurrent tests of controls are not enough to support a low assessment of control risk for specific audit objectives and account balances. To assess control risk as low for one or more audit objectives for some or all revenue cycle accounts, the auditor performs additional tests of controls. Such tests usually require substantial audit effort, and therefore the auditor generally performs them only when he or she believes they will significantly reduce the amount of substantive testing required.

Specific control objectives and typical control procedures applicable to sales of goods and services and to payments received for them are described in Figures 12.2 and 12.3, respectively. The accounting system assumed to be in operation in the figures is a sophisticated computerized system. As discussed in Chapter 8, the tests of controls that the auditor would perform include an appropriate combination of inquiring about the client's control procedures, observing that the procedures have been placed in operation, and examining evidence that they are designed and operating effectively. Also as discussed in Chapter 8, reperformance may be used in tests of controls; but if that becomes necessary, the auditor usually determines it is more efficient to perform substantive tests. In addition to testing control procedures specific to a particular transaction cycle, in order to assess control risk as low the auditor would also need evidence of the effectiveness of general control procedures.

The third class of transactions in the revenue cycle, goods returned by and claims received from customers, is usually less significant than sales and payments received. Accordingly, additional tests of controls generally are not performed. If return transactions were significant, however, the auditor might perform additional tests of controls like the following:

Inquire about and observe

- Control procedures designed to ensure that all goods returned by customers are appropriately documented.
- Procedures for accounting for the numerical sequence of documents supporting goods returned by customers, claims made, and credit memos, including the way errors are investigated and resolved.
- Procedures for authorizing adjustments to the account.

Examine the following documents or reports to support inquiries and observations:

- Receiving reports.
- Credit memos.
- Exception reports for missing or duplicate items.

When performing tests of controls, the auditor should be aware of audit objectives other than completeness, accuracy, existence, and cutoff that may be affected by those tests. An audit objective frequently considered when testing controls in the revenue cycle is valuation. When tests of controls are performed, the auditor usually tests credit department approval procedures; the results of those tests help in evaluating the client's allowance for uncollectible accounts. For example, amounts due from sales made to potentially high-credit-risk customers close to year-end would be classified as "current" in the accounts receivable aged trial balance, which normally would not indicate a potential collection problem. In the absence of control procedures relating to granting credit, however, the auditor may consider it necessary to test the collectibility of "current" receivables. The auditor might do this by extending the review of collections in the post-balance-sheet period.

In evaluating the results of tests of controls (including tests of general control procedures), the auditor considers whether the control structure policies and procedures, taken as a whole, are appropriately designed to achieve the control objectives and are operating effectively. This will determine whether the expected assessment of control risk as low was attained for specific accounts and audit objectives and, thus, whether the auditor can significantly reduce substantive testing. Results differing from those anticipated when developing the audit testing plan require the auditor to reconsider the nature, timing, and extent of planned substantive tests—not only for revenue cycle accounts, but also for other accounts that may be affected. For example, ineffective control procedures to ensure completeness of recorded sales may also affect inventory and cost of sales.

SUBSTANTIVE TESTS

If the auditor has assessed control risk for some or all revenue cycle accounts as low for specific audit objectives, substantive tests addressing those audit objectives may, except for the need to confirm some accounts receivable, be limited to analytical procedures. The auditor will also consider whether evidence obtained from tests directed at other audit objectives is relevant to these audit objectives too. For example, the confirmation of accounts receivable is directed toward the existence audit objective, but provides some evidence about accuracy as well. Control risk is seldom assessed as low with respect to the cutoff, valuation, rights and obligations, and presentation and disclosure objectives, and therefore substantive tests of details are usually performed for these objectives.

Accounts Receivable

Before performing substantive tests directed toward the other audit objectives, the auditor should be reasonably assured that the accounts receivable trial balance contains all sales transactions that remain uncollected at year-end. If the results of tests of controls provide evidence about the completeness of the

Figure 12.2 Sales of Goods and Services

	Control Objectives					
	Transaction Processing					
	Authorization	*Completeness of Input*	*Accuracy of Input*	*Completeness and Accuracy of Updating*[a]	*File*	*Asset Protection*
Specific Control Objectives	All recorded sales transactions represent actual shipments of goods or rendering of services to nonfictitious customers of the entity and are approved.	All sales transactions are input and accepted for processing.	Sales are correctly recorded as to amounts, quantities, dates, and customers; are recorded in the proper period; are accurately converted into computer-readable form; and are accurately input to the computer.	All sales transactions input and accepted for processing are accurately updated to the sales and accounts receivable data files.	The integrity of individual accounts receivable in the subsidiary ledger and the general ledger accounts receivable and sales accounts, after sales transactions have been accumulated in them, is preserved.	Only authorized personnel have access to accounts receivable records or data stored on them.
Typical Control Procedures	Reporting and resolving orders rejected because customers, prices, or credit or other terms were not contained on, or were outside the preestablished limits on, customer and	Accounting for the numerical sequence of shipping or work orders input to the computer. Determining that a sales invoice was generated for each executed ship-	Completeness of input control procedures for shipping or work orders also address the accuracy of input for quantities and descriptions. Mailing of customer state-	Comparing total sales input with the total updated to the sales and accounts receivable files.	Ensuring that the correct version of the file is being used for processing. Balancing of the subsidiary ledger (previous balance plus sales less receipts, compared with the	Restricting access to accounts receivable files and files used in processing receivables.

price master files. Approving changes to master files for customers, terms, credit limits, and sales prices. Approving new customers on the files or changed customer information, such as shipping address or billing address.	ping or work order. Reporting and resolving missing, unmatched, or duplicate shipping orders or invoices by individuals independent of shipping functions. Reporting and resolving long-outstanding items on the open shipping or work order file. Resolving reports of executed shipping and work orders rejected as not matching against the open file by individuals independent of shipping functions.	ments, and investigating and resolving disputes or inquiries, by individuals independent of the invoicing function.		current total). Reconciling the subsidiary ledger to the control account in the general ledger. Reporting and resolving discrepancies.

[a]Completeness of updating and accuracy of updating have been combined, because typically the same control procedures apply to both objectives.

Figure 12.3 Payments Received for Goods and Services

	Control Objectives					
	Transaction Processing					
	Authorization	*Completeness of Input*	*Accuracy of Input*	*Completeness and Accuracy of Updating*[a]	*File*	*Asset Protection*
Specific Control Objectives	All cash receipts from customers are approved for application against specified invoices.	All payments received are input and accepted for processing.	Receipts are correctly recorded as to amounts, dates, and customers; are recorded in the proper period; are accurately converted into computer-readable form; and are accurately input to the computer.	All receipts input and accepted for processing are accurately updated to the cash receipts and accounts receivable data files.	The integrity of individual accounts receivable in the subsidiary ledger and the general ledger accounts receivable and cash accounts, after receipts have been updated to them, is preserved.	Only authorized personnel have access to receipts and accounts receivable records or data stored on them. Receipts are promptly deposited in the entity's bank account.
Typical Control Procedures	Reporting and resolving differences as to the appropriate invoice being paid.	Prelisting of cash received. Comparing bank advice (e.g., validated deposit slip)	Reporting and resolving cash receipts not matched against an unpaid invoice on	Comparing total cash input with the totals updated to the cash receipts and accounts	Same control procedures as described in Figure 12.2, "Sales of Goods and	Receiving and prelisting cash by individuals independent of recording cash receipts.

Reporting and resolving differences as to the amount of the receipt and the amount of the invoice.	with the total of the prelistings and the total receipts input, by individuals independent of receiving, prelisting, or recording cash receipts. Investigation of past-due receivables by individuals independent of receiving or recording cash receipts.	the accounts receivable subsidiary ledger by individuals independent of other receipt functions. Mailing of customer statements, and investigating and resolving disputes or inquiries, by individuals independent of receiving or recording cash receipts, posting to the accounts receivable subsidiary ledger, or authorizing write-offs of receivables.	receivable files.	Services.'' Reconciling the bank statement to the general ledger cash account by personnel independent of receiving and recording cash receipts (and of accounts payable and cash disbursements functions).	Restrictive endorsement of checks on receipt. Deposit of receipts intact daily. Individuals involved in the receipt and deposit function are not authorized check signers. Restricted access to accounts receivable files and files used in processing cash receipts.

[a]Completeness of updating and accuracy of updating have been combined, because typically the same control procedures apply to both objectives.

trial balance, substantive tests of the completeness of accounts receivable will generally be limited to analytical procedures, as discussed later in this chapter.

To achieve the cutoff objective, it is often more efficient for the auditor to perform substantive tests of details, particularly in the case of those companies that are not concerned about precise cutoffs on a month-to-month basis. Companies may, however, implement special control procedures at the end of the year (or possibly quarterly if quarterly earnings are published), which the auditor may decide to test. Also, control structure policies and procedures designed to ensure completeness of input and update may be effective in ensuring that transactions are recorded in the proper period. For example, the design of the accounting system itself may reduce control risk for cutoff.

Cutoff Tests of Shipments and Collections. Cutoff tests are intended to ascertain that all significant transactions have been recorded in the proper period. In the absence of control structure policies and procedures directed toward cutoff, the sooner accounts are closed after year-end, the greater the likelihood that there will be unrecorded sales invoices. Thus, examining files of unmatched shipping reports and unrecorded invoices, the sales journal, the cash receipts journal, and other relevant records for a period after year-end is an almost universal auditing procedure.

If the basic transaction documents are in numerical sequence, the auditor can note the number of the last shipping report and the last sales invoice recorded and also compare the date of the last entry in the cash receipts journal with the date those receipts were deposited in the bank. For clients that do not perform a wall-to-wall inventory at year-end, the auditor may examine perpetual inventory records, the sales journal, and the listing of unmatched shipping reports for evidence that goods sold and shipped before year-end have been removed from inventory. The auditor should apply the same procedures to obtain assurance that sales, shipments, and cash receipts applicable to the following year were not recorded in the year under audit. If the basic transaction documents are not prenumbered, it may be necessary to examine supporting documents for transactions with near-year-end dates and large amounts, selected from the sales journal, cash receipts journal, perpetual inventory records, and shipping reports both before and after the cutoff date to obtain sufficient evidence that the cutoff was properly made.

Cutoff tests of shipments are usually coordinated with the auditor's observation of the client's physical inventory count. When physical inventories are taken at a date other than year-end, it is important that shipment cutoff tests be made at the same date. Cutoff errors are compounded when perpetual inventory records and the general ledger inventory account are adjusted for differences between book and physical amounts (see Chapter 14, "Auditing the Production Cycle, Cost of Sales, and Inventory Balances").

Confirming Accounts Receivable. One of the most widely used substantive tests for determining the existence and, to a lesser extent, the accuracy of accounts receivable is direct communication by the auditor with customers, commonly referred to as ''confirmation.'' Confirmation by the auditor of individual sales transactions or accounts receivable balances by direct communication with customers is one of only a few procedures that are designated as ''generally accepted auditing procedures.'' Statement on Auditing Standards (SAS) No. 1 (AU Section 331.01 and .03) states

> Confirmation of receivables and observation of inventories are generally accepted auditing procedures. The independent auditor who issues an opinion when he has not employed them must bear in mind that he has the burden of justifying the opinion expressed.
>
> Confirmation of receivables requires direct communication with debtors either during or after the period under audit; the confirmation date, the method of requesting confirmations, and the number to be requested are determined by the independent auditor. Such matters as the effectiveness of internal control structure policies and procedures, the apparent possibility of disputes, inaccuracies or irregularities in the accounts, the probability that requests will receive consideration or that the debtor will be able to confirm the information requested, and the materiality of the amounts involved are factors to be considered by the auditor in selecting the information to be requested and the form of confirmation, as well as the extent and timing of his confirmation procedures.

Confirmation of receivables has been required by the profession since 1939, when Statement on Auditing Procedure No. 1 was adopted by the AICPA as a direct result of the McKesson & Robbins fraud. In the intervening years, confirmation has been the subject of extensive authoritative and other professional pronouncements. As discussed in Chapter 5, evidence obtained from third parties, such as confirmation of accounts receivable, is generally more reliable than evidence obtained from within the entity. However, confirmation is only one substantive procedure among several, just as substantive tests produce one kind of audit evidence among several.

Auditors should not blindly accept confirmation replies; they should be aware that many traditional auditing procedures, including confirming receivables, do not in all circumstances produce the assurance they were intended to provide. In its *Report, Conclusions, and Recommendations*, the Commission on Auditors' Responsibilities (Cohen Commission) pointed out that ''. . . in several cases, outsiders either ignored incorrect information that was clearly shown in confirmations or actively cooperated with management in giving incorrect confirmation'' (p. 40).

Moreover, while confirmation produces evidence about the existence and (to some extent) the accuracy of accounts receivable, other procedures are needed to establish their collectibility. The most direct evidence regarding collectibility of receivables is subsequent customer payments. Those payments also provide reliable evidence about existence and accuracy, because it is highly unlikely that a customer will pay a balance that is not owed or is overstated.

Only the accuracy of the date the sale took place is not substantiated by a subsequent customer payment. Confirmation may, however, reveal the improper application of customer payments to older, disputed invoices, perhaps to conceal an unfavorable aging schedule. In practice, the auditor often uses a combination of confirmation, examination of subsequent customer payments, and other procedures to test the existence and accuracy of accounts receivable.

The auditor must make a decision regarding the confirmation date. If there were no deadline for the client to issue financial statements, confirming at year-end would be most effective. In today's business environment, however, there is usually a deadline, and accordingly the auditor often confirms receivables (and performs many other auditing procedures as well) at an earlier date. If early substantive testing is done, the auditor will have to obtain satisfaction that the risk of material misstatement occurring is low during the intervening period, as discussed in Chapter 9.

Substantive tests sometimes provide evidence about control structure policies and procedures, if errors or irregularities disclosed by those tests are investigated and found to result from a control deficiency or breakdown. Specifically, confirmation procedures may provide evidence of control structure effectiveness with respect to the revenue cycle. Accordingly, many auditors consider receivable confirmations as a source of evidence about the effectiveness of the control structure as well as a source of evidence about the existence and accuracy of accounts receivable.

Confirmation Procedures

Before selecting accounts for confirmation, the auditor should be sure the accounts receivable trial balance reconciles to the related control account. Normally the client routinely compares general ledger control account balances with the totals of individual accounts receivable, investigates discrepancies between the two, and makes appropriate adjustments. The auditor should compare the accounts receivable trial balance with the general ledger account and test the arithmetical accuracy of the trial balance (which is often done using audit software) or should test general control procedures for evidence that the trial balance is mathematically accurate. Reasons for recurring discrepancies between the control account and subsidiary ledger should be investigated.

The paragraphs below describe the procedures involved in confirming receivables.

Selecting Accounts for Confirmation. Depending on the audit testing plan and the results of tests of controls, the auditor should decide whether all or only part of the accounts should be confirmed and, if the latter, the basis for selecting them. The selection should exclude debtors from whom replies to requests for confirmation cannot reasonably be expected, such as certain governmental agencies, foreign concerns, and some large industrial and commercial enterprises that use an open invoice or decentralized accounts payable processing system that makes confirmation impracticable.

An experienced auditor usually confirms accounts that appear unusual. Accounts with zero or credit balances should also be considered for confirmation. A credit balance suggests the possibility of an incorrect entry, especially if control structure policies and procedures are not effective.

To preserve the integrity of the confirmation process, the auditor should control the selection, preparation, mailing, and return of the confirmations. If the client does not wish statements or confirmation requests to be sent to certain debtors, the auditor should be satisfied that there is an adequate reason before agreeing to omit them. If such accounts are material, the auditor should use alternative procedures to obtain satisfaction that the accounts exist and are accurate. If the results of the alternative procedures are satisfactory, the client's request not to confirm directly would not be considered a scope limitation.

Processing Confirmation Requests. After selecting the accounts for confirmation, the auditor should observe the procedures below in processing the requests. They are applicable to both negative and positive confirmations (which are described and compared in later sections of this chapter).

- Names, addresses, and amounts shown on statements of accounts selected for confirmation or on the confirmation letters should be compared with the debtors' accounts and reviewed for reasonableness.
- The auditor should maintain control over confirmations until they are mailed; this does not preclude assistance from appropriate client personnel, under the auditor's supervision.
- Requests for confirmation, together with postage-paid return envelopes addressed to the auditor, should be mailed in envelopes showing the auditor's address as the return address. If the client objects to using the auditor's address, returns may be addressed to the client at a post office box controlled by the auditor; the post office should be directed to forward mail to the auditor after the box is surrendered.
- All requests should be mailed by the auditor; the client's mail room may be used for mechanical processing under the control of the auditor, who should deposit the completed requests at the post office.
- Undelivered requests returned by the post office should be investigated, corrected addresses obtained, and the requests remailed by the auditor.

The purpose of those procedures is not so much to protect against possible fraud on the part of the client (although that possibility is clearly implied) as to preserve the integrity of the confirmation procedure. The audit evidence obtained from confirmation is less reliable if there is the possibility of accidental or purposeful interference with direct communication with debtors; the auditor should take all reasonable steps to minimize that possibility.

Negative Confirmations. A negative confirmation is a request that a debtor communicate directly with the auditor only if the statement balance is considered in any way incorrect. It is most frequently used for clients with a large number of low-value accounts. Since debtors are asked to reply only if they wish to report differences, the auditor may conclude, in the absence of any reason to believe the contrary, that no reply signifies a debtor's acceptance of the balance.

Figure 12.4 Positive Confirmation Letter

[Name and Address of Debtor]

Dear Sirs:

In accordance with the request of our auditors [name and address of auditors], we ask that you kindly confirm to them your indebtedness to us at [date] which, according to our records, amounted to [amount].

If the amount shown is in agreement with your records, please so indicate by signing in the space provided below and return this letter directly to our auditors in the enclosed envelope. Your prompt compliance will facilitate the examination of our accounts.

If the amount is not in agreement with your records, please inform our auditors directly of the amount shown by your records, with full details of differences.

Remittances should not be sent to the auditors.

Very truly yours,

[Name of Client]

The above stated amount is correct as of [date].

____
[Debtor of Client]

____
[Title or Position]

It is important to impress on debtors the necessity for communicating directly with the auditor when discrepancies exist. If the auditor has reason to believe that the negative form of confirmation request will not receive consideration, sending out that form of confirmation request does not constitute compliance with generally accepted auditing standards. In that respect, SAS No. 1 (AU Section 331.05) states, in part,

> The negative form is useful particularly when the assessed level of control risk is low, when a large number of small balances are involved, and when the auditor has no reason to believe the persons receiving the requests are unlikely to give them consideration. If the negative rather than the positive form of confirmation is used, the number of requests sent or the extent of the other auditing procedures applied to the receivable balance should normally be greater in order for the independent auditor to obtain the same degree of satisfaction with respect to the accounts receivable balance.

If statements of account are not ordinarily mailed at the time confirmations are requested, or if statements are not to be sent to debtors, the auditor may send a letter form of request. With appropriate changes of language to express the negative form, the positive confirmation letter shown in Figure 12.4 may be used.

If statements are sent to debtors, they may be rubber-stamped or have a sticker affixed reading somewhat as follows:

PLEASE EXAMINE THIS STATEMENT CAREFULLY.

If it is not correct, please write promptly, using the enclosed envelope and giving details of all differences, to our auditors,

[Name and Address of Auditors],

who are now making their periodic audit of our accounts.

Unless you promptly report a difference to our auditors, they will assume that you consider the statement to be correct.

Remittances should not be sent to the auditors.

It should be noted that the request is worded as coming from the client. Even though the auditor drafts the request, prepares it, and selects the accounts, all confirmation requests should be made in the client's name because the relationship exists between client and customer and information about it should not be given out to a third party without the client's authorization.

Depending on the circumstances of an engagement, negative confirmation requests may be supplemented by requests for positive confirmations, particularly of larger balances.

Positive Confirmations. A positive confirmation is a request that a debtor reply directly to the auditor stating whether the account balance is correct. Positive confirmations may be used for all accounts, a sample of accounts, or selected accounts, such as those with larger balances, those representing unusual or isolated transactions, or others for which an auditor needs greater specific assurance of existence and accuracy. The positive form of confirmation is called for if there are indications that a substantial number of accounts may be in dispute or inaccurate or if the individual receivable balances are unusually large or arise from sales to a few major customers. The request may be conveyed by a letter or directly on the statement by means of a rubber stamp or sticker. To facilitate replies, a postage-paid envelope addressed to the auditor should be enclosed.

Because the form of the request specifically asks for a reply, an auditor may not assume that failure to reply means the debtor agrees with the stated balance. Second requests should be sent, and sometimes third requests by registered mail. Replies to "positive" requests may be facilitated if the auditor furnishes the details of the individual items included in the balances, usually by providing a copy of the client's detailed customer statement. That may be particularly helpful if the debtor's accounting system does not readily permit identification of account balances. If the auditor fails to receive positive confirmation, alternative auditing procedures should be employed, as described later in the chapter.

It is impracticable for an auditor to determine the genuineness or authenticity of signatures on replies to confirmation requests. If the client has appropriate control structure policies and procedures, particularly with respect to the acceptance of customer orders, and if the auditor has considered the reasonableness of the addresses on the confirmations, signature authenticity is usually not a concern. If, however, the auditor has determined that the risk of material misstatement in a particular customer account is high, the client should be asked to request an officer of the debtor to sign the confirmation reply. The auditor may then wish to communicate with that officer by telephone or other means to corroborate the authenticity of the confirmation.

Experience has shown that a form of positive request, whether made by letter or a sticker affixed to the statement, that requires a minimum of effort on the part of the recipient produces more responses. The letter form, illustrated in Figure 12.4, is designed so that, when the amount shown agrees with the debtor's records, the individual need only sign in the space provided and return the letter in the envelope enclosed with the request.

If statements of account prepared by the client are to be used for positive confirmation requests, they may be sent in duplicate, with an appropriately worded request (often imprinted on the statement) that the debtor acknowledge the correctness of the statement by returning the duplicate, duly signed, directly to the auditor. A variation is the use of a monthly statement in which the balance and the name of the debtor appear in two places, separated by perforations. One part may be torn off, signed by the debtor, and returned directly to the auditor.

Confirmation Procedures as Affected by Certain Accounting Systems. Replies to confirmation requests are sometimes difficult to obtain if a debtor's accounts payable processing is decentralized or uses an open invoice system, which is increasingly the case in a number of governmental departments and agencies as well as many large industrial and commercial enterprises. In an open invoice system, the debtor processes invoices individually and does not summarize them by vendor. Therefore, the debtor can identify whether or not an individual invoice has been paid, but cannot determine the total amount owed to any particular vendor. In many instances, however, such difficulties can be overcome with care and ingenuity; for example, an auditor may supply details of the balance to be confirmed, such as invoice dates, numbers (including customer purchase order numbers), and amounts, or may confirm specific transactions rather than an account balance.

The auditor can often make effective use of a client's computerized accounts receivable system. Sample selection can be programmed and the files of detail accounts searched automatically, lists and analyses can be prepared, and the confirmation request can be printed. General-purpose computer programs designed to aid in the confirmation process are available and are discussed in Chapter 11.

Exceptions to Confirmation Requests. Exceptions disclosed by the confirmation process should be carefully scrutinized by the auditor. The auditor should evaluate all exceptions and decide whether they represent isolated situations (such as a customer's not receiving goods, the client's not receiving a payment, or the wrong customer's being credited for a payment) or indicate a pattern of disputed sales or payments involving more than one customer. Debtors' responses indicating that payments were sent but not recorded by the client may signal misappropriations of cash and "lapping" of receivables (discussed below). If so, the situation should be thoroughly investigated to determine the amount of the misappropriation, and receivables should be reduced (since the client received the payment) and a loss recorded in the amount of the misappropriation. In addition, the auditor should bring the matter to management's attention and should consider its effect on his or her other auditing procedures.

In many instances, differences reported by debtors on accounts receivable confirmation requests do not have audit significance. Those differences are generally the result of either payments in transit at the confirmation date or delays in recording goods received by the debtor. The auditor should corroborate debtor assertions involving those kinds of differences by examining the cash receipts records and remittance advices for debtor payments received after the confirmation date to determine that the payments were for receivables existing at the confirmation date, and by examining bills of lading or other evidence of shipment. (Differences that are appropriately reconciled in this manner are not exceptions.) Those procedures are often performed on a sample basis. Other reported exceptions, usually involving small amounts, may result from disputes over allowances, discounts, shipping charges, or returned merchandise. These exceptions are usually neither material in amount nor indicative of serious deficiencies in the control structure. After the auditor has made a copy or other record for control purposes, investigation of replies may properly be turned over to a responsible client employee whose regular responsibilities do not involve cash, receivables, or credit functions. The auditor should review the employee's findings and, if considered necessary, perform additional procedures to obtain satisfaction about the balance.

Procedures in Lieu of Confirmation

If replies to confirmation requests cannot reasonably be expected or if the number and character of replies to positive confirmation requests are not satisfactory, the auditor should try to obtain satisfaction about the existence and accuracy of receivable balances by alternative procedures. These include examining relevant contracts, shipping documents, and subsequent cash receipts as evidence that the customer has received the shipment.

Lapping

Lapping is a way of concealing a cash shortage by manipulating credits to the accounts receivable subsidiary ledger. To accomplish lapping, an employee must have access to incoming cash receipts, the cash receipts records, and the detailed accounts receivable records. Accordingly, if there is not appropriate segregation of duties, the auditor should consider the possibility of lapping and other irregularities.

Lapping is perpetrated in the following manner: An employee receives a customer's payment on an account receivable and misappropriates the cash, recording neither the cash receipt nor the reduction of the customer's account. Subsequent cash collections from another customer are later credited to the customer from whom the original collection was misappropriated, to prevent that customer's paid account from appearing as outstanding for more than a short time. Lapping is made easier when customers make periodic payments on their accounts, particularly in round amounts, rather than pay for specific invoices. Even if customers designate that remittances apply to specific invoices, the difference in amount between the second customer's remittance and the amount misappropriated from the first customer's remittance can be concealed by depositing additional cash if the subsequent payment is smaller or by making an additional credit to the first account, or even another account, if the subsequent payment is larger. Obviously, the lapping must continue indefinitely or until the cash shortage is replenished. Accordingly, the auditor should inquire about employees who are rarely absent from work or who do not take vacations that would require someone else to perform their work.

Control structure policies and procedures that should prevent or detect lapping include proper segregation of duties, required vacations for personnel responsible for handling cash and posting credits to customer accounts, mailing monthly statements to customers that show all activity in the accounts by dates, and reviewing entries to customers' accounts for unusual amounts.

The confirmation process, including careful attention to client explanations for delays in posting remittances when a customer states that the amount to be confirmed was paid before the confirmation date, should reveal lapping if it is present. If lapping is strongly suspected, the auditor may want to perform additional procedures. For example, comparing customer remittance advices with credits in the accounts receivable subsidiary ledger, individual amounts on deposit slips with individual amounts posted to the cash receipts records, and individual amounts in the cash receipts records with credits to individual customer accounts (in each case, scrutinizing the dates of the entry or posting) may also uncover lapping. The auditor should be aware, however, of the possibility of altered bank deposit slips and may wish to confirm the accuracy of individual deposit slips with banks.

Tests for Valuation

To achieve the valuation audit objective, the auditor should review the collectibility of receivable balances to determine that the client's allowance for uncollectible accounts is adequate, that is, that receivables are stated at their net realizable value as of the balance sheet date. Before making the review, the auditor should determine whether the client's method of estimating the allowance is reasonable and consistent with prior years and, if so, whether any current business or economic conditions might make the method inappropriate in the current year. For example, if the client estimates an allowance for uncollectible accounts based on the historical relationship of write-offs to total sales (percent of sales method), a significant economic downturn may require a revision of the historical percentage. That same circumstance may also make it inappropriate to develop an allowance for uncollectible accounts by applying historical percentages to groupings of an aged trial balance. For example, usually only a small percentage of accounts receivable less than 30 days old become uncollectible; however, a large percentage of those balances may have to be considered in developing the allowance if the customer mix has changed in a time of economic distress.

Reviewing the Aged Trial Balance. The usual starting point for an auditor's tests of valuation is an aged trial balance. The client should prepare periodic aging analyses as a routine procedure; if that is not done, the auditor should ask the client to prepare one. The auditor may be able to provide the client with a general-purpose computer program for aging accounts receivable. The auditor should compare the total shown on the analysis with the total receivables in the ledger and should obtain an understanding of how the aging was prepared. If it is produced by a computer software package, the auditor needs to know what options in the software the client uses. (This may be done during tests of controls.) Depending on the auditor's risk assessment, he or she may test to establish the accuracy of the analysis.

In reviewing an aging analysis, the most obvious aspect to evaluate is the number and dollar amount of overdue accounts. The auditor should probe more deeply than that, however, and scrutinize a number of accounts closely for evidence that might indicate collectibility problems. The auditor's purpose in inquiring into those matters is not to judge the collectibility of each individual account examined, but to gather evidence that the client's investigation and evaluation of individual accounts (usually performed by the credit manager) were adequate and that the overall allowance for uncollectible accounts is reasonable.

The auditor should review past-due receivable balances and other unusual balances with the credit manager to obtain information on which to base an opinion regarding their collectibility. Files of correspondence with collection agents and debtors should be examined. Past experience in collecting overdue accounts should be used as a guide in deciding the probable collectibility of current balances. Changes in the number and size of overdue accounts and possible changes in business conditions affecting collectibility should be discussed with the credit manager. As a result of those reviews and discussions, the auditor should understand the basis for the client's estimate of the allowance for uncollectible accounts and be able to judge whether the allowance is reasonable. Auditing accounting estimates is discussed further in Chapter 9.

Other Procedures. The auditor should also scan revenue and receivable transactions after the balance sheet date, including sales, cash receipts, discounts allowed, rebates, returns, and write-offs. Those transactions—or their absence or an unusual increase or decrease in them—may reveal abnormal conditions affecting valuation at the balance sheet date. Events after the close of the fiscal period are often the best proof of whether the receivable balances at the balance sheet date are actually what they purport to be. Approvals for notes and accounts receivable written off during the year should be examined.

Notes receivable, whether past due or current, may themselves signal doubtful collectibility if they were received for overdue accounts receivable. The origin of notes should be determined because current notes may sometimes represent renewals of matured notes. If usual trade practice is to obtain notes from debtors of poor credit standing, the collectibility of the notes should be considered in the same way as other receivables.

The collectibility of notes that collateral has been pledged against may depend on the value of the collateral. If the collectibility of significant collateralized notes is in question, the auditor may find it desirable to have an independent appraiser value the collateral.

The auditor should be particularly attentive to revenue transactions that the client has entered into that include contingent sales agreements, customer rights of return, repurchase agreements, or other "special" terms that call into question the collectibility of the receivable and even the entity's legal rights to the revenue. The possibility of misapplication of GAAP increases when those revenue transactions are with related parties. Many audit failures were caused by the auditor's not sufficiently understanding the nature of the client's business and the substance of transactions the enterprise entered into. Detecting unusual and complex revenue transactions is particularly difficult if management consciously withholds information from the auditor. Understanding the client's industry and the transactions the client enters into is an essential first step in determining the proper accounting for and reporting of these types of transactions.

The auditor should pay particular attention to large or unusual transactions recorded at or near year-end. The auditor may also scrutinize the appropriate journals for unusual entries, and should ask management whether transactions like those described above exist. Also, the auditor should perform analytical procedures in the overall review stage of the audit, as required by SAS No. 56, *Analytical Procedures* (AU Section 329). Generally, those are the same procedures (described earlier) as performed during the planning stage, but based on year-end data.

Tests of Rights and Obligations, and Presentation and Disclosure

Receivables from affiliates, directors, officers, and employees should be reviewed to determine that they have been properly authorized and are actually what they purport to be. If loans have been made over a long period of time, past experience often provides evidence of the debtors' intentions. It is good practice to review those receivable accounts even though they appear to have been settled before the balance sheet date, especially to see whether the loans were renewed after the balance sheet date. Receivables that in fact represent advances or loans should be segregated and so described. Disclosure on the balance sheet of receivables from affiliates, directors, officers, and employees does not reflect on the integrity of those debtors.

Proper presentation and disclosure of accounts receivable and sales also require that liens, security interests, and accounts receivable pledged as loan collateral be identified. Accordingly, the auditor should review debt and lease agreements; confirmation replies, particularly from financial institutions; and minutes of directors' meetings. The auditor should also inquire of management about those items.

Throughout the audit, the auditor should be alert for transactions or issues that affect the audit objectives of rights and obligations, and presentation and disclosure. The auditor considers all evidence related to other audit objectives in determining whether the recorded receivables are the legal rights of the entity and all necessary disclosures have been made. In particular, many of the "other procedures" (described above) used to test valuation also address these audit objectives.

Other Substantive Tests

In some circumstances, even though receivable balances have been confirmed, the auditor may consider it advisable to compare, on a test basis, billings, shipping documents, and other data with recorded transactions in accounts receivable for some period. (Those comparisons, if made for a period immediately before and after the fiscal year-end, also help determine that a proper sales cutoff was made. Improper cutoffs may result from errors or from intentional recording of sales in an improper period because of bonus arrangements, sales quotas, royalty agreements, income tax considerations, or other reasons.) Comparisons made on a test basis spread throughout the period help to achieve the completeness and accuracy objectives.

Substantive tests to provide assurance about the completeness of invoicing of goods shipped and recording of goods invoiced may consist primarily of analytical procedures applied to revenue cycle accounts, plus an analysis of the size and direction of adjustments to recorded inventory quantities as a result of the client's physical inventory count. Analytical procedures are helpful in providing assurance that sales and accounts receivable are neither understated nor overstated. Tests of the reasonableness of recorded sales and analytical comparisons of accounts and relationships may provide much assurance about completeness of sales and receivables. In addition, if there are few instances where perpetual inventory quantities must be reduced as a result of the physical count, the risk of unbilled or unrecorded receivables may be sufficiently reduced to the point where analytical procedures may provide most of any additional assurance needed about the completeness of recorded revenues and receivables.

The auditor usually examines credit memos issued during a period after the close of the fiscal year to determine that reported sales were not inflated by recording unauthorized sales in one year and issuing credit memos to eliminate them in the next year, and that proper provision has been made in the year under audit for any such credit memos and for applicable discounts, returns, and allowances. The auditor should be alert for sales under terms permitting customers to return unsold merchandise.

Analytical procedures are particularly helpful in substantiating certain types of revenues. For example, the auditor can usually substantiate dues, tuition, and similar revenues rather easily by comparing receipts with membership or registration records. Sometimes the substantiation can be done on an overall basis: number of members or students multiplied by annual dues or tuition. At other times it is necessary to compare (usually on a test basis) individual items from the accounting records with the membership or registration rolls. In auditing revenues from services, there is often independently generated statistical data, such as numbers of rooms cleaned, beds made, meals served, and the like, that can be used to corroborate revenues.

AUDITING PROCEDURES: SPECIAL CONSIDERATIONS FOR PARTICULAR TYPES OF REVENUES

For the most part, the auditing procedures described so far in this chapter are adaptable to the great variety of circumstances encountered in practice. One auditing procedure may take on greater significance than another, or certain procedures may be used more extensively, but on the whole auditing procedures for many accounts in the revenue cycle are basically similar. Some of the more common revenue sources that require emphasis on particular procedures are the following:

- Cash sales.
- Interest, rents, and similar fixed payments for the use of property.
- Royalties, production payments, and similar variable revenues.
- Gifts and donations.
- Deferred income or unearned revenue.
- Revenues from long-term contracts.

Chapter 16 discusses auditing procedures for income from marketable securities and other investments.

Cash Sales

If cash sales are significant, asset protection control procedures are especially important. Cash sales are characteristic of relatively small unit value goods, which often are easily converted to cash and at the same time are difficult to keep under strict physical and accounting control. In many situations involving cash sales, segregating duties between access to merchandise and access to cash receipts is difficult, if not impossible, and enterprise management will often devise creative control procedures to compensate. Often, those procedures involve bringing the customer into the enterprise's control structure, possibly by creating incentives for the customer to demand a receipt for amounts paid (which is generated only when the sale is recorded) —perhaps to qualify for a prize or premium or to support a later merchandise return or exchange. Control over cash after it has been received and recorded is discussed in Chapter 15.

Interest, Rents, and Similar Fixed Payments for the Use of Property

Revenues from fixed payments can usually be substantiated fairly easily by an overall computation of amounts due and a comparison with amounts recorded. Usually, the client prepares a list of the properties, loans, and so on, and the related income; the auditor should test the list by examining leases, loan agreements, and similar contractual bases for revenues, noting and evaluating all special terms that have financial statement implications. The auditor may also assess control procedures applied to the receipt and recording of revenues, including measures for controlling and accounting for the vacancy rate in rental properties, and should note and evaluate delinquencies and arrearages and their implications for the realization of the related assets. Some or all significant loans receivable should be confirmed; the auditor may also wish to confirm leases and similar contractual obligations.

In particular, the auditor will be concerned about audit risk relating to revenue and cash flow from leased assets owned by a lessor. In obtaining an understanding of control structure policies and procedures and assessing control risk relating to leases, the auditor should focus on the completeness and accuracy of recorded revenue. This may require the auditor to evaluate how management arrived at the salvage value of leased property. For example, if a lessor leases a newly manufactured piece of equipment for a period of ten years, management may be required, depending on the equipment and the terms of the lease, to estimate the value of the equipment at the end of the ten years in order to properly record revenue from the transaction. In this situation, the auditor would need to know how management estimated salvage value and what factors it considered.

The auditor of the lessor is also concerned with the existence audit objective. Since the leased asset is not on the client's premises, the auditor is unable to determine its existence and condition by physical inspection. Most often the auditor will achieve the existence objective by direct confirmation with the lessee and by applying analytical procedures. The auditor should obtain evidence that the accounting classification, measurement, and disclosure requirements for lessors, as specified in Statement of Financial Accounting

Standards No. 13 and related pronouncements (Accounting Standards Section L10), have been followed.

Royalties, Production Payments, and Similar Variable Revenues

Many kinds of revenues are based on a stipulated variable, such as production or sales. Usually, the buyer of a right subject to variable payments for its use is required to report to the seller from time to time the amount of the variable and the computation of the resulting payment. If the amount of revenue is not significant, most companies simply accept the payer's statement after a superficial scrutiny for reasonableness. In that event, the auditor can do much the same, by examining the agreement on which the payment is based, comparing receipts with those of the prior year, and possibly requesting confirmation that all amounts due have been reported and paid. If amounts are significant, contracts usually provide for an independent audit of the accounting for the variable, either by the seller's auditor or by an independent auditor acceptable to the seller. Satisfactory audit reports on the payments ordinarily provide reasonable assurance that the related revenues are complete.

Gifts and Donations

Accountability for donations can be a problem because they are rarely covered by contract and they lack a delivery of goods or services to provide evidence that the revenue is due. If gifts are received centrally—as in development offices of colleges, hospitals, museums, and similar institutions—reasonably effective control procedures can be established: properly supervised opening of mail and recording of receipts; segregation of duties among handling, acknowledging, and recording; and early accountability through means such as issuing prenumbered receipt forms that also serve as documentation for tax purposes. The auditor can test those policies and procedures in the same way as conventional cash receipts.

If donations are received by numerous volunteers—as in many agencies financed by "annual drives"—the control structure is likely to be ineffective because management may feel it is impolitic or impossible to ask volunteers to submit to control procedures. In those cases, the auditor may have to make it clear in the audit report that he or she cannot express an opinion that all donations were recorded, and that the report covers only "recorded receipts."

It is possible, however, to establish an adequate control structure for volunteer solicitations, as the methods used in many United Way drives have proven. Solicitation forms are prepared in advance, and their issuance to volunteers, processing, and return are controlled. The possibility of abuse is thus minimized though not eliminated. When those policies and procedures are in effect, the auditor can test them and usually obtain reasonable assurance that gift revenue is complete.

Deferred Income or Unearned Revenue

Sometimes the accounting system provides trial balances of detailed items supporting deferred income or unearned revenue balances, for example, students' advance payments of tuition. In those cases, the auditor can obtain the necessary assurance by reviewing the trial balance and comparing it with the control account, and examining individual items.

More often, transactions flowing through unearned revenue accounts are not controlled in detail. The input to the account may be on one basis—for example, ticket sales or subscription receipts—and the relief of the account may be on a different basis—a statistical measure of service delivered such as revenue per passenger mile or per issue delivered. In those cases, the client makes a periodic analysis or ''inventory'' of the account balance. That inventory consists of scrutinizing the detail of underlying data, for example, of subscription records or of transportation tickets subsequently ''lifted.'' It can often be an extremely arduous and time-consuming effort, comparable in many ways to physically counting inventories. For that reason, the date selected is usually based on practicality and convenience, and seldom coincides with the fiscal year-end.

The auditor's observation of and participation in the analysis should be similar to the observation and testing of physical inventory procedures. The auditor should observe and test the client's procedures and evaluate the results. If control procedures appear adequate and the resulting adjustment of the account balance is small enough to indicate that the method of relieving the account is reasonably accurate, the auditor can be satisfied with applying analytical procedures to activity and balances between the test date and year-end.

Revenues from Long-Term Contracts

Audit evidence for revenues from long-term contracts is obtained from confirmations and the various means management uses to monitor and control fulfillment of contract terms and the allocation of revenues to fiscal periods. The client should provide the auditor with an analysis of each contract and the change orders that act as amendments. In many instances, an analysis prepared for management purposes will suffice, but in others an analysis will have to be prepared especially for audit purposes. Depending on the size and significance of the contracts, the auditor can compare the analysis with underlying data, including the contract itself, and review the accounting for costs incurred to date, the estimates of cost to complete each contract, and the amounts of revenue recorded in the period under audit. Such reviews should be done with operating personnel responsible for performance, as well as accounting and financial personnel.

Revenues from long-term contracts are usually accounted for by the percentage-of-completion method. Under that method, revenues and receivables are recognized in proportion to the degree of completion of a contract. Accordingly, the auditor's primary objective is to obtain evidence about the reasonableness of the client's estimate of the degree of completion of the project. The client's estimate may be made by relating costs incurred to date to the estimated total cost to complete the contract (the cost-to-cost method), by obtaining an architect's or engineer's estimate of the state of completion, or by physical measurement (usually accompanied by the auditor's observation) of the stage of completion, such as the number of production units completed. Further discussion of auditing accounting estimates is presented in Chapter 9.

After reviewing the client's documentation supporting the estimated total cost to complete a project, the auditor should compare the estimate with the contract price. If the estimated total cost to satisfy contract requirements exceeds the total contract price, a loss should usually be recognized. The auditor should also review the client's financial statement presentation, including disclosures, for conformity with the recommendations for long-term contracts found in the latest edition of the AICPA audit and accounting guide, *Construction Contractors*.

Review Questions

12-1. Specify the transaction classes that make up the revenue cycle.

12-2. What are the objectives of accounting systems and control procedures for sales of goods and services? Be specific.

12-3. With respect to invoice data, what control procedures should exist to ensure accuracy and completeness?

12-4. What are some typical misstatements that could occur in the absence of effective control procedures for the invoicing and billing steps in the revenue cycle?

12-5. How is good internal control achieved over cash receipts?

12-6. Explain the use and advantage of a lockbox system.

12-7. On what basis, and by whom, should credit memos be issued?

12-8. What are the audit objectives for the revenue cycle? Be specific.

12-9. In developing an audit strategy for the revenue cycle, what information should the auditor obtain?

12-10. What are the control objectives for payments received for goods and services?

12–11. Distinguish between negative confirmations and positive confirmations of accounts receivable and indicate when each would be used.

12–12. What procedures should the auditor observe when processing accounts receivable confirmation requests?

12–13. What alternative procedures can be used when confirmation is not possible?

12–14. What are typical follow-up procedures for confirmation differences?

12–15. What procedures should be followed for the period between the interim date and year-end when confirmations were sent at the interim date?

12–16. What is lapping? How is it perpetrated? How can it be detected?

12–17. What procedures might the auditor use to determine that unearned revenue is properly relieved?

12–18. In performing analytical procedures on the collectibility of receivables, what steps should be considered?

12–19. What would the effect on the audit be if the analytical procedures revealed that the number of days' sales in the receivable balance is increasing?

12–20. What procedures might the auditor follow in auditing revenue from long-term contracts?

12–21. What control procedures can be employed for gifts received by institutions?

Discussion Questions

12–30. Mathews, CPA, is auditing the financial statements of a manufacturing company with a significant amount of trade accounts receivable. Mathews is satisfied that the accounts are properly summarized and classified and that allocations, reclassifications, and valuations are made in accordance with generally accepted accounting principles. Mathews is planning to use accounts receivable confirmation requests to satisfy the third standard of field work regarding trade accounts receivable.

Required:

a. Identify and describe the two forms of accounts receivable confirmation requests and indicate what factors Mathews will consider in determining when to use each.

b. Assume Mathews has received a satisfactory response to the confirmation requests. Describe how Mathews could evaluate collectibility of the trade accounts receivable.

(AICPA adapted)

12–31. Items 1 through 4 are based on the following information:

The following sales procedures were encountered during the annual audit of Ben's Wholesalers, Inc.

Customer orders are received by the sales order department. A clerk computes the dollar amount of the order and sends it to the credit department for approval. Credit approval is stamped on the order and returned to the sales order department. An invoice is prepared in duplicate and the order is filed in the "customer order" file.

The "customer copy" of the invoice is sent to the billing department and held in the "pending" file awaiting notification that the order was shipped.

The "shipping copy" of the invoice is routed through the warehouse and the shipping department as authorization for the respective departments to release and ship the merchandise. Shipping department personnel pack the order and prepare a three-copy bill of lading. The original copy is mailed to the customer, the second copy is sent with the shipment, and the third copy is filed in sequence in the "bill of lading" file. The invoice "shipping copy" is sent to the billing department.

The billing clerk matches the received "shipping copy" with the customer copy from the "pending" file. Both copies of the invoice are priced, extended, and footed. The customer copy is then mailed directly to the customer, and the "shipping copy" is sent to the accounts receivable clerk.

The accounts receivable clerk enters the invoice data in a sales and accounts receivable journal, posts the customer's account in the "subsidiary customers' accounts ledger," and files the "shipping copy" in the "sales invoice" file. The invoices are numbered and filed in sequence.

1. In order to gather audit evidence concerning the proper credit approval of sales, the auditor would select a sample of transaction documents from the population represented by the
   a. "Customer order" file.
   b. "Bill of lading" file.
   c. "Subsidiary customers' accounts ledger."
   d. "Sales invoice" file.
2. In order to determine whether the internal control structure operated effectively to minimize misstatements caused by failure to post invoices to the customers' accounts ledger, the auditor would select a sample of transactions from the population represented by the
   a. "Customer order" file.
   b. "Bill of lading" file.
   c. "Subsidiary customers' accounts ledger."
   d. "Sales invoice" file.
3. In order to determine whether the internal control structure operated effectively to minimize misstatements caused by failure to invoice a shipment, the auditor would select a sample of transactions from the population represented by the
   a. "Customer order" file.
   b. "Bill of lading" file.
   c. "Subsidiary customers' accounts ledger."
   d. "Sales invoice" file.
4. In order to gather audit evidence that uncollected items in customers' accounts represented valid trade receivables, the auditor would select a sample of items from the population represented by the
   a. "Customer order" file.
   b. "Bill of lading" file.
   c. "Subsidiary customers' accounts ledger."
   d. "Sales invoice" file.

(AICPA adapted)

12-32. How would you determine that all trade accounts receivable pledged as collateral are identified and disclosed?

12–33. The Colonial Park Homeowners Association utilizes the services of J & B Management Co. to oversee the operation of its clubhouse and recreation facilities, maintain and repair the property's common areas, and collect the monthly assessments for membership. Membership is not mandatory and some homeowners are not members. Homeowners are instructed to make payments directly to a lockbox account maintained at a local bank. The bank records the deposits and provides the management company with a monthly statement of receipts. Money is transferred periodically from the lockbox account to an operating checking account at the request of the management company. The management company follows up delinquent assessments by telephone and requests the homeowner to bring the delinquent payment directly to its clubhouse office. The management company's contract is renewed once a year at the annual meeting of the board of directors of the Homeowners Association. The directors have no other involvement in the operations during the year.

Required:

a. Discuss the strengths and deficiencies of internal control structure policies and procedures for collecting assessments.
b. What auditing procedures would you use to test the cash receipts function of the Colonial Park Homeowners Association?

12–34. What do you do when there is no response to second requests sent for positive confirmations?

12–35. Briefly describe auditing procedures that would be uniquely applicable in the audit of

1. Tuition income of private schools.
2. Rental income of office buildings.
3. Annual dues of golf clubs.
4. Donations to charity organizations.

12–36. In connection with an audit of the financial statements of Blackwell Company for the year ended June 30, 1991, a CPA performs several cutoff tests.

Required:

a. 1. What is a cutoff test?
   2. Why must cutoff tests be performed for both the beginning and the end of the audit period on initial engagements?
b. The CPA wishes to test Blackwell's sales cutoff at June 30, 1991. Describe the steps that should be included in this test.

(AICPA adapted)

12–37. Generally accepted auditing standards call for confirmation of receivables by direct correspondence with the debtors, when practicable and reasonable. However, the usefulness to the auditor of receivable confirmations varies from client to client.

Required:

a. What are the purposes for which the auditor confirms receivables?
b. Briefly indicate why the usefulness of the replies might vary.
c. What should the auditor consider in arriving at a decision on whether to confirm all receivables or to confirm on a sample basis? What should the auditor consider in determining the extent of the sample?

d. Under what conditions would the auditor consider it impracticable to confirm receivables?

12-38. Taylor, CPA, has been engaged to audit the financial statements of Johnsons Coat Outlet, Inc., a medium-sized mail-order retail store that sells a wide variety of coats to the public.

Required:

Prepare the "Shipments" segment of Taylor's internal control questionnaire. Each question should elicit either a yes or no response.

Do *not* prepare questions relating to the cash receipts, sales returns and allowances, billing, inventory control, or other segments.

(AICPA adapted)

12-39. Professional Products, Inc. specializes in the sale of standardized software programs, principally to the accounting and legal professions. Its operation is located on the East Coast but it solicits sales through a network of independent commissioned salespeople throughout the country. On receiving an order, a salesperson notifies the sales department, which processes all orders from the East Coast location. Professional also offers a "trouble-shooter" service whereby customers can call a toll-free number and get expert answers to questions and problems concerning their software systems. This service is billed to customers based on the length of the phone conversation at a standard rate per minute.

Required:

What procedures should be followed to ensure that all time incurred for the "trouble-shooter" service is properly billed and recorded?

AICPA Multiple Choice Questions

These questions are taken from the Auditing part of Uniform CPA Examinations. Choose the single most appropriate answer.

12-40. Confirmation is most likely to be a relevant form of evidence with regard to assertions about accounts receivable when the auditor has concerns about the receivables'

a. Valuation.
b. Classification.
c. Existence.
d. Completeness.

12-41. For effective internal control, the billing function should be performed by the

a. Accounting department.
b. Sales department.
c. Shipping department.
d. Credit and collection department.

12–42. Cash receipts from sales on account have been misappropriated. Which of the following acts would conceal this defalcation and be *least* likely to be detected by an auditor?

a. Understating the sales journal.
b. Overstating the accounts receivable control account.
c. Overstating the accounts receivable subsidiary ledger.
d. Understating the cash receipts journal.

12–43. At which point in an ordinary sales transaction of a wholesaling business would a lack of specific authorization *least* concern the auditor conducting an audit?

a. Determining discounts.
b. Selling goods for cash.
c. Granting credit.
d. Shipping goods.

12–44. When a customer fails to include a remittance advice with a payment, it is a common practice for the person opening the mail to prepare one. Consequently, mail should be opened by which of the following four employees?

a. Credit manager.
b. Receptionist.
c. Sales manager.
d. Accounts receivable clerk.

12–45. An auditor confirms a representative number of open accounts receivable as of December 31, 1989, and investigates respondents' exceptions and comments. By this procedure the auditor would be most likely to learn of which of the following?

a. One of the cashiers has been covering a personal embezzlement by lapping.
b. One of the sales clerks has *not* been preparing charge slips for credit sales to family and friends.
c. One of the EDP control clerks has been removing all sales invoices applicable to his account from the data file.
d. The credit manager has misappropriated remittances from customers whose accounts have been written off.

12–46. During the process of confirming receivables as of December 31, 1989, a positive confirmation was returned indicating the "balance owed as of December 31 was paid on January 9, 1990." The auditor would most likely

a. Determine whether there were any changes in the account between January 1 and January 9, 1990.
b. Determine whether a customary trade discount was taken by the customer.
c. Reconfirm the zero balance as of January 10, 1990.
d. Verify that the amount was received.

12–47. Cooper, CPA, is auditing the financial statements of a small rural municipality. The receivable balances represent residents' delinquent real estate taxes. The internal control structure at the municipality is weak. To determine the existence of the accounts receivable balances at the balance sheet date, Cooper would most likely

a. Send positive confirmation requests.
b. Send negative confirmation requests.

c. Examine evidence of subsequent cash receipts.
d. Inspect the internal records such as copies of the tax invoices that were mailed to the residents.

12-48. To determine whether the internal control structure operated effectively to minimize misstatements caused by failure to invoice a shipment, the auditor would select a sample of transactions from the population represented by the

a. Customer order file.
b. Bill of lading file.
c. Open invoice file.
d. Sales invoice file.

12-49. Which of the following procedures would ordinarily be expected to best reveal unrecorded sales at the balance sheet date?

a. Compare shipping documents with sales records.
b. Apply gross profit rates to inventory disposed of during the period.
c. Trace payments received subsequent to the balance sheet date.
d. Send accounts receivable confirmation requests.

12-50. Customers having substantial year-end past-due balances fail to reply after second request forms have been mailed directly to them. Which of the following is the most appropriate auditing procedure?

a. Examine shipping documents.
b. Review collections during the year being audited.
c. Intensify the tests of the client's internal control structure with respect to receivables.
d. Increase the balance in the accounts receivable allowance (contra) account.

12-51. An auditor selects a sample from the file of shipping documents to determine whether invoices were prepared. This test is performed to satisfy the audit objective of

a. Accuracy.
b. Completeness.
c. Control.
d. Existence.

12-52. An aged trial balance of accounts receivable is usually used by the auditor to

a. Verify the completeness of recorded receivables.
b. Ensure that all accounts are promptly credited.
c. Evaluate the results of tests of controls.
d. Evaluate the provision for bad debt expense.

Problems and Cases

12-60. You are engaged in auditing the financial statements of Perskill Corporation for the year ended December 31, 1990. In connection with your review of the adequacy of the allowance for uncollectible accounts, the balance of which on December 31, 1989, was

$45,000 (no amount has been provided for uncollectible accounts for 1990), the following data is submitted to you:

	Net Sales		*Uncollectible Accounts*
Year Ended	*For Credit*	*For Cash*	*Charged Off*
December 31, 1987	$ 718,500	$52,200	$26,100
December 31, 1988	774,000	68,000	28,400
December 31, 1989	967,000	83,000	35,900
December 31, 1990	1,345,000	94,000	43,000

The aging schedule at December 31, 1990, shows $75,000 as being past due. However, this is considered by management to be a temporary seasonal situation and in line with previous years.

Required:

a. What auditing procedures would you perform to determine the adequacy of the allowance for uncollectible accounts?
b. What provision for uncollectible accounts do you believe necessary (before considering the results of your audit work) to ensure the adequacy of the allowance for uncollectible accounts?

12-61. The United Charities organization in your town has engaged you to audit its statement of receipts and disbursements. United Charities solicits contributions from local donors and then apportions the contributions among local charitable organizations.

The officers and directors are local bankers, professionals, and other leaders of the community. A cashier and a clerk are the only full-time salaried employees. The only records maintained by the organization are a cashbook and a checkbook. The directors prefer not to have a system of pledges.

Contributions are solicited by a number of volunteer workers. The workers are not restricted as to the area of their solicitation and may work among their friends, neighbors, coworkers, and the like, as convenient for them. To ensure blanket coverage of the town, new volunteer workers are welcomed.

Contributions are in the form of cash or checks. They are received by United Charities from the solicitors, who personally deliver the contributions they have collected, or directly from the donors by mail or by personal delivery.

The solicitors complete official receipts, which they give to the donors when contributions are received. These official receipts have attached stubs that the solicitors fill in with the names of the donors and the amount of the contributions. The solicitors turn in the stubs with the contributions to the cashiers. No control is maintained over the number of blank receipts given to the solicitors or the number of receipt stubs turned in with the contributions.

Required:

Discuss the control procedures you would recommend for greater assurance that all contributions received by the solicitors are turned over to the organization. (Do not discuss the control of the funds in the organization's office.)

(AICPA adapted)

12-62. The Sodium Drug Co. has recently been notified by the Food and Drug Administration (FDA) that its product, "Lull-A-Bye Tablets," an aid for insomnia, contains an excessive amount of salt and is a danger to people with high blood pressure. The FDA has instructed Sodium Drug Co. to recall all of the Lull-A-Bye tablets sold during the past year. As a result of the national publicity the case has received, returns of Lull-A-Bye tablets have started to pour in from around the country. The returns are from stores and individuals in the form of both unopened cases and boxes and half-empty individual bottles. Customers are demanding credit against existing accounts receivable or refunds. Mr. Gilbert, president of Sodium Drug Co., has requested your help in setting up procedures to handle this situation in an economical and efficient manner.

Required:

a. List the procedures you would recommend to handle the recall of Lull-A-Bye tablets from receipt of the returns to the granting of credit or refunds.
b. Assuming that you are also the auditor for Sodium Drug Co. and the recall occurred in the middle of the fiscal year, what potential audit problems would you face for the year-end audit and what auditing procedures would you perform?

12-63. During the year, Fowler & Company began to encounter cash flow difficulties, and a cursory review by management revealed receivable collection problems. Fowler's management engaged Dowling, CPA, to perform a special investigation. Dowling studied the billing and collection cycle and noted the following:

The accounting department employs one bookkeeper, who receives and opens all incoming mail. This bookkeeper is also responsible for depositing receipts, filing remittance advices on a daily basis, recording receipts in the cash receipts journal, and posting receipts in the individual customer accounts and the general ledger accounts. There are no cash sales. The bookkeeper prepares and controls the mailing of monthly statements to customers.

The concentration of functions and the receivable collection problems caused Dowling to suspect that a systematic defalcation of customers' payments through a delayed posting of remittances (lapping of accounts receivable) is present. Dowling was surprised to find that no customers complained about receiving erroneous monthly statements.

Required:

Identify the procedures Dowling should perform to determine whether lapping exists. *Do not discuss deficiencies in the internal control structure.*

(AICPA adapted)

12-64. Your client is the Indian Heights Shopping Center, Inc., a shopping center with 30 store tenants. All leases with the store tenants provide for a fixed rent plus a percentage of sales, net of sales taxes, in excess of a fixed dollar amount computed on an annual basis. Each lease also provides that the landlord may engage a CPA to audit all records of the tenant for assurance that sales are being properly reported to the landlord.

You have been requested by your client to audit the records of the Shore House Restaurant to determine that the sales totaling $390,000 for the year ended December 31, 1989 have been properly reported to the landlord. The restaurant and the shopping center entered into a five-year lease on January 1, 1989. The Shore House Restaurant offers only table service. No liquor is served. During mealtimes, there are four or five waitresses in attendance who prepare handwritten prenumbered restaurant checks for the customers. Payment is made at a cash register, manned by the proprietor, as the customer leaves. All sales are for cash. The proprietor also is the bookkeeper. Complete files are kept of restaurant checks and cash register tapes. A daily sales book and general ledger are also maintained.

Required:

List the auditing procedures that you would employ to substantiate the total annual sales of the Shore House Restaurant. (Disregard vending machine sales and counter sales of chewing gum, candy, etc.)

(AICPA adapted)

12-65. The aged trade accounts receivable trial balance on page 519 was prepared by the controller of International Electronics, Inc. for use by the independent auditors during their audit of International's financial statements as of and for the year ended December 31, 1990. All procedures performed by the staff accountant on the aged trial balance were noted on the working paper and explained in the "Legend and Comments" section.

The "customer confirmation responses" listed below and on page 520 represent information received directly by the staff accountant. The working paper entitled "Customer Confirmation Responses: Auditing Procedures Performed" on page 520 indicates the procedures applied by the staff accountant to the confirmation responses and the conclusions reached. The working paper was properly initialed, dated, and indexed and then submitted to the auditor in charge of the engagement for review. The risk of material misstatement of accounts receivable was assessed as being below maximum.

As the auditor in charge, you have the following information that was not known to the staff accountant:

1. Company M is also a supplier. The $16,000 balance results from a netting of accounts receivable and accounts payable.
2. The working papers prepared during the physical inventory observation on December 31, 1990, indicated that merchandise for customer H was segregated and not included in inventory because the customer was expected to pick up the merchandise within a few days.

Required:

a. For each of the customer confirmation responses, indicate whether you agree or disagree with the auditing procedures performed and conclusions reached by the staff accountant. If you disagree, specify what procedures should have been applied or conclusions reached.
b. What essential auditing procedures were not noted as having been performed by the staff accountant?

Customer	*Customer Confirmation Responses*
A	"A check for $5000 was given to your salesman on November 15, 1990."
C	"Returned by post office, marked 'address incorrect, addressee unknown.'"
F	"No balance is due since merchandise was shipped on consignment and goods have not been sold."

International Electronics, Inc.
Aged Trade Accounts Receivable Trial Balance
December 31, 1990

Customer	Total		Current Under 30 days	31-60 Days	Past Due 61-90 Days	Over 90 Days	Customer Confirmation Response
A	25000	S	20000	5000			"A check for $5,000 was given to your salesman on November 15, 1990
B	15000		7000	5000	3000		
C	7500	S				7500	"Returned by post office, marked address incorrect, addressee unknown."
D	12000		2500		5000	4500	
E	(11000)	S1				(11000)	
F	30000	S	15000		7500	7500	"No balance is due since merchandise was shipped on consignment and goods have not been sold."
G	45000	S	45000				"Agree"
H	5000	S	(10000)	15000			"The $10,000 represents an advance payment against a future purchase."
I	75000	S	50000	10000	10000	5000	"Cannot confirm - accounts payable utilizes the voucher system."
J	22000	S	15000		7000		"We cannot identify invoice for $7000 - please send duplicate."
K	14000				14000		
L	8100		2700	2700	2700		
M	16000	S	21000	18000	(23000)		"Our records indicate a balance due of $39,000."
N	17000			17000			
O	27000	S	22000			5000	"A credit is due for $5000 for merchandise returned on January 12, 1991 for incorrect model
TOTALS	$307600		$190200	$72700	$26200	$18500	
	WTZ		W	W	W	W	

Legend and Comments:

S1 = Selected for positive confirmation: however, the client indicated that this credit balance was due to a duplicate payment and requested that a confirmation not be sent. Auditor concurs but will perform alternative auditing procedures.

S = Selected for positive confirmation; confirmation includes specific invoice numbers and amounts.

T = Agreed to general ledger.

W = Totals footed.

Z = Totals crossfooted.

65-814

G	"Agree."
H	"The $10,000 represents an advance payment against a future purchase."
I	"Cannot confirm—accounts payable utilizes the voucher system."
J	"We cannot identify invoice for $7000—please send duplicate."
M	"Our records indicate a balance due of $39,000."
O	"A credit is due for $5000 for merchandise returned on January 12, 1991, for incorrect model."

INTERNATIONAL ELECTRONICS, INC.
Trade Accounts Receivable
December 31, 1990

Customer Confirmation Responses: Auditing Procedures Performed

Customer	*Auditing Procedures Performed*
A	Determined that the $5000 payment was given to the salesman and subsequently deposited into the company's cash account on January 7, 1991; no exception.
C	Reviewed shipping documentation to ensure that receivable is valid. No exception.
E	Examined cash receipts journal and noted that $11,000 in payments were received on August 7 and September 21; no exception.
F	Examined invoices, shipping documentation, and consignment listing and determined that customer was correct. Determined that the consigned merchandise was included in the year-end inventory; no exception.
G	No additional auditing procedures necessary since account was confirmed as correct; no exception.
H	Determined that customer response was correct by examining cash receipts journal in December and an invoice dated January 31, 1991. The January invoice was offset against the advance payment; no exception.
I	Examined invoices and subsequent cash receipts of $25,000 in January; no exception.
J	The $7000 invoice was found to have been charged to customer J in error. The shipping records indicated that customer G received the merchandise and was never billed for it. Client will send bill and correct their records. Since the sale was recorded, there is no misstatement of the books and records and therefore this is not considered an error.
M	Determined that the $23,000 was related to the purchase of merchandise by examination of the related invoice, purchase order, and receiving documentation; no exception.
O	Examined receiving report and client approval for merchandise received in January. This requires an adjustment to reduce sales and accounts receivable by $5000; exception.

12–66. The flowchart on page 522 depicts the activities relating to the shipping, billing, and collecting processes used by Precise Plumbing Parts, Inc.

Required:

Identify deficiencies in the internal control structure relating to the activities of (a) warehouse clerk, (b) bookkeeper #1, (c) bookkeeper #2, and (d) collection clerk.

(AICPA adapted)

12-67. ***Quinn Hardware*** (Revenue Cycle: Overview Flowchart)
This problem is a continuation of the Quinn Hardware case that starts in Chapter 6. The following material describes Quinn's revenue cycle.

Shipments

Sales orders are accepted by customer service representatives who take information over the phone and record it on a sales order form. Orders are also received via the mail.

The sales input clerks enter the sales orders via CRT throughout the day. An on-line edit is performed and customer number and product number must match the information on the system for an order to be accepted. An order acknowledgment is printed and sent to the customer for accepted orders, and an open order file is created. Clerks may override the prices on the price master file. These overrides are reported on a daily price override report, which is forwarded to the sales manager for approval. If an order puts a customer over his or her approved credit limit, the input clerk must provide an override code for the transaction to be entered. All such transactions are reported on an exception report that is forwarded to the credit manager for daily review and approval. Any orders for goods not in stock are reported on the daily backorder report. The backorder report is forwarded to purchasing and customer service for review and action.

Twice a day, the system generates a pick list that summarizes all orders entered since the previous summarization except for backorders, generating a bill of lading for each order. The order is flagged on the open order file as having generated a bill of lading. The appropriate goods are pulled and staged for shipment. When this process is complete, a shipping clerk compares the staged order to the bill of lading and the order is shipped. The shipping input clerk keys the information from the bill of lading into the system via CRT and indicates that the order was shipped. The system matches the data from the bill of lading to the data in the open order file. Differences between the quantity shipped and the order quantity are reported on a shipping variance report, which is reviewed by the sales and production departments. One copy of the bill of lading is retained in the shipping department and the other copy is forwarded to accounting for filing with the invoice.

Daily, the system generates an unmatched bill of lading report, which lists bills of lading that have been generated but not confirmed as shipped. The items on the unmatched bill of lading report are investigated by the accounts receivable clerks. The report is received and approved by Mickey Galer, accounts receivable supervisor.

Upon confirmation of shipment, the system generates an invoice that is numerically sequenced and flags the order on the open order file as having been invoiced. A shipping control report and a daily shipments detail report are generated for items invoiced.

Remittances

Payments on open accounts receivable are received by a lockbox at a major bank in Chicago. The bank provides Quinn Hardware with a magnetic tape that summarizes the information included on the remittance advices that accompanied the previous

PRECISE PLUMBING PARTS, INC.
Flowchart—Shipping, Billing, and Collecting

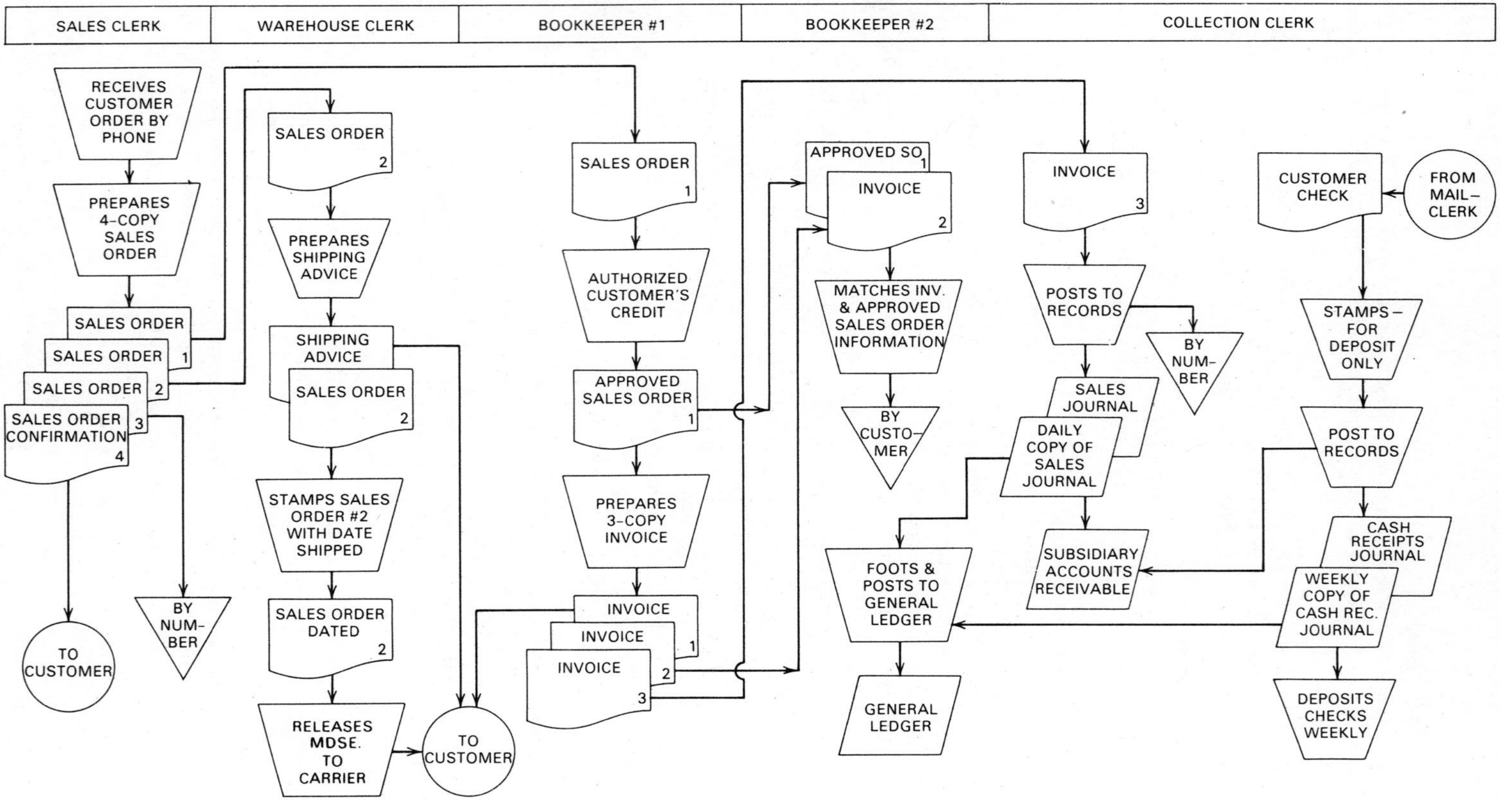

SALES CLERK

RECEIVES CUSTOMER ORDER BY PHONE
PREPARES 4-COPY SALES ORDER
SALES ORDER 1
SALES ORDER 2
SALES ORDER 3
SALES ORDER CONFIRMATION 4
BY NUM-BER
TO CUSTOMER

WAREHOUSE CLERK

SALES ORDER 2
PREPARES SHIPPING ADVICE
SHIPPING ADVICE
SALES ORDER 2
STAMPS SALES ORDER #2 WITH DATE SHIPPED
SALES ORDER DATED 2
RELEASES MDSE. TO CARRIER
TO CUSTOMER

BOOKKEEPER #1

SALES ORDER 1
AUTHORIZED CUSTOMER'S CREDIT
APPROVED SALES ORDER 1
PREPARES 3-COPY INVOICE
INVOICE 1
INVOICE 2
INVOICE 3

BOOKKEEPER #2

APPROVED SO 1
INVOICE 2
MATCHES INV. & APPROVED SALES ORDER INFORMATION
BY CUSTO-MER
FOOTS & POSTS TO GENERAL LEDGER
GENERAL LEDGER

COLLECTION CLERK

INVOICE 3
POSTS TO RECORDS
BY NUM-BER
SALES JOURNAL
DAILY COPY OF SALES JOURNAL
SUBSIDIARY ACCOUNTS RECEIVABLE
FROM MAIL-CLERK
CUSTOMER CHECK
STAMPS—FOR DEPOSIT ONLY
POST TO RECORDS
CASH RECEIPTS JOURNAL
WEEKLY COPY OF CASH REC. JOURNAL
DEPOSITS CHECKS WEEKLY

day's remittances. The tape is processed through an edit routine. The invoice numbers on the remittance advice must match an open invoice on the A/R master file and the customer number must match the customer master file. Any unmatched items are reported on the unidentified cash report. The system also identifies the occasional partial payments, which are reported on the partial payments report. Both of these reports are cumulative; the data is maintained on the unmatched remittance file. The unidentified cash report and partial payments report are generated nightly. The totals of these reports along with the total of accepted remittances are reconciled by a remittance clerk to the lockbox deposit control report received from the bank.

Kara Feular, remittance clerk, reviews the unidentified cash and partial payments reports daily. She resolves problems by calling the customer or refers the issue to customer service if there is a dispute. For each item she notes the reason for the rejection and the status of the investigation, initials the report, and sends it to Rosa Fume, supervisor. Rosa approves resolved items for correction. After approval Kara reinputs the corrections for processing.

Update of Accounts Receivable Files

Nightly, the A/R master and Sales master files are updated. The system generates a number of control and detail reports, which are reconciled. In particular, the A/R posting summary is reconciled to the daily shipments detail and the remittance detail reports. This reconciliation is performed by the accounts receivable control clerk, Dave Clark.

A credit limit threshold report and a report that identifies invoices more than 60 days old are forwarded to the credit department. The credit department staff contacts all customers with accounts past due more than 60 days. At month-end, the clerks investigating the past-due items make notations on the aged accounts receivable trial balance for review and approval by the credit manager, Eileen Dover. Eileen also reviews the credit limit threshold report and forwards it to the sales manager daily.

Jim Miller, controller, reviews daily reports of sales and cash collection activity in order to manage cash flow. He prepares a cash flow management worksheet, making notations of reasons for major fluctuations. He identifies unexpected fluctuations based on his knowledge of the company and its current activity. The treasurer reviews Jim's fluctuation explanations in conjunction with cash flow information from the bank.

Monthly Reports and General Ledger Update

Monthly, the general ledger is updated and a number of reconciliation procedures are performed. Specifically, the A/R aged trial balance is reconciled to the general ledger by Dave Clark or the accounts receivable supervisor when Dave is on vacation. Dave reviews a summary of manual adjusting journal entries, contacts the originator if necessary, corrects the entry if necessary, and writes an explanation for each reconciling item on the reconciliation worksheet. Several times a year there are no reconciling items. The reconciliation is forwarded to Jim Miller by the fifth working day of the month for his review and approval. Jim receives all supporting documentation with the reconciliation and reviews all information for propriety. He signs the reconciliation when he is satisfied that it is correct and that all appropriate adjustments have been made. When Jim is absent, the Vice President of Finance performs the review.

In addition, Dave Clark reconciles monthly sales and remittance summaries to the general ledger reports and sends the reconciliation to Jim Miller for review and approval.

Required:

Prepare an overview flowchart for Quinn Hardware's revenue cycle. Remember to document key files, transactions, and processes as well as reports of accounting significance.

12-68. ***Quinn Hardware*** (Revenue Cycle: Uncollectible Accounts)
This problem is a continuation of the Quinn Hardware case that starts in Chapter 6. The revenue cycle narrative appears in Problem 12-67. Accounts receivable data is provided below.

For purposes of this problem, assume the following:

- Control risk for completeness and accuracy was assessed as low based on the tests of controls.
- Quinn's revenues are evenly distributed between its wholesale operation, which sells heavy mining and industrial equipment, as well as building materials, and the retail hardware business, which has six company-owned stores and over 200 franchised dealers. Refer to Problem 6-62 for further data on sales distribution and number of customers.
- The valuation of accounts receivable from franchises and related parties was identified as an audit risk earlier in the engagement.
- Accounts receivable and sales have increased significantly in 1991 due to the success of the new gardening supply product lines.

QUINN HARDWARE, INC.
SELECTED DATA FOR THE FOLLOWING YEARS:
(000s Omitted)

	1987	*1988*	*1989*	*1990*	*1991*
Sales	$191,444	$225,895	$230,118	$255,426	$292,701
A/R	23,891	31,446	31,973	38,574	51,208
Less: Allowance	1,200	1,400	1,400	1,500	1,800
A/R, Net	$ 22,691	$ 30,046	$ 30,573	$ 37,074	$ 49,408
Bad Debt Expense	$ 620	$ 680	$ 825	$ 894	$ 1,000

COMPOSITION OF YEAR-END BALANCES (AGING)

	1987	*1988*	*1989*	*1990*	*1991*
Current	$13,877	$17,812	$15,479	$19,327	$24,485
30-59 Days	4,481	4,567	5,515	6,426	7,968
60-89 Days	3,410	5,825	6,585	8,615	11,369
Over 90 Days	2,123	3,242	4,394	4,206	7,386
	$23,891	$31,446	$31,973	$38,574	$51,208

Required:

Identify factors to consider in determining the adequacy of Quinn Hardware's provision for uncollectible accounts at May 31, 1991 (do not develop an audit program).

In developing your solution, recognize that the following information is available from the client:

1. Detailed listing of aged accounts receivable by customer for each year.
2. Summary of written-off balances for each year.
3. Discussion with the controller at interim indicated that he was very confident of the adequacy of the year-end balance and that any variances from prior years were "strictly temporary."

13

Auditing the Buying Cycle

This chapter covers the "buying cycle": the acquisition of goods and services in exchange for cash or promises to pay cash. The buying cycle is part of the larger "expenditure cycle" that comprises all transactions in which assets are produced or acquired, expenses are incurred, and payments are made to discharge liabilities incurred. Since the expenditure cycle is too broad to be covered in a single chapter and because it is usually more efficient to divide the cycle into more manageable segments when performing an audit, the expenditure cycle is discussed in several chapters. The discussion in this chapter is limited to auditing transactions involving purchases of and payments for goods and services generally, including human resources, and accounts related to those transactions. Accounts encompassed by the buying cycle are defined and described. Typical buying transactions, accounting systems, and control procedures are then presented in detail, including those for payrolls, followed by a discussion of audit objectives, risk assessment, and the audit testing plan for the buying cycle. Subsequent sections of the chapter present specific tests of controls and substantive tests that may be used in auditing buying cycle transactions and related account balances.

ACCOUNTS RELATED TO THE BUYING CYCLE

Transactions that are part of the buying cycle affect numerous balance sheet and income statement accounts. The term "accounts payable" is used to describe specific amounts owed by an entity, usually arising from purchases of goods or services. It represents amounts due to suppliers of merchandise, materials, supplies, or services, and evidenced by vendors' invoices. Buying activities that generate accounts payable involve purchases of merchandise or raw materials and the incurring of selling, general, administrative, and other expenses.

Depending on their purpose, expenditures for payroll may be recorded as assets, expenses, or both. Amounts withheld from employees' gross pay for such items as federal and state income taxes and miscellaneous authorized deductions are recorded as agency obligations (amounts held in trust for third parties) until such time as the liabilities are paid. Similar obligations arise from payroll taxes and fringe benefits paid by employers. At the end of an accounting period, salaries and wages earned but not yet paid are recorded as an accrued payroll liability. Other related accruals must be recorded for certain compensated absences and rights to severance pay. Agency obligations and accrued liabilities are discussed in Chapter 16.

Selling expenses include expenditures for sales personnel salaries, commissions, and expenses, and other costs of selling goods and services, such as advertising, delivery, and sales department overhead. Also classified as selling expenses are warehousing costs for inventory pending sale, estimated losses from uncollectible accounts, and credit and collection expenses.

General and administrative expenses include executive salaries and costs associated with an enterprise's general offices and departments, corporate expenses such as business licenses and fees, costs of reports to stockholders, and legal and auditing fees. Charges related to the occupancy of buildings, like rent, depreciation, utilities, maintenance, taxes, and insurance, are usually allocated among manufacturing, selling, general, and administrative activities. Other expense accounts affected by transactions in the buying cycle include research and development, maintenance and repairs, and travel and entertainment.

T-accounts are presented in Figure 13.1 to show the various transactions and accounts in a typical buying cycle.

TYPICAL TRANSACTIONS, ACCOUNTING SYSTEMS, AND CONTROL PROCEDURES

The procedures involved in buying goods and services in most contemporary businesses can be classified into three typical classes of transactions.

- Acquisition of goods and services.
- Payments made for goods and services.
- Goods returned to suppliers.

Conceptually, payrolls are part of the buying cycle, but the related control procedures are somewhat unique. Accordingly, two additional classes of transactions are often identified.

- Payroll processing.
- Payment of wages.

Acquisition of Goods and Services

The process of acquiring goods and services includes the following steps:

- Determining needs.
- Ordering.
- Receiving, inspecting, and accepting goods.
- Recording.

In considering the accounting system that processes buying transactions and the control procedures applied to them, the auditor is interested mainly in procedures to ensure that all purchase transactions that actually occurred are

Figure 13.1 Buying Cycle Accounts

Balance Sheet Accounts

Cash

Beginning balance	Cash purchases Payments to suppliers Payments to employees Payments of agency obligations

Accounts Payable

Payments to suppliers Goods returned to suppliers	Beginning balance Purchases on account Various expenses incurred on account Ending balance

Salaries and Wages Payable

Payments to employees	Net salaries and wages payable

Agency Obligation Accounts

Payments of agency obligations	Payroll taxes and fringe benefits Amounts withheld for taxes and other deductions

Income Statement Accounts

Purchases of Raw Materials (Net)

Cash purchases Purchases on account	Discounts granted for prompt payment Goods returned to suppliers

Selling, General, and Administrative and Other Expenses

Various expenses incurred on account	

Compensation Expense

Salaries and wages Payroll taxes and fringe benefits	

authorized and are recorded accurately; that is, that the control objectives of completeness, accuracy, and authorization for transaction processing and files are met. Those control objectives are closely related to the audit objectives of completeness, accuracy, and existence of buying cycle accounts, particularly purchases and accounts payable. Other control procedures, while not directly related to those audit objectives, may also be of interest to the auditor. For example, management reviews of open purchase orders may generate reports the auditor can use in evaluating whether there are unrealized losses on open purchase commitments, which affects the valuation audit objective.

The paragraphs that follow describe the various activities involved in the purchase of goods and services, and the control procedures typically applied in processing the transactions. (Later sections discuss the audit relevance of those procedures.)

Determining Needs. The buying cycle starts when someone identifies a need, which may occur in several different ways. For example,

- Raw material inventory replenishment needs may be determined by a person or automatically when stock on hand reaches a reorder point or when a bill of materials for a job order is prepared. Some computerized systems may identify needs by reference to records of quantities on hand or production orders and simultaneously execute some of the steps in the buying process, for example, selecting vendors and preparing purchase orders. In certain sophisticated systems, raw material needs are identified and the order is placed with the vendor without any human intervention. The company's computer communicates directly with the vendor's computer.
- Needs for occasional goods and services are identified and described by the user, usually on a requisition form that is then approved by the person (who may be the same as the user) with authority over the user's department or the particular type of purchase.
- The need for some services that are provided on a recurring basis by the same vendor, such as utilities, telephone, periodicals, or maintenance services, is usually determined initially and thereafter provided continuously until the end of the contract period or until it is determined that the service is no longer needed or a different supplier is selected.
- Determining the need for specialized services, like insurance, advertising, and legal and auditing services, is ordinarily the responsibility of designated individuals.
- Needs for fixed assets are usually identified by a capital budgeting process.

Control procedures for requisitions typically include review and authorization by a responsible individual and accounting for the numerical sequence of prenumbered requisition forms. Those control procedures are designed to ensure that only necessary goods and services are ordered and that all items requisitioned are actually ordered. While the purpose of these procedures is more closely related to management's decision making than to financial statement assertions, the procedures may have an effect on certain financial statement accounts. For example, if review and authorization procedures for requisitions are absent or ineffective, inventory may become overstocked and eventually obsolete, thereby reducing its value.

Ordering. In most large enterprises, trained purchasing agents rather than personnel from user departments determine sources, negotiate terms, and place orders. Vendor selection and monitoring can be important control procedures affecting both accounts payable and inventory. A separate purchasing function can provide cost savings to the company and enhance control over purchases by providing a division of duties.

When the purchasing department receives a requisition, typically it first determines that the amount and type of goods or services being requisitioned have been approved by an individual with the appropriate authority. The requisition then serves as the source document for inputting the order or, in a manual system, preparing the purchase order. In a computerized system, the requisition information may be input and matched against vendor, price, and (if applicable) inventory master files to assist in vendor selection, evaluating quoted prices, and determining the accuracy of product numbers or descriptions. After all of the specific information about the purchase, such as time and method of delivery, specifications for materials, and quantity and price, have been determined, a purchase order is generated and the open purchase order file is updated. The purchase order authorizes a vendor to deliver goods or services and bill on specified terms, and also authorizes the receiving department to accept the goods described. Since purchase orders authorize execution of transactions, control procedures for issuing them are generally in place. Typically, access to unissued purchase orders is restricted to prevent unauthorized personnel from initiating purchase transactions. Vendors may not be aware of or may not verify whether orders are placed by authorized individuals. While this may not have a financial statement impact, it could result in overstocking or the purchase of unnecessary items.

Prenumbering purchase orders and subsequently accounting for the numerical sequence help ensure that company personnel are aware of all open purchase commitments. That awareness is necessary to ensure that appropriate provisions for losses on purchase commitments are recorded.

Control procedures directed toward the accuracy and authorization of purchase orders typically include comparing them with requisition forms and reviewing them for approval by an authorized individual. These procedures are performed before orders are placed with vendors. An additional control procedure directed toward the accuracy of orders may be giving requisitioners copies of the purchase orders for them to review for conformity with their expectations. Purchase orders with small dollar amounts or routine characteristics may be subjected to a less detailed review.

Some specialized goods and services cannot be handled by a purchasing department because the technical and performance requirements are too specialized or in some cases cannot be specified in advance. For example, the purchase of property and casualty insurance generally requires an insurance risk analysis. This analysis and the subsequent negotiations with an independent insurance agent or broker require special skill and training. Such specialized purchases must be negotiated directly between representatives of the responsible department and the vendor. Bypassing the purchasing department is likely to be a persistent and sometimes highly sensitive problem for most companies because of the conflict between the need for control procedures that a centralized purchasing function can provide, and the desires of individual users, who may believe they can get better quality and service by dealing directly with vendors. Deciding where to draw the line between operating autonomy and centralized purchasing varies from company to company, but even in companies with highly centralized purchasing functions some specialized services are allowed to bypass them. In those situations, control procedures typically include requirements that agreements be in writing, goods be approved on receipt, and the user approves the invoices.

Receiving, Inspecting, and Accepting Goods. In many enterprises the volume of receiving is so large that the receiving function is carried out in a specially organized department separate from the requisitioning, purchasing, and accounting departments. A separate receiving department enhances control over purchases by providing a division of duties.

The receiving function typically inspects goods for conformity with specifications on purchase orders. Quantities are verified by counting, weighing, or measuring. To improve the likelihood that receiving personnel will independently determine quantities, some systems provide for omitting quantities from the copy of the purchase order sent to the receiving department or, in a computerized system, restricting receiving personnel's access to quantity information on the open order file. The receivers also determine the quality of goods as far as possible, including whether or not there is shipping damage. Inspection of incoming goods is an essential control procedure for management's purposes. Laboratory or technical analysis of goods may be necessary in some cases to determine that their quality meets specifications. This requires specialized technical skills and is usually assigned to an appropriately staffed inspection department.

The purchasing and accounting departments are notified of the receipt and acceptance of shipments. Receiving personnel generally document receipts on a receiving report, a packing slip sent with the goods by the vendor, or a copy of the purchase order. The information provided includes vendor, date received, quantity and condition of goods received, and sometimes the carrier. The document is signed by whoever received the goods. In a computerized system, the receiver may input the information directly into the system, which then updates the open purchase order file, indicating that all or a portion of the order was received; generates a receiving report and an open receiving report file; and sometimes also updates the perpetual inventory file. Receipts that cannot be matched with an open purchase order may not be accepted by the receiving department; if they are accepted, they are reported on an exception report for investigation and follow-up, which are typically performed by accounting personnel. Whether prepared manually or by computer, receiving reports are generally prenumbered and their numerical sequence is subsequently accounted for. This control procedure is designed to ensure that goods received are reported completely and on a timely basis to prevent understatement of accounts payable and costs or inventory.

Services and some goods do not arrive through the receiving department but are received directly by users. While formal procedures may be prescribed for users to originate receiving reports, more often the vendor's invoice for the service or goods is forwarded to the user for approval and acknowledgment of receipt.

Recording. An asset or expense and the related liability are most often recorded by people independent of the ordering and receiving functions on the basis of a vendor's invoice that has been matched to an approved purchase order, and of evidence that goods were received or services performed. In some computerized systems, perpetual inventory records are posted when the receiving department inputs the receipt; alternatively, the accounting department may post the inventory records using a copy of the receiving report. Receiving reports not matched with invoices at the end of a period should generate an entry to record a liability for goods received but not billed.

Failure to apply control procedures to vendors' invoices as soon as they are received is a common control structure deficiency, particularly if many invoices must be routed for approval to operating personnel whose main interests are directed elsewhere. The resulting delay in recording invoices may, depending on the accounting system and related control procedures, cause accounts payable and the related asset or expense accounts to be misstated and may result in the loss of discounts for prompt payment. (A large number of unmatched invoices or receiving reports that have not been approved and recorded may indicate deficiencies, breakdowns, or delays in the procedures for processing and approving invoices.)

In a manual system, invoices may be listed in a log upon receipt and the log subsequently reviewed for invoices that were not returned to the accounting department for processing. In a computerized system, invoices may not be specifically approved, but may be recorded based on the authorization of the related purchase orders and on evidence that receiving reports are properly matched to purchase orders. The invoices would then be matched to the open receiving report file; invoices that did not match would be reported on an exception report and updated to a temporary file of unmatched invoices.

Once invoices have been authorized for recording, the transactions are recorded in a manual or computerized purchases journal and are then summarized and posted. Before recording transactions in a manual system, a clerk usually recomputes the calculations on the invoices and compares them with amounts on the purchase orders. The account distribution is reviewed and entered (sometimes an initial account distribution is noted on the purchase order) to prevent transactions from being misclassified. Cutoff procedures to ensure that invoices are recorded in the proper period include reviewing the receiving report file, with attention to the dates goods were received.

The process of authorizing invoices for recording may be reviewed and approved by supervisors. Alternatively, invoices may be approved by supervisors when checks for payment are prepared or when they are signed. Supervisory review and approval are sometimes performed on only a representative sample of vendors' invoices or on specific types of invoices, most commonly if the entity has a large volume of low-dollar-value transactions and effective control procedures.

File control procedures consist primarily of supervising reconciliations of accounts payable subsidiary ledgers to control accounts. If the entity does not maintain accounts payable subsidiary ledgers, as is the case in some manual systems, the reconciliation of total open (unpaid) invoices to the accounts payable control account is subjected to supervisory review. The resolution of errors detected by the reconciliation and review processes is also adequately supervised. Segregating the duties of those who approve invoices, post the detailed inventory and accounts payable records, maintain control accounts, perform the reconciliations and reviews, and resolve errors also enhances the effectiveness of control procedures.

Payments Made for Goods and Services

Control procedures relating to the cash disbursements process—the second transaction class in the buying cycle—are intended to ensure that no unauthorized payments are made, that accurate records are made of each payment, and that unclaimed checks are adequately identified, controlled, and ultimately voided. Other procedures, more closely related to management decision making than to financial statement assertions, are designed to ensure that all liabilities are paid in ways that meet cash flow and vendor relationship objectives, including taking all available discounts for timely payment.

To prevent unauthorized payments, approvals are required for all requests for payment, and invoices and receiving documents are canceled after the related checks have been signed, so that those documents cannot be submitted for processing again. Control procedures to accomplish those objectives may be manual or computerized, and are enhanced if there is division of duties between those who prepare checks and those who originate requests for payment. The check signer should have evidence, at the time the check is signed, that the payment has been authorized. Computerized systems may prevent checks from being printed unless the invoice matches the appropriate purchase files. Asset protection control procedures require the signer to mail or handle signed checks in a way that makes them inaccessible to the people who authorize or process payments; unissued checks are safeguarded, and spoiled checks are mutilated or otherwise controlled.

If the number of employees is limited and the same person performs duties that are incompatible from a strict internal control viewpoint, some measure of control can be achieved by involving the supervisor in the processing. For example, sometimes the same person records payments to vendors and draws the checks. In this situation, the supervisor who signs the checks might require that all supporting evidence accompany the checks presented for signature and might assign someone other than the processor to cancel the supporting documents and mail the checks directly to the vendors.

Checks are drawn specifically to the order of the creditors being paid or to custodians of imprest funds being reimbursed, not to "cash" or "bearer." Drawing checks to the order of a specific entity or individual limits their negotiability and provides an acknowledgment of receipt through payees' endorsements.

Countersignatures are an effective control procedure only if each signer makes an independent examination of checks and supporting documents. Although a countersignature affixed with proper understanding and discharge of assigned responsibility provides effective control, signature by a single employee after careful examination of supporting documents offers greater protection than superficial countersignatures, which create an illusion of control and could result in reliance by one person on functions not performed by another.

Control procedures to ensure that all acknowledged liabilities are paid in time to take advantage of cash discounts, promote good relations with suppliers, and maintain the enterprise's credit rating are more closely related to management's decision making than to financial statement assertions. Timely payments are ensured by periodic reviews of files of unmatched receiving reports and invoices and by the aging of open accounts payable.

Complete and accurate recording of payments is controlled by prenumbering checks, maintaining a detailed check register, accounting for the numerical sequence of checks entered in the register, and comparing paid checks returned by the bank with the check register as part of the periodic reconciliation of cash in banks. After appropriate inquiry into the reasons for long-outstanding checks, payment is stopped at the bank and the accounts are adjusted either to reverse the original entries or to record the items in a separate liability account.

Supervision of the cash disbursements process is provided by the check signer's review of supporting documentation, the review of bank reconciliations, and the reconciliation and review of the accounts payable trial balance.

Goods Returned to Suppliers

Every credit due an enterprise because goods are returned or an allowance is negotiated is an asset equivalent to a receivable, although its recording is usually different, as discussed below. It is important, therefore, that these claims be adequately controlled, even though they are likely to be nonroutine and infrequent. Many companies also have policies and procedures for processing their own internally generated debit memos.

Returns for credit must be prepared for shipment to the vendor; the shipping department usually has procedures for notifying the accounts payable and purchasing departments at the time items are returned. Policies and procedures similar to those used for sales can be used, for example, requiring all shipping documents and supporting materials to be accompanied by a numerically controlled debit memo, usually prepared by the purchasing department and recorded in a debit memo journal by the accounting department. (Chapter 12, "Auditing the Revenue Cycle," discusses those policies and procedures.) Control of freight claims can usually be achieved in a similar manner.

When a credit memo is received from a vendor, it is matched to the related debit memo, if any, shipping documents, or other relevant internally generated documents. Quantities returned, prices, dates, vendor's name, extensions, and footings are compared by personnel independent of the purchasing, shipping, and inventory control functions. If companies have formal debit memo procedures, credits and claims are often deducted immediately from the next vendor payment without waiting for a vendor credit memo.

Claims for allowances, adjustments, and occasional returns that are not subject to the above procedures are subject to some procedure for notifying the accounting and purchasing departments of a dispute or claim due. Since there are no positive means for controlling compliance with that type of procedure, knowledgeable personnel throughout the company are periodically asked about the existence of outstanding claims or allowances.

Payroll Processing

Payroll processing is the one function most likely to have similar characteristics from one entity to another, which is one reason that payroll processing is the service most commonly offered by data processing service organizations. Over the years, payroll transaction processing has become increasingly systematized and generally well controlled. The typical payroll transaction is distinguished from other buying cycle transactions by the withholding of amounts to cover various types of employee obligations (for example, taxes and insurance premiums) and by different control procedures. Payroll processing includes

- Authorizing employment.
- Recording time worked or output produced.
- Calculating gross pay and deductions.

Authorizing Employment. Documents authorizing employment are prepared independently of the prospective employee's immediate supervisor and those responsible for preparing the payroll. Preferred practice is to lodge that responsibility in the personnel department, which, in the formal hiring process, creates records authorizing employment, the rate of pay, and payroll deductions. The personnel department also prepares pay rate changes and employee termination notices.

The employment records contain data of a permanent or semipermanent nature, which is referred to as "standing data." Standing data, such as employee name, social security number, rate of pay, authorized deductions, and tax exemptions, is used for calculating gross pay and deductions each time a payroll is processed. Consequently, errors in standing data are usually more significant than errors in data relating to a single pay period (referred to as "transaction data"), such as hours worked. The completeness, accuracy, and authorization of standing data, which is not changed frequently, should be controlled by periodic review by the personnel department of recorded payroll standing data and of changes thereto.

Recording Time Worked or Output Produced. Evidence of performance of services (including overtime) is produced in the form of time reports or clock cards, which should be controlled by supervisory review and approval. If pay is based on production quantity rather than time, as with piecework or commissions, the quantity should be similarly approved and reconciled to recorded production or sales data.

Calculating Gross Pay and Deductions. Calculating gross pay and deductions involves matching the transaction data (that is, the records of time or output for the payroll period) and standing data for each employee. The computation of pay may be simple or exceedingly complex; it may be done manually or by computer. In a manual system, control procedures consist of reviewing the payroll journal and recalculating the gross pay (including the rates used) if part or all of the payroll is calculated on an hourly rather than a straight salary basis, or using control totals derived from a separate calculation of the aggregate payroll amount. In either event, the payroll should be approved by a responsible official based on evidence that control procedures have been performed. Where payrolls are calculated by a computer program, a responsible official reviews the gross payroll and deductions for reasonableness and approves the amounts. The self-interest of employees and their ready access to the personnel department also act to limit the risk of underpayment. Normally the risk of overpayment is reduced by specifying the maximum amount of a payroll check or establishing payroll grade levels with maximum salaries for each level. Control is also facilitated by comparing payroll costs with standards or budgets or by reconciling payroll costs to production cost or job order records.

Accounting distribution for financial statement purposes is ordinarily not difficult to control because the wages of most employees are charged to the same account from one period to another. Detailed cost accounting systems may call for distributing the total amount among cost centers; in those cases, control over the completeness of the distribution is usually exercised by comparing the amount distributed with the total payroll. The accuracy of the distribution is ensured by investigating differences revealed by variance analyses.

The computation of payroll deductions is governed either by statute (in the case of payroll taxes) or contract (union agreement, group insurance contract, or agency agreements with charitable organizations or credit unions). The authorization to deduct amounts from an employee's pay is given by the individual in writing and is ordinarily obtained and maintained by the personnel department. Cumulative records of deductions are required for each employee. Control procedures for payments of withheld amounts are similar to those for payments of recorded accounts payable.

As previously noted, many companies contract with a data processing service organization for the actual calculation of gross pay and deductions, based on appropriately approved standing and transaction data. If this is done, the output from the service bureau should be reviewed in the same manner as discussed earlier. (See Chapter 6 for a discussion of the auditor's responsibilities in this situation.)

In most organizations, the recognized advantages of segregation of duties in payroll processing are not difficult to achieve. The duties of the personnel and accounting departments are separated, and the person who approves time records is independent of both departments. All of those functions are separate from the handling of payroll checks or cash, as discussed below.

Payment of Wages

Payment of the net payroll amount may be accomplished by check, direct deposit into the employee's bank account, or, in increasingly rare instances, cash payment. Approval of payroll checks, which are often prepared as an integral part of the payroll calculation, usually includes comparing the total of all checks with the total of the payroll summary. Segregation of duties related to payroll disbursements made by check should be the same as for other cash disbursements. It is especially important to segregate duties if the checks are distributed rather than mailed. For example, employees' checks should be distributed by people who do not have responsibility for preparing or approving the payroll.[1]

Unclaimed wages are listed at once, safeguarded, investigated with the personnel department to determine the existence of the employees, and returned to cash if unclaimed within a short time.

[1]Internal auditors may observe a payroll distribution to provide assurance that payments are not made to nonexistent personnel. At one time, it was not uncommon for external auditors to perform the same test, but, except for special "fraud audits," it is rarely done today.

DETERMINING THE AUDIT STRATEGY

The audit strategy for each account balance and class of transactions in the buying cycle is based primarily on the auditor's assessment of inherent and control risk relating to the specific audit objectives and on efficiency considerations.

Audit Objectives

The audit objectives applicable to accounts in the buying cycle are

Completeness

- Accounts payable represent all amounts owed by the entity at the balance sheet date with respect to the purchase of goods or services.
- All goods or services received, less goods returned, during the period covered by the financial statements are reflected in the financial statements.
- All employee wages for services performed during the period covered by the financial statements are reflected in the financial statements; accrued payroll represents all amounts owed to employees at the balance sheet date.

Accuracy

- Purchase transactions are based on correct prices and quantities and are accurately computed and classified in the appropriate general ledger and accounts payable subsidiary ledger accounts.
- Invoice summarizations and postings to the accounts payable subsidiary ledger and purchases account are correct.
- The accounts payable subsidiary ledger is mathematically correct and agrees with the general ledger.
- All payroll amounts are based on correct wage rates and hours, and are accurately computed, summarized, and classified in the appropriate general ledger accounts.

Existence/Occurrence

- Recorded accounts payable represent amounts owed by the entity at the balance sheet date.
- Recorded purchase transactions represent goods or services actually received during the period covered by the financial statements.
- Recorded payroll transactions represent wages for services actually performed during the period covered by the financial statements.

Cutoff

- Purchase transactions, accounts payable, returns, and payroll transactions are recorded in the proper period.

Valuation

- Accounts payable and accrued payroll are stated at the correct amount the entity owes.
- All expenses and losses applicable to the period have been recognized, including unrealized losses on unfavorable purchase commitments.

Rights and Obligations

- Accounts payable and accrued payroll are legal obligations of the entity at the balance sheet date.

Presentation and Disclosure

- Accounts payable, accrued payroll, and expenses are properly described and classified in the financial statements.
- Loss contingencies related to purchase commitments are properly disclosed.

The auditor achieves these objectives by performing substantive tests or a combination of substantive tests and tests of control structure policies and procedures. The auditor often tests an entity's control procedures to obtain evidence that they are designed and operating effectively as a basis for significantly reducing the assurance needed from substantive tests directed at the completeness, accuracy, and existence audit objectives. The auditor generally achieves the remaining audit objectives (with the exception of cutoff) by performing substantive tests, supplemented by the evidence obtained through assessing the entity's inherent risk conditions, control environment, and accounting system. For example, the auditor's awareness of fluctuations in foreign currency exchange rates may cause concern about the valuation audit objective for accounts payable denominated in foreign currencies.

The auditor usually finds it efficient to perform substantive tests to achieve the cutoff objective, particularly if the client has not established control procedures related to cutoff. If management has implemented special control procedures designed to achieve proper cutoff at year-end, the auditor may decide to test those special control procedures in conjunction with other tests of control structure policies and procedures.

Liabilities are more likely to be understated or omitted from the accounts than overstated because the account balances consist of items that have been scrutinized and acknowledged before being recorded, and any inclination to improve financial statement presentation may be reflected in that process. Therefore, auditing procedures in the buying cycle concentrate heavily on seeking evidence of omitted or understated liabilities, although the possibility of overstatement is not ignored.

Risk Assessment

As discussed in Chapter 8, the auditor gathers or updates information about various aspects of the client and its business as a basis for assessing inherent and control risk.

Analytical Procedures. Analytical procedures frequently highlight relationships between accounts and risks not otherwise apparent during the risk assessment phase of the audit. Analytical procedures can, for example, indicate trends in expenses that may assist the auditor in assessing risk. Relationships among expense accounts and between expense and other accounts should be reviewed and compared with those of prior periods and those anticipated in budgets or forecasts. The account balances themselves are often compared from month to month and with the corresponding period of the prior year. Trends and fluctuations (seasonal and other) should be noted and explanations sought for unusual patterns.

The auditor should consider management's performance of analytical procedures as part of its reviews of reports and other internal documentation. The auditor may consider using the results of those procedures, to the extent appropriate, to supplement his or her own analytical procedures.

Management typically reviews various internal expense and budgetary reports and data, such as the following:

- Actual gross profit compared with historical trends and budgets or forecasts.
- Actual expenses, including payroll, compared with historical trends and budgets.
- Trends of returns and debit memos.
- Accounts payable aging.
- Open purchase commitments.

Management's review of reports like these may help identify material misstatements in the processing of purchase transactions. For example, investigation of significant differences between reported expenses and budgeted and historical expenses could identify incomplete updating of invoices to the general ledger.

The way the client responds to the auditor's inquiries resulting from analytical procedures may give some indication of the quality of the client's control environment. For example, prompt, logical, and meaningful answers to questions about differences between current-year expenses and budgeted amounts as of an interim date or corresponding prior-year amounts would provide some indication, in the absence of evidence to the contrary, that the company's management is "in control" and that the accounting system and control procedures appear to be functioning as intended. Analytical procedures, however, may also indicate trends, even in well-controlled companies, that may lead the auditor to extend substantive tests. Analytical procedures performed as substantive tests are discussed later in this chapter.

Control Risk. The auditor also is required, at a minimum, to obtain an understanding of the entity's control structure sufficient to plan the audit. This understanding is used to identify the types of misstatements that might occur and the risk of their occurring, and to design substantive tests. The understanding is obtained, or updated, by considering previous experience with the entity, reviewing prior-year audit results, interviewing client personnel, observing personnel as they perform their duties, reviewing client-prepared descriptions of policies and procedures, and inspecting documents and records. These procedures normally reveal information about all significant cycles and account balances.

In addition to information about the client's overall control environment, how transactions are processed (manually or by computer) and how sophisticated these systems are, and other general characteristics of the control structure, the auditor should consider the following types of information, as appropriate, related to the buying cycle:

- The volume, dollar amount, and types of purchases, and the number of vendors the entity buys from.
- The flow of buying cycle transactions through the accounting system.

The auditor should also obtain an understanding of control procedures applied to purchase orders, receiving documents, invoices, and cash disbursements, and the extent to which duties are segregated among the people performing those procedures. Based on all the above information, the auditor determines whether control structure policies and procedures for specific classes of transactions are appropriately designed and have been placed in operation.

In the course of obtaining the understanding of the control structure, the auditor may perform concurrent tests of controls (either incidental or planned) and thereby obtain evidence that control structure policies and procedures have been properly designed and are operating effectively. That evidence would enable the auditor to assess control risk at below the maximum for relevant audit objectives. For example, when inquiring about management's review of reported expenses, the auditor may also observe personnel performing the review or examine reports or documents that provide evidence of it. If operating effectively, management's review provides some evidence with respect to the completeness and accuracy of expenses. The auditor considers the level of detail reviewed and the likelihood that the reviewer would detect a material misstatement.

The auditor next considers whether he or she wishes to obtain additional evidence of the effectiveness of policies and procedures as a basis for a low assessment of control risk, and then whether such evidence is likely to be available and efficient to obtain. If so, the auditor would usually perform additional tests of controls for specific audit objectives—commonly, completeness, accuracy, and existence/occurrence of accounts payable, purchases, and payroll.

Audit Testing Plan

As discussed in Chapter 5, the basic audit strategy decision the auditor makes for each significant account balance is whether to perform additional tests of controls to support a low assessed level of control risk for specific audit objectives, or to perform substantive tests directed at all relevant audit objectives, without significant restriction based on tests of controls.

Professional judgment is needed to assess risks and translate that assessment into the various decisions that determine the audit plan. The following two situations describe the testing decisions an auditor might make in developing an appropriate audit strategy for the buying cycle.

The first situation is a small manufacturing company with a manual accounting system for purchases and cash disbursements. The volume of transactions is low. The user determines the need to purchase goods or services; for example, the production supervisor determines that the supply of a particular part is low. The user prepares a purchase order, including the item, quantity, vendor, shipping terms, and price. The user determines this information by calling various vendors for quotes. The purchase orders are prenumbered, but the numbers are not accounted for since many individuals have access to and use the forms.

Purchase orders are approved by appropriate individuals in the various departments. For example, the production manager approves the production supervisor's order. Various individuals have the authority to purchase items up to certain dollar amounts. Frequently, the user obtains verbal approval for orders. For example, the production supervisor may tell the production manager that certain items are needed and, based on vendors' quotes, will cost $X. The manager gives the supervisor verbal approval to order the items. The supervisor places the order over the phone. Later, the supervisor completes a purchase order for the manager to sign. Sometimes purchase orders are not completed because the user simply forgets to do so.

Inventory items are received by the production department at the receiving dock, and items like supplies are received by the receptionist. A copy of the purchase order is given to the receiving dock personnel or the receptionist. Typically, the purchase order copy is used only if there is some question about who ordered the goods or if there is no packing slip with the merchandise. The individual receiving the goods counts the items received and indicates the quantity on the packing slip or purchase order copy and signs it. The person who ordered the goods is then notified that they are in, and the packing slip or purchase order copy is forwarded to the accounting department.

The packing slip or purchase order is filed in an open receiving order file until the invoice is received. The accounting clerk then matches the invoice to the packing slip or purchase order and forwards them both to the appropriate individual for approval. If the invoice cannot be matched to a packing slip or purchase order, the accounting clerk tries to identify the person who ordered the goods to determine whether they were received, and then forwards the invoice package to that person for approval.

When approved invoice packages are returned to the accounting clerk, they are filed by expected payment date, but the purchases are not recorded. Each week, the accounting clerk pulls the invoices to be paid that week, types the checks, and lists the account distribution on the invoices. The checks and the invoice packages (collectively usually referred to as "vouchers") are then given to the controller for review and signature. The checks and any items to be sent with them, for example, a copy of the invoice or remittance advice, are given to the receptionist to mail. The check copies and the invoice packages are returned to the accounting clerk, who then records the purchases and the cash disbursements in the check register and files the check copies and the invoice packages.

At the end of the month, the accounting clerk totals the check register and posts the monthly entry to the ledger. The clerk also totals the unpaid invoices and prepares an entry to record the liability for unpaid purchases and the related expense or inventory. (This entry is reversed at the beginning of the following month.) The controller approves all entries before the accounting clerk posts them to the ledger.

The accounting clerk also performs the monthly reconciliations and prepares the financial statements. The financial statements are reviewed by management, and any unexpected results are investigated.

The accounting system for payroll in this company would be similar to that for purchases in general. Gross pay, net pay, and withholdings are calculated manually. The postings to the general ledger are similar to those for purchases, except that the amounts come from the payroll journal and the processing and recording are done by the payroll clerk.

In this situation, the auditor, based on his or her understanding of the control structure and any concurrent tests of controls performed, would probably assess control risk at below the maximum and decide not to perform additional tests of controls. Substantive tests of details would be directed at all assertions. In addition to the substantive tests described later in the chapter, the auditor might need to perform additional tests with respect to the accuracy of accounts payable, accrued payroll, and purchases. Those tests might include determining that the account distributions are proper and that the posting to the subsidiary and general ledgers was done correctly. The tests of details would be performed as of year-end.

The above strategy decisions are based on the following factors:

- Low transaction volume, which makes substantive testing efficient.
- Manual accounting system, which increases the risk of random errors.
- Ineffective division of duties.
- Limited control procedures; for example, there is no review of the invoice package before it is given to the controller, and the invoice package is not canceled or stamped "paid" after the controller signs the check.

The auditor's decision might have been different if the company had

- A higher volume of transactions.
- A computerized accounting system that used packaged software developed and maintained by third-party vendors.
- Increased segregation of duties, for example, if the person responsible for matching invoices to the packing slips or purchase orders and investigating missing orders were independent from the person who recorded payments, typed checks, and performed reconciliations.
- Effective transaction processing and file control procedures, for example, accounting for the numerical sequence of purchase orders, matching of purchases to receiving reports and purchase orders, investigation of unmatched items by accounting clerks, and investigation of long-outstanding orders by the production department.

In those circumstances, the auditor might have decided to perform additional tests of control procedures to reduce the assurance needed from substantive tests for the completeness, accuracy, and existence/occurrence audit objectives.

In the second situation, the client is a large manufacturing company with a computerized accounting system for purchases and cash disbursements. The company has a large, highly skilled EDP department with effective general control procedures and division of duties. The EDP department typically develops software internally, but sometimes modifies packaged software. Control procedures for implementing new systems, maintaining existing systems, and the operations functions are effective, as are program and data file security control procedures. (These general control procedures are discussed in detail in Chapter 11.) Control procedures applied to purchases and cash disbursements are designed to ensure that authorized transactions are completely and accurately input and updated.

In this situation, the auditor will likely have performed tests of controls concurrently with obtaining an understanding of the control structure. The auditor is also likely to consider it efficient to perform additional tests of controls relating to the completeness, accuracy, and authorization control objectives for purchase and cash disbursements transactions, as a basis for assessing control risk as low. If the additional tests of controls support a low assessment of control risk, substantive tests directed at the completeness, accuracy, and existence/occurrence audit objectives could be reduced. They might even be limited to analytical procedures. The auditor would be likely to perform any tests of details prior to year-end.

If the client did not have effective program and data file security control procedures, the auditor might revise the strategy to include more substantive tests directed at the existence audit objective for accounts payable. Ineffective security control procedures increase the risk of unauthorized alterations to programs and data. The ability to manipulate accounts payable data might make it possible for an employee to initiate payment of a check to himself or herself and conceal the defalcation.

ADDITIONAL TESTS OF CONTROLS

Concurrent tests of controls often provide evidence to support an assessment of control risk at below the maximum for one or more audit objectives. However, concurrent tests of controls are generally directed mainly at policies and procedures that are part of the control environment and accounting system, as opposed to specific control procedures, and therefore usually relate to several audit objectives and affect several accounts. Thus, concurrent tests of controls are not enough to support a low assessment of control risk for specific audit objectives and account balances. To assess control risk as low for one or more audit objectives for some or all buying cycle accounts, the auditor performs additional tests of controls. Such tests usually require substantial audit effort, and therefore the auditor generally performs them when he or she believes they will significantly reduce the amount of substantive testing required.

Specific control objectives and typical control procedures applicable to acquisitions of goods and services, payments made for them, and calculating and recording payroll are described in Figures 13.2, 13.3, and 13.4, respectively. The accounting system assumed to be in operation in the figures is a sophisticated computerized system. As discussed in Chapter 8, the tests of controls the auditor would perform include an appropriate combination of inquiring about the client's control procedures, observing that the procedures have been placed in operation, and examining evidence that they are designed and operating effectively. Also as discussed in Chapter 8, reperformance may be used in tests of controls; but if that becomes necessary, the auditor usually determines it is more efficient to perform substantive tests. In addition to testing control procedures specific to a particular transaction cycle, in order to assess control risk as low the auditor would also need evidence of the effectiveness of general control procedures.

In evaluating the results of tests of controls (including tests of general control procedures), the auditor considers whether the control structure policies and procedures, taken as a whole, are appropriately designed to achieve the control

Figure 13.2 Acquisitions of Goods and Services

	Control Objectives					
	Transaction Processing					
	Authorization	*Completeness of Input*	*Accuracy of Input*	*Completeness and Accuracy of Updating*[a]	*File*	*Asset Protection*
Specific Control Objectives	All recorded purchase transactions represent actual receipts of goods and services and are approved.	All purchase transactions are input and accepted for processing.	Purchases are correctly recorded as to amounts, quantities, dates, vendors, and general ledger account; are recorded in the proper period; are accurately converted into computer-readable form; and are accurately input to the computer.	All purchase transactions input and accepted for processing are accurately updated to the general ledger and accounts payable data files.	The integrity of individual accounts payable in the subsidiary ledger and the general ledger accounts, after purchase transactions have been accumulated in them, is preserved.	Only authorized personnel have access to accounts payable records and data stored on them.
Typical Control Procedures	Approval of requisitions and purchase orders. Matching invoices for goods and services received to receiving reports and purchase	Accounting for the numerical sequence of requisitions and purchase orders input to the computer. Reporting and resolving missing or duplicate	Counting, where appropriate, and inspecting goods received, by personnel independent of purchasing and accounting functions.	Comparing total purchases input with the total updated to the purchases and accounts payable files.	Ensuring that the correct version of the file is being used for processing. Balancing of the subsidiary ledger (previous balance plus purchases	Restricting access to accounts payable files and files used in processing payables.

orders by individuals independent of purchasing and receiving functions. Reporting and resolving invoices and receiving reports that do not match against approved purchase orders.	items by individuals independent of receiving and purchasing functions. Reporting and resolving long-outstanding items on the aged open purchase order file, and receipts and invoices rejected as not matching against the open purchase order file. Accounting for the numerical sequence of receiving reports. Reporting and resolving missing or duplicate items by individuals independent of receiving and cash disbursements functions.	Completeness of input control procedures for purchase orders also address the accuracy of input for vendor, prices, and descriptions; completeness of input procedures for receiving reports also address the accuracy of input for date, quantities, and descriptions. Reporting and resolving unmatched items by individuals independent of receiving and purchasing functions. Review of account classifications.		less payments, compared with the current total). Reconciling the subsidiary ledger to the control account in the general ledger; reporting and resolving discrepancies.

[a]Completeness of updating and accuracy of updating have been combined, because typically the same control procedures apply to both objectives.

Figure 13.3 Payments Made for Goods and Services

	Control Objectives					
	Transaction Processing					
	Authorization	*Completeness of Input*	*Accuracy of Input*	*Completeness and Accuracy of Updating*[a]	*File*	*Asset Protection*
Specific Control Objectives	All recorded cash disbursements are for actual purchases of goods and services and are approved.	All payments made are input and accepted for processing.	Disbursements are correctly recorded as to amounts, dates, and payees; are recorded in the proper period; are accurately converted into computer-readable form; and are accurately input to the computer.	All disbursements input and accepted for processing are accurately updated to the cash disbursements and accounts payable data files.	The integrity of individual accounts payable in the subsidiary ledger and the general ledger accounts, after purchase transactions have been updated to them, is preserved.	Only authorized personnel have access to cash, unissued checks, and accounts payable files or data stored on them.

Typical Control Procedures	Approving payment (before checks are signed) by officials independent of purchasing, receiving, and accounts payable functions. Examination by signatory, at time of signing checks, of supporting documentation (e.g., invoices, receiving reports, purchase orders). Canceling supporting documentation to prevent resubmission for payment.	Accounting for the numerical sequence of checks, both used and unused. Reporting and investigating missing or duplicate checks. Reporting and investigating long-outstanding checks by individuals independent of accounts payable and cash disbursements functions.	Matching disbursements records against accounts payable/open invoice files. Reporting and resolving differences by individuals independent of accounts payable and cash disbursements functions.	Comparing total disbursements input with the totals updated to the cash disbursements and accounts payable files.	Same control procedures as described in Figure 13.2, "Acquisitions of Goods and Services." Reconciling the bank statement to the general ledger cash account by personnel independent of accounts payable and cash disbursements functions (and receiving and recording cash receipts).	Mailing of checks by individuals independent of recording accounts payable. Authorized check signers are independent of cash receipts functions. Physically protecting mechanical check signers and signature plates. Restricting access to accounts payable files and files used in processing cash disbursements.

[a]Completeness of updating and accuracy of updating have been combined, because typically the same control procedures apply to both objectives.

Figure 13.4 Calculating and Recording Payroll

	Control Objectives					
	Transaction Processing					
	Authorization	*Completeness of Input*	*Accuracy of Input*	*Completeness and Accuracy of Updating*[a]	*File*	*Asset Protection*
Specific Control Objectives	All recorded transactions for employee wages are for actual services performed and are approved.	All employee wages for services performed are input and accepted for processing.	Employee wages are correctly recorded as to wage rate, hours, and time period; are properly calculated as to gross wages, withholdings, and net pay; are recorded to the correct general ledger accounts; are accurately converted into machine-readable form; and are accurately input to the computer.	All employee wage transactions input and accepted for processing are accurately updated to the payroll register and individual payroll files.	The integrity of the individual employee payroll records and the payroll summary and general ledger accounts for payroll withholdings is preserved.	Only authorized personnel have access to payroll files and data stored on them.

Typical Control Procedures	Approving changes to master files for wage and salary rates. Approving changes to master files for new employees and deleted employees. Approving processing of pay for employees with hours in excess of a predetermined limit.	Comparing total hours (in batch form) with total hours input to the computer. Reporting and investigating employees on master file for whom no hours worked have been input.	Completeness of input control procedures for total hours also addresses the accuracy of input. Matching employee data to comparable master file data—employee name, number, and so on. Reporting and investigating mismatched items. Reporting hours worked in excess of a predetermined limit.	Comparing total hours and number of employees input with the totals updated to the payroll register.	Ensuring that the correct version of the file is being used for processing. Reconciling the employee subsidiary ledger to the control accounts in the general ledger; reporting and resolving discrepancies.	Restricting access to payroll files and data stored on them. Distribution of checks by persons independent of recording and approving the payroll. Physically protecting mechanical check signers and signature plates.

[a]Completeness of updating and accuracy of updating have been combined, because typically the same control procedures apply to both objectives.

objectives and are operating effectively. This will determine whether the expected assessment of control risk as low was attained for specific accounts and audit objectives and, thus, whether the auditor can significantly reduce substantive testing. Results differing from those anticipated when developing the audit testing plan require the auditor to reconsider the nature, timing, and extent of planned substantive tests—not only for buying cycle accounts, but also for other accounts that may be affected. For example, ineffective control procedures to ensure completeness of recorded purchases may also affect inventory and cost of sales.

SUBSTANTIVE TESTS

If the auditor has assessed control risk for some or all buying cycle accounts as low for specific audit objectives, substantive tests addressing those audit objectives may be limited to analytical procedures. This is more likely to be done for expense and payroll accounts than for accounts payable and other liability accounts. The auditor will also consider whether evidence obtained from tests directed at other audit objectives is relevant to these audit objectives too. For example, tracing accounts payable to supporting documentation is directed toward the accuracy audit objective, but provides some evidence about existence as well. Control risk is seldom assessed as low with respect to the cutoff, valuation, rights and obligations, and presentation and disclosure objectives, and therefore substantive tests of details are usually performed for these objectives.

Accounts Payable

Before performing substantive tests directed toward the other audit objectives, the auditor should be reasonably assured that the accounts payable trial balance contains all purchase transactions that remain unpaid at year-end. Evidence about the completeness of the trial balance is often provided largely by the results of tests of controls.

To achieve the cutoff objective, it is usually more efficient for the auditor to perform substantive tests of details, particularly in the case of those companies that are not concerned about precise cutoff on a month-to-month basis. Companies may, however, implement special control procedures at the end of the year, which the auditor may decide to test. Also, control structure policies and procedures designed to ensure completeness of input and update may be effective in ensuring that transactions are recorded in the proper period. For example, the design of the accounting system itself may reduce control risk for cutoff.

Cutoff tests are intended to ascertain that all significant transactions have been recorded in the proper period. In the absence of control structure policies and procedures directed toward cutoff, the sooner the accounts are closed after year-end, the greater the likelihood that there will be unrecorded vendors' invoices. Thus, examining files of unmatched receiving reports and unrecorded invoices, the purchases journal, and the cash disbursements journal, and other relevant records for a period after year-end is an almost universal auditing procedure. (Cutoff tests of the receipt of goods and recording of inventory are usually coordinated with the auditor's observation of the client's physical inventory count; those tests are discussed in Chapter 14.)

If the basic transaction documents are in numerical sequence, the auditor can note the number of the last receiving report, and the last check issued (or other basic transaction documents) prior to year-end. The auditor can examine perpetual inventory records, the year-end accounts payable trial balance, and the listing of unmatched receiving reports to determine whether goods received at or near year-end are included. Similarly, the last check issued can be traced to the cash disbursements records and the list of outstanding checks in the bank reconciliation. The auditor should apply the same procedures to obtain assurance that receipts and invoices applicable to the following year were not recorded in the current year. If the basic transaction documents are not prenumbered, it may be necessary to examine relevant documents, with emphasis on transaction dates and large amounts, selected from the various sources both before and after the cutoff date to obtain sufficient evidence that the cutoff was properly made.

Confirmation of accounts payable balances does not have the widespread acceptance as a substantive test that confirmation of accounts receivable has. Evidence about the existence of payables is usually obtained through tests of control procedures for ordering and receiving goods and for recording invoices, through analytical procedures, and through the substantive tests discussed below; only rarely is confirmation an effective or efficient means of obtaining the necessary assurance that accounts payable have been properly authorized and recorded. Reviewing purchase and disbursement records subsequent to year-end (commonly referred to as unrecorded liability tests) addresses the completeness of payables. (Confirming a few payables as a test of controls, however, may provide the auditor with useful evidence about the effective operation of control policies and procedures directed toward the completeness, accuracy, and proper cutoff of purchases from and disbursements to vendors.) Confirmation (as a substantive test) may be called for if there are deficiencies in control procedures or if the results of other substantive tests indicate that payables may be incomplete or otherwise misstated. If undertaken, the confirmation procedure is like that described in Chapter 12 for confirming accounts receivable, except that an additional step of circularizing known suppliers with zero balances may be included. In extreme situations, if the auditor is still not satisfied as to possible unrecorded liabilities or the accuracy of recorded balances, the client may be requested to deliver the mail, unopened, to the auditor daily for a reasonable period after year-end, so that the auditor can search for vendors' invoices and statements applicable to the year under audit.

Substantive tests directed at the existence and accuracy of recorded accounts payable normally consist of

- Tracing selected entries in the accounts payable subsidiary ledger or trial balance to subsequent cash disbursements or other supporting documents, such as vendors' invoices; examining evidence that the client has matched all invoices to purchase orders and receiving reports; and reperforming the matching procedure (on a test basis if appropriate) to determine that all aspects of the transaction appear reasonable (e.g., that suppliers' invoices are addressed to the client).
- Tracing to appropriate supporting documentation, adjusting items in the client's reconciliation of the subsidiary ledger to the control account. The auditor should also test the mathematical accuracy of the client's accounts payable subsidiary ledger or trial balance and the reconciliation.
- Investigating the underlying causes of debit balances in accounts payable. They may represent overpayments; if so, the auditor should consider whether they are collectible. They may also represent purchases that were not recorded but were nevertheless paid; in that event, the auditor should ascertain why the purchases were not recorded.

Losses from purchase commitments may arise in connection with commodity purchases, forward transactions, or purchase commitments in excess of short-term requirements. If material losses could arise from unfulfilled purchase commitments, the commitments should be identified and the auditor should assess the potential need for a loss provision. This may be accomplished by examining open purchase order records, inquiring of employees who make purchase commitments, or requesting major suppliers to provide details of any purchase commitments outstanding as of year-end. If the auditor is uncertain whether all commitments have been identified, it may be appropriate to review suppliers' invoices and receiving reports for a period after year-end for evidence of purchases above prevailing prices or in quantities in excess of current requirements (by reviewing perpetual inventory records for evidence of goods that are slow-moving or obsolete), which may indicate unfavorable purchase commitments at year-end. Also, since major purchase commitments generally require the approval of the board of directors, examination of minutes of board meetings may help the auditor discover such purchase commitments.

Salaries, Wages, and Payroll Taxes

Substantive tests directed at the completeness and accuracy of accrued payroll and related liabilities consist primarily of analytical procedures and examining the subsequent payment of the liability in the following year. The auditor should obtain an analysis of accrued salaries and wages and test its mathematical accuracy; totals should be agreed to the payroll records. If the company has recorded an estimate (e.g., proration of the payroll for the overlapping period) rather than an exact computation, the appropriateness and consistency with prior years of the method of estimating should be ascertained. The auditor should also review the general ledger accounts relating to payroll expense. Analytical procedures can be helpful in this regard; for instance, the number of employees and the average salary per employee can be compared with the prior year. Any material unusual entries, unusual fluctuations in normal recurring entries in the payroll summaries, and payroll amounts capitalized in fixed asset accounts should be investigated. Substantive tests of details are normally not performed on payroll expense account balances unless control structure policies and procedures are extremely ineffective or the results of other procedures, primarily analytical procedures, indicate the need for additional assurance from detail testing.

Based on materiality and risk assessment, the auditor may examine subsequent payments of agency obligations. Comparing current year-end balances with those of the prior year may indicate unusual items. For accounts like unclaimed wages, the auditor should examine and test a trial balance reconciling the details to a control account and should scrutinize the underlying details for unusual items. If old unclaimed wages have been written off, potential liability under state escheat or unclaimed property laws should be considered.

Accrued commissions should be substantiated by examining sales reports submitted by sales personnel, commission schedules, and contracts with sales personnel. If accrued commissions are significant, the auditor should consider confirming amounts due and commissions earned during the year directly with sales personnel. The overall reasonableness of commission expense for the year may be tested by multiplying commission rates by sales.

The year-end liability for vacation pay, sick pay, and other compensated absences should be reviewed for compliance with Statement of Financial Accounting Standards (SFAS) No. 43 (Accounting Standards Section C44). If vacation periods are based on length of service, normally the client prepares a detailed computation of the accrued liability. The auditor should review the method used and the computation to determine that the amount accrued is appropriate.

A published statement of company policy may create liabilities for rights that accrue to employees even without formal labor contracts. Opinion of counsel may sometimes be necessary to determine whether there is a legal liability at the balance sheet date. Contracts and policies of that nature do not always clearly indicate whether employees' rights accrue ratably over a period or come into existence in their entirety at a specific date. The auditor must also be alert for possible liabilities arising from employee benefits so customary as to constitute an implied promise. Sick pay, severance pay, and some kinds of bonuses and pensions are examples.

Costs and Expenses

Audit evidence with respect to the income statement is based mainly on auditing procedures applied to balance sheet accounts, correlation of amounts on the income statement with balances on the balance sheet, analytical procedures such as the review of performance indicators, and, where applicable, tests of controls. If control risk has not been assessed as low, procedures like correlating income statement amounts with balances in the balance sheet become more important. Many income statement items can be correlated with balance sheet accounts, such as interest with loan balances. In addition, the auditor can assess the reasonableness of the amounts, for example, by comparing the percentage of selling, general, and administrative expenses in relation to sales from period to period. In computerized systems, computer software can facilitate these tests.

When the procedures outlined above have been completed, there may still be income statement accounts the auditor needs further assurance about. Tests should be designed to provide such assurance, normally in one of the following forms:

- If further assurance is needed about the occurrence or accuracy of specific expense accounts (like travel expense or maintenance expense), the auditor should request or prepare an analysis of the account in question or, at least, of the material items in it, and examine supporting documentation for enough items to gain assurance that there is no material misstatement. For example, an auditor may obtain a list of employees with expense accounts and make appropriate tests to determine whether all expenses have been reported and recorded in the accounts in the proper period, and may test related post-balance-sheet entries to determine whether a proper cutoff was made.
- If the auditor is concerned about the possibility of misstatement associated with a particular type of transaction rather than with particular account balances (as might be the case when control structure policies and procedures relating to certain types of payments are ineffective), the areas in the expense accounts that might be affected should be isolated. For example, if certain payments are supported by receiving reports and other payments are not, the auditor need perform substantive tests only for the payments that are not supported by receiving reports. In this situation, the auditor would select a sufficient number of accounts that might be misstated and examine them to the extent necessary to obtain assurance that no material misstatement had occurred.

Other Auditing Procedures

In addition to the specific substantive tests described above, the auditor typically performs procedures designed to detect other unrecorded liabilities, like insurance claims and other loss contingencies, as well as receives a letter of representation from management and a letter from the company's counsel. Those topics are covered in detail in Chapter 17. The remainder of this section describes other procedures the auditor should perform to detect unrecorded liabilities.

The auditor should read minutes of meetings of stockholders, directors, and appropriate committees for the period under audit and up to the date of the audit report. Those minutes may reveal contracts, commitments, and other matters requiring investigation. The auditor should also examine contracts, loan agreements, leases, correspondence from taxing or other governmental agencies, and similar documents. Reviewing such documents may disclose unrecorded liabilities as of the balance sheet date.

One of the auditor's most difficult tasks is identifying liabilities for which no direct reference appears in the accounts. Clues to those obligations may be discovered in unexpected places, and the auditor should be constantly alert for them. For example,

- The auditor should review responses to bank confirmation requests in addition to analyzing interest expense to determine if there are any unrecorded bank loans.
- Responses to requests for confirmation of bank loans may list as collateral securities or other assets that do not appear in the records. They may be borrowed from affiliated companies or others.
- Manufacturers of machinery and equipment often sell their products at prices that include cost of installation. The auditor should determine that the estimated cost of completing the installation of equipment sold has been recorded in the same period as the sale of the equipment.

In a decentralized environment, the possibility of unrecorded liabilities may be more significant than in a centralized environment and may warrant a procedure for formal inquiry of department heads, supervisors, and other responsible officials regarding knowledge of unprocessed invoices, unrecorded commitments, or contingent liabilities. This procedure may apply in a loosely controlled centralized environment as well.

The auditor should take a broad look at the client's operations to determine whether all types of expenses and the related liabilities, if any, that are expected have been recorded and appear to be reasonable. Familiarity with the client's operations should disclose whether such items as royalties, commissions, interest, consignments, and the myriad of taxes most businesses are subject to have been properly recorded.

The search for unrecorded liabilities cannot, of course, bring to light liabilities that have been deliberately withheld from the auditor's attention. The auditor's responsibility regarding irregularities and illegal acts is discussed in Chapter 4. The receipt of a client representation letter, as discussed in Chapter 17, does not relieve the auditor of professional responsibilities in this area.

Finally, transactions with affiliated entities often are not conducted on the same basis as transactions with outsiders; thus, they deserve special attention from the auditor. For example, charges for services rendered may not be billed on a timely basis. Whenever feasible, the auditor should review a reconciliation of the amount due to or from an affiliate by reference to both sets of records. If this cannot be done, the balance should be confirmed.

Review Questions

13–1. What types of activity are generally considered part of the buying cycle?

13–2. What is the financial statement significance of having effective control structure policies and procedures for requisitions?

13–3. What are the objectives of control procedures for purchase orders and how are they implemented?

13–4. What are the responsibilities of a receiving department?

13–5. What are the accounting requirements at the end of an accounting period with respect to receiving reports not matched with invoices?

13–6. What documents are normally included in an invoice package that has been approved for payment?

13–7. What control procedures can be used to help ensure that disbursements are completely and accurately recorded?

13–8. What measures should be taken to prevent duplicate payments?

13–9. What supervisory control procedures should be established for the summarizing and posting of purchases and disbursements?

13–10. What is standing data as related to payroll? Give examples of control procedures for standing data related to payroll.

13–11. What are the audit objectives for the buying cycle?

13–12. What characteristics of a client's buying cycle would indicate that less substantive testing could be performed?

13–13. What control procedures would the auditor expect to find relating to the acquisition of goods and services?

13–14. What control procedures would the auditor expect to find relating to payments for goods and services?

13–15. What is the purpose of performing receiving cutoff tests? How are cutoff tests in the buying cycle performed?

13–16. When may it be desirable to confirm accounts payable?

13–17. What substantive tests are generally performed with respect to accrued liabilities?

13–18. What procedures can an auditor perform that may reveal unrecorded liabilities at year-end?

Discussion Questions

13-30. The audit of trade accounts payable requires a different audit strategy and different procedures than the audit of trade accounts receivable. Answer the following questions in the light of this statement:

1. Why are trade accounts payable auditing procedures heavily weighted toward unrecorded liabilities?
2. What typical auditing procedures are applied to discover unrecorded liabilities?
3. How do the procedures applied to discover unrecorded liabilities assist the auditor in substantiating account balances for recorded liabilities?
4. In your review of the detailed trade accounts payable listing, you noted that there are several significant debit balances and long overdue payables. What transactions could have caused these situations? What auditing procedures should be performed?
5. What representations should be obtained from management related to trade accounts payable? Why?
6. What accounts should be reviewed in connection with fluctuations in trade accounts payable balances from period to period?

13-31. A company received, recorded, and paid the invoice for advertising brochures, but the receiving report was not attached to the paid invoice package. The unmatched receiving report remained in the unpaid file and served as the basis for a year-end adjusting entry for supplies received, not billed. What journal entry will be needed at year-end to correct the error? What auditing procedures might uncover the error?

13-32. A company received and paid for 100 items of part number 616, although the purchase order called for part number 661. It cannot use part number 616 and will be able to recover only 25 percent of the cost. Discuss the effect of the discovery on the audit strategy and auditing procedures.

13-33. Describe briefly several different methods to which dishonest employees may resort in manipulating payrolls. (Do not give variations of the same method.)

13-34. Forman, CPA, is the auditor of the Cardinal Company. Forman is considering the audit work to be performed in the accounts payable area for the current year's engagement.

The prior year's working papers show that confirmation requests were mailed to 100 of Cardinal's 1000 suppliers. The selected suppliers were based on Forman's sample that was designed to select accounts with large dollar balances. A substantial number of hours were spent by Cardinal and Forman resolving relatively minor differences between the confirmation replies and Cardinal's accounting records. Alternative auditing procedures were used for those suppliers who did not respond to the confirmation requests.

Required:

a. Identify the accounts payable audit objectives that Forman must consider in determining the auditing procedures to be followed.
b. Identify situations in which Forman should use accounts payable confirmations and discuss whether Forman is required to use them.
c. Discuss why the use of large dollar balances as the basis for selecting accounts

payable for confirmation might not be the most effective approach and indicate what more effective procedures could be followed when selecting accounts payable for confirmation.

(AICPA adapted)

13-35. While examining paid invoice packages, an auditor noticed that a vendor invoice called for 60 items whereas the receiving report showed only 40 had been received. Payment for 60 items had been made and charged to inventory. Discuss the effect of the discovery on the audit strategy and auditing procedures to be followed.

AICPA Multiple Choice Questions

These questions are taken from the Auditing part of Uniform CPA Examinations. Choose the single most appropriate answer.

13-40. For control purposes the quantities of materials ordered may be omitted from the copy of the purchase order which is

a. Forwarded to the accounting department.
b. Retained in the purchasing department's files.
c. Returned to the requisitioner.
d. Forwarded to the receiving department.

13-41. Which of the following is an internal control procedure that would prevent a paid disbursement voucher from being presented for payment a second time?

a. Vouchers should be prepared by individuals who are responsible for signing disbursement checks.
b. Disbursement vouchers should be approved by at least two responsible management officials.
c. The date on a disbursement voucher should be within a few days of the date the voucher is presented for payment.
d. The official signing the check should compare the check with the voucher and should deface the voucher documents.

13-42. Which of the following *best* explains why accounts payable confirmation procedures are *not* always used?

a. Inclusion of accounts payable balances in the management representation letter received from the client allows the auditor to refrain from using confirmation procedures.
b. Accounts payable generally are insignificant and can be audited by utilizing analytical procedures.
c. The auditor may feel certain that the creditors will press for payment.
d. Reliable externally generated evidence supporting accounts payable balances is generally available for audit inspection on the client's premises.

13–43. An auditor performs a test to determine whether all merchandise for which the client was billed was received. The population for this test consists of all

a. Merchandise received.
b. Vendors' invoices.
c. Canceled checks.
d. Receiving reports.

13–44. Which of the following is the most effective control procedure to detect vouchers that were prepared for the payment of goods that were *not* received?

a. Count goods upon receipt in storeroom.
b. Match purchase order, receiving report, and vendor's invoice for each voucher in accounts payable department.
c. Compare goods received with goods requisitioned in receiving department.
d. Verify vouchers for accuracy and approval in internal audit department.

13–45. The mailing of disbursement checks and remittance advices should be controlled by the employee who

a. Signed the checks last.
b. Approved the vouchers for payment.
c. Matched the receiving reports, purchase orders, and vendors' invoices.
d. Verified the mathematical accuracy of the vouchers and remittance advices.

13–46. Which of the following is the best auditing procedure for determining the existence of unrecorded liabilities at year-end?

a. Examine a sample of invoices dated a few days prior to and subsequent to year-end to ascertain whether they have been properly recorded.
b. Examine a sample of cash disbursements in the period subsequent to year-end.
c. Examine confirmation requests returned by creditors whose accounts appear on a subsidiary trial balance of accounts payable.
d. Examine unusual relationships between monthly accounts payable balances and recorded purchases.

13–47. An auditor would consider internal control procedures for a client's payroll system to be ineffective if the payroll department supervisor is responsible for

a. Hiring subordinate payroll department employees.
b. Having custody over unclaimed paychecks.
c. Updating employee earnings records.
d. Applying pay rates to time tickets.

13–48. The purpose of segregating the duties of hiring personnel and distributing payroll checks is to separate the

a. Operational responsibility from the record keeping responsibility.
b. Responsibilities of recording a transaction at its origin from the ultimate posting in the general ledger.
c. Authorization of transactions from the custody of related assets.
d. Human resources function from the controllership function.

13-49. Tracing selected items from the payroll register to employee time cards that have been approved by supervisory personnel provides evidence that

a. Internal control procedures relating to payroll disbursements were operating effectively.
b. Payroll checks were signed by an appropriate officer independent of the payroll preparation process.
c. Only bona fide employees worked and their pay was properly computed.
d. Employees worked the number of hours for which their pay was computed.

13-50. An auditor who is testing EDP controls in a payroll system would most likely use test data that contains conditions such as

a. Deductions *not* authorized by employees.
b. Overtime *not* approved by supervisors.
c. Time tickets with invalid job numbers.
d. Payroll checks with unauthorized signatures.

Problems and Cases

13-60. Green, CPA, has been engaged to audit the financial statements of Star Manufacturing, Inc. Star is a medium-sized entity that produces a wide variety of household goods. All acquisitions of materials are processed through the purchasing, receiving, accounts payable, and treasury functions.

Required:

Prepare the ''Purchases'' segment of the internal control questionnaire to be used in the assessment of Star's internal control procedures. Each question should elicit either a yes or a no response.

Do *not* prepare the receiving, accounts payable, or treasury segments of the internal control questionnaire.

Do *not* discuss internal control procedures for purchases.

(AICPA adapted)

13-61. Speedy Service Company has 100 branch offices. Each office has a manager and four or five subordinates who are employed by the manager. Branch managers prepare the weekly payroll, including their own salaries, and pay employees from cash on hand. The employee signs the payroll sheet, signifying receipt of the salary. Hours worked by hourly personnel are inserted in the payroll sheet from time cards prepared by the employees and approved by the manager.

The weekly payroll sheets are sent to the home office, along with other accounting statements and reports. The home office compiles employee earnings records and prepares all federal and state salary reports from the weekly payroll sheets.

Salaries are established by home office job-evaluation schedules. Salary adjustments, promotions, and transfers of full-time employees are approved by a home office salary committee based on the recommendations of branch managers and area supervisors. Branch managers advise the salary committee of new full-time employees and terminations. Part-time and temporary employees are hired without referral to the salary committee.

Required:

a. Based on your review of the payroll system, how might funds for payroll be diverted?
b. Prepare a payroll audit program to be used in the home office to audit the branch office payrolls of the Speedy Service Company.

(AICPA adapted)

13-62. A CPA's audit working papers contain the narrative description presented below of *a segment* of the Tigger Corporation's factory payroll system and an accompanying flowchart, shown on page 566.

NARRATIVE

The internal control structure with respect to the personnel department is well-functioning and is *not* included in the accompanying flowchart.

At the beginning of each work week, payroll clerk no. 1 reviews the payroll department files to determine the employment status of factory employees and then prepares time cards and distributes them as each individual arrives at work. This payroll clerk, who is also responsible for custody of the signature stamp machine, verifies the identity of each payee before delivering signed checks to the supervisor.

At the end of each work week, the supervisor distributes payroll checks for the preceding work week. Concurrent with this activity, the supervisor reviews the current week's employee time cards, notes the regular and overtime hours worked on a summary form, and initials the aforementioned time cards. The supervisor then delivers all time cards and unclaimed payroll checks to payroll clerk no. 2.

Required:

a. Based on the narrative and accompanying flowchart, what are the deficiencies in the internal control structure?
b. Based on the narrative and accompanying flowchart, what inquiries should be made with respect to clarifying the existence of *possible additional deficiencies* in the internal control structure?

Note: Do not discuss the internal control structure of the personnel department.

(AICPA adapted)

13-63. At the beginning of your annual audit of Superior Products' financial statements, the company president confides in you that an employee, Barney Coleman, is living on a scale in excess of that which his salary would support.

Coleman has been a buyer in the purchasing department for six years and has charge of purchasing all general materials and supplies. He is authorized to sign purchase orders for amounts up to $200. Purchase orders in excess of $200 require the countersignature of the general purchasing agent.

The president understands that the usual audit of financial statements is not designed, and cannot be relied on, to disclose fraud or conflicts of interest, although their discovery may result. The president authorizes you, however, to expand your regular auditing procedures and to apply additional auditing procedures to determine whether there is any evidence that Coleman has been misappropriating company funds or has engaged in activities that were a conflict of interest.

Tigger Corporation: Factory Payroll System

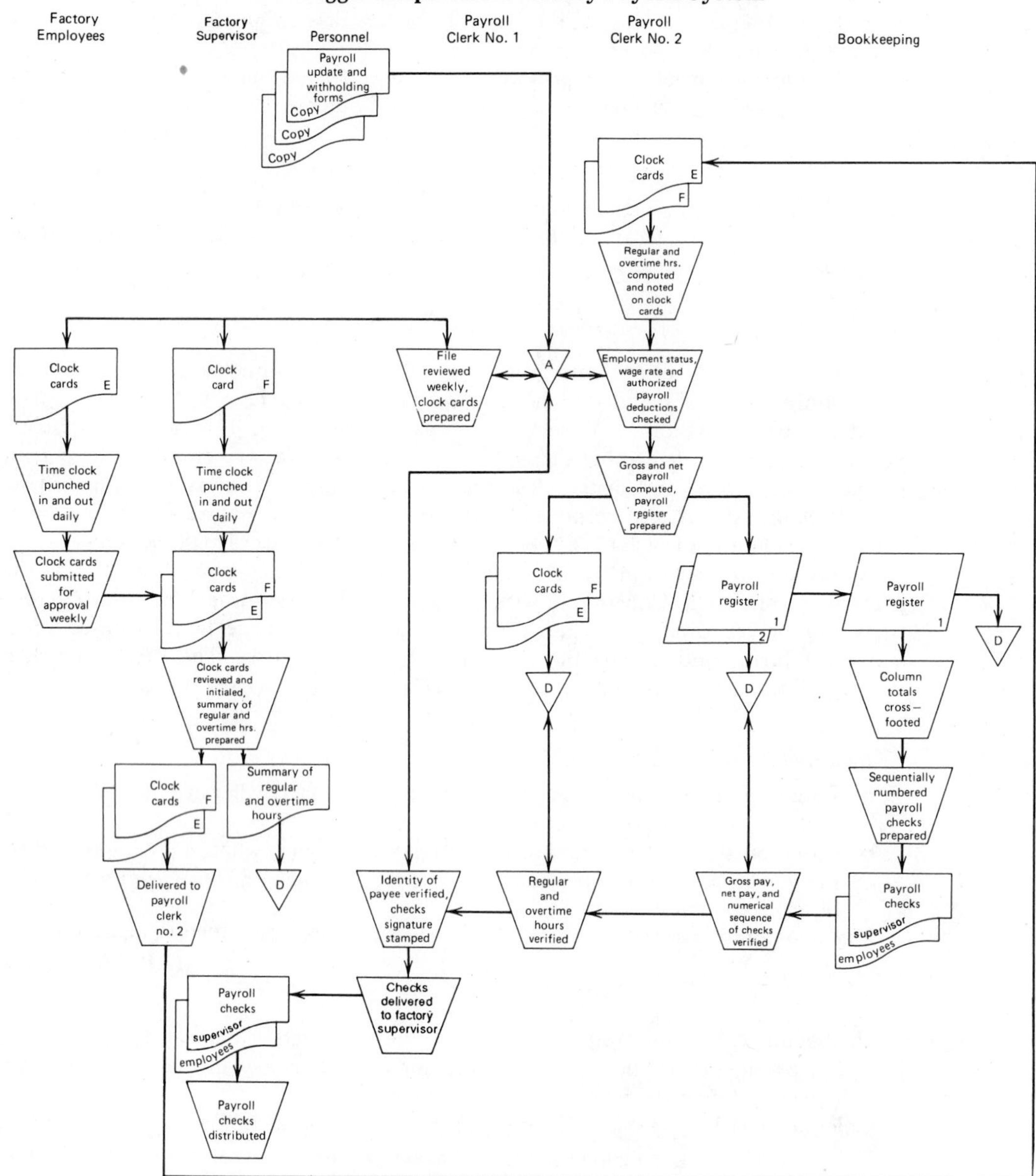

Required:

a. List the auditing procedures that you would apply to the company records and documents in an attempt to
   1. Discover evidence within the purchasing department of defalcations being committed by Coleman. Give the purpose of each auditing procedure.
   2. Provide leads regarding possible collusion between Coleman and the suppliers. Give the purpose of each auditing procedure.

b. Assume that your investigation disclosed that some suppliers have been charging Superior Products in excess of their usual prices and apparently have been making "kickbacks" to Coleman. The excess charges are material in amount. What effect, if any, would the defalcation have on (1) the financial statements that were prepared before the defalcation was uncovered, and (2) your auditor's report? Discuss.

(AICPA adapted)

13-64. The accounts payable schedule on page 568 was obtained from the accounting department of Elwood Services Corp. by the independent auditors for the audit of the December 31, 1989, financial statements. An audit assistant has performed certain auditing procedures that are noted on the schedule and has prepared the schedule of subsequent disbursements on page 569. The working papers were properly initialed, dated, and indexed and then submitted to the auditor for review. The audit strategy does not call for tests of specific internal control procedures.

Required:

a. What essential auditing procedures were not noted as having been performed on the accounts payable schedule?
b. What auditing procedures performed on the January cash disbursements schedule were deficient?

13-65. For each of the following auditing procedures applied to the *buying cycle* (performed using sampling when appropriate), indicate

a. Whether the procedure is *most likely* to be a test of controls or is *most likely* to be a substantive test.
b. The primary audit objective(s) that the procedure is designed to achieve (if the procedure is a substantive test) *or* the control objective(s) met by the control procedure(s) being tested (if the auditing procedure is a test of controls). (Be specific.)
c. The possible errors or irregularities that the procedure may uncover. (Be specific. For example, answering that the error is the "failure to achieve the control objective" is insufficient.)

Procedures

1. Review purchasing orders for proper authorization and supporting requisition.
2. Review and test investigation of computer-generated reports of receiving reports for which no invoice has been received.
3. Trace unmatched receiving reports at year-end to subsequent cash disbursements.
4. Account for the sequence of prenumbered checks issued during the period and on hand at the end of the period; examine voided checks.

Date Prepared 2/10/90
Prepared by: a) C & L ___ b) Client and Examined by BB
Reviewed by C & L SR/SUP ___

Elwood Services Corp.
Schedule of Account Payable
10/31/89

	Invoice Number	Invoice Date	Amount	
Dee Catering	–	10/31/89	1,027.50	
Plasticar	092222	9/15/89	56,922.46	
Ace Construction	823	12/10/89	353,173.00	
Rogers Moldings	60111	12/15/89	120,825.77	
" "			44,803.15	
Brown Leasing	XY1025	12/8/89	12,228.10	
Dean Packaging	79126	12/30/89	15,233.33	
Clavie Hardware	N/A	12/23/89	2,188.00	
Chemcor	89433	11/20/89	47,826.10	
"	89599	12/20/89	30,222.00	
"	A88430	12/8/89	<3,826.15>	
World Travel	N/A	12/16/89	2,123.00	
American Distributors	88-122	12/1/89	124,261.86	
" "	402318	12/2/89	<50,114.60>	
" "	88-189	12/20/89	624,800.00	
AK Trucking	L-124	12/20/89	5,000.00	
Pace Electronics	1925	12/14/89	27,840.53	
" "	1983	12/21/89	10,810.16	
Pacific Motors	18803	12/1/89	12,334.05	
Westfield Supplies	801	12/15/89	5,186.10	
Industrial Suppliers	1103	6/10/89	57,552.18	
Temp Service	N/A	12/15/89	5,123.48	
Bell Telephone	N/A		1,876.52	
City Chemicals	12704	12/17/89	83,411.50	
Excel	188653	12/20/89	6,110.14	
Walter Landscaping	1400	12/15/89	2,500.00	
H. L. Lee	N/A	12/31/89	5,000.00	
Total			1,604,438.18	b
Reconciling item			58,160.00	
Balance per general ledger			1,546,278.18	a
Accounts payable at 12/31/88			1,204,642.83	

a Agreed to the general ledger
b Footed

Date Prepared	2/11/90
Prepared by: a) C & L	BB
b) Client and Examined by	
Reviewed by C & L SR/SUP	

Elwood Services Corp.
January Cash Disbursements
12/31/89

	Check #	Check Date	Amount	Year of Acquisition or Expense ③
SK Chemicals	1022	1/3/90	45726 45	1990 ⑤
Pacific Motors	1023	1/3/90	12334 05	1989 ②
American Distributors	1024	1/3/90	124261 86	1989 ②
" "	1025	1/3/90	624800 00	1989 ②
Bell Telephone	1026	1/7/90	1876 52	1989 ④②
Rogers Moldings	1027	1/10/90	120825 77	1989 ②
RL Corp.	1028	1/10/90	58727 00	1990 ①⑤
Payroll	1029	1/15/90	67126 40	1990 ⑤
Pace Electronics	1030	1/15/90	27840 53	1990 ⑤
Chemcor	1031	1/15/90	47826 10	1989 ②
First National Bank	1032	1/15/90	50000 00	1990 ⑤
Excel	1033	1/20/90	6110 14	1989 ②
Diversified Inc.	1034	1/20/90	32223 75	1990 ⑤
Russell Stationers	1035	1/20/90	3126 50	1990 ⑤
World Travel Agency	1036	1/20/90	2123 00	1989 ②
Davis Metals	1037	1/27/90	1822 43	1990 ⑤
Ace Construction	1038	1/27/90	353173 00	1989 ②
Chemcor	1039	1/31/90	3207 00	1990 ⑤
Payroll	1040	1/31/90	68410 60	1990 ⑤
Wright Trucking	1041	1/31/90	1687 16	1990 ⑤

Note: Selected disbursements greater than $1,000 from the January check register

① Inventory was shipped 12/30/89 with terms FOB shipping point, and was received by the client on 1/3/90

② Agreed to 12/31/89 accounts payables listing.

③ Examined invoice, receiving reports and other supporting documentation noting year expense applies to

④ Examined invoice noting that phone bill is for the period 11/3/89 - 12/2/89, thus properly included in 1989 accounts payable.

⑤ Noted that items were properly excluded from the 12/31/89 accounts payable schedule.

5. Examine vouchers (invoice packages) for proper attachments (and related data): invoice, approved purchase order, and receiving report.
6. Examine documentation supporting disbursements for the first ten days in the subsequent year.
7. Confirm accounts payable with known vendors with whom the client deals.
8. Examine vouchers (invoice packages) for cancellation of supporting documents.

Note: Organize your answer as follows:

Procedure (1–8)	*Type of Test*	*Specific Control Objective or Audit Objective*	*Possible Error or Irregularity*

13–66. The Electronic Hearth Company is a wholesaler of kitchen appliances. It typically buys from fewer than six manufacturers. The accounting system and control procedures related to the buying cycle are described below.

Inventory orders are initiated by the warehouse supervisor, who prepares a preprinted, prenumbered purchase requisition form for goods needed to restock inventory. The warehouse supervisor determines that goods are needed when quantities on hand are at a predetermined reorder point. The warehouse manager approves the forms and forwards them to the purchasing agent. The forms designate only the quantity of goods to be ordered. The purchasing agent ascertains the quoted price from the vendor and obtains the treasurer's authorization for prices outside the approved amounts. This data is then entered into the accounts payable system by a purchasing clerk via a CRT. This updates the open purchase order master file and generates a sequentially numbered four-part purchase order. The clerk compares the requisition form with the purchase order. Discrepancies noted in quantity of goods or price are resolved and corrected immediately. Copies of the purchase order are distributed to the vendor, the receiving department (two copies), and the accounting department.

When the inventory is received, the receiving clerk examines the condition of the merchandise, compares the bill of lading with the goods received and the descriptions on the purchase order copy, signs the bill of lading, and records on his purchase order copy the quantity and date received and initials it. This copy of the purchase order then serves as the receiving report. Another clerk enters, via a CRT, the purchase order number, the quantity of goods, and the date received, thereby creating a receiving report master file.

The receiving clerk files a copy of the receiving report by date of receipt. The file is maintained on site for one year and is then destroyed. The other copy is sent to accounting.

Each night, a program is run based on the information input via CRT by the receiving clerk that generates a "transactions processed" report. The receiving clerk compares the "transactions processed" report with the prior day's receiving reports, matching each line item and receiving report and checking for accuracy. Any corrections are reentered to the accounts payable system.

When the accounting department receives vendors' invoices, the accounts payable clerk enters the vendor number and name, purchase order number, invoice number, and payment data (quantity and price per unit) into the accounts payable system. The clerk must perform this step twice. The first time, the information is entered for purposes of file update. The second time, the system does a one-for-one check of the data entered. If there are discrepancies, the clerk cannot proceed to the next invoice until the discrepancy is resolved. Once the matching has been completed, an open invoice transaction file is created. The system uses the accounts payable master file for reference to vendor data (e.g., name, address, and vendor number).

A comparison is then performed by the computer between the data on the receiving documents maintained in the receiving report master file and the invoice data. This comparison ensures that only items received will be paid. Next, a comparison of the open invoice transaction file with the open purchase order master file is performed by the computer. This comparison ensures that authorized prices are paid by Electronic Hearth. If there are no discrepancies, the accounts payable transaction file, receiving report master file, and open purchase order master file are updated. Discrepancies are updated to a suspense file until resolved.

Exception reports ("invoiced goods not received," "invoice price discrepancies," and the "suspense file status") are reviewed by Mr. Price, the Controller.

The treasurer wishes to pay all suppliers within the 30-day discount period. Therefore, once a week Mr. Price reviews a cash requirements report, which is generated by reference to the accounts payable master file. He identifies the invoices to be paid that week and forwards the report to the accounts payable clerk, who reviews all open invoice items on the CRT and enters an "X" next to those invoices that Mr. Price authorized for payment. This transaction will generate the checks to vendors and a check register. The accounts payable transaction file is generated daily for invoice activity.

Checks generated from the accounts payable system are attached to the invoice, the receiving report, and the purchase order and are forwarded to Mr. Price for his signature. The treasurer's signature is required for payments greater than $50,000. Once signed, the treasurer's or the controller's secretary mails the checks.

Accounts payable and inventory transactions are accumulated on separate transaction files during the month. These files update the general ledger master file at the end of the month.

The accounts payable subsidiary ledger is generated monthly from the updated accounts payable master file. In addition, an open receiving report listing is generated from the receiving report master file.

The accounts payable subsidiary ledger is reconciled by the general ledger clerk to the accounts payable balance in the general ledger. This reconciliation is approved by Mr. Price, who reviews the open receiving report listing and the month-end suspense file and prepares a journal entry for any accruals required.

Required:

a. Identify the procedures in place in Electronic Hearth's buying cycle and the control objectives related to each control procedure.

b. Identify deficiencies in the control structure related to Electronic Hearth's buying cycle. In addition, identify any alternative procedures performed by Electronic Hearth that could compensate for the deficiencies noted.

13-67. ***Quinn Hardware*** (Buying Cycle: Relating Control Procedures to Control Objectives and Identifying Reportable Conditions)
This problem is a continuation of the case on the ordering and receiving segment of Quinn Hardware's buying cycle, which was presented in Problem 8-68.

Required:

a. Based on the narrative presented in Problem 8-68, identify the *specific* procedures used by Quinn to achieve the control objectives related to its ordering and receiving segment. (Refer to Figure 13.2 for a summary of the relevant control objectives and typical control procedures to achieve those objectives.)
b. Identify reportable conditions in the ordering and receiving segment of Quinn Hardware's buying cycle that should be communicated to management and the audit committee.

13-68. ***Quinn Hardware*** (Buying Cycle: Interviewing Client Personnel and Examining Evidence)
This problem is a continuation of the ordering and receiving segment of Quinn Hardware's buying cycle, which was presented in Problem 8-68. Your response to the requirements stated below should be based on the narrative in Problem 8-68.

Required:

a. You wish to interview several of the individuals involved in the ordering and receiving segment, focusing on their duties with respect to the various reports that the system generates. Prepare a list of questions for the following individuals who have responsibilities with respect to the specified reports:
    1. The buyer responsible for reviewing the SRR (steps 1 and 2).
    2. The warehouse clerk, with respect to the reconciliation of the Receipts Update Report and the Daily Edit Report (steps 9-11).
    3. The warehouse supervisor, with respect to the reconciliation of the Receipts Update Report and the Daily Edit Report (steps 9-12).
    4. The expediter, with respect to his or her use of the weekly listing of outstanding purchase orders (steps 13 and 14).
    5. The buyer, with respect to his or her use of the weekly listing of outstanding purchase orders (steps 13-15).
b. You want your assistant to examine evidence that control procedures were appropriately performed with respect to the Daily Edit Report and the Receipts Update Report. Prepare a program for your assistant to follow in examining that evidence. The program should be based on the information in the narrative.

14

Auditing the Production Cycle, Cost of Sales, and Inventory Balances

The production cycle and inventories are often among the most significant and difficult areas in auditing. Service-based enterprises as well as manufacturers, retailers, and wholesalers maintain significant amounts of inventory. The auditor's primary objective in this area is to gather evidence to support management's assertions about the existence, ownership, pricing, and valuation of inventory.

Since the production cycle is normally associated with manufacturing enterprises, this chapter is written primarily from that perspective. Much of the discussion in the chapter, however, applies to other types of enterprises as well, like retailers and wholesalers that purchase and hold inventory for future sale, and various types of service organizations that consume inventory in the process of generating revenues. Accounts encompassed by the production cycle are defined and described. Typical production transactions, accounting systems, and control procedures are then presented in detail, followed by a discussion of audit objectives, risk assessment, and the audit testing plan for the production cycle. Subsequent sections of the chapter present specific tests of controls and substantive tests that may be used in auditing production cycle transactions and related account balances.

ACCOUNTS RELATED TO THE PRODUCTION CYCLE

The production cycle deals with tangible personal property manufactured for sale in the ordinary course of business. The term "inventory" is used to refer to items held for sale, in process of production, or to be converted or consumed in the production of goods or services. Inventory is usually characterized as either merchandise, raw materials, work in process, or finished goods. Merchandise refers to goods acquired for resale by dealers, who incur little or no additional cost preparing them for resale. Raw materials are items or commodities converted or consumed in the production process. Work in process represents products in intermediate stages of production. Finished goods represent the end products of the manufacturing process. Both finished goods and work in process normally have material, labor, and overhead components. The classification of inventory depends on the entity holding it and the nature of its operations. For example, coil steel is a finished product to a steel mill, but a raw material to an appliance manufacturer.

Cost of sales (also called cost of goods sold) includes all costs directly associated with purchasing and producing goods sold. Material costs assignable to inventory include merchandise, raw materials, and component parts used in the production process or purchased for resale, net of purchase returns, discounts, and other allowances. All direct costs incurred in the purchasing process, like inbound transportation (freight in), duties and taxes, and warehousing, are also included. In complex procurement systems that are expensive to operate, a separate purchasing overhead account may be maintained and included in material costs.

Other costs associated with production include direct labor and related costs, like employee fringe benefits, and manufacturing overhead. Manufacturing overhead comprises costs that cannot be directly assigned to specific units of production but are nonetheless directly associated with the production process, for example, indirect labor, supervision, occupancy costs, utilities, repairs and maintenance, and depreciation. Operating supplies and other materials that do not become parts of products, like oils for lubricating machinery, normally are also included in overhead.

Cost of sales may include additional items such as losses from writing inventories down to market value, royalties paid for the right to manufacture a product or use a patented process or equipment, and amortization of preproduction and tooling costs. Cost of sales is often reduced by sales of byproducts and the disposal value of scrap. Estimated costs of warranties, guarantees, and other commitments for future expenditures are usually included in cost of sales, although sometimes they are included in other expense categories.

The term "operating expenses" is sometimes used to describe costs and expenses incurred in generating revenues from the sale of services.

T-accounts are presented in Figure 14.1 to illustrate the transactions and accounts encompassed by a typical production cycle.

TYPICAL TRANSACTIONS, ACCOUNTING SYSTEMS, AND CONTROL PROCEDURES

There are essentially two major kinds of cost accounting systems—a job order system, in which goods are made in the quantities and to the specifications called for by a particular order, and a process system, in which goods are produced repetitively according to a schedule. The number of classes of transactions in the production cycle of either system depends on the complexity of the production process. Among the transactions typically found in a production cycle are issuing raw materials for use in production, allocating labor and overhead costs, computing piecework and incentive pay, receiving materials directly into production, processing customers' materials, and transferring completed products to inventory. The production cycle also includes policies and procedures for storing raw materials, component parts, and finished goods, and for shipping goods produced.

There are virtually unlimited combinations and sequences that may occur in connection with producing goods for sale and storing raw materials and finished goods. The operating, accounting, and control procedures associated with production appear in many forms because of the technological diversity of

Figure 14.1 Production Cycle Accounts

Balance Sheet Accounts

Inventory of Raw Materials

Debit	Credit
Beginning inventory Purchases Ending inventory	Raw materials used

Inventory of Work in Process

Debit	Credit
Beginning inventory Raw materials used Direct labor costs incurred Manufacturing overhead costs incurred Ending inventory	Cost of goods finished during the period

Inventory of Finished Goods

Debit	Credit
Beginning inventory Cost of goods finished during the period Ending inventory	Cost of goods sold

Various Asset and Liability Accounts

Debit	Credit
	Direct labor costs incurred Manufacturing overhead costs incurred

Income Statement Accounts

Cost of Sales

Debit	Credit
Cost of goods sold	

modern manufacturing operations. The discussion in this chapter of typical transactions, accounting systems, and control procedures provides only a generalized suggestion of the kinds of conditions that may be encountered in the three major transaction classes in the production cycle.

- Producing goods for sale.
- Storing raw materials (including component parts) and finished goods.
- Shipping goods produced.

Producing Goods for Sale

The process of producing goods for sale generally includes the following activities:

- Identifying production needs, and planning and scheduling production.
- Producing goods.
- Accounting for production costs.
- Accounting for work in process.

In considering the accounting system through which production transactions are processed and the control procedures applied to them, the auditor is interested primarily in procedures to ensure that incurred production costs are authorized and are accurately recorded and accumulated; that is, that the control objectives of completeness, accuracy, and authorization of transaction processing and files are met. Those control objectives are closely related to the audit objectives of completeness, accuracy, and existence of accounts that are part of the production cycle—most significantly, raw materials, work-in-process, and finished goods inventories, and cost of sales. Other control procedures, while not directly related to those audit objectives, may also be of interest to the auditor. For example, the fact that production is carefully planned to meet anticipated sales may provide evidence the auditor can use in evaluating the adequacy of the allowance for obsolete inventory, which affects the valuation audit objective relating to inventory.

Control procedures for the production process are also important to management because errors in production and inventory data can result in wrong decisions. For example, inaccurate inventory records can result in poor purchasing or production planning decisions. Overstocking can lead to higher inventory carrying costs and a greater risk of obsolescence; understocking can lead to stock-outs, production downtime, and lost sales. Effective procedures to control inventory levels also reduce the probability of errors in accounting data and other data used by management in running the business, thereby contributing to operating effectiveness.

Identifying Production Needs, and Planning and Scheduling Production. In a process system that produces finished goods inventory, identifying production needs may be an integral part of the system and may be accomplished by evaluating existing inventory levels in relation to sales projections. The need may be signaled by a periodic matching of physical or recorded inventory levels against a predetermined minimum. Computerized inventory records offer the opportunity for sophisticated forecasting and modeling computations.

After a need has been identified, a production requisition is initiated, which, after review and approval, becomes the authorization to produce. Product specifications and time and cost estimates are usually developed as part of the production planning and scheduling process. In particular, cost estimates give management a basis for informed scrutiny of actual costs. The result of planning and scheduling is a production order—the detailed execution instructions listing the operations and the desired results.

Poor product specifications (as well as poor inspection procedures) can cause rework, unsalable goods, or returned merchandise. Poor estimates and poor scheduling can give rise to excess cost in inventory, especially overruns on contracts. An auditor who understands the role of planning and scheduling in the production process will be able to more effectively assess the inherent and control risks associated with inventory and cost of sales.

Producing Goods. Raw materials may be moved into the production process on the basis of a document (like an authorized bill of materials supporting an approved production order, an approved materials requisition, or a report of production orders scheduled to start), or electronically when an authorized production order is entered into the system. In either event, an appropriately authorized document or file should be created to account for the movement of materials, for both operational and accounting purposes. Often these documents or files may serve as authorization to update the perpetual inventory records for issues of materials to production. The documents, which are usually prenumbered, are accounted for or open files are reviewed periodically as part of procedures to ascertain that all transactions have been processed and recorded. If material is ordered directly for production, the production order, sometimes supported by an accompanying purchase order, alerts those concerned to the expected delivery date.

Setup time for machines used in the production process may or may not be accounted for separately, depending on management's informational needs. Tools and dies are sometimes charged as direct costs, particularly in job order production systems in which tools are likely to have been designed especially for a particular order and sometimes are paid for by the customer. Most often, though, tools and dies are capitalized because they can be reused on other work or production runs at other times. Usually, documents are prepared to record these processing steps: a time report or job ticket for the setup time and an issues slip or production order for the tool requirements. The documents are then reviewed and approved by supervisory personnel.

Measuring production quantities is a problem in a great many operations.

Both production managers and cost accountants want accurate production counts, but in many cases the large number of units, the inaccuracy of measuring devices, and the problems of distinguishing between acceptable and unacceptable units make it difficult or uneconomical to measure production precisely.

Production is often inspected at several stages and levels. Operators inspect for signs of problems as they complete their work; supervisors may inspect output on a test basis. There may be specialists in quality control, or it may be necessary to employ the special skills and equipment of a laboratory to test the quality of production. Control procedures related to measuring and inspecting production output provide evidence of the salability of the inventory and the level of warranty costs that may be incurred after the sale.

Accounting for Production Costs. The accounting aspects of the production cycle are manifested in the entity's cost accounting system. Cost accounting systems employed by manufacturing concerns vary widely, and range from very simple systems, which account for ending inventory balances annually, to very well-developed standard cost systems, which account for all materials handling, production in process, and completed production, and generate analyses of related variances from predetermined standard costs. A well-developed cost system should provide the details of transfers between raw materials and work in process and between work in process and finished goods, and of the distribution and accumulation of material, labor, and overhead costs by cost centers, job orders, or production runs.

Depending on the structure of the cost accounting system, raw materials may be charged to a job order or to a materials usage account in a process system. If a standard cost system is used, materials may be charged to production at standard quantities and prices, with resulting variances between standard and actual costs subsequently allocated to inventory and cost of sales.

Issues of raw materials may be recorded from a report of production orders scheduled to start, which is compared with production orders reported as actually started, or from raw materials storeroom issue slips whose numerical sequence is accounted for. Occasionally, especially in computerized systems, raw materials usage may be measured by periodically—usually monthly—pricing the ending raw materials inventory and adjusting the account balance through a charge to production.

The total cost of production payroll is accounted for through the buying cycle (covered in Chapter 13). Payroll costs are distributed to detailed cost accounts from payroll records or production reports. The aggregate labor cost distributed to production or other expense accounts is reconciled to a control total from the payroll records to ensure that all labor costs have been allocated to either job order or departmental expense accounts. The system may provide detailed accounts for idle time, waiting time, setup time, cleanup time, rework time, and so on. When a standard cost system is used, production labor is computed at standard rates and hours and, by comparison with actual costs, labor rate and efficiency variances are produced.

Many different kinds of costs enter into overhead, and they are accumulated in descriptive accounts as charges originate. The basis for charging overhead to job orders, departments, or work-in-process inventory is usually some measure of activity, such as direct labor hours or dollars. There are likely to be different overhead rates for different departments, based on accounting or engineering studies. Entries to record overhead absorption may be originated as a separate accounting procedure, but most often they are integrated with entries for the data—payroll or materials usage—on which the absorption rate is based.

In a standard cost system, overhead may be charged through several intermediate accounts before eventually ending up in work in process, finished goods, and cost of sales to produce price, efficiency, and volume variances for management purposes. Overabsorbed overhead is removed from inventories to prevent stating them in excess of actual cost; underabsorbed overhead is generally allocated to inventories, unless it arises from costs that should be written off as incurred. Some companies establish and allocate separate overheads for materials handling (purchasing, receiving, inspecting, and storing), as distinguished from manufacturing overhead, when those costs are significant.

Production rejected as a result of inspection is reported for cost accounting purposes. Sometimes the time spent reworking faulty items to meet specifications is also reported separately. Minimizing the amount of scrap and rework is an important management objective; identifying and accounting for the cost of scrap and rework help achieve that objective. Once scrap has been created, it is subject to custodial procedures and disposed of in a way that maximizes cost recovery and thereby minimizes production costs. Cost accounting is improved if scrap is identified with the operations or products creating it, but that is often impossible. Control procedures for gathering, protecting, weighing, recording, storing, and disposing of scrap are sometimes as important as those for other assets.

Accounting for Work in Process. Movement of production between departments during the manufacturing process is reported for operational purposes, but may or may not be recorded for accounting purposes. Work in process is credited and finished goods are charged when production is complete, on the basis of completed production orders, inspection reports, or finished goods receiving tickets that have been authorized. In addition, most entities have procedures for documenting evidence of inspection according to quality control standards.

Physical inventory counts of work in process are often difficult because a great many items in many different stages of completion must be identified. Goods may be scattered or in hoppers, vats, or pipelines where access, observation, or measurement is difficult, or they may be in the hands of outside processors. Adequate production management, however, requires that someone know the location and stage of completion of each item. The more difficult controlling production is, the more essential it is to have a means of ensuring that excess or "lost" costs do not build up in the work-in-process account.

Storing Raw Materials and Finished Goods

Raw materials and component parts are accounted for and controlled from the time of their receipt through their use in the manufacturing process. Procedures for accomplishing this include protecting the inventory by restricting access to it to authorized personnel, issuing materials to production only upon proper authorization, crediting the perpetual inventory records for issuances to production, and periodically counting materials on hand and agreeing the results to those records.

After production has been completed and has passed final inspection, it goes either to a warehouse or to a storage area to await shipment to customers. The notice to production management may be a copy of the completed production order, or it may be an inspection report or a warehouse receiving report. The completeness of charges to finished goods is controlled by accounting for the numerical sequence of production or receiving reports.

The primary control procedures for inventories in most companies are physical counts of quantities on hand and periodic reconciliations to perpetual inventory records or general ledger balances. Perpetual inventory records of varying degrees of sophistication are found in practice. Some companies maintain perpetual records that reflect both inventory quantities and costs; others keep perpetual records in quantities only. Companies with simple operations and relatively few inventory items frequently do not maintain perpetual records at all.

Physical inventories are part of an effective internal control structure. In entities with an effective control structure, a physical inventory is taken at least annually and sometimes more often, depending on the type of business and the nature of the inventory. The term "physical inventory" includes not only physically counting items but also translating the quantities into dollars, summarizing the dollars, and comparing the results with the accounts. A complete count of the inventory of a company, plant, or department may be made at one time while operations are suspended (sometimes referred to as a wall-to-wall inventory) or, if perpetual inventory records are maintained and other conditions are satisfactory, periodic counts of selected items may be made at various times during the year (known as a cycle count inventory). In the latter instance, all items in the inventory are generally counted at least once each year. Sometimes both types of inventory-taking are used. Since the two methods involve somewhat different techniques, they are discussed separately below.

Inventories Taken at One Time. Taking a complete inventory requires the cooperation of production, accounting, and storekeeping personnel since it often involves suspending or significantly reducing production, shipping, and receiving operations, and physically rearranging inventory to facilitate counting. Often an "inventory committee" is organized, consisting of management representatives of production departments, the controller's office, the general or cost accounting department, the shipping and receiving departments, and the internal audit department, and the independent auditors. It is usually desirable for someone from production management to assume responsibility for rearranging the inventory and making available employees who are familiar with it to assist in the physical inventory procedures.

A physical inventory may be taken during the vacation period for factory employees, when production is stopped for some other reason, at a time when inventories are at a low level, at year-end, or at a convenient month-end prior to the balance sheet date. Inventory-taking before the balance sheet date is advisable, however, only if there are adequate procedures to safeguard the inventory and to control and document inventory movements between the physical inventory and balance sheet dates.

The counts may be made by production, clerical, or accounting personnel; storekeepers; internal auditors; or an outside inventory service. Count teams often include at least one individual from the production department. Such an arrangement provides an added degree of control while utilizing the production department employee's familiarity with the inventory. However the initial counting is organized, the counts are verified. Some companies have a complete recount by independent teams. Others assign production supervisors or internal auditors to make random test counts. These test counts are documented to provide adequate evidence of their performance and to establish responsibility for them.

An almost invariable requirement for a good physical inventory is preparing a written program in advance. An effective program includes instructions about how to

1. Physically arrange the inventory in a way that simplifies the counts.
2. Identify and describe the inventory properly, including stage of completion and condition, when appropriate.
3. Segregate or properly identify slow-moving, obsolete, or damaged goods.
4. Identify and list inventory belonging to others.
5. Numerically control inventory tags or sheets.
6. Record and verify individual counts.
7. Obtain a proper cutoff of receipts and shipments and interdepartmental movements, and the related documentation.
8. Determine and list goods in the hands of others.
9. Correct errors discovered as a result of the counts.

In addition to instructions for controlling and recording the inventory, the program would include instructions to the accounting department for summarizing quantities, costing (pricing), extending (multiplying quantity by price), and summarizing the priced inventory. Special procedures may be required for consignments in or out, goods in transit, and goods in public warehouses or at branches. Adequate supervision helps to ensure that procedures for arranging and counting the inventory, pricing, and summarizing the counts are properly followed.

The mechanics of counting vary. Seldom, if ever, can all individual items in an inventory be seen and counted; often they are in the packages or cartons they were purchased or are to be shipped in, or are located in bins or stockpiles in large numbers that cannot be physically weighed or counted. General practice is to count a reasonable number of items; some packages are opened and some items inspected, particularly if there are any unusual circumstances.

Differences between physical and recorded inventories are investigated, and the possibility of leakage or pilferage needs to be considered. The records may be right and the count wrong; significant adjustments are not made without a thorough investigation.

Cycle Counts. Instead of a wall-to-wall inventory, cycle counts may be made throughout the year if there are adequate perpetual inventory records and control procedures for physical inventory movements and cutoff. Procedures used in making periodic counts differ from those for inventories taken at one time. Rather than large numbers of production and other personnel rearranging and counting all the inventory in a plant, periodic counts are usually made by relatively small groups of employees who are independent of the accounting function and who soon become expert at counting inventories.

Cycle count results are reported to accounting personnel and compared with the perpetual inventory records. Discrepancies between them are identified, investigated, and resolved. Discrepancies may result from improper physical counts, clerical errors, cutoff problems, and improper inputting of transactions. Identifying and correcting the causes of discrepancies are important aspects of a cycle counting system. Procedures to ensure the accuracy of cycle counts are similar to those used in wall-to-wall counts. When periodic counts are made and found to be reliable, the perpetual records may serve as the equivalent of a complete physical inventory and are priced, extended, and summarized for comparison with general ledger accounts at or near year-end.

Inventories in Public Warehouses. Control procedures generally include a preliminary investigation and continuing evaluation of the performance of the custodian. Statement on Auditing Standards (SAS) No. 1, as amended by SAS No. 43 (AU Section 901.26–.27), suggests the following procedures:

Consideration of the business reputation and financial standing of the warehouseman.

Inspection of the physical facilities.

Inquiries as to the warehouseman's internal control structure policies and procedures and whether the warehouseman holds goods for his own account.

Inquiries as to type and adequacy of the warehouseman's insurance.

Inquiries as to government or other licensing and bonding requirements and the nature, extent, and results of any inspection by government or other agencies.

Review of the warehouseman's financial statements and related reports of independent auditors.

Review and update [of] the information developed from the investigation described above.

Physical counts (or test counts) of the goods, wherever practicable and reasonable (may not be practicable in the case of fungible goods).

Reconcilement of quantities shown on statements received from the warehouseman with the owner's records.

Shipping Goods Produced

When finished goods are shipped to customers, the transfer of costs from the finished goods account to cost of sales (if the detailed perpetual records reflect both inventory quantities and costs) is based on executed shipping orders. The process of executing orders and recording shipments and related control procedures are described in Chapter 12, "Auditing the Revenue Cycle." As discussed there, the complete and accurate recording of accounts receivable and sales is ensured by requiring appropriate supporting documentation before executed shipping orders are input to the sales transaction file. Simultaneously inputting those orders to the cost of sales transaction file (if perpetual records reflect both inventory quantities and costs) ensures the complete recording of charges to cost of sales and the reduction of finished goods inventory. Periodically, the detailed perpetual inventory records are adjusted to agree with physical counts, are costed (if only unit records are kept) and aggregated, and any difference between their total and the control account balance is charged to cost of sales. Significant or recurring differences are investigated to determine their causes, and corrective action is taken as necessary.

DETERMINING THE AUDIT STRATEGY

The audit strategy for each account balance and class of transactions in the production cycle is based primarily on the auditor's assessment of inherent and control risk relating to specific audit objectives and on efficiency considerations.

Audit Objectives

The audit objectives applicable to the production cycle and inventories are

Completeness

- Inventories represent all raw materials, work in process, and finished goods that the enterprise owns, including those on hand, in transit, or on the premises of others.
- All shipments (and returns) of goods during the period covered by the financial statements are reflected in cost of sales.

Accuracy

- The detailed perpetual inventory records are mathematically correct and agree with the general ledger inventory control account.
- Costs associated with inventories have been properly classified and accumulated.
- Cost of sales is based on correct costs and quantities, is properly summarized and posted to the costs of sales and inventory control accounts, and, if appropriate, is credited in the perpetual inventory records.

Existence/Occurrence

- Recorded inventories physically exist in salable condition and represent property held for sale in the ordinary course of business.
- Recorded cost of sales represents goods actually shipped during the period covered by the financial statements.

Cutoff

- Production costs incurred and charged to work in process, transfers to finished goods, and cost of sales (and returns) are recorded in the proper period.

Valuation

- Costs associated with inventory and cost of sales are determined and accumulated using generally accepted accounting principles consistently applied.
- Inventories (including slow-moving and obsolete items) are stated at not more than their net realizable value.

Rights and Obligations

- The entity has legal title or ownership rights to the inventory; inventory excludes goods that are the property of others or have been billed to customers.

Presentation and Disclosure

- Inventories and cost of sales are properly described and classified in the financial statements.
- All encumbrances against inventory are adequately disclosed.

The auditor achieves these objectives by performing substantive tests or a combination of substantive tests and tests of control structure policies and procedures. The auditor frequently tests an entity's control procedures to obtain evidence of the effectiveness of their design and operation as a basis for significantly reducing the assurance needed from substantive tests directed at the completeness, accuracy, and existence objectives. The cutoff objective for cost of sales is typically achieved concurrently with the cutoff objective for sales, as described in Chapter 12. The auditor generally achieves the remaining audit objectives by performing substantive tests, supplemented by the evidence obtained through assessing the entity's inherent risk conditions, control environment, and accounting system. For example, the auditor's awareness of an economic decline in the client's industry may cause concern about the salability of inventory and hence its valuation.

Risk Assessment

As discussed in Chapter 8, the auditor gathers or updates information about the client and its business as a basis for assessing inherent and control risk. The audit risks associated with inventories vary based on the nature of an enterprise's inventory and its materiality to the financial statements. For example, there is a high level of inherent risk associated with inventories like precious metals or gems that have relatively high value and can be easily converted to cash. Accordingly, such inventories require more effective control procedures. Or, in estimating net realizable value, there is a higher level of risk associated with a product that must meet very strict technical standards or composition requirements than with a commodity that is generally acceptable to many potential users.

Analytical Procedures. Analytical procedures often highlight relationships between accounts and reveal risks not otherwise apparent during the risk assessment phase of the audit. Analytical procedures can, for example, indicate trends that may help the auditor assess risk. Such trends may involve

- The relationship among the components of production cost.
- Production usage and price variances.
- Finished goods inventory turnover (the ratio of cost of sales to average finished goods inventory).

The auditor should review those relationships and compare them with those of prior periods and those anticipated in budgets or forecasts. The ratios and the account balances themselves are often compared from month to month and with the corresponding period of the prior year. The auditor should note trends and fluctuations (seasonal and other) and seek explanations for unusual patterns.

The auditor should consider management's performance of analytical procedures as part of its reviews of reports and other internal documentation. The auditor may consider using the results of those procedures, to the extent necessary, to supplement his or her own analytical procedures. Management typically reviews various internal production and inventory reports and data, like the following:

- Actual production and inventory levels in relation to historical trends and budgets or forecasts.
- Material, labor, and overhead standard cost variances.
- Actual gross margins compared with historical trends and budgets.
- Write-offs of obsolete and otherwise unsalable inventory and other write-downs compared with budgets and historical data.
- Trends in inventory turnover.

Management's review of reports such as these may help identify material misstatements in processing or recording production costs or cost of sales. For example, investigating significant differences between reported and budgeted production costs could identify incomplete recording of production costs in the general ledger.

The way the client responds to the auditor's inquiries resulting from analytical procedures may give some indication of the quality of the client's control environment. For example, prompt, logical, and meaningful answers to questions about fluctuations in inventory turnover ratios from the prior to the current year would provide some indication, in the absence of evidence to the contrary, that the company's management is "in control" and that the accounting system and control procedures appear to be functioning as intended. Analytical procedures, however, may also indicate trends, even in well-controlled companies, that may lead the auditor to extend substantive tests; for example, trends that raise questions about the realizability of recorded inventory values. Analytical procedures performed as substantive tests are discussed later in this chapter.

Control Risk. The auditor also is required, at a minimum, to obtain an understanding of the entity's control structure sufficient to plan the audit. This understanding is used to identify the types of misstatements that might occur and the risk of their occurring, and to design substantive tests. The understanding is obtained or updated by considering previous experience with the entity, reviewing prior-year audit results, interviewing client personnel, observing personnel as they perform their duties, reviewing client-prepared descriptions of policies and procedures, and inspecting documents and records. These procedures normally reveal information about all significant cycles and account balances.

In addition to information regarding the client's overall control environment, the predominant means of processing transactions (manually or by computer) and the level of its sophistication, and other general characteristics of the control structure, the auditor should consider the following types of information, as appropriate, related to the production cycle:

- Liquidity of the inventory, that is, how easily it can be converted into cash.
- Number of items in the inventory.
- What judgments enter into the inventory valuation (e.g., judgments about inventory obsolescence).
- Susceptibility of major products to technological obsolescence, spoilage, or changes in demand.
- Availability of materials critical to the production process, number of vendors able to supply such materials, price stability of the materials, and ability of the client to pass along price increases to its customers.
- Historical trends of applicable inventory turnover ratios, net realizable value, and inventory obsolescence problems.
- The cost accounting system in use and how well it reflects the actual production process and how it reports the production costs incurred, the application of overhead, and the transfer of production costs to finished goods inventory and cost of sales.
- The accounting methods used to value inventory.
- Current-year production cost variances from standards or budgets.

The auditor should also obtain an understanding of control procedures applied to producing and shipping goods and storing raw materials and finished goods inventories, and how duties are segregated in performing those procedures. Based on this information, the auditor determines whether control structure policies and procedures for specific classes of transactions are appropriately designed and have been placed in operation.

In the course of obtaining the understanding of the control structure, the auditor may perform concurrent tests of controls (either incidental or planned) and thereby obtain evidence that control structure policies and procedures have been properly designed and are operating effectively. That evidence would enable the auditor to assess control risk at below the maximum for relevant audit objectives. For example, when inquiring about management's review of production reports, the auditor may also observe the performance of the review or examine reports or documents that provide evidence of the review. If operating effectively, management's review provides some evidence with respect to the completeness and accuracy of costs charged to production. The auditor considers the level of detail reviewed and whether the individual performing the review would be likely to detect a material misstatement.

The auditor next considers whether he or she wishes to obtain additional evidence of the effectiveness of policies and procedures as a basis for a low assessment of control risk, and then whether such evidence is likely to be available and efficient to obtain. If so, the auditor would usually perform additional tests of controls for specific audit objectives—commonly, completeness, accuracy, and existence/occurrence of inventory, cost of sales, and production costs.

Audit Testing Plan

As discussed in Chapter 5, the basic audit strategy decision the auditor makes for each significant account balance is whether to perform additional tests of controls to support a low assessed level of control risk for specific audit objectives, or to perform substantive tests directed at all relevant audit objectives without significant restriction based on tests of controls. Factors affecting that decision are described below.

Whether to perform additional tests of controls in the production cycle should be determined separately for each transaction class, for each segment of the inventory (raw materials, work in process, and finished goods), and for the price and quantity components of inventory values. For example, the auditor may decide to obtain assurance about the quantity of items on hand by observing and testing the physical count of the items. The auditor may decide, however, that control procedures for pricing the inventory are effective enough to warrant testing them, and that it would be efficient to do so.

Although audit strategy decisions must always be tailored to specific client circumstances, it is possible to make some general observations about what conditions might lead the auditor to either perform or not perform additional tests of controls. Such tests are likely to be effective and efficient if the assessment of inherent risk and the understanding of the control structure, including any concurrent tests of controls performed, indicated that the client had

- Effective production planning, budgeting, and management information systems.
- Effective general control procedures as well as transaction processing and file control procedures for production and inventory.
- Adequate segregation of duties between personnel who produce and store inventory and those responsible for the related accounting, and between

personnel who store inventory and those responsible for receiving and shipping.

- Adequate asset protection control procedures for all significant inventories.
- A policy of taking physical inventories regularly to ensure the existence, accuracy, and salable condition of recorded inventories.
- An effective accounting system and related control procedures for accumulating all production costs and properly allocating them to inventory.
- Adequate control procedures to ensure proper cutoffs in the receiving and shipping departments.

Moreover, the auditor would probably be able to perform a significant portion of substantive testing before the balance sheet date, provided that activity during the period between early substantive testing and year-end could be adequately tested. For example, it might be more difficult to test activity during the intervening period for a large number of low-cost items than for a small number of high-cost items. Early testing may be particularly efficient if the client desires the audit report relatively close to year-end, since substantive procedures for inventory balances are often fairly extensive.

On the other hand, in the absence of the above effective control structure factors, or if the auditor's inherent risk assessment suggests the client may have potential motives for overstating inventories, the audit strategy should emphasize substantive testing, probably as of the balance sheet date.

The auditor's assessment of control risk, along with the results of early substantive testing and the length of time between those tests and year-end, will also affect how the auditor obtains the necessary assurance as to the year-end inventory balance if the client takes its physical inventory before year-end or uses cycle counting procedures. The required low level of audit risk can be achieved through an appropriate combination of procedures, including tests of supervisory procedures and special procedures implemented by the client for the intervening period; reviews of the client's method of calculating ending inventory and cost of sales if inventory activity is not recorded on a perpetual basis; reviews of production and sales reports generated for management decision-making purposes; analytical procedures; and tests of details of purchase, sale, and production activity during the intervening period.

ADDITIONAL TESTS OF CONTROLS

Concurrent tests of controls often provide evidence to support an assessment of control risk at below the maximum for one or more audit objectives. However, concurrent tests of controls are generally directed mainly at policies and procedures that are part of the control environment and accounting system, as opposed to specific control procedures, and therefore usually relate to several audit objectives and affect several accounts. Accordingly, tests of controls performed concurrently with obtaining the understanding of the control structure are not sufficient to support a low assessment of control risk for specific audit objectives and account balances. To assess control risk as low for one or more audit objectives for some or all production cycle accounts, the auditor performs additional tests of controls. Such tests usually require substantial audit effort, and therefore the auditor generally performs them only when he or she believes they will significantly reduce the amount of substantive testing required. This principle is particularly applicable to inventories, because the minimum substantive testing necessary to achieve the existence and accuracy (pricing) audit objectives is often extensive.

Specific control objectives and typical control procedures applicable to producing goods for sale and storing inventory are described in Figure 14.2. The accounting system assumed to be in operation in the figure is a sophisticated computerized system. As discussed in Chapter 8, the tests of controls that the auditor would perform include an appropriate combination of inquiring about the client's control procedures, observing that the procedures have been placed in operation, and examining evidence that they are designed and operating effectively. Also as discussed in Chapter 8, reperformance may be used in tests of controls; but if that becomes necessary, the auditor usually determines it is more efficient to perform substantive tests. In addition to testing control procedures specific to a particular transaction cycle, in order to assess control risk as low the auditor would also need evidence of the effectiveness of general control procedures.

When performing tests of controls, the auditor should be aware of audit objectives other than completeness, accuracy, existence, and cutoff that may be affected by those tests. For example, the auditor frequently considers the valuation objective when testing controls in the production cycle. Tests of the client's procedures for pricing inventory components used in production are performed primarily to obtain evidence of the accuracy of the costs. The results of those tests, however, will also help the auditor determine whether the inventory is valued in accordance with the entity's inventory pricing method. For example, if the entity uses the FIFO method of pricing inventory, the auditor could determine from testing the procedures used in charging costs during the various stages of production whether finished goods are valued according to the FIFO assumption.

The underlying data supporting inventory valuation is derived mainly from the buying cycle, described in Chapter 13. If tests of controls for purchase and payroll transactions produce evidence that related accounting data is reliable, it can be relied on for inventory valuation purposes as well, often with little additional testing. This is particularly true if tests of controls in the buying cycle are planned and performed with production cycle audit objectives in mind as well. For example, tests of controls of payroll can easily be expanded

Figure 14.2 Producing Goods for Sale and Storing Inventory

	Control Objectives					
	Transaction Processing					
	Authorization	*Completeness of Input*	*Accuracy of Input*	*Completeness and Accuracy of Updating*[a]	*File*	*Asset Protection*
Specific Control Objectives	All recorded production costs and transfers of production within work in process and to finished goods represent actual activity and are approved.	All production costs (materials, labor, and overhead) and transfers to and from work in process are input and accepted for processing.	Charges to production for materials, labor, and overhead, and transfers within work in process and transfers of completed production to finished goods are correctly recorded in the proper period as to quantities, descriptions, amounts, and dates in the general ledger control accounts and perpetual inventory records; are accurately converted into computer-readable form; and are accu-	All production costs and transfers input and accepted for processing are accurately updated to the work-in-process and finished goods data files.	The integrity of the perpetual inventory records and the general ledger inventory accounts, after production costs have been accumulated and transferred, is preserved.	Only authorized personnel have access to raw materials, work-in-process, and finished goods inventories and the related accounting records or data stored on them.

			rately input to the computer.			
Typical Control Procedures	Approval of materials, labor, and overhead charged to production, including determination of standard costs and overhead application rates, and of transfers within work in process and to finished goods. Review of materials requisitions and labor distribution by department and/or job number. Approval of changes to standard costs and overhead application rates. Approval of new products on the files.	Accounting for the numerical sequence of requisitions of materials and component parts issued to and returned from production. Reporting and resolving missing or duplicate (unmatched) items by people independent of the materials handling function. Reconciliation of records of labor and overhead charges to payrolls and overhead cost incurred, including reporting and resolving differences. Accounting for the numerical sequence of production reports or other	Completeness of input control procedures for missing or duplicate materials requisitions, records of labor and overhead charges, and transfers within work in process and to finished goods also address the accuracy of input for the fields matched or reconciled. Counting work-in-process and finished goods inventories and reconciling to the perpetual records. Review of period-end cutoff procedures by personnel other than those who maintain related perpetual	Comparing total costs input with the total updated to the work-in-process and finished goods files.	Ensuring that the correct version of the file is being used for processing. Balancing of the raw materials, work-in-process, and finished goods records (previous balance plus additions less transfers out, compared with the current total). Counting raw materials, work-in-process, and finished goods inventories and adjusting the perpetual records. Reconciling the perpetual records to the general ledger control accounts and approving adjustments, by	Adequate physical control procedures to prevent unauthorized access to inventories and related documents (requisitions, production reports) and inventory files and files used in processing production activity.

Figure 14.2 Continued

	Control Objectives					
	Transaction Processing					
	Authorization	*Completeness of Input*	*Accuracy of Input*	*Completeness and Accuracy of Updating*[a]	*File*	*Asset Protection*
Typical Control Procedures (Continued)		records of finished production and transfers within work in process; reconciliation of those reports to quantities recorded, including investigation and resolution of missing documents and differences. Review and approval of monthly summarizing entries.	inventory or other accounting records or safeguard inventories. Reporting adjustments to the perpetual inventory records as a result of inventory counts. Reporting and resolving production costs and inventory transfers recorded in the wrong period.		personnel other than those responsible for maintaining related perpetual records or for safeguarding inventories.	

[a]Completeness of updating and accuracy of updating have been combined, because typically the same control procedures apply to both objectives.

to include the distribution of labor costs to specific production lots or units in the perpetual inventory records. This may provide evidence about the accuracy of unit costs reflected in the perpetual inventory records as a basis for pricing the inventory.

Highly developed cost systems often generate data that provides the details of

- Transfers between raw materials and work in process and between work in process and finished goods.
- Distribution of material, labor, and overhead expenses to cost centers, job orders, or production runs.
- Stages of completion of work in process.
- Variance accounts (in the case of standard cost systems) identifying differences between actual and standard.
- Differences between actual and budgeted costs.

An effective cost accounting system usually generates reports that analyze and explain standard cost variances or differences between actual and budgeted amounts. If management reviews these reports, the auditor may test the accuracy of the analyses and review management's explanations for variances.

In evaluating the results of tests of controls (including tests of general control procedures), the auditor considers whether the control structure policies and procedures, taken as a whole, are appropriately designed to achieve the control objectives and are operating effectively. This will determine whether the auditor can achieve the expected reduction in the assessed level of control risk for specific accounts and audit objectives and, thus, whether the auditor can significantly reduce substantive testing. Results differing from those anticipated require the auditor to reconsider the nature, timing, and extent of planned substantive tests. The auditor should reconsider the planned substantive tests not only for production cycle accounts, but also for other accounts that may be affected. For example, ineffective control procedures to ensure completeness of recorded shipments to customers may affect sales revenue as well as inventory and cost of sales.

SUBSTANTIVE TESTS

If the auditor has assessed control risk for some or all production cycle accounts as low for the audit objectives of completeness, accuracy, and existence, substantive tests addressing those audit objectives may, except for the need to observe physical inventory counts, be limited to analytical procedures. The auditor will also consider the relevance to those audit objectives of evidence obtained from tests directed at other audit objectives and other accounts.

For example, tests that provide evidence of the completeness of accounts payable also provide some evidence about the existence and accuracy of raw materials inventory. The auditor seldom assesses control risk as low for the cutoff, valuation, rights and obligations, and presentation and disclosure objectives, and therefore generally performs substantive tests of details for these objectives. (As noted earlier, cutoff tests for cost of sales are typically performed concurrently with cutoff tests for sales.)

Observation of Physical Inventories

Since the *McKesson & Robbins* case precipitated the issue in 1939, the observation of physical inventories has been a required auditing procedure and one of the principal substantive tests of inventories. For a long time after 1939, auditors were expected to make voluminous and extensive test counts, sometimes virtually taking the physical inventory side-by-side with client personnel. In recent years, the emphasis has shifted to observation and testing of the client's procedures for physical counts of inventories.

The official position of the profession is now stated in SAS No. 1 (AU Section 331.09), as follows:

> It is ordinarily necessary for the independent auditor to be present at the time of count and, by suitable observation, tests, and inquiries, satisfy himself respecting the effectiveness of the methods of inventory-taking and the measure of reliance which may be placed upon the client's representations about the quantities and physical condition of the inventories.

AU Section 331.12 goes on to state

> When the independent auditor has not satisfied himself as to inventories in the possession of the client through the procedures [of a physical count], tests of the accounting records alone will not be sufficient for him to become satisfied as to quantities; it will always be necessary for the auditor to make, or observe, some physical counts of the inventory and apply appropriate tests of intervening transactions.

Planning the Inventory Observation. The client has the primary responsibility for planning and taking the physical inventory. Because of the auditor's participation, however, the planning should be a joint effort. The client and auditor should agree on the timing of the inventory after considering the following factors: The inventory should be counted at year-end if it is subject to significant volatility of movement or quantities, or if the control procedures for accounting for movement are ineffective. If those procedures are effective, the count can be taken before year-end or, if the client uses cycle counts, on a staggered basis throughout the year; if the inventory is taken at one time, both client and auditor usually prefer a month in the last quarter of the fiscal year.

Unless the client has effective control procedures that address proper cutoff, the auditor should discourage the client from taking inventories of different departments (especially sequential work-in-process departments) over a period of several days, because double-counting of inventory could result. Alternative control procedures to prevent double-counting are rarely cost-effective.

The auditor should review and comment on the written instructions or memorandum of inventory plans. Often the client executive responsible for the inventory holds one or more instructional meetings with those who are to supervise the inventory-taking. The auditor's presence at the meetings usually facilitates the plans for observing the inventory.

The need for a large number of auditors to be present is naturally greater if a complete physical inventory is taken at one time than if cycle counts or staggered inventories are taken. Audit staffing requirements must be determined based on the timing of inventories at various locations, the difficulty of observing them, and the number of counting teams the client provides.

Observing the Physical Inventory. The auditor must keep in mind the objectives of observing a physical inventory: to ascertain that the inventory exists and to observe that the count and description of the inventory and its condition are accurate and properly recorded. An auditor is neither a taker of inventory nor an expert appraiser of inventory quality, quantities, or condition; nonetheless, he or she cannot neglect the intelligent application of common sense. Well-arranged inventory is more likely to be accurately counted than is poorly arranged inventory. Signs of age and neglect are often obvious, for example, dust on cartons or rust and corrosion of containers, and they naturally raise questions about the inventory's usefulness and salability. The condition of the inventory is particularly important if the product must meet strict technical specifications. For example, in the aerospace industry, a metal part may have to possess specific size, weight, and shape characteristics, as well as conform to standards for a particular alloy mix. Failure to meet the specifications in the smallest way can mean that the part should be valued as scrap. Before observing the inventory, the auditor should know enough about the client's business to be able to recognize, at least in broad terms, the product under observation and the measures appropriate to determining its quality and condition. Thus, an auditor should spend some time examining the inventory being counted; however, the client, and everyone else concerned, should recognize that the auditor is not acting as an expert appraiser.

The auditor should spend most of the time observing the client's procedures in operation. The diligence of the counting teams should be noted: how carefully they count, weigh, and measure; how well they identify and describe the inventory; what methods they use to make sure no items are omitted or duplicated. The auditor should also observe whether supervisory personnel are present, how planned recounting procedures are executed, whether cutoff procedures are performed, how inventory count documents are controlled,

how individual areas or departments are controlled and "cleared," and whether instructions are followed.

The auditor should make some test counts, both to confirm the accuracy of the client's counting and to record corroborative evidence of the existence of the inventory for later tracing to the inventory summarization. Recorded client counts should be selected and reperformed to test their accuracy; in addition, inventory items should be selected and independently counted and compared with quantities recorded by the client. This provides evidence that all items on hand are accurately included in the client's recorded counts.

The auditor must use judgment in determining how many test counts to perform. In the absence of specific reasons to do otherwise, the auditor usually performs a small number of test counts in relation to the total number of items in the inventory. If the auditor's counts disclose an unacceptable number of errors in a particular location, the client would ordinarily recount the inventory. The auditor should record the test counts for subsequent tracing to the inventory summarization.

Client inventory counts are commonly recorded at least in duplicate, with one copy retained at the scene of the count and another gathered for summarization. The client normally controls the summarization process, and the auditor makes notations of tag or count sheet numbers or other control data on a test basis for later tracing to summarized records to provide corroborative evidence that the process was adequately controlled, that is, that all tags or count sheets were accounted for and none was added later.

As part of the review of plans and observation of the physical inventory procedures, the auditor should note and evaluate the procedures followed in separately identifying and counting items moved from place to place (such as from department to department or from receiving area to storage area) and goods on hand belonging to others, such as consignments, bailments, goods on approval, and property of customers returned for repair or held awaiting delivery instructions. All items belonging to others should be counted and recorded separately, both because they should be subject to control and to preclude their mistaken or purposeful substitution for the client's inventory.

Adequately identifying work in process, especially its stage of completion, is likely to be difficult and may be impossible without a bill of materials or similar document. Production or operating personnel must be able to identify items in process and their condition or stage of completion in order to control the production process, and so they should be able to do so for physical count purposes as well. If they cannot, the auditor may find any of a number of practical ways to deal with the problems of identifying and valuing work in process. On the basis of experience and common sense, the auditor can make assumptions that clearly cannot be materially in error: Goods in a given department can be assumed to have passed through an average stage of completion; the variety of goods in a given department can be assumed to be of an average size, formula, or character; tote boxes, bales, or coils can be assumed to be of an average weight.

Cycle Counts. All procedures applicable to wall-to-wall physical inventory observation can be readily adapted to cycle count observation. The auditor can review the cycle counting schedules, plans, and instructions, and observe the physical arrangement and condition of the inventory, and the diligence and proficiency of the inventory count teams in counting and identifying inventory, controlling records of test counts, preventing omissions or duplications, and identifying and segregating slow-moving, obsolete, or damaged goods. Because the entire inventory is not being counted at one time, the auditor must take steps to ensure that the items counted are properly identified. The auditor can make a few test counts either independently or with the count teams and can observe and, if desired, participate in reconciling the counts to perpetual records and investigating differences.

Effective cycle counting depends on effective control procedures for inventory quantities and timely recording throughout the production process. Having tested the effectiveness of the client's procedures for controlling inventory quantities and related cycle counting, the auditor can choose to observe and test physical inventory procedures at any convenient time, including, if necessary, before or after the period under audit.

The auditor also needs evidence that the cycle counting procedures observed were functioning before and can be expected to function after they were observed and that they are applied to substantially all inventory items. A formal schedule of counts and specific assignments (covering both personnel to perform the counts and supervisory responsibility) is preferable. Many companies, however, operate under a loose policy of ''counting all items at least once a year'' and assign the counting to the stockkeepers to do as time allows. In those instances, the auditor can review work sheets, entries in the perpetual inventory records, and other evidence of the regularity of test counting, and can evaluate the results. Evidence of proper count procedures includes frequent counting; absence of substantial differences between counts and records over a period of time; adequate cutoff of receipts, shipments, and transfers (at the date of each count); quality of investigation of differences that occur (including segregation of duties between personnel performing initial counts and those investigating differences); and quality of storeroom housekeeping and inventory identification.

Difficult Inventories. Certain types of material—for example, logs in a river, piles of coal and scrap metal, vats of chemicals—by their nature may be difficult to count, and an auditor may have to use ingenuity to substantiate quantities on hand. Measurement of a pile of metals may be difficult for a number of reasons: The pile may have sunk into the ground to an unknown depth; the metals may be of varying weights, precluding the use of an average; or the pile may be of uneven density. The quality of chemicals and similar materials may be impossible to determine without specialized knowledge, and the auditor may find it necessary to draw samples from various levels of holding tanks and send them for independent analysis. Irregularities have been perpetrated by substituting water for materials stored in tanks.

Clients sometimes use photographic surveys, engineering studies, and similar specialized techniques to take physical inventories, and an auditor can observe how carefully they are conducted. In such situations, the auditor should consider the need for an expert or specialist to help take or evaluate the inventory. Guidance on the use of specialists is contained in Chapter 6.

In some circumstances, the auditor may be guided by the client's system of handling receipts and disbursements from the piles. For example, the client may use a pile rotation or exhaustion system, in which material received is placed in other piles until a pile is exhausted, at which time errors in the accounts are disclosed. If the pile rotation system functions satisfactorily, the auditor may be willing to consider the accounting records, to a certain extent, as a source of evidence.

Alternative Procedures If Observation of Physical Inventories Is Not Practicable. The auditor should not decide lightly that observation of inventories is impracticable or impossible. If the client does not or cannot take a physical inventory, however, or if the auditor cannot be present at the inventory-taking, the auditor may be able to form an opinion regarding the reasonableness of inventory quantities by applying alternative procedures. Those alternative procedures fall into the following two basic categories:

Examining other physical evidence that may be tantamount to observing physical inventories.

Substantiating inventories through further examination of accounting documents and records.

As an example of the first category, if the auditor is engaged after the physical inventory has been taken, subsequent physical tests (before or after year-end) may be a satisfactory substitute for observing the inventory-taking. The auditor may also examine written instructions for the inventory-taking, review the original tags or sheets, and make suitable tests of the summarization.

In any event, the auditor must examine or observe some physical evidence of the existence of the inventory and make appropriate tests of intervening transactions or control procedures applied to them. If, on the basis of those tests, the auditor is satisfied that inventories are fairly stated, he or she is in a position to express an unqualified opinion. On the other hand, there may be no practicable substitute for observation of inventory-taking, and an auditor may have to express a qualified opinion or disclaimer, depending on the materiality of the inventories and on whether the failure to observe was unavoidable or resulted from management's decision to limit the scope of the audit.

Sometimes procedures for substantiating inventories must be based on examining other accounting documents and records. For example, in an initial audit, the auditor generally will not have observed the physical inventory at the previous year-end, which is a principal factor in determining cost of sales for the current year. If reputable independent accountants expressed an unqualified opinion on the prior-year statements, a successor auditor may accept that opinion and perhaps merely review the predecessor auditor's working papers supporting the prior-year balances. If no audit was made for the preceding year, the auditor may have no alternative but to substantially expand the tests of accounting records to attempt to obtain reasonable assurance about the beginning inventories in order to be able to express an opinion on the current year's results of operations.

Those expanded tests may include a detailed examination of physical inventory sheets and summaries, including review and testing of cutoff data, examination of perpetual inventory records and production records, and review of individual product and overall gross profit percentages. In connection with the latter procedures, cost accumulations for selected inventory items should be tested and significant changes in unit costs directly traced to factors such as technological changes, mass buying economies and freight rate "breaks," changes in labor costs, and changes in overhead rates. Changes in gross profit percentages should be further related to changes in unit sales prices and changes in the profitability of the sales mix, if applicable.

An auditor who is unable to form an opinion on the opening inventory may decide to qualify the audit opinion or disclaim an opinion with respect to results of operations for the year under audit.

Testing Ownership and Cutoff

The auditor must determine that the client holds title to the inventories. In many cases, this is relatively straightforward. Theoretically, the accounting for purchases and sales in transit at year-end is determined by the FOB terms (shipping point or destination), which determine title. Unless financial statements would otherwise be misleading, however, the legal test of title is often disregarded based on materiality considerations: Purchases are generally recorded when received, and sales when shipped.

The primary focus for determining ownership is on proper control of receiving and shipping activities and cutoffs at year-end and, if different, at the physical inventory date. Control over sales cutoff at an early physical inventory date is particularly important because sales cutoff errors at that date—as compared with year-end—are compounded when perpetual inventory records and control account balances are adjusted for differences between recorded and physical inventory. Since cutoff errors correct themselves in the following period when the sales and cost of sales are recorded in the normal course of transaction processing, a reduction of inventory and increase in cost of sales, if goods were shipped before the physical count but not recorded until after the physical count, will be recorded twice. The effect in that situation is to misstate gross profit by the full cost of the inventory involved in the cutoff error. On the other hand, a sales cutoff error at year-end (when the physical inventory has been taken at an earlier date) will result in a misstatement of gross profit only to the extent of the gross profit on the sale.[1]

At the time of the inventory observation, the auditor should visit the receiving and shipping departments, record the last receiving and shipping document numbers, and ascertain that each department has been informed that no receipts after or shipments before the cutoff date should be included in inventory. The auditor should review the records of those departments after the inventory date and compare the last receiving and shipping numbers with accounting department records to ensure that a proper cutoff was achieved. Special care should be taken to control the movement of inventory when manufacturing operations are not suspended during the physical inventory.

If there are consignment inventories, inventories in public warehouses, or customer inventories, those procedures must be expanded. Inventory held by others should be substantiated by direct confirmation in writing with the custodians. If such inventory is material, the auditor should apply one or more of the following procedures, in accordance with SAS No. 1, as amended by SAS No. 43 (AU Section 331.14), to obtain reasonable assurance with respect to the existence of the inventory:

a. Test the owner's procedures for investigating the warehouseman and evaluating the warehouseman's performance.
b. Obtain an independent accountant's report on the warehouseman's control procedures relevant to custody of goods and, if applicable, pledging of receipts, or apply alternative procedures at the warehouse to gain reasonable assurance that information received from the warehouseman is reliable.
c. Observe physical counts of the goods, if practicable and reasonable.
d. If warehouse receipts have been pledged as collateral, confirm with lenders pertinent details of the pledged receipts (on a test basis, if appropriate).

If merchandise is billed to customers and held for them, care must be exercised to exclude that merchandise from inventory and to determine that the customers have authorized billing before delivery. Goods belonging to customers or others should be counted and, if significant in amount, should be confirmed with their owners. The auditor should be alert to the possibility of such goods and should make certain that the client has a system for controlling the goods and that they are properly identified and segregated.

[1]Cutoff errors involving receipt of goods at the physical inventory date also misstate gross profit by the full cost of the inventory involved; cutoff errors involving receipt of goods at year-end (when the physical inventory has been taken at an earlier date) have no effect on gross profit, except in the rare situation in which the merchandise was also sold.

The auditor should also be alert for liens and encumbrances against the inventories. These are normally evident from reading minutes and agreements, or as a result of confirmations with lenders relating to loans or loan agreements. It may be necessary to investigate whether additional liens and encumbrances have been filed with state or local governmental authorities.

Inventory Costing and Summarization

Inventory costing and summarization may be based on the physical inventory results or the perpetual inventory records (if those records have been determined to be reliable); in either case, the results are compared with the recorded amounts. The procedures performed in testing the summarization of the physical inventory quantities are as follows:

1. The inventory tags are tested to determine that all tags used for the physical counts and only those tags are included in the physical inventory summaries. The auditor should also ascertain that tags that were voided during the physical count have been properly accounted for. If count sheets were used for recording physical inventory results, the auditor should ascertain that unused spaces have not been filled in after the physical count was completed.
2. The inventory summaries are compared with the auditor's record of counts and with the client's count sheets or tags; conversions and summarizations of units are tested.
3. Quantities are compared with perpetual records, if they exist, on a test basis, and differences and client dispositions are reviewed; this is particularly important when inventories are taken prior to year-end and perpetual records will be the basis for year-end inventory valuation.
4. Cutoff procedures are tested.
5. Customers' materials on hand and client's inventories in the hands of others are reviewed and confirmed.
6. Raw materials, labor, and overhead costs to be applied to inventories are tested to determine that they are reasonably computed in accordance with an acceptable and consistent accounting method.
7. The multiplication of prices and inventory quantities and the resulting footings and summarizations are tested.

How extensively the auditor performs each of the above procedures depends on the auditor's knowledge of and experience with the client, information obtained when observing the physical inventory count, understanding of the control structure, and the results of any tests of controls performed. Errors noted when testing the summarization should be given particular consideration in assessing whether client procedures are effective and whether additional testing is necessary.

In testing the costing of merchandise inventories and inventories of simple manufacturing operations, the auditor can often relate costs directly to specific vendor invoices and labor summaries. In more complex manufacturing operations, evaluating material, labor, and overhead allocations may be more difficult. An example is the manufacturing operation of a steel mill where the raw materials ore, coal, and limestone are converted into finished steel. Allocating costs is less objective and requires an understanding of process costing and an in-depth knowledge of the manufacturing process. It may be difficult for the auditor to obtain satisfaction regarding the costing of inventory without obtaining some evidence that the client's procedures for product costing and tracking inventory through the various stages of completion are effective.

Accountants have long recognized the conceptual problems associated with allocating overhead to work in process based on activity such as direct labor hours or dollars. Changes in the manufacturing environment—in particular increased automation and computerization, reduced levels of inventories of raw materials and component parts through the use of just-in-time techniques, and direct labor becoming a smaller portion of production costs—have called into question the appropriateness of commonly used overhead allocation bases. Some enterprises have considered new techniques to generate cost accounting data that both better reflects the results of management's decisions and produces financial statements acceptable for financial reporting. The auditor should consider the client's overhead allocation methods to ensure that they generate inventory and cost of sales values that are in conformity with GAAP appropriate to the enterprise's circumstances, and that those methods are not merely routine or mechanical applications of traditional techniques that do not reflect the enterprise's manufacturing environment.

The accounting method used to price inventory also affects the substantive tests to be performed. The differences in the procedures used under different valuation methods relate mainly to the sources of cost information and the mechanics of the pricing calculations. For example, pricing tests of inventory valued on a FIFO basis normally include a comparison of costs to most recent invoice prices for purchased merchandise and most recent unit production costs for manufactured goods. Pricing tests of LIFO inventories normally include procedures to test consistency of base-year prices between years, comparisons of base-year costs for new items with current-year costs, recalculation of indices used to value current-year LIFO increments, and an overall review of the accuracy of the LIFO application.

LIFO presents opportunities, not available under other inventory costing methods, for the client to manage earnings. Those opportunities often involve transactions, usually entered into near year-end, that would charge portions of the beginning inventory to cost of sales or, depending on management's reporting objectives, prevent a liquidation of the beginning inventory from being charged to cost of sales. Management could accomplish these income-managing objectives by entering into accommodation purchases or sales that, pursuant to an undisclosed resale agreement, would later be reversed. The auditor should be alert to the possibility of such transactions, which may be discovered by scanning the records for unusual transactions early in the next accounting period, particularly transactions with known related parties.

Inventory Valuation

Generally accepted accounting principles require that inventories be reported at the lower of historical cost (using an acceptable flow-of-cost assumption) or market (current replacement cost by either purchase or production), except that the carrying value should not exceed net realizable value (estimated selling price minus costs of completion and disposal) or be lower than net realizable value reduced by the normal profit margin. (Net realizable value is frequently referred to as the "ceiling," and net realizable value reduced by the normal profit margin is frequently referred to as the "floor.") To achieve the valuation objective for inventories, the auditor should test the inventory costing as indicated above, and should also

- Review and test procedures for identifying obsolete or slow-moving items.
- Review the costing of damaged or obsolete items to determine that the assigned value does not exceed net realizable value.
- Review and test the determination of market prices to determine whether market is lower than cost.

In reviewing for obsolete items in inventory, the auditor should consider not only finished goods but also work in process and raw materials that will eventually become finished goods. The auditor may compare quantities with those in previous inventories on a test basis to identify slow-moving items or abnormally large or small balances. Comparing inventory quantities with sales forecasts is an effective test for obsolete items. Reviews of usage records can provide further indications of slow-moving items. If the client does not maintain perpetual records, the auditor may examine purchase orders or production orders to determine how recently certain items of inventory were acquired. Many companies have formulas or rules of thumb that translate overall judgments on obsolete inventory into practical detailed applications, like all items over a year's supply, all items that have not moved within six months, or all items bearing certain identifying numbers with regard to date or class of product. The auditor must review whether the rules are realistic and comprehensive enough as well as whether they are fully and accurately applied. In addition to reviewing and testing the client's rules, the auditor must evaluate, based on an understanding of the client's business, whether, for each segment of the inventory, market conditions might raise questions about its realizability in the normal course of operations. The auditor may also inquire of sales and marketing executives about the salability of the inventories. Past experience can be the best guide to the net realizable value of items that must be disposed of at salvage prices. When certain finished goods are declared obsolete (or severe markdowns are required), related raw materials and work-in-process inventories (unless usable for other products) may also need to be written down.

Testing the client's application of the lower of cost or market principle is one of the more difficult and subjective aspects of the audit. In most situations, the auditor's assessment of inherent risk is particularly important in determining the extent of substantive testing. For example, if the risk of defective production or of the acceptance of incoming shipments of defective merchandise is high, the auditor may need to expand testing of the condition of inventories. Companies usually apply the lower of cost or market test on an exception basis when a problem is identified. Accordingly, the auditor has limited opportunity to test control procedures in this area. The greater audit risk is that not all problems have been identified, not that an identified problem may lead to a misstatement in the financial statements.

The auditor should test the client's calculation of net realizable value of individual or major groups of products. Estimated selling prices may be compared with recent sales invoices—or preferably with the latest customer orders—and evaluated for possible trends in prices. Estimated costs of completion and disposal may be tested for reasonableness by an overall computation. The auditor ordinarily need not determine the value of inventory at reproduction or replacement costs if there is acceptable evidence that, for individual or groups of products, the range between net realizable value and the market floor is not great. If necessary, however, the auditor may test replacement costs by reference to cost records, current invoices, or purchase contracts. Reproduction costs may be tested in a similar manner, supplemented by discussions with production and accounting employees.

Auditing Cost of Sales

In planning the audit, the auditor often views the income statement as the residual effect of changes in the balance sheet. The primary focus is on auditing balance sheet accounts at the beginning and end of the year. The audit opinion on results of operations, however, requires that the auditor perform auditing procedures to obtain satisfaction that transactions are properly accounted for and classified in the income statement.

Substantive tests of cost of sales are usually limited for two reasons. First, the audit plan is likely to include tests of controls in the production cycle. Second, if the auditor performs substantive tests of the beginning and ending inventory balances and obtains evidence about the completeness, accuracy, and authorization of purchases of goods and services (including their proper classification) by testing controls that are part of the buying cycle, he or she has significant amounts of evidence about the "residual" cost of sales figure. Accordingly, substantive tests of cost of sales can normally be limited to analytical procedures that test the proper classification of costs by focusing on expected or traditional relationships among various components of cost of sales and obtaining explanations for fluctuations in expense account balances. Often overhead and other variances are also analyzed as part of substantive tests of cost of sales. Typical analytical procedures are discussed later in this section.

If results of the above procedures indicate that additional evidence is needed to support the cost of sales balance, the auditor may also examine selected invoices for material and overhead costs and test the allocation of payroll costs, together with testing the summarization of detailed amounts in the account balances that enter into cost of sales. The auditor would probably perform analytical procedures as well.

Purchase Commitments

Losses from purchase commitments may arise in connection with commodity purchases, forward transactions, or purchase commitments in excess of short-term requirements. If material losses could arise from unfulfilled purchase commitments, the auditor should identify the commitments and assess the potential need for a loss provision. This may be accomplished by examining open purchase order records, inquiring of employees who make purchase commitments, or requesting major suppliers to provide details of any purchase commitments outstanding at year-end. If there is doubt regarding whether all commitments have been identified, it may be appropriate to review suppliers' invoices and receiving reports for a period after year-end for evidence of purchases above prevailing prices or in quantities exceeding current requirements (by reviewing perpetual inventory records for evidence of goods that are slow-moving or obsolete), which may indicate unfavorable purchase commitments at year-end. Also, since major purchase commitments generally require the approval of the board of directors, examining minutes of board meetings may be helpful in discovering such commitments. Chapter 17 contains a discussion of the statements about purchase commitments that should be included in the client's representation letter.

Analytical Procedures

Auditing inventories challenges an auditor's knowledge and analytical skills more than almost any other audit activity. The better the auditor understands the client's business, its operating problems, and the market and other economic conditions it operates in, the greater the ability to determine that the inventory is fairly stated in conformity with generally accepted accounting principles. That understanding can be applied to specific judgments in designing analytical procedures.

Both internal and external data is abundantly available for designing and testing statistical, ratio, and other kinds of analyses. The auditor should make every effort to use analytical procedures unique to the client, but only on the basis of a thorough understanding. The following paragraphs describe only those analytical procedures that are likely to apply to most inventories.

If standard cost systems or budgetary systems produce variance reports, the system has, in effect, performed a large part of the analytical procedure by identifying the variances. The auditor can then read the variance reports carefully and analyze reasons for variances. If variances are small, the auditor can infer that standards approximate actual costs and can significantly reduce price testing.

The auditor may compare purchases, usage reports, and production costs from month to month, and investigate and obtain explanations for fluctuations. Significant ratios may be computed and compared from month to month and with the prior year. The ratios of cost of sales to inventory and to sales are universally considered informative. They must be used with caution in a period of changing prices, however, as results under FIFO will differ, perhaps significantly, from those under LIFO. In a great many industries, the computation of the ratio of total units to total value—that is, average unit cost—is valid and informative, but if the "mix" of unit costs is likely to vary substantially, explaining fluctuations in average unit costs may not be cost effective. If they are valid, average unit costs can be computed for sales, purchases, and inventory balances.

If available, sales forecasts and marketing plans can provide important information about salability and net realizable value of inventories. For example, marketing plans for a "new line" can effectively render obsolete an inventory that otherwise appears salable at normal profit margins. Sales forecasts and marketing plans, however, are often not well organized or in written form, and thus the auditor must take care not to waste time searching for material that is nonexistent or inconclusive. An auditor who has an adequate understanding of the client will know what to expect and of whom to inquire.

Analytical procedures must be particularly intensive between an interim inventory date and year-end. Often the audit effort during this period is directed primarily toward tests of controls, with minimal substantive testing of intervening activity or the year-end balance. Analytical procedures provide an excellent means of identifying changes in conditions that may require additional substantive tests or, in conjunction with the results of related tests of controls and other substantive tests, of providing the needed assurance regarding the year-end balances.

Management Representation Letter

It is standard practice for the auditor to request management to include certain matters relating to inventory in the representation letter. The focus of the letter is on judgments made by management in the financial accounting process; the letter includes representations relating to agreements to repurchase inventory or the absence thereof, net realizable value judgments, pledging of assets, and the nature of significant inventory purchase commitments. Management representation letters are discussed in Chapter 17.

Review Questions

14–1. What is meant by the production cycle?

14–2. What are the audit objectives for the production cycle?

14–3. What audit risk factors are considered in determining the audit testing plan for the production cycle?

14–4. What control procedures should be in effect for raw materials and component parts from receipt to utilization?

14–5. Companies and their auditors must make reviews to discover slow-moving, obsolete, or damaged goods. Why?

14–6. Given the significance of inventory and the production cycle to many businesses, management reviews are often performed to ensure operational efficiency. Cite examples of management reviews related to inventory and production.

14–7. What are the audit objectives associated with variances generated by a standard cost system?

14–8. Why are physical inventory counts of work in process often difficult? What recommendations can an auditor make in this regard?

14–9. Distinguish between wall-to-wall and cycle count inventory taking. When is each appropriate?

14–10. What evidence does the auditor need when the client uses cycle count procedures?

14–11. Briefly outline the instructions a client's physical inventory program should contain.

14–12. Briefly outline the procedures an auditor's physical inventory program should contain.

14–13. What alternative procedures should an auditor follow if physical inventory observation is impracticable?

14–14. What factors should the auditor consider in determining whether to perform additional tests of controls in the production cycle?

14–15. Under what conditions should the auditor emphasize substantive testing in lieu of testing control procedures in auditing the production cycle?

14–16. What factors influence the nature, timing, and extent of substantive tests?

14–17. What control procedures are generally used for producing goods and storing inventory?

14–18. How are tests of controls in the buying cycle related to those in the production cycle?

14–19. Who has the primary responsibility for planning and conducting the physical inventory? What factors affect the timing of the physical inventory?

14–20. What should the auditor do when observing inventory taking?

14–21. Why does an auditor make test counts during the physical inventory?

14–22. What substantive tests should be performed with respect to consignment inventories, inventories in public warehouses, and inventory held for customers?

14–23. What analytical procedures are applied in the audit of inventories? When should they be applied?

14–24. What matters relating to inventory should be included in the management representation letter?

Discussion Questions

14–30. State what steps you would take to substantiate the book balance of the physical quantities of inventories in each of the following cases:

a. A large, outdoor pile of coal.
b. Grain in an elevator.
c. A large quantity of nails, dumped in a bin, the book inventory being carried in pounds.

The book balances are obtained as the result of a continuous record of receipts, withdrawals, and arithmetically computed balances.

(AICPA adapted)

14–31. Often an important aspect of a CPA's audit of financial statements is the observation of the taking of the physical inventory.

Required:

a. What are the general objectives or purposes of the CPA's observation of the taking of the physical inventory? (Do not discuss the procedures or techniques involved in making the observation.)
b. For what purposes does the CPA make and record test counts of inventory quantities during the observation of the taking of the physical inventory? Discuss.

(AICPA adapted)

14–32. State the procedures you would follow if a significant number of adjustments were necessary arising from differences between amounts shown on the perpetual inventory records and

a. The client's cycle counts.
b. The client's year-end counts.
c. Your test counts.

Consider each case separately.

14–33. Top & Co. determines its inventories by means of a complete physical inventory count at year-end. Actual costs are used for pricing. You attended the year-end physical count and observed that the count procedures were satisfactory. What additional steps should you take to satisfy yourself concerning the quantities and value of the inventories?

14–34. The auditor should review and comment on the client's written instructions to personnel responsible for taking a physical inventory. What matters should be covered in those instructions? (Do not discuss procedures the auditor should follow in observing the physical inventory.)

14–35. The client's cost system is often the focal point in the CPA's audit of the financial statements of a manufacturing company.

Required:

a. For what purposes does the CPA review the cost system?
b. Streamline, Inc. employs standard costs in its cost accounting system. List the auditing procedures that you would apply to satisfy yourself that Streamline's cost standards and related variance amounts are acceptable and have not distorted the financial statements. (Confine your auditing procedures to those applicable to materials.)

(AICPA adapted)

14–36. Walton, CPA, is performing an audit of the financial statements of Stein's Wholesalers for the year ended December 31, 1990. Stein's has been in business for many years and has never had its financial statements audited. Walton has gained satisfaction with respect to the ending inventory and is considering alternative auditing procedures to gain satisfaction with respect to management's representations concerning the beginning inventory, which was not observed.

Stein's sells only one product (bottled brand X beer), and maintains perpetual inventory records. In addition, Stein's takes physical inventory counts monthly. Walton has already confirmed purchases with the manufacturer and has decided to concentrate on evaluating the reliability of perpetual inventory records and performing analytical procedures to the extent that the prior year's unaudited records will enable such procedures to be performed.

Required:

What are the audit tests, including analytical procedures, that Walton should apply in evaluating the reliability of perpetual inventory records and gaining satisfaction with respect to the January 1, 1990 inventory?

(AICPA adapted)

14–37. In an annual audit at December 31, 1990, you find the following transactions near the closing date:

1. A packing case containing products costing $816 was standing in the shipping room when the physical inventory was taken. It was not included in the inventory because it was marked "Hold for shipping instructions." Your investigation revealed that the customer's order was dated December 18, 1990, but that the case was shipped and the customer billed on January 10, 1991. The product was a stock item of your client.

2. A special machine, fabricated to order for a customer, was finished and in the shipping room on December 31, 1990. The customer was billed on that date and the machine excluded from inventory, although it was shipped on January 4, 1991.
3. Merchandise costing $1822 was received on January 3, 1991, and the related purchase invoice recorded January 5. The invoice showed the shipment was made on December 29, 1990, FOB destination.
4. Merchandise costing $625 was received on December 28, 1990, and the invoice was not recorded. You located it in the hands of the purchasing agent; it was marked "on consignment."
5. Merchandise received on January 6, 1991, costing $720 was entered in the purchase register on January 7, 1991. The invoice showed that the merchandise was shipped FOB supplier's warehouse on December 31, 1990. Since it was not on hand at December 31, it was not included in inventory.

Required:

a. State whether the merchandise should be included in the client's inventory.
b. Give the reason for your decision on each item in (a).

(AICPA adapted)

14–38. While reviewing purchase commitments, an auditor discovered that the purchase price in an unauthorized purchase commitment exceeded the current market price for that item at the time of the order. Discuss the effect of the discovery on audit strategy and auditing procedures to be followed.

14–39. Steve Jackson, CPA, is engaged in the audit of the financial statements of Old World Furniture Corporation for the year ended June 30, 1990. Old World's inventories at year-end include merchandise on consignment with consignees and merchandise held in public warehouses. The merchandise held in public warehouses is pledged as collateral for outstanding debt.

Required:

Normal inventory and notes payable auditing procedures have been satisfactorily completed. Describe the specific additional auditing procedures that Jackson should undertake with respect to

a. Consignments out.
b. Merchandise in public warehouses pledged as collateral for outstanding debt.

(AICPA adapted)

AICPA Multiple Choice Questions

These questions are taken from the Auditing part of Uniform CPA Examinations. Choose the single most appropriate answer.

14–40. The primary objective of a CPA's observation of a client's physical inventory count is to

a. Discover whether a client has counted a particular inventory item or group of items.

b. Obtain direct knowledge that the inventory exists and has been properly counted.
c. Provide an appraisal of the quality of the merchandise on hand on the day of the physical count.
d. Allow the auditor to supervise the conduct of the count so as to obtain assurance that inventory quantities are reasonably accurate.

14–41. The physical count of inventory of a retailer was higher than shown by the perpetual records. Which of the following could explain the difference?

a. Inventory items had been counted but the tags placed on the items had *not* been taken off the items and added to the inventory accumulation sheets.
b. Credit memos for several items returned by customers had *not* been recorded.
c. No journal entry had been made on the retailer's books for several items returned to its suppliers.
d. An item purchased "FOB shipping point" had *not* arrived at the date of the inventory count and had *not* been reflected in the perpetual records.

14–42. A CPA is engaged in the annual audit of a client for the year ended December 31, 1990. The client took a complete physical inventory under the CPA's observation on December 15 and adjusted its inventory control account and detailed perpetual inventory records to agree with the physical inventory. The client considers a sale to be made in the period that goods are shipped. Listed below are four items taken from the CPA's sales-cutoff-test worksheet. Which item does *not* require an adjusting entry on the client's books?

	Date (Month/Day)		
	Shipped	*Recorded as Sale*	*Credited to Inventory Control*
a.	12/10	12/19	12/12
b.	12/14	12/16	12/16
c.	12/31	1/2	12/31
d.	1/2	12/31	12/31

14–43. When outside firms of nonaccountants specializing in the taking of physical inventories are used to count, list, price, and subsequently compute the total dollar amount of inventory on hand at the date of the physical count, the auditor will ordinarily

a. Consider the report of the outside inventory-taking firm to be an acceptable alternative procedure to the observation of physical inventories.
b. Make or observe some physical counts of the inventory, recompute certain inventory calculations, and test certain inventory transactions.
c. *Not* reduce the extent of work on the physical count of inventory.
d. Consider the reduced audit effort with respect to the physical count of inventory as a scope limitation.

14–44. An auditor would be *most* likely to learn of slow-moving inventory through

a. Inquiry of sales personnel.
b. Inquiry of stores personnel.

c. Physical observation of inventory.
d. Review of perpetual inventory records.

14–45. Instead of taking a physical inventory count on the balance sheet date the client may take physical counts prior to the year-end if the internal control structure is adequate and

a. Computerized records of perpetual inventory are maintained.
b. Inventory is slow-moving.
c. EDP error reports are generated for missing prenumbered inventory tickets.
d. Obsolete inventory items are segregated and excluded.

14–46. After accounting for a sequence of inventory tags, an auditor traces a sample of tags to the physical inventory listing to obtain evidence that all items

a. Included in the listing have been counted.
b. Represented by inventory tags are included in the listing.
c. Included in the listing are represented by inventory tags.
d. Represented by inventory tags are bona fide.

14–47. The auditor's use of analytical procedures will be facilitated if the client

a. Uses a standard cost system that produces variance reports.
b. Segregates obsolete inventory before the physical inventory count.
c. Corrects material deficiencies in the internal control structure before the beginning of the audit.
d. Reduces inventory balances to the lower of cost or market.

14–48. When auditing merchandise inventory at year-end, the auditor performs a purchase cutoff test to obtain evidence that

a. All goods purchased before year-end are received before the physical inventory count.
b. No goods held on consignment for customers are included in the inventory balance.
c. No goods observed during the physical count are pledged or sold.
d. All goods owned at year-end are included in the inventory balance.

14–49. Which of the following is a question that the auditor would expect to find on the production cycle section of an internal control questionnaire?

a. Are vendors' invoices for raw materials approved for payment by an employee who is independent of the cash disbursements function?
b. Are signed checks for the purchase of raw materials mailed directly after signing without being returned to the person who authorized the invoice processing?
c. Are all releases by storekeepers of raw materials from storage based on approved requisition documents?
d. Are details of individual disbursements for raw materials balanced with the total to be posted to the appropriate general ledger account?

14–50. Independent internal verification of inventory occurs when employees who

a. Issue raw materials obtain material requisitions for each issue and prepare daily totals of materials issued.
b. Compare records of goods on hand with physical quantitites do *not* maintain the records or have custody of the inventory.
c. Obtain receipts for the transfer of completed work to finished goods prepare a completed production report.
d. Are independent of issuing production orders update records from completed job cost sheets and production cost reports on a timely basis.

14–51. An auditor generally tests physical security control procedures related to inventory by

a. Test counts and cutoff procedures.
b. Examination and reconciliation.
c. Inspection and recomputation.
d. Inquiry and observation.

Problems and Cases

14–60. An auditor is conducting an audit of the financial statements of a wholesale cosmetics distributor with an inventory consisting of thousands of individual items. The distributor keeps its inventory in its own distribution center and in two public warehouses. An inventory computer file is maintained on a computer disk and at the end of each business day the file is updated. Each record of the inventory file contains the following data:

- Item number
- Location of item
- Description of item
- Quantity on hand
- Cost per item
- Date of last purchase
- Date of last sale
- Quantity sold during year

The auditor is planning to observe the distributor's physical count of inventories as of a given date. The auditor will have available a computer tape of the data on the inventory file on the date of the physical count and a general-purpose computer software package.

Required:

The auditor is planning to perform basic inventory auditing procedures. Identify the basic inventory auditing procedures and describe how the use of the general-purpose software package and the tape of the inventory file data might be helpful to the auditor in performing such auditing procedures.

Organize your answer as follows:

Baic Inventory Auditing Procedure	*How General-Purpose Computer Software Package and Tape of the Inventory File Data Might Be Helpful*
1. Observe the physical count, making and recording test counts where applicable.	Determining which items are to be test-counted by selecting a random sample of a representative number of items from the inventory file as of the date of the physical count.

(AICPA adapted)

14-61. Indicate the misstatements, if any, in financial position at September 30, and in operating results for the year ended September 30, arising from the following situation:

Assumptions: Physical inventory was taken August 31 and book inventory amount was adjusted to physical. Fiscal year ends September 30.

Case I

Item	*Selling Price*	*Cost to Manufacture*	*Date Goods Shipped*	*Date Sale and Cost of Sale Recorded*
A	$ 80,000	$50,000	9/3	8/29
B	120,000	80,000	9/27	10/2
C	50,000	30,000	8/25	8/29
D	60,000	36,000	8/29	9/5
E	100,000	64,000	8/15	9/1

Case II

Item	*Cost of Raw Materials*	*Date Goods Received*	*Date Purchase Recorded*
A	$60,000	9/29	10/1
B	50,000	8/26	9/3
C	20,000	9/2	8/29

14-62. PDQ Inc. does not conduct a complete annual physical count of purchased parts and supplies in its principal warehouse but uses statistical sampling instead to estimate the year-end inventory. PDQ maintains a perpetual inventory record of parts and supplies and believes that statistical sampling is both highly effective in determining inventory values and sufficiently reliable to make a physical count of each item of inventory unnecessary.

Required:

a. Identify the auditing procedures that should be used by the independent auditor *that change or are in addition to* normal required auditing procedures when a client utilizes statistical sampling to determine inventory value and does not conduct a 100 percent annual physical count of inventory items.

b. List at least ten normal auditing procedures that should be performed *to substantiate physical quantities* whenever a client conducts a periodic physical count of all or part of its inventory.

(AICPA adapted)

14-63. The Powder Puff Company packages two cosmetics items that it stores at various warehouses. The company employs a perpetual inventory accounting system under which the finished goods inventory is charged with production and credited for sales at standard cost. The detail of the finished goods inventory is maintained on magnetic tape by the Tabulating Department in units and dollars for the various warehouses.

Company procedures call for the Accounting Department to receive copies of daily production reports and sales invoices. Units are then extended at standard cost and a summary of the day's activity is posted to the Finished Goods Inventory general ledger control account. Next, the sales invoices and production reports are sent to the Tabulating Department for processing. Every month the control and detailed tab records are reconciled and adjustments recorded. The last reconciliation and adjustments were made on November 30, 1989.

Your CPA firm observed the taking of the physical inventory at all locations on December 31, 1989. The inventory count began at 4:00 P.M. and was completed at 8:00 P.M. The company's figure for the physical inventory is $331,400. The general ledger control account balance at December 31 was $373,900, and the final inventory tape showed a total of $392,300.

Unit cost data for the company's two products are as follows:

Product	*Standard Cost*
A	$2.00
B	3.00

A review of December transactions disclosed the following:

1. Sales invoice #1301, 12/2/89, was priced at standard cost for $11,700, but was listed on the Accounting Department's daily summary at $11,200.
2. A production report for $23,900, 12/15/89, was processed twice in error by the Tabulating Department.
3. Sales invoice #1423, 12/9/89, for 1200 units of Product A, was priced at a standard cost of $1.50 per unit by the Accounting Department. The Tabulating Department noticed and corrected the error but did not notify the Accounting Department of the error.
4. A shipment of 3400 units of Product A was invoiced by the Billing Department as 3000 units on sales invoice #1504, 12/27/89. The error was discovered by your review of transactions.
5. On December 27, the Nashville warehouse notified the Tabulating Department to remove 2200 unsalable units of Product A from the finished goods inventory, which it did without receiving a special invoice from the Accounting Department. The Accounting Department received a copy of the Nashville warehouse notification on December 29 and made up a special invoice, which was processed in the normal manner. The units were not included in the physical inventory.
6. A production report for the production on January 3 of 2500 units of Product B was processed for the Wilmington plant as of December 31.

7. A shipment of 300 units of Product B was made from the Bloomington warehouse to Guinevere's Beauty Supplies, at 8:30 P.M. on December 31 as a rush order for a special promotion. The sales invoice was processed as of December 31. The client prefers to treat the transaction as a sale in 1989.
8. The working papers of the auditor observing the physical count at the Detroit warehouse revealed that 700 units of Product B were omitted from the client's physical count. The client concurred that the units were omitted in error.
9. A sales invoice for 600 units of Product A shipped from the Seattle warehouse was mislaid and was not processed until January 5. The units involved were shipped on December 30.
10. The physical inventory of the Dallas warehouse excluded 350 units of Product A that were marked "reserved." On investigation, it was ascertained that this merchandise was being stored as a convenience for Helen's Beauty Aids, a customer. This merchandise, which has not been recorded as a sale, is billed as it is shipped.
11. A shipment of 10,000 units of Product B was made on December 27 from the Seattle warehouse. The shipment arrived on January 6 but had been excluded from the physical inventories.

Required:

Prepare a worksheet to reconcile the balances for the physical inventory, Finished Goods Inventory general ledger control account, and Tabulating Department's detail of finished goods inventory ("Tab Run").

The following format is suggested for the worksheet:

	Physical Inventory	*General Ledger Control Account*	*Tabulating Department's Detail of Inventory*
Balance per client	$331,400	$373,900	$392,300

(AICPA adapted)

14-64. Review the case study provided and answer the questions concerning inventory valuation.

ARCTIC REFRIGERATION CORP.

The Arctic Refrigeration Corp. is engaged in the manufacture of refrigerator display units under specific contracts and in accordance with the customers' specifications. Customers are required to advance 25 percent of the contract price. The company records sales on a shipment basis and accumulates costs by job orders. The normal profit margin over the past few years has been approximately 5 percent of sales, after providing for sales commissions of 10 percent that are paid at the time of delivery. Management values its inventory at the lower of cost or net realizable value.

Among the jobs you are reviewing in the course of your annual audit of the company's December 31 financial statements is Job 1468, calling for delivery of a refrigerator display unit at a firm contract price of $50,000. Costs accumulated for the job at year-end aggregated $30,250. The company's engineer estimated that the job was approximately 55 percent complete at that time. You have carried out the following procedures to date:

1. Examined all contracts, noting pertinent provisions.
2. Observed physical inventory of work in process and reconciled details to job order accounts.
3. Tested labor, material, and overhead charged to the various jobs to determine that such charges were authentic and had been posted correctly.
4. Confirmed customers' advances at year-end.
5. Balanced work-in-process job ledger with control account at year-end.

Required:

With respect to Job 1468:

a. State what additional auditing procedures, if any, you would follow and explain the purposes of the procedures.
b. Indicate the value at which you would include Job 1468 on the balance sheet. You are to assume that no adjustment in the total selling price for this job is possible and that costs to completion will be incurred on the basis experienced to date.

14-65. The inventory detail schedule on page 620 was prepared by the controller of the Walk-About Sound Company for use by the independent auditors during their audit of Walk-About's year-end financial statements. In addition, the audit assistant prepared the schedule of purchase cutoff shown on page 621. All auditing procedures performed and conclusions reached are listed below. Each schedule was properly initialed, dated, and indexed and then submitted to a senior member of the audit staff for review. The internal control structure is considered to be satisfactory. Walk-About uses FIFO for determining cost. Perpetual records are kept for units only.

Required:

a. For each of the auditing procedures performed, indicate whether the conclusions reached by the audit assistant are appropriate. If they are inappropriate, state why they are inappropriate.
b. What essential auditing procedures were not noted as having been performed by the audit assistant?

Auditing Procedures Performed and Conclusions Reached

1. Agreed quantities to counts taken at the physical inventory observation on 12/31/90. No exceptions noted.
2. Confirmed merchandise held at public warehouses. One exception noted on working paper; adjustment proposed.
3. Agreed unit cost with vendor invoices. No exceptions noted.
4. Footed inventory schedule. No exceptions noted.
5. Agreed total to general ledger. No exceptions noted.
6. Determined that a proper cutoff was achieved at year-end. No exceptions noted.
7. Determined that the average selling price of all inventory items exceeded the respective unit cost, therefore substantiating that inventory valuation is the lower of cost or market. No exceptions noted.

Date Prepared ______
Prepared by
a) C & L ______
b) Client and Examined by ______
Reviewed by C & L SR/SUP ______

WALK-ABOUT SOUND COMPANY
INVENTORY DETAIL SCHEDULE
DECEMBER 31, 1990

PRODUCT	PURCHASE DATE	QUANTITY ON HAND	UNIT COST	TOTAL COST	Y-T-D SALES	Y-T-D UNITS SOLD	AVERAGE SELLING PRICE
RADIO	6/17/90	2500 T	$ 18.62	P $46,550	$ 26,551	978	$ 27.15
RADIO/ CASSETTE PLAYER	11/12/90	6000 } T	25.10	P 150,600	} 1,253,879	28,818	43.51
	12/18/90	4700 }	27.75	P 130,425			
TELEVISION	10/17/90	1200 } TW	93.19	P 111,828	} 613,040	4860	126.14
	11/25/90	1500 }	95.27	P 142,905			
DELUXE CASSETTE PLAYER	10/12/90	3200 T	47.19	P 151,008	627,968	7040	89.20
CASSETTE PLAYER	6/17/90	4200 T	22.98	S 96,516	1,132,994	38,511	29.42
CD PLAYER	8/10/90	800 C	112.30	P 89,840	} 1,245,143	6257	199.00
	12/30/90	1500 T	118.57	P 177,855			
CASSETTE PLAYER/ TELEVISION	6/15/90	250 T	672.20	P 168,050	189,840	120	1,582.00
				1,265,577 FG	5,089,415 F		

W = PERPETUAL INVENTORY RECORDS INDICATED THAT 3000 UNITS WERE IN INVENTORY AT YEAR-END. CONTROLLER COULD NOT RECONCILE DIFFERENCE.

S = PRODUCT IS IMPORTED AND COST EXCLUDES DUTY, FREIGHT AND INSURANCE COSTS OF $4 PER UNIT. DUTY AND INSURANCE IS CHARGED TO EXPENSE WHEN INCURRED.

P = UNIT COST AGREES WITH VENDOR INVOICE.

C = CONFIRMED WITH PUBLIC WAREHOUSE. WHICH INDICATED THAT 710 UNITS WERE ON HAND ON JANUARY 6, 1991. SALES CUTOFF SCHEDULE [NOT INCLUDED IN THIS PROBLEM] INDICATES THAT 90 UNITS WERE SHIPPED ON 1/4/91. JOURNAL ENTRY PROPOSED TO RECOGNIZE THE COST OF SALE AND REDUCE INVENTORY (AJE No. 13) AND TO RECOGNIZE THE RECEIVABLE AND THE SALE (AJE No. 14).

T = AGREES WITH PHYSICAL INVENTORY COUNTS

F = TOTALS FOOTED

G = TOTALS TRACED TO GENERAL LEDGER

65-814

WALK-ABOUT SOUND COMPANY
PURCHASE CUTOFF TEST
DECEMBER 31, 1990

VENDOR	INVOICE NUMBER	SHIPPING AND INVOICE DATE	PRODUCT	QUANTITY	TOTAL COST	DATE RECEIVED	DATE DEBITED TO INVENTORY CONTROL ACCOUNT
ACME	97852	12/16/90	RADIO CASSETTE PLAYER	4700	130 425	12/18/90	12/22/90
BARNES	5754	12/28/90	CD PLAYER	1500	177 855	12/28/90	12/30/90
KENDEL	86-352	12/30/90	TELEVISION	1200	115 824	12/30/90	1/4/91
MARTIN	16725	12/29/90	DELUXE CASSETTE PLAYER	1400	67 550	1/2/91	1/5/91
ACME	98102	12/31/90	RADIO CASSETTE PLAYER	1000	27 750	*	N/A
JONES	2669	1/3/91	CASSETTE PLAYER	800	25 048	1/5/91	1/7/91
ACME	98897	1/9/91	RADIO CASSETTE PLAYER	3000	83 250	1/12/91	1/15/91
KENDEL	87-122	1/15/91	TELEVISION	1100	105 182	1/15/91	1/17/91

- SHIPPING TERMS FROM ALL VENDORS ARE FOB: SHIPPING POINT
- THE ABOVE SAMPLE WAS TAKEN FROM PURCHASE JOURNAL ENTRIES POSTED FROM 12/15/90–1/15/91

* = SHIPMENT WAS DELIVERED DIRECTLY TO CUSTOMER. BILL OF LADING INDICATED SHIPMENT DATE WAS 12/31/90

65-814

14–66. ***Quinn Hardware*** (Cutoff Procedures)

At Quinn's warehouses, the physical inventory is performed prior to year-end. The accountant in charge of the Quinn Hardware engagement has asked you to develop procedures to test the cutoff at Quinn's Chicago warehouse, one of three locations where the auditors will perform an inventory observation.

Required:

a. List the detailed substantive tests to be performed at the time of the physical inventory that are necessary to ensure that Quinn has achieved a proper inventory cutoff.
b. List the detailed substantive tests that could be performed at year-end with respect to the cutoff objective.
c. Specify analytical procedures that could be performed to reduce the extent of, or replace, substantive tests of details at year-end.

15

Auditing Cash Balances and Property, Plant, and Equipment

INTRODUCTION

Most of an enterprise's transactions arise from buying, producing, and selling goods and services, and paying and collecting cash in connection with those activities. Those transactions are reflected in the revenue, expense, asset, and liability accounts that were discussed in the three preceding chapters on the revenue, buying, and production cycles. Other financial statement accounts typically reflect a relatively small number of material transactions (such as financing and investing activities) and events (such as allocations of revenues and expenses between periods).

This and the following chapter consider auditing procedures for financial statement accounts that in commercial and industrial enterprises are typically not derived from transaction cycles or that, even if they are, for efficiency reasons are typically audited by performing substantive tests. The auditor's purpose for considering a class of transactions as a cycle is to increase audit efficiency by testing control structure policies and procedures and then restricting substantive tests from those that would otherwise be required. That strategy may be appropriate, even for the transactions and accounts considered in this and the following chapter, if in a particular enterprise the volume of transactions is large and policies and procedures applied to those transactions appear to be designed and operating effectively. That strategy is clearly not appropriate, however, when only a few transactions affect an account in a year, or if certain audit objectives can be achieved more efficiently by performing substantive tests.

This chapter considers two financial statement accounts, cash and property, plant, and equipment, for which the auditor is generally not likely to adopt a strategy of performing tests of controls. The following chapter treats four other groups of accounts—investments, prepayments and accruals, income taxes, and debt and equity accounts—that are usually audited by performing substantive tests. This is not to suggest that in auditing those accounts the auditor has necessarily assessed the risk of material misstatement occurring at the maximum. Before performing substantive tests, the auditor will have gathered or updated sufficient information about the client to make preliminary materiality judgments and to assess inherent and control risk. Those assessments, which are based in part on an understanding of the control environment, the accounting procedures used to process transactions, and the reports generated by those procedures, are likely to permit the auditor to restrict substantive tests from those that would otherwise be required. The discussions in this and the following chapter assume that, principally because of the small number of transactions involved or because of the assessed risk of material misstatement occurring, the auditor has determined that it would not be efficient to perform tests of controls in order to restrict substantive tests significantly. But, as will be evident from the examples presented, that is far from suggesting that a 100 percent examination of all transactions or balances is appropriate or that none of the work can be performed before year-end.

CASH BALANCES

The following discussion is based on the assumption that the auditor, through the appropriate combination of risk assessment activities and substantive tests, will have reduced audit risk to an appropriately low level with regard to cash receipts from customers, cash disbursements to vendors, and other cash transactions. Because cash is so liquid and transferable, the risk of theft is greater than for any other asset. Accordingly, the auditor focuses on how responsive the client's control structure policies and procedures—particularly relating to asset protection, segregation of duties to safeguard cash balances, and reconciliations to meet the file control objective—are to that inherent risk characteristic.

Failure to detect cash defalcations is, at a minimum, frequently a source of embarrassment to the auditor. Often, it may be the basis for litigation, particularly if it involves material fraud that a plaintiff contends should have been detected by an auditor following a testing plan that gave appropriate consideration to the inherent risk associated with cash and the client's response to that risk. Cash defalcations may result in nonexistent assets being reported on the balance sheet, which would be the case if a theft was not concealed and the cash account not reduced by the amount stolen. Often, however, cash defalcations are concealed by unauthorized charges to income statement accounts, resulting in an appropriate balance sheet presentation for cash, but an income statement containing misclassified or fictitious expenses, along with possibly deficient disclosures.

The nature, timing, and extent of substantive tests of cash are strongly influenced by the auditor's assessment of inherent and control risk. For example, the auditor may merely review the client's bank reconciliations, rather than perform one or more reconciliations, if he or she has obtained evidence that bank reconciliations are performed regularly and there is proper segregation of duties within the various cash functions. The effectiveness of control procedures also affects the timing of substantive tests. For example, public companies often have early earnings release dates, so that the auditor may wish to perform early substantive tests of cash. If segregation of duties and asset protection control procedures have been tested and found adequate, they may provide evidence that the control objectives are met in the period between the early testing date and year-end.

Other control structure policies and procedures may affect the nature and extent of substantive tests. For example, management personnel or the internal auditors may receive monthly bank statements directly from the banks, review the statements for unusual transactions, and examine the signatures on the returned checks. Those procedures provide the auditor with additional evidence of the effectiveness of the control structure regarding cash.

Audit Objectives

The objectives of auditing cash are to obtain reasonable assurance that

- Recorded cash, on hand and in financial institutions, exists, and is accurate and complete, and the client has legal title to it at the balance sheet date.
- All items properly included as part of cash are realizable in the amounts stated; for example, foreign currency on hand or on deposit in foreign countries is properly valued.
- Cash restricted as to availability or use is properly identified and disclosed.
- Cash receipts, disbursements, and transfers between bank accounts are recorded in the proper period.

Meeting the cutoff objective with respect to cash receipts from customers and disbursements to vendors is important to prevent end-of-period "window dressing" of working capital accounts. Recording bank transfers in the wrong period could be indicative of a defalcation, as discussed under "Bank Transfer Schedule" later in this chapter.

Substantive Tests of Cash Balances

Substantive tests that are frequently performed in auditing cash balances fall into the following categories:

- Testing completeness, accuracy, and existence of ending balances.
    - Confirming balances and other information with banks and other financial institutions.
    - Preparing, reviewing, or testing bank reconciliations.
    - Cash counts.
- Testing bank transfer cutoff.
- Reviewing restrictions on cash balances and related disclosures.

Confirming Bank Balances and Other Information

Bank Balances. The auditor should ordinarily confirm balances at year-end by direct correspondence with all banks the client has conducted business with during the year, regardless of whether all year-end reconciliations are reviewed or tested. Usual practice is to confirm all bank accounts open at any time during the year under audit. The auditor should ask the client to request the financial institution to communicate directly with the auditor. In the past, auditors ordinarily requested confirmations of bank balances and various aspects of indebtedness to banks by using a standard confirmation form, appropriately signed by the client, approved by the AICPA and the Bank Administration Institute; some auditors still use this form. With the increase in the number of services provided by banks and the number of different people in positions to confirm various items (in both banks and other financial institutions), the practicality of using a form that combines a number of requests for confirmation has become questionable. At the time of this writing, the AICPA is considering revisions to the standard form that would make it appropriate only for confirming bank balances.

Indebtedness, Compensating Balances, and Other Arrangements. Banks may have arrangements with or provide services to the client other than maintaining deposits or granting loans. For example, banks may require borrowers to keep certain amounts on deposit (compensating balances) as a condition for a loan. Banks may also hold, as agent or trustee, securities or other items in safekeeping or for collection for the account of the client. Other arrangements—such as oral and written guarantees, commitments to buy foreign currencies, repurchase or reverse repurchase agreements, and letters of credit and lines of credit—may create contingent liabilities.

Auditors typically confirm client indebtedness to banks and other financial institutions, as well as related financial arrangements such as compensating balances, by requesting the client to send confirmation requests to specific officials of those institutions who are knowledgeable about the transactions or arrangements. Thus, the auditor might ask the client to address letters to a number of bank officials asking for information about various debt and other arrangements, like automatic investment services, bank acceptances, cash management services, commitments to purchase foreign currencies, lines of credit, letters of credit, and loan agreements and related covenants.

Bank Reconciliations. Periodic reconciliations of cash receipts and disbursements to amounts shown on bank statements are key control procedures to meet the asset protection objective for cash. The reconciliation procedure will be more effective if, in addition to reconciling the balances, the detailed items listed on the bank statement are reconciled to the detailed items recorded in the accounts during the period covered by the bank statement. The latter step ensures that all items recorded in the accounts, including offsetting items within receipts or disbursements, are also recorded on the bank statement and vice versa. The preferred reconciliation procedure is the "proof of cash," which is described in detail later in this chapter.

Effective segregation of duties requires that the person responsible for reconciling bank balances to account balances not have functions relating to cash receipts, cash disbursements, or preparing or approving vouchers for payment. It also requires that the person performing the reconciliation obtain the bank statements directly from the bank and make specific comparisons, like comparing paid checks and other debits and credits listed on the bank statement with entries in the accounts, examining checks for signatures and endorsements, and reconciling bank transfers.

The client's reconciliation of bank accounts, and the appropriate division of duties with respect to cash balances and transactions, are key control procedures. The auditor's assessment of how effective the client's reconciliations are determines the nature, timing, and extent of many of the substantive tests of cash. The adequacy of the accounting system, the competence of employees doing the reconciliations, and the segregation of duties are the major factors in that assessment. The more effective the auditor finds the client's reconciliations to be, that is, the lower the assessed level of control risk, the less detailed the auditor's reconciliation procedures have to be. Those procedures may range from simply reviewing the client's reconciliations at year-end, if control risk has been assessed as low, to performing independent reconciliations covering the entire year using the proof of cash form (discussed later). Generally, performing proof of cash reconciliations for the entire year is considered necessary only in special situations, such as when a defalcation is believed to have occurred. Between those two extremes, the auditor may review and test the client's reconciliations, or may perform independent reconciliations at year-end (either using the proof of cash form or not). The various audit approaches to bank reconciliations are described below.

Review of Client's Reconciliations. If the auditor has assessed control risk as low, then merely reviewing the client's reconciliations at year-end may be appropriate. The steps in reviewing a client's bank reconciliation are

1. Obtain copies of the client's bank reconciliations and establish their mathematical accuracy.
2. Reconcile the total of the bank balances on the reconciliations to the general ledger balance. This will generally require using a summary of the individual cash account balances in the general ledger account.
3. Scan the bank reconciliation for significant unusual reconciling items and adjustments, and obtain evidence to support them by inquiry or examination of appropriate documents.

Review and Test of Client's Reconciliations. In addition to the review procedures described above, the auditor may decide to test the client's reconciliations. The tests may be performed at an interim date, if the auditor has assessed that the client's reconciliations are subject to effective supervisory control procedures. If supervision during the intervening period is not considered effective, the auditor would probably perform the tests at year-end. If he or she has determined that segregation of duties and asset protection control procedures are effective, the extent of testing of reconciliations may be limited. In addition, depending on these same considerations, the auditor might ask the client to request the bank to send directly to the auditor a bank statement and related canceled checks for the "cutoff period" (usually a week or two immediately following the balance sheet date) or for the following month. Alternatively, the auditor may use the client's bank statement for the following month, if the reconciliation is tested at an interim date.

In addition to steps 1 and 2 above, the procedures below are typically performed in testing the client's reconciliations. These procedures assume that the testing is performed as of the balance sheet date and that cutoff statements for a reasonable period after the balance sheet date are obtained from the bank.

1. Determine that paid checks, deposits, and debit and credit advices appearing on the cutoff bank statements and issued on or before the balance sheet date appear on the year-end reconciliations.
2. Trace to the cash disbursements records outstanding checks listed on bank reconciliations but not returned with the cutoff statements.
3. Trace deposits in transit on the bank reconciliations to the cutoff bank statements and the cash receipts records, and determine whether there are any unusual delays between the date received per the books and the date deposited per the bank statements.
4. Trace other reconciling items to supporting documentation and entries in the cash records.
5. Investigate old or unusual reconciling items. If checks remain uncashed after a specified period of time, the reason should be determined and the amounts either restored to the cash account or disposed of according to state escheat law.
6. Determine the exact nature of items on the year-end bank statements not accounted for by the reconciliation procedures, such as debits or credits followed by offsetting entries of identical amounts that appear to be, or are represented by the client to be, bank errors and corrections not so coded. If information in the client's records is inadequate, clarification should be requested from the bank. In these circumstances, the auditor should consider performing a "proof of cash" reconciliation (described below) if the client's reconciliation process does not include one.

Some companies experiencing cash flow difficulties follow a practice of preparing, recording, and then "holding" checks and releasing them as cash balances become available. The client may believe it is easier to "hold" the checks than to void them and replace them when cash becomes available. Although clients should be urged to prepare checks only when they can be released, the auditor may encounter this situation when checks are routinely prepared by computer at the time invoices are processed based on predetermined invoice due dates. Accordingly, the auditor should inquire whether any checks drawn before year-end were released after year-end and should consider obtaining the numbers of the last checks written for the current fiscal year. If the amount of "held" checks is potentially significant at the balance sheet date, the auditor should plan to examine them at that date and subsequently determine that the amount of such checks has been reinstated by appropriate adjusting entries in the cash account (and related liability accounts) at that date.

Independent "Proof of Cash" Reconciliations. A proof of cash reconciliation (also known as a "four-column reconciliation") summarizes and controls the examination of cash records for a selected period. An advantage of the proof of cash is that it provides a reconciliation of balances at the beginning and end of the period and, with little additional effort, also reconciles transactions recorded in the accounts during the period to those reflected on the bank statement. An auditor preparing a proof of cash is thus able to "prove" the propriety of recorded transactions in the accounts to an independent source (the bank statement). Any other audit tests applied to the receipts, disbursements, or balances can also be described on the form. A proof of cash working paper is illustrated in Figure 15.1.

A proof of cash reconciliation involves performing the steps described above for reviewing and testing the client's reconciliations (which may or may not be in the form of a proof of cash), plus the procedures described below. Procedures already performed need not be performed again.

1. Enter the totals from the bank statement on the proof of cash form.
2. Obtain the client's reconciliation as of the close of the preceding period and compare balances shown on that reconciliation with the corresponding amounts shown by the accounts and the bank statement; substantiate outstanding checks at the close of the preceding period by examining paid checks returned by the bank in the current period and investigating any still outstanding; and substantiate deposits in transit and other reconciling items at the close of the preceding period by referring to the current bank statement, bank notifications of charges and credits, and other supporting documents.
3. Compare daily totals of recorded cash receipts shown in the cash journal with daily deposits appearing on the bank statement. If there are time lags between the receipt, recording, and depositing of collections, investigate any that appear unreasonable in light of the company's usual practices. (Delay in depositing receipts constitutes inefficient cash management and exposes cash items on hand to risk of loss or misuse, such as "lapping" collections of accounts receivable—a method of continuously concealing a defalcation by crediting later collections to accounts whose collections were not previously recorded.) Enter unmatched cash receipts items or deposit items on the proof of cash form.
4. Compare paid checks returned with the bank statement with the disbursements records for check number, date, payee, and amount. The comparison determines not only which checks have not cleared the bank during the period but also that dates, payees, and amounts of disbursements as shown by the paid checks agree with recorded disbursements.

Figure 15.1 Proof of Cash

Date Prepared: 1/26/9-
Prepared By:
a) C&L PLD
b) Client and Examined By ______
Reviewed By:
C&L Sr Sup SAC

XYZ Corporation
Proof of Cash-Month of December
12/31/9-

	1 Balance Beginning of period	2 Receipts	3 Disbursements	4 Balance End of period
Per bank statement	$31268 A	$42687 A	$46560 A	$27395 C ✓A
Deposits in transit:				
Beginning	1000 T	(1000)		
End		2000		2000 T
Outstanding checks:				
Beginning	(3917)		(2817) ø	(1100) y
End			3460	(3460) ø
Unrecorded charges and credits:				
Collection from customer on note, credited by bank during period, entered on books after end of period		(2078)		(2078) CM
Per Books	$28351 A	$41609 A	$47203 A	22757 ✓A
	✓	✓	✓	✓
Audit adjusting entry #1:				
Collection of customer note				2078
Per books as adjusted				$24835
				✓

Legend of audit procedures:
✓ = Footed & cross-footed
A = Agreed with amounts shown on bank statement/books
C = Balance confirmed with bank; see bank confirmation on W/P—
T = Traced to subsequent bank statement
ø = Checks cleared on subsequent bank statement
y = Check #895 dated 11/27/9- for $1,100 is still outstanding. Examined purchase order, receiving report and vendor invoice. The purchase made and paid by this check appears proper. No adjusting entry proposed
CM = Examined bank credit memo

List checks outstanding at the end of the period, foot the list, and enter the total on the proof of cash form.

5. Account for all checks issued in the sequence between the first and last checks drawn on the bank account during the period.
6. Determine that the reconciliation foots and cross-foots. All items appearing in either of the balance columns and bank errors corrected in the same period must also appear appropriately in either the receipts or disbursements column (as additions or subtractions) so that both activity and balances are reconciled. A later entry in the accounts that apparently offsets an item in a reconciliation is not necessarily proof of its correctness. The propriety of reconciling items or adjusting entries is not established merely by the fact that including them makes it possible to reconcile the balances.
7. Compare deposits in transit and outstanding checks revealed by the reconciliation with a subsequent bank statement and accompanying paid checks. Substantiate checks outstanding at the date of the reconciliation that are not returned with the subsequent bank statement, if material in amount, by referring to properly approved vouchers or other available documents.

As noted earlier, the auditor may, in special situations, consider it necessary to perform proof of cash reconciliations throughout the year. In that event, following up reconciling items (step 7 above) would ordinarily not be required, because the client's procedures in that area would have been tested in step 2.

Count of Cash on Hand. Cash funds on hand, normally constituting one or more petty cash funds, are seldom significant in relation to the overall cash balance, except in retail operations. Therefore, auditors generally do not perform substantive tests of the year-end balance of cash on hand. They may nevertheless wish to perform tests of control procedures relating to the day-to-day operation of cash funds to obtain evidence that the activity in the funds has been authorized and is completely and accurately recorded. Ineffective control procedures could result in improperly classified expenses in the income statement.

Some circumstances require physical counting of currency and other cash items on hand. If cash funds on hand and undeposited receipts are significant in relation to the overall cash balance, and if control procedures are ineffective, there may be no alternative to a year-end cash count. If the auditor concludes that a cash count is required, it should be coordinated with the examination or confirmation of negotiable assets such as marketable securities, notes receivable, and collateral held as security for loans to others. In addition, the auditor should take appropriate steps to ensure that a cash shortage at a particular location cannot be concealed by the conversion of negotiable assets or the transfer of cash from another location. If simultaneous physical examination of negotiable assets on hand is not practicable, the auditor should establish control over all such assets to avoid the possibility of a shortage in one group being covered up by other assets already examined. Less active negotiable assets—such as notes receivable and marketable securities—may be counted in advance and placed under seal until all counts are completed. Occasionally it is necessary to permit movement of assets under seal; the auditor should control and record all such transactions. Totals of funds and other negotiable assets counted or confirmed should be reconciled to general ledger controlling accounts as of the date of the examination.

An auditor should not assume responsibility for custody of cash or negotiable assets in a physical count, but should insist on continuous attendance by a representative of the client while those assets are being examined. After the count has been completed, the client's representative should be asked to acknowledge its accuracy. Auditors should never count funds in the absence (even if temporary) of the custodian, and should always obtain a written acknowledgment from the client's representative that the funds have been returned intact. If the count discloses an overage or shortage in the fund, the auditor should ask for a recount and acknowledgment by the client's representative of the accuracy of the count.

Bank Transfer Schedule. To ensure there has been a proper cutoff at year-end, the auditor should determine whether significant transfers of funds occurred among the client's various bank accounts near the balance sheet date. All transfers of funds within the organization should be considered—whether among branches, divisions, or affiliates—to make sure that cash is not "double counted" in two or more bank accounts and that "kiting" (explained below) has not occurred. The auditor should determine (1) that each transaction represented as a transfer is in fact an authorized transfer; (2) that debits and credits representing transfers of cash are recorded in the same period; and (3) that the funds are actually deposited in the receiving bank in the appropriate period.

Kiting is a way of concealing a cash shortage caused by a defalcation, such as misappropriating cash receipts, that was perpetrated previously. It involves the careful and deliberate use of the "float" (the time necessary for a check to clear the bank it was drawn on). Kiting is effected by drawing a check on one bank, depositing it in another bank just before year-end so that the deposit appears on the bank statement, and not recording the transfer in the cash receipts or cash disbursements journals until after year-end. The float period will cause the check not to clear the bank it was drawn on until after year-end, and the amount transferred is included in the balances of both bank accounts. Since the transfer is not recorded as a receipt or a disbursement until the following year, it will not appear as an outstanding check or a deposit in transit on the reconciliation of either bank account. The effect is to increase receipts per the bank statement; if the misappropriation of cash receipts and the kiting take place in the same period, receipts per the bank statement will agree with receipts per the cash receipts journal at the date of the bank reconciliation. (If

Figure 15.2 Bank Transfer Schedule

	Disbursement (Transfer Out)		*Receipt (Transfer In)*	
Check Number	*Date Recorded in Books*	*Date Paid by Bank*	*Date Recorded in Books*	*Date Received by Bank*
A	12/28/89	01/03/90	12/28/89	12/29/89
B	12/29/89	01/05/90	12/29/89	01/03/90
C	12/30/89	01/03/90	01/02/90	01/02/90
D	01/02/90	01/05/90	01/02/90	12/29/89
E	01/04/90	01/10/90	01/04/90	01/08/90

the misappropriation of cash receipts takes place in the period before the kiting, a proof of cash may also reveal the kiting.) Kiting requires that the transfer process be repeated continually until the misappropriated funds have been restored.[1]

A bank transfer schedule is an efficient and effective tool that assists the auditor in determining that all transfers of funds among bank accounts near the balance sheet date are recorded in the books in the proper accounting period, that cash has not been double-counted, and that there is no apparent kiting. The schedule should indicate, for each transfer, the date the check effecting the transfer was recorded as a cash disbursement, the date it was recorded as a cash receipt, the date it cleared the bank it was drawn on, and the date it cleared the bank it was deposited in. The list of bank transfers should be compiled from both originating documents (paid checks or bank advices) returned with the subsequent bank statement and the client's cash receipts and disbursements records. A bank transfer schedule is illustrated in Figure 15.2.

The dates on the bank transfer schedule should be obtained from the cash records and the dates on the check showing when it was received by the bank it was deposited in and when it was canceled by the bank it was drawn on. The date the check was recorded as a disbursement should be compared with the date it was recorded as a receipt; the dates should be the same. If they are not and the entries are in different fiscal years, an adjusting entry may be necessary to prevent double-counting of cash, depending on the offsetting debit or credit to the entry that was made in the year being audited. Then, for each transfer, the bank dates (paid and cleared) should be compared with the corresponding dates the transaction was recorded in the books (received and disbursed). If those dates are in different accounting periods, the transfer should appear on the bank reconciliation as a reconciling item—an outstanding

[1]Banks and other financial institutions use the term "kiting" in a wider sense, to include writing checks against inadequate funds with the intent of depositing sufficient funds later, but before the checks clear the bank.

check if the check cleared the disbursing bank in a later period than it was recorded, and a deposit in transit if it cleared the receiving bank in a later period than the receipt was recorded. Lastly, unusually long time lags between dates recorded and dates cleared should be investigated for possible holding of checks at year-end—a cutoff problem.

In Figure 15.2, there are no double-counting problems with the transfers involving checks A, B, and E because the transfer out of one bank account was recorded in the same period as the transfer into the other bank account. Transfers A and B should appear as outstanding checks on the reconciliation of the disbursing bank's account. Transfer B should also appear as a deposit in transit on the reconciliation of the receiving bank's account. Transfer E should not affect either the books or the reconciliations, because it occurred in the following year and all dates are in the same accounting period.

The other transfers in the figure require further analysis. Transfer C should appear on the reconciliation of the disbursing bank's account as an outstanding check at December 31, 1989. If it does, the balance per the books will not be in error. If it does not, the total of outstanding checks will be understated and the balance per the books will be overstated, possibly covering up an unrecorded check drawn on that account that already cleared the bank.

Transfer D is an example of possible kiting. That transfer should appear as an outstanding check on the reconciliation of the disbursing bank's account; it should also appear as a recording error (an omitted disbursement) on the reconciliation. If kiting were taking place, it is unlikely that the preparer of the reconciliation would be aware that a check was outstanding that should be included on the outstanding check list; nor would the person doing the kiting call the "recording error" to anyone's attention. The funds transferred would thus be counted twice—once in the bank account the check was drawn on and once again in the account it was deposited in. Transfer D would result in a misstatement, though not from kiting, if the delay in recording was the result of an oversight or an attempt to conceal an overdraft at the bank.

Reviewing Cash Restrictions and Related Disclosures. The auditor should review the evidence previously obtained and, if necessary, perform further procedures to ensure that all appropriate disclosures related to cash have been made. Bank confirmations, responses to inquiry letters, loan agreements, minutes of board of directors' meetings, and bond indentures may indicate restrictions on the availability or use of cash that should be disclosed. Inquiries of client management may also indicate the need for disclosures of cash balances that are restricted or the property of others. (If the latter, the related liability should be recorded.) If the entity has substantial funds in other countries or in foreign currencies, the auditor should determine whether there are any restrictions on their availability and that appropriate disclosures have been made.

PROPERTY, PLANT, AND EQUIPMENT

Most businesses use property, plant, and equipment in the process of generating revenues. The term "property, plant, and equipment" generally refers to noncurrent tangible assets, including those held under capital leases, used by a business to create and distribute its goods and services. The term "fixed assets" is also used (although not as much as in the past) to describe the property, plant, and equipment accounts. Related accounts that are audited in the same manner as property, plant, and equipment are leasehold improvements and construction in progress.

Expenditures to maintain or improve property, plant, and equipment are normal following their acquisition. A major audit consideration is whether such expenditures should be accounted for as expenses of the current period or reflected on the balance sheet as either an addition to the cost of the asset or a reduction of the related accumulated depreciation. As a general rule, an expenditure should be capitalized if it benefits future periods by extending the useful or productive life of the asset. The distinction between the two categories of expenditures frequently is not clear-cut. Enterprises usually have stated policies defining which expenditures are to be capitalized, and the auditor must exercise judgment in determining whether the policies are appropriate and are being complied with.

Audit Objectives

The objectives of auditing property, plant, and equipment and related accounts are to obtain reasonable assurance that

- Property, plant, and equipment recorded in the accounts exist and are owned or leased under capital leases by the company.
- All additions to and disposals of property, plant, and equipment have been properly authorized and accurately recorded.
- No material items were charged to expense that should have been capitalized.
- The cost or other basis of initially recording property, plant, and equipment is appropriate.
- Appropriate methods of depreciation have been properly applied, on a basis consistent with the previous year, to all items of property, plant, and equipment that should be depreciated.
- The carrying value of property, plant, and equipment is appropriate in periods subsequent to acquisition, considering such factors as utilization, geographic location, laws and regulations, and technological changes.
- Property, plant, and equipment pledged as collateral are identified and disclosed, along with other necessary disclosures.

The auditor may meet some of these objectives through procedures performed in connection with other aspects of the audit or tests of other accounts. For example, the pledging of property, plant, and equipment is generally discovered through reading and analyzing loan documents and minutes of meetings of the board of directors or other management groups. Property acquired under capital leases may be determined by reading minutes and analyzing lease or rental expense accounts. Similarly, the auditor may determine the continued existence of recorded property, plant, and equipment (though often not specifically or explicitly) as he or she moves about the facilities in the course of observing physical inventories and performing other audit tasks. Auditors often review charges to repair and maintenance accounts for items that should have been capitalized, and test the calculation and summarization of depreciation.

Determining the cost or other basis of recording property, plant, and equipment usually presents few problems, because most assets are acquired individually in short-term credit transactions. The auditor must exercise judgment, however, about the appropriate cost in situations involving business combinations, self-constructed assets, capitalized leases, and nonmonetary transactions. While they are not usually a major audit concern, the auditor must be alert for changes in laws or general business conditions that might make it impossible to recover the remaining costs of property through revenue generated or outright sale. Also, the auditor should be aware of conditions that might require reevaluation of the remaining depreciable lives of property, plant, and equipment.

Many businesses also incur expenditures for the acquisition of intangible assets. The audit objectives for such assets are similar to those for property, plant, and equipment. The audit emphasis for intangible assets should be on determining that the carrying value of those assets can be fully recovered, that there has not been a permanent impairment of their value, and that the remaining period of amortization is appropriate.

Substantive Tests of Balances

As with other areas of the audit, the audit testing plan should be based on an analysis of inherent risk factors associated with property, plant, and equipment transactions and accounts and on the entity's internal control structure. Efficiency considerations, however, often lead the auditor to rely principally on substantive tests to reduce audit risk, even if the control structure is strong. Many of the substantive tests described below can be traced to a "Summary of Property, Plant, & Equipment & Accumulated Depreciation," frequently referred to as a "lead schedule," an example of which is shown in Figure 15.3.

Assessing Risk. Most companies do not have a large volume of transactions in their property accounts, and most transactions are of high dollar value.

Figure 15.3 Property, Plant, and Equipment Lead Schedule

Date Prepared 1/23/9_
Prepared by
a) C & L
b) Client and Examined by S
Reviewed by C & L SR/SUP HRJ

ACE Enterprises Inc.
Summary of Property, Plant, & Equipment & Accumulated Depreciation
12/31/9_

Classification	Balance at Beginning of period	Additions	Disposals	Other	Balance at End of period
Cost	Ⓐ	Ⓑ Ⓒ	Ⓓ	Ⓔ	TB
Buildings	10,745,986.43 ʃ	98,723.66	9,161.31 Ⓕ	(3,347.83)	10,832,200.95 TB
Machinery & Equipment	2,088,816.57 ʃ	337,937.01	1,962.22 Ⓖ		2,424,791.36 TB
Furniture & Fixtures	58,077.06 ʃ	6,684.91		3,347.83	68,109.80 TB
	12,892,880.06 ✓✓	443,345.58 ✓✓	11,123.53 ✓✓	-0- ✓✓	13,325,102.11 ✓✓ ✓✓
Accumulated Depreciation	Ⓐ	Ⓗ		Ⓔ	Ⓐ
Buildings	3,007,975.34 ʃ	214,929.27	9,161.31 Ⓕ	(167.35)	3,213,575.95 TB
Machinery & Equipment	743,567.95 ʃ	104,549.57	1,758.46 Ⓖ		846,359.06 TB
Furniture & Fixtures	18,521.18 ʃ	5,927.33		167.35	24,615.86 TB
	3,770,064.47 ✓✓	325,406.17 ✓✓	10,919.77 ✓✓	-0- ✓✓	4,084,550.87 ✓✓ ✓✓

Legend

ʃ = Traced to prior year work papers
✓✓ = Footed & cross-footed
TB = Agreed to trial balance
Ⓐ = Agreed to fixed asset subsidiary ledger
Ⓑ = Supported by detail listing of fixed asset additions. See work papers — to — where additions were vouched
Ⓒ = See W/p — For calculation of investment tax credit
Ⓓ = See W/p — For calculation of investment tax credit recapture
Ⓔ = Reclassification for light fixtures erroneously classified as building
Ⓕ = Write off obsolete and scrapped items
Ⓖ = Sale of miscellaneous M & E - No further audit work deemed necessary
Ⓗ = See W/p's — To — where reasonableness of client's calculation of depreciation was tested using the firm's computer audit program for estimating depreciation

Thus, the auditor can generally obtain evidence about the existence of particular assets from informal walk-throughs of client facilities or from observing and testing the client's fixed asset physical inventory counts. Because of the permanent nature of the assets, there is less likelihood of unrecorded transactions remaining undetected.

Property, plant, and equipment are recorded and carried in the financial statements at amounts equal to the costs identified with specific assets; net realizable values of productive assets are normally not relevant to the values at which assets are carried. After acquisition and recognition as an asset, the cost of property, plant, and equipment enters into the determination of periodic income through depreciation. A misstatement of income resulting from the property accounts would normally occur only through depreciation errors (including unrecognized premature obsolescence) or misclassification of expenditures between the asset account and the repairs and maintenance account.

The auditor may have obtained some evidence of the effectiveness of policies and procedures relating to property transactions from tests of controls performed concurrently with developing an understanding of the control structure. To reduce substantive tests significantly, however, the auditor would have to perform additional tests of controls to obtain evidence to support a low assessment of control risk. In the property accounts, it is generally more efficient to use an audit testing plan that emphasizes substantive tests. Exceptions occur in highly capital-intensive companies that have a large volume of property transactions. For example, utilities generally have an effective accounting system for processing and recording property transactions, most of which are for the acquisition or repair of utility properties. In any event, the auditor considers the assessed level of control risk and the assessment of inherent risk conditions in developing the audit testing plan.

Existence and Ownership of Assets. If financial statements are being audited for the first time, the auditor must decide to what extent it is necessary to examine property and other noncurrent asset accounts before the beginning of the year or years under audit. Since assets acquired in prior years and related accumulated depreciation are likely to be significant in the current balance sheet and income statement, the auditor must have a basis for believing that both are fairly stated in conformity with generally accepted accounting principles. If financial statements for earlier years have been audited and reported on by independent auditors, reviewing the other auditors' working papers and the client's records should be sufficient to provide the necessary understanding of the accounting principles, policies, and methods employed.

In an initial engagement, the auditor should seek evidence that tangible and intangible assets exist and are, in fact, the property of the company. If a company's record keeping is adequate, deeds, purchase contracts, and other evidence of ownership will be on file and retrievable. Sometimes, however, those documents get mislaid over the years as successive generations of management come and go and files are moved, rearranged, or culled. If no other evidence can be found, the auditor can ask management to seek representations from counsel concerning legal title to properties.

On subsequent audits, tests directed at the existence and ownership of property, plant, and equipment, and intangible assets and deferred charges normally consist of reviewing the company's procedures for maintaining detailed records and for periodically comparing those records with the assets themselves, and examining selected additions, disposals, and allocations during the year. If the company's detailed records are accurate, and if the auditor has performed tests of the client's physical inspections and control procedures related to existence and ownership of property, plant, and equipment, substantive procedures can be limited to reviews of selected major additions and disposals and periodic allocations.

If the company periodically compares its detailed records with the actual assets but the auditor has not performed tests of those procedures, the procedures set forth below should be carried out as of the date selected for testing.

- Review the company's procedures for conducting the physical inspection and comparison.
- Consider whether to observe those procedures.
- Review the actions taken to investigate discrepancies disclosed and to propose necessary adjustments to the records.

The auditor should determine that the company's comparison of assets with records is performed by a person who is independent of the custody of the assets and of maintaining the detailed property records. If the comparison is performed by a person who has custodial responsibility for or other access to the assets, the auditor should consider testing the client's comparison more extensively.

The comparison of the accounting records with the assets themselves should also be used to determine whether the carrying value of property, plant, and equipment requires adjustment because the assets are no longer in use or in good condition. The auditor should review the comparison to determine if obsolete or damaged assets on hand have been included and whether these assets are carried at an amount in excess of what can be recovered through revenue generated or outright sale.

If the company does not compare assets with the accounting records, the auditor should consider requesting the client to perform a complete or partial comparison, depending on such factors as susceptibility to loss, theft, or destruction. Alternatively, the auditor may make the comparison, although that may be a very inefficient use of audit time. If equipment is easily damaged, lost, stolen, or subject to personal use, such as in the case of small tools, the auditor should determine if the depreciation rate used by the company considers those factors and, if not, should consider physically inspecting such assets, if material.

In many instances, the auditor may obtain evidence of the existence and condition of a major portion of the company's property, plant, and equipment through observation during physical inventory observations or routine plant tours. Other evidence may also be available regarding the existence of major property items; for example, continued sales of specific products provide evidence that the assets used to produce the products are still in existence and operating effectively. Conversely, discontinuance of a product or product line should raise questions as to the carrying value of the related production facilities. Continued full occupancy of a hotel facility, for example, might also provide evidence regarding the existence and condition of the furniture and equipment used in the facility and might preclude the need for an annual physical inspection of those assets. The auditor should consider, however, the risk of material misstatements arising in the property accounts if incorrect conclusions are drawn.

In selecting procedures for substantiating the existence and ownership of real property, if transactions are usually few and of high value, the auditor should consider inspecting documents of title (or confirming that such documents are held by proper custodians—normally banks or other lending institutions) for all or a substantial proportion of the properties, to ascertain that the company has valid title and that the assets have not been pledged. In addition, the auditor may examine title insurance policies, confirm with title insurance companies, or, in some cases, examine recorded deeds. Schedules of property covered by casualty insurance policies may be compared with recorded assets, as may schedules used for property tax records. Documentation and confirmations relating to notes payable and long-term debt should be reviewed for indications of assets that have been pledged as collateral. These procedures are normally performed at the balance sheet date.

Acquisition of Assets. Substantive tests of property, plant, and equipment additions normally include the following (the extent of testing depends on the assessed level of control risk):

- Examining properly authorized agreements, architects' certificates, deeds, invoices, and other documents. For a purchase of land and buildings as a complete unit, the auditor should test the purchase price by comparing the data with the purchase agreement.
- Examining work orders and other supporting documentation for the company's own materials and labor. The auditor should review the percentage added for overhead to ensure that only factory overhead, as appropriate, has been allocated to the addition.
- Reviewing the minutes of meetings of the board of directors or other committees to determine whether major additions were appropriately authorized.

Evaluating whether additions were appropriately approved should be based on the auditor's understanding of the authorization procedures and the level of the individuals authorized to approve acquisitions. If written authorizations are not obtained, unneeded assets may be acquired or portions of cost overruns that should be expensed may be capitalized. The approval process may not be adequate if authorizations do not include the reason for the expenditure, the estimated amount, the allocation between capital expenditures and charges to current operations, and procedures for comparing estimated amounts with actual expenditures. If these are lacking, the auditor should consider expanding the substantive tests, for example, by reviewing with senior company officials the usefulness of assets acquired during the year or reasons for budget overruns, to obtain satisfaction that the recorded additions are appropriate.

Disposition of Assets. The auditor should test entries removing assets from the accounts by examining evidence of approval, comparing acquisition cost with underlying records, recomputing accumulated depreciation and the resulting gain or loss, and evaluating the reasonableness of removal costs and recovery from scrap or salvage. If there is a properly controlled work order system or if numerous assets are disposed of at the same time, as in the case of a sale or an abandonment of a plant, the auditor can usually test the entries using a sample of the individual transactions.

As with acquisitions of assets, the auditor should also be familiar with the company's procedures for recording dispositions and with the levels of the people who approve them. If the company's procedures for recording new assets that replace existing assets do not identify the related retirement or disposal, the auditor may need to expand the testing of asset dispositions. The auditor should review additions for the year to determine if they are replacements for other assets and, if so, should ascertain that the replaced asset has been correctly accounted for. Also, miscellaneous income accounts should be reviewed for evidence of sales or disposals of assets.

Classification of Expenditures. If tests of controls provide evidence that control procedures for classifying expenditures between capital expenditures and current-period expenses are effective, the auditor may limit testing of classifications to scanning the charges to repair and maintenance accounts for significant or unusual items, reviewing fluctuations, and other substantive tests of additions. Ordinarily, however, the auditor will perform further substantive tests, on at least a limited basis, even if control risk has been assessed as low. Those tests may include

- Reviewing capitalizations, disposals, and repair and maintenance expense for reasonableness in relation to budgets and to the previous year, and obtaining explanations for any large or unusual fluctuations.
- Reviewing whether all major additions and disposals during the year are properly classified.
- Reviewing significant charges to repair and maintenance expense.

The auditor might vary the extent of these tests depending on whether the classification of expenditures is approved by a designated official.

A company may routinely expense the cost of small-dollar items to reduce the clerical effort involved in maintaining detailed asset records. In reviewing charges to repair and maintenance accounts, the auditor should consider whether such items in the aggregate could have a material effect on the financial statements. Also, the auditor must recognize that determining whether an expenditure should be capitalized or charged to current operations may be subjective and highly judgmental. Even in a company with effective control structure policies and procedures, differences of opinion may arise over the nature and proper recording of a particular expenditure.

Carrying Values. Property, plant, and equipment are typically carried on the balance sheet at amortized (depreciated) cost. Cost includes all expenditures necessary to make an asset ready for its intended use, including freight and taxes, and interest incurred during construction. Determining whether the client has appropriately capitalized costs requires the auditor to have extensive expertise in evaluating accounting principles selected and applied to asset acquisitions.

The auditor is concerned with recoverable value of noncurrent assets only in considering whether there has been a material permanent decline in value. Depreciable assets are, in effect, "realized" in the normal course of business by charging depreciation to income, and thus provision for a decline in value may be necessary only if future income from an asset is unlikely to equal or exceed its carrying value. This can normally be calculated only for a complete production unit or similar group of assets.

Depreciation and Salvage Values. Substantive testing of depreciation accounts should start with a review of the company's methods and policies. Policies preferably should be systematically documented, but if they are not, they can be inferred from the computations and work sheets of prior and current years. Depreciation rates, salvage values, and useful lives may be compared with those in general use by similar enterprises. Computations of depreciation expense should be tested, which in many cases may be accomplished by making approximations on an overall basis.

The auditor should consider the reasonableness of useful lives and whether known factors require reducing or extending the lives of any categories of plant assets. This can be accomplished by observing the pattern of gains and losses on disposition; consistent gains or consistent losses could suggest that the lives used are too short or too long or that salvage values used are inappropriate. For assets depreciated on the composite method, the auditor should review the relationship of the balances of allowance accounts to those of asset accounts. Ratios are, of course, affected by the pattern of additions, but after an auditor allows for unusually high or low additions in certain years, a significant upward or downward trend in the ratio of an allowance account to a related asset account should indicate whether useful lives are too short or too long. If either seems possible, an analysis of actual useful lives is called for.

The auditor should also be aware of changing business conditions that might suggest the client should revise the estimated remaining lives of assets upward or downward for purposes of future depreciation charges. For example, leasehold improvements are depreciated over the estimated useful life of the improvements or over the original term of the lease, whichever is shorter, without regard to renewal options until those options are actually exercised or it becomes obvious they will be exercised. Significant expenditures for additional improvements with a life considerably longer than the remaining original lease might indicate management's intention to exercise a renewal option. Conversely, the auditor might learn that management intends to replace within the next two years computer equipment with a remaining depreciable life of four years. In these situations, the auditor must assess management's justification for changing or not changing the remaining depreciable life.

In practice, estimated lives, salvage values, and depreciation methods are not commonly reviewed, by either clients or auditors. Once established for particular assets, these items are usually left unchanged unless events or circumstances arise that call them into question. Auditors usually do not have the expertise to evaluate the remaining life of an asset and generally rely on other experts when necessary. Formal, in-depth reviews are usually made only for tax purposes, as part of acquisition reviews, or in industries in which depreciation has a significant effect on earnings, such as equipment leasing. The auditor's risk assessment process should include determining whether such an evaluation is appropriate.

If the reasonableness of the depreciation charges cannot be determined by making approximations on an overall basis for each class of assets, the auditor should test the individual computations and the balances in the subsidiary ledgers, compare the totals with the control account, and investigate any difference at year-end.

Intangible Assets. Substantive tests of intangible assets focus on the bases for determining their cost and the amortization periods for intangible assets that have been capitalized. Substantiating the valuation of intangible assets requires extensive auditor judgment; documentation for an account balance seldom provides conclusive evidence of value. Occasionally, it may be desirable to confirm the existence of certain material intangible assets by direct correspondence with third parties.

Review Questions

Cash balances

15–1. List the types of substantive tests available for auditing cash balances.

15–2. Why are all bank balances usually confirmed regardless of their size?

15–3. State the alternative audit approaches to bank reconciliations.

15–4. What procedures are typically performed in reviewing and testing a client's bank reconciliations?

15–5. What is a cutoff bank statement? What use does the auditor make of a cutoff bank statement?

15–6. What is a proof of cash and what is its purpose?

15–7. Define kiting and suggest ways in which an auditor may uncover it.

15–8. What is the objective of performing bank transfer tests?

Property, plant, and equipment

15–9. What are the objectives of auditing property, plant, and equipment? Give examples of how these objectives can be achieved through auditing other accounts.

15–10. Why are prior-year transactions involving fixed asset accounts of concern in an initial audit of financial statements?

15–11. What auditing procedures are necessary to obtain assurance about the existence and ownership of the opening balances of fixed asset accounts?

15–12. How can an auditor obtain evidence of the existence and condition of property, plant, and equipment?

15–13. What substantive tests may be performed for the acquisition and disposition of assets?

15–14. How does the auditor obtain assurance concerning correct classification of expenditures?

15–15. What tests are appropriate for depreciation?

Discussion Questions

Cash balances

15–30. Outline, in detail, what the auditor should do in performing substantive tests with respect to a client's bank reconciliation. Your answer should address the following areas:

1. Bank account balance.
2. Listing of outstanding checks.
3. Checks that cleared in the subsequent bank statement.
4. Deposits in transit.
5. Bank statements for the reconciliation date and subsequent period.
6. Other possible items on the reconciliation.

15–31. In relation to the audit of a client's bank reconciliation,

1. What is a cutoff bank statement?
2. Why would the auditor be interested in the dates of the outstanding checks that were returned with the cutoff statement?
3. How might the auditor determine if any checks had been recorded but not issued at the reconciliation date?

15–32. Briefly discuss some of the circumstances or types of activity that might be indicative of irregularities involving cash.

Questions 15–33 and 15–34 are based on the following:

Miles Company
Bank Transfer Schedule
December 31, 1990

Check	*Bank Accounts*			*Date disbursed per*		*Date deposited per*	
Number	*From*	*To*	*Amount*	*Books*	*Bank*	*Books*	*Bank*
2020	1st Natl.	Suburban	$32,000	12/31	1/5 ♦	12/31	1/3 ▲
2021	1st Natl.	Capital	21,000	12/31	1/4 ♦	12/31	1/3 ▲
3217	2nd State	Suburban	6,700	1/3	1/5	1/3	1/6
0659	Midtown	Suburban	5,500	12/30	1/5 ♦	12/30	1/3 ▲

15–33. The tick mark ♦ most likely indicates that the amount was traced to the

a. January cash receipts journal.
b. Outstanding check list of the applicable bank reconciliation.
c. January cash disbursements journal.
d. Year-end bank confirmations.

(AICPA adapted)

15–34. The tick mark ▲ most likely indicates that the amount was traced to the

a. Deposits in transit of the applicable bank reconciliation.
b. January cash disbursements journal.
c. January cash receipts journal.
d. Year-end bank confirmations.

Property, plant, and equipment

15–35. The extent of audit work to determine the existence of property, plant, and equipment depends on whether physical inspection has been carried out by the client.

1. What auditing procedures would you perform in the fiscal year in which the client makes a physical inspection?
2. What auditing procedures would you perform when no inspection has ever been made?

15–36. Discuss the effect each of the following items has in determining the audit testing plan for property, plant, and equipment:

1. A large volume of small-dollar transactions.
2. Property accounting records that are decentralized and maintained at various locations.
3. Prior-year tests of controls that indicate deficiencies in the control structure relating to property.
4. Adoption by the client during the current year of a new computerized property accounting system.

15-37. How would you determine that there are no significant items charged to expense that should have been capitalized, or vice versa?

15-38. The auditor should determine whether appropriate rates of depreciation have been properly applied to all items of property, plant, and equipment that should be depreciated, and that the method used is consistent with the previous year.

1. What are "appropriate" rates of depreciation?
2. What is "proper application"?
3. How would you determine that appropriate rates of depreciation have been properly applied?

15-39. How would you determine whether property, plant, and equipment have been pledged as collateral?

AICPA Multiple Choice Questions

These questions are taken from the Auditing part of Uniform CPA Examinations. Choose the single most appropriate answer.

Cash balances

15-40. To gather evidence regarding the balance per bank in a bank reconciliation, an auditor would examine all of the following *except*

a. Cutoff bank statement.
b. Year-end bank statement.
c. Bank confirmation.
d. General ledger.

15-41. The auditor's count of the client's cash should be coordinated to coincide with the

a. Assessment of the internal control structure with respect to cash.
b. Close of business on the balance sheet date.
c. Count of marketable securities.
d. Count of inventories.

15-42. Which of the following is one of the better auditing techniques that might be used by an auditor to detect kiting between intercompany banks?

a. Review composition of authenticated deposit slips.
b. Review subsequent bank statements received directly from the banks.
c. Prepare a schedule of bank transfers.
d. Prepare year-end bank reconciliations.

15-43. For the most effective internal control procedures, monthly bank statements should be received directly from the banks and reviewed by the

a. Controller.
b. Cash receipts accountant.
c. Cash disbursements accountant.
d. Internal auditor.

15–44. On receiving the bank cutoff statement, the auditor should trace

a. Deposits in transit on the year-end bank reconciliation to deposits in the cash receipts journal.
b. Checks dated prior to year-end to the outstanding checks listed on the year-end bank reconciliation.
c. Deposits listed on the cutoff statement to deposits in the cash receipts journal.
d. Checks dated subsequent to year-end to the outstanding checks listed on the year-end bank reconciliation.

Property, plant, and equipment

15–45. In violation of Company policy, the Jefferson City Company erroneously capitalized the cost of painting its warehouse. The CPA auditing Jefferson City's financial statements most likely would learn of this by

a. Reviewing the listing of construction work orders for the year.
b. Discussing capitalization policies with the Company controller.
c. Observing, during the physical inventory observation, that the warehouse had been painted.
d. Examining in detail a sample of construction work orders.

15–46. Which of the following is the *best* evidence of real estate ownership at the balance sheet date?

a. Title insurance policy.
b. Original deed held in the client's safe.
c. Paid real estate tax bills.
d. Closing statement.

15–47. The auditor may conclude that depreciation charges are insufficient by noting

a. Insured values greatly in excess of book values.
b. Large amounts of fully depreciated assets.
c. Continuous trade-ins of relatively new assets.
d. Excessive recurring losses on assets retired.

15–48. An auditor determines that a client has properly capitalized a leased asset (and corresponding lease liability) as representing, in substance, an installment purchase. As part of the auditor's procedures, the auditor should

a. Substantiate the cost of the property to the lessor and determine that this is the cost recorded by the client.
b. Evaluate the propriety of the interest rate used in discounting the future lease payments.
c. Determine that the leased property is being amortized over the life of the lease.
d. Evaluate whether the total amount of lease payments represents the fair market value of the property.

15–49. When there are numerous property and equipment transactions during the year, an auditor planning to assess control risk at the minimum level usually plans to obtain an understanding of the internal control structure and to perform

a. Tests of controls and extensive tests of property and equipment balances at the end of the year.
b. Extensive tests of current year property and equipment transactions.
c. Tests of controls and limited tests of current-year property and equipment transactions.
d. Analytical procedures for property and equipment balances at the end of the year.

15-50. Which of the following internal control procedures would most likely allow for a reduction in the scope of the auditor's tests of depreciation expense?

a. Review and approval of the periodic equipment depreciation entry by a supervisor who does *not* actively participate in its preparation.
b. Comparison of equipment account balances for the current year with the current-year budget and prior-year actual balances.
c. Review of the miscellaneous income account for salvage credits and scrap sales of partially depreciated equipment.
d. Authorization of payment of vendors' invoices by a designated employee who is independent of the equipment receiving function.

15-51. Which of the following procedures is most likely to prevent the improper disposition of equipment?

a. A separation of duties between those authorized to dispose of equipment and those authorized to approve removal work orders.
b. The use of serial numbers to identify equipment that could be sold.
c. Periodic comparison of removal work orders with authorizing documentation.
d. A periodic analysis of the scrap sales and the repairs and maintenance accounts.

15-52. Property acquisitions that are misclassified as maintenance expense would most likely be detected by an internal control procedure that provides for

a. Investigation of variances within a formal budgeting system.
b. Review and approval of the monthly depreciation entry by the plant supervisor.
c. Segregation of duties of employees in the accounts payable department.
d. Examination by the internal auditor of vendor invoices and canceled checks for property acquisitions.

Problems and Cases

Cash balances

15-60. MLG Company's auditor received, directly from the banks, confirmations and cutoff statements with related checks and deposit tickets for MLG's three general-purpose bank accounts. The auditor determined that internal control procedures for cash were satisfactory and assessed control risk as low. The proper cutoff of external cash receipts and disbursements was established. No bank accounts were opened or closed during the year.

Required:

Prepare the audit program of substantive procedures to substantiate MLG's bank balances. Ignore any other cash accounts.

(AICPA adapted)

15-61. Your client, who sells on credit, has several bank accounts. A reconciliation of one of these accounts as of the balance sheet date appears as follows:

Balance per bank, December 31	$10,000
Add—Deposit in transit	2,000
Total	12,000
Less—Outstanding checks	100
Balance per books, December 31	$11,900

Required:

As to the $2000 shown as a deposit in transit

a. Briefly describe the major possibilities of error or irregularity.
b. List the auditing procedures that might be followed in an annual audit that would help to establish the validity and accuracy of the deposit in transit. Explain how each of those procedures would help to detect a possible error or irregularity.

15-62. When you arrived at your client's office on January 11, 1990 to begin the December 31, 1989 audit, you discovered that the client had been drawing checks as creditors' invoices became due but not necessarily mailing them. Because of a working capital shortage, some checks have been held for two or three weeks.

The client informed you that unmailed checks totaling $55,200 were on hand at December 31, 1989. You were told these December-dated checks had been entered in the cash disbursements book and charged to the respective creditors' accounts in December because the checks were prenumbered. Heavy collections permitted the checks to be mailed before your arrival.

The client wants to adjust the cash balance and accounts payable at December 31 by $55,200 because the cash account had a credit balance. The client objects to submitting to the bank your audit report showing an overdraft of cash.

Required:

a. Prepare an audit program indicating the procedures you would use to satisfy yourself of the accuracy of the cash balance on the client's statements.
b. Discuss the acceptability of reversing the indicated amount of outstanding checks.

(AICPA adapted)

15-63. The Courtney Corporation maintains two bank accounts. General ledger balances at year-end are as follows:

City Trust Co.	$50,000
Greene County Bank	(20,000) overdraft

The company's balance sheet presentation in the current assets section is as follows:

Cash $30,000

Required:

State your position concerning the propriety of this presentation. In your discussion mention additional questions you may wish to raise and any auditing procedures you consider necessary.

15-64. In tracing checks to the cash disbursements book you find a series of ten checks unentered in the last month of the year under audit, none of which has been returned by the bank. Inquiry reveals that the checks in question were signed in blank by the treasurer and given to the vice president in charge of sales, who was making an extended business trip that ended two weeks after the close of the fiscal year. The vice president had requested the signed checks, which required only a countersignature, to avoid carrying a large amount of cash customarily expended on such trips for the usual traveling expenses and for entertaining customers and prospects.

Required:

a. What auditing procedures would you follow in view of this practice?
b. What recommendations would you make to your client to accommodate the vice president's desires?

15-65. In connection with your audit of Kent & Sons at December 31, 1990, you were given the following bank reconciliation prepared by a company employee:

Balance per bank	$30,534
Deposits in transit	37,856
	68,390
Checks outstanding	42,756
Balance per books	$25,634

As part of your audit you obtained the bank statement and canceled checks from the bank on January 15, 1991. Checks issued from January 1 to January 15, 1991 per the books were $22,482. Checks returned by the bank on January 15 amounted to $58,438. Of the checks outstanding December 31, $9600 were not returned by the bank with the January 15 statement, and of those issued per the books in January 1991, $7200 were not returned.

Required:

a. Prepare a schedule showing this data in proper form.
b. Suggest four possible explanations for the condition existing here and state what your action would be in each case, including any necessary journal entries.

(AICPA adapted)

15-66. You are engaged in an audit of the financial statements of the Speedy Service Corporation for the year ended December 31, 1989. In the course of your interim work conducted early in the fall, you selected June as a test month for review of cash records and procedures.

Client's bank reconciliation—*May 31, 1989*

General ledger and cash book balance			$12,777
Deduct:			
Bank service charges for May		$ 15	
Deposit of May 31, 1989 in transit		4,350	4,365
			8,412
Add:			
Note of J. Smith collected by the bank May 30, 1989, $4000, less collection fee of $7 (debit and credit memos attached), recorded June 6, 1989			3,993
Outstanding checks			
#	*Date*	*Amount*	
25044	10/19/88	$ 55	
27918	2/03/89	2,500	
28887	5/30/89	2,692	
28888 (certified)	5/31/89	1,391	
28890	5/31/89	45	5,292
Balance per bank statement			$17,697

Client's bank reconciliation—*June 30, 1989*

General ledger and cash book balance			$19,072
Deduct:			
Deposit of June 29, 1989 in transit		$3,592	
Bank error: check #28890 cleared as $145 instead of $45		100	
Bank error: check of Burns Corp. incorrectly charged to our account		870	4,562
			14,510
Add:			
Outstanding checks			
#	*Date*	*Amount*	
25044	10/19/88	$ 55	
27918	2/03/89	2,500	
28888 (certified)	5/31/89	1,391	
28902 (certified)	6/22/89	736	
28907	6/25/89	118	
28910	6/26/89	1,505	
28911	6/26/89	762	4,940
Balance per bank statement			$19,450

Other data available

	Period *June 1–30, 1989*
Total credited by the bank	$13,449
Cash receipts per books	16,691
Cash disbursements per books	10,396

A comparison of paid checks accompanying the June bank statement with the disbursements book and the May 31 reconciliation revealed that the following checks had cleared the bank: #28887, #28890 (cleared as $145), all of the checks drawn in June except #28902 $736 (certified June 2), #28907 $118, #28910 $1505, #28911 $762. A check for $870 drawn on the Burns Corporation also cleared the account during this period. The deposit in transit at May 31 was credited by the bank on June 2; the June 29 deposit was credited on July 2. The bank was notified of its errors on July 15. Corrections were recorded on the July bank statement.

Required:

From the information given, prepare a proof of cash for the month of June. (*Note:* When banks certify checks, they charge the company's account immediately.) Indicate all auditing procedures applied.

Property, plant, and equipment

15-67. While auditing a trucking company, you encounter the following situation:

1. You have reviewed an authorization for the purchase of five engines to replace the engines in five trucks.
2. The cost of the old engines was removed from property and that of the new engines properly capitalized. The work was done in the company garage.
3. You find no credits for salvage and none for the sale of any scrap metal at any time during the year. You have been in the garage and did not see the old engines.
4. The accountant is also treasurer and office manager. She is an authorized check signer and has access to all cash receipts. On inquiry, she says she does not recall the sale of the old engines or of any scrap metal.

Required:

Assuming that the engines were sold as scrap, outline all steps that this fact would cause you to take in connection with your audit. Give consideration to steps beyond those related directly to this one item.

(AICPA adapted)

15-68. You have been assigned as a staff accountant for a new client, Luxury Car Rental. The business involves primarily the rental and leasing of automobiles for personal and business use. The company continually purchases and disposes of automobiles throughout the year, with approximately 1500 acquisitions annually.

Required:

Discuss the risk factors and audit strategy for this client relative to the property accounts. Include a discussion of procedures you would consider necessary to examine opening balances.

15-69. Gamon, CPA, is the auditor for a manufacturing company with a balance sheet that includes the caption "Property, Plant, and Equipment." Gamon has been asked by the company's management whether audit adjustments or reclassifications are required for the following material items that have been included in or excluded from "Property, Plant, and Equipment."

1. A tract of land was acquired during the year. The land is the future site of the client's new headquarters, which will be constructed in the following year.

Commissions were paid to the real estate agent used to acquire the land, and expenditures were made to relocate the previous owner's equipment. These commissions and expenditures were expensed and are excluded from "Property, Plant, and Equipment."

2. Clearing costs were incurred to make the land ready for construction. These costs were included in "Property, Plant, and Equipment."
3. During the land clearing process, timber and gravel were recovered and sold. The proceeds from the sale were recorded as other income and are excluded from "Property, Plant, and Equipment."
4. A group of machines was purchased under a royalty agreement that provides for royalty payments based on units of production from the machines. The cost of the machines, freight costs, unloading charges, and royalty payments were capitalized and are included in "Property, Plant, and Equipment."

Required:

a. Describe the general characteristics of assets, such as land, buildings, improvements, machinery, equipment, fixtures, and so on, that should normally be classified as "Property, Plant, and Equipment," and identify audit objectives in connection with the audit of "Property, Plant, and Equipment." *Do not discuss specific auditing procedures.*
b. Indicate whether each of the foregoing items numbered 1 to 4 requires one or more audit adjustments or reclassifications, and explain why such adjustments or reclassifications are required or not required.

Organize your answer as follows:

Item Number	*Is Audit Adjustment or Reclassification Required?* *Yes or No*	*Reasons Why Audit Adjustment or Reclassification Is Required or Not Required*

(AICPA adapted)

15–70. In connection with a recurring audit of the financial statements of George's Machinery, Inc. for the year ended December 31, 1990, you have been assigned the audit of the Manufacturing Equipment, Manufacturing Equipment—Accumulated Depreciation, and Repairs to Manufacturing Equipment accounts. Your review of George's policies and procedures has disclosed the following pertinent information:

1. The Manufacturing Equipment account includes the net invoice price plus related freight and installation costs for all the equipment in George's manufacturing plant.
2. The Manufacturing Equipment and Accumulated Depreciation accounts are supported by a subsidiary ledger that shows the cost and accumulated depreciation for each piece of equipment.
3. An annual budget for capital expenditures of $1000 or more is prepared by the budget committee of the board of directors and approved by the full board of

directors. Capital expenditures over $1000 that are not included in this budget must be approved by the board of directors and variations of 20 percent or more must be explained to the board. Approval by the supervisor of production is required for capital expenditures under $1000.

4. Company employees handle installation, removal, repair, and rebuilding of the machinery. Work orders are prepared for these activities and are subject to the same budgetary control as other expenditures. Work orders are not required for external expenditures.

Required:

a. Cite the major objectives of your audit of the Manufacturing Equipment, Manufacturing Equipment—Accumulated Depreciation, and Repairs to Manufacturing Equipment accounts. Do not include in this listing the auditing procedures designed to accomplish these objectives.
b. Prepare the portion of your audit program applicable to the review of 1990 additions to the Manufacturing Equipment account.

(AICPA adapted)

15-71. While on a plant tour of Shoreline Company, it was brought to your attention that a specialized inventory order preparation machine, which had been put into service three years earlier, is now sitting idle. You inquired of the controller as to the company's intentions regarding the future use of this machine and she informed you of management's intentions to dismantle the machine and sell it for scrap.

Required:

Discuss the appropriate auditing procedures you would employ in this situation.

16

Auditing Investments, Prepayments and Accruals, Income Taxes, and Debt and Equity Accounts

This chapter continues the discussion of financial statement accounts that are typically audited by performing substantive tests. As noted in the introduction to Chapter 15, the choice of particular substantive tests and their timing and extent will be determined by the auditor's assessment of the risk of material misstatement occurring. Accordingly, not all the procedures described in this chapter need be performed on a particular engagement, on 100 percent of the transactions and accounts under audit, or only after the client's accounting year has ended.

INVESTMENTS AND RELATED INCOME

"Investments" is a broad term used to describe nonoperating, income-producing assets of a commercial or industrial enterprise that are held either as a means of using excess cash or to accomplish some special purpose. The term "securities" is commonly used interchangeably with investments, as it is in this chapter. Often, the description of investment assets in the financial statements gives further insight into the specific reasons they are held.

"Short-term investments" usually consist of marketable securities acquired for income-producing purposes by temporarily using excess cash. In a classified balance sheet, short-term investments are classified as current. The term "investments" without any modifier often identifies assets held for long-term yield and market appreciation and consequently classified as noncurrent assets.

The phrase "marketable securities" indicates a high degree of liquidity, that is, securities for which an organized and active market exists. Such securities may be held in either a current or long-term investment account and may consist of equity or other securities. It is important to identify marketable equity securities, since they are required by Statement of Financial Accounting Standards (SFAS) No. 12, *Accounting for Certain Marketable Securities* (Accounting Standards Section I89), to be carried in the financial statements at the lower of aggregate cost or market.

"Long-term investments," "investments in affiliates," or "investments" may also represent holdings of securities for purposes of control, affiliation, or financing of enterprises related to the investing company's operations. Those investments, which are classified as noncurrent assets, may require using the equity method of accounting. Sinking funds, building funds, and other funds accumulated for special purposes may consist of investments in securities and are classified as noncurrent assets.

Income statement accounts related to investments are generally "interest revenue" (including amortization of premium and discount, as appropriate), "dividend revenue," "realized gain or loss on sale of securities," "unrealized gain or loss from holding marketable equity securities," and "earnings or losses from investments accounted for by the equity method." Market value adjustments made for long-term marketable equity securities are reflected in the equity section of the balance sheet and not on the income statement.

Particularly in recent years, investment bankers and securities underwriters have created an ever-growing array of new types of investments, sometimes referred as "new financial products" or "new financial instruments." Several notorious instances of significant investor losses suggest that many buyers of these rather exotic investments have little understanding of the nature and extent of the various risks they have undertaken. For example, in the mid-1980s several municipalities bought from a bond dealer securities that were either issued or guaranteed by the U.S. Treasury, and simultaneously entered into a contract to sell the securities back to the dealer the next day (to earn extra interest). These transactions, referred to as repurchase agreements (or "repos," for short), were widely believed to be extremely safe. As a result, the municipalities in several cases did not take possession of the securities because it was not practical to do so, and left them with the dealer for safekeeping. The bond dealer used the municipalities' bonds for fraudulent purposes and then went bankrupt. While the securities were guaranteed by the U.S. government, the contract with the bond dealer was not, and the municipalities found, often to their surprise, that their status was little more than that of unsecured creditors—the municipalities had in effect made unsecured loans to the bond dealer.

The auditor in this and similar situations needs to understand clearly the nature of the transaction that the client has entered into and the attendant risks. The auditor also needs to know how those risks affect management's assertions, particularly with regard to legal rights and asset valuations. The nature and extent of those risks may well affect the selection of accounting measurement and disclosure principles (e.g., the need to provide for possible losses and to disclose the substance of repo transactions as unsecured loans). The complexity of many of these new financial products makes the auditor's task particularly difficult.

Audit Objectives

The auditor should design tests to provide reasonable assurance that

- Investments exist and the client has legal title to them at the balance sheet date. Establishing the existence (in either certificate form, electronic or "book entry" form, or a custodial account) and ownership of investments is paramount to the audit process, particularly because many securities are readily negotiable.
- All investments owned by the client at the balance sheet date are included in the investment accounts.
- The values at which investments are carried in the financial statements are appropriate and are adequately disclosed.
- The investments are properly classified between current and noncurrent components.

- Investments pledged as collateral or otherwise restricted are appropriately identified and disclosed.
- Income from investments, including gains and losses on sales and adjustments in valuation allowances, is appropriately reflected in the financial statements.

Substantive Tests of Balances

Many of the substantive tests of investments and related income are documented on a summary working paper similar to that shown for notes receivable and interest income in Figure 5.7 in Chapter 5.

Existence, Ownership, Accuracy, and Completeness. Evidence of the existence and ownership of investments, as well as some assurance about the accuracy and completeness of the investment accounts, is normally obtained by confirmation or inspection. The auditor should agree the securities confirmed or inspected to the client's detailed records. Whether these procedures are performed at year-end or at an interim date will be based on the auditor's assessment of control risk with respect to asset protection and segregation of duties and on efficiency considerations.

Physical protection of securities is vital because many marketable securities are readily negotiable; moreover, documents evidencing legal ownership have value even if securities are not readily negotiable. Therefore, restricted access and segregation of duties are particularly important aspects of the control structure for investments. Securities are generally kept in a vault or safe deposit box, or entrusted to a financial institution for safekeeping. The custodian and other personnel who have access to the securities would be independent of the functions of authorizing investment transactions, keeping investment records, handling cash, maintaining the general ledger; preferably each of those employees would be independent of all the others.

Counts of Portfolios. If an investment portfolio is relatively large and active (as in banks, insurance companies, investment companies, and stock brokerages), the count of securities may be a major undertaking requiring extensive planning, precise execution, and a large staff of auditors. In contrast, most industrial and commercial companies do not own numerous securities, and physical inspection is not difficult. The auditor usually obtains a list of securities supporting the general ledger balance at the date of the count and arranges to visit the place where the securities are kept, accompanied by the custodian. The auditor examines the securities and compares them with the list. This process normally provides the auditor with evidence about the control structure; for example, an accurate security list, proper endorsement or evidence of ownership on the securities, proper division of duties between custodian and record keeper, adequate physical safeguards (such as use of a bank's safe deposit vault), and requirements that two people be present for access to the securities are all indications of an effective control structure.

Generally, the auditor should count the securities at the balance sheet date; if it is done at another date, the vault or safe deposit box should be sealed during the intervening period. Banks ordinarily seal a safe deposit box on a client's request and subsequently confirm to the auditor that no access to the box was granted during the specified period. Securities should be counted simultaneously with cash and other negotiable assets. A count is considered "simultaneous" if the securities are sealed or otherwise controlled until all negotiable assets have been examined.

The auditor should maintain control over the securities from the start of the count until it has been completed, the results have been compared with the list of securities, and all exceptions have been investigated to the extent possible at the time. Responsible officers and employees of the client should be present during the count to reduce the possibility of later questions about the handling of securities, and should acknowledge, in writing, the return of the securities intact upon conclusion of the count.

The auditor should note that stock certificates and registered bonds are in the name of the client or an accredited nominee or, if they are not, that certificates are appropriately endorsed or accompanied by powers of attorney. Bonds with interest coupons should be examined to determine that coupons not yet due have not been detached. If coupons presently coming due are not attached to the bonds, the auditor should ask where they are and either inspect them or confirm them with the holders. Likewise, explanations should be obtained and evaluated for any coupons past due that are attached and have not been presented for payment. Interest in default should be noted in the working papers for consideration in connection with the audit of accrued income and carrying amounts of investments.

The auditor should investigate reasons for differences between the count and the list of securities. Certain types of differences are normal and expected, for example, securities held by others and securities in transit. The holders of securities in other locations should be identified and requests for confirmation sent. In-transit items should be related to recent transactions; outgoing in-transit items should be confirmed with recipients. Securities received by the client through the mail for a few days following the date of the count should be examined to substantiate items in transit. Once the auditor is satisfied that all items on the security list have been counted or their location elsewhere has been confirmed and all differences have been reconciled, he or she may "release" control over securities.

The auditor should not overlook the possibility of substitutions. If, for example, examinations are being made of one or more trust accounts handled by the same trustee, securities in all accounts should be counted at the same time. Similarly, if different auditors are employed to examine several accounts, they should make their counts simultaneously. Otherwise, material shortages may be concealed by temporary transfers from accounts whose securities are not being counted. If a client is reluctant to permit an auditor to count securities of other accounts or is unwilling or unable to arrange for a simultaneous count by all auditors concerned, the auditor may identify securities owned by the client by accounting for certificate numbers of stocks and bonds; however, that procedure is difficult and time-consuming for a large portfolio with numerous purchases and sales. Securities owned or held as collateral or for safekeeping should also be counted simultaneously with cash funds and cash equivalents, undeposited receipts, notes receivable, and other negotiable assets if there is a possibility of substitution of one item for another.

Confirmation of Securities Not on Hand. Items on the list of securities owned at the count date but not counted should be confirmed with the holders. If a client's entire portfolio is held by a custodian, confirmation procedures usually take the place of the security count.

Items not on hand ordinarily include securities held by banks as collateral for loans, securities left with broker-dealers as custodians for safekeeping, securities with transfer agents, and securities that exist on computerized files in "book entry" form. The auditor should determine the location of those securities at the examination date, the appropriate responsible person acting as custodian, and the reasons they are held by the custodian. (If the securities are held by people or organizations unknown to the auditor, he or she may consider it necessary to inspect them physically rather than confirm them.)

If the client's entire portfolio of securities is held in custody by a well-known, reliable financial institution independent of the client, the custodian should be requested to furnish directly to the auditor a list of securities held for the client at the examination date. The confirmation request should also ask whether the client has clear title to the securities. The auditor should compare the list with the client's security records and account for differences noted. It is sometimes desirable to corroborate the custodian's confirmation by counting the securities, for example, if the portfolio is large in relation to the custodian's assets or if the auditor seeks assurance about the adequacy of the custodian's procedures. A letter from the custodian's auditor addressing its internal control structure can also provide that assurance. Joint counts with other auditors having a similar interest are possible.

If securities are in the custody of an affiliate or are under the control of a person or group of people who take an active part in the management of the client, the auditor is not justified in relying solely on written confirmation from the custodian. Instead, the auditing procedures outlined above for counting securities under the client's control should be followed.

Tests of Carrying Values. Cost of securities purchased and proceeds from securities sold are normally supported by brokers' advices. The auditor should examine these documents to substantiate the basis for initially recording those transactions. Additionally, the auditor should review the client's method of determining cost (first in, first out, average, or specific identification) of securities sold and ascertain that it is consistent during the year and with prior years. Periodic valuation of investments is necessary for management decision-making purposes; it is also required so that market or fair value can be determined for financial statement purposes. If investments are few, relatively short-term, and not significant to a company's operations, the valuation process is sometimes performed informally by the officer responsible for investments. If investments are significant, the valuation should be formally executed and documented. The frequency of valuation depends on the amount of investment activity and how often financial statements are issued. (Some active investment portfolios are under virtually continual valuation.)

The auditor should test the client's identification of marketable equity securities that are required to be carried at the lower of aggregate cost or market and should determine that market values have been appropriately applied to those securities. Normally, this is accomplished by comparing values with published sources. The auditor should also determine that any necessary valuation allowance adjustment is properly reflected in the financial statements. The client's support for fair values of investments that are determined on a basis other than published values should be tested for propriety and consistency. The auditor should be alert to any indication that declines in market value below cost may be other than temporary.

The auditor should consider evidence related to the degree of influence or control the client can exercise over an investee, to evaluate whether the equity method of accounting or consolidation is appropriate in the circumstances. In addition, the auditor should exercise appropriate professional care to ensure that transactions involving investments are accounted for in accordance with their substance, regardless of their form.

If there are investments accounted for by the equity method and if the investee enterprise is audited by other auditors, the auditor will have to use the report of the investee's auditors to be able to report on the client investor's equity in the investee's underlying net assets and its share of the investee's earnings or losses and other transactions. This places the auditor in the position of a principal auditor who is using the work and reports of other auditors. The work and reports of other auditors may also serve as evidence with respect to investments carried on the cost basis or at the lower of cost or market, which would similarly place the auditor in the position of a principal auditor. The procedures to be followed in those instances are discussed in Chapter 6; reporting aspects of using the work and reports of other auditors are discussed in Chapter 18.

Tests of Investment Income. Accounting for income from publicly traded marketable securities is usually straightforward: Interest is accrued periodically and dividends are recorded as received (or when the shares first trade "ex-dividend"). Published records of interest, dividends, and other distributions are compared with recorded income periodically to ensure that all income has been received on a timely basis. That procedure is more effective if it is exercised by a person other than those responsible for initially recording investments and cash receipts from investment income. If an investment is accounted for on the equity method, copies of financial statements of the investee are needed to determine the appropriate earnings or losses to record.

The auditor should determine that all income earned has been appropriately recorded and either collected or recognized as a receivable, and that all accrued income receivable has in fact been earned. The auditor usually obtains evidence about investment income and collection dates by referring to dates of purchase and disposal of investments, interest rates, and published dividend records. In testing income from investments, the auditor can often perform analytical procedures, for example, analyzing the rate of return or gross investment income on a month-to-month or quarter-to-quarter basis, or comparing income with budgeted or prior-year data. Fluctuations in investment income that do not conform to the auditor's expectations would indicate that recorded investments might not exist or that investments exist that have not been recorded.

Tests of Classification and Presentation. If the balance sheet is classified, the auditor should determine that the investments are properly classified between the current and noncurrent categories. The auditor should also ascertain that the financial statements contain all required disclosures regarding investment carrying values and realized and unrealized gains and losses. In addition, minutes, confirmation replies, loan agreements, bond indentures, and other appropriate documents should be reviewed to determine whether investments have been pledged as collateral or whether there is evidence of commitments to acquire or dispose of investments, both of which may require disclosures.

Financial statement classification of investments depends largely on management's objectives and intentions. The auditor can ascertain management's objectives through inquiry and by reviewing minutes of meetings of the board of directors and its investment committee. It may be desirable to include a statement of management's intent in the client representation letter (discussed in Chapter 17). To evaluate management's representations about its intentions, the auditor should consider whether they are reasonable in light of the enterprise's financial position, working capital requirements, debt agreements, and other contractual obligations. For example, the client's needs may indicate a reasonable presumption that marketable securities will have to be sold to meet operating requirements and that therefore they should be classified as current assets.

PREPAID EXPENSES, ESTIMATED AND ACCRUED LIABILITIES, AND RELATED EXPENSES

Prepaid expenses are assets, most often in the form of services (but sometimes for goods such as stationery and supplies), that have been acquired as part of the buying cycle but that apply to future periods or to the production of future revenues—for example, unexpired insurance, rent paid in advance, and prepaid taxes other than those on income. The distinction between prepaid expenses and deferred charges is based mainly on whether the asset is current or noncurrent. How precisely that distinction is made depends on custom and materiality considerations. Prepaid insurance, for example, and many types of deposits do not expire and are not realized within one year or the enterprise's operating cycle, but are traditionally classified as current. The prepaid expense account is seldom material to the financial statements, and noncurrent items that are not material are included in prepaid expenses for convenience. If deferred costs (such as debt issuance costs) are material and will expire over several years, they are properly classified as noncurrent deferred charges.

Accrued liabilities, often referred to as accrued expenses, are items for which a service or benefit has been received and for which the related liability is acknowledged and reasonably determinable, but that are not yet payable (either because of the terms of the commitment or because the invoice has not been received). Most accrued liabilities accrue with the passage of time—for example, interest, rent, and property taxes—or with some service or activity, for example, payrolls, vacation pay, royalties, sales commissions, and payroll taxes. Deferred credits (such as unearned revenue and deferred income accounts) result from the receipt of revenues in advance of the related delivery of goods or services and are discussed in Chapter 12.

Agency obligations, such as payroll withholdings and deductions, are funds collected for others for which accountability must be maintained until the funds are turned over at the required time to the agency for whom they are held in trust. Those obligations result from transactions that are part of the buying cycle and the revenue cycle.

Many similarities exist among prepaid expenses, accrued liabilities, and agency obligations and among the underlying transactions that affect these accounts. For example, similar types of transactions may result in prepaid insurance or accrued insurance expense; the same is true for rent and property taxes. Items such as insurance premiums and various deposits are often held as agency obligations. All three categories of accounts are frequently subjected to similar types of control structure policies and procedures, and the general audit approach employed is also similar.

Audit Objectives

The auditor should approach prepaid assets and accrued liabilities with the view that liabilities are more likely to be understated or omitted from the accounts than overstated and, conversely, assets are more likely to be overstated than understated. Therefore, audit objectives should focus on ascertaining that prepaid assets are not overstated and that accrued liabilities are not understated, but without ignoring the possibility that the opposite may occur.

In specifying audit objectives for prepaid expenses, the auditor should focus on obtaining reasonable assurance that

- All amounts reported as assets were acquired in authorized transactions and were properly recorded at the time of acquisition.
- The balance of the expenditure carried forward can be reasonably expected to be recovered from future income.
- The basis of amortization is reasonable and consistent with prior years and the related expenses are properly classified.

Principal audit objectives related to accrued expenses and other liabilities are to obtain reasonable assurance that

- All material accrued expenses, agency obligations, and other liabilities existing at the balance sheet date have been recorded and properly measured.
- The amounts recorded for accrued expenses, agency obligations, and other liabilities have been authorized and are properly measured.
- Related expenses have been recognized and properly measured on a consistent basis.

Substantive Tests of Balances

Tests of controls in the buying cycle are often sufficiently comprehensive to encompass all purchases and expenses, including those that involve prepayments, deferred charges, or accruals. If those tests have met their objectives, and if warranted by audit risk and materiality considerations, substantive tests of prepayments and accruals often are limited. In many cases, analytical procedures are the only type of substantive tests performed on prepaid and accrued accounts. For that reason, they are discussed first in this section.

Analytical Procedures. Balances in prepaid and accrued accounts and the related expense accounts should be compared with the prior-year balance sheet and income statement amounts. The underlying causes of trends, fluctuations, and unusual transactions noted should be understood thoroughly and evaluated for their implications for other accounts.

If they exist, variance reports and analyses of actual costs and expenses compared with budgeted amounts may be examined. The auditor should critically evaluate explanations of variances, both for their adequacy and for evidence they may provide about the accuracy and authorization of the accounts.

In a stable business, predictable relationships often exist among certain accounts, and changes in those relationships may signal conditions requiring accounting recognition. The auditor should compute pertinent ratios and compare them with corresponding ones for prior periods. For example, comparing selling expense with sales might lead the auditor to discover sales commissions that should be but were not accrued. Unexplained changes in ratios involving revenue and expense accounts may indicate possible misstatements of related prepayments and accruals.

Analytical procedures applied to related expense accounts can provide additional assurance about the reasonableness of prepayments and accruals. The auditor may review expense account activity for missing or unusual entries that may indicate unrecorded liabilities or the failure to amortize prepayments. Substantive tests of details are normally not performed on expense account balances unless the control structure is extremely ineffective or the auditor wants additional assurance in high-risk or sensitive areas (such as legal expense).

Substantive Tests of Specific Accounts. Control risk for prepaid assets and accrued liabilities is not usually assessed as low; therefore the auditor will often perform substantive testing beyond analytical procedures. Substantive testing usually consists of examining the contractual, statutory, or other basis for prepaid expenses or accrued liabilities; ascertaining that the method of calculating periodic amortization or accrual is appropriate; and recomputing the amortization or accrual and the balance as of the dates selected for testing (either interim or year-end). For many accrued liabilities and some prepaid expenses, the accrual or prepayment is based on an estimate of a liability or a future benefit that cannot be determined precisely. In that case, the basis and rationale for the estimate should be reviewed, compared with prior experience, and evaluated in the light of related circumstances. The related expense account is usually audited (at least in part) in connection with the aforementioned amortization or accrual.

Prepaid Insurance. Most well-controlled companies maintain an insurance register that indicates, for each policy, the insurance company, policy number, type and amount of coverage, policy dates, premium, prepayments, expense for the period, and any coinsurance provision. From this register or from the insurance policies themselves, a schedule of prepaid insurance should be prepared, preferably by the client's staff. The auditor should test the data shown on the schedule and examine insurance policies and vouchers supporting premiums. In addition, the auditor should note beneficiaries and evidence of liens on the insured property.

If original insurance policies are not available for inspection, the auditor should determine the reason. Since lenders often retain insurance policies on property that collateralizes loans, the absence of policies may indicate the existence of liens on the property. The auditor should request the client to obtain the policies (or copies of them) and should examine them. Depending on his or her assessment of control risk, the auditor may request confirmations from the insurance companies or brokers.

Prepaid liability and compensation insurance, if premiums are based on payrolls, may be compared with payrolls to determine that charges to expense appear proper. Premiums due may exceed advance payments so that at the end of a period there may be a liability rather than a prepayment. Total prepaid insurance per the insurance register or schedule of prepaid insurance should be compared with the general ledger.

An auditor is usually not an expert in determining insurable values and has no responsibility for management's decisions concerning insuring risks and coverage, but may render helpful service to the client by calling attention to differences among the amount of coverage, the insurable value (if available), and the recorded amount of insured property.

Prepaid and Accrued Property Taxes. The auditor should determine that the amount of prepaid taxes is actually an expense applicable to future periods, and should refer to local tax bills and laws because state and local tax statutes vary widely in their proration provisions. The related expense account should be examined closely and compared with prior years' accounts. Since taxes are generally computed by multiplying a base by a rate, the auditor can analyze the two components and seek explanations for fluctuations.

Prepaid and Accrued Commissions. The auditor should investigate whether prepaid or accrued commissions are proper. If commission expense is material, the auditor may wish to examine contracts with salespeople or obtain from management an authoritative statement of the employment terms. He or she may review sales reports, commission records, or other evidence of commissions earned, or may trace amounts in sales reports to commission records and cash records. If there are many salespeople, the auditor may, depending on the risk assessment, limit the examination to only a few accounts or to the entries for only a limited period. Transactions in the last month of the period may be reviewed to determine that commissions have been allocated to the proper period. The auditor should be satisfied that prepayments will be matched with revenues of future periods and are not current-period compensation. If amounts are significant, the auditor should consider confirming directly with salespeople the amounts due them and the commissions they earned during the year, and should test—for example, by applying commission rates against sales—the overall reasonableness of commission expense for the year. If there is a subsidiary ledger for prepaid or accrued commission accounts, the auditor should compare the balance of the general ledger account with the trial balance of the subsidiary ledger and investigate differences.

Travel and Entertainment Advances. Advances to employees for expenses may be tested by examining cash disbursements, expense reports, and cash receipts. If employees are advanced amounts as working funds on an imprest basis, the auditor may examine reimbursements in the month following the end of the period to determine whether material expenditures prior to the end of the period have been reimbursed. The auditor may review related entries after period-end to determine whether any should have been recorded in the period under audit. Advances may be confirmed by correspondence with employees. The general ledger account should be compared with the subsidiary ledger and differences investigated; the individual balances may be aged and long outstanding balances scrutinized. The auditor should identify unusual advances to officers and examine evidence that they were authorized.

Accrued Professional Fees. The auditor should consider including in the audit inquiry letters to lawyers a request for the amounts of unpaid or unbilled charges, which can then be compared with the recorded liability.

Royalties Payable. In evaluating the amount of royalties payable, the auditor should examine royalty and licensing contracts and extract important provisions for the permanent files. Many contracts provide for a minimum royalty payment regardless of whether a liability for royalties accrues on a unit basis. If royalty payments are based on sales, the auditor may compare computations with recorded sales; statements of royalties due may be tested to substantiate recorded amounts. If royalty payments are based on the quantity or value of goods produced, rather than on sales, the auditor should review documents on file supporting amounts accrued and test the underlying data. If accounting records are not kept in sufficient detail to furnish the required information, it may be necessary to analyze production records.

If lessors or vendors possess the only data on which royalties are based, statements of liability under royalty agreements may be secured from them. A request for confirmation may produce evidence of important differences in interpretation of contract provisions.

Provisions for Warranty Costs. Through inquiry and reading contracts and similar documents, the auditor should obtain an understanding of the client's warranty policies as a first step in evaluating whether the estimated liability for warranty claims is adequate. Auditing procedures in this area commonly include examining documentation supporting open warranty claims, reviewing claims settled after the balance sheet date, and considering past activity in the account in the light of relevant changes (such as new products or changes in warranty periods)—all for the purpose of determining whether the estimated liability at the balance sheet date is adequate. The auditor should also apply the procedures discussed under "Auditing Accounting Estimates" in Chapter 9.

Suspense Debits and Credits. Every chart of accounts contains a place for debit and credit items whose final accounting has not been determined. The person responsible may not have decided which expense account should be charged; the job order, cost center, or subaccount may not have been opened yet; or there may be some other unresolved question about the handling or propriety of the item. Although most suspense debit and credit accounts may be quite active during the year, all material issues should be resolved by year-end. The auditor should understand the nature of suspense items and how they arose, since their existence, even at an interim date, could indicate a deficiency in the client's control structure.

The auditor may want to test balances at an interim date and inquire into the disposition of items. This may contribute considerably to understanding the kinds of accounting problems that can occur and their implications for the auditor's risk assessment. In the rare instance of balances remaining at the end of the year, the auditor should age the items and inquire into the reasons why the proper distribution has not been determined. Particularly in the case of suspense debits, a client commonly and understandably often wishes to carry in the balance sheet disputed items that someone in management "just doesn't want to give up on." If those debits are significant, the auditor needs evidence that they are likely to have a realizable value or to benefit future operations, and are therefore properly classified as assets.

Accrued Pension Costs. To ascertain that the liability for pension costs and the related expense have been determined in conformity with GAAP, as set forth in SFAS No. 87, *Employers' Accounting for Pensions* (Accounting Standards Section P16), the auditor must understand the contractual and other arrangements giving rise to pension costs and be aware of the requirements of the Employee Retirement Income Security Act of 1974 (ERISA). SFAS No. 87 prescribes precisely the way to calculate pension costs. The significance of pension costs to most companies, and the effect of a possible misstatement of them on the financial statements, often calls for substantive testing. The extent of testing will depend on the auditor's risk assessment and on materiality considerations.

Many of the basic calculations required by SFAS No. 87 are actuarial calculations that should be considered the work of a specialist, and the auditor should apply the provisions of SAS No. 11, *Using the Work of a Specialist* (AU Section 336), in auditing those amounts. This does not require the auditor to reperform the actuary's calculations. Rather, the auditor needs to be satisfied that the methods and assumptions the actuary used are in conformity with GAAP. It is particularly important for the auditor to understand the reasons for fluctuations in pension information from one period to the next.

Under SAS No. 11, the auditor should reach an understanding with the client and the actuary about the nature of the actuary's work. This understanding should cover

- The objectives and scope of the actuary's work.
- The actuary's representations regarding his or her relationship, if any, to the client.
- The methods and assumptions to be used.

- A comparison of those methods and assumptions with the ones used in the preceding period.
- The actuary's understanding of how the auditor will use the actuary's findings to corroborate the representations in the financial statements.
- The form and content of the actuary's report needed by the auditor.

SAS No. 11 requires the auditor to evaluate the actuary's qualifications, reputation, and relationship (if any) to the client. The auditor is also required to make appropriate tests of the accounting data the client provided to the actuary. The auditor should also be satisfied that the actuary's methods and assumptions conform with the provisions of SFAS No. 87. The auditor should not rely on an actuary's conclusion about whether the actuarially computed amounts conform with GAAP; such a conclusion requires a skilled and experience-based knowledge of accounting principles.

Other suggested procedures are set forth below. They are not intended to be all inclusive or to apply to all situations. Selecting auditing procedures appropriate for a particular situation is a matter of judgment.

- Identify the client's pension plans, and obtain an understanding of the nature, coverage, and other relevant matters pertaining to each plan.
- Compare pension cost and related balance sheet and disclosure amounts and other information with the prior year for reasonableness and changes affecting comparability. Trace amounts to the actuary's report and to any supporting schedules or working papers used in connection with other auditing procedures.
- Evaluate compliance with ERISA.
- Determine whether plan asset and obligation amounts have been computed as of the measurement date and whether plan assets have been measured at their fair value.
- Examine the client's records to determine that the basic data (e.g., size, age, and sex distribution of the work force) used by the actuary is appropriate and that employees ultimately entitled to participate in the plan have been included in the actuarial calculations. Trace (normally in summary form) the employee data tested to the actuary's report or confirm it directly with the actuary.
- Review the actuary's report to determine whether all plan terms have been properly reflected in it and that the actuarial cost method is appropriate.
- Determine whether pension cost and related amounts have been computed on a consistent basis and recognized and disclosed in conformity with GAAP.
- Review the period from the measurement date to the company's year-end (and beyond, to the extent necessary) to determine whether any signifi-

cant events (e.g., changes in plan provisions) have occurred that would materially affect the computation of the provision for pension costs. If such events have occurred, consult with the actuary and obtain an estimate of the dollar effect on the provision.

Bonuses, Profit Sharing, and Compensated Absences. Amounts due officers and employees under plans for profit sharing and compensated absences become a liability in the period during which the profits are earned or service is rendered. The auditor should determine that the liability is computed in accordance with the authorization and the plans in effect and in conformity with applicable authoritative accounting pronouncements.

INCOME TAXES

Income tax differs from other costs and expenses because it is largely a dependent variable, based on revenue received and costs and expenses incurred by an enterprise. Management often has the ability to control the timing and amount of tax payments by controlling the related underlying transactions, particularly in closely held enterprises where minimizing taxes currently payable is often a significant management objective.

The issues associated with accounting for income taxes fall principally into two broad categories: determining the tax provision in the income statement and the timing of its payment. Those two issues complicate presentation of the current tax liability and deferred tax accounts on the balance sheet and the expense on the income statement. The actual liability is difficult to determine because of the complexities of federal and state tax statutes and regulations. The accounting is further complicated by the number and variety of differences between generally accepted accounting principles (GAAP) and the treatment permitted or required by tax laws and related rulings and regulations of the various taxing jurisdictions an entity is subject to. For multinational companies, income taxes levied in foreign countries under the laws and regulations of those countries must also be evaluated to determine their treatment under U.S. accounting pronouncements.

Audit Objectives

The objectives in auditing income tax accounts are to obtain reasonable assurance that all tax liabilities (or refunds receivable), tax provisions, and deferred tax accounts are included in the financial statements; that they are properly measured, classified, and described; and that all necessary disclosures are made in the financial statements. The basic auditing procedures are to test the accuracy of the computation of the current and deferred tax liability or asset accounts and the charge or credit to expense for the period.

This requires that the auditor determine that the underlying data is complete and accurate. The amounts involved are likely to be significant, and the issues affecting them numerous, complex, and often debatable. The discussion that follows suggests some of the specific objectives the auditor must meet in auditing income taxes.

In addition to obtaining reasonable assurance that the tax liability accounts accurately reflect the company's current tax obligations (including interest and penalty charges, which should be accounted for separately from the tax expense and liability accounts), the auditor must determine that probable loss contingencies that are reasonably estimable are provided for. Such contingencies may result from existing disagreements with taxing authorities or from the possibility that future disagreements may arise over positions taken by a company in its current tax return that may be interpreted differently by the Internal Revenue Service (IRS). Guidance for dealing with contingencies of this nature is contained in SFAS No. 5, *Accounting for Contingencies* (Accounting Standards Section C59). Further, the auditor should obtain reasonable assurance that deferred tax liabilities and assets are properly classified as to current and noncurrent amounts. The auditor should also determine that the total tax provision in the income statement is properly classified as to currently payable and deferred amounts. In addition, the auditor must ascertain that the tax effects of extraordinary items, discontinued operations, and changes in accounting principles have been properly calculated and reflected in the income statement.

Required disclosures relating to income taxes contain information of particular interest to financial statement users. Those disclosures include the nature of and changes in the composition of deferred taxes, variations from statutory tax rates (including treatment of investment tax credits), operating loss and tax credit carryforwards, and information about tax aspects of subsidiaries or investments. The auditor must also be satisfied that tax exposures not provided for in the financial statements but requiring disclosure under SFAS No. 5 are properly set forth in the notes to the financial statements. In addition, public companies are subject to specific disclosure requirements of the Securities and Exchange Commission.

The efficiency of the audit of income tax accounts can be enhanced by collecting, in the course of examining other accounts, data that may be useful in examining the tax accrual. Examples include collecting tax depreciation data when auditing fixed asset accounts, and gathering officer compensation data when testing the payroll accounts. The auditor should analyze significant nonrecurring transactions to determine their impact on the tax accrual. Equally important from a client service standpoint, the auditor should be alert to tax planning and tax savings opportunities, and can help the client plan transactions to result in the most favorable tax treatment.

Taxes are usually audited through substantive tests; however, some control structures may be effective enough to allow the auditor to limit substantive tests or to perform certain substantive tests at an interim date.

Substantive Tests of Balances

Background Information. The auditor should review the tax returns and related correspondence for all "open" years (for a recurring engagement this means reviewing the most recent year and updating the understanding of earlier years). Often the review can be combined with the auditor's participation in the preparation of the prior year's tax return or the technical review of the client's preparation. If a revenue agent's examination is in process, the auditor should request from the client reports and memorandums related to the examination and should review and evaluate any issues set forth in them. The auditor should also ask the client about any other adjustments proposed by the agent. The auditor should determine whether the status of "open" tax years has been affected by extensions of the statute of limitations granted by the client.

An auditor is expected to have sufficient knowledge of the major taxing statutes to be able to evaluate the accrued liabilities for the various taxes a company is subject to. Accordingly, on a recurring engagement, the auditor must review changes in the tax laws and regulations and court decisions since the preceding audit and consider whether they apply to the company. It is extremely important that the auditor have sufficient expertise in tax matters to resolve all questions that arise; how much a tax specialist needs to be involved in the audit varies with the circumstances.

Summary Account Analysis. As the starting point in the audit of the tax accounts and to provide an orderly framework for testing, the auditor usually requests analyses of the tax accounts for the year. The analyses may be prepared as of an interim date and later updated to year-end, and should show, for each kind of tax (including each type of deferred tax) and for each year still "open," the beginning balance, accruals, payments, transfers or adjustments, and the ending balance. An example of an analysis of federal income taxes payable appears in Figure 5.6 in Chapter 5.

The auditor can then review the analyses, examine documents supporting transactions (to determine their existence or occurrence), and determine that prior-year overpayments and underpayments are properly identified (completeness), that deferred taxes are properly identified and computed (completeness and valuation), and that amounts currently payable are identified and scheduled for payment on the due dates (completeness and presentation). The appropriateness of the tax and accounting principles used and the mechanics of their application should also be substantiated (valuation). The level of detail the auditor examines in support of account balances and the extent to which normal business transactions (generated from other transaction cycles) are reviewed will depend on the auditor's assessment of inherent and control risk and the materiality of the accounts.

Often the auditor obtains or prepares a comparative summary of income and other tax account balances, ascertains that the summary is mathematically accurate, agrees the totals to the general ledger trial balance and the previous year's working papers, and traces significant reconciling items to supporting documentation.

Income Tax Payments and Refunds. Tax payments should be tested by examining assessment notices, correspondence with taxing authorities, canceled checks, and receipts, if available. The auditor should ascertain whether appropriate estimated taxes were paid during the year; support for refunds received should also be examined. In addition, the auditor should determine that the client reviewed assessments before making payments and that the payments were made on the due dates. If interest has been charged for late payment of tax, the period of charge should be ascertained and the calculations reviewed. The auditor should also compare taxes payable or refundable as shown on the tax returns filed for the previous year with the amounts recorded for that year and ascertain that any necessary accounting adjustments have been made. A schedule of carryover items from prior years should be prepared and the current impact of the items considered.

Income Tax Expense, Deferred Taxes, and Related Disclosures. The auditor should obtain or prepare a schedule showing the computation of the tax provision. The current and deferred tax liability accounts should be tested against the current and deferred tax computation. As mentioned earlier, it is normally efficient to gather the information required to prepare or review tax computations during the course of audit work on other accounts. Such information includes differences in tax and financial statement bases of many asset and liability accounts. For example, basis differences can be assembled when reviewing book and tax depreciation during the audit of fixed assets. Tax credits (such as foreign tax credits) and deductions (such as accelerated depreciation) based on special provisions of the law should be scrutinized and tested for compliance with the Internal Revenue Code. The auditor should test the mathematical accuracy of the schedule and determine that it includes consideration of all matters affecting the computation of income taxes currently payable or refundable. Beginning and ending balances should be traced to the summary of income taxes payable, and significant reconciling items should be traced to supporting documentation.

The schedule supporting the tax calculations should include a reconciliation of accounting income to taxable income; differences should be individually identified. The auditor should be particularly concerned about permanent differences, because of their direct effect on the amounts included in the provision for income taxes. In addition, if differences are significant, the auditor may review their nature and amounts for propriety and consistency with the prior year, agree amounts to supporting documentation in the working papers, and determine that the differences are accounted for properly.

The auditor should determine that the client has complied with requirements related to special tax status that may have been claimed. For example, favorable tax treatment may be available to certain entities, like real estate investment trusts, financial institutions, S Corporations, regulated investment companies, and Foreign Sales Corporations (FSCs). If the client claims status as one of those or similar types of enterprises, the auditor should ascertain that the client has in fact met the relevant eligibility requirements. Similarly, the auditor should test for compliance with federal tax documentation requirements regarding travel and entertainment expenditures, expenditures for charitable purposes, and other similar deductions.

In addition, the auditor should inquire about the status of all IRS examinations, examine revenue agents' reports for their effect on the prior and current years' tax provisions and financial statements (including necessary disclosures), and review the status of all tax disagreements. Adjustments to tax provisions for a previous year determined as a result of examinations by taxing authorities should be tested by examining the previous year's computations and any related correspondence.

The auditor must evaluate the adequacy of financial statement disclosures relating to income taxes as well as the propriety of the principles used to recognize and measure income taxes. Disclosures of accounting changes and significant uncertainties related to tax issues may be particularly sensitive matters. In addition, auditors of public companies must consider SEC disclosure requirements.

Estimated and Contingent Liabilities. It is often necessary to provide in the accounts for possible additional liability that might result from revenue agents' examinations of the current year's and prior years' returns. Although such liability may not become payable for a long time, it should be included in the tax liability and the provision for income taxes in the income statement, in accordance with SFAS No. 5. Prior-year estimates of tax provisions should be reassessed based on recent IRS or court decisions or interpretations. The amount of any "cushion" should be supported by a detailed listing of possible tax questions and potential liabilities. The auditor should evaluate the propriety of contingent amounts and assess the adequacy of the tax accrual in light of all pending tax matters.

The auditor, by exercising judgment and consulting tax specialists, must reach a conclusion about each of the issues affecting the tax liability. While the function of a tax specialist may end with the estimate of the liability, the auditor's responsibility goes further. The auditor must evaluate the adequacy of the evidence supporting the decisions made—whether any data or matters affecting taxes have been overlooked and whether the evidence is adequate in the circumstances. If the treatment and disclosure of taxes in the financial statements depend significantly on the intentions of management, it is generally appropriate to obtain written representation of those intentions in the client representation letter. For example, evidence of management's intentions may be needed to support a decision to provide or not to provide for taxes on the undistributed earnings of subsidiaries. Also, evidence must be present to support the tax basis of assets purchased in an acquisition in which the purchase price must be allocated.

The auditor's need to obtain sufficient competent evidence to support the income tax accrual has several implications. First, a mere statement of management's intentions that might affect the tax accrual is insufficient evidence. Management must have specific plans that the auditor can evaluate to determine that they are reasonable and feasible. Second, client restrictions that limit the auditor's access to information necessary to audit the tax accrual, possibly out of concern over IRS access to tax accrual working papers, may constitute a scope limitation and affect the auditor's ability to issue an unqualified opinion. (See an auditing interpretation of Section 326, *Evidential Matter* [AU Section 9326.06–.12], and the further discussion of IRS access to tax accrual working papers in Chapter 3.) Third, the opinion of the client's outside or in-house legal counsel on the adequacy of the tax accrual is not sufficient competent evidence to support an opinion on the financial statements. According to the auditing interpretation of Section 326 (AU Section 9326.13–.17), the auditor should not rely on a specialist in another discipline if the auditor possesses the necessary competence to assess the matter.

State and Local Taxes. Accruals for state and local income taxes (including franchise taxes based on income) are reviewed in much the same way as federal income tax accruals. The auditor should obtain or prepare an analysis for the year of deferred and accrued state and local income taxes, showing the computation of the provisions for the current year. He or she should test the mathematical accuracy of the analysis and trace applicable amounts to the general ledger, trial balance, and prior year's working papers. Significant reconciling items should be traced to supporting documentation. Support for payments made and refunds received during the year should be examined. The auditor should also compare the liability per the returns filed for the preceding year, the estimated liability recorded for that year, and the payments made to discharge that liability; evaluate the reasons for any differences; and determine that they have been appropriately accounted for. All state and local tax examinations should be reviewed, and the auditor should determine that appropriate provisions have been made for unresolved assessments.

DEBT AND EQUITY; INTEREST AND DIVIDENDS

The traditional distinction between debt and equity is clear in most businesses. Equity arises from owners' invested funds plus earnings retained and reinvested; debt is the result of borrowing funds for specific periods, both short and long term, although the individual loans are often renewed indefinitely. The distinctions among debt, equity, and other financing arrangements are often blurred, however. It is more realistic to view various debt, equity, lease, and other contractual arrangements as an array of alternatives that financial managers use to enhance the company's earnings record as well as its financial strength. Common stock is as much a financing instrument as bank loans, and convertible debt may have as many equity characteristics as preferred stock. Financial managers may adjust the legal characteristics of an instrument, whether formally designated as debt or equity, to achieve a desired (or required) balance between protecting principal and income and sharing the risks and rewards of ownership. Financial instruments may be designed to reconcile an enterprise's need for financial resources at minimal cost with investors' preferences for safety and rewards. The result is a virtually continuous spectrum of financing instruments, ranging from straight borrowing to borrowing with equity features, borrowing with variable income features, stock with preferences as to income and principal, common stock, and even promises of future stock. The Securities and Exchange Commission (SEC) and the Internal Revenue Service have from time to time addressed the distinctions among debt, equity, and other financing arrangements, and the subject continues to be of interest to those agencies and to auditors and users of financial statements.

The amount, type, and classification of financing appearing in a company's balance sheet are of concern to investors, lenders, bond rating agencies, and others who influence the supply of financial resources. It is therefore important to financial management. Over the years, a great deal of ingenuity has gone into designing financing that looks like something else, like disguising what were actually asset acquisitions as off-balance-sheet operating lease transactions. The Financial Accounting Standards Board (FASB) and its Emerging Issues Task Force (EITF) have since addressed many of those transactions, but auditors must constantly be alert to discern the substance of each transaction. If form is allowed to rule over substance, one or more audit objectives may not be achieved.

Transactions and accounts related to debt and equity include lessee accounting for capital leases, interest expense, debt discount and premium, early extinguishment of debt (including gain or loss thereon), debt defeasance (and "in substance" defeasance), troubled debt restructuring, product financing arrangements, cash and stock dividends, stock splits, stock warrants, options and purchase plans, and treasury stock transactions. Many of these transactions and accounts involve special accounting measurement, presentation, and disclosure principles that require particular audit attention. Other matters with audit implications include short-term debt expected to be refinanced, debt covenants and security, compensating balance arrangements, debt conversion features, mandatory stock redemption requirements, and stock conversion features.

Audit Objectives

The auditor's objectives in examining debt and equity transactions and accounts are to obtain reasonable assurance that

- All obligations for notes payable, long-term debt, and capitalized leases and all equity accounts have been properly valued, classified, described, and disclosed.
- All off-balance-sheet obligations have been identified and considered (e.g., operating leases, product financing arrangements, take-or-pay contracts, and throughput contracts).
- All liability and equity transactions, accounts, and changes therein have been properly authorized and are obligations of the entity or ownership rights in the entity.
- Interest, discounts, premiums, dividends, and other debt-related and equity-related transactions and accounts have been properly valued, classified, described, and disclosed.
- All terms, requirements, instructions, commitments, and other debt-related and equity-related matters have been identified, complied with, and disclosed, as appropriate.

Substantive Tests of Balances

The following discussion applies to all kinds of financing transactions unless clearly inapplicable in the context or specified in the discussion. A convenient way to document substantive tests of the various kinds of financing transactions and accounts is an account analysis working paper, that is, a list of the notes, debt issues, or equities outstanding at the beginning of a period, and the additions, reductions, and outstanding amounts at the end of the period. Often the list can be carried forward from year to year if changes are infrequent. It may incorporate all pertinent information about the financing instruments, or that information may be summarized separately. The auditor should compare the list with the accounts and reconcile the total to the general ledger. The list can also be used to document other audit tests performed.

Tests of details of debt and equity transactions and balances consist of obtaining confirmations from third parties, reperforming computations, and examining documents and records. The following are some examples:

Confirmations—debt payable and terms with holder; outstanding stock with holder and registrar; authorized stock with the Secretary of State of the state in which the entity is incorporated; treasury stock with safekeeping agent; and dividend and interest payments with disbursing agent.

Reperformance of computations—debt discount or premium, interest, gains or losses on debt extinguishment, stock issuances and purchases, and dividends.

Examining documents and records—debt and stock issuances and retirements, and interest and dividend payments to registrar; unissued debt and stock instruments (as partial substantiation of the completeness of recorded outstanding instruments).

Common Substantive Tests of Debt and Equity Accounts. The auditor should trace authorization for all types of financing to a vote of the board of directors. If the directors have delegated authority for the details of financing, individual transactions should be traced to the authorizing officer's signature.

The auditor should read financing instruments carefully to be sure that the financing is properly classified and described in the financial statements. The instruments should be examined for commitments, which often accompany financing arrangements, and evidence of rights given or received, which might require accounting recognition and/or disclosure. Often an instrument is designed to achieve a desired accounting and tax result; it is good practice for clients to seek the auditor's interpretation of accounting and disclosure implications of financing instruments before they are executed. Once the accounting and disclosure implications have been analyzed and understood, it is usually possible to set up a worksheet that can be carried forward from year to year for computing and documenting compliance with pertinent commitments and covenants.

If financing is in the form of a lease, the terms must be evaluated to determine whether it should be accounted for as an operating or a capital lease. If leases are capitalized, the auditor should test computations of the carrying amounts of assets and debt, and compare the terms with the underlying lease contract.

The auditor should trace the recording of cash receipts and payments from financing and related activities into the accounts and compare those transactions with the authorization and terms of the instrument for timing and amount. Paid notes should be examined for evidence of proper authorization, documentation, and cancellation; the mathematical accuracy of interest expense, accrued interest, and dividends declared should be tested; in some circumstances, the auditor may recompute the amounts.

The auditor often confirms outstanding balances, usually at year-end, with holders of notes and issuers of lines of credit, trustees under bond and debenture indentures, and registrars and transfer agents for stock issues. Authorized stock often must be recorded with the Secretary of State in the state of incorporation, and the auditor may request confirmation from that office. Treasury stock should be confirmed with the custodian, or, if there is no custodian, the auditor should examine the certificates in the presence of client personnel.

If several types of financing are outstanding, the auditor should compare transactions in each with restrictions and provisions of the others. Dividend payments may be restricted by bond and note indentures; dividends on common stock may be affected by the rights of preferred stockholders or their rights may change with changes in capital structure or retained earnings accounts; certain transactions may require the consent of holders of senior securities, and so on. It is essential that the client determine and the auditor review the restrictive provisions of the various agreements and determine whether disclosure in the financial statements is appropriate.

The client's reconciliation of detailed stock ledgers to the control account should be reviewed and tested. Accounting for unissued, issued, and canceled certificates should be similarly tested.

The auditor may reperform computations of shares reserved for issuance on exercise of options and warrants or conversion of convertible securities and of the basis for valuing stock dividends and splits. In testing those computations, the auditor should pay close attention to the interrelated effects of one issue on another and on the total amount of each issue authorized and outstanding. The accuracy of accounting for warrants, options, and conversion privileges exercised can often be reviewed by an overall computation based on the terms of the related instruments.

If the interest rate of a financing instrument is not clearly the going market rate for that type of instrument at time of issuance, the auditor should evaluate the reasonableness of the interest rate in terms of the requirements of APB Opinion No. 21, *Interest on Receivables and Payables* (Accounting Standards Section I69), and document the evaluation in the working papers. If the interest rate must be imputed, the documentation for the imputed rate may be carried forward from year to year.

Debt Covenants. Debt agreements often contain covenants or provisions requiring the borrower to meet certain standards (e.g., specified levels of working capital and income) and to provide the lender with periodic information. These provisions are referred to as positive covenants. Positive covenants may also require the borrower to provide the lender with periodic financial statements, market values of pledged properties, or other internally generated reports. In addition, the borrower is often required to comply with various negative covenants (like limitations on capital expenditures, officers' salaries, and dividends) and to present its financial statements in accordance with generally accepted accounting principles (GAAP). Some debt agreements may contain cross-default provisions, which could result in acceleration of the lender's right of repayment because of default under or violation of other agreements. Violations of covenants or provisions, unless waived by the lender, usually require the borrower to classify the debt obligation as a current liability. The auditor should test for compliance with debt covenants at all applicable dates during the year, as well as at year-end.

Initial Audits. In an initial audit, the auditor should review the corporation's charter or articles of incorporation, bylaws, and all pertinent amendments. The articles of incorporation contain information about the classes of stock the enterprise is empowered to issue and the number of authorized shares in each class. Once this information is obtained, it can be kept in a permanent file; the articles of incorporation need not be read each year. How extensively the auditor reviews prior years' minutes of meetings of the board of directors and stockholders, other documents, and capital stock accounts depends on the circumstances and whether the financial statements were previously audited.

The auditor should also analyze the additional paid-in capital and retained earnings accounts from the corporation's inception to determine whether all entries were in conformity with GAAP then prevailing. If, however, previous audits have been made, the procedures may be limited to a review of analyses made by the predecessor auditors. Entries in those accounts should also be reviewed for consistency of treatment from year to year. The analyses of additional paid-in capital accounts should segregate the balances by classes of stock outstanding.

Permanent Files. The auditor should include in the permanent working paper files information about the kinds of stock authorized, the number of shares of each class authorized, par or stated values, provisions concerning dividend rates, redemption values, priority rights to dividends and in liquidation, cumulative or noncumulative rights to dividends, participation or conversion privileges, and other pertinent data. The auditor should also retain the analyses of additional paid-in capital and retained earnings in the permanent files so that changes in the current year may be readily compared with those in previous years.

Tests Unique to Stockholders' Equity Accounts. Since analyses of stockholders' equity accounts appear in the financial statements and are subject to detailed scrutiny by security analysts and others, the auditor should ordinarily perform detailed substantive tests of changes in those accounts. Some entries, like appropriations of retained earnings, are simply traced to the authorization by the board of directors. Other entries summarize a large volume of individual transactions and can be tested by means of an overall computation based on the authorizing instrument or vote of the directors. Still other entries—the most common example is the exercise of stock options that were granted in the past at various times and prices—are an aggregation of unique transactions and are best audited by examining the underlying authorization of the transactions and reperforming the calculations, as well as reconciling beginning and ending balances with the activity for the year. Each type of entry should be evaluated for compliance with loan agreements or other restrictive covenants or commitments.

The auditor should review the terms of outstanding stock subscriptions and perform enough tests of activity and balances to obtain reasonable assurance that they are being complied with. Outstanding stock subscriptions receivable preferably should be confirmed. Such receivables (whether for shares already issued or to be issued) typically are deducted from capital stock issued or subscribed, as appropriate, and additional paid-in capital; this accounting is required for SEC registrants.

Tests Unique to Dividends. The auditor should determine whether cash dividends, stock dividends and splits (including reverse splits), dividends payable in scrip, and dividends payable in assets other than cash have been properly accounted for. One of an auditor's responsibilities is to form an opinion on whether the intentions of the board, as indicated in the resolutions authorizing dividends, are properly reflected in the financial statements.

Covenants of debentures and other debt and equity instruments often restrict the payment of cash dividends in some way (e.g., to earnings subsequent to the date of the instrument). The auditor should ascertain that dividend declarations do not exceed the amount of retained earnings available for dividends, and that the amount of unrestricted retained earnings has been properly calculated in accordance with the debt covenants or other restrictions and has been appropriately disclosed.

Review Questions

Investments

16–1. State the audit objectives for investment accounts.

16–2. What income statement accounts should be considered when auditing investments?

16–3. What are some typical reasons for differences between the count of securities and the list of securities prepared by the client?

16–4. What actions should an auditor take if (a) past-due interest coupons are still attached to bonds, or (b) coupons are missing when the bonds are inspected?

16–5. What procedures should the auditor follow if the entire portfolio of securities is in the custody of a reliable financial institution?

16–6. What procedures should be followed to determine whether securities have been pledged as collateral?

Prepaid expenses, estimated and accrued liabilities, and related expenses

16–7. What characteristics distinguish prepaid expenses from deferred charges?

16–8. How do agency obligations differ from accrued liabilities?

16–9. What are the audit objectives for prepaid expenses? For accrued liabilities?

16–10. With respect to prepaid expenses and accrued liabilities

What types of substantive tests of details are performed?
What types of analytical procedures are applicable?

16–11. What auditing procedures are generally applied to prepaid insurance?

16–12. What responsibility does the auditor have with respect to insurance coverage?

16–13. Explain the auditing procedures generally followed with respect to

a. Prepaid and accrued property taxes.

b. Prepaid and accrued commissions.
c. Employee advances.

16–14. What auditing procedures are generally followed with respect to royalties payable?

16–15. What are suspense accounts and how does the auditor deal with them?

16–16. What auditing procedures are generally followed with respect to accrued pension costs?

Income taxes

16–17. What are the audit objectives with respect to income taxes?

16–18. Describe in general terms auditing procedures that are typically applied in evaluating the appropriateness of a company's income tax liability.

16–19. Why is it important for an auditor to examine prior years' tax returns examined by taxing authorities (and agents' reports)? Those not yet examined by taxing authorities?

16–20. Briefly describe the auditing procedures used with respect to state and local tax accruals.

Debt and equity; interest and dividends

16–21. What are the audit objectives with respect to debt and equity accounts?

16–22. Why are debt covenants significant to accountants and auditors?

16–23. What are the major substantive tests of details used for debt and equity accounts?

16–24. Of what concern to an auditor is the interest rate of a financing instrument?

16–25. What information related to equity accounts should be included in the permanent working paper files?

Discussion Questions

Investments

16–30. Give substantive procedures for the audit of the transactions in a sinking fund for the redemption of bonds, if the fund is in the custody of an independent trustee.

16–31. A corporation temporarily invested some of its excess funds in stocks of other companies listed on established exchanges. In the course of your preliminary audit work you ascertain that all such stocks were acquired through a brokerage firm at various dates during the year under audit, and that the stock certificates are in the name of the corporation (your client) but are being held in safekeeping by the brokerage firm. The corporation does not maintain an investment ledger.

Required:

Outline the auditing procedures for stocks and income therefrom.

16–32. Explain how you would obtain evidence that all investment income to which a company is entitled has been recorded. Assume that the company has a sizable portfolio of marketable stocks and bonds (some of which do not have market prices) invested to utilize excess working capital, and a fairly good internal control structure. Explain how you would determine appropriate valuations at year-end, indicating the sources you would use.

Prepaid expenses, estimated and accrued liabilities, and related expenses

16-33. In an audit of the financial statements of a manufacturing company, what types of information, obtained from an examination of fire insurance policies (in which your client is named as the insured) and the company's insurance register, would you include in your working papers?

For what purpose or purposes should the auditor examine fire insurance policies?

16-34. If a client's accrual for property taxes is based on estimates, what audit steps can be performed to substantiate the amount of the liability?

16-35. Why would an auditor want to audit individual accrued liability accounts even though the account balances were insignificant?

16-36. What are some possible auditing procedures that would help the auditor address the completeness audit objective for accrued liability balances?

Income taxes

16-37. Your client has not provided for deferred taxes on the difference between accelerated depreciation (which is used for tax purposes) and straight-line depreciation (which is used for financial statement purposes). This position is based on the theory that when the same type of temporary differences recur in subsequent periods (thus offsetting the reversal of earlier differences), the practical effect is an indefinite postponement of taxes. Hence, the effect is similar to a permanent difference and no interperiod allocation is required.

What is your position regarding this practice? What effect will your position have on your audit of the provision for income taxes?

16-38. The provision for possible additional tax liabilities that might result from revenue agents' examinations is normally included in the current liability account even though it may not be payable for some time.

a. Why is this appropriate?
b. Discuss the appropriate treatment of this ''cushion'' when the revenue agent's examination of tax returns for all prior years has been completed with no additional assessment required.

Debt and equity; interest and dividends

16-39. Outline the auditing procedures for substantiating the issued capital stock of a corporation that does not employ an outside registrar or transfer agent, which you are auditing for the first time.

AICPA Multiple Choice Questions

These questions are taken from the Auditing part of Uniform CPA Examinations. Choose the single most appropriate answer.

Investments

16–40. Which of the following is *not* one of the auditor's primary objectives in auditing marketable securities?

a. To determine whether securities are authentic.
b. To determine whether securities are the property of the client.
c. To determine whether securities actually exist.
d. To determine whether securities are properly classified on the balance sheet.

16–41. The auditor should insist that a representative of the client be present during the physical examination of securities in order to

a. Lend authority to the auditor's directives.
b. Detect forged securities.
c. Coordinate the return of all securities to proper locations.
d. Acknowledge the receipt of securities returned.

16–42. An auditor would most likely substantiate the interest earned on bond investments by

a. Vouching the receipt and deposit of interest checks.
b. Confirming the bond interest rate with the issuer of the bonds.
c. Recomputing the interest earned on the basis of face amount, interest rate, and period held.
d. Testing the internal controls over cash receipts.

16–43. To establish the existence and ownership of a long-term investment in the common stock of a publicly traded company, an auditor ordinarily performs a security count or

a. Tests the client's internal control structure to obtain reasonable assurance that the control procedures are being applied as prescribed.
b. Confirms the number of shares owned that are held by an independent custodian.
c. Determines the market price per share at the balance sheet date from published quotations.
d. Confirms the number of shares owned with the issuing company.

16–44. Which of the following is the most effective audit procedure for substantiating dividends earned on investments in marketable equity securities?

a. Tracing deposit of dividend checks to the cash receipts book.
b. Reconciling amounts received with published dividend records.
c. Comparing the amounts received with preceding year dividends received.
d. Recomputing selected extensions and footings of dividend schedules and comparing totals to the general ledger.

Prepaid expenses, estimated and accrued liabilities, and related expenses

16–45. The audit procedures used to substantiate accrued liabilities differ from those employed for accounts payable because

a. Accrued liabilities usually pertain to services of a continuing nature while accounts payable are the result of completed transactions.
b. Accrued liability balances are less material than accounts payable balances.

c. Evidence supporting accrued liabilities is nonexistent while evidence supporting accounts payable is readily available.
d. Accrued liabilities at year-end will become accounts payable during the following year.

16–46. Which of the following audit procedures is *least* likely to detect an unrecorded liability?

a. Analysis and recomputation of interest expense.
b. Analysis and recomputation of depreciation expense.
c. Mailing of standard bank confirmation form.
d. Reading of the minutes of meetings of the board of directors.

16–47. The auditor is *most* likely to substantiate accrued commissions payable in conjunction with the

a. Sales cutoff review.
b. Verification of contingent liabilities.
c. Review of post balance sheet date disbursements.
d. Examination of trade accounts payable.

Debt and equity; interest and dividends

16–48. When a company has treasury stock certificates on hand, a year-end count of the certificates by the auditor is

a. Required when the company classifies treasury stock with other assets.
b. Not required if treasury stock is a deduction from stockholders' equity.
c. Required when the company had treasury stock transactions during the year.
d. Always required.

16–49. In connection with the audit of a current issue of long-term bonds payable, the auditor should

a. Determine whether bondholders are persons other than owners, directors, or officers of the company issuing the bond.
b. Calculate the effective interest rate to see if it is substantially the same as the rates for similar issues.
c. Decide whether the bond issue was made without violating state or local law.
d. Ascertain that the client has obtained the opinion of counsel on the legality of the issue.

16–50. An auditor's client has violated a minor requirement of its bond indenture, which could result in the trustee requiring immediate payment of the principal amount due. The client refuses to seek a waiver from the bond trustee. Request for immediate payment is *not* considered likely. Under these circumstances the auditor must

a. Require classification of bonds payable as a current liability.
b. Contact the bond trustee directly.
c. Disclose the situation in the auditor's report.
d. Obtain an opinion from the company's attorney as to the likelihood of the trustee's enforcement of the requirement.

16–51. An auditor's program for the audit of long-term debt should include steps that require the

a. Inspection of the accounts payable subsidiary ledger.
b. Investigation of credits to the bond interest income account.
c. Verification of the existence of the bondholders.
d. Examination of any bond trust indenture.

16–52. An auditor should trace corporate stock issuances and treasury stock transactions to the

a. Numbered stock certificates.
b. Articles of incorporation.
c. Transfer agent's records.
d. Minutes of the board of directors.

Problems and Cases

Investments

16–60. You were engaged to audit the financial statements of Kallomar Corporation for the year ended June 30, 1990.

On May 1, the Corporation borrowed $500,000 from Mainland Bank to finance plant expansion. Because of unexpected difficulties in acquiring the building site, the plant expansion had not begun at June 30. To make use of the borrowed funds, management decided to invest in stocks and bonds, and on May 16, the $500,000 was invested in securities.

Required:

a. How could you substantiate the security position of Kallomar at June 30?
b. In your audit of investments, how would you accomplish the following?
   1. Substantiate the dividend or interest income recorded.
   2. Determine market value.
   3. Establish the authority for security purchases.

(AICPA adapted)

16–61. On January 1, 1990 your client owned 1000 shares of BBT Corp. capital stock, which were purchased April 15, 1988. During 1990 the following purchases and sales were effected:

Purchases: March 1, 500 shares; June 29, 300 shares
Sales: March 23, 150 shares; September 28, 200 shares.

Examination of a dividend service revealed the following dividend record:

BBT Corp., Cap. (par $0.10)

Amount of Div'd.	*Date Declared*	*Ex-div'd. Date*	*Stock of Record*	*Payment Date*
$0.20	12/21/89	12/28/89	12/30/89	1/13/90
10%[a] stock	2/ 1/90	2/21/90	2/24/90	3/10/90
0.20	3/ 1/90	3/22/90	3/24/90	4/ 7/90
0.25	6/21/90	6/28/90	6/30/90	7/14/90
20%[b] stock	9/20/90	9/28/90	10/ 2/90	10/16/90
0.30	9/20/90	9/28/90	10/ 2/90	10/16/90
0.37-1/2	12/20/90	12/28/90	1/ 2/91	1/15/91

[a]Fractions paid in cash at rate of $0.75 for each 1/10 of a share.
[b]Fractions paid in cash at rate of $1.75 for each 1/5 of a share.

Required:
Prepare a worksheet to calculate the following:

a. Dividend income for the year 1990, on an accrual basis (use ex-dividend date).
b. Cash dividend receipts that should be traced to the books for the 1990 audit.
c. The number of shares for which stock certificates should be examined on the date of the cash count and cutoff, January 12, 1991.

16–62. The schedule on page 690 was prepared by the controller of Hawthorne Corp. for use by the independent auditors during their audit of Hawthorne's year-end financial statements. All procedures performed by the audit assistant were noted at the bottom "legend" section, and the schedule was properly initialed, dated, and indexed and then submitted to a senior member of the audit staff for review. The internal control structure was tested and assessed to be effective.

Required:

a. What information that is essential to the audit of marketable securities is missing from this schedule?
b. What essential auditing procedures were not noted as having been performed by the audit assistant?

(AICPA adapted)

16–63. In connection with her audit of the financial statements of Greentrees, Inc., Kathy Lansing, CPA, is considering the necessity of inspecting marketable securities on the balance sheet date, May 31, 1989, or at some other date. The marketable securities held by Greentrees include negotiable bearer bonds, which are kept in a safe in the treasurer's office, and miscellaneous stocks and bonds kept in a safe deposit box at First County Bank. Both the negotiable bearer bonds and the miscellaneous stocks and bonds are material to proper presentation of Greentrees' financial position.

Required:

a. What are the factors that Ms. Lansing should consider in determining the necessity for inspecting these securities on May 31, 1989, as opposed to other dates?

Hawthorne Corp.
Marketable Securities
Year Ended December 31, 1990

Description of Security			Serial No.	Face Value of Bonds	Gen. Ledger 1/1	Purch. in 1990	Sold in 1990	Cost	Gen. Ledger 12/31	12/31 Market	Dividends and Interest: Pay Date(s)	Dividends and Interest: Amt. Rec.	Accruals 12/31
Corp. Bonds	***%***	***Yr. Due***											
											1/15	300 b,d	
A	6	00	21-7	10000	9400 a				9400	9100	7/15	300 b,d	275
D	4	91	73-0	30000	27500 a				27500	26220	12/1	1200 b,d	100
G	9	08	16-4	5000	4000 a				4000	5080	8/1	450 b,d	188
Rc	5	95	08-2	70000	66000 a		57000b	66000					
Sc	10	09	07-4	100000		100000 e			100000	101250	7/1	5000 b,d	5000
					106900	100000	57000	66000	140900	141650		7250	5563
					a,f	f	f	f	f,g	f		f	f
Stocks													
											3/1	750 b,d	
P 1000 shs.			1044		7500 a				7500	7600	6/1	750 b,d	
Common											9/1	750 b,d	
											12/1	750 b,d	250
U 50 shs.			8530		9700 a				9700	9800	2/1	800 b,d	
Common											8/1	800 b,d	667
					17200				17200	17400		4600	917
					a,f				f,g	f		f	f

Legends and Comments Relative to Above

a = Beginning balances agreed to 1989 working papers
b = Traced to cash receipts
c = Minutes examined (purchase and sale approved by the board of directors)
d = Agreed to 1099
e = Examined broker's advice
f = Totals footed
g = Agreed to general ledger

b. Assume that Ms. Lansing plans to send a member of her staff to Greentrees' offices and First County Bank on May 31, 1989, to make the security inspection. What instructions should she give to this staff member as to the conduct of the inspection and the evidence to be included in the audit working papers? (*Note*: Do not discuss the valuation of securities, the income from securities, or the examination of information contained in the books and records of the Company.)

c. Assume that Ms. Lansing finds it impracticable to send a member of her staff to Greentrees' offices and First County Bank on May 31, 1989. What alternative procedures may she employ to assure herself that the Company had physical possession of its marketable securities on May 31, 1989, if the securities are inspected (1) May 27, 1989? (2) June 6, 1989?

(AICPA adapted)

Prepaid expenses, estimated and accrued liabilities, and related expenses

16-64. The Convenience Company manufactures household appliances that are sold through independent franchised retail dealers. The electric motors in the appliances are guaranteed for five years from the date of sale of the appliances to the consumer. Under the guarantee, defective motors are replaced by the dealers without charge.

Inventories of replacement motors are kept in the dealers' stores and are carried at cost in the Convenience Company's records. When a dealer replaces a defective motor, the factory is notified and the defective motor is returned to the factory for reconditioning. After the defective motor is received by the factory, the dealer's account is credited with an agreed fee for the replacement service.

When the appliance is brought to the dealer after the guarantee period has elapsed, the dealer charges the owner for installing the new motor. The dealer notifies the factory of the installation and returns the replaced motor for reconditioning. The motor installed is then charged to the dealer's account at a price in excess of its inventory value. In this instance, to encourage the return of replaced motors, the dealer's account is credited with a nominal value for the returned motor.

Dealers submit quarterly inventory reports of the motors on hand. The reports are later verified by factory salespeople. Dealers are billed for inventory shortages determined by comparison of the dealers' inventory reports with the factory's perpetual records of the dealers' inventories. The dealers order additional motors as they need them. One motor is used for all appliances in a given year, but the motors are changed in basic design each model year.

The Convenience Company has established an account, Estimated Liability for Product Guarantees, in connection with the guarantees. An amount representing the estimated guarantee cost prorated by sales unit is credited to the Estimated Liability account for each appliance sold, and the debit is charged to an expense account. The Estimated Liability account is debited for the service fees credited to the dealers' accounts and for the inventory cost of motors installed under the guarantees.

The engineering department keeps statistical records of the number of units of each model sold in each year and the replacements that were made. The effect of improvements in design and construction is under continual study by the engineering department, and the estimated guarantee cost by unit is adjusted annually on the basis of experience and improvements in design. Experience shows that, for a given motor model, the number of guarantees made good varies widely from year to year during the guarantee period, but the total number of guarantees to be made good can be reliably predicted.

Required:

a. Prepare an audit program to satisfy yourself as to the propriety of transactions recorded in the Estimated Liability for Product Guarantees account for the year ended December 31, 1989.
b. Prepare the worksheet format that would be used to test the adequacy of the balance in the Estimated Liability for Product Guarantees account. The worksheet column headings should describe clearly the data to be inserted in the columns.

(AICPA adapted)

16–65. You are engaged in an audit of the financial statements of Millman Company for the year ended December 31, 1990. You have examined all of the insurance policies (as listed) that were in force during the year.

Policy No.	*Kind*	*Coverage*	*Term*	*Premium*
General Casualty Insurance Co.:				
N-30393	Fire on contents	4 million	5/25/90–5/25/91	$ 9,000.00
First Surety Company:				
DF1274027	Forgery	300M	6/8/90–6/8/93	1,725.00
LO31487	Forgery	300M	6/8/89–6/8/90	690.00
Federal Insurance Co.:				
206271[a]	Workmen's compensation		6/26/89–6/26/90	1,824.00 (deposit)
228631	Workmen's compensation		6/26/90–6/26/91	2,436.00 (deposit)
Capitol Insurance Co.:				
3260945	Auto liability	500M–1 million	4/22/90–4/22/91	13,524.00
	Property damage	50M	4/22/90–4/22/91	302.00
Commuters Insurance Co.:				
NY96292	Auto fire, theft, collision	500M	4/25/90–4/25/91	30,000.00[b]

[a]Assessment of $923.00 for year ended 6/26/90 paid 1/8/91.
[b]Return premium of $5,000 received 5/15/90 because of change in rate.

Required:

Prepare a working paper to indicate the auditing procedures applied to the prepaid insurance and insurance expense accounts. Compute prepaid balances to the nearest half month. Indicate all auditing procedures required to be followed.

Income taxes

16–66. You happen to come across an article in the *Wall Street Journal* indicating that the Internal Revenue Service has settled a dispute with a large company regarding its tax treatment of certain items. As a result, the company was assessed a substantial additional tax liability. Your client, Tyngate Corporation, currently uses the same disputed treatment for similar items. Discuss how this situation will affect your audit strategy for taxes for your client.

16–67. Shelley Company does business in all 50 states in the United States. However, you discover while speaking with the controller that state tax returns are filed in only 30 states. Discuss the impact of this finding on the audit of Shelley Company. Describe additional procedures that you feel may be necessary in the circumstances.

Debt and equity; interest and dividends

16–68. You were engaged to audit the financial statements of Kallomar Corporation for the year ended June 30, 1990.

On May 1, 1990, the Corporation borrowed $500,000 from Mainland Bank to finance plant expansion. The long-term note agreement provided for the annual payment of principal and interest over five years. The existing plant was pledged as security for the loan.

Required:

a. What are the audit objectives for long-term debt?
b. Prepare an audit program for the long-term note agreement between Kallomar and Mainland Bank.

(AICPA adapted)

16–69. In auditing a corporation that has a bond issue outstanding, the trust indenture is reviewed and a confirmation as to the issue is obtained from the trustee. List the matters of importance to the auditor that might be found either in the indenture or in the confirmation obtained from the trustee. Explain briefly the reason for the auditor's interest in each of the items.

16–70. You are engaged in the audit of a corporation whose records have not previously been audited by you. The corporation has both an independent transfer agent and a registrar for its capital stock. The transfer agent maintains the record of stockholders, and the registrar is responsible for seeing that there is no overissue of stock. Signatures of both are required to validate stock certificates.

It has been proposed that confirmations be obtained from both the transfer agent and the registrar as to the stock outstanding at the balance sheet date. If such confirmations agree with the books, no additional work is to be performed as to capital stock.

Required:

If you agree that obtaining confirmations would be sufficient in this situation, give the justification for your position. If you do not agree, state specifically all additional steps you would take and explain your reasons for taking them.

16–71. You are assigned to a new client, Fennimore Manufacturing, whose principal business is the manufacture of custom cutting machines for various commercial applications. On a plant tour of its facilities you observe seven high-cost, new tool-and-die machines, which you learn have been acquired during this year. At year-end, you review the client's fixed asset and debt schedules and become aware that the additions do not appear as assets and related liabilities.

Required:

Discuss the client's apparent incorrect treatment of these transactions and the procedures necessary in these circumstances to obtain reasonable assurance that all obligations are properly valued, classified, and disclosed.

16–72. The following covenants are extracted from the indenture of a bond issue. The indenture provides that failure to comply with its terms in any respect automatically advances the due date of the loan to the date of noncompliance (the maturity date is 20 years hence in the absence of any acts of default).

1. "The debtor company shall endeavor to maintain a working capital ratio of 2 to 1 at all times, and in any fiscal year following a failure to maintain said ratio, the company shall restrict compensation of officers to a total of $100,000. Officers for this purpose shall include chairman of the board of directors, president, all vice presidents, secretary, and treasurer."
2. "The debtor company shall keep all property that is security for this debt insured against loss by fire to the extent of 100 percent of its actual value. Policies of insurance comprising this protection shall be filed with the trustee."
3. "The debtor company shall pay all taxes legally assessed against property that is security for this debt within the time provided by law for payment without penalty and shall deposit receipted tax bills or equally acceptable evidence of payment of same with the trustee."
4. "A sinking fund shall be deposited with the trustee by semiannual payments of $300,000, from which the trustee shall, in his discretion, purchase bonds of this issue."

Required:

Give any audit steps or reporting requirements you believe should be taken or recognized in connection with each one of the covenants.

(AICPA adapted)

PART 4

Completing the Work and Reporting the Results

17

Completing the Audit

This chapter deals with auditing procedures and considerations that are part of the completion phase of an audit but are not related to specific transaction cycles or accounts. The completion phase takes place primarily after the balance sheet date. These procedures entail many subjective decisions requiring judgment and experience, and thus are usually performed by the senior members of the engagement team.

The judgments made during this phase of an audit are often crucial to the ultimate outcome of the engagement. Accordingly, the procedures employed should reflect the auditor's assessment of the risks associated with the business and the financial statements. The procedures covered in this chapter often bring to light matters that are of major concern in forming an opinion on the financial statements.

First, procedures performed at the end of the audit, including tests for contingent liabilities, are described, followed by a discussion and illustrations of lawyers' letters (dealing with litigation, claims, and assessments) and client representation letters. The critical process of summarizing and evaluating the audit findings is described next, and two review functions performed during the completion phase of the audit—the working paper review and the review of the financial statements for appropriate disclosure—are discussed. Finally, the auditor's responsibilities for subsequent events are presented, the administrative details that remain to be taken care of at the end of an engagement are described, and communicating with audit committees is discussed.

PROCEDURES PERFORMED AT THE CONCLUSION OF THE AUDIT

Analytical Procedures

As noted in Chapter 9, Statement on Auditing Standards (SAS) No. 56, *Analytical Procedures* (AU Section 329), requires the auditor to perform analytical procedures as a final review of the financial statements at or near the end of the audit. The objective of analytical procedures used at this stage is to help the auditor assess the conclusions reached during the audit and form an opinion on the financial statements. The final review generally includes reading the statements and notes, and considering (a) whether the information and explanations gathered in response to unusual or unexpected balances or relationships previously identified are adequate, and (b) whether there are unusual or unexpected balances or relationships that were not previously identified. The auditor may use a variety of analytical procedures (as described in Chapter 9) in making this overall review. Those procedures may provide added evidence that the financial statements are not materially misstated because of undetected errors or irregularities; or, they may indicate the need for additional auditing procedures before the report on the financial statements is issued.

Reading Minutes of Meetings

Reading the minutes of meetings of the board of directors and its important committees enables the auditor to examine the board's approval of management's significant actions and to determine whether significant decisions that affect the financial statements or require disclosure in the notes have been appropriately reflected. Often the auditor reads minutes of meetings shortly after the meetings or during the early stage of the year-end field work. This allows the auditor to amend the audit testing plan, if necessary, for actions taken by the board or a board committee. For example, the board's authorizing the disposal of a segment of the business could significantly affect the audit testing plan. The auditor should be satisfied that copies of minutes of all meetings held during the period have been provided, including meetings held after year-end but before the date of the audit report. If minutes were not prepared and approved for meetings held shortly before the date of the audit report, the auditor should inquire of the secretary of the board or the committee about actions taken. This inquiry should be documented in the working papers.

Tests for Contingent Liabilities

A contingency may be defined as an existing condition, situation, or set of circumstances involving uncertainty as to possible gain (gain contingency) or loss (loss contingency) that will be resolved when one or more future events occur or fail to occur.

Accounting Overview. Contingencies that might result in gains, such as claims against others for patent infringement, usually are not recorded until realized. They should be adequately disclosed in the notes to the financial statements; however, misleading implications as to the likelihood of their realization should be avoided.

In many cases, the existence of a loss contingency results in a charge to income and the recording of a liability, for example, a probable loss resulting from the guarantee of the indebtedness of others or an obligation relating to a product warranty or defect. In other cases, such as a probable loss from uncollectible receivables, the existence of a loss contingency results in the write-down of an asset (often by means of an allowance account) and a charge to income. Still other loss contingencies result only in financial statement disclosure; an example would be litigation whose outcome is uncertain. (Loss contingencies arising from litigation, claims, and assessments are discussed in detail in the next section of this chapter.) Lastly, some loss contingencies need not be either accrued (recorded) or disclosed, for example, the uninsured risk of property loss or damage from fire or other hazards. The following table summarizes the proper financial accounting and reporting for material loss contingencies.[1]

	Amount of Loss Can Be Reasonably Estimated	
Likelihood of Occurrence	*Yes*	*No*
Probable	Accrue; consider need to disclose	Disclose
Reasonably possible	Disclose	Disclose
Remote	Not accrued or disclosed	

Paragraph 3 of Statement of Financial Accounting Standards (SFAS) No. 5, *Accounting for Contingencies* (Accounting Standards Section C59.104), defines the ranges of likelihood of occurrence, as follows:

- *Probable.* The future event or events are likely to occur.
- *Reasonably possible.* The chance of the future event or events occurring is more than remote but less than likely.
- *Remote.* The chance of the future event or events occurring is slight.

When a material loss contingency involves an *unasserted* claim or assessment, disclosure is not required if there is no evidence that the assertion of a claim is probable. If it is considered probable that the claim will be asserted and there is a reasonable possibility that the outcome will be unfavorable, disclosure is required.

Auditing Procedures. Auditing loss contingencies is one of the most difficult aspects of many audits, and the variety of conditions encountered makes it impossible to describe the auditor's task definitively. Even in the best and most responsibly managed companies, a loss contingency requiring evaluation can be overlooked. Following is a description of the kinds of procedures the auditor usually undertakes to identify material loss contingencies.

The auditor should be alert for possible contingent liabilities while performing tests for unrecorded liabilities, described in Chapter 13. For example, when inspecting the minute books, contracts, and other documents, the auditor should be alert for matters indicating contingencies to be investigated. When inquiring of management about the existence of unrecorded liabilities, the auditor should also consider the possibility of loss contingencies. Management's statement about loss contingencies should be included in the representation letter, discussed later.

[1]Explanatory paragraphs in the auditor's report because of potential losses arising from uncertainties are discussed in Chapter 18.

An entity may have contingent liabilities for accounts receivable it has discounted, with recourse, with banks or other financial institutions. The auditor should be alert when performing other auditing procedures for indications of such transactions, for example, interest payments unrelated to recorded debt obligations, and should investigate them. An entity may also have guaranteed payment of the indebtedness of another entity, which may be an affiliate or a subsidiary or may be unrelated to the guarantor entity. The auditor should review the representation letter from management and corporate minutes and contractual arrangements, and inquire of officials of the guarantor about such contingent liabilities.

Although it is customary to insure against liability for damages claimed by employees and the public, insurance policies usually do not cover unlimited liabilities and not all companies carry adequate insurance against all potential claims. Furthermore, unusual claims for damages may arise from alleged breach of contract, failure to deliver goods, antitrust violations, existence of foreign substances in a company's product, and other causes. The auditor should inquire about possible liabilities of that general character. Possible sources of information include the client's inside and outside attorneys and its risk manager, risk consultants, and insurance agents or brokers who provide insurance coverage.

Auditors ordinarily must perform additional procedures to obtain sufficient competent evidential matter concerning litigation, claims, and assessments. Those procedures are discussed below.

LAWYERS' LETTERS

With respect to one particular group of loss contingencies— litigation, claims, and assessments—the auditor is required by paragraph 4 of Statement on Auditing Standards No. 12, *Inquiry of a Client's Lawyer Concerning Litigation, Claims, and Assessments* (AU Section 337.04), to obtain evidential matter related to the following matters:

a. The existence of a condition, situation, or set of circumstances indicating an uncertainty as to the possible loss to an entity arising from litigation, claims, and assessments.
b. The period in which the underlying cause for legal action occurred.
c. The probability of an unfavorable outcome.
d. The amount or range of potential loss.

The term "litigation, claims, and assessments" includes both pending and threatened litigation, claims, and assessments and unasserted claims and assessments.

Auditing Procedures

Management is responsible for adopting policies and procedures to identify, evaluate, and account for litigation, claims, and assessments. Accordingly, the auditor's procedures with respect to such matters should include

- Inquiring of management about its policies and procedures for identifying, evaluating, and accounting for litigation, claims, and assessments.
- Near the completion of field work, obtaining from management a description and evaluation of litigation, claims, and assessments as of the balance sheet date and during the period from the balance sheet date to the date the information is furnished.
- Examining documents related to litigation, claims, and assessments, including correspondence and invoices from lawyers.
- Requesting management to send a letter of audit inquiry to lawyers who were consulted concerning litigation, claims, and assessments.
- Obtaining assurance from management—preferably in the representation letter, discussed below—that all contingencies, including litigation, claims, and assessments, required to be disclosed by SFAS No. 5 have been disclosed and that all unasserted claims that counsel has advised management are probable of assertion and must be disclosed in accordance with SFAS No. 5 have been disclosed.

Procedures undertaken for different purposes, for example, reading minutes, contracts, agreements, leases, and correspondence with taxing authorities, may also disclose the existence of litigation, claims, and assessments.

Inquiry of a Client's Lawyer

The auditor can readily ascertain the existence of litigation, claims, and assessments when provisions for losses are recorded in the accounts. Also, while making routine audit inquiries and performing tests for unrecorded and contingent liabilities, the auditor may become aware of events that are likely to give or have given rise to litigation, claims, or assessments. Certain events, however, such as patent infringement or price fixing, may be more difficult to detect in an audit. As noted in SAS No. 54, *Illegal Acts by Clients* (AU Section 317.06), many laws or regulations "relate more to an entity's operating aspects than to its financial and accounting aspects, and their financial statement effect is indirect. An auditor ordinarily does not have sufficient basis for recognizing possible violations of such laws and regulations."

SAS No. 12 was issued in January 1976. At about the same time, the American Bar Association (ABA) issued a "Statement of Policy Regarding Lawyers' Responses to Auditors' Requests for Information," which is reproduced in Appendix C to SAS No. 12. These professional standards require the auditor, client, and lawyer all to become involved in determining which litigation, claims, and assessments need to be disclosed. As can be seen from the specimen letters of audit inquiry that appear in Appendix A to SAS No. 12 and in an interpretation of that SAS (AU Section 9337.10–.14), management is the primary source of information concerning litigation, claims, and assessments; the lawyer is expected to corroborate the completeness of the information supplied by management regarding pending or threatened litigation, claims, and assessments.

Specifically, SAS No. 12 (AU Section 337.09) requires, among other things, the following to be included in the client's letter of audit inquiry to the lawyer:

- A list prepared by management (or a request by management that the lawyer prepare a list) that describes and evaluates pending or threatened litigation, claims, and assessments with respect to which the lawyer has been engaged. When the list is prepared by the client, the lawyer's response should state that the list is complete (or identify any omissions) and comment on the client's evaluation.
- A list prepared by management (the lawyer will not prepare this list) that describes and evaluates unasserted claims, if any, that management considers to be probable of assertion, and that, if asserted, would have at least a reasonable possibility of an unfavorable outcome, with respect to which the lawyer has been engaged. The lawyer's response will not comment on the completeness of the list, but should comment on the client's descriptions and evaluations.

The lawyer should be informed in the client's letter of audit inquiry or, with the client's permission, in a separate letter from the auditor (illustrated in Figure 17.1), of management's assurance to the auditor concerning unasserted claims and assessments.

If the lawyer has formed a professional conclusion that the client should consider disclosure of an unasserted possible claim or assessment, the lawyer will, as a matter of professional responsibility to the client, consult with the client concerning the applicable requirements of SFAS No. 5. While the lawyer will not comment on the completeness of the client's list of unasserted claims, he or she will, at the client's request, confirm to the auditor this professional responsibility to the client.

If the lawyer disclaims responsibility for informing the auditor of any changes in the information reported to the auditor from the date of the response to the date of the auditor's report, it may be necessary to send a supplemental letter of audit inquiry. Factors to be considered in determining the need for a supplemental letter of audit inquiry include the length of time between the date of the response and the date of the auditor's report, the number and significance of matters included in the lawyer's response, the probability of more current developments related to matters included in the lawyer's response, and the reliability of the client's policies and procedures for

Figure 17.1 Specimen Letter to Inform Lawyer of Management's Assurance, When Not Included in Client's Letter of Audit Inquiry

[The Auditor's Letterhead]

(Date)

(Name and Address of Lawyer)

Gentlemen:

We are writing to inform you that (name of client) has represented to us that, with respect to the financial statements of (name of client) at (balance sheet date) and for the (period) then ended and excluding any matters listed in the letter of audit inquiry dated (date), (there are no unasserted possible claims or assessments that you have advised them are probable of assertion and must be disclosed in accordance with Statement of Financial Accounting Standards No. 5) or (the only unasserted possible claims or assessments that you have advised them are probable of assertion and must be disclosed in accordance with Statement of Financial Accounting Standards No. 5 are the following: [list]).

Very truly yours,

(The Auditor's Firm)

identifying, evaluating, and accounting for litigation, claims, and assessments. The auditor may determine that a supplemental letter of inquiry is not required, even though the lawyer's response is dated considerably earlier than the auditor's report. In those circumstances, the auditor should ordinarily arrange for an oral update and should document it in the working papers.

The specimen letters of audit inquiry in Appendix A to SAS No. 12 and in the related interpretation include a "response date" that, combined with proper timing in mailing letters of audit inquiry, is intended to minimize the need for supplemental letters of audit inquiry. Letters of audit inquiry should be mailed at a date that provides the lawyer sufficient time to meet the response date (two weeks is ordinarily sufficient time). The response date should allow sufficient time prior to the date of the audit report for the auditor to evaluate the response and make supplemental inquiries, if necessary.

Acceptable Limitations on the Scope of Lawyers' Responses. Several types of limitations on the scope of a lawyer's response to a letter of audit inquiry are acceptable. These limitations, which the lawyer may indicate in the response by either a direct statement or a reference to the ABA Statement of Policy, include

- Limiting the response to matters to which the lawyer has devoted substantive attention on behalf of the client in the form of legal consultation or representation.
- When the letter of inquiry is addressed to a law firm, excluding matters that have been communicated to an individual member or employee of the firm by reason of that individual's serving in the capacity of director or officer of the client.
- Limiting the response to matters that are considered, individually or collectively, to be material to the client's financial statements.
- Disclaiming any undertaking to advise the auditor of changes in the status of litigation, claims, and assessments since the date the lawyer began internal review procedures for purposes of preparing the response.

Sometimes a response from a lawyer contains the phrase "not material" or "would not have a material effect on the financial condition of the company or the results of its operations." Responses containing these or similar phrases are acceptable and do not constitute an audit scope limitation if the response itself provides data sufficient for the auditor to evaluate the lawyer's conclusion. Such responses are also acceptable if materiality guidelines for the lawyer's use on both an individual item and an aggregate basis were included in the letter of audit inquiry from management, as the authors believe should be done. The auditor should be satisfied with the materiality guidelines provided to the client's lawyer. A materiality guideline in the inquiry letter might read as follows: "This request is limited to contingencies amounting to $XXX individually or items involving lesser amounts that exceed $XXX in the aggregate."

Evaluating Lawyers' Responses. In evaluating responses from lawyers, the auditor should consider whether there is any reason to doubt their professional qualifications and reputation. If, as will often be the case, the auditor is familiar with the lawyer's professional reputation, there would be no need to make specific inquiries in this regard. An auditor who is not familiar with a lawyer representing the client in what appears to be a significant case may wish to inquire as to the lawyer's professional background, reputation, and standing in the legal and financial community and to consider information available in such legal publications as the *Martindale-Hubbell Law Directory*. Once satisfied in this regard, the auditor can accept the lawyer's opinion regarding a legal matter, unless it appears to be unreasonable.

The lawyer's response should be read in its totality to ascertain its overall responsiveness to the letter of audit inquiry and to determine whether it conflicts with information otherwise known to the auditor. The language used in responses from lawyers takes many forms, and definitive guidance does not exist on the effect of the language used on the type of opinion the auditor may express. Certain responses, however, ordinarily permit an unqualified opinion, while others may preclude an unqualified opinion.

Responses Permitting a Standard Unqualified Opinion. Responses from lawyers that enable the auditor to render a standard unqualified opinion usually (a) indicate a high probability of a favorable outcome or that the matters in question are not material, and (b) do not indicate that the lawyer has not made a reasonable investigation of the case. The following examples of actual language from lawyers' letters would permit the auditor to render a standard unqualified opinion:

- It is our opinion that if the matter is litigated, it will be successfully defended on behalf of the Company.
- We believe plaintiff's assertions to be without merit.
- In connection with your audit of the financial statements of the Company, please be advised that to the best of our knowledge and belief, there were no material pending claims in which the Company was involved as of (date).
- The possibility of unfavorable outcome is remote (slight).

Responses Leading to an Explanatory Paragraph Because of an Uncertainty. If because of inherent uncertainties a lawyer is unable to indicate whether an unfavorable outcome of material litigation, claims, or assessments is likely or to estimate the amount or range of potential loss, the auditor will ordinarily conclude that an explanatory paragraph should be added to the auditor's report because of a matter involving an uncertainty (SAS No. 12 [AU Section 337.14]). The lawyer may not be able to respond because the factors influencing the likelihood of an unfavorable outcome are not within the competence of lawyers to judge, historical experience of the entity in similar litigation or the experience of other entities may not be relevant or available, or the amount or range of possible loss may vary widely at different stages of litigation. The following examples of actual language from lawyers' letters would, if related to material items that are not remedied, result in an explanatory paragraph (following the opinion paragraph) in the auditor's report:

- No demand for monetary damages has been made in the complaint. Consequently, I am unable to give an estimate as to potential loss.
- In the case of nonpersonal injury claims, the Company should be contacted for further information regarding such claims. Our substantive attention to the claims set forth in the exhibits hereto has been limited either to coordinating activities and communication between the Com-

pany and its risk managers or to a lesser extent facilitating communications between the Company and the various claimants.

In the latter example, the lawyer did not feel that the factors influencing the likelihood of unfavorable outcomes were within his competence to judge. The company then employed a specialist to determine the likelihood of unfavorable outcomes and amounts or ranges of possible losses. The auditor was able to conclude that the specialist's findings were suitable for corroborating the information related to these claims in the financial statements, and a standard unqualified opinion was issued.

Lawyers sometimes use language that is not sufficiently clear as to the likelihood of a favorable outcome. Examples of that kind of language are provided in an interpretation of SAS No. 12 (AU Section 9337.22), as follows:

- This action involves unique characteristics wherein authoritative legal precedents do not seem to exist. We believe that the plaintiff will have serious problems establishing the company's liability under the act; nevertheless, if the plaintiff is successful, the award may be substantial.
- It is our opinion that the company will be able to assert meritorious defenses to this action. (The term "meritorious defenses" indicates that the company's defenses will not be summarily dismissed by the court; it does not necessarily indicate counsel's opinion that the company will prevail.)
- We believe the action can be settled for less than the damages claimed.
- We are unable to express an opinion as to the merits of the litigation at this time. The company believes there is absolutely no merit to the litigation. (If the client's counsel, with the benefit of all relevant information, is unable to conclude that the likelihood of an unfavorable outcome is "remote," it is unlikely that management would be able to form a judgment to that effect.)
- In our opinion, the company has a substantial chance of prevailing in this action. (A "substantial chance," a "reasonable opportunity," and similar terms indicate more uncertainty than an opinion that the company will prevail.)

The interpretation states that an auditor who is uncertain about the meaning of a lawyer's evaluation should request clarification either in a follow-up letter or in a conference with the lawyer and client, which should be appropriately documented. If the lawyer is still unable to give, either in writing or orally, an unequivocal evaluation of the likelihood of an unfavorable outcome, the auditor should consider the effect of the resulting uncertainty on the audit report.

Responses Resulting in Scope Limitations. Responses that indicate or imply that the lawyer is withholding information should ordinarily, if not remedied, be considered an audit scope limitation (SAS No. 58, *Reports on Audited Financial Statements* [AU Section 508.40–.41]). For example, the lawyer may state that the reply is limited because of the policy of the law firm or the impracticability of reviewing the files, or for reasons not given. Normally, such limitations would be considered significant, since the auditor usually cannot evaluate the effect of withheld information.

A response indicating that the newness of a case precludes evaluating it does not provide sufficient evidence to support an unqualified opinion. The following examples of actual language from lawyers' letters would, if related to material items that are not resolved, constitute limitations on the scope of the engagement, requiring modification of the scope paragraph of the audit report, a separate paragraph (preceding the opinion paragraph) describing the limitation, and a qualified opinion:

- The claim has been received by this office only recently, and is being investigated. At this time it is not possible to predict the outcome of the litigation.
- This suit for declaratory judgment by the plaintiff presents some risk for the Bank depending upon the values assigned to parcels of realty transferred to the Bank to reduce a preexisting debt owed by the plaintiff to the Bank. We have not been supplied with sufficient information to determine whether a deficiency existed which warranted the note and mortgage obtained from the plaintiff. At present, we can only assume that the Bank was justified in obtaining this obligation.

Inside Counsel. The duties of an inside counsel may vary from handling specialized litigation to acting as general counsel with supervisory authority in all legal matters, including the selection of outside counsel to represent or advise the client on specific matters.

If inside counsel acts as general counsel, evidential matter gathered by and obtained from inside counsel may provide the necessary corroboration for the auditor. Letters of audit inquiry to outside counsel may be appropriate if inside general counsel has retained outside counsel to represent or advise the client on certain matters. Information provided by inside counsel is not a substitute for information that outside counsel refuses to furnish.

Changes or Resignations of Lawyers. The legal profession's Code of Professional Responsibility requires that, in some circumstances, lawyers must resign if the client has disregarded their advice concerning financial accounting for and reporting of litigation, claims, and assessments. The auditor should be alert for such circumstances and should ensure that he or she understands the reasons for the change or resignation of lawyers, and should also consider the implications for financial statement disclosures concerning litigation, claims, and assessments.

CLIENT REPRESENTATIONS

The auditor is required by SAS No. 19, *Client Representations* (AU Section 333), to obtain a representation letter from management confirming that they are responsible for the financial statements and have made all pertinent information available to the auditor, and stating their belief in the accuracy and completeness of that information. The representation letter provides written evidence that the auditor has made certain inquiries of management; ordinarily it documents oral responses given to the auditor, thus reducing the possibility of errors or misunderstandings. A representation letter is one kind of competent evidence, but it is not sufficient in itself to provide the auditor with a reasonable basis for forming an opinion.

Written Representations

The representation letter illustrated in Figure 17.2 incorporates the written representations that the auditor should ordinarily obtain. The letter should be modified to meet the circumstances of the particular engagement and the nature and basis of presentation of the financial statements. For example, if the auditor is reporting on consolidated financial statements, the written representations obtained from the parent company's management should specify that they pertain to the consolidated financial statements. If the auditor is reporting on the parent company's separate financial statements as well, the letter should also extend to them.

Written representations relating to management's knowledge or intent should be obtained when the auditor believes they are necessary to complement other auditing procedures. For example, even if the auditor has performed tests for unrecorded liabilities and has not detected any, written representation should be obtained to document that management has no knowledge of any liabilities that have not been recorded. Liabilities known to management but not accrued, through oversight, might be brought to the auditor's attention in this manner. Such a written representation, however, does not relieve the auditor of responsibility for planning the audit to identify material unrecorded liabilities. Information may be unintentionally overlooked or intentionally withheld from the auditor. Accordingly, the auditor must still perform all the usual tests to corroborate representations made by management.

In some cases, evidential matter to corroborate written representations is limited. For example, income taxes may not be provided for undistributed income of a subsidiary because management of the parent company represents that it intends to permanently reinvest that income, but the auditor may not be able to obtain sufficient information through other auditing procedures to corroborate that intent. Unless the auditor obtains evidential matter to the contrary, he or she may rely on the truthfulness of management's representations, as discussed in SAS No. 53, *The Auditor's Responsibility to Detect and Report Errors and Irregularities* (AU Section 316.17).

Figure 17.2 Illustrative Client Representation Letter

Quinn Hardware, Inc.

July 10, 1991

[To Independent Auditor]

In connection with your audit of the consolidated financial statements of Quinn Hardware, Inc. and Subsidiary as of May 31, 1991 and for the year then ended for the purpose of expressing an opinion as to whether such financial statements present fairly, in all material respects, the financial position, results of operations, and cash flows of Quinn Hardware, Inc. and Subsidiary in conformity with generally accepted accounting principles, we confirm, to the best of our knowledge and belief, as of July 10, 1991, the date of your report, the following representations made to you during your audit.

1. We are responsible for the fair presentation in the consolidated financial statements of financial position, results of operations, and cash flows in conformity with generally accepted accounting principles.
2. We have made available to you all financial and accounting records and related data and all minutes of the meetings of shareholders, directors, and committees of directors. The most recent meeting held was the June 14, 1991 Board of Directors meeting. We are not aware of any accounts, transactions, or material agreements not fairly described and properly recorded in the financial and accounting records underlying the financial statements.
3. We are not aware of (a) any irregularities involving management or those employees who have significant roles in the internal control structure, or any irregularities involving other employees that could have a material effect on the financial statements, or (b) any violations or possible violations of laws or regulations whose effects should be considered for disclosure in the financial statements or as a basis for recording a loss contingency. (We understand the term "irregularities" to mean those matters described in Statement on Auditing Standards No. 53.) There have been no communications from regulatory agencies concerning noncompliance with or deficiencies in financial reporting practices that could have a material effect on the financial statements. The company has complied with all aspects of contractual agreements that would have a material effect on the financial statements in the event of noncompliance.
4. All cash and bank accounts and all other properties and assets of the company of which we are aware are included in the financial statements at May 31, 1991. The company has satisfactory title to all owned assets, and all liens, encumbrances, or security interests having any important consequence on any asset of the company are disclosed in the statements or notes thereto.

Figure 17.2 ***Continued***

5. The receivables in the aggregate gross amount of $51,208,000 at May 31, 1991 represent bona fide claims against debtors for sales or other charges arising on or before that date and are not subject to discount except for normal cash discounts. These receivables do not include any amounts that are collectible after one year. The amount of $1,800,000 carried as an allowance for uncollectible accounts is sufficient to provide for any losses that may be sustained on realization of the receivables.
6. Inventories at May 31, 1991 in the aggregate amount of $63,570,000 are stated at the lower of cost or market, cost being determined on the basis of FIFO, and consistently with the prior year, and provision was made to reduce all slow-moving, obsolete, or unusable inventories to their estimated net realizable values. Inventory quantities at May 31, 1991 were determined from the company's perpetual inventory records, which have been adjusted on the basis of physical inventories taken by competent employees at March 31, 1991. Liability, if unpaid, for all items included in inventories is recorded at May 31, 1991, and all quantities billed to customers at that date are excluded from the inventory balances.
7. All liabilities of the company of which we are aware are included in the financial statements at May 31, 1991. There are no other material liabilities or gain or loss contingencies that are required to be accrued or disclosed by Statement of Financial Accounting Standards No. 5 and no unasserted claims or assessments that our legal counsel has advised us are probable of assertion and must be disclosed in accordance with that Statement.
8. Commitments for future purchases are for quantities not in excess of anticipated requirements and at prices that will not result in loss. Provision has been made for any material loss to be sustained in the fulfillment of, or from the inability to fulfill, any sales commitments.
9. We have no plans or intentions that may materially affect the carrying value or classification of assets and liabilities.
10. The financial statements and related notes include all disclosures necessary for a fair presentation of the financial position, results of operations, and cash flows of the company in conformity with generally accepted accounting principles, and disclosures otherwise required to be included therein by the laws and regulations to which the company is subject. The following have been properly recorded or disclosed in the financial statements:

    - Related party transactions and related amounts receivable or payable, including sales, purchases, loans, transfers, leasing arrangements, and guarantees. (We understand the term "related party" to include those entities described in Statement of Financial Accounting Standards No. 57.)

Figure 17.2 *Continued*

There are no

- Capital stock repurchase options or agreements or capital stock reserved for options, warrants, conversions, or other requirements.
- Arrangements with financial institutions involving compensating balances, arrangements involving restrictions on cash balances and lines of credit, or similar arrangements.
- Agreements to repurchase assets previously sold.
- Guarantees, whether written or oral, under which the company is contingently liable to a bank or other lending institution.

No matters or occurrences have come to our attention up to the date of this letter that would materially affect the financial statements and related disclosures for the year ended May 31, 1991 or, although not affecting such financial statements or disclosures, have caused or are likely to cause any material change, adverse or otherwise, in the financial position, results of operations, or cash flows of the company.

____

Harvey Quinn, President and Chairman of the Board

____

Ed Green, Vice President, Finance

Materiality. Paragraph 5 of SAS No. 19 (AU Section 333.05) states that "management's representations may be limited to matters that are considered either individually or collectively material to the financial statements, provided management and the auditor have reached an understanding on the limits of materiality for this purpose." The limits of materiality may differ in different circumstances, for example, amounts that affect only the balance sheet versus amounts that affect income. The auditor may wish to request management to specify in the representation letter the materiality limits agreed on.

Definitions. Certain terms used in the letter in Figure 17.2 are defined in the authoritative literature, for example, irregularities (SAS No. 53 [AU Section 316.02-.03]), related party transactions (SFAS No. 57 [Accounting Standards Section R36.101]), and contingencies (SFAS No. 5 [Accounting Standards Section C59.101]). The auditor may wish to furnish the applicable literature to the client and request that management acknowledge in the representation letter that they have received it.

Dating and Signing. The representation letter should be addressed to the auditor and should be dated no earlier than the date of the auditor's report (discussed later), but no later than the report release date. Representation letters should ordinarily be signed by both the chief executive and chief financial officers. Other members of management may sign the letter instead, however, if the auditor is satisfied that they are responsible for and knowledgeable about the matters covered by the representations.

Scope Limitations. In rare instances, management may refuse to furnish a written representation that the auditor believes is essential or may refuse to sign the representation letter. SAS No. 19 (AU Section 333.11) notes that either refusal constitutes a limitation on the scope of the audit sufficient to preclude an unqualified opinion (SAS No. 58 [AU Section 508.40-.41]). An auditor must consider whether management's refusal to furnish a written representation affects the reliability of their other representations. Executives are expected to understand their legal and ethical responsibilities for financial statement representations. Thus, they should also understand that the representation letter only specifies some of those responsibilities but does not increase them. Refusal to sign the letter must be taken as a signal either of withheld evidence or of inadequately understood responsibilities; either destroys the basis for an unqualified opinion.

SUMMARIZING AND EVALUATING THE AUDIT FINDINGS

The discussion of materiality in Chapter 6 noted that auditors frequently maintain a summary of the misstatements found in the course of the various procedures performed throughout the audit. Misstatements include unintentional mistakes, unreasonable accounting estimates, intentional misrepresentations, and intentional or unintentional misapplications of GAAP. Ordinarily, management makes adjustments for some items, leaving the unadjusted differences to be evaluated by the auditor. Normally the summary includes items arising in the current year, but, as discussed below, it may also include waived adjustments from prior years' audits that have an effect on the current year's financial statements.

The summary serves as the central means of evaluating whether the evidence examined by the auditor supports the conclusion that the financial statements are presented fairly, in all material respects, in conformity with generally accepted accounting principles. The auditor should be sure that the items on the summary, either individually or in the aggregate, do not cause the financial statements to be materially misstated. If they do, either the financial statements will have to be revised by the client, or the auditor will have to express a qualified opinion or an adverse opinion because of departures from GAAP. Usually the auditor and the client are able to reach agreement so that a qualified or an adverse opinion is not necessary.

Categories of Misstatements to Be Evaluated

Authoritative auditing literature addresses the auditor's consideration of misstatements. SAS No. 39, *Audit Sampling* (AU Section 350.30), requires the auditor to consider "projected misstatement results for all audit sampling applications and all known misstatements from nonsampling applications" in the aggregate in evaluating whether the financial statements as a whole may be materially misstated. SAS No. 47, *Audit Risk and Materiality in Conducting an Audit* (AU Section 312.27), expands on this concept by stating that "the auditor should aggregate misstatements that the entity has not corrected in a way that enables him to consider whether, in relation to individual amounts, subtotals, or totals in the financial statements, they materially misstate the financial statements taken as a whole." With regard to the amounts to be aggregated, SAS No. 47 states

> The aggregation of misstatements should include the auditor's best estimate of the total misstatements in the account balances or classes of transactions that he has examined (hereafter referred to as likely misstatement), not just the amount of misstatements he specifically identifies (hereafter referred to as known misstatement). . . . Projected misstatement [from audit sampling, if used], along with the results of other substantive tests, contributes to the auditor's assessment of likely misstatement in the balance or class. (para. 28)

As defined in SAS No. 47, likely misstatement includes unreasonable differences between accounting estimates as determined by the client and the amounts supported by audit evidence. SAS No. 47 states

> Since no one accounting estimate can be considered accurate with certainty, the auditor recognizes that a difference between an estimated amount best supported by the audit evidence and the estimated amount included in the financial statements may be reasonable, and such difference would not be considered to be a likely misstatement. However, if the auditor believes the estimated amount included in the financial statements is unreasonable, he should treat the difference between that estimate and the closest reasonable estimate as a likely misstatement and aggregate it with other likely misstatements. (para. 29)

Preparing and Using the Summary

The exact form of the summary used to aggregate misstatements, and even what it is called, varies in practice. Its complexity depends on the complexity of the engagement (e.g., extensive subsidiary operations may require a more complex format) and circumstances (e.g., if significant misstatements are expected or many accounts are considered potentially troublesome, a more structured, formal format may be required). Additionally, professional standards may require specific documentation.

In general, the summary is a multiple-column work sheet. In the extreme left columns, the auditor records the nature of misstatements identified, for example, descriptions of known misstatements from nonsampling procedures and projected misstatements from sampling procedures in the inventory accounts. The amount in question is then "spread" to show its impact on assets, liabilities and owners' equity, and income, such as a failure to record on a timely basis $10,000 of inventory received before year-end that might result in a $10,000 understatement of assets and a $10,000 understatement of liabilities.

A single document that summarizes and accumulates misstatements identified in the various accounts, such as receivables and payables, makes it easier for the auditor to evaluate the overall audit findings. For example, a review of the summary may reveal that individually immaterial misstatements taken together have a material impact on income or some other financial statement element. The summary is helpful in comparing the results of auditing procedures with materiality at the account level, for major groups of accounts (such as current assets), and for the financial statements as a whole. Figure 17.3 illustrates a summary of adjustments.

Aggregating and Netting

The issue of aggregating and netting misstated amounts in the final evaluation of audit evidence is complicated and somewhat controversial. The controversy centers around the appropriateness of netting or offsetting certain misstatements.

In aggregating misstatements affecting the income statement or balance sheet, likely misstatements relating to each line item are considered together to determine whether the line item is not materially misstated. The more "cushion" that exists between the total of likely misstatements and a larger amount that the auditor considers "material" for the line item, the higher the auditor's level of assurance that the item is not materially misstated.

One technique used in practice is to aggregate misstatements within groupings of financial statement components and to assess materiality at that level and at each successively higher logical subdivision of the financial statements. For example, in assessing the fair presentation of assets, the results of the audit of cash and short-term liquid assets might be aggregated to determine whether the sum of those assets, which enters into the computation of the "quick ratio," is reasonable. Other current assets such as accounts receivable might then be added and another assessment made at the current asset level. Finally, these results would be combined with a similar series of aggregations for noncurrent assets to evaluate reported assets in total. The auditor's objective is

Summary of Adjustments

Figure 17.3 Summary of Adjustments

Client PSR Corporation

Year End 12/31/90

Prepared by/Date R.B., 2/28/91

Reviewed by/Date M.C., 3/2/91

Working Paper Ref.	DESCRIPTION OF ADJUSTMENT NEEDED	BALANCE SHEET IMPACT					PRETAX INCOME STATEMENT IMPACT			
		Assets		Liabilities						
		Current	Non-current	Current	Non-current	Equity	Known Mis-statements[1]	Projected[2]	Estimated[3]	Total
53.2	Additional provision for uncollectible accounts	(39,000)							39,000	39,000
53.25	Sales invoice pricing misstatements (underbillings)	34,000						(34,000)		(34,000)
55.2	Physical inventory count adjustments	38,000					(38,000)			(38,000)
55.2	Inventory pricing misstatements	76,000						(76,000)		(76,000)
71.2	Unrecorded liabilities adjustments (invoices received after cutoff date)	47,000		(67,000)			20,000			20,000
72.25	Warranty accruals understatement			(50,000)					50,000	50,000
	TOTAL PRETAX UNADJUSTED MISSTATEMENTS	156,000		(117,000)		(39,000)	(18,000)	(110,000)	89,000	(39,000) (A)
	TAX EFFECTS:									
	Estimated tax impact of unadjusted misstatements			(14,000)		14,000	6,000	38,000	(30,000)	14,000
	TOTAL AFTER-TAX UNADJUSTED MISSTATEMENTS	156,000 (B)	(B)	(131,000) (B)	(B)	(25,000) (B)	(12,000)	(72,000)	59,000	(25,000) (B)
	BALANCE SHEET AMOUNTS	11,193,000 (C)	22,438,000 (C)	5,780,000 (C)	10,354,000 (C)	17,497,000 (C)				
	PERCENTAGE OF MISSTATEMENTS TO BALANCE SHEET AMOUNTS (B) ÷ (C)	1.4%	%	2.3%	%	.1%				
				PRETAX INCOME						3,671,000 (D)
				PERCENTAGE OF PRETAX MISSTATEMENTS TO PRETAX INCOME (A) ÷ (D)						1.1%
				AFTER-TAX INCOME						2,569,000 (E)
				PERCENTAGE OF AFTER-TAX MISSTATEMENTS TO AFTER-TAX INCOME (B) ÷ (E)						1.0%

[1] Misstatements specifically identified in nonsampling applications.

[2] Misstatements relating to the application of audit sampling techniques (includes known misstatements identified in samples examined).

[3] Misstatements determined by the difference between the client's accounting estimate and the closest reasonable amount supported by the audit evidence.

to obtain reasonable assurance that neither the line item itself, subtotals or important ratios of which the line item is a component, or the financial statements as a whole are materially misstated.

The way items are added together or offset against each other can significantly affect evaluations of materiality. Some items or events are more significant than others, implying that they should be evaluated individually while others may be evaluated in groups. For example, many auditors consider it inappropriate to aggregate or offset an individually immaterial overstatement of cash with a misstatement in an unrelated account. The inherent risk associated with the cash account, as well as the potential for determining its value precisely, often precludes an auditor from treating misstatements of cash in the same manner as misstatements in other accounts. Immaterial inventory misstatements and immaterial receivable misstatements, however, are often offset in determining whether the financial statements as a whole may be materially misstated.

Netting separate items to determine the amount to be compared with materiality raises several questions. Is it acceptable, for example, to net the effect of an error against the effect of a change in accounting principle? Clearly, the answer is no. APB Opinion No. 20, paragraph 38 (Accounting Standards Section A06.133), requires that materiality be considered for the separate effects of each accounting change. Also, netting individually material items to obtain an immaterial total would result in inadequate financial statement disclosure. It is acceptable, however, to net immaterial misstatements in a particular component of financial statements or in related accounts.

Quantitative Aspects of Materiality Judgments

The question of how large a "difference" must be before it is material has never been definitively answered in the accounting and auditing literature. Many auditors have developed rules of thumb for setting materiality thresholds, such as some percentage of one or more financial statement totals. Net income is a commonly cited base for assessing materiality, but there are others, such as total assets, equities, or revenues, as well as trends in each of these. As long as investors continue to pay attention to net income in their investment assessments, however, an audit standard of materiality based on net income (or the trend of net income) is likely to be widely used.

A commonly used figure for materiality is 5 percent of the chosen base. That is, if the item is within 5 percent of what it might otherwise be, the difference may be immaterial. Obviously, any rule of thumb, such as 5 percent, must be used with a great deal of caution and careful judgment. Qualitative considerations, as discussed below, can render such a range too broad. Most studies of the subject have generally concluded that a single dollar amount or percentage is not appropriate in all situations. Five to ten percent of net income is frequently used, but is affected in individual cases by nonquantitative criteria. Some examples of quantitative criteria for significance or materiality that have been used by professional and regulatory standard-setting bodies are cited in Table 1 in Appendix C to FASB Statement of Financial Accounting Concepts No. 2. In addition, many auditors assign greater significance to differences that change the client's trend of earnings than to those that do not.

Having established that there may be more than one level of materiality—for example, one level for income statement effects and a higher level in absolute terms for balance sheet effects—the auditor should recognize that a misstatement that affects both statements should be compared with the smaller materiality level in determining whether the misstatement requires correction or can be "waived" as immaterial. For example, a misstated accrual may not materially affect the balance sheet, but may materially affect reported expenses and consequently net income. In that situation, the lower income statement threshold would determine materiality. Misclassifications that affect only balance sheet accounts would be material if they exceeded the balance sheet materiality threshold.

Qualitative Considerations in Assessing Materiality

The types of misstatements found may influence the auditor's evaluation of the audit results. Paragraph 22 of SAS No. 53 (AU Section 316.22) states that the auditor should consider whether misstatements are the result of errors or of irregularities. Because irregularities are intentional, their implications for the audit extend beyond their direct monetary effect, and the auditor must consider those implications in evaluating the audit results. Chapter 4 discusses actions the auditor should take, including disclosures, when an irregularity may have a material effect on the financial statements.

In many cases, known misstatements in an account discovered by applying either sampling or nonsampling procedures are corrected in the accounts and entail no further consideration. Misstatements that arise from projecting the results of a sample to the population are more difficult to deal with. While projected misstatements should be included on the summary of adjustments, correcting the financial statements for them is difficult in practice, since sampling does not help identify all of the specific components, such as the individual accounts receivable, that may be misstated. Additionally, according to sampling theory, the projected misstatement is not the "true" misstatement, but only a presumably close approximation. Therefore, correcting the financial statements for nonspecific "projected" misstatements may create a risk that actual misstatements will be introduced into the financial statements. Sample results may be used, however, to identify aspects of an account (e.g., inventory) that deserve special attention by the client, such as repricing or recounting. If such procedures are performed, the auditor will need to adjust the projected misstatement amount based on the results of the procedures.

Evaluating some types of misstatements involves distinguishing between "hard" and "soft" misstatements and properly characterizing the "soft" ones. A mathematical mistake, omission of a segment of inventory from the total inventory, or an accounting principle misapplication, whether discovered by sampling or nonsampling procedures, may be referred to as a "hard" misstatement. In these cases, the auditor knows there is a problem and can calculate the misstatement. If potential misstatements are based on judgments or estimates that cannot be calculated precisely but must be estimated, they are described as "soft."

Accounting and auditing are not exact sciences, and much judgment often goes into developing the account balances presented in the financial statements. The auditor must evaluate accounts, such as the allowance for uncollectible accounts receivable and liability for product warranties, that are based on estimates and are not subject to absolute determination. (The auditor's responsibility to evaluate management's estimates is discussed in Chapter 9.) Using methods that are appropriate in the circumstances but are not exactly the same ones the client used, the auditor may develop an estimate that differs from the client's. The auditor should develop such estimates carefully and compare them with the client's estimates to determine whether the client's estimates are reasonable. Those considered unreasonable should be included with other likely misstatements and evaluated, and those deemed to be reasonable should be excluded from likely misstatement.

Sometimes the auditor may not be able to arrive at a single estimated amount, but may establish a range of "reasonableness"; if the client's estimate falls within that range, it does not belong on the summary. If the client's estimate falls outside that range, the auditor should enter an item representing the difference between the client's estimate and the nearest point in the range. For example, if a client established a product warranty liability for $150,000 and the auditor, by analyzing past trends and the experience of other companies in similar circumstances, established a reasonable range of product warranty liability of between $200,000 and $300,000, the auditor might include on the summary $50,000 ($200,000 – $150,000) for possible adjustment by the client. This would be a "soft" misstatement; only if the auditor knew the liability must exceed $200,000 could the difference in estimates be called a "hard" or "known" misstatement.

The Commission on Auditors' Responsibilities noted that "the auditor may make many separate evaluations of the appropriateness of accounting principles selected and estimates made by management. On viewing the financial statements as a whole, the auditor may find that most or all of the selections or estimates made by management had the effect of increasing (or decreasing) earnings and that the overall result is a misleading picture of the entity's earning power or liquidity" (page 21). SAS No. 47, *Audit Risk and Materiality in Conducting an Audit* (AU Section 312.29), addresses that possibility, and suggests that "the auditor should also consider whether the difference between estimates best supported by the audit evidence and the estimates included in the financial statements, which are individually reasonable, indicate a possible bias on the part of the entity's management. For example, if each accounting estimate included in the financial statements was individually reasonable, but the effect of the difference between each estimate and the estimate best supported by the audit evidence was to increase income, the auditor should reconsider the estimates taken as a whole."

Other qualitative factors may also influence the auditor's response to likely misstatements in the financial statements. These factors may warrant consideration that goes beyond the quantitative significance of the misstatements. Following are examples of factors that may cause the auditor greater concern and prompt other reactions than the quantitative amounts themselves might indicate:

- *Business conditions*. For example, in a weak economy or in a company with a weak financial condition, materiality is sometimes given special emphasis since the company's future may rest on investors' and creditors' evaluations of the current financial position and recent trends.
- *Contractual arrangements*. Debt covenants, buy-sell agreements, and union contracts may be geared to various financial statement elements or relationships (such as the current ratio).
- *Cause of the misstatement*. Misapplications of GAAP (e.g., recording a purchase of a business as a pooling of interests or failing to accrue vacation pay or product warranties) may have possible long-term effects the auditor should assess, since correcting the misstatement later may erode investors' confidence in the company's financial reporting.
- *Situations in which the "investor-based" materiality rule is difficult to apply*. For entities such as privately owned companies, trusts, and others, the auditor may need to consider who are the likely users of the financial statements and what their interests are, and designate a materiality level appropriate for their needs. Special user needs may tighten customary materiality standards.
- *Susceptibility of an account to misstatement*. Misstatements in the cash and capital accounts are generally unexpected and may warrant further investigation if discovered. The susceptibility of cash and other liquid assets to misuse or misappropriation should naturally heighten auditor concern about likely misstatements in these accounts.
- *Trends in financial statement components*. While it may be unrealistic to use a materiality standard as tight as a small fraction of the yearly change in net income or other financial statement components, longer-range trends or averages of balances or components (e.g., "normal income") may serve as useful signals that users react to. Consequently, auditors should be sensitive to departures from trends or normal expectations. Additionally, in a company with a stable earnings history, smaller variations in cash flow, income, or other financial statement components may have more

impact than in a less stable business environment where wider fluctuations are more common.

Treatment of Prior-Year Waived Adjustments

An issue that often arises in assessing materiality is the treatment in the current year of prior-year waived adjustments. For example, the auditor may have waived a known overstatement of $10,000 in ending inventory and income in 1989, caused perhaps by errors in pricing the inventory, on the grounds that the misstatement was not material. The overstatement of the 1989 ending inventory and income will flow through to 1990 income as an overstatement of cost of sales and an understatement of income. The issue in this case is this: In considering misstatements affecting income in the 1990 financial statements, should the auditor include the $10,000 understatement of 1990 income caused by the waived adjustment of the 1989 misstatement?

Some auditors believe that prior-year waived adjustments should be ignored in considering likely misstatements in the current year; in effect, the "correct" beginning 1990 inventory in the above example is the 1989 ending inventory, with the misstatement in it. Since it was waived, those auditors treat the misstatement as not existing after 1989 and consider that 1990 starts with a "clean slate." Other auditors believe that the reversal in 1990 of the 1989 misstatement should be considered in assessing likely misstatements in 1990.

The issue becomes even more complex when unadjusted misstatements, instead of reversing in the following year as in the above example, build up. Assume that the auditor determines that the estimated warranty liability at the end of 1989 and warranty expense for 1989 are understated by $15,000 because an unreasonable estimate was made by the client. The auditor waived the adjustment because the amount was not material to either the balance sheet or the income statement. In the course of the audit of the 1990 financial statements, the auditor determines that the estimated warranty liability at December 31, 1990, is understated by $35,000—an additional $20,000. In assessing the materiality of the misstatement, the auditor may determine that neither the $35,000 cumulative misstatement on the balance sheet nor the $20,000 impact on current-year income is material and again waive the adjustment. This may continue for several years. At some point, the accumulated misstatement on the balance sheet will become material, and an adjustment will be needed if the financial statements are to be presented fairly in conformity with GAAP. The resulting adjustment may be so large that it will produce a material misstatement in that year's income statement.

SAS No. 47 provides only the broadest guidance on this topic, stating merely that "if the auditor believes that there is an unacceptably high risk that the current period's financial statements may be materially misstated when those prior-period likely misstatements that affect the current period's financial statements are considered along with likely misstatements arising in the current period, he should include in aggregate likely misstatement the effect on the current period's financial statements of those prior-period likely misstatements'' (AU Section 312.30). It does not, however, state how the auditor should include the effect in likely misstatement, and accordingly does not resolve the issues discussed here.

The auditor must plan properly to ensure that sufficient auditing procedures are performed in the various accounts so that he or she can draw appropriate audit conclusions. If there has been a buildup of misstatements in an account from prior years, the auditor may have to do more work to refine the estimate of the present misstatement in the account. More audit work may also be necessary to prevent a materially misstated balance from going undetected. Of course, assessing at the planning stage whether an immaterially misstated account balance from prior years will no longer be misstated, remain similarly misstated, or become misstated in the opposite direction in the current period is difficult. Thus, the auditor's experience with the client, assessment of the possible level of misstatement in the account, and the nature of the account all influence the testing plan for the current period.

Resolving Material Differences

Occasionally, the auditor will conclude after reviewing the summary that one or more financial statement components are materially misstated or cause the income statement or balance sheet in the aggregate to be materially misstated. The auditor then needs to discuss the items in question with the client's management. Management may be able to produce further evidence to justify the initial treatment of some items or may agree to record some of the discovered misstatements in the accounts and to disclose more about the nature of and assumptions used in creating subjectively developed estimates that may be in dispute. The discussions continue until enough items are resolved so that the auditor can conclude that the remaining items do not adversely affect the fair presentation of the financial statements.

Depending on the size and complexity of an organization, the auditor may have to take up each item on the summary with several levels of management. The first consultation, of course, is with the individual directly responsible, who must supply all the facts. Additional conferences may include a supervisor and sometimes a plant or division controller. Often the deciding conference includes top management—the financial vice president and chief executive. If discussions reach that level, two subjects should be probed: how to resolve the current problems so that an unqualified opinion can be given, and how to prevent similar problems from growing to such magnitude in the future. In these conferences, auditors must be careful not to allow factors such as pressing deadlines, heated arguments, or client dissatisfaction to influence them or to compromise their professional objectivity. Diplomacy and tact and an attitude of constructive assistance are obviously important in such situations. Early and thorough consideration of potential problems is the best way to avoid actual problems that may lead to qualified or adverse opinions. In some situations, however, such opinions may be the only appropriate response to a client's unwillingness to correct material financial statement misstatements.

WORKING PAPER REVIEW

Paragraph 11 of SAS No. 22, *Planning and Supervision* (AU Section 311.13), states that "the work performed by each assistant should be reviewed to determine whether it was adequately performed and to evaluate whether the results are consistent with the conclusions to be presented in the auditor's report."

Key Engagement Matters

To facilitate the review process, the audit personnel in charge of the field work should document significant matters relating to the engagement and bring them to the attention of the partner in charge of the engagement. Key engagement matters include, but are not limited to, the following:

1. Significant questions involving accounting principles and auditing procedures, or failure to comply with regulatory requirements, even when the person in charge of the field work is satisfied that the matter has been disposed of properly.
2. Incomplete audit steps or unresolved questions.
3. Matters of significance noted in the previous year's engagement and their disposition.
4. Resolved or unresolved disagreements with the client on accounting and auditing matters.
5. Any information, not otherwise obvious, that should be considered in evaluating the results of the audit or in discussing the financial statements with the client.

It is desirable to address significant matters in one section of the working papers. Those matters may be summarized in the lead working paper binder, with cross-references to the related working papers that contain the details.

Types of Reviews

Generally, two types of reviews of working papers and procedures are performed on audit engagements.

- A review of the completed working papers by the person in charge of the field work to evaluate the audit results and ascertain that all appropriate auditing procedures have been applied.
- A review of the auditing procedures by an individual who did not participate in the field work. This review provides an objective assessment of the procedures applied during the field work and their results, which form the basis of the audit opinion.

The person in charge of the field work is responsible for reviewing all completed working papers to determine that

1. All appropriate auditing procedures have been completed and that the nature and extent of the work performed have been adequately documented in the working papers.
2. The requirements of the audit program were adhered to.
3. The working papers are relevant, clearly presented, orderly, and self-explanatory.
4. All exceptions have been appropriately cleared and documented.

The second review is the responsibility of the partner, who exercises overall supervision but does not usually perform the detailed auditing procedures. Depending on the structure of the audit team, the partner may delegate a portion of the review to a manager who was not involved in preparing the working papers. The partner would then ordinarily focus primarily on the key engagement matters and any areas in which there is a high risk of material misstatement, taking into consideration the dollar amounts involved, the complexity of the problems, and the internal control structure.

The purpose of the review of the working papers and audit program is to ensure that the procedures used are adequate and appropriate, that they have been performed properly, that they generated sufficient evidence to support the auditor's conclusions, that the conclusions reached are objective and logical, and that there is a properly documented basis for an informed opinion. The reviewer must evaluate the completeness of the audit program—including changes made to reflect changes in audit strategy in the course of the audit—in light of the results of the tests, the quality of the work performed by assistants, the quality of management's judgments and decisions, and the adequacy of both the work performed and its documentation by the assistants. The exacting but inconclusive nature of most audit tasks makes it imperative that every piece of work be reviewed for completeness and logic by another qualified professional.

Whatever other purposes the review may have, its primary purpose must be to make sure that the logic of the audit is complete and properly documented. The logic calls for evidence in the working papers that the control structure was understood and inherent and control risks were assessed, and, if appropriate, tests of controls were performed; the understanding and assessment were translated into a program of substantive tests; the results of those tests either corroborated the assertions embodied in the financial statement components or led to a rational exploration of differences; and the results support each item in the financial statements.

The reviewer should be satisfied that the working papers have been integrated with the final financial statements. That is, the reviewer should ascertain that each account analysis in the working papers agrees with the corresponding amount shown on the trial balance, and that those amounts are reconcilable to the amounts shown on the financial statements. Amounts or other data appearing on the financial statements but not reflected on the trial balance (e.g., footnote or supplementary information) must also be agreed to the related working papers.

Regardless of what duties the partner delegates to a manager, the partner should review the auditor's report, related financial statements, and, where applicable, the entire text of the published report. The partner should consider each of the key engagement matters and ensure that the decision reached as to its disposition is appropriate.

Review by a Concurring Partner

Many accounting firms require that all financial statements be reviewed by a concurring (sometimes referred to as a second) partner before the audit report is released. Other firms limit this requirement to audits of specified entities, for example, entities in specialized industries and publicly owned entities.[2] In this review, the concurring partner should be particularly concerned that matters of importance have been appropriately dealt with and that the financial statements and audit report comply with professional standards and firm policies. The concurring partner should discuss with the partner in charge of the engagement questions regarding the consistent application of GAAP, auditing standards, or auditing procedures. The concurring partner may also consider it advisable to review certain working papers. If a concurring-partner review is required, the auditor's report should not be signed until all questions raised by the concurring partner have been disposed of properly.

Aids for Reviewers

The review process is so critical that accounting firms are constantly seeking ways to help reviewers by providing aids such as engagement control checklists, standardized procedures, and policy bulletins. In providing such aids to the

[2]As indicated in Chapter 3, second-partner reviews are required on SEC engagements if the auditor is a member of the SEC Practice Section of the AICPA Division for CPA Firms.

reviewer, accounting firms must try to guard against routinized performance of a highly judgmental task. The quality of the review, and therefore of the audit, rests on the professional diligence and sense of responsibility of the reviewer. Although guided and supported by aids such as those mentioned above, the reviewer cannot and should not be relieved of the responsibility for understanding all that is needed to be able to form an appropriate opinion on the financial statements.

Timing of the Review Process

For the sake of both audit efficiency and good client relations, potentially material issues must be raised at the earliest possible stage. More time for consideration by the partner on the engagement and the client is thus available than if the review is postponed until the final stages of the audit when the report deadline is near.

The real substance of an audit is planning it intelligently and logically, executing it diligently and perceptively, and supervising it so that the review is continuous and active. If an audit is properly planned, executed, and supervised, the working paper review becomes the final control over a result already accomplished—a means of determining that all items of significance have been considered in reaching an audit conclusion.

In practice, the review process rarely works as smoothly as it does in theory. There are delays by client personnel, unexpected auditing or accounting problems, an assistant who falls ill or cannot complete the assignment on time, and innumerable other possible complications. Increasing public pressure for the fastest possible release of significant information causes deadlines to be drawn constantly tighter. The risk of oversight or misjudgment is greatest under the pressure of a deadline. Experienced auditors learn to resist those problems and pressures, and make sure they review an integrated set of financial statements supported by coherent working papers before committing themselves, explicitly or implicitly, to an opinion on the financial statements or to approving release of information drawn from them.

Documentation of Significant Review Findings

During the various working paper reviews, questions usually arise concerning significant unresolved matters. Those questions are commonly referred to as "review notes." They often involve the appropriateness of accounting principles, auditing procedures used, or compliance with regulatory requirements, and may call for further investigation. Some auditors require that the review notes become part of the audit working papers and that a clear and precise record be maintained of how such questions were resolved, including, among other things, such matters as the following (if applicable):

- The additional auditing procedures performed.
- The individuals with whom the matter was discussed.
- The conclusions arrived at and supporting rationale.

Other auditors believe that matters identified in review notes should be adequately disposed of by changes or additions to appropriate working papers and the review notes destroyed.

REVIEW OF FINANCIAL STATEMENTS FOR APPROPRIATE DISCLOSURE

The third generally accepted auditing standard applicable to reporting is

> Informative disclosures in the financial statements are to be regarded as reasonably adequate unless otherwise stated in the report. (SAS No. 1 [AU Section 150.02])

SAS No. 32, *Adequacy of Disclosure in Financial Statements* (AU Section 431), discusses this standard in very general terms. Essentially, material matters regarding the financial statements are to be disclosed in the financial statements or notes; if they are not, the auditor should express a qualified or an adverse opinion and should, if practicable, provide the information in the auditor's report. The auditor's reporting responsibilities with regard to inadequate disclosures are discussed in Chapter 18.

With the proliferation of accounting standards in recent years, many auditors have adopted checklists as a means of enhancing overall quality control. Some auditors have developed separate disclosure checklists for companies subject to SEC reporting requirements and those that are not. Further, separate checklists may be prepared for certain specialized industries, such as banking, insurance, government units, and colleges and universities. A typical arrangement would be to have a series of questions covering all aspects of the financial statements in one column; specific references to the relevant authoritative pronouncement or the auditing firm's preferences in another column (by necessity, the requirements can only be generally stated in the checklist, but the references can make it easier to prepare and review the document); and an indication, in a third column, of whether the item is applicable, and, if so, whether it has been complied with. Space should be allowed for notes or calculations of amounts to demonstrate how materiality considerations entered into disclosure decisions. A completed checklist for an audit can document in one place all reporting and disclosure considerations.

If checklists are used by an auditing firm, it is desirable that a clear statement be appended setting forth the firm's policy on whether they are mandatory for all engagements or only for certain specified engagements, or simply to be used as practice aids. Disclosure checklists should be updated periodically and should also indicate the date produced so that authoritative pronouncements after that date will be considered.

SUBSEQUENT EVENTS

Types of Subsequent Events

Subsequent events are defined in Section 560 of SAS No. 1 (AU Section 560.01–.09) as events or transactions that "occur subsequent to the balance-sheet date, but prior to the issuance of the financial statements and auditor's report, that have a material effect on the financial statements and therefore require adjustment or disclosure in the statements."[3] Subsequent events that occur after the balance sheet date but before the issuance of the financial statements and the auditor's report fall into two categories: those that require adjustment of account balances (and consequently are reflected on the face of the financial statements) and those that should not be recorded but should be disclosed in the financial statements.

The first category of subsequent event is succinctly described in SAS No. 1 (AU Section 560.03), as follows:

> Those events that provide additional evidence with respect to conditions that existed at the date of the balance sheet and affect the estimates inherent in the process of preparing financial statements. All information that becomes available prior to the issuance of the financial statements should be used by management in its evaluation of the conditions on which the estimates were based. The financial statements should be adjusted for any changes in estimates resulting from the use of such evidence.

The second type of subsequent event is one that provides evidence about conditions that did not exist at the balance sheet date but arose afterwards. These events should be reflected in the financial statements of the year in which they occurred, and should not result in adjustment of the statements of the year being reported on. Some of these events, however, may be significant enough that, if they are not disclosed, the prior-year financial statements

[3]The distinction between the discovery of subsequent events before the financial statements are issued and later discovery of facts that existed at the date of the auditor's report, is significant. The latter is discussed in Chapter 18.

would be misleading. They include all transactions and other events and circumstances having significant financial impact. Some examples given in SAS No. 1 are issuance of debt or stock, acquisition of a business, and casualty losses.

Occasionally, an event of that type may be so significant that the auditor's report should call attention to it in an explanatory paragraph. Sometimes adequate disclosure can be made only by means of pro forma data giving effect to the event as if it had occurred at the balance sheet date; major acquisitions, mergers, and recapitalizations are examples.

Section 560 of SAS No. 1 illustrates the distinction between events that reveal or clarify conditions existing at the balance sheet date and those that represent new conditions. The illustration used is a receivable found to be uncollectible after year-end because of a customer's bankruptcy subsequent to that date. This event is in the first category (requiring adjustment of the gross receivable and possibly recalculation of bad debt expense and the allowance for uncollectible accounts) because the debtor's poor financial condition existed at the balance sheet date. A similar receivable found to be uncollectible because of a disaster occurring to the debtor after the balance sheet date is a new condition and falls in the second category, requiring disclosure in the notes to the financial statements rather than adjustment of the accounts. The SAS notes that making the distinction requires "the exercise of judgment and knowledge of the facts and circumstances" (AU Section 560.04).

The distinction is often a fine one and the judgment difficult to make. For example, deteriorating market conditions subsequent to year-end could be a new condition that merely requires disclosure, or it could be evidence of a condition that was inherent in the inventory at year-end, which calls for adjusting it to net realizable value. Similarly, a subsequent event that reveals that estimated expenses are insufficient because of conditions occurring after the balance sheet date should be disclosed. On the other hand, if the reason for the insufficiency is newly discovered evidence of conditions that existed at the balance sheet date, that evidence should be reflected in the expense and related asset or liability accounts on the face of the statements.

There is a third type of subsequent event—one occurring after year-end that requires neither adjustment nor disclosure in the financial statements. Events that do not affect the interpretation of financial statements should not be disclosed because describing them in notes could cause misleading or confusing inferences. Since every event may have a financial impact, it is often extremely difficult to distinguish between events that should and those that should not be disclosed in the financial statements. Strikes, changes in customers or management, and new contracts and agreements are examples of events that ordinarily should not be disclosed in the financial statements, although management may have a responsibility to make public disclosure apart from the financial statements. If the events occur before the annual report to shareholders is printed, the president's letter is often used as a convenient method of communication.

Auditor's Responsibility for Subsequent Events

The auditor's responsibility for subsequent events depends on whether they occurred before or after the date of the auditor's report. The auditor's responsibility for events occurring in the period between the client's year-end and the audit report date (called the subsequent period) is defined in Section 560 of SAS No. 1. Auditors have no responsibility to seek any additional evidence in the period (typically a rather short time) between the date of the auditor's report and the date the financial statements and auditor's report are issued. Nevertheless, many auditors believe that while they have no responsibility to seek additional evidence during that period, they do have a responsibility not to ignore information that comes to their attention.

Auditing Procedures in the Subsequent Period

Paragraphs 10–12 of Section 560 of SAS No. 1 (AU Section 560.10–.12) define the auditor's responsibility to determine whether relevant subsequent events have occurred and discuss auditing procedures performed in the subsequent period. That work generally falls into two major categories—procedures performed for the purpose of keeping current with respect to events occurring in the subsequent period, and completion of auditing procedures performed for other purposes.

The latter category consists of substantive tests and other auditing procedures that involve reviewing transactions occurring in the subsequent period as part of the audit of year-end account balances. These procedures, which have been discussed earlier in this book, include tests of the client's cash cutoffs and sales and purchase cutoffs, and reviews of collections and payments after year-end. As previously noted, however, the auditor has no responsibility to carry out any auditing procedures for the period after the report date.

The procedures for keeping current with respect to events occurring in the subsequent period are specified in AU Section 560.12 and may be summarized as follows:

Read all available information relating to the client's financial affairs: interim financial statements; minutes of meetings of stockholders, directors, and any appropriate committees; pertinent variance and other management reports, and the like. An auditor who understands the client knows which areas are sensitive or volatile and what information about them is likely to be available.

Make inquiries—the more specific the better—about such things as financing activities, unusual entries or adjustments in the accounts, and potential problems discovered during the audit. An auditor who has developed a close working relationship with the client can make those inquiries easily and expeditiously.

Inquire of client's legal counsel concerning litigation, claims, and assessments.

Obtain a letter of representation from client officers describing subsequent events or disclaiming knowledge of any.

In addition, as part of the subsequent-period review, the auditor may compare the latest available interim financial statements with the financial statements being reported on, as well as making other comparisons considered appropriate in the circumstances.

It is sometimes necessary in the subsequent period to perform analytical procedures or other substantive tests in a recognized problem area. Usually, their purpose is to form an opinion on whether a client has measured the impact of a subsequent event reasonably, for example, the impact of a decision to discontinue a line of business made subsequent to year-end. Sometimes, however, tests are required to satisfy the auditor that a possible subsequent event did not occur; an example is tests of the net realizable value of inventories due to changed market conditions subsequent to year-end.

Dating the Report

SAS No. 1 (AU Section 530.01) states that the auditor's report generally should be dated the date when the audit field work is completed, that is, when the auditor has completed substantially all the tests of the accounting records and all other auditing procedures considered necessary in the circumstances of the particular engagement. Matters that may require follow-up with the client, particularly if performed off the client's premises, generally do not affect the date of the auditor's report.

The date of the auditor's report establishes the end of the subsequent period—the period during which an auditor has responsibility for events occurring after the client's year-end—unless the auditor agrees or is required to perform additional procedures, as for example, in filings with the SEC under the Securities Act of 1933, discussed later in this chapter. The higher levels of responsibility that auditors are now being held to, the increased demands of users for reliable financial information, and the fact that the report date signifies the end of the period of the auditor's responsibility for that information have all imparted greater significance to the date of the auditor's report.

The report date is seldom the last day the auditors are on the client's premises. Ancillary matters often require the audit team's presence after the completion of field work. For example, various regulatory reports, covenant letters, and communications to management may have to be prepared or completed. Separate audits may be required for employee benefit plans or related foundations.

A report date about 25 to 45 days after the end of the fiscal year is common for publicly held commercial and manufacturing companies; 15 to 20 days is usual for commercial banks. It then may take several weeks for the published annual report containing the financial statements to be prepared, printed, and mailed, but the auditor's report carries the date on which agreement on the financial statements was reached (unless new information is incorporated in the statements—see the discussion under "Dual Dating," below).

Audit Planning Considerations. If an audit report must be issued within two or three weeks of year-end, the amount of auditing that can take place after year-end is obviously limited. Thus, much of the auditor's work must be essentially completed by year-end. This usually requires that the client have an effective internal control structure and always requires careful planning by the auditor. As indicated in Chapter 9, there are several strategies under which an auditor can perform substantive tests before the balance sheet date and have a reasonable basis for "rolling forward" conclusions from those tests to the balance sheet date.

Many companies, however, cannot or do not choose to seek such early publication of their financial statements. Also, depending on risk assessment, the auditor may find it necessary to perform much of the substantive testing after the balance sheet date, or problems may be encountered in making necessary valuations, estimates, and judgments. It may take 8 to 12 weeks, or even longer, for the audit to be completed. During that time, the auditor must "keep current" with client affairs so as to have a basis for an opinion that subsequent events are properly reflected or disclosed in the financial statements.

Dual Dating. As described earlier, subsequent events that occur after the date of the auditor's report but before the report is issued and that come to the auditor's attention may require adjustment or disclosure in the financial statements. If such an event is disclosed, the auditor can either redate the report as of the date of that event or use "dual dating." In practice, unless the time period is very short, dual dating is more common because of the additional work (discussed above) necessary for the extended period if the report is redated.

An auditor may be required or requested to reissue a report after it was first issued. If the auditor is aware of subsequent events that occurred after the date of the original report, several alternatives are possible. For events that require adjustment of the previously issued financial statements, the report should be dual dated. For events that require disclosure only, the auditor may dual date the report, or the disclosure may be included in an additional (usually the last) note to the financial statements that is labeled "unaudited." When dual dating is used, it usually appears as "January 25, 19X9, except as to Note ___, for which the date is March 1, 19X9."

The Securities Act of 1933

Auditors' SEC practice is dealt with in entire volumes and is beyond the scope of this work. As mentioned in SAS No. 37, *Filings Under Federal Securities Statutes* (AU Section 711.02), "the accountant's responsibility, generally [when reporting on financial statements included in a filing with the SEC], is in substance no different from that involved in other types of reporting." A critical consideration in a 1933 Act filing, however, is that the independent auditor's responsibility with respect to subsequent events extends *to the effective date* of the registration statement and does not terminate at the date of the audit report. This situation results from Section 11(a) of the 1933 Act, which provides for substantial liabilities to those involved in the preparation of a registration statement found to contain untrue statements or material omissions. As pointed out in SAS No. 37 (AU Section 711.10), "To sustain the burden of proof that he has made a 'reasonable investigation,' . . . as required under the Securities Act of 1933, an auditor should extend his procedures with respect to subsequent events from the date of his audit report up to the effective date or as close thereto as is reasonable and practicable in the circumstances."

Subsequent Event Procedures for Keeping Current. The procedures already discussed for keeping current with respect to subsequent events through the date of the auditor's report should be extended to the effective date of the registration statement. In addition, the auditor generally should read the entire prospectus and other pertinent sections of the registration statement.

Letters for Underwriters. The procedures for keeping current that were discussed above are separate and distinct from any procedures that may be required by underwriters in connection with a 1933 Act filing, even though they may frequently be performed at the same time. Letters for underwriters, commonly called "comfort letters," are the subject of SAS No. 49, *Letters for Underwriters* (AU Section 634).

ADMINISTRATIVE WRAP-UP

After the audit has been completed and the working papers have been reviewed and filed, there are both technical and administrative loose ends to wrap up. Special reports, tax returns, and similar matters are likely to have due dates that act as a professional discipline, but it is easy to let administrative matters slide. Tight administrative controls are necessary to prevent that from happening.

Time analyses must be completed and budget variances analyzed. Billings must be prepared and processed. The audit program should be revised in preliminary preparation for the next year's engagement. Ideally, the next year's engagement should be planned with the client as part of the current wrapping-up process. On many well-organized engagements, the end of one engagement constitutes the beginning of the next.

COMMUNICATION WITH AUDIT COMMITTEES

Auditors usually acquire information in the course of an audit that may help the audit committee of the board of directors meet its responsibility for overseeing the entity's financial reporting process, including the audit itself. Various Statements on Auditing Standards require the auditor to communicate certain matters to the audit committee, or to determine that management has appropriately reported them. Those matters include material errors and irregularities, illegal acts, and significant deficiencies in the design or operation of the internal control structure that the auditor became aware of in the course of the audit, including deficiencies related to the preparation of interim financial information. The SEC Practice Section of the AICPA Division for CPA Firms requires the auditor to communicate to the audit committee fees received for management advisory services.

SAS No. 61, *Communication With Audit Committees* (AU Section 380), requires the auditor to determine that certain additional matters related to the conduct of an audit are communicated to those who have responsibility for financial reporting; generally, this means the audit committee. The required communications are applicable to all SEC engagements (as defined in Chapter 3) and to other entities that have an audit committee or equivalent group with formally designated oversight of the financial reporting process. Among the items that should be communicated are

- The level of responsibility the auditor assumes under GAAS for the financial statements and for considering the entity's internal control structure.
- Significant accounting policies that the entity has selected for new or unusual transactions, and changes in those policies.
- The process management used to formulate particularly sensitive accounting estimates, and the basis for the auditor's conclusion that they were reasonable.
- Significant adjustments to the financial statements that resulted from the audit and that have a significant effect on the entity's financial reporting process.
- The auditor's responsibility for other information in documents, such as annual reports to shareholders, containing audited financial statements (see the discussion in the section, "Material Inconsistency Between Fi-

nancial Statements and Other Information Reported by Management," in Chapter 18).

- Disagreements with management over the application of accounting principles, the scope of the audit, and the wording of the auditor's report.
- The auditor's views on auditing and accounting matters that management consulted other auditors about (see the discussion in Chapter 3).
- Major issues regarding the application of accounting principles and auditing standards that the auditor and management discussed in connection with the auditor's initial or recurring retention.
- Serious difficulties encountered in dealing with management related to the performance of the audit, such as unreasonable delays in permitting the start of the audit or in providing needed information, unreasonable timetables, or not making needed client personnel available.

As noted earlier, these matters may be communicated either by the auditor or by management, but the communications must be timely. Some matters should logically be discussed with the audit committee before the auditor's report is drafted, because the discussion may help the auditor form the appropriate conclusion about the financial statements. Others could occur after the report has been issued. The communication of recurring matters need not be repeated every year.

Review Questions

17-1. Define the term contingency, describe the two general types of contingencies that may arise, and briefly discuss how they are accounted for.

17-2. What authoritative pronouncement governs the treatment of contingencies in financial statements?

17-3. Describe the three ranges of likelihood of a contingency occurrence and the appropriate financial statement treatment in each case.

17-4. With respect to loss contingencies related to litigation, claims, and assessments, list the matters for which the auditor is required to obtain evidence. What auditing procedures are used to obtain this evidence?

17-5. What factors should the auditor bear in mind when evaluating lawyers' responses to audit inquiries?

17-6. What course of action should an auditor take when a lawyer's response is incomplete or equivocal?

17-7. What is a client representation letter and when is it required?

17-8. What matters are usually covered in a representation letter? When, and by whom, is it signed?

17-9. How does the auditor resolve items on the summary of adjustments?

17-10. What purpose does the review of working papers serve?

17–11. Describe and distinguish between the two levels of working paper reviews.

17–12. Why is a second-partner review necessary? What are the primary concerns in a second-partner review?

17–13. Name and describe the different types of subsequent events auditors must consider.

17–14. How does an auditor's responsibility with respect to subsequent events on a 1933 Act engagement differ from that on other engagements?

Discussion Questions

17–30. During the audit of the annual financial statements of Waterstone, Inc., the company's president, M. Aldrich, and Williams, the auditor, reviewed matters that were supposed to be included in a written representation letter. On receipt of the following client representation letter, Williams contacted Aldrich to state that it was incomplete.

To D. R. Williams, CPA:

In connection with your audit of the balance sheet of Waterstone, Inc., as of December 31, 1990, and the related statements of income, retained earnings, and cash flows for the year then ended, for the purpose of expressing an opinion as to whether the financial statements present fairly, in all material respects, the financial position, results of operations, and cash flows of Waterstone, Inc. in conformity with generally accepted accounting principles, we confirm, to the best of our knowledge and belief, the following representations made to you during your audit. There were no

- Plans or intentions that may materially affect the carrying value or classification of assets and liabilities.
- Communications from regulatory agencies concerning noncompliance with or deficiencies in financial reporting practices.
- Agreements to repurchase assets previously sold.
- Violations or possible violations of laws or regulations whose effects should be considered for disclosure in the financial statements or as a basis for recording a loss contingency.
- Unasserted claims or assessments that our lawyer has advised are probable of assertion and must be disclosed in accordance with Statement of Financial Accounting Standards No. 5.
- Capital stock repurchase options or agreements or capital stock reserved for options, warrants, conversions, or other requirements.
- Compensating balance or other arrangements involving restrictions on cash balances.

M. Aldrich, President
Waterstone, Inc.
March 14, 1991

Required:

Identify the other matters that Aldrich's representation letter should specifically confirm.

(AICPA adapted)

17–31. What should the reviewer look for during the detailed review of the working papers, and what pitfalls should the reviewer be on guard against?

17–32. How should the auditor in charge of field work prepare for the partner's review of the working papers?

17–33. Bowman, a CPA, is nearing the completion of an audit of the financial statements of Island Products Corp. for the year ended December 31, 1990. Bowman is currently concerned with ascertaining the occurrence of subsequent events that may require adjustment or disclosure essential to a fair presentation in conformity with generally accepted accounting principles.

Required:

a. Briefly explain what is meant by the phrase subsequent event.
b. How do those subsequent events that require financial statement adjustments differ from those that require financial statement disclosure?
c. What procedures should be performed in order to ascertain the occurrence of subsequent events?

(AICPA adapted)

17–34. For items 1 to 6 below, assume that Jane Stevens, CPA, is expressing an opinion on Magical Properties, Inc.'s financial statements for the year ended September 30, 1990, that she completed field work on October 21, 1990, and that she now is preparing her opinion to accompany the financial statements. In each item a "subsequent event" is described. Each event was disclosed to Stevens either in connection with her review of subsequent events or after the completion of the field work. You are to indicate in each case the required financial statement adjustment or disclosure of the event. Each of the six cases is independent of the other five and is to be considered separately. *Your answer choice for each item 1 to 6 should be selected from the following responses:*

a. No financial statement disclosure necessary.
b. Disclosure in a footnote to the financial statements.
c. Adjustment of the financial statements for the year ended September 30, 1990.
d. Disclosure by means of supplemental, pro forma financial data.

1. A large account receivable from CCC Construction Corp. (material to financial statement presentation) was considered fully collectible at September 30, 1990. CCC suffered a plant explosion on October 25, 1990. Since CCC was uninsured, it is unlikely that the account will be paid.
2. A large account receivable from Turner Brothers (material to financial statement presentation) was considered fully collectible at September 30, 1990. Turner filed for bankruptcy on October 17, 1990 as a result of its deteriorating financial condition.
3. Based on a directors' resolution on October 5, 1990, Magical Properties' common stock was split 3-for-1 on October 10, 1990. Magical Properties' earnings per share have been computed based on common shares outstanding at September 30, 1990.
4. Magical Properties' manufacturing division, whose assets constituted 75 percent of the company's total assets at September 30, 1990, was sold on November 1, 1990. The new owner assumed the bonded indebtedness associated with this property.

5. On October 15, 1990, a major investment adviser issued a pessimistic report on Magical Properties' long-term prospects. The market price for Magical Properties' common stock subsequently declined by 50 percent.
6. At its October 5, 1990, meeting, Magical Properties' Board of Directors voted to double the advertising budget for the coming year and authorized a change in advertising agencies.

(AICPA adapted)

17-35. Young, CPA, is considering the procedures to be applied concerning a client's loss contingencies relating to litigation, claims, and assessments.

Required:

What substantive procedures should Young apply when testing for loss contingencies relating to litigation, claims, and assessments?

(AICPA adapted)

AICPA Multiple Choice Questions

These questions are taken from the Auditing part of Uniform CPA Examinations. Choose the single most appropriate answer.

17-40. Which of the following auditing procedures is ordinarily performed last?

a. Reading of the minutes of the directors' meetings.
b. Confirming accounts payable.
c. Obtaining a management representation letter.
d. Testing of the purchasing function.

17-41. The primary objective of analytical procedures used in the final review stage of an audit is to

a. Obtain evidence from details tested to corroborate particular assertions.
b. Identify areas that represent specific risks relevant to the audit.
c. Assist the auditor in assessing the validity of the conclusions reached.
d. Satisfy doubts when questions arise about a client's ability to continue in existence.

17-42. In an audit of contingent liabilities, which of the following procedures would be *least* effective?

a. Reviewing a bank confirmation letter.
b. Examining customer confirmation replies.
c. Examining invoices for professional services.
d. Reading the minutes of the board of directors.

17-43. The auditor's primary means of obtaining corroboration of management's information concerning litigation is a

a. Letter of audit inquiry to the client's lawyer.
b. Letter of corroboration from the auditor's lawyer upon review of the legal documentation.

c. Confirmation of claims and assessments from the other parties to the litigation.
d. Confirmation of claims and assessments from an officer of the court presiding over the litigation.

17–44. An attorney responding to an auditor as a result of the client's letter of audit inquiry may appropriately limit the response to

a. Items which have high probability of being resolved to the client's detriment.
b. Asserted claims and pending or threatened litigation.
c. Legal matters subject to unsettled points of law, uncorroborated information, or other complex judgments.
d. Matters to which the attorney has given substantive attention in the form of legal consultation or representation.

17–45. When obtaining evidence regarding litigation against a client, the CPA would be *least* interested in determining

a. An estimate of when the matter will be resolved.
b. The period in which the underlying cause of the litigation occurred.
c. The probability of an unfavorable outcome.
d. An estimate of the potential loss.

17–46. When considering the use of management's written representations as audit evidence about the completeness assertion, an auditor should understand that such representations

a. Complement, but do *not* replace, substantive tests designed to support the assertion.
b. Constitute sufficient evidence to support the assertion when considered in combination with a test of controls.
c. Are *not* part of the evidential matter considered to support the assertion.
d. Replace tests of controls as evidence to support the assertion.

17–47. A written understanding between the auditor and the client concerning the auditor's responsibility for the discovery of illegal acts is usually set forth in a (an)

a. Client representation letter.
b. Letter of audit inquiry.
c. Management letter.
d. Engagement letter.

17–48. Which of the following statements ordinarily is included among the written client representations obtained by the auditor?

a. Sufficient evidential matter has been made available to permit the issuance of an unqualified opinion.
b. Compensating balances and other arrangements involving restrictions on cash balances have been disclosed.
c. Management acknowledges responsibility for illegal actions committed by employees.
d. Management acknowledges that there are *no* material weaknesses in the internal control structure.

17-49. Hall accepted an engagement to audit the 1989 financial statements of XYZ Company. XYZ completed the preparation of the 1989 financial statements on February 13, 1990, and Hall began the field work on February 17, 1990. Hall completed the field work on March 24, 1990, and completed the report on March 28, 1990. The client's representation letter normally would be dated

a. February 13, 1990.
b. February 17, 1990.
c. March 24, 1990.
d. March 28, 1990.

17-50. The audit work performed by each assistant should be reviewed to determine whether it was adequately performed and to evaluate whether the

a. Audit procedures performed are approved in the professional standards.
b. Audit has been performed by persons having adequate technical training and proficiency as auditors.
c. Auditor's system of quality control has been maintained at a high level.
d. Results are consistent with the conclusions to be presented in the auditor's report.

17-51. "Subsequent events" for reporting purposes are defined as events that occur subsequent to the

a. Balance sheet date.
b. Date of the auditor's report.
c. Balance sheet date but prior to the date of the auditor's report.
d. Date of the auditor's report and concern contingencies that are not reflected in the financial statements.

17-52. An auditor issued an audit report that was dual dated for a subsequent event occurring after the completion of field work but before issuance of the auditor's report. The auditor's responsibility for events occurring subsequent to the completion of field work was

a. Limited to the specific event referenced.
b. Limited to include only events occurring before the date of the last subsequent event referenced.
c. Extended to subsequent events occurring through the date of issuance of the report.
d. Extended to include all events occurring since the completion of field work.

17-53. Which of the following procedures would an auditor most likely perform to obtain evidence about an entity's subsequent events?

a. Reconcile bank activity for the month after the balance sheet date with cash activity reflected in the accounting records.
b. Examine on a test basis the purchase invoices and receiving reports for several days after the inventory date.
c. Review the treasurer's monthly reports on temporary investments owned, purchased, and sold.
d. Obtain a letter from the entity's attorney describing any pending litigation, unasserted claims, or loss contingencies.

17–54. Karr has audited the financial statements of Lurch Corporation for the year ended December 31, 1990. Although Karr's field work was completed on February 27, 1991, Karr's auditor's report was dated February 28, 1991, and was received by the management of Lurch on March 5, 1991. On April 4, 1991, the management of Lurch asked that Karr approve inclusion of this report in their annual report to stockholders, which will include unaudited financial statements for the first quarter ended March 31, 1991. Karr approved of the inclusion of this auditor's report in the annual report to stockholders. Under the circumstances Karr is responsible for inquiring as to subsequent events occurring through

a. February 27, 1991.
b. February 28, 1991.
c. March 31, 1991.
d. April 4, 1991.

17–55. Subsequent events affecting the realization of assets ordinarily will require adjustment of the financial statements under audit because such events typically represent

a. The culmination of conditions that existed at the balance sheet date.
b. The final estimates of losses relating to casualties occurring in the subsequent events period.
c. The discovery of new conditions occurring in the subsequent events period.
d. The preliminary estimate of losses relating to new events that occurred subsequent to the balance sheet date.

Problems and Cases

17–60. You were in the process of completing your audit of the financial statements of General Circuitry Company for the year ended December 31, 1990, when on December 1, 1990, the Pentagon announced that it had been investigating the suitability of certain microcircuits made by General Circuitry and suspended the authorization for defense contractors to use these circuits in weapons and military communications devices, pending the results of its investigation.

Several large defense contractors have stated that, in light of this investigation, they will cease purchasing the microcircuits and have instituted proceedings to recover cost overruns due to the additional costs of alternative materials needed to complete their defense contracts, plus damages. The company estimates that these suits could result in awards of not less than $1 million or more than $3 million, exclusive of estimated legal costs of $500,000.

At present, General Circuitry has approximately $800,000 of the microcircuits in question in finished goods inventory and is committed to purchase $200,000 of raw materials used solely for the manufacture of these microcircuits.

Assume that the company has litigation insurance but with a deductible amount of $500,000 and that a disclaimer of opinion is *not* appropriate.

Required:

a. Define the audit problems and cite applicable professional pronouncements.
b. Determine the approach you would propose toward the solution of the problems, including the evidence or other data you would want to review.

c. Indicate the factors you would consider in determining the impact on the audit budget and related timing of year-end field work.

17-61. In connection with her audit of Grimm Industries for the year ended December 31, 1990, Carol Rogers, CPA, is aware that certain events and transactions that took place after December 31, 1990, but before she issued her report dated February 28, 1991, may affect the company's financial statements.

The following material events or transactions have come to her attention:

1. On January 3, 1991, Grimm received a shipment of raw materials. The materials had been ordered in October 1990 and shipped FOB shipping point in November 1990.
2. On January 15, 1991, the company settled and paid a personal injury claim of a former employee as the result of an accident that occurred in March 1990. The company had not previously recorded a liability for the claim.
3. On January 25, 1991, the company agreed to purchase for cash the outstanding stock of United Plumbing, Inc. The acquisition is likely to double the sales volume of Grimm.
4. On February 1, 1991, a plant owned by Grimm was damaged by a flood, resulting in an uninsured loss of inventory.
5. On February 5, 1991, Grimm issued and sold to the public $2 million of convertible bonds.

Required:

For each of these events or transactions, indicate the auditing procedures that should have brought the item to the attention of the auditor, and the form of disclosure in the financial statements (including the reasons for such disclosure).

Arrange your answer in the following format.

Item No.	*Auditing Procedures*	*Required Disclosures and Reasons*

(AICPA adapted)

17-62. The following are unrelated events that occurred after the balance sheet date but before the audit report was prepared:

1. The granting of a retroactive pay increase.
2. Determination by the federal government of additional income tax due for a prior year.
3. Filing of an antitrust suit by the federal government.
4. Declaration of a stock dividend.
5. Sale of a fixed asset at a substantial profit.

Required:

a. Explain how each of the items might have come to the auditor's attention.
b. Discuss the appropriate accounting recognition or disclosure for each of these events.

(AICPA adapted)

17–63. The auditor in charge of the field work proposed to you, the manager on the engagement, the following adjustments to the December 31, 1989 financial statements of York Products, Inc., as a result of the recently completed audit. Assume that there are no prior-period unadjusted likely misstatements and that you have reviewed the relevant working papers and agree with the auditor's conclusions. Assume also that the client will strongly resist making any adjustments that are not absolutely necessary to avoid a qualified audit opinion.

1. Per working paper 55.2, ending inventory is known to be understated by $25,000 as a result of errors in the physical count.
2. Per working paper 55.3, ending inventory is projected to be understated by $49,000 as a result of inventory pricing errors discovered in a sampling application.
3. Per working paper 71.5, known year-end unrecorded expenses and liabilities identified in nonsampling applications amount to $47,500. A projection from sampling procedures indicates that an additional $20,000 should be recorded.
4. Per working paper 53.2, the allowance for uncollectible accounts is $79,000 below the lowest reasonable estimate of what the balance should be.
5. Per working paper 23.19, the balance in the pension liability account at December 31, 1986, was discovered to be understated by $95,000. This was not a self-correcting error, and it was not discovered until this year's audit.
6. Per working paper 53.25, a sample of sales transactions revealed that errors in pricing sales invoices are projected to lead to a $164,000 understatement of sales revenue.
7. Per working paper 52.3, $150,000 of cash receipts from collection of accounts receivable was incorrectly included in 1990 cash receipts; another $45,800 of cash receipts from cash sales was incorrectly recorded in 1990 cash receipts. The cost of those sales, also recorded in the wrong period, is $20,000.
8. Per working paper 53.6, year-end cutoff tests of sales indicated that sales on open account in the amount of $865,000 are known to be incorrectly recorded in 1989. They should have been recorded in 1990. The cost of those sales, also recorded in the wrong period, is $415,000.

Financial statement totals (before audit adjustments) are as follows:

Assets	$19,193,000
Liabilities	10,760,000
Owners' equity	8,433,000
Income before taxes	3,793,000

The partner on the engagement has set balance sheet materiality at $400,000 and income statement materiality (pretax) at $150,000. The effective ordinary income tax rate is 45 percent.

Required:

a. Prepare a summary of audit differences that summarizes proposed audit adjustments. For the balance sheet, consider the impact on assets, liabilities, and owners' equity. For the income statement, distinguish among known misstatements, projected misstatements, and misstatements from unreasonable estimates.
b. What adjustments, if any, would you require the client to make in order that an unqualified opinion could be issued? Explain.

17-64. For each of the following attorney's responses, indicate the likelihood of an unfavorable outcome (i.e., probable, reasonably possible, or remote) or indicate if a response needs further clarification or information.

1. "Discovery has been completed and we believe the company will be able to defend this action successfully."
2. "We believe the company will be unable to defend this action."
3. "We believe the action can be settled for less than the damages claimed."
4. "We are of the opinion that this action will not result in any liability to the company."
5. "We believe that the plaintiff's case against the company is without merit."
6. "We feel that our client has meritorious defenses against the aforementioned lawsuit."
7. "We are of the opinion the company will be liable for the full amount of the alleged damages."
8. "It is our opinion that the possible liability to the company in this proceeding is nominal in amount."

17-65. ***Quinn Hardware*** (Year-End Procedures)

Part A

You have been assigned the responsibility for year-end auditing procedures relating to Quinn's inventory account balances. During the inventory observation procedures at interim, it was noted that a large section at the Houston warehouse contained a herbicide product that showed signs of water damage.

Upon further investigation, management informed you that the warehouse has had problems with a leaking roof and significant damage occurred to the supply of bagged Lorax herbicide that was being stored. In some areas the roof leaked so badly that runoff water had to be routed through a drainage system, contaminating the local water supply. You learned that moisture damage ruins herbicides; therefore, bags that have been damaged will not be salvageable and will have to be disposed of. The total cost of the inventories is $1.2 million. It has been estimated that three-quarters of the stock has been damaged and no reserve has been recorded.

Required:

a. What should you consider in valuing the Lorax?
b. What other matters merit consideration regarding potential risks?
c. If the damage occurred subsequent to year-end but before issuance of the report, how might this affect the financial statements?

Part B

The information on page 745 relates to inventories of Quinn. You are performing analytical procedures to identify potential valuation risks.

Required:

What inquiries would you make of client management based on your review of this information?

Part C

Based on your analysis of the information in Part B and further discussions with the client, you determined the reason for the lower than anticipated turnover in lawn and garden supplies is due primarily to problems with one line of fertilizer, FertiGro.

	May 31, 1991 Inventory (in Millions)	*Actual Fiscal 1991 Inventory Turnover*	*Budgeted Fiscal 1991 Inventory Turnover*
Housewares	$10.4	2.9	2.7
Sporting goods	4.7	2.8	2.5
Hand tools	7.2	3.2	3.1
Machine tools	9.5	3.3	3.1
Building materials	6.2	2.6	2.5
Architectural supplies	3.1	2.3	2.5
Paint	3.4	2.4	2.3
Plumbing materials	5.3	2.1	2.4
Lawn and garden supplies (new product line introduced in March 1990)	13.8	1.9	3.0
	$63.6	2.6	2.9

Quinn, in their efforts to start their lawn and garden line, stocked up heavily on FertiGro, a relatively new product. Inventory cost at May 31, 1991 is approximately $2 million. Shortly after the initial purchase, various environmental concerns were raised regarding the use of FertiGro. Reports published in the *U.S. Agricultural Reporter*, a trade publication, have stated that use of FertiGro has been linked to cancer and possible birth defects. Reports have indicated that the government may ban the use of the fertilizer. Quinn has discontinued sale of the product. Due to the problems, FertiGro's manufacturer has filed for bankruptcy, and Quinn is unable to return the products.

Required:

a. What questions or concerns should you raise in the valuation of FertiGro?
b. Assume there are three viable options management is considering.
    - Selling the product to a company that can extract certain chemical components usable in other products. They are willing to buy all quantities on hand for $500,000.
    - Contracting with a processing company to reprocess the product at an additional cost of $1.2 million to remove the cancer-causing component, after which it is anticipated the product could be sold for $2.4 million. Additional shipping and repackaging costs would be $200,000.
    - Disposing of the product, which would result in additional disposal costs of $100,000.

As of the date of the audit work, management has still not decided which option to take. Even though contracting out for reprocessing would minimize the loss, the publicity from the sales of FertiGro has hurt Quinn's public image, and management is considering selling to the extracting company to disassociate Quinn from the product. Because of this indecision, management has not yet adjusted the inventory for the possible loss.

As the auditor, determine a proposed write-down, along with rationale, for your discussion with the controller.

18

The Auditor's Report

An auditor's report is the formal result of all the effort that goes into an audit. There are many other results—for example, the direct and indirect impact of audits on the control, accountability, and public reporting practices of companies—and some people maintain that these are more significant, but the report is the specific, identifiable focal point for the auditor and for all those who rely on the audit.

This chapter covers the standard report (often called an unqualified or "clean" report or opinion), matters that require explicit attention in issuing a report, and the handling of variations from the standard report. Those variations fall into two categories—*explanatory language* in the standard report that does not constitute a qualified opinion, and *departures* from the standard report to express other than an unqualified opinion. The three types of departures from unqualified opinions—qualified opinions, adverse opinions, and disclaimers of opinion—what each conveys, and the circumstances in which each is appropriate are examined in detail, with illustrations. The chapter also includes a discussion of the auditor's responsibilities after the report date.

STANDARD REPORTS

The auditor's report that appears in Figure 18.1 indicates the wording of the standard report prescribed by SAS No. 58, *Reports on Audited Financial Statements* (AU Section 508), issued in 1988.

Organization and Wording

The following paragraphs explain the language used in the standard report and its organization.

Title. The title should include the word "independent," as in the phrase "Independent Auditor's Report." This is intended to remind the reader of the credibility an audit adds to the financial statements because of the auditor's independence.

Introductory Paragraph. The opening paragraph of the report identifies the financial statements that were audited and states that management is responsible for them.[1] The auditor's responsibility is to give an opinion on those

[1]Many publicly traded companies include reports by management in their financial statements. Those reports usually contain a statement of management's responsibility for the financial statements. An auditing interpretation of SAS No. 58 (AU Section 9508.51) indicates that the statement about management's responsibility for the financial statements that appears in the introductory paragraph of the auditor's standard report should not be further elaborated on nor should it refer to a management report. Such modifications of the auditor's report might lead to unwarranted assumptions that the auditor was providing assurance about representations made by management about its responsibility for financial reporting, internal control, and other matters that might be discussed in the management report.

Figure 18.1 Auditor's Standard Report

Report of Independent Accountants

To the Stockholders and Board of Directors of NYNEX Corporation:

We have audited the accompanying consolidated balance sheets of NYNEX Corporation and its subsidiaries as of December 31, 1988 and 1987, and related consolidated statements of income, changes in stockholders' equity, and cash flows for each of the three years in the period ended December 31, 1988. These consolidated financial statements are the responsibility of NYNEX Corporation's management. Our responsibility is to express an opinion on these consolidated financial statements based on our audits.

We conducted our audits in accordance with generally accepted auditing standards. Those standards require that we plan and perform the audit to obtain reasonable assurance about whether the consolidated financial statements are free of material misstatement. An audit includes examining, on a test basis, evidence supporting the amounts and disclosures in the consolidated financial statements. An audit also includes assessing the accounting principles used and significant estimates made by management, as well as evaluating the overall consolidated financial statement presentation. We believe that our audits provide a reasonable basis for our opinion.

In our opinion, the consolidated financial statements referred to above present fairly, in all material respects, the consolidated financial position of NYNEX Corporation and its subsidiaries as of December 31, 1988 and 1987, and the results of their operations and their cash flows for each of the three years in the period ended December 31, 1988, in conformity with generally accepted accounting principles.

Coopers & Lybrand

New York, New York
February 7, 1989

statements based on the results of the audit. The phrase "we have audited" implies that the auditor is providing the highest level of assurance that can be given. (Lower levels of assurance can be provided in other types of engagements, such as "reviews.") The introductory paragraph also specifies the dates of and periods covered by the financial statements that were audited.

It is important that the reader of the document in which the financial statements appear know precisely what is covered by the auditor's report and, by inference, what is not. Since an annual report or prospectus contains much more than the financial statements, the reader must be told specifically what has been audited (the financial statements and the related notes that are, as stated on each page of the body of the financial statements, an "integral part of the financial statements") and what, by implication, has not been audited, such as the letter from the president and chairman of the board, financial ratios, and information about stock prices.

Scope Paragraph. The scope paragraph describes the auditor's basis for forming the opinion on the financial statements. Telling the reader that the audit was conducted in accordance with generally accepted auditing standards is the equivalent of saying that the auditor has complied with the standards established by the auditing profession for performing an audit. The auditor's objective in performing an audit is to gather enough evidence to enable him or her to provide *reasonable* assurance, but not a guarantee, that the financial statements do not contain material misstatements. (A misstatement is considered material if it is probable that the judgment of a reasonable person relying on the financial statements would have been changed or influenced by the misstatement.)

The scope paragraph includes a thumbnail sketch of what an audit entails. It notes that evidence about the accounting measurements and disclosures in the financial statements was obtained only on a test basis. To do otherwise would be economically prohibitive and would entail costs that society as a whole would not be willing to pay. The report specifically states that assessing the client's accounting principles, the estimates that are part of the financial statements, and the overall financial statement presentation are key elements of an audit. Last, the auditor explicitly states that the evidence obtained and evaluated in the course of the audit was sufficient to support the opinion given.

Opinion Paragraph. The opinion paragraph of the auditor's report—usually the third, and final, paragraph—states the auditor's conclusions reached from the work performed. The auditor's opinion represents a judgment made after evaluating evidence about the assertions implicit in the financial statements; the phrase "in our opinion" is intended to convey this element of judgment, as opposed to a statement of fact. (As discussed later, in some cases the auditor may be unable to form an opinion.)

The conclusion the auditor reaches in most audits of financial statements is that the financial statements "present fairly . . . in conformity with generally accepted accounting principles."[2] The opinion illustrated here is technically called an unqualified opinion—that is, it is not qualified by any exceptions. A less technical term for an unqualified opinion is a "clean" opinion. Although authoritative AICPA literature describes other types of opinions (qualified opinions, adverse opinions, and disclaimers of opinion), the usual expectation is that the auditor will be able to render a positive, unqualified opinion. Anything less is usually undesirable, and often unacceptable either to the client or to regulatory bodies. Users of financial statements are best served if the client's financial statements do "present fairly . . . in conformity with generally accepted accounting principles." Thus, auditors have a responsibility to both the public and their clients to assist clients in receiving an unqualified opinion by seeking to improve their financial reporting practices, when that may be necessary.

Until 1988, generally accepted auditing standards required a reference to consistency in the auditor's report. That requirement was eliminated by SAS No. 58, which requires the auditor to report only a *lack* of consistency in the application of GAAP.

The Meaning of Fair Presentation in Conformity with GAAP

The first standard of reporting states

> The report shall state whether the financial statements are presented in accordance with generally accepted accounting principles.

Generally accepted accounting principles provide a consistent frame of reference against which each of management's assertions that are implicit in the financial statements can be evaluated. Obviously, an auditor must be thoroughly familiar with generally accepted accounting principles to comply responsibly with this standard. The literature is vast on accounting principles and the meaning of "generally accepted." Nevertheless, the accounting profession has been criticized for failure to promulgate GAAP that would provide even more detailed guidance.

Despite acknowledged deficiencies in generally accepted accounting principles, aggravated by some misunderstanding by nonaccountants, the phrase is generally understood by practitioners and many users of the report as well. Paragraph 138 of APB Statement No. 4, *Basic Concepts and Accounting Principles Underlying Financial Statements of Business Enterprises*, defines generally accepted accounting principles as "the conventions, rules, and procedures necessary to define accepted accounting practice at a particular time." The Commission

[2]Note that the illustrative opinion is about the financial statements, not about individual account balances. The auditor may express an opinion about specific accounts, rather than about the financial statements taken as a whole, in a "special report," which is discussed in Chapter 19.

on Auditors' Responsibilities (Cohen Commission) noted that generally accepted accounting principles

> Are not limited to the principles in pronouncements of authoritative bodies such as the Financial Accounting Standards Board (FASB). They also include practices that have achieved acceptance through common usage as well as principles in nonauthoritative pronouncements of bodies of recognized stature such as the Accounting Standards Division of the American Institute of Certified Public Accountants. Too narrow a view of the scope of those principles by auditors and preparers has contributed to the criticism of both generally accepted accounting principles and auditors. (p. 15)

SAS No. 5, *The Meaning of "Present Fairly in Conformity With Generally Accepted Accounting Principles" in the Independent Auditor's Report*, as amended (AU Section 411), also suggests that in addition to the accounting principles covered by Rule 203 of the AICPA Code of Professional Conduct (FASB Statements, FASB Interpretations, APB Opinions, AICPA Accounting Research Bulletins, and Statements and Interpretations of the Governmental Accounting Standards Board [GASB]), there are other possible sources of GAAP. These other sources include AICPA industry audit and accounting guides and Statements of Position, FASB and GASB Technical Bulletins, AICPA Accounting Interpretations, prevalent industry accounting practices, and other accounting literature, such as APB Statements, AICPA Issues Papers and Practice Bulletins, minutes of the FASB Emerging Issues Task Force, FASB and GASB Concepts Statements, and Statements of the International Accounting Standards Committee, as well as accounting textbooks and articles. SAS No. 5 also notes that

> On occasion, established accounting principles may not exist for recording and presenting a specific event or transaction because of developments such as new legislation or the evolution of a new type of business transaction. In certain instances, it may be possible to account for the event or transaction on the basis of its substance by selecting an accounting principle that appears appropriate when applied in a manner similar to the application of an established principle to an analogous event or transaction.

Accountants generally agree that, unlike Newton's laws in physics, the accounting principles referred to in the first standard of reporting and in the auditor's opinion are not fundamental truths or comprehensive laws from which the details of practice are derived. As a result, accountants over the years have wrestled with specific situations arising in practice and have developed and adopted numerous rules, conventions, and doctrines, which are now called principles. Some of those principles have been promulgated formally by an authoritative body of the profession (such as the FASB, the GASB, or the APB) or by the SEC, but often they represent a consensus of professional bodies, prominent writers, and eminent practitioners. As suggested earlier, all of those accepted conventions constitute the body of GAAP.

There have been efforts to expand the first reporting standard to require auditors to report on "fairness" separately from GAAP. The reason for these attempts is a belief in some quarters that it is possible to prepare financial statements that conform with GAAP but that nevertheless are not presented fairly and may in fact be misleading. Unfortunately, there has been some basis for that view in the past, principally because some preparers and auditors took a much narrower view of what constitutes GAAP than was explained earlier. SAS No. 5 (AU Section 411) clarified the situation by setting forth what the term "generally accepted accounting principles" encompassed (essentially, what was described earlier), and by noting that the auditor's judgment concerning the fairness of financial statement presentation should be applied within that frame of reference. Clearly, "fairness" is too loose a term to be practical or useful unless it is defined within a specific frame of reference, that is, GAAP. Some auditors believe that the word "fairly" should be removed from the auditor's opinion; that proposal has met strong resistance, particularly from the SEC.

The SAS also enumerated the various judgments that the auditor must make before rendering an unqualified opinion. The auditor's positive opinion about fair presentation in conformity with generally accepted accounting principles implies a belief that the financial statements have the following qualities:

1. The accounting principles selected and applied have general acceptance;
2. The accounting principles are appropriate in the circumstances;
3. The financial statements, including the related notes, are informative on matters that may affect their use, understanding, and interpretation;
4. The information presented in the financial statements is classified and summarized in a reasonable manner, that is, neither too detailed nor too condensed; and
5. The financial statements reflect the underlying events and transactions in a manner that presents financial position, results of operations, and cash flows stated within a range of acceptable limits—that is, limits that are reasonable and practicable to attain in financial statements. (SAS No. 5 [AU Section 411.04])

Routine Variations in the Standard Report

Routine variations in the wording of the standard report include the party or parties to whom it is addressed, the identification of the statements reported on, the period(s) covered, and the date of the report. An auditor should not alter the standard report unless there are problems or unusual conditions to be highlighted—and then the alterations should follow the carefully drawn rules referred to in the following sections of this chapter—because any departure from the standard words is usually regarded as some sort of warning to the reader.

Addressing the Report. The report may be addressed to the client company itself or to its board of directors or stockholders. The authors believe auditors have a responsibility to the owners of a business enterprise and therefore that the report should be addressed to the stockholders, board of directors and stockholders, partners, or proprietor. The authors also believe reports generally should not be addressed solely to the board of directors, unless the company is closely held. An auditor's ultimate responsibility is to the stockholders rather than to the company or its management.

Sometimes an auditor is retained to audit the financial statements of a nonclient company on behalf of a client. In that case, the report should be addressed to the client and not to the company being audited or its directors or stockholders (but see the discussion about confidentiality in Chapter 3, concerning the necessity for making sure that all parties involved understand the auditor's responsibility).

Identifying the Statements. The statements should be clearly identified, usually in the introductory paragraph. The exact name of the company should be used and the statements audited should be enumerated. Generally, these are the balance sheet, the statement of income and retained earnings, and the statement of cash flows. If any other statements are covered by the report, they should also be enumerated; for example, some companies present a separate statement of changes in stockholders' equity accounts.

Periods Covered. The periods reported on should also be specified. In annual reports it is common to report on two years for comparative purposes. Companies whose securities are registered with the SEC are, however, required to present audited comparative income statements and statements of cash flows for three years and balance sheets for two years. A continuing auditor should update his or her report on the individual financial statements of the one or more prior periods presented on a comparative basis with those of the current period by referring to those statements in the introductory and opinion paragraphs.[3]

Dating the Report. Inevitably, an auditor's report is issued on a date later than the end of the period being reported on because it takes time to close the books, prepare financial statements, and complete final auditing procedures. The selection of the appropriate date is discussed in Chapter 17.

[3]SAS No. 58 (AU Section 508) states in a footnote to paragraph 74

> An updated report on prior-period financial statements should be distinguished from a reissuance of a previous report . . . since in issuing an updated report the continuing auditor considers information that he has become aware of during his audit of the current-period financial statements . . . and because an updated report is issued in conjunction with the auditor's report on the current-period financial statements.

See also the discussion later in this chapter, "Different Reports on Comparative Financial Statements Presented."

EXPLANATORY LANGUAGE ADDED TO THE STANDARD REPORT

There are several circumstances that while not affecting the auditor's unqualified opinion may require that the auditor add an explanatory paragraph (or other explanatory language) to the standard report. Those circumstances are discussed in the following paragraphs.

Opinion Based in Part on Report of Another Auditor

Chapter 6 discusses audit planning considerations when part of an engagement is carried out by another auditor. The auditor who serves as the principal auditor may decide not to refer to that circumstance in the report, thus assuming responsibility for the work of the other auditor. If the principal auditor does refer to the work of the other auditor, the standard report is expanded to indicate the division of responsibility and the magnitude of the portion of the financial statements audited by the other auditor. Normally, this is done by noting the percentage or dollar amount of total assets and total revenues audited by the other auditor. Sometimes, other appropriate criteria, such as the percentage of net income, may be used. The other auditor usually is not named. When other auditors are named, their express permission must be obtained and their reports must be presented together with that of the principal auditor.

If the other auditor's report contains explanatory language or a departure from an unqualified opinion (see the later discussion), the principal auditor should decide whether the cause of the explanatory language or departure is of such a nature and significance, in relation to the financial statements the principal auditor is reporting on, that it requires explanatory language or a departure from an unqualified opinion in the principal auditor's report. If the subject of the explanatory language or departure is not material to the overall financial statements, and if the other auditor's report is not presented, the principal auditor need not refer to the explanatory language or departure. If the other auditor's report is presented, the principal auditor may nevertheless wish to make reference to the explanatory language or departure and its disposition.

An example of an unqualified report (on comparative financial statements) in which the work of another auditor has been used and is referred to follows[4]:

> We have audited the consolidated balance sheets of ABC Company as of December 31, 19X2 and 19X1, and the related consolidated statements of income,

[4]SAS No. 58 (AU Section 508.08) specifies that a title that includes the word "independent" is one of the basic elements of the standard audit report. The illustrative standard reports in AU Section 508 use the title "Independent Auditor's Report." This and subsequent illustrative audit reports present only the body of the report and omit the title, as well as the date of the report and signature of the auditor's firm.

> retained earnings, and cash flows for the years then ended. These financial statements are the responsibility of the Company's management. Our responsibility is to express an opinion on these financial statements based on our audits. We did not audit the financial statements of B Company, a wholly-owned subsidiary, which statements reflect total assets of $ _____ and $ _____ as of December 31, 19X2 and 19X1, respectively, and total revenues of $ _____ and $ _____ for the years then ended. Those statements were audited by other auditors whose report has been furnished to us, and our opinion, insofar as it relates to the amounts included for B Company, is based solely on the report of the other auditors.
>
> We conducted our audits in accordance with generally accepted auditing standards. Those standards require that we plan and perform the audit to obtain reasonable assurance about whether the financial statements are free of material misstatement. An audit includes examining, on a test basis, evidence supporting the amounts and disclosures in the financial statements. An audit also includes assessing the accounting principles used and significant estimates made by management, as well as evaluating the overall financial statement presentation. We believe that our audits and the report of other auditors provide a reasonable basis for our opinion.
>
> In our opinion, based on our audits and the report of other auditors, the consolidated financial statements referred to above present fairly, in all material respects, the financial position of ABC Company as of December 31, 19X2 and 19X1, and the results of its operations and its cash flows for the years then ended in conformity with generally accepted accounting principles.

The disclosure is lengthy and somewhat awkward and much expanded from reporting practice of some years ago when it was customary only to state that part of the engagement had been carried out by other auditors. Employing more than one auditor is an acceptable practice, but inevitably results in divided responsibility and risk of misunderstanding or omission. The practice is sometimes followed, however, to take advantage of specialized expertise or when the principal auditor is not located in areas served by other auditors. Chapter 6 includes a discussion of additional procedures the principal auditor may follow when the work of other auditors is used.

Also as discussed in Chapter 6, an auditor may obtain and use a report by another auditor on internal control at a service organization that is used by the client to execute or record certain transactions or to process certain data. The auditor's report on the financial statements should not refer to the report of the auditor who reported on the service organization's internal control. As stated in AU Section 324.24, "The service [organization's] auditor's report is used in the audit, but the service [organization's] auditor is not responsible for examining a portion of the financial statements. . . . Thus, there cannot be a meaningful indication of a division of responsibility for the financial statements."

Departures from a Promulgated Accounting Principle with Which an Auditor Agrees

Since 1964, members of the AICPA have been expected to treat departures from accounting principles promulgated in the Opinions of the APB and in the predecessor Accounting Research Bulletins as departures from GAAP, leading to a qualified or an adverse opinion. That expectation is now incorporated in Rule 203 of the AICPA Code of Professional Conduct and the related interpretations; it also applies to the pronouncements of the FASB and the GASB. It is covered as a special case in paragraphs 14 and 15 of SAS No. 58 (AU Section 508).

In rare and unusual circumstances, a departure from an accounting principle promulgated by the APB, the FASB, or the GASB may be required to present a particular transaction or other event or circumstance in a manner that is not misleading. If the auditor and client agree that a certain treatment that departs from such a promulgated principle is required in order to make the statements not misleading, it is permissible for the financial statements to reflect the departure, provided the departure and its effect are disclosed both in a note to the financial statements and in the auditor's report. The reason for believing that the departure from a promulgated standard is justified should be stated, and the auditor should then express an unqualified opinion.

Predecessor Auditor's Report Not Presented

When comparative financial statements are presented and the prior year's statements were audited by another auditor, the successor auditor and the client have two options concerning the auditor's report. Under the first option, the client could make arrangements with the predecessor auditor to reissue the report on the financial statements of the prior period, provided the predecessor auditor performs the procedures described in paragraph 80 of SAS No. 58 (AU Section 508). Paragraph 80 requires that before reissuing a previously issued report, a predecessor auditor should consider whether the previous opinion is still appropriate. To do that,

> A predecessor auditor should (a) read the financial statements of the current period, (b) compare the prior-period financial statements that he reported on with the financial statements to be presented for comparative purposes, and (c) obtain a letter of representations from the successor auditor.

The predecessor auditor should not refer in the reissued report to the report of the successor auditor. The successor auditor should report only on the current year's financial statements.

Under the second option, the predecessor auditor's report is not presented.[5] In this case, pursuant to paragraph 83 of SAS No. 58,

> The successor auditor should indicate in the introductory paragraph of his report (a) that the financial statements of the prior period were audited by another auditor, (b) the date of his report, (c) the type of report issued by the predecessor auditor, and (d) if the report was other than a standard report, the substantive reasons therefor.

An example of a successor auditor's report when the predecessor auditor's report is not presented follows:

> We have audited the balance sheet of ABC Company as of December 31, 19X2, and the related statements of income, retained earnings, and cash flows for the year then ended. These financial statements are the responsibility of the Company's management. Our responsibility is to express an opinion on these financial statements based on our audit. The financial statements of ABC Company as of December 31, 19X1, were audited by other auditors whose report dated March 31, 19X2, expressed an unqualified opinion on those statements.
>
> [*Same second paragraph as the standard report*]
>
> In our opinion, the 19X2 financial statements referred to above present fairly, in all material respects, the financial position of ABC Company as of December 31, 19X2, and the results of its operations and its cash flows for the year then ended in conformity with generally accepted accounting principles.

If the predecessor auditor's report was other than a standard report, the successor auditor should describe the nature of and reasons for any explanatory paragraphs or opinion qualifications.

Report on a Balance Sheet Only

In certain instances, an auditor may be asked to report only on a client's balance sheet, rather than on all of the financial statements. This may occur in filings under debt or credit agreements. The following is an example (from AU Section 508.48) of a report on a balance sheet only:

> We have audited the accompanying balance sheet of X Company as of December 31, 19XX. This financial statement is the responsibility of the Company's management. Our responsibility is to express an opinion on this financial statement based on our audit.

[5]SEC proxy Rule 14c-3 permits the separate report of the predecessor auditor to be omitted in the annual report to securityholders, provided the registrant has obtained a reissued report from the predecessor auditor. The separate report of the predecessor auditor is, however, required in filings with the Commission.

We conducted our audit in accordance with generally accepted auditing standards. Those standards require that we plan and perform the audit to obtain reasonable assurance about whether the balance sheet is free of material misstatement. An audit includes examining, on a test basis, evidence supporting the amounts and disclosures in the balance sheet. An audit also includes assessing the accounting principles used and significant estimates made by management, as well as evaluating the overall balance sheet presentation. We believe that our audit of the balance sheet provides a reasonable basis for our opinion.

In our opinion, the balance sheet referred to above presents fairly, in all material respects, the financial position of X Company as of December 31, 19XX, in conformity with generally accepted accounting principles.

Material Inconsistency Between Financial Statements and Other Information Reported by Management

An enterprise may publish a document, such as an annual report, that contains information in addition to audited financial statements and the auditor's report. That information, which is referred to in professional pronouncements (SAS No. 8, *Other Information in Documents Containing Audited Financial Statements* [AU Section 550]) as "other information," includes such items as a ten-year financial summary and an analysis of financial data in the president's letter. It also includes management's discussion and analysis of operations (for the three most recent years) and of changes in financial position and liquidity (during the two most recent years), as required of enterprises whose securities are registered with the SEC. In addition, an auditing interpretation (AU Section 9550.01-.06) indicates that statements made in a report by management on the entity's internal control structure are "other information" covered by SAS No. 8.

The auditor has no responsibility to corroborate "other information," but SAS No. 8 specifies that the auditor does have a responsibility to read it and consider whether it is materially inconsistent with information appearing in the financial statements. If it is, the auditor should request the client to revise the other information. If the other information is not revised to eliminate the inconsistency, the auditor should consider whether to withhold the audit report, withdraw from the engagement, or include an explanatory paragraph describing the inconsistency. The auditor's opinion would still be unqualified, since the deficiency would not be in the audited financial statements. Such instances are, as might be expected, extremely rare, since even management that is prone to "puffery" of its accomplishments is likely to retreat in the face of the possibility of an explanatory comment in the auditor's report.

Another problem arises when the auditor, on reading the other information, determines (on the basis of knowledge obtained in the course of the audit) that there is a material misstatement of fact that is not related to information in the audited financial statements. Beyond suggesting that the auditor consult others, including legal counsel, and notify the client, the authoritative literature provides scant guidance; nor does the literature require the auditor to disclose the misstatement. The Cohen Commission recommended (page 69) that the auditor be required to read the other information to ensure that it is not inconsistent with *anything* the auditor knows, as a result of the audit, about the company and its operations and that the auditor modify the report to describe the misstatement if management does not correct it. At the date of this writing, no professional standard-setting body has acted on this recommendation.

Supplementary Information Required by FASB or GASB Pronouncements

Supplementary information required by the FASB or the GASB differs from other types of information outside the basic financial statements. This is because the FASB or the GASB considers the information an essential part of the financial reporting of certain entities and has, therefore, established guidelines for the measurement and presentation of the information. The only supplementary information presently required by the FASB or the GASB is oil and gas reserve information (SFAS No. 69, *Disclosures about Oil and Gas Producing Activities*) and ten-year historical trend pension information by public employee retirement systems and state and local governmental employers (GASB Statement No. 5, *Disclosure of Pension Information by Public Employee Retirement Systems and State and Local Government Employers*).

The AICPA has established limited procedures to be applied by the auditor to this information. In addition, AU Section 558.08 provides for exception reporting. That is, the auditor is required to report, in an additional explanatory paragraph (a) deficiencies in or the omission of such information, (b) an inability to complete the prescribed limited procedures, or (c) the inability to remove substantial doubts about whether the supplementary information conforms to prescribed guidelines.

Uncertainties

Management is expected to evaluate and reach a reasoned conclusion on all matters materially affecting financial position and results of operations, and an auditor is expected to review and form an opinion on those conclusions. Sometimes, however, the financial statements are affected by uncertainties concerning future events, such as a lawsuit whose outcome cannot be reasonably estimated by either management or the auditor. Such uncertainties may give rise to explanatory paragraphs in the auditor's report, or possibly even to disclaimers when the uncertainties are pervasive (see discussion of disclaimers later in this chapter).

SFAS No. 5 (Accounting Standards Section C59.104) requires that potential losses due to uncertainties be classified as "probable," "reasonably possible," or "remote." If a loss is probable, management must provide for it in the financial statements, either by accruing it if the amount is susceptible to reasonable determination or by disclosing it if the amount cannot be reasonably estimated. No explanatory language is needed in the auditor's standard report if the auditor agrees that the provision or disclosure is appropriate; if the amount cannot be reasonably estimated, however, the auditor should add an explanatory paragraph to the report because of the uncertainty. Likewise, a "remote" uncertainty would not require an explanatory paragraph in the standard report. If a material loss is "reasonably possible," however, management is required to disclose the uncertainty in the notes to the financial statements, including an estimate of the amount, and the auditor would normally add an explanatory paragraph to the report.

For instance, if the outcome of a matter having an impact on the financial statements depends on the decisions of others, it may be impossible for management and the auditor to reach a valid conclusion about it because competent evidential matter simply does not exist. The most common events of that kind are lawsuits and tax disputes. The mere existence of an unresolved question does not relieve management or the auditor of the responsibility for forming a judgment about the outcome, if at all possible; for many disputed tax issues, for example, the outcome can be reasonably determined by an informed analysis. In some cases, however, the best possible efforts result in a judgment that no valid conclusion can be formed. In that event, the auditor should describe the uncertainty in a separate explanatory paragraph following the opinion paragraph of the report, along with an indication that its outcome cannot presently be determined. The separate paragraph may be shortened to refer to disclosures made in a note to the financial statements.

SAS No. 58 (AU Section 508.32) gives an example of the wording of a report containing an explanatory paragraph describing an uncertainty affecting the financial statements.

> [*Separate paragraph following the opinion paragraph*]
>
> As discussed in Note X to the financial statements, the Company is a defendant in a lawsuit alleging infringement of certain patent rights and claiming royalties and punitive damages. The Company has filed a counteraction, and preliminary hearings and discovery proceedings on both actions are in progress. The ultimate outcome of the litigation cannot presently be determined. Accordingly, no provision for any liability that may result upon adjudication has been made in the accompanying financial statements.

The Likelihood and Materiality of Uncertainties. The auditor must use professional judgment in considering whether a loss resulting from the resolution of an uncertainty is sufficiently likely and material to require adding an explanatory paragraph in the report.

If the likelihood of a material loss is only remote, no explanatory paragraph would be necessary. If it is probable (likely) that a material loss will occur, but management cannot make a reasonable estimate of the amount or range of the potential loss and thus cannot accrue the loss in the financial statements, the auditor should add an explanatory paragraph. If the chance of a material loss is "reasonably possible" (that is, more than remote but less than probable), whether or not an explanatory paragraph should be added depends on the likelihood of the loss occurring (for example, whether that likelihood is closer to remote or to probable) and on by how much the possible loss exceeds the auditor's materiality threshold.

SAS No. 58 (AU Section 508.28–.30) offers the following guidance regarding materiality considerations in situations where uncertainties exist:

> Materiality judgments involving uncertainties are made in light of the surrounding circumstances. Some uncertainties relate primarily to financial position, while others more closely relate to results of operations or cash flows. Thus, for purposes of evaluating the materiality of a possible loss, the auditor should consider which, if any, of the financial statements is the more appropriate base in the circumstances.
>
> Some uncertainties are unusual in nature or infrequent in occurrence and thus more closely related to financial position than to normal, recurring operations (for example, litigation relating to alleged violations of antitrust or securities laws). In such instances, the auditor should consider the possible loss in relation to shareholder's equity and other relevant balance sheet components such as total assets, total liabilities, current assets, and current liabilities.
>
> In other instances, the nature of an uncertainty may be more closely related to normal, recurring operations (for example, litigation with a party to a royalty agreement concerning whether a royalty fee should be paid on certain revenues). In such circumstances, the auditor should consider the possible loss in relation to relevant income statement components such as income from continuing operations.

Going Concern. One specific type of uncertainty the auditor must consider is the client's continued existence as a "going concern." An entity is a going concern when it has the ability to continue in operation and meet its obligations. The concept that financial statements are prepared on the basis of a going concern is one of the basic tenets of financial accounting. Because the going concern assumption is so basic, the standard auditor's report does not make reference to it.

When the entity can continue in operation and meet its obligations only by selling substantial amounts of its assets outside the ordinary course of business or by its creditors' willingness to forgive or restructure its debt, such circumstances should raise doubts about whether the enterprise is a going concern. Doubts about the entity's continued existence should also raise questions about realizable value of assets, the order of payment of liabilities, the proper classification and carrying amounts of both, and the appropriateness of necessary financial statement disclosures. If the auditor concludes there is substantial doubt about the entity's ability to continue as a going concern for a reasonable period of time (not to exceed one year from the date of the financial statements), he or she should determine that this is appropriately disclosed in the financial statements and should include an explanatory paragraph in the auditor's report to reflect that conclusion.

SAS No. 59, *The Auditor's Consideration of an Entity's Ability to Continue as a Going Concern* (AU Section 341), provides guidance to the auditor for meeting an explicit responsibility to evaluate whether there is substantial doubt about the entity's ability to continue as a going concern for a reasonable period of time. This is done through the following steps:

1. *Consider whether the results of procedures performed in planning, gathering evidence relative to the various audit objectives, and completing the audit identify conditions and events that, when considered in the aggregate, indicate there could be substantial doubt about the entity's ability to continue as a going concern for a reasonable period of time.*

In a properly planned audit, it should not be necessary to design auditing procedures specifically directed at the going concern issue. The results of auditing procedures designed and performed to achieve other audit objectives should be sufficient for that purpose. For example, conditions and events that could raise doubts may be identified through some of the following procedures: analytical procedures; review of subsequent events; review of compliance with the terms of debt and loan agreements; reading of minutes of meetings of stockholders, board of directors, and important committees of the board; inquiry of the entity's lawyers about litigation, claims, and assessments; and confirmation with related and third parties of the details of arrangements to provide or maintain financial support.

In considering the evidence provided by those procedures, it may be necessary for the auditor to obtain additional information about conditions and events identified that could create substantial doubt about the entity's ability to continue as a going concern. Their significance will depend on the circumstances. SAS No. 59 (AU Section 341.06) gives the following examples of such conditions and events, some of which are interrelated:

Negative trends—for example, recurring operating losses, working capital deficiencies, negative cash flows from operating activities, adverse key financial ratios.

Other indications of possible financial difficulties—for example, default on loan or similar agreements, arrearages in dividends, denial of usual trade credit from suppliers, restructuring of debt, noncompliance with statutory capital requirements, need to seek new sources or methods of financing or to dispose of substantial assets.

Internal matters—for example, work stoppages or other labor difficulties, substantial dependence on the success of a particular project, uneconomic long-term commitments, need to significantly revise operations.

External matters that have occurred—for example, legal proceedings, legislation, or similar matters that might jeopardize an entity's ability to operate; loss of a key franchise, license, or patent; loss of a principal customer or supplier; uninsured or underinsured catastrophe such as a drought, earthquake, or flood.

2. *If substantial doubt exists about the entity's ability to continue as a going concern for a reasonable period of time, obtain information about management's plans that are intended to mitigate the adverse effects of the conditions or events that gave rise to the doubt, and assess the likelihood that such plans can be effectively implemented.*

Those plans might include plans to dispose of assets, reduce or delay expenditures, borrow money or restructure debt, or increase ownership equity. In evaluating those plans, the auditor should consider whether there is adequate evidence supporting management's ability to carry out the plans. For example, plans to dispose of assets could be difficult or impossible to accomplish if there are restrictive covenants in loan agreements limiting such disposals. When prospective financial information is particularly significant to management's plans, the auditor should request management to provide that information and should consider whether there is adequate support for the significant assumptions underlying it.

3. *After evaluating management's plans, conclude whether substantial doubt exists about the entity's ability to continue as a going concern for a reasonable period of time.*

If the auditor concludes there *is* substantial doubt, he or she should then consider the adequacy of financial statement disclosure about the entity's possible inability to continue as a going concern *and include an explanatory paragraph* (following the opinion paragraph) in the audit report to reflect that conclusion. (If the entity's disclosures with respect to its ability to continue as a going concern are inadequate, a departure from generally accepted accounting principles exists and would result in either a qualified or an adverse opinion, as explained later in this chapter.) An example of such a paragraph from SAS No. 59 (AU Section 341.13) follows:

> The accompanying financial statements have been prepared assuming that the Company will continue as a going concern. As discussed in Note X to the financial statements, the Company has suffered recurring losses from operations and has a net capital deficiency that raise substantial doubt about its ability to continue as a going concern. Management's plans in regard to these matters are

also described in Note X. The financial statements do not include any adjustments that might result from the outcome of this uncertainty.[6]

Financial statement disclosures about the entity's ability to continue as a going concern might include the following information (as described in SAS No. 59 [AU Section 341.10]):

- Pertinent conditions and events giving rise to the assessment of substantial doubt about the entity's ability to continue as a going concern for a reasonable period of time.
- The possible effects of such conditions and events.
- Management's evaluation of the significance of those conditions and events and any mitigating factors.
- Possible discontinuance of operations.
- Management's plans (including relevant prospective financial information).
- Information about the recoverability or classification of recorded asset amounts or the amounts or classification of liabilities. . . .

If, after considering management's plans, substantial doubt about the entity's ability to continue as a going concern does *not* exist, the auditor should still consider whether the principal conditions and events that initially generated the doubt need to be disclosed. The consideration of disclosure should include the possible effects of those conditions and events and any mitigating factors, including management's plans.

SAS No. 59 (AU Section 341.04) notes that

> The auditor is not responsible for predicting future conditions or events. The fact that the entity may cease to exist as a going concern subsequent to receiving a report from the auditor that does not refer to substantial doubt, even within one year following the date of the financial statements, does not, in itself, indicate inadequate performance by the auditor. Accordingly, the absence of reference to substantial doubt in an auditor's report should not be viewed as providing assurance as to an entity's ability to continue as a going concern.

Operating in Bankruptcy or Liquidation. Companies that continue operations while in bankruptcy and prepare financial statements on a "going

[6]SAS No. 59 provides the following guidance when substantial doubt that formerly existed no longer exists:

> If substantial doubt about the entity's ability to continue as a going concern for a reasonable period of time existed at the date of prior period financial statements that are presented on a comparative basis, and that doubt has been removed in the current period, the explanatory paragraph included in the auditor's report (following the opinion paragraph) on the financial statements of the prior period should not be repeated.

concern basis'' are also subject to the requirements of SAS No. 59. In that situation, the financial statements would ordinarily include extensive disclosures about the enterprise's legal status, and the auditor's report would ordinarily contain an explanatory paragraph conveying the existence of substantial doubt about the entity's ability to continue as a going concern and referring the reader to the disclosures in the financial statements. If the enterprise is in liquidation, or if liquidation appears probable, a liquidation basis of accounting would be considered GAAP. If the liquidation basis of accounting has been properly applied and adequate disclosures made, the auditor's report should be unqualified, with the addition of explanatory language stating that the entity is being liquidated. An auditing interpretation (AU Section 9508.33–.38) provides reporting guidance in this situation.

Lack of Consistency

The second standard of reporting is

> The report shall identify those circumstances in which . . . [generally accepted accounting] principles have not been consistently observed in the current period in relation to the preceding period.

The consistency standard requires an auditor to inform readers in the report if GAAP have not been applied consistently from period to period; consistency within a period and between periods is presumed unless otherwise disclosed. The objective is to ensure that changes in accounting principles that materially affect the comparability of financial statements between periods are highlighted in the auditor's report as well as in the financial statements. Of course, factors other than consistent application of accounting principles also affect the comparability of financial statements between periods. For example, changed conditions that necessitate changes in accounting and changed conditions that are unrelated to accounting may exist. The effect of those other factors normally requires disclosure in the financial statements (covered by the third standard of reporting) but not explanatory language in the auditor's report. In requiring other effects on comparability to be disclosed only under the more general third standard, the profession has singled out the consistency of accounting principles for separate attention. The reason for the different treatment lies in the nature of alternative accounting principles: Alternatives that are considered generally accepted may in some cases be substituted one for another, thus changing accounting results without any change in the underlying economic substance—a sound and sometimes necessary practice that is obviously susceptible to abuse.

Changes in accounting principles occur fairly often. Companies from time to time change managements, operating philosophies, or judgments about which accounting principles are most appropriate for the company. Also, authoritative FASB and GASB pronouncements may change the way that various transactions or other events and circumstances are to be measured or reported.

Any significant change in accounting principle or method of applying a principle must be referred to in the auditor's report in an explanatory paragraph (following the opinion paragraph). That paragraph should identify the change and refer to the note in the financial statements that discusses the change. An example of an appropriate explanatory paragraph would be[7]

> As discussed in Note X to the financial statements, the Company changed its method of computing depreciation in 19X2.

The auditor's concurrence with a change is implicit unless he or she takes exception to it in the opinion.

Accounting Principles Board Opinion No. 20, *Accounting Changes* (Accounting Standards Sections A06 and A35), provides standards for accounting for and disclosing accounting changes in financial statements. Section 420, "Consistency of Application of Generally Accepted Accounting Principles," of SAS No. 1 (AU Section 420) provides guidelines for determining which accounting changes affect consistency and, therefore, require an explanatory paragraph in the auditor's report.

Identifying Changes in Accounting Principles. Both the Opinion and SAS No. 1 distinguish changes in accounting principles from changes in accounting estimates or changes in the reporting entity. The three kinds of changes, called collectively "accounting changes," are further distinguished from other factors affecting the comparability of financial statements between periods, including errors in previously issued statements, changes in statement classification, initial adoption of an accounting principle to recognize an event occurring for the first time, and adoption or modification of an accounting principle necessitated by transactions that are clearly different in substance from previous transactions. Of all classes mentioned, only changes in accounting principles and, sometimes, changes in the reporting entity require an explanatory paragraph in an auditor's report under the second standard of reporting. Of course, the others may have to be either disclosed or commented on under the third standard of reporting.

[7]SAS No. 58 (AU Section 508.36) notes that

> The addition of this explanatory paragraph in the auditor's report is required in reports on financial statements of subsequent years as long as the year of the change is presented and reported on. However, if the accounting change is accounted for by retroactive restatement of the financial statements affected, the additional paragraph is required only in the year of the change since, in subsequent years, all periods presented will be comparable.

An explanatory paragraph is also not required when a change in accounting principle that does not require a cumulative effect adjustment is made at the beginning of the earliest year presented and reported on.

Justification for Changes in Accounting Principles. An important advance in disclosure standards was the requirement in APB Opinion No. 20 (Accounting Standards Section A06), issued in 1971, that a change in accounting principle be justified by a clear explanation by management of why the newly adopted principle is preferable and that the justification be disclosed in the financial statements. Requiring that changes in accounting principles be justified was a significant step toward expecting issuers of financial statements to explain the "why" of their accounting as well as the "what." It should be noted, however, that while Opinion No. 20 prescribes that a note to the financial statements explain clearly why a newly adopted accounting principle is preferable, the authoritative literature of the profession does not explicitly require the auditor to be satisfied as to that preferability. The authoritative literature requires only that the auditor determine that a reasonable justification of preferability was properly disclosed. The SEC, however, requires the auditor to submit a "preferability letter" stating that the auditor is satisfied with the justification provided by the company when an accounting change has been made.

Emphasis of a Matter

The foregoing discussion of explanatory language added to the standard report covered situations in which such language is required. Although it does not occur often, sometimes the auditor wishes to emphasize a matter regarding the financial statements, even though he or she is expressing an unqualified opinion. SAS No. 58 (AU Section 508.37) states: "For example, he may wish to emphasize that the entity is a component of a larger business enterprise or that it has had significant transactions with related parties, or he may wish to emphasize an unusually important subsequent event or an accounting matter affecting the comparability of the financial statements with those of the preceding period." Such explanatory language should be presented in a separate paragraph of the auditor's report. The opinion paragraph should not refer to the explanatory paragraph.

DEPARTURES FROM UNQUALIFIED OPINIONS

The fourth standard of reporting (AU Section 150.02) reads as follows:

> The report shall either contain an expression of opinion regarding the financial statements, taken as a whole, or an assertion to the effect that an opinion cannot be expressed. When an overall opinion cannot be expressed, the reasons therefor should be stated. In all cases where an auditor's name is associated with financial statements, the report should contain a clear-cut indication of the character of the auditor's work and the degree of responsibility the auditor is taking.

The standardized language of the unqualified report fosters precision in meeting this standard. The professional literature, both at the time of publication of the fourth standard of reporting and since then, has attempted to provide similar precision in describing departures from the standard report. Authoritative pronouncements on the fourth standard of reporting, including SAS No. 58, are set forth in AU Section 500 of *AICPA Professional Standards.* It calls for explaining all departures from an unqualified opinion in one or more separate paragraphs preceding the opinion paragraph.

SAS No. 58 classifies departures from the standard unqualified report, sometimes referred to as a "clean" opinion, as qualified opinions, adverse opinions, and disclaimers of opinion. These departures are discussed in the following paragraphs.

Qualified Opinions

There are two basic reasons for qualifying an opinion: limitations on the scope of the audit and departures from GAAP.

Scope Limitations. An audit can be limited by circumstances beyond the client's control that preclude the auditor from employing the auditing procedures that would otherwise be considered necessary, or it can be limited by client-imposed restrictions.

Circumstances Precluding Necessary Auditing Procedures. Sometimes an auditor is not able to carry out procedures that customarily are considered necessary in the circumstances as a basis for rendering an unqualified opinion. In most instances, the auditor is able to design and perform alternative procedures that provide sufficient assurance that the relevant audit objectives have been achieved. The most common instances in which the auditor might not be able to perform alternative procedures are when conditions make it impracticable or impossible to confirm accounts receivable or observe inventories. Other examples of such scope limitations involve noncontrolling investments in affiliated companies, when the auditor is unable to either (1) obtain audited financial statements of an investee or apply auditing procedures to unaudited financial statements of an investee, or (2) examine sufficient evidence that unrealized profits and losses resulting from transactions between the investor and the investee have been eliminated.

If an auditor cannot obtain satisfaction by means of alternative auditing procedures when circumstances preclude conventional procedures, the auditor should describe the problem and modify the standard report. If the auditor decides to express a qualified opinion (rather than disclaim an opinion), the problem should be described in a separate paragraph and referred to in both the scope paragraph and the opinion paragraph.

A scope limitation should always be described entirely within the auditor's report, in contrast to the treatment of qualifications related to information presented in the financial statements, which are usually described in a note to the statements and only referred to in the report. That is because a qualification based on a scope limitation arises from the auditor's activities, and limitations on them, not from the financial statements themselves, which are the representations of management. The qualification itself should be stated in terms of the scope limitation. SAS No. 58 (AU Section 508.44) presents an example regarding an investment in a foreign affiliate (the example assumes that the effects of the scope limitation do not cause the auditor to conclude that a disclaimer of opinion is appropriate).

> [*Same first paragraph as the standard report*]
>
> Except as discussed in the following paragraph, we conducted our audits in accordance with generally accepted auditing standards. Those standards require that we plan and perform the audit to obtain reasonable assurance about whether the financial statements are free of material misstatement. An audit includes examining, on a test basis, evidence supporting the amounts and disclosures in the financial statements. An audit also includes assessing the accounting principles used and significant estimates made by management, as well as evaluating the overall financial statement presentation. We believe that our audits provide a reasonable basis for our opinion.
>
> We were unable to obtain audited financial statements supporting the Company's investment in a foreign affiliate stated at $ _____ and $ _____ at December 31, 19X2 and 19X1, respectively, or its equity in earnings of that affiliate of $ _____ and $ _____, which is included in net income for the years then ended as described in Note X to the financial statements; nor were we able to satisfy ourselves as to the carrying value of the investment in the foreign affiliate or the equity in its earnings by other auditing procedures.
>
> In our opinion, except for the effects of such adjustments, if any, as might have been determined to be necessary had we been able to examine evidence regarding the foreign affiliate investment and earnings, the financial statements referred to in the first paragraph above present fairly, in all material respects, the financial position of X Company as of December 31, 19X2 and 19X1, and the results of its operations and its cash flows for the years then ended in conformity with generally accepted accounting principles.

Client-Imposed Restrictions. The most common client-imposed restrictions are limitations preventing observation of physical inventories, confirmation of accounts receivable, or examination of a significant subsidiary. Usually, if scope is limited by client-imposed restrictions, an auditor should disclaim an opinion (see later discussion) because the client's election to limit the auditor's scope implies also an election to limit the auditor's responsibility. On rare occasions, if a client-imposed scope limitation applies to an isolated transaction or a single account, a qualified opinion may be acceptable.

Departures from GAAP. The standard report makes the positive assertion that the financial statements are presented in conformity with generally accepted accounting principles; thus, any departures from GAAP must be noted as "exceptions" to that assertion. Such departures are rare in practice because most companies believe that an auditor's opinion qualified because of a departure from GAAP carries intolerable implications, and so they use accounting principles that are generally accepted. Also, only rarely are such qualified opinions acceptable in SEC filings. Nevertheless, instances of departures sometimes occur; the most common ones are described and examples presented in the following paragraphs.

Departures from Measurement Principles. SAS No. 58 (AU Section 508.53) gives the following example of an auditor's report that is qualified because of the use of an accounting principle that is at variance with GAAP:

> [*Same first and second paragraphs as the standard report*]
>
> The Company has excluded, from property and debt in the accompanying balance sheets, certain lease obligations that, in our opinion, should be capitalized in order to conform with generally accepted accounting principles. If these lease obligations were capitalized, property would be increased by $ _____ and $ _____, long-term debt by $ _____ and $ _____, and retained earnings by $ _____ and $ _____ as of December 31, 19X2 and 19X1, respectively. Additionally, net income would be increased (decreased) by $ _____ and $ _____ and earnings per share would be increased (decreased) by $ _____ and $ _____, respectively, for the years then ended.
>
> In our opinion, except for the effects of not capitalizing certain lease obligations as discussed in the preceding paragraph, the financial statements referred to above present fairly, in all material respects, the financial position of X Company as of December 31, 19X2 and 19X1, and the results of its operations and its cash flows for the years then ended in conformity with generally accepted accounting principles.

If the pertinent facts are disclosed in the notes to the financial statements, the separate paragraph preceding the opinion paragraph would read as follows:

> As more fully described in Note X to the financial statements, the Company has excluded certain lease obligations from property and debt in the accompanying balance sheets. In our opinion, generally accepted accounting principles require that such obligations be included in the balance sheets.

Departures from Disclosure Principles. Under the third standard of reporting (AU Section 150.02),

> Informative disclosures in the financial statements are to be regarded as reasonably adequate unless otherwise stated in the report.

SAS No. 32, *Adequacy of Disclosure in Financial Statements* (AU Section 431), is general about what constitutes informative disclosures. Some specific disclosures required in financial statements are contained in various pronouncements that constitute GAAP, for example, Statements of the FASB and the GASB, Opinions of the Accounting Principles Board, and Accounting Research Bulletins. Specific industry disclosures are often called for in AICPA industry audit and accounting guides. Those pronouncements, however, cover only the topics addressed, and not the vast area of financial information on which no pronouncement has been issued. Identifying matters of potential interest to financial statement users, deciding whether and how they should be disclosed, and then demonstrating the appropriateness of the conclusion to the client place great demands on an auditor's skill and judgment.

The intent of the third standard of reporting is to establish that issuers of financial statements and auditors have a responsibility to ensure that disclosures are adequate, regardless of whether a requirement, convention, or precedent covers the matter. Some issuers of financial statements, however, take the approach of "no rule, no disclosure." Court cases and items appearing in the press indicate that a disclosure policy based on this attitude is dangerous, not to mention its not being in the public interest. Deciding what should be disclosed beyond what is specifically required in authoritative pronouncements, however, requires a balancing of diverse interests. On the one hand, management may believe that certain disclosures are likely to result in a competitive disadvantage or other detriment to the company or its stockholders. On the other hand, directors, management, auditors, and their legal counsel need to consider the possibility that a detrimental disclosure not made may be a basis for litigation in the wake of subsequent difficulties, even if the cause of the difficulties is completely unrelated to the undisclosed matter.

Disclosure is never a substitute for the proper recognition and measurement of transactions and other events and circumstances in conformity with GAAP. In practice, a temptation on the part of issuers and auditors sometimes exists to resolve a difficult problem by presenting information in a footnote rather than by adjusting the financial statements. For example, a contingency that is likely to occur and for which an estimate of loss is known must be accrued in the financial statements according to GAAP; mere disclosure of such an item is not an acceptable alternative.

An auditor who believes that disclosures in the financial statements are inadequate is required to so state and to make the necessary disclosures in the auditor's report, if it is practicable to do so and unless the omission from the auditor's report is recognized as appropriate in a specific SAS. Since most clients choose to make the necessary disclosures rather than to have them appear in the auditor's report, this type of disclosure in an auditor's report is extremely rare. SAS No. 58 (AU Section 508.56) contains the following example of a report qualified for inadequate disclosure:

> [*Same first and second paragraphs as the standard report*]
>
> The Company's financial statements do not disclose [*describe the nature of the omitted disclosures*]. In our opinion, disclosure of this information is required by generally accepted accounting principles.

> In our opinion, except for the omission of the information discussed in the preceding paragraph, . . .

There are two exceptions to the requirement that when informative disclosures are omitted from the financial statements, the auditor should make the necessary disclosures in the auditor's report. The two exceptions, specifically sanctioned in the SASs (AU Sections 435.10 and 508.58), pertain to omitted segment information that is required by GAAP and to the statement of cash flows. The auditor should qualify the report if an entity declines to present the necessary segment information or a statement of cash flows, but the auditor is not required to provide the omitted segment information or to prepare the statement of cash flows and include it in the report.

An example of a report qualified because of the absence of a statement of cash flows follows:

> We have audited the accompanying balance sheets of X Company as of December 31, 19X2 and 19X1, and the related statements of income and retained earnings for the years then ended. These financial statements are the responsibility of the Company's management. Our responsibility is to express an opinion on these financial statements based on our audit.
>
> [*Same second paragraph as the standard report*]
>
> The Company declined to present a statement of cash flows for the years ended December 31, 19X2 and 19X1. Presentation of such statement summarizing the Company's operating, investing, and financing activities is required by generally accepted accounting principles.
>
> In our opinion, except that the omission of a statement of cash flows results in an incomplete presentation as explained in the preceding paragraph, the financial statements referred to above present fairly, in all material respects, the financial position of X Company as of December 31, 19X2 and 19X1, and the results of its operations for the years then ended in conformity with generally accepted accounting principles.

Departures Related to Accounting Changes. SAS No. 58 requires the auditor to evaluate a change in accounting principle to be satisfied that (a) the newly adopted accounting principle is GAAP, (b) the method of accounting for the effect of the change is in conformity with GAAP, and (c) management's justification for the change is reasonable. APB Opinion No. 20, paragraph 16 (Accounting Standards Section A06.112), states

> The presumption that an entity should not change an accounting principle may be overcome only if the enterprise justifies the use of an alternative acceptable accounting principle on the basis that it is preferable.

If management has not provided reasonable justification for the change, or if the change does not meet both of the other conditions mentioned above, the auditor should express a qualified opinion or, if the effect of the change is sufficiently material, express an adverse opinion on the financial statements.

AU Section 508.61 contains an example of a report qualified because management has not provided reasonable justification for a change in accounting principles.

> [*Same first and second paragraphs as the standard report*]
>
> As disclosed in Note X to the financial statements, the Company adopted, in 19X2, the first-in, first-out method of accounting for its inventories, whereas it previously used the last-in, first-out method. Although use of the first-in, first-out method is in conformity with generally accepted accounting principles, in our opinion the Company has not provided reasonable justification for making this change as required by generally accepted accounting principles.[8]
>
> In our opinion, except for the change in accounting principle discussed in the preceding paragraph, the financial statements referred to above present fairly, in all material respects, the financial position of X Company as of December 31, 19X2 and 19X1, and the results of its operations and its cash flows for the years then ended in conformity with generally accepted accounting principles.

Accounting changes that result in qualified or adverse opinions should also trigger similar opinions in future years as long as the change continues to have a material effect on either the financial statements of subsequent years or the financial statements of the year of the change when presented for comparative purposes.

Adverse Opinions

An adverse opinion expresses a belief that financial statements are not presented fairly in conformity with generally accepted accounting principles or otherwise do not present fairly what they purport to present. It is required when an auditor believes that one or more departures from GAAP are sufficiently material to make the statements as a whole misleading. The auditor cannot sidestep an adverse opinion by disclaiming an opinion.

When an adverse opinion is issued, the opinion paragraph should include a reference to a separate paragraph in the auditor's report that discloses all the reasons for the adverse opinion, including any reservations the auditor may have regarding fair presentation in conformity with GAAP other than those that gave rise to the adverse opinion. The separate paragraph (or paragraphs, if appropriate) should also disclose the effects of the departures from GAAP on the financial statements, or state that such a determination is not possible.

Adverse opinions are rare. It is obviously better for all concerned to correct the conditions before such an opinion is issued, and it is usually within the client's power to correct them. Adverse opinions are sometimes issued on

[8]Because this paragraph contains all of the information required in an explanatory paragraph on consistency, a separate explanatory paragraph (following the opinion paragraph) is not necessary in this instance.

financial statements showing appraised values of property. Occasionally, an adverse opinion is issued on the financial statements of a regulated company that are prepared in accordance with a basis of accounting prescribed by a governmental agency and are presented other than in filings with the agency. In that situation, AU Section 544 indicates that the auditor generally should issue either a qualified or an adverse opinion, depending on the materiality of the departures from GAAP, and also, in an additional paragraph of the report, express an opinion on whether the financial statements are presented in conformity with the prescribed basis of accounting.

An example of an adverse opinion, taken from SAS No. 58 (AU Section 508.69), follows:

> [*Same first and second paragraphs as the standard report*]
>
> As discussed in Note X to the financial statements, the Company carries its property, plant and equipment accounts at appraisal values, and provides depreciation on the basis of such values. Further, the Company does not provide for income taxes with respect to differences between financial income and taxable income arising because of the use, for income tax purposes, of the installment method of reporting gross profit from certain types of sales. Generally accepted accounting principles require that property, plant and equipment be stated at an amount not in excess of cost, reduced by depreciation based on such amount, and that deferred income taxes be provided.
>
> Because of the departures from generally accepted accounting principles identified above, as of December 31, 19X2 and 19X1, inventories have been increased \$ _____ and \$ _____ by inclusion in manufacturing overhead of depreciation in excess of that based on cost; property, plant and equipment, less accumulated depreciation, is carried at \$ _____ and \$ _____ in excess of an amount based on the cost to the Company; and deferred income taxes of \$ _____ and \$ _____ have not been recorded; resulting in an increase of \$ _____ and \$ _____ in retained earnings and in appraisal surplus of \$ _____ and \$ _____, respectively. For the years ended December 31, 19X2 and 19X1, cost of goods sold has been increased \$ _____ and \$ _____, respectively, because of the effects of the depreciation accounting referred to above and deferred income taxes of \$ _____ and \$ _____ have not been provided, resulting in an increase in net income of \$ _____ and \$ _____, respectively.
>
> In our opinion, because of the effects of the matters discussed in the preceding paragraphs, the financial statements referred to above do not present fairly, in conformity with generally accepted accounting principles, the financial position of X Company as of December 31, 19X2 and 19X1, or the results of its operations or its cash flows for the years then ended.

Disclaimers of Opinion

If an auditor does not have enough evidence to form an opinion, the appropriate form of report is a disclaimer of opinion. A disclaimer can result from an inability to obtain sufficient competent evidential matter because the scope of the audit was seriously limited. In addition, while SAS No. 58 indicates that the addition of an explanatory paragraph to the auditor's report serves adequately to inform financial statement users when there are uncertainties, an auditor may nevertheless decide to decline to express an opinion in some cases involving uncertainties.

SAS No. 58 (AU Section 508.71) states that the reasons for a disclaimer must be given in a separate paragraph of the report. The auditor is also required to disclose in a separate paragraph any reservations about fair presentation in conformity with GAAP. It would be misleading for an auditor to issue a disclaimer if a basis for an adverse or a qualified opinion existed. Adverse opinions and disclaimers of opinion are never interchangeable, nor can an auditor's report contain both an adverse opinion and a disclaimer of opinion. A report may, however, contain an opinion that is qualified for more than one reason. For example, an opinion may be qualified because of a scope limitation and because of a departure from GAAP.

An example of a report (AU Section 508.71) disclaiming an opinion resulting from a scope limitation follows:

> We were engaged to audit the accompanying balance sheets of X Company as of December 31, 19X2 and 19X1, and the related statements of income, retained earnings, and cash flows for the years then ended. These financial statements are the responsibility of the Company's management.
>
> [*Second paragraph of standard report should be omitted.*]
>
> The Company did not make a count of its physical inventory in 19X2 or 19X1, stated in the accompanying financial statements at $ _____ as of December 31, 19X2, and at $ _____ as of December 31, 19X1. Further, evidence supporting the cost of property and equipment acquired prior to December 31, 19X1, is no longer available. The Company's records do not permit the application of other auditing procedures to inventories or property and equipment.
>
> Since the Company did not take physical inventories and we were not able to apply other auditing procedures to satisfy ourselves as to inventory quantities and the cost of property and equipment, the scope of our work was not sufficient to enable us to express, and we do not express, an opinion on these financial statements.

Note that, as required in a footnote to AU Section 508.72,

> The wording in the first paragraph of the auditor's standard report is changed in a disclaimer of opinion because of a scope limitation. The first sentence now states that "we were engaged to audit" rather than "we have audited" since, because of the scope limitation, the auditor was not able to perform an audit in accordance with generally accepted auditing standards. In addition, the last sentence of the first paragraph is also deleted, because of the scope limitation, to eliminate the reference to the auditor's responsibility to express an opinion.

The most frequently encountered examples of disclaimers because of scope limitations arise in initial engagements for new clients. In those circumstances, an auditor may begin work well after the beginning of the year under audit. If the opening inventory has a material effect on income for the year (as it usually does in most manufacturing and commercial enterprises), an auditor must gather evidence on which to base an opinion on the opening inventory in order to issue an unqualified opinion. If this is not possible, which often occurs, the auditor should, in the authors' opinion, disclaim an opinion on the income statement and statement of cash flows. When the auditor is able to form an opinion on the opening inventory—which ordinarily happens when another reputable auditor is succeeded—there is no need to cover the point in the report. (Chapter 14 discusses appropriate auditing procedures in this situation.)

As an alternative, the auditor could be asked to report on the balance sheet only. Such an engagement does not involve a scope limitation if the auditor's access to information is not limited and if the auditor applies all procedures appropriate in the circumstances. An example of a report on a balance-sheet-only audit was presented on pages 758–759. (That report assumed that the auditor was satisfied as to the consistent application of GAAP.) If an income statement and statement of cash flows accompany the balance sheet, a disclaimer on them will be required.

While an auditor must stand ready to serve a client in any way appropriate, limited reporting engagements in which only a balance sheet is presented may not best meet the client's needs. Engagements likely to lead to a disclaimer on the income statement and statement of cash flows when a full set of financial statements is presented (other than when the auditor is appointed after year-end) should be approached reluctantly because of the risk that incorrect inferences about the auditor's responsibilities will be drawn by the client and other users. Consideration should be given to whether a client's needs can be better served by a review of financial statements performed in accordance with SSARS No. 1 or by designing a special engagement in which responsibilities can be spelled out explicitly. Various special reports are discussed in Chapter 19.

Piecemeal Opinions

Piecemeal opinions (opinions on certain identified financial statement items) are prohibited by SAS No. 58. A piecemeal opinion is the complement of a qualified opinion: That is, a qualified opinion gives an opinion on the financial statements as a whole and makes exceptions for certain items, whereas a piecemeal opinion disclaims or is adverse on the financial statements as a whole and gives an opinion on certain items. In the past, piecemeal opinions were not uncommon, but they presented so many problems that they are now prohibited.

SAS No. 58 (AU Section 508.73) states as a reason that "piecemeal opinions tend to overshadow or contradict a disclaimer of opinion or an adverse opinion." In addition, piecemeal opinions took specific items out of the context of the financial statements as a whole, thus implying a greater degree of precision about those items under conditions that usually entailed a lesser degree of certainty. Also, the defect in the financial statements as a whole that caused the disclaimer or adverse opinion tended to destroy or call into question the interrelated, corroborative nature of accounts on which the audit logic depended. When all of these deficiencies were balanced against the limited usefulness of piecemeal opinions, the profession was well advised to abandon them.

Adverse Opinions Versus Disclaimers

There is a fundamental difference between departures from GAAP, which affect the quality of the financial statements, and scope limitations, which affect the sufficiency and competence of audit evidence. Departures from GAAP call for a qualified opinion because of the auditor's reservations about the quality of the financial statements. If departures from GAAP become so great as to make the financial statements useless, an adverse opinion is called for. On the other hand, scope limitations affect the degree of assurance contained in the opinion, whether the limitations are client imposed or the result of circumstances, and call for a qualification in both the scope and opinion paragraphs. If scope limitations are so pervasive that the auditor cannot form an opinion, a disclaimer of opinion may be called for. The following tabulation helps keep in perspective the distinctions among qualified opinions, adverse opinions, and disclaimers of opinion.

	Degree of Materiality or Pervasiveness	
Condition	*Less*	*More*
Departures from GAAP	Qualified opinion	Adverse opinion
Scope limitations	Qualified opinion	Disclaimer of opinion

Distinguishing Among Situations Involving Scope Limitations, Uncertainties, and Departures from GAAP

Distinguishing between situations that require an explanatory paragraph because of an uncertainty and those that require departures from an unqualified opinion because of a scope limitation or a departure from GAAP can sometimes be difficult.

SAS No. 58 (AU Section 508.18) notes that

> A matter involving an uncertainty is one that is expected to be resolved at a future date, at which time sufficient evidential matter concerning its outcome

would be expected to become available. A qualification or disclaimer of opinion because of a scope limitation is appropriate when sufficient evidential matter does or did exist but was not available to the auditor for reasons such as management's record retention policies or a restriction imposed by management.

Departures from generally accepted accounting principles involving uncertainties usually involve inadequate disclosure of the uncertainty, the use of inappropriate accounting principles in making accounting estimates, or unreasonable accounting estimates themselves. These situations would require a qualified or an adverse opinion because of a departure from GAAP.

To distinguish among the various types of auditors' reports that are possible in situations involving uncertainties, consider the following example. As discussed in Chapter 21, SAS No. 12, *Inquiry of a Client's Lawyer Concerning Litigation, Claims, and Assessments* (AU Section 337), requires the auditor to obtain corroborating evidence from the client's legal counsel about the completeness of the information supplied by management regarding pending or threatened litigation, claims, and assessments. If the client refuses to request its lawyer to communicate with the auditor, or if the lawyer refuses to furnish information concerning the likelihood of an unfavorable outcome of material litigation, claims, or assessments, an audit scope limitation exists that would, depending on the potential materiality of the unresolved items, lead to a scope qualification or a disclaimer of opinion, along with a separate explanatory paragraph preceding the opinion or disclaimer. If the lawyer is unable to respond concerning the likelihood of an unfavorable outcome of the uncertainty or the amount or range of potential loss, an uncertainty exists that would lead to an explanatory paragraph, assuming that the uncertainty is appropriately disclosed in the notes to the financial statements. If, however, after both the client and the lawyer acknowledge the uncertainty, the client refuses to make the appropriate disclosures, a qualified or an adverse opinion because of a GAAP departure (along with a separate explanatory paragraph preceding the opinion paragraph) would be required. In practice, distinguishing among these three situations is not always easy.

Different Reports on Comparative Financial Statements Presented

An auditor may express a qualified or an adverse opinion, disclaim an opinion, or include an explanatory paragraph with respect to one or more financial statements of one or more periods presented and issue a different report on the other financial statements presented. Following is an example of a report (AU Section 508.76) on comparative financial statements, consisting of a standard report on the current-year financial statements with a disclaimer of opinion on the prior-year statements of income, retained earnings, and cash flows:

> We have audited the accompanying balance sheets of ABC Company as of December 31, 19X2 and 19X1, and the related statements of income, retained earnings, and cash flows for the years then ended. These financial statements are the responsibility of the Company's management. Our responsibility is to express an opinion on these financial statements based on our audits.
>
> Except as explained in the following paragraph, we conducted our audits in accordance with generally accepted auditing standards. Those standards require that we plan and perform our audit to obtain reasonable assurance about whether the financial statements are free of material misstatement. An audit includes examining, on a test basis, evidence supporting the amounts and disclosures in the financial statements. An audit also includes assessing the accounting principles used and significant estimates made by management, as well as evaluating the overall financial statement presentation. We believe that our audits provide a reasonable basis for our opinion.
>
> We did not observe the taking of the physical inventory as of December 31, 19X0, since that date was prior to our appointment as auditors for the Company, and we were unable to satisfy ourselves regarding inventory quantities by means of other auditing procedures. Inventory amounts as of December 31, 19X0, enter into the determination of net income and cash flows for the year ended December 31, 19X1.
>
> Because of the matter discussed in the preceding paragraph, the scope of our work was not sufficient to enable us to express, and we do not express, an opinion on the results of operations and cash flows for the year ended December 31, 19X1.
>
> In our opinion, the balance sheets of ABC Company as of December 31, 19X2 and 19X1, and the related statements of income, retained earnings, and cash flows for the year ended December 31, 19X2, present fairly, in all material respects, the financial position of ABC Company as of December 31, 19X2 and 19X1, and the results of its operations and its cash flows for the year ended December 31, 19X2, in conformity with generally accepted accounting principles.

SAS No. 58 also provides guidance for situations when an auditor becomes aware, during the current audit, of circumstances or events that affect the financial statements of a prior period. For example, the subsequent restatement of prior-period financial statements on which the auditor had issued a qualified or an adverse opinion would cause the auditor to express an unqualified opinion in an updated report on the financial statements of the prior period. In these circumstances, SAS No. 58 (AU Section 508.78) requires that all the substantive reasons for the different opinion be disclosed in a separate explanatory paragraph(s) preceding the opinion paragraph of the report. According to SAS No. 58, the explanatory paragraph should include

(a) the date of the auditor's previous report, (b) the type of opinion previously expressed, (c) the circumstances or events that caused the auditor to express a different opinion, and (d) that the auditor's updated opinion on the financial statements of the prior period is different from his previous opinion on those statements.

SUMMARY: PRINCIPAL VARIATIONS FROM STANDARD REPORTS

Figure 18.2 summarizes the principal causes of variations from the standard, unqualified report and how they affect the report. In deciding whether a variation from the standard, unqualified report is appropriate, the auditor considers the materiality of the condition or circumstance in question. A materiality test must be applied in determining not only whether to depart from a standard, unqualified opinion but also whether the appropriate variation is to include explanatory language or to issue a qualified opinion on the one hand, or to issue an adverse opinion or a disclaimer of opinion on the other. As noted earlier, a departure from GAAP that is sufficiently material could lead to an adverse opinion, and scope limitations that are sufficiently material could lead to a disclaimer of opinion.

Authoritative auditing literature provides scant guidance for deciding whether the effects of a particular condition or circumstance are sufficiently material to require explanatory language, a qualified opinion, or either an adverse opinion or a disclaimer. Paragraph 50 of SAS No. 58 suggests several factors to be considered in determining the materiality of the effects of a departure from GAAP, namely, the dollar magnitude of the effects, the significance of an item to a particular enterprise, the pervasiveness of the misstatement, and the impact of the misstatement on the financial statements taken as a whole. As previously noted, paragraphs 28–30 of SAS No. 58 provide some guidance regarding materiality considerations when uncertainties exist. There is no guidance in the authoritative literature concerning scope limitations.

RESPONSIBILITIES AFTER THE REPORT DATE

Discovery of Information After the Report Date

Chapter 17 discusses an auditor's responsibility to obtain knowledge about subsequent events up to certain dates. Clearly, the auditor is not obligated to "keep current" indefinitely; as explained in Chapter 17, the responsibility ends with the issuance of the financial statements and the auditor's report, with the exception of a 1933 Act filing with the SEC. In that situation, the responsibility extends to the effective date of the registration statement.

Figure 18.2 Summary of Principal Variations from Standard Reports

Type of Variation	*Report Treatment*
Situations Requiring Unqualified Opinions with Explanatory Language	
Opinion based in part on report of another auditor	Add explanatory language in the introductory and opinion paragraphs.
Departure from an authoritative pronouncement with which the auditor agrees	Add an explanatory paragraph describing and justifying the departure.
Predecessor auditor's reports on prior year's comparative statements not presented	Add explanatory language in the introductory paragraph.
Report on a balance sheet only	Refer only to balance sheet in introductory, scope, and opinion paragraphs.
Material inconsistency between financial statements and other information reported by management	Add an explanatory paragraph describing the inconsistency. (The auditor should also consider withholding the audit report or withdrawing from the engagement.)
Exceptions regarding supplementary information required by FASB or GASB	Add an explanatory paragraph describing the circumstances.
Existence of a material uncertainty affecting the financial statements	Add an explanatory paragraph after the opinion paragraph (disclaimer of opinion is permissible but not required).
Lack of consistency in application of accounting principles	Add an explanatory paragraph after the opinion paragraph.
Auditor wishes to emphasize a matter	Add an explanatory paragraph.
Situations Requiring Departures from Unqualified Opinions	
Scope limitation	Qualify the scope paragraph (''except as''); describe the scope limitation in a separate paragraph preceding the opinion paragraph; qualify the opinion (''except for'') or disclaim an opinion, depending on circumstances and materiality.
Departure from GAAP	Describe the departure in a separate paragraph preceding the opinion paragraph; qualify the opinion (''except for'') or give an adverse opinion, depending on materiality.

After the financial statements and audit report have been issued, however, an auditor may become aware of new information regarding the client. If the new information refers to a condition that did not exist at the date of the audit report, or if it refers to final resolutions of contingencies or other matters disclosed in the financial statements or the auditor's report, the auditor has no further obligation. The new information may, however, relate to facts existing at the date of the audit report that might have affected the financial statements or auditor's report had the auditor been aware of them. For example, the auditor may learn on April 14, 19X2, after the financial statements for 19X1 were issued, that a large receivable on the December 31, 19X1, balance sheet believed at that date to be collectible was in fact uncollectible because the customer had declared bankruptcy on December 5, 19X1. In those circumstances, the auditor is obligated to pursue the matter. According to an auditing interpretation (AU Section 9561.01), that obligation exists even if the auditor has resigned or has been discharged.

While the distinction between the two kinds of new information is conceptually clear, in practice it is often difficult to tell, at least initially, whether the new information refers to a new condition or a preexisting one. The new information is often fragmentary, hearsay, or otherwise suspect, and may come from inside or outside the entity. Regardless of its source, the auditor should ordinarily discuss the information with the client and request that the client make any necessary investigations. There may be situations in which the auditor may find it desirable to seek the advice of legal counsel.

SAS No. 1 (AU Section 561) provides guidance to the auditor on subsequent steps to be taken. If the client cooperates and the information is found to be reliable and to have existed at the date of the auditor's report, the client should be advised to disclose the newly discovered facts and their effect on the financial statements by issuing revised financial statements and auditor's report. The reasons for the revisions should be described in a note to the financial statements and referred to in the auditor's report. An auditor's report accompanying revised financial statements would read (in part) as follows: "In our opinion, the financial statements referred to above, revised as described in Note X, present fairly . . . ." If financial statements for a subsequent period are about to be issued, the revision may be incorporated in those statements, as long as disclosure of the revision is not thereby unduly delayed. The auditor's report on the comparative financial statements need not refer to the revision provided there is appropriate disclosure. The auditor may, however, include an explanatory paragraph to emphasize the revision.

Sometimes, determining the effect on the financial statements requires prolonged investigation, or the information is so significant that no delay is tolerable. In those circumstances, the client should notify all persons likely to be relying on the financial statements of the problem under investigation. Usually, that would include stockholders, banks, and, for publicly held companies, the SEC, stock exchanges, regulatory agencies, and the press.

If the client's management refuses to make the appropriate disclosures, the auditor should obtain the advice of legal counsel and should notify each member of the client's board of directors of that refusal and of the subsequent steps the auditor will take to prevent future reliance on the audit report. Unless the auditor's counsel recommends otherwise, the auditor should notify the client that the auditor's report is no longer to be associated with the financial statements. In addition, the auditor should notify the SEC, stock exchanges, and any other regulatory agencies involved of the situation and the withdrawal of the report and request that steps be taken to accomplish the necessary public disclosure (usually this notification is made public at once). The auditor should also notify in writing any others who are known to be currently relying or who are likely to rely on the financial statements and the related auditor's report. The public disclosure following notification of the SEC is intended to take care of all unknown interested parties.

The disclosures made by the auditor to regulatory agencies and other parties should, if possible, describe the information and its effect on the financial statements and the auditor's report. The description should be precise and factual and should avoid references to conduct, motives, and the like. SAS No. 1 (AU Section 561.09) describes the appropriate disclosure if precise and factual information is not available, as follows:

> If the client has not cooperated and as a result the auditor is unable to conduct a satisfactory investigation of the information, his disclosure need not detail the specific information but can merely indicate that information has come to his attention which his client has not cooperated in attempting to substantiate and that, if the information is true, the auditor believes that his report must no longer be relied upon or be associated with the financial statements. No such disclosure should be made unless the auditor believes that the financial statements are likely to be misleading and that his report should not be relied on.

Consideration of Omitted Procedures After the Report Date

The auditor may, subsequent to issuing an audit report, conclude that one or more auditing procedures considered necessary in the circumstances were omitted during the audit. For example, as part of its internal quality review program, a CPA firm may discover that no physical inspection was performed of a significant quantity of a client's inventory stored at a remote location. The actions to be taken by the auditor in this and similar situations vary depending on the circumstances, and the auditor should be guided by the advice of legal counsel. SAS No. 46, *Consideration of Omitted Procedures After the Report Date* (AU Section 390), provides guidance in this area.

The auditor should, as a first step, assess the importance of the omitted procedure in relation to his or her ability to support the previously issued opinion. On further investigation (such as, for example, review of working papers and inquiry of members of the engagement team), the auditor may decide that other procedures that were performed compensated adequately for the omitted procedure. In this instance, the auditor usually does not take any further steps. If, however, the auditor concludes that the omission of the auditing procedure significantly impairs his or her ability to support the previously issued opinion and believes there are persons currently relying or likely to rely on the report, additional procedures necessary to provide an adequate basis for the opinion issued should be performed promptly. Those procedures may be the omitted procedure or appropriate alternatives designed to compensate adequately for it.

The performance of those procedures may disclose facts that existed at the date of the audit report that would have affected the opinion rendered had the auditor been aware of them at the time. In such circumstances, the auditor should follow the steps outlined in the preceding section of this chapter.

Situations may arise, however, when because of the passage of time or other reasons, the auditor is unable to perform the previously omitted or alternative procedures. In such instances, the auditor should seek the advice of legal counsel before deciding on the appropriate course of action. In any event, strong consideration should be given to notifying the client regarding the problem and the proposed action.

Review Questions

18-1. What are the four standards of reporting?

18-2. Describe the organization of the standard audit report. What "messages" are intended to be conveyed by the standard report?

18-3. When the principal auditor decides to refer to the audit of a subsidiary by another auditor, how is this indicated in the report? When is this reference necessary?

18-4. When comparative financial statements are presented, and the prior year's statements were audited by another auditor, what are the two alternatives the successor auditor and the client have?

18-5. What is the auditor's responsibility concerning additional information published by the client in the same document as the audited financial statements (as, for example, in an annual report to stockholders)?

18-6. What are the three types of departures from the standard unqualified report?

18-7. What are the two reasons for qualifying an opinion?

18-8. Why does explanatory language concerning an uncertainty ordinarily not constitute a qualification of the auditor's opinion?

18-9. What conditions must be met in order for the auditor to express a "clean" or unqualified opinion when there is a change in accounting principle?

18-10. What is a scope limitation? Give an illustration, and indicate when a disclaimer would be necessary.

18-11. When informative disclosures are omitted from the financial statements, the auditor should usually make the necessary disclosures in the auditor's report. What are the two exceptions to this requirement?

18-12. Describe the process by which the auditor evaluates whether there is substantial doubt about an entity's ability to continue as a going concern for a reasonable period of time.

18-13. Distinguish between an adverse opinion and a disclaimer of opinion.

18–14. What is a piecemeal opinion? What restrictions are there on piecemeal opinions?

18–15. What are the auditor's responsibilities with regard to "new information" about a client that becomes available after the report date?

18–16. Why should limited engagements (other than compilations and reviews) that are likely to lead to disclaimers be approached with reluctance by an auditor?

Discussion Questions

18–30. Your client's president has requested that you confine your audit work to the balance sheet at the year-end and render an opinion on the balance sheet only. The president contends that if the balance sheet is audited, and you have previously audited the balance sheet at the close of the preceding year, then the net income for the year must be the difference, and thus there is no necessity for spending the time to audit the income statement.

Required:

a. Is it permissible to express an opinion on the balance sheet alone?
b. What reasons would you advance for the desirability of auditing the income and expense accounts in sufficient detail to permit an opinion on the income statement? (Disregard any income tax considerations.)

18–31. Your client is issuing comparative financial statements. During the year under audit, the client was named as a defendant in a material lawsuit relating to the sale of a division that occurred during the current period.

The attorney's letter indicates that the client's outside counsel is unable to render any opinion at this time as to the outcome of the litigation. In the absence of an opinion from legal counsel, or of other evidence, what effect, if any, would this have on the audit report?

18–32. There are circumstances in which auditors should qualify their opinions in reporting on financial statements and other circumstances in which they should disclaim an opinion on the financial statements. Explain the general nature of the circumstances that would make each course necessary.

18–33. What would be the effect of each of the following conditions on the auditor's report?

a. Accounts receivable are significant in amount. The client refused to permit their confirmation by direct correspondence and no other satisfactory means of establishing the substantial correctness of the total were available.
b. The client refused to permit the auditor to examine the minutes of board of directors' meetings.

18–34. In the current year a client changes its method of valuing inventory from the first-in, first-out (FIFO) to the last-in, first-out (LIFO) method.

a. What effect, if any, would this have on the audit report for the current year?
b. How would the change in principle affect the audit report in the next year,

assuming the auditor is reporting on comparative financial statements including the year in which the change was made?

18-35. You are the accountant in charge of field work for a new client that has never been audited. Your audit report will cover only the current year. There has been no observation of the opening inventory and you are unable to satisfy yourself as to the opening inventory balance by means of alternative auditing procedures. Inventory represents about 45 percent of the total assets. What effect, if any, would these circumstances have on the audit opinion?

18-36. Assume the same situation as in Question 18-35 but, in addition, the client's records are insufficient to enable you to determine the accounting principles applied in the prior year. What additional effect, if any, would this circumstance have on the audit opinion?

18-37. You are newly engaged by Josephson, Inc., a northwestern manufacturer with a sales office and warehouse located in Tennessee. The Josephson audit must be made at the peak of your busy season, when you will not have a senior auditor available for travel to Tennessee. Furthermore, Josephson is reluctant to bear the travel expenses of an out-of-town auditor.

Required:

a. Under what conditions would you, the principal auditor, be willing to accept full responsibility for the work of, and not make reference in your report to, another auditor?
b. What procedures should you follow regardless of whether you accept full or divided responsibility, that is, regardless of whether you decide to make reference to the audit of another auditor?
c. What reference, if any, would you make to the other auditor in your report if you did not assume full responsibility for the other auditor's work?

(AICPA adapted)

AICPA Multiple Choice Questions

These questions are taken or adapted from the Auditing part of Uniform CPA Examinations. Choose the single most appropriate answer.

18-40. In which of the following situations would the auditor appropriately issue a report that did not contain a separate explanatory paragraph concerning consistency?

a. A change in the method of accounting for specific subsidiaries that comprise the group of companies for which consolidated statements are presented.
b. A change from an accounting principle that is *not* generally accepted to one that is generally accepted.
c. A change in the percentage used to calculate the provision for warranty expense.
d. Correction of a mistake in the application of a generally accepted accounting principle.

18-41. When financial statements are presented that are *not* in conformity with generally accepted accounting principles, an auditor may issue a

	Qualified opinion	*Disclaimer of opinion*
a.	Yes	No
b.	Yes	Yes
c.	No	Yes
d.	No	No

18-42. An auditor who qualifies an opinion because of an insufficiency of evidential matter should describe the limitation in an explanatory paragraph. The auditor should also refer to the limitation in the

	Scope paragraph	*Opinion paragraph*	*Notes to the financial statements*
a.	Yes	No	Yes
b.	No	Yes	No
c.	Yes	Yes	No
d.	Yes	Yes	Yes

18-43. When the financial statements contain a departure from generally accepted accounting principles, the effect of which is material, the auditor should

a. Qualify the opinion and explain the effect of the departure from generally accepted accounting principles in an explanatory paragraph.
b. Qualify the opinion and describe the departure from generally accepted accounting principles within the opinion paragraph.
c. Disclaim an opinion and explain the effect of the departure from generally accepted accounting principles in an explanatory paragraph.
d. Disclaim an opinion and describe the departure from generally accepted accounting principles within the opinion paragraph.

18-44. In which of the following circumstances would an auditor be most likely to express an adverse opinion?

a. The statements are *not* in conformity with the FASB Statements regarding the capitalization of leases.
b. Information comes to the auditor's attention that raises substantial doubt about the entity's ability to continue in existence.
c. The chief executive officer refuses the auditor access to minutes of board of directors' meetings.
d. The auditor concludes that the entity's internal control structure is so poor that control risk is at the maximum.

18-45. When unable to obtain sufficient competent evidential matter to determine whether certain client acts are illegal, the auditor would most likely issue

a. An unqualified opinion with a separate explanatory paragraph.
b. Either a qualified opinion or an adverse opinion.

c. Either a disclaimer of opinion or a qualified opinion.
d. Either an adverse opinion or a disclaimer of opinion.

18–46. A limitation on the scope of an audit sufficient to preclude an unqualified opinion will always result when management

a. Prevents the auditor from reviewing the working papers of the predecessor auditor.
b. Engages the auditor after the year-end physical inventory count is completed.
c. Fails to correct a material internal accounting control weakness that had been identified during the prior year's audit.
d. Refuses to furnish a management representation letter to the auditor.

18–47. Ajax Company's auditor concludes that the omission of an audit procedure considered necessary at the time of the prior audit impairs the auditor's present ability to support the previously expressed unqualified opinion. If the auditor believes there are stockholders currently relying on the opinion, the auditor should promptly

a. Notify the stockholders currently relying on the previously expressed unqualified opinion that they should *not* rely on it.
b. Advise management to disclose this development in its next interim report to the stockholders.
c. Advise management to revise the financial statements with full disclosure of the auditor's inability to support the unqualified opinion.
d. Undertake to apply the omitted procedure or alternative procedures that would provide a satisfactory basis for the opinion.

18–48. The auditor would most likely issue a disclaimer of opinion because of

a. The client's failure to present supplementary information required by the FASB.
b. Inadequate disclosure of material information.
c. A client-imposed scope limitation.
d. The qualification of an opinion by the other auditor of a subsidiary where there is a division of responsibility.

18–49. Subsequent to the issuance of the auditor's report, the auditor became aware of facts existing at the report date that would have affected the report had the auditor then been aware of such facts. After determining that the information is reliable, the auditor should next

a. Notify the board of directors that the auditor's report must *no* longer be associated with the financial statements.
b. Determine whether there are persons relying or likely to rely on the financial statements who would attach importance to the information.
c. Request that management disclose the effects of the newly discovered information by adding a footnote to subsequently issued financial statements.
d. Issue revised pro forma financial statements taking into consideration the newly discovered information.

18–50. When reporting on comparative financial statements where the financial statements of the prior period have been audited by a predecessor auditor whose report is *not* presented, the successor auditor should indicate in the introductory paragraph

a. The reasons why the predecessor auditor's report is *not* presented.
b. The identity of the predecessor auditor who audited the financial statements of the prior year.
c. Whether the predecessor auditor's review of the current year's financial statements revealed any matters that might have a material effect on the successor auditor's opinion.
d. The type of opinion expressed by the predecessor auditor.

18–51. An auditor concludes that there is a material inconsistency in the other information in an annual report to shareholders containing audited financial statements. If the auditor concludes that the financial statements do *not* require revision, but the client refuses to revise or eliminate the material inconsistency, the auditor may

a. Issue an "except for" qualified opinion after discussing the matter with the client's board of directors.
b. Consider the matter closed since the other information is *not* in the audited financial statements.
c. Disclaim an opinion on the financial statements after explaining the material inconsistency in a separate explanatory paragraph.
d. Revise the auditor's report to include a separate explanatory paragraph describing the material inconsistency.

18–52. An auditor did not observe a client's taking of beginning physical inventory and was unable to become satisfied about the inventory by means of other auditing procedures. Assuming *no* other scope limitations or reporting problems, the auditor could issue an unqualified opinion on the current year's financial statements for

a. The balance sheet only.
b. The income statement only.
c. The income and retained earnings statements only.
d. All of the financial statements.

18–53. An auditor may *not* issue a qualified opinion when

a. A scope limitation prevents the auditor from completing an important audit procedure.
b. The auditor's report refers to the work of a specialist.
c. An accounting principle at variance with generally accepted accounting principles is used.
d. The auditor lacks independence with respect to the audited entity.

18–54. An auditor may reasonably issue an "except for" qualified opinion for

	Inadequate disclosure	*Scope limitation*
a.	Yes	Yes
b.	Yes	No
c.	No	Yes
d.	No	No

18–55. If a publicly held entity declines to include in its financial report supplementary information required by the FASB, the auditor should issue

a. An unqualified opinion with a separate explanatory paragraph.
b. Either a disclaimer of opinion or an adverse opinion.
c. Either an "except for" qualified opinion or a disclaimer of opinion.
d. Either an adverse opinion or an "except for" qualified opinion.

18–56. When a client declines to include a statement of cash flows in its financial report, the auditor's report will usually

a. Contain a qualified opinion.
b. Include a separate paragraph that summarizes the company's financing, investing, and operating activities.
c. Refer to a footnote that contains an auditor-prepared statement of cash flows.
d. Refer to the scope limitation.

18–57. When financial statements are prepared on the basis of a going concern and the auditor believes that there is substantial doubt about the client's ability to continue as a going concern, the auditor should issue

a. A qualified opinion.
b. An unqualified opinion with an explanatory paragraph following the opinion paragraph.
c. An unqualified opinion.
d. An adverse opinion.

18–58. Approximately 90 percent of Helena Holding Company's assets consist of investments in wholly owned subsidiary companies. The CPA auditing Helena's financial statements has satisfied himself that changes in underlying equity in these investments have been properly computed based upon the subsidiaries' unaudited financial statements, but he has not audited the subsidiaries' financial statements. The auditor's report should include

a. An adverse opinion.
b. An "except for" opinion.
c. A "subject to" opinion.
d. A disclaimer of opinion.

18–59. An auditor includes an explanatory paragraph in an unqualified report in order to emphasize that the entity being reported upon is a subsidiary of another business enterprise. The inclusion of this explanatory paragraph

a. Is appropriate and would *not* negate the unqualified opinion.
b. Is considered a qualification of the report.
c. Is a violation of generally accepted reporting standards if this information is disclosed in footnotes to the financial statements.
d. Necessitates a revision of the opinion paragraph to include the phrase "with the foregoing explanation."

Problems and Cases

18-60. Items 1 through 4 are based on the following information:

The auditor's report must contain an expression of opinion or a statement to the effect that an opinion cannot be expressed. Four types of opinions or statements that meet these requirements are generally known as

a. An unqualified opinion.
b. A qualified opinion.
c. A disclaimer of opinion.
d. An adverse opinion.

For each of the situations presented in items 1 through 4, indicate the type of opinion or statement that should be rendered, by reference to the appropriate letter from the above list, and give reasons for your answer.

1. Subsequent to the close of Lane & Company's fiscal year, a major debtor was declared bankrupt due to a rapid series of events. The receivable is significantly material in relation to the financial statements and recovery is doubtful. The debtor had confirmed the full amount due to Lane & Company at the balance sheet date. Since the account was good at the balance sheet date, Lane & Company refuses to disclose any information in relation to this subsequent event. The CPA believes that all accounts were stated fairly at the balance sheet date.
2. Gallagher Enterprises is a substantial user of electronic data processing equipment and has used an outside service bureau to process data in past years. During the current year Gallagher adopted the policy of leasing all hardware and expects to continue this arrangement in the future. This change in policy is adequately disclosed in footnotes to Gallagher's financial statements, but uncertainty prohibits either Gallagher or the CPA from assessing the impact of this change on future operations.
3. The president of Janis Corporation would not allow the auditor to confirm the receivable balance from one of its major customers. The amount of the receivable is material in relation to the financial statements of Janis Corporation. The auditor was unable to obtain satisfaction as to the receivable balance by alternative procedures.
4. Chester Company issued financial statements that purported to present financial position and results of operations but omitted the statement of cash flows.

(AICPA adapted)

18-61. You have received the attorney's letter on the following page three days before you are to issue the audit opinion. Assume all amounts are material.

After reading the attorney's letter you contact Buttonwood Industries' management and it discloses the following:

1. Buttonwood Industries has filed a counteraction for libel, and preliminary hearings and discovery proceedings are just beginning.
2. Management believes the company has a good chance of prevailing but the outcome cannot presently be determined.
3. No provision for any liability has been made in the financial statements.

C.S. BRODERICK
2525 First Street
Binghamton, New York 13901

February 8, 1990

Re: Buttonwood Industries, Inc.

Samuel & Butler
600 Fulton Avenue
Syracuse, New York 13202

Dear Sir or Madam:

This letter is in response to the audit inquiry letter of Buttonwood Industries, Inc. (''Company'') concerning your audit of the financial statements of the Company as of December 31, 1989.

While this firm represents the Company, our engagement has been limited to specific matters as to which we were consulted by them. On February 1, 1990, the Company was sued by Dormer Corporation in the United States District Court for the Southern District of New York. The complaint alleges that the Company negligently provided defective electronics components to Dormer in 1989 and the latter subsequently included such components in equipment sold to third parties. Dormer asked for relief, jointly and severally in the amount of $5 million. The matter has not been fully investigated at this time; accordingly, we are not able to form an opinion at this time as to the ultimate outcome of this matter.

Referring to the Company's request that we furnish to you a description of any other matters of which we are aware involving a possible actual or contingent liability of the Company at the audit date or subsequent thereto, please be advised that we are not in a position to comment on matters other than claims which to our knowledge have been actually made or threatened against the Company or its subsidiaries and which have been referred to us in a manner so as to require legal advice and, where appropriate, legal representation.

The information contained in this letter is as of the date of this letter, and we assume no obligation to provide you with any changes, whether material or not, which come to our attention after the date of this letter. This response is limited by, and in accordance with, the ABA Statement of Policy Regarding Lawyers' Responses to Auditors' Requests for Information (December 1975); without limiting the generality of the foregoing, the limitations in such Statement on the scope and use of this response (paragraphs 2 and 7) are specifically incorporated herein by reference and any description herein of any ''loss contingencies'' is qualified in its entirety by paragraph 5 of the Statement and the accompanying Commentary (which is an integral part of the Statement). Consistent with the last sentence of paragraph 6 of the ABA Statement of Policy and pursuant to the Company's request, this will confirm as correct the Company's understanding, as set forth in its audit inquiry letter to us, that whenever, in the course of performing legal services for the Company with respect to a matter recognized to involve an unasserted possible claim or assessment that may call for financial statement disclosure, we have formed a professional conclusion that the Company must disclose or consider disclosure concerning such possible claim or assessment, we, as a matter of professional responsibility to the Company, will so advise the Company and will consult with the Company concerning the question of such disclosure and the applicable requirements of Statement of Financial Accounting Standards No. 5.

Very truly yours,

C.S. Broderick

Required:

a. Determine what impact, if any, this will have on the financial statements and on the auditor's report.
b. Prepare the modifications, if any, to the auditor's report and the footnote required to disclose this situation.

18–62. New Designs Corp., an audit client of yours, is a manufacturer of consumer products and has several wholly owned subsidiaries in foreign countries that are audited by other independent auditors in those countries. The financial statements of all subsidiaries were properly consolidated in the financial statements of the parent company, and the foreign auditors' reports were furnished to your CPA firm.

You are now preparing your auditor's opinion on the consolidated financial statements for the year ended June 30, 1990. These statements were prepared on a comparative basis with those of the prior year.

Required:

a. How would you evaluate and accept the independence and professional reputation of the foreign auditors?
b. In what circumstances may a principal auditor assume responsibility for the work of another auditor to the same extent as if the principal auditor had performed the work?
c. Assume that in both the prior year and this year you were willing to utilize the reports of the other independent auditors in expressing your opinion on the consolidated financial statements but were unwilling to take full responsibility for performance of the work underlying their opinions. Assuming your audit of the parent company's financial statements would allow you to render an unqualified opinion, prepare the necessary disclosures to be contained in the auditor's report.
d. What modification(s), if any, would be necessary in your auditor's report if the financial statements for the prior year were unaudited?

(AICPA adapted)

18–63. The Toy Factory is engaged in the manufacture and wholesale distribution of children's toys. Its operations have been very successful for a number of years. Because of the increased demand for video games, however, Toy Factory's sales volume declined sharply following a bad Christmas sales period in 1989, and a significant loss was reported for that year. Early in 1990, the company contracted for the purchase of electronic components and modified its production facilities to provide for the assembly of both toys and video games.

In October 1990, you and the audit manager met with Toy Factory's President to finalize plans for the audit for the year ending December 31, 1990. You were informed that although the company reduced its loss for the first nine months of the year as compared with the same period in the prior year, the amount of the loss was still substantial. The financial condition of the Toy Factory as of September 30, 1990, is summarized as follows:

		$000s Omitted
Current assets:		
Cash		$ 5
Accounts receivable		800
Inventories		650
		1,455
Fixed assets less depreciation		1,200
		$2,655
Current liabilities:		
Notes payable to bank		$1,000
Accounts payable and current portion of bonds payable		950
		1,950
Long-term bonds (payable over five years)		350
		2,300
Stockholders' equity:		
Common stock		250
Retained earnings at Dec. 31, 1989	$955	
Loss for nine months ended Sept. 30, 1990	(850)	105
		355
		$2,655

The President further informed you that Silverline Bank had increased the company's line of credit from $800,000 to $1.2 million on September 1, 1990, based on the company's forecast of future cash flow. This forecast indicated that this line of credit would be required until September 1, 1991.

You pointed out to the President that the company had already had to increase its borrowings from the bank to $1 million by September 30 and that she had indicated to you that the customary Christmas season sales increase to retailers during August and September had not improved the cash flow problems of the company. The President assured you she is confident that the company's cash flow will improve and that the problems of 1989 have been overcome because the demand for the new video games will increase and justify higher margins than for the toys. She believes that the company will not have to borrow funds in excess of the present bank limit because cash requirements for the remainder of 1990 and the first half of 1991 will be relatively small.

Required:

a. Define the audit problems and cite applicable professional pronouncements, if any.
b. Determine the approach you would propose to the partner on the engagement for the solution of the problems, including the evidence or other data you would want to review.
c. Indicate the factors you would consider in determining the impact on the audit budget and timing of field work.

18–64. Various types of accounting changes can affect the second standard of reporting. This standard reads, "The report shall identify those circumstances in which such principles have not been consistently observed in the current period in relation to the preceding period."

Assume that the following list describes changes that have a material effect on a client's financial statements for the current year.

1. A change from the completed-contract method to the percentage-of-completion method of accounting for long-term construction contracts.
2. A change in the estimated useful life of previously recorded fixed assets based on newly acquired information.
3. Correction of a mathematical error in inventory pricing made in a prior period.
4. A change from prime costing to full absorption costing for inventory valuation.
5. A change from presentation of statements of individual companies to presentation of consolidated statements.
6. A change from deferring and amortizing preproduction costs to recording such costs as an expense when incurred because future benefits of the costs have become doubtful. The new accounting method was adopted in recognition of the change in estimated future benefits.
7. A change to including the employer's share of FICA taxes as "retirement benefits" on the income statement from including it with "other taxes."
8. A change from the FIFO method of inventory pricing to the LIFO method of inventory pricing.

Required:

Identify the type of change described in each item, state whether explanatory language should be added to the auditor's standard report as it relates to the second standard of reporting, and state whether the prior year's financial statements should be restated when presented in comparative form with the current year's statements. Organize your answer as shown in the chart on page 797.

For example, a change from the LIFO method of inventory pricing to the FIFO method of inventory pricing would appear as shown.

Item No.	*Type of Change*	*Should Explanatory Language Be Added to Standard Report?*	*Should Prior Year's Statements Be Restated?*
Example	An accounting change from one generally accepted accounting principle to another generally accepted accounting principle.	Yes	Yes

(AICPA adapted)

18–65. Watkins, CPA, has completed the audit of the financial statements of Glenview Corporation as of and for the year ended December 31, 1990. Watkins has also audited and reported on the Glenview financial statements for the prior year. Watkins drafted the following report for 1990.

March 14, 1991

We have audited the accompanying balance sheet of Glenview Corporation as of December 31, 1990, and the related statements of income and retained earnings for the year then ended. These financial statements are the responsibility of the Company's management.

We conducted our audit in accordance with generally accepted accounting standards. Those standards require that we plan and perform the audit to obtain assurance about whether the financial statements are accurate. An audit includes examining, on a test basis, evidence supporting the amounts and disclosures in the financial statements. An audit also includes assessing the accounting principles used and significant estimates made by management, as well as evaluating the overall financial statement presentation.

In our opinion, the financial statements referred to above are fairly presented, in all material respects, in conformity with generally accepted accounting principles in effect at December 31, 1990.

Watkins, CPA
(Signed)

Other Information:

- Glenview is presenting comparative financial statements.
- Glenview does not wish to present a statement of cash flows for either year.
- During 1990, Glenview changed its method of accounting for long-term construction contracts and properly reflected the effect of the change in the current year's financial statements and restated the prior year's statements. Watkins is satisfied with Glenview's justification for making the change. The change is discussed in footnote 12.
- Watkins was unable to perform normal accounts receivable confirmation procedures but alternative procedures were used to satisfy Watkins about the existence and accuracy of the receivables.
- Glenview Corporation is the defendant in a litigation, the outcome of which is highly uncertain. If the case is settled in favor of the plaintiff, Glenview will be

required to pay a substantial amount of cash, which might require the sale of certain fixed assets. The litigation and the possible effects have been properly disclosed in footnote 11.

- Glenview issued debentures on January 31, 1989, in the amount of $10,000,000. The funds obtained from the issuance were used to finance the expansion of plant facilities. The debenture agreement restricts the payment of future cash dividends to earnings after December 31, 1990. Glenview declined to disclose this essential data in the footnotes to the financial statements.

Required:

a. Identify and explain any items included in "Other Information" that need *not* be referred to or otherwise be part of the *auditor's report*.

b. Explain the deficiencies in Watkins' report as drafted (including omissions). (Do *not* rewrite the report.)

18–66. This is the conclusion of the Quinn Hardware case that began in Chapter 6. The complete set of financial statements, including footnotes, for the years ended May 31, 1991 and 1990 follows. (*Note*: An adverse outcome of the litigation described in Note 9 would have a significant effect on the Company.) Field work was completed on July 10 and the report is to be issued on July 20, 1991.

Required:

Prepare the audit report.

QUINN HARDWARE, INC. AND SUBSIDIARY
CONSOLIDATED BALANCE SHEETS
May 31, 1991 and 1990
(in 000s)

ASSETS

	1991	1990
Current assets:		
Cash and cash equivalents	$ 3,382	$ 12,919
Accounts receivable, net of allowance for uncollectible accounts of $1,800 in 1991 and $1,500 in 1990	49,408	37,074
Merchandise inventory	63,570	48,637
Other current assets	5,989	6,675
Total current assets	122,349	105,305
Property, plant, and equipment:		
Land	2,206	1,804
Buildings and improvements	44,423	44,749
Furniture and fixtures	112,874	92,530
Automotive equipment	17,860	14,780
	177,363	153,863
Less accumulated depreciation	75,092	66,819
	102,271	87,044
Building and improvements held for sale	7,450	5,772
Total assets	$232,070	$198,121

LIABILITIES AND STOCKHOLDERS' EQUITY

	1991	1990
Current liabilities:		
Short-term borrowings	$ 7,055	$ 6,559
Accounts payable	13,160	11,818
Accrued liabilities	18,893	17,917
Income taxes payable	1,424	1,431
Current portion of long-term indebtedness	5,010	3,351
Total current liabilities	45,542	41,076
Long-term debt less current portion	42,329	28,468
Other liabilities	2,054	1,812
Deferred income taxes	14,500	13,400
	58,883	43,680
Commitments and contingencies		
Stockholders' equity:		
Preferred stock, $1.00 par value; nonparticipating, 9% cumulative preference, 500,000 shares authorized, 250,000 shares issued and outstanding	250	250
Common stock, no par value; 1,250,000 shares authorized, 500,000 shares issued and outstanding	5,000	5,000
Additional paid-in capital	27,168	27,168
Retained earnings	95,227	80,947
Total stockholders' equity	127,645	113,365
Total liabilities and stockholders' equity	$232,070	$198,121

The accompanying notes are an integral part of the consolidated financial statements.

QUINN HARDWARE, INC. AND SUBSIDIARY
CONSOLIDATED STATEMENTS OF INCOME
for the years ended May 31, 1991 and 1990
(in 000s)

	1991	*1990*
Sales	$292,701	$255,426
Cost of goods sold	212,743	186,684
Gross profit	79,958	68,742
Other costs and expenses:		
General and administrative expenses	45,442	40,732
Operating profit	34,516	28,010
Interest expense	2,305	2,462
Income before provision for income taxes	32,211	25,548
Provision for income taxes	13,851	12,000
Net income	$ 18,360	$ 13,548

The accompanying notes are an integral part of the consolidated financial statements.

QUINN HARDWARE, INC. AND SUBSIDIARY
CONSOLIDATED STATEMENTS OF STOCKHOLDERS' EQUITY
for the years ended May 31, 1991 and 1990
(in 000s)

	Preferred Stock		*Common Stock*				
	Number of Shares	*Amount*	*Number of Shares*	*Amount*	*Additional Paid-in Capital*	*Retained Earnings*	*Total Stockholders' Equity*
Balance, June 1, 1989 as previously reported	250	$250	500	$5,000	$27,168	$67,280	$ 99,698
Adjustment (Note 6)						1,750	1,750
Balance, June 1, 1989 as restated	250	250	500	5,000	27,168	69,030	101,448
Net income						13,548	13,548
Cash dividends declared on common stock, $2.00 per share						(1,000)	(1,000)
Cash dividends declared on preferred stock, $2.524 per share						(631)	(631)
Balance, May 31, 1990	250	250	500	5,000	27,168	80,947	113,365
Net income						18,360	18,360
Cash dividends declared on common stock, $5.58 per share						(2,790)	(2,790)
Cash dividends declared on preferred stock, $5.16 per share						(1,290)	(1,290)
Balance, May 31, 1991	250	$250	500	$5,000	$27,168	$95,227	$127,645

The accompanying notes are an integral part of the consolidated financial statements.

QUINN HARDWARE, INC. AND SUBSIDIARY
CONSOLIDATED STATEMENTS OF CASH FLOWS
for the years ended May 31, 1991 and 1990
(Decrease) Increase in Cash and Cash Equivalents
(in 000s)

	1991		*1990*	
Cash flows from operating activities:				
Net income		$18,360		$13,548
Adjustments to reconcile net income to net cash provided by operating activities:				
Depreciation	$ 3,126		$ 2,923	
Provisions for losses on accounts receivable	1,000		894	
Change in assets and liabilities:				
(Increase) in accounts receivable	(13,334)		(3,501)	
(Increase) Decrease in merchandise inventory	(14,933)		4,378	
Decrease (Increase) in other current assets	686		(835)	
Increase in short-term borrowings	496		1,647	
Increase in accounts payable	1,342		482	
Increase in accrued liabilities	976		5,782	
(Decrease) Increase in income taxes payable	(7)		200	
Increase in other liabilities	242		189	
Increase in deferred taxes	1,100		3,040	
Total adjustments		(19,306)		15,199
Net cash provided by operating activities		(946)		28,747

Cash flows from investing activities:				
Capital expenditures	(20,031)		(13,872)	
Net cash used in investing activities		(20,031)		(13,872)
Cash flows from financing activities:				
Proceeds from long-term indebtedness	19,000			
Principal payments on long-term indebtedness	(3,480)		(9,864)	
Dividends paid	(4,080)		(1,631)	
Net cash used in financing activities		11,440		(11,495)
Net (decrease) increase in cash and cash equivalents		(9,537)		3,380
Cash and cash equivalents at beginning of year		12,919		9,539
Cash and cash equivalents at end of year		$ 3,382		$12,919
Supplemental disclosures of cash flow information:				
Income taxes paid		$14,321		$9,172
Interest paid		$3,081		$3,134

The accompanying notes are an integral part of the consolidated financial statements.

QUINN HARDWARE, INC. AND SUBSIDIARY
NOTES TO CONSOLIDATED FINANCIAL STATEMENTS

1. Accounting Policies

Principles of Consolidation

The consolidated financial statements include the accounts of Quinn Hardware, Inc. (the Company) and its wholly owned subsidiary. All intercompany transactions have been eliminated.

Merchandise Inventory

Merchandise inventory is stated at the lower of cost or market, based on the FIFO (first-in, first-out) method.

Property, Plant, and Equipment

Property, plant, and equipment is stated at cost. Depreciation of buildings and improvements is provided over the estimated useful lives of the assets using the straight-line method. Automotive equipment, furniture, and fixtures are depreciated using the sum-of-the-years'-digits method.

Stock Options

Proceeds from the sale of common stock issued under stock options are credited to common stock. There are no charges to income with respect to these options.

Franchise Fee Revenue

Franchise fee revenue from the sale of individual franchises is recognized when all significant services and conditions have been satisfied by the Company, generally at the time the franchisee commences operations. No new franchises were sold or opened during fiscal 1991 or 1990. Continuing franchise fee revenue is based on a percentage of the net sales of the franchisees and is recorded when earned.

Income Taxes

Deferred income taxes are recorded to reflect the tax consequences on future years of differences between the tax bases of assets and liabilities and their financial reporting amounts at each year-end.

The Company adopted the liability method of accounting for income taxes pursuant to Financial Accounting Standards Board Statement of Financial Accounting Standards No. 96 (SFAS No. 96), *Accounting for Income Taxes* (issued December 1987). Although SFAS No. 96 is effective for annual financial statements for fiscal years beginning after December 15, 1991, earlier application is permitted. The Company previously used the deferred method.

The Company accounts for investment tax credits under the flow-through method.

Cash Equivalents

For purposes of the consolidated Statement of Cash Flows, the Company considers marketable securities and interest-bearing deposits with maturities of three months or less to be cash equivalents.

QUINN HARDWARE, INC. AND SUBSIDIARY
NOTES TO CONSOLIDATED FINANCIAL STATEMENTS
(Continued)

Account Classification

Various income statement and balance sheet accounts for 1990 have been reclassified to conform to the classifications used in the 1991 financial statements, with no effect on previously reported results of operations.

2. Buildings and Improvements Held for Sale

Buildings and improvements held for sale consist of two warehouses located in Dallas, Texas, and Scottsdale, Arizona. These properties are carried at net book value which approximates estimated net realizable value.

3. Long-Term Debt

Long-term debt, less current portion, at May 31, 1991 and 1990, consists of the following:

	1991	*1990*
8.45% senior note, due 1994—annual sinking fund requirements of $700,000	$ 4,400,000	$5,100,000
9.88% note payable to bank due in installments of $1,556,000 beginning in 1993 through 2002	14,000,000	
Industrial Revenue Bonds, interest at rates from 5¾% to 9%, due in varying installments from 1993 through 2003	6,769,000	7,269,000
Miscellaneous notes payable at interest rates from 9% to 9¾%	4,394,000	4,359,000
Industrial Development Bonds due in annual installments of $1,329,000 to $1,671,000 through 1996 and decreasing amounts thereafter to 2004 plus interest at rates from 5% to 9¾%	12,766,000	11,740,000
Total	$42,329,000	$28,468,000

Certain long-term debt agreements contain, among other covenants, requirements on maintenance of working capital, limitations on additional long-term indebtedness, payment of cash dividends, and purchase of the Company's stock. At May 31, 1991 there were no restricted retained earnings.

Annual maturities of long-term indebtedness are approximately $4,515,000, $3,779,000, $4,654,000, and $4,510,000 in the years 1993 through 1996, respectively.

QUINN HARDWARE, INC. AND SUBSIDIARY
NOTES TO CONSOLIDATED FINANCIAL STATEMENTS
(Continued)

4. Leases

The Company operates certain of its stores and office locations under noncancelable leases that are generally for initial periods of five years and contain provisions for renewal options (for up to an additional aggregate period of 20 years). In addition, certain store and delivery equipment is leased over periods ranging from 5 to 10 years.

Future minimum rental payments required under noncancelable operating leases consisted of the following at May 31, 1991:

Year Ending May 31,	*Minimum Operating Leases*	*Minimum Sublease Income*	*Net Minimum Annual Rentals*
1992	$1,080,000	$150,000	$ 930,000
1993	878,000	69,000	809,000
1994	104,000	30,000	74,000
1995	104,000	30,000	74,000
1996	101,000	30,000	71,000
Thereafter	25,000	20,000	5,000
Total minimum payments	$2,292,000	$329,000	$1,963,000

Net rental expense for operating leases for the years ended May 31 comprises

	1991	*1990*
Rent expense	$3,060,000	$3,156,000
Less sublease income	900,000	680,000
Net rent expense	$2,160,000	$2,476,000

5. Preferred and Common Stock

The preferred stock may be redeemed by the Company at any time for $1.00 per share, plus accrued and unpaid dividends.

The stock option plan approved by the Company's shareholders provides for the granting of 150,000 options to employees for purchase of the Company's common stock at prices equal to 100% of the fair market price at the dates the options are granted. All options are exercisable in full after one year from the date of grant. Options exercisable at May 31, 1991 and 1990 were 67,000 and 24,000, respectively. During 1991 and 1990 no options were exercised.

Options to employees under this plan are as follows:

	Shares	*Price Per Share*
Balance at June 1, 1989	47,500	$5.00 to $6.00
Granted	48,000	6.50 to 8.50
Canceled	(23,500)	5.75 to 6.00
Balance at May 31, 1990	72,000	5.00 to 8.50
Granted	25,000	9.75
Canceled	(4,600)	5.00
Balance at May 31, 1991	92,400	$5.25 to $9.75

QUINN HARDWARE, INC. AND SUBSIDIARY
NOTES TO CONSOLIDATED FINANCIAL STATEMENTS
(Continued)

6. Income Taxes

The Company adopted the liability method of accounting for income taxes under Statement of Financial Accounting Standards No. 96 (SFAS No. 96), *Accounting for Income Taxes*. Although SFAS No. 96 is effective for annual financial statements for fiscal years beginning after December 15, 1991, earlier application is permitted. The Company previously used the deferred method.

The consolidated financial statements at, and for the years ended, May 31, 1990 and 1989 (not presented) have been restated, as permitted by SFAS No. 96, to reflect the Statement's new provisions. This accounting change increased retained earnings at June 1, 1989 by $1,750,000. In addition, this accounting change increased the 1991 and 1990 consolidated statements of income by $1,125,000 and $1,190,000, respectively.

The components of the provision for income taxes on income are as follows:

	1991	*1990*
	(in 000s)	
U.S. federal:		
Current tax provision	$ 9,867	$ 8,565
Deferred tax provision:		
Effect of a change in enacted tax laws or tax status	1,125	1,190
Other	909	750
Deferred tax provision	2,034	1,940
U.S. federal income tax provision	11,901	10,505
State and local:		
Current tax provision	1,884	1,435
Deferred tax provision	66	60
State and local income tax provision	1,950	1,495
Total income tax provision on income from continuing operations	$13,851	$12,000

The Company's effective tax rate on pretax income from operations differs from U.S. federal statutory regular tax rate as follows:

	Percent of Income Before Income Taxes	
	1991	*1990*
Normal statutory rate	34.0%	34.0%
Investment tax credits	—	(.5)
State and local taxes, net of federal tax benefit	9.6	11.0
Other	(.6)	2.5
	43.0%	47.0%

The Internal Revenue Service (IRS) is currently conducting an examination of the Company's federal income tax returns for the years 1988 to 1990. Although no report has been rendered, informal discussions between management and the IRS have indicated that any adjustments arising from this examination will not have a material effect on the consolidated financial statements.

QUINN HARDWARE, INC. AND SUBSIDIARY
NOTES TO CONSOLIDATED FINANCIAL STATEMENTS
(Continued)

7. Transactions with Related Parties

During 1991 the Company, in the ordinary course of business, sold merchandise to an entity in which the Company's President is a significant stockholder. The Company's sales to this entity were $19,000,000 for the year ended May 31, 1991. These are paid upon receipt and there is no receivable balance at May 31, 1991.

Three of the Company's stores are leased from the Company's President. Aggregate rentals charged and paid with respect to these leases totaled $1,670,000 and $1,630,000 for 1991 and 1990, respectively.

8. Pension Plan

The Company has a defined contribution plan covering substantially all its full-time employees who meet certain eligibility requirements. Contributions and costs, which are determined based on a percentage of each covered employee's salary, totaled $1,304,000 and $1,110,000 in 1991 and 1990, respectively.

9. Contingencies

In September 1990 Key Lumber, Alpha Inc., and Syntex Co. filed suit against the Company in the United States District Court. The suit seeks damages that the plaintiffs claim resulted from the Company's nonperformance of certain contractual obligations.

In view of the preliminary nature of this proceeding, it is not possible for the Company to predict the outcome or the range of potential loss, if any, that may result from this proceeding. As a result no provision for loss has been made in the consolidated financial statements. The Company's intention is to deny the allegation and to defend the actions vigorously.

10. Subsequent Event

On July 17, 1991, the Company entered into a term loan agreement with an insurance company, which provides for the borrowing of $6,000,000 (at the prime interest rate plus 1½%) to finance the expansion of its franchise system. The agreement provides for a commitment fee of ½ of 1% of the unused amount.

19

Responsibilities in Other Engagements

The increased sophistication of our society and of the business environment, coupled with a better understanding by the public of auditors' skills and experience, has created a demand for a variety of services far beyond audits of financial statements. The work accountants in public practice may be asked to perform, the diversity of resulting reports and letters that may be issued, and the reporting problems these create are literally infinite. Standard-setters have tried to keep pace with this explosion in the demand for special services. Their efforts are reflected in the series of attestation standards as well as in the Statements on Auditing Standards and Statements on Standards for Accounting and Review Services. These standards and statements address a number of special reporting situations and nonaudit services—among them compilations, reviews, interim reviews, a variety of special reports, reporting on information accompanying basic financial statements, reports on internal control, reports on compliance with contractual agreements, letters for underwriters, reports on various attest engagements (including those relating to pro forma and prospective financial statements), and reports on compliance with laws and regulations. Both the procedures employed in providing those and other services and the reports issued are discussed in this chapter.

Some of the issues addressed in this chapter arise because nonaudit engagements do not require obtaining sufficient competent evidence to provide the relatively high level of assurance an audit opinion demands. In those situations, both the professional literature and this chapter refer to a person who undertakes the engagement and issues a report as an "accountant," a "certified public accountant" (CPA), or a "practitioner." The term "auditor" is reserved for a person who undertakes to perform an audit in accordance with generally accepted auditing standards (GAAS) and expresses an opinion based on the results of that audit.

NONAUDITS, COMPILATIONS, AND REVIEWS

Association with Financial Data

SAS No. 26 (AU Section 504.03) provides that "when an accountant submits to his client or others financial statements that he has prepared or assisted in preparing, he is deemed to be associated even though the accountant does not append his name to the statements." A practitioner is *directly associated* with financial data whenever he or she is engaged to perform a compilation, review, or audit, or to apply agreed-upon procedures to specified elements, accounts, or items of a financial statement. When a practitioner is directly associated with financial data, he or she has a duty to clearly indicate the character of the work done and the degree of responsibility taken. The practitioner's objective is to prevent readers from misinterpreting his or her role and association with the data. Thus for each type of engagement, there is a standard reporting format that conveys the appropriate level of assurance.

Practitioners may be *indirectly associated* with financial data by virtue of special services provided to clients. These services can range from merely typing financial statements to various types of accounting services such as preparing a trial balance or assisting in adjusting the accounts. When a practitioner is indirectly associated with financial data, he or she needs to be aware that third parties may infer an unwarranted level of assurance based on knowledge of the practitioner's involvement. Because of this, the profession has provided guidance in some areas where a practitioner may be indirectly associated with financial data. For example, a form of indirect association with financial statements of a nonpublic company that was permitted at one time but is now generally prohibited is referred to as a "plain paper" engagement. This is an engagement to prepare and submit to the client, for management's use only, financial statements without any accompanying report or other direct association of the CPA and without meeting the requirements for a compilation service.

Compilations of Financial Statements

To address clients' needs for accountants' services that would not entail providing any assurance on financial data, the Accounting and Review Services Committee of the AICPA has established a level of professional service for nonpublic companies called a compilation. This service involves presenting information, consisting of management's representations in the form of financial statements, without expressing any assurance on them. The accountant is not required to make inquiries or perform other procedures to corroborate or review the information supplied by the client. The accountant does, however, have certain other duties and responsibilities, specified in Statement on Standards for Accounting and Review Services (SSARS) No. 1 (AR Section 100).

Compilation Procedures. At the outset, the accountant should establish an understanding, preferably in writing, with the client as to the nature and limitations of the service to be performed, and the type of report to be rendered. Before beginning the work, the accountant should have or acquire a knowledge of the accounting principles and practices of the client's industry and a general understanding of the nature of the client's business transactions, the form of its accounting records, the qualifications of its accounting personnel, the accounting basis used, and the form and content of the financial statements. The accountant should read the financial statements to see if they are free from obvious material errors, such as arithmetical or clerical mistakes, misapplication of accounting principles, and inadequate disclosures.

The accountant should discuss with the client any items of concern that arise from performing the foregoing procedures. The client should be asked to revise the financial statements, as appropriate; if the client does not comply, the accountant should modify the report. At the extreme, the accountant should withdraw from the engagement if modifying the report is not adequate to communicate the deficiencies.

Form of Reporting. The accountant's report on a compilation engagement explicitly disclaims an opinion and gives no other form of assurance about the financial statements. The standard form of compilation report, as suggested in SSARS No. 5, *Reporting on Compiled Financial Statements* (AR Section 500), for a nonpublic company follows:

> We have compiled the accompanying balance sheet of XYZ Company as of December 31, 19XX, and the related statements of income, retained earnings, and cash flows for the year then ended, in accordance with standards established by the American Institute of Certified Public Accountants.
>
> A compilation is limited to presenting in the form of financial statements information that is the representation of management (owners). We have not audited or reviewed the accompanying financial statements and, accordingly, do not express an opinion or any other form of assurance on them.

Each page of the financial statements should include a reference such as "See Accountant's Compilation Report." If substantially all disclosures are omitted, the accountant's report should highlight this fact to alert users of the financial statements.

Reviews of Financial Statements

A review of financial statements, as described in SSARS No. 1 (AR Section 100), involves inquiry and analytical procedures intended to provide the accountant with a reasonable basis for expressing limited assurance that there are no material modifications that should be made to the financial statements in order for them to be in conformity with GAAP or some other comprehensive basis of accounting.[1] Like compilations, reviews generally may be performed only for nonpublic entities.

Paragraph 4 of SSARS No. 1 (AR Section 100.04) compares a review with a compilation and an audit, as follows:

> The objective of a review differs significantly from the objective of a compilation. The inquiry and analytical procedures performed in a review should provide the accountant with a reasonable basis for expressing limited assurance that there are no material modifications that should be made to the financial statements. No expression of assurance is contemplated in a compilation.

[1]Comprehensive bases of accounting other than GAAP are described and discussed later in this chapter. Hereafter, reference to GAAP in this section of the chapter includes, where applicable, another comprehensive basis of accounting.

The objective of a review also differs significantly from the objective of an audit of financial statements in accordance with generally accepted auditing standards. The objective of an audit is to provide a reasonable basis for expressing an opinion regarding the financial statements taken as a whole. A review does not provide a basis for the expression of such an opinion because a review does not contemplate obtaining an understanding of the internal control structure or assessing control risk, tests of accounting records and of responses to inquiries by obtaining corroborating evidential matter through inspection, observation or confirmation, and certain other procedures ordinarily performed during an audit. A review may bring to the accountant's attention significant matters affecting the financial statements, but it does not provide assurance that the accountant will become aware of all significant matters that would be disclosed in an audit.

Review Procedures. In a review engagement, either the accountant or the client prepares the financial statements from the entity's records. As with a compilation engagement, the accountant should have or acquire a knowledge of the client's industry and business. If the client prepares the financial statements, the accountant should ascertain that they are supported by formal accounting records.

The accountant should ordinarily make inquiries about

- The entity's accounting principles, practices, and methods of applying them.
- Procedures for recording, classifying, and summarizing transactions and accumulating information for financial statement disclosures.
- Actions taken at meetings (such as of stockholders or the board of directors) that could affect the financial statements.
- Whether the financial statements have been prepared in conformity with GAAP consistently applied.
- Changes in business activities or accounting principles and practices.
- Subsequent events that could have a material effect on the financial statements.
- Matters on which questions have arisen during the conduct of the review.

The accountant should perform analytical procedures to identify relationships between account balances and other fluctuations that appear unusual because they do not conform to a predictable pattern (e.g., changes in sales and in accounts receivable and expenses that ordinarily fluctuate with sales). The accountant should also make comparisons with prior-period financial statements and with budgets and forecasts, if any. SSARS No. 1 also suggests that the accountant may wish to obtain a representation letter from the client to confirm the oral representations made in the course of the review.

Form of Reporting. The accountant's report on reviewed financial statements expresses limited assurance. The opinion is in the form of "negative assurance" that the accountant is not aware of any material modifications that should be made to the financial statements in order for them to be in conformity with GAAP. The standard form of review report to be issued, as specified in SSARS No. 1 (AR Section 100.35), follows:

> We have reviewed the accompanying balance sheet of XYZ Company as of December 31, 19XX, and the related statements of income, retained earnings, and cash flows for the year then ended, in accordance with standards established by the American Institute of Certified Public Accountants. All information included in these financial statements is the representation of the management (owners) of XYZ Company.
>
> A review consists principally of inquiries of company personnel and analytical procedures applied to financial data. It is substantially less in scope than an audit in accordance with generally accepted auditing standards, the objective of which is the expression of an opinion regarding the financial statements taken as a whole. Accordingly, we do not express such an opinion.
>
> Based on our review, we are not aware of any material modifications that should be made to the accompanying financial statements in order for them to be in conformity with generally accepted accounting principles.

Material departures from GAAP should cause the accountant to modify the standard review report. Each page of the financial statements should include a reference such as "See Accountant's Review Report."

Reporting When the Accountant Is Not Independent

Lack of independence precludes an accountant from issuing a review report. The accountant may, however, issue a report on a compilation engagement for a nonpublic company with respect to which the accountant is not independent, provided the report includes language specifically stating the lack of independence. The reason for lack of independence should not be described.

INTERIM REVIEWS

A review of interim financial information is intended to provide the accountant with a basis for reporting whether material modifications should be made to such information in order for it to conform with GAAP. The accountant does this by applying a knowledge of financial reporting practices to significant accounting matters that come to his or her attention through inquiries and analytical procedures.

An accountant may be requested to perform a preissuance review of interim financial information for a client for a number of reasons. The client may wish to include a representation that the information has been reviewed in a document issued to stockholders or third parties or in Form 10-Q, a quarterly report required to be submitted to the SEC pursuant to Section 13 or 15(d) of the Securities Exchange Act of 1934. Such representation may also be included or incorporated by reference in a registration statement. Larger, more widely traded companies meeting specified criteria are also required by Item 302(a) of SEC Regulation S-K to include selected quarterly financial data in their annual reports or other documents filed with the SEC that contain audited financial statements. The selected quarterly financial data is required to be reviewed, on either a preissuance or retrospective basis.

Companies that include quarterly financial information with their audited annual financial statements may want their accountants to review the information periodically throughout the year, rather than retrospectively at year-end. There are a number of tangible benefits to this approach. First, a preissuance review helps bring accounting problems to light early enough to avoid year-end "surprises." Second, there may be some offsetting reductions in the audit fee for the year because, even though the review does not entail actual audit tests, it involves procedures that, if the work is coordinated, the auditor can utilize in performing the audit. Finally, it may prevent the need to publish at year-end quarterly financial information that differs from amounts previously reported during the year.

The National Commission on Fraudulent Financial Reporting (Treadway Commission) recommended that "the SEC should require independent public accountants to review quarterly financial data of all public companies before release to the public." At the time of this writing, the SEC staff has issued a concepts release on timely reviews of interim financial information. This release asks for comments on whether the SEC should propose a requirement that (1) interim financial data of registrants be reviewed by independent accountants before it is filed with the SEC, and (2) a report issued by the independent accountant be included in the registrant's Form 10-Q and any registration statements that include the interim financial information.

SAS No. 36, *Review of Interim Financial Information* (AU Section 722), sets forth the procedures established by the profession for a review of interim financial information. Those procedures are similar to the procedures previously discussed for a review engagement, with one main exception. In an engagement to review interim financial information, as contrasted with an ordinary review engagement, the accountant should normally obtain written representations from management stating its responsibility for the financial information, completeness of minutes, subsequent events, and other matters for which the accountant believes written representations are appropriate in the circumstances.

The report on a review of interim financial information is similar to the review report presented above.

SPECIAL REPORTS

An auditor may be asked to audit and report on financial information other than financial statements prepared in conformity with GAAP. This section covers auditors' reports issued in connection with financial statements prepared on a basis of accounting other than GAAP and in connection with parts of a financial statement. It also discusses reports on client compliance with aspects of contracts or regulations.

Non-GAAP Financial Statements

Some organizations believe they do not need financial statements based on GAAP or that non-GAAP financial statements would be more informative in a particular situation. Those organizations that do not find the extra effort and cost to prepare accrual basis statements worthwhile believe they are better served by a comprehensive basis of accounting other than GAAP. Typical of these organizations are some not-for-profit entities, certain nonpublic companies, regulated companies that must file financial statements based on accounting principles prescribed by a government regulatory agency, and entities formed for special purposes, such as certain partnerships and joint ventures. A special report containing an unqualified opinion on financial statements prepared in accordance with a comprehensive basis of accounting other than GAAP is a useful, practical alternative for companies that prepare statements on such a basis and wish an audit.

SAS No. 62, *Special Reports*, paragraph 4 (AU Section 623.04), defines a comprehensive basis of accounting other than GAAP as one of the following:

- A basis of accounting that the reporting entity uses to comply with the requirements or financial reporting provisions of a governmental regulatory agency to whose jurisdiction the entity is subject.
- A basis of accounting that the reporting entity uses or expects to use to file its income tax return for the period covered by the financial statements.
- The cash receipts and disbursements basis of accounting, and modifications of the cash basis having substantial support, such as recording depreciation on fixed assets or accruing income taxes.
- A definite set of criteria having substantial support that is applied to all material items appearing in financial statements, such as the price-level basis of accounting.

The key element of a special report on a comprehensive basis of accounting other than GAAP is a paragraph stating what the basis of presentation is and that it is a comprehensive basis of accounting other than GAAP. The paragraph also refers to a note to the financial statements that describes the basis of presentation and how it differs from GAAP. (These differences need not be quantified, however.)

The financial statements should be titled using terms that are not generally associated with financial statements intended to present financial position, results of operations, or cash flows in conformity with GAAP. For example, "statement of assets and liabilities arising from cash transactions" should be used instead of "balance sheet." If the financial statements are not suitably titled, the auditor should disclose his or her reservations in an explanatory paragraph of the report and qualify the opinion.

Illustrations of reports on financial statements prepared in accordance with a comprehensive basis of accounting other than GAAP can be found in SAS No. 62 (AU Section 623.08). One example, that of a report on financial statements prepared on the entity's income tax basis, follows:

> We have audited the accompanying statements of assets, liabilities, and capital—income tax basis of ABC Partnership as of December 31, 19X2 and 19X1, and the related statements of revenue and expenses—income tax basis and of changes in partners' capital accounts—income tax basis for the years then ended. These financial statements are the responsibility of the Partnership's management. Our responsibility is to express an opinion on these financial statements based on our audits.
>
> [*Standard scope paragraph*]
>
> As described in Note X, these financial statements were prepared on the basis of accounting the Partnership uses for income tax purposes, which is a comprehensive basis of accounting other than generally accepted accounting principles.
>
> In our opinion, the financial statements referred to above present fairly, in all material respects, the assets, liabilities, and capital of ABC Partnership as of December 31, 19X2 and 19X1, and its revenue and expenses and changes in partners' capital accounts for the years then ended, on the basis of accounting described in Note X.

Reports on Parts of a Financial Statement

An auditor may be engaged to audit and express an opinion on one or more specified elements, accounts, or items of a financial statement.[2] The audit might be performed as a separate engagement or, more commonly, in conjunction with an audit of financial statements taken as a whole. For example, the report might be on the amount of sales for the purpose of computing rentals,

[2]In a different type of engagement, discussed later in this section of the chapter, an accountant may be engaged to apply agreed-upon procedures to specified elements, accounts, or items of a financial statement. An accountant may also be asked to provide a review of one or more specified elements, accounts, or items of a financial statement. For that type of engagement, the auditor should refer to the attestation standards (AT Section 100).

royalties, a profit participation, or the adequacy of a provision for income taxes in financial statements. SAS No. 62 (AU Section 623) provides guidance on these kinds of engagements.

Materiality. Since the auditor expresses an opinion on each specified element, account, or item of a financial statement covered by the report, the measurement of materiality should be related to each individual element, account, or item rather than to the aggregate thereof or to the financial statements taken as a whole. Thus, an audit of only specified parts of a set of financial statements is usually more extensive than an audit of those same parts if they are included in a full set of audited financial statements. Items that are interrelated with those the auditor has been engaged to express an opinion on must also be considered. Examples of interrelated financial statement elements are sales and receivables, inventories and payables, and property, plant, and equipment, and depreciation.

Similarly, evaluating the reasonableness of a provision for income taxes requires broad knowledge of a company's business transactions and of the content of many individual accounts. For that reason, a report on the adequacy of a provision for income taxes in financial statements should not be issued unless the auditor has audited the complete financial statements in which the provision appears. Similarly, the auditor should have audited the complete financial statements before issuing an opinion on a specified element, account, or item based on an entity's net income or equity.

Forms of Reporting. If the specified elements, accounts, or items are prepared in accordance with the requirements or financial reporting provisions of a contract or agreement that results in a presentation not in conformity with GAAP or other comprehensive basis of accounting, the auditor's report should contain a paragraph restricting distribution of the report to those within the entity and parties to the contract or agreement.

The form of report depends on the purpose of the audit and the elements, accounts, or items audited. Although the form of report varies, there are characteristics common to all reports on specified elements, accounts, or items. One illustration of a report of this type (a report relating to royalties) follows. Other examples are presented in SAS No. 62 (AU Section 623.18).

> We have audited the accompanying schedule of royalties applicable to engine production of the Q Division of XYZ Corporation for the year ended December 31 19X2, under the terms of a license agreement dated May 14, 19XX, between ABC Company and XYZ Corporation. This schedule is the responsibility of XYZ Corporation's management. Our responsibility is to express an opinion on this schedule based on our audit.
>
> We conducted our audit in accordance with generally accepted auditing standards. Those standards require that we plan and perform the audit to obtain reasonable assurance about whether the schedule of royalties is free of material

misstatement. An audit includes examining, on a test basis, evidence supporting the amounts and disclosures in the schedule. An audit also includes assessing the accounting principles used and significant estimates made by management, as well as evaluating the overall schedule presentation. We believe that our audit provides a reasonable basis for our opinion.

We have been informed that, under XYZ Corporation's interpretation of the agreement referred to in the first paragraph, royalties were based on the number of engines produced after giving effect to a reduction for production retirements that were scrapped, but without a reduction for field returns that were scrapped, even though the field returns were replaced with new engines without charge to customers.

In our opinion, the schedule of royalties referred to above presents fairly, in all material respects, the number of engines produced by the Q Division of XYZ Corporation during the year ended December 31, 19X2, and the amount of royalties applicable thereto, under the license agreement referred to above.

This report is intended solely for the information and use of the boards of directors and managements of XYZ Corporation and ABC Company and should not be used for any other purpose.

Applying Agreed-Upon Procedures to Specified Elements, Accounts, or Items of a Financial Statement. An accountant may be asked to apply agreed-upon procedures to one or more specified elements, accounts, or items of a financial statement that are not sufficient to allow expressing an opinion on them. Even though the scope of the engagement is limited, the accountant may accept such an engagement provided the parties involved have a clear understanding of the procedures to be performed, and distribution of the accountant's report is restricted to the named parties involved.

The content of the accountant's report on the results of applying agreed-upon procedures varies with the circumstances. Certain characteristics, however, are common to all such reports. The report should identify the specified elements, accounts, or items to which the agreed-upon procedures were applied; enumerate the procedures performed; state the accountant's findings; specify the intended distribution of the report; state that the report relates only to the elements, accounts, or items specified and does not extend to the entity's financial statements taken as a whole; and disclaim an opinion with respect to such elements, accounts, or items. Distribution of the report is restricted to parties that have a clear understanding of the procedures performed. If the accountant has no adjustments to propose, negative assurance may be expressed to that effect. The negative assurance and disclaimer are illustrated below.

Because the above procedures do not constitute an audit conducted in accordance with generally accepted auditing standards, we do not express an opinion on any of the accounts or items referred to above. In connection with the procedures referred to above, no matters came to our attention that caused us to believe that the specified accounts or items should be adjusted. Had we performed additional procedures or had we conducted an audit of the financial statements in accordance with generally accepted auditing standards, matters might have come to our attention that would have been reported to you. This report relates only to the accounts and items specified above and does not extend to any financial statements of Y Company, Inc., taken as a whole. (AU Section 622.06)

Reports on Compliance with Aspects of Contractual Agreements or Regulatory Requirements

Determining a client's compliance with contractual agreements or regulatory requirements is integral to an audit of financial statements. If noncompliance with contracts or statutes could have a material effect on a client's financial statements, the auditor should determine the extent of compliance with them. For example, an auditor should determine that the client has conformed with the restrictive covenants in a long-term bond agreement, since a violation of those covenants could make the entire issue due and payable at the lender's option and require the debt to be classified as a current rather than a long-term liability.

Companies may be required by a contractual agreement or regulatory agency to furnish a report on compliance with aspects of the agreement or regulatory requirements. For example, a loan agreement may call for assurance from an independent auditor that the borrower has complied with covenants in the agreement relating to accounting or auditing matters, or a state regulatory agency may require assurance that the enterprise has complied with certain accounting provisions specified by the agency. This section discusses engagements where the auditor has been requested to provide explicit assurance about the client's compliance with contractual agreements or regulatory requirements.

SAS No. 62 (AU Section 623) provides guidance on reports on compliance with aspects of contractual agreements or regulatory requirements related to audited financial statements. Special reports of this type should be issued only if the auditor has audited the financial statements to which the contractual agreement or regulatory requirements relate. The report usually contains negative assurance relative to the applicable covenants of the agreement or the applicable regulatory requirements, and a statement that the audit of the financial statements was not directed primarily toward obtaining knowledge about compliance. Furthermore, since the matters the auditor is reporting on are set forth in a document that generally would not be publicly available, the auditor's report should contain a paragraph restricting distribution to those within the entity and the parties to the contract or agreement or for filing with any applicable regulatory agency. The report on compliance may be given in a separate report or in one or more paragraphs following the opinion paragraph of the auditor's report accompanying the financial statements. An example of a separate report on compliance is presented below.

Report on Compliance with Contractual Provisions

We have audited, in accordance with generally accepted auditing standards, the balance sheet of XYZ Company as of December 31, 19X2, and the related statements of income, retained earnings, and cash flows for the year then ended, and have issued our report thereon dated February 16, 19X3.

In connection with our audit, nothing came to our attention that caused us to believe that the Company failed to comply with the terms, covenants, provisions, or conditions of sections XX to XX, inclusive, of the Indenture dated July 21, 19X0, with ABC Bank insofar as they relate to accounting matters. However, our audit was not directed primarily toward obtaining knowledge of such non-compliance.

This report is intended solely for the information and use of the boards of directors and managements of XYZ Company and ABC Bank and should not be used for any other purpose.

The report illustrated above is issued based on the audit of the entity's financial statements. In other situations, the auditor may be engaged to test and report on specific compliance with laws and regulations. Such engagements are described later in this chapter under "Compliance Auditing" and generally relate to governmental entities or other recipients of federal financial assistance.

REPORTING ON INFORMATION ACCOMPANYING BASIC FINANCIAL STATEMENTS

Information such as additional details or explanations of items in the basic financial statements, historical summaries of items extracted from the basic financial statements, and other material, some of which may be from sources outside the accounting system or outside the entity, may be presented in a document, like an annual report, that also includes basic audited financial statements. That information is not considered necessary for the fair presentation of financial position, results of operations, or cash flows in conformity with GAAP.

Such additional information, often referred to as "other information," may be included in a *client-prepared document* like the annual report to shareholders. Alternatively, additional information could be included in an *auditor-submitted document.* For example, the auditor could present the client with a document bound in the CPA's own cover and including not only the basic financial statements and auditor's report, but also a schedule of general and administrative expenses. The auditor's responsibility for additional information in auditor-submitted documents is discussed later in this section.

Additional Information in Client-Prepared Documents

The auditor's responsibility for other information included in a client-prepared document is set forth in SAS No. 8 (AU Section 550) and is discussed in Chapter 18. That chapter also discusses a specific type of other information for which AU Section 558 prescribes additional performance and exception reporting responsibilities. That type of information is supplementary information *required* by FASB or GASB pronouncements. Some entities may *voluntarily* include in documents containing audited financial statements, certain supplementary information that is required by the FASB or the GASB to be presented by other entities. In that situation, the additional responsibilities set forth in AU Section 558 do *not* apply, provided it is clear that the information is not covered by the auditor's report. This may be accomplished by a statement by the entity that the auditor has not applied any procedures to the information or by the auditor's including in the report a disclaimer on the information.

Additional Information in Auditor-Submitted Documents

The auditor may be requested to include a variety of material in addition to the basic financial statements in a document submitted to the client. For example, the document might include details of the subaccounts composing financial statement captions, statistical data, consolidating data, explanatory comments, financial analyses, possibly some operational data, and occasionally a description of the auditing procedures applied to specific items in the financial statements. The account details, analytical comment, and audit scope explanations might be combined under appropriate account headings, or these subjects might be separated and presented in different sections of the document.

The auditor has a responsibility to report—by a disclaimer or otherwise—on all information in a document containing audited financial statements that is submitted to the client. The auditor is not obligated, however, to apply auditing procedures to information presented outside the basic financial statements in such a document; in that event, the auditor should disclaim an opinion on the additional information. Alternatively, the auditor may choose to modify or redirect certain of the procedures applied in the audit so as to be able to express an opinion on the accompanying information rather than disclaim an opinion on it. SAS No. 29, *Reporting on Information Accompanying the Basic Financial Statements in Auditor-Submitted Documents* (AU Section 551), contains reporting guidelines, as well as examples, for information accompanying the basic financial statements in an auditor-submitted document. The auditor's report on the accompanying information may be either added to the standard report on the basic financial statements or presented separately. In either case, the report should

- State that the audit has been conducted for the purpose of forming an opinion on the basic financial statements taken as a whole.
- Identify the accompanying information.
- State that the accompanying information is presented for purposes of additional analysis and is not a required part of the basic financial statements.
- Include either an opinion on whether the accompanying information is fairly stated in all material respects in relation to the basic financial statements taken as a whole or a disclaimer of opinion, depending on whether the information has been subjected to the auditing procedures applied in the audit of the basic financial statements. (The auditor may express an opinion on a portion of the accompanying information and disclaim an opinion on the remainder.)

For purposes of reporting in this manner, the measurement of materiality is the same as in forming an opinion on the basic financial statements taken as a whole. Accordingly, the auditor need not apply procedures as extensive as would be necessary to express an opinion on a separate presentation of the information, as would be true for a report on parts of a financial statement, as described earlier in this chapter.

REPORTS ON INTERNAL CONTROL

Financial statement users have become increasingly interested in the effectiveness of an entity's internal control structure since passage of the Foreign Corrupt Practices Act of 1977 (FCPA) (see Chapter 7) and the events that led to it. In the 1970s, both the Commission on Auditors' Responsibilities (Cohen Commission) and the Financial Executives Institute endorsed the publication of a report by enterprise management on, among other matters, the enterprise's internal control. In response to these developments, numerous public companies included a report of management in their annual report to shareholders. An example of a management report taken from the 1988 annual report to shareholders of American Telephone and Telegraph Company, signed by both the chairman of the board and the chief financial officer, is found in Figure 19.1.

Figure 19.1 Report of Management

Report of Management

The accompanying financial statements, which consolidate the accounts of American Telephone and Telegraph Company and its subsidiaries, have been prepared in conformity with generally accepted accounting principles.

The integrity and the objectivity of the data in these financial statements, including estimates and judgments relating to matters not concluded by year-end, are the responsibility of management as is all other information included in this Annual Report unless indicated otherwise. To this end, management maintains a system of internal controls. Our internal auditors monitor compliance with it in connection with an annual plan of internal audits. The system of internal controls, on an ongoing basis, is reviewed, evaluated and revised as necessary in view of the results of constant management oversight, internal and independent audits, changes in the Company's business, and other conditions and changes. Management believes that the Company's internal control system, taken as a whole, provides reasonable assurance that (1) financial records are adequate and can be relied upon to permit the preparation of financial statements in conformity with generally accepted accounting principles and (2) access to assets occurs only in accordance with management's authorizations. Recorded assets are compared with existing assets at reasonable intervals and appropriate action is taken with respect to any differences. As a part of the system of internal controls, management establishes organization structures, carefully selects key personnel to provide an appropriate division of responsibility, and uses informational programs designed to assure that its policies, standards, and managerial authorities are understood throughout the organization.

These financial statements have been audited by Coopers & Lybrand, Independent Certified Public Accountants. Their audits are conducted in accordance with generally accepted auditing standards and include selective tests of transactions and a review of internal controls.

The Audit Committee of the Board of Directors, which is composed of Directors who are not employees, meets periodically with management, the internal auditors, and the independent auditors to review the manner in which they are performing their responsibilities and to carry out its oversight role with respect to auditing, internal controls, and financial reporting matters. Both the internal auditors and the independent auditors periodically meet alone with the Audit Committee and have access to the Audit Committee, and its individual members, at any time.

Morris Tanenbaum
Vice Chairman and Chief Financial Officer

Robert E. Allen
Chairman of the Board and Chief Executive Officer

Providing Assurance on the Internal Control Structure

As discussed in Chapter 8, auditors are required to communicate to the audit committee (or its equivalent) matters coming to their attention in the course of the audit that represent material weaknesses or other reportable conditions. Sometimes, however, audit committee members, as well as members of management, want more information and request auditors to provide assurance on an entity's internal control structure.

SAS No. 30, *Reporting on Internal Accounting Control*[3] (AU Section 642), provides guidance to auditors in connection with engagements to express an opinion on an entity's internal control structure, or a part thereof, and similar types of engagements. The scope of such an engagement is more extensive than that in a financial statement audit, although some of the procedures are similar. Paragraphs 13–34 of SAS No. 30 (AU Section 642.13–.34) specify that engagements under that standard involve planning the scope of the engagement, reviewing the design of the internal control structure, performing tests of controls, and evaluating the results.

AU Section 642 also specifies the forms of reporting on the internal control structure for various types of engagements. The main elements of the standard report expressing an unqualified opinion on an entity's internal control structure are

- A description of the scope of the engagement.
- The date to which the opinion relates.
- A statement that establishing and maintaining the internal control structure are the responsibility of management.
- A brief explanation of the broad objectives and inherent limitations of an internal control structure.
- The auditor's opinion on whether the entity's control structure policies and procedures meet the objectives of an internal control structure pertaining to preventing or detecting errors or irregularities that would be material to the financial statements (material weaknesses).

If the auditor's procedures disclose conditions that, individually or in combination, result in one or more material weaknesses, the auditor's report should be modified to describe the material weaknesses, the general nature of potential errors or irregularities that might occur as a result of the weaknesses, and whether the weaknesses arose from a lack of control structure policies and procedures or a breakdown in adhering to specific control procedures. If the auditor issues the opinion on the internal control structure in conjunction with or as part of an audit of the entity's financial statements, the report should state that the material weaknesses were considered in determining what audit tests to apply in conducting the financial statement audit.

[3]The terminology and concepts in SAS No. 30 have not been conformed to those in SAS Nos. 53 through 61 at the time of this writing. An ASB task force is considering substantive amendments to SAS No. 30.

Reports on Internal Control at Service Organizations

Service organizations may record transactions, process related data, or even execute and account for transactions on behalf of others. Companies that provide such services include, for example, trust departments of banks (which invest and hold securities for others), computer service centers (which process data for others), and securities depositories (which hold and account for securities for others). A service organization may seek a special-purpose report from an auditor on the design of its internal control structure or on both the design of the structure and the tests directed at specified control objectives. SAS No. 44, *Special-Purpose Reports on Internal Accounting Control at Service Organizations*[4] (AU Section 324), provides guidance on the responsibilities of an auditor who issues that type of special-purpose report. Those reports are frequently used by auditors of the enterprises whose transactions are executed or processed by the service organization (see the discussion in Chapter 6); the SAS also provides guidance on the auditor's decision to obtain a report on the internal control structure at a service organization and on considerations in using that type of report.

OPINIONS ON ACCOUNTING PRINCIPLES

An auditor is often requested by an *audit client* to give a formal opinion on an accepted or preferred method of accounting, either for a hypothetical situation or for a specific proposed or completed transaction. Notable examples of this type of opinion are the "preferability letter" required by the SEC when a company changes an accounting principle, and by the New York Stock Exchange (NYSE) in connection with the accounting for a business combination as a pooling of interests.

Paragraph 16 of Accounting Principles Board (APB) Opinion No. 20, *Accounting Changes* (Accounting Standards Section A06.112), requires enterprise management to justify using an alternative accounting principle on the basis that it is preferable. The SEC requires companies subject to its reporting regulations that make a discretionary accounting change to obtain concurrence, in a "preferability letter," from their independent public accountants that the change is to a principle that is preferable in the circumstances.

The auditor should review the reasonableness of the client's justification for a change. This requires considering the client's business as well as industry conditions, and the recent history of the client's changes applicable to the same circumstances. If the justification for the change is based on a desire to

[4]The terminology and concepts in SAS No. 44 (AU Section 324) have not been conformed to those in SAS Nos. 53 through 61 at the time of this writing. An ASB task force is considering substantive amendments to SAS No. 44.

conform with industry practice, the auditor should corroborate the client's position that the new accounting method is prevalent in the industry. Citing one or two instances of its use in a large industry would not necessarily indicate that the new method is prevalent in the industry.

Since the adoption of APB Opinion No. 16, *Business Combinations* (Accounting Standards Section B50), the NYSE has requested each company listing shares to be issued in a business combination accounted for as a pooling of interests to furnish the Exchange with a letter setting forth the requirements for pooling of interests accounting and indicating that the contemplated transaction meets each of those requirements. The NYSE requires that the other party to the business combination assent to the letter as an indication of its agreement with the specified terms of the transaction. In addition, the NYSE asks that the auditors of the corporation issuing stock in the transaction also furnish a letter to the Exchange indicating that they have reviewed the transaction and expressing their opinion that the combination meets the requirements for pooling accounting set forth in Opinion No. 16.

An accountant (the "reporting accountant") may be asked by a nonaudit client (the "requester") to give an opinion on the appropriate accounting for recording a hypothetical, proposed, or consummated transaction. The requester may be, among others, an investment banker that has created a new type of financial product and wants to include an opinion from the reporting accountant (sometimes called a "generic letter") in its promotional material, an investment banker representing another auditor's client that is contemplating a specific transaction, or another auditor's (the "continuing accountant") client seeking a "second opinion" on a proposed or consummated transaction. The requester may have only the purest motives for seeking the advice of a CPA other than its own auditor, perhaps based on a belief that its auditor lacks the expertise to evaluate the appropriate accounting for a new financial product. Or the requester may be "opinion shopping," seeking an opinion that can be used to intimidate its auditor to accede to its preferences or risk losing the engagement.

The profession has long been concerned with opinion shopping and has tried to prevent it. SAS No. 50, *Reports on the Application of Accounting Principles* (AU Section 625), specifies standards, for both performance and reporting, that should be followed by the reporting accountant when providing advice (either written or oral) on accounting matters or on the appropriate type of opinion on an entity's financial statements. The performance standards include a requirement that the reporting accountant seek permission from the requester to consult with the continuing accountant and ask the requester to authorize the continuing accountant to respond fully to the reporting accountant's inquiries. That requirement serves two purposes. The first, not explicitly stated in the SAS, is to discourage opinion shopping. The second is to provide the reporting accountant with information that the continuing accountant may have and that might not otherwise be available.

LETTERS FOR UNDERWRITERS

The SEC's requirements for disclosures to be made in prospectuses and registration statements are complicated and periodically undergo significant changes. Accordingly, all parties to an SEC filing go to great lengths to ensure that the contents of those filings comply with the applicable requirements. In particular, as part of their ''due diligence'' duties, underwriters have had a long-standing practice of seeking specific assurance from lawyers and accountants that the SEC rules and regulations have been complied with. A common practice for underwriters has long been to seek ''comfort'' from an auditor on financial information in registration statements that is not covered by the auditor's report and on events subsequent to the report date.

As public expectations have grown and been reflected in legal and other attacks on those associated with disclosures, underwriters and their counsel have sought to obtain more and more ''comfort'' from auditors, which is formally expressed in a letter called a comfort letter. (Some lawyers still use the phrase common in earlier, more austere times: ''cold comfort'' letter.) While the comfort letter may originally have been an informal or semiformal helpful gesture on the part of an auditor, it is now a significant formal communication. In drafting comfort letters, formally called ''letters for underwriters,'' auditors must therefore be especially careful not to assume unwarranted responsibility, either explicitly or implicitly.

SAS No. 49, *Letters for Underwriters*[5] (AU Section 634), provides guidelines intended to minimize misunderstandings in connection with comfort letters. The importance attached to comfort letters is reflected in the length and details of the numerous paragraphs in the Statement. It covers the kinds of matters that may properly be commented on by auditors in comfort letters and how the matters should be phrased, suggests forms of letters and how to prepare them, and recommends ways of reducing or avoiding misunderstanding about responsibility. To avoid the possibility of misunderstanding about the purpose and intended use of the comfort letter, it is customary to conclude the letter with a paragraph along the following lines:

> This letter is solely for the information of the addressees and to assist the underwriters in conducting and documenting their investigation of the affairs of the company in connection with the offering of the securities covered by the registration statement, and it is not to be used, circulated, quoted, or otherwise referred to within or without the underwriting group for any other purpose, including, but not limited to, the registration, purchase, or sale of securities, nor is it to be filed with or referred to in whole or in part in the registration statement or any other document, except that reference may be made to it in the underwrit-

[5]At the time of this writing, an ASB task force is reconsidering the guidance in SAS No. 49, which was issued in 1984, because of possible inconsistencies between it and the attestation standards, issued in 1986, as well as possible practice problems in applying SAS No. 49.

ing agreement or in any list of closing documents pertaining to the offering of the securities covered by the registration statement.

ATTESTATION ENGAGEMENTS

In recent years, clients have increasingly requested accountants to express opinions about various representations unrelated to an audit of historical financial statements. CPAs were usually able to seek guidance by referring to AICPA auditing pronouncements or by applying the concepts underlying them. As the range of requests for attest services expanded, it became increasingly difficult to look to the existing standards for guidance, and the need for new standards that would be responsive to the changing environment became apparent.

Consequently, attestation standards were developed to establish a broad framework for addressing engagements to provide assurance on a wide variety of client assertions. The standards set boundaries around the types of attest services a CPA in the practice of public accounting (referred to hereafter as a practitioner) may perform, and also provide a guide for the AICPA in promulgating future interpretive pronouncements.

Statement on Standards for Attestation Engagements (SSAE), *Attestation Standards* (AT Section 100) (the Statement), was issued jointly by the Auditing Standards Board and the Accounting and Review Services Committee in 1986. In December 1987, the Management Advisory Services (MAS) Executive Committee issued an SSAE, *Attest Services Related to MAS Engagements* (AT Section 100.71–.76), which effectively extended the applicability of the attestation standards to MAS services. Two other statements have been issued that rely on the attestation standards for their authority. *Reporting on Pro Forma Financial Information* (AT Section 300) was issued in 1988; it provides interpretive guidance based on the standards. The other statement, *Financial Forecasts and Projections* (AT Section 200), was actually issued shortly before the first SSAE, but it too draws on the attestation standards as a basis for its interpretive guidance. All of those pronouncements are discussed in this section.

Definitions

The Statement (AT Section 100.01) defines an attest engagement as "one in which a practitioner is engaged to issue or does issue a written communication that expresses a conclusion about the reliability of a written assertion that is the responsibility of another party." The definition uses the term "practitioner," which according to the Statement includes not only CPAs but full- or part-time employees of a public accounting firm. Thus, an employee of a CPA firm who is not a CPA, such as a management advisory services consultant, is required to comply with the provisions of the Statement if the engagement meets the definition of an attest engagement.

Services Covered by Standards

Attest engagements might include examining or reviewing, and reporting on

- Descriptions of an entity's internal control structure.
- Descriptions of computer software products to be marketed.
- Investment performance statistics.
- Antitrust case data.
- Insurance claims data.
- Labor data for union contract negotiation.
- Audience and circulation data for broadcasters and publishers.
- Occupancy, enrollment, and attendance data for universities.
- Cost justification for a utility rate increase.
- Productivity indicators.
- Pension plan obligations of a target company in a buy–sell agreement.

By contrast, the following professional services typically provided by practitioners, in addition to the other types of engagements described in this chapter, are *not* attest engagements:

- Management consulting engagements in which the practitioner provides advice or recommendations to a client.
- Engagements in which the practitioner is engaged to advocate a client's position—for example, concerning tax matters being reviewed by the Internal Revenue Service.
- Tax engagements in which a practitioner prepares tax returns or provides tax advice.
- Engagements in which the practitioner's role is solely to assist the client—such as preparing information other than financial statements.
- Engagements in which a practitioner is engaged to provide an expert opinion or to testify as an expert witness in accounting, auditing, taxation, or other matters, given certain stipulated facts.

The distinguishing characteristic of the above services that are not attest engagements is that the services involve providing advice, recommendations, or assistance to a client on the basis of a practitioner's experience and expertise in a particular area. They do not require the practitioner to express a conclusion about an assertion.

Standards for Attestation Engagements

Figure 19.2 shows the 11 attestation standards and compares them with the 10 auditing standards. The attestation standards are broader in scope than the ten generally accepted auditing standards because of the distinction between an audit engagement and an attest engagement. In its most basic form, auditing is concerned only with an enterprise's historical financial statements measured against a set of criteria known as generally accepted accounting principles. Because of the range of services that might qualify as an attest engagement, however, it is not possible to establish a single set of criteria for only one kind of assertion. In one instance, the attestor may be asked to express a conclusion about the reliability of audit software, and in the next instance, the conclusion may relate to whether management's assumptions provide a reasonable basis for a financial forecast.

In adopting the Statement, the AICPA pointed out that the attestation standards did not supersede any existing standards. That is, the practitioner should first look to Statements on Auditing Standards or Statements on Standards for Accounting and Review Services for guidance, before looking to the attestation standards.

Some of the attestation standards are analogous to the auditing standards and related interpretations. Other attestation standards, however, are based on concepts that differ from their counterparts in an auditing environment. These concepts are explained in the remainder of this section of the chapter.

Independence in Attest Engagements. The Statement (AT Section 100.23) notes that "practitioners performing an attest service should not only be independent in fact, but also should avoid situations that may impair the appearance of independence." All personnel assigned to the engagement, as well as those to whom members of the engagement team report or with whom they consult, are required to be independent of the client. This contrasts with an audit engagement, where the CPA firm as a whole is required to be independent of the client.

The Need for Reasonable Criteria. AT Section 100.12 states that "the attest function should be performed only when it can be effective and useful. Practitioners should have a reasonable basis for believing that a meaningful conclusion can be provided on an assertion." This means that the assertion cannot be so subjective that it is meaningless or possibly misleading. To meet this condition, *reasonable criteria* should exist that competent persons could use to reach substantially similar estimates or measurements, though not necessarily the same conclusion. For example, attesting to a software product characterized as the "best" or attesting to the competence of management would not meet this condition for an attest function, since it is unlikely that reasonable criteria exist against which "best" and "competent" can be consistently measured.

Figure 19.2 Attestation Standards Compared with Generally Accepted Auditing Standards

Attestation Standards	*Generally Accepted Auditing Standards*
General Standards	
1. The engagement shall be performed by a practitioner or practitioners having adequate technical training and proficiency in the attest function.	1. The audit is to be performed by a person or persons having adequate technical training and proficiency as an auditor.
2. The engagement shall be performed by a practitioner or practitioners having adequate knowledge in the subject matter of the assertion.	
3. The practitioner shall perform an engagement only if he or she has reason to believe that the following two conditions exist: • The assertion is capable of evaluation against reasonable criteria that either have been established by a recognized body or are stated in the presentation of the assertion in a sufficiently clear and comprehensive manner for a knowledgeable reader to be able to understand them. • The assertion is capable of reasonably consistent estimation or measurement using such criteria.	
4. In all matters relating to the engagement, an independence in mental attitude shall be maintained by the practitioner or practitioners.	2. In all matters relating to the assignment, an independence in mental attitude is to be maintained by the auditor or auditors.
5. Due professional care shall be exercised in the performance of the engagement.	3. Due professional care is to be exercised in the performance of the audit and the preparation of the report.
Standards of Fieldwork	
1. The work shall be adequately planned and assistants, if any, shall be properly supervised.	1. The work is to be adequately planned and assistants, if any, are to be properly supervised.
	2. A sufficient understanding of the internal control structure is to be obtained to plan the audit and to deter-

Figure 19.2 *Continued*

Attestation Standards	*Generally Accepted Auditing Standards*
	mine the nature, timing, and extent of tests to be performed.
2. Sufficient evidence shall be obtained to provide a reasonable basis for the conclusion that is expressed in the report.	3. Sufficient competent evidential matter is to be obtained through inspection, observation, inquiries, and confirmations to afford a reasonable basis for an opinion regarding the financial statements under audit.
Standards of Reporting	
1. The report shall identify the assertion being reported on and state the character of the engagement.	
2. The report shall state the practitioner's conclusion about whether the assertion is presented in conformity with the established or stated criteria against which it was measured.	1. The report shall state whether the financial statements are presented in accordance with generally accepted accounting principles.
	2. The report shall identify those circumstances in which such principles have not been consistently observed in the current period in relation to the preceding period.
	3. Informative disclosures in the financial statements are to be regarded as reasonably adequate unless otherwise stated in the report.
3. The report shall state all of the practitioner's significant reservations about the engagement and the presentation of the assertion.	4. The report shall either contain an expression of opinion regarding the financial statements, taken as a whole, or an assertion to the effect that an opinion cannot be expressed. When an overall opinion cannot be expressed, the reasons therefor should be stated. In all cases where an auditor's name is associated with financial statements, the report should contain a clear-cut indication of the character of the auditor's work and the degree of responsibility the auditor is taking.
4. The report on an engagement to evaluate an assertion that has been prepared in conformity with agreed-upon criteria or on an engagement to apply agreed-upon procedures should contain a statement limiting its use to the parties who have agreed upon such criteria or procedures.	

Source: Adapted from Statement on Standards for Attestation Engagements, *Attestation Standards* (AT Section 100.77).

The SSAE (AT Section 100.15) defines reasonable criteria as "those that yield useful information." They may be criteria established by a recognized body such as the FASB or GASB, which are authoritative and therefore need only be referred to in the presentation of the assertion. (These are referred to as *established criteria*.) Other criteria, such as standards prepared by an industry association, even though they do not have authoritative support, may also pass the "reasonableness" test. If the assertion is to be evaluated against the latter type of criteria, they must be stated in the presentation of the assertion, as indicated by the third general attestation standard. (These are referred to as *stated criteria*.) Still other criteria are reasonable for evaluating an assertion, but only by a limited number of specified users who participated in establishing the criteria. (These are referred to as *agreed-upon criteria*.)

Engagement Planning and Performance. Planning an attest engagement involves developing an overall strategy and designing a program of procedures that is consistent with the level of assurance to be provided. When planning those procedures, the practitioner considers a number of factors, including the nature and complexity of the assertions, the criteria against which the assertions will be evaluated, preliminary judgments about materiality, the anticipated level of attestation risk related to the assertions, and the level of assurance that the practitioner has been engaged to provide in the attest report.

Attestation risk, which is similar to the concept of audit risk as described in SAS No. 47, *Audit Risk and Materiality in Conducting an Audit* (AU Section 312), is the risk that the practitioner may unknowingly fail to appropriately modify his or her attest report on an assertion that is materially misstated. The level of attestation risk the practitioner is willing to accept varies inversely with the level of assurance the practitioner plans to provide on the presentation of assertions. In an attest engagement designed to provide the highest level of assurance (an "examination"), the practitioner should plan and perform procedures to generate sufficient evidence to limit attestation risk to an appropriately low level for the high level of assurance that may be imparted. Those procedures generally involve search and verification (for example, inspection, confirmation, and observation) as well as internal inquiries and comparisons of internal information. In a limited assurance engagement (a "review"), the practitioner's objective is to accumulate sufficient evidence to limit attestation risk to a moderate level. This can ordinarily be achieved by internal inquiries and analytical procedures.

Reports on Attest Engagements

A report for public distribution on an attest service may be based on either an examination or a review. The high level of assurance provided in a report on an examination is referred to as positive assurance; in a report on a review, the moderate level of assurance expressed is in the form of negative assurance.

When expressing positive assurance, the practitioner states a conclusion about whether the assertions are presented in conformity with established or stated criteria. In providing negative assurance, the practitioner states only whether information has come to his or her attention that indicates the assertions are not presented in conformity with those criteria.

Reports expressing positive assurance based on an examination or negative assurance based on a review may be issued for general distribution, provided the assertions on which the auditor provides assurance are based on established or stated criteria. Examination and review reports may also be based on specified criteria agreed upon by the asserter and the user(s); in that event, use of the report is limited to those parties, because other parties may not understand the criteria or the assurance expressed in the report. For example, the assertion may be based on contractual terms known only by the specified users who participated in negotiating the contract.

When the presentation of assertions has been prepared in conformity with specified criteria agreed to by the asserter and the user, the report should contain

a. A statement limiting use of the report to the specified parties.
b. An indication, when applicable, that the presentation of assertions differs materially from what would have been presented if criteria for the presentation of such assertions for general distribution had been followed. (For example, financial information prepared in accordance with criteria specified in a contract may differ materially from information prepared in conformity with generally accepted accounting principles [GAAP].)

A practitioner may also perform attest services based on agreed-upon procedures; in those services, the reports are also restricted to the parties that agreed to the procedures.

An overview of each of the three attest services (including examples of reports) follows.

Examination. When expressing a positive opinion, the practitioner should clearly state whether, in his or her opinion, the presentation of assertions is in conformity with established or stated criteria. Examination reports may be qualified or modified for some aspect of the presentation or the engagement. In addition, they may emphasize certain matters relating to the attest engagement or the presentation of assertions. The following is an illustrative examination report that expresses an unqualified opinion on a presentation of assertions:

> We have examined the accompanying Statement of Investment Performance Statistics of XYZ Fund for the year ended December 31, 19X1. Our examination was made in accordance with standards established by the American In-

stitute of Certified Public Accountants and, accordingly, included such procedures as we considered necessary in the circumstances.

[*Additional paragraph(s) may be added to emphasize certain matters relating to the attest engagement or the presentation of assertions.*]

In our opinion, the Statement of Investment Performance Statistics referred to above presents the investment performance of XYZ Fund for the year ended December 31, 19X1, in conformity with the measurement and disclosure criteria set forth in Note 1.

Review. In providing negative assurance, the practitioner's conclusion should state whether any information came to his or her attention on the basis of the work performed that indicates the assertions are not presented in all material respects in conformity with established or stated criteria. The following illustrative review report expresses negative assurance where no exceptions have been found:

We have reviewed the accompanying Statement of Investment Performance Statistics of XYZ Fund for the year ended December 31, 19X1. Our review was conducted in accordance with standards established by the American Institute of Certified Public Accountants.

A review is substantially less in scope than an examination, the objective of which is the expression of an opinion on the Statement of Investment Performance Statistics. Accordingly, we do not express such an opinion.

[*Additional paragraph(s) may be added to emphasize certain matters relating to the attest engagement or the presentation of assertions.*]

Based on our review, nothing came to our attention that caused us to believe that the accompanying Statement of Investment Performance Statistics is not presented in conformity with the measurement and disclosure criteria set forth in Note 1.

Agreed-Upon Procedures. A practitioner's conclusion on the results of applying agreed-upon procedures to a presentation of assertions should be in the form of a summary of findings, negative assurance, or both. The level of assurance provided in a report on the application of agreed-upon procedures depends on the nature and scope of the practitioner's procedures as agreed to by the specified parties to whom the report is restricted. Furthermore, such parties must understand that they take responsibility for the adequacy of the attest procedures (and, therefore, the amount of assurance provided) for their purposes.

Following is an illustrative agreed-upon procedures report that enumerates the procedures performed and includes both a summary of findings and negative assurance. Either the summary of findings, if no exceptions are found, or negative assurance could be omitted.

To ABC Inc. and XYZ Fund

We have applied the procedures enumerated below to the accompanying Statement of Investment Performance Statistics of XYZ Fund for the year ended December 31, 19X1. These procedures, which were agreed to by ABC Inc. and XYZ Fund, were performed solely to assist you in evaluating the investment performance of XYZ Fund. This report is intended solely for your information and should not be used by those who did not participate in determining the procedures.

[*Include paragraph enumerating procedures and findings.*]

These agreed-upon procedures are substantially less in scope than an examination, the objective of which is the expression of an opinion on the Statement of Investment Performance Statistics. Accordingly, we do not express such an opinion.

Based on the application of the procedures referred to above, nothing came to our attention that caused us to believe that the accompanying Statement of Investment Performance Statistics is not presented in conformity with the measurement and disclosure criteria set forth in Note 1. Had we performed additional procedures or had we made an examination of the Statement of Investment Performance Statistics, other matters might have come to our attention that would have been reported to you.

Modifications to Standard Report. If the practitioner has any reservations about the engagement or the presentation of assertions (e.g., restrictions on the scope of the engagement or concerns about conformity of the presentation with stated criteria), the report should be modified. A detailed discussion of modified reports is included in the Statement.

Pro Forma Financial Information

Pro forma financial information presents the significant effects on historical financial information of "what might have been," had a consummated or proposed transaction or event occurred at an earlier date. It is commonly used to show the effects of

- Business combinations.
- Changes in capitalization.
- Dispositions of a significant portion of a business.
- Changes in the form of a business organization or in its status as an autonomous entity.
- Proposed sales of securities and the application of the proceeds.

Pro forma financial information is sometimes included in prospectuses, proxy statements, and other public documents, and more often in less widely circulated, special-purpose statements. It is frequently the only way to illustrate the effects of a particular contemplated transaction. An important business decision may be impossible to describe intelligibly without the use of pro forma data. An SSAE on *Reporting on Pro Forma Financial Information* (AT Section 300) provides guidance to a practitioner who is engaged to examine or review and to report on pro forma financial information. Pro forma financial information includes historical financial information and pro forma adjustments that are applied to the historical data to show the effect of the proposed transaction or event. The historical information, adjustments, and resulting pro forma amounts are commonly presented in columnar form. Pro forma adjustments are based on assumptions reflecting, to the best of management's knowledge and belief, the conditions it expects would have existed and the course of action it would have taken had the proposed transaction or event occurred at an earlier date. Assumptions typically included in a presentation of pro forma financial information are

- Bank borrowings and related interest rates.
- Fixed asset purchases and disposals.
- Business combinations and divestitures, including cash layouts and proceeds, respectively.

There are three conditions that must be met for a practitioner to examine or review, and report on, pro forma financial information.

- The document containing the pro forma financial information should include (or incorporate by reference) complete historical financial statements of the entity or entities for the most recent year.
- The historical financial statements on which the pro forma financial information is based must have been audited or reviewed. The level of assurance that may be provided on the pro forma financial information cannot exceed the level of assurance provided on the accompanying historical financial information.
- The practitioner should have an appropriate level of knowledge of the accounting and financial reporting practices of the entity or entities.

The SSAE on pro forma information requires that

- The pro forma financial information be appropriately distinguished from the historical financial information. (The column of pro forma amounts in the financial statements is usually labeled "pro forma.")
- The transaction or event reflected in the pro forma financial information be described, along with the source of the historical financial information on which it is based.

- The significant assumptions used in developing the pro forma adjustments, together with any significant uncertainties about those assumptions, be disclosed.
- The pro forma financial information include statements to the effect that it should be read in conjunction with the related historical financial information and that it is not necessarily indicative of the results that would have been attained had the transaction or event actually taken place earlier.

The objective of *examination* procedures applied to pro forma financial information is to limit attestation risk to an appropriately low level to allow the practitioner to provide positive assurance about whether

- Management's assumptions provide a reasonable basis for presenting the significant effects directly attributable to the underlying transaction or event.
- The related pro forma adjustments give appropriate effect to those assumptions.
- The pro forma column reflects the proper application of the adjustments to the historical financial statements.

In a *review*, the procedures should be sufficient to limit attestation risk to a moderate level, so that the practitioner can provide negative assurance with respect to the three items stated above.

Reports on examinations and reviews of pro forma information incorporate those assurances in the opinion paragraph; in other respects they are analogous to other reports on attest engagements.

Prospective Financial Information

The usefulness of prospective financial information has become widely recognized, and such information is in demand by the financial community, including investors and potential investors. Prospective financial information is presently used in a wide variety of situations, ranging from public offerings of bonds or other securities and arrangements for bank or similar financing, to internal microcomputer "spreadsheet" software programs designed to facilitate the preparation of various financial analyses, including short-range plans (budgets), long-range plans, cash flow studies, capital improvement decisions, and other plans.

Prospective financial information is any financial information about the future. The information may be presented as complete prospective financial statements or limited to one or more elements, items, or accounts. To qualify as *prospective financial statements*, the presentation must meet minimum presentation guidelines. Other, more limited presentations of prospective financial information that do not meet those guidelines are referred to as *partial presentations*. (Partial presentations are ordinarily not appropriate for general use and are not discussed in this chapter.)

Carried to an extreme, almost any financial presentation could arguably be deemed to be prospective financial information, since many amounts contained in historical financial statements are calculated in light of future expectations. For practical purposes, presentations that contain dollar amounts based on assumptions of future events in each of a number of future years generally fall under the definition of prospective financial information. On the other hand, financial information based on historical values, such as annual depreciation expense or scheduled principal payments of debt, would not be considered prospective financial information. Also, information based on assumptions of future events that is used only in determining current values typically would not be considered prospective financial information.

The AICPA has developed the following guidance on the preparation and presentation of prospective financial information, along with guidance for practitioners associated with that information.

- AICPA Statement on Standards for Accountants' Services on Prospective Financial Information, *Financial Forecasts and Projections* (AT Section 200). The statement specifies the procedures to perform and the reports to issue and sets forth "minimum presentation guidelines" for prospective financial statements.
- AICPA *Guide for Prospective Financial Statements*, which is a companion document to the statement.
- AICPA Statement of Position (SOP), *Questions Concerning Accountants' Services on Prospective Financial Statements*, which clarifies and expands on certain reporting and procedural guidance in the guide.

Prospective financial statements are either financial forecasts or financial projections that present financial position, results of operations, and cash flows, and include summaries of significant assumptions and accounting policies.

Financial forecasts are prospective financial statements that present, to the best of management's[6] knowledge and belief, an entity's expected financial position, results of operations, and cash flows. A financial forecast is based on management's assumptions reflecting *conditions it expects to exist* and the *course of action it expects to take*. A financial forecast may be expressed in specific monetary amounts as a single-point estimate of forecasted results or as a

[6]Prospective financial statements, including the underlying assumptions, are the responsibility of the "responsible party," usually the client's management. In certain circumstances, this may be a party outside the entity being reported on (for example, a party considering acquiring the entity).

range. In the latter instance, management selects key assumptions to form a range within which it reasonably expects the item or items subject to the assumptions to fall. For example, forecasted financial statements that present expected results for a proposed apartment complex may contain a range showing the sensitivity of the forecast to variations in occupancy rates. The range must not be selected in a biased or misleading manner, for example, a range in which one end is significantly less expected than the other.

Financial projections are prospective financial statements that present, to the best of management's knowledge and belief, given one or more *hypothetical assumptions*, an entity's expected financial position, results of operations, and cash flows. A financial projection is sometimes prepared to present one or more hypothetical courses of action for evaluation, as in response to a question such as, "What would happen if . . . ?" A financial projection is based on management's assumptions reflecting conditions it expects would exist and the course of action it expects would be taken, given one or more hypothetical assumptions. For instance, a financial projection of a company's operations and cash flows may be based on assumptions about the construction of an additional plant facility. A projection, like a forecast, may be expressed as a range.

Commonly presented prospective financial statements include

- Forecasts in feasibility studies and preliminary feasibility studies. These studies may cover hospitals, sports complexes, homes for the elderly, real estate ventures, and so on. Generally, they involve various types of capital expenditures.
- Forecasts or projections relating to new or expanded projects or operations or existing operations of an entity over specified future periods. The prospective financial statements may be, for example, forecasts of target companies the client is considering acquiring, forecasts of the client company for purposes of conducting discussions with lenders, forecasts prepared on behalf of creditors (for example, in troubled financial situations, such as bankruptcies), or forecasts for the client company in contemplation of a refinancing or eliminating a line of business.
- Forecasts filed in connection with applications for government assistance grants.
- Rate studies for municipalities and public utilities, reported in financial statement format.
- Forecasts prepared in connection with a revenue bond issue.

Prospective financial statements may be prepared for either general use or limited use. *General use* refers to use of the statements by persons with whom management is not negotiating directly, for example, in an offering statement of an entity's debt or equity interests. Because recipients of prospective financial statements distributed for general use are unable to communicate directly with management, the most useful presentation for them is one that portrays, to the best of management's knowledge and belief, the expected results. Thus, only *a financial forecast* is appropriate for general use.

Limited use of prospective financial statements refers to use of the statements by management alone or by management and third parties with whom it is negotiating directly. Examples include use in negotiations for a bank loan, submission to a regulatory agency, and use solely within the entity. Third-party recipients of prospective financial statements intended for limited use can ask questions of and negotiate terms directly with management. Any type of prospective financial statements that would be useful in the circumstances would normally be appropriate for limited use. Thus, the presentation may be either *a financial forecast* or *a financial projection.*

Types of Services. There are three services practitioners may apply to prospective financial statements for use by third parties—compilation, examination, and application of agreed-upon procedures. The practitioner is required to perform one of the three services whenever a third party, including specified users (see below), might reasonably be expected to use prospective financial statements that the practitioner assisted in assembling.[7] (The AICPA statement does not permit practitioners to review prospective financial statements.)

Examinations of and application of agreed-upon procedures to prospective financial statements correspond to those services for attest engagements generally. Compilations of prospective financial statements are not attest engagements, because they do not result in the expression of a conclusion on the reliability of the assertions contained in the financial statements. Compilations are covered by the statement and guide, however, because they are valuable professional services involving a practitioner's expertise as an accountant, though not as an attestor.

Compilation. A compilation of a financial forecast or projection involves

- Assembling the prospective data, to the extent necessary, based on the responsible party's assumptions.
- Obtaining satisfaction that the underlying assumptions are not obviously inappropriate.
- Reading the prospective data and considering whether it appears to be presented in conformity with the AICPA presentation guidelines.

[7]The SEC staff has expressed concern about a practitioner's independence regarding prospective financial statements or historical financial statements covering the forecast period when a practitioner has assisted in preparing the prospective financial statements. Accordingly, the practitioner should consider the issue of independence if he or she is requested to assist in preparing prospective financial statements for an SEC registrant or for an entity that may become an SEC registrant during the forecast period.

Since in a compilation the practitioner does not provide assurance on the prospective data or the underlying assumptions, the practitioner's procedures are limited, consisting principally of obtaining background knowledge of the industry and the entity, making inquiries, reading the data, and confirming with management the latter's responsibility for the assumptions.

Examination. An examination of a financial forecast or projection is the highest level of service offered by a practitioner with regard to prospective financial statements. An examination involves evaluating the

- Preparation of the forecast or projection.
- Support underlying the assumptions.
- Presentation for conformity with the AICPA presentation guidelines.

In examining a projection, the practitioner need not obtain support for the hypothetical assumptions, but should consider whether they are consistent with the purpose of the presentation.

Applying Agreed-Upon Procedures. When a practitioner applies agreed-upon procedures to a financial forecast or projection, specified users of the forecast or projection participate in establishing the nature and scope of the engagement and take responsibility for the adequacy of the procedures to be performed. Generally, those procedures may be as limited or extensive as the specified users desire, as long as the users take responsibility for the adequacy of the procedures. Mere reading of the prospective financial statements, however, is not in itself a sufficient procedure. Consistent with other attest engagements involving the application of agreed-upon procedures, distribution of the practitioner's report when agreed-upon procedures are applied to a financial forecast or projection is restricted to the specified users. The report enumerates the procedures performed and states the practitioner's findings; it may not express any form of negative assurance on the financial statements taken as a whole.

Reporting on Prospective Financial Statements. The statement and guide set forth reporting standards for compilations, examinations, and engagements to apply agreed-upon procedures.

Standard Compilation Report. A practitioner's standard report on a compilation of a forecast that does not contain a range follows:

> We have compiled the accompanying forecasted balance sheet, statements of income, retained earnings, and cash flows of XYZ Company as of December 31, 19XX, and for the year then ending, in accordance with standards established by the American Institute of Certified Public Accountants.

> A compilation is limited to presenting in the form of a forecast information that is the representation of management and does not include evaluation of the support for the assumptions underlying the forecast. We have not examined the forecast and, accordingly, do not express an opinion or any other form of assurance on the accompanying statements or assumptions. Furthermore, there will usually be differences between the forecasted and actual results, because events and circumstances frequently do not occur as expected, and those differences may be material. We have no responsibility to update this report for events and circumstances occurring after the date of this report.

For a projection, the practitioner's report would include a separate paragraph describing the limitations on the usefulness of the presentation.

If the practitioner compiles prospective financial statements for an entity with respect to which he or she is not independent, the practitioner may issue the standard compilation report. The report should specifically disclose the lack of independence; however, the reason for the lack of independence should not be described.

Standard Examination Report. Following is the practitioner's standard report on an examination of a forecast that does not contain a range:

> We have examined the accompanying forecasted balance sheet, statements of income, retained earnings, and cash flows of XYZ Company as of December 31, 19XX, and for the year then ending. Our examination was made in accordance with standards for an examination of a forecast established by the American Institute of Certified Public Accountants and, accordingly, included such procedures as we considered necessary to evaluate both the assumptions used by management and the preparation and presentation of the forecast.
>
> In our opinion, the accompanying forecast is presented in conformity with guidelines for presentation of a forecast established by the American Institute of Certified Public Accountants, and the underlying assumptions provide a reasonable basis for management's forecast. However, there will usually be differences between the forecasted and actual results, because events and circumstances frequently do not occur as expected, and those differences may be material. We have no responsibility to update this report for events and circumstances occurring after the date of this report.

When a practitioner examines a projection, the opinion regarding the assumptions should be predicated on the hypothetical assumptions; that is, the practitioner should express an opinion on whether the assumptions provide a reasonable basis for the projection given the hypothetical assumptions. Also, the report should include a separate paragraph that describes the limitations on the usefulness of the presentation. An example of an opinion paragraph that meets this requirement follows:

> In our opinion, the accompanying projection is presented in conformity with guidelines for presentation of a projection established by the American Institute

of Certified Public Accountants, and the underlying assumptions provide a reasonable basis for management's projection assuming the granting of the requested loan for the purpose of expanding XYZ Company's plant as described in the summary of significant assumptions. However, even if the loan is granted and the plant is expanded, there will usually be differences between the projected and actual results, because events and circumstances frequently do not occur as expected, and those differences may be material. We have no responsibility to update this report for events and circumstances occurring after the date of this report.

COMPLIANCE AUDITING

Laws and governmental regulations play an integral part in an entity's operations, and failure to comply with them may affect its financial statements. Management is responsible for ensuring that the entity complies with applicable laws and regulations. To meet that responsibility, management identifies those laws and regulations and establishes internal control structure policies and procedures designed to provide reasonable assurance of compliance. The auditor's responsibility for testing and reporting on compliance with laws and governmental regulations varies according to the type of entity being audited and the terms of the engagement.

During the mid-1980s, reports of illegal activities caused concern in Congress and among the public and raised questions about auditors' responsibility for detecting and reporting violations of laws and governmental regulations—referred to as illegal acts. In response, the Auditing Standards Board issued two new Statements on Auditing Standards (SASs): No. 53, *The Auditor's Responsibility to Detect and Report Errors and Irregularities* (AU Section 316), and No. 54, *Illegal Acts by Clients* (AU Section 317). Together they define the auditor's responsibilities in this area under generally accepted auditing standards (GAAS).

Those responsibilities, including those related to illegal acts, apply to *all* audits performed under GAAS. A governmental entity, not-for-profit organization, or business enterprise may engage an auditor, however, to audit its financial statements in accordance with government auditing standards issued by the Comptroller General of the United States or, in certain circumstances, in accordance with the federal Single Audit Act of 1984. In performing an audit in accordance with those requirements, the auditor assumes responsibilities beyond those encompassed by GAAS. To fully understand how the consideration of illegal acts affects the scope of such audits, the auditor must be familiar with the requirements of government auditing standards and the Single Audit Act of 1984 as well as GAAS. This section discusses each of these sources of audit guidance regarding an entity's compliance with laws and regulations.

Generally Accepted Auditing Standards

The auditor's responsibilities with respect to illegal acts under GAAS are to design the audit to provide reasonable assurance of detecting illegal acts that could have a *direct and material* effect on financial statement amounts, and to make the audit committee aware of any illegal acts that come to the auditor's attention. Those responsibilities are described in Chapter 4. If the auditor concludes that noncompliance with laws and regulations could have a direct and material effect on the financial statements, he or she must design the audit to obtain reasonable assurance that noncompliance will be detected: He or she should assess the control structure as it applies to compliance with laws and regulations and, if necessary, based on that assessment, design substantive tests of compliance. SAS Nos. 53 and 54 do not require the auditor to issue a report on the client's compliance with laws and regulations.

SAS No. 54 states that an audit conducted in accordance with GAAS does not ordinarily include auditing procedures specifically designed to detect illegal acts that might have only an *indirect* effect on financial statements. Those kinds of illegal acts (which SAS No. 54 refers to simply as "illegal acts") may come to the auditor's attention, however, through procedures performed to support the audit opinion, for example, reading minutes and inquiring of management and legal counsel concerning litigation, claims, and assessments. In addition, the auditor may inquire of management about compliance with laws and regulations, its policies for preventing illegal acts, and whether it issues directives and obtains periodic representations from management concerning compliance with laws and regulations. Any of these or other procedures may point to the possibility of an illegal act. SAS No. 54 provides additional guidance with respect to detecting and reporting illegal acts generally, and is discussed in Chapter 4.

In auditing a governmental entity, compliance with laws and regulations is particularly important, because governmental organizations are usually subject to more specific rules and regulations than other business entities. The audit risk of failing to detect instances of noncompliance is correspondingly greater. Since many of those rules and regulations may have a *direct and material* effect on the determination of financial statement amounts, the auditor should take them into consideration when designing procedures to reduce overall audit risk—the risk that the financial statements are materially misstated—to the appropriately low level required by professional standards.

To determine an appropriate audit testing plan, the auditor considers preliminary judgments about materiality in addition to the assessment of inherent and control risk. In a governmental audit, the auditor needs to consider materiality not only in relation to the individual fund balances, but also in relation to federal financial assistance programs. Failure to consider this in the planning stages may cause a duplication of efforts later in the audit. The auditor's understanding of a governmental entity client should include consideration of the possible financial statement effects of laws and regulations that auditors generally recognize as having a direct and material effect on the financial statements of governmental entities. The auditor should also assess whether management has identified those laws and regulations, by considering knowledge obtained in prior-year audits; inquiry of management, legal counsel, appropriate oversight organizations, and program administrators; obtaining written representations from management; reading relevant agreements; reviewing minutes of meetings of relevant legislative bodies; and reviewing other relevant information. Furthermore, two statements should be added to the management representation letter required by SAS No. 19.

- A statement that management acknowledges its responsibility for the entity's compliance with applicable laws and regulations.
- A statement that management has identified and disclosed all laws and regulations having a direct and material effect on the determination of financial statement amounts.

As discussed below, government auditing standards require that "a test should be made of compliance with applicable laws and regulations." In planning and conducting the necessary tests of compliance, the auditor should

- Determine which laws and regulations could, if not complied with, have a direct and material effect on the financial statements.
- Assess, for each significant law or regulation, the risk that material noncompliance could occur. This includes assessing the internal control structure policies and procedures the entity has placed in operation to ensure compliance with laws and regulations.
- Based on that assessment, design procedures to test compliance with laws and regulations to provide reasonable assurance that intentional or unintentional instances of noncompliance that could have a material effect on the financial statements have not occurred.

In developing the audit testing plan for a governmental entity, the auditor should consider all the applicable performance and reporting requirements in combination, to design the most efficient plan. There are three sources—GAAS, government auditing standards, and the Single Audit Act—each with different requirements, that the auditor needs to be aware of when considering a governmental entity's compliance with laws and regulations. Because the provisions of these three sources overlap, the Auditing Standards Board issued SAS No. 63, *Compliance Auditing Applicable to Governmental Entities and Other Recipients of Governmental Financial Assistance*, which provides guidance for applying SAS Nos. 53 and 54, government auditing standards, and the Single Audit Act, as they apply to compliance with laws and regulations.

Government Auditing Standards

In 1988, the U.S. General Accounting Office (GAO) issued a revised edition of *Government Auditing Standards—Standards for Audit of Governmental Organizations, Programs, Activities, and Functions* (often referred to as the "Yellow Book"). The Yellow Book prescribes generally accepted governmental auditing standards (GAGAS), which are applicable for audits of state and local governmental units; not-for-profit organizations, like universities and hospitals, that receive government aid or grants; and mortgage companies subject to the provisions of Housing and Urban Development audit guides. Certain laws, like the Single Audit Act, and regulations, like Office of Management and Budget (OMB) Circulars, also require public accountants to follow the standards in the Yellow Book for financial audits. The standards do not apply to providers of goods and services to the government unless specifically required by the supply contract between the parties.

The Yellow Book contains standards for two types of governmental audits, financial and performance. This chapter discusses only financial audits, since they are the type an independent auditor is more likely to perform. Generally accepted governmental auditing standards incorporate GAAS and include some additional standards. Like GAAS, GAGAS are divided into three categories: general, field work, and reporting standards. Among the additional standards an auditor must adhere to when performing an audit in accordance with GAGAS are

- Certain education and training requirements.
- A lower materiality level and/or threshold of acceptable risk than in similar-type audits in the private sector.
- Participation in an external quality control review program.
- A documentation requirement that the audit program be cross-referenced to the working papers.
- Tests of compliance with applicable laws and regulations; that is, laws and regulations that could have a direct and material effect on the financial statements. (This standard does not extend the auditor's responsibility beyond SAS Nos. 53 and 54; however, entities subject to the provisions of the Yellow Book are likely to be subject to extensive laws and regulations.)

The additional reporting standards under GAGAS designed to satisfy the unique needs of governmental financial audits are

- A statement in the auditor's report that the audit was conducted in accordance with GAGAS as well as GAAS.
- A report on the entity's compliance with laws and regulations that could, if not complied with, have a direct and material effect on the financial statements. This report should include all material instances of non-

compliance. The auditor expresses positive assurance on items tested for compliance and negative assurance on items not tested.

- A written report on the auditor's understanding of the entity's internal control structure and the assessment of control risk made as part of a financial audit.

The additional reporting requirements for audits conducted under the Yellow Book are discussed in SAS No. 63.

Single Audit Act

Before the enactment of the Single Audit Act of 1984 (the Act), a federal agency that issued a grant to a state or local government had the authority to establish its own audit guidelines. There was no oversight body or any other means of controlling the scope or number of audits required for a particular agency or other entity receiving federal financial assistance. Often the federal assistance came from several different federal agencies. As a result, the same internal control procedures and transactions often were tested more than once, frequently by different independent auditors, and sometimes even simultaneously. These duplicative audits caused organizational inefficiencies and led to increased audit costs.

The Single Audit Act created a single, coordinated audit (often called a "single audit," "organization-wide audit," or "entity-wide audit") of all federal financial assistance provided to a recipient agency during a fiscal year. The Act emphasizes audits of those federal financial assistance programs that the federal government has defined as "major." The objectives of the Act are to

- Promote the efficient and effective use of audit resources.
- Improve state and local governments' financial management of federal financial assistance programs through more effective auditing.
- Establish uniform requirements for audits of federal financial assistance provided to state and local governments.
- Ensure that federal departments and agencies, to the greatest extent practicable, are audited in accordance with the requirements of the Single Audit Act.

The Office of Management and Budget is responsible for setting policies regarding the frequency and scope of audits required for federal agencies to meet government auditing standards. In 1985 the OMB issued Circular A-128, "Audits of State and Local Governments," to facilitate the implementation of the Single Audit Act. Together, Circular A-128 and the Act require (1) an audit of the entity's general-purpose or basic financial statements, (2) the performance of additional audit tests for compliance with applicable laws and regulations related to grants received, and (3) tests of control structure policies and procedures designed to ensure compliance with laws and regulations of applicable federal financial assistance programs. In addition, Circular A-128 prescribes the responsibilities for monitoring those requirements.

In 1976, the OMB issued Circular A-110, which set forth audit requirements for institutions of higher education, hospitals, and other nonprofit organizations receiving federal grants. However, the audit requirements were not clear and were often misunderstood. At the time of this writing, the OMB has proposed Circular A-133, "Audits of Higher Education and Other Nonprofit Agencies," which, when issued, would extend to colleges and universities and nonprofit agencies receiving federal financial assistance, requirements similar to those contained in Circular A-128. Hospitals, other than those associated with a university, are specifically excluded from Circular A-133.

Auditing Compliance with Specific Requirements of Major Federal Financial Assistance Programs. Under the Single Audit Act, the auditor must report on whether the entity has complied with laws and regulations that have a material effect on each *major* federal financial assistance program. The Act defines a major federal financial assistance program based on the total expenditures of federal financial assistance during a program year. These major programs are listed in the *Catalog of Federal Domestic Assistance*; examples include the National School Lunch program and Headstart programs.

Management is responsible for identifying those federal financial assistance programs from which it receives funding. On a single audit, it is the auditor's responsibility to test for compliance with the specific requirements of every applicable major federal financial assistance program. This is in addition to the GAGAS requirement to design tests to assess the risk that noncompliance with laws and regulations could have a direct and material effect on the financial statements. The Single Audit Act requirement is much more stringent; thus, after testing compliance with the requirements of the Single Audit Act, the auditor may often consider that no further testing of compliance with laws and regulations is necessary to fulfill the GAGAS requirement.

The single audit must include the selection and testing of a representative number of charges from each major federal financial assistance program identified. The extent and selection of items to be tested depends on the auditor's professional judgment. For *all* major programs, Circular A-128 requires the auditor to specifically consider

- *Types of Services Allowed*—Is the entity using financial assistance to purchase goods and services allowed by the program?
- *Eligibility*—Were the recipients of the goods and services eligible to receive them?
- *Matching Requirement*—Did the entity contribute the necessary amount from its own resources toward projects paid for with financial assistance?

- *Reporting*—Did the entity file all the reports required by the federal financial assistance program?
- *Special Tests and Provisions*—Are there other federal provisions with which noncompliance could materially affect the federal financial assistance programs?

The details of these items vary with each federal financial assistance program. To help the auditor determine which federal compliance requirements should be tested, the OMB publishes the *Compliance Supplement for Single Audits of State and Local Governments* (the *Compliance Supplement*), which specifies program compliance requirements and suggests auditing procedures for the larger federal financial assistance programs.

In addition to the specific requirements that recipient agencies must comply with and that the auditor must test, Circulars A-128 and the proposed A-133 require that independent auditors determine whether

- Financial reports and claims for advances and reimbursements contain information that is supported by the books and records used to prepare the basic financial statements.
- Amounts claimed or used for matching were determined in accordance with the particular grant requirements.

Materiality and Risk Assessment Under the Single Audit Act. The concept of materiality for financial statements covered by the Act differs somewhat from that prescribed by GAAS. Under the Act, materiality is considered in relation to each major federal financial assistance program. Also, a material amount pertaining to one major program may not be considered material to another major program of a different size or nature.

Risk assessment in an audit performed under GAGAS is identical to that under GAAS. Under the Single Audit Act, however, the auditor has responsibilities over and above those of GAAS and GAGAS, namely, testing and reporting on the entity's compliance with the specific requirements of a particular program and the general requirements that apply to all programs. Thus, in assessing risk in a compliance audit of a major federal program, the auditor must also consider the risk that he or she may fail to appropriately modify his or her opinion on compliance with such a program. Like audit risk, this risk has three aspects.

- Inherent risk—the risk that material noncompliance with requirements applicable to a major federal financial assistance program could occur assuming there were no related control structure policies or procedures.
- Control risk—the risk that material noncompliance that could occur in a major federal financial assistance program will not be prevented or

detected on a timely basis by the entity's internal control structure policies and procedures.

- Detection risk—the risk that the auditor's procedures will lead him or her to conclude that noncompliance that could be material to a major federal financial assistance program does not exist when in fact such noncompliance does exist.

Nonmajor Programs. The discussion of the Single Audit Act thus far has related to those programs defined as major federal financial assistance programs. Many state and local governments, however, receive some or all of their federal financial assistance from programs that do not meet the federal definition of major programs. These programs are referred to as nonmajor programs. The procedures required to be performed on nonmajor programs are substantially more limited in scope than those for major programs. As part of the audit of the financial statements or of considering the internal control structure, the auditor may have selected for testing some transactions from nonmajor programs; if so, he or she should test those transactions for compliance with the applicable requirements. The auditor is not required to address compliance with the general requirements or the specific requirements of other transactions from the nonmajor program.

SAS No. 63 cites, in paragraph 86, an example of the extent of testing necessary for a nonmajor program.

> If in the audit of the general-purpose or basic financial statements an auditor examined a payroll transaction that was charged to a nonmajor program, the auditor should determine that the position could reasonably be charged to that program and that the individual's salary was correctly charged to that program.

Reporting Under the Single Audit Act. The reporting requirements of the Single Audit Act are more extensive than those under GAAS and GAGAS. In addition to the report required by GAAS on the financial statements and the reports required by GAGAS on the internal control structure and on compliance with laws and regulations, the auditor performing a single audit must issue reports on

- Compliance with specific requirements applicable to major federal financial assistance programs.
- Compliance with the general requirements applicable to those programs. Those general requirements prohibit use of federal funds for political activity; payment of wages in construction contracts at less than the prevailing wage; civil rights discrimination; and withdrawal of cash in excess of immediate needs. They also require payments to households and

businesses displaced by property acquisition, and periodic submission of specified reports.

- Compliance with requirements applicable to nonmajor federal financial assistance programs.
- A supplementary schedule of federal financial assistance.
- The internal control structure, based on the additional tests relating to systems used in administering federal financial assistance programs.

SAS No. 63 provides examples of such reports.

Review Questions

19–1. Explain what is meant by a CPA's association with financial data.

19–2. What is a compilation and what kind of report is given?

19–3. What is a review and what kind of report is given?

19–4. Would lack of independence preclude the issuance of a review report? A compilation report?

19–5. What are some of the benefits to a company from having the auditor make a preissuance review of interim financial information?

19–6. Compare and contrast an ordinary review engagement with an interim review engagement, including procedures followed and report issued.

19–7. Describe the most significant element in a special report on a comprehensive basis of accounting other than GAAP.

19–8. How should the auditor report on additional information accompanying the basic financial statements in an auditor-submitted document?

19–9. What are the main elements of a special report expressing an unqualified opinion on an entity's internal control structure?

19–10. What is a comfort letter and when is it used?

19–11. What is an attestation engagement? Give some examples of attestation engagements.

19–12. What are pro forma financial statements? When are they usually presented?

19–13. Distinguish between a financial forecast and a financial projection.

19–14. What key elements must be contained in reports on attestation engagements?

19–15. List the attestation standards.

19–16. What are "reasonable criteria" against which assertions in attestation engagements must be capable of being evaluated? Give some examples.

19–17. What standards, in addition to GAAS, must an auditor adhere to when performing an audit in accordance with generally accepted governmental auditing standards?

19–18. What is the Single Audit Act of 1984, and what are its objectives?

Discussion Questions

19–30. In recent years there has been an increasing trend toward the furnishing of compilation or review services for small, growing, nonpublic companies. Discuss the opportunities, desirability, and standards concerning these services from the following standpoints:

a. When would you recommend these services? Can there be a combination of them, such as monthly compilations and annual reviews?
b. What recommendation would you make if a company was growing rapidly and might go public in a few years?
c. What are the differences in reporting between compilations and reviews?
d. What effect does the CPA's independence have on the issuance of these reports?

19–31. Benson, CPA, who has audited the financial statements of Greystone, Inc., a publicly held company, for the year ended December 31, 1989, was asked to perform a limited review of the financial statements of Greystone, Inc. for the period ending March 31, 1990. The engagement letter stated that a limited review does not provide a basis for the expression of an opinion.

Required:

a. Explain why Benson's limited review will *not* provide a basis for the expression of an opinion.
b. What are the review procedures that Benson should perform, and what is the purpose of each procedure? Structure your response as follows:

Procedure	*Purpose of Procedure*

(AICPA adapted)

19–32. The following cases involve auditors' reports issued in connection with financial statements prepared on a comprehensive basis of accounting other than generally accepted accounting principles:

1. The financial statements of a retail grocery store operated as an individual proprietorship are prepared on the basis of cash receipts and disbursements. The statements do not purport to present the financial position and results of operations of the company.
2. The financial statements of a private nonprofit hospital are prepared in accordance with the principles and practices of accounting recommended in an AICPA industry audit and accounting guide for hospitals.
3. The financial statements of an insurance company are prepared in accordance with the principles and practices of uniform accounting prescribed by a state insurance commission. The statements purport to present the financial position and results of operations of the insurance company.

Required:
Discuss the type of opinion the auditor should give in each of these cases.

(AICPA adapted)

19–33. An accountant is sometimes called on by clients to report on or assemble prospective financial statements for use by third parties.

Required:

a. 1. Identify the types of engagements that an accountant may perform under these circumstances.
   2. Explain the difference between "general use" of and "limited use" of prospective financial statements.
   3. Explain what types of prospective financial statements are appropriate for "general use" and what types are appropriate for "limited use."

b. Describe the contents of the accountant's standard report on a compilation of a financial projection.

(AICPA adapted)

AICPA Multiple Choice Questions

These questions are taken from the Auditing part of Uniform CPA Examinations. Choose the single most appropriate answer.

19–40. Which of the following statements with respect to an auditor's report expressing an opinion on a specific item on a financial statement is correct?

a. Materiality must be related to the specified item rather than to the financial statements taken as a whole.
b. Such an opinion can be expressed only if the auditor is also engaged to audit the entire set of financial statements.
c. The attention devoted to the specified item is usually less than it would be if the financial statements taken as a whole were being audited.
d. The auditor who has issued an adverse opinion on the financial statements taken as a whole can never express an opinion on a specified item in these financial statements.

19–41. In performing a compilation of financial statements of a nonpublic entity, the accountant decides that modification of the standard report is not adequate to indicate deficiencies in the financial statements taken as a whole, and the client is not willing to correct the deficiencies. The accountant should therefore

a. Perform a review of the financial statements.
b. Issue a special report.
c. Withdraw from the engagement.
d. Express an adverse audit opinion.

19–42. Information accompanying the basic financial statements in an auditor-submitted document should *not* include

a. An analysis of inventory by location.
b. A statement that the allowance for doubtful accounts is adequate.
c. A statement that the depreciable life of a new asset is 20 years.
d. An analysis of revenue by product line.

19–43. Inquiry of the entity's personnel and analytical procedures are the primary bases for the issuance of a (an)

a. Compilation report on financial statements for a nonpublic company in its first year of operations.
b. Auditor's report on financial statements supplemented with price level information.
c. Review report on comparative financial statements for a nonpublic company in its second year of operations.
d. Management advisory report prepared at the request of the client's audit committee.

19–44. If the auditor believes that financial statements prepared on the entity's income tax basis are *not* suitably titled, the auditor should

a. Issue a disclaimer of opinion.
b. Explain in the notes to the financial statements the terminology used.
c. Issue a compilation report.
d. Modify the auditor's report to disclose any reservations.

19–45. Inquiry and analytical procedures ordinarily performed during a review of a nonpublic entity's financial statements include

a. Analytical procedures designed to identify material weaknesses in internal control procedures.
b. Inquiries concerning actions taken at meetings of the stockholders and the board of directors.
c. Analytical procedures designed to test the accounting records by obtaining corroborating evidential matter.
d. Inquiries of knowledgeable outside parties such as the client's attorneys and bankers.

19–46. Which of the following best describes the auditor's reporting responsibility concerning information accompanying the basic financial statements in an auditor-submitted document?

a. The auditor should report on all the information included in the document.
b. The auditor should report on the basic financial statements but may *not* issue a report covering the accompanying information.
c. The auditor should report on the information accompanying the basic financial statements only if the auditor participated in the preparation of the accompanying information.
d. The auditor should report on the information accompanying the basic financial statements only if the document is being distributed to public shareholders.

19–47. If requested to perform a review engagement for a nonpublic entity in which an accountant has an immaterial direct financial interest, the accountant is

a. Not independent and, therefore, may issue a review report, but may *not* issue an auditor's opinion.
b. Not independent and, therefore, may *not* issue a review report.
c. Not independent and, therefore, may *not* be associated with the financial statements.

d. Independent because the financial interest is immaterial and, therefore, may issue a review report.

19–48. In which of the following reports should an accountant *not* express negative or limited assurance?

a. A standard review report on financial statements of a nonpublic entity.
b. A standard compilation report on financial statements of a nonpublic entity.
c. A standard comfort letter on financial information included in a registration statement of a public entity.
d. A standard review report on interim financial statements of a public entity.

19–49. An auditor's report would be designated as a special report when it is issued in connection with financial statements that are

a. For an interim period and are subjected to a limited review.
b. Unaudited and are prepared from a client's accounting records.
c. Prepared in accordance with a comprehensive basis of accounting other than generally accepted accounting principles.
d. Purported to be in accordance with generally accepted accounting principles but do *not* include a presentation of the statement of cash flows.

19–50. When providing limited assurance that the financial statements of a nonpublic entity require *no* material modifications to be in accordance with generally accepted accounting principles, the accountant should

a. Understand the entity's internal control structure.
b. Test the accounting records that identify inconsistencies with the prior year's financial statements.
c. Understand the accounting principles of the industry in which the entity operates.
d. Develop audit programs to determine whether the entity's financial statements are fairly presented.

19–51. Green, CPA, is requested to render an opinion on the application of accounting principles by an entity that is audited by another CPA. Green may

a. Not accept such an engagement because to do so would be considered unethical.
b. Not accept such an engagement because Green would lack the necessary information on which to base an opinion without conducting an audit.
c. Accept the engagement but should form an independent opinion without consulting with the continuing CPA.
d. Accept the engagement but should consult with the continuing CPA to ascertain all the available facts relevant to forming a professional judgment.

19–52. The underwriter of a securities offering may request that an auditor perform specified procedures and supply certain assurances concerning unaudited information contained in a registration statement. The auditor's response to such a request is commonly called a

a. Report under federal security statutes.
b. Comfort letter.

c. Review of interim financial information.
d. Compilation report for underwriters.

19–53. The party responsible for assumptions identified in the preparation of prospective financial statements is usually

a. A third-party lending institution.
b. The client's management.
c. The reporting accountant.
d. The client's independent auditor.

19–54. An accountant may accept an engagement to apply agreed-upon procedures to prospective financial statements provided that

a. Distribution of the report is to be restricted to the specified users involved.
b. The prospective financial statements are also examined.
c. Responsibility for the adequacy of the procedures performed is taken by the accountant.
d. Negative assurance is expressed on the prospective financial statements taken as a whole.

19–55. Under which of the following circumstances could an auditor consider rendering an opinion on pro forma statements that give effect to proposed transactions?

a. When the proposed transactions are subject to a definitive agreement among the parties.
b. When the time interval between the date of the financial statements and consummation of the transactions is relatively long.
c. When certain subsequent events have some chance of interfering with the consummation of the transactions.
d. When the pro forma statements include amounts based on financial projections.

19–56. Prospective financial information presented in the format of historical financial statements that omit either revenue or cost of sales is deemed to be a

a. Partial presentation.
b. Projected balance sheet.
c. Financial forecast.
d. Financial projection.

19–57. Given one or more hypothetical assumptions, a responsible party may prepare, to the best of its knowledge and belief, an entity's expected financial position, results of operations, and cash flows. Such prospective financial statements are known as

a. Pro forma financial statements.
b. Financial projections.
c. Partial presentations.
d. Financial forecasts.

19–58. Which of the following bodies promulgates standards for audits of federal financial assistance recipients?

a. Governmental Accounting Standards Board.
b. Financial Accounting Standards Board.

c. General Accounting Office.
d. Governmental Auditing Standards Board.

Problems and Cases

19-60. Nicholaus, CPA, received a telephone call from Tory, the sole owner and manager of a small corporation. Tory asked Nicholaus to prepare the financial statements for the corporation and told Nicholaus that the statements were needed in two weeks for external financing purposes. Tory was vague when Nicholaus inquired about the intended use of the statements. Nicholaus was convinced that Tory thought Nicholaus' work would constitute an audit. To avoid confusion, Nicholaus decided not to explain to Tory that the engagement would only be to prepare the financial statements. Nicholaus, with the understanding that a substantial fee would be paid if the work were completed in two weeks, accepted the engagement and started the work at once.

During the course of the work, Nicholaus discovered an accrued expense account labeled "professional fees" and learned that the balance in the account represented an accrual for the cost of Nicholaus' services. Nicholaus suggested to Tory's bookkeeper that the account name be changed to "fees for limited audit engagement." Nicholaus also reviewed several invoices to determine whether accounts were being properly classified. Some of the invoices were missing. Nicholaus listed the missing invoice numbers in the working papers with a note indicating that there should be a follow-up on the next engagement. Nicholaus also discovered that the available records included the fixed asset values at estimated current replacement costs. Based on the records available, Nicholaus prepared a balance sheet, income statement, and statement of stockholders' equity. In addition, Nicholaus drafted the footnotes but decided that any mention of the replacement costs would only mislead the readers. Nicholaus suggested to Tory that readers of the financial statements would be better informed if they received a separate letter from Tory explaining the meaning and effect of the estimated replacement costs of the fixed assets. Nicholaus mailed the financial statements and footnotes to Tory with the following note included on each page:

> The accompanying financial statements are submitted to you without complete audit verification.

Required:

Identify Nicholaus' inappropriate actions and indicate what Nicholaus should have done to avoid each one. Organize your answer as follows:

Inappropriate Action	*What Nicholaus Should Have Done to Avoid Inappropriate Action*

(AICPA adapted)

19-61. In order to obtain information that is necessary to make informed decisions, management often calls on the independent auditor for assistance. This may involve a request that the independent auditor apply certain auditing procedures to specific accounts of a company that is a candidate for acquisition and report upon the results. In such an engagement, the agreed-upon procedures may constitute a scope limitation.

At the completion of an engagement performed at the request of Ocean Products Company, which was limited in scope as explained, the following report was prepared by an audit assistant and was submitted to the partner for review.

> To the Board of Directors of Marine Instruments, Inc.:
>
> We have applied certain agreed-upon procedures, as discussed below, to accounting records of Marine Instruments, Inc. as of December 31, 1989, solely to assist Ocean Products Company in connection with the proposed acquisition of Marine Instruments, Inc.
>
> We have audited the cash in banks and accounts receivable of Marine Instruments, Inc. as of December 31, 1989, in accordance with generally accepted auditing standards and, accordingly, included such tests of the accounting records and such other auditing procedures as we considered necessary in the circumstances.
>
> In our opinion, the cash and receivables referred to above are fairly presented, in all material respects, as of December 31, 1989, in conformity with generally accepted accounting principles. We therefore recommend that Ocean Products Company acquire Marine Instruments, Inc. pursuant to the proposed agreement.
>
> [signature]

Required:

Comment on the proposed report, describing those assertions that are

a. Incorrect or should otherwise be deleted.
b. Missing and should be inserted.

19-62. For the year ended December 31, 1990, Morris & Winfred, CPAs, audited the financial statements of Towson, Inc. and expressed an unqualified opinion dated February 27, 1991.

For the year ended December 31, 1991, Morris & Winfred were engaged by Towson, Inc. to review Towson's financial statements, that is, to "look into the company's financial statements and determine whether there are any obvious modifications that should be made to the financial statements in order for them to be in conformity with generally accepted accounting principles."

Morris & Winfred made the necessary inquiries, performed the necessary analytical procedures, and performed certain additional procedures that were deemed necessary to achieve the requisite limited assurance. Morris & Winfred's work was completed on March 3, 1992, and the financial statements appeared to be in conformity with GAAP that were consistently applied. The report was prepared on March 5, 1992. It was delivered to Anderman, the controller of Towson, on March 9, 1992.

Required:

Prepare the properly addressed and dated report on the comparative financial statements of Towson, Inc. for the years ended December 31, 1990 and 1991.

(AICPA adapted)

19-63. Modern Office Services, Inc., is a corporation that furnishes temporary office help to its customers. Billings are rendered monthly based on predetermined hourly rates. You have audited the company's financial statements for several years. Following is an abbreviated statement of assets and liabilities on the modified cash basis as of December 31, 1990:

Assets:	
Cash	$40,000
Advances to employees	2,000
Equipment and autos, less accumulated depreciation	50,000
Total assets	92,000
Liabilities:	
Employees' payroll taxes withheld	16,000
Bank loan payable	20,000
Estimated income taxes on cash basis profits	20,000
Total liabilities	56,000
Net assets	$36,000
Represented by:	
Common stock	$ 6,000
Cash profits retained in the business	30,000
	$36,000

Unrecorded receivables were $110,000 and payables were $60,000.

Required:

a. Prepare the report you would issue covering the statement of assets and liabilities as of December 31, 1990, as summarized, and the related statement of revenue collected and expenses paid for the year ended on that date.
b. Briefly discuss and justify your modifications of the conventional report on accrual basis statements.

(AICPA adapted)

19-64. The report on page 862 was drafted by a staff assistant at the completion of the calendar year 1989 review engagement of RLG Company, a continuing client. The 1988 financial statements were compiled. On March 6, 1990, the date of the completion of the review, the report was submitted to the partner with client responsibility. The financial statements for 1988 and 1989 are presented in comparative form.

Required:

Identify the deficiencies in the draft of the proposed report. Group the deficiencies by paragraph. Do *not* redraft the report.

(AICPA adapted)

To the Board of Directors of RLG Company

We have reviewed the accompanying financial statements of RLG Company for the year ended December 31, 1989, in accordance with standards established by Statements on Standards for Auditing and Review Services.

A review consists principally of analytical procedures applied to financial data. It is substantially more in scope than a compilation, but less in scope than an examination in accordance with generally accepted auditing standards, the objective of which is the expression of an opinion regarding the financial statements taken as a whole.

Based on our compilation and review, we are not aware of any material modifications that should be made to the 1988 and 1989 financial statements in order for them to be consistent with the prior year's financial statements.

The accompanying 1988 financial statements of RLG Company were compiled by us and, accordingly, we do not express an opinion on them.

March 6, 1990

Appendix A:
TABLES FOR DETERMINING SAMPLE SIZE: ATTRIBUTES SAMPLING

Reliability Levels of 60, 80, 90, and 95 Percent

Appendix A: Table 1 Determination of Sample Size (Reliability = 60%)

Expected Deviation Rate	*Tolerable Deviation Rate (Percent)*														
(Percent)	*1*	*2*	*3*	*4*	*5*	*6*	*7*	*8*	*9*	*10*	*12*	*14*	*16*	*18*	*20*
0.00	95	50	35	25	20	15	15	15	10	10	10	10	10	5	5
0.50	310	110	70	55	40	35	30	25	25	20	20	15	15	15	10
1.0		160	70	55	40	35	30	25	25	20	20	15	15	15	10
2.0			140	80	40	35	30	25	25	20	20	15	15	15	10
3.0				140	65	55	30	25	25	20	20	15	15	15	10
4.0					150	70	45	25	25	20	20	15	15	15	10
5.0						140	60	40	35	20	20	15	15	15	10
6.0							150	65	50	35	30	15	15	15	10
7.0								160	70	45	30	15	15	15	10
8.0									170	75	35	25	20	15	10
9.0										180	45	25	20	15	10
10.0											70	30	20	20	10

Appendix A: Table 2 Determination of Sample Size (Reliability = 80%)

Expected Deviation Rate	*Tolerable Deviation Rate (Percent)*														
(Percent)	*1*	*2*	*3*	*4*	*5*	*6*	*7*	*8*	*9*	*10*	*12*	*14*	*16*	*18*	*20*
0.00	170	80	55	40	35	30	25	20	20	20	15	15	10	10	10
0.50		150	100	75	60	50	45	40	35	30	25	25	20	20	15
1.0		280	100	75	60	50	45	40	35	30	25	25	20	20	15
2.0			340	140	85	50	45	40	35	30	25	25	20	20	15
3.0				400	160	95	60	55	35	30	25	25	20	20	15
4.0					450	150	95	70	50	45	25	25	20	20	15
5.0						500	180	100	60	55	35	30	20	20	15
6.0								190	100	70	45	30	30	20	15
7.0									200	120	55	40	30	25	15
8.0										230	75	50	35	25	25
9.0											130	55	45	30	25
10.0											240	80	50	30	30

Note: These tables are designed for one-sided tests. To determine the relevant table to use for two-sided estimation, double the one-sided test table indicated sampling risk. For example, the 95 percent reliability table implies a 5 percent sampling risk; doubling the sampling risk to 10 percent indicates that this table can also be used for a 90 percent reliability two-sided estimation sample.

Appendix A: Table 3 Determination of Sample Size (Reliability = 90%)

Expected Deviation Rate (Percent)	*Tolerable Deviation Rate (Percent)*														
	1	*2*	*3*	*4*	*5*	*6*	*7*	*8*	*9*	*10*	*12*	*14*	*16*	*18*	*20*
0.00	230	120	80	60	45	40	35	30	25	25	20	20	15	15	15
0.50		200	130	100	80	65	55	50	45	40	35	30	25	25	20
1.0		400	180	100	80	65	55	50	45	40	35	30	25	25	20
2.0				200	140	90	75	50	45	40	35	30	25	25	20
3.0					240	140	95	65	60	55	35	30	25	25	20
4.0						280	150	100	75	65	45	40	25	25	20
5.0							320	160	120	80	55	40	35	30	20
6.0								350	190	120	65	50	35	30	25
7.0									390	200	100	60	40	30	25
8.0										420	140	75	50	40	25
9.0											230	100	65	45	35
10.0											480	150	80	50	40

Appendix A: Table 4 Determination of Sample Size (Reliability = 95%)

Expected Deviation Rate (Percent)	*Tolerable Deviation Rate (Percent)*														
	1	*2*	*3*	*4*	*5*	*6*	*7*	*8*	*9*	*10*	*12*	*14*	*16*	*18*	*20*
0.00	300	150	100	75	60	50	45	40	35	30	25	20	20	20	15
0.50		320	160	120	95	80	70	60	55	50	40	35	30	25	25
1.0			260	160	95	80	70	60	55	50	40	35	30	25	25
2.0				300	190	130	90	80	70	50	40	35	30	25	25
3.0					370	200	130	95	85	65	55	35	30	25	25
4.0						430	230	150	100	90	65	45	40	25	25
5.0							480	240	160	120	75	55	40	35	30
6.0									270	180	100	65	50	35	30
7.0										300	130	85	55	45	40
8.0											200	100	75	50	40
9.0											350	150	90	65	45
10.0												220	120	70	50

Appendix B: TABLES FOR EVALUATING SAMPLE RESULTS: ATTRIBUTES SAMPLING

Reliability Levels of 60, 80, 90, and 95 Percent

Note: Only upper deviation limits are obtainable using these tables.

Appendix B: Table 1 Evaluation of Results Based on Number of Observed Deviations (Reliability = 60%)

Sample Size	Achieved Upper Deviation Rate Limit (Percent)																
	1	*2*	*3*	*4*	*5*	*6*	*7*	*8*	*9*	*10*	*12*	*14*	*16*	*18*	*20*	*25*	*30*
5														0			
10									0						1		2
15						0						1			2		3
20					0					1			2			3	4
25				0				1			2			3		5	6
30				0			1			2		3		4		6	7
35			0			1			2		3		4	5		7	9
40			0		1			2			3	4	5		6	8	10
45		0			1		2			3	4	5		6	7	10	12
50		0			1		2		3		4	5	6	7	8	11	13
55		0		1		2		3		4	5	6	7	8	9	12	15
60		0		1		2	3		4		5	7	8	9	10	13	16
65		0		1	2		3	4		5	6	7	9	10	11	14	18
70		0	1		2	3		4	5		7	8	9	11	12	16	19
75		0	1		2	3	4		5	6	7	9	10	12	13	17	20
80		0	1	2		3	4	5		6	8	9	11	12	14	18	22
85		0	1	2	3		4	5	6	7	8	10	12	13	15	19	24
90		0	1	2	3	4	5	6		7	9	11	13	14	16	21	25
95	0		1	2	3	4	5	6	7	8	9	12	13	15	17	22	26
100	0		1	2	3	4	5	6	7	8	10	12	14	16	18	23	28
110	0	1	2	3	4	5	6	7	8	9	11	14	16	18	20	25	31
120	0	1	2	3	4	6	7	8	9	10	12	15	17	19	22	28	34
130	0	1	2	3	4	6	7	8	10	11	14	16	19	21	24	30	37
140	0	1	3	4	5	7	8	9	11	12	15	17	20	23	26	33	40
150	0	1	3	4	5	7	9	10	11	13	16	19	22	25	28	35	43
160	0	2	3	5	6	8	9	11	12	14	17	20	24	26	30	38	45
170	0	2	3	5	7	8	10	12	13	15	19	22	25	29	32	40	48
180	0	2	4	5	7	9	11	13	14	16	19	23	26	30	34	42	51
190	0	2	4	6	8	9	11	13	15	17	21	25	28	32	36	45	54
200	1	2	4	6	8	10	12	14	16	18	22	26	30	34	37	47	58
210	1	3	5	7	9	11	13	15	17	19	23	27	32	36	39	50	61
220	1	3	5	7	9	11	14	15	18	20	24	28	33	37	41	52	64
230	1	3	5	7	10	12	14	16	18	21	26	30	34	39	43	55	67
240	1	3	5	8	10	13	15	17	20	22	26	32	36	41	45	58	70
250	1	3	6	8	10	13	16	18	20	23	28	32	37	42	47	60	73
260	1	3	6	8	11	13	16	19	21	24	29	34	39	45	49	63	76
270	1	4	6	9	11	14	17	20	22	25	30	35	41	46	51	65	79
280	1	4	7	9	12	15	17	20	23	26	32	37	43	48	54	68	82
290	1	4	7	10	12	16	18	21	24	27	32	39	44	49	56	70	85
300	1	4	7	10	13	16	19	22	25	28	33	40	45	51	58	73	88

Appendix B: Table 2 Evaluation of Results Based on Number of Observed Deviations (Reliability = 80%)

Sample Size	*Achieved Upper Deviation Rate Limit (Percent)*																
	1	*2*	*3*	*4*	*5*	*6*	*7*	*8*	*9*	*10*	*12*	*14*	*16*	*18*	*20*	*25*	*30*
5																	0
10													0				1
15											0				1		2
20								0					1			2	3
25							0				1			2		3	5
30						0				1		2		3		4	6
35					0				1		2		3		4	6	7
40				0				1			2	3		4	5	7	9
45				0			1			2	3		4	5	6	8	10
50				0		1			2		3	4	5	6	7	9	11
55			0			1		2		3	4	5		6	7	10	13
60			0		1		2		3		4	5	6	7	8	11	14
65			0		1		2		3		5	6	7	8	9	12	15
70			0		1		2	3		4	5	6	8	9	10	13	17
75			0	1		2		3	4		6	7	8	10	11	15	18
80		0		1		2	3		4	5	6	8	9	10	12	16	20
85		0		1	2		3	4		5	7	8	10	11	13	17	21
90		0		1	2		3	4	5	6	7	9	10	12	14	18	22
95		0		1	2	3	4		5	6	8	9	11	13	15	19	24
100		0	1		2	3	4	5	6		8	10	12	14	16	20	25
110		0	1	2	3		4	5	6	7	9	11	13	15	17	23	28
120		0	1	2	3	4	5	6	7	8	10	13	15	17	19	25	31
130		0	1	2	3	4	6	7	8	9	11	14	16	19	21	27	34
140		0	2	3	4	5	6	8	9	10	13	15	18	20	23	30	36
150		1	2	3	4	6	7	8	10	11	14	16	19	22	25	32	39
160	0	1	2	3	5	6	7	9	10	12	15	18	21	24	27	34	42
170	0	1	2	4	5	7	8	10	11	13	16	19	22	25	29	37	45
180	0	1	3	4	6	7	9	10	12	14	17	20	24	27	30	39	48
190	0	1	3	4	6	8	9	11	13	14	18	22	25	29	32	41	51
200	0	1	3	5	6	8	10	12	14	15	19	23	27	30	34	44	54
210	0	2	3	5	7	9	11	13	15	16	20	24	28	32	36	46	56
220	0	2	4	5	7	9	11	13	15	17	21	25	30	34	38	49	59
230	0	2	4	6	8	10	12	14	16	18	22	27	31	35	40	51	62
240	0	2	4	6	8	10	12	15	17	19	24	28	33	37	42	53	65
250	0	2	4	6	9	11	13	16	18	20	25	29	34	39	44	56	68
260	0	2	5	7	9	11	14	16	19	21	26	31	36	41	46	58	71
270	0	3	5	7	9	12	14	17	20	22	27	32	37	42	47	60	74
280	0	3	5	8	10	12	15	18	20	23	28	33	39	44	49	63	77
290	1	3	5	8	10	13	16	19	21	24	29	35	40	46	51	65	79
300	1	3	6	8	11	14	16	19	22	25	30	36	42	47	53	68	82

Appendix B: Table 3 Evaluation of Results Based on Number of Observed Deviations (Reliability = 90%)

Sample Size	Achieved Upper Deviation Rate Limit (Percent)																
	1	*2*	*3*	*4*	*5*	*6*	*7*	*8*	*9*	*10*	*12*	*14*	*16*	*18*	*20*	*25*	*30*
5																	
10																0	
15													0			1	
20											0				1	2	
25									0				1		2	3	4
30								0				1		2		4	5
35							0				1		2		3	5	6
40						0				1		2	3		4	6	7
45					0				1		2		3	4	5	7	9
50					0			1			2	3	4	5		8	10
55					0		1			2	3		4	5	6	9	11
60				0			1		2		3	4	5	6	7	10	13
65				0		1		2		3	4	5	6	7	8	11	14
70				0		1		2		3	4	5	6	8	9	12	15
75			0			1	2		3		4	6	7	8	10	13	16
80			0		1		2		3	4	5	6	8	9	10	14	18
85			0		1		2	3		4	5	7	8	10	11	15	19
90			0		1	2		3	4		6	7	9	11	12	16	20
95			0	1		2	3		4	5	6	8	10	11	13	17	22
100			0	1		2	3	4	5		7	9	10	12	14	19	23
110			0	1	2	3		4	5	6	8	10	12	14	16	21	26
120		0		1	2	3	4	5	6	7	9	11	13	15	17	23	29
130		0	1	2		3	4	6	7	8	10	12	15	17	19	25	31
140		0	1	2	3	4	5	6	7	9	11	13	16	18	21	27	34
150		0	1	2	3	4	6	7	8	9	12	15	17	20	23	30	37
160		0	1	2	4	5	6	8	9	10	13	16	19	22	25	32	40
170		0	1	3	4	5	7	8	10	11	14	17	20	23	26	34	42
180		0	2	3	4	6	7	9	11	12	15	18	22	25	28	37	45
190		1	2	3	5	6	8	10	11	13	16	20	23	26	30	39	48
200		1	2	4	5	7	8	10	12	14	17	21	24	28	32	41	51
210		1	2	4	6	7	9	11	13	15	18	22	26	30	34	44	54
220		1	3	4	6	8	10	12	14	15	19	23	27	31	35	46	56
230		1	3	5	6	8	10	12	14	16	20	25	29	33	37	48	59
240		1	3	5	7	9	11	13	15	17	21	26	30	35	39	50	62
250	0	1	3	5	7	9	11	14	16	18	23	27	32	36	41	53	65
260	0	2	4	6	8	10	12	15	17	19	24	28	33	38	43	55	68
270	0	2	4	6	8	10	13	15	18	20	25	30	35	40	45	57	70
280	0	2	4	6	8	11	13	16	18	21	26	31	36	41	47	60	73
290	0	2	4	7	9	11	14	17	19	22	27	32	37	43	48	62	76
300	0	2	4	7	9	12	14	17	20	22	28	33	39	45	50	64	79

Appendix B: Table 4 Evaluation of Results Based on Number of Observed Deviations (Reliability = 95%)

Sample Size	*Achieved Upper Deviation Rate Limit (Percent)*																
	1	*2*	*3*	*4*	*5*	*6*	*7*	*8*	*9*	*10*	*12*	*14*	*16*	*18*	*20*	*25*	*30*
5																	
10																	0
15															0		1
20												0				1	2
25											0			1		2	3
30										0			1		2	3	4
35									0			1		2		4	5
40								0			1		2		3	5	6
45							0				1	2		3	4	6	8
50						0				1		2	3	4	5	7	9
55						0			1		2	3	4		5	8	10
60					0			1			2	3	4	5	6	9	11
65					0			1		2	3	4	5	6	7	10	13
70					0		1		2		3	4	5	7	8	11	14
75				0			1		2		4	5	6	7	8	12	15
80				0		1		2		3	4	5	7	8	9	13	16
85				0		1		2	3		5	6	7	9	10	14	18
90				0		1	2		3	4	5	6	8	9	11	15	19
95				0	1		2	3		4	5	7	9	10	12	16	20
100			0		1		2	3	4		6	8	9	11	13	17	22
110			0		1	2	3		4	5	7	9	10	12	14	19	24
120			0	1		2	3	4	5	6	8	10	12	14	16	21	27
130			0	1	2	3	4	5	6	7	9	11	13	15	18	24	30
140			0	1	2	3	4	5	6	7	10	12	14	17	19	26	32
150		0		1	2	4	5	6	7	8	11	13	16	18	21	28	35
160		0	1	2	3	4	5	7	8	9	12	14	17	20	23	30	38
170		0	1	2	3	4	6	7	9	10	13	16	19	22	25	32	40
180		0	1	2	3	5	6	8	9	11	14	17	20	23	26	35	43
190		0	1	3	4	5	7	8	10	11	15	18	21	25	28	37	46
200		0	1	3	4	6	7	9	11	12	16	19	23	26	30	39	48
210		0	2	3	5	6	8	10	12	13	17	20	24	28	32	41	51
220		0	2	3	5	7	8	10	12	14	18	22	25	29	33	44	54
230		1	2	4	5	7	9	11	13	15	19	23	27	31	35	46	57
240		1	2	4	6	8	10	12	14	16	20	24	28	33	37	48	59
250		1	2	4	6	8	10	12	15	16	21	25	30	34	39	50	62
260		1	3	5	7	9	11	13	15	17	22	26	31	36	41	53	65
270		1	3	5	7	9	11	14	16	18	23	28	33	37	42	55	68
280		1	3	5	7	10	12	14	17	19	24	29	34	39	44	57	71
290	0	1	3	6	8	10	12	15	18	20	25	30	35	41	46	60	73
300	0	1	4	6	8	11	13	16	18	21	26	31	37	42	48	62	76

Appendix C: TABLES FOR TWO-STAGE SEQUENTIAL SAMPLING PLANS: ATTRIBUTES SAMPLING

Reliability Levels of 80, 85, 90, and 95 Percent

Appendix C: Table 1 Two-Stage Sequential Sampling Plan (Reliability = 80%)

Tolerable Deviation Rate (Percent)	*Initial Sample Size*	*Second-Stage Sample Size*
10	17	22
9	19	24
8	21	30
7	24	36
6	29	36
5	35	43
4	46	45
3	62	59
2	97	77

Appendix C: Table 2 Two-Stage Sequential Sampling Plan (Reliability = 85%)

Tolerable Deviation Rate (Percent)	*Initial Sample Size*	*Second-Stage Sample Size*
10	20	22
9	22	26
8	25	29
7	29	31
6	34	37
5	41	44
4	54	45
3	71	65
2	113	79

Appendix C: Table 3 Two-Stage Sequential Sampling Plan (Reliability = 90%)

Tolerable Deviation Rate (Percent)	*Initial Sample Size*	*Second-Stage Sample Size*
10	23	29
9	26	30
8	30	30
7	35	32
6	41	38
5	51	39
4	64	49
3	89	56
2	133	87

Appendix C: Table 4 Two-Stage Sequential Sampling Plan (Reliability = 95%)

Tolerable Deviation Rate (Percent)	*Initial Sample Size*	*Second-Stage Sample Size*
10	31	23
9	34	29
8	39	30
7	45	33
6	53	38
5	65	42
4	84	46
3	113	60
2	169	94

Decision Rules for Two-Stage Sequential Sampling Plans

	No Deviations	*One Deviation*	*Two or More Deviations*
Initial sample	Stop—achieved goal	Go to next stage	Stop—failed
Second stage	Stop—achieved goal	Stop—failed	Stop—failed

Index

Answers to Multiple Choice AICPA Questions

Ch1
1-40. C
1-41. A
1-42. B

Ch2.
2-40 B
2-41 B
2-42 D
2-43 D
2-44 B

Ch3.
3-40. B
41. A
42. B
43. C
44. D
45. D
46. D
47. B
48. D
49. A
50. C
51. B
52. D
53. B
54. D
55. D

Ch4.
4-40 B
41 A
42 B
43 A
44 D
45 C
46 A
47 B
48 B
49 C
50 C
51 ADA
52 C
53 D
54 BBC
55 C
56 B

Ch5
5-40 C
41 A
42 B
43 A
44 A
45 C

Ch6
6-40 D
41 D
42 D
43 C
44 D
45 D
46 C
47 D

Ch7
7-40 A
41 D
42 A
43 B
44 C
45 D
46 A
47 A
48 C
49 C
50 D

Ch8
8-40 A
41 C
42 A
43 B
44 C
45 D
46 A
47 D
48 B
49 C
50 D
51 D

Ch9
9-40 C
41 D
42 D
43 A
44 C
45 D
46 D
47 D
48 A
49 B

Ch10
10-40 D
41 D
42 A
43 D
44 B
45 A
46 C
47 C
48 A
49 D
50 D
51 B
52 C
53 D

Ch11
11-40 A
41 B
42 B
43 B
44 B
45 B
46 A
47 C
48 C
49 D
50 D

Ch12
12-40 C
41 A
42 A
43 B
44 B
45 A
46 D
47 A
48 B
49 A
50 A
51 B
52 D

Ch13
13-40 D
41 D
42 D
43 B
44 B
45 A
46 B
47 B
48 C
49 D
50 C

Ch14
14-40 B
41 B
42 A
43 B
44 D
45 A
46 B
47 A
48 D
49 C
50 B
51 D

h15 15-40
41
42
43
44
45
46
47
48
49
50
51
52

h16 16-40
41
42
43
44
45
46
47
48
49
50
51
52

Ch17 17-40
41
42
43
44
45
46
47
48
49
50
51
52
53
54
55

Ch18 18-40 C
41 A
42 C
43 A
44 A
45 C
46 D
47 D
48 C
49 B
50 D
51 D
52 A
53 D
54 A
55 A
56 A
57 BB?
58 D
59 A

Ch19 19-40 A
41 C
42 B
43 C
44 D
45 B
46 A
47 B
48 B
49 C
50 C
51 D
52 B
53 B
54 A
55 A
56 A
57 B
58 C